Toward Social Change

Caryl Sutton, editor-coordinator, Lee S. Allen, Ted J. Alves, Sheila Bacharach, Ronald Bayne, Rene Borboa, Eileen Brass, Harry D. Brass, Elisha Butler, Lynn Cadwallader, Genevieve M. Campbell, Alan Carlson, Betsy Chandler, John Stuart Chang, James L. Chenney, Jorge Cortés, Dan Daly, Jean G. Davidson, William R. Dougherty, John Duff, Linda Dunson, Steve Elgar, Susan Fantus, John R. Farrell, Ellen Feldheyn, Suzanne M. Fleck, John Forrester, Harold Fox, Jr., Karen Friedland, Jean Frazier, Marshall Fuss, Thomas Gamez, Jeff Gaudet, Betsi Goff, Michael R. Goff, Ellen A. Goldman, Doreen Hamilton, Roy R. Harmon, Mary K. Harrington, James E. Hartung, Jr., John Heald, Sandra A. Hickey, Gregory Hollidge, Douglas R. Horner, Hector R. Javkin, Krisida Jones, Sandra Kallerup, Kevin Keogan, Margaret Kerr, Robert D. Links, Gerald William Lucker, Robert J. P. Maginnis, Guy Mansfield, Terje Martinsen, Paul Matz, Robert K. McCann, James Carlson McKenzie, Ellen Melchoir, Robert J. Nichols, Robert Oshita, Kenneth Patton, Paul A. Pickering, Rachel Posner, Jane B. Rockwood, Jim Rosenfield, Valentine N. Sengebau, Susan Tilya Shuirman, Madelyn Silver, Joe deSousa, Elizabeth Stephens, Richard Stephens, Dave Stoltze, Patrick D. Tamayo, Ted Tanaka, Julian F. Tosky, Hillary Turner, Bart Wander, Judy Wanschura, Joshua Wattles, Vicki Lynn Weisblat, James Williams.

Toward Social Change

a handbook for those who will

edited by Robert Buckhout and
81 concerned Berkeley students

HARPER & ROW, PUBLISHERS
New York, Evanston,
San Francisco, London

Come writers and critics
Who prophecies with your pen
And keep your eyes wide
The chance won't come again.
And don't speak too soon
For the wheel's still in spin
And there's no tellin' who
That it's namin'
For the loser now
Will be later to win
For the times they are a-changin'.

Contents

Foreword

The idea for a handbook on social change edited primarily by students grew during the winter of 1969 in Berkeley as my research assistant Caryl Sutton and I pondered innovations in undergraduate education. I was scheduled to teach a course in Social Problems during the spring 1970 quarter—a course which seemed like a natural framework within which teams of students could function as research groups oriented toward analyzing specific problems and making recommendations for change which could be taken seriously by the people and agencies who are able to change things.

Thus began a series of one-hour meetings with interested students during which ideas could be exchanged and people shanghaied into the project. We called it Project SAP —an acronym for Social Action Project—and began to approach publishers with the idea of gaining a publisher so that the students would be oriented to the tangible goal of editing a published work.

The aim of the book which evolved from these meetings was for students to speak to students on their views about social problems which affect *their* lives. My role as a professor was that of catalyst, deadline-watcher, and senior editor. We implored those who signed up for the "course" to meet in social problem interest groups—either suggested by me or generated by them—and be prepared to work on their own to collect information. Our guidelines were to find sharp critiques, overviews, interviews, pictures, cartoons, songs, poetry, and any other material which would help to shape a specific point of view about the social problem. They were to use these materials to write an introduction and specific conclusions aimed at social change. Our models were the teams of "Nader's Raiders" who have done so much to promote social change by using information as an instrument for stirring the public.

This was the beginning of one of the most exciting, creative periods I have ever enjoyed as a teacher. It was a time in which I, as a teacher, learned more, perhaps, than did the students.

Some eighty students signed up, dividing themselves into twelve research teams in such areas as violence, education, reform, drugs, etc. One group joined us with their own project—white community involvement. Each team scheduled meetings either in Project SAP headquarters (a hastily converted laboratory) or in one of their own homes. Despite the absence of formal class hours or grade pressures, most students ended up working harder on Project SAP than on any of their other courses. Caryl Sutton or I met with each team twice during the first couple of weeks but after that they were on their own.

The students—of all ages from 17 to 35—responded magnificently. Where the teams found gaps, confusion, or blandness in the literature, they went out, got information, and wrote their own material. Taking advantage of facilities and knowledgeable people in the San Francisco Bay area, they conducted interviews or did site visits to new drug treatment centers. A full-time policeman added an unusual dimension to the violence team (especially at Berkeley). The students uncovered a number of recent unpublished papers which are more pointed than most published works! Most were highly moved by the writing and example set by my good friend Ed Sampson, whose paper, "Evolution versus Revolution in Psychological Character: Mechanicus or Man?" is featured in Chapter 1. Chaos and humor were frequent, highlighted by the fact that the leader of the population group had a baby boy shortly after turning in the manuscript.

The hectic work did not go entirely smoothly. The students had to live through a period of intense social change brought on by the invasion of Cambodia and the deaths at Kent State and Jackson State in May, 1970. These events had a profound effect on all of us as many of us put our work aside to help out in the antiwar effort. The Berkeley campus was reconstituted into a major antiwar center which emphasized constructive political work in the community and through the system. Many of our student editors played key roles in this movement, while to our delight, they continued to work on the book. This proved to be a painful division of energy for most, and the impact of these events can be clearly seen in the tone and content of the book. The initial optimism of the students gave way to more sober reflection and a decision on their part that a book on social change was needed more desperately than ever before.

Some readers (particularly instructors) may find the contrasting editorial styles and McLuhanesque media in the chapters to be distracting. For this we offer no apologies. We determined from the beginning that the students in each team would tell it like they saw, heard, and felt it. We are convinced that the student readers will understand and appreciate the honesty and ingenuity of their Berkeley compatriots. As concerned people with strong convictions they sought to inform, to promote genuine social change, and to be taken seriously. They owe no allegiance to any government body, foundation, profession, or tradition. Indicative of their concern, they and I agreed before we started work, to donate 60 percent of the royalties from the book to the Fund for the College of Malcolm X, an organization backing an ethnic studies college at the University of California, Santa Cruz (see "For Those Who Would Change Things Now" in the back of the book).

Of the eighty-one young people who made indispensable contributions to the book, it is difficult to single out individuals. I know for a start that our efforts would have been impossible were it not for the outstanding efforts of Caryl Sutton who served as coordinator, editor, and trouble-shooter from beginning to end. Hillary Turner deserves special thanks for devoting a great deal of energy and time to over-all editing, typing, and detail work in addition to her creative leadership on the drug team.

Volunteers with talent appeared at crucial moments as needs arose. Joshua Wattles contributed his fine talents as a photographer covering most of the teams' activities. Jorge Cortés drew original cartoons filling the request of various team members. Jeff Gaudet—an American Indian on the Third World Experience team—was our pilot in a rented aircraft for a rapid visit to the Mendocino drug treatment program. Brenda Johnson, Margaret Kerr, John Chang, and Jean Frazier deserve thanks for typing and editorial work far beyond the normal call of duty. I also want to thank Harrison Gough, Chairman of the Department of Psychology, for a number of adjustments in business as usual which aided in the book's completion.

To Judith Kahn and Jack Ellis, I give special thanks for their devoted work as the Harper & Row editorial and design team whose enthusiasm and hard work made all of us feel that our team had an extension of itself in New York. The collective effort with all these people was a truly beautiful experience.

Finally, I owe a great deal of gratitude to George Middendorf, executive editor at Harper and Row for backing this most unusual project and for demonstrating his faith in me on numerous occasions.

We hope that readers interested in bringing about social change will find the Handbook a useful aid in joining us in that effort.

BOB BUCKHOUT

June 26, 1970

Toward Social Change

Introduction

Robert Buckhout

One alternative to the usual fare in social problems books which touch on revolution is to turn to the people who are either creating or are most likely to participate in any revolution. In this handbook, we present the judgments on social change of some eighty undergraduate students from the University of California, Berkeley, whose main qualification is social concern. The book is addressed to the mover, the shaker, the concerned. As students of social problems, the students speak of those problems which will affect *their* lives. Their aim was to select readings and make specific suggestions for change which would be understood by their peers and be acted upon by those who will.

At least two major revolutions are underway in the United States —a phenomenon which is unique in the world history of revolutions. More social than political, more subtle than dramatic, the revolutions may take place without the emergence of a visible ruling dynasty. Or, they may lead to chaos.

The two revolutions differ in terms of black and white. The black revolution began with the participation of white liberals in the civil rights movement and persists with blacks and other minorities trying to complete it on their own. The white revolution, a more diffuse phenomenon, broke from the silence of the younger generation in the 1950s to become the mixture of alienation, reform movements, and militant revolutionary groups which are alarmingly visible to the adults on the upper end of the "generation gap" in white, affluent America.

Predictably, the revolutionary factions are minorities which speak primarily to potential joiners. The revolutionary movements are also chronicled in second-hand manner in the press and by the social scientists in the journals. Seldom do we find the substance of the revolution printed in "respectable" media such as texts or journals.

The reaction of the American establishment to these twin revolutions ranges from uncritical pandering on one end to violent repression on the other. It is an inevitable clash of those who want change against those who fear change. But whether you approach the answer from the smug confidence of the young revolutionary or the hapless sense of resignation of the old guard, the word is the same: The times are changing.

No state reflects these social changes more than California; perhaps no urban area more than the San Francisco Bay Area. California is filled with people in transition, people seeking change in their personal life space; movements being born and dying; a place condemned as the opposite pole by the "Okies from Muskogee."

Berkeley, the world head-quarters of student unrest, functions like a living laboratory of environmental and social change. It is physically beautiful; it is an ever-stimulating place to be in; if the United States has two revolutions, Berkeley has twenty. But, even Berkeley doesn't work. Try as we might to keep our book on social change from becoming Berkeleyized or Californianized, we could not escape the influence. For, tragically, only an area so rich in beauty, wealth, intelligence, and resources could drive home the points shared by all of us with Marcuse: that our society is failing and its problems are multiplying; that we lack the sense of urgency to act to manage those inescapable movements toward social change.

To live in Berkeley in the last few years has been to experience the closest thing to urban guerrilla warfare the U.S. has to offer. *Everyone* in town has a war story about being gassed, clubbed, or jailed whether they were involved in the disputes or not. Such a climate forces most people either to choose sides or to reinforce a brand of apathetic withdrawal, which most observers of the Berkeley scene have missed. Without resorting to homilies about "a raucous minority," it is true that

1

the majority of students at Berkeley, like most students throughout the country, have not been directly involved in provoking violence. Students understand the violence and even tacitly support it, because there is generally little disagreement on the ills of society among the socially concerned young.

As John Holt expresses it:

... the students do not find out from S.D.S alone in what desperate shape our society and civilization find themselves. . . . They find this out in our T.V., newspapers and mass media. Nobody seriously believes that we are likely to solve or are even moving toward a solution to any of the most urgent problems of our times. . . . We do not think any more that we can really make the world a fit and happy and beautiful place for people to live. . . . Only when we talk to students do we talk as if these problems were not real or serious or urgent. Only to the young do we keep saying that daddy knows best. But it is no good; they hear us talking to each other.[1]

The key event for most of the young in the 1960s was the Democratic National Convention in Chicago. To participate in or witness the cynicism of the establishment in Chicago was to convince many young people that striving for social change within the system was doomed to failure. Despite a mandate to the Democratic party to end the disastrous war in Vietnam, the answer was clear: LBJ would save his face by any means necessary.

Alienation is not peculiar to the younger generation in America. Political observers point out that there is evidence of a falling off of political interest and involvement in the organizational end of party politics. As one columnist indicated, more and more people are turned off by everything and anything to do with politics.[2] Paradoxically, in spite of an overwhelming amount of information and political analysis in every conceivable media, voters seem to be "tuning out."

Perhaps those on the upper end of the generation gap will recognize the feelings of those who have the options of dropping out or turning to revolutionary activities—and exercise them. An instructive analysis of the depth of alienation in America can be found in Studs Terkel's remarkable book, *Division Street, U.S.A.* Deliberately excluding teachers, students, and other leaders (who have vocal outlets) from his sample, Terkel interviewed ordinary people—the "silent majority." He found—in different words —alienation, frustration, and a sense of impotence with the bigness of society which paralleled the findings of most studies of the younger generation. While few of his respondents can be expected to turn on, many have and will tune out.

And into this morass comes the revolutionary, the concerned, the activist, the politician, the muckraker, the *tumula.*

Too often, the activist confronts an apathetic, perhaps sleeping society. He may characterize the people as ignorant, unfeeling, "don't give a damn" boobs; as pigs; as out of it; as people who need to be awakened.

To a society bored to death with political rhetoric and overloaded with undigested and contradictory information, the *tumula* shouts: Wake up!

To a society made up of some of the most blasé churchgoers in the world, whose irreverence is a basic cultural trait, our hero cries out: Repent!

To people whose effective control of *anything* in the system affecting their lives barely extends beyond the walls of their home, the revolutionary says: Change it!

When the results of such efforts are predictably marginal, too often our social changer writes off the system, takes up a more violent approach to change, or possibly becomes himself a victim of the system he hopes to change.

Yet things *are* changing. People are concerned. Polarization, alleged to be a precursor to revolution, is undeniably here. So why the confusion? Why the malaise among many of those whose lives have been committed to social change?

Let's return to the two-revolution idea. The black (or third world) revolution is more like the great revolutions of history in that the model of an oppressed people rising up against a colonial or dominant force is relatively clear. Black and other third world people constitute a minority (less than 20 percent) of the American population whose grievances have been articulated by a succession of well-known spokesmen, a literature explosion, and a linkage with emergent third world peoples all over the world. All share the experience of being on the outside; they are excluded from the sources of affluence and power. The revolutionary leader can articulate his people's desire to gain the material affluent life they have been denied.

When the third world revolutionary takes as his bible Frantz Fanon's *The Wretched of the Earth,* the stark analysis has a ring of truth which applies as well to America as it does to Africa. The young black militant who has seen the assassinations of Martin Luther King and Malcolm X listens when Fanon writes:

. . . if whole regimes, even your non-violent ideas, are conditioned by a thousand-year-old oppression, your passivity serves only to place you in the ranks of the oppressors.[3]

Translated into the American cliché: "If you're not a part of the solution, you're part of the problem."

Thus the third world revolution is ideological, possessed of a historical imperative, cast often in terms of a Marxian analysis, and aimed ultimately at basically changing or destroying the system which sustains oppression.[4] Speaking of Europe—the ultimate colonizer—Fanon says:

So, comrades, let us not pay tribute to Europe by creating states, institutions and societies which draw their inspiration from her. . . . For Europe, for ourselves, and for humanity, comrades, we must turn over a new leaf, we must work out a new concept, and try to set afoot a new man.

Enter the white revolutionary. In the United States, his people have it made. The perspective of those who have grown up in relatively affluent circumstances differs dramatically from the perspective of the third worlder. The evils of society stem more from excess than poverty, from overpopulation rather than genocide, from purposeless consumption rather than frustrated desire, from inconsistent hypocrisy rather than blatant discrimination, from authoritarian pressures to take *certain* roads to success rather than an absence of opportunity. Despite some exceptionally good alliances, the black and white revolution-

---

[1] John Holt, "The Radicalization of a Guest Teacher at Berkeley," *The New York Times Magazine,* February 22, 1970.

[2] D. S. Broder, *San Francisco Chronicle,* July 23, 1970.

[3] Frantz Fanon, *The Wretched of the Earth,* New York, Grove, 1967.

[4] The tone of Chapter 3, "Out of the Third World Experience," edited by third world people, is uncompromising, bitter, and largely aimed at stirring awareness of the problem.

aries are on two separate pathways.

In 1969, an incident occurred in the booming ecology movement which underscores this point. In order to drive home the message that the automobile is not only the major cause of air pollution but is an extravagance, white ecology activists held a public "funeral" at which an undriven new car was to be buried. They became flustered and backed off when black students interrupted the "service" and called it a waste of a useful car, denying transportation to those who needed it.[5]

But, as a study of relationships between the new left and the Black Panthers will reveal, the white revolutionary has often vicariously adopted the model for change advocated by the third world despite its irrelevance to the major concerns of white social changers. Among young activists, this phenomenon is often based on a sincere desire to be brothers and sisters in a common cause.

But at the tactical level, it has produced aping of the black life style (e.g., White Panthers), shared rhetoric (right on!), unresolvable guilt, cop-outs by whites who run while a black group stands and fights, etc. Inevitably, there has been a move to militant violence—a great deal of which has been inappropriate or incredibly poorly timed in terms of political effect. Unfortunately, some of my friends in the movement have felt themselves obliged to prove their manliness by engaging in violence, only to find themselves scorned not only by white society but also by blacks, who question their judgment.[6] The result is a level of distrust between the races which extends across all types of social change efforts in the United States.

One friend of mine came back from his hitch with the Venceremos Brigade in Cuba, where he cut sugar cane for a few weeks, side by side with the Cubans who succeeded in their revolution. But it's a long way from the Sierra

Maestre to the high Sierras. He brings back a model of a third world revolution against colonial *oppression* to a country beset by *repression*. His poster of the dead Che Guevara is not matched by an equivalent American hero who can lead a revolution here. In short, he has adopted the wrong model—and deep down he knows it—but can't face it.

Back home he is a part of the problem of the third world revolutionary. He is a part of the affluent majority. He is, de facto, as much an oppressor as are his parents, teachers, and friends. He is as convinced as his third world brothers that the society must be changed. But to admit to the apocalyptic vision of Fanon is to doom himself as well. In a large, complex, interdependent (overdeveloped) society with a highly literate populace, neither simple analyses or simple answers are going to go down. More white Americans have read or seen *Catch*-22 than will ever read Fanon.[7]

These observations do not necessarily sustain the conventional establishment wisdom purveyed in the bible of those who would contain social change—Daniel Bell's *The End of Ideology*. The tumultuous events of the 1960s should have convinced most people that ideology is far from dead. But, as many an ecology activist has learned, the validity of a systems analysis of society is asserted every time a change proposal is advanced. For every change in an eco-system, a price is exacted. It is equally true in a social system.

In short, the lesson for those who will change this society is that one must do his homework: to assess the consequences of any proposed change. This is true whether one works for change from within or outside the system. Mistakes in social policy can be costly and possibly fatal to society.

To the white revolutionary, I would have to say—as Tom Hayden did recently in *The Trial* —that you cannot have a revolution of the type proposed by the third world because your problems are unique to the times and to your culture. You cannot accept the charge that working within the system is a cop-out—because

le système c'est moi, you are the "system."

While you have every reason to be skeptical of how much activism and dissent will be tolerated in America, let us not pretend that we have exhausted the possibilities of using creative alternatives to an Armageddon confrontation with society as it stands. The year 1970 saw the emergence of Ralph Nader as a model revolutionary (and I mean to use that term) who used the system against itself by using the skills of hundreds of dedicated volunteers committed to forcing social change.

Their weapon is information. Their trump card is knowing more about the social problem than the forces of inertia. They mince no words. They avoid the stigma of copping out by sticking to private sources of financing. They aim at the sources of power in this society—large corporations, government, etc. They would rather provoke an outcry in Congress than in the streets. But, at least for the moment, Naders Raiders are provoking social change and are feared by those in power.

In my opinion this and similar approaches can be started by students and young people throughout the country right in their own backyard, focusing on their own social problems. As the events following the Cambodian invasion in May, 1970, demonstrated, mobilized students on campuses throughout the country are a force to be reckoned with. As the students found out when many of them went out in the community, there are many concerns that they share in common with the silent majority, especially in regard to larger issues like the war in Indochina.

Despite their minority status, students can do a great deal to articulate the complexities of social problems and attempt to promote change through the imaginative use of channels which all too often are not used. Failing this, they will be better prepared for more dramatic steps when they become necessary.

Where does all of this leave the third world revolution? Frankly, I think it leaves it freer of the interference of well-intentioned white radicals, who cannot help but overwhelm this very different undertaking by their sheer numbers and inherent stake in the system. If all the concerned white students organized to work in the ghettos, they would probably subvert the growth of local leadership

---

[5] Several papers in the *Handbook* attack some of the sacred cow liberal causes in bitter terms. See "Ecology Is a Racist Shuck" by Robert Chrisman (chap. 10) and "Community Mental Health as a Pacification Program" by James Statman (chap. 9).

[6] Saul Alinsky (chap. 12) homes in on this point with his belief that white radicals should stick to their own backyard to affect social change and cease the prevalent cow-towing to black militants.

[7] The popularity of existential works like *Catch*-22 breeds a small ray of hope about the psyche of Americans capable of enjoying the paradoxical, irreverent message of this work. It has always been a kind of bible to socially concerned people.

so vital to independence.[8] While whites and third world people can work together on common causes, the third world people must direct their own revolution and the whites theirs.[9]

At times, this will mean that the white radical will find himself unwelcome; and, at times the white radical will have to shrug off the scorn of the black militant who questions *his* priorities.

Clarity begins at home.

Against this background, the book *Toward Social Change* was born.

When I spoke to students about the idea for a social change book with an emphasis on specific positive recommendations for change, I was not prepared for the level of malaise I ran into. The then active radical students avoided joining in on the book project, as expected. The editors who did participate would probably be called moderates or even "liberals" by the radicals. But the tone of those who did join was still highly skeptical. As will be evident in each chapter, a consensus was more readily achieved among the student editors on an imaginative critical analysis—telling it like it is—than on specific change proposals.

While my biases and judgments undoubtedly had some impact on the book, it remains very much the net judgment of the students, who selected most of the articles and wrote introductions and conclusions for each chapter. The resulting work is somewhat more pessimistic than I would have done on my own, but it is undoubtedly a more genuine reflection of what students are really thinking about social problems.

What has pleased me immensely is the fact that each chapter has a very clear message despite the very eclectic sources of material which were consulted. Instead of reifying only those articles (there are damned few of them) written by professional social scientists in "respectable" journals, the coverage runs the gamut of the underground press,

radio commercials, sociology, anthropology, philosophy, psychology, and recent popular books. The readers may not agree with the messages presented, but they will at least know where the editors stand.

The pessimistic tone can be seen in selections such as the classic "Student as a Nigger," Paul Ehrlich's unequivocably stated alarm on the population explosion, the bitter commentary of most of the selections in the third world experience chapter, and the passages on mental health by Ken Kesey. Still, after stating their criticisms in no uncertain terms, the editors came forth with a series of very concrete alternatives in the interest of promoting social change. The following edited partial list will give the reader some idea of where these student editors were heading:

1. Training of social scientists by the universities to fill professional roles in their *own* communities—white or third world.
2. Reeducation of the American people to the true history of their nation as one which grew out of violence, dissent, and exploitation of minorities in the hope that facing the truth about ourselves will permit us to face the need for change.
3. Establishment of drug education programs and counselors at all educational levels.
4. Repeal of existing legal restrictions on possession, manufacture, and free distribution of drugs.
5. Guarantee of legal immunity to drug addicts who turn themselves in for treatment.
6. Development of community mental health centers which provide preventative (in- and outpatient) mental health care.
7. Employment of nonprofessionals, para-professionals, and volunteers in the mental health and drug fields to alleviate the chronic shortage of trained professionals.
8. Repeal of all existing legal restrictions on abortion; encouragement of a favorable attitude toward a norm of the two-child family in order to stabilize population growth.

In addition, the students did some pioneering in analyzing social problem areas which are relatively new. The chapter on alternative life styles (chap. 6) studies some of the problems encountered by people who have rejected the

usual cultural norms and priorities. If it can be said that most American students become alienated or turn into existentialists, then there may be some hope in the experimentation with new religious, ecological, communal, and rural life styles. I should footnote this chapter by observing that few of the student editors had their own heads in the place of the people they observed, that is, they were somewhat more conventional students undergoing changes of their own, who were observing phenomena which have engendered a considerable amount of commitment to change on the part of some young people. The largely apolitical, almost tribal alternative life styles have, in turn, had major effects on the surrounding society, invoking repression in some cases. Their philosophy seems to be that we must change our heads before we can change society.

A corollary to alternate life styles is the chapter on encounter groups (chap. 8) which have become a nationwide pastime. Since most of our student editors have had group experience, the cautionary note they sound is worth listening to. My personal feeling is that the creative use of the encounter group tactic has yet to be tried in the area of social problem solving. I was particularly pleased with an effort at Berkeley which saw topic and task oriented encounter groups created between students and townspeople. The students and I tend to share some skepticism about the therapeutic value of sensitivity training.

We are hopeful that the chapter on the psychological consequences of population control (chap. 10) will be something of an answer to the questions raised by Wayne R. Bartz in his article "While Psychologists Doze On." His point about the neglect of the population explosion by psychologists is well taken. I have been concerned about the lack of a sense of urgency on this and other social problems by my colleagues in the psychology profession. One may view Chapter 2 as a frank call for more psychologists (and other social scientists) to follow the example of constructive involvement in social action set by Ralph Nader.

Finally, a few last words by the senior editor who finds himself with eighty genuine colleagues as coeditors of a book.

This collective effort was not a panacea for producing recom-

[8] An object lesson can be found in the pacification program in Indochina, which has employed thousands of white Americans in a futile effort to teach a whole culture to be good Vietnamese—which means loyalty to a government they have good reason to despise.

[9] See Chapter 12 for a case study of a white group who set out to affect social change in their own community—a lily-white suburb.

mendations for social change. It was, in part, an educational experience for me as well as the students. It was a model for training social scientists to assemble information quickly, synthesize it, ascertain a point of view, and make concrete proposals in spite of the dynamic changing nature of social problems. I often asked the students to role play an appearance before a congressional committee to which they were expected to recommend legislation.

The recommendations came only with considerable strain as the students fought in themselves a much conditioned habit of reacting to a complex social problem by equivocation. I and my colleagues must take the blame for this since we have taught neutral objectivity (the art of saying nothing eloquently) to many generations of students, reinforced by our own modeling behavior.

The shock of the Cambodian invasion and subsequent murders of students at Kent State and Jackson State brought the moderates at Berkeley out into the open as leaders of a concerted political effort to try and stop the war. For a few brief weeks, business as usual was swept aside as the silent majority of moderates reconstituted classes, campaigned for peace candidates, compiled facts on the war, and went out into the community to speak honestly about the issues.

It was a time of renewed hope as students committed to work for social and political change within the system found allies among an awakened faculty and some administrators. The vast resources of Berkeley and several hundred other universities were mobilized behind efforts to elect peace candidates and in the soliciting of support for congressional efforts to limit the president's ability to prolong the Indochina war.

It is too early to tell if these efforts will promote change or simply provoke more repression from an already threatened establishment. But, the students are largely the children of the ruling elite in America. There is a joke among activists, that marijuana will be legalized when enough sons of politicians get busted for possession. But maybe I'm just a little more optimistic than my students.

This Handbook is aimed largely at those who *will* promote social change. Realistically, most of you are out there somewhere in the white majority. If you can change society to something like the world envisioned by the white radical, perhaps it will provide a worthwhile goal for the third world to aspire to rather than to destroy in their revolution. Perhaps then, history—with all of its violence and successions of one oppressor class for another—need not repeat itself.

DO IT!

Part 1
Basic Assumptions

... I can imagine nothing we could do that would be more relevant to human welfare and nothing that could pose a greater challenge to the next generation of psychologists, than to discover how best to give psychology away.

George A. Miller
(Presidential Address to the American Psychological Association, September, 1969.)

In this part of the book, some basic assumptions about social change are explored. Discussion of the basic question of the possibility of social change and the desire of society to experience change raises some of the philosophical issues which come up repeatedly in later chapters in reference to specific social problems.

The question of the possibility of social change suggests the acute concern of many people as to whether the American society stands on the brink of revolution. No definite answer can be given to this question, but the desire of the editors to promote social change is clear. In their opinion, change is both possible and desirable, and if efforts toward constructive change are blocked, revolution, in its least effective sense, may occur. The drift of the editors' recommendations is to revolutionize the nature of man, to change social priorities toward more humanistic ends, and to use effectively or modify radically "the system" in such a way as to promote human welfare.

The second chapter deals with a way to effect change. It examines the position of the advocate of social change within the system. Inspired by the example of Ralph Nader within the legal profession, the authors here consider the possibility of innovators' changing society from their position in the social science profession. The prognosis is not good. Serious criticism is directed at the lack of social relevance in research and practice; the absence of a social science "Nader" is noted. Some specific suggestions are offered to those in the profession who would attempt to lead efforts toward change.

Is Social Change Possible and Do We Want It?

EDITED BY:

Eileen Brass   James Carlson McKenzie

Harry D. Brass   Kenneth Patton

George III was the symbol against which our Founders made a revolution now considered bright and glorious. . . . We must now realize that today's Establishment is the new George III. Whether it will continue to adhere to his tactics, we do not know. If it does, the redress, honored in tradition, is also revolution.

William O. Douglas, Justice
of the U.S. Supreme Court

INTRODUCTION

Is social change possible? In view of past social performance and especially in view of recent events, it is becoming increasingly more difficult to answer this question, positively or otherwise. We are now witnessing, in the United States, the effects of our policies of repression of dissent and the disregard of our environment. The type of social structure which permits and promotes such policies must be changed. The goals of society should be to provide for the common good of all men.

Such a society could not morally permit one man to starve, one man to be degraded, one man's opinion to be suppressed, one man to be killed, or one man to lose his pride in the beauty of the countryside. Here in the U.S. there are ten million starving poor, along with another twenty million people who are just at the subsistence level. Our minority people suffer from substandard education, lack of job opportunities, and inadequate living quarters in the urban ghettos. Dissenting voices are now being silenced by violence with the tacit approval of even the President and Vice-President. Pollution of air, land, and water has reached critical, if not irreversible levels. If we desire to have a more beneficial society, then we must change from the present destructive social policies

to more moral and humanistic ones. The time for constructive steps toward change has come and may well be passing rapidly. As people, we are in great danger of becoming the *"homo mechanicus"* which Sampson describes in one of the papers presented below. To change society we must change institutions. To change mankind we must change ourselves. To change the social trends of 10,000 years of human evolution will not be easy. Learned and inherited tolerances and intolerances are not so easily remolded.

How will we change society and its institutions? Functionally, there seem to be only two alternatives. Either we can work through the channels open to us in our present social structure or we can rid ourselves of the old social order and establish a new one. The latter alternative may necessitate a violent revolution. Both alternatives are beset by a mass of problems. If change is to be effected through institutions, there must first be large support and specifically articulated goals. It is because of the lack of support and confusion over goals that many attempts at social change have failed. Another problem which prevents effective use of the means within institutions is the fact that channels for use by the people are either inefficient or simply nonexistent. Still a third problem is trying to keep the downtrodden people patient while you chip away at the monoliths of social structure. Perhaps the most frustrating problem is the reluctance of the power structure to act.

Dixon, Calif. UPI

A fourth-grade girl wrote a letter to President Nixon complaining she could "smell the sewage" when she went on a hike.

"I think you should do something about the pollution," 9-year-old Pamela Cross told the Chief Executive.

Her reply came from the Department of Health, Education and Welfare. It was signed by Thomas J. Burns, acting associate commissioner for elementary and secondary education.

"Pay attention to your own learning activities, and let the President take care of decisions on national and international affairs," the response said in part. "He is equipped to do this. Good luck in your studies."

Pamela wasn't sure what the answer meant, so she asked her mother.

"It means mind your own business," the mother replied.

"I felt kind of miserable," the girl said. "We are supposed to be interested in affairs and write the President about them, and then we are told to mind our own business."[1]

These are only some of the problems. Many of the same problems also apply to the alternative of violent revolution. If the contention of the supporters of revolution—that radical social changes will be met by the real ruling structure of our society (the corporate power elite) with the violence necessary to maintain their positions and profits—is correct, then the result of social change initiatives will be bloody. It is probable that the power elite will win out, simply because it controls the economic and military power. The great "silent majority" cannot be counted on for aid for, although they may resent and react to the undisguised and over-all violence of the government, they will also fear the revolution, because they will face losing the material wealth they have worked all of their lives to gain. The United States is neither geographically, demographically, nor socially disposed to revolution in the classic historical sense. Furthermore, if revolution should succeed, the old objection is still valid—the new power elite may find itself impotent to regulate any type of government without the same force used by the current power structure. Violent revolution is not an alternative taken up by choice. Third world people in the ghettos feel very strongly that their hands have been forced by a social and political structure unresponsive to their problems. The revolution for them has already begun. How far it will have to go depends on how far the power structure will force it.

It seems clear that changing society by changing institutions (through either alternative) will not succeed or endure if man does

[1] *San Francisco Chronicle*, May 20, 1970.

not change mankind. Reform will mean nothing if the social behavior of mankind which allowed the immoral social structures to exist does not change. This will necessitate a reevaluation of basic human values and needs. The science of psychology has given us a somewhat effective means of controlling human behavior and suggests the possibility of establishing new societies.

However, we must be aware of the danger involved in continuing to perceive man's nature as controllable. The danger is in forever losing our potential for becoming existential beings. It is our being that is at stake, not an arbitrary set of rules and mores. This is deadly serious, not to be taken lightly, for to do so implies that we still have a choice not to act, and not to act means that we may not survive as human beings.

We present in this first chapter, several sweeping analyses directed toward the question of whether social change is possible. The authors vary in their degree of hope and despair. All of them want change as do we.

The Rogers-Skinner debate is quite old but the issues raised are as vital now as they were in 1956. Skinner, as always erudite, as always one who generalizes to the universal nature of man, discusses the positive and negative aspects of behavior control, but asserts optimistically that "the methods of science, now for the first time being applied to human affairs, may mean a new and exciting phase of human life to which historical analogies will not apply. . . ."

Rogers raises the questions of who shall control and who shall be controlled and in the pursuit of what end or value will control be exercised. He concludes that science cannot come into being without a personal choice of the values we wish to achieve. While Rogers and Skinner represent the polarization of psychology, it is probable that this debate touches on the basic division between all people who wish to promote social change.

1.1
Some Issues Concerning the Control of Human Behavior

A SYMPOSIUM

Carl R. Rogers and
B. F. Skinner

I [Skinner]

Science is steadily increasing our power to influence, change, mold —in a word, control—human behavior. It has extended our "understanding" (whatever that may be) so that we deal more successfully with people in nonscientific ways, but it has also identified conditions or variables which can be used to predict and control behavior in a new, and increasingly rigorous, technology. The broad disciplines of government and economics offer examples of this, but there is special cogency in those contributions of anthropology, sociology, and psychology which deal with individual behavior. Carl Rogers has listed some of the achievements to date in a recent paper (1). Those of his examples which show or imply the control of the single organism are primarily due, as we should expect, to psychology. It is the experimental study of behavior which carries us beyond awkward or inaccessible "principles," "factors," and so on, to variables which can be directly manipulated.

It is also, and for more or less the same reasons, the conception of human behavior, emerging from an experimental analysis which most directly challenges traditional views. Psychologists themselves often do not seem to be aware of how far they have moved in this direction. But the change is not passing unnoticed by others. Until only recently it was customary to deny the possibility of a rigorous science of human behavior by arguing, either that a lawful science was impossible because man was a free agent, or that merely statistical predictions would always leave room for personal freedom. But those who used to take this line have become more vociferous in expressing their alarm at the way these obstacles are being surmounted.

Now, the control of human be-

Reprinted by permission from *Science*, *124* (November 30, 1956), 1057–1066. Copyright 1956 by the American Association for the Advancement of Science.

havior has always been unpopular. Any undisguised effort to control usually arouses emotional reactions. We hesitate to admit, even to ourselves, that we are engaged in control, and we may refuse to control, even when this would be helpful, for fear of criticism. Those who have explicitly avowed an interest in control have been roughly treated by history. Machiavelli is the great prototype. As Macaulay said of him, "Out of his surname they coined an epithet for a knave and out of his Christian name a synonym for the devil." There were obvious reasons. The control that Machiavelli analyzed and recommended, like most political control, used techniques that were aversive to the controllee. The threats and punishments of the bully, like those of the government operating on the same plan, are not designed— whatever their success—to endear themselves to those who are controlled. Even when the techniques themselves are not aversive, control is usually exercised for the selfish purposes of the controller and, hence, has indirectly punishing effects upon others.

Man's natural inclination to revolt against selfish control has been exploited to good purpose in what we call the philosophy and literature of democracy. The doctrine of the rights of man has been effective in arousing individuals to concerted action against governmental and religious tyranny. The literature which has had this effect has greatly extended the number of terms in our language which express reactions to the control of men. But the ubiquity and ease of expression of this attitude spells trouble for any science which may give birth to a powerful technology of behavior. Intelligent men and women, dominated by the humanistic philosophy of the past two centuries, cannot view with equanimity what Andrew Hacker has called "the specter of predictable man" (2). Even the statistical or actuarial prediction of human events, such as the number of fatalities to be expected on a holiday weekend, strikes many people as uncanny and evil, while the prediction and control of individual behavior is regarded as little less than the work of the devil. I am not so much concerned here with the political or economic consequences for psychology, although research following certain channels may well suffer harmful effects. We ourselves, as intelligent men and women, and as exponents of

Western thought, share these attitudes. They have already interfered with the free exercise of a scientific analysis, and their influence threatens to assume more serious proportions.

Three broad areas of human behavior supply good examples. The first of these—*personal control*—may be taken to include person-to-person relationships in the family, among friends, in social and work groups, and in counseling and psychotherapy. Other fields are *education* and *government*. A few examples from each will show how nonscientific preconceptions are affecting our current thinking about human behavior.

Personal Control

People living together in groups come to control one another with a technique which is not inappropriately called "ethical." When an individual behaves in a fashion acceptable to the group, he receives admiration, approval, affection, and many other reinforcements which increase the likelihood that he will continue to behave in that fashion. When his behavior is not acceptable, he is criticized, censured, blamed, or otherwise punished. In the first case the group calls him "good"; in the second, "bad." This practice is so thoroughly ingrained in our culture that we often fail to see that it is a technique of control. Yet we are almost always engaged in such control, even though the reinforcements and punishments are often subtle.

The practice of admiration is an important part of a culture, because behavior which is otherwise inclined to be weak can be set up and maintained with its help. The individual is especially likely to be praised, admired, or loved when he acts for the group in the face of great danger, for example, or sacrifices himself or his possessions, or submits to prolonged hardship, or suffers martyrdom. These actions are not admirable in any absolute sense, but they require admiration if they are to be strong. Similarly, we admire people who behave in original or exceptional ways, not because such behavior is itself admirable, but because we do not know how to encourage original or exceptional behavior in any other way. The group acclaims independent, unaided behavior in part because it is easier to reinforce than to help.

As long as this technique of control is misunderstood, we cannot judge correctly an environment in which there is less need for heroism, hardship, or independent action. We are likely to argue that such an environment is itself less admirable or produces less admirable people. In the old days, for example, young scholars often lived in undesirable quarters, ate unappetizing or inadequate food, performed unprofitable tasks for a living or to pay for necessary books and materials or publication. Older scholars and other members of the group offered compensating reinforcement in the form of approval and admiration for these sacrifices. When the modern graduate student receives a generous scholarship, enjoys good living conditions, and has his research and publication subsidized, the grounds for evaluation seem to be pulled from under us. Such a student no longer *needs* admiration to carry him over a series of obstacles (no matter how much he may need it for other reasons), and, in missing certain familiar objects of admiration, we are likely to conclude that such *conditions* are less admirable. Obstacles to scholarly work may serve as a useful measure of motivation—and we may go wrong unless some substitute is found—but we can scarcely defend a deliberate harassment of the student for this purpose. The productivity of any set of conditions can be evaluated only when we have freed ourselves of the attitudes which have been generated in us as members of an ethical group.

A similar difficulty arises from our use of punishment in the form of censure or blame. The concept of responsibility and the related concepts of foreknowledge and choice are used to justify techniques of control using punishment. Was So-and-So aware of the probable consequences of his action, and was the action deliberate? If so, we are justified in punishing him. But what does this mean? It appears to be a question concerning the efficacy of the contigent relations between behavior and punishing consequences. We punish behavior because it is objectionable to us or the group, but in a minor refinement of rather recent origin we have come to withhold punishment when it cannot be expected to have any effect. If the objectionable consequences of an act were accidental and not likely to occur again, there is no point in punishing. We say that the individual was not "aware of the consequences of his action" or that the consequences were not "intentional." If the action could not have been avoided—if the individual "had no choice"—punishment is also withheld, as it is if the individual is incapable of being changed by punishment because he is of "unsound mind." In all these cases—different as they are—the individual is held "not responsible" and goes unpunished.

Just as we say that it is "not fair" to punish a man for something he could not help doing, so we call it "unfair" when one is rewarded beyond his due or for something he could not help doing. In other words, we also object to wasting *reinforcers* where they are not needed or will do no good. We make the same point with the words *just* and *right*. Thus we have no right to punish the irresponsible, and a man has no right to reinforcers he does not earn or deserve. But concepts of choice, responsibility, justice, and so on, provide a most inadequate analysis of efficient reinforcing and punishing contingencies because they carry a heavy semantic cargo of a quite different sort, which obscures any attempt to clarify controlling practices or to improve techniques. In particular, they fail to prepare us for techniques based on other than aversive techniques of control. Most people would object to forcing prisoners to serve as subjects of dangerous medical experiments, but few object when they are induced to serve by the offer of return privileges—even when the reinforcing effect of these privileges has been created by forcible deprivation. In the traditional scheme the right to refuse guarantees the individual against coercion or an unfair bargain. But to what extent *can* a prisoner refuse under such circumstances?

We need not go so far afield to make the point. We can observe our own attitude toward personal freedom in the way we resent any interference with what we want to do. Suppose we want to buy a car of a particular sort. Then we may object, for example, if our wife urges us to buy a less expensive model and to put the difference into a new refrigerator. Or we may resent it if our neighbor questions our need for such a car or our ability to pay for it. We would certainly resent it if it were illegal to buy such a car (remember Prohibition); and if we find we cannot actually afford it, we may resent governmental control of the price through tariffs and taxes. We resent it if we discover that we cannot get the car because the manufacturer is holding the model in deliberately short supply in order to push a model we do not want. In all this we assert our democratic right to buy the car of our choice. We are well prepared to do so and to resent any restriction on our freedom.

But why do we not ask *why* it is the car of our choice and resent the forces which made it so? Perhaps our favorite toy as a child was a car, of a very different model, but nevertheless bearing the name of the car we now want. Perhaps our favorite TV program is sponsored by the manufacturer of that car. Perhaps we have seen pictures of many beautiful or prestigeful persons driving it—in pleasant or glamorous places. Perhaps the car has been designed with respect to our motivational patterns: the device on the hood is a phallic symbol; or the horsepower has been stepped up to please our competitive spirit in enabling us to pass other cars swiftly (or, as the advertisements say, "safely"). The concept of freedom that has emerged as part of the cultural practice of our group makes little or no provision for recognizing or dealing with these kinds of control. Concepts like "responsibility" and "rights" are scarcely applicable. We are prepared to deal with coercive measures, but we have no traditional recourse with respect to other measures which in the long run (and especially with the help of science) may be much more powerful and dangerous.

Education

The techniques of education were once frankly aversive. The teacher was usually older and stronger than his pupils and was able to "make them learn." This meant that they were not actually taught but were surrounded by a threatening world from which they could escape only by learning. Usually they were left to their own resources in discovering how to do so. Claude Coleman has published a grimly amusing reminder of these older practices (3). He tells of a schoolteacher who published a careful account of his services during 51 years of teaching, during which he administered: ". . . 911,527 blows with a cane; 124,-010 with a rod; 20,989 with a ruler; 136,715 with the hand; 10,-295 over the mouth; 7,905 boxes on the ear; [and] 1,115,800 slaps on the head. . . ."

Progressive education was a humanitarian effort to substitute positive reinforcement for such aversive measures, but in the search for useful human values in the classroom it has never fully replaced the variables it abandoned. Viewed as a branch of behavioral technology, education remains relatively inefficient. We supplement it, and rationalize it, by admiring the pupil who learns *for himself;* and we often attribute the learning process, or knowledge itself, to something *inside* the individual. We admire behavior which seems to have inner sources. Thus we admire one who *recites* a poem more than one who simply *reads* it. We admire one who *knows* the answer more than one who *knows where to look it up.* We admire the *writer* rather than the *reader.* We admire the arithmetician who can do a problem in his head rather than with a slide rule or calculating machine, or in "original" ways rather than by a strict application of rules. In general we feel that any aid or "crutch"—except those aids to which we are now thoroughly accustomed—reduces the credit due. In Plato's *Phaedus,* Thamus, the king, attacks the invention of the alphabet on similar grounds! He is afraid "it will produce forgetfulness in the minds of those who learn to use it, because they will not practice their memories. . . ." In other words, he holds it more admirable to remember than to use a memorandum. He also objects that pupils "will read many things without instruction . . . [and] will therefore seem to know many things when they are for the most part ignorant." In the same vein we are today sometimes contemptuous of book learning but, as educators, we can scarcely afford to adopt this view without reservation.

By admiring the student for knowledge and blaming him for ignorance, we escape some of the responsibility of teaching him. We resist any analysis of the educational process which threatens the notion of inner wisdom or questions the contention that the fault of ignorance lies with the student. More powerful techniques which bring about the same changes in behavior by manipulating *external* variables are decried as brainwashing or thought control. We are quite unprepared to judge *effective* educational measures. As long as only a few pupils learn much of what is taught, we do not worry about uniformity or regimentation. We do not fear the feeble technique; but we should view with dismay a system under which every student learned everything listed in a syllabus—although such a condition is far from unthinkable. Similarly, we do not fear a system which is so defective that the student must *work* for an education; but we are loath to give credit for anything learned without effort—although this could well be taken as an ideal result—and we flatly refuse to give credit if the student already knows what a school teaches.

A world in which people are wise and good without trying, without "having to be," without "choosing to be," could conceivably be a far better world for everyone. In such a world we should not have to "give anyone credit"—we should not need to admire anyone—for being wise and good. From our present point of view we cannot believe that such a world would be admirable. We do not even permit ourselves to imagine what it would be like.

Government

Government has always been the special field of aversive control. The state is frequently defined in terms of the power to punish, and jurisprudence leans heavily upon the associated notion of personal responsibility. Yet it is becoming increasingly difficult to reconcile current practice and theory with these earlier views. In criminology, for example, there is a strong tendency to drop the notion of responsibility in favor of some such alternative as capacity or controllability. But no matter how strongly the facts, or even practical expedience, support such a change, it is difficult to make the change in a legal system designed on a different plan. When governments resort to other techniques (for example, positive reinforcement), the concept of responsibility is no longer relevant and the theory of government is no longer applicable.

The conflict is illustrated by two decisions of the Supreme Court in the 1930's which dealt with, and disagreed on, the definition of control or coorcion (4, p. 233). The Agricultural Adjustment Act proposed that the Secretary of Agriculture make "rental or benefit payments" to those farmers who agreed to reduce production. The government agreed that the Act would be unconstitutional if the farmer had been *compelled* to reduce production but was not, since he was merely *invited* to do so. Justice Roberts (4) expressed the contrary majority view of the court that "The power to confer or withhold unlimited benefits is the power to coerce or destroy." This recognition of positive reinforcement was withdrawn a few years later in another case in which Justice Cardozo (4, p. 244) wrote "To hold that motive or temptation is equivalent to coercion is to plunge the law in endless difficulties." We may agree with him, without implying that the proposition is therefore wrong. Sooner or later the law must be prepared to deal with all possible techniques of governmental control.

The uneasiness with which we view government (in the broadest possible sense) when it does not use punishment is shown by the reception of my utopian novel, *Walden Two* (4a). This was essentially a proposal to apply a behavioral technology to the construction of a workable, effective, and productive pattern of government. It was greeted with wrathful violence. *Life* magazine called it "a travesty on the good life," and "a menace . . . a triumph of mortmain or the dead hand not envisaged since the days of Sparta . . . a slur upon a name, a corruption of an impulse." Joseph Wood Krutch devoted a substantial part of his book, *The Measure of Man* (5), to attacking my views and those of the protagonist, Frazier, in the same vein, and Morris Viteles has recently criticized the book in a similar manner in *Science* (6). Perhaps the reaction is best expressed in a quotation from *The Quest for Utopia* by Negley and Patrick (7):

"Halfway through this contemporary utopia, the reader may feel sure, as we did, that this is a beautifully ironic satire on what has been called 'behavioral engineering.' The longer one stays in this better world of the psychologist, however, the plainer it becomes that the inspiration is not satiric, but messianic. This is indeed the behaviorally engineered society, and while it was to be expected that sooner or later the principle of psychological conditioning would be made the basis of a serious construction of utopia —Brown anticipated it in *Limanora*—yet not even the effective satire of Huxley is adequate preparation for the shocking horror of the idea when positively presented. Of all the dictatorships espoused by utopists, this is the most profound, and incipient dictators might well find in this utopia a guidebook of political practice."

One would scarcely guess that the authors are talking about a world in which there is food, clothing, and shelter for all, where everyone chooses his own work and works on the average only 4 hours a day, where music and the arts flourish, where personal relationships develop under the most favorable circumstances, where education prepares every child for the social and intellectual life which lies before him, where—in short—people are truly happy, secure, productive, creative, and forward-looking. What is wrong with it? Only one thing: someone "planned it that way." If these critics had come upon a society in some remote corner of the world which boasted similar advantages, they would undoubtedly have hailed it as providing a pattern we all might well follow—provided that it was clearly the result of a natural process of cultural evolution. Any evidence that intelligence had been used in arriving at this version of the good life would, in their eyes, be a serious flaw. No matter if the planner of *Walden Two* diverts none of the proceeds of the community to his own use, no matter if he has no current control or is, indeed, unknown to most of the other members of the community (he planned that, too), somewhere back of it all he occupies the position of prime mover. And this, to the child of the democratic tradition, spoils it all.

The dangers inherent in the control of human behavior are very real. The possibility of the misuse of scientific knowledge must always be faced. We cannot escape by denying the power of a science of behavior or arresting its development. It is no help to cling to familiar philosophies of human behavior simply because they are more reassuring. As I have pointed out elsewhere (8), the new techniques emerging from a science of behavior must be subject to the explicit countercontrol which has already been applied to earlier and cruder forms. Brute force and deception, for example, are now fairly generally suppressed by ethical practices and by explicit governmental and religious agencies. A similar countercontrol of scientific knowledge in the interests of the group is a feasible and promising possibility. Although we cannot say how devious the course of its evolution may be, a cultural pattern of control and countercontrol will presumably emerge which will be most widely supported because it

is most widely reinforcing.

If we cannot foresee all the details of this (as we obviously cannot), it is important to remember that this is true of the critics of science as well. The dire consequences of new techniques of control, the hidden menace in original cultural designs—these need some proof. It is only another example of my present point that the need for proof is so often overlooked. Man has got himself into some pretty fixes, and it is easy to believe that he will do so again. But there is a more optimisitic possibility. The slow growth of the methods of science, now for the first time being applied to human affairs, *may* mean a new and exciting phase of human life to which historical analogies will not apply and in which earlier political slogans will not be appropriate. If we are to use the knowledge that a science of behavior is now making available with any hope of success, we must look at human nature as it is brought into focus through the methods of science rather than as it has been presented to us in a series of historical accidents.

If the advent of a powerful science of behavior causes trouble, it will not be because science itself is inimical to human welfare but because older conceptions have not yielded easily or gracefully. We expect resistance to new techniques of control from those who have heavy investments in the old, but we have no reason to help them preserve a series of principles that are not ends in themselves but rather outmoded means to an end. What is needed is a new conception of human behavior which is compatible with the implications of a scientific analysis. All men control and are controlled. The question of government in the broadest possible sense is not how freedom is to be preserved but what kinds of control are to be used and to what ends. Control must be analyzed and considered in its proper proportions. No one, I am sure, wishes to develop new master-slave relationships or bend the will of the people to despotic rulers in new ways. These are patterns of control appropriate to a world without science. They may well be the first to go when the experimental analysis of behavior comes into its own in the design of cultural practices.

II [Rogers]

There are, I believe, a number of

matters in connection with this important topic on which the authors of this article, and probably a large majority of psychologists, are in agreement. These matters then are not issues as far as we are concerned, and I should like to mention them briefly in order to put them to one side.

Points of Agreement

I am sure we agree that men—as individuals and as societies—have always endeavored to understand, predict, influence, and control human behavior—their own behavior and that of others.

I believe we agree that the behavioral sciences are making and will continue to make increasingly rapid progress in the understanding of behavior, and that as a consequence the capacity to predict and to control behavior is developing with equal rapidity.

I believe we agree that to deny these advances, or to claim that man's behavior cannot be a field of science, is unrealistic. Even though this is not an issue for us, we should recognize that many intelligent men still hold strongly to the view that the actions of men are free in some sense such that scientific knowledge of man's behavior is impossible. Thus Reinhold Niebuhr, the noted theologian, heaps scorn on the concept of psychology as a science of man's behavior and even says, "In any event, no scientific investigation of past behavior can become the basis of predictions of future behavior" (9). So, while this is not an issue for psychologists, we should at least notice in passing that it is an issue for many people.

I believe we are in agreement that the tremendous potential power of a science which permits the prediction and control of behavior may be misused, and that the possibility of such misuse constitutes a serious threat.

Consequently Skinner and I are in agreement that the whole question of the scientific control of human behavior is a matter with which psychologists and the general public should concern themselves. As Robert Oppenheimer told the American Psychological Association last year (10) the problems that psychologists will pose for society by their growing ability to control behavior will be much more grave than the problems posed by the ability of physicists to control the reactions of matter. I am not sure whether psychologists generally recognize this. My impression is that by and large they hold a laissez-faire atti-

tude. Obviously Skinner and I do not hold this laissez-faire view, or we would not have written this article.

Points at Issue

With these several points of basic and important agreement, are there then any issues that remain on which there are differences? I believe there are. They can be stated very briefly: Who will be controlled? Who will exercise control? What type of control will be exercised? Most important of all, toward what end or what purpose, or in the pursuit of what value, will control be exercised?

It is on questions of this sort that there exist ambiguities, misunderstandings, and probably deep differences. These differences exist among psychologists, among members of the general public in this country, and among various world cultures. Without any hope of achieving a final resolution of these questions, we can, I believe, put these issues in clearer form.

Some Meanings

To avoid ambiguity and faulty communication, I would like to clarify the meanings of some of the terms we are using.

Behavioral science is a term that might be defined from several angles but in the context of this discussion it refers primarily to knowledge that the existence of certain describable conditions in the human being and/or in his environment is followed by certain describable consequences in his actions.

Prediction means the prior identification of behaviors which then occur. Because it is important in some things I wish to say later, I would point out that one may predict a highly specific behavior, such as an eye blink, or one may predict a class of behaviors. One might correctly predict "avoidant behavior," for example, without being able to specify whether the individual will run away or simply close his eyes.

The word *control* is a very slippery one, which can be used with any one of several meanings. I would like to specify three that seem most important for our present purposes. *Control* may mean: (i) The setting of conditions by B for A, A having no voice in the matter, such that certain predictable behaviors then occur in A. I refer to this as external control. (ii) The setting of conditions by B for A, A giving some degree of consent to these conditions, such

that certain predictable behaviors then occur in A. I refer to this as the influence of B on A. (iii) The setting of conditions by A such that certain predictable behaviors then occur in himself. I refer to this as internal control. It will be noted that Skinner lumps together the first two meanings, external control and influence, under the concept of control. I find this confusing.

Usual Concept of Control of Human Behavior

With the underbrush thus cleared away (I hope), let us review very briefly the various elements that are involved in the usual concept of the control of human behavior as mediated by the behavioral sciences. I am drawing here on the previous writings of Skinner, on his present statements, on the writings of others who have considered in either friendly or antagonistic fashion the meanings that would be involved in such control. I have not excluded the science fiction writers, as reported recently by Vandenburg (11), since they often show an awareness of the issues involved, even though the methods described are as yet fictional. These then are the elements that seem common to these different concepts of the application of science to human behavior.

1) There must first be some sort of decision about goals. Usually desirable goals are assumed, but sometimes, as in George Orwell's book *1984*, the goal that is selected is an aggrandizement of individual power with which most of us would disagree. In a recent paper Skinner suggests that one possible set of goals to be assigned to the behavioral technology is this: "Let men be happy, informed, skillful, well-behaved and productive" (12). In the first draft of his part of this article, which he was kind enough to show me, he did not mention such definite goals as these, but desired "improved" educational practices, "wiser" use of knowledge in government, and the like. In the final version of his article he avoids even these value-laden terms, and his implicit goal is the very general one that scientific control of behavior is desirable, because it would perhaps bring "a far better world for everyone."

Thus the first step in thinking about the control of human behavior is the choice of goals, whether specific or general. It is necessary to come to terms in some way with the issue, "For what purpose?"

2) A second element is that, whether the end selected is highly specific or is a very general one such as wanting "a better world," we proceed by the methods of science to discover the means to these ends. We continue through further experimentation and investigation to discover more effective means. The method of science is self-correcting in thus arriving at increasingly effective ways of achieving the purpose we have in mind.

3) The third aspect of such control is that as the conditions or methods are discovered by which to reach the goal, some person or some group establishes these conditions and uses these methods, having in one way or another obtained the power to do so.

4) The fourth element is the exposure of individuals to the prescribed conditions, and this leads, with a high degree of probability, to behavior which is in line with the goals desired. Individuals are now happy, if that has been the goal, or well-behaved, or submissive, or whatever it has been decided to make them.

5) The fifth element is that if the process I have described is put in motion then there is a continuing social organization which will continue to produce the types of behavior that have been valued.

Some Flaws

Are there any flaws in this way of viewing the control of human behavior? I believe there are. In fact the only element in this description with which I find myself in agreement is the second. It seems to me quite incontrovertibly true that the scientific method is an excellent way to discover the means by which to achieve our goals. Beyond that, I feel many sharp differences, which I will try to spell out.

I believe that in Skinner's presentation here and in his previous writings, there is a serious underestimation of the problem of power. To hope that the power which is being made available by the behavioral sciences will be exercised by the scientists, or by a benevolent group, seems to me a hope little supported by either recent or distant history. It seems far more likely that behavioral scientists, holding their present attitudes, will be in the position of the German rocket scientists specializing in guided missiles. First they worked devotedly for Hitler to destroy the U.S.S.R. and the United States. Now, depending on who captured them, they work de-votedly for the U.S.S.R. in the interest of destroying the United States, or devotedly for the United States in the interest of destroying the U.S.S.R. If behavioral scientists are concerned solely with advancing their science, it seems most probable that they will serve the purposes of whatever individual or group has the power.

But the major flaw I see in this review of what is involved in the scientific control of human behavior is the denial, misunderstanding, or gross underestimation of the place of ends, goals or values in their relationship to science. This error (as it seems to me) has so many implications that I would like to devote some space to it.

Ends and Values in Relation to Science

In sharp contradiction to some views that have been advanced, I would like to propose a two-pronged thesis: (i) In any scientific endeavor—whether "pure" or applied science—there is a prior subjective choice of the purpose or value which that scientific work is perceived as serving. (ii) This subjective value choice which brings the scientific endeavor into being must always lie outside of that endeavor and can never become a part of the science involved in that endeavor.

Let me illustrate the first point from Skinner himself. It is clear that in his earlier writing (12) it is recognized that a prior value choice is necessary, and it is specified as the goal that men are to become happy, well-behaved, productive, and so on. I am pleased that Skinner has retreated from the goals he then chose, because to me they seem to be stultifying values. I can only feel that he was choosing these goals for others, not for himself. I would hate to see Skinner become "well-behaved," as that term would be defined for him by behavioral scientists. His recent article in the *American Psychologist* (13) shows that he certainly does not want to be "productive" as that value is defined by most psychologists. And the most awful fate I can imagine for him would be to have him constantly "happy." It is the fact that he is very unhappy about many things which makes me prize him.

In the first draft of his part of this article, he also included such prior value choices, saying for example, "We must decide how we are to use the knowledge which a science of human behavior is now making available." Now he has dropped all mention of such choices, and if I understand him correctly, he believes that science can proceed without them. He has suggested this view in another recent paper, stating that "We must continue to experiment in cultural design . . . testing the consequences as we go. Eventually the practices which make for the greatest biological and psychological strength of the group will presumably survive" (8, p. 549).

I would point out, however, that to choose to experiment is a value choice. Even to move in the direction of perfectly random experimentation is a value choice. To test the consequences of an experiment is possible only if we have first made a subjective choice of a criterion value. And implicit in his statement is a valuing of biological and psychological strength. So even when trying to avoid such choice, it seems inescapable that a prior subjective value choice is necessary for any scientific endeavor, or for any application of scientific knowledge.

I wish to make it clear that I am not saying that values cannot be included as a subject of science. It is not true that science deals only with certain classes of "facts" and that these classes do not include values. It is a bit more complex than that, as a simple illustration or two may make clear.

If I value knowledge of the "three R's" as a goal of education, the methods of science can give me increasingly accurate information on how this goal may be achieved. If I value problem-solving ability as a goal of education, the scientific method can give me the same kind of help.

Now, if I wish to determine whether problem-solving ability is "better" than knowledge of the three R's, then scientific method can also study those two values but *only*—and this is very important—in terms of some other value which I have subjectively chosen. I may value college success. Then I can determine whether problem-solving ability or knowledge of the three R's is most closely associated with that value. I may value personal integration or vocational success or responsible citizenship. I can determine whether problem-solving ability or knowledge of the three R's is "better" for achieving any one of these values. But the value or purpose that gives meaning to a particular scientific endeavor must always lie outside of that endeavor.

Although our concern in this

symposium is largely with applied science, what I have been saying seems equally true of so-called "pure" science. In pure science the usual prior subjective value choice is the discovery of truth. But this is a subjective choice, and science can never say whether it is the best choice, save in the light of some other value. Geneticists in the U.S.S.R., for example, had to make a subjective choice of whether it was better to pursue truth or to discover facts which upheld a governmental dogma. Which choice is "better"? We could make a scientific investigation of those alternatives but only in the light of some other subjectively chosen value. If, for example, we value the survival of a culture, then we could begin to investigate with the methods of science the question of whether pursuit of truth or support of governmental dogma is most closely associated with cultural survival.

My point then is that any endeavor in science, pure or applied, is carried on in the pursuit of a purpose or value that is subjectively chosen by persons. It is important that this choice be made explicit, since the particular value which is being sought can never be tested or evaluated, confirmed or denied, by the scientific endeavor to which it gives birth. The initial purpose or value always and necessarily lies outside the scope of the scientific effort which it sets in motion.

Among other things this means that if we choose some particular goal or series of goals for human beings and then set out on a large scale to control human behavior to the end of achieving those goals, we are locked in the rigidity of our initial choice, because such a scientific endeavor can never transcend itself to select new goals. Only subjective human persons can do that. Thus if we chose as our goal the state of happiness for human beings (a goal deservedly ridiculed by Aldous Huxley in *Brave New World*), and if we involved all of society in a successful scientific program by which people became happy, we would be locked in a colossal rigidity in which no one would be free to question this goal, because our scientific operations could not transcend themselves to question their guiding purposes. And without laboring this point, I would remark that colossal rigidity, whether in dinosaurs or dictatorships, has a very poor record of evolutionary survival.

If, however, a part of our scheme is to set free some "planners" who do not have to be happy, who are not controlled, and who are therefore free to choose other values, this has several meanings. It means that the purpose we have chosen as our goal is not a sufficient and a satisfying one for human beings but must be supplemented. It also means that if it is necessary to set up an elite group which is free, then this shows all too clearly that the great majority are only the slaves—no matter by what high-sounding name we call them—of those who select the goals.

Perhaps, however, the thought is that a continuing scientific endeavor will evolve its own goals; that the initial findings will alter the directions, and subsequent findings will alter them still further, and that science somehow develops its own purpose. Although he does not clearly say so, this appears to be the pattern Skinner has in mind. It is surely a reasonable description, but it overlooks one element in this continuing development, which is that subjective personal choice enters in at every point at which the direction changes. The findings of a science, the results of an experiment, do not and never can tell us what next scientific purpose to pursue. Even in the purest of science, the scientist must decide what the findings mean and must subjectively choose what next step will be most profitable in the pursuit of his purpose. And if we are speaking of the application of scientific knowledge, then it is distressingly clear that the increasing scientific knowledge of the structure of the atom carries with it no necessary choice as to the purpose to which this knowledge will be put. This is a subjective personal choice which must be made by many individuals.

Thus I return to the proposition with which I began this section of my remarks—and which I now repeat in different words. Science has its meaning as the objective pursuit of a purpose which has been subjectively chosen by a person or persons. This purpose or value can never be investigated by the particular scientific experiment or investigation to which it has given birth and meaning. Consequently, any discussion of the control of human beings by the behavioral sciences must first and most deeply concern itself with the subjectively chosen purposes which such an application

of science is intended to implement.

Is the Situation Hopeless?

The thoughtful reader may recognize that, although my remarks up to this point have introduced some modifications in the conception of the processes by which human behavior will be controlled, these remarks may have made such control seem, if anything, even more inevitable. We might sum it up this way: Behavioral science is clearly moving forward; the increasing power for control which it gives will be held by someone or some group; such an individual or group will surely choose the values or goals to be achieved; and most of us will then be increasingly controlled by means so subtle that we will not even be aware of them as controls. Thus, whether a council of wise psychologists (if this is not a contradiction in terms), or a Stalin, or a Big Brother has the power, and whether the goal is happiness, or productivity, or resolution of the Oedipus complex, or submission, or love of Big Brother, we will inevitably find ourselves moving toward the chosen goal and probably thinking that we ourselves desire it. Thus, if this line of reasoning is correct, it appears that some form of *Walden Two* or of *1984* (and at a deep philosophic level they seem indistinguishable) is coming. The fact that it would surely arrive piecemeal, rather than all at once, does not greatly change the fundamental issues. In any event, as Skinner has indicated in his writings, we would then look back upon the concepts of human freedom, the capacity for choice, the responsibility for choice, and the worth of the human individual as historical curiosities which once existed by cultural accident as values in a pre-scientific civilization.

I believe that any person observant of trends must regard something like the foregoing sequence as a real possibility. It is not simply a fantasy. Something of that sort may even be the most likely future. But is it an inevitable future? I want to devote the remainder of my remarks to an alternative possibility.

Alternative Set of Values

Suppose we start with a set of ends, values, purposes, quite different from the type of goals we have been considering. Suppose we do this quite openly, setting them forth as a possible value choice to be accepted or rejected. Suppose we select a set of values that focuses on fluid elements of process rather than static attributes. We might then value: man as a process of becoming, as a process of achieving worth and dignity through the development of his potentialities; the individual human being as a self-actualizing process, moving on to more challenging and enriching experiences; the process by which the individual creatively adapts to an ever-new and changing world; the process by which knowledge transcends itself, as, for example, the theory of relativity transcended Newtonian physics, itself to be transcended in some future day by a new perception.

If we select values such as these we turn to our science and technology of behavior with a very different set of questions. We will want to know such things as these: Can science aid in the discovery of new modes of richly rewarding living? more meaningful and satisfying modes of interpersonal relationships? Can science inform us on how the human race can become a more intelligent participant in its own evolution—its physical, psychological and social evolution? Can science inform us on ways of releasing the creative capacity of individuals, which seem so necessary if we are to survive in this fantastically expanding atomic age? Oppenheimer has pointed out (14) that knowledge, which used to double in millennia or centuries, now doubles in a generation or a decade. It appears that we must discover the utmost in release of creativity if we are to be able to adapt effectively. In short, can science discover the methods by which man can most readily become a continually developing and self-transcending process, in his behavior, his thinking, his knowledge? Can science predict and release an essentially "unpredictable" freedom?

It is one of the virtues of science as a method that it is as able to advance and implement goals and purposes of this sort as it is to serve static values, such as states of being well-informed, happy, obedient. Indeed we have some evidence of this.

Small Example

I will perhaps be forgiven if I document some of the possibilities along this line by turning to psychotherapy, the field I know best.

Psychotherapy, as Meerloo (15) and others have pointed out, can be one of the most subtle tools for the control of A by B. The therapist can subtly mold individuals in imitation of himself. He can cause an individual to become a submissive and conforming being. When certain therapeutic principles are used in extreme fashion, we call it brainwashing, an instance of the disintegration of the personality and a reformulation of the person along lines desired by the controlling individual. So the principles of therapy can be used as an effective means of external control of human personality and behavior. Can psychotherapy be anything else?

Here I find the developments going on in client-centered psychotherapy (16) an exciting hint of what a behavioral science can do in achieving the kinds of values I have stated. Quite aside from being a somewhat new orientation in psychotherapy, this development has important implications regarding the relation of a behavioral science to the control of human behavior. Let me describe our experience as it relates to the issues of this discussion.

In client-centered therapy, we are deeply engaged in the prediction and influencing of behavior, or even the control of behavior. As therapists, we institute certain attitudinal conditions, and the client has relatively little voice in the establishment of these conditions. We predict that if these conditions are instituted, certain behavioral consequences will ensue in the client. Up to this point this is largely external control, no different from what Skinner has described, and no different from what I have discussed in the preceding sections of this article. But here any similarity ceases.

The conditions we have chosen to establish predict such behavioral consequences as these: that the client will become self-directing, less rigid, more open to the evidence of his senses, better organized and integrated, more similar to the ideal which he has chosen for himself. In other words, we have established by external control conditions which we predict will be followed by internal control by the individual, in pursuit of internally chosen goals. We have set the conditions which predict various classes of behaviors—self-directing behaviors, sensitivity to realities within and without, flexible adaptiveness—which are by their very nature unpredictable in their specifics. Our recent research (17) indicates that our predictions are to a significant degree corroborated, and our commitment to the scientific method causes us to believe that more effective means of achieving these goals may be realized.

Research exists in other fields—industry, education, group dynamics—which seems to support our own findings. I believe it may be conservatively stated that scientific progress has been made in identifying those conditions in an interpersonal relationship which, if they exist in B, are followed in A by greater maturity in behavior, less dependence on others, an increase in expressiveness as a person, an increase in variability, flexibility and effectiveness of adaptation, an increase in self-responsibility and self-direction. And, quite in contrast to the concern expressed by some, we do not find that the creatively adaptive behavior which results from such self-directed variability of expression is a "happy accident" which occurs in "chaos." Rather, the individual who is open to his experience, and self-directing, is harmonious not chaotic, ingenious rather than random, as he orders his responses imaginatively toward the achievement of his own purposes. His creative actions are no more a "happy accident" than was Einstein's development of the theory of relativity.

Thus we find ourselves in fundamental agreement with John Dewey's statement: "Science has made its way by releasing, not by suppressing, the elements of variation, of invention and innovation, of novel creation in individuals" (18). Progress in personal life and in group living is, we believe, made in the same way.

Possible Concept of the Control of Human Behavior

It is quite clear that the point of view I am expressing is in sharp contrast to the usual conception of the relationship of the behavioral sciences to the control of human behavior. In order to make this contrast even more blunt, I will state this possibility in paragraphs parallel to those used before.

1) It is possible for us to choose to value man as a self-actualizing process of becoming; to value creativity, and the process by which knowledge becomes self-transcending.

2) We can proceed, by the methods of science, to discover the conditions which necessarily precede these processes and, through continuing experimentation, to discover better means of achieving these purposes.

3) It is possible for individuals or groups to set these conditions, with a minimum of power or control. According to present knowledge, the only authority necessary is the authority to establish certain qualities of interpersonal relationship.

4) Exposed to these conditions, present knowledge suggests that individuals become more self-responsible, make progress in self-actualization, become more flexible, and become more creatively adaptive.

5) Thus such an initial choice would inaugurate the beginnings of a social system or subsystem in which values, knowledge, adaptive skills, and even the concept of science would be continually changing and self-transcending. The emphasis would be upon man as a process of becoming.

I believe it is clear that such a view as I have been describing does not lead to any definable utopia. It would be impossible to predict its final outcome. It involves a step-by-step development, based on a continuing subjective choice of purposes, which are implemented by the behavioral sciences. It is in the direction of the "open society," as that term has been defined by Popper (*19*), where individuals carry responsibility for personal decisions. It is at the opposite pole from his concept of the closed society, of which *Walden Two* would be an example.

I trust it is also evident that the whole emphasis is on process, not on end-states of being. I am suggesting that it is by choosing to value certain qualitative elements of the process of becoming that we can find a pathway toward the open society.

The Choice

It is my hope that we have helped to clarify the range of choice which will lie before us and our children in regard to the behavioral sciences. We can choose to use our growing knowledge to enslave people in ways never dreamed of before, depersonalizing them, controlling them by means so carefully selected that they will perhaps never be aware of their loss of personhood. We can choose to utilize our scientific knowledge to make men happy, well-behaved, and productive, as Skinner earlier suggested. Or we can insure that each person learns all the syllabus which we select and set before him, as Skinner now suggests. Or at the other end of the spectrum of choice we can

choose to use the behavioral sciences in ways which will free, not control; which will bring about constructive variability, not conformity; which will develop creativity, not contentment; which will facilitate each person in his self-directed process of becoming; which will aid individuals, groups, and even the concept of science to become self-transcending in freshly adaptive ways of meeting life and its problems. The choice is up to us, and, the human race being what it is, we are likely to stumble about, making at times some nearly disastrous value choices and at other times highly constructive ones.

I am aware that to some, this setting forth of a choice is unrealistic, because a choice of values is regarded as not possible. Skinner has stated: "Man's vaunted creative powers . . . his capacity to choose and our right to hold him responsible for his choice—none of these is conspicuous in this new self-portrait (provided by science). Man, we once believed, was free to express himself in art, music, and literature, to inquire into nature, to seek salvation in his own way. He could initiate action and make spontaneous and capricious changes of course. . . . But science insists that action is initiated by forces, impinging upon the individual, and that caprice is only another name for behavior for which we have not yet found a cause" (*12*, pp 52–53).

I can understand this point of view, but I believe that it avoids looking at the great paradox of behavioral science. Behavior, when it is examined scientifically, is surely best understood as determined by prior causation. This is one great fact of science. But responsible personal choice, which is the most essential element in being a person, which is the core experience in psychotherapy, which exists prior to any scientific endeavor, is an equally prominent fact in our lives. To deny the experience of responsible choice is, to me, as restricted a view as to deny the possibility of a behavioral science. That these two important elements of our experience appear to be in contradiction has perhaps the same significance as the contradiction between the wave theory and the corpuscular theory of light, both of which can be shown to be true, even though incompatible. We cannot profitably deny our subjective life, any more than we can deny the objective description of that life.

In conclusion then, it is my contention that science cannot come into being without a personal choice of the values we wish to achieve. And these values we choose to implement will forever lie outside of the science which implements them; the goals we select, the purposes we wish to follow, must always be outside of the science which achieves them. To me this has the encouraging meaning that the human person, with his capacity of subjective choice, can and will always exist, separate from and prior to any of his scientific undertakings. Unless as individuals and groups we choose to relinquish our capacity of subjective choice, we will always remain persons, not simply pawns of a self-created science.

III [Skinner]

I cannot quite agree that the practice of science *requires* a prior decision about goals or a prior choice of values. The metallurgist can study the properties of steel and the engineer can design a bridge without raising the question of whether a bridge is to be built. But such questions are certainly frequently raised and tentatively answered. Rogers wants to call the answers "subjective expression suggests that we have had to abandon more rigorous scientific practices in order to talk about our own behavior. In the experimental analysis of other organisms I would use other terms, and I shall try to do so here. Any list of values is a list of reinforcers—conditioned or otherwise. We are so constituted that under certain circumstances food, water, sexual contact, and so on, will make any behavior which produces them more likely to occur again. Other things may acquire this power. We do not need to say that an organism chooses to eat rather than to starve. If you answer that it is a very different thing when a man chooses to starve, I am only too happy to agree. If it were not so, we should have cleared up the question of choice long ago. An organism can be reinforced by—can be made to "choose"—almost any given state of affairs.

Rogers is concerned with choices that involve multiple and usually conflicting consequences. I have dealt with some of these elsewhere (*20*) in an analysis of self-control. Shall I eat these delicious strawberries today if I will then suffer an annoying rash to-morrow? The decision I am to make used to be assigned to the province of ethics. But we are now studying similar combinations of positive and negative consequences, as well as collateral conditions which affect the result, in the laboratory. Even a pigeon can be taught some measure of self-control! And this work helps us to understand the operation of certain formulas—among them value judgments—which folk-wisdom, religion, and psychotherapy have advanced in the interests of self-discipline. The observable effect of any statement of value is to alter the relative effectiveness of reinforcers. We may no longer enjoy the strawberries for thinking about the rash. If rashes are made sufficiently shameful, illegal, sinful, maladjusted, or unwise, we may glow with satisfaction as we push the strawberries aside in a grandiose avoidance response which would bring a smile to the lips of Murray Sidman.

People behave in ways which, as we say, conform to ethical, governmental, or religious patterns because they are reinforced for doing so. The resulting behavior may have far-reaching consequences for the survival of the pattern to which it conforms. And whether we like it or not, survival is the ultimate criterion. This is where, it seems to me, science can help—not in choosing a goal, but in enabling us to predict the survival value of cultural practices. Man has too long tried to get the kind of world he wants by glorifying some brand of immediate reinforcement. As science points up more and more of the remoter consequences, he may begin to work to strengthen behavior, not in a slavish devotion to a chosen value, but with respect to the ultimate survival of mankind. Do not ask me why I want mankind to survive. I can tell you why only in the sense in which the physiologist can tell you why I want to breathe. Once the relation between a given step and the survival of my group has been pointed out, I will take that step. And it is the business of science to point out just such relations.

The values I have occasionally recommended (and Rogers has not led me to recant) are transitional. Other things being equal, I am betting on the group whose practices make for healthy, happy, secure, productive, and creative people. And I insist that the values recommended by Rogers are transitional, too, for I can ask him

the same kind of question. Man as a process of becoming—*what*? Self-actualization—for what? Inner control is no more a goal than external.

What Rogers seems to me to be proposing, both here and elsewhere (*1*), is this: Let us use our increasing power of control to create individuals who will not need and perhaps will no longer respond to control. Let us solve the problem of our power by renouncing it. At first blush this seems as implausible as a benevolent despot. Yet power has occasionally been foresworn. A nation has burned its Reichstag, rich men have given away their wealth, beautiful women have become ugly hermits in the desert, and psychotherapists have become nondirective. When this happens, I look to other possible reinforcements for a plausible explanation. A people relinquish democratic power when a tyrant promises them the earth. Rich men give away wealth to escape the accusing finger of their fellowmen. A woman destroys her beauty in the hope of salvation. And a psychotherapist relinquishes control because he can thus help his client more effectively.

The solution that Rogers is suggesting is thus understandable. But is he correctly interpreting the result? What evidence is there that a client ever becomes truly *self*-directing? What evidence is there that he ever makes a truly *inner* choice of ideal or goal? Even though the therapist does not do the choosing, even though he encourages "self-actualization" —he is not out of control as long as he holds himself ready to step in when occasion demands— when, for example, the client chooses the goal of becoming a more accomplished liar or murdering his boss. But supposing the therapist does withdraw completely or is no longer necessary— what about all the other forces acting upon the client? Is the self-chosen goal independent of his early ethical and religious training? of the folk-wisdom of his group? of the opinions and attitudes of others who are important to him? Surely not. The therapeutic situation is only a small part of the world of the client. From the therapist's point of view it may appear to be possible to relinquish control. But the control passes, not to a "self," but to forces in other parts of the client's world. The solution of the therapist's problem of power cannot be *our* solution, for we must consider *all*

the forces acting upon the individual.

The child who must be prodded and nagged is something less than a fully developed human being. We want to see him hurrying to his appointment, not because each step is taken in response to verbal reminders from his mother, but because certain temporal contingencies, in which dawdling has been punished and hurrying reinforced, have worked a change in his behavior. Call this a state of better organization, a greater sensitivity to reality, or what you will. The plain fact is that the child passes from a temporary verbal control exercised by his parents to control by certain inexorable features of the environment. I should suppose that something of the same sort happens in successful psychotherapy. Rogers seems to me to be saying this: Let us put an end, as quickly as possible, to any pattern of master-and-slave, to any direct obedience to command, to the submissive following of suggestions. Let the individual be free to adjust himself to more rewarding features of the world about him. In the end, let his teachers and counselors "wither away," like the Marxist state. I not only agree with this as a useful ideal, I have constructed a fanciful world to demonstrate its advantages. It saddens me to hear Rogers say that "at a deep philosophic level" *Walden Two* and George Orwell's *1984* "seem indistinguishable." They could scarcely be more unlike—at any level. The book *1984* is a picture of immediate aversive control for vicious selfish purposes. The founder of *Walden Two*, on the other hand, has built a community in which neither he nor any other person exerts any *current* control. His achievement lay in his original *plan*, and when he boasts of this ("It is enough to satisfy the thirstiest tyrant") we do not fear him but only pity him for his weakness.

Another critic of *Walden Two*, Andrew Hacker (*21*), has discussed this point in considering the bearing of mass conditioning upon the liberal notion of autonomous man. In drawing certain parallels between the Grand Inquisition passage in Dostoevsky's *Brothers Karamazov*, Huxley's *Brave New World*, and *Walden Two*, he attempts to set up a distinction to be drawn in any society between conditioners and conditioned. He assumes that "the conditioner can be said to be autonomous in the traditional liberal sense." But then he notes: "Of course the conditioner has been conditioned. But he has not been conditioned by the conscious manipulation of another *person*." But how does this affect the resulting behavior? Can we not soon forget the origins of the "artificial" diamond which is identical with the real thing? Whether it is an "accidental" cultural pattern, such as is said to have produced the founder of *Walden Two,* or the engineered environment which is about to produce his successors, we are dealing with sets of conditions generating human behavior which will ultimately be measured by their contribution to the strength of the group. We look to the future, not the past, for the test of "goodness" or acceptability.

If we are worthy of our democratic heritage we shall, of course, be ready to resist any tyrannical use of science for immediate or selfish purposes. But if we value the achievements and goals of democracy we must not refuse to apply science to the design and construction of cultural patterns, even though we may then find ourselves in some sense in the position of controllers. Fear of control, generalized beyond any warrant, has led to a misinterpretation of valid practices and the blind rejection of intelligent planning for a better way of life. In terms which I trust Rogers will approve, in conquering this fear we shall become more mature and better organized and shall, thus, more fully actualize ourselves as human beings.

REFERENCES AND NOTES

1. C. R. Rogers, *Teachers College Record* 57, 316 (1956).
2. A. Hacker, *Antioch Rev.* 14, 195 (1954).
3. C. Coleman, *Bull. Am. Assoc. Univ. Professors* 39, 457 (1953).
4. P. A. Freund *et al., Constitutional Law: Cases and Other Problems,* vol. 1 (Little, Brown, Boston, 1954).
4a. B. F. Skinner, *Walden Two* (Macmillan, New York, 1948).
5. J. W. Krutch, *The Measure of Man* (Bobbs-Merrill, Indianapolis, 1953).
6. M. Viteles, *Science* 122, 1167 (1955).
7. G. Negley and J. M. Patrick, *The Quest for Utopia* (Schuman, New York, 1952).
8. B. F. Skinner, *Trans. N.Y. Acad. Sci.* 17, 547 (1955).
9. R. Niebuhr, *The Self and the Dramas of History* (Scribner, New York, 1955), p. 47.
10. R. Oppenheimer, *Am. Psychol.* 11, 127 (1956).
11. S. G. Vandenberg, *ibid.* 11, 339 (1956).
12. B. F. Skinner, *Am. Scholar* 25, 47 (1955–56).
13. ——, *Am. Psychol.* 11, 221 (1956).
14. R. Oppenheimer, *Roosevelt University Occasional Papers* 2 (1956).
15. J. A. M. Meerloo, *J. Nervous Mental Disease* 122, 353 (1955).
16. C. R. Rogers, *Client-Centered Therapy* (Houghton-Mifflin, Boston, 1951).
17. —— and R. Dymond, Eds., *Psychotherapy and Personality Change* (Univ. of Chicago Press, Chicago, 1954).
18. J. Ratner, Ed., *Intelligence in the Modern World: John Dewey's Philosophy* (Modern Library, New York, 1939), p. 359.
19. K. R. Popper, *The Open Society and Its Enemies* (Rutledge and Kegan Paul, London, 1945).
20. B. F. Skinner, *Science and Human Behavior* (Macmillan, New York, 1953).
21. A. Hacker, *J. Politics* 17, 590 (1955).

If the earlier promise was that knowledge would make man free, the contemporary reality seems to be that more men are manipulated without their consent for more purposes by more techniques by fewer men than at any time in history.

Harold D. Laswell
(Address to the American Psychological Association, September, 1969.)

Professor Sampson presents a dichotomy of man as mechanical and man as existential in his critique of the American society. Warning of the perils of waiting out evolution, he calls for a psychological revolution—a transformation of character which must precede political revolution. *Homo mechanicus*—the present character—is well suited to adapt to an oppressive society in a polluted environment. He is trained from birth to want to follow orders from a corporate society. As one who is controlled, *mechanicus* is likely to fill the role of the controller in the scenario envisioned by Rogers and Skinner. Existential man does not submit passively to adaptation to and oppression by external forces. He assumes, rather than surrenders, personal responsibility for his own life and therefore must act to create an external environment consistent with his internal principles. Sampson sees the existential character as one possibly hopeful outcome of a revolution in education and thinking.

1.2
Evolution Versus Revolution in Psychological Character: Mechanicus or Man?

Edward E. Sampson

I. Introduction

Our time is short, our need is great, and our task is enormous. The survival of the species known as man depends on a radical revolution in his fundamental character, a revolution in his concept of himself and of his place in life.

Some call today for a political revolution; I speak of a psychological revolution, a transformation in character that must *precede* any political revolution. For without a new conception *by* man *of* man, any political revolution will merely replace one perversion, one evil with another.

Some warn today of an ecological devastation; I speak of a far more insidious psychological devastation. Clean air to breathe and unpolluted water to drink, though vital, have little value if the species man is destroyed in the process.

Every species has its natural enemies; man's enemies are unnatural. They are his own inventions, his own constructions, his own products. They are his social institutions, his forms of government, his manner of organizing his life in efficient ways that comfort and soothe on the surface while extinguishing his human essence just beneath.

Even now as I speak, trends begun just decades ago are spiraling upwards in an escalating cycle of human exploitation, destruction, and debasement. If we await evolution to take its natural course, we shall indeed see a new psychological character evolve. But that character will not be the human species as we knew it once and as its potential could be; rather, that evolved character will be a mechanistic creature, a *homo mechanicus,* a form of life well suited to a cybernetic age. That species will not be man. That evolved character will be one who can live off poison and pollution in crowded conditions without privacy, who thinks minimally and follows orders dutifully—a *mechanicus,* not a *sapiens.* It will be as unlike man as the chimpanzee is or as Neanderthal man was.

Our hope for man requires radical action and radical transformation; we do not have the luxury of time to wait.

II. An Analogy

I wish to merge some 19th Century thought with some 21st Century science fiction. The image that emerges from this blend is of an enormous, pervading, all encompassing social organism—somewhat like a huge corporate beehive. Individual men will participate as parts of this social organism. They will have specific roles and routines to carry out—routines of work, routines of sex, routines of leisure and of play, routines of birth, of growth, of retirement, and of death. Everything will be directed by the need to keep that corporate giant alive and well. Individuals will be trained from birth to *want* to do just what the social organism insists that they do. And in this picture, man will aptly be called *mechanicus.* As though he were actually a piece of mechanical equipment, he will have given up his will and his initiative, lost his capacity to make choices, abandoned his responsibility, and denied his rationality. But man will *not* experience himself as this cog, for he will have abandoned even his imagination, and will come to see as *inevitable* everything that is and will define as *freedom* each routine and role. The transformation will be complete; and at that moment, man will have died and *mechanicus* will be alive and well and a drone in the corporate beehive.

III. Two Types of Man-in-Society

I have not based my remarks thus far on idle armchair speculation. My worries stem from real events that are taking place today, especially but not exclusively in the United States. Recently, I had the opportunity to conduct a small scale but intensive study of several young Americans. In evaluating the results of that study, I was struck by the two character types that emerged. The one, the Ameri-

can ideal of today, the emerging *mechanicus* of tomorrow, already predominates in this society. The other, by contrast, lives his shadow existence in the minority. We esteem the former while casting aside the latter. Yet, it is this latter being who embodies those qualities of character that are essential if man is to prevail.

Mechanical man has evolved slowly and dutifully in accordance with those principles of socialization that characterize a highly populated and technologically advanced setting, one in which man has become *superfluous.* He was trained to fit an efficient corporate society that cares little for people. He adjusts himself all too readily to expansionistic wars. He has learned to fear and distrust himself and others. He has adopted a consumer mentality that each day wants more quantity. He supports the principle of apathetic democracy through his membership in the esteemed silent majority.

The latter character, our modern non-hero, has not evolved, but has burst forth like a mutant strain, an alien being who grew in spite of these dehumanizing and will-destroying principles of socialization. He is a misfit: he dreads war and will not kill; he is not guided by fear and distrust to distance himself from others or to shelter himself within a protective shield of hate. His life style is nonconventional and apparently unAmerican, for he refuses to purchase more goods than anyone but a demanding little child could reasonably need. His living conflicts with the over-controlled, rationalized imperatives of technological social organization: he insists on being involved and in participating—apathy and silence are distasteful to him. A modern misfit whose character is an outline of man's potential greatness.

Let me be more specific and paint two portraits, one for the American hero, mechanical man; the other, for today's lonely and isolated misfit, but tomorrow's hope, existential man. This portrait will cover six psychological factors including (1) a concept of masculinity and femininity; (2) a view of responsibility of accountability; (3) a capacity for empathy; (4) relationships with authority and with intimates; (5) ability to experience feelings; and finally, (6) an overall orientation to life.

IV. A Portrait of Mechanicus

From out of the pioneer West our mechanical man came riding; our American ideal with his faithful

wife tagging dutifully along to the rear. He conquered everything in view—the native Indians were slaughtered in the name of progress; the mountains were carved, their peaks were breached, their majesty diminished; the wilderness was cast aside. He paved over a land and built large urban complexes in which to live out his time on earth. He defined the term masculine for himself—bold, brash, aggressive, manly—and feminine for his little woman— the petite and delicate homebody. He packaged his world neatly into sex-typed categories: men's work *vs.* women's work; men's clubs *vs.* women's clubs; men's fashions *vs.* women's fashions; men's talk *vs.* women's gossip. Those not fitting the categories were "sissies," "queers," "tomboys," "dykes."

Like so many who seek to conquer, to be conquered is likewise psychologically pleasing. This hero of ours needs to live in a hierarchy of relationships with others, in superior-subordinate, master-slave contexts. He functions best when he can be the one with power over others at one moment, while submitting to another's power over him at the next. He is at once the master and next the slave. While loudly proclaiming his independence and freedom, he thrives in hierarchy, control and dependence and grows confused and fearful when he cannot be placed somewhere into a power-and-control system.

Emotionally, our hero is insensitive and non-empathic. He has minimal control over his impulses and manifests what I call the *sorry-too-late* pattern. He never knows the strength of a rope until it breaks, nor the harm done to others until the harm is done; and then he's sorry, but it's too late. He arrives *after* the damage is done and graciously offers to help pick up the pieces. He seems incapable of exercising human forethought to guarantee that no damage will be done for which he must be sorry, but too late.

He finds it far preferable to deny his feelings than to experience them. He is neither rational or irrational, but rather is non-rational, because he is unable to use his human feelings and emotions as guideposts to action. Yet just beneath this thin veneer of non-rationality, and barely in control, there exists a seething volcano of frustration, hate, and anger, just waiting to erupt in violence with minimal provocation. We see this eruption, for example, when our modern hero gets behind the wheel of his automobile and carries out his fantasies of conquest, seeking to win on the highway what he has lost at home and work. He uses his horn and accelerator as substitutes for his oft-silenced voice, screeching out in defiance and creating a rate of death and destruction beyond relief.

He cherishes being cold, precise, and callous; he deals with others as though they were objects to be manipulated and exploited rather than people to be understood. He expects to be dealt with by them in a similarly manipulative manner. Callous and without empathy, he easily divides his work into "we" and "us" *versus* "you" and "they." He dehumanizes his relationships with people: they are pointers on a map, subjects in an experiment, patients to be treated, students to be processed, victims to be counted, but rarely persons to be known. In Martin Buber's terms, he relates to others as an *I* to an *It* rather than forming more intimate *I-Thou* bonds. And soon, he comes even to dehumanize himself, creating a world of vacuous relationships of *It-to-It*. Objects, not people, face-off for their daily encounters. As many have noted, even sex becomes mechanical and dehumanized. It was Rollo May in commenting on *Playboy* magazine, who noted how two vacuous *Its* confronted one another—the suave, uninvolved bachelor and the distant, bland and sexless centerfoldout. As May comments, *"Playboy* has . . . shifted the fig leaf from the genitals to the face."

Of all the qualities of character, one most frightening in its implications, is our mechanical man's sense of personal non-responsibility. The American ideal of today unfortunately shares much in common with the German of World War II.

In prisons, mental hospitals, and other forms called *total institutions*, one's entire life is programmed and controlled. The consequences of total institutionalization are many; but one striking outcome is the destruction of the human will that systematically takes place. The person, once active and thoughtful, is stripped of his humanity, is treated in a child-like, dependent manner, is made into a do-nothing, care-nothing, apathetic, will-less being.

What if a society itself becomes like a total institution? In such a setting, the individual comes to see himself more the pawn in someone's chess game than the origin who makes his own moves and decides his own fate. He serves when called and kills when asked, and readily blames his government, the President, his superiors, Congress, his upbringing: never once does he conceive of himself as a thinking being with choices to make and responsibilities for those choices. Rather, like the mechanical being that he has become, he views himself as a small cog in a large machine. And who could blame the cog? He is not an agent of himself. He *is* his role. And Nobody is responsible.

How often do we hear people proclaim loudly, "I *had* to do that!" and thereby seek to absolve themselves of all responsibility for their actions? And how often have we accepted their non-responsibility, granting them freedom from the charge of being morally accountable? How often have we ourselves said to our students or friends, "If only I were not a Dean, if only I were not a professor; my *role* demands things of me and I must do them." This translates roughly in Eichmann's terms into: "I am not responsible; it is *my role* that has acted; I am just taking orders, just following role-expectations." And what is worse, we believe it. We deny ourselves the very responsibility that makes man the potential being that he is. And in this denial, we affirm the reality of *mechanicus*. In my comments here, I am not denying the reality of role demands; I am emphasizing the individual's choice to obey those demands or not, and thus the individual's personal responsibility for what follows.

A final touch to this portrait of the mechanical man: he acts as though he were a *visitor* and rarely a *caretaker*. Picture a park. Our visitor arrives and passes his day there, never concerning himself with others or with the future of that park. He is just there for himself, a visitor using up facilities for his own benefit. No caretaker is he; no concern for the future of the park; no concern for others. Imagine further that his whole life on earth is spent as though he were a visitor never recognizing the fundamental interdependence of all mankind. He watches out for his own. He seeks to maximize his personal comfort. He lives for his life today and cares nought for anyone else or for tomorrow. A visitor, not a caretaker. And with the orientation and attitudes of a visitor, he exploits and destroys, undoubtedly assuming, if he cares at all, that someone else will be the caretaker; he's too busy with himself to care.

V. A Portrait of Existential Man

The portrait of existential man is difficult to paint for he is an enduring rarity on the face of the earth. Whenever and wherever he has appeared, he has been a misfit in the eyes of the majority, to be destroyed or to be ignored as some strange character with peculiar ideas. He is the man who once preached love and understanding and met death while still a youth. He is the man in the concentration camp whose every freedom was removed, who yet remained free to choose and to be responsibile while all others gave up and went quietly or became savage, inhuman beasts no better than their captors. He is the man who in German-occupied France said, "Rather death than remain silent"; who more recently in Hungary and in Czechoslovakia said, "Rather death than not protest"; who in today's Greece of the Colonels, says, "Rather death than . . ."; and in the United States, says, "Rather death than not fight injustice; Hell no, I won't go!" He is the man whose every action is a declaration of his independence, a statement that recognizes his essential human quality; to have choice and to be responsible even when all seems lost and at an end.

On each of the six dimensions by which I have characterized mechanical man, the existential man falls at the opposite extreme. He is not trapped by narrow or rigid concepts of masculine and feminine, but rather grants to each person his chance to find and express his own potentials. For him, there is not men's work and women's work: there is work. There are not men's fashions and women's fashions: there are fashions to be worn as one chooses. There is not men's talk and women's gossip: there is conversation and communication between people.

His is not a world of hierarchy. He wishes to be neither master nor slave. As a slave, he rebels; yet, he refuses to be a master if another's relation to him is that of slave. He does not approach others in contexts of superior-to-subordinate, but rather sees each man as an equal among others. Clearly, he has difficulty in fitting into most modern organizations; likewise, he has trouble being a student where the teacher acts as a superior rather than as a colleague in the educational adventure.

Our existential man tends to be sensitive and empathic. He identifies with the human condition: your pain is his pain, your oppression is his. He denies few of his feelings. He *owns up* to his loves and hates, and recognizes them as both very human and as his, not as some foreign element dwelling within to be covered over or cast out. He has great difficulty in dehumanizing others, in making them objects of his scrutiny. "After all," he proclaims, "they are people, just as you and I." He cannot kill simply because they are subhuman, slant-eyed gooks.

Existential man places a personal burden of responsibility on his every deed. He and he alone is responsible. He cannot take the cop-out and claim that he was merely following orders and therefore should not be held accountable, or that his role demanded that he act in such-and-such a way. No, he recognizes that it was *his choice* to follow those orders rather than to defy them; that it was *his decision* to remain in that role and enact its requirements. A heavy burden indeed, for he is obliged now to be actively involved in the affairs of his community and world: inaction is as much a decision-choice as action. And, as a responsible, accountable being, he *must* act.

It follows then, that our existential man sees himself to be more of a caretaker than a visitor. He is concerned for the future and does not simply live out his life in the jungle of now and today. He fully recognizes the interdependence of all persons and all life everywhere. His personal assignment through life is to be the caretaker of himself, his family, his community, his society, his earth.

Note well that young people who protest, who have made headlines scream with their angry cries, are not by those actions alone, in this view, existential men. If anything, they are as much mechanical men as their parents and as the rest of the nation. In spite of what the media lead us to believe, few persons protest today; and of those few, only a minuscule number could rightly fall into this vision of existential man. For much as I would like to characterize today's youth as the saviors of mankind, I fear that the vast majority are merely a slight bit further along the evolutionary rather than the revolutionary chain of human development. Although those who first spoke out may have shared much in common with this existential view, most of those who followed simply hopped aboard the bandwagon and went where the action was.

Like the adults around them, few rose from that mediocre mass to transform *themselves* in a revolutionary way. Being young is no guarantee, for like sheep, they, too, dutifully and blindly march the route to *mechanicus*.

VI. A Declaration of Psychological Independence

People often ask, "Tell me, where would the revolution take us?" This existential man I have briefly described embodies the qualities of character that outline the *goals* of this psychological revolution. This view offers us a Declaration of Psychological Independence. The original American Revolution demanded that men of compassion and vision don the paraphernalia of war and take to the streets to do battle with a known and uniformed enemy. The new American Revolution—this psychological transformation—still requires men of compassion and vision; but unlike its predecessor, it can never be fully accomplished by force of arms or battles in the streets—though these undoubtedly will be essential at various times. This new revolution demands herculean efforts of both a personal and an institutional sort. It requires a radical transformation of self-image from pawn to origin, from apathy to activity, from nonrational to rational, from nonresponsible to responsible, from hierarchy to equality, from denial to affirmation, from insensitivity to empathy, from visitor to caretaker.

A transformation of this depth and magnitude cannot occur by means of slick advertising campaigns presented by the media; nor can it be legislated by governmental action. These merely substitute one external form of control for another; a change so fundamental cannot be imposed and still be meaningful. There are no magical potions, pink pills, scholarly incantations or behavior modification reinforcement schedules that can *zap* an instantaneous cure and transform man into this new being. This psychological revolution requires more effort than most are willing to give, more daring than most will try. For after all, being mechanical is far easier and seemingly less risky than being human, so why even bother! The man who tries not, however, has little basis to complain when he cannot safely walk the streets at night; when he sees more chaos than order; when he

finds no uncrowded, unpolluted, unlittered spot to rest a moment; when his sons are called to die in meaningless wars.

VII. Achieving the Transformation

I say that this new American Revolution, this psychology transformation, requires efforts of both a personal and an institutional sort. The key to one's personal liberation is to be found in a continuing process of *unmasking*, of bringing into awareness the variety of unconscious personal, social, economic, and historical determinants of one's life. The basic encounter whereby such unmasking is possible involves *disconfirming* confrontations or challenges, *met openly*, which compel the person to examine himself rather than to dismiss the challenger. The person is never freer than when once concealed forces are revealed, when alternatives are thereby seen; thus when intelligent choice becomes a known reality.

To see the several tinted lenses we each wear that color our view is to see as we've never seen before. But, if you are born blind, how can you know what it is to see a sunset? And can it ever really be described to you by someone else? Those socialized from birth on to be a *mechanicus* are likewise blind and likewise have great difficulty in understanding the views and options that can await them should new vision occur.

Paddy Chayefsky's play, *The Tenth Man*, tells of a deaf man who passes by a house in which a wedding party is being held. This deaf man looks in the window and sees everyone cavorting and dancing about. Not hearing the music, however, he imagines them all to be insane, jumping about so. Just because *you* are deaf, does it follow then that *we* are crazy?

Vision through the tinted lenses, through our own forms of deafness, requires a continuing openness, a willingness to explore ourselves, to refuse to deny possibilities of self-deception and blindness. Such vision requires a willingness to face each encounter without fear. Fear stifles knowledge; it inhibits freedom and destroys man's potential for growth. And those who today play upon man's fears—the Reagans, the Agnews, the Wallaces—tragically contribute thereby to the crippling rather than the growth of man's great potential.

Let me now be more specific and briefly examine the kinds of societal opportunities and experiences which provide these disconfirming challenges that can give rise to existential man. Ideally, communication—by travel, by the media, especially T.V., and between generations—offers each of us an opportunity to experience an encounter that can unmask cultural and personal myths and thereby clarify our often muddied vision.

Our educational institutions, from grade school through the university, offer another potential means of transforming man's character. In theory, but seldom in practice, educational institutions are not around merely to pour so-called facts into empty brains so that after 16 years and a B.A., one's vessel is now full. Rather, education should force a confrontation; it should thrust each person up against alternatives and thereby compel him to look at himself, at his society, at his generation, at history. Education should be subversive, not mollifying; it should upset, not soothe; it should question, not answer. Education should allow participation in all its facets, for only in that manner can an individual try out various possibilities and obtain the experiences necessary to gain perspective and self-awareness.

Instead, our educational institutions have become training and skill centers. The structure of most schools and colleges, the form of faculty organization and professionalization, the standard model of the classroom, all militate against any encounter that might cast the individual student back upon himself and shed light on who he is and why and where. And this is no mere accident; for after all, who really wants anything but mechanical men cranked out?

Those who say "No!" to this treatment have made a declaration of psychological independence that we all need closely to examine. More of us should be saying "No!" as well. For there are none so blind as those who pretend to teach and counsel others while never having seen and understood themselves clearly.

In the broader context of the society itself, existential men are likely to develop only in a fully open society, one that welcomes a variety of ideas and styles of life, one that provides opportunities for all persons to share and partici-

pate in all aspects of the culture. And I mean all persons: men, women, children, Blacks, Chicanos, Asians, Native Americans, Whites, poor and rich alike.

The formula for creating *mechanicus* is rather simple: minimize an individual's opportunities to participate meaningfully in the running of his own life; fortify the illusion of freedom, but carefully channel people into predetermined slots; conceal the iron fist of fascism under the velvet glove of corporate democracy; make consumer exploitation the norm but disguise it under the rubric of free enterprise; make corporate expansionism in overseas markets a national goal, but conceal it under the motherhood-banner of making the world safe for democracy; educate for skills, not for critical thinking; discriminate carefully on the basis of age, sex, and race, permitting minimal participation of those too young (i.e., below 30—keep them in school), of those too old (i.e., above 60—put them to pasture in retirement villages), of the wrong sex (i.e., female—mollify their liberation demands by changing hemlines every six months), or of the wrong color (i.e., black or brown—offer them the Southern strategy with some benign neglect).

VIII. An Act of Will

Although I have pointed to communications, education, and general societal openness as crucial to this psychological transformation, in my view, the one fundamental key to this revolution more vital than anything else, involves a personal, willful commitment to transform oneself. Waiting for someone else to change social institutions so that future generations will be better reared, or waiting for scientists to create that new magical invention of technological wonderment that will solve all of our problems while creating none worse than it solves (waiting thusly) will only guarantee that we shall usher in the dawning of the age of *mechanicus*.

The psychological revolution demands that each individual reaffirm his existence each day, each moment, as a living, thinking, choosing, responsible, free being. Change must begin at home and at work and on the most personal level first. One must *act*, not simply spend endless hours complaining of impotence or thinking about acting. Too often, inundated by incessant barrages of informa-

tion—the true opiate of modern man—we become narcotized into inaction, believing that having *heard* and *thought*, we have thereby done. No personal transformation has ever occurred without enactment; no change without action; and no action without the will to try.

By way of conclusion, let me anticipate a question some of you may wish to ask me: "Do you really think that this psychological revolution will occur?" I wish I could smile knowingly and say, "Yes, man will prevail." But I cannot. The time is short; the need, great; and the task, enormous. And I am not confident that we'll make it. Though as long as one man lives, there is hope. Our own will to try must be fueled by this hope.

I don't predict an end to the world, not even an ecological devastation. No, that's not it. When *mechanicus* reigns, *homo sapiens* will have died, and man's great potential will be lost *forever*. It saddens and disturbs me when I think of what could have been, but may never be.

I truly wish my words and thoughts were merely idle speculations and that there was nothing really serious to concern ourselves with. But as I know, and as I'm sure deep down you all know, that just isn't so.

The task *is* enormous: a psychological revolution in character.

The time *is* short: we are already far along an exponential curve running away to *mechanicus* faster with each passing day.

And the need *is* great: that man shall prevail.

Can we do it? If *we* here cannot; if each of *you* cannot; it will not be done.

The standard social science viewpoint is that man is the product of his culture; that from birth he passively undergoes manipulation to make him internalize the goals, rewards, punishments, and world view given to him by his society. If he doesn't fit in, then he is sick. Ironically, the "sick" person is then held to be personally responsible for his "illness."

There is something very wrong with this oversocialized view of normalcy. Etzioni questions it and suggests that there may be basic human needs that are crosscultural and universal. These basic needs transcend cultural and consequently relativistic modes of organization and imply that a social system may thwart these needs. The deviant individual may be the healthy one in a sick society. Anomie and confusion may be normal. Fitting in may be sick. We believe the question to be a crucial one, for if "existential man" is to emerge dominant he must have a suitable ecological niche in which to survive.

1.3
Man and Society: The Inauthentic Condition

Amitai Etzioni

Among sociologists and social psychologists the concept of "basic human needs" is held in low regard. Inkeles (1964), in reviewing the field, said:

Man's *"original nature"* is seen largely in neutral terms, as neither good nor bad. It is, rather, a potential for development, and the extent to which the potential is realized depends on the time and society into which a man is born and on his distinctive place in it. If it does not quite treat him as a "tabula rasa," modern sociology, nevertheless, regards man as a flexible form which can be given all manner of content.

Socialization, the process of learning one's culture while growing out of infant and childhood dependency, leads to internalization of society's values and goals. People come to want to do what from the point of society they must do. Man is, therefore, seen, in his inner being, as mainly moral, by and large accepting and fulfilling the demands society makes on him [p. 50, italics added].

Cohen (1966) stated recently:

Nobody has ever been able to formulate an inventory of original or unsocialized tendencies that has commanded more than scattered and temporary agreement. In the second place, the very meaning of "original human nature," in any other sense

Reprinted by permission of the author and Plenum Publishing Co. Ltd from a revised version of an Invited Address presented to the Division of Personality and Social Psychology at the Annual Meeting of the American Psychological Association, Washington, D.C., September 1, 1969. Copyright 1970 Tavistock Institute of Human Relations.

than a range of possibilities, each of them dependent upon specific experiences for its development or maturation, has always proved exceedingly elusive and obscure [p. 60].

Basic Human Needs Debate

This is not to suggest that these disciplines do not recognize the existence of tensions between social roles (modes of conduct which are socially prescribed and reinforced) and personal needs or preferences. But the discrepancies between a person's inclination and that which is socially expected are accounted for by imperfect socialization, inadequate social control, or conflicting social demands, all *social* factors. True, these sociologists and social psychologists will concede, we do encounter what seems like a conflict between a person's private self and his public self (or between a person and his fellow men), but since the private self is shaped by previous socializations, this conflict really amounts to a clash between the *social* past and the present. One cannot even retreat, grant that private selves are "socialized" and that all that is "socialized" is by definition a social product, and suggest that unsocialized elements in the infant's conduct are indicative of basic human needs. This is because sociologists and social psychologists will be quick to point out that unsocialized conduct is animal-like (illustrated by studies of children adopted by a wolf or left in attics) or like a free-floating libido, which has no shape of its own. The *human* element, they stress, is socially provided, and the "animal" needs—the physiological requirements for nourishment, liquids, and slumber—can be provided for in such a wide variety of socially approved ways that they set only very lax limits on that which is socially feasible. This is where the collective wisdom of mainstreams of modern sociology and much of social psychology stand; the concept of basic human needs cannot be used to account for tensions between specific attributes of private and public selves.

The counterarguments—and we are dealing with debates among schools rather than with findings of "critical" experiments—advance the proposition that human nature is significantly less malleable than these disciplines tend to assume, that unsocialized beings have *specific* needs. When social arrangements run counter to these needs, human beings can be made

to "adapt" to them, but the fact that adaptations had to be made can be learned from the level of personal "costs" inflicted, such as mental disorganization and psychosomatic illness. Modern industrial society is often depicted as such a frustrating structure, one which causes various kinds of neurosis, interpersonal violence, and craving for charismatic leadership. Excessively "instrumental" (or "cold"), it is said to provide only inadequate opportunities for "expressive" (or "warm") relations.

A second set of costs is social rather than personal. It manifests itself, we suggest, in that efforts which must be spent to socialize men into roles or cultures which are unresponsive to basic human needs are much greater than those needed to socialize men into more responsive ones. The same holds, as we see it, with regard to the costs of social control; that is, those expenditures required to keep men in frustrating roles and to prevent them from being altered are higher than those which would be required to keep men in less frustrating roles. It seems more costly, for instance, to educate a man to be a good bureaucrat (e.g., one who disregards family, friendship, and political bonds and allows his decisions and acts to be governed by abstract and "universalisitic" criteria) than to be a public servant who follows the opposite rules; that is, we suggest that it is more natural to be "particularistic."[1] The same difference is expected to be found between roles which require substantial deferment of gratification versus those which allow more frequent gratification, even if there is no difference in the sum total of rewards received.

Evidence that some social roles and cultural patterns are less "natural" as compared to some others may be gleaned from cross-cultural comparative studies, which show that certain modes of required conduct generate frustration in a large variety of societies, which suggests that such conduct violates a universal set of human needs. The frustration found could not be caused by a specific socialization, cultural pattern, or institutional structure of any one society, for these vary greatly among the societies compared. Austerity, for instance, is found

[1] We draw here on the well-known opposition between universalistic and particularistic orientations presented by Parsons (1951).

objectionable (and generates pressure to overcome it) in as different situations as the Soviet Union a decade after the revolution, contemporary Israeli kibbutzim, and Catholic orders a generation after their foundation.

The implications for critical view and social research of these two divergent views of the malleability of human nature are extensive. By the first view, persons who do not accept the social prescriptions are "deviants." Even when no moral connotations are attached to the term, attention focuses on the factors which generated the deviancy and the ways these factors can be altered to engender conformity to social prescriptions. In contrast, the second view implies that a society is the "deviant" if it sets prescriptions which are contrary to human nature. According to this view, it is society that ought to be altered, to make it more responsive to man.

While this debate, as briefly outlined, is often viewed as one between the "integration" school (of which G. H. Mead and Talcott Parsons are main proponents) and the "conflict" or alienation school (whose representatives are numerous), scholars of the Marxist branch of the conflict school tend to reject human nature conceptions even more resolutely than those of the "integration" school. This is because they see the concept of a universal set of basic human needs as ahistorical. Conflicts, the Marxist writers stress, are determined by technological and economic relations which have grown apart from other social relations in the process of history. They are not due to personality variables. Actually, the notion of basic human needs and of historical processes can be quite readily reconciled. Human needs, such as a need for regular and frequent affection and recognition, may be universal, while the social conditions, which determine the degree to which they are satisfied, may be historically shaped.

From Alienation to Inauthenticity

If we ask the extent of responsiveness of society in the present historical stage, and limit our answer to Western societies, a rather central transformation from past stages suggests itself. This is the transformation from scarcity and the alienation generated by instrumentality toward rising inauthenticity of affluence and pseudo-

expressive relations. Before this trend can be explored, a note on the place of participation in our conceptual scheme is necessary. Of the many definitions of alienation, the following seems the most essential: A social condition is alienating if it is unresponsive to the basic needs of men in that condition; if it is beyond their understanding and control. The question arises as to how a responsive social structure may be generated. How are the members' needs and preferences to be related to societal forms? The answer seems to us to lie in the members' participation in shaping and reshaping these forms. Maximal societal responsiveness will be attained under the utopian condition in which all the members participate in the shaping of all aspects of their societal life. Even this condition would be expected to encounter some alienation (which Marcuse, 1955, refers to as irreducible), the result of the fact that not all members' needs are mutually complementary, and hence the compromises inevitably worked out leave each less than fully satisfied. Participation, though, provides the most effective way to reach such compromise; any other procedure, for example, a wise and open-minded monarch taking his country's needs into account, would be expected to leave a greater residue of alienation than broadly based participation. This is because under such a system upward communication of members' needs would be both more accurate and more powerful as compared to any other system. While maximal participation is utopian, we may compare social systems in terms of the extent to which they are participatory, and expect that those which are relatively more participatory will also be relatively less alienating.

This brings us to the historical stage and situation in which we find ourselves. In contrast to previous ages of scarcity, the contemporary period, for industrialized societies, has been characterized as one of abundance (at least for the private sector and the "upper" two-thirds of the members). The lower the level of scarcity, the lower the extent of irreducible alienation. This is because the more basic needs of members can be satisfied without necessarily depriving anyone.

When a society lives close to the subsistence level, existing allocative patterns often entail the deprivation of the most basic hu-

man needs to some categories or groups of members—baby girls or minorities, for instance. Here, reallocation aimed at improving the lot of these members may entail inflicting such deprivation on some other segment of the membership. In the age of affluence, reallocation is aimed at creating a society which satisfies the basic needs of all members and which does not inflict deprivation of basic needs on any member; it can draw on "slack"; that is, rather than redistribute the burden of societal alienation, the total level can be reduced. Moreover, it is not only that material needs can be more widely satisfied, but also that more time and energy can be freed for expressive pursuits. For example, all other things being equal, the mother who need not labor to add to the family's income will find it easier to provide affection for both her husband *and* her children, reducing the rivalry between them over this overscarce "commodity." In *this* period of affluence the role of participation becomes more crucial; if alienation is not reduced here, this can be attributed more to exclusion and unresponsiveness than to objective inability to respond, as compared to *much* less affluent earlier periods or other societies.

The difference between our own and earlier societies, it may be argued, is much smaller than we suggest, because scarcity is a state of mind as well as of the economy. For a suburban matron, inability to acquire a new fur, when all her friends acquire them, may be as frustrating as a Burmese village matron's inability to fill her rice bowl with rice or any other food. But, even if there are no "real" (physiological) differences, and if the status race has no level of satiation, it will must be noted that the basic reason the suburban matron is caught in a status race is lack of authentic expressive relations, while the sources of hunger in the Burmese village are at least in part economic and technological. The suburban "scarcity" can be treated to a large extent by providing for authentic participation; the hunger in Burma can be so treated only to a very limited degree.

Sources of Societal
Unresponsiveness

The resistance to making affluent societies more responsive, to reallocating, and to opening the society to extensive participation has both "real" and symbolic sources. In part, this resistance draws on existing privileged power and economic positions, which would be undermined in such a societal change. While there is, on the one hand, a rise in and a spread of societal consciousness and of the capacity to act politically among the deprived collectivities due to the mass education and means of communication, there is also in contemporary industrialized society an increasing capacity of those in power to manipulate. This is because of the communication revolution and the growing utility of social science, especially market and voting research. Aside from sustaining the existing pattern of privileges and restricted participation, mass manipulation is said to provide for the unloading of the ever-increasing produce the affluent economy manufactures. The ultimate manipulation, some empirical evidence for which is cited below, is found in sustaining the legitimacy of a system that is unresponsive to the basic needs of its members, in that it offers a sense of participation—and, more broadly, of responsiveness—where there is only a pittance.

In pursuing the idea of alienation with the eyes of a sociologist, our attention focuses first on the array of societal institutions. In earlier writings on unresponsiveness attention would typically focus on work and economic institutions as the source of alienation. But in seeking to understand the affluent age, attention ought to focus on the main source of inauthentic participation, the politics of pluralistic, democratic societies. On the face of it all, authentic democracy is assured by the structure of the government interests and by the values of all members. It is asserted that these can find their way into the political give-and-take, out of which consensual policies and acceptable structures emerge. These claims tend to minimize or view as temporary the unresponsiveness of this political system to those significant segments of the population which have no effective vote, the role played by the mass media and the elites in producing endorsement of unresponsive policies (policies which are against the interests of the members and which they would reject if they were better informed and less tranquilized), and the fact that the political alternatives among which choice is offered constitute a narrow range, one which excludes many options—especially for fundamental changes leading

to increased responsiveness on the society-wide level. The 1964 choice between the Vietnam policy Senator Goldwater advocated and the rather similar one President Johnson followed up to the election (let alone after it) is a case in point.

Pluralism by itself, without substantial equality in power among the political contenders, does not provide for a responsive political system. Groups of citizens (such as classes or ethnic groups) have a say in accordance with their assets, power, and, above all, extent of organization for political action, such as lobbying and campaigning. As these resources are unevenly distributed among groups of citizens, the consensus produced is about as responsive to the needs of the weaker members as an agreement between an international oil company and a street-corner gasoline-pump owner. Pluralism "works" not mainly via elections, but via private and public interest groups (McConnell, 1966). New administrative policies and major pieces of legislation are "cleared" with the "relevant" groups, that is, labor and management, churches, and civic associations. In the process those interests which are not organized (and part of their deprivation is their relative lack of the educational background and experience which organization necessitates) are neglected. Farm hands, excluded from the minimum-wage legislation in the United States, are a typical case in point.

Inauthenticity in other institutional areas is frequently reported. Studies of education show the stress which is placed on a uniform personality format, the "rounded personality" capable of smooth handling of others. This is a format which, first, does not provide for expression of the variety of personality needs young men exhibit, and which, second, promotes relations among men which are devoid of deep affection and adequate releases (Freidenberg, 1965). Studies of suburbia have shown the pseudoquality of the *Gemeinschaft* generated. Here, it is reported, the instrumental orientation penetrates even the relation between mother and child, the former using the latter to score points in a status race, disregarding the child's deeper needs (e.g., to get dirty sometimes), and failing to provide authentic, unconditional affection (Seeley, 1956). Studies of "human relations" training programs for

management show programs whose aim is to teach supervisory personnel how to provide their underlings with a sense of participation in industrial decision making without real sharing of power or interest in responsiveness (Bendix & Fisher, 1961), and of labor unions which are so committed to industrial peace and cooperation that they serve much more as a mechanism of downward control (part of the labor relations department of the plant"), than of upward representation of workers' needs (Whyte, 1955).

Inauthenticity in one area sustains that in others. "Rounded" education prepares for pseudoparticipation in the realm of work (with "don't rock the boat" as the prime tenet). Consumer races provide an outlet for an avalanche of products which answer no authentic need, but produce the demand to work, even at alienating conditions, in order to obtain them. Inauthentic politics close the circle by not providing an opportunity to mobilize for fundamentally different systems, and the mass culture provides "escapes" which drain protest and which, in turn, serve to conceal the "flatness" (Marcuse, 1964) of the mass-society, consumption-and-work world.

The total effect is one of a society which is not committing, to which members are not "cathected," one which provides no effective channels for expression of frustrations, grievances, and needs. Hence, the rise of demonstration democracy, as men take to the streets to express, release, or communicate feelings upward; the rise in wildcat strikes, as labor unions become part of the managerial structure;[2] the rise in *middle class* dropouts among students; and the rise in the number of demonstrators and the increasingly "respectable" kinds of social groups which take to the streets (teachers, social workers, and, at least in one case, doctors).[3] More deeply, the high rate of alcoholism, neuroses, divorce, addiction, and other such symptoms seem traceable in part to the noncommitting social world. The best evidence that lack of involvement is

[2] On the nature of wildcat strikes, see Raskin (1967); for engineers on the picket line, see *American Engineer News* (January 1968, p. 13).

[3] Doctors demonstrated in front of the automobile displays at Columbus Circle in New York City to call attention to unsafe cars.

a major factor in causing these personal "costs" and societal problems is that when social life becomes more committing—as for the members of a social movement —there is a sharp decline in these symptoms.[4] It seems that not only are members of such movements less likely to be alcoholics, have fewer "breakdowns," etc., when compared to other less-involved citizens of similar class, ethnic, and educational background, but also that the same persons—for instance, Malcolm X—experience a sharp decline in particular symptoms and/or asocial behavior when they are authentically activated.[5] In the final analysis, even the members of a social movement are, of course, not free of their society, and only a society which would become more active and less inauthentic could expect to overcome these problems on a broader base.

Psychological Focus on Alienation and Inauthenticity

Shifting from a sociological focus to a psychological one, the difference between alienation and inauthentic involvement seems to lie first in the difference between

having a clear and external target for aggression and keeping aggression at least in part "bottled up" inside. The "purely" alienated person—barred from voting, joining a labor union, or attending a university—may feel "shut out," as if facing a heavy locked door in a passage he seeks to travel. He can, with relative ease, identify an "enemy" and release part of his frustration by anger and even physical violence against the "bosses," the Establishment, etc. The inauthentically involved person is allowed to vote, to organize, to join; but all of this does not make the system more responsive to his needs. It is like being caught in an invisible nylon net. He is often unable to identify the sources of his frustrations. He frequently has a sense of guilt because had he not played along it would have been impossible to sustain the system and he would not have ended up being manipulated. His resentment against being caught is in part a resentment against himself for allowing himself to be taken.

Rejection, which lies at the root of both conditions, is much more impersonal and hence less psychologically damaging in the pure alienating situation as compared to the inauthentic one. Jews, usually excluded during the Middle Ages from the political and economic power centers of society, could make a comparatively healthy psychological adjustment by focusing their identity on the ingroup and limiting their expressive ties to other Jews. But with emancipation, as Jews were allowed, for instance, to study at German universities, they lowered their defenses and moved emotionally closer to non-Jews. When rejection came here, it was often more damaging to self-identity and emotional security (Wirth, 1957). Similar experiences are now the fate of educated Negroes in the United States. More technically it may be said that pure alienation exists when the social distance scale is great and encompasses all the major expressive relations; authentic relations reduce the scale to a minimum; inauthentic ones stand midway on the scale and are "uneven," allowing for closer relations in some expressive areas, and less in others, a particularly strained imbalance. Much more needs to be found out about the differences in the psychological problems and dynamics of persons who live in these two kinds of social conditions. Are there differences in psy-

chosomatic illness, for instance? Do alienated persons have more speech defects while inauthentic ones have more asthma and ulcers? etc.

Conclusion

I conclude with a brief note on the conditions under which alienation and inauthenticity may be reduced. In part these are "structural" conditions, as, for instance, those under which a more equal distribution of political power among the members of society can be brought about. These, in turn, are a prerequisite of more widely distributed opportunity for participation and thus for a more broadly based responsiveness. Here the central question is does not the very structure of inequality which generated excluded and underprivileged groups also prevent their effective mobilization for societal change, which such a redistribution of power would constitute. The answer, which cannot be spelled out here, seems to be that while the existing structure does make it more difficult, if only because of differential access to education, for some groups to mobilize themselves, other factors prevent control from being watertight. The spread of education (which the economy's needs foster) and the unbalanced upward mobility of those groups which did gain admittance (e.g., the Jews in the United States) are among these factors (see Etzioni, 1968).

In addition, there are psychological factors. The fear to challenge the existing social structure or its rhetoric, for example, has some roots in the reality of experiences in earlier periods or even present ones (e.g., where political activeness on the side of change, as in parts of the South, causes loss of one's job, land, or life); but it may also be grossly magnified because of internal weakness or lack of a tradition of collective action (Wilson, 1960).

Attempts by those who share similar fears, underprivileged statuses, *and* the social sources of alienation to confront their difficulties serve, first, to reduce the inauthenticity by more clearly marking the true opportunities for participation and by pointing out the false ones. They then serve to make the system less alienating by promoting some reallocation of resources and power, which, in turn, makes society somewhat more participatory and responsive. Whether this leads to a continual

[4] A study of narcotics addiction among Negroes in the United States for a decade by the Federal Bureau of Narcotics (quoted in *The New York Times*, March 6, 1957) showed a 15% decline (27,321 as compared to 29,482) from 1955 to 1965; the first factor listed among four was "growing racial pride among Negroes has accompanied the fight for civil rights." See also Clark, 1965, pp. 101, 216. On similar evidence for Los Angeles, see Druz, 1967, p. 131. It is said that rates of neurosis were much lower during the London Blitz, and that those mobilized by a social movement had a low criminal record. See also Rude, 1964, especially chap. 15, pp. 195–268. See also Reid, 1961. It is necessary, though, to use as indicators antisocial behavior as defined by a social science model and not by the middle class or the alienating society. Thus, it is not clear at all that the smoking of marihuana (as distinct from heroin or opium) is more antisocial than moderate drinking. Its prevalence in a mobilized group is not a sign that activation does not reduce deviancy. But interpersonal violence, for instance, seems more antisocial, and we would expect a lower rate in active groups, unless this happens to be a pattern the group picks up as its rebelling symbol. The question of an absolute base for the study of deviant behavior will be explored further in a later publication.

[5] For a story of a deviant who becomes a political innovator through mobilization, see *The Autobiography of Malcolm X* (1965).

reformation of society, until it gradually becomes a highly responsive one, or leads to full-fledged confrontation between the rising collectivities and those who see their interest in preserving the status quo it is too early to tell. In either case, should mobilization of the uninvolved lead to a gradual transformation or a showdown, inauthenticity—the mark of the affluent society—will be much reduced.

REFERENCES

Bendix, R., & Fisher, L. The perspectives of Elton Mayo. In A. Etzioni (Ed.), *Complex organizations.* New York: Holt, Rinehart & Winston, 1961.

Clark, K. B. *Dark ghetto dilemmas of social power.* New York: Harper & Row, 1965.

Cohen, A. K. *Deviance and control.* Englewood Cliffs, N.J.: Prentice-Hall, 1966.

Druz, E. *The big blue line.* New York: Coward, McCann, 1967.

Etzioni, A. *The active society: A theory of societal and political processes.* New York: Free Press, 1968.

Friedenberg, E. Z. *Coming of age in America.* New York: Random House, 1965.

Inkeles, A. *What is sociology?* Englewood Cliffs, N.J.: Prentice-Hall, 1964.

Malcolm X. *The autobiography of Malcolm X.* New York: Grove Press, 1965.

Marcuse, H. *Eros and civilization.* Boston: Beacon Press, 1955.

Marcuse, H. *One-dimensional man.* Boston: Beacon Press, 1964.

McConnell, G. *Private power and American democracy.* New York: Knopf, 1966.

Parsons, T. *The Social system.* New York: Free Press, 1951.

Raskin, A. H. Why labor doesn't follow its leaders. *The New York Times,* January 8, 1967.

Reid, D. D. Precipitating proximal factors in the occurence of mental disorders: Epidemiological evidence. In, *Causes of mental disorders: A review of epidemiological knowledge, 1959.* New York: Milbank Memorial Fund, 1961.

Rude, G. *The crowd in history.* New York: Wiley, 1964.

Seeley, J. R. *Crestwood Heights.* New York: Basic Books, 1956.

Whyte, W. F. *Money and motivation.* New York: Harper, 1955.

Wilson, J. Q. *Negro politics.* New York: Free Press, 1960.

Wirth, L. *The ghetto.* Chicago: University of Chicago Press, 1957.

The "psychological revolution" as Miller sees it, is changing people's conceptions of themselves by giving them the means to practice psychology among themselves. This may be a way to achieve Sampson's existential man. However, due to the inherent power of behavior mechanics, this proposition raises some important moral questions. "Who will be controlling whom?" Perhaps existentialism attained in this way will be only an artificial state of grace. Education would seem to be the only practical way of giving psychology away to the people. However, this process will necessarily be a long one. Miller implies that the psychological revolution will be speeded up if there are fundamental changes in the outlook of the psychological profession.

1.4
Psychology as a Means of Promoting Human Welfare

George A. Miller

Revolutionary Potential of Psychology

I will begin by stating publicly something that I think psychologists all feel, but seldom talk about. In my opinion, scientific psychology is potentially one of the most revolutionary intellectual enterprises ever conceived by the mind of man. If we were ever to achieve substantial progress toward our stated aim—toward the understanding, prediction, and control of mental and behavioral phenomena—the implications for every aspect of society would make brave men tremble.

. . . Anyone who claims that psychology is a revolutionary enterprise will face a demand from his scientific colleagues to put up or shut up. Nothing that psychology has done so far, they will say, is very revolutionary. They will admit that psychometric tests, psychoanalysis, conditioned reflexes, sensory thresholds, implanted electrodes, and factor analysis are all quite admirable,

but they can scarcely be compared to gunpowder, the steam engine, organic chemistry, radio-telephony, computers, atom bombs, or genetic surgery in their revolutionary consequences for society.

. . . I believe that the real impact of psychology will be felt, not through the technological products it places in the hands of powerful men, but through its effects on the public at large, through a new and different public conception of what is humanly possible and what is humanly desirable.

I believe that any broad and successful application of psychological knowledge to human problems will necessarily entail a change in our conception of ourselves and of how we live and love and work together. Instead of inventing some new technique for modifying the environment, or some new product for society to adapt itself to however it can, we are proposing to tamper with the adaptive process itself. Such an innovation is quite different from a "technological fix." I see little reason to believe that the traditional model for scientific revolutions should be appropriate.

Consider, for example, the effect that Freudian psychology has already had on Western society. It is obvious that its effects, though limited to certain segments of society, have been profound, yet I do not believe that one can argue that those effects were achieved by providing new instrumentalities for achieving goals socially agreed upon. As a method of therapy, psychoanalysis has had limited success even for those who can afford it. It has been more successful as a method of investigation, perhaps, but even there it has been only one of several available methods. The impact of Freud's thought has been due far less to the instrumentalities he provided than to the changed conception of ourselves that he inspired. The wider range of psychological problems that Freud opened up for professional psychologists is only part of his contribution. More important in the scale of history has been his effect on the broader intellectual community and, through it, on the public at large. Today we are much more aware of the irrational components of human nature and much better able to accept the reality of our unconscious impulses. The importance of Freudian psychology derives far less from its scientific validity than from the effects it has had on our shared image of man himself.

I realize that one might argue that changes in man's conception of himself under the impact of advances in scientific knowledge are neither novel nor revolutionary. For example, Darwin's theory changed our conception of ourselves, but not until the past decade has it been possible to mount a truly scientific revolution based on biological science. One might argue that we are now only at the Darwinian stage in psychology, and that the real psychological revolution is still a century or more in the future. I do not find this analogy appropriate, however.

To discover that we are not at the center of the universe, or that our remote ancestors lived in a tree, does indeed change our conception of man and society, but such new conceptions can have little effect on the way we behave in our daily affairs and in our institutional contexts. A new conception of man based on psychology, however, would have immediate implications for the most intimate details of our social and personal lives. This fact is unprecedented in any earlier stage of the Industrial Revolution.

The heart of the psychological revolution will be a new and scientifically based conception of man as an individual and as a social creature. When I say that the psychological revolution is already upon us, what I mean is that we have already begun to change man's self-conception. If we want to further that revolution, not only must we strengthen its scientific base, but we must also try to communicate it to our students and to the public. It is not the industrialist or the politician who should exploit it, but Everyman, every day.

The enrichment of public psychology by scientific psychology constitutes the most direct and important application of our science to the promotion of human welfare. Instead of trying to foresee new psychological products that might disrupt our existing social arrangements, therefore, we should be self-consciously analyzing the general effect that our scientific psychology may have on popular psychology. As I try to perform this analysis for myself, I must confess that I am not altogether pleased with the results.

I would like now to consider briefly some of the effects we are having and where, in my view, our influence is leading at the present time. Let me begin with a thumbnail sketch of one major

message that many scientific psychologists are trying to communicate to the public.

Control of Behavior

One of the most admired truisms of modern psychology is that some stimuli can serve to reinforce the behavior that produces them. The practical significance of this familiar principle arises from the implication that if you can control the occurrence of these reinforcing stimuli, then you can control the occurrence of adaptive behavior intended to achieve or avoid them. This contingency between behavior and its consequences has been demonstrated in many studies of animal behavior, where environmental conditions can be controlled, or at least specified, and where the results can be measured with some precision.

Something similar holds for the human animal, of course, although it is complicated by man's symbolic proclivities and by the fact that the disparity between experimenter and subject changes when the subject is also a man. Between men, reinforcement is usually a mutual relation and each person controls the other to some extent. This relation of mutual reinforcement, which man's genius for symbols has generalized in terms of money or the promise of money, provides the psychological basis for our economic system of exchange. Psychologists did not create this economic system for controlling behavior, of course. What we have tried to do is to describe its psychological basis and its limits in terms sufficiently general to hold across different species, and to suggest how the technique might be extended to educational, rehabilitative, therapeutic, or even political situations in which economic rewards and punishments would not normally be appropriate. Once a problem of behavior control has been phrased in these terms, we may then try to discover the most effective schedule of reinforcements.

My present concern has nothing to do with the validity of these ideas. I am concerned with their effect on the public at large, for it is there, if I am right, that we are most likely to achieve a psychological revolution.

In the public view, I suspect, all this talk about controlling behavior comes across as unpleasant, if not actually threatening. Freud has already established in the public mind a general belief that all

behavior is motivated. The current message says that psychologists now know how to use this motivation to control what people will do. When they hear this, of course, our scientific colleagues are likely to accuse us of pseudoscientific claims; less scientific segments of the public are likely to resent what they perceive as a threat to their personal freedom. Neither reaction is completely just, but neither is completely unjustifiable.

I believe these critics see an important truth, one that a myopic concentration on techniques of behavior control may cause us to overlook. At best, control is but one component in any program for personal improvement or social reform. Changing behavior is pointless in the absence of any coherent plan for how it should be changed. It is our plan for using control that the public wants to know about. Too often, I fear, psychologists have implied that acceptable uses for behavior control are either self-evident or can be safely left to the wisdom and benevolence of powerful men. Psychologists must not surrender the planning function so easily. Humane applications of behavior control must be based on intelligent diagnosis of the personal and social problems we are trying to solve. Psychology has at least as much, probably more, to contribute to the diagnosis of personal and social problems as it has to the control of behavior.

Regardless of whether we have actually achieved new scientific techniques of behavior control that are effective with human beings, and regardless of whether control is of any value in the absence of diagnosis and planning for its use, the simple fact that so many psychologists keep talking about control is having an effect on public psychology. The average citizen is predisposed to believe it. Control has been the practical payoff from the other sciences. Control must be what psychologists are after, too. Moreover, since science is notoriously successful, behavior control must be inevitable. Thus the layman forms an impression that control is the name of the road we are traveling, and that the experts are simply quibbling about how far down that road we have managed to go.

Closely related to this emphasis on control is the frequently repeated claim that living organisms are nothing but machines. A scientist recognizes, of course, that this claim says far more about our rapidly evolving conception of machines than it says about living organisms, but this interpretation is usually lost when the message reaches public ears. The public idea of a machine is something like an automobile, a mechanical device controlled by its operator. If people are machines, they can be driven like automobiles. The analogy is absurd, of course, but it illustrates the kind of distortion that can occur.

If the assumption that behavior control is feasible in some precise scientific sense becomes firmly rooted in public psychology, it could have unfortunate consequences, particularly if it is coupled with an assumption that control should be exercised by an industrial or bureaucratic elite. Psychologists must always respect and advocate the principle of *habeas mentem*—the right of a man to his own mind (Sanford, 1955). If we really did have a new scientific way to control human behavior, it would be highly immoral to let it fall into the hands of some small group of men, even if they were psychologists.

Perhaps a historical analogy would be appropriate. When the evolution of species was a new and exciting idea in biology, various social theorists took it up and interpreted it to mean that capitalistic competition, like the competition between species, was the source of all progress, so the great wealth of the new industrialists was a scientifically necessary consequence of the law of the survival of the fittest. This argument, called "social Darwinism," had unfortunate consequences, both for social science and for society generally (Hofstadter, 1944).

If the notion should now be accepted that it is a scientifically necessary consequence of the law of reinforcement that industrialists or bureaucrats must be allowed the same control over people that an experimenter has over his laboratory animals, I fear that a similar period of intolerable exploitation might ensue—if, indeed, it has not already begun.

The dangers that accompany a science of behavior control have been pointed out many times. Psychologists who study motivation scientifically are usually puzzled by this widespread apprehension that they might be successful. Control is not something invented by psychologists. Everyone is "controlled" all the time by something or other. All we want is to discover how the controls work. Once we understand that, society can use the knowledge in whatever manner seems socially advantageous. Our critics, on the other hand, want to know who will diagnose our problems, who will set our social goals, and who will administer the rewards and punishments.

All that I have tried to add to this familiar dialogue is the observation that the social dangers involved need not await the success of the scientific enterprise. Behavior control could easily become a self-fulfilling prophecy. If people generally should come to believe in the scientific control of behavior, proponents of coercive social programs would surely exploit that belief by dressing their proposals in scientific costumes. If our new public conception of human nature is that man's behavior can be scientifically controlled by those in positions of power, governments will quickly conform to that conception. Thus, when I try to discern what direction our psychological revolution has been taking, some aspects of it disturb me deeply and lead me to question whether in the long run these developments will really promote human welfare.

This is a serious charge. If there is any truth to it, we should ask whether any other approaches are open to us.

Personally, I believe there is a better way to advertise psychology and to relate it to social problems. Reinforcement is only one of many important ideas that we have to offer. Instead of repeating leads to control, I would prefer to emphasize that reinforcement can lead to satisfaction and competence. And I would prefer to speak of understanding and prediction as our major scientific goals.

In the space remaining, therefore, I want to try to make the case that understanding and prediction are better goals for psychology than is control—better both for psychology and for the promotion of human welfare—because they lead us to think, not in terms of coercion by a powerful elite, but in terms of the diagnosis of problems and the development of programs that can enrich the lives of every citizen.

Public Psychology: Two Paradigms

It should be obvious by now that I have somewhere in the back of my mind two alternative images of what the popular conception of human nature might become under the impact of scientific advances in psychology. One of these images is unfortunate, even threatening; the other is vaguer, but full of promise. Let me try to make these ideas more concrete.

The first image is the one I have been describing. It has great appeal to an authoritarian mind, and fits well with our traditional competitive ideology based on coercion, punishment, and retribution. The fact that it represents a serious distortion of scientific psychology is exactly my point. In my opinion, we have made a mistake by trying to apply our ideas to social problems and to gain acceptance for our science within the framework of this ideology.

The second image rests on the same psychological foundation, but reflects it more accurately; it allows no compromise with our traditional social ideology. It is assumed, vaguely but optimistically, that this ideology can be modified so as to be more receptive to a truer conception of human nature. How this modification can be achieved is one of the problems we face; I believe it will not be achieved if we continue to advertise the control of behavior through reinforcement as our major contribution to the solution of social problems. I would not wish to give anyone the impression that I have formulated a well-defined social alternative, but I would at least like to open a discussion and make some suggestions.

My two images are not very different from what McGregor (1960) once called Theory X and Theory Y. Theory X is the traditional theory which holds that because people dislike work, they must be coerced, controlled, directed, and threatened with punishment before they will do it. People tolerate being directed, and many even prefer it, because they have little ambition and want to avoid responsibility. McGregor's alternative Theory Y, based on social science, holds that work is as natural as play or rest. External control and threats are not the only means for inspiring people to work. People will exercise self-direction and self-control in the service of objectives to which they are committed; their commitment is a function of the rewards associated with the achievement of their objectives. People can learn not only to accept but to seek responsibility. Imagination, ingenuity, and creativity are widely distributed in the population, although these intellectual potentialities are poorly utilized under the conditions of modern industrial life.

McGregor's Theory X and Theory Y evolved in the context of his studies of industrial management. They are rival theories held by industrial managers about how best to achieve their institutional goals. A somewhat broader view is needed if we are to talk about public psychology generally, and not merely the managerial manifestations of public psychology. So let me amplify McGregor's distinction by referring to the ideas of Varela, a very remarkable engineer in Montevideo, Uruguay, who uses scientific psychology in the solution of a wide range of personal and social problems.

Varela (1970, in press) contrasts two conceptions of the social nature of man. Following Kuhn's (1962) discussion of scientific revolutions, he refers to these two conceptions as "paradigms." The first paradigm is a set of assumptions on which our social institutions are presently based. The second is a contrasting paradigm based on psychological research. Let me outline them for you very briefly.

Our current social paradigm is characterized as follows: All men are created equal. Most behavior is motivated by economic competition, and conflict is inevitable. One truth underlies all controversy, and unreasonableness is best countered by facts and logic. When something goes wrong, someone is to blame, and every effort must be made to establish his guilt so that he can be punished. The guilty person is responsible for his own misbehavior and for his own rehabilitation. His teachers and supervisors are too busy to become experts in social science; their role is to devise solutions and see to it that their students or subordinates do what they are told.

For comparison, Varela offers a paradigm based on psychological research: There are large individual differences among people, both in ability and personality. Human motivation is complex and no one ever acts as he does for any single reason, but, in general, positive incentives are more effective than threats or punishments. Conflict is no more inevitable than disease and can be resolved or, still better, prevented. Time and resources for resolving social problems are strictly limited. When something goes wrong, how a person perceives the situation is

more important to him than the "true facts," and he cannot reason about the situation until his irrational feelings have been toned down. Social problems are solved by correcting causes, not symptoms, and this can be done more effectively in groups than individually. Teachers and supervisors must be experts in social science because they are responsible for the cooperation and individual improvement of their students or subordinates.

No doubt other psychologists would draw the picture somewhat differently. Without reviewing the psychological evidence on which such generalizations are based, of course, I cannot argue their validity. But I think most of you will recognize the lines of research on which McGregor's Theory Y and Varela's second paradigm are based. Moreover, these psychologically based paradigms are incompatible in several respects with the prevailing ideology of our society.

Here, then, is the real challenge: How can we foster a social climate in which some such new public conception of man based on psychology can take root and flourish? In my opinion, this is the proper translation of our more familiar question about how psychology might contribute to the promotion of human welfare.

I cannot pretend to have an answer to this question, even in its translated form, but I believe that part of the answer is that psychology must be practiced by nonpsychologists. We are not physicians; the secrets of our trade need not be reserved for highly trained specialists. Psychological facts should be passed out freely to all who need and can use them. And from successful applications of psychological principles the public may gain a better appreciation for the power of the new conception of man that is emerging from our science.

If we take seriously the idea of a peaceful revolution based on a new conception of human nature, our scientific results will have to be instilled in the public consciousness in a practical and usable form so that what we know can be applied by ordinary people. There simply are not enough psychologists, even including nonprofessionals, to meet every need for psychological services. The people at large will have to be their own psychologists, and make their own applications of the principles that we establish.

Of course, everyone practices

psychology, just as everyone who cooks is a chemist, everyone who reads a clock is an astronomer, everyone who drives a car is an engineer. I am not suggesting any radical departure when I say that nonpsychologists must practice psychology. I am simply proposing that we should teach them to practice it better, to make use self-consciously of what we believe to be scientifically valid principles.

Our responsibility is less to assume the role of experts and try to apply psychology ourselves than to give it away to the people who really need it—and that includes everyone. The practice of valid psychology by nonpsychologists will inevitably change people's conception of themselves and what they can do. When we have accomplished that, we will really have caused a psychological revolution.

How To Give Psychology Away

I am keenly aware that giving psychology away will be no simple task. In our society there are depths of resistance to psychological innovations that have to be experienced to be believed (Graziano, 1969).

Solving social problems is generally considered to be more difficult than solving scientific problems. A social problem usually involves many more independent variables, and it cannot be finally solved until society has been persuaded to adopt the solution. Many who have tried to introduce sound psychological practices into schools, clinics, hospitals, prisons, or industries have been forced to retreat in dismay. They complain, and with good reason, that they were unable to buck the "System," and often their reactions are more violent than sensible. The System, they say, refuses to change even when it does not work.

This experience has been so common that in my pessimistic moments I have been led to wonder whether anything less than complete reform is posssible.

Deutsch (1969) has made an interesting case that competitive and cooperative social relationships tend to be mutually exclusive. He summarizes the result of considerable research in the following terms:

The strategy of power and the tactics of coercion, threat, and deception result from and also result in a competitive relationship. Similarly, the strategy of mutual problem solving and the tactics of persuasion, openness, and mutual enhancement elicit and also are elicited by a cooperative orientation [p. 4].

Each orientation has its own internal consistency; elements of one are not easily injected into the other.

Perhaps a similar pressure toward internal coherence lies at the root of public resistance to many of our innovative suggestions. It often seems that any one of our ideas taken alone is inadequate. Injected into the existing social paradigm it is either a foreign body, incompatible with the other presuppositions that shape our social institutions, or it is distorted and trivialized to fit the preexisting paradigm.

One of the most basic ideas in all the social sciences is the concept of culture. Social anthropologists have developed a conception of culture as an organic whole, in which each particular value, practice, or assumption must be understood in the context of the total system. They tell terrible tales about the consequences of introducing Western reforms into aboriginal cultures without understanding the social equilibria that would be upset.

Perhaps cultural integrity is not limited to primitive cultures, but applies also to our own society here and now. If so, then our attempts at piecemeal innovation may be doomed either to fail or to be rejected outright.

I label these thoughts pessimistic because they imply a need for drastic changes throughout the whole system, changes that could only be imposed by someone with dangerous power over the lives of others. And that, I have argued, is not the way our psychological revolution should proceed.

In my more optimistic moments, however, I recognize that you do not need complete authority over a social organization in order to reform it. The important thing is not to control the system, but to understand it. Someone who has a valid conception of the system as a whole can often introduce relatively minor changes that have extensive consequences throughout the entire organization. Lacking such a conception, worthwhile innovations may be total failures.

For example, if you institute a schedule of rewards and punishments in the psychiatric ward of a Veterans Hospital, you should not be indignant when the American Legion objects on the grounds that you cannot withhold food and clothing from veterans. If you had

had a more adequate understanding of the hospital as a social system, you would have included the interests and influence of the American Legion in your diagnosis of the problem, and you would have formulated a plan to gain their endorsement as part of your task as a social engineer. You should not demand inordinate power just because you made an inadequate diagnosis of the problem. Understanding must come first.

In my optimistic moments I am able to convince myself that understanding is attainable and that social science is already at a stage where successful applications are possible. Careful diagnosis and astute planning based on what we already know can often resolve problems that at first glance seemed insurmountable. Many social, clinical, and industrial psychologists have already demonstrated the power of diagnosis and planning based on sound psychological principles.

Varela has illustrated such applications by his work in Uruguay. Diagnosis involves not only a detailed analysis of the social organization and of the perceptions and goals of all the people caught up in the problem, but also the description of their abilities and personalities. Planning involves the explicit formulation of a series of steps that will lead these people to consider the problem together and will help them to discover a solution that respects everyone's hopes and aspirations. If, in the course of this plan, it becomes necessary to persuade someone, this is not to be accomplished by coercion or by marshaling facts, but by a gradual, step-by-step process that enables him to reduce his reactance little by little as he convinces himself of the virtues of the alternative view and broadens his conception of the range of acceptable solutions (Zimbardo & Ebbeson, 1969, pp. 114–121). This is not the place and I am not the person to describe the ingenuity with which Varela has constructed such plans and carried them out, but such applications give me some reason for optimism.

Diagnosing practical problems and developing detailed plans to deal with them may or may not be more difficult than solving scientific problems, but it is certainly different. Many psychologists, trained in an empiricist, experimental tradition, have tried to serve two masters at once. That is to say, they have tried to solve

practical problems and simultaneously to collect data of scientific value on the effects of their interventions. Other fields, however, maintain a more equitable division of labor between scientist and engineer. Scientists are responsible for the validity of the principles; engineers accept them and try to use them to solve practical problems.

Although I recognize the importance of evaluating an engineer's product, in this domain it is no easy thing to do. Assessing social innovations is a whole art in itself, one that we are only beginning to develop. Economic considerations are relevant, of course, but we must also learn to evaluate the subtler psychological and social implications of our new solutions (Bauer, 1966). Technological assessment in this sense will not be achieved by insisting that every reform should resemble a well-designed experiment. In particular, the need for assessment should not be allowed to discourage those who enjoy and have a talent for social engineering.

We are in serious need of many more psychological technologists who can apply our science to the personal and social problems of the general public, for it is through them that the public will eventually discover the new paradigm that psychologists are developing. That is to say, it is through the success of such practical applications that we have our best hope for revolutionizing public psychology.

Obviously, we must avoid the evils of superficiality; we must continue as scientists to refine, clarify, and integrate our new paradigm. Most importantly, we must self-consciously recognize that it *is* a new and revolutionary conception that we are working toward, so that isolated discoveries can be related to and evaluated in terms of that larger context. But all that would be futile, of course, if the general public did not accept it, or if public psychology were not altered by it.

There is no possibility of legislating the changes I have in mind. Passing laws that people must change their conceptions of themselves and others is precisely the opposite of what we need. Education would seem to be our only possibility. I do not mean only education in the schoolroom, although that is probably the best communication channel presently at our disposal. I have in mind a more ambitious program of educating the general public.

It is critically important to shape this education to fit the perceived needs of the people who receive it. Lectures suitable for graduate seminars are seldom suitable for laymen, and for a layman facing a concrete problem they are usually worse than useless. In order to get a factory supervisor or a ghetto mother involved, we must give them something they can use. Abstract theories, however elegant, or sensitivity training, however insightful, are too remote from the specific troubles they face. In order to get started, we must begin with people where they are, not assume we know where they should be. If a supervisor is having trouble with his men, perhaps we should teach him how to write a job description and how to evaluate the abilities and personalities of those who fill the job; perhaps we should teach him the art of persuasion, or the time and place for positive reinforcement. If a ghetto mother is not giving her children sufficient intellectual challenge, perhaps we should teach her how to encourage their motor, perceptual, and linguistic skills. The techniques involved are not some esoteric branch of witchcraft that must be reserved for those with PhD degrees in psychology. When the ideas are made sufficiently concrete and explicit, the scientific foundations of psychology can be grasped by sixth-grade children.

There are many obvious and useful suggestions that we could make and that nonpsychologists could exploit. Not every psychological problem in human engineering has to be solved by a professional psychologist; engineers can rapidly assimilate psychological facts and theories that are relevant to their own work. Not every teaching program has to be written by a learning theorist; principles governing the design and evaluation of programmed materials can be learned by content specialists. Not every personnel decision has to be made by a psychometrician; not every interview has to be conducted by a clinical psychologist; not every problem has to be solved by a cognitive psychologist; not every reinforcement has to be supervised by a student of conditioning. Psychological principles and techniques can be usefully applied by everyone. If our suggestions actually work, people should be eager to learn more. If they do not work, we should improve them. But we should not try to give people something whose value they cannot recognize, then complain when they do not return for a second meeting.

Consider the teaching of reading, for example. Here is an obviously appropriate area for the application of psychological principles. So what do we do? We assemble experts who decide what words children know, and in what order they should learn to read them; then we write stories with those words and teachers make the children read them, or we use them in programmed instruction that exploits the principles of reinforcement. But all too often the children fail to recognize the value of learning these carefully constructed lessons.

Personally, I have been much impressed with the approach of Ashton-Warner (1963), who begins by asking a child what words he wants. Mummy, daddy, kiss, frightened, ghost, their own names—these are the words children ask for, words that are bound up with their own loves and fears. She writes each child's word on a large, tough card and gives it to him. If a child wants words like police, butcher, knife, kill, jail, and bomb, he gets them. And he learns to read them almost immediately. It is *his* word, and each morning he retrieves his own words from the pile collected each night by the teacher. These are not dead words of an expert's choosing, but words that live in a child's own experience. Given this start, children begin to write, using their own words, and from there the teaching of reading follows naturally. Under this regimen, a word is not an imposed task to be learned with reinforcements borrowed from some external source of motivation. Learning the word is itself reinforcing; it gives the child something he wants, a new way to cope with a desire or fear. Each child decides where he wants to start, and each child receives something whose value he can recognize.

Could we generalize this technique discovered by an inspired teacher in a small New Zealand school? In my own thinking I have linked it with something that White (1959) has called competence motivation. In order to tap this motivational system we must use psychology to give people skills that will satisfy their urge to feel more effective. Feeling effective is a very personal thing, for it must be a feeling of effectiveness in coping with personal problems in one's own life. From that beginning some might want to learn more about the science that helped them increase their competence, and then perhaps we could afford to be more abstract. But in the beginning we must try to diagnose and solve the problems people think they have, not the problems we experts think they ought to have, and we must learn to understand those problems in the social and institutional contexts that define them. With this approach we might do something practical for nurses, policemen, prison guards, salesmen—for people in many different walks of life. That, I believe, is what we should mean when we talk about applying psychology to the promotion of human welfare.

If you tell me that such a program is too ambitious or too foreign to our conception of ourselves as scientists and practitioners, I must agree that I do not know where to place our fulcrum to move the world. My goal is to persuade you that this is the problem we face, and that we dare not leave it for bureaucrats or businessmen to solve. We will have to cope with it however we can, and I hope that someone has better ideas than I about how to do it.

I can see some promise for innovations in particular subcultures. If we apply our new paradigm in particular institutions—in schools, hospitals, prisons, industries—we can perhaps test its validity and demonstrate its superiority. Many such social experiments are already in progress, of course. And much of the recent surge of interest in community psychology (Bennett, 1966) has been stimulated by the realization that we really do have something to contribute to community life. Perhaps all this work will eventually have a cumulative effect.

One trouble, of course, is that we are trying to reverse the natural direction of influence. Ordinarily, an institution or a community models its own subculture more or less automatically after the larger culture in which it is embedded, and new members require little indoctrination in order to understand the tacit assumptions on which the institution is based. Whether the new paradigm will be powerful enough to reverse this direction is, I suppose, a matter for pure speculation at the present time. It seems unlikely that we will succeed, however, if each application of the new paradigm is viewed as unrelated to every other, and no attempt is made to integrate these experiments into a paradigm for society as a whole.

It is possible, however, that our society may not be quite as resistant as we anticipate. The demand for social relevance that we have been voicing as psychologists is only one aspect of a general dissatisfaction with the current state of our society. On every hand we hear complaints about the old paradigm. People are growing increasingly alienated from a society in which a few wise men behind closed doors decide what is good for everyone. Our system of justice based on punishment and retribution is not working. Even those most blessed by economic rewards are asking for something more satisfying to fill their lives. We desperately need techniques for resolving conflicts, and for preventing them from becoming public confrontations from which reasonable retreat is impossible. Anyone who reads the newspapers must realize that vast social changes are in the making, that they must occur if civilized society is to survive.

Vested interests will oppose these changes, of course, but as someone once said, vested interests, however powerful, cannot withstand the gradual encroachment of new ideas. If we psychologists are ready for it, we may be able to contribute a coherent and workable philosophy, based on the science of psychology, that will make this general agitation less negative, that will make it a positive search for something new.

I recognize that many of you will note these ambitions as little more than empty rhetoric. Psychologists will never be up to it, you will say. We should stay in our laboratories and do our own thing. The public will work out its own paradigms without us. Perhaps such skepticism is justified.

On the other hand, difficulty is no excuse for surrender. There is a sense in which the unattainable is the best goal to pursue. So let us continue our struggle to advance psychology as a means of promoting human welfare, each in our own way. For myself, however, I can imagine nothing we could do that would be more relevant to human welfare, and nothing that could pose a greater challenge to the next generation of psychologists, than to discover how best to give psychology away.

REFERENCES

American Psychological Association. Bylaws of the American Psychological Association. *1968 Directory.* Washington, D.C.: Author, 1968.
Ashton-Warner, S. *Teacher.* New York: Simon & Schuster, 1963.
Bauer, R. A. (Ed.) *Social indicators.* Cambridge: M.I.T. Press, 1966.
Bennett, C. C. *Community psychology.* Report of Boston Conference on the Education of Psychologists for Community Mental Health. Boston: Boston University, 1966.
Davis, K. The perilous promise of behavioral science. In, *Research in the service of man: Biomedical knowledge, development, and use.* A conference sponsored by the Subcommittee on Government Research and the Frontiers of Science Foundation of Oklahoma for the Committee on Government, Operations of the U.S. Senate, October 1966. Washington, D.C.: U.S. Government Printing Office, 1967.
Deutsch, M. Reflections on some experimental studies of interpersonal conflict. Presidential Address to the Eastern Psychological Association, New York, April 11, 1969.
Graziano, A. M. Clinical innovation and the mental health power structure: A social case history. *American Psychologist,* 1969, *24,* 10–18.
Hofstadter, R. *Social Darwinism in American thought.* Philadelphia: University of Pennsylvania Press, 1944.
Kuhn, T. *The structure of scientific revolutions.* Chicago: University of Chicago Press, 1962.
Ladd, E. C., Jr. Professors and political petitions. *Science,* 1969, *163,* 1425–1430.
McGregor, D. *The human side of enterprise.* New York: McGraw-Hill, 1960.
Sanford, F. H. Creative health and the principle of *habeas mentem. American Psychologist,* 1955, *10,* 829–835.
Tyler, L. An approach to public affairs: Report of the ad hoc Committee on Public Affairs. *American Psychologist,* 1969, *24,* 1–4.
Varela, J. A. *Introduction to social science technology.* New York: Academic Press, 1970, in press.
White, R. W. Motivation reconsidered: The concept of competence. *Psychological Review,* 1959, *66,* 297–333.
Zimbardo, P., & Ebbeson, E. *Influencing attitudes and changing behavior.* Reading, Mass.: Addison-Wesley, 1969.

Each society has its own peculiar idiosyncrasies. Institutional reform (from roughly within the system) may yet be possible if we act now. There are other channels besides those commonly held to be guaranteed us by the Constitution. If institutional change can be accomplished, it will have an added benefit. The changes necessary to provide justice, decency, and a beneficial society for everyone will become the new institutions, and these institutions will be dynamic. The institutional revolution would require no deaths, no destruction. It would be the humane way to a humane society. Professor Domhoff presents an alternative to violent revolution—psychic guerrilla warfare to replace corporation capitalism with a post-industrial America.

1.5
How to Commit Revolution

William Domhoff

Part I

I am well aware that most of you aren't revolutionaries—that you are mostly upper-middle-class people cutting loose from home by temporarily growing beards or indulging in exotic potions or getting all caught up in doing good things for your less fortunate brethren from the other side of the tracks.

I know that most of you think it is just a matter of a little more time, a little more education, and a little more good will before most of this country's social and economic problems are straightened out, and I suspect that many of you who are currently among the earnest and concerned are going to be somewhere else in a few years, as is that idealistic student group of past years, your parents.

But maybe some day you will wise up to the Square Deals, New Deals, Fair Deals, New Frontiers, and other quasi-liberal gimmicks used to shore up and justify an overdeveloped, inhuman, and wasteful corporation capitalism as it gradually rose to power in the 20th century. Maybe someday a significant number of people, Left and Right, will learn that courage, integrity, and a casual style aren't enough to bring about meaningful, substantial changes, that moral anguish has to be translated into changes in the social structure which do more than make you feel all warm and good and guilt-free inside.

Maybe some day others of you, who are already on the right road, will learn that no matter how militant or violent or critical you may

Reprinted by permission from the *Peninsula Observer.*

be, you are still not your own person and a revolutionary, as long as you merely try to get your leaders to pay attention and better understand, whether it be through letters or sit-ins or time bombs.

Maybe you will learn to ignore the leaders you are harassing and decide to replace them and their system with yourselves and your own system, and on that day you will become revolutionaries instead of militant supplicants appealing to the stuffy Father Figures for a little more welfare and social justice, and a little less war.

Order of Priorities

There are three aspects, I think, to any good revolutionary program for corporate America. These aspects are closely intertwined, and all three must be developed alongside each other, but there is nonetheless a certain logic, a certain order of priorities, in the manner I present them.

First, you need a comprehensive overall analysis of the present-day American system. You've got to realize that the corporation capitalism of today is not the 19th-century individual capitalism that conservatives yearn for. Nor is it the pluralistic paradise that liberals rave about and try to patch up. Nor is it the finance capitalism of the American Communists who are frozen in their analyses of another day.

Second, you need relatively detailed blueprints for a post-industrial America. You've got to show people concrete plans that improve their lot either spiritually or materially. There's no use scaring them with shouts of socialism, which used to be enough of a plan, however general, but which today only calls to mind images of Russia, deadening bureaucracy, and 1984.

And there's no use boring them with vague slogans about participation and vague abstractions about dehumanization. You've got to get down to where people live, and you've got to get them thinking in terms of a better America without the spectre of Russia, rightly or wrongly, driving any thought of risking social change out of their heads.

Third, and finally, you need a plan of attack, a program for taking power. For make no mistake about it—before most people get involved in revolutionary activity they take a mental look way down the road. Maybe not all the way down the road, but a long way down. They want to know what they are getting into, and what the

chances are, and whether there is really anything positive in sight that is worth the gamble.

I suspect that most people just don't fit the formula that seems to be prevalent in America: get people involved in anything—rent strikes, anti-nuclear testing demonstrations, rat strikes, draft demonstrations, whatever, and gradually they will develop a revolutionary mentality. Ponder carefully about this activity for activity's sake. You need a plan of attack, not just some issues like peace or rats. And one thing more on this point: that plan has to come out of your analysis of the present socioeconomic system and out of your own life experience—that is, out of the American experience, and not out of the experiences of Russia, or China, or Cuba, all of which have been different from each other, and are different from the U.S.A.

The world moves, even in America, and as it moves new realities arise and old theories become irrelevant. New methods become necessary. If you expect to be listened to, you will have to look around you afresh and build your own plan, abandoning all the sacred texts on What Is To Be Done.

Analysis Comes First

The name of the system is corporation capitalism. Huge corporations have come to dominate the economy, reaping fabulous, unheard-of profits and avoiding their share of the taxes, and their owners and managers—the corporate rich—are more and more coming to dominate all aspects of American life, including government. Corporate rich foundations—like Ford, Rockefeller, and Carnegie—finance and direct cultural and intellectual innovations; corporate rich institutes and associations—like the Council on Foreign Relations, the Committee for Economic Development, and the Rand Corporation—do most of the economic, political, and military research and provide most of the necessary government experts and consultants.

As for the future, Bell Telephone is undertaking a pilot project in which it will run a high school in a Detroit ghetto, and Larry Rockefeller has suggested that every corporation in New York "adopt" a city block and help make sure that its residents are healthy, happy, and nonriotous. Adopt-a-block may never happen, and corporations may not run many high schools any time soon,

but such instances are symbolic of where we are probably headed—corporate feudalism, cradle to grave dependency on some aspect or another of a corporate structure run by a privileged few who use its enormous rewards to finance their own private schools, maintain their own exclusive clubs, and ride to the hounds on their vast farm lands.

For even agriculture is being corporatized at an amazing rate. Family farmers are in a state of panic as the corporate rich and their corporations use tax loopholes to gobble up this last remaining bastion of 19th-century America.

Much work on this analysis of corporation capitalism, or feudalism, has been done, but more needs to be done. It is a scandal, or, rather, a sign of corporate rich dominance of the universities, that so little social stratification research concerns the social upper class of big businessmen, that so little political sociology research concerns the power elite that is the operating arm of the corporate rich—indeed, that so much of social science in general concerns itself with the workers, the poor, and other countries, namely with things of interest to the corporate rich.

If you want to know anything about the American power structure you have to piece together the hints of journalists, read the few books by the handful of Leftists who are academic outcasts, follow the research reports of two excellent student groups, and listen to and read Dan Smoot.

Dan Smoot? Yes, Dan Smoot. Properly translated, he has a better view of the American power structure than most American political scientists, who of course merely laugh at him. He may not use the same labels I would for the men in charge (he thinks David Rockefeller & Co. are communists or dupes), but at least he knows who's running the show.

It is truly a commentary on American academia that he and one journalist—Establishment journalist Joseph Kraft—have done the only work on the all-important Council on Foreign Relations, one of the most influential policy-forming associations of the corporate rich.

While the professors are laughing at Dan Smoot and equating the business community with the National Association of Manufacturers and the U.S. Chamber of Commerce, Smoot is keeping up with the activities of the richest,

REPRINTED BY PERMISSION OF JULES FEIFFER. © 1970 JULES FEIFFER.

most powerful, the most internationally oriented of American big businessmen, the vanguard of corporate feudalism.

First Revolutionary Act

This really brings you to your first revolutionary act. Research one thing and one thing only—the American power structure. Withdraw your libido from 12th-century Antarctica, historical criticism of Viking poetry, and other such niceties, and get to where you are: here, America, the 20th century.

Just turning the spotlight on the power elite is a revolutionary act, although only Act One. Ideas and analysis are powerful, and they shake people up. The problem of would-be American revolutionaries has not been an overemphasis on ideas, but the use of old ones, wrong ones, and transplanted ones. That is why C. Wright Mills grabbed American students and parts of American academia. He had new, relevant ideas and facts about the here and now—he exploded old clichés and slogans, and I think he created more radicals with his work than any hundred Oakland or Los Angeles policemen with their billy clubs.

A good analysis is essential in developing a program for taking power because it tells you what you can and cannot expect, what you can and cannot do, and what you should and should not advocate. Let me give four examples:

1. Corporation capitalism, if it can continue to corporatize the "underdeveloped" world and displace the cities, may have a lot more room for reforms. In fact, if creature comfort is enough, it may come to satisfy most of its members. Be that as it may, and I doubt if it can solve its problems in a humanly tolerable way, the important point is that no American revolutionary could find himself shocked or irrelevant because the corporate rich agree to nationwide health insurance or guaranteed annual incomes, or pull out of one of their military adventures.

And don't get your hopes up for any imminent collapse. Better to be surprised by a sudden turn that hastens your time schedule than to be disappointed once again by the flexibility of the corporate rich. This means that you should rely on your own program, not depression or war, to challenge the system and to bring about change, and that you should have a flexible, hang-loose attitude toward the future. Predictions of the inevitability of anything, whether collapse or socialism, fall a little flat and leave us a little jaded after comparing earlier predictions with the experience of the 20th century.

2. Corporation capitalism seems to be very much dependent on overseas sales and investments, probably much more so than it is on the military spending necessary to defend and extend the Free World empire. And even if some economists would dispute

that, I think it is 100 percent safe to say that most members of the corporate rich are convinced that this overseas empire is essential—and that is what affects their political and economic and military behavior. Thus, the corporate rich fear—indeed, have utter horror of—isolationism, and that suggests that you revolutionaries should agree with the conservatives about the need for isolationism.

3. The American corporate rich have at their command unprecedented, almost unbelievable firepower and snooping power. This makes it questionable whether or not a violent revolutionary movement has a chance of getting off the ground. It also makes it doubtful whether or not a secret little Leninist-type party can remain secret and unpenetrated for long. In short a nonviolent and open party may be dictated to you as your only choice by the given fact of the corporate leaders' military and surveillance capability, just as a violent and closed party was dictated by the Russian situation.

4. The differences between present-day corporation capitalism and 19th-century individual capitalism must be emphasized again and again if you are to reach those currently making up the New Right. Those people protest corporation capitalism and its need for big government and overseas spending in the name of small business, small government, competition, the marketplace—all those things destroyed or distorted by the corporate system.

You must agree with the New Right that these things have happened and then be able to explain to them how and why they have happened, not due to the communists or labor, or liberal professors, but due to the growing corporatization of the society and the needs of these corporations.

You can't give up on these New Rightists—they know that the Rockefellers, the J. J. McCloys, the Averell Harrimans, the Paul Hoffmans, the Adlai Stevensons, and the John V. Lindsays run American society. (Here I am just naming some of the relatively few multimillionaire businessmen and corporation lawyers known to the American public.) And, like the New Left, the New Rightists don't like it.

It is your job to teach them that the new corporate system is the problem, not the motives and good faith of the corporate rich they call communists and dupes of liberal academics.

Blueprint for New Society

Now, as to our second general need, blueprints for a post-industrial America. Blueprints are first of all necessary to go beyond mere criticism. Any half-way moral idiot can criticize corporation capitalism, anyone can point to slums, unemployment, waste, phony advertising, inflation, shoddy goods, and on and on.

To be revolutionary, you have got to go beyond the militantly liberal act of offering some criticism and then asking people to write their congressman or to sit in somewhere so that the authorities will do something about the problem. And it is necessary for you to self-consciously begin to develop this plan because it is not going to miraculously appear after a holocaust or emanate mystically from the collective mind of that heterogeneous generalization called The Movement.

Individuals are going to have to develop aspects of these blueprints, wild, yea-saying blueprints that you can present with excitement and glee to Mr. and Mrs. Fedup America. It is not enough to be for peace and freedom, which is really only to be against war and racism. It is not positive enough. As a smug little man from the Rand Corporation—a consultant for the other side—once reminded me, everyone, even he, is for peace and justice—the differences begin when you get to specifics.

Blueprints are also necessary to break the Russian logjam in everyone's thinking, revolutionary and non-revolutionary alike. Only by talking about concrete plans, thus getting people reacting to them and thereby developing their own plans, will people forget about Russia—a centralized, bureaucratic, industrializing country that is neither here nor there as far as you are concerned, and has no relevance to either your criticisms or plans.

In short, you have got to show people that your concern is America, that you love America, and that your moral concern is based upon what America could be, as compared with what it is. No one should out-American you. You, as revolutionaries, have a right to that flag. And if you don't feel like grabbing the present American flag right at this juncture, then reach back into American revolutionary history, to the unfinished revolution, for your flags. Like that great snake flag, that phallic message, of the Gadsden Rebellion with its prideful warning hissing out across the centuries: DON'T TREAD ON ME.

Forget Internationalism

The point is that you are Americans and that you want to build a better, a post-industrial America, that you want to use the base your forefathers gave you to realize the American dream. Forget all this internationalism talk. The foreign revolutions some of you hope to copy were fought by men who were fervent nationalists, not bigoted ethnocentrics who believed that no other nationalism was as good or moral as theirs, but nationalists who were of their people, who loved their country and its culture, and who really lived and developed their own heritage.

They talked internationalism, they read widely, they were appreciative and tolerant of many other culture ways, but they were heart and soul products of their land and its traditions.

To throw away the potent psychological force of nationalism because it has been identified in this country with an Americanism that is often parochial and ethnocentric, and especially anti-Semitic, is to ignore, ironically enough, one of the few things you can learn from studying other 20th-century revolutions: a feeling for your country and its little nuances is an intimate and potent part of Western man.

If that sounds too narrow and unfeeling for some of you, I would add that it is probably wrong anyhow to think your international-ism somehow supports foreign revolutionaries. Don't you think the NLF and the Russians and the Chinese are big enough to take care of themselves? Isn't it perhaps a little bit paternalistic to think you are in any way helping those indigenous movements? Your task is here at home, and the way to get to this task is to develop a set of blueprints to go with your critique.

Now, I don't make these statements, and this distinction between nationalism and ethnocentrism, as one who has not considered the problem long and hard. As a Freudian-oriented psychologist, I believe more than anyone, certainly more than you who subscribe to one or other of the environmentalisms that predominate in American social science, that people everywhere have the same basic psyche, the same wishes and fears.

I believe that the transition rites, myths, and rituals from tribes all over the world show that all men and women suffer from fears of separation from mother and group, that all men come to feel rivalry toward father and brother, that all men must go to the desert or the mountain to struggle for independence from their parents, and that all men have a strange sweet ambivalence toward death.

In short, I know that all people have the same problems, but I also know that there are such things as personality and culture —that is, that we all have slightly different ways of handling our wishes and fears. And since I know that these personality and cultural differences are in good part, if not totally, defenses against anxiety and wishes that cause anxiety, I recognize that to attack them, or to ask people to discard them without offering them a new set of defenses, is to invite resistance, is to invite fear and distrust. We are faced with the seeming paradox that men who share the same problems can easily come to mistrust or hate each other if one person's defenses threaten those of the other.

So I am saying that you should bypass these resistances, that as theoretical psychologists you should of course recognize the psychic universality of mankind, but that as revolutionaries you should also recognize that such a general truism is of no use to you in your day-to-day dealings with people if you are not sensitive to and sympathetic toward those individual and group defenses called personality and culture.

You have to recognize that we are all nationalists in the sense of our identity, and work with this fact, trying to bring out the best in your own national tradition.

If this sounds risky to you somehow, as something that might lead to outcomes you don't advocate or to a narrow parochialism, then you have underestimated the importance of blueprints in your revolutionary program. For it is the blueprints that are the key to transcending narrow outlooks and ensuring that only the best in the American national character is more fully manifested.

It is the explicitly stated blueprints which ensure that some implicit retrogressive program does not come to tacitly guide your actions as a revolutionary movement.

Picture of New Society

What could this post-industrial society look like? Naturally, I have a few suggestions, all tentative, and I will mention some of them. It is on this project that so many more people could become totally involved in the revolutionary process.

If it would be by and large intellectuals, academics, and students who would work on the analysis and critique of the growing corporation feudalism, it would be people from all walks of life who would be essential to this second necessity. You need men and women with years of experience—in farming, small business, teaching, city planning, recreation, medicine, and on and on—to start discussing and writing about ways to organize that part of society they know best for a post-industrial America.

You need to provide outlets via forums, discussions, papers, and magazines for the pent-up plans and ideals of literally millions of well-trained, experienced, frustrated Americans who see stupidity and greed all around them but can't do a thing about it.

You need to say, for example, "Look Mr. and Mrs. City Planning Expert trapped in this deadly bureaucracy controlled by big businessmen, draw up a sensible plan for street development, or park development, in your town of 30,-000 people." "Look, Mr. Blue Collar Worker, working for this big corporation, how should this particular plant be run in a sensible society?"

Many Must Be Neutralized

In addition, the neutralization of large masses should be one of the prime goals of a program to develop and present blueprints for a post-industrial America. To this end each person in America should receive a short, simple, one-page handbill especially relevant to his situation or occupation. It would begin, for example, "Policeman, standing here protecting us from Evil at this demonstration, Where Will You Be After The Revolution?"

And then, in a few short sentences you will tell this bewildered soul that there will still be a great need for policemen after the revolution, but that policemen will tend to do more of the things that they like to do—helping, assisting, guiding—rather than the things that get them a bad name—that is, faithfully carrying out the repressive dictates of their power elite masters.

You will tell him you know that some policemen are prejudiced or authoritarian, but you also know that is neither here nor there because orders on whether to shoot or not to shoot come from officials higher up, who are intimately intertwined in the corporate system.

Similar handbills should be prepared for every person. Some would hear good things, like more money and better health. Some would hear things that would surprise them or make them wonder, like "You won't be socialized, Mr. Small Businessman producing a novelty or retailing pets on a local level, because the socialized corporations can produce more than enough; and furthermore, keep in mind that government in a post-industrial America couldn't possibly harass you as much as the big bankers who won't lend you money, the big corporations who undercut you, and the corporate-oriented politicians who overtax you."

Others, for whom there is no good news, would get such cheery messages as "Insurance Man—we hope you have other skills, like gardening or typing." "Corporate Manager—we hope you like working for the anonymous public good as much as you liked working for anonymous millionaire coupon clippers." "CIA man—we hope you are as good at hiding as you are supposed to be at seeking."

Talk to the New Right

Perhaps most of all, there has to be a consideration of the role of Mr. John Bircher, Mr. Physician, Mr. Dentist, and others now on the New Right. These people are put off or ignored by increasing corporatization, and they have to be shown that their major values —individuality, freedom, local determination—are also the values of a post-industrial America.

This does not mean they will suddenly become revolutionaries, but it is important to start them wondering whether they would find things as bad in the new social system as they do in this system, which increasingly annoys them, exasperates them, and ignores them. They must be weaned from the handful of large corporations and multi-millionaires who use them for their own ends by talking competition while practicing monopoly by screaming about taxes while paying very little, and by talking individuality while practicing collectivism.

What would a post-industrial America look like? First of all, it would be certain American institutions writ large—like the Berkeley food co-op, which is locally controlled by consumers, like the Pasadena water and electric systems, which are publically owned, like the Tennessee Valley Authority, which has allowed the beginnings of the sane, productive, and beautiful development of at least one river region in our country.

In simple terms, the system would start from local controls and work up, like it used to before all power and taxes were swept to the national level, mostly by war and the big corporations. And, as you can see, it would be a mixed system, sometimes with control by consumers, sometimes with control by local government, sometimes with control by regional authorities, and sometimes, as should be made clear in the handbill to certain small businessmen, with control in private hands.

For many retail franchises, for many novelty productions, and, I suspect, for many types of farms and farmers, depending on region, crop involved, and other considerations, private enterprise may be the best method of control.

Must Be Flexible

Some people will ask if, by promising some private ownership, we are pandering to a voting bloc. Is it like the old Communist trick of the United Front? The answer is a resounding NO. Any post-industrial society that does not maximize chances for freedom, flexibility, and individuality is not worth fighting for.

Given the enormous capabilities of corporate production, the economic and cultural insignificance of most small businessmen, and the very small number of family farmers, there is simply no economic or political or cultural reason to socialize everything. There is no "kulak" class, there is no "petty bourgeoisie."

Pre-industrial societies may have had to socialize everything to defend their revolutions against hostile forces, but that is only another way in which your situation differs from theirs.

I have left the most obvious change for last. Of course the corporations would be socialized. Their profits would go to all people in lower prices (and thus higher real wages) and/or repair to local, state, and national treasuries in the amounts necessary to have a park on every corner (replacing one of the four gas stations), and medical, dental, educational, recreational, or arts facilities on the other corners (replacing the other three gas stations—there being no need for any but a few gas stations due to the ease of introducing electric cars when a few hundred thousand rich people are not in a position to interfere).

But how to man this huge corporate enterprise? First, with blue collar workers, who would be with you all the way in any showdown no matter how nice some members of the corporate rich have been to them lately. Second, with men from lower-level management positions who have long ago given up the rat race, wised up, and tacitly awaited our revolution.

Fantasy? Perhaps, but don't underestimate the cynicism at minor levels of the technostructure. I have spoken with and to these groups, and there is hope. They are not all taken in, any more than most Americans are fooled by the mass media about domestic matters. They are just trapped, with no place to go but out if they think too much or make a wave.

"Out" is easy enough if you're young and single, but it's a little sticky if you didn't wake up to the whole corporate absurdity until you were long out of college and had a wife and two kids.

Cultivate these well-educated men and women whose talents are wasted and ill-used. Remind them that the most revolutionary thing they can do—aside from feeding you information and money so you can further expose the system and aside from helping to plan the post-industrial society—is to be in a key position in the technostructure when the revolution comes. You may not win a large percentage of them, but then it wouldn't

take many to help you through the transition.

End Duplication

Then too, part of the corporate system would disappear—one computerized system of banking and insurance would eliminate the incredible duplication, paperwork, and nonsense now existent in those "highly profitable" but worthless areas of the corporate economy.

Corporate retails would be broken up and given to local consumer co-ops, or integrated into nationalized producer-retailer units in some cases. Corporate transports (air, rails, buses) would be given in different cases to state, local, and national government, as well as to, on occasion, the retailers or producers they primarily serve.

The public utilities, as earlier hinted, would finally be given to the public, mostly on the local and regional level, probably on the national level in the case of telephones.

The only real problem, I think, is manufacturing, where you have to hold the loyalty of technicians and workers to survive a transition. Blue collar control—syndicalism—may be the answer in some cases, regional or national government control in others. Here, obviously, is one of those questions that needs much study, with blue collar and white collar workers in the various industries being the key informants and idea men.

I have not here presented a final, detailed set of blueprints for a post-industrial America, but I hope I have suggested how important the development of such blueprints is, that I have tossed out a few ideas that might have merit or start you thinking, and that I have made you see how much energy and enthusiasm might possibly be released by taking such a project to Americans in all walks of life.

Part II

Now to a program for taking the reins of government from the power elite in order to carry out the plan developed by revolutionary visionaries. It is on this point that we are likely to find the most disagreement, the most confusion, the most uncertainty, and the most fear.

But I think you do have something very important to go on— the ideas and experiences and successes of the Civil Rights and New Left and Hippie movements

of the past several years. If they have not given you an analysis of corporate capitalism or a set of blueprints, which is their weakness, they have given you the incredibly precious gift of new forms of struggle and new methods of reaching people; and these gifts must be generalized, articulated, and more fully developed.

I have a general term, borrowed from a radical hippie, that I like to use because it so beautifully encompasses what these movements have given to you—psychic guerrilla warfare—the "psychic" part appealing to my psychologist instincts and summarizing all the hard-hitting nonviolent methods, the "guerrilla warfare" part hopefully giving to those who want to take to the hills some satisfaction, so that they will stick around and participate in the only type of guerrilla warfare likely to work in corporate America.

For make no mistake about it, psychic guerrilla warfare is a powerful weapon in a well-educated, sedate, highly industrialized country that has a tradition of liberal values and democratic political processes.

And it is the kind of guerrilla warfare that America's great new acting-out girls can indulge in on an equal basis with any male anywhere. It is the confrontation politics of the New Left—teach-ins, marches, mill-ins, sit-ins, push-ins, love-ins, folk rocks, be-ins. It is the nonviolent, religiously-based, democratically-inspired confrontation morality of Martin Luther King, and it is the unfailing good humor, psychological analysis, and flower power of the Hippie. Together they are dynamite.

Role of Violence

Before I suggest how and where to lay this psychological dynamite, I know I must force myself to say a few words concerning what you are wondering about most, the role of violence. The words aren't easy for me to say, a look at history makes the ground shaky under me, and many will secretly or openly assume that this is cowardly rationalization by an academic.

Despite all this, I reject the lesson of history by claiming that the situation is different in this over-industrialized, sedate country: I don't think violence will work in corporate America, 1968. I don't believe in nonviolence as a way of life as some people do, so I don't argue from any philosophic base. I have never been adverse to violence or denied its necessity in past revolutions.

No, I'm just afraid violence is not a winning strategy in corporate America, and a winning strategy is the primary concern of the revolutionary consultant.

This doubt about the usefulness of violence in corporate America was also the opinion of one of the greatest violent revolutionists of all time, certainly a man who stands as tall in my gallery of revolutionary heroes as any man.

I refer to Che. Indeed, it is almost a tragedy that those who love and admire Che, and at the same time dream of physical guerrilla warfare in the U.S.A., should overlook his very first premise for it— people take to physical guerrilla warfare only when they have lost all hope of nonviolent solutions. Che is said to have laughed long and hard when asked about the possibility of guerrilla warfare in this country. He too apparently believed that what works in the maldeveloped, exploited hinterland does not necessarily apply to the overdeveloped, affluent capitalist center.

System Must Be Tested

Americans have not lost their hope. Furthermore, they are not likely to lose it by any of the means currently being used to escalate physical confrontations, for such confrontations do not "expose" the most fundamental aspects of the political system.

The only way people would lose their faith in the political system, if they are capable of losing it at all, is in a full and open and honest test of its promise.

And if you argue that people won't listen, that they haven't listened in the past few years, then I say it's because you haven't yet brought to them an analysis that rings true enough, that you haven't yet hit them with a program that is exciting enough, and that you haven't yet provided them with a plan of attack that is believable enough to be worth trying.

I say you really haven't turned on with all your intellectual and libidinal resources, that you haven't given them your best shot. What you have done so far is great, but it is only a prelude. You've got to escalate your incredibleness, your audacity, your cleverness, and your playfulness, not your physical encounters, if you are to break through the American malaise.

Enough of such moralizing and breast-beating. Back to psychic guerrilla warfare. How do you direct this dynamite to its task of destroying the ideological cover of the corporate rich?

First, you start a new political party, a wide-open, locally-based political party dedicated to the development of blueprints for a post-industrial America and to the implementation of them through psychic guerrilla warfare. It should be a party open to anyone prepared to abandon all other political affiliations and beliefs—in other words, it would not be an Anti-This-Or-That coalition of liberal Democrats, Communists, Trotskyists, and Maoists.

In fact, ignore those groups. The best members will drop out and join yours. For the rest, they have no constituencies and would soon fall to fighting the Old Fights among themselves anyway—Communist and Anti-Communist, Pro-Soviet and Anti-Soviet, and On and On ad tedium.

No, you don't need that—it would destroy you like it destroyed them. Indeed, they need you, for if you got something going the party would be big enough for all of them to work in without seeing each other or having to defend the Old Faiths.

Before I go on, let me pause to make some things clear. Lenin was great. So was Trotsky. So were Eugene Debs and Thomas Paine, and so are Mao and Fidel, but they have nothing to teach you except guts and perseverence because your situation is different. Honor them for their courage and their example, but most of all, for their ability to let go of sacred texts and do what was necessary in their given society even when it contradicted received doctrine (as it always did).

Your Own Che

If they could forget the sacred texts of their masters, why can't you go beyond theirs? You need your own Lenins, not theirs, your own Ches, not theirs, and I suspect they will be as different as the first is from the second.

So what does your party do besides present a constant withering critique of corporation capitalism and build blueprints of a post-industrial America? It practices all forms of psychic guerrilla warfare whenever and wherever there is a possible convert. Eventually, and on the right occasions, it even enters elections, not to win votes at first, but to win converts. In making its pitch, it doesn't ask men and women to quit their jobs or take to the hills, but rather it asks them to commit their allegiances to new socioeconomic arrangements, to help develop new social and intellectual institutions, to financially support the growth of the party, to read party-oriented newspapers, to convert and neutralize friends and neighbors, and even to stand firm if the corporate rich try something funny.

Neutralize the Army

But what about the military, you ask? Everyone knows that any serious revolution must not only isolate the ruling social class and eliminate its economic base, but it must do away with the army that is its ultimate instrument. How is that possible in America? By keeping it a civilian, draftee army and by infiltrating its officer ranks. As long as the American army is not a standing, professional army, as long as it is made up mostly of civilian recruits serving short terms, then you have control of that army to the degree that you have the loyalty of the majority of citizens.

However, to ensure leadership, at a certain point it would become necessary for party members to sacrifice themselves, not by avoiding the draft, but by joining the ranks of military officers. If that sounds like a very great sacrifice, I agree, but perhaps it will appeal to those among you who like undercover games.

Let me be sure I am being clear. Now is not the time to begin infiltrating the army, but at some point along the line that would become a prime task. The only task of such infiltrators would be to make sure that the corporate rich could never turn military firepower on the nonviolent revolution.

They would do this by advocating one thing and one thing only —the subservience of the military to civilian government, the refusal to take sides in an internal political controversy. In so doing they would be indistinguishable from non-party members within the military who truly accepted this tradition. It may be that there are many of those but that should not be counted on.

Who Are Constituents?

Now who does this party address itself to as its agitators and organizers drive around in open-air trucks, complete with folk rock bands, shouting out their message and distributing their handbills in every town, county fair, ghetto, and shopping center in the country? What is its potential constituency?

The answer is first of all a very general one, but this very generality frees American revolutionaries from trying to duplicate the past or fit into theoretical molds.

You should direct yourself to anyone disgusted with the present system and assume that your potential constituency is everyone not wrapped up in the power elite.

This even includes sons and daughters of the corporate rich who have seen enough and want out—and they've always been there in small numbers on the American Left and Right anyhow, so why pretend differently?

I suggest as follows: the initial base is, as C. Wright Mills said, radical intellectuals and students. The intellectuals have got to start talking like Gene Debs and Malcom X. They have got to blast out of the classroom and clinic like Mills and Benjamin Spock, carrying their revolutionary consultation services to every group in the country that will send them an airplane fare or bus ticket.

What with the protection of tenure and the right of academic freedom, and with lots of universities opening up in Canada, Australia, and New Zealand, professors are the least vulnerable group in American society. They ought to be ashamed of themselves for not raising a hundred times more ruckus than they are now.

These professors and their students also have to continue work on the analysis, and begin involving people in their local community to work on the blueprints. They should form small study-action groups in every university, college, and junior college town in the country.

Youth Is Most Vital

These small study-action groups have to prepare themselves for a psychic blitz of their most important constituency. That constituency is simply called youth— blue collar, white collar, white skin, black skin, who cares? They are pouring out of schools like crazy, affluence has made them somewhat independent and hang-loose, many of them don't communicate with their parents, and they're going to be a majority in a very few years.

Catch them in those years when they are sociologically part of a unique subculture and psychologically looking for something moral and true and meaningful for their lives, and sock it to them with analyses and programs that will make them as wise to the slick McCarthys, Kennedys, and Rockefellers as they are to the Rusks, Johnsons, and Nixons.

If you don't get them the first time around, at least they have something to chew over when they get out there in the boredom of being a clerk-typist, or probation officer, or real estate salesman. I know that right now an amazing number of the young are enamored of the integrity and professorial cool of Eugene McCarthy, but that's all he's got. With no program but a little more of the same, wedded to corporation capitalism, and committed to a party with a reactionary Southern wing and a fistful of New York investment bankers, his time is going to run out if he can't produce.

Young people react to the put-on, they hate to be fooled or talked down to or pandered to, and some day they will have had enough— they will remember Humphrey's sell-out, if you are there to remind them; they will remember Johnson's campaign fibs about his plans for Vietnam, if you never let them forget it; and they will start looking around again.

After youth, the early appeals of the party must be to the disaffected teachers, librarians, nurses, and bureaucrats of the white collar class. They are the ones hit by inflation and hurt by the limitations on government spending, not the unionizing blue-collar workers with their built-in cost-of-living raises. And besides, you've got something immediate for them—thanks to the Hippies, you can teach them how to be happy. Happy? Yes happy.

Get your Hippie friends out of the woods, put a light trim on their beards and hairdos, and start them to work on the poor, wasted paper pushers and people manipulators. I'm serious. They can be had. They're going nowhere, they're restless, and their rage shows how jealous they really are. Their kids—using flower power and psychic guerrilla warfare— can cajole them over the line.

After all, these people raised the turned-on kids. Their emptiness and searching is reflected in their children, who have to resort to modern-day ambrosias and Eastern mystical religions to overcome their boredom. If the kids can be had, the parents can be had, if you handle them with psychological bribery and good-humored taunts rather than threats and insults.

Approach the New Right

As I've implied throughout, an effort has to be made toward those on the Right. I'm under no illusions about the difficulties of this, but I insist that it is necessary to dismiss talk about racism and fascism on the Right: all white Americans are racists, and parts of the blue collar world are probably worse than the Right. As to fascism, if we get a European-style dictatorship in this country, it will probably be more like France anyway, and it will be instituted by the corporate rich presently in power in order to get around their difficulties with Congress and local governments.

So forget all this talk about fascism, which has scared American revolutionaries into the laps of the liberals almost as well as the cry of Communism has scared the Right into the arms of the corporate rich. Old Left and liberal talk about fascism amounts to their fear of angering the corporate masters to the point where they call on their supposed Right-wing shock troops.

See if you can make contact with those people on the New Right, who really have no place to go because there is no turning back now that the huge corporations have destroyed individual capitalism. Of course they don't share your program, but they do share your view of the power structure and your desire for more individuality and local autonomy.

In dealing with the New Right, it is essential to respect individuality and personality. Neither Left nor Right really does this despite their rhetoric. A revolution must transcend personality and respect individuality if it is to get to its task of reaching large masses of people. In fact, personal diversity will be an asset in getting the attention of all types of people. Different religions, different styles and different hair arrangements must be de-emphasized (not changed) and consciously subordinated by self-analysis and devotion to common goals through the mechanism of the blueprints.

The enemy is corporation capitalism, not religion, personality structure, or type of oral indulgent —pot on the Left, alcohol on the Right—used to lessen anxiety and dispel depression.

Leave Blacks Alone

Why haven't I mentioned black people till now? Aren't they important? Am I just another Whitey who doesn't care about the black man? Not at all. I suggest that you do what the black man has told you to: let him do his own thing and you get to work building a party that can unite with him some day far off down the road after you've overcome your racism and he's made up his mind about where he's going and with whom. For now the black man is right—you've got nothing to tell him, and he's got to go it on his own in order to win his manhood. Nobody has ever been given anything worth having. Finally some black men are learning that freeing fact.

Of course black people should be welcome in your party, as should anyone who shares your beliefs, but I suspect it will be a while before many will be along.

One group is going to go a separate and/or violent route. They have had enough and they will have to see some fine action from a revolutionary party before they are going to buy any dreams and hopes again. I don't blame them. I for one will never get uppity or moralistic if some blacks decide to bring the whole mess to the ground. I understand their rage, I feel their rage.

But despite my sympathy I don't mistake the catharsis of wrecking the system for changing it. Revolutionary movements grow more slowly and have positive goals. I hope you can show these black radicals something so they'll work with you, because the ones I've watched have the juice to turn the masses on like nothing I've ever seen. Malcolm X was the finest American agitator since Eugene Debs, and a revolutionary party would need a hundred more like him.

Then there's another group of blacks who are committed to nonviolence but who think John F. Kennedy freed them! Imagine. Like the Socialists of the Old Left, their hangup is a faith in the Democratic Party that knows no bounds, through thick and thin, Raw Deal and Screw Deal. Pictures of JFK abound in their homes. The tragic thing about this group is that they don't know they freed themselves—they pushed that smooth-talking young conservative to the wall before he would make a move.

These people don't know their own power. Nor do they understand the limitations of the present socioeconomic system; they are still hoping it will assimilate them economically. Apparently their faith in God and American democracy even includes corporation capitalism. Many even refuse to talk about the Vietnam war, hoping that their white masters will give them a little more if they keep their traps shut about the repression of other colored peoples.

Blue Collar Workers

What about blue collar workers? First, create a party they have to react to. And don't waste time trying to control or shape labor unions, which are conservative bureaucratic institutions these days, rightfully looking out for the working man in day-to-day battles with the corporate leaders. Confront these people at home, at school, and at play, and get them involved in the party and its activities. In short, don't get caught in Old Left fixations.

Now I know there are many thousands of dedicated and farseeing blue collar workers who would be with you from the start, heart and soul, sweat and tears. But don't get the idea that any great percentage of organized labor will be willing to risk leaving the Democratic Party. Right now they have it relatively good—as long as they are working, or are insulated against automation, or have cost-of-living raises built into their contracts as checks against inflation. But no matter how nicely some of the corporate rich treat blue collar workers in wartime, don't worry, because there is no question about where the blue collar masses would be in a showdown if you have done your homework carefully.

Force a Choice

Let's assume that the party is not snuffed out in its early stages and that it grows. Then the power elite is in a bind; they will have to compete with it, which means a move towards the Welfare State, or, failing that, they would have to repress it, which would be the great watershed for American liberals, liberalism, and democracy.

If you are nonviolent, open, of all religions, and not tied to a foreign power, they would be destroying America to move on you. Liberals would have no course but to join the fight on your side or admit that socioeconomic privileges are more basic than political institutions and values; some might even be annoyed enough to join you in air-conditioned, music-equipped prison cells that the corporate rich are likely to provide. More generally, at that point the masses of people in America would have to draw their own conclusions about what is to be done.

Your job is to force them to make that choice between democracy and corporation feudalism by taking the system on its promise and testing it to its limits. Either way, you win—a democratic, nonviolent takeover or proof to all that when it gets down to the nitty-gritty, even in America, the only way to power is through the barrel of the gun.

How to Begin

To conclude, let me outline what you should do today and tomorrow if you are revolutionaries (if you are in California, wait until after the November elections so as not to undercut your many friends who are working hard in the Peace and Freedom Party). First, start a chapter of a future revolutionary party. Call it, say, the American Revolutionary Party so as to make your intention clear from the start.

Then, to set the sort of tone you want for the thing, print up a membership card, something like, "I, the undersigned, am a card-carrying member of the American Revolutionary Party, dedicated to replacing corporation capitalism with a post-industrial America through psychic guerrilla warfare."

Then start a chapter newsletter in which you invite people to discuss and develop blueprints for your local area—for running its schools, its beaches, its universities, its utilities, and its factories. Send particularly good ideas and articles, especially those relevant to the national level or other cities, to the editorial staff of the nationwide party journal.

At the same time, begin to hold classes in which you teach about the nature of corporation capitalism and discuss blueprints for a post-industrial America. Such educational efforts are a must, one of the best lessons to be learned from the Old Left, and they are the start of the parallel educational structure that each local chapter should strive to develop.

As soon as you have enough people in the chapter who are dedicated and know what it's all about, then you look for opportunities to reach larger numbers of people through confrontation politics—marches, rallies, sit-ins, whatever, but always including explicit mention of the party and its goals.

If there is a local bond issue asking for higher property taxes to support the schools, then that's the time to show in detail how the corporate rich distort the tax structure and force the burden on the middle levels, even to the point of bribing the tax assessors in some cities. Agree with the New Right that taxes are killing them and tell them why, agree with the liberals on the need for better schools and show them how they would be in a post-industrial America.

If the issue is an increase in the gasoline tax, then maybe that's the time to shock conservatives about the price manipulations and tax dodges by the pious oil companies who help finance the New Right.

In short, armed with a real understanding of the present system and the beginnings of plans for a better one, you use every occasion possible to get people's attention and gain converts.

University Not Key

If you bother to go on campus for other than speeches to interested student groups, use picketing not to stop recruiters or Dow Chemical agents but to educate and convert more students and professors. Aside from exposing the complicity of leading universities and research institutes in the machinations of the corporate rich (which ranges from CIA involvement at MIT and Michigan State to overseas economic front men at Stanford Research Institute), your main concern is elsewhere.

The university is not the key structure in the system, and just exposing its uglier aspects is enough to get you a careful hearing from most students, and even some professors.

This advice about dealing with the universities is part of a larger strategy: ignore the corporate rich and their tag-alongs. You have no criticisms or suggestions to offer them. There is nothing they can do to satisfy you, short of joining your party. Don't try to change them and their policies. Leave that for liberals.

Talk to people, don't debate with the power structure.

Now, once the party exists and has distinct identity, you can of course support just causes. You are for anything that makes peoples' lives better. The important thing is to show that you are for these causes without getting so caught up in them that you can't see the forest for the trees. Don't get sidetracked.

Once you have a good-sized local chapter, then add "politics" to your other activities. This consists of developing parallel governments and councils (like shadow cabinets) ready to step in

if and when, and of running for legislative offices in the hopes of winning and thus gaining a better platform from which to reach people.

Loose National Structure

But action would not take place only on the local level. All the while, the many locals would be in contact through social (not, ugh, business) meetings at regional and national levels. Then too, they would contribute representatives and ideas and money to a loose national party structure which would consist mostly, at the outset, of the editorial staff of the nationwide journal and the organizers, agitators, and revolutionary consultants who would travel around the country helping to organize and strengthen locals.

Every chapter would contribute a few members to this national-level effort each year, thus ensuring that a great many members from all over the country get national experience and perspective. This not only cross-fertilizes the locals and helps maintain an overall outlook, but it provides some basis for the selection of candidates for national offices.

During the summer the national organization would also coordinate the Student Organizing Teams who would in groups of 20–30 spend several weeks in every hamlet in the country carrying the message of the party to the hinterlands. The groups would be made up of those with an empathy for and knowledge of rural America, including return-to-the-land type of Hippies.

Their goal would be to develop a chapter, however small, in any settlement or town where people would listen. And listen they might, for the descendants of those people who became Populists in the 1890's and took potshots at local bankers and judges in the 1930's are being had once again by the corporate oligarchy.

What do you do next? What do you do if the infiltration of the army is not very far along and the corporate rich attempt to suppress your fast-growing movement? Well, you can't expect to anticipate everything.

If your analysis is sound, if your blueprints are appealing, and if your psychic guerrilla warfare has blown the minds and ideological cover of the power elite, then you are part of the most exciting, inspiring, and creative thing in human history: an unstoppable mass movement *that can take care of itself*. Masses in action, armed

with ideas and moral fervor, cannot be beaten.

The real problem for you, then, is not how to end. The real problem is how to begin. And good luck.

John Platt presents another alternative to total destruction, the motto of which might be "we have nothing to change but change itself." He proposes task forces for social research and development —full-time interdisciplinary teams —which can develop ideas and technical solutions to problems which stem from science and technology. Platt presents a crisis intensity chart which may stimulate thinking on the question of social priorities to planners and changers.

Social change, peaceful or turbulent, is powered by "what might be" . . . what is needed is an inventive man or group—a social entrepreneur who can connect the pieces and show . . . some present advantage for every participating party. . . . The whole human experiment may hang on the question of how fast we can now press the development of science for survival.

1.6
What We Must Do

John Platt

There is only one crisis in the world. It is the crisis of transformation. The trouble is that it is now coming upon us as a storm of crisis problems from every direction. But if we look quantitatively at the course of our changes in this century, we can see immediately why the problems are building up so rapidly at this time, and we will see that it has now become urgent for us to mobilize all our intelligence to solve these problems if we are to keep from killing ourselves in the next few years.

Reprinted by permission of the author and the American Association for the Advancement of Science from *Science, 166* (November 28, 1969), 1115–1121. Copyright 1969 by the American Association for the Advancement of Science.

The essence of the matter is that the human race is on a steeply rising "S-curve" of change. We are undergoing a great historical transition to new levels of technological power all over the world. We all know about these changes, but we do not often stop to realize how large they are in orders of magnitude, or how rapid and enormous compared to all previous changes in history. In the last century, we have increased our speeds of communication by a factor of 10^7; our speeds of travel by 10^2; our speeds of data handling by 10^6; our energy resources by 10^3; our power of weapons by 10^6; our ability to control diseases by something like 10^2; and our rate of population growth to 10^3 times what it was a few thousand years ago.

Could anyone suppose that human relations around the world would not be affected to their very roots by such changes? Within the last 25 years, the Western world has moved into an age of jet planes, missiles and satellites, nuclear power and nuclear terror. We have acquired computers and automation, a service and leisure economy, superhighways, superagriculture, supermedicine, mass higher education, universal TV, oral contraceptives, environmental pollution, and urban crises. The rest of the world is also moving rapidly and may catch up with all these powers and problems within a very short time. It is hardly surprising that young people under 30, who have grown up familiar with these things from childhood, have developed very different expectations and concerns from the older generation that grew up in another world.

What many people do not realize is that many of these technological changes are now approaching certain natural limits. The "S-curve" is beginning to level off. We may never have faster communications or more TV or larger weapons or a higher level of danger than we have now. This means that if we could learn how to manage these new powers and problems in the next few years without killing ourselves by our obsolete structures and behavior, we might be able to create new and more effective social structures that would last for many generations. We might be able to move into that new world of abundance and diversity and well-being for all mankind which technology has now made possible.

The trouble is that we may not

survive these next few years. The human race today is like a rocket on a launching pad. We have been building up to this moment of takeoff for a long time, and if we can get safely through the takeoff period, we may fly on a new and exciting course for a long time to come. But at this moment, as the powerful new engines are fired, their thrust and roar shakes and stresses every part of the ship and may cause the whole thing to blow up before we can steer it on its way. Our problem today is to harness and direct these tremendous new forces through this dangerous transition period to the new world instead of to destruction. But unless we can do this, the rapidly increasing strains and crises of the next decade may kill us all. They will make the last 20 years look like a peaceful interlude.

The Next 10 Years

Several types of crisis may reach the point of explosion in the next 10 years: nuclear escalation, famine, participatory crises, racial crises, and what have been called the crises of administrative legitimacy. It is worth singling out two or three of these to see how imminent and dangerous they are, so that we can fully realize how very little time we have for preventing or controlling them.

Take the problem of nuclear war, for example. A few years ago, Leo Szilard estimated the "half-life" of the human race with respect to nuclear escalation as being between 10 and 20 years. His reasoning then is still valid now. As long as we continue to have no adequate stabilizing peace-keeping structures for the world, we continue to live under the daily threat not only of local wars but of nuclear escalation with overkill and megatonnage enough to destroy all life on earth. Every year or two there is a confrontation between nuclear powers—Korea, Laos, Berlin, Suez, Quemoy, Cuba, Vietnam, and the rest. MacArthur wanted to use nuclear weapons in Korea; and in the Cuban missile crisis, John Kennedy is said to have estimated the probability of a nuclear exchange as about 25 percent.

The danger is not so much that of the unexpected, such as a radar error or even a new nuclear dictator, as it is that our present systems will work exactly as planned! —from border testing, strategic gambles, threat and counter-threat, all the way up to that "second-strike capability" that is

already aimed, armed, and triggered to wipe out hundreds of millions of people in a 3-hour duel!

What is the probability of this in the average incident? 10 percent? 5 percent? There is no average incident. But it is easy to see that five or ten more such confrontations in this game of "nuclear roulette" might indeed give us only a 50-50 chance of living until 1980 or 1990. This is a shorter life expectancy than people have ever had in the world before. All our medical increases in length of life are meaningless, as long as our nuclear lifetime is so short.

Many agricultural experts also think that within this next decade the great famines will begin, with deaths that may reach 100 million people in densely populated countries like India and China. Some contradict this, claiming that the remarkable new grains and new agricultural methods introduced in the last 3 years in Southeast Asia may now be able to keep the food supply ahead of population growth. But others think that the reeducation of farmers and consumers to use the new grains cannot proceed fast enough to make a difference.

But if famine does come, it is clear that it will be catastrophic. Besides the direct human suffering, it will further increase our international instabilities, with food riots, troops called out, governments falling, and international interventions that will change the whole political map of the world. It could make Vietnam look like a popgun.

In addition, the next decade is likely to see continued crises of legitimacy of all our overloaded administrations, from universities and unions to cities and national governments. Everywhere there is protest and refusal to accept the solutions handed down by some central elite. The student revolutions circle the globe. Suburbs protest as well as ghettoes, Right as well as Left. There are many new sources of collision and protest, but it is clear that the general problem is in large part structural rather than political. Our traditional methods of election and management no longer give administrations the skill and capacity they need to handle their complex new burdens and decisions. They become swollen, unresponsive—and repudiated. Every day now some distinguished administrator is pressured out of office by protesting constituents.

In spite of the violence of some of these confrontations, this may seem like a trivial problem compared to war or famine—until we realize the dangerous effects of these instabilities on the stability of the whole system. In a nuclear crisis or in any of our other crises today, administrators or negotiators may often work out some basis of agreement between conflicting groups or nations, only to find themselves rejected by their people on one or both sides, who are then left with no mechanism except to escalate their battles further.

The Crisis of Crises

What finally makes all of our crises still more dangerous is that they are now coming on top of each other. Most administrations are able to endure or even enjoy an occasional crisis, with everyone working late together and getting a new sense of importance and unity. What they are not prepared to deal with are multiple crises, a crisis of crises all at one time. This is what happened in New York City in 1968 when the Ocean Hill–Brownsville teacher and race strike was combined with a police strike, on top of a garbage strike, on top of a longshoremen's strike, all within a few days of each other.

When something like this happens, the staffs get jumpy with smoke and coffee and alcohol, the mediators become exhausted, and the administrators find themselves running two crises behind. Every problem may escalate because those involved no longer have time to think straight. What would have happened in the Cuban missile crisis if the East Coast power blackout had occurred by accident that same day? Or if the "hot line" between Washington and Moscow had gone dead? There might have been hours of misinterpretation, and some fatally different decisions.

I think this multiplication of domestic and international crises today will shorten that short half-life. In the continued absence of better ways of heading off these multiple crises, our half-life may no longer be 10 or 20 years, but more like 5 to 10 years, or less. We may have even less than a 50-50 chance of living until 1980.

This statement may seem uncertain and excessively dramatic. But is there any scientist who would make a much more optimistic estimate after considering all the different sources of danger

and how they are increasing? The shortness of the time is due to the exponential and multiplying character of our problems and not to what particular numbers or guesses we put in. Anyone who feels more hopeful about getting past the nightmares of the 1970's has only to look beyond them to the monsters of pollution and population rising up in the 1980's and 1990's. Whether we have 10 years or more like 20 or 30, unless we systematically find new large-scale solutions, we are in the gravest danger of destroying our society, our world, and ourselves in any of a number of different ways well before the end of this century. Many futurologists who have predicted what the world will be like in the year 2000 have neglected to tell us that.

Nevertheless the real reason for trying to make rational estimates of these deadlines is not because of their shock value but because they give us at least a rough idea of how much time we may have for finding and mounting some large-scale solutions. The time is short but, as we shall see, it is not too short to give us a chance that something can be done, if we begin immediately.

From this point, there is no place to go but up. Human predictions are always conditional. The future always depends on what we do and can be made worse or better by stupid or intelligent action. To change our earlier analogy, today we are like men coming out of a coal mine who suddenly begin to hear the rock rumbling, but who have also begun to see a little square of light at the end of the tunnel. Against this background, I am an optimist —in that I want to insist that there is a square of light and that it is worth trying to get to. I think what we must do is to start running as fast as possible toward that light, working to increase the probability of our survival through the next decade by some measurable amount.

For the light at the end of the tunnel is very bright indeed. If we can only devise new mechanisms to help us survive this round of terrible crises, we have a chance of moving into a new world of incredible potentialities for all mankind. But if we cannot get through this next decade, we may never reach it.

Task Forces for Social Research and Development

What can we do? I think that

nothing less than the application of the full intelligence of our society is likely to be adequate. These problems will require the humane and constructive efforts of everyone involved. But I think they will also require something very similar to the mobilization of scientists for solving crisis problems in wartime. I believe we are going to need large numbers of scientists forming something like research teams or task forces for social research and development. We need full-time interdisciplinary teams combining men of different specialties, natural scientists, social scientists, doctors, engineers, teachers, lawyers, and many other trained and inventive minds, who can put together our stores of knowledge and powerful new ideas into improved technical methods, organizational designs, or "social inventions" that have a chance of being adopted soon enough and widely enough to be effective. Even a great mobilization of scientists may not be enough. There is no guarantee that these problems can be solved, or solved in time, no matter what we do. But for problems of this scale and urgency, this kind of focusing of our brains and knowledge may be the only chance we have.

Scientists, of course, are not the only ones who can make contributions. Millions of citizens, business and labor leaders, city and government officials, and workers in existing agencies, are already doing all they can to solve these problems. No scientific innovation will be effective without extensive advice and help from all these groups.

But it is the new science and technology that have made our problems so immense and intractable. Technology did not create human conflicts and inequities, but it has made them unendurable. And where science and technology have expanded the problems in this way, it may be only more scientific understanding and better technology that can carry us past them. The cure for the pollution of the rivers by detergents is the use of nonpolluting detergents. The cure for bad management designs is better management designs.

Also, in many of these areas, there are few people outside the research community who have the basic knowledge necessary for radically new solutions. In our great biological problems, it is the new ideas from cell biology and ecology that may be crucial. In our social-organizational problems, it may be the new theories of organization and management and behavior theory and game theory that offer the only hope. Scientific research and development groups of some kind may be the only effective mechanism by which many of these new ideas can be converted into practical invention and action.

The time scale on which such task forces would have to operate is very different from what is usual in science. In the past, most scientists have tended to work on something like a 30-year time scale, hoping that their careful studies would fit into some great intellectual synthesis that might be years away. Of course when they become politically concerned, they begin to work on something more like a 3-month time scale, collecting signatures or trying to persuade the government to start or stop some program.

But 30 years is too long, and 3 months is too short, to cope with the major crises that might destroy us in the next 10 years. Our urgent problems now are more like wartime problems, where we need to work as rapidly as is consistent with large-scale effectiveness. We need to think rather in terms of a 3-year time scale—or more broadly, a 1- to 5-year time scale. In World War II, the ten thousand scientists who were mobilized for war research knew they did not have 30 years, or even 10 years, to come up with answers. But they did have time for the new research, design, and construction that brought sonar and radar and atomic energy to operational effectiveness within 1 to 4 years. Today we need the same large-scale mobilization for innovation and action and the same sense of constructive urgency.

Priorities: A Crisis Intensity Chart

In any such enterprise, it is most important to be clear about which problems are the real priority problems. To get this straight, it is valuable to try to separate the different problem areas according to some measures of their magnitude and urgency. A possible classification of this kind is shown in Tables 1 and 2. In these tables, I have tried to rank a number of present or potential problems or crises, vertically, according to an estimate of their order of intensity or "seriousness," and horizontally, by a rough estimate of their time to reach climactic importance.

Table 1 is such a classification for the United States for the next 1 to 5 years, the next 5 to 20 years, and the next 20 to 50 years. Table 2 is a similar classification for world problems and crises.

The successive rows indicate something like order-of-magnitude differences in the intensity of the crises, as estimated by a rough product of the size of population that might be hurt or affected, multiplied by some estimated average effect in the disruption of their lives. Thus the first row corresponds to total or near-total annihilation; the second row, to great destruction or change affecting everybody; the third row, to a lower tension affecting a smaller part of the population or a smaller part of everyone's life, and so on.

Informed men might easily disagree about one row up or down in intensity, or one column left or right in the time scales, but these order-of-magnitude differences are already so great that it would be surprising to find much larger disagreements. Clearly, an important initial step in any serious problem study would be to refine such estimates.

In both tables, the one crisis that must be ranked at the top in total danger and imminence is, of course, the danger of large-scale or total annihilation by nuclear escalation or by radiological-chemical-biological-warfare (RCBW). This kind of crisis will continue through both the 1- to 5-year time period and the 5- to 20-year period as Crisis Number 1, unless and until we get a safer peace-keeping arrangement. But in the 20- to 50-year column, following the reasoning already given, I think we must simply put a big "?" at this level, on the grounds that the peace-keeping stabilization problem will either be solved by that time or we will probably be dead.

At the second level, the 1- to 5-year period may not be a period of great destruction (except nuclear) in either the United States or the world. But the problems at this level are building up, and within the 5- to 20-year period, many scientists fear the destruction of our whole biological and ecological balance in the United States by mismanagement or pollution. Others fear political catastrophe within this period, as a result of participatory confrontations or backlash or even dictatorship, if our divisive social and structural problems are not solved before that time.

On a world scale in this period,

famine and ecological catastrophe head the list of destructive problems. We will come back later to the items in the 20- to 50-year column.

The third level of crisis problems in the United States includes those that are already upon us: administrative management of communities and cities, slums, participatory democracy, and racial conflict. In the 5- to 20-year period, the problems of pollution and poverty or major failures of law and justice could escalate to this level of tension if they are not solved. The last column is left blank because secondary events and second-order effects will interfere seriously with any attempt to make longer-range predictions at these lower levels.

The items in the lower part of the tables are not intended to be exhaustive. Some are common headline problems which are included simply to show how they might rank quantitatively in this kind of comparison. Anyone concerned with any of them will find it a useful exercise to estimate for himself their order of seriousness, in terms of the number of people they actually affect and the average distress they cause. Transportation problems and neighborhood ugliness, for example, are listed as grade 4 problems in the United States because they depress the lives of tens of millions for 1 or 2 hours every day. Violent crime may affect a corresponding number every year or two. These evils are not negligible, and they are worth the efforts of enormous numbers of people to cure them and to keep them cured—but on the other hand, they will not destroy our society.

The grade 5 crises are those where the hue and cry has been raised and where responsive changes of some kind are already under way. Cancer goes here, along with problems like auto safety and an adequate water supply. This is not to say that we have solved the problem of cancer, but rather that good people are working on it and are making as much progress as we could expect from anyone. (At this level of social intensity, it should be kept in mind that there are also positive opportunities for research, such as the automation of clinical biochemistry or the invention of new channels of personal communication, which might affect the 20-year future as greatly as the new drugs and solid state devices of 20 years ago have begun to affect the present.)

TABLE 1. CLASSIFICATION OF PROBLEMS AND CRISES BY ESTIMATED TIME AND INTENSITY (UNITED STATES).

GRADE	ESTIMATED CRISIS INTENSITY (NUMBER AFFECTED × DEGREE OF EFFECT)		ESTIMATED TIME TO CRISIS*		
			1 TO 5 YEARS	5 TO 20 YEARS	20 TO 50 YEARS
1.		Total annihilation	Nuclear or RCBW escalation	Nuclear or RCBW escalation	⌖ (Solved or dead)
2.	10^8	Great destruction or change (physical, biological, or political)	(Too soon)	Participatory democracy Ecological balance	Political theory and economic structure Population planning Patterns of living Education Communications Integrative philosophy
3.	10^7	Widespread almost unbearable tension	Administrative management Slums Participatory democracy Racial conflict	Pollution Poverty Law and justice	?
4.	10^6	Large-scale distress	Transportation Neighborhood ugliness Crime	Communications gap	?
5.	10^5	Tension producing responsive change	Cancer and heart Smoking and drugs Artificial organs Accidents Sonic boom Water supply Marine resources Privacy on computers	Educational inadequacy	?
6.		Other problems— important, but adequately re- searched	Military R & D New educational methods Mental illness Fusion power	Military R & D	
7.		Exaggerated dangers and hopes	Mind control Heart transplants Definition of death	Sperm banks Freezing bodies Unemployment from automation	Eugenics
8.		Noncrisis problems being "overstudied"	Man in space Most basic science		

* If no major effort is made at anticipatory solution.

Where the Scientists Are

Below grade 5, three less quantitative categories are listed, where the scientists begin to outnumber the problems. Grade 6 consists of problems that many people believe to be important but that are adequately researched at the present time. Military R & D belongs in this category. Our huge military establishment creates many social problems, both of national priority and international stability, but even in its own terms, war research, which engrosses hundreds of thousands of scientists and engineers, is being taken care of generously. Likewise, fusion power is being studied at the $100-million level, though even if we had it tomorrow, it would scarcely change our rates of application of nuclear energy in generating more electric power for the world.

Grade 7 contains the exaggerated problems which are being talked about or worked on out of all proportion to their true importance, such as heart transplants, which can never affect more than a few thousands of people out of the billions in the world. It is sad to note that the symposia on "social implications of science" at many national scientific meetings are often on the problems of grade 7.

In the last category, grade 8, are two subjects which I am sorry to say I must now call "overstudied," at least with respect to the real crisis problems today. The Man in Space flights to the moon and back are the most beautiful technical achievements of man, but they are not urgent except for national display, and they absorb tens of thousands of our most ingenious technical brains.

And in the "overstudied" list I have begun to think we must now put most of our basic science. This is a hard conclusion, because all of science is so important in the long run and because it is still so small compared, say, to advertising or the tobacco industry. But basic scientific thinking is a scarce resource. In a national emergency, we would suddenly find that a host of our scientific problems could be postponed for several years in favor of more urgent research. Should not our total human emergency make the same claims? Long-range science is useless unless we survive to use it. Tens of thousands of our best trained minds may now be needed for something more important than "science as usual."

The arrows at level 2 in the tables are intended to indicate that problems may escalate to a higher level of crisis in the next time period if they are not solved. The arrows toward level 2 in the last columns of both tables show the escalation of all our problems upward to some general recon-

TABLE 2. CLASSIFICATION OF PROBLEMS AND CRISES BY ESTIMATED TIME AND INTENSITY (WORLD).

GRADE	ESTIMATED CRISIS INTENSITY (NUMBER AFFECTED × DEGREE OF EFFECT)		ESTIMATED TIME TO CRISIS*		
			1 TO 5 YEARS	5 TO 20 YEARS	20 TO 50 YEARS
1.	10^{10}	Total annihilation	Nuclear or RCBW escalation	Nuclear or RCBW escalation	✠ (Solved or dead)
2.	10^9	Great destruction or change (physical, biological, or political)	(Too soon)	Famines Ecological balance Development failures Local wars Rich-poor gap	Economic structure and political theory Population and ecological balance Patterns of living Universal education Communications-integration Management of world Integrative philosophy
3.	10^8	Widespread almost unbearable tension	Administrative management Need for participation Group and racial conflict Poverty-rising expectations Environmental degradation	Poverty Pollution Racial wars Political rigidity Strong dictatorships	?
4.	10^7	Large-scale distress	Transportation Diseases Loss of old cultures	Housing Education Independence of big powers Communications gap	?
5.	10^6	Tension producing responsive change	Regional organization Water supplies	?	?
6.		Other problems—important, but adequately researched	Technical development design Intelligent monetary design		
7.		Exaggerated dangers and hopes			Eugenics Melting of ice caps
8.		Noncrisis problems being "overstudied"	Man in space Most basic science		

* If no major effort is made at anticipatory solution.

struction in the 20- to 50-year time period, if we survive. Probably no human institution will continue unchanged for another 50 years, because they will all be changed by the crises if they are not changed in advance to prevent them. There will surely be widespread rearrangements in all our ways of life everywhere, from our patterns of society to our whole philosophy of man. Will they be more humane, or less? Will the world come to resemble a diverse and open humanist democracy? Or Orwell's *1984*? Or a postnuclear desert with its scientists hanged? It is our acts of commitment and leadership in the next few months and years that will decide.

Mobilizing Scientists

It is a unique experience for us to have peacetime problems, or technical problems which are not industrial problems, on such a scale. We do not know quite where to start, and there is no mechanism yet for generating ideas systematically or paying teams to turn them into successful solutions.

But the comparison with wartime research and development may not be inappropriate. Perhaps the antisubmarine warfare work or the atomic energy project of the 1940's provide the closest parallels to what we must do in terms of the novelty, scale, and urgency of the problems, the initiative needed, and the kind of large success that has to be achieved. In the antisubmarine campaign, Blackett assembled a few scientists and other ingenious minds in his "back room," and within a few months they had worked out the "operations analysis" that made an order-of-magnitude difference in the success of the campaign. In the atomic energy work, scientists started off with extracurricular research, formed a central committee to channel their secret communications, and then studied the possible solutions for some time before they went to the government for large-scale support for the great development laboratories and production plants.

Fortunately, work on our crisis problems today would not require secrecy. Our great problems today

are all beginning to be world problems, and scientists from many countries would have important insights to contribute.

Probably the first step in crisis studies now should be the organization of intense technical discussion and education groups in every laboratory. Promising lines of interest could then lead to the setting up of part-time or full-time studies and teams and coordinating committees. Administrators and boards of directors might find active crisis research important to their own organizations in many cases. Several foundations and federal agencies already have inhouse research and make outside grants in many of these crisis areas, and they would be important initial sources of support.

But the step that will probably be required in a short time is the creation of whole new centers, perhaps comparable to Los Alamos or the RAND Corporation, where interdisciplinary groups can be assembled to work full-time on solutions to these crisis problems. Many different kinds of centers will eventually be necessary, including research centers, development centers, training centers, and even production centers for new sociotechnical inventions. The problems of our time—the $100-billion food problem or the $100-billion arms control problem—are no smaller than World War II in scale and importance, and it would be absurd to think that a few academic research teams or a few agency laboratories could do the job.

Social Inventions

The thing that discourages many scientists—even social scientists—from thinking in these research-and-development terms is their failure to realize that there are such things as social inventions and that they can have large-scale effects in a surprisingly short time. A recent study with Karl Deutsch has examined some 40 of the great achievements in social science in this century, to see where they were made and by whom and how long they took to become effective. They include developments such as the following:

Keynesian economics
Opinion polls and statistical sampling
Input-output economics
Operations analysis
Information theory and feedback theory
Theory of games and economic behavior
Operant conditioning and programmed learning
Planned programming and budgeting (PPB)
Non–zero-sum game theory

Many of these have made remarkable differences within just a few years in our ability to handle social problems or management problems. The opinion poll became a national necessity within a single election period. The theory of games, published in 1946, had become an important component of American strategic thinking by RAND and the Defense Department by 1953, in spite of the limitation of the theory at that time to zero-sum games, with their dangerous bluffing and "brinksmanship." Today, within less than a decade, the PPB management technique is sweeping through every large organization.

This list is particularly interesting because it shows how much can be done outside official government agencies when inventive men put their brains together. Most of the achievements were the work of teams of two or more men, almost all of them located in intellectual centers such as Princeton or the two Cambridges.

The list might be extended by adding commercial social inventions with rapid and widespread effects, like credit cards. And sociotechnical inventions, like computers and automation or like oral contraceptives, which were in widespread use within 10 years after they were developed. In addition, there are political innovations like the New Deal, which made great changes in our economic life within 4 years, and the pay-as-you-go income tax, which transformed federal taxing power within 2 years.

On the international scene, the Peace Corps, the "hot line," the Test-Ban Treaty, the Antarctic Treaty, and the Nonproliferation Treaty were all implemented within 2 to 10 years after their initial proposal. These are only small contributions, a tiny patchwork part of the basic international stabilization system that is needed, but they show that the time to adopt new structural designs may be surprisingly short. Our clichés about "social lag" are very misleading. Over half of the major social innovations since 1940 were adopted or had widespread social effects within less than 12 years—a time as short as, or shorter than, the average time for adoption of technological innovations.

Areas for Task Forces

Is it possible to create more of these social inventions systematically to deal with our present crisis problems? I think it is. It may be worth listing a few specific areas where new task forces might start.

1) *Peace-keeping mechanisms and feedback stabilization.* Our various nuclear treaties are a beginning. But how about a technical group that sits down and thinks about the whole range of possible and impossible stabilization and peace-keeping mechanisms? Stabilization feedback-design might be a complex modern counterpart of the "checks and balances" used in designing the constitutional structure of the United States 200 years ago. With our new knowledge today about feedbacks, group behavior, and game theory, it ought to be possible to design more complex and even more successful structures.

Some peace-keeping mechanisms that might be hard to adopt today could still be worked out and tested and publicized, awaiting a more favorable moment. Sometimes the very existence of new possibilities can change the atmosphere. Sometimes, in a crisis, men may finally be willing to try out new ways and may find some previously prepared plan of enormous help.

2) *Biotechnology.* Humanity must feed and care for the children who are already in the world, even while we try to level off the further population explosion that makes this so difficult. Some novel proposals, such as food from coal, or genetic copying of champion animals, or still simpler contraceptive methods, could possibly have large-scale effects on human welfare within 10 to 15 years. New chemical, statistical, and management methods for measuring and maintaining the ecological balance could be of very great importance.

3) *Game theory.* As we have seen, zero-sum game theory has not been too academic to be used for national strategy and policy analysis. Unfortunately, in zero-sum games, what I win, you lose, and what you win, I lose. This may be the way poker works, but it is not the way the world works. We are collectively in a non–zero-sum game in which we will all lose together in nuclear holocaust or race conflict or economic nationalism, or all win together in survival and prosperity. Some of the many variations of non–zero-sum game theory, applied to group conflict and cooperation, might show us profitable new approaches to replace our sterile and dangerous confrontation strategies.

4) *Psychological and social theories.* Many teams are needed to explore in detail and in practice how the powerful new ideas of behavior theory and the new ideas of responsive living might be used to improve family life or community and management structures. New ideas of information handling and management theory need to be turned into practical recipes for reducing the daily frustrations of small businesses, schools, hospitals, churches, and town meetings. New economic inventions are needed, such as urban development corporations. A deeper systems analysis is urgently needed to see if there is not some practical way to separate full employment from inflation. Inflation pinches the poor, increases labor-management disputes, and multiplies all our domestic conflicts and our sense of despair.

5) *Social indicators.* We need new social indicators, like the cost-of-living index, for measuring a thousand social goods and evils. Good indicators can have great "multiplier effects" in helping to maximize our welfare and minimize our ills. Engineers and physical scientists working with social scientists might come up with ingenious new methods of measuring many of these important but elusive parameters.

6) *Channels of effectiveness.* Detailed case studies of the reasons for success or failure of various social inventions could also have a large multiplier effect. Handbooks showing what channels or methods are now most effective for different small-scale and large-scale social problems would be of immense value.

The list could go on and on. In fact, each study group will have its own pet projects. Why not? Society is at least as complex as, say, an automobile with its several thousand parts. It will probably require as many research-and-development teams as the auto industry in order to explore all the inventions it needs to solve its problems. But it is clear that there are many areas of great potential crying out for brilliant minds and brilliant teams to get to work on them.

Future Satisfactions and Present Solutions

This is an enormous program. But there is nothing impossible about mounting and financing it, if we, as concerned men, go into it with commitment and leadership. Yes, there will be a need for money and power to overcome organizational difficulties and vested interests. But it is worth remembering that the only real source of power in the world is the gap between what is and what might be. Why else do men work and save and plan? If there is some future increase in human satisfaction that we can point to and realistically anticipate, men will be willing to pay something for it and invest in it in the hope of that return. In economics, they pay with money; in politics, with their votes and time and sometimes with their jail sentences and their lives.

Social change, peaceful or turbulent, is powered by "what might be." This means that for peaceful change, to get over some impossible barrier of unresponsiveness or complexity or group conflict, what is needed is an inventive man or group—a "social entrepreneur"—who can connect the pieces and show how to turn the advantage of "what might be" into some present advantage for every participating party. To get toll roads, when highways were hopeless, a legislative-corporation mechanism was invented that turned the future need into present profits for construction workers and bondholders and continuing profitability for the state and all the drivers.

This principle of broad-payoff anticipatory design has guided many successful social plans. Regular task forces using systems analysis to find payoffs over the barriers might give us such successful solutions much more often. The new world that could lie ahead, with its blocks and malfunctions removed, would be fantastically wealthy. It seems almost certain that there must be many systematic ways for intelligence to convert that large payoff into the profitable solution of our present problems.

The only possible conclusion is a call to action. Who will commit himself to this kind of search for more ingenious and fundamental solutions? Who will begin to assemble the research teams and the funds? Who will begin to create those full-time interdisciplinary centers that will be necessary for testing detailed designs and turning them into effective applications?

The task is clear. The task is huge. The time is horribly short. In the past, we have had science for intellectual pleasure, and science for the control of nature. We have had science for war. But today, the whole human experiment may hang on the question of how fast we now press the development of science for survival.

─────────────────────

The problems facing society today are exceedingly complex and interrelated. We exist in a social system which, by its very operation, creates and multiplies the dehumanization of our culture. Those groups and factions entrusted with the well being of our society are the very ones guilty of destroying it. It is not unreasonable that they will resist all efforts at social change which would tend to remove them from control. This forms the basis for the logical argument that a revolution may be necessary to bring about changes beneficial to man. The following paper produced by ecology activists presents a third alternative—attacking our social problems at their source, the industrial structure of the United States. The authors repudiate advances in technology as a solution, arguing that industry will take a cosmetic approach, convinced that expansion of progress is inevitable. They call for durable long-lasting products, the end of overproduction of marginally needed goods, and advance calculation of the cost to the environment of any production. Implicit in the text is the theme of a return of power to the people in opposition to the present system of profit for the few.

1.7
The Earth Belongs to the People: Ecology and Power

R. Giuseppi Slater   Dave Widelock
Doug Kitt   Paul Kangas

Pollution: Hot Air and Smokescreens

Government and industry, President Nixon told the country in his 1970 State of the Union message, *are leading the fight against pollution.* The press agreed: the energy and initiative of American private enterprise, directed and funded in the public interest by the watchdog government, is the only solution.

Mr. Nixon's own program is a shining example of how the government tackles this problem. On nationwide TV and radio, with perhaps half the American people tuned in, he proclaimed a $10 billion program just for water pollution—a headline story.

He failed to point out that the federal government's share would be only $4 billion, to be spent over a nine year period. This would make the average yearly expenditure only $455 million, little more than half of what Congress had already appropriated for 1970, and only about a third of what had already been voted for 1971.

Reprinted by permission from *The Earth Belongs to the People,* San Francisco, Peoples Press, 1970, chaps. V, VII, IX. Copyright 1970 by Peoples Press.

Nor did Nixon care to confess that he was refusing to spend over half the money already set aside for 1970 to start fighting water pollution now. His "war on water pollution" is nothing more than a stealthy retreat!

Of course, Nixon didn't compare his proposed spending on water pollution with the $80 billion for the military or the $5 billion for space now featured in his budget.

But this little bit of deception— in front of 100 million people— only hints at the government's real role in the pollution problem.

The same President Nixon who told 100 million Americans about his concern for our environment is pushing the controversial "supertransport" SST, a commercial airliner that will fly faster than the speed of sound. He wants to spend $700 million giving airplane companies like Boeing the money to develop it.

Have you ever lived by an airport? With all the noise, it's a lousy place to live. The SST, trailing thunderous sonic booms, will bring the sounds of airport violence to over 60 million Americans.

Even worse, many scientists fear that the high-flying SST will leave smoke and dirt high in the atmosphere, where it will remain indefinitely and change the chemistry of the air. Such pollution, they believe, could have tremendously harmful effects, ranging from blotting out sunlight to letting through deadly ultra-violet rays that would bombard the earth.

Very few of us will ever be able to afford a ride on the SST. Fares will be several times higher than on regular jets. Who finds it so important that such a destructive and limited aircraft be built? Business executives, for one. They want to be able to cut a few hours flying time off their intercontinental flights. TWA and Pan Am and United like it: it means more business. Boeing and General Dynamics like it: it means a nice, safe government contract on which they can't possibly lose money.

And, evidently, President Nixon likes it.

There are also less obvious ways in which the federal government aids the forces that are ruining America. In southern Florida, for example, the Army Corps of Engineers drained vast areas of swamp and diverted natural waterflow with an elaborate and costly "flood control/irrigation" complex.

Real estate speculators and businessman-farmers who controlled the land made tremendous profits. But the ecology of the entire region has been disturbed; drinking water is being poisoned with pesticides, and now the Everglades are dying from lack of water.

We subsidize the pollution of our own country.

It's not hard to understand why the federal government does these things. Look at the kind of men who hold the major "environment-management" positions. Look at the policies they set.

The Secretary of the Interior is Walter Hickel, a millionaire businessman from Alaska. He's the guy who made a big deal about stopping oil drilling in the Santa Barbara channel after a Union Oil off-shore well blew out and covered hundreds of miles of California coastline with oil—and then he quietly reversed himself and let the drilling continue. Together with President Nixon, he's been trying to force the "Timber Supply Bill" through Congress, which would let lumber companies come in and chop up millions of acres in our National Forests.

Is Hickel more concerned about the environment, or about the profits of the oil and lumber companies?

Can a *businessman* work for the best interests of all of us?

The federal government thinks so, but then most of the top positions in government are held by business executives and corporation lawyers—like Nixon himself.

The January 18 edition of the Los Angeles *Times* carried a short article which demonstrates rather clearly how a businessman's government responds to pollution problems. It pointed out that after the Santa Barbara oil-drilling disaster, Nixon and Hickel appointed a special panel to decide whether or not drilling should be continued in the area. After "long and careful study," this panel decided that Union Oil and the other companies in the channel should resume drilling.

At least five of the eleven members of that panel, observed the *Times,* were working for Union Oil or its partners in the channel! In addition, the paper observed that most of the others also had dealings with the oil industry, such as contracts, or running universities that received large donations from oil companies.

If the federal government allows the wolves to be the shepherds, what do state and local governments do?

Industry Domination

The state of California has been facing pollution problems as bad as any in the nation. Now state officials are talking big about their counterattack, which is supposed to be a model for the nation.

Among California's worst problems is massive pollution of seashores and coastal waters from off-shore oil drilling. If big oil companies had to pay for the messes they make, they might be a little more careful about mucking over our land and water. So that is what the state attorney general, Charles O'Brien, set out to do after the big Union Oil blow-out. But when he tried to help citizens sue the oil companies, he found that the very state agencies set up to protect the people against industries were the strongest supporters of the oil companies!

The state conservation boards, charged Mr. O'Brien, suffer from "industry domination." How often does a public official come out and admit something like that?

But then, it was becoming difficult to cover up. Especially when one of the directors of the state agency most responsible for controlling pollution in the Santa Barbara channel happened to be a Union Oil executive.

So O'Brien turned to the experts in the state's universities. Men who, for the most part, drew their salaries from the taxpayers. The response of these professors was rather interesting.

"The university experts," said Mr. O'Brien, "all seem to be working on grants from the oil industry. There is an atmosphere of fear. The experts are afraid that if they assist in our case on behalf of the people of California, they will lose their oil industry grants."

Does that sound far-fetched? Wilbur H. Somerton, a professor of oil engineering, admitted that he wouldn't testify "because my work depends on good relations with the oil industry. My interest is serving the petroleum industry."

California cities are notorious for their air pollution. What have urban officials done?

In the Bay Area, officials got together and set up a regional authority: the Bay Area Air Pollution Control District (BAAPCD). Read the hand-outs this agency distributes and you'll see how they've cut down on air pollution by vigorous enforcement. Go to San Francisco or Oakland, especially on a sunny, calm day, and your eyes, nose and lungs tell a different story.

What kind of policies does the BAAPCD follow? For one thing, it's very tolerant of industrial pollution. According to BAAPCD regulations, when pollution control devices in factories have breakdowns, companies can be excused for polluting the air.

One study found that the Shell Oil refinery in nearby Martinez reported "breakdowns" on 84 out of 111 days!

The BAAPCD likes to play down air pollution from big industries. They set their standards so low that they don't even conform to state health standards. This way, industries can pollute all they please and still brag to the public, "We're responsible! We're within the safety standards!"

The BAAPCD makes big claims about how it is winning the battle against air pollution. It tells the public how it cut air pollution "34.3%" in 1967 alone. It doesn't confess that this impressive figure really refers to the amount of air pollution it claims to have *prevented*. But *total* air pollution is increasing. "At least things are getting worse a little less quickly" is what the BAAPCD really means.

Things weren't always done this way. Back in 1961, a man by the name of Benjamin Linsky was the main enforcement officer for the BAAPCD. He ordered a series of studies and then concluded that autos were causing only 25% of local air pollution. Mr. Linsky was quietly eased out of office. His replacement was D. J. (Jud) Callaghan, a former PG&E executive. Within a short time, the BAAPCD decided that cars, not industry, were the worst offenders of all.

What kind of ecology-minded people give policy advice about air polluters and landholders in the BAAPCD?

One man works for Standard Oil. Another works for Dow Chemical. A third draws paychecks from the Pacific Gas and Electric Company, one of the major air polluters and landholders in the area. Three of the "advisors" are actually paid consultants for the Bay Area League of Industrial Associations, an organization put together by big companies like Standard Oil and PG&E to apply "friendly pressure" on public officials and tell the public what a great job industry does.

The wolves are the shepherds.

And California is no exception. It is even considered to have the strictest pollution controls in the nation!

In Eugene, Oregon, there was a filter stoppage in the huge Weyerhauser wood-pulp plant. Rather than shut down the plant, the company decided to continue operations, even though they were dumping raw pollutant—*sheer poison*—into the river 100 yards upstream from the city water intake. The company continued production for the two days it took the filter to be fixed, and then paid a small fine for its pollution.

In Tacoma, Washington, the American Smelting Co. paid the grand total of $3,750 for one year of poisoning the area with lethal, stinking sulfur dioxide. The company is now building an 1100 foot high smokestack to spread the poison over an even wider area— and in doing so it gains legal freedom from pollution prosecution!

All over America, penalties and fines like these are nothing but a license for companies to pollute. Check out your own area. If you have a pollution control board, you'll see that people who live near the big, messy factories don't sit on it. Nowhere are the people who are most affected by industrial poison given the chance to control it. Everywhere government works with industry to save them the expense of cleaning up, and to convince us that something is being done.

And if this is how government tackles pollution, it's not hard to guess what industry does.

Industry's Solution

Many companies take a "cosmetic" approach to pollution. If you can't see it, then it's not there.

They mix steam with the crud belching out of their smokestacks so that the plume looks white, and clean, and harmless. Companies that emit too much filth to disguise often do their dirty work at night—an even better ploy.

Oil companies come out with big ads showing how their "special additive" gasolines make car exhaust so clean that a balloon can be filled with exhaust and remain nearly transparent. This is supposed to mean it's no longer dangerous pollution. A better test would be to stick an oil company executive in the balloon along with the fumes for a few minutes, or pump that exhaust through the

company board room while a meeting is in session.

Other companies prefer to juggle statistics. And there are companies, slightly more blatant than most, that revert to outright lies.

If you read *Life*, or *Look*, or *Time*, you've probably seen full-page ads showing crystal-clear rivers flowing through green, unspoiled forests. The Georgia-Pacific Lumber Co. places these ads and tells us how much it believes in conservation. That same company, reported a Portland, Oregon, newspaper, sent letters to its workers attacking conservationists because they were "trying to limit the workers' right to cut trees!" They're also spending huge sums of *money* pushing for the Timber Supply Bill.

It's a good story to remember next time some big corporation tries to tell you how concerned it is about our environment.

What big corporations are really concerned about is money. That's why they go to so much trouble to be sure the government—and even the public—won't tip the applecart. Because the balance sheet is very one-sided about who profits from pollution versus who pays for it. It reads as follows:

In 1969, American corporations spent approximately a billion dollars on pollution control, while amassing after-tax profits of $66 billion. They spent only 1.5% of their profits cleaning up their own mess!

Even these figures are deceptive. The federal and state governments give big tax breaks to corporations for their pollution-control expenses. For every million dollars companies spend, they get back over $700,000. The public pays 70% of their costs. Their break is our burden.

Not only do we quietly pick up the tab for business' own expenses, but the bill for government anti-pollution programs also falls on our shoulders.

The government wants the public to pay over $10 billion for municipal treatment plants over the next five years, while asking industry to spend only $3 billion (tax-deductible) on its own waste water. But industry uses —and dirties—two-thirds of America's water, and farmers account for most of the rest.

The icing on the cake is the simple fact that 40% of all the wastes handled by *public* water plants come from industry! There's another $4 billion we pick up for them.

It's the same story with air pollution. What companies pay they save on tax deductions, or else they raise the prices and pass the costs on to us. We pay extra for smog control devices on our cars, and for modified gasoline.

And garbage: the cost of handling

all the trash from industry, and all the consumer products which can't be disposed of, will be over $40 billion during the next five to ten years. *Forbes Magazine*, a businessman's journal, tells us very clearly just what this means: "Little wonder that businessmen and Wall Streeters alike are drooling. . . . The taxpayer had better steel himself to pay the tab."

In other words corporations want us to pay for their own pollution, while making big profits out of pollution itself. Pollution control is becoming a Big Business. Some of the big companies that rank among the worst of all polluters are buying up pollution control companies. They want to have their cake and eat it.

There should be no doubt now why the Bigwigs tell us that "People Pollute." "Let the public pay!" is their real message.

They get away with it because the role of industry shapes the role of government. All across the nation, big corporations have friends on planning boards, in legislatures, and on pollution commissions. They sponsor the research of university experts. Their interests are well represented. Who represents the interests of the people?

No one can represent our interests when only wealthy people, or people with powerful backers, can get into office; when the nation's newspapers and radio and television stations are controlled by wealthy men and powerful corporations. Very rarely do black or white working people, or non-wealthy housewives, get to become mayors, or city supervisors—or pollution control officials.

But what if more of them did? Suppose there were lots of dedicated politicians, and suppose corporations agreed to cooperate. Then could they stop pollution? How would they do it?

Pollution: The Nature of the Beast

People Don't Pollute

The human race has been around for a million years. Nature engineered us very carefully so we wouldn't interfere with the balance of life, which supports all living things—including humanity.

You breathe in oxygen and breathe out carbon dioxide (CO_2). You give off solid and liquid wastes.

Plants breathe in CO_2, and take in minerals and nitrogen from animal and human waste. They

PHOTO COURTESY OF RICHARD MISRACH.

use sunlight to turn these things into food substance, and they grow.

Animals eat the plants, then humans eat these animals and plants as well. After we die, our bodies decompose, and become food for the plants.

The cycle is closed. Nothing is wasted.

Pollution interferes with this natural cycle of life, a cycle which depends on air, land and water. What pollutes these things?

Pollution is smoke and oil slicks and junk cars and weed-killers. Pollution pours out of smokestacks, exhaust pipes, culverts, dump trucks. Pollution comes from producing things and from the things that are produced.

We've already seen what makes the air so dirty. Cars and industries do an equal job of poisoning the atmosphere.

Water is even more the victim of the factory. Industry uses and pollutes almost two-thirds of our water supply, and agribusiness (big farms using irrigation) accounts for most of the rest.

People themselves use less than 1/7 of all the water consumed in America. Sewage, the waste that humans put into water, can be removed. The oil, acid, ammonia, dissolved metal and pesticides from industry and agribusiness in most cases cannot be removed.

It's the same story with land pollution (garbage). Industrial and commercial waste makes up 60% of the hundreds of millions of tons of garbage discarded annually. The other 40% comes from "people." But look more closely and you find that much unavoidable people garbage—discarded food, paper and the like—breaks down or can be recycled. The problem comes from all the "convenience" packages.

The no-deposit, non-returnable cans and bottles are hard to get rid of. They pile up on the scrap heaps—over 100 *billion* a year—and actually cost us a lot more money than the old returnable types. Each one costs you an extra 30¢ in taxes for disposal, a tab the manufacturer never mentions. That's one reason they started making non-returnable containers in the first place: to slip us the bill for getting rid of them.

All of which leads to one conclusion: pollution is not a people problem. If it was, countries like India which have many more people and less area than America would be dying from pollution. It is the industrial countries of the world that are polluted, but even

among those some are much more polluted than others. And none of them—not even Japan—compares with America.

The cause of pollution is the way machines and technology are used.

Expanding Corporations

In America, most of the machines and technology are controlled by corporations. The goal of these corporations is to make more and more profits. And in order to do this, they have to grow bigger and produce more. This is what determines how they use the machines and technology and land that they own.

Our economy is like a person built leaning forward who must keep running ahead or he will fall over. Businesses can't keep making and selling the same things all the time because people would soon have most of the products they need, and demand would fall off. Which means profits would fall. Then workers get laid off, plants shut down, and you've got a recession or depression. Which makes profits drop more.

Corporations have to make more things, and convince people to buy more, in order to keep making profits. They *must* keep growing.

America has the world's largest "Gross National Product." That means that America makes more things than any other country in the world. And every year, the GNP gets bigger. . . .

What kinds of goods does Business sell us, and what kind of life does it bring?

We spend thousands of dollars on cars, refrigerators, TV sets, stoves and washing machines that can be made (labor included) for a fraction of their price tags. And then, while we're working overtime to keep up with our payments, the things break down. Or some new and jazzier model comes out.

Advertisements are always yammering at us about some new product that's supposed to make us look and feel sexier, or younger, or stronger, or more important. The ads are very clever, being scientifically designed to play on our weaknesses, our desires, our vanities. They're nothing but psychological pick-pockets and purse-snatchers.

Many of us go into debt to buy all the things the ads tell us we need. No matter how much we have, we never have enough. There's always something else we're urged to buy. There's always

a new set of Joneses we're supposed to keep up with.

So consumer goods and military hardware form the heart of the gigantic American economy. Why are these things produced?

Business must keep growing to make profits. Profits come from sales. The critical problem for corporations becomes "How can we increase sales?" They have found several ways.

They build their products to break down in a relatively short time, because this increases turnover. Scholars call this "planned obsolescence." We can call it *waste*.

They spend billions of dollars on advertising (and tack the cost onto the price-tag) to convince us to buy new things, often things we don't really need. This too we can call *waste*.

They back the politicians and newspapers that push for expensive new defense systems, which collect dust for a few years and are replaced. What else could we call it but *waste!*

Our enormous, expanding economy powers itself by creating waste!

Look at all the metal objects which surround you and consider how many of them you really need. While you do this, keep in mind that 650,000 gallons of America's water are degraded making one ton of steel; 130 million tons are produced each year. It's part of the cost—*your cost*—that companies don't tell you about.

Thumb through the daily paper and notice all the advertising pages. You pay for these ads. Not only do the companies tack the cost onto the price-tag, but 240,000 gallons of water and thousands of trees go into making one ton of newspaper. 61% of all newspaper goes for ads, consuming well over 5 million tons of paper each year. That's your cost also. *Waste exhausts the resources of the land—and of the people.*

There are other, less obvious ways in which we pay the price of an illogical system fueled by greed:

To make greater Los Angeles even greater, some of the world's best farmland is being plowed under at the rate of 90,000 acres a year, over 3½ million acres altogether. This is the private property of speculators turned into profit property: motels, hot dog stands, split level houses and industrial parks rise on prime farmland in a world and a country where people are hungry.

To make up for the resulting shortage of cropland, other interests have opened up inferior land in the desert. Taxpayers had to shell out the $1½ billion necessary to irrigate 1,500,000 acres of Central Valley drylands.

But intensive irrigation can ruin land permanently. Salts and minerals can be leached into the soil, poisoning it for life. The corporation farms of Southern California are working the land as hard and fast as possible, and the land is starting to die a salt death.

The oversized cities of Southern California have run out of water, and so the streams and rivers of five states are tapped. And as whole watersheds are diverted, new disasters result.

Water used for irrigation is fully consumed and cannot be reclaimed. And the rivers that fill the irrigation canals become filled with poisonous pesticides and weed killers.

How much better off are we?

Businessmen are much better off. In the last 5 years, big corporations have grown *31 percent*.

But inflation has crippled many of us. It's left us running on a treadmill. Many of us are even going backwards: working people can't even buy as much now with their paychecks as they could 10 years ago.

Many of us are deeply in debt. American consumers are over $98 *billion* in the hole. That works out to over $2000 per family!

And the final price we pay for all the possessions and "conveniences" that they sell us runs a lot higher. The billions and billions of dollars worth of goods America produces every year exact a fearsome ecological toll.

Our cities are crowded, smelly, and ugly. There's less open land each passing year. Our health is deteriorating: more people are getting degenerative diseases—which means their bodies virtually rot—at younger ages. Even life expectancy is decreasing. Our jobs are boring. We work harder and harder to pay our bills and end up making other people rich.

Alternative

Things don't have to be this way.

Suppose America was really run for the benefit of everyone. That would make it possible to plan very carefully how to use our land, resources and technology without ripping up our environment.

We could use things over instead of using them up. People could decide for themselves what their needs are and what should be produced.

Things would be built to last: there's no reason why lightbulbs can't shine for years, and refrigerators run for a lifetime. The know-

how exists right now but most companies know that durable goods compete with fast profits.

We could get a lot of energy from cleaner power sources like solar power or "super-battery" fuel cells. These things aren't used now because they can't deliver the kind of power needed for enormous cities packed with people, or industries which crank out endless heaps of goods. But they would be perfect for smaller, spread-out cities that could be planned and built.

Even if some of the goods we need must be made by dirty methods and with dirty power, making only as much as we really need and not overloading any one area with factories would minimize the damage. Nature has tremendous ability to clean up human messes if she isn't pushed too hard.

The rewards of technology need not be abandoned if technology is used selectively, and carefully. We don't have to go back to the horse and plow to escape death from the smokestack and culvert.

But this sounds like a wild dream. Not because these things are impossible—they could be started immediately. It sounds unreal because the men and the corporations that run the present system, and profit by it, insist that no other way of doing things is as good as what we have now. And they back up these claims with force when people try to change their system.

And yet, these same men, who are now being attacked from so many directions—by people against the war, by people suffering from inflation, by black and brown and poor people—are now leading the parade and carrying the banners for America's new Ecology Crusade. Politicians talk tough and make promises, government officials slip money and supplies to "responsible" students who demonstrate for ecology; businessmen give financial support to the college professors and conservation clubs that are spreading the Word.

But the Word they spread is a lie. And if lies work better than force to keep people confused and keep them from attacking their system, then lie they will. If encouraging people to rally for Ecology discourages others from rallying for decent working conditions, an end to the war in Asia, equal opportunity, and real control over their own lives, then they will make Ecology the watchword of the day. The wolves will pose as shepherds.

The pollution of America is not an accident. It is not a technical oversight, nor is it the fault of the people, or caused by too many people. It will not be cured by a few fancy gadgets or inventions.

Pollution comes from producing too much, producing too sloppily, and waste. There will be pollution as long as things are made for profit, not because people actually need them. There will be pollution until we consider *all* the costs of making something—including the cost to the environment.

There will be pollution and hunger as long as the land and resources of a nation are run for the profit of a few, and at the expense of the many.

Putting It All Together: Vietnam and America's "Ecology Problem"

Lyndon B. Johnson, a now retired American politician, once said that "the best guide to what we do abroad is what we do at home."

One of the things we have been doing at home is spraying farms, lawns, highway medians and vacant lots with herbicides (weedkillers). Something called 2,3,5-T is the most common one used; it has been sprayed on over 5% of the U.S. Unfortunately it does a lot more than kill weeds.

2,3,5-T was being used near Globe, Arizona, in 1965, and some of it drifted over populated areas. Shortly thereafter, one farmer reported that 60% of his goats were born dead or deformed, and his chickens stopped laying. Then trees started to die. Children got sick. And finally women in the area began to have miscarriages; and many had their reproductive organs removed.

Possibly 30% of South Vietnam has now been sprayed with 2,3,5-T *thirteen times more concentrated* than that permitted in America.

The Army says that it "only" wants to defoliate the trees. But it sprays 2,3,5-T directly on "unfriendly" villages. Unfriendly villages are those in which *any* of the people are sympathetic to the Viet Cong. This includes almost all the villages in South Vietnam.

The American government and American corporations are running the Vietnam war. The corporations build the war machine that the government directs. And polluting Vietnam is one of their basic tactics. They attack the people and destroy the ecology of their country.

The poisons they have sprayed to kill trees and destroy crops stay

LIBERTY, ECOLOGY, MODERNITY. PHOTO COURTESY OF JOSHUA WATTLES.

back from Vietnam of stillborn and deformed babies. We may be crippling a whole generation of Vietnamese.

What does the ecological destruction of Vietnam have to do with the ecological destruction of America?

The same government that tells us about its concern for America's environment poisons the environment of Vietnam. The same corporations that pollute America and call it "pollution control" make products to pollute Vietnam and call it "saving Vietnam from the communists."

Saving Vietnam from the communists can be translated as saving Vietnam from the Vietnamese, even if this means destroying the whole country and the people themselves. The same goes for Guatemala, the Dominican Republic, or any country whose people want to get rid of foreign businessmen and take control over their own resources. Politicians and businessmen cry "Communism!" whenever their power over the people and resources of the earth is threatened, either abroad or at home.

Money and power is the real story behind the Vietnam war. Power for American companies to control the wealth of Southeast Asia. Power that will let them keep the money rolling in.

Vietnam and all of Southeast Asia are prized by American businessmen because of the great natural resources of the region, and because control over this area would give them an immense captive market.

American corporations value the resources because they are things that America no longer has, or never had—things like tungsten, antimony, tin.

American corporations need these markets because the American people just cannot keep buying fast enough to keep the corporations growing and profiting.

The Vietnamese know all this. That's why they are fighting back. For over a thousand years, the Vietnamese have been fighting against foreign powers that came to take away the wealth of their country.

How about us?—we have to fight the war, and we have to pay for it. 45,000 lives and over $100 billion dollars, and the war grinds on. We have nothing to gain from this war—we can only lose.

When you get right down to it, we really have much in common with the Vietnamese. The companies that run America make

in the soil. Much of this soil is permanently destroyed. In many places, after the plant cover dies, the bare ground becomes as hard as a rock through a process called "laterization." Generations must pass before laterized soil can again be farmed.

In other places, bamboo weeds grow in after the original plants are killed. So tough and stubborn is the bamboo plant that it is almost impossible to get rid of once it has taken over the land.

American planes have also sprayed herbicides over 100,000 acres of the mangroves which line Vietnam's estuaries. Estuaries are coastline bays and inlets where fresh water mixes with salt and where, in Vietnam, shoreline mangroves provide breeding grounds that yield premium harvests of fish and shellfish. The Vietnamese have always depended on their estuaries for much of their protein supply.

Now the estuaries of Vietnam have been destroyed. The few fish and shellfish that have survived the destruction cannot be eaten. They are so contaminated as to be poison timebombs for humans.

Poisons that get into soil and water also get into humans, even humans that are born years after the poisons were sprayed. As the lesson of Globe, Arizona shows, they are as deadly to people as they are to weeds and forests. One substance in the herbicides has been found to be 10,000 times more harmful than thalidomide. Already there are reports filtering profits off both of us. And both of us are the victims of their ecological crimes.

The Vietnamese have a head-start on us in solving their pollution problem. They know very clearly what causes it. They are attacking the problem at its source.

If we really want to make America a fit place to live in once again, we also have to understand our problem. More of us have to realize that bad ecology cannot be separated from unjust laws, corrupt politics, or unfairly-distributed wealth, unfit housing, high prices, or lousy working conditions, hungry people or wars of aggression. And once we understand these things, it will be clear that there is only one way to deal with our ecology problem:

Attack the problem at its source.

The following statements of social standards for organizations prepared by the Psychologists for Social Action is reprinted here as a guide to institutions which would be more responsive to social problems and to those institutions which would take action to promote human welfare.

1.8
Social Standards for Organizations

Psychologists for Social Action

People

1. *Personnel*. The organization shall work to employ women, black persons, Mexican Americans, Puerto Ricans, American Indians, and members of other oppressed groups, in numbers that correspond, at each job level, to their proportion in the relevant geographical area.

2. *Participation*. The organization shall strive to provide equal influence in determining policies, practices, and administration of the organization to all persons in or affected by it.

3. *Pay*. The organization shall endeavor to pay all its employees

the average national income, and shall work actively to reduce overall income differentials.

Activities

4. *Work*. The organization shall attempt to organize its activity so that all members have jobs that are intrinsically meaningful and personally rewarding, and as equally so as possible.

5. *Purpose*. The organization shall attempt to produce goods and services that serve real (rather than created) needs and desires of people generally, and shall help see that these goods and services are used in beneficial ways.

6. *Distribution*. The organization shall attempt to make its services and products available to all persons equally, employing subsidization and other means to pursue this goal.

Finances

7. *Income*. The organization shall not accept funds from any source for the purpose of oppressive social control.

8. *Expenditures*. The organization shall endeavor not to purchase goods or services from other organizations that do not attempt to follow these standards.

9. *Use of Capital*. The organization shall try to avoid investments, loans, or other use of capital with organizations that do not attempt to follow these standards.

Guarantees

10. *By-Products*. The organization shall examine carefully the possible physical and social by-products of all its activities to insure that there are no ill effects on the health or well-being of any persons.

11. *Disclosure*. The organization shall make all aspects of its operation open to any person in or affected by the organization.

12. *Freedom of Dissent*. The organization shall not discipline or discriminate against any person for speaking against organizational practices or policies.

Our children are being shot by their older brothers on the campuses throughout the nation. Police no

longer wear badges during riots and national guardsmen put adhesive tape over their name patches.

Anonymous, 1970

CONCLUSIONS

This chapter has been concerned with two questions: Is social change possible and desirable? How can social change be effected? The bare statistics of the "Earth" article offer enough data to affirm the desirability of change. There remains the philosophical considerations contingent upon the presumptions of the leadership of the American society in the instigation of any new system. Interlocking relationships are so complex that it is difficult to trace all possible repercussions of any act however small. For the sake of this chapter and those following, we place the burden of conscience upon the reader, freeing ourselves to consider the remaining question pragmatically, to wit—by what means can change be effected?

Obviously, how the change is to be effected depends upon the change desired. A point which is often overlooked, however, is that both of these considerations depend upon the initial situation. If one is sincere in seeking redress of inequalities, then the important consideration is the change, not the method. The question of violence vs. nonviolence becomes less important. Given some definitions of the current state of the Union, nonviolent means would be effective. There are, however, other points of view. That was in essence the function of this chapter: the presentation of various points of view.

Violence places a horrible responsibility upon the revolutionary. He must judge that the benefit to be derived is greater than the harm that must herald the new age. No one becomes a revolutionary by choice. A revolutionary is a doomed man. If he does not feel the imminence of his own personal doom, he could not risk all to change. It is much safer to be passive and concerned than to be active and revolutionary. And yet the time is slipping away. Though barely visible and even so only dimly, a form of revolution, in our opinion, has begun in the United States.

Meaningful change will have to include a change within people, and yet there is a possibility that institutions, functioning as legal but soulless persons, provide structures which are independent of the people who run them. If, as Professor Edward E. Sampson suggests, the age of *homo mechanicus* is upon us, a simple change of bureaucrats will not be enough. By the same token, minor alterations in structure will not change things if control is still effectively in the hands of these mechanized bureaucrats. Government should exist for and through the interest of the people. Such is not now the case. Any candidate can voice the words the populace wants to hear. Election by computer has become a reality. What a man says while campaigning is having increasingly little effect upon his policies once in office. If the system engulfs those who present themselves as its opponents, it is not because of the system or the man alone. Something is wrong with our sense of priorities. We believe that change is possible, that we do want it, but as a people, we have lacked the sense of urgency to make fundamental changes.

Continued failure to change may push those members of our society who suffer most from the status quo to attack the society regardless of the consequences.

"THOSE WHO MAKE PEACEFUL REVOLUTION IMPOSSIBLE, MAKE VIOLENT REVOLUTION INEVITABLE" J.F.K.

Will "Naderism" Spread to the Social Sciences?

EDITED BY:

John Stuart Chang

Marshall Fuss

Susan Tilya Shuirman

INTRODUCTION

This chapter's title is posed in the form of a question which inquires into the possibilities of developing a program of social action within the social sciences.

The term "Naderism" is used to label the germination of such a program. "Naderism" is a conjured word which, if not already legitimized by lexicographers, may well be on its way to becoming a standard American household word in the English language. The term is named in honor of American social critic, Ralph Nader. A national magazine describes him thus:

As the self-appointed and unpaid guardian of the interests of 204 million United States consumers, he has championed dozens of causes, prompted much of United States industry to reappraise its responsibilities and, against considerable odds, created a new climate of concern for the consumer among both politicians and businessmen.[1]

Those who are infused with this activist spirit are described as "Nader's Raiders." Each summer a limited number of college students are recruited as "Nader's Raiders" to assist Nader in gathering the information necessary to initiate change. To some extent, the student teams who edited each chapter of this book functioned much like Nader's Raiders.

The spirit of being "pro-people" which pervades Naderism is par-

[1] *Time Magazine,* December 12, 1969.

ticularly relevant to the field of social sciences. The knowledge acquired in our profession has important social consequences; it is too important to remain on dusty bookshelves without due consideration as to how it may be used constructively for promoting human welfare.

Certainly social scientists, as professionals in the "people business," should be in the forefront among those who declare themselves "pro-people." There is consensus on this point. But are they likely to become the leaders and proponents of social change? This question is crucial in considering the future direction of the field.

This chapter is devoted to the analysis of social change within the social science profession, with particular emphasis upon psychology, an accident of the academic background of most of the editors. As will be seen, the analytical approaches are bounded by prevalent, established approaches. The chapter surveys some of these ideas presented by today's professionals and then offers some specific suggestions for change within the field.

As this chapter's title suggests rhetorically, the field may well be able to accommodate a new, alternative scheme of professional livelihood for future social scientists, a Naderism which revolutionizes the field.

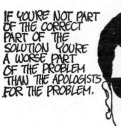

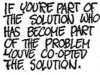

In the beginning . . .
The social science conventions find that they can't be conventional . . .
Shaking up the Psychologists . . .

2.1
Psychologists: Searching for Social Relevance at APA Meeting

Bryce Nelson

"Oh my—another one—oh my," sighed George A. Miller, president of the American Psychological Association (APA), as he learned of yet another disruption at the APA's annual meeting in Washington last week. For the first time the APA had a topic, "Psychology and the Problems of Society," for its annual convention. As it turned out, there was little need for the psychologists to impose a theme on their meeting. Last week, society's problems stormed into the gilded rooms of the Shoreham and the Sheraton-Park hotels to confront the psychologists directly.

According to veteran psychologists, last week marked the first time in the organization's 77-year history that an APA meeting was physically disrupted. Meetings that were more dramatic than usual also marked the annual gathering of the American Sociological Association last week. So far, most of the natural sciences associations have escaped disruption at their meetings. In view of the way things are going, however, the leaders of these organizations would be well advised to begin preparing to cope with the prospect of more boisterous conventions.

The demands of black Americans were again brought to the clear attention of the psychologists when black graduate students in psychology appeared in force at George Miller's presidential address. The students were

Reprinted by permission from *Science, 165* (September 12, 1969), 1101–1104. Copyright 1969 by the American Association for the Advancement of Science.

told that they would be allowed to present their case before the APA council meeting the next morning; Miller was then left to give his presidential address unimpeded.

The next morning, the regular agenda of the APA council was set aside so that the black students could be heard. Twenty-four black students stood shoulder to shoulder at the front of the room confronting the council while their statement and the council's reply were discussed. The black students told the council that it was being allowed 24 hours to come up with its response. Although the council's publicly articulated answer to the students was generally sympathetic, some council members expressed resentment about the confrontation tactics of the students. One of the most activist members of the council, Milton J. Rosenberg of the University of Chicago, told the students that, although "we have our burden to bear in the redemption of the last 200 to 300 years," the council was "beyond racism" and was tired of the "make it hot for whitey routine."

Howard Gruber, a psychology professor at Rutgers but not a member of the APA council, suggested from the audience that the council declare an emergency assessment of $50 or $100 from each person in the 29,000 member APA to improve the opportunities for black people in psychology.

In an impassioned speech, Robert L. Green of the Michigan State University faculty, one of the cochairmen of the Association of Black Psychologists, argued that the APA could afford a $50 commitment from each member. "This can allow APA to become the most meaningful professional organization in the country," Green said. The assessment, he continued, should be made not so that "your building won't be burned down now but rather so that black people can be aided in becoming strong Americans." Green told the council that black psychologists had not been given proper training in universities "to assist black people in liberation," and that "white psychologists and sociologists have shirked their duty to black people and poor people . . . all you have done is attend meetings and read your reports on verbal learning." Green termed such studies "passé."

The idea of a $50 assessment was not mentioned in the request of the Black Students Psychological Association. The students' requests centered around developing

procedures to obtain more black undergraduates, graduate students, and faculty members in psychology; providing community experience for black psychology students; and developing programs that "would equip black students to function in the black community." The students said that APA should provide the "seed money" necessary for research and development on these proposals. The council adopted "in principle" the black students' statement and authorized the establishment of a committee to devise a more concrete set of proposals to present to the APA council meeting on 4 October. The council shied away from setting a specified money figure, but there were private mutterings that anything like a mandatory $50 assessment would drive thousands of APA members out of the organization.

Among APA leaders there seemed to be much more sympathy for the demands of black students and psychologists than for the demands of the radical white psychologists who were also active at the APA meeting. Anne Anastasi, chairman of Fordham's psychology department, commented that she was "depressed" by some of the actions of the white radicals. "The blacks are much more constructive" she said; "we have more faith in their sincerity." Of course, the case of inadequate representation of blacks in psychology has been well documented. A report prepared recently by George W. Albee of Case Western Reserve University indicates that, out of 3767 Ph.D. degrees in psychology granted by the ten most prestigious psychology departments from 1920 to 1966, only eight were given to black psychologists.

The radical white psychologists were also a little bit more difficult to take seriously because of their often playful manner. When the most radical white psychologists, who call themselves the Psychologists for a Democratic Society, took over the stage in the middle of the business meeting, they carried such placards as "Up Against the Wall—APA" and "Produced and Directed by Harold Pinter."

CIA Spooked Away

Radical psychologists were not successful in getting their resolutions acted on by the APA council at this meeting. One of these resolutions involved initiating a committee to study the possibility of eliminating the APA's division of military psychology, and another concerned cutting off business dealings with firms which practice racial discrimination in employment; action on these resolutions was postponed until the APA's October council meeting. Threats by at least one radical psychologist were successful in persuading the APA leaders to ask the Central Intelligence Agency (CIA) to stop its recruiting at the APA meeting. According to APA executive officer Kenneth B. Little, telephone callers had threatened "to bust up the joint" if the CIA remained.

The Psychologists for a Democratic Society and the less radical American Psychologists for Social Action joined forces toward the end of the APA convention to march to the White House to protest the Vietnam war. (One observer asked, "What would a scientific meeting in Washington be these days without a march to the White House?") A couple of hundred marchers struggled through the rain to President Nixon's home. The march illustrated one of the difficulties of achieving relevance—the principal occupant of the White House was sunning himself on the beaches of San Clemente at the time of the march.

Nonetheless, this year's convention was full of statements about the need for psychologists to become more "relevant" to society. Kenneth E. Clark of the University of Rochester told the group, "I believe that if a strong program of participation and involvement does not characterize their work, professional psychologists are no more than run of the mill. . . . The professional psychologist must be a professional activist."

A psychologist-turned-political-leader, Timothy W. Costello, deputy mayor of New York City, said that psychologists "have failed to communicate the value of our science to today's urban decision makers" and urged his fellows to "put aside our professional incest and seek to make friends with politicians, legislators and municipal bureaucrats."

Wiesner Urges New Agency

M.I.T. provost Jerome B. Wiesner told the group that "social and behavioral scientists should get out of their ivory tower." He called for the establishment of a new profession of social engineering to apply the findings of the social sciences to pressing social problems. (Wiesner also said that he

had come to believe in a more centralized system for the federal support of science, since efforts to get the mission-oriented federal agencies sufficiently interested in research support had failed. He urged the creation of a National Institutes of Science similar in structure to the National Institutes of Health, with overall management of scientific funding but with a great deal of autonomy for the individual institutes.)

Why did psychologists express so much concern about social relevance at this year's convention? First, it is obvious that, in an era of mounting social problems, activist students are putting great pressure on their professors to reexamine their attitudes toward their disciplines. Second, it should be remembered that last year's APA convention was held immediately after the violence of the Democratic convention in Chicago. The APA voted, in protest, to move this year's convention from Chicago to Washington, and then decided to devote this year's meeting to the problems of society that had been given such vivid demonstration in Chicago.

George W. Albee, APA president-elect, thinks the concern for social relevance is also related to the historical stage that the psychological profession has now reached. "In the beginning, psychology was concerned with guild building and with establishing legitimacy," Albee noted in an interview. "As these goals are achieved, there is more concern for developing a social consciousness. There is a pervasive awareness that doing psychotherapy with middle-aged neurotics is not the best use of a psychologist's time. The idea of just seeing eight people a day begins to pall after a few years."

George A. Miller of Rockefeller University elaborated similar ideas in an interview. Miller noted that, in the beginnings of the profession of psychology, there had been tensions between the clinicians and the experimentalists, which had become resolved with the increasing respectability of the clinician. Later tensions between academic psychologists and practitioners have also now been resolved, he maintained. "Now, our problem is how to make all these activities relevant to the crisis in our own country," he said.

Miller also pointed out that clinical psychologists are increasingly displacing medical people in "getting out in the community" and working with mental health problems on a large-scale basis.

"More and more they're getting their noses rubbed in real problems," Miller explained, "and they ask what in their psychological training is relevant to their current needs. They come bleeding to our meetings asking frantically for help. They feel that what they were taught in the university **is** *not* what they need to know."

Resistance to Ghetto Research

If the comments at last week's meeting are an accurate indicator, one thing psychologists can avoid doing in their hunt for social relevance is conducting more studies of ghetto residents.

Robert L. Green commented that the black community had served as "a research colony" for social scientists: "Psychologists and sociologists go into the black community and do research but refuse to specify and push major programs of improvement for the black community." In his fiery address to the APA council, Green argued, "Your research has had a negative impact. . . . Do not use us for research efforts any longer. . . . Help us instead to mitigate the effects of white racism."

The warnings against using the ghetto as a "research plantation" were directed against black psychologists as well as white ones. At a scholarly meeting on "the psychology of blackness," a black woman who identified herself as a "nonprofessional" from the inner city told the black psychologists present, "You psychologists come and tell us that we're uneducable. You people shut up and come to listen to us for a change. If you don't, we're going to shut you out of the ghetto. Fortune tellers, that's all you are—a bunch of fortune tellers."

In his talk to the APA, Wiesner criticized social scientists for an "abdication" of responsibility in not protecting the people who are the subjects of their research. "I don't know why the hell social scientists shouldn't defend the people they are talking about," he argued; "I can't understand why the great weight of social sciences can't be put behind worthy causes."

Doubts About Relevance

Not all psychologists want to be "relevant." This was symbolized after the take-over of the business meeting, when a senior psychologist angrily brushed by a student with a placard. The radical asked him, "Aren't you here to promote human welfare?" The senior psychologist heatedly answered, "No, I'm here as a psychologist!"

Although sympathizing with the people who wanted to be socially relevant, George Miller said he was also "fully in sympathy" with the psychologists who maintained that their discipline was a science and who asked "How can we keep it a science if we try to solve everybody's goddamn problems?"

There is also a good deal of doubt among psychologists about how much their discipline has to offer the world. Even among the activists, one heard the statement, as made by one psychologist in a meeting of the Psychologists for a Democratic Society, "Let's face it. We have no answers now. There is no radical psychology yet. We're just trying to get people together."

Psychologist Stanley D. Klein, now a member of the staff of Boston's mayor, said in a paper that his psychological knowledge had been of "limited value" in his political role. He said that psychologists should avoid the fantasy of thinking they "can be especially helpful in social-political situations."

One leading psychologist, Sigmund Koch, a professor at the University of Texas, told *Science* in an interview, "Is psychology socially relevant? I would give an atypical answer. So far as any backlog of scientific knowledge, psychology has very little to offer. Society expects more than we have to provide. It is a very unhappy situation."

Koch, who is a member of the APA council, said he watched with "mixed feelings" the confrontation "with those beautiful black students—these are people who are asking desperately to be taken into our field, but the trouble is that psychology has no answers in respect of the problems that they are concerned about." Koch thinks the main thing psychology can do is to "contribute to our respect for the multiplicity of factors which affect human behavior and the cautions which must be taken into account in describing behavior."

Even if all psychologists were sure how their discipline could be truly relevant to today's social problems, the organization and reward system of their profession, many believe, will have to be drastically changed before much significant work on social issues can be attempted. Kenneth E. Clark pointed out that, in most universities, "the young investigator is taking a grave risk if he takes up a big problem" and that

it usually seems more beneficial to one's career to work on smaller problems. Ernest R. Hilgard of Stanford University said his study indicated that most university departments still respect basic research most highly. Hilgard called for independent graduate schools of applied behavioral sciences. In a small group discussion, one psychologist said to Wiesner, "We all have a social commitment, but our department chairman wants published papers so we have to join our colleagues in running rats so that we can get publishable results."

A difficulty which some psychologists encounter in their quest for social relevance is the feeling that "relevance" is too general a word to give them much direction. What they believe they need is some hard thinking about how to take the small, progressive steps necessary to make their disciplines more socially meaningful.

With the continued pressure from student activists and from the social agonies of our age, there will doubtless be a sustained impulse to change the training given by various disciplines in the social and natural sciences and to alter the role of the professional organizations which represent these disciplines. It may not be entirely true, as Charles W. Thomas told an APA meeting, that "the social revolution has caught social scientists in the wilderness resting on a cot of science for science's sake with their proverbial pants down." But it is safe to say that scientists will be arguing for many years about the types of pants best suited to forays through the tangled thickets of social problems that they feel increasingly pushed to explore.

___

Then it was the psychiatrists turn . . .

2.2
The Psychiatrists and the Protesters

David Perlman

The militant tactics of protest are invading new arenas today—moving from street corners and campuses to forums where tradition and decorous debate have never before been ruffled.

Sex and science were the victims of the new look in controversy a week ago; it may not be long before tectonics, taxonomy and even electron microscopy find themselves beset by alarums and excursions too.

A week ago it was the turn of the American Psychiatric Association, whose members came to town 5000-strong for their annual meeting. They found one research session on problems of human sexuality shattered by an incredible display of uncontrolled temper, mutual abuse and generalized chaos.

Shouting Match

Conflicting shouts in a Sproul Plaza or a Civic Center are no longer news; but when the cries, the tumult and the disruption break up scholarly discussions and set the scholars to shouting back, it may indicate a difficult turn in communication.

Some 600 psychiatrists were attending a panel discussion in Veterans Auditorium when the brouhaha began with a verbal assault by 25 young members of two militant groups: the Women's Liberation Movement and the Gay Liberation Front.

Infuriated by what they perceived as evidence of sexually chauvinistic and insensitive psychiatry, the new popular front heckled the psychiatrists with obscenities and epithets.

Sound and Fury

What astonished everyone else there was the sound and fury of the psychiatrists shouting right back.

"You're a maniac!" shouted one doctor to a vehement homosexual.

"You're a paranoid fool, you stupid bitch!" a distinguished, 65-year-old Viennese born Boston psychiatrist stormed at a Women's Liberation speaker who calls herself simply Judy X.

Cries of "I want my plane fare back!" and "Why don't you idiot girls shut up!" sounded in the auditorium.

Rudeness there was, although it was obvious that to many of the hecklers at the meeting it was actually a successful tactic designed to make the psychiatrists lose their cool and to shock them into seeing new issues.

It was certainly the first scientific meeting in history at which scholars were told off with phrases like "f— you," or their research papers were loudly called "b—s—."

It was also the first to see an angry psychiatrist pointing and cursing in fury at a woman speaker, while the speaker's woman ally shouted: "Don't you point your penis finger at her!"

"Gay Is Good"

The formal psychiatric session at Veterans Auditorium began calmly enough. It ended with a hastily ordered adjournment that interrupted one researcher in midreport, and it continued as a rump session when all the lights went off and someone summoned five policemen.

No one was arrested.

During the official program speakers reported on surgery for transsexuals, conditioned-reflex "aversion therapy" for homosexuals, and the boredom of pornography.

Dr. Nathaniel McConaghy of New Zealand was reporting on experimental use of severe electric shocks and nauseating drugs to condition homosexuals toward heterosexual behavior when the eruption started. A dozen Gay Liberation Front members shouted "torture!" and "barbaric!" and "Gay is good!"

They permitted Dr. McConaghy to finish his paper amid heckling, and then raised a shouting storm of protest over what they called a "tool of fascist psychotherapy."

"Feel Like Scum"

Dr. John P. Brady, professor of psychiatry at the University of Pennsylvania, was chairing the meeting. He tried vainly to calm the shouters, and suggested someone might like five minutes at the microphone.

The young woman called Judy X, who had been talking from the floor, stood up to speak.

She echoed much of the feeling of her friends of both sexes when she described her attitude toward psychiatric concern for sexual identity problems:

"We're made to feel like scum, and we're turned inside out inside ourselves. Why must our shrinks say we're sick when we're not? Why are there no homosexuals on this panel? Why no research by women?"

Priestly Comments

Dr. Evelyn P. Ivey, a New Jersey psychiatrist who was co-chairman of the session, replied:

"I would hope that all this energy could be truly put to liberating women, and that this young vitality would be focused on research."

Then her words were drowned out by a loud "F— you!" from a man in priestly garb who identified himself as Michael F. Itkin of the Evangelical Catholic Communion Church.

After more tumult Dr. Clifford B. Reifler of the University of North Carolina began reading a paper on hard-core pornography (it bores healthy young men to distraction after a while, he said) and Itkin shouted:

"This society is pornographic! The war is pornographic! These papers are pornographic!"

Then Dr. Brady tried to suggest the militants wait and discuss the papers later.

The two dozen hecklers began chanting "We've waited long enough! We've waited long enough."

Dr. Brady finally adjourned the session and practically all the 600 psychiatrists left angrily.

But a couple of dozen stayed, and—to no one's surprise—a serious if brief discussion took place.

One San Francisco Women's Liberation member read an open letter to psychiatrists charging that men "teach us to respond to aggression directed against us with passivity." For too long, she said, men have dominated women, and psychiatrists have become men's allies by telling women their resentments are signs of mental illness or neurosis.

In subhuman primates, she said, male gestures of dominance instinctively elicit "gestures of submission" from females. In humans, however, this submissive response is a pattern of learned behavior—instilled in women over millennia by the men who control the culture. Dominance and submission have no rightful place in human culture, she argued.

Then Marie De Santis, a 25-year-old graduate in chemistry and sociology, told the few psychiatrists who stayed for the impromptu rap session:

"People of our age are really caught in a bind. We're victims of cultural change that's coming on us so fast it's no wonder so many of us come to you asking for help.

"But it's very important in your therapy now that you allow your patients to discuss the social aspects of their problems, because the nature of the world today has really strong effects on people's heads."

Listen, Listen

Dr. Jo Ann Gardner, a Pittsburgh psychologist, defended the disruption at the meeting this way:

"When you're at the forefront of a new movement you have to make yourself heard anyway you can. You psychiatrists must rise above the anxiety of disruptions like this so you can really listen to new voices saying things in new ways."

Among the psychiatrists who stayed to listen until the lights went out was Dr. George H. Hogle of Palo Alto.

"You know," he reflected sadly afterwards, "this could have been a serious encounter, a useful exchange of ideas among people who are far apart.

"Maybe these kids are immature, but maybe they're using shock tactics just to be heard by other people. After all, when they meet on their own no one's listening except themselves.

"I think we could have used our psychiatric skills to keep the full meeting going, and not chicken out because of some shouting. It's too bad, because we really need to know whatever is happening inside people."

And Dr. Maxwell N. Weisman of Johns Hopkins University, another psychiatrist who listened, added:

"What we saw here were people with legitimate grievances who were unable to handle their own rage.

"We saw signs of this on both sides, and the result was chaos. How much better it would have been for these people, with something important to tell us, to have told the whole group instead of this emotionally disturbed rump session. Scenes like this fill me with despair at the hopelessness of confrontation."

Alan Wolfe tells it like it regrettably is. This is one of many disturbing inside looks at the professional mores of academics. He explodes the myth of free scholarship in today's university which too often functions like a corporation. Wolfe describes a system which takes in a young person and forces him into a game which is not conducive to training an academic to be an independent innovator.

2.3
The Myth of the Free Scholar

Alan Wolfe

In *White Collar*, C. Wright Mills pointed out that while American society was becoming increasingly complex, an archaic rhetoric of smallness and competitiveness remained. Nor was this an accident; the divorce between rhetoric and reality served political purposes: "Nobody talks more of free enterprise and competition and of the best man winning than the man who inherited his father's store or farm." I wish to discuss a similar discrepancy, one that takes place in a university setting. My point, simply put, is that while American scholarship and university life are becoming increasingly bureaucratized and standardized, the image of the free scholar freely pursuing his freely chosen subject in a free university setting is continually put forward. Furthermore, this image is designed to mask reality so that those who have succeeded to power in the university can maintain that power without being questioned. No one defends free scholarship, the open pursuit of ideas, and academic freedom as much as the physicist on a government contract, the college president facing an obstructive demonstration, or the social scientist who has never had a critical thought in his life.

In order to build support for my thesis that the modern university uses the imagery of freedom to cover the existence of unfreedom and power, I believe I must do three things. First, unfreedom in the university must be shown to

Reprinted by permission from the July 1969 issue of *The Center Magazine*, a publication of The Center for the Study of Democratic Institutions in Santa Barbara, California.

exist. Second, the connections between the advocates of freedom and the practitioners of unfreedom must be demonstrated. And third, an alternative model of university and scholarly life must be advanced.

Unfreedom exists in at least three different places in the modern university. The university itself is a social institution with interests of its own. It exists in a society where power is valued, and far from being disinterested and neutral, it is an active participant in the struggle for that power. James Ridgeway has documented that aspect of university life in his book *The Closed Corporation*. Another area of unfreedom is the dependence of both the university and its scholars on government and corporate contracts, as well as their patriotic desires to help their country in times of stress, an area explored by Noam Chomsky in *American Power and the New Mandarins*. Finally, the individual located in the university doing his research is subject to limitations of an institutional kind. Far from being a free scholar, he is subject to a series of restraints imposed by his department, his profession, and his society, though not necessarily in that order. Because the first two types of unfreedom have been discussed at length, I would like here to concentrate on the third as evidence for my first charge that little freedom exists in the modern American university.

The image of the free scholar conjures up simplicity, beauty, and harmony. Widely read, he chooses something to concentrate on that particularly strikes his imagination. Examining that item in great detail, he fashions a series of hypotheses about it, and then, going directly to the sources of the problem, gathers all the data on the subject available. With these in hand, the hypothesis is accepted or rejected and the preliminary results presented to like-minded members of the scholar's own discipline in a yearly meeting of people who get together for the purpose of exchanging information on the new boundaries of knowledge. After discussion with his colleagues, he publishes his findings in a disinterested scholarly journal. Other free scholars note its presence there and take his findings into account in their own search. On and on the process is repeated until the truth emerges. All this activity takes place inside universities where job security and the fellowship of disinterested

scholars provide an atmosphere highly conducive to the work of the academic community.

This model has about as much relevance to the reality of twentieth-century American scholarly life as the laissez-faire model has to economic life. First of all, most scholars are not widely read. Their training and the conditions of their lives militate against reading in all areas, including even their own areas of specialization, where skimming or abstracting by research assistants is the rule. Nor does the scholar pick something which strikes his imagination. His primary interest is picked for him by one of his senior professors in graduate school. Further research interests are determined by the conditions of his work. If the picking were left to his imagination, it would probably never be picked. Moreover, the hypotheses are usually selected before the detailed examination is begun. The examination is rarely so detailed that the hypothesis will be rejected. There is too much of a vested interest in having it accepted. To turn to the scholarly get-togethers, the best that can be said is that their purpose is to tantalize. The researcher does not wish to divulge too much lest someone else beat him to publication. And most people have gotten together not to share information but to drink and find a job. Scholarly journals are far from disinterested. They have an ideology (nearly always a conservative one) and they shape their expectations of what is publishable upon that ideology. Other scholars do not read the article, if only because the journals are unreadable. They have it abstracted and place it in proper alphabetical order into their own bibliographies. In short, truth does not emerge. A consensus among like-minded researchers as to what is a correct interpretation does, however, emerge. The university, then, is not conducive to the free-scholar ideal. It is, rather, conducive to an unfree-scholar model. The highly political and insecure nature of university life is in part a response to the standardization and bureaucratization of scholarly life.

I know of no particular way to "prove" the charges I have just made, since we are dealing with abstractions and ideal types. Let me try to complete the picture by examining the career pattern of a young scholar, trying to isolate where the pressures and commitments that destroy the free-scholar model come in.

When he enters graduate school the young political scientist (this being my "field," I have some familiarity with it) is often about twenty-one years old, especially if, like me, he has avoided the draft. He knows that there are certain names which win favorable responses from certain professors. He noticed this in college where a well-placed "Dahl" or "Almond" was easily worth an A. The first two years of graduate school, devoted to course work, become an elaboration of the importance of those names. He can, however, no longer expect that simple mention will get him anywhere; the competition has intensified. Now what he must do is build research designs which take an obscure sentence from one of the masters and build it into a paper from which may eventually come a thesis. Meanwhile, he is expected to distribute the courses he takes among certain subfields, like public administration, international relations, political theory, and so forth. In each sub-field, he notices the same thing. There is a "school" which dominates thinking in that field. The members of that school consider themselves value-free scientists who would undermine their authority if they attempted to deal with politics rather than political science. If the student is sharp, he may also notice that this is a sham, for the leading scholars within each field actually do take political positions and these political positions are supportive of the basic assumptions of the status quo. But chances are he will not notice that, since he is set on becoming a member of that school.

Course work is followed by comprehensive examinations which reflect the division of political science into sub-fields. A comprehensive examination is a form of human activity in which people with a vested interest in doing things a certain way obtain assurances from other people that if permitted to do these things, they too will do them in the same way. At the same time, the presence or absence of knowledge is also searched for. Knowledge is the degree to which the person can manipulate with ease the names of the masters and the ideas associated with those names. If the student has the knowledge, and if he indicates by his answers a sympathy for acknowledged ways of doing things, he passes and is permitted to write a thesis. If he has neither, he is usually permitted two more chances to obtain them.

Now he must write his thesis. It suddenly dawns on him, if it hadn't already, that soon he will be out of graduate school and in the real world. This realization is often the result of his department's decision to stop subsidizing him with fellowships, most of which only last for two or three years. Since he may well have taken on a wife and baby, the decision is important. But all is not lost. One of his professors, coincidentally one who was impressed by his manipulation of the masters' names, or maybe even one of the masters himself, has a grant to deal with "Nonnmilitary Aspects of Civilian Infrastructure in Six New Haven Suburbs," while the student's major interest has been with black insurgency in the inner-city, a reflection of his undergraduate liberalism. Again, all is not lost. Meeting the master (or his disciple) in the hall between conferences, they work out a compromise by which the student can study "Negro Support Building in Six New Haven Suburbs." He masters the jargon necessary for the grant and gets down to work.

The requirement that a thesis has to be published has been taken care of by University Microfilms, Inc., a subsidiary of Xerox Corporation. But not completely. He must plan for his first job, which requires immediate publication, usually from the thesis. Therefore, the thesis is written with two audiences in mind: the specific men on his committee who must approve it, and the men in charge of the journals who must publish it. This is not an enormous problem since these may be the same men, or if not, they are similar men. The point is that he does not write the thesis to support an inner craving of his own but the outer craving of others. Formal and informal guidelines are available for him to master in deciding what those others want. The end result, neither too long nor too short, too theoretical nor too empirical, too stylistic nor too dull, is presented to his committee with the sponsorship of the grant-giver, and after adjustments to mollify the idiosyncratic desires of the committee members are made, he is passed and given his degree. He is now a practicing member of his profession.

What has he learned in graduate school? Much. He has learned the formula for academic success and the futility of his idealism. Remember that he came to graduate school with liberal notions; he wanted to make the world a better place. He has learned that it is permissible to entertain such notions, provided that they remain entertained. For example, his finished thesis resembles his professor's views much more than it resembles his own undergraduate liberalism. He lost in that compromise, as indeed he will lose in many more. He thought when he entered graduate school that academic life was an isolated enclave in a competitive, managerial, corrupt society. As long as he holds that belief he could never exist in the petty, specialized, and conservative world of the modern university. The graduate school experience, then, teaches him a great deal. It is a watershed, socializing him into the new world he is now certified to enter.

University life is departmental life. His senior professor called his attention to an opening at Blank University in the field of urban politics, an opening for which his thesis research suits him perfectly. After meeting with the tenured members of that department and saying to them substantially the same things he said in his comprehensive examination, he is offered a three-year contract as an assistant professor with a nine-hour teaching load. Now a variety of choices is open to him. He can publish (over the next six years) one book and three articles, or six articles, or two books. That is by and large the extent of the choice. If he didn't know it before, he learns quickly enough that publication, and only publication, counts in his career. A survey of political scientists indicates that ninety percent have come to that realization.

Departmental success is defined by time. Normally, a new Ph.D. is granted two three-year contracts before the "up or out" tenure decision is made. At most schools, a decision about the second three-year contract is made a year or more in advance. This means that the new assistant professor must demonstrate his competence within at most a two-year period after obtaining his degree. Demonstrating competence usually means that he has had at least one scholarly article accepted by a reputable journal. Hence, since the time period is too short to start something new, he must dig something out of his thesis. This is usually easy to do because his thesis was written for that purpose, so let us assume that his contract is renewed. This means that his period of grace before tenure is extended to four and a half to five years after his first appointment. But in the greater time period, greater output is expected. Departments are loathe to establish specific quantitative requirements, but an average requirement for tenure is two units, in which a unit is defined as either a book (a written one, not an edited one), three articles, or two edited books. These do not have to be published when the tenure decision is made, but acceptance letters and signed contracts should be presented. In addition, letters of reference from tenured professors in other departments are usually solicited. If he passes all these tests, our scholar, six years older but hardly wiser, is promoted to associate professor and given tenure.

At this point he realizes the value of graduate education. In fact, he has become so educated that he no longer sees himself in conflict with the rules for success. They are merely the conditions of his work; he accepts them and goes about trying to satisfy them. He simply does not have time to challenge them. To be sure, he can take a year or even more off and escape into the field to do research on a foundation grant. But there is little opportunity there to reflect on the type of person he has become because he feels obliged to give the granters a return on their investment. The years rush by. Those who cannot adjust to the pace drop into the inferior college or non-college positions. Those who can maintain and internalize it become successful scholars. The greater the extent our young scholar can make these values his own, the more successful he is.

In case he has still persisted in his illusions about academic life, a tenured position should free him to do those things he always wanted to do. Rarely does this happen. Instead, he has to concern himself with the pressure being exercised by young members of his department who are envious of his prerogatives. This pressure, which generally takes the form of a vicious cycle in which younger men try to outproduce older men only to be outproduced in their turn by people still younger, is combined with a certain amount of pressure from above. A tenured position is a valued slot in the academic department, valued by the chairman and the dean, both of whom are on the lookout for someone who will make the school known. Let our scholar rest on his laurels and he will find his privileges rapidly curtailed. Introductory courses, political science for

business administration students, no secretarial help—these become his lot. With tenure, in other words, the pressure does not cease; if anything, it intensifies. No wonder that few can stand it. At this stage in his career our scholar formally becomes what he already actually was, an administrator. There are so many high-level administrative positions in the modern university that it is fairly easy to promote a nonproducing tenured professor upstairs if you fail to make life miserable enough for him downstairs. Little of this infighting, it should be pointed out, is particularly harmful. Our scholar really did not enjoy his scholarly work too much anyway (who could?) and he gracefully settles for an administrative position.

If he decides to turn down the administrative position and continue producing, he must concern himself with his status in the profession. Both the American Political Science Association and its *Review* tend to share their rewards with like-minded people who adjust to and succeed in the world I have described. The desire to have the so-called high-powered men in the field serve on panels at the annual meetings of the A.P.S.A. is so strong that one man will often have to serve on more than one panel. In addition, older scholars of international repute who rose to full professorships before scholarly life closed itself so tightly often find themselves uninvited to serve on panels no matter how well known they are. Meanwhile, the *American Political Science Review*, although it has in the last few years accepted articles critical of established doctrines, serves to reinforce the situation in the departments through an arbitrary definition of what proper scholarship is, a definition that excludes as inherently inferior anything containing explicit value statements, anything written in the first person (except a Presidential address), or anything written from a point of view totally at odds with the prevailing one in the field. In short, some of the same forces impinging on freedom of scholarly choice which exist in the departments exist also in the profession. Operating together, one detecting possible rejects which might have slipped through the other, these two institutions can almost guarantee that anything faintly resembling the free scholar I described earlier will not rise to a position of prominence or influence in their academic world.

We have now arrived at a definition of a successful scholar. He is a person who constantly reiterates different aspects of the same idea in a manner determined for him by others without being critical of the conditions which have shaped his life.

There is not much difference, I have been arguing, between the scholarly way of life and any other bureaucratic activity taking place in our organizational society. Yet in this one form of human activity, the idea still persists that people are operating freely, making their own personal choices. At a time when the laissez-faire model is totally discredited as a description of economic reality, it is remarkable that the same laissez-faire model is accepted as a description of the not very different scholarly reality.

Laissez-faire served to convince more than one generation of Americans that the reality they perceived around them was itself somehow unreal. It blinded people to reality in order to insure that economically powerful individuals could exercise their power with little criticism. Similarly, as Grant McConnell has shown, the concept of grass-roots democracy was used by powerful local-interest groups that were as undemocratic as they could be, in order to maintain their monopolistic and oligarchic power over public funds. What I am arguing here is that the free-scholar model focuses attention away from realities of the situation and enables those who have succeeded in the system to maintain their power and control over the system. Since this is a procedure which maximizes free choice, the free-scholar advocates argue, anything that attacks it could seriously endanger academic freedom. And since academic freedom is what makes the American university so strong and important, one is accused of being destructive toward the entire process of higher education when one attacks the free-scholar notion as unreal.

"Academic freedom" thus becomes a term like "free enterprise" around which defenders of the status quo are expected to rally. It enables powerful individuals to do "their own thing" without being subject to public review. Just as freedom of choice was used by the Supreme Court in *Lochner vs. New York* to insure industrial slavery, academic freedom is used to justify not only secret research on military matters and the secret proceedings of trustee meetings but the entire system of scholarly slavery. Nor do the ironies end here. While all these unfree activities are justified by "academic freedom," those for whom the term was at one time developed—people with unorthodox political views—remain unprotected. Nearly all the professors who have been fired for their political views in recent years have been charged, not with the possession of an unpopular political ideology, but with unscholarly behavior; that is, they failed to accept the premises under which modern scholarly life is organized and so were deemed unworthy of receiving its benefits. It should now be clear, then, how academic freedom could mean to over one hundred professors at Harvard University that the elimination of a course in riot control from the curriculum is more dangerous than the teaching of a course in riot control.

We should be suspicious of any system when its beneficiaries tell us how well it works. As Jacques Ellul says of man, that "he is most enslaved when he thinks he is comfortably settled in freedom," I would argue that an indication of how unfree our universities are is the constancy with which we are told how free they are. To make this argument—to maintain that what impedes academic freedom is our belief that it has already been won—is to assume the burden of developing an alternative. I would advance the thesis that as socialism is the major alternative to laissez-faire, the social university is the alternative to what we have now. The social university is not primarily concerned with the abstract pursuit of scholarship, but with the utilization of knowledge obtained through scholarship to obtain social change. Therefore, it does not recognize the right of its members to do anything they wish under the name of academic freedom; instead it assumes that all its members are committed to social change. To give an example, a course in riot control would simply be declared out of place in such a university, while a course in methods of rioting might be perfectly appropriate.

Most people who accept the idea that there are limitations on the businessman's right to do as he pleases will find it hard to accept an argument that a university might choose to impose similar limitations on its professors. So I fully expect this notion to be roundly denounced by many. Let

me, then, say something in its defense and in so doing make an attempt to tie together the themes I have touched on in this article.

I would argue that our universities are in disastrous condition because of the laissez-faire pluralism which has been allowed to exist there. My indictments are essentially two. The first is that the adherence to a spurious free-scholar model has obscured reality to the point where academic establishments can almost totally define what will pass for scholarly research. This adherence is used to justify the power these individuals have and serves to remove from the university people who do not coöperate. The result is that the university differs from other institutions only in being a little more hypocritical. Secondly, academic pluralism has insured the predominance of conservative scholarship in a conservative society. The concept of a social university would work toward the elimination of both those problems; by recognizing the unfreedom of the modern scholar, it could free him to channel his energies into social change, and by substituting judgment for pluralism, it could free the university from its dependence on the status quo and transform it into something better than the modern corporation, supermarket, or migrant labor camp.

The social university need not be put off until the arrival of the socialist society. We have in this country at the present time universities which impose limits on the conduct of the professors within them. Many religious colleges and those junior and business colleges which fill the academic freedom violations section of the A.A.U.P. *Journal*, the *lumpenproletariat* institutions of higher education, explicitly impose a conservative or reactionary orthodoxy on their teachers. Our multiversities also impose limits, conservative ones hidden under a different name, like liberalism. With nearly every institution of higher learning in the United States supporting the status quo, the creation of social universities at this time would merely redress an imbalance in an alleged pluralism which has never really existed.

But I am not content to rest the case there. Without having made up my mind on the question, I realize that the concept of the social university undermines the entire tradition of liberal arts education as we know it. I say this, not

in condemnation of the idea, but as a way of forcing all of us to consider alternative methods of education. Liberal arts education is a product of liberalism. If we are to be sincere in our dissatisfaction with liberalism, we must reëvaluate all its tenets, even those which—like academic freedom or the liberal arts—either benefit us to provide us with our livelihood. Without such a reëvaluation, the radical political thought we manage to assemble will be incomplete at best and without impact at worst.

Professor Walker gave this address to the Midwestern Psychological Association in Chicago one year after the Democratic National Convention. It represented a break in the tradition of these conventions in which the president normally talks about his research. Addressing himself to the establishment (the experimental branch) of psychology, Walker stresses that science is a social enterprise, but, if a man is a scientist, he has little time for social activism. In summing up, Walker argues that experimental psychology has the responsibility to interpret its basic research to society, to step up its attack on pressing social problems, and to oppose political climates which inhibit free inquiry.

2.4
Experimental Psychology and Social Responsibility

Edward L. Walker

Experimental psychology is a social enterprise. It is an effort to attack problems of behavior in a controlled and rigorous fashion. The goal is the accumulation of data that are reproducible and the development of principles that

Reprinted by permission of the author and the American Psychological Association from "Experimental Psychology and Social Responsibility," *American Psychologist*, 24, 9 (1969), 862–868. Copyright 1969 by the American Psychological Association.

work. These goals are common to any discipline with scientific aspirations.

Science is a social enterprise. Any effort to examine the problem of experimental psychology and social responsibility must place the problem in a context of the social responsibility of all science. In so doing, it becomes apparent to me that psychology has special problems in the realm of social responsibility that are not shared by other scientific disciplines. This paper is an attempt to explore the problems of social responsibility in an effort to begin the task of the development of a set of guiding principles. Those principles should preserve the integrity of experimental psychology while providing a basis for discussion and decision with respect to particular social realities when psychology is inescapably confronted with them or chooses to respond out of urgent necessity.

Science flourishes to the extent to which it receives social support, and its products may have profound social consequences. I believe that scientists have the responsibility for protecting, encouraging, and guiding social support of their disciplines. Since the products of science may have profound social consequences, I think that the problem of the scientist's responsibilities for the uses to which scientific principles are put requires reexamination.

The Roles of Scientist and Human Being

Some feel that the social responsibility of scientists extends far beyond the realm of the application of principle of science to human affairs. In a recent interview Noam Chomsky (1968) is quoted as saying, "I would not criticize a person as a physicist, in Nazi Germany, if he did only physics. But I'd criticize him as a human being. My argument would be that by being complacent and quiescent he's not preventing oppression and destruction."

There are at least two major difficulties with Chomsky's statement. (a) The first is that the roles of scientist and human being may not be as completely disassociable as Chomsky implies. (b) The second is that the tasks he prescribes for the individual scientist may be physically and psychologically impossible.

While it may be clarifying in some respects to make the distinction between the role as scientist and the role as human being, the difficulty appears to me to arise from the quite unnecessary and invalid assumption that the two roles are in all respects different rather than merely being in some respects different. Specifically, it implies that the scientific enterprise is and should be free of social values. I believe this proposition to be false, and the belief in it to have arisen from false considerations.

There is sometimes confusion between the application of research findings and applied research. The first of these problems is the one that became traumatic for the atomic physicists. Is the individual scientist responsible for the nature of the use that is made of the knowledge he acquires? There is presumably nothing good or bad about knowledge of the structure of the atom. Atomic energy can be used for good purposes (power) and bad purposes (nuclear warfare). Yet individual physicists could not escape a feeling of profound guilt concerning Hiroshima and Nagasaki. The distinction, while useful for some purposes, turned out to be a specious one for individual physicists. Thus the answer the physicist has given us is that the individual scientist does, in fact, share the responsibility for the manner in which his knowledge is used, and physicists have created organizations in response to this problem.

It is often claimed that the criteria of social value are not relevant to basic research as they are to applied and socially relevant research in any discipline. It is implied that basic research is different from applied research in that its values are intrinsic rather than extrinsic. I believe this argument to be specious as well. The intrinsic value of research is independent of the dimension of basic versus applied. An applied problem can possess all of the features of intellectual intrigue of the most esoteric of basic conundrums. Among the various characteristics that might be used to distinguish between basic and applied research, the functionally significant one may be remoteness of applicability. It is argued that basic research must be protected from close scrutiny because the greatest advances in knowledge frequently arise from research from which the potential applicability of the results is not foreseen or foreseeable. This is a value in the strategy of research in which I believe, yet it has certain limits.

The dimension has basic research at one end and at the other end it has research that can be described as applied, relevant, or simply intelligible to the ordinary layman. Applied research is research that offers no mystery to any reasonably intelligent and well-educated individual. He can see how the results may be applied, and he can see the social implications of the results as well as the scientist who was responsible for the acquisition of the knowledge. A basic research study is one that the layman is not able to judge. The judgment must be made by colleagues.

I would argue that in judging the merit of basic research, colleagues have an obligation to evaluate the research in terms of relevance and social need in the broadest sense. The problem is similar to one addressed by Lytton (1863) about a century ago. He said, "In science, address the few, in literature, the many. In science, the few must dictate opinion to the many; in literature, the many, sooner or later, force their opinion on the few." By analogy, the basic research scientist must address himself to his colleagues, the few. The applied scientist, doing relevant research, must address himself to the many as well. And because he must address the many, he is subject to having the opinion of the many forced upon him.

I would argue that basic research enjoys a freedom from accountability in terms of social values that is based on ignorance and is therefore unwarranted. However remote that applicability, I believe that ultimate human usefulness is the primary criterion on which the social support of psychological research should be based. I believe that the individual scientist should take social value into consideration in choosing his problems, and I believe that his colleagues should take social value into consideration in judging the merit of his work. Someone, either the individual scientist or his colleagues, must take the responsibility for assessing the potential social value of the research in question.

Failure to perform this task adequately has led to the charge that experimental psychology too frequently addresses itself to *trivial* problems. I do not think the charge is just. I do, however, believe that the charge is a symptom of two failures on the part of scientific psychology. The first is that we have failed to interpret basic research in terms of social relevance declaring it to be impossible. I would agree that it is difficult, but I would argue that it is necessary. It is the responsibility of the scientist himself or his colleagues, since they are the only ones who understand the research, to perform the task, however difficult it may appear.

The second failure is a disproportionate emphasis on basic research at the expense of applied, or relevant, research. I think this occurs because basic research is not available to public scrutiny and its implications are not clear. It is therefore more comfortable to work on problems where the threat of public controversy is small. If there was more relevant research, there would be less of a tendency to regard basic research as trivial. I think scientific psychologists need to be supported in their basic research, but they also need to be encouraged to tackle the more controversial but more urgent problems.

Finally, it seems reasonable that the physicist can keep his work separate from his daily, non-professional life on the grounds that his scientific work involves inanimate matter and that his work is not therefore relevant to human affairs. However, knowledge is a human attribute, and the physicist could not be a physicist if he was not also human. Thus theoretical physics is a human, social form of behavior whether the immediate object of the theoretical physicist's work is living or nonliving. The inanimate character of his object of study does not make his work asocial in any significant sense. Thus the argument is that the work of a scientist working in physics is a social enterprise because all knowledge is social and of value only because of its social implications.

What *is* true is that the scientist working on nonliving matter enjoys a freedom of choice of problem and procedure that is not enjoyed by the scientist whose immediate subject matter is a living organism. Thus, the psychologist has an additional social dimension in his work in that his object of study is usually human. Therefore, he works under a set of varying social proscriptions that affect what he can and cannot do as a scientist. He may not carry out experiments that are obviously harmful to his subject, a proscription he shares with medicine.

In summary, then, I would argue that science cannot proceed as if the individual's roles as scientist and as human being are completely separate. In some respects, they are inseparable. No part of science is categorically free of social values. The scientist shares the responsibility for the uses that are made of his discoveries. Intrinsic values are equally applicable to basic and applied research, and social values are applicable to them in the same manner although they differ in remoteness of that applicability. The social difference between research on atoms and humans is a matter of social restrictions applicable when the object of the research is human but does not imply that one class of object of study makes science a social activity and the other asocial.

The Individual Scientist and the Scientific Organization

The second major difficulty in Chomsky's position is that, if a man is to be a social activist, it is very difficult for him to be a scientist. If a man is to be a scientist, he has little time and energy for social activism.

The successful scientist is often an individual who devotes an enormous number of hours to his scientific pursuits. He achieves a high level of scientific productivity by sacrificing a great many activities in which he would otherwise be engaged. He is likely to forego most social activities. He may neglect his family. He may teach sparingly and without substantial preparation. He may avoid involvement in committees and in administrative responsibilities. He attends meetings of scientific societies solely to exchange scientific information. He may do so even though he enjoys social affairs, has great affection for his family, believes in the need and value of teaching, realizes the necessity of administrative activities, and enjoys a party at the meetings as well as the next man. However, he loves science more than any of these, and his single-minded devotion to scientific enterprise is a choice among positively valenced activities. The same man may have deep concerns for social problems and issues, whether they appear to affect his scientific prospects or not. Yet he can no more devote himself to the solution to social problems than he can devote himself to effective university administration. There is only so much time in the day, and that time must be devoted to the scientific problem at hand, if progress is to be made. He cannot *do* science and *promote* science within the limits of his time and energy.

Furthermore, there is not always complete agreement among individual members of a discipline on what should be regarded as oppression that should therefore be opposed. For example, there may be in this audience some individuals who feel that the rabble in the park represented oppression and destruction so redolent of insurrection and threat of assassination that any preventive measures the Chicago police chose to take would be wholly justified. There may also be in this audience some who regard the behavior of the Chicago police as being so oppressive and destructive that very strong opposing action is required.

The only solution that I can see to this problem is for an organization or association of scientific psychologists to act for the individual psychologist. Such an association can determine the majority opinion of its constituency and it could act in the name of the individual scientist who has the will but not the time to devote to social action. . . .

Social Support for Psychology

Few numbers are required to document the enormous growth of psychology as a science in less than a century. The Midwestern Psychological Association grew from a very small organization in 1926 to its present membership of about 3,500 members today. The American Psychological Association has grown from a small group in 1892 to a membership of over 35,000 in a matter of 77 years. Such growth requires massive social support. That support has come in the form of very rapidly mounting commitments from colleges and universities to staff in psychology, documented in turn by heavy enrollments in psychology from undergraduates and graduate students. The income from salaries of academic psychologists is a very large sum of money. One would have to agree that this constitutes massive social support. When one adds the amount of research support from the various branches of the Federal Government and from private foundations as well as fellowship support for students of psychology, the annual investment in psychology becomes staggering.

In the span of my own academic lifetime there has been a complete change in the forces determining the character of scientific psychology. When I was a graduate student, support came almost exclusively from university budgets. One's choice of problem was almost entirely a matter of individual interest. Now psychology is so heavily subsidized by Federal funds that much of the decision has been removed from the local scene and placed in the hands of a decision-making apparatus located in Washington. . . .

Social and Political Obligations of Experimental Psychology

In a recent speech, excerpts of which appeared in *Science*, Representative Daddario (1968) (D–Conn.) cited an Italian philosopher as saying, "There is nothing more difficult to take in hand, more perilous to conduct, or more uncertain of its success than to take the lead in the introduction of a new order of things." Yet my commitment to talk on this subject has led me to that perilous position. I would like to propose a new order of things for scientific psychology.

I have tried to argue that the new order of things with respect to the involvement of scientific psychology in certain political and social affairs is a task for a formal organization of scientists. The individual scholar must be left to pursue knowledge through individual scientific inquiry, for no organization originates knowledge. Some organizations *must* meet these obligations if we are to survive.

I would like to propose four sets of obligations experimental psychology owes to itself and to society as a whole. They amount to a preliminary formulation of a set of social and political goals, and I believe that an organization of psychologists should use every available means to advance the welfare of scientific psychology within that set of goals.

1. The first is a matter of communication. A convention such as this one provides a means of communication between scientist and scientist. It does not provide communication between scientist and layman. Such communication is an obligation of the profession and means must be developed to accomplish it. In brief, *experimental psychology has the responsibility to interpret its basic research to society as a whole.*

2. The second is the problem posed by the need for social support of experimental psychology. Representative Daddario (1968) sets this problem as a paradox. He says: "science is obviously affected by funding, funding is dependent on public policy, so science must affect public policy. The paradox is that science is characteristically aloof from politicking, feeling that it is in the best interests of the functioning of the scientific method to ignore the exigencies of politics." He also cites the outcome of a meeting that George Wald of Harvard helped to organize in August 1968 at Woods Hole. The problem was to discuss what action could be taken on Federal cutbacks in research support. The meeting seemed to produce the consensus that "the only way for scientists to work effectively for their cause is to become more active politically." I believe, then, that *experimental psychology has the responsibility to encourage its own social support through political action.*

3. The third goal has to do with pressing social problems. In the public mind, psychology, of all disciplines, should have something to offer that would aid in dealing with them. How can a discipline that has the scientific study of learning as one of its provinces be unable to offer any solution to the problem of educating children in such a manner that they do not turn to violence in the streets and punishment in the courts? How can a discipline that purports to include the scientific study of motivation be unable to provide understanding and control of the will to order the indiscriminate destruction of life that is modern war? Pressing social problems, such as the urban ghetto, police excesses, irrational violence in the name of dissent, racism, and poverty, are clearly matters of the execution of extremely stupid and irrational behavior on the part of intelligent and rational men. If the science of human behavior has too little to offer in the solution to these problems, then we had better reexamine our directions. It is not necessary for experimental psychology to take sides on controversial issues, but it is necessary for experimental psychology to provide the data and principles in terms of which rational solutions can be reached. The third goal is: *Experimental psychology must find a means of stepping up its attack on pressing social problems.*

4. The final goal that I would propose is perhaps the most remote from life in the laboratory, but perhaps the most important of all. Experimental psychology cannot survive in a repressive political atmosphere. It shares this vulnerability with other scientific and scholarly pursuits. However, political ideologies frequently contain dogma that is in direct conflict with the principle of freedom of inquiry with respect to human behavior. Thus there are forms of political milieu in which physics and mathematics can prosper and in which psychology cannot. Thus psychology, of all scientific disciplines, must remain alert to political weather signals and it must act within its power as a political force for freedom of scientific inquiry. Thus my fourth and final goal, and final words of the day are: *Experimental psychology has the responsibility to oppose political climates that would inhibit the progress of free psychological inquiry and to encourage political climates that permit or encourage such progress.*

REFERENCES

Chomsky, N. Quotation in *New York Times*, October 27, 1968.
Daddario, E. Q. Academic science and the federal government. *Science*, 1968, *162*, 1249–1251.
Lytton, E. B. *Caxtoniana: A series of essays on life, literature, and manners.* Edinburgh and London: W. Blackwood and Sons, 1863.
Pitzer, K. S. University integrity. *Science*, 1968, *162*, 228–230.
Seitz, F. Science, government and the university. *Stanford Alumni Almanac*, 1968, *7*, 5–6.

Professor Pilisuk, coauthor of *The Triple Revolution*, talks frankly of his own activist role as a researcher who aspires to conduct research which is both rigorous and relevant. His story is told against the background of the 1969 People's Park disturbances in Berkeley. His research, the description of a local power elite, revealed insights which are useful in describing the tragic misuse of power and breakdown of trust which contributed to the People's Park episode. He credits his transformation as a researcher to lessons learned from his students. A telling footnote is the fact that this research, like so many highly relevant efforts, was not funded by any agency.

2.5
People's Park, Power and the Calling of the Social Sciences

Marc Pilisuk

I am continually amazed by the capacity of people to adjust themselves to harsh and punishing environments. Even when people have known something better, which is not the case unfortunately for the majority of the world's population, there is apparently tremendous capability of individuals to deny the scope of extreme adversity, to minimize the extent of stressful changes and to believe that things will once again revert to normalcy. Everett Hughes in his study of German residents following the end of World War II shows how prevalent was the feeling during Hitler's ascendancy in the 1930's that things just couldn't possibly be as bad as they were (Hughes, 1964). The attitude of "but we are a civilized people" or "something like that just couldn't happen here" protected people from a realization of the horrible happenings which took place among their neighbors and themselves.

Recognizing this very ample capability to deny and to adapt in myself as well as in others around me, I have often wondered what kind of objective indicators I might use in the event that I felt that fascism or some other brutal and oppressive rule were coming to dominate my own country and my life. With only a modest amount of discomfort I have been able to accommodate to the dismissal of colleagues apparently for reasons of their political activities, to the imprisonment and even to the slaying of essentially non-violent civil rights demonstrators, to the waging of a war of attrition by this nation in support of a dictatorial puppet regime, and to the apparent centralization of military, governmental and industrial power in the United States. Whatever my discomfort with such occurrences, I was still able to persist with a deep-felt belief that I, personally, was a man free to make my own deci-

sions, to go about my work without fear of repression and even to do something in my work which I felt would have a constructive influence upon the directions of society.

The People's Park controversy in the City of Berkeley in 1969 shook some of my confidence and (before my capacities for adjustment and denial take over once again) I feel the need for a re-appraisal of the relevance of what I, as one psychologist, am doing to the scene around me. For about three weeks Berkeley was a city under military occupation. As I drove to my office I could see the large convoys of drab colored trucks and jeeps carrying armed Guardsmen to their stations on and around the Berkeley campus. Governor Ronald Reagan's announced "state of extreme emergency" made automatic the deployment of large numbers of California Highway Patrolmen and police from outside of the Berkeley area, all under the absolute direction of the Sheriff of Alameda County.

Assembling groups of more than six people on or off the campus was illegal. Children were tear gassed on their way to or from elementary schools; people were warned by officers not to distribute handbills or to hold silent vigils in public places. A small group of Quakers conducting such a silent vigil were poked with bayonets while being asked to leave. Students and faculty members were clubbed and subjected to gassing, many while attempting to perform their normal duties on campus. Medics in white coats whose only function was to care for victims were subjected to similar treatment from some of the police.

The opening salvos of the controversy, which occurred after a cyclone fence had been placed around the Park which local residents had developed, involved what can only be described as a sanctioned loss of control by law enforcement officers. In confrontation with an angry crowd of people, a very small number of whom threw rocks and soda bottles (which police threw back), the police raised their rifles against an unarmed crowd of people and fired buckshot. One man was killed, hundreds were wounded. In the weeks following, the police presence was ubiquitous. Tear gas was used consistently and helicopters hovered over the city continuously relaying signals to police officers on the

rooftops of buildings.

On one occasion a large group of students and faculty were refused, at bayonet point, permission to conduct a silent memorial march through the streets of Berkeley in honor of the man who had died. The campus Chief of Police issued a statement urging the group to return to the steps of Sproul Hall where they would be permitted to conduct a silent vigil. I, myself, urged people through a bullhorn to avoid possible bloodshed and return. After this, people were granted permission to enter Sproul Plaza through a narrow corridor of Guardsmen. They were not, however, permitted to leave the Plaza until immediately before an army helicopter came flying over, without official warning, at treetop level distributing huge clouds of noxious CS gas which had been developed for use in Vietnam. On another occasion all of the people who could be rounded up on a street in the business section of Berkeley were placed under arrest. The charges against them were trivial and were later, in almost all cases, dropped by the police. This did not take place, however, before the victims of the arrest had been sent to Santa Rita prison and subjected to severe physical abuse during a period of booking which lasted in many cases over seven hours. The abuse was later explained by Alameda County Sheriff Madigan and Governor Reagan as resulting from the fact that many of the guards were Vietnam veterans who looked upon anti-war demonstrators as no better than Viet Cong. The degree of dehumanization revealed by such rationale was forecast by the Society for the Psychological Study of Social Issues (SPSSI) Council in describing consequences of our immunization to the atrocities of Vietnam. It suggests a disease process not unlike the one which incubated in Germany in the 1930's.

It is not necessary to labor or even to discuss the justice of the issue over which this horrible military occupation and chemical aerial attack on an American city occurred. A vast majority of the student population both by direct poll and through the student government made known their support for People's Park. A strong majority of faculty in the University Senate also made known their support of the People's Park idea and their opposition to police tactics in the community. But whatever the justice of the issue, it was clear that students, faculty and even city government officials had no control over the state of occupation. It is also clear that the actions performed during that occupation by constituted authorities are not pardonable.

What does a psychologist or anyone else do in such a situation, when he looks out of his window and sees a battalion of police officers chasing a small group of students across the campus? How does he evaluate the relevance of his work and his life? I have long felt that many aspects of my work have been at least as useful to society as they have been enjoyable and rewarding to myself. But under the test of what has happened in Berkeley I now have doubts. They derive from what I believe is the basis of the Governor's popularity in handling the particular case and the prognostication that such handling will become increasingly the pattern in this country. With this in mind, the utility of most of my work is in serious question. There is, however, one area of my research work which does hold some promise for standing up under the harsher test of relevance to existing conditions and it is this project that I would like to discuss further.

The context in which I should like to review this work deals with three objects of choice. One is the target of study, two is the method for studying that target population, and three is the nature of the client, i.e., foundation, agency, federal bureau or what have you, under whose auspices the research is being conducted and for whom the findings are prepared. Most of the social scientists who are able to give facile accounts of the relevance of their work to the existing world of problems have selected a target population for study which is in some way either disadvantaged or disenfranchised or both. We accept, almost as given, that our studies of Black and Brown minorities, of the needs of the very poor, of the conditions of students and their education, of emotionally and physically disturbed persons, will serve either to document a severe social need or to point in the direction of constructive attempts to ameliorate or resolve it. As good scientists, we develop a design which is as rigorously controlled as circumstances permit and a method of assessment which provides for a maximum of reliability, prediction and control. We then publish our findings or turn them in as a re-port to the agency which has provided the financial sponsorship which made possible the research.

There is one example of this model of research which exposes its practical limitations. It was an evaluation study of Head Start (Impact of Head Start, 1969). Of all the programs designed as outgrowths of the originally proposed War on Poverty, it is the Head Start programs which have perhaps fired the most enthusiastic participation by groups of indigenous poor people. With the costs of the Vietnam war imposing a great scrutiny on all non-defense expenditures, the Office of Economic Opportunity decided to subject the Head Start program to a careful evaluation to determine whether the programs were in fact having the intended effect upon the youngsters who had been through it. Were the children who had been through a Head Start program actually better motivated to study, better able to read, more suited to meet the requirements of our elementary school system than those of similar backgrounds who had not enjoyed the benefits of a Head Start? The study used a carefully matched sample and employed as good objective indicators of the children's achievement and motivation as were available. The results were clear. By the criteria established for success of the program Head Start did not work.

Like any other finding, the implication for action is always double-edged. When a technical system such as the Polaris submarine or the underground Minute Man ballistic missiles fails to provide the invulnerable deterrence which it had promised, the implication is usually that we need more of the same, and from the sources which promised the original (note the source of advocacy for ABM). Notwithstanding the possibility that the results of the Head Start activity may have been used to support a similar conclusion, i.e., that a year's work of pre-school enrichment might be inadequate to overcome the deficiencies of many years of deprivation, the study has been used, with some effectiveness, to cut the meager funds available to Head Start programs.

One thing is patently clear in this research and it is that the criteria for the success of Head Start were assumed to be given by the people who designed the program and by the schools and other institutions of middle class society which were not to be subjected to question. The investigators learned of these criteria for the Head Start programs by an entirely different research procedure and an important one even to the most diehard experimentalist. They read their newspapers and journals, they discussed Head Start objectives with their colleagues, with the heads of their departments, with their friends, with the directors of agencies and with the organization which sponsored their research. If they were astute, as I believe they were, they used their own capabilities as extremely sensitive instruments for registering information about other people to obtain a very close understanding of the values, objectives and purposes of these successful others. The information they found is being used by these same peers and superiors in their efforts at the prediction and control of the behavior of children from disadvantaged families. I have already suggested that cutting Head Start funds is a misapplication of the findings of this study. It seems also true that such misapplication is not a mere accident but is rather a natural product of choices that the investigators made regarding methods, target population and sponsorship of their study.

All of us who have attempted a scientific study of one sort or another have been familiar with the needs for reliability, for prediction and for control. All of us who have managed to survive in our social environments have made ample use as well of our clinical intuitions, our insights, our abilities to exchange ideas with colleagues, with the directors of our universities, departments, agencies and sources of funding in order to determine an understanding of the limitations of what can and cannot be supported by existing sources of revenue. In the main, we have used our more rigorous scientific skills to study students, prison inmates, disturbed people, minority group members and others in need, and have developed great amounts of information relevant to the *prediction and control* of their behavior. By and large, we have used our clinical and intuitive skills to obtain an *understanding* of people who range from our colleagues to our superiors in the Establishment. I would like to suggest that this procedure may on several counts be wrong, that we should perhaps be using our clinical and intuitive skills to listen more carefully to what disadvantaged people are saying, to gain an understanding of their needs and desires and to direct our more rigorous research efforts to the prediction and control of those people among our colleagues and superiors whose decisions and practices are in large measure responsible for the distress of those whom we have been traditionally studying. Had there been an adequate understanding of what the children in the Head Start programs and their parents wanted and were getting from these programs, the question of reading readiness skills may not have been a fundamental one.

There are examples, some very striking, of the rich clinical study of people whose needs run counter to the grooves provided by society. Eliot Leibow's *Tally's Corner* is one of the better known. Recently, Edward Sampson has conducted a rich clinical study of the depth of conviction of men who chose prosecution as draft refusers rather than cooperate with the U.S. war in Vietnam (Sampson, 1968). This unsponsored research is expected to be of use in the court cases of defense of these young men. How would our society look if the men of *Tally's Corner* or the draft resistors could sponsor research into the behavior of those segments of the society which they would like to predict and control?

The project I wish to discuss then is one which reverses some of our traditional methodology by trying to gain some understanding of what the disadvantaged person wants, and by applying more rigorous techniques to a study which could make the prediction and control of the behavior of decision-making elites more possible. The study took place in a midwestern community of approximately 50,-000 persons.[1] The research was not sponsored but was conducted as part of a graduate course. A few of the faculty members and graduate students associated with this course did in fact spend some time hanging around the most impoverished areas of the city, talking to people in their houses, in the Negro bars and in the poor churches. We did all too little of this, but enough to give us a feeling of how far removed these people were from the events of decision-making in the community. Research cannot by itself provide such people with money or with a

[1] A fuller and more detailed report of the findings has been prepared (see Perrucci and Pilisuk, 1969).

sense of potency which they sorely lack. But perhaps with a small staff of research personnel they could identify the men who run the community which treats them so badly. The importance of the study to this discussion was in its promise for illustrating the way in which decision-makers can be studied through more rigorous techniques than are usually applied to them.

The particular focus of this research dealt with the theoretical controversy between pluralism and elitism in the study of American communities. The elitist view holds that a rather small number of men completely dominate the economic and political life of a community, leaving very little room for any form of citizen participation in local government. The pluralist view sees power to be distributed among a number of different organizations within a community with domination shifting according to issue. It seems clear from studies of actual citizen participation in community decision-making that whether there is one elite group, as the elitists would have us believe, or several, as the pluralists would argue, in either case very few people are actually involved in the major decisions that affect their lives (Presthus, 1964). Still, the question has theoretical interest and the study was designed to distinguish between these two competing views of community power.

What elitists have traditionally done, in similar studies in the past, is to examine the reputation of individuals for power in the community and have found a high degree of convergence. What pluralists have conventionally done is to examine actual participation in decision-making and have found that the same individuals did not necessarily take part in decisions across issue areas. The weakness in this latter method is that it relies very heavily upon overt community controversies to define the arena of decision-making while the major decisions may be those which go on before something is permitted to emerge as an issue. For example, an elimination of the national defense budget is not an item on the agenda of national decision-making, but at the same time the absence of this item is a critical decision accounting for the greatest expenditure in the national budget. If a self-serving elite which is able to dominate policy does exist, one of its most certain

functions would be to safeguard the current directions of policy which have led to the formation and continuation of that elite and its interests. The examination of actual participation in the making of community decisions, while it has a strong empirical flavor, may be actually missing the covert workings of an elite group if one should exist. Further, if the interests continually represented in community decisions are the same, what does it matter if the same individual represents them each time? One major problem in both traditions of research is that while power is defined in both cases as an organizational variable or a variable of the social structure, it is inevitably measured as a characteristic of individuals, that is as an individual's reputation, the convergence of choices upon a single individual, the number of places that an individual actively gets himself involved, etc. This particular study sought to make the measurement consistent with the conception that power is embedded in organizations and we sought for our indication of this embeddedness the positions that are held by individuals at a decision-making level in one or more of the organizations which operate in a community.

Our idea was that while no individual himself would have the resources necessary to bear upon every important decision in a modern heterogeneous community, that an individual with an executive level position in several organizations would be able to bring to bear the resources of those organizations in the activation of a particular policy. If there were in fact a single power elite, as the elitists have claimed, then we would expect to find a number of individuals who hold interlocking affiliations at an executive or decision-making level in a number of organizations and we would tend also to find that these individuals were linked organizationally to each other within a closed network in which all the operating elite organizations held some shared executive level personnel. The individual who is part of such a power resource network should, we believed, be found to have a greater reputation for power in the community and also, if we can define a community issue which cuts deeply enough into the financial and political structure of the community, should in fact be one which shows the greater or more critical participation in determining the outcome of the decision. Thus the person who may be a bank president or an officer in the parent-teachers organization who also has positions on three other community organizations should be more powerful than another bank president or parent-teacher organization officer who does not hold overlapping decision-making positions.

With this idea about how power resources are spread through the community and how they can be brought to bear on community decision-making we offered four hypotheses. The first hypothesis was that we would find a small and clearly identifiable group of interorganizational leaders or persons who held high executive positions in a number of organizations. Second, we hypothesized that a matched group of organizational leaders, that is persons who held equally high positions but in fewer organizations, would be less frequently identified by their peers as either the most reputed powerful leaders of the community or those who had actually taken part in some critical community decision. Third, we hypothesized that the interorganizational leaders, the people with the high overlaps, would show greater value homophyly, or similarity among values, and more primary social ties among each other than would the organizational leaders. And fourth, we hypothesized that those interorganizational leaders who were part of the same resource network would be judged most powerful by their peers and would show the greatest value homophyly and the most frequent social ties.

The original study then set out to determine whether interorganizational linkages when exposed would reveal either a pluralist or elitist distribution. From a list of 1,677 persons with official positions in organizations in this midwestern community of 50,000 persons, a group of 26 were selected for their presence in executive level of four or more organizations in the community. A matching sample (matched on prime vocation but lacking overlapping organizational affiliations) was also selected. The two groups were interviewed to discover (a) demographic contrasts (there were no important differences), (b) actual participation in a critical community conflict involving the distribution of scarce resources (the group with overlapping ties were

far more frequently involved in a determining manner), (c) the reputation for influence and power in the community (the group with overlapping affiliations was again far more frequently named), (d) the values of the interviewees (the overlapping group were somewhat less conservative but, more important, showed more value homophyly than the matched group), (e) a sociometric mapping of business and social acquaintances among the interviewees (the interorganizational leaders had significantly more social as well as business ties to each other), (f) a ranking of the ten most powerful men in the community (both groups selected ten from among the 26 with four or more interorganizational ties).

The twenty-six leaders represented seven lawyers, six bankers, five industrialists, two city officials, two real estate men, two school officials and one newspaper owner. From among this group a plot was made of the actual organizational ties which connected these particular individuals. Beginning arbitrarily with any organization with several high overlap individuals, the network was depicted through all possible interconnections with the hope of discovering closed cycles of interconnectedness, i.e., organizations each connected with each other through these twenty-six individuals, but not connected with organizations outside of the cycle. One such cycle existed containing eleven of the twenty-six interorganizational leaders. This list was matched with the ten most powerful leaders cited in the questionnaire. There were eight men (all interorganizational leaders) who were listed both as among the ten most powerful in the community and who were found to be part of this exclusive resource network. These eight were examined for value homophyly and social acquaintance. Almost all knew each other socially as well as through business ties and the group was even closer in values than the twenty-six interorganizational leaders from whom they were selected. The conclusion of this study is obvious.

While I believe that the methods in this study were somewhat better suited to uncover a local power elite than those which have so far appeared in the literature, it must certainly be pointed out that the use of these methods in other communities will not necessarily

produce the same result. In a somewhat larger community of over 100,000 persons a partial replication of this study has found a very different picture of community power. The important thing, however, is that the method can be used to uncover the frequently covert arrangements which are available to assist elite groups in constraining the agenda of public policy in ways that preserve the interests of the elite and preclude radical challenges to it. These interests, I believe, were challenged in the People's Park controversy.

The challenge involved an attack upon the assumption that political appointees with industrial management backgrounds (the Regents) can determine the best interests of the University community better than can the personnel of that community. The failure of any legitimate channels to process such a challenge was evidenced by the University Chancellor's decision, after weeks of occupation, to recommend that the city, *but not the University,* take over the property for a user-developed park. The Mayor then tossed the albatross back to the University saying that the University, *but not the City,* should provide such a park. The Regents in their wisdom have since decided that there will be no park on the site and the failing policies of urban renewal—the removal of people who look different or live differently—is now in practice (Gans, 1965). State Assemblyman Donald Mulford voices the policy in his commendation to the police for "clearing out an element which has been too close to the gate of the University for too long" (Outcry, 1969). Given such a deaf ear to the legitimacy of popular demand it seems not unreasonable that young people, schooled in the belief that governments derive their just powers from the consent of the governed, scorned the University and set out to remove the fence secretly (and in violation of a promise to the contrary) erected around their park in the middle of the night. Such are the instances of "violence" which can provide an almost unaccountable elite with the rationale for a total military occupation of an American city. The type of closely interconnected power structure in the smaller midwestern community maintains law and order and precludes any such overt challenge to the elites which, we have shown, have exclusive control over a reserve of organized activity and resources needed to insure an outcome favorable to their own interests in the event of any genuine conflict over major policy.

So much for the eight big wheels of this moderate sized midwestern community. The goal of the study was to find information about the power structure of the community and to continue doing so as a service project, on the part of the research team, to what we had hoped to see flourish as an indigenous newspaper of the poor people in the community. Individuals living separately and isolated by poverty would come to see (through their newspaper) that their dissatisfactions with the police, with job opportunities, with the landlords, with food and drug costs, and with the extremely limited health and welfare facilities of the community were shared by other individuals. In addition, we could help them to identify those most directly responsible for the state of affairs. It seemed only fair that the impoverished should have as good a file on their ruling elite as the elite have on them through their credit ratings, police and school records and tests for jobs or for welfare.

Precisely what would be done with such information is an open question. In 1963, a nineteen-year-old Negro youth from Savannah, using some of the same sources for information about bankers which we used in our study, walked into the main office of Chase Manhattan Bank and asked to see David Rockefeller. He wanted to know why Chase Manhattan served as paying agent on Savannah bond issues which were floated to build segregated facilities. When faced first with a denial, and then with a refusal to examine the bank's investment records, the young man was able to react with a picket line which served to embarrass Chase Manhattan Bank at the very time that Governor Nelson Rockefeller, the brother of the bank's chief executive officer, was declaring loudly, as part of his campaign for the Republican presidential nomination, that racial discrimination must end (Minnis, 1964).

Control by social scientists is a somewhat ephemeral concept. We can recognize it in its more virulent forms as when psychologists assist in the writing of police manuals which give directions on how to so disorient a suspect that he will confess to a crime (in many cases to a crime which he

has not done) (Zimbardo, 1966), or when social scientists help to institute an interfamilial spying system as part of a program to pacify the Vietnamese people (Nicholaus, 1966). Apparently, less directly noxious (until one recalls the Hitler Youth Corps) is the use of the military as the agency for programs of rehabilitation for youth alienated from our society. This military program has been facilitated by social scientists (Little, 1968; Pilisuk, 1968). Is it any wonder then that some young people are suspicious of psychologists and other social scientists? The warning of one occupied American city seems to me sufficient and I do not think it is necessary to wait for the sounds of boots clicking toward the door of my office or my home to consider seriously the charges by young people of complicity with a social order capable of great malevolence.

I believe we have something important to learn from many of these alienated and rebellious youths of our society. We share with them, as psychologists, a sincere and devoted concern for the well-being of our fellow man, but perhaps we have not become sufficiently alienated from the society or gained sufficient distance to study it objectively and to see its limitations in providing for human needs. It is obviously a hard thing to discover that many of my activities as a psychologist, including most of my research activities, do not stand up to the test of social relevance to the conditions of this society at the current time. I do believe, however, that the research strategy described in this article has promise in this regard and I should point out that it is one which I learned from my students. In closing I would like to quote from one of my former students, a research assistant, who told me many years ago that my research on the resolution of international conflict was probably irrelevant to the achievement of any such resolution. He delivered the following remarks as a speaker in the first peace march on Washington, D.C., ever to take place in this country.

What kind of system is it that disenfranchises people in the South, leaves millions . . . impoverished and excluded from the mainstream and promise of American society, that creates faceless and terrible bureaucracies . . . that consistently put material values before human values—

and still persists in calling itself free and in finding itself fit to police the world? What place is there for ordinary men in that system and how are they to control it, make it bend itself to their wills rather than bending themselves to it? We must name that system, we must name it, describe it, analyze it, understand it, and change it.[2]

With the memory of what happened in the city of Berkeley still fresh in my mind, I believe that he has named the task which is indeed worthy of the efforts of psychologists, scientists and educators.

REFERENCES

American media baronies: A modest Atlantic atlas. A report by the editors of the *Atlantic*, 1969, *221*, No. 1, 82–86, 90–94.

Domhoff, G. W. *Who Rules America?* Englewood, N.J.: Prentice-Hall, 1967.

Draper, Theodore. The roots of the Dominican crisis. *The New Leader*, May 24, 1965.

Gans, Herbert J. The failure of urban renewal: A critique and some proposals. *Commentary*, 1965, *39*, 29–37.

Goff, Fred, and Locker, Michael. The violence of domination: U.S. power and the Dominican Republic. In Gerassi, J. (Eds.) *Latin American Radicalism*, Vintage, 1969, 244–291.

Goldin, Hyman H. The television overlords. *Atlantic*, 1969, *221*, No. 1, 87–89.

Horowitz, David, and Kolodney, David. The foundations (charity begins at home). *Rumparts*, 1969, *7*, No. 11, 38–48.

Hughes, Everett C. Good people and dirty work. *Social Problems*, 1964, *10*, 3–11.

Impact of Head Start: An evaluation of the effects of Head Start on children's cognitive and affective development. Westinghouse Learning Corporation, Ohio University, June 12, 1969, Vols. I, II, Appendices A–J.

Little, Roger W. Basic education and youth socialization in the armed forces. *American Journal of Orthopsychiatry*, 1968, *38*, 869–876.

Jacobs, Paul. How the CIA makes liars out of union leaders. *Ramparts*, 1967, *5*, No. 10, 25–28.

Minnis, Jack. The care and feeding of power structures. *New University Thought*, 1964, *4*, 73–79.

Nicholaus, Martin. The professor, the policeman and the peasant. *Viet Report*, February, 1966, *2*, 16–21.

Outcry from occupied Berkeley. Report by Radical Student Union, Berkeley, May, 1969.

Perlo, Victor. *Militarism and In-*

[2] The remarks are those of K. Paul Potter at the Washington Monument on April 17, 1965.

dustry. New York: International Publishers, 1963.

Perrucci, Robert, and Pilisuk, Marc. Leaders and ruling elites: The interorganizational basis of community power. Unpublished paper.

Pilisuk, Marc. Basic education and youth socialization anywhere else: A reply to Roger Little. *American Journal of Orthopsychiatry,* 1968, 38, 877–881.

Presthus, Robert. *Men at the Top: A Study in Community Power.* New York: Oxford, 1964.

Sampson, E., Fisher, L., Angel, A., Mulman, A., and Sullins, C. Two profiles: The draft resister and the ROTC cadet. Paper presented at the American Orthopsychiatric Association, New York, April, 1969.

Who Rules Columbia? North American Congress on Latin America, New York, 1968.

Zimbardo, Phillip G. Coercion and compliance: The psychology of police confessions. Paper presented at American Psychological Association, New York, September, 1966.

This paper presents a rare story of a psychologist who served as a special assistant to the Mayor of Boston. Klein, a trained group psychotherapist, found himself able to influence decisions which affected people's lives because of his central political position, even though he owed allegiance to the Mayor and his policies. He stresses that person-to-person trust and understanding is a necessary ingredient if the psychologist is to be invited into the social action arena.

2.6
Psychologist at City Hall— A Problem of Identity

Stanley D. Klein

In recent times, citizens have become increasingly aware of the social problems within society. Along with this awareness has come the wish on the part of indi-

Reprinted by permission of the author and the American Psychological Association from "Psychologist at City Hall—A Problem of Identity," *American Psychologist,* 25 (1970), 195–199. Copyright 1970 by the American Psychological Association.

viduals and groups to actively "do something" about these problems. The call for involvement on the part of psychologists is heard within professional meetings and on the pages of professional journals. In fact, the theme of the 1969 Convention of the American Psychological Association was "Psychology and the Problems of Society."

Psychology as a body of scientific knowledge about behavior and professional psychologists as individuals would appear to have some part to play in solving social problems.

How applicable is psychological knowledge? The answer may seem obvious: Since psychologists know about human behavior and the solving of problems, they are ideally suited to confront today's social problems.

This article describes my personal experiences as a representative of the Mayor of Boston. More specifically, it reviews the identity conflicts I experienced as I tried to utilize my knowledge and experience as a psychologist in a new role and in new situations.

Professionally I identify myself as a clinical psychologist, dividing my time between undergraduate teaching and private psychotherapeutic practice with children and young adults. As a private citizen living in Boston, I have been active in local politics.

In the spring of 1968, I was appointed to the staff of Mayor Kevin H. White of Boston as a special assistant, charged with the responsibility of "taking care of the hippie situation." This appointment evolved from discussions between city officials and myself about the expected influx of young people to Boston in the coming summer. It is important to note that these discussions occurred primarily because I was known personally and politically at city hall, rather than because of any judgment by city officials of my professional competence as a psychologist. That is, I had been a working colleague of a number of individuals who were now key city officials because I had served in an administrative capacity in Mayor White's election campaign in 1967. The fact that I was a responsible and loyal political worker was both a key factor in my appointment and a source of some of the subsequent identity conflicts on the job.

City officials felt that a psychologist familiar with young people and their problems would be help-

ful in dealing with "hippies." I implicitly agreed and felt that my experience as a teacher and a therapist would be applicable, because I expected to serve principally as a liaison person between the Mayor's Office and the various individuals and groups involved in the hippie situation. I expected to be a listener and a communicator, both familiar roles. Furthermore, I expected that my psychologist's behavioral style (which, of course, is part of my own personality style) would be relevant to the situations.

In the months that followed, hundreds of young people, all labeled hippies by the mass media, came to Boston. The complexities of problems for the city administration exceeded the springtime expectations. It was necessary for many departments within the executive branch of city government, such as Parks and Recreation, Law, Housing Inspection, Health and Hospitals, Youth Opportunities, and Police, to become directly involved. In addition, private agencies and citizens' groups involved themselves. As a result, as the representative of the Mayor's Office, I had to face a wide range of situations, some of which had not been anticipated. Some, such as coping with runaway adolescents, challenged my psychological knowledge about such behavior. Others, such as coping with the grievances of irate citizens' groups, challenged my political skills. Finally, some crises, such as observing a midnight demonstration on the Boston Common, and visiting demonstrators in jail a few hours later, challenged my physical stamina.

As the summer progressed, I realized that my role was much more that of politician than psychologist. I had expected my psychological knowledge to be particularly helpful; however, I discovered that my knowledge and my style were of limited value. As a representative of the Mayor, it was necessary for my orientation to shift from helper or teacher to negotiator, judge, detective, manipulator, and sometimes defender of "hippies," or police, or politicians. While my professional training was helpful to me in some ways in this political role, most of the decisions that I made were based primarily upon political, rather than psychological, considerations. To my disappointment, I found that my psychological knowledge was, at best, secondary to my understanding of the politics of the situations.

My role at city hall proved to be different from my previous professional roles as teacher, researcher, or therapist in four ways.

First, in these traditional psychologist's roles, one's primary responsibility is to the welfare of the client, who usually invites the psychologist to provide a specific service in an area in which the psychologist is an expert. In my role at city hall, my clientele seemed to include "hippies," private citizens, police officers, and many others, individually and collectively, but my primary responsibility was to the welfare of my boss—the Mayor.

Second, in the protective confines of my office or classroom, my clientele come to me and I am in charge. What I say represents my point of view, and my clientele and I are the only ones who observe my behavior. In contrast, as a representative of city hall, I went wherever the "action was." I had to present and defend policies that did not always represent my point of view. Furthermore, I was always subject to public as well as private scrutiny.

Third, my function as a teacher and a therapist is relatively clear to me, my students, and the people who consult me for psychotherapy. However, on my city job, not only did I experience some confusion about my role, but I was perceived in a variety of conflicting ways: To conservative police officials, I was a hippie or hippie advocate; to some hippies, I was a plainclothes police officer; to radicals, I was a "fascist pig"; to the press, I was a "psychologist advising the Mayor," or "doing research on hippies."

Fourth, as a teacher or therapist, my goal is to facilitate change within individuals. The direction of the change is usually mutually agreeable. As a representative of the Mayor's Office, I could direct external environmental change, and sometimes the direction of the change might be totally disagreeable to some of my constituency.

These four role differences are not mutually exclusive, nor do they exhaust the possible ways of conceptualizing my particular experiences. The conceptual framework itself evolved after the summer of 1968. Nonetheless, it has proven personally functional because it has decreased my identity conflict as I have continued to work in 1969 as a member of Mayor White's staff—as a politician with the credentials of a professional psychologist.

Utilizing the role differences as points of departure and keeping in mind the issue of the value of psychological knowledge, I will describe some of my specific experiences during the summer of 1968.

Welfare of Client (Mayor)

To be primarily concerned with the political welfare of the Mayor, rather than the personal welfare of an individual client or the social welfare of a community group, was difficult and distasteful, and the most important role change. This reorientation away from the recipients of service pervaded all the other role changes.

My "street work" illustrates this issue. Some social workers and most police officers have experience working with their "clients" on the street. My role, as I toured the Boston Common and the surrounding areas where the young people were "making the scene," included the friendly, helpful, observer type roles of these two professions. However, the implications of my activities for my actual client remained my primary concern.

My experience in relating to young people and my therapists tolerance of unusual behavior made it relatively easy to maintain personal contact with the hippies. While I knew the language and customs of the group, I also knew that I did not have to adopt them in order to be an acceptable person. Most importantly, I knew how to listen and how to try to understand. At the same time, I represented the Establishment and had the responsibility of assessing the situation; that is, I had to judge the level of tension of the situation and, if necessary, notify law enforcement officials of any potential trouble. Here, my clinical training was helpful in enabling me to judge the reliability of some of my "informants." However, this detectivelike role was strange to me and I had to gain my experience "on the job."

In the street-work setting, confidentiality of communication—a sacred commandment for me as a psychotherapist—was a complex issue. Here, I experienced conflict concerning the use of information that was given in trust, particularly when it involved illegal activities. Once, at a time of high tension on the Common, two youths gave me concealed weapons (knives) that they had allegedly found. Frequently, I observed the sale and use of illegal drugs and acquired knowledge of the whereabouts of runaways. Violence, drugs, runaways, and similar problems are perplexing to me clinically. However, in this context, they represented unlawful behavior, potential danger for large numbers of people, and a bad scene politically.

Public Self and Self-Determination

As a psychologist, I have enjoyed relative autonomy in my professional career. Supervisors and department chairmen notwithstanding, I am accustomed to deciding what I teach, what I research, or how I therapize. In addition, I usually perform these functions in safe, relatively private places. In contrast, going wherever "the action was" was part of my political job.

A number of times during the summer, I was confronted by large unruly groups in meetings as well as in organized public demonstrations against the Establishment. In the confines of my office, I am prepared to be harassed by an individual or a family who feels it is not getting what it wants. Furthermore, in individual or group psychotherapy, and in teaching to some extent, interpersonal struggle, tension, and similar phenomena are part of the process and occur in the context of the transaction between people who have some kind of relationship with one another. Possibly, mass meetings and public demonstrations also evolve according to particular processes. Generally, my knowledge of individual and group dynamics did not seem applicable in these confrontation situations. Although at times I could demonstrate my understanding of "their side," the value of such empathy seemed short-lived. For the most part, I felt that all I could do was to "maintain my cool" and try to figure a safe way out politically and physically for myself and others.

Often, my job was to communicate administration policy. Sometimes, in the process of policy formation, my personal recommendations did not prevail. Subsequently, I had to present and defend the policies. Thus, before large groups and occasionally in response to queries from the press, I had to restrain my "academic freedom" and "therapeutic honesty."

Clarity of Role

It is comforting to know one's own role, and it is usually helpful if others understand it. As has been suggested previously, I was often unclear about my role. In addition, I seemed to be perceived differently by different groups with whom I had contact. Furthermore, my role in relation to different groups changed over the course of the summer.

In the early part of the summer, I attended many meetings of separate groups of businessmen, police officials, hippies, "hippie helpers," and others. Here, particularly in the beginning of the summer, I was acceptable to myself and to the groups as an information gatherer and observer. Later on, as individuals and groups began to demand action from me, it was difficult to know how and when and to what kinds of demands to be responsive. I found that it was essential to know the background of the varous groups' relationships with the city government in order to assess their demands. Such knowledge could only come from discussions with other city officials, not from my particular background or knowledge.

Some of these separate groups were in conflict with each other. I had information about each group that the other groups wished they had. For example, I knew about planned demonstrations as well as police operational procedures Here again, I tried to retain my professional commitment to confidentiality of communication. Political considerations often threatened this commitment.

At administrative policy meetings, my role and function was again perplexing. Some of my colleagues at city hall perceived me as the psychologist "hippie expert." According to this percept, I was expected to deliver certain statistical information on numbers (how many hippies are there?), psychopathology (how many of them are crazy?), and other matters. As a scientist, I had insufficient data. As a clinician, I had decided that it would be both ethically inappropriate and socially destructive for me to discuss the psychopathology of individual young people. I had gathered some information and was expected to report on it. The problem was how to communicate in an understandable and helpful manner while clarifying my role for others and for myself.

I found that some psychological knowledge could be communicated in a useful manner at policy meetings. For example, I successfully argued against confrontation by suggesting that many youths unconsciously (and some consciously) were desirous of a destructive encounter with the police. Therefore, the Establishment would be "giving them what they wanted" while thinking it would be resisting their wishes.

Psychological knowledge was pertinent to policy formation in two other ways. First, stereotyping was popular among all groups. Over time, I was able to describe and differentiate different groups within the so-called "hippie" group stereotype. This enabled the administration to develop policies that accounted for these differences. In my work with the youth, I tried to undo stereotypes about "politicians" and "cops." Second, I advised against the use of affect-laden words in public statements. Thus, we tried to substitute "closing hour" for "curfew" and "youth" for "hippies."

Within policy discussions, I altered some of my own stereotypes. For example, I learned that public policy decision making often involves far more than the content of the situation. Also, I vividly experienced that there are more than two sides to many questions. In addition, I gained an appreciation of the power struggles that take place between different city agencies—struggles that may be unrelated to the social problem itself. Retrospectively, my work with families and groups should have prepared me to expect such power struggles as well as to appreciate the many sides of a question. However, I was unable to make this transfer of learning until after I had experienced it.

Change Agent

Facilitating change, be it in individuals, groups, or systems, is an important function of applied psychology. With my particular background as therapist and teacher, I knew something about the facilitation of internal change. For the most part, I had to abandon my theoretical orientation, which tends to emphasize internal change as a prerequisite for external change. Instead, my energies were directed toward the manipulation of external factors with the diffuse goal of a "cool scene."

In the interests of this goal, I organized and led a weekly meeting of representatives of all groups involved—"straight" citizens, hippies, hippie helpers, police, city officials, and others. It was at these meetings that my psychological background was of particular value. I knew that communication between individuals could occur in a group setting. I also knew that such meetings were potentially constructive or destructive to individuals and/or groups, and would require careful leadership.

In early June, I met separately with the different groups involved with the youth. This provided me with an opportunity to understand points of view and to note key individuals within each group. Next, I invited representatives of each of these groups to meet together. At the first meeting, small discussion groups were formed with representatives of each faction in each small group. Later these small groups reported to the entire group. This format worked successfully as an initial encounter as individuals had an opportunity to talk with each other as individuals. Apparently, it made it possible for individuals with different points of view to meet with one another as human beings and to share their ideas. The meeting format was then changed to a large group meeting, which I chaired. The invitations to attend were broadened. As a result, about 40 people attended weekly meetings through July and August. The meetings were a principal vehicle for communication among the various groups and factions within groups.

Although these meetings were incorrectly labeled group therapy by some participants, my experience as a group therapist was helpful in this setting. I was able to keep the meetings focused on problem solving while allowing intensive expression of affect. These meetings were exciting, frightening, informative, and sometimes comical. Often, threats and counterthreats, accompanied by illustrative profanity, were tenuously balanced by understanding, firmness, and consistency. As a trained group psychotherapist, I was prepared to accept hostility. Often I invited such hostility toward myself as the Mayor's representative in order to channel it away from other protagonists. In addition, I was prepared to respond to "hidden agendas," unconscious communiqués, and nonverbal messages, while not becoming trapped by verbal content. For example, in the midst of a heated argument between youth and police, I interrupted the discussion to point out the pleasant, friendly greeting exchanged between a police officer and a young person who had just arrived. I was thereby able to illustrate that such relationships are possible.

Once again, because I also had the role of communicator of city policy, political considerations intruded on my group leadership style. I had powers that were quite different from the powers of the group therapist. I could influence decisions that could affect the lives of the participants outside of the group setting, especially because what they said during the group sessions might well be used against them by me or by others. In addition, I was not unbiased. Rather, I had to be prepared to present a relatively united position of city officials and to avoid an open conflict between officials of the Mayor's Office and other city agencies. Any such conflicts had to be settled elsewhere.

As a scientist, I lack specific criteria to evaluate the impact of these meetings as a factor in change, internal or external. Much tension continued; there were troublesome events. But the feedback from participants indicated that the meetings were helpful to them and to their groups.

Conclusion

In the previous example of the group meetings, my psychological background was particularly relevant. In the other examples, my psychological knowledge was helpful sometimes. In retrospect, it had been naive of me to think that my professional background had adequately prepared me for the particular situations in which I found myself.

My personal identity problem was determined in part by my inability to define my area of competence ahead of time. Erroneously, I had generalized my experience on some matters pertaining to youth to a broad community setting. By the time I realized the need for setting limits on myself, I had committed myself to certain responsibilities beyond my own limits and could not retreat without putting myself or the Mayor in an embarrassing position. In time, I resolved my identity problem in a way that was somewhat unsatisfactory to me as a psychologist. I identified myself as a politician

serving the city, and, specifically, the Mayor.

My experience suggests that the psychologist has some knowledge that may be helpful in the social action arena. However, the psychologist should be extremely cautious in accepting the willingness of society, including some psychologists, to perpetuate two fantasies; first, that the psychologist "knows everything" about people; and second, following from this omniscient position, that the psychologist can be especially helpful in social-political situations.

I have described my activities as an assistant to the Mayor of Boston within a framework of role differences between my usual role as a psychologist and my role at city hall. However, I am concerned that the focus of this article was such that the key factor in my entry into the political system might be overlooked. As I noted at the beginning of the article, I was a trusted political worker, known personally to key city officials. I am not suggesting that such partisan political activity is the only way into the system. Instead, I wish to conclude by emphasizing that person-to-person trust and understanding, although it may not be sufficient, is necessary if the psychologist or any other human science specialist is to be invited to have the opportunity to "do his thing" within the social action arena.

In this very pointed article, Professor Reiff describes professionals as elitist humanists with a basically middle class type of thinking which hampers their ability to promote human welfare. Today the income bracket of the professional's clients serves as a measure of his status and competence. This leads to a diminishment of the difference between science, profession, and a business. As to the political neutrality claimed by many scientific professionals, a cursory survey shows that "whenever society was faced with war, organized psychology presented arms and surrendered its professional neutrality." Reiff observes that organized psychology responds primarily when the

social context resembles a crisis. Social irrelevancy of psychological research increases in between crisis periods when business is as usual. He concludes that, "It is not professionalism which must be the organizing force of professional life but the social and political condition of man must become the organizing force of professionalism."

2.7
Professionalism and the Promotion of Human Welfare

Robert Reiff

In the past three decades there have been profound changes in the nature of professionalism in this country. These changes can be largely attributed to two major social and economic conditions. The first is the growth of a large enough and wealthy enough middle-class to buy up all the human services offered by professionals leaving nothing for the poor and disadvantaged. The second is the professions have become the major path of upward social mobility in society.

As a consequence of these conditions there has been a growth in size, wealth and influence of the professions which has made them the modern economic, social and political organized expression of the middle-class, replacing the old petit-bourgeois. They have become, in effect, a new middle-class "estate" in the affairs of our society.

Historically, organized professions have regarded themselves as the institutions responsible for the application of a science or body of knowledge for the promotion of human welfare. Society has agreed to assign to the professions this moral task and has expected them to function as "social guardians" of their particular field of knowledge in the interest of the public good.

The assignment of this responsibility to the professions has been called by Everett Hughes a "moral division of labor."[1] As such, it im-

By permission of the author.

[1] E. C. Hughes, *Men and Their Work*, Glencoe, Ill.: Free Press, 1958, p. 80.

poses certain social obligations on professions and promotes certain expectations on the part of the public.

The public's expectation is that the interests of the profession and the interests of the public will normally be the same, and that when they differ, the profession will act in the interest of the public good regardless of its own interest.

The public expects that the professional is obliged to render his service to all alike regardless of economic status and solely on the basis of need. Society, on the other hand, agrees that the professional is entitled to sufficient rewards for his services so that he may be free of any economic or social incumbrances. They, therefore, endow him with a comfortable living and a great social prestige and status.

The professional is expected to render his services free of political influence. As a citizen he is free to be as politically partisan as he is capable. But in the dispensing of his professional services he must be non-partisan.

In the last three decades this moral divison of labor, this social contract between society and the professions has become more a matter of mere rhetoric than fact.

During the last few decades, the old upper-class elitist, humanist spirit and noblesse oblige morality of the professions has gradually eroded and a new middle-class entrepreneural morality has taken its place. I would like to show how this transformation took place. There is no implication here that the old was better than the new. I am concerned only with the nature of the transformation and its implication for the promotion of human welfare.

It may be useful to look at social history as a series of periods in the life of a nation each of which is characterized by a dominant social theme. The dominant social theme of each period finds expression in every aspect of economic, social and political life. The theme in a sense expresses the desires, the hopes and the goals of the people, the psychological stance from which the daily economic, social and political activities of the nation are played out. This is not a conscious process of decision-making but rather the psychological expression of the social process. One might call it an aspect of the social mind.

After World War II, the social theme in American life was up-ward social mobility. This was reflected in every aspect of economic, social and political life. The movement to suburbia, the rise in the gross national product, the production of new Ph.D.s, even the popularity of the psychological concept of self-actualization were all expressions of the social theme of this period. During this period, the professions became the major path of upward social mobility. It was a period of explosive growth and expansion of professions in the United States. It seemed like almost everyone wanted to be a professional and almost every occupation wanted to be viewed as a profession and began to act like one. This resulted in the ranks of the middle-class being swelled by people who either were in fact professionals or people who thought they were and assimilated the professional ideology.

A significant segment of society, however, who did not have the necessary means or prerequisites to travel that path were unable to participate in this upward movement and were left behind to shift for themselves. Millions of poor, black and white, were ignored and forgotten or, at best, considered part of the undeserving, the criminal or the socially sick. The professional services either ignored them or were alienated from them, treating them in an alms-house fashion, providing, on rare occasions, what has been called "cheap lines for slender purses."

In the past few years, we have witnessed a reaction to the theme of upward social mobility. The hippie's costume and preferred mode of living may be perceived as a mockery of that theme, the student's rejection of a future filled with unlimited entrepreneurial opportunities but void of meaning is a reaction to it. The concept of the non-professional is a direct attack on upward social mobility through the professions. Certain aspects of the new career movement are also attacks on this, while others represent the attempt to "buy-in" on the professionalization process. Looking back over the last ten years one can see the growing momentum of a new social theme sparked by the Civil Rights movement, which can best be characterized as "social justice." We can see this theme beginning to invade every aspect of economic, social and political life—citizen participation, community control, black power and

black capitalism are aspects of it and advocacy, accountability and community psychology and psychiatry are professional responses to it. A new "social mind" is in the process of being developed and its major preoccupation is with "social justice."

But we are in a transition stage where the new is competing with the old as the dominant theme of the next period in our history. Social justice is the theme mainly of the social reform and radical movements. The major purpose of this paper is to look at the developing conflict between these two themes and its implications for the nature of professionalism.

Modern professionalism has developed from a basically upper-class, elitist dominated group to a middle-class dominated group. The upper-class elitist elements brought to the professions their elitist psychology and noblesse oblige notions about human service.

When we consider the professions in their elitist state the social rank and prestige of their members was consonant with their role as social guardians. In their social position entrepreneurism was a taint just exactly in the same sense that you didn't expect the sons of the landed gentry starving and bankrupt as they may be to turn their hands to a trade. It was corrupting of their social prestige position.

According to the old elitist humanist tradition the natural foe of the professions in private life was commercialism and its natural foe in public life was politics.

During the past several decades those sons and daughters of the middle-class who might otherwise have gone into the market place as a career went into the professions and began to transform them.

When the members of the professions came to be drawn from the petit-bourgeois, they brought to the professions their middle-class entrepreneurial way of thinking.

The professionals began to act like petit-bourgeois in their practice and went into business for themselves. Many of the techniques of business became accepted professional practice. The production lines in the offices of doctors and dentists is one expression. The practice of turning unpaid bills over to a collection agency was unheard of in professional practice before this period. Among some professionals, this entrepreneurial-orientation found its expression in the development of the art of grantsmanship. And much of social system theory is simply the application of the cost-effective techniques of big business to professional services.

In the days of the old elitist tradition, the professional who had a good reputation was sought after by the affluent and though he may have been subject to the criticism of commercialism, it was his professional competence and status which in part determined the income bracket from which his clients come. But today, the reverse is true. It is the income bracket from which his clients come that often is the measure of a professional's status and competence. In the days of the old elitism, it was a common practice for professionals to give a certain proportion of their time to rendering free service to the poor. The higher fees they could charge their more affluent clients were justified on the basis that it was equitable to expect the wealthier clients to contribute towards the professional's service to the poor. This practice has practically become extinct. Today, the poor must rely on public institutions for services and public institutions must compete with private practice income in order to recruit staff.

When the morals of the market place replaced the morals of the elite, the professions came to look and act more like corporate entities for the welfare of their stockholders rather than institutions for the promotion of human welfare.

The differences between a science, a profession, and a business began to dissolve. Many scientific and professional enterprises became, in fact, big business, and the thinking of the average professional with regard to the services he was offering was similar in many respects to the business-hungry attitude of the petit-bourgeois shopkeeper and entrepreneur, albeit couched in the rhetoric of humanism and public service.

It is not accidental that the great expansion and new office in society which accrued to the professions during the period of the "middle-classizing" of the professions was accompanied by an erosion of the noblesse oblige humanist tradition and a deterioration of its traditional moral role in society. It was the inevitable consequence of a social process in which the morals of the middle-class spirit of entrepreneurism became institutionalized and established hegemony over the morals of the spirit of elitist humanism.

Historically, the medical profession is the prototype of all modern professions. This development is therefore clearly and obviously evident in the medical profession, but no profession has escaped the consequences of this social process. It has infected the many new professions which have been created as well as the old traditional ones.

The entrepreneurial orientation of the professions has affected every aspect of the moral division of labor. In the political area entrepreneurism may be said to have converted the concept of professional neutrality into the middle-class attitude that business is business, politics is politics.

In the eyes of the public the non-partisan obligation of the professions applied only to the rendering of service. The public never expected the professions to be neutral about social issues. In fact, as Hughes has pointed out,[2] in times of social crises, professional detachment appears to the public as the most perilous deviation of all, the one least to be tolerated. The professional mind in such a case appears as a perversion of the common sense of what is urgent and what is less urgent. The professions have, indeed, perverted their obligation of neutrality in the area of service into the principle of "scientific objectivity" in the area of public affairs, insisting that they cannot take sides on matters of public policy.

I thought it would be interesting to see how the principle of professional neutrality in matters of public policy has been practiced during the last few decades, especially during periods of social crisis. I elected to survey the interests and activities of one profession during periods of social crisis in the last fifty years. I selected psychology, first, because I am more familiar with psychology than any other profession and, second, because professional psychologists almost more than any other practitioners still cling to the myth that they are objective scientists. However, it should be understood that the basic observations about psychology are also true of all organized human service professions.

[2] *Ibid.*, p. 83.

The survey revealed that whenever society was faced with war organized psychology presented arms and surrendered its professional neutrality. No matter how severe the social crisis, no matter how pressing the social problems, unless they occurred within the context of a major war, organized psychology remained a "business as usual" enterprise. Neither depression, marked institution change, radical conflict, or the war against poverty has produced the same response as war. Furthermore, war *itself* as a social problem has never been responded to by organized psychology *during a war*.

From 1942 until 1945 most psychological activity was directly related to the war. Psychologists conducted many studies dealing with minority group problems within the army and the effect of rumor within the civilian population. Psychological warfare was an important activity. Propaganda policy was determined by psychologists. They monitored foreign broadcasts and designed training programs in the field of international relations. They conducted surveys of public needs and popular attitudes and studied and recommended programs to cope with the psychological problems of wartime economy. A number of psychologists addressed their research to the training of democratic leaders in occupied territories. There were studies to remedy deficiencies in production and to increase worker productivity. Public opinion polls were conducted by psychologists to provide civilian intelligence to government and military officials.

The legitimacy of influencing government programs and policies was taken for granted by the American Psychological Association. Psychologists served as consultants and program planners in every branch of government. Some even assumed responsibility for top government and military policies.

In contrast to the war years, the interest and activity of psychologists during the years of the great depression and recovery period reflect a lack of concern with the social problems and needs of that period. Between 1929 and 1937, the period of the great depression, Psychological Abstracts lists 10 studies on prohibition and 39 studies on unemployment in contrast to 83 child development studies, 174 animal studies and a total of 665 papers on learning!

Why was psychology able to advise the government on Negro-White relations to prevent demoralization during the war, but seems reluctant or timid or even opposed to educating the public or advising the government or assisting black and white organizations to prevent a holocaust in the present social crisis?

The conclusion is inescapable that it is not the public policy itself but the social context in which it occurs which determined whether or not organized psychology responded.

Once this is understood it becomes clear that the question no longer is should the professions be neutral but rather what are the social conditions, what are the social contexts which determine whether or not organized professions will respond to social problems or insist on their neutrality.

In a major war every sector of society comes under the domination of the political-military interests of the country. The demand on professions is part of a monolithic demand on every available resource in society and all of society is united in its interest in meeting the demand. Under such conditions professions respond with immediate mobilization of their resources, internal tensions and conflicts are suppressed, and a new level of cooperative and integrated activity takes place.

But in times of other kinds of social crisis, such as depression, the war against poverty, racial conflict, or the failure of our education system, the country is divided. There is no monolithic demand. There are conflicting interests and points of view.

Social problems become social issues and it is impossible to respond to them without taking sides. This is not to say that in the war professions did not have to take a stand. But taking a stand when everybody is on the same side is vastly different from taking a stand in a divided society marked by controversy and confrontation.

It is evident from professional behavior that there is really no fixed "fundamental" or "principled" professional neutrality. Although the issues are often debated in this way, history shows us that the definition of the "legitimate" role of professions does not rest on some "ideal" set of values but shifts with the social context in which the issues arise.

When this is a context of controversy, professions as an organized institution retreat to the sidelines. It is a rather interesting morality for a professional to find it permissible to take a stand on social problems when there is social consensus but to insist on the necessity to be neutral on social problems about which society is divided.

If the promotion of human welfare is the primary responsibility of the professions, how can they discharge their obligation by abstaining from social issues? The promotion of human welfare is a social concept. It cannot be understood or evaluated except in the context of the social conditions of the time. The professions assume that there is always a course of action possible in the interest of the public which transcends the social, political and economic differences between the various segments of the public. Promoting human welfare implies that there is such a thing as "a public" which is above and beyond the various ways in which society is divided into classes, organizations, political parties, etc. But the only way to create such a public is to make a particular issue so general and abstract that it becomes meaningless as a guide to action for the promotion of human welfare. It is only on the rarest occasions that there is consensus among all groups in society on a particular professional issue. In such cases the public is not that which truly exists in the reality of everyday life, but is most often an ideological abstraction reflecting the abstractness of the level on which the issue has been put by the professions. The reality is that any decision as to what is in the interest of the *public* good is, in fact, in the interest of one or more various groups or "publics" in society. The more there is consensus among the various groups, the more the position is likely to be considered as one promoting human welfare. If, in fact, every decision about a course of action to promote human welfare is tantamount to taking sides, it is easy to see why professions find it possible to mobilize themselves on those issues where there is consensus but retreat to a self-deceptive neutrality on those issues where society is divided. It is self-deceptive because every failure to make a decision may also benefit one or more groups of society. It is necessary, therefore, for professions to recognize that, except on the rarest occasions, no matter what they do, every course of action or failure to take a course of action is, in effect, taking sides and results in the profession's acting for or against the interest of one or more groups in society. Once this fact of life is accepted by the professions the task of promoting human welfare will be less a passive response to the vicissitudes of social forces but an active and purposive partisan intervention in the course of human affairs.

Hughes has observed that social unrest often shows itself precisely in questioning the prerogatives of the leading professions.[3] In times of crisis there may arise a general demand for more complete conformity of professionals to the lay ideology about professions. He points out that the typical reform movement is often a restless attempt to redefine the values or at least change the nature and tempo of a professional action. The movement may simply push for faster or more drastic action or it may be a direct attack on the philosophy of the profession or professionalism in general. The present social crisis supports this observation. Almost every element described above is present in the demands of the present social reform movement in this country. The poor are attacking the profession's ideology on the following points.

First, the poor are challenging the traditional moral division of labor. They are no longer content to allow the professions the sole responsibility as social guardians of a science or body of knowledge for the promotion of human welfare. Their bitter experiences has taught them that the professions have identified the promotion of human welfare with the interests of the middle-class with great cost to them. They have lost their trust and they are now demanding that they share the social guardian role and that the nature of the relationship of the professions to society be fundamentally changed so that they, the poor, can participate in the task of guarding how a profession advances the application of its science or body of knowledge. This is the essence of the demand for greater accountability. The poor are not asking to control the doctors in each case of individual treatment. As individuals, they want a doctor to be in charge of their treatment, but they feel that their treatment would be better if, as a group, they could control the institution of doctoring.

[3] *Ibid.*, p. 83.

Secondly, the poor are frustrated and angry at professional policies which in theory are for the protection of the client but in practice protect the professional against the client. They have seen that professional self-interest takes precedent over the interest of the client. There are a number of studies to show that when there is a conflict of interests between an agency and a client invariably the professional will decide in the interest of the agency.

The poor are also reacting to the professionals' propensity to favor one group of clients over another. Basically this is a challenge to the entrepreneurial professional ideology in which professionals tend to sell all their services to the affluent and make no provisions for the poor to receive their share of the best.

They are also reacting to that aspect of professional ideology in which status and competence are judged by the criteria of the affluence of one's clients and which in fact has tended to relegate the "second and third raters" to take care of the poor. To remedy these grievances they are demanding greater client responsibility.

Thirdly, the poor are challenging the professional's ideology with regard to the hierarchal structure of the roles, skills, functions and competencies of their professionals and their ancilaries. They are demanding a restructuring of the professions with regard to roles, functions, skills and competencies and are not willing to leave this restructuring up to the professions but want to participate in it.

These are but a few of the major issues raised by the social reform movement of our time. Those that I have mentioned are issues that apply to all professions. But each profession has its own unique set of issues which relate to its specific practice and to the substantive nature of the body of knowledge on which its practice is based.

It is apparent from the issues cited above that they represent a challenge to some of the fundamental concepts and principles of both traditional professionalism and its modern entrepreneurial form. But it is a challenge not only to the form of professionalism but to its very essence. It is a demand to radically change the nature of professionalism, that is, to radically change the relationship of the professions not only to the poor but to society as a whole.

If professionals are to respond to these demands, it will require a movement among all professions to radically change some of the fundamental concepts and principles of professionalism as well as radically change the nature of the relationship between all professions and society. The times are calling for a radical professionalism. Radical because it takes a stand on the side of the poor and sees their grievances as socially just. Radical because it understands that meeting the needs of the poor cannot be achieved without challenging some of the fundamental concepts and principles of the professions and their relationship to society. Professional because it seeks to make a professional response to the social crisis. The lay public is less informed, less knowledgeable and less aware about a science and its possibilities than the professions. The poor feel aggrieved and they want equity. If it's good enough for Rockefeller they say, it's good enough for us. But what works for Rockefeller may not work for them so long as they are not in Rockefeller's shoes. What the poor want is often derived from what they do not have, not from an informed consideration and choice of the possibilities. In the first place that information and knowledge is not made available to them and in the second place, if it were, and they were able to choose the best of all possibilities there would still be many constraints on their ability to get it. As Lisa Peattie[4] has pointed out the poor as a public are much clearer and more homogeneous when it comes to expressing what they are against. Their list of grievances are generally realistic and accurately reflect what it is they want to change from. But they are less clear and less homogeneous when it comes to expressing how and what it is they want to change to. That is why it is so important for professionals in their desire to respond to the poor not to identify with them so completely that they lose their professional identity. There is a real social need for a professional response. Simply making an individual response and devoting one's time to giving service to the poor may be laudable but it is inadequate, even futile, because under present social conditions there will never be enough individuals giving service to the poor until the nature of pro-

[4] L. R. Peattie, Reflections on advocacy planning, *Journal of the American Institute of Planners*, 34, 2 (March, 1968), 80–88.

fessionalism changes. Radical professionalism must face the dilemma which modern professionalism has imposed on society. How is society going to solve the problem of the economic burden created by a large and powerful caste which renders a service essential to the welfare of all people in society, but which produces no wealth yet at the same time extracts such a high price for its services that only the wealthy can afford them? It seems to me that any social or economic program such as, for example, "health insurance" cannot work if it is based on the present entrepreneurial professional ideology of a "fee for service" basis. Only if the professions change their ideology and morality can an effective social program be designed to meet the needs of all the people.

In each profession there already are groups striving to change professional concepts and practices, innovate new roles and functions, develop new social programs and a new professional philosophy which will constitute a professional response to the present social crisis. I have pointed out what appears to be developing as a common conceptual framework for a radical professional program which can serve as the basis on which a constituency can be developed among the professions, the students and the lay public. Radical professionalism is a philosophy, a morality, a set of goals and aims and a point of view that is at one and the same time a model of what the professions might look like in the future and a transforming process. For as professionals act in accordance with such a new model this in itself will stimulate the transformation of the professions.

In the final analysis this transformation can take place only if professionals develop a broader view than that of technologists who see the social and political problems of society as an arena for the aggrandizement of their technology. Professionalism is not an end in itself, an ultimate goal that society cannot do without. It is not professionalism which must be the organizing force of professional life, but the social and political condition of man must become the organizing force of professionalism. In this sense "the professional man" must become "the political man" if professionalism is to truly promote human welfare.

2.8
Advocacy and Democracy: The Long View

Alan E. Guskin and
Robert Ross

The last few years of urban crisis have generated a new concern about the citizen's role in the planning process. Given the complexity of the issues and growing sophistication of techniques in urban and social planning, many writers have argued that community groups, especially in low income neighborhoods, need the expertise of professionals to defend their interests in the policy process. From this perspective, the idea of planners who are advocates for low income communities has generated a great deal of interest, especially within the planning and health professions, and a great deal of commentary on the part of social scientists, policy makers, and others interested in the inner city. The phrase "advocate planner" has become current in discussing the role of a professional who is acting as advisor and sometimes spokesman for poor people's organizations in the inner city policy process.

The most typical justification and argument for advocacy can be gleaned from a document of one of the most experienced and dedicated advocate groups in the country—Urban Planning Aid in Boston. In one of their fund-raising documents they state the following:

Government planning without community participation helps to destroy democratic values. It can produce feelings of impotence and fierce struggles for power and self-determination by those at the bottom of the urban system.

The groups with power and those able to present their case forcefully are the ones reckoned with, while the needs of the poor and the black community are rather easily neglected.

One way to correct this is through the processes which planners are beginning to talk about as *advocacy planning*. The advocate planner tries to make public planning less one-sided by providing special help to the groups which tend to get passed over. (UPA, 1969, p. 1)

The setting for these assertions is a contemporary urbanism and urban government which are notable for the extreme complexity of

Reprinted by permission from *American Journal of Orthopsychiatry*, 41, 1 (1971), 43–57. Copyright © 1971 by The American Orthopsychiatric Association, Inc.

factors, layers of organization, and the specialized knowledge needed to make the system operate. The scale and scope of government responsibility alone is huge. From air pollution to rat control, the policy-making apparatus is a maze of bureaucracy and data; the specialists who are able to make their way through this maze are very few, and the demand for their skills are very high.

The scope of the problems facing municipal (and other) governments create, in turn, an objective necessity for advance planning. Correspondingly, a decision-making process emerges which takes into account as much of the relevant data as possible. Dependence on computers, various kinds of social data collection, and the ability to project into the near future (when the policy or program under consideration actually becomes operative) generates very esoteric specialties. And, the length of lead-times stretches further and further into the future (Michael, 1968).

In the face of these developments, the ordinary citizen finds the details of the city planning processes quite beyond his ken. Passive acquiescence serves as consent for many whose basic interests are more or less served; apathy or frustrated rage (its near relative) is the response of those who do not comprehend the processes and who feel their interests are excluded from the process of tacit representation.

The advocate's role responds, then, to two major themes in contemporary community development and reform. On the one hand, it seems to accept the idea of a pluralism of contesting interest groups in American society as a defective, but more or less adequate way of understanding the political process in America; it asserts, though, that the poor, black, and minority ethnic groups are left out of the process by which other groups contend, generally successfully, in order to advance or defend their vital interests. The title of the key document in the discussion of advocacy, for example, is Paul Davidoff's article: "Advocacy and Pluralism in Planning" (Davidoff, 1965).

On the other hand, addressed as it is to planning and the provision of service in the inner city, the movement for advocacy intimates another aspect of American political life besides that of interest group contests; namely, the increasing importance of technical

expertise in the management of the policy-making apparatus of an advanced industrial capitalism.

In this context the demands for community participation in black communities and elsewhere and the rise of the notion of advocacy take on their important historical meaning. The black community is attempting to gain, from the affluent capitalism which surrounds it, fundamental changes—especially those concerning land development, housing, and, of course, schools. The demand for participation in planning—for whatever service or project is underway—is a reflex of its sense that only the black community or its direct agents can be trusted to represent itself.

But black citizens, like all of us, confront some key problems. For example, average time, until recently, for the development of one type of nonprofit subsidized housing was 44 months. In order to make that work literally countless layers of governmental and financial negotiation must be encountered: full time work of sophisticated corporate managers are required (Goldston, 1969). The estimation of traffic potential on newly routed streets, to take another example, is not likely to be in the repetoire of skills of most community activists, especially in areas whose schools do not generate high numbers of trained personnel in residence. So the need to put technical ability at the service of what are called "client" populations has emerged from the social and technological trends of the Sixties.

In the last five or six years, the concept of community control, linked historically to community action, has become associated with advocacy. It was thought that by decentralizing power and authority, in some cases, to the neighborhood level, citizen's interests would be weighed in the decision-making process. A number of obstacles have made clear that, by itself, this is an inadequate strategy for reallocating power alignments and the representation of interests. Two of them are relevant here: first, once on various committees or boards, the residents of low income communities were often manipulable, for the issues were presented to them by experts or political professionals, and it was beyond their ability to deal with technical terms; second, community control is a relatively undifferentiated concept, especially in the black community where, because of residential segregation, there are frequently conflicting class interests internal to the black community as a whole.

Emerging from these insights into some inadequacies of the community control and community action ideas, then, came the notion of advocacy *for* the community on the part of professionals who are responsible to the community, not to an agency of the city government or other groups. But in order to respond fully to the need to redistribute power, the advocate must address himself to the nontechnical as well as technical problems faced by his community client: community organization is one; education about what he, the advocate, can actually offer is another. We shall return later to problems which arise in the course of meeting these needs. At this point it is necessary to indicate what all this implies for American democracy.

The Myth of Political Pluralism

Growing up through the Fifties, the most widely accepted view of American power and political processes was, as we noted, that of "pluralism" (Dahl, 1967). As we must necessarily be brief, that argument may be summarized thus: while town-meeting democracy was both mythic and inadequate to the tasks of governing a highly complex society, there developed by a process of virtual representation through a variety of interest groups, the individual citizen's interests being advanced by the interplay of more or less equally powerful groups. Such groups were, at least, able to veto each other and the government actions which would be deeply threatening to the individual's ability to survive or prosper.

Of course, this view of American politics came under attack from a variety of sources. C. W. Mills, for example, argued that this horse-trading of interest-lobbyists took place only at the "middle levels" of (Congressional) power, whereas real priorities, such as Cold War, or monopoly expansion, took place among "power elite." E. E. Schatt-schneider, a political scientist, argued that the process of lobbying in Washington was very much a process of settling disputes between the already affluent and established—leaving out, basically, the working class, and the strata below it, in wealth and power. (See Gamson, 1968, for a review of some of these perspec-

tives.) And Gabriel Kolko has shown the persistence over time of inequalities of wealth and power, despite various reforms (1962).

In the Sixties it became clear that government processes were not in fact inclusive in their pluralism. For example, groups like the poor, black, and third world minorities did not have the resources to compete successfully in the influence process. Further, it also became clear that as a regulator of other basic processes of an advanced technological state, the political capitalism of the post-War era did not protect the white middle class consumer of drugs, food, mass media, or, for that matter, air. (See Kolko, 1970, for an explanation of the term "political capitalism.") Advocacy, seen in this light, is a way to compensate for an imperfect pluralism.

As the theories of pluralism were blooming, so too, another generation of political theory appeared which justified existing power. This family of perspectives had as its institutional and intellectual base the reform-minded liberalism of the late Fifties and early Sixties. It was in these years that the theory of the democratic Chief Executive, who should be unencumbered by a stalemated or conservative Congress, was elaborated and celebrated. Building on the traditions of the New Deal and the charismatic leftovers of FDR, reforming liberalism associated itself with a political style best understood as "deference to the executive." (See, e.g., Burns, 1963.) The Bricker amendment, Congressional opposition to trade with Communist nations, and even the highly questionable basis upon which the Gulf of Tonkin resolution was passed, all were defeated or passed respectively in the name of giving the President "freedom of action."

The development of this deference to society's executives seems to emerge as the social order in which we live becomes more highly technological, and sophistication—technical, scientific, and political—needed to run it becomes an ever more demanding prerequisite for those who would guide the destiny of cities, states, regions, and nations. A commonplace truism, this, but in it is hidden a whole process of ideological and political developments which form the guiding precepts of the managers of the society and their academic colleagues.

Commanding the heights of the public and private organs which

make social policy are men who are talented in management—or trained in it—if we are to believe their apologists and academic theorists.

The professional manager has emerged as a new focus of social order, or social mores, and of individual aspirations. The manager is the agent of economic and social development. . . . For the manager is the carrier of our new capacity or organize. (Drucker, 1959, p. 57)

Among the key skills held by these managers is the judicious use of technical, scientific, and professional advice bearing upon the problems which the political leadership must act—or decide—upon. The managerial perspective may be seen as another way to "patch up" pluralism. By manipulation of groups from the top of executive hierarchies, groups or interests not served or defended by "normal" political processes may be linked to power. "Experts" within the hierarchy come to stand as surrogates for the contending groups themselves. (See Moynihan, 1969, for his account of this process in the War on Poverty.)

The War on Poverty, and even before that, urban renewal, has gone a long way to create a sense that these professionals—sometimes called planners, sometimes called advisors or researchers—are the key factors in what is called "innovation." Given the complexity of the task of simply maintaining livable conditions in the cities, the expert's perspective becomes increasingly visible and valued.

Therefore, another force in the managers attempt to "provide" for the people by using professional advice is the advent of "social engineering" perspectives. Hauser states that social engineering is neither "liberal" nor conservative. Rather,

. . . the social engineer, as yet represented by a pathetically few professions—e.g., the public administrator, the city manager, the social workers, the educator, the criminologist, the planner, the professional businessman—is emerging to apply the knowledge of social-science to the solution of social problems, in the same manner as the electronics engineer applies the knowledge of physics to electronics problems, of the biological engineer, the physician, applies the knowledge of the life sciences to problems of ill health. (Hauser, 1969, p. 14)

Hauser, mindful that we live in a nominally democratic society, qualified the implicit authoritarianism in his doctor-patient analogy with the following:

Although a majority of the people must fix the goals of a society, the social scientist and the social engineer are in a strategic position to participate in goal formation. *They must work closely with political and other leaders* to help develop a broad spectrum of choices. . . . (*Ibid.,* p. 15, emphasis ours)

Quoting sociologist Hauser should not imply that this sort of perspective is limited to his discipline, or even his particular role in his discipline. As the ideology of pluralism and democratically elected bodies waned in effectiveness in the Sixties, similar perspectives began to emerge rapidly and universally.

Writing in the February, 1970, *Transaction* magazine (p. 23) Allen Schick of the Brookings Institution characterizes the emerging "cybernetic state"; the cybernetic state, he says, is one which *succeeds* first the administrative and then the bureaucratic state. It is cybernated in that it responds automatically, he projects, to categorical situations: Politics "withers away." For example, if you haven't adequate income, then there are preprogrammed steps for that money (or services in kind) to be delivered unto you. One might reasonably ask of this programmed state of affairs, who writes the program?

Brzezinski seems to provide us with an answer.

. . . the rapid pace of change will put a premium on anticipating events and planning for them. Power will gravitate into the hands of those who control the information, and can correlate it most rapidly. [In] pre-crisis management institutions the tasks . . . will be to identify in advance likely social crises and to develop programs to cope with them. This could encourage tendencies during the next several decades towards a technocratic dictatorship, leaving less and less room for political procedures as we know them. (1967, p. 16)

American innovation is most strikingly seen in the manner which the meritocratic elite is taking over American life, utilizing the universities, exploiting the latest techniques of communications, harnessing as rapidly as possible the recent technological devices. . . . (1967, p. 23; for another aspect of this perspective see Galbraith, 1967, passim, especially Chapter XXV)

Our analysis thus far has brought us to this point: pluralism as a reigning perspective on American society was weakened vitally in the course of the ferment of both social and intellec-

tual attacks even while at the height of its success; emerging in its place is the notion of social engineering, a notion, of course, which takes us to the very outer boundaries of political thinking which could be called democratic. What has this all to do with advocacy, in planning or elsewhere?

Recent Reforms

A new generation of social programs succeeded the urban renewal and public housing reforms of the first wave of post-War concern with the slums of the inner city. Spurred by the militant civil rights movement and the black liberation radicalism which succeeded it, "Community Action" of various forms, followed by Model Cities, and now by black capitalism have been the reforming vehicles of the last few years. These very programs were generated from professionals and social scientist-engineers who dwell in the middle layers of formal and informal government. Of course, these plans are delivered into the hands of the publicly celebrated executives upon whom the media focus political attention; but their genesis indicates to us the nature of transformation going on in what we increasingly see as post-democratic America. (See Moynihan, 1969.)

Basically these developments presume that solutions to social problems can be engineered through the application of management techniques—which, to be sure, may be participatory—for the objectives which applied social scientists have identified as "strategic"—that is, objectives which have some decisive impact over a broader range of what is defined by various policy elites as deviant behavior. However, the reality of experience tends to dampen the glowing hope in these words.

As Marris and Rein (1967) and Moynihan (1969) have demonstrated, rather than consensus between community and political and business leadership which the Ford Foundation social scientists envisioned in its "gray areas" programs, poor people once in control of some organizational resources would tend to oppose what they saw as an Establishment, despite its protestations of benevolence. Similarly, it is becoming increasingly evident that many of the Model Cities programs will result in little more than the creation of model plans with little commitment to them on the part of community residents, and almost no hope at all of implementation

through a public sector which is financially committed to subsidizing other apparently deserving needs—like highways, airports, and through the ABM, defense electronic firms.

And here we have the crux of the matter. Pluralism cannot be considered outside of the context of class inequality. Some will compete more successfully, more powerfully, over time than others. A combination of wealth and bureaucratic access appear to be the chief components of success in the competition for the resource of the public sector. The same holds true for competition for the scarce resource of technical skills and planning capacity in the society: if knowledge is power, then it tends to flow to the already powerful, defined and utilized in the ways most expeditious to their purposes. This is the political conclusion of processes which have as their base an oligarchic economy; it is the reality facing all reform effort.

What we have been pointing to is that the movement towards advocacy in a number of professions is not merely about the delivery of more or better service to disadvantaged populations in an unequal society. Rather, the *need* that calls forth the phenomenon reflects deep-seated trends in the development of the social system —trends which we have come to conceive of as post-democratic. We have felt compelled to raise these matters in the context of advocacy programs, for too often such projects are seen as subjects for the so-called "nitty-gritty" practical problems of the practicing professional. Yet, these general trends in our social system place great restrictions on the efficacy of advocacy programs. As we turn now to some of these problems—of role conflict, of professional identity, of relations with community clients, and so forth—these trends should be kept in mind. In the latter part of this paper we shall return to them, for our understanding of the problems faced by advocates—be they in medicine, mental health, planning, architecture, law, media, etc., is intimately associated with our sense of the strategic directions needed by those who would redress the inegalitarian distribution of resource and amenity in social life.

Roles of Advocate Planners

From the point of view of the advocate planners their actions reflect the realization that it is mainly by means of political and technical advocacy that past and present abuses can be attacked. Also evident to these planners has been the lack of success of past planning efforts to either effect equitable change in a city-wide or specific community basis. (See Hatch, 1968.)

Advocate planning can best be defined in terms of the work or role(s) the advocate planners perform. While much of what they do differs in many respects from the work of the traditional planners and professionals, the advocate planner or advocate professional still does utilize his skills as a physical planner or architect or health planner or psychologist. Along with community members, the advocate planner does attempt to develop program alternatives to those being pursued by the city planners or politicians and attempt to assess the differential costs and benefits of each of these programs for the poor and the residents of the ghetto. This might involve developing plans for alternate highway routes, or to indicate the type of rehabilitation program that can be an alternative to building demolition. Given the nature of the city-wide policy process frequently this means the advocate is not merely creating "alternatives," but also is *oppositional* to the existing municipal administration or its agencies.

But, one of the basic problems for a planner who attempts to advocate ghetto community interests through alternative plans is that in many communities the poor *are unorganized* and often unable to articulate issues in ways amenable to the formulation of actual proposals. As a result, some advocate planners have seen their major task as creating organizations of the poor which could articulate and support the community's concern. These advocates raise such questions as, how do you get people to be involved as model city program representatives? How do you effectively involve poor people on decision-making boards for planning urban renewal sites (e.g., Edelston and Kolodner, 1968)? The result of this community organization frequently involves a confrontation strategy where the community attempts to fight the plans laid down by the city agencies. The oppositional tone of this activity reflects both the substantive inequities perceived by the organizations and a sense of formal impotence. As well, it is symptomatic of the defensive nature of much of this work: "they" initiate a proposal,

for example, a school location; "the community" and its advocates "oppose" it.

The problems of the community organization role of the advocate planner are similar to those experienced generally by organizers: the uncertain boundaries of the community, the lack of participation of certain community groups, the community leaders' fear of visibility and increased vulnerability, and the fact that the community's experience has taught it to reject the plans of others rather than develop alternatives.

Related to the advocate planner's role as community organizer is his function as a liaison-spokesman for his client with city planners or political-bureaucratic decision makers. This role naturally develops as the next step after unilateral and effective political protest and after communities are better able to present a somewhat unified voice. Often such a role brings the advocate planner into direct confrontation with conventional planning concerned with city-wide issues.

The liaison role may be seen by the establishment oriented city planners as "constructive" when there is some concern by the city government for developing the ghetto areas. In such situations the liaison-spokesman role of the advocate planner becomes an important middleman function between the poor and the city's planning department. Provided the advocate is a trained planner, he may be able to talk the "language" of the city planner while being committed to the interests of the poor. This role may be particularly difficult for the advocate planner who may be seen by the poor as an under-cover agent of the city agencies. This may be acute when the advocate himself is from a different ethnic background or the community is not well organized. A great difficulty related to his being suspect is that in the non-homogeneous black communities there may not be a consensus community interest to represent.

Moreover, the problem of the role of advocate as liaison-contact person is not merely one of perception or trust by the community with which he is working. The process of negotiation, the discussion of "feasibility," the exchange of notes and memos, all these may, in fact, result in *a pacification of discontent* which is grounded not merely in perception but in objective conditions of life. Thus, the advocate may find himself torn between two realities:

that of bureaucratic and technical detail which is necessary, and that of anger and anguish which is just.

Another role that has been performed by some advocate planners is that of the social scientist who collects data to support protests (e.g., abusive policies and actions of government agencies, or private groups, census information, surveys of facilities, conditions, and opinion). The particular effectiveness of this role is that it deals with city agencies on their own terms. Thus, respectable social scientists become advocates for the poor (i.e., their clients) with the agencies that are affecting them and use their data for purposes of changing proposed plans. A peculiar problem for the social scientist in this role is that he may believe he is representing the poor by his collection of data about and from the poor (this is especially true when he's working for an agency which is a nominal advocate for the poor, e.g., OEO, Model Cities) but in actuality he may be seen by the poor as not advocating for them and surely not part of them (see Kaplan, 1969). This problem has some similarity to the more general advocate planner problem where the poor perceive them as establishment agents or manipulators.

Here, too, the advocate as researcher faces two realities. The official processes need (or sometimes merely want) certain data for the sake of budgets, proposals to Washington, etc. But, the poor and black community has had experience of these studies, they say: *they want action, not questionnaires*. The result is frequently quite mechanical: a survey is done which, predictably enough, indicates that "the people" want good housing, better transport, protection from criminal violence, and, always, decent schools and jobs. Occasionally, of course, such work will be an important guide to policy which is beneficial to a community: problems unrecognized may be found (for example, infant lead poisoning from peeling paint); densities may be found to be higher than realized because of undetected illegal subdivisions and conversions; or surface quiescence may be found to hide deep anger. Nevertheless, even the sincere advocate researcher has most typically had to face the quandry of giving trivial information to elites about the poor, rather than, for example, getting significant intelligence back to the community. This latter function has most often been performed by activist students who have occasionally done situationally valuable investigation of land-holding, political corruption, etc. (The flow of information is thus usually *upwards*, enabling elites to plan for *their* objectives with more accurate data than otherwise available. Communities thus served are planned *for;* the opposite of this "Surrogate pluralism" would be for detailed data and reconnaissance about the elites and their plans to flow *down*, enabling communities to plan for themselves.)

So far, the advocate planner role has been viewed as that of a physical planner or architect, a community organizer, a liaison-advocate (spokesman) for the poor with government agencies, and a social scientist. Because of the necessity for performing more than one of these roles, advocacy planning often is practiced by a team of people who have all or most of the skills needed to carry out these functions. One of the best examples of this team effort is the Urban Planning Aid (UPA) group of Boston. The group includes faculty members in architecture, city planning, and sociology, an urban anthropologist as well as such practicing professionals as a civil engineer-architect, community organizer-sociologist, lawyer, and transportation planner.

These roles, however, do potentially create some shared problems for the advocate planner. Probably the single most important problem is that of *trust* by the client group. This relationship probably reaches its greatest test when the planner begins negotiating with the target agency. Since the client usually is a minority group and the advocate usually a white upper-middle-class professional, the suspicion can be considerable—especially if any compromise is proposed.

The client's fears of being manipulated by the advocate planners are further stimulated by existing funding arrangements. If the target of protest is a city agency (e.g., Redevelopment) and the advocate planner's salary is paid by another city/federal agency (e.g., OEO or Model Cities), the client may feel their interests will be compromised in favor of the "establishment." This role ambiguity has required some advocate planners to prove themselves through a heightened *verbal militancy* in an attempt to prove commitment to the client. The implications of this for relationships between advocate planners and

convention planners, or city-wide or region-wide planners are considerable.The need to be militant on an issue could lead advocates to reject, for the moment, all longer range issues in order to fulfill the long-range organizational requisites of immediate action and success, even if such desires do not adequately resolve the structural problems facing the community.

Generally, we would anticipate that this need to continually prove oneself may take a large psychological toll on full-time advocate planners. Along with objective financial problems, it may also lead planners who are interested in such work to do it on a part-time or even voluntary basis, thereby enabling them to maintain their professional integrity in the eyes of other planners without totally compromising what they see as the dictates of their conscience. On the other hand, this might lead the less thick skinned and more professional-oriented planner to not follow these dictates directly but to work on long range issues less directly related to the immediate demands of poor communities. Our sense of these factors gives us the impression that the advocate planners tend to be the more risk-oriented, less professionally integrated, younger and less technically, trained planners. There is some indication that this is, at present, the case. (See AIP Newsletter, September, 1968.)

Ideology of Advocate Planners

The key factor that may determine a professional's choice to be an advocate planner, as against another type of planner, probably is his ideological orientation and commitment. In a role (or roles) which is so highly politicized the planner's values become most critical. This is especially so from the point of view of the poor—the main client group of advocate planners.

The most salient value-orientation that seems to be common to *all* advocate planners and the communities they serve is a strong belief in the participation of the poor and citizens generally in decisions (i.e., plans) which directly affect their lives. This participation is seen by some as a right, an end state in itself, and only secondarily as an instrumental act for the purpose of making plans more effective. It reflects a commitment to perfect pluralism. Much of the activities of the advocate planner

are based on the implementation of this value. Hatch, the founder of ARCH, states this "participation ethic" most strongly when he says that

We must recognize that the salvation of the ghetto and of the nation lies not so much in the provision of a little more goods and services . . . but in the new sense of manhood which comes out of controlling the institutions which now make decisions on behalf of black people. . . . A respect for these special psychological needs and a sense of guilt at the disservice which the architectural and planning professions have done to the poor underlie the new profession of advocacy—and *it* must be sensitive to the need for black leadership. (1968, p. 73)

The priority placed on "participation ethic" by advocate planners clearly separates them from all other types of planners, though not, nowadays, from the use of this particular rhetoric. It thus has important implications for the type of people who will become advocate planners and the type of plans around which advocate planners will attempt to organize the poor: that is, if the poor are to be involved as key decision makers then all plans must deal with what the poor consider most important. Given the defensive and oppositional setting of the inner city communities their desires for immediate payoffs will be primary. They have critical needs which must be filled if they are to think about broader community-wide issues. Those who, like James Q. Wilson (1968) identify the city-wide elite as the bearers of progressive change will see this as "obstructionist."

A second major value orientation of many advocate planners is their belief in the necessity of some short range payoffs. While some advocate planners have longer range perspectives, the nature of the overwhelming needs and conditions of the poor lead them and the communities they serve to seek as many immediate victories as possible. These victories, in turn, strengthen the cohesiveness of the community. Rather than representing a faulty analysis of the ultimate needs of the society, this seems to reflect a major concern for an immediate reorientation of the present urban decision-making processes which fail to take into account the poor. It also reflects a need of the advocate planner to prove his worth to the poor.

A third critical value orientation which most advocate planners hold is a distrust of the established decision makers in public and private bureaucracies (Peattie, 1968). This distrust is probably most evident in matters relating to urban renewal. It is also very prominent in their clients' targets of protest. Most advocacy planning groups spend a good deal of their time in fights with such agencies. If they were not distrustful before they began their work, they quickly get that way from an identification with their clients' problems or from their realization of the reality of establishment "repression." The egalitarian ideological underpinning of these planners attitudes is, of course, an implicit base for this distrust.

Advocate planners also seem to distrust government bureaucracies because they have been and are relatively resistant to change, because they often place major emphasis on organizational efficiency rather than on analysis of the client's problems and because of the irrelevancy of traditional planning, embedded in these bureaucracies, in dealing with the present social crises. Finally, the high saliency of the participation ethic makes the advocate planner suspicious of decisions emanating from the top.

Finally, advocate planners seem to strongly believe that there is no separation between planning and politics or planning and values. They correctly understand planning decisions as being made within a context of competing vested interests and value orientations, albeit among only certain sectors of society. The recognition of this and the frequent use of conflict or contest strategies to deal with it clearly distinguishes advocate planners from other types of planners.

Thus, the primary goal of the advocate planners' clients and, therefore, their own commitment is to improve the quality of the client's community and individual life. This leads the advocate planner to propose, organize, plan, and fight for the interests of a particular community as against those of other interests or communities in the city. This is based on a belief by the clients and the advocate planner that there are limited resources in the city which are being denied them and which they need. The strategies of change that the advocate planner and his clients utilize revolve around the inherent conflict in the interests of different community groups in the city and the need to organize in their own community to attain their own interests. There is also the implicit assumption that the resources they need can be attained in the particular community through the assertion of their power. Hence there is a strong behavioral commitment to the belief that democratic strategies inherent in the advocate planner/community relationship can achieve the resources that the community needs. The problem with this commitment to a democratic strategy at the community level is that many of the most critical needs of the poor are not related to their immediate community but reflect city-wide, regional, and national power centers. Hence, the advocate planners are attempting to perfect a political pluralism in a government which is increasingly centralized and which has limited its pluralism to only certain sectors of society.

The Limits of Community Reform

An unequal pluralism, technocratic trends, and certain inherent strains in the role and training of planners, these are the problems this paper has delineated thus far. But the concept of professional advocacy for the poor, or any other group seeking redress, must address itself to still other structural realities of contemporary society. Chief among these is that the strategic levers of power—for many service-oriented objectives are not located at the neighborhood level. This should not need lengthy explication after a generation of Big Government, but brief illustration of some key variables will indicate the nature of the problem faced by community planners.

Resources availability in the public sector under present taxation and fiscal policies does not in any way depend on the direct actions of an affected neighborhood. Obviously this applies to the budgetary and legislative process in Washington. The corporate economy entails the proposition that though government will grow, the kinds of public allocations, or the kinds of programs so subsidized, are subject to a political process in which national elites, not locally mobilized citizens, are the most important actors. An illustration using one key regulatory agency is the Federal Reserve Board. Its action in raising or lowering prime interest rates, for example, is more decisive in employment and unemployment than almost any Model Cities proposal could be, unless, of course, one envisions advocates as speaking for one set of deprived contestants over and against another within a single city system. Similarly, welfare service and renewal kinds of programs all compete with one another in the budgeting process, and they compete as well with health programs, farm subsidies, etc.; that is, they compete within the roughly one-half of the federal budget which is "left over" from defense allocations. In turn defense allocations are the least amenable to public reaction, debate, etc. of all the contestants in the federal arena. Community planners have come up against the symptoms of this problem again and again: they design programs which cannot be funded.

Of course, the relevant arena is not only federal; the city-wide fiscal situation is bleak. A basically regressive real property tax base is being eroded rapidly, and the bonded indebtedness alternatives are limited and lead to further regressive budgetary practices. Thus, the alternatives which are practically open to even the most progressive or liberal city administration are relatively limited. The two pincers, policy set nationally and limited resource locally, are illuminated and exacerbated by the suburbanization of industry and the way the governments involved have sought to deal with this basic trend.

As industry and middle class whites have moved out of the inner city, the basic governmental response of the last fifteen years has been to build high speed highways to give commuters access to their downtown jobs and to give industry needed transport facility. But the poor family without a car, or the working class family with more than one wage earner and only one car, has not been serviced with the public transport to take them to jobs or to other sections of the city in a cheap, attractive, efficient mass transit system. In the course of building these highways housing for the poor has been eliminated, the objective impact of the outlay of public monies has been redistributive, favoring the affluent, and industry has been further encouraged to move out of reach of inner city job seekers. Meanwhile federal housing programs encouraged segregated suburbs, and public housing intensified inner city segregation. In this complex mix of policy and basic social trends any given community has had little leverage—

even if mobilized and adequately equipped with technincal advice.

Marris and Rein summarized the failure of community organizations they studied in this way:

Since the promotion of a national policy to reallocate services and jobs to benefit the poor lay beyond their scope, the projects naturally emphasized other aspects of poverty that lay more within their means. Any approach to reform must accept some practical limit to its aims, and work within a setting that partly frustrates its ideals. But by ignoring the wider issue, the projects risked deceiving both themselves and others as to what they could achieve, and provoking a corresponding disillusionment. The difficulties of younger people from the ghettos in mastering the demands of employment, or the insensitivity of schools and social agencies, only became crucial as the resources to provide decent jobs and training were assured. Forced to apply their remedies without the backing of complementary national reforms on which any wide-spread success depended, the projects could only act as pioneers, exploring the means to implement a policy that had to be undertaken. And even as pioneers, they were handicapped by lack of any forseeable funds adequate to the need. The competition for scarce resources accentuated institutional rivalries; unemployment and the improverishment of social services embittered relations between poor neighborhoods and any official source of help. Thus the search for an enlightened, rational plan to promote change, endorsed by the whole community, set out to confront problems aggravated by a vacuum of national policy it could do nothing to fill. (1967, p. 91–92)

Thus, the role of advocacy planning or any community oriented strategy must face the reality of its limited resources to change policies and decision-making structures at state, regional, and national level.

Advocates and Partisans

The literature on the problems of the inner city and poverty and of advocacy in various professions is remarkable for the fact that almost nowhere is the realistic scope of the political and social structures facing the advocate analytically delineated. A countertrend, among young planners loosely associated with the new left, has begun a reconceptualization of their first attraction to advocacy and community planning. The response has been a political one. The Urban Underground in New York, for example, is a group of planners who, according to their best judgment of the interests of the people, have taken to

surfacing their accusations of corruption and maldistribution of public favors at public hearings (Urban Underground, 1969). Radical caucuses are appearing in professional groups and meetings such as that among social workers, and the caucus of Radicals in Mental Health who first appeared at the AOA in 1969.

These seem to us predictable responses to the dilemmas of reform we have been discussing. A "national" nation requires national bases of power to mobilize the energy necessary to redistribute resources. To the extent that conditions of life in neighborhoods and communities are at stake, of course, community organizations and the technical help they need are important components in a general social movement which is still developing. But one prediction is that more and more professionals who identify as advocates will move towards identifying themselves as partisans in an ideological sense. The categories of thought which create such self-identification are apt to be diverse at first. Some will think in terms of capitalism and socialism; others will think in terms of national welfare rights organizations and the mobilization of clients on a national, not just city or state level. Eventually though, that which created the ferment— the struggles for equality and social justice as seen by both the participants and their advocates— seems to be recovering from the centrifugal tendencies of intense neighborhood preoccupation which has been the case until recently.

What does this portend? First, the professionals so engaged may very well find that in order to do work in the *general* interests which motivate them, the *particular* neighborhood focus of their work will be deserted, modified, or transformed into the notion of national political movements. Besides the indications mentioned earlier, Paul Davidoff's latest contribution to the discussion of advocacy in planning is a symptom of this shift (Davidoff, 1970). From the beginning, he asserts, ideological advocacy was seen as part of the conception of the advocate: the general interest is the client; the planner's idea of what serves it, the program; the theaters of operations are the relevant legislative, community, or media arenas. Similarly, the Student Health Organization is a national group of liberal-to-radical medical students and health services students who are organized

nationally as professionals, even though many of their best programs are designed to bring services to local communities. Ronald Caines, Director of Advocacy Programs of the American Institute of Planners has just written an article putting "national" programs at the "top of a ladder of advocacy" (1970).

As citizens and as social analysts, then, we are predicting and suggesting the advocates begin to see themselves as a national movement; this implies the creation of national organizations— both of clients and advocates. Eventually, in fact, it implies a new partnership in a new partisanship. There is not evidence now to say whether this will be liberal or radical, reformist or socialist; but there is strong evidence that it will, one way or the other, have to overcome the weak theory it started with in terms of the possibilities of a perfected pluralism in a class society, and will have to deal with the scope of the power needed to solve problems in a nationally engineered society.

BIBLIOGRAPHY

"Advocacy planning: What it is, how it works," *P/A,* September, 1968, pp. 102–115.

AIP Newsletter (American Institute of Planners), 3, 9 (September, 1968); 3, 10 (October, 1968); 3, 11 (November, 1968).

Burns, James MacGregor. *The Deadlock of Democracy.* Englewood Cliffs, N.J.: Prentice-Hall, 1963.

Caines, Ronald. "Advocacy for the seventies will aim at public policies," *AIP Newsletter,* January, 1970.

Dahl, Robert. *Pluralist Democracy in the United States: Conflict and Consent.* Chicago: Rand-McNally, 1967.

Davidoff, Paul. "Advocacy and pluralism in planning," *Journal of the American Institute of Planners,* 31, 4 (November, 1965), 331–337.

Davidoff, Paul and Linda, and Neil Newton Gold, "Suburban action advocate planning for an open society," *Journal of the American Institute of Planners,* 36, 1 (January, 1970), 12–21.

Drucker, Peter. *The Landmarks of Tomorrow.* New York: Harper & Row, 1959.

Edelston, H. C., and F. K. Kolodner. "Are the poor capable of planning for themselves?" in H. C. Spiegel (ed.), *Citizen Participation in Urban Development.* Washington, D.C.: National Institute for Applied Behavioral Science, 1969.

Galbraith, John Kenneth. *The New Industrial State.* Boston: Houghton Mifflin, 1967.

Gamson, William. "Stable unrepresentation in American society,"

American Behavioral Scientist, 12, 2 (November/December, 1968).

Goldston, Eli. "BURP and make money," *Harvard Business Review,* September/October, 1969.

Hatch, C. Richard. "Some thoughts on advocacy planning," *FORUM,* June, 1968, pp. 72, 73, 103, 109.

Hauser, Phillip. "The chaotic society: Product of the social morphological revolution," *American Sociological Review,* 34, 1 (February, 1969).

Kaplan, Marshall. "The role of the planner in urban areas," in H. C. Spiegel, *Citizen Participation in Urban Development,* vol. II. Washington, D.C.: National Institute for Applied Behavioral Science, 1969.

Kolko, Gabriel, *Wealth and Power in America.* New York: Praeger, 1962.

Kolko, Gabriel. "Power in America in the twentieth century," in J. David Colfax and Jack Roach (eds.), *Radical Sociology,* New York: Basic Books, 1970.

Marris, Peter, and Martin Rein. *Dilemmas of Social Reform.* New York: Atherton, 1967.

Michael, Donald. *The Unprepared Society.* New York: Basic Books, 1968.

Moynihan, Daniel P. *Maximum Feasible Misunderstanding.* New York: The Free Press, 1969.

Peattie, Lisa R. "Reflections on advocacy planning," *Journal of American Institute of Planners,* 34, 3 (March, 1968), 80–88.

Urban Planning Aid, Fund-Raising Proposal; Development of Advocacy Planning, July 30, 1968.

"Urban underground resurfaces." Testimony at New York City Planning Commission, February 19, 1969. Available from MOS, 225 Lafayette Street, New York, N.Y. 10012.

Wilson, James Q. "Planning and politics: Citizen participation in urban renewal," in H. C. Spiegel (ed.), *Citizen Participation in Urban Development,* vol. I, Washington, D.C.: National Institute for Applied Behavioral Science, 1969.

COMMENTARY: THE DIALECTICS OF PROFESSIONALISM

Like the other professionals in the business world, social science intellectuals organize their world to promote their interests, exchange specialized knowledge, and establish contacts among themselves. Social scientists, too, have their professional fraternities, such as the American Psychological Association, the American Psychiatric Association, and the American Sociological Association. These societies seek to promote the interests of their professional members. These professional faternities have no coherent political ideology, but

this does not mean they are non-ideological. In fact, they are most ideological in terms of their outlook, interests and privileged position. This combination comprises the ideology of professionalism. This subtle ideology has effects upon their limited role as agents of social change and upon their biased analytical approach.

Within the profession, the professional intellectuals have engaged in little self-criticism of their self-interests as a well-to-do, privileged group which, because of its relatively safe and secure position, can afford the luxury of stagnation. Critiques like those of Noam Chomsky of his fellow intellectuals are few in number. Certainly, the repressive policy of political blacklisting does not encourage criticalness among social scientists who like to see their field as being one without political consequences and aseptic to contamination by society's turmoil. The result of minimal self-criticism is a virtual running away from oneself; this denial of oneself helps to explain the pretense of a nonideological orientation so popular among academics today. The price of the nonideological, non-self-critical antiseptic posture, in human terms, is a total loss of understanding of the urgency with which social problems impinge upon social scientists. Hence, it is not surprising that many professionals feel less intensely, if at all, the anger and indignation expressed by protesters against war, racial injustice, and poverty.

What *is* surprising is the less-than-professional way this inertia is hidden and even justified as "professional conduct." There is little doubt about one characteristic of the social crisis today: Those who are most susceptible to injustices are the most ardent and vocal in their demands. Those who must fight in a controversial war, those who are the victims of racism, and those who must withstand hunger are among those in the forefront of advocating radical change. The professionals as a class are not subject to these physical indignities. In this light, the charge of their residence in an "ivory tower" appears justified.

Those who must suffer abuses can be expected to get excited, to have their adrenalin flowing, and to engage in boisterous physical activity. The turbulence of their lives is the result of a society which injects turbulence into their lives.

For the professional class, this turbulence is lacking. Some even

justify this privileged position in their very analysis of the problem. Some social scientists are continually amazed at the emotionalism which characterizes demonstrators. A few would even label such outbursts as "emotionally disturbed" behavior, a biased analysis which obscures the interests of the professional analyzer whose own life style is far removed from those he analyzes.

Related to this ideological bias of professionals is a second bias. This bias is one against the radical perspective. This bias, which borders on prejudice, reflects the same bias which this society holds tenaciously. In this sense, the professionals have not transcended their own cultural ethnocentricity, but rather have incorporated it into their outlook.

Reflecting society's stagnant predicament, the social science professions have many conservatively-oriented people but few who are radically-oriented. Newspaper accounts of governmental blacklisting of scientific panel members illustrates the political strait-jacket into which the professional is bound. This strait-jacketing is essentially political and has nothing to do with science.

Another kind of strait-jacketing occurs within the profession. The very structure of the professional organization, with its status quo philosophy, has much to do with the political limitations of its members. Within the confines of this structure, any radicalism is treated more as a malignancy than as a valid political perspective.

The older general consensus among psychologists is that they should serve not as a professional organization, but only as individuals and in an advisory capacity. As the situation now stands, radicals within the profession do not have much say or sway over these professional societies, which are not formed to take on the task of implementing change and certainly have not moved in the direction of radical reconstruction. Professional organizations like the American Psychological Association may respond when pressured, but they have generally remained "neutral." Within the profession, only smaller groups—with less resources—are more inclined toward activism, e.g., Psychologists for a Democratic Society and the less radical American Psychologists for Social Action.

Significant change within these hallowed and tradition-bound professional associations is nil; they

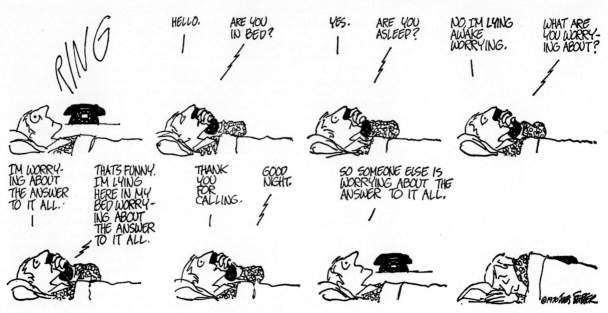

REPRINTED BY PERMISSION OF JULES FEIFFER. © 1970 JULES FEIFFER.

remain traditional organizations which are ingrown in terms of membership and ossified ideologically.

The current condition of professional societies does not suggest radical change from within because the radical professional, like other radicals in society, is an outmaneuvered minority member. Radicalism within the professions is in an embryonic state. Professional societies are still structured so that tradition triumphs over change.

The best that may be expected from within the professions is reform piecemeal in nature. These reforms will not alter society significantly but will reflect society's own piecemeal reforms.

This chapter has surveyed some of the problems and positions presented by one particular group of professionals, the social science intellectuals. In the process, hopefully, one view of society has been made more clear. Nevertheless, there is a need for continuous clarification since society's image is always changing. The suggestion of this commentary may be concisely stated as the need for further clarifications.

Indeed, the major social responsibility of social scientists is to generate innovative ideas and present clearer visions of society. This idea is similar to George M. Miller's suggestion to "give" psychology away. However, thoughtful analysis alone is insufficient to implement change. Correlated to thought is concerted action. This action, in the service of social change, is political by nature. As in politics, the risks and sacrifices are great.

CONCLUSIONS

If we can now address ourselves to the individual social science professional we can perhaps be more positive. For, if Naderism is to spread to the social sciences, it will take individual Nader-like decisions to pave the way. If enough people make such a decision we will have a better profession and perhaps a better society.

To the academic social scientist we can point to their home base—the university or college—as the place where social change can begin. Instead of the usual pattern of individuals selling their services as consultants to agencies, a few in a department can create a community service base in their clinic. They can offer a suicide prevention service to the community. They can run community-university, police-student, police-ghetto dweller or any other type of encounter group which would promote better understanding. They could offer better in-service training by incorporating a multiservice clinical-counseling center, partially staffed by low-paid or volunteer graduate students who receive credit for field training.

Another "Nader's Raiders" adaptation would be the creation of social problem task forces whose job it would be to investigate, expose, or constructively criticize existing social service agencies. As independent groups they could provide the community with unwhitewashed facts on the effectiveness of mental health, welfare, and other social services.

But these and other ideas which will be presented in subsequent chapters will all be worth very little unless the social scientists undergo a fundamental change in their ideology. If they remain dependent upon existing institutions to define their priorities for them, if they remain neutral observers who merely attempt to analyze the workings of the existing social structure, they are likely to have a minimal influence on social change. We must abandon the concept of neutrality, prepare to take a position, and, yes, even be prepared to be wrong, if we are to engage in social action. What made Nader succeed was his willingness to act on what he believed was right, a decision which only history could (and did) vindicate.

In the social sciences, we may not need a single Nader, but rather a coalescing of those rare individuals who see that a redirected social science profession would go a long way toward the promotion of human welfare.

Part II
The Roots

And will you try and tell us that
You been too long at school—
That knowledge is not needed—
That power does not rule—
That war is not the answer—
That young men should not die?
Sit down young stranger:
I wait for your reply.
The answer is not easy,
For souls are not reborn.
To wear the crown of peace,
You must wear the crown of thorns.
If Jesus had a reason,
I'm sure he would not tell.
They treated him so badly,
How could he wish them well?

The parlor now is empty
There's nothing left to say.
My father has departed;
My mother's gone to pray.
There's rockets in the meadow and
Ships out on the sea.
The answer's in the forest
Carved upon a tree:
John loves Mary, does anyone love
*   me?*

Gordon Lightfoot
(From "Sit Down Young Stranger."
By permission of Warner
Brothers Records, Inc.)

In this part of the book, we present some of the roots of some of America's social problems. The tone of this section is deliberately impressionistic rather than analytical. There are forces and feelings underlying social problems which cannot be intellectualized. In song, poetry, prose, picture, cartoon, and discourse, the editors present their impressions of the third world experience—violence, alienation, and the search for a new life style.

Unity in diversity might describe the strong message of the chapter on third world experience. The editors of this chapter represent all races, especially the four principle minority groups in California—Black, Asian-American, Chicano, and Native American. While each group has its special problems, the root cause is seen as the reaction of a white majority to people whose experience is neither understood nor respected. There is not much optimism in the judgments presented.

The editors of the chapter on violence lived through a period of time when violence at the Berkeley campus was an everyday occurrence; then came the Cambodian invasion and the murders at Kent State and Jackson State. They saw the Berkeley campus reconstituted into a center for non-violent political activity against the Indochina War. In struggling to understand this shift, they urge social changes in the direction of promoting communication, creative use of the law to aid oppressed people, civilian control of the police, and a cessation of the arms race.

The chapter on alienation examines several of the ways man is dehumanized by his own culture. The sad commentary shows that alienation is prevalent in the society which can afford the maximum in material things and leisure time. From the lyrics of Elinor Rigby to the words of Paul Goodman, the under current of alienation in America remains as it did when Riesman wrote *The Lonely Crowd* in 1952.

The final chapter is an attempt to capture the spirit of those adventurers who would create an entirely new style of living— whether they are alienated from the old or unspoiled by it. This phenomenon, which is centered in California, touches the lives of all of the editors. New life styles are experiments which leave one a little more hopeful after the unrelieved pessimism of the three preceding chapters.

Out of the Third World Experience

EDITED BY:

Lee S. Allen	Gregory Hollidge
Elisha Butler	Krisida Jones
Linda Dunson	Robert Oshita
Harold Fox, Jr.	Patrick D. Tamayo
Thomas Gamez	Ted Tanaka
Jeff Gaudet	

The line it is drawn, the curse it is cast
The slow one now will later be fast
As the present now will later be past
The order is rapidly fading
And the first one now will later be last
For the times they are a changin'.

Bob Dylan
(From "The Times They Are A-Changin'." © 1963 by M. Whitmark & Sons. Used by permission of Warner Bros. Music. All rights reserved.)

Step into my shoes; wear my skin;
See what I see; feel what I feel
And then you shall know,
Who I am, what I am, and why I am.

Patrick Tamayo

INTRODUCTION

The experiences of all nonwhites in the U.S. have been crucial factors in the economic, political and social life in this country. Afro-Americans, Mexican-Americans (Chicanos), Asian-Americans, and Native-Americans (Indians) have contributed to the development of this nation since its inception. Yet, today, a man of color knows that his color or origin represents agony, suffering, and degradation at the hands of the white man.

The system by which this nation operates is constructed in such a way that blacks cannot be economically, socially, or politically equal. There has always been a tremendous economic gap between blacks and whites with 29 percent of all black families today still existing below the poverty level as compare to 8 percent of all whites. The black man who complete college has a median income of $7,154 compared to $8,754 for the white who has only four years of high school. Blacks in urban centers as well as in rural areas suffer inordinately from poor health care, resulting in higher mortality rates; from atrocious educational systems and educational theorists who postulate theories of genetic inferiority; from social welfare systems which constitute an attack on the family structure. While the optimists wave statistics to show that the blacks position in America is improving, more realistic minds point to the increased polarization as well as to the relationships between white gains and black gains which then add up to regression rather than real progress.

These factors have fomented a new awakening among large numbers of blacks, thereby resulting in reformulations of the old concepts of Garvey, DuBois, and other black intellectuals of the past. The new intellectuals like Carmichael, Malcolm X, and Cleaver, are more activist. They perceive the situation in a more personal light and they may be America's last hope for reform.

Robert S. Browne in his provocative presentation of "The Case for Black Separatism" asks whether the new black consciousness can be reconciled with the larger American society which accepts racism and its accompanying violence and attempts to export these two evils to the rest of the world via wars, threats of war, and economic subjugation. Browne says that "partition offers one way out of this tragic situation." Partition (into two separate nations) may very well be the only alternative to continuing conflict and escalation of the conflict to a Final Solution.

Browne states further:

Divorce is an inherent aspect of the American tradition. It terminates the misery of an enforced but unhappy union, relieves the tension and avoids the rush of more serious consequences. It is increasingly apparent to Blacks and whites alike that their national marriage has been a failure. Consequently, in the search for ways to remedy this tragic situation, divorce should obviously not be ruled out as a possible solution. The Black Power Conference resolution (in this chapter) asks Americans to do no more than give it serious consideration.

There may be other solutions to these problems accompanying the racial situation in America. This handbook for social change is operating from the premise that changes can be made.

The Mexican-Americans (Chicanos) suffer under similar handicaps. In some southwestern states, Mexican-Americans suffer greater discrimination than blacks in the same area. Many Spanish-speaking children are handicapped by schools taught in English. IQ tests administered to Spanish-speaking children in California show them scoring consistently lower than their "Anglo" counterparts. In a Southern California school district 22 percent of all Spanish-speaking school children were classified as mentally retarded. When these children were retested in Spanish, their scores were significantly higher. Behind this episode of ruined lives lay a bureaucratic fact which saw $500 payments go to school districts for each "retarded" child— to be added to the general operating budget. Thus, the state rewarded injustice with dollars which benefited the white majority.

Thousands of Mexican-American migrant farmworkers labor under appalling conditions which have been widely documented, but the conditions prevail. Mexican-American children suffer ill health, malnutrition, and inferior educational experiences, and constant exposure to toxic pesticides. Many are doomed to follow their parents into living a life of exploitation. The following article gives a graphic expression of the farm-worker's experience:

In the Beginning was the word and the word was "No!" Manuelito got spanked for speaking Spanish the very first day of school. He wasn't spanked hard; he was only six years old. Some kids weren't even spanked; they were only scolded.

He wondered why.

"No Spanish even on the playground," was what Mrs. Sinclair had said. It must be bad to speak Spanish. Mother and Father spoke it and they were always telling him about being good and nice and to share everything with others. Maybe they didn't know Spanish was bad, because they had told him to do everything the teacher told him. Manuelito was confused.

When he got home, he told them.

"You must have been *malcreado* [naughty]; no one spanks a child for speaking any language. What did you do?" More confusion.

He didn't feel like a bad boy. But maybe he was. Everyone thought so.

Right after Christmas a little German girl entered Manuelito's class. She had pretty, pretty blue eyes and blonde hair just like the Baby Jesus that the San Antonio statue held. He wished he could warn her because she might get spanked if she spoke German, which was all she seemed to know.

At recess time he quit fearing for the pretty little girl. Mrs. Sinclair was taking her by the hand and presenting her to all the other teachers. A German-speaking, pretty little girl. They all thought it was absolutely precious. Absolutely precious.

Manuelito's confusion was thrice confounded.

Today Hildegarde [which turned out to be her name] is in the eleventh grade and still precious. She gets B's in Spanish because her parents had taught her French which served as a base.

Manuel [no longer Manuelito] is not going back to his second year in the ninth grade because the wood shop classes that his counselor told him to take and the auto mechanics classes aren't very interesting. His memories of the past 11 years aren't either. The kids laughing about his lunch—tortillas, chile. Who ever heard of taking tortillas to school? Your father must be either lazy or

careless if he can't give you a dollar for the Halloween party. The day all the kids were naming their father's occupation he had lied. How can you say, "My father is a grape picker?" Everyone would have laughed. He told them he was a fireman. He had wanted to be the prince of the Cinderella play but Kenneth got it because Mrs. Roberts said the image called for a red-blooded American something-or-another.

Mr. Johnson thought he should join the Job Corps. Manuel thinks he probably should pick apricots and wait for the draft.

Vietnam. American . . . and RED-BLOODED.

In order to overcome some of the educational deficits, the La Raza Studies Program has been formed at some colleges and universities in California, a good example of diverse groups working together. The main idea of this program is for Chicano people to unite in recognizing themselves as a unique and preservable cultural entity. To arrive at this end, all points of friction are ignored and all efforts are made to insure the gathering of information that will enforce the credibility of their belief.

Perhaps one of the assets of La Raza Studies is the total dependence of the people of each other and a slowly dwindling area of ignorance about each other's separate subgroups. As they grow in knowledge of their diverse cultures because of their own discoveries, they easily identify with their findings as a whole. Unlike many ethnic groups that have been studied prior to their own investigations, very little written data exists on Chicanos in the United States. In his article, "Goodbye Revolution—Hello Slum," Romano mentions the absence of Mexican-American social scientists. The La Raza Studies Program is aimed at filling such gaps.

Asian-Americans suffer from the problems arising from what might be called pseudoassimilation. Dwarfed in a society which condescendingly paternalizes the more affluent and barely tolerates the poor, the Asian segment of America's population experiences a wide range of problems. Even in professional positions, Asians are channeled into what has been termed "houseboy" work. In the technical professions, Chinese- and Japanese-Americans are continually "cleaning up the MAN's house" while the more provocative assignments are given to the white counterparts.

The apathetic, affluent middle-

class Americans have become mute to the problems of their people. Often they openly exploit the poor. For example, there are sweatshops in San Francisco's Chinatown where immigrant women are forced to work for less than 90 cents an hour for ten hours a day, for as much as seven days a week. Substandard housing, health, and educational facilities are further examples of the exploitation and "benign neglect" of the Asian people. Because of this, Chinatown has the highest rate of tuberculosis *and* suicide in the nation.

Similarly, the Filipino community of San Francisco was once a bustling area of shops and homes called Manilatown. This area was in the heart of the city. Constant encroachment has caused Manilatown to dwindle to one block. Now the Redevelopment Agency has decided to raze the area leaving many elderly Filipinos homeless, an example of the agency's ignorance of the cultural, historical, and social importance of the area to its residents. This chapter includes two articles dealing with the emerging Asian consciousness, especially among the young.

From the first European settlers' arrival to the present, American Indians have suffered one of the most traumatic of all third world experiences. They have been the victims of a nearly successful genocide attempt. It is undeniable that the cultural genocide has produced the facts of a high suicide rate for young Indians, a school dropout rate which causes few Indians to complete high school, gross mismanagement of Indian affairs by the Bureau of Indian Affairs, the breaking of many treaties and the illegal circumvention of others. These problems have caused a depression of the Indian people which is now being lifted. This awakening of the Indians is underscored by the following article.

American Indians want the right to be Indians, to preserve their tribal identities and tribal lands, to make their own mistakes, to have a say about their destiny. That, in essence, is the message that emerged from the meeting in Denver of 40 Indian leaders from all parts of the nation to see whether a common program could be worked out to improve the status of the nation's oldest and poorest minority. The fact that they met together at all was remarkable. Indians do not view themselves as a single group, so jealous are they of their tribal, linguistic, cultural and territorial backgrounds. The significance of the Denver meeting is that they decided to look at their problems to-gether and be heard as a group. If it works, the meeting may prove to be of historic importance in the long effort of America to solve its "Indian problem."

The message of Denver itself is not an unfamiliar one, from Ameri-can Indians or other ethnic groups. But few White Americans have listened in the past when Indians spoke—a reflection of a general national feeling that assimilation and absorption into the contemporary American "mainstream" is the ulti-mate answer for this country's first inhabitants. The Indians made it clear that they are not buying this answer. They want the option to remain on their lands and work out ways of improving their economic and social condition within the tribal framework. Some will leave as many thousands have done. But they do not want to be compelled to go and there is no good reason why they should be.

The group declared that the strength of America lies in its "plural society made up of different races and ethnic groups." In effect, they were saying that their cause is not too startlingly different from the cause of black Americans, Mexican Americans, Puerto Ricans and other ethnic minorities that have been voicing their desires to maintain group identification. Spurred by the Community Action Program, the political arm of our national anti-poverty effort, this has become a respectable and accepted goal for urban dwellers. Why not for Indians, too?

By coincidence, the Denver group assembled while administration officials concerned with Indian matters were meeting at State Line, Nevada, with some selected Indian representatives. Both meetings re-vealed the existence of deep distrust of the administration's intentions, part of it the historic distrust of the white man and part a fear that the Republican administration will go back to the old program of "termi-nation," of forcing Indians off their lands. The sounds being made by the administration spokesmen are not reassuring in this regard. Interior Secretary Hickel has suggested that the Indians must "cut the cord" of dependence on the reservation sooner or later and other officials have sug-gested that it may be desirable to transfer specific Indian programs to the states.

The Indian effort to improve their lot needs to be encouraged. With Indian participation at every level, ways should be found to better the existence of the nation's 600,000 Indians, to improve their health, their education, their economic con-ditions—both on and off the reserva-tion, and without destroying their identity as Indians.[1]

The articles presented in this

[1] *Washington Post,* August 29, 1969.

chapter are an attempt to give a brief overview of the experiences of the major ethnic groups in this country. They are by no means complete. They are simply to ac-quaint the reader with some of the problems that must be dealt with before this country can become the pluralistic nation it was origi-nally conceived to be.

Black Consciousness

I am for violence if non-violence means we continue postponing a solution to the American black man's problem—just to *avoid* violence. I don't go for non-violence if it also means a delayed solution. To me a delayed solution is a non-solution.

Malcolm X
1965

3.1
Initial Reactions on the Assassination of Malcolm X

Eldridge Cleaver

Folsom Prison,
June 19, 1965

Sunday is Movie Day at Folsom Prison and I was sitting in the darkened hulk of Mess Hall No. 1—which convicts call "The Fol-som Theatre"—watching Victor Buono in a movie called *The Strangler,* when a convict known as Silly Willie came over to where I was sitting and whispered into my ear:

"Brother J sent me in to tell you it just came over the TV that Mal-colm X was shot as he addressed a rally in New York."

For a moment the earth seemed to reel in orbit. The skin all over my body tightened up. "How bad?" I asked.

"The TV didn't say," answered Silly Willie. The distress was obvi-ous in his voice. "We was around back in Pipe Alley checking TV when a special bulletin came on. All they said was Malcolm X was shot and they were rushing him to the hospital."

"Thanks," I said to Silly Willie. I felt his reassuring hand on my shoulder as he faded away in the darkness. For a moment I pon-

From *Soul on Ice* by Eldridge Cleaver. Copyright © 1968 by Eldridge Cleaver. Used with permission of McGraw-Hill Book Company.

dered whether to go outside and get more information, but some-thing made me hang back. I re-member distinctly thinking that I would know soon enough. On the screen before me, Victor Buono had a woman by the throat and was frantically choking the last gasping twitches of life out of her slumping body. I was thinking that if Malcom's wounds were not too serious, that if he recovered, the shooting might prove to be a blessing in disguise: it would focus more intensified attention on him and create a windfall of sympathy and support for him throughout America's black ghettos, and so put more power into his hands. The possibility that the wounds may have been fatal, that as I sat there Malcolm was lying already dead, was ex-cluded from my mind.

After the movie ended, as I filed outside in the long line of convicts and saw the shocked, wild expres-sion on Brother J's face, I still could not believe that Malcolm X was dead. We mingled in the crowd of convicts milling around in the yard and were immediately surrounded by a group of Mus-lims, all of whom, like myself, were firm supporters of Malcolm X. He's dead, their faces said, al-though not one of them spoke a word. As we stood there in silence, two Negro inmates walked by and one of them said to us, "That's a goddam shame how they killed that man! Of all people, why'd they kill Malcolm? Why'n't they kill some of them Uncle-Tomming m.f.'s? I wish I could get my hands on whoever did it." And he walked away, talking and cursing to his buddy.

What does one say to his comrades at the moment when The Leader falls? All comment seems irrelevant. If the source of death is so-called natural causes, or an accident, the reaction is predictable, a feeling of impotence, humbleness, helplessness before the forces of the universe. But when the cause of death is an assassin's bullet, the overpowering desire is for vengeance. One wants to strike out, to kill, crush, destroy, to deliver a telling counterblow, to inflict upon the enemy a reciprocal, equivalent loss. But whom does one strike down at such a time if one happens to be in an anonymous, amorphous crowd of convicts in Folsom Prison and The Leader lies dead thousands of miles away across the continent?

"I'm going to my cell," I told the tight little knot of Muslims. "Allah is the Best Knower. Everything will be made manifest in time. Give it a little time. *As-Salaam Aliakum.*" . . .

So now Malcolm is no more. The bootlickers, Uncle Toms, lackeys, and stooges of the white power structure have done their best to denigrate Malcolm, to root him out of his people's heart, to tarnish his memory. But their million-worded lies fall on deaf ears. As Ossie Davis so eloquently expressed it in his immortal eulogy of Malcolm:

If you knew him you would know why we must honor him: Malcolm was our manhood, our living, black manhood! This was his meaning to his people. And, in honoring him, we honor the best in ourselves. . . . However much we may have differed with him—or with each other about him and his value as a man, let his going from us serve only to bring us together, now. Consigning these mortal remains to earth, the common mother of all, secure in the knowledge that what we place in the ground is no more now a man—but a seed—which, after the winter of our discontent will come forth again to meet us. And we will know him then for what he was and is—a Prince—our own black shining Prince!—who didn't hesitate to die, because he loved us so.

We shall have our manhood. We shall have it or the earth will be leveled by our attempts to gain it.

PHOTO COURTESY OF EVE ARNOLD, MAGNUM.

3.2
White Power: The Colonial Situation

Stokely Carmichael and Charles V. Hamilton

> *The dark ghettos are social, political, educational and—above all—economic colonies. Their inhabitants are subject peoples, victims of the greed, cruelty, insensitivity, guilt, and fear of their masters.*
>
> Dr. Kenneth B. Clark,
> *Dark Ghetto*, p. 11.

> *In an age of decolonization, it may be fruitful to regard the problem of the American Negro as a unique case of colonialism, an instance of internal imperialism, an underdeveloped people in our very midst.*
>
> I. F. Stone,
> *The New York Review of Books*
> (August 18, 1966), p. 10.

What is racism? The word has represented daily reality to millions of black people for centuries, yet it is rarely defined—perhaps just because that reality has been such a commonplace. By "racism" we mean the predication of decisions and policies on considerations of race for the purpose of *subordinating* a racial group and maintaining control over that group. That has been the practice of this country toward the black man; we shall see why and how.

Racism is both overt and covert. It takes two, closely related forms: individual whites acting against individual blacks, and acts by the total white community against the black community. We call these individual racism and institutional racism. The first consists of overt acts by individuals, which cause death, injury or the violent destruction of property. This type can be recorded by television cameras; it can frequently be observed in the process of commission. The second type is less overt, far more subtle, less identifiable in terms of *specific* individuals committing the acts. But it is no less destructive of human life. The second type originates in the operation of established and respected forces in the society, and thus receives far less public condemnation than the first type.

When white terrorists bomb a black church and kill five black children, that is an act of individual racism, widely deplored by most segments of the society. But when in that same city—Birmingham, Alabama—five hundred black babies die each year because of the lack of proper food, shelter and medical facilities, and thousands more are destroyed and maimed physically, emotionally and intellectually because of conditions of poverty and discrimination in the black community, that is a function of institutional racism. When a black family moves into a home in a white neighborhood and is stoned, burned or routed out, they are victims of an overt act of individual racism which many people will condemn—at least in words. But it is institutional racism that keeps black people locked in dilapidated slum tenements, subject to the daily prey of exploitative slumlords, merchants, loan sharks and discriminatory real estate agents. The society either pretends it does not know of this latter situation, or is in fact incapable of doing anything meaningful about it. We shall examine the reasons for this in a moment.

Institutional racism relies on the active and pervasive operation of anti-black attitudes and practices. A sense of superior group position prevails: whites are "better" than blacks; therefore blacks should be subordinated to whites. This is a racist attitude and it permeates the society, on both the individual and institutional level, covertly and overtly.
. . .

Colonial subjects have their political decisions made for them by the colonial masters, and those decisions are handed down directly or through a process of "indirect rule." Politically, decisions which affect black lives have always been made by white people—the "white power structure." There is some dislike for this phrase because it tends to ignore or oversimplify the fact that there are many centers of power, many different forces making decisions. Those who raise that objection point to the pluralistic character of the body politic. They frequently overlook the fact that American pluralism quickly becomes a monolithic structure on issues of race. When faced with demands from black people, the multi-faction whites unite and present a common front. . . .
The black community perceives the "white power structure" in very concrete terms. The man in

the ghetto sees his white landlord come only to collect exorbitant rents and fail to make necessary repairs, while both know that the white-dominated city building inspection department will wink at violations or impose only slight fines. The man in the ghetto sees the white policeman on the corner brutally manhandle a black drunkard in a doorway, and at the same time accept a pay-off from one of the agents of the white-controlled rackets. He sees the streets in the ghetto lined with uncollected garbage, and he knows that the powers which could send trucks in to collect that garbage are white. When they don't, he knows the reason: the low political esteem in which the black community is held. He looks at the absence of a meaningful curriculum in the ghetto schools—for example, the history books that woefully overlook the historical achievements of black people—and he knows that the school board is controlled by whites.[1] He is not about to listen to intellectual discourses on the pluralistic and fragmented nature of political power. He is faced with a "white power structure" as monolithic as Europe's colonial offices have been to African and Asian colonies.

. . . the white power structure rules the black community through local blacks who are responsive to the white leaders, the downtown, white machine, not to the black populace. These black politicians do not exercise effective power. They cannot be relied upon to make forceful demands in behalf of their black constituents, and they become no more than puppets. They put loyalty to a political party before loyalty to their constituents and thus nullify any bargaining power the black community might develop. Colonial politics causes the subject to muffle his voice while participating in the councils of the white power structure. The black man forfeits his opportunity to speak forcefully and clearly for his race, and he justifies this in terms of

[1] Studies have shown the heavy preponderance of business and professional men on school boards throughout the country. One survey showed that such people, although only fifteen percent of the population, constituted seventy-six percent of school board members in a national sample. The percentage of laborers on the boards was only three percent. William C. Mitchell, *The American Polity: A Social and Cultural Interpretation*, Glencoe, Illinois: Free Press, 1962.

expediency. Thus, when one talks of a "Negro Establishment" in most places in this country, one is talking of an Establishment resting on a white power base; of hand-picked blacks whom that base projects as showpieces out front. These black "leaders" are, then, only as powerful as their white kingmakers will permit them to be. This is no less true of the North than the South.

. . . Before Congressman William O. Dawson (black Congressman from the predominantly black First Congressional District of Southside Chicago) was co-opted by the white machine, he was an outspoken champion of the race. Afterward, he became a tool of the downtown white Democratic power structure. Note the result, as described in Silberman's *Crisis in Black and White:*

Chicago provides an excellent example of how Negroes can be co-opted into inactivity. . . . Dawson surrendered far more than he has obtained for the Negro community. What Dawson obtained were the traditional benefits of the big-city political machine: low-paying jobs for a lot of followers; political intervention with the police and with bail bondsmen, social workers, housing officials, and other bureaucrats whose decisions can affect a poor constituent's life; and a slice of the "melon" in the form of public housing projects, welfare payments, and the like.

Dawson, and countless others like him, have an answer to this criticism: this is the proper way to operate; you must "play ball" with the party in order to exact maximum benefits. We reject this notion. It may well result in particular benefits—in terms of status or material gains—for individuals, but it does not speak to the alleviation of a multitude of social problems shared by the masses. They may also say: if I spoke up, I would no longer be permitted to take part in the party councils. I would be ousted, and then the black people would have neither voice nor access. Ultimately, this is, at best, a spurious argument, which does more to enhance the security of the individual person than it does to gain substantial benefits for the group.

In time, one notes that a gap develops between the leadership and the followers. The masses, correctly, no longer view the leaders as their legitimate representatives. They come to see them more for what they are, emissaries sent by the white society. Identity between the two is lost. . . .

This process of co-optation and a subsequent widening of the gap between the black elites and the masses is common under colonial rule. There has developed in this country an entire class of "captive leaders" in the black communities. These are black people with certain technical and administrative skills who could provide useful leadership roles in the black communities but do not because they have become beholden to the white power structure. These are black school teachers, county agents, junior executives in management positions with companies, etc. . . .

It is crystal clear that most of these people have accommodated themselves to the racist system. They have capitulated to colonial subjugation in exchange for the security of a few dollars and dubious status. They are effectively lost to the struggle for an improved black position which would fundamentally challenge that racist system. John A. Williams tells in *This is My Country Too* of how he went to Alabama State College (the state college for black people) in 1963 to interview a black professor, who brusquely told him: "Governor Wallace pays my salary; I have nothing to say to you. Excuse me, I have a class to get to" (p. 62).

When black people play colonial politics, they also mislead the white community into thinking that it has the sanction of the blacks. A professor of political science who made a study of black people in Detroit politics from 1956–1960 has concluded:

The fact that the Negro participates in the system by voting and participating in the party politics in the North should not lead us to conclude that he has accepted the popular consensus of the society about the polity. His support and work for the Democratic party is more a strategic compromise in most cases than a wholehearted endorsement of the party. . . .[2]

. . . More than a handful of black people will admit privately their contempt for insincere whites with whom they must work and deal. (In all likelihood, the contempt is mutual.) They feel secure in articulating their true feelings only when out of hearing range of "the man."

[2] A. W. Singham, "The Political Socialization of Marginal Groups." Paper presented at the 1966 meeting of the American Political Science Association, New York City.

Those who would assume the responsibility of representing black people in this country must be able to throw off the notion that they can effectively do so and still maintain a maximum amount of security. Jobs will have to be sacrificed, positions of prestige and status given up, favors forfeited. It may well be—and we think it is—that leadership and security are basically incompatible. When one forcefully challenges the racist system, one cannot, at the same time, expect that system to reward him or even treat him comfortably. Political leadership which pacifies and stifles its voice and then rationalizes this on grounds of gaining "something for my people" is, at bottom, gaining only meaningless, token rewards that an affluent society is perfectly willing to give.

A final aspect of political colonialism is the manipulation of political boundaries and the devising of restrictive electoral systems. The point is frequently made that black people are only ten percent of the population—no less a personage than President Johnson has seen fit to remind us of this ratio. It is seldom pointed out that this minority is geographically located so as to create potential majority blocs—that strategic location being an ironic side-effect of segregation. But black people have never been able to utilize fully their numerical voting strength. Where we could vote, the white political machines have gerrymandered black neighborhoods so that the true voting strength is not reflected in political representation. . . .

The decision-makers are most adept at devising ways of utilizing existing factors to maintain their monopoly of political power.

The economic relationship of America's black communities to the larger society also reflects their colonial status. The political power exercised over those communities goes hand in glove with the economic deprivation experienced by the black citizens.

. . . Exploiters come into the ghetto from outside, bleed it dry, and leave it economically dependent on the larger society. As with the missionaries, these exploiters frequently come as the "friend of the Negro," pretending to offer worthwhile goods and services, when their basic motivation is personal profit and their basic impact is the maintenance of racism. Many of the social welfare agencies—public and private—frequently pretend to offer "uplift" services; in reality, they end up creating a system which dehumanizes the individual and perpetuates his dependency. Conscious or unconscious, the paternalistic attitude of many of these agencies is no different from that of many missionaries going into Africa.

Professor Kenneth Clark described the economic colonization of the *Dark Ghetto* as follows:

The ghetto feeds upon itself; it does not produce goods or contribute to the prosperity of the city. It has few large businesses. . . . Even though the white community has tried to keep the Negro confined in ghetto pockets, the white businessman has not stayed out of the ghetto. A ghetto, too, offers opportunities for profit, and in a competitive society profit is to be made where it can.

In Harlem there is only one large department store and that is owned by whites. Negroes own a savings and loan association; and one Negro-owned bank has recently been organized. The other banks are branches of white-owned downtown banks. Property—apartment houses, stores, businesses, bars, concessions, and theaters—are for the most part owned by persons who live outside the community and take their profits home. . . .

When tumult arose in ghetto streets in the summer of 1964, most of the stores broken into and looted belonged to white men. Many of these owners responded to the destruction with bewilderment and anger, for they felt that they had been serving a community that needed them. *They did not realize* that the residents were not grateful for this service but bitter, as natives often feel toward the functionaries of a colonial power who in the very act of service, keep the hated *structure of oppression intact* [pp. 27–28].

It is a stark reality that the black communities are becoming more and more economically depressed. In June, 1966, the Bureau of Labor Statistics reported on the deteriorating condition of black people in this country. In 1948, the jobless rate of non-white[3] males between the ages of fourteen and nineteen was 7.6 percent. In 1965, the percentage of unemployment in this age group was 22.6 percent. The corresponding figures for unemployed white male teen-agers were 8.3 percent in 1948, and 11.8 percent in 1965. . . .

[3] Non-white in this and subsequent statistics includes Puerto Ricans, but the vast majority of non-whites are black people.

Again, as in the African colonies, the black community is sapped senseless of what economic resources it does have. Through the exploitative system of credit, people pay "a dollar down, a dollar a week" literally for years. Interest rates are astronomical, and the merchandise—of relatively poor quality in the first place—is long since worn out before the final payment. Professor David Caplovitz of Columbia University has commented in his book, *The Poor Pay More*, "The high markup on low-quality goods is thus a major device used by merchants to protect themselves against the risks of their credit business" (p. 18). Many of the ghetto citizens, because of unsteady employment and low incomes, cannot obtain credit from more legitimate businesses; thus they must do without important items or end up being exploited. They are lured into the stores by attractive advertising displays hawking, for example, three rooms of furniture for "only $199." Once inside, the unsuspecting customer is persuaded to buy lesser furniture at a more expensive price, or he is told that the advertised items are temporarily out of stock and is shown other goods. More frequently than not, of course, all the items are overpriced.

The exploitative merchant relies as much on threats as he does on legal action to guarantee payment. Garnishment of wages is not particularly beneficial to the merchant—although certainly used—because the employer will frequently fire an employee rather than be subjected to the bother of extra bookkeeping. And once the buyer is fired, all payments stop. But the merchant can hold the threat of garnishment over the customer's head. Repossession is another threat; again, not particularly beneficial to the merchant. He knows the poor quality of his goods in the first place, and there is little resale value in such goods which have probably already received substantial use. In addition, both the methods of garnishment and repossession give the merchant a bad business image in the community. It is better business practice to raise the prices two to three hundred percent, get what he can—dogging the customer for that weekly payment—and still realize a sizeable profit. At the same time the merchant can protect his image as a "considerate, understanding fellow." . . .

This is why the society does nothing meaningful about institutional racism: because the black community has been the creation of, and dominated by, a combination of oppressive forces and special interests in the white community. The groups which have access to the necessary resources and the ability to effect change benefit politically and economically from the continued subordinate status of the black community. This is not to say that every single white American consciously oppresses black people. He does not need to. Institutional racism has been maintained deliberately by the power structure and through indifference, inertia and lack courage on the part of white masses as well as petty officials. Whenever black demands for change become loud and strong, indifference is replaced by active opposition based on fear and self-interest. The line between purposeful suppression and indifference blurs. One way or another, most whites participate in economic colonialism.

Indeed, the colonial white power structure has been a most formidable foe. It has perpetuated a vicious circle—the poverty cycle—in which the black communities are denied good jobs, and therefore stuck with a low income and therefore unable to obtain a good education with which to obtain good jobs. They cannot qualify for credit at most reputable places; they then resort to unethical merchants who take advantage of them by charging higher prices for inferior goods. They end up having less funds to buy in bulk, thus unable to reduce overall costs. They remain trapped.

In the face of such realities, it becomes ludicrous to condemn black people for "not showing more initiative." Black people are not in a depressed condition because of some defect in their character. The colonial power structure clamped a boot of oppression on the neck of the black people and then, ironically, said "they are not ready for freedom." Left solely to the good will of the oppressor, the oppressed would never be ready.

And no one accepts blame. And there is no "white power structure" doing it to them. And they are in that condition "because they are lazy and don't want to work." And this is not colonialism. And this is the land of opportunity, and the home of the free. And people should not become alienated.

But people *do* become alienated.

The operation of political and economic colonialism in this country has had social repercussions which date back to slavery but did not by any means end with the Emancipation Proclamation. Perhaps the most vicious result of colonialism—in Africa and this country—was that it purposefully, maliciously and with reckless abandon relegated the black man to a subordinated, inferior status in the society. The individual was considered and treated as a lowly animal, not to be housed properly, or given adequate medical services, and by no means a decent education. . . . Here, we shall concentrate on the human and psychological results of social colonialism, first as it affected white attitudes toward blacks and then the attitude of black people toward themselves.

As we have already noted, slaves were brought to this land for the good of white masters, not for the purpose of saving or "civilizing" the blacks. . . .

The fact of slavery had to have profound impact on the subsequent attitudes of the larger society toward the black man. The fact of slavery helped to fix the sense of superior group position. Chief Justice Taney, in the Dred Scott decision of 1857, stated ". . . that they (black people) had no rights which the white man was bound to respect; and that the negro might justly and lawfully be reduced to slavery for his benefit." The emancipation of the slaves by legal act could certainly not erase such notions from the minds of racists. They believed in their superior status, not in paper documents. And that belief has persisted. When some people compare the black American to "other immigrant" groups in this country, they overlook the fact that slavery was peculiar to the blacks. No other minority group in this country was ever treated as legal property. . . .

Woodrow Wilson proclaimed that this country entered World War I "to make the world safe for democracy." This was the very same President who issued executive orders segregating most of the eating and rest-room facilities for federal employees. This was the same man who had written in 1901:

An extraordinary and very perilous state of affairs had been created in the South by the sudden and absolute emancipation of the Negroes, and it was not strange that the Southern legislatures should deem it necessary to take extraordinary steps to guard against the manifest and pressing dangers which it entailed. Here was a vast "laboring, landless, homeless class," once slaves; now free; unpracticed in liberty, unschooled in self-control; never sobered by the discipline of self-support; never established in any habit of prudence; excited by a freedom they did not understand, exalted by false hopes, bewildered and without leaders and yet insolent and aggressive; sick of work, covetous of pleasure—a host of dusky children untimely put out of school.[4]

". . . dusky children untimely put out of school," freed too soon —it is absolutely inconceivable that a man who spoke in such a manner could have black people in mind when he talked of saving the world (i.e., the United States) for democracy. Obviously, black people were not included in Woodrow Wilson's defense perimeter. Whatever the life of blacks might have been under German rule this country clearly did not fight Germany for the improvement of the status of black people —under the saved democracy—in *this* land. . . .

World War II was basically little different. The increased need for manpower in defense industries slowly opened up more jobs for black people as a result of the war effort, but as Professor Garfinkel has pointed out in *When Negroes March*, "When defense jobs were finally opened up to Negroes, they tended to be on the lowest rungs of the success ladder." Garfinkel also tells of how the President of the North American Aviation Company, for example, issued this statement on May 7, 1941:

While we are in complete sympathy with the Negroes, it is against company policy to employ them as aircraft workers or mechanics . . . regardless of their training. . . . There will be some jobs as janitors for Negroes [p. 17].

This country also saw fit to treat German prisoners of war more humanely than it treated its own black soldiers. On one occasion, a group of black soldiers was transporting German prisoners by train through the South to a prisoner-of-war camp. The railroad diner required the black American soldiers to eat in segregated facilities on the train—only four at a time and with considerable delay —while the German prisoners

4 Woodrow Wilson, "Reconstruction in the Southern States," *Atlantic Monthly* (January, 1901).

(white, of course) ate without delay and with other passengers in the main section of the diner!

. . .

The social and psychological effects on black people of all their degrading experiences are also very clear. From the time black people were introduced into this country, their condition has fostered human indignity and the denial of respect. Born into this society today, black people begin to doubt themselves, their worth as human beings. Self-respect becomes almost impossible. Kenneth Clark describes the process in *Dark Ghetto*:

Human beings who are forced to live under ghetto conditions and whose daily experience tells them that almost nowhere in society are they respected and granted the ordinary dignity and courtesy accorded to others will, as a matter of course, begin to doubt their own worth. Since every human being depends upon his cumulative experiences with others for clues as to how he should view and value himself, children who are consistently rejected understandably begin to question and doubt whether they, their family, and their group really deserve no more respect from the larger society than they receive. These doubts become the seeds of a pernicious self- and group-hatred, the Negro's complex and debilitating prejudice against himself.

The preoccupation of many Negroes with hair straighteners, skin bleachers, and the like illustrates this tragic aspect of American racial prejudice—Negroes have come to believe in their own inferiority [pp. 63–64].

In a manner similar to that of the colonial powers in Africa, American society indicates avenues of escape from the ghetto for those individuals who adapt to the "main-stream." This adaptation means to disassociate oneself from the black race, its culture, community and heritage, and become immersed (dispersed is another term) in the white world. What actually happens, as Professor E. Franklin Frazier pointed out in his book, *Black Bourgeoisie*, is that the black person ceases to identify himself with black people yet is obviously unable to assimilate with whites. He becomes a "marginal man," living on the fringes of both societies in a world largely of "make believe." This black person is urged to adopt American middle-class standards and values. As with the black African who had to become a "Frenchman" in order to be accepted, so to be an American, the black man must strive to become

"white." To the extent that he does, he is considered "well adjusted"—one who has "risen above the race question." These people are frequently held up by the white Establishment as living examples of the progress being made by the society in solving the race problem. Suffice it to say that precisely because they are required to denounce—overtly or covertly—their black race, *they are reinforcing racism in this country*.

In the United States, as in Africa, their "adaptation" operated to deprive the black community of its potential skills and brain power. All too frequently, these "integrated" people are used to blunt the true feelings and goals of the black masses. They are picked as "Negro leaders," and the white power structure proceeds to talk to and deal only with them. Needless to say, no fruitful, meaningful dialogue can take place under such circumstances. Those hand-picked "leaders" have no viable constituency for which they can speak and act. All this is a classic formula of colonial co-optation.

At all times, then, the social effects of colonialism are to degrade and to dehumanize the subjected black man. White America's School of Slavery and Segregation, like the School of Colonialism, has taught the subject to hate himself and to deny his own humanity. The white society maintains an attitude of superiority and the black community has too often succumbed to it, thereby permitting the whites to believe in the correctness of their position. Racist assumptions of white superiority have been so deeply engrained into the fiber of the society that they infuse the entire functioning of the national subconscious. They are taken for granted and frequently not even recognized. As Professors Lewis Killian and Charles Grigg express it in their book, *Racial Crisis in America*:

At the present time, integration as a solution to the race problem demands that the Negro foreswear his identity as a Negro. But for a lasting solution, the meaning of "American" must lose its implicit racial modifier, "white." Even without biological amalgamation, integration requires a sincere acceptance by all Americans that it is just as good to be a black American as to be a white American. Here is the crux of the problem of race relations—the redefinition of the sense of group position so that the status advantage of the white man is no longer an advantage, so that an

American may acknowledge his Negro ancestry without apologizing for it. . . . They [black people] live in a society in which to be unconditionally "American" is to be white, and to be black is a misfortune [pp. 108–9].

The time is long overdue for the black community to redefine itself, set forth new values and goals, and organize around them.

3.3
Rallying Round the Flag

Eldridge Cleaver

I distinguished between two colonialisms, between a domestic one, and an external one. Capitalism at home is domestic colonialism.

Osagyefo Kwame Nkrumah,
Consciencism.

Five years ago, even the most audacious visionary would not have dared predict the slashing do-or-die desperation and the sizzling up-tempo beat which has exploded into our politics, into our daily conversation, and into our nightmares and dreams. The ferment beneath the surface of our formal politics and public debate has grown more important in the last five years than at any time since the years preceding the Civil War. The parapolitics of the first Johnson Congress which, in contrast to most of its predecessors, seemed to resemble the dynamiting of a logjam, was actually sluggish, compromising, and drag-footish in terms of the pressing social problems which are feeding the conflagration raging in America's soul; problems which can no longer be compromised or swept cleverly under that national rug of self-delusion. The possibility of concealment no longer exists, and the only ones deceived are the deceivers themselves. Those who are victimized by these "social problems"—Negroes, the aged, unemployed and unemployable, the poor, the miseducated and dissatisfied students, the haters of war and lovers of man—have flung back the rug in outraged rebellion, refusing to be silenced

until their grievances are uncompromisingly redressed. America has come alive deep down in its raw guts, and vast contending forces of revolutionary momentum are squaring off in this land for decisive showdowns from which no one can purchase sanctuary.

Americans are becoming increasingly polarized right and left, with the great body of the people in the middle confused and, sometimes to mask their confusion, feigning indifference. "Extremism of the right," "extremism of the left"—not since the '30s and the cringing McCarthy era have these slogans been armed with the power to kill. On the lips of articulate people today, "right" and "left" are verbal razor blades in a sense unparalleled in American history. California's former Governor Brown issued the ominous warning that "the stench of fascism is in the air." The last Republican presidential candidate was branded a right-wing extremist. And the FBI's J. Edgar Hoover, America's flattest foot, periodically issues grave reminders that left-wingers, having mastered deceit, are almost succeeding in subverting *this*, and are busily boring from within to take over *that*.

Both right and left claim to love their country. The Ku Klux Klan, John Birch Society, American Nazi Party, conservative Republicans, Minutemen, even the Hell's Angels—all wrap themselves up in the American flat and solemnly call themselves patriots. Their enemies and critics, seeing that the right wing would not disappear when spoofed as kooks, nuts, and little old ladies in tennis shoes, surprised and frightened by their potential strength as indicated by the 26,000,000 votes cast for Goldwater, now grant them *de facto* political status by applying to them such sophisticated labels as "neo-fascist" and "right-winger."

As for the left, all red-blooded Americans who love TV and gentle toilet tissue know that the Negro revolution was conceived in Moscow (scratch Moscow, insert Peking) and launched by left-wing fanatics, and that the growing mass movement in opposition to America's war in Vietnam is "Communist inspired, manipulated and controlled."

It is not an overstatement to say that the destiny of the entire human race depends on the outcome of what is going on in America today. This is a staggering reality to the rest of the world; they must feel like passengers in a super-

sonic jet liner who are forced to watch helplessly while a passle of drunks, hypes, freaks, and madmen fight for the controls and the pilot's seat. Whether America decisively moves to the right or to the left is the fundamental political problem in the world today; and the most serious question now before the American people is who now, in this post–civil rights era, are the true patriots, the new right or the new left?

The question of the Negro's place in America, which for a long time could actually be kicked around as a serious question, has been decisively resolved: he is here to stay. But the Negro revolution is the real bedrock of the battleground on which the new right and the new left are contending. In a sense, both the new left and the new right are the spawn of the Negro revolution. A broad national consensus was developed over the civil rights struggle, and it had the sophistication and morality to repudiate the right wing. This consensus, which stands between a violent nation and chaos, is America's most precious possession. But there are those who despise it.

The task which the new right has feverishly undertaken is to erode and break up this consensus, something that is a distinct possibility since the precise issues and conditions which gave birth to the consensus no longer exist.

On the other hand, the task of the new left has been to hold the consensus together during the period of transition from the civil rights struggle to the post–civil rights era, which may see the growth of a broader movement challenging the structure of political and economic power in America.

The fact that Johnson adopted Goldwater's foreign policy has severely disillusioned a significant sector of the consensus; many felt it was a betrayal of trust. This nation had just begun to relax after fighting a battle for its moral life, a battle which gave birth to a trust that became a holy cause; and the betrayal of this trust, this cause, may one day be looked upon as having laid the foundation of cynicism and political depravity that prepared the way for America's Hitler. Nevertheless, in seeking to hold the consensus together, the left is aided tremendously by the enemies it makes, and more so by the enemies it inherited from the civil rights struggle. The lewd spectacle of Dixiecratic dinosaurs denouncing the protestants of the war in Vietnam can only infuriate and educate large sectors of the public who lost their bearings during the period of transition. All the new left need do is point: Look, there's old scurvy X, and dig who's with him—that filthy Y! Remember what they said about Selma?

At the same time, the link between America's undercover support of colonialism abroad and the bondage of the Negro at home becomes increasingly clearer. Those who are primarily concerned with improving the Negro's condition recognize, as do proponents of the liquidation of America's neo-colonial network, that their fight is one and the same. They see the key contradiction of our time.

We conceal something of the truth by saying that the new left merely opposes America's foreign policy. That is a euphemism for their support of national liberation in those areas of the world still under *de jure* colonial rule and those under the thumb of neo-colonial puppet regimes. The United States has the yes-or-no power of decision over all colonialism in the world today. There is not a colonial regime on the face of the earth today that could survive six months if the U.S. opposed it; and in many cases, without the active military and economic support of the U.S., the exploiting, murderous regimes would be dashed to bits by the exploited people themselves. The new left understands this thoroughly. It also knows that America's support of colonialism must be shattered before the resources and administrative machinery of the nation can be freed for the task of creating a truly free and humanistic society here at home. It is at this point, at the juncture of foreign policy and domestic policy, that the Negro revolution becomes one with the world revolution. Those who most bitterly oppose Negro progress are also the most ardent advocates of a belligerent foreign policy, the most violent castigators of critics of American escalation of war against the Vietnamese people, the hardest to die of the diehard enthusiasts of armed intervention in the internal affairs of the Dominican Republic and Latin America generally.

It is no coincidence that such political cavemen and fossilized intellects as Senator Stennis of Mississippi and Strom Thurmond of South Carolina were the first to speak out against the Vietnam

1970, The Register and Tribune Syndicate

CONRAD ©THE LOS ANGELES TIMES, 1970.

REPRINTED BY PERMISSION OF THE REGISTER AND TRIBUNE SYNDICATE, INC.

Day demonstrations and protest marches held throughout America in October 1965. They who once spoke out so vehemently against the Negro revolution are still fighting the same war; they have merely retreated to different terrain. The massive upsurge of the Negro people and the support and sympathy aroused in the white community beat the dinosaurs back from their first line of defense: the color line. But these opponents of the Negro revolution, routed on the issue of civil rights, have by no means folded up their tents and slinked away disgracefully in defeat. They have regrouped and entrenched themselves on a new front. They understand that the Negro's basic situation cannot really change without structural changes in America's political and economic system.

What the Negro now needs and consciously seeks is political and economic power. And ultimately we shall witness the merging of the Negro revolution with a broader movement demanding disarmament and conversion of the economy to peaceful purposes.

This prospect, of an alliance between the Negro revolution, the new left and the peace movement, fills the power structure with apprehension: witness the furious reaction provoked by Martin Luther King when he called for the cessation of American bombings of North Vietnam, negotiations with the National Liberation Front, and admission of China into the UN.

The fight against the Negro revolution, as long as this was possible, was waged in the name of the flag and the Constitution. Now, in this new stage of the struggle, the opposition is again employing as weapons the very same tools with which they have once been defeated. They are the only weapons remaining to the right-wing forces—short of naked terror and military repression to which they would eagerly resort if they saw no other way. Curiously, on this new level of struggle, they have much brighter hopes of success. The issues are more clouded. The moral issue has not yet become clear-cut as it was in the civil rights struggle. And the right is able to manipulate the people by playing upon the have-gun-will-travel streak in America's character, coupled with the narcissistic self-image as friend of the underdog. Americans think of themselves collectively as a huge rescue squad on twenty-four-hour call to any spot on the globe where dispute and conflict may erupt.

It does not make sense to the American people to fight a war half-heartedly. Goldwater knew this when he campaigned for President, and the right knows it today. If America is at war in Vietnam, then it makes sense to Americans when the right wing indignantly demands the application of more and more force, increased bombings, gas, napalm, and even nuclear weapons, the use of any and all effective weapons to kill and defeat the enemy and get it over with. Americans like to get a job done, and what they hate most of all is to drag out a job when they have the means in their hands of completing it.

The Johnson administration feels obligated to obfuscate the issue by refusing to clarify to the American people the true nature of the Vietnam conflict. By interpreting the Vietnam situation as a war between two sovereign nations, the Communist North having invaded the peace-loving, democratic South, LBJ is able to pose as a courageous do-gooder coming to the aid of a weak underdog, while a cynical world, as usual, looks on and refuses to help Uncle Sam do his good deed. The power structure cannot publicly recognize that the Vietnamese conflict is a civil war, because such an acknowledgement would reveal us as an aggressor intervening on a favored side in a civil conflict. In fact, America's intervention has transformed a civil war into a war of national liberation.

The President cannot afford to tell the truth to the American people because he knows they would not support the war if they really understood. It is only by keeping them confused and hysterical—the job of the vast, centralized, collusive mass media—that LBJ is able to get away with it. And this is the source of Johnson's great fear of the teach-ins and protest demonstrations. The truth is electric and it spreads, spreads, spreads. What galls Johnson and the new right is the fear that the mounting protests against their policy will awaken the American people. They know that masses of Americans would

come out to demonstrate against LBJ. Mass embarrassment—at such obviously hypocritical actions as the American intervention in the Dominican Republic on the bloody side of a right-wing military *junta*—might turn to mass anger.

The world capitalist system has come to a decisive fork in the road, and this is at the heart of our national crisis. The road to the left is the way of reconciliation with the exploited people of the world, the liberation of all peoples, the dismantling of all economic relations based upon the exploitation of man by man, universal disarmament, and the establishment of international rule of law with effective means of enforcement. The road to the right is refusal to submit to the universal demand for national liberation, economic justice, peace, and popular sovereignty. To walk this last path, the decision-makers must be prepared to unleash worldwide genocide, including the extermination of America's Negroes. The people within these countries who try to stand against the will of the overwhelming majority of the human race must be willing to forgo the last traces of their own liberty and see their governments turned into totalitarian regimes tolerating no dissent. The rage of the American power structure over the exercise of the constitutional right to dissent, to assemble and peacefully petition against Johnson's war in Vietnam, is only a mild taste of the hemlock the people will be forced to swallow if they allow their country to go down the death-seeking branch of the fork.

President Kennedy gave the distinct impression of commitment to the path of reconciliation, and it was the source of much of his appeal. What frightens people about President Johnson is that he seems to be trying to walk down both roads simultaneously. But he cannot play his double game for long. Sooner or later he and his successors will have to choose.

The new right and the new left in America, each trying to lead the nation down the diverging branches of the fork, have between them the fate of the world and the hopes of a tortured, bleeding humanity—forever seeking life and almost always receiving betrayal and death from the outstretched hand of the seducer.

In the next articles we present two views of the Black Panther Party, the first written by a white, middle-class radical and the second by a Black man.

3.4
The Black Panthers: A White Man's View

Gregory Hollidge

It is quite true that the Black Panther Party poses a threat to the "American Way of Life." They *are* dangerous and White people are justified in their fear of the party. The question is, though, *why* do they threaten America? Is it because they are Black racists, attempting to kill all White people? Is it because they are a Communist-inspired organization whose purpose is to overthrow the government so that Russia can take over? Are they murderous anarchists who glory in wreaking havoc and destruction for the sheer joy of death and chaos? Are they demagogues who are seeking to take power away from the people so they can take all benefits for themselves? Or are they, in final desperation trying to win, for all Black people in particular, and for oppressed people in general, the human rights which were supposedly guaranteed all men in the Constitution of the United States? I think that the latter answer is correct. The Black Panthers say that political power grows out of the barrel of a gun. If the White people will not open their eyes to the blatant institutional racism imbedded in our culture and allow the poverty-stricken to share in their due, the gun is the only way to obtain power—if it is consistently denied through all other means. The White people of America are afraid of the Black Panthers because they do not want to give up what they have. The White people are afraid of the Black Panthers because they believe that they are racist, Communist, anarchist, etc. They refuse to believe that this "wonderful land of the free" is institutionally racist, and instead, blame the poverty of the Blacks on their "shiftlessness, laziness, stupidity, etc." The authors of *Institutional Racism in America* point out that White children have always been miseducated about the Blacks, as well as all other minority ethnic groups. The Whites abhor the violent methods that the Black Panthers propose to use while at the same time ignoring the violence which is aimed at the Blacks: physical, mental, economic, social, political, etc. The Panthers *do* pose a threat to White people, especially those in power, and the only way that the Panther's proposed method—Revolution—will prove unnecessary will be if they offer the Blacks the *right* of self-determination. If this does not occur, and rapidly, the future of our nation looks dark indeed.

When Huey Newton and Bobby Seale started the Black Panther Party for Self-Defense, both of them had begun to realize that the Black people in the United States needed a revolutionary movement which could liberate the people from the oppression of the power structure. They drew up a platform which articulated the demands of the Black people:

1. We want freedom. We want power to determine the destiny of our Black Community.

2. We want full employment for our people.

3. We want an end to the robbery by the White man of our Black Community.

4. We want decent housing, fit for shelter of human beings.

5. We want education for our people that exposes the true nature of this decadent American society. We want education that teaches us our true history and our role in the present-day society.

6. We want all Black men to be exempt from military service.

7. We want an immediate end to POLICE BRUTALITY and MURDER of Black people.

8. We want freedom for all Black men held in federal, state, county, and city prisons and jails.

9. We want all Black people when brought to trial to be tried in court by a jury of their peer group or people from their Black communities, as defined by the Constitution of the United States.

10. We want land, bread, housing, education, clothing, justice, and peace. And as our major political objective, a United Nations-supervised plebiscite to be held throughout the Black colony in which only Black colonial subjects will be allowed to participate, for the purpose of determining the will of Black people as to their national destiny.[1]

All of these points echo the speeches of Malcolm X, who was not a racist or a fascist or a Communist, but merely demanded that Black people have their human rights *now!*

Huey Newton formed his beliefs from the writings of Frantz Fanon, Mao, and Malcolm X. It was from Fanon that the concept of the "colonized people" within the "mother country" was derived. In pooling his own beliefs and experiences with those of Fanon, Mao, and Malcolm X, Huey Newton developed the guiding principles and ideology of the Black Panther Party. The basis for the freedom of the oppressed Black man is political power. He wrote:

The only way he can become political is to represent what is commonly a military power—which the Black Panther Party for Self-Defense calls

[1] These statements and others have been taken from the Black Panther Party newspaper—a source too seldom consulted by those who write about Black Power.

Self-Defense power. Black people can develop Self-Defense power by arming themselves from house to house, block to block, community to community, throughout the nation. Then we will choose a political representative and he will state to the power structure the desires of the Black masses. If the desires are not met, the power structure will receive a political consequence.

What this represents—and what is so repugnant to the Establishment—is a very activist stance towards liberation. It *is* a threat, but it is one which *must* be made. History has shown—as Malcolm X pointed out—that singing "We Shall Overcome" and marching in protest parades which were engineered by Whites and Uncle Toms will not move the power structure to meaningful and immediate action. This nation is coming to understand *only* militarism and violence—witness the extraordinarily large portion of the budget which is spent on "defense." In order to combat this, Huey writes:

This racist United States operates with the motive of profit. He lifts the gun and escalates the war for profit

reasons. *We will make him lower the guns because they will no longer serve his profit motive.*

The controllers of the economic system are obligated to furnish each man with a livelihood. If they cannot do this or if they will not do this, they do not deserve the position of administrators. The means of production should be taken away from them and placed in the people's hands, so that . . . [they can] choose capable administrators motivated by their sincere interest in the people's welfare and not the interest of private property.

The Panther ideology is based upon the premise that racism and capitalism go hand in hand.

The Black Panther Party feels that this government and the institutions necessary to make the government function are illegitimate because they are not relating to the people. . . . With the technology that exists in AmeriKKKa there is no excuse in these modern times for people to be without food or other basic necessities of life.

In a speech at Stanford University following Reagan's *refusal* to allow credit for Sociology 139X, Eldridge Cleaver, Minister of Information of the Black Panther Party, spoke about the current political conditions and their relation to the Black Panthers. I shall quote some of that speech here, along with my comments on it:

Everyone accuses the Black Panther Party of having a police hangup— the only thing we can do is sit around, ambush policemen, and call them pigs. Those are just some of the things we can do. That's not all. That's not all.

The White press loves to get stories on the Black Panthers which depict them as raving nihilists. The White community is simply not ready to accept the concept of institutional racism. When the Panthers point this out, it simply goes right by them. The press never talks about the free breakfast programs and the other community projects in which the Panthers are active. They would much rather see the Panthers as destroyers of all that "Freedom Has Accomplished." Of course, the quotation above *does* have an ominous tone to it also. It is a warning to Whites that the Black Panthers are not playing games.

Speaking about economic problems facing the Blacks, Cleaver discussed the ghetto:

We're dealing with community imperialism. The Black community is ruled by racist, exploiting elements who live in the White community: a coalition of White, avaricious businessmen, politicians, who are backed up by the gestapo police departments. They've turned the Black community into a market: not any longer for cheap labor so much, but a market where they take welfare checks, they take the loot that we can steal and rob from the affluent White people in this country, and they suck it back through profits, and they leave us there. On top of us, we have a very vicious Black bourgeoisie."

In this statement, he has made three assertions: (1) The Black revolution does not consist of the oppressed workers as such. This opposes the notion that it is "Communist-inspired," (2) the White people feel that any money that the Blacks *do* get is robbery; and (3) the White man is not the only oppressor.

Eldridge Cleaver clarified the Black Panther Party position on the matter of representation— Black and White—by the following:

I want to say "all power to the people. Black power to Black people, White power to White people." And do you get uptight about that, because you haven't had White power, you've had pig power? You haven't had any White power. We say, power to the people, all people should have the power to control their own destiny.

The Black Panthers are opposed to the police oppression of Black people and dissenters. They feel that the power structure is too arrogant, that the leaders think they own the people and the country. They are pointing out that there is no democracy in the United States, and that if it takes war to eliminate the oppression of the people by the state, then a war will occur. Their motto comes from Mao Tse-Tung's *Little Red Book:*

We are advocates of the abolition of war; we do not want war; but war can only be abolished through war; and in order to get rid of the gun it is necessary to pick up the gun.

Unless there is freedom for all— in fact, as well as in print—there will be a revolution.

3.5
A Black Panther's Funeral

Frank A. Jones

A panther is a black cat.

History teaches that slavery, regardless of its form, always provokes a war of liberation. A few years ago, two young Black men got together to act in response to the provocations of slavery, according to the records of history. They organized a clique of Blacks around a ten-point program. They took on the name of Black Panther Party. The panther was chosen as their symbol, not because of its blackness, but because of its defensive nature. Their goal was defense, not aggression.

After looking at a record of "justifiable" homicides by the Oakland, California, police, this group labeled the established police force as murderers. They loudly publicized the fact that five Black men were killed in one week by the Oakland Police Department. Along with the anger that had built up in them, there was also resolution to bring an immediate end to this "outright murder."

These young Blacks went into the streets of the hardcore ghetto recruiting Blacks with relative ease. They found in propagating their ten-point program and recruiting members that most of the people of the ghetto were in total agreement with them.

Huey Newton, Minister of Defense, and Bobby Seale, Chairman, realized that a theory in a book is nothing more than a theory in a book unless it is applied. Hence, they implemented their program of counter-policing the Oakland Police Department. During the first month of this program, they claimed that police brutality was at a standstill. As they continued policing the established police force in the execution of its duties, the police felt harassed and decided to destroy this "gang of hoodlums" from its leadership down.

The police establishment took this surveillance of their duties to be an insult. They took it to mean a suspicion of their moral integrity. The Panthers openly said they not only doubted their ethics but believed they were non-existent. They attached the name of "pigs" to the police to denote their low opinion of these officers of the law. The police department refused to be policed or observed by the citizens, who were paying them. The conflicts between Panthers and the police increased. The Panthers were cited on trivial and non-existent violations. They were stopped and detained without reasonable explanations.

As conflicts with the police increased, their organization's membership grew by two's and three's. And with negative news coverage, they became national. The police establishment was determined to destroy the functioning leadership. The news media gave attention to minute incidents and whitewashed them as "The Black Panthers Again in Conflict with the Police!"

The "Battle on 28th Street" was a police blunder. After all the harassing of the Panthers for their peccadillos, the police now attempted to destroy one of the biggest Panther leaders, Eldridge Cleaver. It had been apparent to the crudest of minds that the pattern of events which had occurred was planned precisely for the obliteration of the Panthers. The papers had killed them psychologically in the public's mind; the battle on 28th Street was to be their physical destruction.

Whatever the setting was, whether it be as the Panthers testified—a Black man, member of their group, hiding behind an auto to urinate and fired upon by the police—or, as the police testified—a Black with a gun behind an auto firing upon them—the outcome was clear for all to behold: Bobby Hutton, a seventeen year-old boy, dead with ten bullet holes in his young body; a house on 28th Street with countless bullet holes and the odor of tear gas; a basement afire; Eldridge Cleaver and Wells, another member of the Panthers, both with bullet wounds, and a police officer with a bullet wound.

My attitude toward the Panthers had been formed, as I assume many others had, by the negative coverage of the news media. So I decided that I would go to this funeral to see, if possible, firsthand. I must confess that this was the turning point in my view of the Panthers. I had thought, as the news media had directed me to, that the Panthers were nothing more than a group of hoodlums and foolhardy rabble-rousers who were making it harder on Blacks by their actions. No really intelligent person would join that group. I went to espy the scene. And at this meeting (funeral) a profound sense of awareness took control of me.

At the Holiness Church, where the funeral was held, the fervor of suffering was felt. The auditorium was packed and only standing room was left. Eulogies were many and diverse; The Reverend E. E. Cleaveland, pastor of the church, said, "This young man saw that a hog was in the pond polluting the water. He tried to get the hog out, and it took his life . . . We older people, too, had a part in his death; we failed to get the hog out of the pond that he might have clean water!"

The awareness of what was happening began to envelop me as I marched around to look at the body of Bobby Hutton; a boy young and tender, yet aware of a morose history of Blacks being abused, was disfigured with bullet holes from the lower back to the head, all totaling ten to twelve bullets; a body beyond embalmer's repair. Marching around the church with the silent others, I looked on the parents of this seventeen year old child and felt their hurt, resolution, helplessness, and anger. I called to mind the death and funeral of Jerome Cook, whom the police had killed, seemingly without cause; I remembered the holes in his face, and his mother who attended the same little Holiness Church I had attended. I thought how she tried with all the strength in her to understand, saying, "It's the Lord that giveth and the Lord that taketh." As I looked at the Huttons, I remembered Mrs. Hutton's futile attempt not to hate or feel anger toward those who had ruthlessly "murdered" another young Black boy. I recalled her voice in testimony services, how she tried to hide that inner hostility and utter resentment, that intestinal chaos that urges one to seek revenge in every form, that drives dying men to live, that a vicious vendetta might be accomplished. She reiterated the Biblical encyclical "Vengeance is mine, saith the Lord." She was comforted that "whatever is right the Lord will repay." I remembered, as I stood there looking on the Huttons, how I had stood at Jerome Cook's funeral and watched, trying to read the obituary, young children in their impressionable years weeping sorely over a dead brother; young men being taken away from the corpse as they looked on weeping unashamedly and uttering vengeance with their lips and meaning it in their hearts. I recalled looking at these five children, ranging from seven to twelve years, in their infantile inner fears and psychic altering chaotic states, how the beauty of their young and innocent countenances was shattered by this bewildering nightmarish episode. They stood over a dead brother, tense, scared, confused, and embittered. I watched, as they stared at the body, their radiant and energetic faces, along with their total persons, being disfigured as they screamed and wept horribly, calling, "Mama! Mama!" Their little muscles tightened, their throats full, they wept bitterly and screamed unabatedly, refusing to be comforted other than by their mother who also needed solace.

I understood what was happening. I felt that same lump in my stomach that they were now feeling in theirs; that same fullness also enclosed me as it did them. I realized that this was a painful lesson that they had to learn as had too many Blacks before them and too many after them shall learn—a senseless and brutal lesson that will forever be imprinted on a child's mind; a psychic transmutation that would deform him and his attitudes toward Whites. I understood the emotions engendered. I understood the funky sensation of helplessness that was hurled upon them! I understood! I understood! I understood traumatically that this was the fruit of knowledge that was to enlighten them to the sin of Blackness and the denial of a Black man's right to be alive in this land. From the Great Lakes to the Mississippi and on, this land had been declared a White man's land. Blacks were sojourners and mere workers with limited benefits and no insurance. He was pissed on daily, and if he complained it was too funky, he was thrust into a state where it ceased to smell at all. Because I understood this and was aware of this nauseating awareness enslaving the children at such a tender and impressionable age, I wept bitterly and was unable to read the obituary properly.

I relived all of these distraught moments, and it provoked a certain something in me of which I had never been aware. I felt I wanted to go out and force a bigoted populace to see the savage and brutal murders that they were paying these swine to commit. I felt I wanted to make every sane and insane White person see what

Blacks have seen much too long. I felt like letting emotions, rather than reason, prevail; I felt like joining the Panthers, the Black Guard, U.S. or an organization that was going to actively kill White people, kill cops, kill honkies, KILL, KILL, KILL, until the Black life taken was avenged! I said within myself, "Kill those who have killed, maim those who have maimed!"

I walked outside and there I saw Bobby Seale, a young man, a chain smoker. I understood, having come from a home of smokers, what it meant when cigarette after cigarette was lit and only smoked partially. There, I saw a young man who had just come back from the funeral of Dr. Martin Luther King now at the funeral of another slain human rights warrior, surrounded by older women who were showing him that they cared, loved, and respected him for risking his life for their sake as well as the whole community.

I went in a caravan to the house on 28th Street after the funeral. It was two weeks after the shoot-out and the tear gas was still strong enough to make those weep who went inside. Bullet holes everywhere. In the top of the house, in the bottom of the house and everywhere. I went to the basement and looked at the rubbish—a basement that was burned and tear gassed and heavily punctured with police bullets. An auto outside was shot up as one would picture in an Al Capone movie. The house next door had police bullet holes also. As I stood looking, flashes of Vietnamese huts came into my mind. This place looked worse than an American-bombed hut. I walked around weeping from an overdose of tear gas, remembering Bobby Seale's nervousness and fear. I thought on this place and pictured his face in my mind, realizing for the first time exactly what the Panthers were attempting to do. I finally understood that these young men were, in fact, putting their lives on the altar for the sake of the police-harassed and murdered Black community. I felt guilty because I had not only been unaware of this risk but totally ungrateful as many other Blacks were.

I went from that place for the first time in my life with an intelligent understanding of what the Black Panther Party was about.

3.6
Credo of Black Students

Black Student Organization

Dear Black Brothers and Sisters, there is no need for continued analysis and questioning of our position in American society.

All over the country our people are under siege as the system becomes more repressive in its response to our people's determined efforts to achieve relief from the burden of economic exploitation, political oppression, and the violence of racism.

We all know what is happening: the man is moving with massive military preparation to violently repress and if need be exterminate Black people in America.

It is time to unite and organize to survive. We must move collectively against our oppressor in organized action on all fronts. We have met in conference after conference, only to compare the smoothness of our raps. Now, we call for a moratorium on inspirational oratory. History affords us what may well be our last chance to maximize our commitment to the liberation of our people and consolidation of our Black Nation.

On April 12–14, 1968, a group of brothers and sisters met at Holly Knolls, Virginia, to consider a proposal to form a National Black Student Organization. We concluded that our vital interests dictate the necessity of such an organization.

We adopted the following as a credo for Black students:

We believe that freedom, justice, and equality are the human rights of all peoples and nations;

We believe that Afro-Americans are a nation defined by common experiences. The Black experience profoundly proclaims the human condition;

We believe in the beauty of Blackness and the celebration of Soul. All people must love what they are and celebrate themselves;

We believe in love and the spiritual reality of the universe. The essence of our cultural reality is an expression of the universal spirit of life;

We believe that Black people must be independent as a cultural nation and must be united to build their own cultural institutions;

We believe that together, Black men and women must express the dignity of Black culture in the family, the home, and the community;

We believe that the role of Black students is to build Black educational institutions that service the needs of the Black Community, that are actively involved in the struggle to liberate Black people from racist oppression and that engage in the job of building the Black nation;

We believe that Afro-Americans are in a common struggle with people in Asia, Africa, and Latin America. We believe that oppression can be defeated and new societies erected, based on self-determination and cooperation;

Therefore:

WE DEDICATE OUR LIVES TO THE LIBERATION OF ALL MEN BY WORKING FOR THE LIBERATION OF THE BLACK COMMUNITY.

It is from this context that we call upon you to join with other brothers and sisters from all over this country to organize a strong, disciplined Black Student Organization.

Chicano Consciousness

3.7
"Tío Taco Is Dead"

Newsweek

It is impossible to ignore the handwriting on the wall—the enormous, angular jottings that spill over imaginary margins. Across the peeling faces of neo-Victorian buildings, on littered sidewalks, anywhere where there is a decent-size blank space, young *chicanos* scrawl their names, their slogans, their dreams. Often the graffiti ends with the mystic "*con safos*," a charm-like incantation that is supposed to protect the scribbling from defacement. On the ash-gray bricks of one nameless liquor store deep in the heart of the East Los Angeles barrio, someone has written a footnote to American history. "Tío Taco is dead," it says. "Con safos."

Tío Taco—or Uncle Taco, the stereotype Mexican-American, sapped of energy and ambition, sulking in the shadow of an Anglo culture—*is* dead. The point needs no "con safos" to drive home its essential irreversibility. From the ghettos of Los Angeles, through the wastelands of New Mexico and Colorado, into the fertile reaches of the Rio Grande valley in Texas, a new Mexican-American militancy is emerging. Brown has become aggressively beautiful. And the name of the game is pride and power. A Los Angeles poet named A. Arzate has captured the mood that grips young chicanos:[1]

Thus far
The image *de me raza* [of my people]
Comes from gringo hands . . .

Reprinted by permission from *Newsweek*, June 29, 1970, pp. 22–28. Copyright Newsweek, Inc., 1970.

[1] Mexican-Americans. The term has been traced to the Indians of Mexico who pronounced *Mexicano* "Mehchee-cano" and then shortened it to "chicano."

Now must be the time to change,
And with my forming hands, create
  my real self.
I slap the clay,
My clay,
Upon the wheel and begin.
And the clenched fist I use
To smash and crush the gringo's
  vision
Of what I should be . . .

But once the gringo's vision is shattered, what will take its place? And where will this search for identity take the Mexican-Americans? There are no pat answers. For like other dark-skinned minority groups in the U.S., the chicanos are caught in a curious limbo, suspended between two cultures, torn between assimilation and ethnic isolation—and uncertain whether a tenable middle ground even exists. The uncertainty hasn't impaired the momentum of the Mexican-American movement—but it has left the chicanos unsure of their real goals.

There are 5.6 million Mexican-Americans in the United States, divided roughly into two subgroups. The first is made up of descendants of settlers who arrived in the Southwest before the Mayflower hove to off the shores of the New World. The forefathers of these Spanish-Americans, as they prefer to be called, founded California and gave Los Angeles its name—*El Pueblo de Nuestra Señora la Reina de Los Angeles de Porciúncula.* Today, they live in rural communities scattered across New Mexico and Colorado, relatively cut off from the mainstream of American life.

Way Station

The second, and larger, subgroup is made up of more recent immigrants from Mexico and their descendants. Substantial migration to the U.S. began with the Mexican Revolution and went on through the boom days of the

1920s, '50s and '60s, with Texas serving as the way station to the great urban ghettos of San Antonio, Los Angeles, Denver and points farther north. Characteristically, the immigrants from Mexico thought of their move to the States as an expedient; unlike immigrants from czarist Russia or Germany or Ireland, they deluded themselves into thinking that they could always go home again at relatively modest psychic and financial cost if things didn't work out. Largely because of this psychic crutch, the Mexican immigrants never really cut their ties with Mexico, and only halfheartedly committed themselves to American culture.

This ambivalence was reinforced by the racial and class prejudices of the white majority in the country, which rebuffed Mexican-Americans wherever and whenever the two cultures met. Taken together, these two elements—Mexican-American ambivalence and white rejection—combined to place the country's second-largest minority on the lowest rung of the social ladder. Through the Southwest today, where 90 per cent of the Mexican-Americans live, a third of them are below the official poverty line—that is, they make do on less than $3,000 a year. In some sections of Texas, poverty-stricken Mexican-Americans live in unbelievably primitive conditions. Countrywide, the unemployment rate among chicanos is twice as high as the unemployment rate among Anglos. And the vast majority of Mexican-Americans who are employed work at unskilled or low-skilled, low-paying jobs. Mexican-Americans average four years less schooling than Anglos, and two years less than Negroes.

Health statistics are generally hard to come by, mainly because Mexican-Americans are usually lumped together with whites. But a recent survey in Colorado showed that persons with Spanish surnames had a life expectancy of only 56.7 years—ten years less than the life expectancy of Colorado whites. "Come down here and look at the bloated bellies and watery eyes," says José Angel Gutiérrez, 25, one of the brightest—and most aggressive—chicano leaders in the country today. "This kind of thing is found all over the Southwest."

Statistics tell only part of the story. On top of the poverty, Mexican-Americans have long been subjected to violence by the authorities. For years, law-enforcement agencies in the Southwest acted as if it was open season on *muchachos*. "There's a lot to the saying that all Texas Rangers have Mexican blood," one witness told the U.S. Commission on Civil Rights. "They have it on their boots." Just as often, the Anglo attitude has been more subtle—and more crippling. Guidance counselors in Mexican-American schools, for example, regularly steer students into "realistic" vocational programs, advice that just about locks young chicanos into the poverty cycle. Over-all, the insensitivity of Anglos—whether in government, in education or simply on a person-to-person basis—has amounted to psychological oppression of incalculable dimensions. "Why do they persecute us?" asks Bob Castro, a chicano activist in Los Angeles. "Why do they beat us and throw us into prison? Why do they insult our language and our culture and our history? Why do they call us names? Why do they deny us jobs?" And Castro pauses before adding: "Why do they hate us?"

Cycle

Given the plight of the Mexican-Americans, the only surprising thing about the *movimiento chicano* is that it took so long to get started. This was due, in large measure, to the fact that the overwhelmingly majority of Mexican-Americans are devout Roman Catholics. "The emphasis the church places on misery and penance and suffering does nothing but buttress the condition we're in—and it's one hell of a condition," says José Gutiérrez. And once the movement was under way, its most distinctive trait quickly became its crippling fragmentation; from the start, chicanos tended to develop regional leadership and set regional goals. Behind this regionalization were honest and hard-to-resolve-differences over the best way to break the cycle of poverty and discrimination in which Mexican-Americans are trapped.

Cesar Chavez, 42, the only Mexican-American leader to achieve national recognition, decided early on that the best way to break the cycle was to put more money directly into chicano jeans. Accordingly, in 1962, he began his long, drawn-out drive to unionize California grapepickers, the majority of whom are Mexican-Americans. For years the vineyard

owners have held out, but the strike—backed by a nationwide boycott of California grapes—has been partially successful. By last week, Chavez's union had signed contracts (setting a minimum wage of $2 an hour, 40 cents more than most nonunion growers pay) with fifteen firms—and more are on the way. And early this month Chavez began expanding his activities, calling Coachella Valley melon workers out of the fields to force their employers to pay union wages.

But there are some Mexican-Americans who argue that putting more money in chicano pockets is not enough; there are simply too many mouths to feed in the average chicano family, these critics say, for a direct economic approach to have more than a superficial impact on Mexican-American life. Following this reasoning, a number of chicano groups have focused on improving the educational opportunities of young Mexican-Americans to speed them on their way into the middle class. The drive to improve education has been particularly forceful—and successful—in Los Angeles. As a result of pressure from the Mexican-American community there, the Board of Education has established a Mexican-American Education Commission, essentially a lobby to exert pressure on behalf of chicanos. In January, 1969, the commission managed to get IQ tests eliminated for Mexican-American children through the fifth grade on the ground that their low scores were the result of difficulty with the English language rather than a measure of low intelligence. The commission has also taken a hand in selecting administrators for Mexican-American schools, designing and appraising programs specifically aimed at Mexican-American children and monitoring the over-all performance of schools in Mexican-American neighborhoods.

Secession

Other Mexican-American leaders have opted for yet another approach. In New Mexico, a fiery chicano activist named Reies López Tijerina, 43, has mustered a local following behind what amounts to a secessionist scheme aimed at giving Mexican-Americans their own land. Tijerina, who enjoys a reputation as something of a romantic revolutionary as a result of a 1967 shoot-out at the Rio Arriba County courthouse in

Tierra Amarilla, is now serving a two-year prison term for assaulting two forest rangers. Undaunted by a stretch in prison, he has laid claim to millions of acres originally owned by Mexican settlers under Spanish land grants that were conveniently lost, destroyed or ignored by the Anglo authorities. At stake are New Mexico, Arizona, Nevada, Utah, Texas, parts of Colorado, at last half of California and a slice of Wyoming. Most historians concede Tijerina's point—that the land was wrested illegally from the original Mexican owners after the Mexican-American war. But the issue has yet to be taken up by Congress or the courts, and the chance that the land will ever be parceled out to the heirs of the original owners is all but nonexistent.

Tijerina's quixotic crusade—designed among other things, to give Mexican-Americans pride in their heritage—has found an echo in Denver. There, another local chicano leader, Rodolfo (Corky) Gonzáles, 41, has called for chicanos to "unite in a new nation [on] the land that once belonged to us."

Still others have taken the political route in an effort to crack the cycle. But nothing has been more frustrating—and more unsuccessful—for Mexican-Americans than their search for political leverage. On a national scale, chicanos are represented by only four congressmen and one senator—Joseph Montoya of New Mexico. There is only one chicano in the California Legislature, and not a single chicano councilman in Los Angeles, where some 1 million Mexican-Americans live. For years chicanos in L.A. have voted a straight Democratic ticket—and received next to nothing in the way of patronage jobs. So in 1965, they rallied around Ronald Reagan —and then received precious little from the Republicans when he won the governorship. "He hasn't done a thing," complains Francisco Bravo, a wealthy chicano physician who is one of the most influential Mexican-American figures in the city. "In fact, he's made it worse. He promised more Mexican-American appointees and he appointed even less than [former Gov. Edmund] Brown."

Now, under the leadership of the Congress of Mexican-American Unity, which represents 200 chicano organizations, the Mexican-Americans are looking into the possibility of organizing a common front with blacks or, if that fails, getting something in return for delivering their votes. The situation is much the same in Texas. "Two, three, four years back, we heard one thing," explains Joe J. Bernal, the only Mexican-American in the Texas Senate, " 'pull the big lever for the Democrats.' In Spanish, we call it *la palanca.*' It means lever. You don't go in and jump around on the ballot. You just pull the big lever. But sophistication is coming into politics for the chicano. As a Democrat, I can tell you there is going to be less and less of a chance to tell the people, 'pull la palanca.' I tell you that for sure. Whoever is running is going to have to give some reasons. There's going to have to be some compromises made."

Some of the bolder Mexican-Americans are abandoning the Democrats and Republicans altogether and striking out on their own. The most dramatic example of this is in South Texas, where José Gutiérrez has organized a third party, *La Raza Unida.* Operating on a shoestring budget out of a cluttered, two-room office in Crystal City, Gutiérrez and the activists around him are fielding their own candidates in three Texas counties this year—counties in which 85 per cent of the residents are Mexican-Americans. And Gutiérrez, who has an M.A. in political science and knows the rules of the road, makes clear that La Raza Unida intends to gain control of *everything* in those counties—judgeships, county-commissioner posts, Chamber of Commerce seats, even the Boy Scouts. If this drive proves successful, Gutiérrez plans to send his organizers into 21 other Texas counties where Mexican-Americans make up the majority of the population. Ultimately, he hopes to create a Mexican-American island in the middle of Texas, with every lever of economic and political power in chicano hands.

Key Questions

Gutiérrez is taking an obvious path—rallying the majority where he is fortunate enough to have a majority. But this approach is not applicable to the thousands of towns and counties across the Southwest where chicanos are very much in the minority. Gutiérrez—indeed, the whole chicano movement as it exists today—is really begging the key questions:

how are the Mexican-Americans to come to terms with the white majority? And what is the role of such a minority in America today?

Some experts, among them Dr. Leo Grebler, a UCLA economist who directed the most comprehensive study on Mexican-Americans made thus far, claim that the chicanos—most of whom live in cities—have a great potential for assimilation. "They have had less time to become assimilated than the Jews or Poles or Irish," says Grebler, whose study, "The Mexican-American People: The Nation's Second Largest Minority," will be published this summer. "But if they keep going the way they are, the Mexican-Americans will proceed along the same path as the Jews and Poles and Irish—accumulating middle-class values and properties and outlook."

What Grebler is suggesting is a middle ground called cultural pluralism, in which minority groups conform to American norms (such as material achievement) while retaining traces of their distinctive cultural identity. Generally speaking, this is what the Polish-Americans or Irish-Americans do when they blend into middle-class America 364 days a year and dress up in national costumes for a parade down New York City's Fifth Avenue on the 365th. The idea attracts a good many Mexican-Americans. "I resent the term 'brown power'," says Dr. Hector P. García, a veteran chicano crusader and the founder of the American GI Forum, one of the oldest Mexican-American rights organizations in the country. "That sounds as if we were a different race. We're not. We're white. We should be Americans. But we should eat enchiladas and be proud of our names."

Madness

But for many Mexican-Americans, cultural pluralism is an uncomfortable middle ground. In the wake of the frustrations of the black civil-rights movement, young chicanos tend to believe that middle-class American values are not all that desirable—and certainly not worth the price of their own cultural identity. "I hate the white ideal," says David Sánchez, 21, the prime minister of the Los Angeles-based Brown Berets, a militant group patterned after the Black Panthers. "It's a disease leading to madness." For all their radical rhetoric, the central thrust

of the Brown Berets is to throw up a cultural wall around the chicano community to insulate it from the heat of the American melting pot.

And so the Mexican-American community is torn between the advantages of assimilation and the attractions of cultural isolation, between joining and resisting. The result is uncertainty and indirection. The ambivalence is symbolized by the way chicano posters leap from English to Spanish in a medley of Mex-Tex: "Valentine Dance. 8 p.m. in the Latin-American club in Cotulla. 50 cents for *hombres y* 25 cents for *mujeres.*" And again: "*Para justicia en los campos*—support the grape boycott."

Patsy

But if the chicanos are moving uncertainly, they are still moving. Says Peter Torres Jr., 36, an activist lawyer in San Antonio: "Many Mexican-Americans believe you can't fight City Hall. You don't question the patrón. You don't question police brutality. I grew up in a poor section of west San Antonio and I saw people beaten in the streets. If you were poor, you said '*Que puede hacer uno?*'—What can one do? Well, the young people today aren't going to play patsy for the establishment. There's an awareness of something among the young people that is either going to make this country and take us on to greater glories—or destroy us." Con safos.

We offer a portion of the transcript of Case No. 40331 of the Superior Court of the State of California in and for the county of Santa Clara, September 2, 1969, 10:25 a.m.

3.8
Statements of the Court

IN THE SUPERIOR COURT OF THE STATE OF CALIFORNIA IN AND FOR THE COUNTY OF SANTA CLARA

JUVENILE DIVISION

HONORABLE GERALD S. CHARGIN,
Judge   Courtroom No. 1

———

In the Matter of

PAUL PETE CASILLAS, JR.,

a minor.

No. 40331

———

STATEMENTS OF THE COURT

San Jose, California
                    September 2, 1969

———

APPEARANCES:

For the Minor:
          FRED LUCERO, ESQ.
          Deputy Public Defender
For the Probation Department:
          WILLIAM TAPOGNA, ESQ.
          Court Probation Officer
Official Court Reporter:
          SUSAN K. STRAHM, C.S.R.

THE COURT: There is some indication that you more or less didn't think that it was against the law or was improper. Haven't you had any moral training? Have you and your family gone to church?
          THE MINOR: Yes, sir.
          THE COURT: Don't you know that things like this are terribly wrong? This is one of the worst crimes that a person can commit. I just get so disgusted that I just figure what is the use? You are just an animal. You are lower than an animal. Even animals don't do that. You are pretty low.

I don't know why your parents haven't been able to teach you anything or train you. Mexican people, after 13 years of age, it's perfectly all right to go out and act like an animal. It's not even right to do that to a stranger, let alone a member of your own family. I don't have much hope for you. You will probably end up in State's Prison before you are 25, and that's where you belong, any how. here is nothing much you can do.

I think you haven't got any moral principles. You won't acquire anything. Your parents won't teach you what is right or wrong and won't watch out.

Apparently, your sister is pregnant; is that right?
          THE MINOR'S FATHER, MR. CASILLAS: Yes.

THE COURT: It's a fine situation. How old is she?
          THE MINOR'S MOTHER, MRS. CASILLAS: Fifteen.
          THE COURT: Well, probably she will have a half a dozen children and three or four marriages before she is 18.

The County will have to take care of you. You are no particular good to anybody. We ought to send you out of the country—send you back to Mexico. You belong in prison for the rest of your life for doing things of this kind. You ought to commit suicide. That's what I think of people of this kind. You are lower than animals and haven't the right to live in organized society—just miserable, lousy, rotten people.

There is nothing we can do with you. You expect the County to take care of you. Maybe Hitler was right. The animals in our society probably ought to be destroyed because they have no right to live among human beings. If you refuse to act like a human being, then, you don't belong among the society of human beings.
          MR. LUCERO: Your Honor, I don't think I can sit here and listen to that sort of thing.
          THE COURT: You are going to have to listen to it because I consider this a very vulgar, rotten human being.
          MR. LUCERO: The Court is indicting the whole Mexican group.
          THE COURT: When they are 10 or 12 years of age, going out and having intercourse with anybody without any moral training —they don't even understand the Ten Commandments. That's all. Apparently, they don't want to.

So if you want to act like that, the County has a system of taking care of them. They don't care about that. They have no personal self-respect.
          MR. LUCERO: The Court ought to look at this youngster and deal with this youngster's case.
          THE COURT: All right. That's what I am going to do. The family should be able to control this boy and the young girl.
          MR. LUCERO: What appalls me is that the Court is saying that Hitler was right in genocide.
          THE COURT: What are we going to do with the mad dogs of our society? Either we have to kill them or send them to an institution or place them out of the hands of good people because that's the theory—one of the theories of punishment is if they get to the position that they want to

act like mad dogs, then, we have to separate them from our society.

Well, I will go along with the recommendation. You will learn in time or else you will have to pay for the penalty with the law because the law grinds slowly but exceedingly well. If you are going to be a law violator—you have to make up your mind whether you are going to observe the law or not. If you can't observe the law, then, you have to be put away.

———

3.9
Chale con el Draft!

Rosalio Munoz

Today, the sixteenth of September, the day of independence for all Mexican peoples, I declare my independence of the Selective Service System.

I accuse the government of the United States of America of genocide against the Mexican people. Specifically, I accuse the draft, the entire social, political, and economic system of the United States of America, of creating a funnel which shoots Mexican youth into Vietnam to be killed and to kill innocent men, women and children.

I accuse the education system of the United States of breaking down the family structure of the Mexican people. Robbing us of our language and culture has torn the youth away from our fathers, mothers, grandfathers and grandmothers. Thus, it is that I accuse the educational system of uneducating Chicano youth. Generally, we are ineligible for higher education, and thus are ineligible for higher education, and thus are ineligible for the draft deferments which other college age youth take for granted, which is genocide.

I accuse the American welfare system of taking the self-respect from our Mexican families, forcing our youth to see the army as a better alternative to living in our community than with their own families, which is genocide.

I accuse the law enforcement agencies of the United States of instilling greater fear and insecurity in the Mexican youth than the Viet Cong could ever, which is genocide.

I accuse the United States Congress and the Selective Service System which they have created, of recognizing these weaknesses they have imposed on the Chicano community, and of drafting their laws so that many more Chicanos are sent to Vietnam, in proportion to the total population, than they sent any of their own white youth.

I accuse the entire American social and economic system of taking advantage of the machismo of the Mexican-American male, widowing and orphaning the mothers, wives and children of the Mexican-American community, sending the Mexican men onto the front lines, where their machismo has given them more congressional medals, purple hearts, and many times more deaths and casualties than any of the other racial or ethnic groups in the nation, which is genocide.

I accuse the legislature of the United States of gerimandering the Mexican people out of their proper representation in the political system.

I have my induction papers, but I will not respect them UNTIL the government and the people of the United States begin to use the machismo of the Mexican male and the passion and suffering of the Mexican female to the benefit of themselves and of their own heritage, deferring all Chicano youth who serve our people, and providing the money and support that would make such work meaningful in social, political and economic terms.

I will not respect the papers UNTIL the United States government and people can provide the

funds and the willingness to improve the educational system so that all Mexican youth, the intelligent, the mediocre, and the tapados, just like the white youth, the intelligent, the mediocre, and the tapados, have the opportunity to go to college and get deferments.

I will not respect the papers UNTIL the welfare and other community agencies of the United States foster and allow for self-respect in the Mexican-American community so that our youth can stay home and be men amongst our own families and friends.

I will not respect the papers UNTIL the systematic harassment of the law enforcement agencies has ended, and these agencies begin truly to protect and serve the

Mexican-American community as well.

I will not respect the papers UNTIL the legislatures of the United States discontinue gerimandering the Mexican-American people out of their representation in the political system.

I will not respect the papers UNTIL the Armed Forces, the largest domestic consumer of California table grapes, recognizes the United Farm Workers' Organizing Committee. Until that time, I cannot recognize the Armed Forces, or any of its political uses of the American people. Until they begin to boycott the sellers and growers of California table grapes, I must boycott them.

CHALE CON EL DRAFT!

Asian-American Consciousness

3.10
Making It

Toshio Oshita

Today the Asians who feel they have made it in society continue to prove and over-prove themselves by behaving ultra-American. This has aptly been called 200 per cent Americanism. What is most striking is the overwhelming majority of Japanese-Americans who gain a false sense of security from their mortgaged material possessions.

Money in a capitalistic system is thought to be the great equalizer. Thus, it is not too uncommon to find Asians with middle and upper class living standards identifying more with the White oppressors (the winners) than with those of their own color who have

By permission of the author.

not "made it." Recently, I had the opportunity to ask members of the Freedom Troupe (a group of young Black performers who advocate social change through understanding) how Blacks viewed the Japanese-American people and community. At first they said they knew very little. This in itself said much, for the Japanese community has existed in its present San Francisco site since 1906, and has always been a significant minority. For these young San Francisco Blacks, many of whom were raised in the same Western Addition district, to say they knew nothing simply mirrored the apathy of the Japanese people. Finally, after some discussion the director of the group rose and said, "As long as I can remember, the Japanese-Americans have always sided with the winners." By this, he meant the Whites.

This false sense of security

which makes the affluent Asians side with the winners is also the reason why Asians have long been placed by the MAN on a pedestal among the people of color. We Asians have been held above other people of color as the ideal minority. Surprisingly, many Asians believe this.

Asians are stereotyped as being hard-working, industrious, quiet people who don't complain because "they know their place." Little do many of us realize that these "good" qualities which the

MAN attributes to us were the very same ones he condemned us for in the early periods of Asian settlement in the United States, and even more so during World War II. Recall if you will the sneaky, ruthless, stab-you-in-the-back JAP. There is obviously a very thin and very permeable line separating "ideal" qualities from those that would liken the Japanese-Americans (and other Asians as well, for Whites do not normally differentiate nationalities) to the scum of the universe.

What is even more surprising is the apathy found in those Asians of lower socio-economic status. Here I would use the term fear instead of apathy, for there is an intense suppressed fear of the awesome power of the White power structure. A while back I spoke with an Issei (elderly Japanese) lady about advocating social change. She answered (translated and paraphrased): "It is the people on top with all the money who create wars and exploit poor people to make more money. It is

The following document is an item in the historical development of racism in America. Published in *Life* Magazine in 1941, it contributed to a climate of opinion which permitted the U.S. government to imprison thousands of Japanese-Americans in concentration camps during World War II. This hysterical abridgement of basic freedoms was carried off without any substantial reaction from civil libertarians.

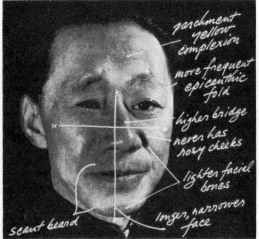

Chinese public servant, Ong Wen-hao, is representative of North Chinese anthropological group with long, fine-boned face and scant beard. Epicanthic fold of skin above eyelid is found in 85% of Chinese. Southern Chinese have round, broad faces, not as massively boned as the Japanese. Except that their skin is darker, this description fits Filipinos who are often mistaken for Japs. Chinese sometimes pass for Europeans; but Japs more often approach Western types.

Japanese warrior, General Hideki Tojo, current Premier, is a Samurai, closer to type of humble Jap than highbred relatives of Imperial Household. Typical are his heavy beard, massive cheek and jaw bones. Peasant Jap is squat Mongoloid, with flat, blob nose. An often sounder clue is facial expression, shaped by cultural, not anthropological, factors. Chinese wear rational calm of tolerant realists. Japs, like General Tojo, show humorless intensity of ruthless mystics.

HOW TO TELL JAPS FROM THE CHINESE

ANGRY CITIZENS VICTIMIZE ALLIES WITH EMOTIONAL OUTBURST AT ENEMY

In the first discharge of emotions touched off by the Japanese assaults on their nation, U. S. citizens have been demonstrating a distressing ignorance on the delicate question of how to tell a Chinese from a Jap. Innocent victims in cities all over the country are many of the 75,000 U. S. Chinese, whose homeland is our stanch ally. So serious were the consequences threatened, that the Chinese consulates last week prepared to tag their nationals with identification buttons. To dispel some of this confusion, LIFE here adduces a rule-of-thumb from the anthropometric conformations that distinguish friendly Chinese from enemy alien Japs.

To physical anthropologists, devoted debunkers of race myths, the difference between Chinese and Japs is measurable in millimeters. Both are related to the Eskimo and North American Indian. The modern Jap is the descendant of Mongoloids who invaded the Japanese archipelago back in the mists of prehistory, and of the native aborigines who possessed the islands before them. Physical anthropology, in consequence, finds Japs and Chinese as closely related as Germans and English. It can, however, set apart the special types of each national group.

The typical Northern Chinese, represented by Ong Wen-hao, Chungking's Minister of Economic Affairs (*left, above*), is relatively tall and slenderly built. His complexion is parchment yellow, his face long and delicately boned, his nose more finely bridged. Representative of the Japanese people as a whole is Premier and General Hideki Tojo (*left, below*), who betrays aboriginal antecedents in a squat, long-torsoed build, a broader, more massively boned head and face, flat, often pug, nose, yellow-ocher skin and heavier beard. From this average type, aristocratic Japs, who claim kinship to the Imperial Household, diverge sharply. They are proud to approximate the patrician lines of the Northern Chinese.

Chinese journalist, Joe Chiang, found it necessary to advertise his nationality to gain admittance to White House press conference. Under Immigration Act of 1924, Japs and Chinese, as members of the "yellow race," are barred from immigration and naturalization.

Tall Chinese brothers, full length, show lanky, lithe build of northern anthropological group that has suffered most in China's recent history from flood, famine and war with Japs. Average height of Northern Chinese is 5 ft. 7 in., sometimes exceeds 6 ft. Most Chinese in America come from southern and coastal cities, Canton and Shanghai. They are shorter than Northern Chinese, but retain the slight proportions of the young men shown here. When middle-aged and fat, they look more like Japs.

Short Japanese admirals, full length, exhibit the squat, solid, long torso and short stocky legs of the most numerous Japanese anthropological group. Since Navy is relatively new and junior service, Jap naval officer corps numbers fewer Samurai, has more of the round-faced, flat-nosed peasant type. Over 6 ft. tall, Admiral Nomura shows traits of the big, fair-skinned hairy Ainu, aborigines who still live on reservations in Northern Japan. Special Emissary Kurusu, also atypical, looks European.

FROM "HOW TO TELL JAPS FROM CHINESE," *LIFE* MAGAZINE, DECEMBER 22, 1941, © TIME INC.

useless for us to try to do anything because they would only eliminate us." She had used the death of the student demonstrators and her own World War II incarceration as examples of eliminating agitation.

What we as Asians must realize is that we have not made it nor will we or any people of color ever make it as long as all the wealth and power are on top. Think! Eight per cent of this nation's population controls over 50 per cent of the wealth, and the other half indirectly. We must realize there is institutionalized in the American way of life a racist doctrine which has and will continue to function to oppress all people of color. Because of this, change will never be instigated by those who profit from the perpetuation of the system. Asian people must come off their lowly pedestals and work collectively towards social change. If you still feel we Asians have made it, remember, "Those who make peaceful change impossible make violence inevitable."

3.11
The Need for a United Asian-American Front

Alex Hing

The most politically aware of the Asians in America are usually those who have reached a high level of assimilation into the White Mother Country's culture. This is because of two reasons: 1) The frustrations which Asian-Americans encounter while trying to assimilate have educated them on the impossibility of attaining entry into the so-called "American main-stream" because of the racism inherent in this society. 2) The most assimilated of the Asians in America are usually native born citizens and, as such, they cannot be deported by the immigration authorities for political reasons.

On the other hand, the large masses of Asians in America are totally unassimilated into American culture. 70% of the population of San Francisco's Chinatown can speak no English, with the majority of its inhabitants being recent

Reprinted by permission from *AION*, Spring, 1970, pp. 9–11.

immigrants from Hong Kong and Formosa. These people are the most exploited and most oppressed segment of the Asians in America. These are the workers who earn as little as 70¢ an hour toiling 12 hours a day, 6 days a week. These are the families who are crammed into one or two room apartments with kitchen and toilet facilities shared with the other occupants of their building. These are the people with the highest suicide and tuberculosis rates in the nation. These are the people who take all of this shit without one cry of outrage so that their children can go to college and be successful in business.

Most of the politically aware Asians are students who are undergoing identity crises. They realize that they cannot fit into White society, yet at the same time they are also rebelling against the strict, Confucian ideas instilled into them by their parents. The contradiction caused by trying to assimilate into two cultures at one time can be resolved not by rejecting one and assimilating more into the other, but by rejecting the bad elements in both cultures and building a revolutionary culture from the best elements of both.

It has become apparent, however, that the so-called "American culture" is so decadent that it is totally beyond salvation. It has the blood of the Third World and the now more recent blood of the Mother Country's own young on her hands. We must become Asians and we should be clear on exactly what that means. First of all, Asians have the longest unbroken civilization in history. Secondly, Asia is the vanguard of the Third World Liberation Struggle against Yankee Imperialism.

The situation in the Asian communities is so deplorable that a Marxist-Leninist Party must begin to take firm root among the people. It is necessary that this party does not alienate the people or create any factions among the budding Asian-American Movement as we do not even make up 1% of the total population of America. The purpose of this party is to educate the people on the fact that the Asian communities in America are included in the genocidal American foreign policy in Asia. If America ever enters into a war with China, the Asians in America will pay the price in blood.

In respect to the Chinese community in San Francisco, there is an apparent contradiction between organizing a Marxist-Leninist Party in an area where the population consists of refugees from a Socialist Revolution. This contradiction will resolve itself as the people realize that the desperate imperialist policies of the United States in Asia are reflected by the ever-increasing fascism at home.

The universities must be made to respond to the needs of the community. Therefore, Asian Studies programs are necessary. Also, the campuses provide a mass base for organizing Asians to fight imperialism. But students should realize that their knowledge must be used as a weapon for the masses to wield in their struggle for liberation—that their knowledge is genuine only if it is put into practice in order to serve the people. There has been very little research on the power structures of the Asian communities, particularly in Chinatown. This research is best handled by students and should be made available for mass distribution.

Also, as Asians, we must become more sensitive to our environment. We must realize that the affluency of American society is nothing but a joy ride on nature, and that within thirty years, unless we are able to sanely control our environment, ecological disaster will occur. Given expert ecological data on the amount of time we, as human beings, have left to save our environment from total collapse, we must realize the urgency of our task and begin to work much harder.

Because of the San Francisco Bay Area's political climate and because San Francisco's Chinatown is the largest Asian community outside of Asia, the Bay Area is the most logical place for a massive Asian-American Movement to begin. In fact, the Bay Area has already made steps in that direction with the formation of the Asian-American Political Alliance (AAPA), the Inter-Collegiate Chinese for Social Action (ICSA), the Filipino-American Collegiate Endeavor (PACE) and the Red Guard. There are also a few Asian-Americans in the Bay Area with a revolutionary perspective who do not belong to any organized group. It is extremely important that these diverse elements of political Asians in America come together to fight our common oppressor.

In other words, a United Front of Asians in America must be formed to combat fascism and imperalism. This United Front must be led by Marxists-Leninists and develop into a strong organization which serves the Asian people. The United Front should bring forth a program which relates to the needs of Asians in America and not become issue oriented. The United Front should not rely on demonstration-type, symbolic confrontations but build mass support through hard, thorough work among the people, which is not as glamorous as demonstrating but a lot more rewarding in terms of building a revolution.

Communications must develop on two levels. We must build an efficient communications system among the various Asian groups and we must have a smooth flow of information between the masses and the Asian-American Movement. One possible way to further develop communications would be to combine our efforts into producing one community oriented newspaper. This would also avoid duplication of labor and conserve our resources which are scarce. We must also begin to learn our native tongues and put our knowledge of them into practice in the community.

The main emphasis of all Asian-American political groups must be intensive political education. The lack of such an education is, unfortunately, characteristic of the whole Asian-American Movement. Without painstaking study we will not be able to properly analyze our situation and develop the proper strategy and tactics for it. Without political education, a general political line for the Asian-American Movement will not be developed; and as a result, factionalism will occur. We must all become teachers and pupils at the same time.

Every Asian in the Movement should also be educated on first-aid and self-defense—which includes fire arms handling and safety. Qualified teachers and materials are available providing each cadre is willing to accept the discipline of studying and attending classes. This knowledge is necessary for survival in America's urban environment.

A legal defense program must be set up in order to provide legal assistance for those of us who will be ripped off by the pigs. At this stage of American fascism it would be foolish for us to disregard this task. The Red Guards have experienced over thirty arrests since they began to organize a scant nine months ago. The legal defense program must include a bail fund, bail contacts,

legal defense fund and lawyer contacts.

In our relations with other groups, we must always make a class analysis to determine who are our friends and who are our enemies. It would be absurd to believe that Asians alone could seize state power in America. We must link up with the Third World and White revolutionaries throughout the country and establish international contacts, especially in Asia, with those who are struggling against Yankee Imperialism.

The time has come for us to break out of the stereotypes imposed upon us by the racists. We are not docile, complacent, obedient and self-sufficient Orientals. We are Asians, and as such, identify ourselves with the baddest motherfuckers alive. We can no longer be a witness to the daily slaughter of our people in Asia nor to the oppression of the Asians here in America and be afraid of death or prison. We must fight because that's what Asians are all about.

3.12
Encounter and the Marginal Man—A Search for Identity: The Psychological Aspects

Alan S. Wong

There is a dire need to look into the validity or obsolescence of theories about the "melting pot," the "marginal man," the impact of culture on personality, and the consequences of cultural contact between diverse populations. If some groups never truly integrate, the factors which hinder their absorption can be isolated and known.

The marginal man is the product of a dual set of social forces at work moulding his behavior, norms, values and traits—one set pertains to the ghetto, while the other belongs to the larger society. Associated with ghettos is the concept of marginality, compounded of feelings of frustration, anxiety, hostility, fear, insecurity and other distorted emotional, economic, social and intellectual reactions.

It is in this context that I wish to share my observations. Many of

By permission of the author.

us use the terms "Chinese-Americans or "American-Chinese." "Chinese-Americans" carries the connotation of the descendants of a racial and cultural group against whom prejudical and discriminatory acts have been directed. With this meaning the term "Chinese-Americans" is more commonly used, as they are considered Chinese before they are Americans. This expression implies that they are second-class Americans and do not enjoy fully the rights and privileges accorded by the society to its citizens.

The term "American-Chinese" is used by those who are more enlightened and are attempting to correct the distorted areas of social relations between ethnic and cultural groups. Fair treatment must apply to Americans of Chinese ancestry; they represent one aspect of the belief in cultural and racial pluralism. Unfortunately, they are seldom thought of as American per se, without reference to their antecedents, regardless of the number of generations they have lived with Americans.

It should be reiterated that the native-born of Chinese ancestry want to be called citizens and thought of as Americans rather than as "marginal" men and assigned a minority status. It cannot be denied that the subtle connotations underlying the two terms symbolize as well as contribute to the confusion the Americans of Chinese ancestry undergo when thinking of themselves. They are Americans like others born in similar circumstances, and they very much want to be integrated into the American society without reservations. Yet they are forced through various social contacts to be conscious of their different racial and cultural heritage.

The terms "Chinese-Americans" and "American-Chinese" influence the manner in which they play their roles and how they meet the expectations, demands and norms of two racially and culturally distinct groups: the Protestant-Caucasoid and the Chinese-Mongoloid. They cannot be totally Chinese, because over-manifestation of loyalty to the Chinese group inevitably leads to criticism and questions regarding their place in the American society. Then, if they reject Chinese culture and their racial group, the Chinese chastise them severely for not joining them in the struggle for the greater racial and social equality. They are forced to concede that the larger society has heaped various injustices upon the Chinese throughout the century of their settlement. Hence, they vacillate between two ways of life, two cultural heritages and two racial groups, each of which is diametrically opposed to the other.

The possession of distinctive racial features adds to their difficulties because these physical characteristics arouse the prejudices of the dominant society who thinks of and treats them as a group rather than as individuals. This difference invokes curiosity, often hostility, whenever a racial minority interacts with other groups. As race is an immutable fact, the dominant group utilizes it as a criterion for membership in social groups, occupational selection and mobility, marriage, educational opportunities, residence and the conferring or denial of rights and privileges. Problems related to these areas of life confront the American-Chinese as they seek accommodation to the multi-racial social situations in which they find themselves. In turn, their marginality is heightened, the fate of most marginal men.

Some "American-Chinese" are declaring rather badly that they should think of themselves as "Americans" only, since it is in this frame of mind that they will best integrate and succeed in the wider "American" community. This thinking implies that "American-Chinese" have no interests in and no knowledge of mainland China, Formosa, her culture, history, people, and customs. There is no desire or love for the "old" country, so to speak. All of us are "unembarrassed pseudo-orientals."

The question is raised, "Do we really have a double heritage to draw from?" Are we hanging on to a "floating" culture? What values do we keep and practice and which do we reject? These conflicts are caused largely by our own ambivalences by our constant battle to be loyal to a group and an attempt to seek individual fulfillment.

A large number of us are confronted with the reality that we will be unable to bring up our children either to speak or write the Chinese language, for so many of us are already ill-equipped to do so ourselves! Is all of Chinese culture that we are to pass on to our children the color of our skin, which they will not thank us for?

Is removing the psychological obstacle, our conception of ourselves as "Chinese" our solution? Will thinking of ourselves merely as "American" enable us to begin reaching for higher goals, and equip us for greater self-development and cause us to remove the self-erected barriers?

It is an erroneous assumption that we can consciously acquire some easily obtainable universal culture called "American." Ask, what is it to think like an "American-Italian-Japanese-Irish-Polish," and so on. It is foolish to tell a Negro to stop being a Negro and be an "American," as if he cannot be an "American" without rejecting himself. There is no average "American" standard of thought or pattern of culture, as there is likewise no "average" man commonly referred to in statistics. To graphically point this problem out, a recent news article stated that a legislator complained of the varied definitions of the word "American" in the dictionaries.

This nation is a single, unified, political and geographical entity; it is, however, inhabited by "Americans" who represent many and divergent nationalities, races, religions, and cultures. To become an "American" would mean assuming the characteristics of a cross-sectional composite of all said factors.

A large number of us are children of parents born over-seas. Psychology and sociology teaches us that we are all products of our environment. Thus, we are already inculcated with some degree of Chinese traditions, customs, mores, and culture. The attempt to repudiate our Chinese background is tantamount to denying the actuality and an escape from reality. It would be frustration to the individual who can never reject what he is.

The alleged purpose of the repudiation of the Chinese heritage is to secure "full citizenship." Is the prejudice for these individuals a "self-erected barrier"? Is it reasonable that those being discriminated against are themselves causing said prejudice by mere knowledge of the Chinese language and customs? I doubt that those who are prejudiced would stop their discriminatory practice merely because the "American-Chinese" unilaterally renounced the "Chinese" part of their dual heritage. Discriminatory practices will lessen as we enter more actively into the main-stream of society and in our own community.

From an affirmative standpoint, there are definite values in learning the Chinese language, customs knowing only English has no place in our rapidly dwindling world. Language deficiencies have been recognized nationally as the U.S. has shockingly few personnel who speak the native language of that nation which he is assigned to work with.

More important to us is the growing international focus in Asia and Russia in relationship to world affairs. It is a challenge to "American-Chinese" that we must be able to communicate and interpret for both the Western and Asiatic cultures.

Our culture speaks well of us in the area of juvenile delinquency and care of the aged. The close family ties and strict discipline exerted has served in curbing a higher rate of delinquency among our ethnic group. Filial piety expressed in respect for our elders resulted in our community in a concern for the care of the aged.

The richness of Chinese culture, philosophy, history, art and language should be studied, per se, as another form of knowledge. We decendents of the China-born parents have certainly more to pass on to our children than merely the color of our skin.

The Chinese cultural pattern is imperfect and stagnant if it is not innovated by today's "American-Chinese." All of us here are what sociology terms "marginal" people. We stand on a line between our ancestral culture and that of the country in which we live.

We "American-Chinese" have a political advantage. We have a duty and obligation to select the worthwhile aspects of our Chinese and Westernized American cultures to be passed on to our children. America's greatness has been the total contribution of each ethnic and national group of its finest cultural offerings into the "melting pot" of America.

A rejuvenation of Chinese culture can be made by us who, instead of binding together for mere security and social reasons, should try to build cultural bonds with the help of students from overseas. We should continue to hold conferences, seminars, such as you are doing, and participate together in cultural projects.

Above all, it is important that we individually define Chinese culture for ourselves. Be proud that we are "American-Chinese"!

Native-American Consciousness

. . . They have assumed the names and gestures of their enemies but have held onto their own, secret soul, and in this there is a resistance and an overcoming, a long outwaiting.

M. Scott Momaday
(From *House Made of Dawn*.)

3.13
Laws of the Lodge

Be hospitable. Be kind. Always assume that your guest is tired, cold, and hungry. If even a hungry dog enter your lodge, you must feed him.

Always give your guest the place of honour in the lodge, and at the feast, and serve him in reasonable ways. Never sit while your guest stands.

Go hungry rather than stint your guest. If he refuses certain food, say nothing; he may be under vow.

Protect your guest as one of the family; feed his horse, and beat your dogs if they harm his dog.

Do not trouble your guest with many questions about himself; he will tell you what he wishes you to know.

In another man's lodge, follow his customs, not your own.

Never worry your host with your troubles.

Always repay calls of courtesy; do not delay.

Give your host a little present on leaving; little presents are little courtesies and never give offence.

Say "Thank you" for every gift, however small.

Compliment your host, even if you must strain the facts to do so.

Never come between anyone and the fire.

Never walk between persons talking. Never interrupt persons talking.

In council, listen attentively to the other man's words as though they were words of wisdom, however much they may be otherwise.

Let not the young speak among those much older, unless asked.

When you address the council, carry a green bough in your hand, that yours may be living words.

Always give place to your seniors in entering or leaving the lodge. Never sit while your seniors stand.

Never force your conversation on anyone.

Speak softly, especially before your elders or in presence of strangers.

Do not touch live coals with a steel knife or any sharp steel.

Do not break a marrow bone in the lodge; it is unlucky.

The women of the lodge are the keepers of the fire, but the men should help with the heavier sticks.

When setting up the tepees, keep the camp circle with its opening to the east, the door of each tepee to the sunrise.

Let each tepee be in its place, as long ago appointed by the old men—the wise ones—the nigh kin near each other, and the clans of different totems facing across the circle. In this wise the young men shall see that they must marry across the circle of the camp, never with their close kin in the nearer tepees.

3.14
What Would Happen If the Moon Had People

OR "PROMISE THE MOON" AS WE DID THE INDIANS

Art Buchwald

The only one I know who isn't excited about the upcoming moonshot is an American Indian friend of mine who I'll call Joe.

Joe showed me a picture the other day of the plaque which the astronauts are going to leave on the moon which said, "We came in peace . . ."

"That," said Joe, "is what they said to us about 400 years ago. We've been taking it on the chin ever since."

"Things are different now, Joe. The space program is specifically designed for peaceful exploration."

"That's because they're certain no one is on the moon. I wonder what would happen if they knew there were tribes of Moon People?"

Joe continued: "If the treatment of the American Indian can be used as an example, this is what would happen:

"The first astronauts would land and express feelings of warmth and friendship for the Moon People. They probably would bring gifts with them to give to the Moon People, and the Moon People would give them gifts in exchange. The astronauts would ask permission to set up a base on the moon for scientific study, and since there were only three of them, the Moon People would agree. They would allot them several acres near the Sea of Tranquillity.

"With this base of operations more and more people would start coming to the moon—first scientists, then tourists, then businessmen looking for ore and oil. The Earth People would need more land and would start pushing out from the Sea of Tranquillity with housing and moon farms.

"The moon people would protest that they had only agreed to a small settlement on the Sea of Tranquillity and the Earth People were encroaching on their land.

"The Earth People would call for troops to protect them from the hostile Moon People, and the air cavalry would be sent up to the moon to protect the settlers.

"The Moon People would decide to push out the settlers, but due to lack of fighting equipment, they would be thrown back. Finally, a peace treaty would be signed with the Moon People promising them all the land beyond the Sea of Fertility, in exchange for letting the Earth People settle on the Sea of Tranquillity.

"But in 20 years, the Earth People would discover that there was water under the Sea of Fertility; so, despite the treaty, they would force the Moon People out of the Sea of Fertility. In exchange, the Earth People would give them all the lands facing the earth on the Sea of Crisis, for their sons and their sons and their sons for time immemorial.

"Then in a few years they would discover gold under the Sea of Crisis, and they'd send in the cavalry to move the Moon People who were left after the fighting was over to the Ocean of Storms. This would be given to them in perpetuity for as long as the moon revolved around the earth and the earth revolved around the sun.

"But then they'd discover natural gas in the Ocean of Storms, and they'd make all the Moon People pack up and move to the other side of the moon so the Earth People wouldn't have to look at their poverty."

"If what you say is true, Joe, we are indeed fortunate that there is no life on the moon," I said. "But I can't understand why you're so uptight about it."

"There's been some talk about taking over our reservation for a resort area, and the last rumor was that they're going to make it up to us by giving us the same amount of land on the moon."

REPRINTED COURTESY OF SAWYER PRESS, L.A., CALIF.

3.15
America's Colonial Service

David R. Maxey

We were poor conquerors. A more ruthless culture would have killed all the Indians, chivied them out of all their land, not just part of it, and assimilated any survivors into the dominant white bloodstream.

Instead, juggling our consciences and our urge to expand, we made deals. There are more than 2,000 regulations, 350 treaties, 5,000 statutes, 2,000 Federal-court decisions and 500 opinions of the Attorney General that apply to Indians. Every session of Congress considers more bills on Indian matters than on almost any other topic. And we have in the Department of the Interior our own brand of colonial service, the Bureau of Indian Affairs. The BIA employed some 15,000 people in 1969 and spent nearly $240 million. And the sum of it, all those deals, all those bills, all that money, is that we do not quite have a history-book Indian, interesting for his past, dead culture. We have only an angry, threatened species. And our guilt. The Bureau of Indian Affairs is 146 years old, and paternalism is its birthright. Quite literally, the BIA reaches into every segment of Indian life. Indian land is held in trust by the Secretary of the Interior, and Indians must clear with the Bureau before selling or leasing it. The few Indians who receive any amount of formal education do so mostly at BIA boarding schools, often far from home and family. The list of things done for and to Indians is endless.

In this age, when departments of Government regularly get criticism for being "slaves" to their constituencies (e.g., the Department of Agriculture has become the captive of the farmers), the problem at BIA is just the opposite. The Bureau pays lavish attention to the wishes of the House and Senate Interior committees, and relatively little to the voices of Indians that filter through the layers of BIA bureaucracy. And that is because there are few rewards for the bureaucrat who listens to Indians.

BIA's past unresponsiveness to Indian wishes tempts congressional liberals to try moving the Bureau out of the Interior Department on the argument that Interior is a land-and-resource department not interested in human beings, and that over half the BIA budget goes for education. Therefore, they reason, why not derrick BIA into the Department of Health, Education, and Welfare? Liberals charge the Interior Department with conflict of interest, notably in the matter of Indian legal services. Now, when a conflict over Indian land arises between the BIA and Interior's Bureau of Reclamation, the Interior Department's solicitor's office winds up representing both parties. And, critics charge, when the argument is between a pork-fat reclamation project and the land or water rights of Indians, the Indians lose. Just like in the movies.

But there is a picket line blocking the transfer of BIA. The Indians. The most obscene word you can say to an Indian leader is "termination," the name for the idea that the special relationship between Indians and the Federal Government should be snapped. This policy was last tried in the Eisenhower years under the leadership of Sen. Arthur Watkins of Utah. He used the rhetoric of "giving Indians first-class citizenship." Watkins hustled several relatively wealthy tribes onto the terminated list, which soon left them headed for the first-class citizenship of the white folks' welfare rolls.

Ever since, Indian groups have dug in their heels at suggestions that BIA should be moved or done away with. A classic love-hate relationship. A new berth at HEW, Indians say, would leave them scrambling for Federal money against politically more powerful blacks. The BIA's critics are sure the Bureau encourages those Indian worries. Sen. Walter Mondale: "I'm convinced the BIA scared the gizzard out of the Indian leadership with talk of termination."

Mondale points out that the Kennedy Subcommittee on Indian Education left out of its November, 1969, report the recommendation that BIA shift quarters to HEW. "We couldn't very well complain about BIA paternalism and then recommend ourselves something the Indians wouldn't agree to."

Enter the Nixon Administration. Secretary of the Interior Walter Hickel came out of Alaska nursing a low opinion of the BIA, based on his experiences with it while Governor. BIA Commissioner Robert Bennett resigned after being pushed, claiming that the Nixon Administration cared nothing for Indians. That set off a months' long search by Hickel for the Man Who: a) Was an Indian; b) Was qualified to be Commissioner; c) Was a Republican. Surfacing a Republican Indian was about as easy as bridling a unicorn, but Hickel overcame. He found Louis Rooks Bruce, Mohawk and Oglala Sioux, packing a GOP card in the wilds of Greenwich Village. Indian militants muttered

that Bruce was an Apple: red on the outside, white on the inside. But Bruce got the job.

Soon after Bruce became Commissioner, he, Hickel and Assistant Secretary for Public Land Management Harrison Loesch began to peck at the order of things in the BIA hierarchy. Proclaiming an Executive Realignment last January, they pushed 17 top executives out of their jobs, and replaced them with temporary men pulled in from BIA field offices.

Then they began a curious search for new men to man the BIA. They consulted earnestly with the National Congress of American Indians and other Indian groups, laying emphasis on finding Indians for many of the 17 jobs. Some Indians were already making too much money. Others, still tussling with their ambivalence about the BIA, listened to their friends say that working for the Bureau would be a sellout. Still others tired of waiting while the list of 17 was completed. The Moccasin Telegraph, BIA code for the Indian community's gossip mill, thrummed with rumors, criticisms and suggestions for job appointments. As this issue of *Look* went to press, Bureau spokesmen were saying that there would be seven, eight or nine Indians taking over high-level jobs at the BIA.

Well. More Indians, and all new men running the BIA. Will that make the Bureau more responsive to Indian desires and ambitions? Assistant Secretary Loesch, who says he is only a small-town Colorado lawyer, brought his horror of Big Government with him, and he knows better than to confuse reorganization with action. He is prepared to go further, notably in the direction of contracting services formerly performed by the BIA to the Indians themselves. A recent example of the contracting idea: the Navajo from Ramah, N.M., signed a $368,000, three-year contract with BIA to run their own high school. The money is equivalent to what the BIA has been spending to educate the 167 children from the Ramah area. The differences: The school will be Indian-controlled, and the children will not be scattered over three states at BIA boarding schools. Loesch thinks a great many Indian schools can be similarly treated.

Looking down the BIA's organizational ladder, Loesch can see the Bureau's Area Offices changing their role from Father in Residence to technical assistance

groups that help Indians do what Indians want.

Loesch also sees a good chance that BIA will get its own legal service, to tilt with the land- and water-consuming bureaus of the Interior Department. Secretary Hickel is reportedly committed to making the Bureau's head man Assistant Secretary of Indian and Insular Affairs, giving BIA more sinew to defend the Indian position.

But the best reason to believe that BIA will do better is the rise of Indian militancy. No more Uncle Tomahawk, to hear young Indians talk. Strangely, one BIA hand hears them. He sat in one of the cluttered old offices off the sallow hall in the BIA building and ruminated: "I just looked at a new school code one of the tribes drew up. *Sorry* goddamn thing, from a legal point of view, but it works better than the *Code Napoléon*. Because it's *theirs*, don't you see. . . . You know, if we don't talk about termination—and don't *do* termination, why they'll take the BIA away from us. They'll kick us out!" He looked as if he liked the idea.

3.16
America's Indians: Reawakening of a Conquered People

William Hedgepeth

A buzzard floated in the reservation's scorched air. "Know what I want to be?" asked 12-year-old Hector, looking up. "A bus driver. A Greyhound bus driver. So I could see everything. And go *reeel* fast." Behind stared gaunt cactuses and the adobe hut, decorated with plastic flowers, where he lived with his aunt. About an hour later, operating the trigger with his toe, muffling the noise with his mouth, little Hector quietly passed a load of buckshot through his head. Indian boys often pay the price of culture clash. They feel they are not "manly," either in relation to Indian traditions or the marketplace mentality of the Anglo world. Like their parents

Reprinted by permission from *Look* Magazine, June 2, 1970, p. 23. Copyright 1970 by Cowles Communications, Inc.

before them, they are publicly schooled to see themselves as a dirty, lazy subspecies, out of synch with the rest of the country, which officially conceives itself as a vast middle-class suburb. The crisis of Indian identity is shared by Anglos. The average white cherishes the thought of a taciturn race living in "poverty and pride" on wonderfully colorful reservations—yet remaining, essentially, a mass of social misfits, chiefly appreciated as wooden figures in front of cigar shops. Even those who have some level of concern view the Indians in terms of impoverished blacks and what-can-we-do-for-them-to-make-them-just-like-us. No one really knows what to do with the Indian people themselves. The Government has forever vacillated, with typical bureaucratic cretinism, between extermination and assimilation, each of which has amounted to the systematic eradication of Indian self-respect.

The relationship of Indians to the U.S. Government is that of a ward and an addlepated trustee who keeps repeating, in essence, "Live like we *expect* you to live, goddamnit!" Generally, those Indians who somehow refuse to succumb to benevolent white washing are expected to lie back silently on their reservations—prisoners of forgotten wars in the remnants of an old world—to witness the steady dissipation of their land and, whenever the spirit moves them (if not sooner), to manage somehow simply to fade away. But Indians—perceiving today a certain falling apart of our society— are becoming freshly attuned to their own culture and old sayings. The upshot is a wholly new thing: pan-Indian nationalism—the thinking of themselves as *Indians*, rather than as Sioux or Crow or Navajo. And with this new awareness has grown new militancy—a determination to judge life according to their own values, as well as to retain an Indian identity while participating in an industrial economy. All of this requires not merely new policies but a different ordering of reality in the matter of Indians vis-à-vis whites. Obviously, though, public compassion among politicians doesn't pay off right now, with the tenor of the times being what it is. An Administration that draws upon a sullen, silent majority for its moral inspiration can't possibly be expected to pay much mind to the most silent of minorities—as long as that minority remains silent.

But perceptions are changing. Stereotypes are fading into sepia. The reawakened Indian today is already a long, long way from the cigar store.

3.17
"Sometimes We Feel We're Already Dead"

Charles Mangel

We talk, and the anguish goes on. We spend half a billion dollars each year on "the Indian problem" (enough to give each Indian family in the land a direct income of $6,000), yet three times as many Indian infants as white still die, more than twice as many children still quit school convinced they— not we—are dumb, ten times as many adults can't find work.

We don't even know where they all are. The 745 Cocopah Indians in Southwestern Arizona were not "discovered" by the Bureau of Indian Affairs until two years ago (although Selective Service had found them for World War II and conflicts since). The Cocopah may be the poorest tribe in the nation. Most still live in the ancestral mud-and-twig huts. Floors are dirt. Tree branches serve as fuel. Diseases the white man licked a generation ago are uncontrolled. The Cocopah continue to die young.

No road exists to link them to anything. You drive along the dirt bank of an irrigation canal. (During one rainstorm, an expectant mother had to get out of the ambulance bringing her to the hospital and help push the vehicle out of the mud.) The canal itself, conduit for the valuable water flowing to farmers inland, is neatly cemented and fenced, sharp contrast to the shanties lining its side. The desert grit cuts your eyes and seeps into your mouth and nose even after the car windows roll shut. The kids wipe uselessly at running noses with their sleeves. (Without adequate shelter, clothing, diet or medicine, Indian children remain the number-one victims of the respiratory infections that other Americans no longer

consider dangerous.)

Jimmy Star lives in a hut 9 feet by 12 feet—about the size of a small rug—made of flattened cardboard cartons. The six-foot-high roof is cardboard, too, held down solely by two bald automobile tires. His income is $67 a month from welfare. The floor is the desert. He has no water, no toilet. A power line stands 50 feet from his paper door, but he doesn't have the $20 required to have it run to his home.

His neighbor, Bill Santez, is as desolate. Bill, 14, has just quit school. A quick boy with sensitive eyes, he could no longer accept the taunts of the white kids in Yuma, where he had attended public school. ("I don't drink. Why do they call me those names?") Abandoned by their parents, he and a brother a year younger, Bob, live with their grandmother. Bob has also quit school. ("Why stay there? I know a couple of Indians who went to college. They still can't get jobs.")

The nights are cold on the desert in the winter months, even in Arizona. Flames from a small fire in the center of the shack don't reach far. "We go to bed early," Bill says. "If you lay very still, it gets warm." Their house—mud and sticks on three sides and cardboard on the fourth—holds an old refrigerator. But it isn't used. "We just leave the food on the table," Bill explained. "It's cold enough."

Bill doesn't think he will go back to school. "They don't worry about us, just about the white ones. I asked a question one day. The teacher said, 'Stay in class and find out.' I told another teacher I was going to quit. He said, 'It's your own affair.'"

The two boys and their shrunken grandmother exist on an $85 monthly welfare check and the Federal Government's surplus-food program. Their diet is chiefly pinto beans, tortillas and potatoes. They rarely eat meat or fruit. I asked Bill about certain vegetables by name. He had not heard of half. "Don't you get tired of potatoes?" I asked. "Not as long as it fills my stomach." (Obesity is a major Indian problem, disguising malnutrition; the bulk of the Indian diet is starch.) A cough shook his body as he talked with me. He had had a cold for about four weeks. (With no exception, every one of the dozens of Cocopah children I found suffered from a respiratory illness; there is just no way it can be prevented.)

Two calendars from 1963 decorated the walls. A Bible lay on a bed. "It's my brother's," Bill said. "He really believes in it."

The Indian belief in the Christian God is visible in the small Cocopah cemetery. Most of the graves are marked with simple wooden crosses. (Eight have carved head-markers. They are for veterans of our wars; the Veterans Administration paid for the stones.) The average age of the men lying there was 36. A Cocopah woman, chairman of the small tribal council, walked with me and told me about some of the men: Robert San Raphael, 36. "He died in a car accident." John Flower, 31. "He was my uncle. He was drinking too much. He died from that, I guess." (The average American Indian dies at 44, 20 years before the rest of us. The major cause of death: accidents—usually car accidents, believed related to drinking—followed by flu and pneumonia.) Woodrow Porrell, 26. "He drowned when he fell in the irrigation canal. He was drunk. He was my father." Henry Flower, John's brother, 39. "He shot himself. I think he was just tired of living." The oldest man in the cemetery was 54.

If anything, the Cocopah far exceed most of the "average" Indians in miseries. Their unemployment is an incredible nine out of ten men. Welfare keeps them alive, with a family income of about $1,000. Among the adolescents, virtually everyone I met had quit school. They desperately seek release from boredom and poverty. Indians have the highest suicide rate in the nation. Two young Cocopah killed themselves the month before I arrived. One was 16, the other, 18. Both had left school years before.

Timidity clouds the Cocopah future. Penniless, disorganized, they are uncertain of their own direction or of where to turn for aid. The BIA, under new and tougher local leadership, is beginning to stir, but slowly. (Ten houses—abandoned when a Marine air base was closed—have been trucked in to one of the three different sites that comprise the Cocopah reservation.) The bedrock problems of schools and job training and employment remain untouched. Cocopah men and women, like Indians elsewhere, are slow to leave the reservations for jobs even if they have the skills and the perseverance to withstand employer prejudice (33 Indian men went to Yuma two years ago to enroll with the Federal employment office; not one has yet been offered a job). The public schools to which most Indian children today are assigned clearly are failing them (eight Indians from one local school attempted junior college in the past few years; none could handle it).

The reticent, quiet Indian is getting angry. "The white man likes to meet and talk about our problems," says Henry Montague, Sr., tribal chairman of the neighboring Quechan, a larger tribe that tries to help the Cocopah as well as itself. "They call us once a year and listen and then send us home until next year."

Montague, a handsome, articulate man, stalked out of a recent meeting called by a platoon of Government people. "We have a one-inch pipe that brings water into our reservation," Montague says. "At the end of the line, there just is no pressure. We have had to stand by helplessly while several houses there have burned."

The Quechan had been pushing for ten months to get a larger line installed. "At this meeting, the talk went around and around. I finally got up and said, 'You are wasting my time. All you want to do is pass the buck.'" The Quechan have been battling Federal authorities on the basics of land and water for more than a generation. The 95,000 acres granted them by Government treaty in 1883 shrank to 50,000 the following year and to the present 9,000 nine years later. (Of 138 million acres held by American Indians in 1887, only 55 million remain in their hands today. The Sioux lost the Black Hills in South Dakota, for example, soon after prospectors discovered gold there.) The 1893 land grab from the Quechan was simply handled. The Federal Government decided the land should be held by individual tribe members, rather than the tribe as a whole. Leaders refused. They were jailed, beaten—and gave in. In the process of transfer from tribal to individual ownership (ten acres for each tribe member), 41,000 acres somehow became transferred to Government control. The tribe has been trying since then to get 9,000 of those acres back.

Water, in the form of brimming irrigation canals, dissects the Quechan reservation. Yet the tribe cannot get more of it for itself. A carpet manufacturer, ready to employ 150 in a proposed plant on the reservation, had to be turned away because the Quechan could not promise the amount he needed. A private water supplier has a pipeline that has run through Quechan land for 40 years. He has no permission for a right-of-way and pays no fee. When the tribe's water pump broke down for two days last year, Montague had to get water from this man. The tribe paid $150.

Bill Santez passes the day playing mumblety-peg. He rarely lifts his eyes from his shoes. He will not go back to school, yet he has no plan of what he will do. He listens as a BIA man tells his grandmother that she will get a new house ("When?" she asks. "Maybe two years." "Oh, I die before then.") and then tells me, "Sometimes we feel we're already dead."

The young principal of one of the schools the Indian children attend whips off his coat and flops alongside me on a wooden chair. "These kids come to school at age five or six, and their eyes sparkle. About the sixth grade, the dullness begins to creep in, and I know we've lost them."

We are losing most of our American Indians. And the question, unanswered since they and we put down our weapons, remains: What are we going to do about it? We still have not decided. We talk.

3.18
The Invasion of Alcatraz

The Editors

Who needs it? This is the natural reaction of most people who view the bleak island of Alcatraz, which once housed the maximum security prison in San Francisco Bay. But on November 9, 1969, the Indians landed.

Led by Richard Oakes, a Mohawk, close to 100 Native-Americans laid claim to the island, demanding that the U.S. government turn it into a Native-American Cultural center. They offered to buy the island from the U.S. for $24 in glass beads and cloth, and, rubbing it in, told of a Bureau of Caucasian Affairs to make wards of any whites on the island. Conscious of the physical deterioration on Alcatraz, the Indians thought of it as comparable to the marginal land and poverty common to the reservations their people are forced to live on.

But the meaning of Alcatraz is more important as the opening round of new militancy and all-Indian consciousness among the 600,000 Native-Americans of the U.S. Oakes felt that it might also wake up the conscience of the white majority. The island is governed by a seven-man council known as the Indians of All Tribes. While the U.S. Interior department has stalled on responding to proposals specific to Alcatraz, the invasion has done more to publicize the plight of the Indian than any other event. Whether the unity of the hundreds of tribes will lead to effective political action remains to be seen. But no one remotely connected with Native-American affairs—and no Native-American will forget the invasion of Alcatraz.

3.19
Alcatraz Visions

Coyote 2

Coast Guard boats circling the
  island,
Navy helicopters hovering like
  vultures,
military American melting pot
with Liberty and Justice, they say,

> creatures of wonder are the
>   children
> as they run across the con-
>   crete fields,
> young eaglets of an Indian
>   tomorrow
> children of all tribes, here on
>   Alcatraz.

Government officials squirming,
red-eared at the sounds of a suck-
  ing child,
Alcatraz mother who must be
  there
for the words of her child's tomorrow.

> Boatload of new arrivals,
> Navajo, Sioux, Hoopa, Pomo,
> spirit, heart, eyes and feet
> testing the grounds of unity.

Reprinted from the Alcatraz Indians
of All Tribes Newsletter, *1, 2 (February, 1970). For information write
to 4339 California Street, San Francisco, California 94118.*

San Francisco so close to us,
vertical fabrications erase the
  rounded hills,
bright lights and sounds and
  smells of decay,
drift to this turtle island.

> Sunday sailboats clustered
>   close,
> snapping sails and wind and
>   voices,
> Tim studies this scene of
>   white gaiety
> and says, "Once, it was our
>   people our there."

A warship pushes swiftly by,
a jet screams in mechanical rage;
when dugout and birchbark
  canoes glide,
rage is not the call of snow birds.

> Steel bridges all around this
>   Bay,
> connecting land in bumper to
>   bumper pain,
> dreams of Alcatraz are of a
>   different bridge,
> fashioned of sunlight and
>   soft voices.

My father hunted the giant
  mammoth
and I am only five hundred years
  old,
who can still remember the blood
  of Montezuma
and the crying at Wounded Knee.

And I am only five hundred years
  old
who yesterday was herded on a
  Trail of Tears
and a hundred Sand Creek's flow
through veins my Indian heart
  feeds,

And I am only five hundred years
  old
and my dream is just now beginning,
as the drums of Alcatraz throb my
  spirit
and all the people do a round
  dance,

And our Earth Mother is in round
  dance
and all the stars circle our eagle
  dreams,
and the children of Alcatraz run
  and play
and glad I am to be a youth of
  only five hundred years.

3.20
A Native American's Reflections on Thanksgiving

James L. West

This morning, I have been asked to relate part of a worship service to you that took place last Wednesday at Plymouth Rock. This particular part of the service is very close to me for two reasons: The first one's pretty obvious—I happen to have given this particular part of the service on Wednesday. The second reason is obvious to some and not so much to others—for my part of the worship service was to represent my people, the American Indians, as they look at Thanksgiving—a tradition based on the beginning of the "great American dream."

The service is over and that moment is past. But, the purpose of that service is very meaningful for us as we begin the season of Advent, as we begin preparation for another great tradition in our lives: Christmas. You see, that worship service at Plymouth Rock was dedicating a "fast" for Thanksgiving. A fast in which people were asked to think about the tradition before them. The fast did not attempt to judge Thanksgiving in a personal way. I'm sure that each of us finds much strength in gathering with friends and loved ones in fellowship. Rather, people were asked to sacrifice this fellowship to look more closely at the tradition in which the fellowship is based. People were asked to really look at Thanksgiving; to look behind Thanksgiving to the mentality it represents and see what that tradition means in light of Vietnam, in light of blacks in the ghettoes of this country, in light of Mexican-Americans in California, in light of American Indians on the Reservations and in the red ghettoes of this country. What we learn from this past experience, still fresh in our minds, might help us to look forward to the coming season with new insight and understanding.

I must also admit a personal struggle to you. I struggle between two responsibilities this morning: A responsibility to you. As a spiritual leader of this congregation, I must seek to educate, to help and to learn from you as effectively and with as much compassion as I can. But, I also have a responsibility to my people: A responsibility to my tribe, the Cheyenne; a responsibility to my brothers in blood. This is a responsibility that I cannot help but deal with because it is a part of me. I want to use this struggle in my sermon by sharing some of that responsibility with you. I want you to hear me in a special way this morning. I want you to hear me in the same way I have had to hear you most of my life: as an Indian at-

By permission of the author and the
Andover Newton Quarterly *in which
the article will be reprinted.*

tempting to deal with the white viewpoint and way of life, I must ask you to accept the Indian point of view and attempt to deal with it, because I have no choice. As I face this last Thanksgiving and the many traditions that are a part of the American way of life, I face them the only way I can—as an American Indian.

Sermon by James West, delivered Sunday, November 30, 1969, at the First Church in Newton.

My people have grown weary of hearing the songs of Thanksgiving. My people have grown weary of looking back at that first winter when the white man came and singing songs of praise to a white man's God who has blessed the new experiment in the "bleak wilderness" where no man had set foot. My people have grown weary of a celebration that can speak over and over again of a great tradition and a great nation "born under God" for the good of all mankind; which can turn men's hearts and minds over years of building a Great American dream without turning their hearts and minds to the blood and death upon which that dream is built.

My people do not grow weary because we do not wish to share in a dream or because we do not wish to gather as families in thanks to God. We only grow weary of a celebration which not only excludes us, but which in fact attempts to emasculate us. Thanksgiving brings back many memories to us, also. But, memories of thanks and good will are not to be ours. Our memories are filled with blood and sickness and hate.

We remember very well that Masasoit helped to save those first white men by teaching them to survive in the wilderness they feared so much. But, we also remember that he could not teach them that their "red brothers" were more than animals. We remember that two generations later in King Philip's War, Masasoit's own people fought back at these white men who had no regard for our humanity or civilization.[1] We remember the Mohigans, a tribe whose territory included much of what is now eastern Massachusetts and who roamed in these woods long before any white man set his foot here. We remember

that the campaign of genocide was so complete and so careful that there is not a single Mohigan left to take part in this "great American dream." We remember this brother with pride and envy for he died an Indian and may now be better off than some of us.

Yes, the natives of this country remember the coming of the great American experiment. We remember the blankets deliberately filled with small pox and other diseases by the white man which killed first the children, then the women, and, finally the men whose preparation as proud warriors did not equip them for this first glimpse of biological warfare. What better way to wipe out large portions of Indian people than through the introduction of wretched diseases which spread the same death a bullet brought? The white man had discovered that many diseases which had plagued him for centuries were unknown in this country before his coming. He also discovered that this lack of contact with such diseases left the Native American with very little natural immunity. The distinguished British General, Jeffrey Amherst, of French and Indian War fame knew these same facts in his war with Pontiac, famous Ottawa war chief. During his campaign he wrote the following correspondence to one of his colonels in Pennsylvania, Henry Bouguet:

"Could it be contrieved to send the small pox among the disaffected tribes of Indians? We must on this occasion use every strategem in our power to reduce them." When Bouguet replied that he would try to follow the British general's advice, and added that he would even like to hunt "the Vermin" with dogs, Amherst wrote him again, "you will do well to try to inoculate the Indians by means of blankets, as well as to try every other method that can serve to extirpate this execrable race. I should be glad your scheme for hunting them down by dogs could take effect, but England is at too great a distance to think of that at present."[2]

We must assume that General Amherst was confident of the results this tactic would have on noncombatant as well as warriors.

My own people, the Cheyenne, remember the so-called battles, also, such as the Battle of Sand Creek. It took place on Sand Creek near Denver, Colorado, where Colonel Chivington and his men

arrived looking for a raiding war party of hostile Indians. This band of southern Cheyennes led by one of our more outstanding leaders, Black Kettle, happened to have made peace several weeks earlier. However, Chivington does not seem to have been concerned with what Indians had been raiding and for what reason or that this band of Cheyenne was not responsible for these raids. In the small hours of dawn 200 of our brothers and sisters were killed as the pony soldiers rode forth killing every man, woman and child that they could find. And they seem to have found more old men and women and children than warriors. This so-called battle is recorded as one among many which were "fought" against the "savages" who lived in the great wilderness that God was going to give to "his people."[3]

Thanksgiving—you ask for the Indian people to join in Thanksgiving? You ask my people to join hands on their reservations and in their ghettoes and sing praises to God for the founding and success of this great American dream? You ask me to share in the celebration of the death of my people!

It is not difficult to draw some very interesting parallels between the development of the "great American dream" on this continent and this same dream's development in Latin America or in Vietnam. Look at Guatemala or a half dozen other countries in Latin America. Who has taken the land in these countries? Where does the capital from the sweat of these natives go? It is not hard for the Indian to understand, as we look from the reservation and the ghetto and see the ties form between these governments and Washington, D.C., much as some of our people must relate to Washington through the Bureau of Indian Affairs.

It is not difficult for the Indian to understand the trial of a white soldier who has allegedly killed 109 Vietnamese as if they were stock in a slaughterhouse. It is not difficult for the Indian, who has been called "savage," "beast," and "barbarian" to understand how the title of "communist," "pinko," or "red"—"red," mind you—supplies the fear that is necessary for the American people to condone genocide and dehumanization for the protection of that great Ameri-

[1] Alden T. Vaughan, *New England Frontier: Puritans and Indians, 1620–1675* (Boston: Little, Brown and Company, 1965); S. C. Bartlett, *Sketches of the Missions of the American Board* (Boston: Published by the Board, 1964), p. 176.

[2] Alvin M. Josephy, Jr., *The Patriot Chiefs: A Chronicle of American Indian* (U.S.A.: The Colonial Press, 1961), pp. 122–123.

[3] Stan Hoig, *The Sand Creek Massacre* (Norman: University of Oklahoma Press, 1961); Donald J. Berthrong, *The Southern Cheyennes* (Norman: University of Oklahoma Press, 1963), pp. 195–223.

can dream. And through this fear not only support this effort, but rationalize these human beings right out of their minds, just as they have rationalized the American Indian out of their history and their conscience.

There is a voice crying in the wilderness! Not the wilderness you tamed and civilized, but a wilderness you created! Your genocide was not successful in America; and even though you have isolated us as far from your life as you physically can, we have watched white society in America and we have heard the echoes of our own cries as they come from black ghettoes, from California, from Latin America, from Vietnam. Yes, the Indian people are watching and they are listening, but luckily, from a distance. Our existence on reservations and in ghettoes which are far from the mainstream of American society has helped us remain a people—a part of America, yet so separated that we still possess much of our own culture. Not so separated, however, that we feel no kinship with those people who are brothers in oppression.

There is a voice crying in the wilderness, but it is no longer crying for pity: not for blankets, not for land, not for a poverty existence from the charity of the Bureau of Indian Affairs. No, it's a war cry of a people who will not become "white-washed" so that they can be acceptable in your sight. It's a war cry that is growing stronger as our people realize that the meaning that has gone from our lives won't come back to us as whites. It is a war cry against the average life expectancy of 44 years, against the suicide rate of teenagers on reservations that is three times that of teenagers in general, against the alcoholism rate, against the arrest rate, against all the ills that won't be cured by the soothing medicine of self-pity and acceptance as whites in a white world.[4] It's a war cry of a people who seek their humanity, the right to be human beings, and who must have that humanity as whole persons—whole persons who are *Indian*.

We must all realize that the great blot of oppression on my people is worse today than it was yesterday. Yesterday, my people

REPRINTED COURTESY OF SAWYER PRESS, L.A., CALIF.

were a proud people, a people who could share what we were or fight for what we were. In those days, when you considered us far worse off in all our barbaric heathenism, we were a whole people, proud and free! Yesterday, there might have been much we could have learned, but there might have been much that we could have taught you about life. For instance, we could have taught you that all life was so dear that when a hunter killed an animal he prayed a prayer of forgiveness and thanks that the animal had given of himself to feed the empty stomaches of Cheyenne people. Or we could have taught you of a man's social commitment to his community that was so strong and real that when he became too old to contribute to his community, he would sing his death song and die rather than be a burden to his people. Yes, we were a whole people that could have contributed much, but because we were red, because we were different, and because we would not become white, you attempted to destroy us!

So, listen, listen well! The Afro-Americans of this country have tried to teach us much in the last few years. I am not sure some of

us have learned much in these years, but the test is coming. The Indian people are gathering to test our learning, and along with our brothers in oppression we are prepared to give refresher courses in human rights to those who have not learned well. I hope you have learned. I hope you have learned that people cannot ask politely for their own human rights any more. I hope you have learned that people who are different still hold the rights of whole personhood. I hope you have learned that whole persons are not necessarily white persons.

Finally, I hope you have learned that you did not and cannot destroy us, although you have tried through attempted genocide and now through the attempted emasculation of the very Indianness which makes us whole. This attempted process of emasculation is very real today as our ceremonies become "circus acts" in your eyes and our people "freaks." My people often "prostitute" themselves for charity and "handouts" to relieve them from the abject poverty you subject them to. Without our identity as a people and isolated from the mainstream of American life, we might have had very little today in

[4] Peter Collier, "The Red Man's Burden," *Ramparts*, vol. 8, no. 8 (February, 1970); "The Angry American Indian: Starting Down the Protest Trail," *Time*, vol. 95, no. 6 (February, 9, 1970), pp. 14–20.

which we could find meaning. But, we are a *people!* We are the Cheyenne, the Kiowa, the Sioux, the Iroquois, the Seneca, · the Yakima, the Klamath, the Navajo, the Pueblo, the Chickasaw, the Seminole! We are Indian and it is in our Indianness that we must still find the meaning that gives us our rights as human beings; the meaning that gives us the courage to raise our war cry against the establishments that seek to destroy us as a whole people! Whether that war cry leads to another Watts, another Detroit, or another Vietnam, or whether that war cry leads to understanding, and acceptance,

and responsibility is up to white America.

Thus, I offer this lesson from our common past. This lesson concerns a tradition called Thanksgiving and its meaning. This lesson presents an underlying hope that as we prepare for this tradition each year, we will open our minds anew and not be unconscious of those around us who are a part of this tradition and yet so separated from it. May our minds move behind the tradition to a gracious God who has so much to give to white Americans, to Afro-Americans, to Vietnamese, to Mexican-Americans and to Native Americans.

White Unconsciousness

3.21

It's Either Brain Damage or No Father

THE FALSE ISSUE OF DEFICIT VS. DIFFERENCE MODELS OF AFRO-AMERICAN BEHAVIOR

Charles A. Valentine

Theory and Current Research

Apparent themes of this symposium include the argument that a psychological deficit model or normative approach to Afro-Americans rules educational theory and practice, perpetuating both scientifically untenable beliefs and destructive institutional policies. Against this is placed the contention that a cultural-difference model or relativistic anthropological approach, presently absent from the educational scene, should be fostered because it is scientifically more adequate and will produce more constructive results, especially for Afro-American children.

My own somewhat different view of these problems is derived

By permission of the author. An adaptation of this article appears in *Harvard Educational Review*, May, 1971.

in part from a current ethnographic study of poverty and Afro-American subcultures in a large northern city. This ongoing research, which has been in progress for nearly fourteen months, is being carried out by a family team consisting of myself, my wife, and our two-year-old son (Valentine and Valentine, 1970a, 1970b).[1]

My thesis is threefold: (1) both the deficit model and the difference formulation are already well established in ghetto educational theory and practice; (2) both models are in serious need of scientific revision; and (3) both are extremely pernicious as presently applied. Moreover, we are convinced that these same models are producing equally destructive results through the ghetto interventions of other mainstream institutions controlled by dominant social strata. Preeminent among these institutions are psychiatric clinics and hospitals. In all probability, however, the deficit and difference formulas are projected

[1] This research has been supported in part by P.H.S. research grant MH 16866-01 from a division of the National Institute of Mental Health.

upon Afro-Americans by all major institutions of the wider society from the mass media to official anti-poverty programs. In other words, both models really belong to certain aspects of mainstream culture which impinge most directly on Afro-American ghetto communities.

Anthropological training and experience, plus more than a passing acquaintance with the psychological and sociological literature on Afro-Americans, convince us that the deficit theory is largely undemonstrated. Any theory of class or racial deficits of biological origin is quite undemonstrable— indeed scientifically untestable— in an ethnically plural and structurally discriminatory society. The necessary separation of biological and socio-cultural factors is methodologically impossible in this setting. Writings which put forward biochemical genetic determination, or social selection in the evolutionary sense, as explanations for group differences in behavior must therefore be dismissed as psuedo-scientific nonsense.

On the other hand, environmentally imposed and biologically mediated group deficits can probably be demonstrated. Life in Black communities today (and no doubt among poor non-Blacks as well) presents one with much evidence that poverty and ghettoization subject the human organism to repeated biological assaults such as malnutrition, poisoning, and physical traumas from intrauterine life until death. These phenomena are structured by the social class system, but there is probably no social category which suffers more from them than Afro-Americans except perhaps American Indians. Long-term immersion in ghetto conditions leaves one vastly impressed with the amount of organic punishment human beings can absorb without crippling impairment.

The area in which the clearest choice can be made between deficit and difference formulations is the realm of cultural differences, researched by anthropologists and linguists and emphasized in this symposium. It is both untenable and unjust to characterize Afro-American culture patterns as merely deficient or pathological versions of mainstream American culture. Indeed, systematic research guided by hypotheses derived in part from a cultural-difference model may reveal unexpectedly rich ethnic variation. Our current field work in a single urban community has so far pro-

foster family, other local relatives, playmates, and additional neighborhood associates. (2) Weekly or more frequent visits with the patient during a recent psychiatric hospitalization of three and a half months, including observation of most of his daily activities in the hospital. (3) A very full week of interviews and observations in the region of the patient's birth, including intensive contact with all ten of his most significant surviving relatives, all members of his former foster family, all fourteen medical, welfare, law-enforcement, and correctional professionals who had important contact with the patient or his close relatives. At this time we also collected full medical, legal, police, and newspaper records from all sources known to be relevant. (4) Later we were also granted access to the records of the case in two Northern hospitals where the youngster became a psychiatric patient.

The findings from the retrospective evidence can be summarized briefly. All medical and family history data indicate a normal pregnancy and birth, followed by an organically normal early childhood: no serious fevers, no bad falls, no unconsciousness or other obviously pathogenic effects from the physical traumas which it will become clear the boy did receive. With one exception, no other member of the extended family has ever received psychiatric diagnosis or treatment. The exception is the patient's father who experienced a brief psychotic break several months after having been imprisoned for murdering the patient's mother. By the time we talked with this man in May, 1969, he had been returned to the prison as normal, and our impressions accorded with this evaluation.

The boy's early childhood was dominated by an extremely hostile and punitive father and a very passive, indulgent mother. During this period the patient also spent much time in the poor but stable, warm, strict household of his maternal grandparents, spending many long visits there with his mother and his siblings. One of the father's chief impositions, evidentally based on intense sexual jealousy, was to keep his wife and children isolated from all other social contacts. Thus the boy had little or no direct experience of the outside world beyond his grandparents' home. Five of the patient's older and younger siblings have lived continuously in this same grandparental household in the South for the last two to three years. All of them appear to be normal and are reported doing well in school. All reliable evidence, including eye-witness testimony from the patient's older adolescent siblings, consistently indicates that the boy was not present when his mother died during his sixth year. Indeed, he was shielded by the family from the knowledge of her death until circumstances, including the father's arrest for murder, made this impossible some two months later. On the other hand, the child certainly did both witness and receive many severe beatings from his father during the first five and a half years of his life. From early childhood on, this boy was regarded by all who knew him as decidedly hyperactive, highly intelligent, somewhat aggressive and disobedient, but otherwise quite happily related to peers and to adults other than his father. No one in his various family and neighborhood settings regarded him as uncontrollable, and it never occurred to any known relative or associate to label him as mentally ill.

All available family and professional sources directly knowledgeable as to the facts agree that this youngster made a happy adjustment to life in a Southern rural Afro-American foster home during the year following his mother's death. After the initial grief of bereavement, there is no indication of lasting behavioral change in family or neighborhood settings at any time during this year. During this same period, however, the boy received his first exposure to larger social institutions. Here a pattern emerged which appears to represent the roots of the patient's later difficulties. As long as his early experiences with larger institutions were mediated by his guardians or other adults in the foster family, for example in regular church attendance, everything went smoothly. When the boy was exposed alone to impersonal, bureaucratic, mainstream institutional settings, on the other hand, problems arose immediately. The middle-class and generally White authority figures in these settings saw his hyperactivity and tendency to disobedience as disruptive and uncontrollable. Teachers in a summer Headstart program for pre-schoolers remember this child chiefly as one who would not sit still in his assigned seat and be quiet. When he was taken to a large hospital for minor surgery, he was sent home a day ahead of the post-operative schedule because the nurses could not make him stay in his bed or keep up with his whereabouts within the institution. These institutional problems did not disturb the warm relationships within the foster home. When we met the boy's former guardians some two years later, they were obviously hungry for news of him, spontaneously reminisced about what an appealing child he was, and asked if we could help them get him back.

We interpret this retrospective evidence in the following way. The child suffered considerable emotional deprivation and disturbance of primary object relations during his first six years. This deprivation was substantially compensated by healthy relationships in the grandparents' household and further reduced by nurturance in the first foster family. In this connection, it should be noted that within Afro-American subcultures there appear to be both a structural fact and a socially learned expectation that family attachments are quite diversified and flexible in comparison with the rather narrow and rigid focus on specific parent-figures which is the mainstream norm. (While we do not feel that we fully understand the psychodynamics of this subcultural pattern at the present stage of our research, we are gaining the impression that it functions quite positively in the settings of variable household composition which often stem from economic fluctuations and other recurrent stresses of poverty and minority status.) During this period the boy was adjusted, quite within normal limits, to Afro-American family and micro-institutional settings. Here his rambunctious hyperactive style was easily tolerated and controlled without difficulty whenever necessary by subcultural standards. Because of the family's social isolation during early years when biculturation normally begins, the child received very little preparation for mainstream macro-institutional settings. His behavior style was not tolerated in these settings. Yet there was neither any close personal relationship nor any subculturally appropriate approach available among the institutional personnel. Under these conditions the already delayed biculturation process again failed to function. So the mainstream educators and health specialists were unable to calm the youngster down or keep him under control within limits acceptable to them. In the patient's history to this point we find no evidence of psychosis, organic deficit, or other serious psychopathology.

We turn now to more current evidence. As we observed this boy during the first three months of the present year, he showed a continuation of previously noted trends. He was clearly hyperactive, notably aggressive, strongly but never uncontrollably disobedient, and warmly attached to his new urban Northern foster parents, who are also relatives with the same Southern Afro-American background. The boy was clearly capable of stable relationships with his neighborhood peers, successful in learning a new physical and social environment, and able to perform such organized activities as periodic work for small payments and participation in small neighborhood institutions like a locally modified cub scout troop.

Nevertheless, the boy was found by the local public school to be incapable of learning and dangerously uncontrollable. Teachers reported that he refused to obey them and that he disrupted classes with various kinds of outbursts, including fights with other youngsters. The same guidance counselor mentioned earlier was called in and decided the boy was deeply disturbed by a tragically unstable family life. This man placed in the record the fatefully erroneous statement that the boy had seen his father murder his mother. Precisely what misunderstanding led to this error is unknown, for none of the patient's kinsmen or associates in the North were acquainted with the circumstances surrounding the mother's death. The boy himself never alleged to us or anyone we know in the community that he had witnessed a killing. Until our trip to the boy's former homes, the actual facts were unknown outside the Southern branch of the family and a small circle of professionals in the South. Nevertheless, this nonexistent trauma was invoked as the source of deep psychopathology by every educator, psychiatrist, and social worker who subsequently dealt with the child. The counselor and the school principal contrived to have the boy excluded from school without the legally required suspension hearing. By this time the youngster had become a psychiatric out-patient at a nearby hospital. After interviews and tests, the hospital personnel recorded their diagnosis of childhood schizophrenia with mental retardation and probable organic damage. Tranquilizing medication was prescribed. After the expulsion from school, institutional interest in the case dropped away, and nothing further was done.

The boy then spent several months freely and successfully living the life of the ghetto streets each weekday, while his foster parents literally worked day and night at minimally remunerative jobs to support the whole family. Over a period of two years in the urban North, the child's adaptation to home and community settings had been well within tolerable limits as defined by his Afro-American foster family and neighborhood associates. No one in these settings saw him as abnormal or impossible to control. Nevertheless, his relationship to home and community became decidedly stressful for obvious reasons as soon as he was excluded from school and defined by external authorities as mentally sick. Among other things, his guardians worried about his safety in the streets and tried without success to get him back into school.

We first met this youngster after the school expulsion and heard his story from him, his foster parents, and other neighbors. With the permission and encouragement of the guardians, we naively turned to local school and hospital personnel for clarification. Before we knew it, there was suddenly a move afoot at the nearby hospital to have this long-forgotten child involuntarily committed to a state mental hospital immediately. Although there had been no change in the boy's behavior or situation, the plan for commitment was justified by a psychiatrist on the grounds that the patient was an imminent danger to himself and everyone around him. Local community leadership became aware of this plan and prevented it from being carried out. As the compromise among local power centers worked out, the boy was temporarily hospitalized in another institution for so-called "independent" evaluation. It was soon clear that because of the interlocking professional associations of psychiatrists and others between the two institutions the alleged "independence" of the new evaluation was thoroughly compromised.

By anthropological hook or crook we gained access to the operations and records of the institution where our young friend was now confined. We soon discovered that hospital staff people at all levels felt extremely threatened because out of the circumstances surrounding this patient's admission they had concocted an image of the researchers, and even of the little boy himself, as "civil rights agitators" out to expose the institution by accusing it of anti-Black discrimination. While this posed certain methodological problems for us, it made life for the little boy even more miserable than it would otherwise have been. Lower echelon staff in particular were openly hostile and punitive, to the extreme of confinement in a strait-jacket for hours at a time. During visits to our friend we found the same child we had known before, with two significant additions. First, it was obvious that the boy actively hated the conditions of enforced confinement. Second, he was so heavily influenced by what the hospital staff referred to as a "chemical strait-jacket" that often he acted like a zombie.

Despite much bureaucratic and professional resistance, we managed to interview and observe all hospital staff with major responsibilities in relation to this patient. We soon found that the staff had projected such destructive power onto this 8-year-old that they talked about him as if he were about to destroy the hospital by physically assaulting its personnel and creating general chaos throughout the institution. Next we found that the middle-class White upper-echelon staff so often misunderstood verbalizations by our young Afro-American friend that they added "speech pathology" to the many strikes against him which they had accepted from the earlier diagnosis by the psychiatrist who originally tried to have him put away in a state institution. The hospital personnel were very largely ignorant of the boy's life before his admission. What little information they had of this nature came from his earlier psychiatric record plus a family history composed by hospital social workers. Both these sources were filled with significant errors and distortions.

Eventually two lengthy staff conferences were held to decide what to do with this troublesome patient. A clinical psychologist presented the finding that on the WISC our little friend scored a so-called "borderline IQ," but as soon as he was given a chance to learn the arcane secrets of the Bentor Visual Retention Test he immediately demonstrated a capacity to learn rapidly. Findings reported from Rorschach and other projective tests indicated what the psychologist described as good reality testing, normal intelligence, and no evidence of psychosis of any kind. The neurologist reported no hard signs of organic deficit and only such minor soft signs that she concluded significant organic pathology must be regarded as unproven.

In spite of all this, two senior psychiatrists insisted that the patient was certainly psychotic, probably brain-damaged, and evidently retarded. The more they insisted, the more the psychologist, neurologist, and lesser staff tended to reinterpret their findings along lines more in accord with the assertion of deep pathology. At one point a suggestion was made that the patient's tranquilizing medication be reduced or discontinued to make possible psychological and neurological retests. This provoked a burly male recreation aid, who probably weighs four times as much as the patient, to almost beg that if the boy were taken off drugs he should be locked up in continuous isolation. The proceedings reached such irrational extremes that ordinary experiences described by the young patient, which we know by observation were perfectly real, were presented as evidence of hallucination. The outcome was perhaps even more illogical than the proceedings which led up to it. The patient was to be released to his foster parents with an expressed professional evaluation that he probably could not make it in the outside world and therefore would soon be back in the hospital. It was made clear that wherever this little boy went in the world of macro-institutions he would be followed by a certified record attesting that he is dangerously insane.

The child was indeed returned to his foster home a few weeks ago. Personnel of the releasing institution have conveyed to the foster parents a strong message that the child is irremediably pathological. An additional message from the same source is the threat that the alleged pathology will sooner or later get the foster parents into trouble which may lead to serious legal sanctions. As might be expected, the youngster's guardians are by now quite anxious and confused. Our sad expectation is that within weeks or months the boy will be confined to a state institution from which he may never escape.

Our interpretation of these recent and current data can be summarized as follows. The patient received another developmental setback in the object loss occasioned by his move from the first foster family to his present guard-

ians' household. Fortunately these new parents are warm and responsible people who are devoted to the child's welfare. Beyond these individual characteristics, the culturally conditioned flexibility of Afro-American domestic relations is again relevant. For these and perhaps other reasons, the boy was able to adjust normally to the family and neighborhood dimensions of his new situation Associates and intimates in these settings have found him no more than mildly undersocialized or immature, sometimes a nuisance but nothing more.

Yet the earlier difficulties, stemming from circumstantially arrested biculturation, have increased to crisis proportions. The personnel of mainstream macro-institutions now regard this patient as essentially without internalized controls. For the same reasons as earlier, these mainstream caretakers have been unable to produce any improvement in the patient's behavior. Out of feelings ranging from anxiety over disruption of institutional routines to fear of racial conflict and stereotyped aversions against ghetto people, these caretakers have projected upon this small child the image of a powerful monster threatening chaos. They have evidently concluded that such a menace must be restrained by custodial and punitive confinement, lest its destructive potential become even more frightening.

So the whole local educational and medical apparatus operated in such a way as to continue preventing crucial gaps in the child's socialization from being filled in. Today as he nears his 9th birthday, the boy remains illiterate and he is becoming accustomed to institutional failure and rejection. His guardians are nearing the end of their capacity to resist authoritarian mainstream pressure to give up and accept the official diagnosis which their own experience has never supported. Unless some new factor enters the situation, these conditions can be expected to injure or sever the remaining parental ties which presently offer the only hope that this boy might still grow up as a biculturally normal Afro-American. Starting with a relatively minor disability attributable to his family history, over the past three years the patient has been effectively prevented from achieving healthy biculturation by the very nature and workings of mainstream institutions. Despite the damage al-

ready done, we can still find no convincing evidence that the case supports findings of psychosis, organic pathology, or retardation other than the institutionally induced illiteracy. Today the child still illustrates how tough the human organism is and how much it can take. Soon the self-fulfillment of mainstream prophecies, enshrined in both the deficit and difference models, may become irreversible and permanent.

Wider Implications

During the course of the case history just described, we had occasion to discuss the patient at length with nearly a dozen medical, clinical, and social work specialists directly or indirectly involved in the case. In fact, we provided them with all our evidence, discussed our interpretations of the data, and made several recommendations. These discussions revealed over and over again that the thinking of these professionals is ruled by highly standardized assumptions embodying both the difference and deficit models of Afro-American psychology. We attempted to stimulate their interest in cultural phenomena by presenting the difference model in much the way it is being presented at this symposium. The standard reply was, in essence, "Oh, yes of course, that's just the problem!" One senior psychiatrist went on to volunteer his considered calculation that within our community and adjacent ghettos there are 30,000 Black children who are just as sick as the patient described earlier. (This statistical opinion casts a depressing light on the question of how large a universe of Afro-Americans is represented by our case history.) The implicit assumption evident in all these conversations is that Afro-American culture is not only distinct but pathogenic, thus neatly combining the deficit and difference theories. This is perhaps not surprising, considering the outpouring of both specialized and popular literature campaigning for just this point of view. (Even Black psychiatrists are gaining the limelight by portraying their own people as a pathological group [Grier and Cobbs, 1968; cf. Valentine, 1969].). What has impressed us, however, is the rigidity with which this view is held by relevant professionals and the strength of emotional commitment to it which one senses in such specialists. At no time in these conversations were we able to detect any recognition that a mainstream institution might bear the slightest responsibility for the patient's problems, nor even any interest in the question what effect the various schools and hospitals might have had. On the contrary, the ruling implicit assumption was that all sources of difficulty must lie within the family or the non-institutional community. In short, there was no hint that any of the institutions might have acted in any way other than just as they did.

To us who know the patient well in his home milieu of Afro-American subculture, he looks entirely different from the image that institutional specialists have of him. We know that he functions well in his own subcultural world. From this perspective, it seems obvious that, even after months in a punitive custodial institution, the child shows none of the dire pathology attributed to him. The significant professionals in the boy's case, however, have never even seen his home and have no direct experience of Black ghetto life whatever. These men make it clear that they regard themselves as experts on Black children. Yet they make it equally clear, usually without intending to, that they have no understanding of the child's cultural milieu—or even any real interest in it, beyond the derogatory stereotypes carried by the difference and deficit theories. One senior clinician admitted that we might well be right in our contention that the patient was functionally well-adapted to his home environment. This doctor insisted, however, that what goes on in the home or community is totally irrelevant to the problems of diagnosis and disposition: medical diagnosis and therapy are determined strictly within the clinical setting without consideration of extraneous data from the outside world. Such institution-bound professionals have insulated themselves from any understanding of cultural factors, except again the stereotypes in the literature.

Both the theoretical significance and the policy implications of the case history described here now seem clear. This youngster's problems can be understood primarily as a mainstream institutional failure in the process of biculturation. In spite of a stressful and deprived early childhood, the patient succeeded in adapting sufficiently well to his Afro-American subcul-

tural environment. Now the macro-institutional problems are threatening his adaptation to his third Afro-American home and community. The failure of the macro-institutional settings has been manifold. Not only was it in these settings that the patient's difficulties first became evident, but these same institutions have been unable to do anything constructive about his problems. The prognosis appears to be that a basically healthy child will end up being forced into one or more of the delinquent, mentally sick, or functionally illiterate roles defined by the society's major institutions.

This is not to say that the initial home setting played no part in the etiology of this case. Without attempting any psychological analysis of the original parents, it is plain that the father actively inflicted, with the mother's passive complicity, a double disadvantage on their son. Not only was his early maturation compromised by emotional deprivation and injury, but his potential biculturation was initially arrested by parentally imposed or allowed isolation. Yet it is precisely such intra-family problems which the so-called "helping professions" of mainstream culture—social work, guidance counseling, clinical psychology, and psychiatry—are supposed to resolve or at least mitigate. In this case, a long series of these professionals, plus their colleagues in education and hospital management, have done nothing but make the boy's problems worse for so long that they are now the principal source of the present unhappy situation. One or two reasonably sensitive and humane teachers or clinicians, willing to assert themselves against institutional norms almost anywhere in this long sad story, could probably have changed the course of events decisively and averted the impending tragedy. Diligent study has not disclosed a single individual of this quality among all the professionals involved in the case.

The individual aspects of this case are quite enough to make anyone who knows or cares about the people involved both sad and angry. If one contemplates the wider implications, however, one begins to appreciate the dimensions of our society's intergroup tragedy. Reflecting upon a powerful psychiatrist's clear implication that some 30,000 children in one part of a single American city should be treated as this child has been treated, the imagination recoils from the obvious inferences.

It seems imperative to recognize that men capable of such projects cannot be made into humanitarians by preaching the difference model to them. When it is remembered that the cultural-difference theory has already been assimilated by these people and made to support their existing approach, the futility, or worse, of communicating with them about subcultural contrasts must be apparent.

The practical and policy implications of biculturation theory, at least with respect to Afro-American communities, are radical and stringent in each of the several senses of both terms. Much impairment of Afro-American personalities is directly traceable to the standard operations of mainstream institutions which inhibit or entirely block vital portions of the biculturation process. It therefore appears that no amount of dedication by Afro-Americans to mainstream ideals, and no extremes of assimilationist effort by Negroes, can make these institutions function to the advantage of Black people. The group-destructive tendencies of these settings are too deeply built in to be susceptible to rational reform. Certainly nothing will be accomplished by trying to teach professionals respect for subcultural systems when all their other training and experience has already taught them to regard these same subcultures as impersonally pathogenic and personally threatening.

At least two alternatives remain. One is for Afro-Americans to avoid mainstream institutions, as far as possible, and build their own parallel organizations for social services of all kinds. This is essentially the Black Nationalist orientation. For reasons of the existing power relations within our society, this is an approach fraught with problematical practical issues of its own. The other alternative is a radical alteration of the existing dominant institutions with respect to the values, attitudes, and interests which they serve. Nothing like this can be realistically expected short of revolutionary innovations in the national social structure as a whole. This obviously involves equally problematical practical issues and power questions. From these perspectives, everything depends upon the presently unknown potential strength of Black pride and Black power as cultural revitalization movements, the rebellion of American youth, and perhaps a few other national tendencies. It would appear to be in these quarters that some reason for hope may lie. Certainly it must be clear that the debate between deficit theorists and difference proponents is of no practical or humane significance. This debate should be confined within the ivied walls where privileged people can still play intellectual games without regard to the consequences for the unprivileged people outside the walls.

As is already clear, I believe a biculturation model is preferable to other formulations discussed here. This is not only because a bicultural theory more adequately represents Afro-American realities than the distorting notions of deficit or the oversimplified difference concept. Recognition of bicultural processes is also more congruent with desirable changes in the practice of service institutions operating in Black ghettos. It is important that educators and health specialists not only recognize the legitimacy and creativity of ethnic subcultures, but also appreciate that Afro-Americans are already more conversant with and competent in mainstream culture than most non-Black Americans believe or admit. Indeed the latter point is more likely to neutralize mainstream ethnocentrism than a simple difference model. The bicultural conception calls attention to a kind of psychocultural adequacy which mainstream Americans can respect *in spite of* their ethnocentrism if they will only accept its reality. Out of this could perhaps come the beginnings of a more realistic and humane basis for service institutions changing to serve Afro-American needs and interests.

Finally, however, there must be a word of caution on the relationship between theoretical ideas and social action. Intensive immersion in ghetto life makes one tend to feel that expecting new concepts in psychology to alter the nittygritty practicalities of major institutions is a romantic form of philosophical idealism. Let us assume that good scientists who are also real humanitarians can achieve intellectual ascendancy for the difference model, the theory of biculturation, or other better concepts. Let us even assume that this outlook dominates the training of a whole new breed of service professionals. What will happen when this new wave hits the bulwarks of established macroinstitutions in the ghetto? We must be prepared for at least three depressing possibilities. Some of

the new caretakers will shortly have their idealism shattered against the established stone walls and openly revert to the rationalizations of old hands. A second group may slip into a cynical hypocrisy in which the new ideals are given lip-service but the practitioner acts on his realization that bureaucratized professionals are rewarded for following existing institutionalized routines. Perhaps the remaining group will simply compartmentalize their theoretical training in a separate section of their consciousness from the practical exigencies of institutional practice. These possibilities seem all too plausible, unless the assumed conceptual changes are accompanied by radical shifts in power relationships and other factors conditioning the present functions of dominant institutions in the context of the class system and race.

There are many discouraging precedents and analogies to support these prognostications, and worse. Consider, for example, the implications of the following quotation from a recent paper advocating the difference model discussed in this symposium.

> In conclusion, we are hoping for a complete reevaluation of the assumptive base of most of the literature on the Afro-American. . . . We wish us as a profession and a society, not to seek integration, nor separation, but acculturation. Acculturation which does not seek to destroy the ties that bind black Americans together. We wish to recognize that acculturation is a two-way street— that we, the white society, have something to learn from the black community and that we, too, can change as a result of those learnings. (Baratz, 1968)

This quotation expresses well the anthropologically fostered doctrine of respect for worldwide cultural variety outside our own society, which has been absorbed by two generations of liberally educated Americans. The concept of acculturation itself describes the influence of dominant European societies on non-Western peoples through the impositions of colonialism. The one outstanding present-day outcome of these historical processes is the war in Vietnam. The American participation in this war is being administered by the very Americans who have been steeped in the liberal tradition of respect for foreign cultures. Nevertheless, the war is destroying Vietnamese society and culture. There are today many intimations of an internal Vietnam

within the United States. If the internal war lasts long enough, perhaps it will be administered by White Americans who have gained from the difference model a new appreciation for the culture of their adversaries. Will they be any less likely to destroy that culture or those who live by it?

REFERENCES

Baratz, Stephen S. 1968. Social science strategies for research on the Afro-American. Paper prepared for American Psychological Association Annual Meeting.

Grier, William H., and Cobbs, Price M. 1968. *Black Rage*. New York: Basic Books.

Hannerz, Ulf. 1969a. Review of Valentine, 1968. *In* Valentine *et al.*, 1969.

Hannerz, Ulf. 1969b. What ghetto males are like: another look. *For* Witten and Szwed, 1970.

Hannerz, Ulf. 1969c. *Soulside: Inquiries into Ghetto Culture and Community*. Stockholm: Almqvist and Wiksell.

Leacock, Eleanor, ed. 1970. *The Culture of Poverty: a Critique*. New York: Simon and Schuster. In press.

Polgar, Steven, 1960. Biculturation of Mesquakie teenage boys. *American Anthropologist*, 62:217-235.

Stewart, William. 1967. Nonstandard speech patterns. *Baltimore Bulletin of Education*, 43:2-4:52-65.

Valentine, Charles A. 1968. *Culture and Poverty: Critique and Counterproposals*. Chicago: University of Chicago Press.

Valentine, Charles A. 1969. Incomplete diagnosis: review of *Black Rage* by Grier and Cobbs. *The Nation*, 208:1:24-26.

Valentine, Charles A. 1970. The "culture of poverty," its scientific significance and its implications for action. *In* Leacock, 1970.

Valentine, Charles A., and Valentine, Betty Lou. 1970a. Ghetto ethnography: a preliminary report of research. *In* Weaver and White, 1970.

Valentine, Charles A., and Valentine, Betty Lou. 1970a. Making the scene, digging the action and telling it like it is: anthropologists at work in a dark ghetto. *In* Whitten and Szwed, 1970.

Valentine, Charles A., *et al.* 1969. Culture and Poverty: a CA book review. *Current Anthropology*, 10:181-201.

Weaver, Thomas, and White, Douglas, eds. 1970. Urban Anthropology. *Human Organization Monographs*. In press.

Whitten, Norman E., and Szwed, John, eds. 1970. *Afro-American Anthropology: Contemporary Perspectives*. New York: Free Press. In press.

CONCLUSIONS

Two interrelated concepts have brought about the oppression of third world people on this earth: racism and imperialism. The two are tied up in the white man's inexorable missionary "burden." In deciding, from his pure white pedestal, that third world people are inferior, the white man has posited two goals: to make over the cultures of nonwhites and to use their resources for the aggrandizement, perpetuation, and expansion of his lands. In 1970, the feelings of third world people are being expressed in rage and anguish:

For those seeking a solution to this horror, we say to all Third World people—unite, and take back what is rightfully yours. This will not occur without violence, and we grieve for this, but the Man will not give up without a fight.

Anonymous

In order to realize this or any aim, unity is a paramount concern. Third world people must unite around the common goals while attempting to preserve the integrity of each individual group. This involves putting away the ethnic animosities that separate us as third world people. From this unity, we will gain the strength of numbers and the strength of sharing in a creative, dynamic endeavor. Further, we must not be separated by political ideologies. Our goals are too similar to allow ourselves to be fragmented by the wording of our political theories.

Further, the research colonialism of white educators must be ended. Many social scientists have made their fame and fortunes by compiling titillating statistics concerning third world people and not making any recommendations for solutions. We must end the colonizing of our communities. Colonialism can take many forms including economic exploitation, academic research colonialism, perpetuation of ignorance and disease, maintenance of occupying armies of police or military organizations.

Colonialism is good business. It creates a vast pool of consumers who have no means of producing goods to satisfy their own needs. In the economic and political climate, small businesses operated by the colonized are doomed to fail. By controlling the educational system, the oppressor does not allow the majority of the oppressed to attain the economic status necessary for minimal standard of living. Oppression takes more extreme forms as in South Africa, some parts of South America, Rhodesia, and Vietnam where masses of people must suffer and die in order for the economic system to be maintained. If the consumers in the United States were to begin boycotting companies who make a profit from the death of third world people, those companies might find a way of modifying their practices. The U.S. in its commitment to justice has never seen its way clear to effect an embargo on South Africa, although its Cuban embargo effected changes in Soviet policy. The U.S. with the support of the "silent majority" calmly goes about exporting the practices designed to dehumanize third world people as has been done in this country.

The educational system for third world people produces those who are fit for menial, low paying jobs. Those programs like the Educational Opportunity Program (EOP) which are designed to help students to enter colleges are subject to political whims of governors like Governor Reagan who has recently vetoed EOP funding in the state universities. It is ridiculous that the richest state (California) in the world's richest nation must cut off the funds by which the poor are aided in college in a program which has proven that third world students in college earn an academic average slightly better than their more affluent counterparts. This kind of political manipulation of the lives and futures of a generation of people must be ended.

Another educational system evil is the research conducted by white "scholars" among third world people. These people, completely ignorant of the diversity of cultural values, come in and formulate theories which serve to enrich the researcher both economically and socially. P. Moynihan formulated a report dealing with blacks which has now been found largely invalid in its conclusions. Yet, Moynihan is the highest ranked and most influential social scientist in the U.S. His latest theory calls for "benign neglect" of blacks causing many of us to feel that the past must have been filled with "malevolent neglect." Researchers coming into black, Chicano, Asian, or Native American communities must leave their biases behind. Moreover, the universities should train people to fill professional roles in their *own* communities, white or third world.

Finally, whites have admitted that the society is not designed either to allow equal participation of the masses of third world people or to allow them self-determination. As students, those willing to work for social change can begin by educating people in their own communities to the injustices and dangers of holding thirty million people in subjugation. The growing use of deadly force in putting down domestic dissent and the frequency of foreign intervention both are preludes to a loss of freedom for all. In addition, students can bring pressure on government and on corporations by exercising their rights such as voting, discussions, or selective buying. The racial problem has been one which has been a torment to third world people since the first settlers arrived from Europe and perhaps only a change in the ethnic composition of America can thwart further problems.

Repatriation to native lands for third world people, partition of America, and genocide are three commonly discussed solutions, but none speak to the problem of the remainder of the planet which is largely nonwhite. The war in Southeast Asia, which has been going on for more than two decades, indicates that land wars cannot bring people to subjugation any more. The only weapon left for the U.S. is ultimately the total annihilation of atomic or biological warfare. Unless changes can be made with regard to domestic and foreign policy, our common future is nonexistent.

Violence

EDITED BY:

Betsy Chandler
Joe deSousa
William R. Dougherty
James E. Hartung, Jr.
Robert D. Links

Robert J. P. Maginnis
Robert K. McCann
Ellen Melchoir
Valentine N. Sengebau
James Williams

*Come Senators, Congressmen, please
   heed the call
Don't stand in the doorway, don't
   block up the hall
For he that gets hurt will be he who
   has stalled
The battle outside raging
Will soon shake your windows and
   rattle your walls
For the times they are a-changin'.*

Bob Dylan
(From "The Times They Are
A-Changin'." © 1963 by M. Witmark
& Sons. Used by permission
of Warner Bros. Music. All rights
reserved.)

INTRODUCTION

The existence of violence in American, and more generally Western, culture can not be taken as proof that man has an intrinsically violent nature. Studies of man's closest animal relatives, the primates, and his early existence through the Paleolithic age give no evidence of any innate instinct for aggressive, violent behavior. Perhaps the only way man has made it this far has been through his unique cultural capacity to help his fellow man. Perhaps it was the development of this capacity that led to the Neolithic revolution ten thousand years ago, when man developed agriculture, domesticated animals, built villages, and multiplied. However, these early argicultural-pastoral communities and their successors, such as Western civilization, confronted each other violently. The communities became larger, the technologies became more sophisticated, and violence increased in proportion. From Babylon to Genghis Khan to Hitler and to the second World War, certain segments of the human species (no-

tably the West) have been perpetrating acts of violence in ever increasing amounts, and now have perfected weapons which are capable of exterminating all life on the planet. If this catastrophe is to be averted, some basic changes will probably have to be made in our violent culture.

In our society today, babies are fed a daily pablum of violent television programing, children swing through a jungle of violence-oriented toys, and adolescents rock out to movies which are cele-

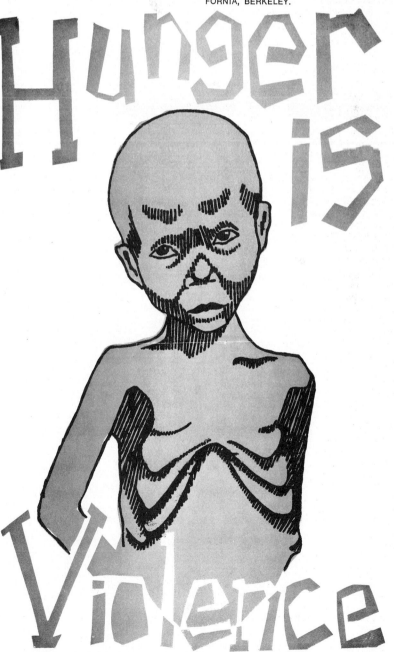

Hunger is Violence

brations of violence. A recent study showed that the average child television viewer sees 12,000 TV deaths before he's 14 years old. And adults, who have not become desensitized by these early massive doses of violence, are barraged with daily newspaper articles and television reports of war, crime in the streets, police brutality, urban riots, student rebellions, assassinations, and many other growing sores of violence.

But while we can easily criticize the people who produce violence-oriented entertainment programs and movies, we cannot lightly dismiss the statistics that tell us that our society is becoming more violent with each passing day. Experts say that there are between 50 and 200 million guns in the United States; assaults with such weapons in this country increased by 77 percent from 1964 to 1967. The number of gun murders each year in the United States is 48 times the combined total of gun homicides committed in England, Japan, and Germany (collectively, these nations have an equivalent sized population).

In this chapter, we will explore the origins of violence, law and order, institutionalized violence in the prisons, violence in the mass media, and the exporting of violence, to support our conclusions.

Origins of Violence

We begin with Arthur Schlesinger's overview of violence in present-day America—a bad inheritance from our violent past:

> We began, after all, as a people who killed red men and enslaved black men. . . . [N]o nation . . . could act as we did without burying deep in itself—in its customs, its institutions, and its psyche—a propensity toward violence.

Schlesinger touches all of the bases—crime, interpersonal violence, police violence, media, the assassination of presidents—to support a point once expressed in more graphic terms by Rap Brown, that violence is as American as cherry pie.

4.1
The Dark Heart of American History

Arthur Schlesinger, Jr.

The murders within five years of John F. Kennedy, Martin Luther King, Jr., and Robert F. Kennedy raise—or ought to raise—somber questions about the character of contemporary America. One such murder might be explained away as an isolated horror, unrelated to the inner life of our society. But the successive shootings, in a short time, of three men who greatly embodied the idealism of American life suggest not so much a fortuitous set of aberrations as an emerging pattern of response and action—a spreading and ominous belief in the efficacy of violence and the politics of the deed.

Yet, while each of these murders produced a genuine season of

From *Violence: America in the Sixties* by Arthur Schlesinger, Jr. Copyright © 1968 by Arthur Schlesinger, Jr. Reprinted by arrangement with The New American Library, Inc., New York.

national mourning, none has produced a sustained season of national questioning. In every case, remorse has seemed to end, not as an incitement to self-examination, but as an escape from it. An orgy of sorrow and shame becomes an easy way of purging a bad conscience and returning as quickly as possible to business as usual.

"It would be . . . self-deceptive," President Johnson said after the shooting of Robert Kennedy, "to conclude from this act that our country is sick, that it has lost its balance, that it has lost its sense of direction, even its common decency. Two hundred million Americans did not strike down Robert Kennedy last night any more than they struck down John F. Kennedy in 1963 or Dr. Martin Luther King in April of this year."

I do not quarrel with these words. Of course two hundred million Americans did not strike down these men. Nor, in my judgment, is this a question of a "sick society" or of "collective guilt." I do not know what such phrases mean, but I am certain that they do not represent useful ways of thinking about our problem. . . . Obviously most Americans were deeply and honestly appalled by these atrocities. Obviously most Americans rightly resent being told that they were "guilty" of crimes they neither willed nor wished.

Still, it is not enough to dismiss the ideas of a sick society and of collective guilt and suppose that such dismissal closes the question. For a problem remains—the problem of a contagion of political murder in the United States in the 1960s unparalleled in our own history and unequaled today anywhere in the world. . . .

Self-knowledge is the indispensable prelude to self-control; and self-knowledge, for a nation as well as for an individual, begins with history. We like to think of ourselves as a peaceful, tolerant, benign people who have always lived under a government of laws and not of men. . . . Most Americans probably pay this respect most of their lives. Yet this is by no means the only strain in our tradition. For we also have been a violent people. . . .

We began, after all, as a people who killed red men and enslaved black men. No doubt we often did this with a Bible and a prayer book. But no nation, however righteous its professions, could act as we did without burying deep in itself—in its customs, its institutions, and its psyche—a propensity toward violence. However much we pretended that Indians and Negroes were subhuman, we really knew that they were God's children too.

Nor did we confine our violence to red men and black men. We gained our freedom, after all, through revolution. The first century after independence were years of incessant violence—wars, slave insurrections, Indian fighting, urban riots, murders, duels, beatings. Members of Congress went armed to the Senate and House. In his first notable speech, in January 1838, before the Young Men's Lyceum of Springfield, Illinois, Abraham Lincoln named internal violence as the supreme threat to American political institutions. He spoke of "the increasing disregard for law which pervades the country; the growing disposition to substitute the wild and furious passions, in lieu of the sober judgment of Courts; and the worse than savage mobs, for the executive ministers of justice." . . .

So the young Lincoln named the American peril—a peril he did not fear to locate within the American breast. Indeed, the sadness of America has been that our worst qualities have so often been the other face of our best. Our commitment to morality, our faith in experiment: these have been sources of America's greatness, but they have also led Americans into our error. For our moralists have sometimes condoned murder if the cause is deemed good. . . .

America, Martin Luther King correctly said, has been "a schizophrenic personality, tragically divided against herself." The impulses of violence and civility continued after Lincoln to war within the American breast. The insensate bloodshed of the Civil War exhausted the national capacity for violence and left the nation emotionally and psychologically spent. For nearly a century after Appomattox, we appeared on the surface the tranquil and friendly people we still like to imagine ourselves to be. . . . There were still crazy individuals, filled with grievance, bitterness, and a potential for violence. . . . These years of stability, a stability fitfully recaptured after the First World War, created the older generation's image of a "normal" America.

Yet even in the kindly years we did not wholly eradicate the propensity toward violence which history had hidden in the national unconscious. In certain moods, indeed, we prided ourselves on our violence; we almost considered it evidence of our virility. "Above all," cried Theodore Roosevelt, "let us shrink from no strife, moral or physical, within or without the nation, provided we are certain that the strife is justified." That fatal susceptibility always lurked under the surface, breaking out in Indian wars and vigilantism in the West, in lynchings in the South, in labor riots and race riots and gang wars in the cities.

It is important to distinguish collective from individual violence —the work of mobs from the work of murderers; for the motive and the effect can be very different. There can, of course, be murder by a mob. But not all mobs aim at murder. Collective violence—rioting against what were considered illegal British taxes in Boston in 1773, or dangerous Papist influence sixty years later, or inequitable draft laws in New York in 1863, or unfair labor practices in Chicago in 1937—is more characteristically directed at conditions than at individuals. In many cases (though by no means all), the aim has been to protest rather than protect the status quo; and the historian is obliged to concede that collective violence, including the recent riots in black ghettos, has often quickened the disposition of those in power to redress just grievances. . . . Violence, for better or worse, *does* settle some questions, and for the better. Violence secured American independence, freed the slaves, and stopped Hitler.

But this has ordinarily been the violence of a society. The individual who plans violence is less likely to be concerned with reforming conditions than with punishing persons. On occasion the purpose is to protect the status quo by destroying men who symbolize or threaten social change. A difference exists in psychic color and content between spontaneous mass convulsions and the premeditated killing of individuals. The first signifies an unstable society, the second, a murderous society. America has exhibited both forms of violence.

Now in the third quarter of the twentieth century, violence has broken out with new ferocity in our country. . . . What is it about the climate of this decade that suddenly encourages—that for some evidently legitimatizes— the relish for hate and the resort to violence? Why, according to the Federal Bureau of Investigation, have assaults with a gun in-creased 77 per cent in the four years from 1964 through 1967? . . .

We talk about the tensions of industrial society. No doubt the ever-quickening pace of social change depletes and destroys the institutions which make for social stability. But this does not explain why Americans shoot and kill so many more Americans than Englishmen kill Englishmen or Japanese kill Japanese. England, Japan, and West Germany are, next to the United States, the most heavily industrialized countries in the world. Together they have a population of 214 million people. Among these 214 million, there are 135 gun murders a year. Among the 200 million people of the United States there are 6,500 gun murders a year—about *forty-eight times* as many.

We talk about the fears and antagonisms generated by racial conflict. Unquestionably this has contributed to the recent increase in violence. The murders of Dr. King and Senator Kennedy seem directly traceable to ethnic hatreds. Whites and blacks alike are laying in arms, both sides invoking the needs of self-defense. Yet this explanation still does not tell us why in America today we are tending to convert political problems into military problems. . . .

The New Left tells us that we are a violent society because we are a capitalist society—that capitalism is itself institutionalized violence; and that life under capitalism inevitably deforms relations among men. This view would be more impressive if the greatest violence of man against man in this century had not taken place in noncapitalist societies— in Nazi Germany, in Stalinist Russia, in precapitalist Indonesia. The fact is that every form of society is in some sense institutionalized violence. . . .

One reason surely for the enormous tolerance of violence in contemporary America is the fact that our country has now been more or less continuously at war for a generation. The experience of war over a long period devalues human life and habituates people to killing. And the war in which we are presently engaged is far more brutalizing than was the Second World War or the Korean War. It is more brutalizing because the destruction we have wrought in Vietnam is so wildly out of proportion to any demonstrated involvement of our national security or any rational assessment of our national interest. In the other wars we killed for need. In this war we are killing beyond need, and, as we do so, we corrupt our national life. When violence is legally sanctioned for a cause in which people see no moral purpose, this is an obvious stimulus to individuals to use violence for what they may maniacally consider moral purposes of their own.

A second reason for the climate of violence in the United States is surely the zest with which the mass media, and especially television and films, dwell on violence. One must be clear about this. The mass media do *not* create violence. But they *reinforce* aggressive and destructive impulses, and they may well *teach* the morality as well as the methods of violence. . . .

For a time, the television industry comforted itself with the theory that children listened to children's programs and that, if by any chance they saw programs for adults, violence would serve as a safety valve, offering a harmless outlet for pent-up aggressions. . . . Experiments show that such programs, far from serving as safety valves for aggression, attract children with high levels of aggression and stimulate them to seek overt means of acting out their aggressions. Evidence suggests that these programs work the same incitement on adults. And televiolence does more than condition emotion and behavior. It also may attenuate people's sense of reality. Men murdered on the television screen ordinarily spring to life after the episode is over: all death is therefore diminished. A child asked a man last June where he was headed in his car. "To Washington," he said. "Why?" he asked. "To attend the funeral of Senator Kennedy." The child said, "Oh yeah—they shot him again." And such shooting may well condition the manner in which people approach the perplexities of existence. On television the hero too glibly resolves his problems by shooting somebody. The *Gunsmoke* ethos, however, is not necessarily the best way to deal with human or social complexity. It is hardly compatible with any kind of humane or libertarian democracy.

The problem of electronic violence raises difficult questions of prescription as well as of analysis. It would be fatal to restrain artistic exploration and portrayal, even of the most extreme and bitter aspects of human experience. No rational person wants to re-estab-

lish a reign of censorship or mobilize new Legions of Decency. Nor is there great gain in making the electronic media scapegoats for propensities which they reflect rather than create—propensities which spring from our history and our hearts.

Yet society retains a certain right of self-defense. Is it inconceivable that the television industry might work out forms of self-restraint? Beyond this, it should be noted that the networks and the stations do *not* own the airwaves; the nation does; and, if the industry cannot restrain itself, the Communications Act offers means, as yet unused, of democratic control.

We have a bad inheritance as far as violence is concerned; and in recent years war and television have given new vitality to the darkest strains in our national psyche. How can we master this horror in our souls before it rushes us on to ultimate disintegration?

There is not a problem of collective guilt, but there is a problem of collective responsibility. Certainly two hundred million Americans did not strike down John Kennedy or Martin Luther King or Robert Kennedy. But two hundred million Americans are plainly responsible for the character of a society that works on deranged men and incites them to depraved acts. There were Lee Harvey Oswalds and James Earl Rays and Sirhan Bishara Sirhans in America in the Thirties— angry, frustrated, alienated, resentful, marginal men in rootless, unstable cities like Dallas and Memphis and Los Angeles. But our society in the Thirties did not stimulate such men to compensate for their own failure by killing leaders the people loved.

Some of the young in their despair have come to feel that the answer to reason is unreason, the answer to violence, more violence; but these only hasten the plunge toward the abyss. The more intelligent disagree. They do not want America to beat its breast and go back to the golf course. *They do want America to recognize its responsibility.* They want us to tell it like it is—to confront the darkness in our past and the darkness in our present. They want us to realize that life is not solid and predictable but infinitely chancy, that violence is not the deviation but the ever-present possibility, that we can therefore never rest in the effort to prevent unreason from rending the skin of civility.

They want our leaders to *talk* less about law and order and *do* more about justice.

The view of man as being instinctual and innately violent has undergone a revitalization of sorts recently, largely due to the writings of Robert Ardrey (*African Genesis* and *The Territorial Imperative*) and Konrad Lorenz (*On Aggression*). This is the so-called Hobbesian view of man which was an integral part of the thinking of the Social Darwinists. Freud called it the death instinct, something since repudiated by most psychoanalysts. But the lay public has never given the idea up. The layman sees wars, hatred, and the looming possibility of nuclear holocaust. When Ardrey and Lorenz began to publish, the public was ready to accept what they said; it gave the public an answer; a reason they could point to.

However, most experts, especially in anthropology, feel that Ardrey (a playwright by profession) and Lorenz (a famous animal behaviorist) are wrong in their view of man. It is the conclusion of many in the behavioral sciences that man does not have instincts. Man is an animal capable of a high degree of generalized learning. Man evolved to be able to function with maximum efficiency within a cultural setting.

There is another possible explanation as to why there has been such a receptivity to these views of "innate aggression." In a culture where violence occurs, it is somehow absolving to be told that it is not your fault, that this is man's "animal nature." If you are born thus, you cannot help yourself. Somehow, you are not really responsible for your violent acts. It must have been somewhat the same motives which led the authors of the Bible to proclaim man as basically a sinner, with an evil nature.

Two articles in this section discuss the sources of violent behavior in man. The first, "The New Litany of Innate Depravity, or Original Sin Revisited," by M. F. Ashley Montagu, deals with man's basic nature as seen by an anthropologist. The second, "Violence and Man's Struggle to Adapt," written by Marshall Gilula and D. N. Daniels, is a psychiatric view of the adaptiveness of violence in the modern world.

4.2
The New Litany of "Innate Depravity," or Original Sin Revisited

M. F. Ashley Montagu

It is said that when the Bishop of Worcester returned from the Oxford meeting of the British Association in 1860, he informed his wife, at tea, that the horrid Professor Huxley had declared that man was descended from the apes. Whereupon the dear lady is said to have exclaimed, "Descended from the apes! Let us hope it is not true, but if it is, let us pray that it will not become generally known."

It would seem that the last forty years of anthropological research and discovery in the field and in the laboratory, taken together with the findings of the behavioral sciences, place us in much the same position as the Bishop's lady, for while the findings of these disciplines are wholly opposed to the deeply entrenched view that man is an innately aggressive creature, most people tend to dismiss these findings out of hand or ridicule them as a rather eccentric idealistic heterodoxy, which do not deserve to become generally known. In preference to examining the scientific findings they choose to cast their lot with such "authorities" as William Golding who, in his novel *Lord of the Flies*,[1] offers a colorful account of the allegedly innate nastiness of human nature, and Robert Ardrey who, in *African Genesis*[2] and more recently in *The Territorial Imperative*,[3] similarly seeks to show that man is an innately aggressive creature.

The first part of *African Genesis*

is devoted to a demonstration, which the author brings off quite convincingly and with éclat, of the validity of Professor Raymond Dart's claims for an osteodontokeratic culture among the australopithecines. It is in the second part that Mr. Ardrey makes one of the most remarkable extrapolations from the first part I have ever encountered in any work. Mr. Ardrey argues that since the australopithecines made use of tools, and employed some of them as implements with which to bash in the skulls of baboons, the australopithecines were therefore "killers," and that *therefore* human beings are "killers" by nature! Mr. Ardrey's book constitutes, perhaps, the most illuminating example of the manner in which a man's prejudices may get in the way of his reason and distort his view of the evidence. Mr. Ardrey refers to some of his early personal experiences of violence which convinced him of the murderousness of human nature. Hence, when through the distorting glass of his prejudgments he looks at a tool it becomes not simply a scraper but a weapon, a knife becomes a dagger, and even a large canine tooth becomes "the natural dagger that is the hallmark of all hunting mammals," while in "the armed hunting primate" it becomes "a redundant instrument." "With the advent of the lethal weapon natural selection turned from the armament of the jaw to the armament of the hand."

But the teeth are no more an armament than is the hand, and it is entirely to beg the question to call them so. Virtually all the members of the order of primates, other than man, have large canine teeth, and these animals, with the exception of the baboons, are predominantly vegetarians, and it is because they are vegetarians that they require large canine teeth; that such teeth may, on occasion, serve a protective purpose is entirely secondary to their main function, which is to rip and shred the hard outer coverings of plant foods. Primates are not usually belligerent unless provoked, and the more carefully they are observed the more remarkably revealing do their unquarrelsomeness and cooperativeness become. The myth of the ferocity of "wild animals" constitutes one of Western man's supreme rationalizations, for it not only has served to "explain" to him the origins of his own aggressiveness, but also to relieve him of the responsibility for

it—for since it is "innate," derived from his early apelike ancestors, he can hardly, so he rationalizes, be blamed for it! And some have gone so far as to add that nothing can be done about it, and that therefore wars and juvenile delinquents, as Mr. Ardrey among others tells us, will always be with us! From one not-so-minor error to another Mr. Ardrey sweeps on to the grand fallacy.

At this point it needs to be said that Mr. Ardrey's views are firmly based on and derived from those of Professor Raymond Dart, who in an article entitled, "The Predatory Transition from Ape to Man,"[4] published in 1953, argued that man's animal ancestry was carnivorous, predatory, and cannibalistic in origin, and went on to add that "The blood-bespattered, slaughter-gutted archives of human history from the earliest Egyptian and Sumerian records to the most recent atrocities of the Second World War accord with early universal cannibalism, with animal and human sacrificial practices or their substitutes in formalized religions and with the world-wide scalping, head-hunting, body-mutilating and necrophiliac practices of mankind in proclaiming this common blood-lust differentiator, this predaceous habit, this mark of Cain that separates man dietetically from his anthropoidal relatives and allies him rather with the deadliest of Carnivora."[5]

Mr. Ardrey puts this in the following words: "The human being in the most fundamental aspects of his soul and body is nature's last if temporary word on the subject of the armed predator. And human history must be read in these terms."

In furtherance of this argument "tools" for Mr. Ardrey are not only identified as "weapons," but, he goes on to imply, nay, indeed, he states, "that when any scientist writes the word, 'tool,' as a rule he refers to weapons. This is a euphemism" (p. 306).

Perhaps this opportunity should be taken to assure Mr. Ardrey that when scientists write the word "tool" they mean exactly what they say, and that euphemisms are not, as Mr. Ardrey says, "normal to all natural science" (p. 306). Some tools may be used as weapons and even manufactured

Reprinted by permission of the author from M. F. Ashley Montagu, *Man and Aggression*, Oxford University Press, 1968, pp. 3–17. Copyright 1968 by Ashley Montagu.

[1] William Golding, *Lord of the Fies*, New York: Harcourt, Brace & World, 1954.

[2] Robert Ardrey, *African Genesis*, New York: Atheneum, 1961.

[3] Robert Ardrey, *The Territorial Imperative*, New York: Atheneum, 1966.

[4] Raymond A. Dart, "The Predatory Transition from Ape to Man," *International Anthropological and Linguistic Review*, vol. I, 1953, pp. 201–8.

[5] *Ibid.*, pp. 207–8.

as such, but most tools of prehistoric man, from his earliest days, were most certainly not designed primarily to serve as weapons. Knives were designed to cut, scrapers to scrape, choppers to chop, and hammers to hammer. That such tools could be used as weapons is true, but to serve as weapons was not their primary purpose nor the reason for which they were devised.

"Man," Mr. Ardrey tells us, "is a predator whose natural instinct is to kill with a weapon" (p. 316). But man has no instincts, and if he had, they could hardly include the use of weapons in their psychophysical structure.

Early man's hunting, according to Mr. Ardrey, was due to instinctive belligerence, not to the hunger for food. "When the necessities of the hunting life encountered the basic primate instincts, then all were intensified. Conflicts became lethal, territorial arguments minor wars. . . . The creature who had once killed only through circumstance now killed for a living" (p. 317). This was "the aggressive imperative."

The evidence does not support Mr. Ardrey's theories. Whatever "the basic primate instincts" may be, they are not what Mr. Ardrey implies. Indeed, when he forgets himself, he writes of "the non-aggressive, vegetarian primate," which is precisely what all primates tend to be. But Mr. Ardrey would have us believe the contrary: the basic primate instincts according to him are aggressive. And, of course, with the assumption of hunting as a way of life, these, according to him, would become intensified. But in previous pages, and at greater length elsewhere, I have given the evidence for the contrary view. This evidence renders Mr. Ardrey's interpretations quite unacceptable. Everything points to the non-violence of the greater part of early man's life, to the contribution made by the increasing development of cooperative activities, the very social process of hunting itself, the invention of speech, the development of food-getting and food-preparing tools, and the like. These facts are never once mentioned by Mr. Ardrey, except perhaps obliquely as a doctrine which scheming scientists have foisted upon an unsuspecting world. The truth is that Mr. Ardrey is arguing a thesis. It is the thesis of "innate deprivity." It is an unsound thesis, and it is a dangerous one, because it perpetuates unsound views which justify, and even tend to

sanction, the violence which man is capable of learning, but which Mr. Ardrey erroneously believes to be inherited from man's australopithecine ancestors.

When man hunts he is the predator and the hunted animal is the prey. But prehistoric man did not hunt for pleasure, in order to satisfy his "predatory instincts." He hunted for food, to satisfy his hunger, and the hunger of those who were dependent upon him. He did not hunt because he was a "killer," any more than contemporary men are "killers" who kill animals in abattoirs so that others may eat them. Prehistoric man was no more a "killer" than we are "killers" when we sit down at table to consume a chicken or a steak which, by proxy, someone else has "killed" for us. It would be interesting to know who are the "murderers," the men who are paid to slaughter the animals we eat, or we who pay the cashier at the supermarket? Or perhaps it is really the owner of the store in which we buy meat who is the "murderer," the "killer"? Prehistoric man hunted because he desired to live—*that* hardly makes him a killer, any more than our continuing in the habit of eating meat makes us killers.

When Mr. Ardrey admiringly presents us with *West Side Story* as a "vivid portrait of natural man," in which "we watch our animal legacy unfold its awful power," in the form of juvenile delinquents in their "timeless struggle over territory, as lunatic in the New York streets as it is logical in our animal heritage," we can only say, "in police parlance," that it is worthy of William Golding's *Lord of the Flies,* in which a similar view of the depravity of human nature is unfolded. In Golding's novel two groups of children, abandoned on an island, take to hunting each other to the death. This novel has a wide readership on American college campuses, and it has recently been made into a film. Its appeal to young people is not strange, for in the world of violence in which they live Golding's novel supplies them with an easy "explanation." I understand that the novel is used in some sociology courses as a good illustration of "innate depravity," of the alleged natural nastiness of man. It could hardly be expected to be otherwise.[6]

[6] For a critical examination by various authors of Golding's thesis, see William Nelson (ed.), *William Golding's Lord of the Flies: A Source Book,* New York: Odyssey, 1963.

Mr. Ardrey has further elaborated his views in a book entitled *The Territorial Imperative,*[7] published in August 1966. In this work Mr. Ardrey endeavors to show that man's aggressiveness is based on his allegedly innate territorial nature. Man, he argues, has an innate compulsion to gain and defend exclusive territory, preserve or property. The territorial nature of man, he says, is genetic and ineradicable.

Mr. Ardrey devotes the greater part of his book to a discussion of territoriality in many different kinds of animals. He attempts to show that territoriality in animals is innately determined. The informed student of these matters would be interested in knowing why the evidence has not been considered which leads to the opposite conclusion. Mr. Ardrey writes that "The disposition to possess a territory is innate. . . . But its position and borders will be learned" (p. 25). Certainly it is biologically and socially valuable for many animals to possess their own special territory, and certainly there are strong drives in most animals to defend their territory against trespassers, but such drives are not necessarily innate. They may be learned in just the same way in which animals learn the position and borders of their territory. Territory is defined as an area defended by its occupant against competing members of the same species. But there are many animals that do not exhibit such behavior. The California ground squirrel, adult male long-tailed field mice, she-wolves, the red fox, the Iowan prairie spotted skunk, the northern plains red fox, and in the superfamily to which man belongs, the Hominoidea, the orang-utan, the chimpanzee, and the gorilla, as well as many other animals. As Bourlière has observed in his admirable book, *The Natural History of Animals,* "It would seem that territorial behavior is far from being as important in mammals as in birds."[8] Somehow, Ardrey manages to neglect to consider the significance of these many exceptional cases. And while he does mention the chimpanzee, he omits any reference to the orang-utan[9] and the gorilla.[10]

[7] Robert Ardrey, *The Territorial Imperative.*

[8] François Bourlière, *The Natural History of Animals,* New York: Knopf, 1954, pp. 99–100.

[9] Barbara Harrisson, *Orang-Utan,* New York: Doubleday, 1963.

On the naturally amiable chimpanzee's non-territoriality he comments, "The chimpanzee has demonstrated, I presume, that we must reckon on some degree of innate amity in the primate potential; but as I have indicated, it is a very small candle on a very dark night" (p. 222).

On the contrary, the non-territoriality of great apes constitutes, one would have thought, a very bright beacon in a cloudless sky, for if, as is evident, man's nearest collateral relatives are wanting in anything resembling an inborn territorial drive, it is highly improbable that any form of man was ever characterized by such a drive. Arguments based on fish, birds, and other animals are strictly for them. They have no relevance for man. "The otherwise admirable animal," the chimpanzee, is for Mr. Ardrey, "an evolutionary failure" (p. 223), while the aggressive baboon is "an outrageous evolutionary success" (p. 222).

Apparently evolutionary failure or success is to be measured by the yardstick of population number. The baboons are many, the great apes are few and are threatened with extinction. There is little evidence that the great apes were ever numerous, but that they are today few in number and threatened with extinction is all too tragically true. The diminishing numbers of these animals is due not to their lack of territoriality, but to the encroachments upon both their habitats and their lives by men with weapons against which they are utterly defenseless. No matter how highly developed their territorial sense might have been, they could never have withstood these onslaughts.

What we are witnessing in Mr. Ardrey's "territorial imperative" is a revival in modern dress of the good old "Instinct of Property" which, together with such oddities as the "Instinct of Philoprogenitiveness" and other such curiosities were repudiated by scientists half a century ago.[11]

Mr. Ardrey deplores the rejection of "instinct" in man, and actually goes so far as to suggest that "a party line" has appeared in American science designed to perpetuate the "falsehood" that instincts do not exist in man. Mr. Ardrey needs the concept of "open instincts," of innate factors, to support his theorizing. But that requirement constitutes the fatal flaw in his theory, the rift in the playwright's lute, for man is man because he has no instincts, because everything he is and has become he has learned, acquired, from his culture, from the man-made part of the environment, from other human beings. Mr. Ardrey declines to accept that fact, being more enamored of his theories than he is of facts. This is rather a pity because he would serve himself and us all a great deal more worthily if he would only realize that a scientist is not interested in proving or in disproving theories, in believing or in disbelieving, but in discovering what *is*. Thomas Henry Huxley once remarked of Herbert Spencer that his idea of a tragedy was a beautiful theory killed by an ugly fact. In Mr. Ardrey's case the beautiful facts render his ugly theories otiose.

What is the explanation of the appeal such books have for so many people? Golding's novel is a rattling good story. Ardrey's books are excitingly written and hold the reader spellbound. But these qualities are not the secret of their appeal. What, then, is?

Such books are both congenial to the temper of the times and comforting to the reader who is seeking some sort of absolution for his sins. It is gratifying to find father confessors who will relieve one of the burdensome load of guilt we bear by shifting the responsibility for it to our "natural inheritance," our "innate aggressiveness."

If it is our "nature" to be what we are, if we are the lineal descendants of our "murderous" ancestors, we can hardly be blamed or blame ourselves for the sin of being little more than made-over apes. Our orneriness is explained, and so is the peccant behavior of children, juvenile delinquency, crime, rape, murder, arson, and war, not to mention every other form of violence. It is all simply explained: it is due to man's innate aggressiveness.

There is nothing new in all this. We have heard it before. During the latter half of the 19th century, and during the early part of the

20th century, this viewpoint formed the foundation for the doctrine of "Social Darwinism." It was implied in such ideas as "The Survival of the Fittest" and "The Struggle for Existence," and in such phrases as "The weakest go to the wall," "Competition is the life-blood of a nation," and the like.

Such ideas were not merely taken to explain, but were actually used to justify, violence and war. As General von Bernhardi put it in 1912, "War is a biological necessity . . . it is as necessary as the struggle of the elements in Nature . . . it gives a biologically just decision, since its decisions rest on the very nature of things."[12] One wonders what von Bernhardi would have said after the "biologically just" defeat of Germany in two World Wars? No doubt, the general would have had little difficulty in finding an "explanation."

The new liturgy of "innate aggression," as an explanation of man's proclivities to violent behavior, does not seek to justify that behavior, but by thus "explaining" it to point the direction in which we must proceed if we are to exercise some measure of control over it. Toward this end, Dr. Konrad Lorenz, one of the founders of the modern science of ethology—the study of behavior under natural conditions of life—has dedicated himself in his latest book, *On Aggression*, published in April 1966.[13]

In *On Aggression* Lorenz has set out his views at length. In many respects they parallel those of Ardrey.

Ardrey's and Lorenz's views suffer from the same fatal defect, namely, extrapolation from other animals to man.

Why do reasonable beings behave so unreasonably, asks Lorenz. And he answers, "Undeniably, there must be superlatively strong factors which are able to overcome the commands of individual reason so completely and which are so obviously impervious to experience and learning" (p. 237). "All these amazing paradoxes, however, find an unconstrained explanation, falling into place like the pieces of a jigsaw puzzle, if one assumes that human behavior, far from being de-

[10] George Schaller, *The Mountain Gorilla: Ecology and Behavior*, Chicago: University of Chicago Press, 1963; and the same author's *The Year of the Gorilla*, Chicago: University of Chicago Press, 1964.

[11] L. L. Bernard, *Instinct*, New York: Holt, 1924; Otto Klineberg, *Social Psychology*, New York: Holt, 1954, pp. 63–75; David Krech and Richard S. Crutchfield, *Theory and Problems of Social Psychology*, New York: McGraw-Hill, 1948.

[12] Friedrich von Bernhardi, *Germany and the Next War*, New York: Longmans, 1912.

[13] Konrad Lorenz, *On Aggression*, New York: Harcourt, Brace & World, 1966.

termined by reason and cultural tradition alone, is still subject to all the laws prevailing in all phylogenetically adapted instinctive behavior. Of these laws we possess a fair amount of knowledge from studying the instincts of animals" (p. 237).

It is in these sentences that the flaws in Lorenz's argument are exhibited. First he assumes that man's frequent irrational behavior is phylogenetically based. Second, this enables him to conclude that the "laws" derived from the "study of the instincts of animals" are applicable to man.

There is, in fact, not the slightest evidence or ground for assuming that the alleged "phylogenetically adapted instinctive" behavior of other animals is in any way relevant to the discussion of the motive-forces of human behavior. The fact is, that with the exception of the instinctoid reactions in infants to sudden withdrawals of support and to sudden loud noises, the human being is entirely instinctless.

Those who speak of "innate aggression" in man appear to be lacking in any understanding of the uniqueness of man's evolutionary history. Unacquainted with the facts or else undeterred by them they insist on fitting whatever facts they are acquainted with into their theories. In so doing they commit the most awful excesses. But, as is well known, nothing succeeds like excess. Lorenz's assumptions and interpretations are typical.

"There is evidence" he writes, "that the first inventors of pebble tools—the African Australopithecines—promptly used their new weapon to kill not only game, but fellow members of their species as well" (p. 239). In fact there is not the slightest evidence for such a statement.

Lorenz continues, "Peking Man, the Prometheus who learned to preserve fire, used it to roast his brothers: beside the first traces of the regular use of fire lie the mutilated and roasted bones of Sinanthropus pekinesis himself" (p. 239).

Lorenz's interpretation of the "evidence" is one he shares with many others, but it is gravely doubted whether it is sound. The cracked bones of Peking man may represent the remains of individuals who died during a famine and who may well have been eaten by their surviving associates. This sort of thing has been known to occur among most peoples of whom we have any

knowledge. There is, however, no record of any people, prehistoric, nonliterate, or anywhere in the annals of human history, who made a habit of killing their fellow men in order to dine off them. It is absurd to suggest that Peking man used fire "to roast his brothers." Does Lorenz seriously believe that Peking man made a practice of "roast brother"? As another possibility it does not appear to have occurred to Lorenz that, like some contemporary peoples, burning the corpse may have been Peking man's way of disposing of the dead.

Lorenz writes, "One shudders at the thought of a creature as irascible as all pre-human primates are, swinging a well-sharpened hand-ax" (pp. 241–242). For a serious student of animal behavior Dr. Lorenz appears to be singularly ill-informed on the temperaments of prehuman primates. It is not "irascibility" which is the term most frequently used to describe the temperaments of "prehuman primates" by those who know them best, but "amiability." The field studies of Schaller on the gorilla, of Goodall on the chimpanzee, of Harrisson on the orangutan, as well as those of others,[14] show these creatures to be anything but irascible. All the field observers agree that these creatures are amiable and quite unaggressive, and there is not the least reason to suppose that man's prehuman primate ancestors were in any way different. Captured monkeys and apes in zoos and circuses are not the best examples from which to deduce the behavior of such creatures under natural conditions.

Lorenz writes of early man faced with "the counter-pressures of hostile and neighboring hordes" (p. 243). Again, there exists not the slightest evidence of hostility between neighboring hordes of early man. The populations of early man were very small, a few score or a few hundred individuals at most. "Neighboring hordes"

[14] Jane Goodall, "My Life among Wild Chimpanzees," *National Geographic*, vol. 124, 1963, pp. 272–308; George B. Schaller, *The Mountain Gorilla*; Barbara Harrisson, *Orang-Utan*; Charles H. Southwick (ed.), *Primate Social Behavior*, Princeton, N.J.: Van Nostrand, 1963; Irven DeVore (ed.), *Primate Behavior*, New York: Holt, Rinehart & Winston, 1965; Allan M. Schrier, Harry F. Harlow & Fred Stollnitz (eds.), *Behavior of Nonhuman Primates*, 2 vols., New York: Academic Press, 1965.

would have been few and far between, and when they met it is extremely unlikely that they would have been any less friendly than food-gathering hunting peoples are today.

"The hostile neighboring tribe," writes Lorenz, "once the target at which to discharge phylogenetically programmed aggression, has now withdrawn to an ideal distance, hidden behind a curtain, if possible of iron. Among the many phylogenetically adopted norms of human social behavior, there is hardly one that does not need to be controlled and kept on a leash by responsible morality" (p. 253).

And there we have it: man's aggressiveness is "phylogenetically programmed," and can be kept within bounds only by moral controls.

Lorenz knows a great deal about the behavior of animals, but with respect to man he apparently knows very little else that is not in the realm of nineteenth-century desk anthropology. Like Ardrey, he extrapolates his dubious interpretations of animal behavior to still more dubious conclusions concerning man.

Since all instincts, according to Lorenz, are characterized by "spontaneity," and it is this spontaneity which makes "the aggression drive" so dangerous, one would have thought that he would have provided the reader with some convincing examples of such spontaneous aggression in man. But all that Lorenz can do is to cite the "very exact psychoanalytical and psycho-sociological studies on Prairie Indians, particularly the Utes" of Sydney Margolin (p. 244). According to these "very exact" studies the Prairie Indians "led a wild life consisting almost entirely of war and raids," and that therefore, "there must have been an extreme selection pressure at work, breeding extreme aggressiveness." Since Doctors Omer Stewart and John Beatty have independently shown how utterly erroneous this account is of the Prairie Indians in general and of the Utes in particular, it only needs to be remarked that Lorenz's example of spontaneous aggression in man has not a leg to stand upon, and that the alleged "excess of aggression drive" "may have produced changes in the hereditary pattern" (p. 244) of the Utes are statements which derive no support whatever from the facts.

But Lorenz chooses to see aggression his way. Nowhere, for example, does he deign to consider how other scientists have looked at aggression. He neglects, for example, to discuss the possibility that a considerable proportion of aggressive behavior represents a reaction to frustration.[15] Nor does he pay the least attention to the view that in many instances aggressive behavior is situational, provoked by situations and conditions which have nothing whatever to do with anything "phylogenetically" or otherwise "programmed" in the individual. As a general and outstanding example of the spontaneity of instinctive aggression in man Lorenz cites "militant enthusiasm" which can be "elicited with the predictability of a reflex" when the proper environmental stimuli are available (p. 272). The possibility that "militant enthusiasm" may be learned behavior is not even considered by Lorenz. Lorenz's declarative statements are no substitute for the hard evidence that militant enthusiasm, like every other kind of enthusiasm, is learned.

The roles of learning and experience in influencing the development and expression of aggression are largely ignored by Lorenz. Yet the evidence is abundant and clear, both for animals and man, that learning and experience play substantive roles in the history of the individual or of the group in relation to the development of aggression. Where aggressive behavior is unrewarded and unrewarding, as among the Hopi and Zuñi Indians, it is minimally if at all evident.

"Let dogs delight to bark and bite, it is their nature to." Lorenz, who has written a charming book on dogs,[16] feels it is the nature, too, of men. Is it? What is human nature?

What is most important to understand in relation to that question is man's unique evolutionary history, the manner in which an ape was gradually transformed into a man as he moved from a dimension of limited capacity for learning into an increasingly enlarging zone of adaptation in which he became entirely dependent upon learning from the man-made part of the environment, *culture*, for his development as a functioning human being; that his brain, far from containing any "phylogenetically pro-

grammed" determinants for behavior, is characterized by a supremely highly developed generalized capacity for learning; that this principally constitutes his innate *hominid* nature, and that he has to learn his *human* nature from the human environment, from the culture that humanizes him, and that therefore, given man's unique educability, human nature is what man learns to become as a human being.

As we trace the details of man's evolutionary history we see that it is with the development of culture that man's brain began to grow and develop in a simultaneous feedback interaction with culture as an organ of learning, retrieval, and intelligence. Under the selection pressures exerted by the necessity to function in the dimension of culture, instinctive behavior would have been worse than useless, and hence would have been negatively selected, assuming that any remnant of it remained in man's progenitors. In fact, I also think it very doubtful that any of the great apes have any instincts. On the contrary, it seems that as social animals they must learn from others everything they come to know and do. Their capacities for learning are simply more limited than those of *Homo sapiens*.

As Clifford Geertz has put it,

Recent research in anthropology suggests that the prevailing view that the mental dispositions of man are genetically prior to culture and that his actual capabilities represent the amplification or extension of these pre-existent dispositions by cultural means is incorrect. The apparent fact that the final stages of the biological evolution of man occurred after the initial stages of the growth of culture implies that "basic," "pure," or "unconditioned," human nature, in the sense of the innate constitution of man, is so functionally incomplete as to be unworkable. Tools, hunting, family organization, and, later, art, religion, and "science" molded man somatically; and they are, therefore, necessary not merely to his survival but to his existential realization. It is true that without men there would be no cultural forms; but it is also true that without cultural forms there would be no men.[17]

Given the limits set by his genetic constitution, whatever man is he learns to be.

Throughout the two million years of man's evolution the

highest premium has been placed on cooperation, not merely *intra*group cooperation, but also upon *inter*group cooperation, or else there would be no human beings today.[18] Intra- or intergroup hostilities, in small populations, would have endangered the very existence of such populations, for any serious reduction in numbers would have made the maintenance of such populations impossible. There is not the slightest evidence nor is there the least reason to suppose that such conflicts ever occurred in human populations before the development of agricultural-pastoral communities, not much more than 12,000 years ago.

The myth of early man's aggressiveness belongs in the same class as the myth of "the beast," that is, the belief that most if not all "wild" animals are ferocious killers. In the same class belongs the myth of "the jungle," "the wild," "the warfare of Nature," and, of course, the myth of "innate depravity" or "original sin." These myths represent the projection of our *acquired* deplorabilities upon the screen of "Nature." What we are unwilling to acknowledge as essentially of our own making, the consequence of our own disordering in the man-made environment, we saddle upon "Nature," upon "phylogenetically programmed" or "innate" factors. It is very comforting, and if, somehow, one can connect it all with findings on greylag goslings, studied for their "releaser mechanisms," and relate the findings on fish, birds, and other animals to man, it makes everything all the easier to understand and to accept.

What, in fact, such writers do, in addition to perpetuating their wholly erroneous interpretation of human nature, is to divert attention from the real sources of man's aggression and destructiveness, namely, the many false and contradictory values by which, in an overcrowded, highly competitive, threatening world, he so disoperatively attempts to live. It is not man's nature, but his nurture, in such a world, that requires our attention.

[18] Ashley Montagu, *Darwin, Competition and Cooperation*, New York: Schuman, 1952; Ashley Montagu, *The Human Revolution*, New York: Bantam Books, 1967.

[15] John Dollard *et al.*, *Frustration and Aggression*, New Haven: Yale University Press, 1935.

[16] Konrad Lorenz, *Man Meets Dog*, Boston: Houghton Mifflin, 1955.

[17] Clifford Geertz, "The Growth of Culture and the Evolution of Mind," in Jordan Scher (ed.), *Theories of the Mind*, New York: Free Press, 1962, p. 736.

4.3
Violence and Man's Struggle to Adapt

Marshall F. Gilula and
David N. Daniels

Violence surrounds us, and we must try to understand it in the hopes of finding alternatives that will meet today's demand for change. Do we benefit from violence? Or is violence losing whatever adaptive value it may once have had? We present two theses. (i) Violence can best be understood in the context of adaptation. Violence is part of a struggle to resolve stressful and threatening events—a struggle to adapt. (ii) Adaptive alternatives to violence are needed in this technological era because the survival value of violent aggression is diminishing rapidly.

The shock of Robert F. Kennedy's death prompted the formation of a committee on violence (3) in the Department of Psychiatry, Stanford University School of Medicine. We committee members reviewed the literature on violence and then interpreted this literature from the point of view of psychiatrists and psychologists. We discussed our readings in seminars and sought answers to our questions about violence. This article presents a synthesis of our group's findings and observations and reflects our view of adaptation theory as a unifying principle in human behavior.

We here define aggression (4, 5) as the entire spectrum of assertive, intrusive, and attacking behaviors. Aggression thus includes both over and covert attacks, such defamatory acts as sarcasm, self-directed attacks, and dominance behavior. We extend

Reprinted by permission from *Science,* 164 (April 25, 1969), 396–405. Copyright 1969 by the American Association for the Advancement of Science. This article represents a preliminary summary statement by the Committee on Violence of the Department of Psychology, Stanford University School of Medicine. The material from which the article is drawn is revised and greatly expanded in a book edited by D. N. Daniels, M. F. Gilula, and F. M. Ochberg, *Violence and the Struggle for Existence,* Boston, Little, Brown, 1970.

aggression to include such assertive behaviors as forceful and determined attempts to master a task or accomplish an act.

By adaptation we mean the behavioral and biological fit between all species and the environment from the process of natural selection (8, 9). In man, adaptation increasingly involves modifying the environment as well. Here we want to stress that behavior, especially group-living behavior in higher social species like man, is a crucial element in natural selection (10). Adaptive behaviors are those that enhance species survival and, in most instances, individual survival. In contrast, we define adjustment as behavior of a group or individual that temporarily enhances the way we fit with the immediate situation. By definition, adjustment is often a passive rather than active process and does not result in an enduring alteration of behavior structure or patterns (4, 11). In fact, adjustment may have biologically maladaptive consequences in the long run. In addition, rapid environmental change or extraordinary environmental circumstances may render formerly adaptive behaviors largely maladaptive (10), that is, behaviors appropriate to past environmental conditions can work against survival in "new" or unusual environments.

Aggression has helped man survive. Aggression in man—including behaviors that are assertive, intrusive, and dominant as well as violent—is fundamental and adaptive. Violence is not a result of aggression but simply a form of aggression. Nor is all violence necessarily motivated by destructive aggression. For instance, in the sadistic behavior of sexual assaults, violence is evoked in part by sexual motives. In other instances, violence can occur accidentally or without conscious intent, as in many auto accidents. Currently there are three main views of aggression—all involving adaptation—but each suggests a different solution to the problem of violent behavior. Broadly labeled, these theories are (i) the biological-instinctual theory, (ii) the frustration theory, and (iii) the social-learning theory.

1) *The biological-instinctual theory* (14–16) holds that aggressive behavior, including violence, is an intrinsic component of man resulting from natural selection: Man is naturally aggressive. It is hard to imagine the survival of man without aggressiveness, namely because aggression is an

element of all purposeful behavior and, in many cases, provides the drive for a particular action. This theory says that aggression includes a wide variety of behaviors, many of which are constructive and essential to an active existence. Stimulus-seeking behavior (for example, curiosity or the need to have something happen) is certainly at least as important a facet of human behavior as avoidance behavior and need-satisfaction. Seeking the novel and unexpected provides much of life's color and excitement. Aggression can supply much of the force and power for man's creative potential.

Psychiatric and psychoanalytic case studies are one source of evidence supporting this theory (14–17). Examples range from individuals with destructive antisocial behavior who express violent aggression directly and often impulsively, to cases of depression and suicide in which violent aggression is turned against the self, and to seriously inhibited persons for whom the expression of aggression, even in the form of assertion, is blocked almost entirely. Psychiatrists and other mental-health professionals describe many disordered behaviors as stemming from ramifications and distortions of the aggressive drive (14).

Animal studies (6, 15, 18) (including primate field studies), studies of brain-damaged humans, and male-female comparisons provide behavioral, anatomical, and hormonal data illustrating the human predisposition to aggression. Among nonhuman mammals, intraspecies violence occurs less frequently than with humans (7). When violent aggressive behaviors do occur among members of the same species, they serve the valuable functions of spacing the population over the available land and maintaining a dominance order among the group members. Uncontrolled aggression in animals generally occurs only under conditions of overcrowding. Aggression in humans, even in the form of violence, has had similar adaptive value historically.

The biological-instinctual theory suggests that since aggression is inevitable, effective controls upon its expression are necessary, and reduction of violence depends upon providing constructive channels for expressing aggression.

2) *The frustration theory* (19) states that aggressive behavior comes from interfering with ongoing purposeful activity. A per-

son feels frustrated when a violation of his hopes or expectations occurs, and he then tries to solve the problem by behaving aggressively. Frustrations can take various forms: threats to life, thwarting of basic needs, and personal insults. This theory often equates aggression with destructive or damaging violent behavior. Major factors influencing aggressive responses to frustration are the nature of the frustration, previous experience, available alternatives for reaction (aggression is by no means the only response to frustration), the person's maturity, and the preceding events or feelings. Even boredom may provoke an aggressive response. As a response to frustration, aggression is often viewed as a learned rather than an innate behavior. According to this theory, frustration-evoked aggression aims at removing obstacles to our goals; hence the frustration theory also ties in with adaptation. The aggressive response to frustration often is a form of coping behavior that may have not only adjustive but also long-range consequences.

The frustration theory suggests that control or reduction of violence requires reducing existing frustrations as well as encouraging constructive redirection of aggressive responses to frustration. This reduction includes removing or improving frustrating environmental factors that stand between personal needs and environmental demands. Such factors include violation of human rights, economic deprivation, and various social stresses.

3) *The social-learning theory* (20) states that aggressive behavior results from child-rearing practices and other forms of socialization. Documentation comes from sociological and anthropological studies and from observing social learning in children. Aggressive behavior can be acquired merely by watching and learning —often by imitation—and does not require frustration. Aggressive behaviors rewarded by a particular culture or subculture usually reflect the basic values and adaptive behaviors of the group. In American culture, where achievement, self-reliance, and individual self-interest are valued highly, we also find a relatively high emphasis on military glory, a relatively high incidence of personal crime, and a society characterized by a relatively high degree of bellicosity. Similar patterns occur in other cultures. From this theory we infer that as long as a nation values

and accepts violence as an effective coping strategy, violent behavior will continue.

The social-learning theory of aggression suggests that control and reduction of violence require changes in cultural traditions, child-rearing practices, and parental examples. Parents who violently punish children for violent acts are teaching their children how and in what circumstances violence can be performed with impunity. Other changes in cultural traditions would emphasize prevention rather than punishment of violent acts and, equally important, would emphasize human rights and group effort rather than excessive and isolated self-reliance. The first step toward making the changes that will reduce violence is to examine our values. We must decide which values foster violence and then begin the difficult job of altering basic values.

In reality, the three theories of aggression are interrelated. Proclivities for social learning and for frustration often have a biological determinant. For example, the biology of sex influences the learning of courting behavior. Regarding violence, from these theories of aggression we see that the many expressions of violence include man's inherent aggression, aggressive responses to thwarted goals, and behavior patterns imitatively learned within the cultural setting. All three theories of aggression and violence fit into the adaptation-coping explanation. Violence is an attempt to cope with stressful situations and to resolve intolerable conflicts. Violence may have short-run adjustive value, even when the long-run adaptive consequences may in fact be adverse. It is the sometimes conflicting natures of adjustment and adaptation that are confusing and insufficiently appreciated. In some instances violence emerges when other more constructive coping strategies have failed. In other instances violence is used to enhance survival. Our species apparently has overabsorbed violence into our cultures as a survival technique. Children and adolescents have learned well the accepted violent behaviors of their elders.

Changing Nature of Human Adaptation: Some Speculations

Violence is unique to no particular region, nation, or time (55). Centuries ago man survived primarily as a nomadic hunter relying on

violent aggression for both food and protection. Even when becoming agricultural and sedentary, man struggled against nature, and survival still required violent aggression, especially for maintaining territory when food was scarce.

Then in a moment of evolution man's energies suddenly produced the age of technology. Instead of adapting mainly by way of biological evolution, we are now increasingly subject to the effects and demands of cultural evolution. Instead of having to adapt to our environment, we now can adapt our environment to our needs. Despite this potential emancipation from biological evolution, we retain the adaptive mechanisms derived from a long history of mammalian and primate evolution, including our primitive forms of aggression, our violence, bellicosity, and inclination to fight in a time of emergency. Where these mechanisms once responded more to physical stress, they now must respond more to social, cultural, and psychological stresses, and the response does not always produce adaptive results. Where violent aggressive behavior once served to maintain the human species in times of danger, it now threatens our continued existence.

In this new era, culture changes so rapidly that even time has assumed another dimension—the dimension of acceleration. Looking to the past becomes less relevant for discerning the future.

In the current rapidly expanding technological era, many once useful modes of adaptation are transformed into threats to survival. Territorial exclusivity is becoming obsolete in an economy of abundance. Vast weapons, communication, and transportation networks shrink the world to living-room size and expand our own backyard to encompass a "global village." Yet war and exclusivity continue. Our exploitation of natural resources becomes maladaptive. Unlimited reproduction, once adaptive for advancing the survival of the species, now produces the overcrowded conditions similar to those that lead to destructive and violent behavior in laboratory experiments with other species.

The rate at which we change our environment now apparently exceeds our capacity for adapting to the changes we make. Technological advances alter our physical and social environments, which in turn demand different adaptive strategies and a reshaping of culture. The accelerated civilization of technology is crowded, complex, ambiguous, uncertain. To cope with it, we must become capable of restructuring knowledge of our current situation and then applying new information adaptively. Several factors give us reason to hope that we can succeed.

1) Our social organization and intellectual abilities give us vast potential for coping. Knowledge and technology can be harnessed to serve goals determined by man. Automation makes possible the economics of abundance, but only our cultural values can make abundance a reality for all people. Medicine permits us to control life, but we have not yet seen fit to use this power to determine the limits of population. The technologies of communication and travel shrink the world, but man has not yet expanded the horizon of exclusion. We can learn to unite in goals that transcend exclusivity and direct cultural evolution in accordance with adaptive values and wisdom. The past need not be master of our future.

2) Violence can be understood and controlled. The crisis is one of violence, not of aggression, and it is violence that we must replace. Aggression in the service of adaptation can build and create rather than destroy. The several theories of aggression and current issues of violence suggest many complementary ways of controlling and redirecting aggression. We have suggested some in this article. Furthermore, our brief review of theory and issues points to many possibilities for multidimensional research—an approach that we believe is needed rather than "one note" studies or presentations.

3) Greater attention can be focused on both social change and adaptation processes. Cultural lag in the technological era produces not stability but a repetitious game of "catch up" characterized by one major social crisis after another and by behaviors that are too often only adjustive in that they bring relief of immediate problems while doing little to provide long-range solutions. Expanding our knowledge of the processes of social change and understanding resistance to change are of highest priority. Unforeseen change produces intolerable stress, anxiety, and increased resistance to rational change. These reactions inhibit solution-seeking behavior; evoke feelings of mistrust, loss, and helplessness; and lead to attacks on the apparent agents of change. We must develop the ability to foresee crises and actively meet them. We must dwell more on our strengths, assets, and potential as the really challenging frontier.

Conclusion

The current examples of violence and the factors encouraging it reflect our vacillation between the anachronistic culture of violence and the perplexing culture of constant change. We feel alienated and experience social disruption. Current demands for change are potentially dangerous because change activates a tendency to return to older, formerly effective, coping behaviors. Social disruption caused by change tends to increase violence as a means of coping at a time when violence is becoming a great danger to our survival.

America's current crises of violence make it difficult for us to cope with our changing world. Today's challenge, the crisis of violence, is really the crisis of man. This crisis is especially difficult because violence, a once useful but now increasingly maladaptive coping strategy, seems to be firmly rooted in human behavior patterns. We conquer the elements and yet end up facing our own image. Adaptation to a changing world rests on how effectively we can understand, channel, and redirect our aggressive energies. Then man can close his era of violence.

Summary

We are uniquely endowed both biologically and culturally to adapt to our environment. Although we are potentially capable of consciously determining the nature of our environment, our outmoded adaptive behavior—our violent aggression—keeps us from doing so.

Aggression is viewed as multidetermined. It is inherent, caused by frustration, or learned by imitation. Violent aggression is a form of attempted coping behavior that we in America, as others elsewhere, use despite its potentially maladaptive and destructive results. Current examples of violence and the factors fostering it include assassination, the mass media, mental illness and homicide, firearms and resistances to restrictive gun legislation, and collective and sanctioned violence. These examples are considered from the perspectives of the changing nature of adaptation and the opportunities they offer for research. Among recommendations for resolving or reducing violence, the need for thoughtful research by behavioral scientists is stressed. But the major obstacle to removing violence from our society is our slowness to recognize that our anachronistic, violent style of coping with problems will destroy us in this technological era.

REFERENCES AND NOTES

1. L. Eiseley, *The Immense Journey* (Random House, New York, 1946).
2. D. N. Daniels, M. F. Gilula, F. M. Ochberg, Eds., *Violence and the Struggle for Existence* (Little, Brown, Boston, in press).
3. Dr. T. Bittker, C. Boelkins, Dr. P. Bourne, Dr. D. N. Daniels (co-chairman); Dr. J. C. Gillin, Dr. M. F. Gilula, Dr. G. D. Gulevich, Dr. B. Hamburg, Dr. J. Heiser, Dr. F. Ilfeld, Dr. M. Jackman, Dr. P. H. Leiderman, Dr. F. T. Melges, Dr. R. Metzner, Dr. F. M. Ochberg (co-chairman); Dr. J. Rosenthal, Dr. W. T. Roth, Dr. A. Siegel, Dr. G. F. Solomon, Dr. R. Stillman, Dr. R. Taylor, Dr. J. Tinklenberg, Dr. Edison Trickett, and Dr. A. Weisz.
4. *Webster's Third New International Dictionary* (Merriam, Springfield, Mass., 1966).
5. J. Gould and W. L. Kolb, *A Dictionary of the Social Sciences* (Free Press, New York, 1964); L. E. Hinsie and R. J. Campbell, *Psychiatric Dictionary* (Oxford Univ. Press, ed. 3, New York, 1960).
6. R. C. Boelkins and J. Heiser, "Biological aspects of aggression," in *Violence and the Struggle for Existence*, D. N. Daniels, M. F. Gilula, F. M. Ochberg, Eds. (Little, Brown, Boston, in press).
7. *The Natural History of Aggression*, J. D. Carthy and F. J. Ebling, Eds. (Academic Press, New York, 1964).
8. Th. Dobzhansky, *Mankind Evolving* (Yale Univ. Press, New Haven, 1962).
9. G. G. Simpson, "The study of evolution: Methods and present states of theory," in *Behavior and Evolution*, A. Roe and G. G. Simpson, Eds. (Yale Univ. Press, New Haven, 1958).
10. D. A. Hamburg, "Emotions in the perspective of human evolution," in *Expression of the Emotions in Man*, P. D. Knapp, Ed. (International Universities Press, New York, 1963).
11. C. Kluckhohn. "The limitations of adaptation and adjustment as concepts for understanding cultural behavior," in *Adaptation*, J. Romano, Ed. (Cornell Univ. Press, Ithaca, New York, 1949).
12. E. Silber, D. A. Hamburg, G. V. Coelho, E. B. Murphey, M. Rosen-

berg, L. I. Pearlin, *Arch Gen. Psychiat.* 5, 354 (1961).

13. D. A. Hamburg and J. E. Adams, *ibid.* 17, 277 (1967).

14. O. Fenichel, *The Psychoanalytic Theory of Neurosis* (Norton, New York, 1945).

15. K. Lorenz, *On Aggression* (Harcourt, Brace and World, New York, 1966).

16. A. Storr, *Human Aggression* (Atheneum, New York, 1968).

17. G. F. Solomon, "Case studies in violence," in *Violence and the Struggle for Existence,* D. N. Daniels, M. F. Gilula, F. M. Ochberg, Eds. (Little, Brown, Boston, in press).

18. J. P. Scott, *Aggression* (Univ. of Chicago Press, Chicago, 1958).

19. L. Berkowitz, *Aggression: A Social-Psychological Analysis* (McGraw-Hill, New York, 1962); J. Dollard, L. W. Doob, N. E. Miller, O. H. Mowrer, R. R. Sears, *Frustration and Aggression* (Yale Univ. Press, New Haven, 1939).

20. A. Bandura and R. H. Walters, *Social Learning and Personality Development* (Holt, Rinehart, & Winston, New York, 1963); F. Ilfeld, "Environmental theories of aggression," in *Violence and the Struggle for Existence,* D. N. Daniels, M. F. Gilula, F. M. Ochberg, Eds. (Little, Brown, Boston, in press); M. E. Wolfgang and F. Ferracuti, *The Sub-Culture of Violence* (Barnes and Noble, New York, 1967).

21. R. Taylor and A. Weisz, "The phenomenon of assassination," in *Violence and the Struggle for Existence,* D. N. Daniels, M. F. Gilula, F. M. Ochberg, Eds. (Little, Brown, Boston, in press).

22. L. Z. Freedman, *Postgrad Med.* 37, 650 (1965); D. W. Hastings, *J. Lancet* 85, 93 (1965); *ibid.,* p. 157; *ibid.,* p. 189; *ibid.,* p. 294.

23. "It's Russian roulette every day, said Bobby," San Francisco *Examiner* (6 June 1968).

24. J. Cottrel, *Anatomy of an Assassination* (Muller, London, 1966).

25. A. E. Siegel, "Mass media and violence," in *Violence and the Struggle for Existence,* D. N. Daniels, M. F. Gilula, F. M. Ochberg, Eds. (Little, Brown, Boston, in press); O. N. Larsen, Ed., *Violence and the Mass Media* (Harper & Row, New York, 1968).

26. E. A. Maccoby, "Effects of the mass media," in *Review of Child Development Research,* L. W. Hoffman and M. L. Hoffman, Eds. (Russell Sage Foundation, New York, 1964).

27. L. Berkowitz, *Psychol. Today* 2 (No. 4), 18 (1968).

28. H. T. Himmelweit, A. N. Oppenheim, P. Vince, *Television and the Child* (Oxford Univ. Press, New York, 1958).

29. W. Schramm, J. Lyle, E. B. Parker, *Television in the Lives of Our Children* (Stanford Univ. Press, Stanford, Calif., 1961).

30. A. Bandura, D. Ross, S. Ross, *J. Abnorm. Soc. Psychol.* 63, 575 (1961); *ibid.* 66, 3 (1963).

31. F. Wertham, *A Sign for Cain* (Macmillan, New York, 1966).

32. G. Mirams, *Quart. Film Radio Television* 6, 1 (1951).

33. Purdue Opinion Panel, *Four Years of New York Television* (National Association of Educational Broadcasters, Urbana, Ill., 1954).

34. Associated Press report of 25 July 1968; *Christian Science Monitor* article; *New York Times* (29 July 1968).

35. G. D. Gulevich and P. Bourne, "Mental illness and violence," in *Violence and the Struggle for Existence,* in D. N. Daniels, M. F. Gilula, F. M. Ochberg, Eds. (Little, Brown, Boston, in press).

36. L. H. Cohen and H. Freeman, *Conn. State Med. J.* 9, 697 (1945).

37. H. Brill and B. Malzberg, *Mental Hospital Service (APA) Suppl. No. 153* (August 1962).

38. J. R. Rappaport and G. Lassen, *Amer. J. Psychiat.* 121, 776 (1964).

39. C. Bakal, *No [sic] Right to Bear Arms* (Paperback Library, New York, 1968).

40. C. A. deLeon, "Threatened homicide—A medical emergency," *J. Nat. Med. Assoc.* 53, 467 (1961).

41. J. C. Gillin and F. M. Ochberg, "Firearms control and violence," in *Violence and the Struggle for Existence,* D. N. Daniels, M. F. Gilula, F. M. Ochberg, Eds. (Little, Brown, Boston, in press).

42. D. N. Daniels, E. J. Trickett, J. R. Tinklenberg, J. M. Jackman, "The gun law controversy: Issues, arguments, and speculations concerning gun legislation," in *Violence and the Struggle for Existence,* D. N. Daniels, M. F. Gilula, F. M. Ochberg, Eds. (Little, Brown, Boston, in press).

43. Criminal Division, U.S. Department of Justice, *Firearms Facts* (16 June 1968); based in large part on the Federal Bureau of Investigation, *Uniform Crime Reports* (1967) (U.S. Government Printing Office, Washington, D.C., 1968).

44. F. Zimring, "*Is Gun Control Likely To Reduce Violent Killings?*" (Center for Studies in Criminal Justice, Univ. of Chicago Law School, Chicago, 1968).

45. *Congressional Quarterly,* "King's murder, riots spark demands for gun controls" (12 April 1968), pp. 805–815.

46. R. Harris, *The New Yorker* 44 (20 April 1968), p. 56.

47. E. Cleaver, *Ramparts* 7 (15 June 1968), p. 17.

48. *Amer. Rifleman* 116 (Nos. 2–5) (1968), various writings.

49. W. W. Herlihy, *ibid.* 116 (no. 5), 21 (1968).

50. T. E. Bittker, "The choice of collective violence in intergroup conflict," in *Violence and the Struggle for Existence,* D. N. Daniels, M. F. Gilula, F. M. Ochberg, Eds. (Little, Brown, Boston, in press).

51. P. Lowinger, E. D. Luby, R. Mendelsohn, C. Darrow, "Case study of the Detroit uprising: The troops and the leaders" (Department of Psychiatry, Wayne State Univ. School of Medicine, and the Lafayette Clinic, Detroit, 1968); C. Darrow and P. Lowinger, "The Detroit uprising: A psychosicial study," in *Science and Psychoanalysis, Dissent,* J. H. Masserman, Ed. (Grune and Stratton, New York, 1968), vol. 13.

52. J. Spiegel, *Psychiat. Opinion* 5 (No. 3), 6 (1968).

53. J. D. Frank, *Sanity and Survival: Psychological Aspects of War and Peace* (Random House, New York, 1967); I. Ziferstein, *Amer. J. Orthopsychiat.* 37, 457 (1967).

54. D. Freeman, "Human aggression in anthropological perspective," in *The Natural History of Aggression,* J. D. Carthy and F. J. Ebling, Eds. (Academic Press, New York, 1964).

55. L. F. Richardson, *Statistics of Deadly Quarrels* (Boxwood Press, Pittsburgh, 1960).

56. F. Ilfeld and R. Metzner, "Alternatives to violence: Strategies for coping with social conflict," in *Violence and the Struggle for Existence,* D. N. Daniels, M. F. Gilula, F. M. Ochberg, Eds. (Little, Brown, Boston, in press).

57. We thank Dr. D. A. Hamburg and Dr. A. Siegel for their review and critique of this paper and M. Shapiro, C. DiMaria, and R. Franklin for their contributions in preparing this manuscript.

Law and Order

4.4
Violence and the Police

William A. Westley

Brutality and the third degree have been identified with the municipal police of the United States since their inauguration in 1844. These aspects of police activity have been subject to exaggeration, repeated exposure, and virulent criticism. Since they are a breach of the law by the law-enforcement agents, they constitute a serious social, but intriguing sociological, problem. Yet there is little information about or understanding of the process through which such activity arises or of the purposes which it serves.[1]

Reprinted by permission of the author and the University of Chicago Press from "Violence and the Police," The American Journal of Sociology, 59 (July, 1953), 34–41. Copyright 1953 by the University of Chicago.

[1] The writer is indebted to Joseph D. Lohman for his assistance in making contact with the police and for many excellent suggestions as to research procedure and insights into the organization of the police.

This paper presents part of a larger study of the police by the writer. For

This paper is concerned with the genesis and function of the illegal use of violence by the police and presents an explanation based on an interpretative understanding of the experience of the police as an occupational group.[2] It shows that (a) the police accept and morally justify their illegal use of violence; (b) such acceptance and justification arise through their occupational experience; and (c) its use is functionally related to the collective occupational, as well as to the legal, ends of the police.

The analysis which follows offers both an occupational perspective on the use of violence by the police and an explanation of policing as an occupation, from the perspective of the illegal use of violence. Thus the meaning of

the complete study see William A. Westley, "The Police: A Sociological Study of Law, Custom, and Morality" (unpublished Ph.D. dissertation, University of Chicago, Department of Sociology, 1951).

[2] Interpretative understanding is here used as defined by Max Weber (see The Theory of Social and Economic Organization, trans. Talcott Parsons [New York: Oxford University Press, 1947], pp. 88).

this use of violence is derived by relating it to the general behavior of policemen as policemen, and occupations in general are illuminated through the delineation of the manner in which a particular occupation handles one aspect of its work.

The technical demands of a man's work tend to specify the kinds of social relationships in which he will be involved and to select the groups with whom these relationships are to be maintained. The social definition of the occupation invests its members with a common prestige position. Thus, a man's occupation is a major determining factor of his conduct and social identity. This being so, it involves more than man's work, and one must go beyond the technical in the explanation of work behavior. One must discover the occupationally derived definitions of self and conduct which arise in the involvements of technical demands, social relationships between colleagues and with the public, status, and self-conception. To understand these definitions, one must track them back to the occupational problems in which they have their genesis.[3]

The policeman finds his most pressing problems in his relationships to the public. His is a service occupation but of an incongruous kind, since he must discipline those whom he serves. He is regarded as corrupt and inefficient by, and meets with hostility and criticism from, the public. He regards the public as his enemy, feels his occupation to be in conflict with the community, and regards himself to be a pariah. The experience and the feeling give rise to a collective emphasis on secrecy, an attempt to coerce respect from the public, and a belief that almost any means are legitimate in completing an important arrest. These are for the policeman basic occupational values. They arise from his experience, take precedence over his legal responsibilities, are central to an understanding of his conduct, and form the occupational contexts within which violence gains its meaning. This then is the background for our analysis.[4]

[3] The ideas are not original. I am indebted for many of them to Everett C. Hughes, although he is in no way responsible for their present formulation (see E. C. Hughes, "Work and the Self" in Rohrer and Sherif, Social Psychology at the Crossroads [New York: Harper & Bros., 1951]).

[4] The background material will be developed in subsequent papers which

The materials which follow are drawn from a case study of a municipal police department in an industrial city of approximately one hundred and fifty thousand inhabitants. This study included participation in all types of police activities, ranging from walking the beat and cruising with policemen in a squad car to the observation of raids, interrogations, and the police school. It included intensive interviews with over half the men in the department who were representative as to rank, time in service, race, religion, and specific type of police job.

Duty and Violence

In the United States the use of violence by the police is both an occupational prerogative and a necessity. Police powers include the use of violence, for to them, within civil society, has been delegated the monopoly of the legitimate means of violence possessed by the state. Police are obliged by their duties to use violence as the only measure adequate to control and apprehension in the presence of counterviolence.

Violence in the form of the club and the gun is for the police a means of persuasion. Violence from the criminal, the drunk, the quarreling family, and the rioter arises in the course of police duty. The fighting drunk who is damaging property or assailing his fellows and who looks upon the policeman as a malicious intruder justifies for the policeman his use of force in restoring order. The armed criminal who has demonstrated a casual regard for the lives of others and a general hatred of the policeman forces the use of violence by the police in the pursuit of duty. Every policeman has some such experiences, and they proliferate in police lore. They constitute a common-sense and legal justification for the use of violence by the police and for training policemen in the skills of violence. Thus, from experience in the pursuit of their legally prescribed duties, the police develop a justification for the use of violence. They come to see it as good, as useful, and as their own. Furthermore, although legally their use of violence is limited to the requirements of the arrest and the protection of themselves and the community, the contingencies of their occupation lead them to

enlarge the area in which violence may be used. Two kinds of experience—that with respect to the conviction of the felon and that with respect to the control of sexual conduct—will illustrate how and why the illegal use of violence arises.

1. The conviction of the felon. —The apprehension and conviction of the felon is, for the policeman, the essence of police work. It is the source of prestige both within and outside police circles, it has career implications, and it is a major source of justification for the existence of the police before a critical and often hostile public. Out of these conditions a legitimation for the illegal use of violence is wrought.

The career and prestige implication of the "good pinch"[5] elevate it to a major end in the conduct of the policeman. It is an end which is justified both legally and through public opinion as one which should be of great concern to the police. Therefore it takes precedence over other duties and tends to justify strong means. Both trickery and violence are such means. The "third degree" has been criticized for many years, and extensive administrative controls have been devised in an effort to eliminate it. Police persistence in the face of that attitude suggests that the illegal use of violence is regarded as functional to their work. It also indicates a tendency to regard the third degree as a legitimate means for obtaining the conviction of the felon. However, to understand the strength of this legitimation, one must include other factors: the competition between patrolman and detectives and the publicity value of convictions for the police department.

The patrolman has less access to cases that might result in the "good pinch" than the detective. Such cases are assigned to the detective, and for their solution he will reap the credit. Even where the patrolman first detects the crime, or actually apprehends the possible offender, the case is likely to be turned over to the detective. Therefore patrolmen are eager to obtain evidence and make the arrest before the arrival of the detectives. Intimidation and actual

violence frequently come into play under these conditions. This is illustrated in the following case recounted by a young patrolman when he was questioned as to the situations in which he felt that the use of force was necessary:

One time Joe and I found three guys in a car, and we found that they had a gun down between the seats. We wanted to find out who owned that gun before the dicks arrived so that we could make a good pinch. They told us.

Patrolmen feel that little credit is forthcoming from a clean beat (a crimeless beat), while a number of good arrests really stands out on the record. To a great extent this is actually the case, since a good arrest results in good newspaper publicity, and the policeman who has made many "good pinches" has prestige among his colleagues.

A further justification for the illegal use of violence arises from the fact that almost every police department is under continuous criticism from the community, which tends to assign its own moral responsibilities to the police. The police are therefore faced with the task of justifying themselves to the public, both as individuals and as a group. They feel that the solution of major criminal cases serves this function. This is illustrated in the following statement:

There is a case I remember of four Negroes who held up a filling station. We got a description of them and picked them up. Then we took them down to the station and really worked them over. I guess that everybody that came into the station that night had a hand in it, and they were in pretty bad shape. Do you think that sounds cruel? Well, you know what we got out of it? We broke a big case in ———. There was a mob of twenty guys, burglars and stick-up men, and eighteen of them are in the pen now. Sometimes you have to get rough with them, see. The way I figure it is, if you can get a clue that a man is a pro and if he won't co-operate, tell you what you want to know, it is justified to rough him up a little, up to a point. You know how it is. You feel that the end justifies the means.

It is easier for the police to justify themselves to the community through the dramatic solution of big crimes than through orderly and responsible completion of their routine duties. Although they may be criticized for failures in routine areas, the criticism for the failure to solve big crimes is more intense and sets off a criticism of their work in noncriminal areas.

---

will analyze the occupational experience of the police and give a full description of police norms.

[5] Policemen, in the case studied, use this term to mean an arrest which (*a*) is politically clear and (*b*) likely to bring them esteem. Generally it refers to felonies, but in the case of a "real" vice drive it may include the arrest and *conviction* of an important bookie.

VIOLENCE IN BERKELEY. PHOTOS COURTESY OF JOSHUA WATTLES.

The pressure to solve important cases therefore becomes strong. The following statement, made in reference to the use of violence in interrogations, demonstrates the point:

If it's a big case and there is a lot of pressure on you and they tell you you can't go home until the case is finished, then naturally you are going to lose patience.

The policeman's response to this pressure is to extend the use of violence to its illegal utilization in interrogations. The apprehension of the felon or the "good pinch" thus constitutes a basis for justifying the illegal use of violence.

2. *Control of sexual conduct.*—The police are responsible for the enforcement of laws regulating sexual conduct. This includes the suppression of sexual deviation and the protection of the public from advances and attacks of persons of deviant sexual tendencies. Here the police face a difficult task. The victims of such deviants are notoriously unwilling to cooperate, since popular curiosity and gossip about sexual crimes and the sanctions against the open discussion of sexual activities make it embarrassing for the victim to admit or describe a deviant sexual advance or attack and cause him to feel that he gains a kind of guilt by association from such admissions. Thus the police find that frequently the victims will refuse to identify or testify against the deviant.

These difficulties are intensified by the fact that, once the community becomes aware of sexual depredations, the reports of such activity multiply well beyond reasonable expectations. Since the bulk of these reports will be false, they add to the confusion of the police and consequently to the elusiveness of the offender.

The difficulties of the police are further aggravated by extreme public demand for the apprehension of the offender. The hysteria and alarm generated by reports of a peeping Tom, a rapist, or an exhibitionist result in great public pressure on the police; and, should the activities continue, the public becomes violently critical of police efficiency. The police, who feel insecure in their relationship to the public, are extremely sensitive to this criticism and feel that they must act in response to the demands made by the political and moral leaders of the community.

Thus the police find themselves caught in a dilemma. Apprehension is extremely difficult because of the confusion created by public hysteria and the scarcity of witnesses, but the police are compelled to action by extremely public demands. They dissolve this dilemma through the illegal utilization of violence.

A statement of this "misuse" of police powers is represented in the remarks of a patrolman:

Now in my own case when I catch a guy like that I just pick him up and take him into the woods and beat him until he can't crawl. I have had seventeen cases like that in the last couple of years. I tell that guy that if I catch him doing that again I will take him out to those woods and I will shoot him. I tell him that I carry a second gun on me just in case I find guys like him and that I will plant it in his hand and say that he tried to kill and that no jury will convict me.

This statement is extreme and is not representative of policemen in general. In many instances the policeman is likely to act in a different fashion. This is illustrated in the following statement of a rookie who described what happened when he and his partner investigated a parked car which had aroused their suspicions:

He [the partner] went up there and pretty soon he called me, and there were a couple of fellows in the car with their pants open. I couldn't understand it. I kept looking around for where the woman would be. They were both pretty plastered. One was a young kid about eighteen years old, and the other was an older man. We decided, with the kid so drunk, that bringing him in would only really ruin his reputation, and we told him to go home. Otherwise we would have pinched them. During the time we were talking to them they offered us twenty-eight dollars, and I was going to pinch them when they showed me the money, but my partner said, "Never mind, let them go."

Nevertheless, most policemen would apply no sanctions against a colleague who took the more extreme view of the right to use violence and would openly support some milder form of illegal coercion. This is illustrated in the statement of another rookie:

They feel that its okay to rough a man up in the case of sex crimes. One of the older men advised me that if the courts didn't punish a man we should. He told me about a sex crime, the story about it, and then said that the law says the policeman has the right to use the amount of force necessary to make an arrest and that

in that kind of a crime you can use just a little more force. They feel definitely, for example, in extreme cases like rape, that if a man was guilty he ought to be punished even if you could not get any evidence on him. My feeling is that all the men on the force feel that way, at least from what they have told me.

Furthermore, the police believe, and with some justification it seems, that the community supports their definition of the situation and that they are operating in terms of an implicit directive.

The point of this discussion is that the control of sexual conduct is so difficult and the demand for it so incessant that the police come to sanction the illegal use of violence in obtaining that control. This does not imply that all policemen treat all sex deviants brutally, for, as the above quotations indicate, such is not the case. Rather, it indicates that this use of violence is permitted and condoned by the police and that they come to think of it as a resource more extensive than is included in the legal definition.

Legitimation of Violence

The preceding discussion has indicated two ways in which the experience of the police encourages them to use violence as a general resource in the achievement of their occupational ends and thus to sanction its illegal use. The experience, thus, makes violence acceptable to the policeman as a generalized means. We now wish to indicate the particular basis on which this general resource is legitimated. In particular we wish to point out the extent to which the policeman tends to transfer violence from a legal resource to a personal resource, one which he uses to further his own ends.

Seventy-three policemen, drawn from all ranks and constituting approximately 50 percent of the patrolmen, were asked, "When do you think a policeman is justified in roughing a man up?" The intent of the question was to get them to legitimate the use of violence. Their replies are summarized in Table 1.

An inspection of the types and distribution of the responses indicates (1) that violence is legitimated by illegal ends (A, C, E, F, G) in 69 per cent of the cases; (2) that violence is legitimated in terms of purely personal or group ends (A) in 37 per cent of the cases (this is important, since it is

TABLE 1. BASES FOR THE USE OF FORCE NAMED BY 73 POLICEMEN[a]

TYPES OF RESPONSE	FRE-QUENCY	PERCENT-AGE
(A) Disrespect for police	27	37
(B) When impossible to avoid	17	23
(C) To obtain information	14	19
(D) To make an arrest	6	8
(E) For the hardened criminal	5	7
(F) When you know man is guilty	2	3
(G) For sex criminals	2	3
Total	73	100

[a] Many respondents described more than one type of situation which they felt called for the use of violence. The "reason" which was either (a) given most heatedly and at greatest length and/or (b) given first was used to characterize the respondent's answer to the question. However, this table is exhaustive of the types of replies which were given.

the largest single reason for the use of violence given); and (3) that legal ends are the bases for legitimation in 31 per cent of the cases (B and D). However, this probably represents a distortion of the true feelings of some of these men, since both the police chief and the community had been severely critical of the use of violence by the men, and the respondents had a tendency to be very cautious with the interviewer, whom some of them never fully trusted. Furthermore, since all the men were conscious of the chief's policy and of public criticism, it seems likely that those who did justify the use of violence for illegal and personal ends no longer recognized the illegality involved. They probably believed that such ends fully represented a moral legitimation for their use of violence.

The most significant finding is that at least 37 per cent of the men believed that it was legitimate to use violence to coerce respect. This suggests that policemen use the resource of violence to persuade their audience (the public) to respect their occupational status. In terms of the policeman's definition of the situation, the individual who lacks respect for the police, the "wise guy" who talks back, or any individual who acts or talks in a disrespectful way, deserves brutality. This idea is epitomized in admonitions given to the rookies such as, "You gotta make them respect you" and "You gotta act tough." Examples of some of the responses to the preceding question that fall into the "disrespect for the police" category follows:

Well, there are cases. For example, when you stop a fellow for a routine questioning, say a wise guy, and he starts talking back to you and telling you you are no good and that sort of thing. You know you can take a man in on a disorderly conduct charge, but you can practically never make it stick. So what you do in a case like that is to egg the guy on until he makes a remark where you can justifiably slap him and, then, if he fights back, you can call it resisting arrest.

Well, it varies in different cases. Most of the police use punishment if the fellow gives them any trouble. Usually you can judge a man who will give you trouble though. *If there is any slight resistance,* you can go all out on him. You shouldn't do it in the street though. Wait until you are in the squad car, because, even if you are in the right and a guy takes a poke at you, just when you are hitting back somebody's just likely to come around the corner, and what he will say is that you are beating the guy with your club.

Well, a prisoner deserves to be hit when he goes to the point where he tries to put you below him.

You gotta get rough when a man's language becomes very bad, when he is trying to make a fool of you in front of everybody else. I think most policemen try to treat people in a nice way, but usually you have to talk pretty rough. That's the only way to set a man down, to make him show a little respect.

If a fellow called a policeman a filthy name, a slap in the mouth would be a good thing, especially if it was out in the public where calling a policeman a bad name would look bad for the police.

There was the incident of a fellow I picked up. I was on the beat, and I was taking him down to the station. There were people following us. He kept saying that I wasn't in the army. Well, he kept going on like that, and I finally had to bust him one. I had to do it. The people would have thought I was afraid otherwise.

These results suggest (1) that the police believe that these private or group ends constitute a moral legitimation for violence which is equal *or superior* to the legitimation derived from the law and (2) that the monopoly of violence delegated to the police, by the state, to enforce the ends of the state has been appropriated by the police as a personal resource to be used for personal and group ends.

The Use of Violence

The sanctions for the use of violence arising from occupational experience and the fact that policemen morally justify even its illegal use may suggest that violence is employed with great frequency and little provocation. Such an impression would be erroneous, for the actual use of violence is limited by other considerations, such as individual inclinations, the threat of detection, and a sensitivity to public reactions.

Individual policemen vary of course in psychological disposition and past experience. All have been drawn from the larger community which tends to condemn the use of violence and therefore have internalized with varying degrees of intensity this other definition of violence. Their experience as policemen creates a new dimension to their self-conceptions and gives them a new perspective on the use of violence. But individual men vary in the degree to which they assimilate this new conception of self. Therefore, the amount of violence which is used and the frequency with which it is employed will vary among policemen according to their individual propensities. However, policemen cannot and do not employ sanctions against their colleagues for using violence,[6] and individual men who personally condemn the use of violence and avoid it whenever possible[7] refuse openly to condemn acts of violence by other men on the force. Thus, the collective sanction for the use of violence permits those men who are inclined to its use to employ it without fear.

All policemen, however, are conscious of the dangers of the illegal use of violence. If detected, they may be subject to a lawsuit and possibly dismissal from the force. Therefore, they limit its use to what they think they can get away with. Thus, they recognize that, if a man is guilty of a serious crime, it is easy to "cover up" for their brutality by accusing him of resisting arrest, and the extent to which they believe a man guilty tends to act as a precondition to the use of violence.[8]

[6] The emphasis on secrecy among the police prevents them from using legal sanctions against their colleagues.

[7] Many men who held jobs in the police station rather than on beats indicate to the interviewer that their reason for choosing a desk job was to avoid the use of violence.

[8] In addition, the policeman is aware that the courts are highly critical of confessions obtained by violence and that, if violence is detected, it will "spoil his case."

The policeman, in common with members of other occupations, is sensitive to the evaluation of his occupation by the public. A man's work is an important aspect of his status, and to the extent that he is identified with his work (by himself and/or the community) he finds that his self-esteem requires the justification and social elevation of his work. Since policemen are low in the occupational prestige scale, subject to continuous criticism, and in constant contact with this criticizing and evaluating public, they are profoundly involved in justifying their work and its tactics to the public and to themselves. The way in which the police emphasize the solution of big crimes and their violent solution to the problem of the control of sexual conduct illustrate this concern. However, different portions of the public have differing definitions of conduct and are of differential importance to the policeman, and the way in which the police define different portions of the public has an effect on whether or not they will use violence.

The police believe that certain groups of persons will respond only to fear and rough treatment. In the city studied they defined both Negroes and slum dwellers in this category. The following statements, each by a different man, typify the manner in which they discriminate the public:

In the good districts you appeal to people's judgment and explain the law to them. In the South Side the only way is to appear like you are the boss.

You can't ask them a question and get an answer that is not a lie. In the South Side the only way to walk into a tavern is to walk in swaggering as if you own the place and if somebody is standing in your way give him an elbow and push him aside.

The colored people understand one thing. The policeman is the law, and he is going to treat you rough and that's the way you have to treat them. Personally, I don't think the colored are trying to help themselves one bit. If you don't treat them rough, they will sit right on top of your head.

Discriminations with respect to the public are largely based on the political power of the group, the degree to which the police believe that the group is potentially criminal, and the type of treatment which the police believe will elicit respect from it.

Variations in the administration and community setting of the police will introduce variations in their use of violence. Thus, a thoroughly corrupt police department will use violence in supporting the ends of this corruption, while a carefully administered nonpolitical department can go a long way toward reducing the illegal use of violence. However, wherever the basic conditions here described are present, it will be very difficult to eradicate the illegal use of violence.

Given these conditions, violence will be used when necessary to the pursuit of duty or when basic occupational values are threatened. Thus a threat to the respect with which the policeman believes his occupation should be regarded or the opportunity to make a "good pinch" will tend to evoke its use.

Conclusions

This paper sets forth an explanation of the illegal use of violence by the police based on an interpretative understanding of their occupational experience. Therefore, it contains a description and analysis of *their* interpretation of *their* experience.

The policeman uses violence illegally because such usage is seen as just, acceptable, and, at times, expected by his colleague group and because it constitutes an effective means for solving problems in obtaining status and self-esteem which policemen as policemen have in common. Since the ends for which violence is illegally used are conceived to be both just and important, they function to justify, to the policeman, the illegal use of violence as a general means. Since "brutality" is strongly criticized by the larger community, the policeman must devise a defense of his brutality to himself and the community, and the defense in turn gives a deeper and more lasting justification to the "misuse of violence." This process then results in a transfer in property from the state to the colleague group. The means of violence which were originally a property of the state, in loan to its law-enforcement agent, the police, are in a psychological sense confiscated by the police, to be conceived of as a personal property to be used at their discretion. This, then, is the explanation of the illegal use of violence by the police which results from viewing it in terms of the police as an occupational group.

The explanation of the illegal use of violence by the police offers an illuminating perspective on the social nature of their occupation. The analysis of their use of brutality in dealing with sexual deviants and felons shows that it is a result of their desire to defend and improve their social status in the absence of effective legal means. This desire in turn is directly related to and makes sense in terms of the low status of the police in the community, which results in a driving need on the part of policemen to assert and improve their status. Their general legitimation of the use of violence *primarily* in terms of coercing respect and making a "good pinch" early points out the existence of occupational goals, which are independent of and take precedence over their legal mandate. The existence of such goals and patterns of conduct indicates that the policeman has made of his occupation a preoccupation and invested in it a large aspect of his self.

We present here two views of campus violence—one a personal account by a policeman, the other a defense of the political validity of violence by a socialist. Officer Maginnis, a student as well as an officer, pours out feelings of fear, confusion, and revulsion against violence from either side. Arneson gives a reasoned political analysis of the value of violence in the same demonstration that Officer Maginnis was involved in. His point is summarized in his conclusion:

In order to eliminate violence from this society, it will be necessary for the ordinary people of this society to revolutionize that defective social structure—by any means necessary.

4.5
I Wear Two Hats

Robert Maginnis
Police Officer, San Leandro, California, and Student, University of California, Berkeley

Disorders span a wide spectrum of types; they are seen in the form of

By permission of the author.

racially oriented riots, labor management disputes, anti-war demonstrations, and as of late, the weekly confrontations on the college campus.

In the United States the years 1960–1969 had more varied types of civil disorders than any other decade in the 193-year history of this country. The loss of life has numbered into the hundreds, the property damage into the billions of dollars and the scars that were left behind are irreparable.

A number of in-depth studies, sponsored, censored and published by the government, have flooded the book stores and reading racks in the last five to seven years. The McCone Report, the Kerner Report, the Walker Report and the Report to the President's Commission on Crime and Civil Disorder are but a few examples of the current ones on the market. Once you read these reports, it becomes noticeable that there is a system to them all; that is, each has an introduction loaded with political names, a discussion of the causes, reactions of the involved, "casting": rioters, police, local lawmakers, news-media and the victims, a section on criticism and related evaluation, all of which is rounded out into a well laid conclusion. After reading all of these reports, it begins to remind the reader of a broken record.

None of these reports takes the time to delve into the individuals that are involved and none of these reports was written by any of those persons that were directly related by involvement or whatever in the disorders. A number of people that were involved wrote or gave oral "canned" supplements, resulting in each side placing the blame for the causes upon the other. While the theme of these reports is supposed to be accurate, little is printed about the individual. Who is this person? As I see him, he is like you and me; student, non-student, faculty member, policeman, national guardsman, SDS, RSU, TWLF, PLP, newsman, cameraman, the left, the right, plainclothesman, the list is unlimited. Looking over this list, it brings to mind the long cast credits prior to seeing a spectacular movie. Although these reports fail to mention such, these people and the reasons for being involved are as important, if not more so, than the issue at hand.

Keeping this in mind and based upon the dual role that I have at the University of California at Berkeley, I offer this paper as an attempt to view not only the issues, but to show what it is like to see the disorders from the police officer's position as I do. The area of concentration will be the latest disruptions at UC, since February, 1970, and reflections of past experiences that I have had in Berkeley.

It is imperative that the reader keep in mind that this paper does not offer any solutions, will not come to a theoretical conclusion, but will strive to tell it like it is. The research area was somewhat limited as it consists mainly of my personal reflections, those of my fellow officers and fellow students.

I wrote this paper for the purpose of letting someone know how a policeman feels about being involved in campus disruptions. I have tried to put into writing what this position is like without a philosophical stand on the legality of demonstrations or a defense of the use of police.

I first enrolled as a student at UC in the summer of 1969, as a junior, and I have been attending full time in the School of Criminology. The police department for which I work requires all of the officers to pursue a degree, of at least two years of college, in any field. I am twenty-eight, married, and have one daughter, seventeen months old. Politically, I am, what you might call a liberal. I am against the war in Vietnam and the recent expansion into Cambodia. In fact, I am against all wars.

During my three years with the Department, I have responded to mutual aid to the following locations: Oakland Induction Center, 1967, San Francisco State, 1968, College of San Mateo, 1968, and UC, 1968, 1969 and 1970.

My first appearance in Berkeley as a police officer was during the Third World Liberation Front Movement in 1968–69. Nine other officers and I went to the campus and then out into the streets. I will never forget as long as I live the scene in Berkeley as I walked in a line of twenty officers down Durant Avenue toward Telegraph.

As I recall it was on a Wednesday and I was home, my wife was fixing dinner. At 5:30 the phone rang. An hour later I was in the line walking down Durant Avenue. I am sure to those who could see the line moving, we looked like twenty uniformed, inhuman robots. Ugly brown helmets with odd-shaped plexi-glass face shields cover faces with no identity. Each one wearing a dark brown bulky nylon jacket, with large, heavy fur collars, which turn upward

to protect the back of the neck. We all carry a 36″ riot baton, which is held across the chest. My left hand is even with the badge, which in the nighttime reflects the street lamps and the numbers 55 are easily read. My right hand is even with the large brown belt around my waist. This belt carries the service revolver, a container of MACE, a pair of handcuffs, a small portable radio, and two odd-looking pouches which carry 18 rounds. There is an odd-colored sack that hangs along my left leg and inside the sack is the gas mask. Hanging from the two straps that hold the gas mask are four gas grenades; two are the instantaneous blast type and two are the continuous type, all are CS (containing an irritant). As I walk the cans clink against one another, and between the clinking noises, one can strikes the brass baton ring and a ringing sound is added to the concerto of strange noises. The clinging and the ringing rhyme with the footsteps and the keys that are jangling from the large brown belt. Multiplying these sounds by twenty produces an eerie almost frightening noise as we walk down Durant toward Telegraph. Unconsciously listening to the sounds of the moving men, I glance down the line, and I can see the reactions from the gas that is kicked up as we walk, for some officers have removed their helmets and are putting their gas masks on. The line stalls for a moment, but once the masks are in place, we all move on. Those of us that are not wearing masks begin to breathe a bit heavier; partially due to the wandering, lost clouds of gas and partly due to nervousness. As we get closer to the intersection, I can hear yelling, the sounds of glass breaking and the cracking of shotguns firing tear-gas cannisters. The heavy breathing has caused a circular form of fog on the inside of the face shield.

We are almost in the intersection and what I thought to be a simple fire is now a blazing inferno located directly in the center of the intersection. There is no one in sight, at least that I can see, except a shop owner who is matching four by twelve foot sections of thick, heavy plywood to the metal shells which used to hold the glass front to his shop. Walking now in the gutter, I hear crushing noises and looking down I note that I'm walking in a sea of broken glass. A street sweeper has just passed through the intersec-

tion and the water on the shattered glass mirrors the flames that are leaping, licking at the night from this large fire that is located, as if by design, dead center in the intersection. This fire, a symbol of defiance, is as disorganized as its makers; bus benches, garbage cans, clothing, newspapers and their racks all adding to the twenty- to thirty-foot flames that alight the area.

Stunned by the sight, and as if magically possessed, we all stop. No people, no cars, no animals, just twenty policemen staring at this pile of flame. The scene reminded me, as it did others, of a scene from an old World War II movie, which shows a bombed-out, deserted town, with all of its people gone and the only sign of life—a fire, with the ashes and burnt debris that surrounds it.

Once on Telegraph Avenue, we turn toward campus avoiding the fire. The noise of our presence was beginning to bring people to their windows and suddenly people were appearing everywhere. Some were speechless, some swore and others were content to simply look, and wonder why.

We were almost to the campus and walking along I kicked an empty tear gas cannister, black from emitting its gas, out into the street. It reminded me of playing kick-the-can when I was young.

As we approach Bancroft, the gas is much heavier and is choking those of us who don't have on masks. Must be CS gas rather than the milder CN. The street sweeper is making another pass which will disturb the gas on the ground and prompt masks on the rest of us.

We complete our sweep up to Bancroft, and that is as far as we were to go. Then, as if we had scored the winning goal, we left the area, returned to our cars and departed from Berkeley.

At 9:30 P.M. I was home again eating the postponed dinner wondering what it was all about.

Ever since this experience I have asked myself why? Why the disorder? Why police? Why the burning? Why the destruction, the waste? Now that I am more involved—involved as a student—I think that I can attack this "why" and rationalize an answer.

Being on campus and rapping with students, I now see that student organizations have grievances or differences of opinion that clash with university policy. The Free Speech Movement, anti-ROTC and anti-war demonstrations, Free Huey, TWLF are examples, just to name a few. As a student I cannot see why the diverse opinions cannot come to some sort of an agreement. Yet it seems that each time a group raises an issue, the University's response is a negative one. For example, in late 1968, the TWLF supporters wanted their own college. The response from the University was quite emphatic—NO! There is no form of collective bargaining, no conferring in good faith by which the matter could be settled to the satisfaction of both sides.

Frustrated by the attitude of the administration, the group will turn to Sproul Plaza and the weapon of the "noon rally." With the chiming of the Campanile, as the hands mark the noon hour, the rally begins. In order for it to be a success it must be illegal. Illegal rallies invariably draw larger crowds. The rally with its variety of speakers lasts until one or one-fifteen. At this time, the rally ends and marches begin and quite frequently the rocks fly.

Flying rocks lead to broken windows and broken windows mean police, and with the appearance of police, a number of events take place. The campus police, if unable to contain the situation, call for mutual aid. More police are poured into the area, arriving in great numbers. (There is an agreement among the Police Departments in the Bay area to provide any number of men directed by the Sheriff of the County.) Then, in response, the original crowd is swelled by numbers of high school students and off-campus people that are attracted by the opportunity to throw a rock or two. The police become the target of the demonstrators and the rocks, and the initial issue takes a temporary second place. The battle cry of "ROTC off campus" changes to "PIGS off campus."

Many of the students and non-student participants view the use of police as a political tool of the administration who are present to enforce University laws, rules, political ideals or to protect University interests. Yet no one is called to protect the ideals of those demonstrating; save the demonstrators themselves!

After a period of rock throwing, the police advance, their shot-guns launching tear gas cannisters. The gas begins to fill the Plaza and the crowd dissipates and the cat and mouse tactics begin. The police advance, some demonstrators are arrested, some clubbed, both sides

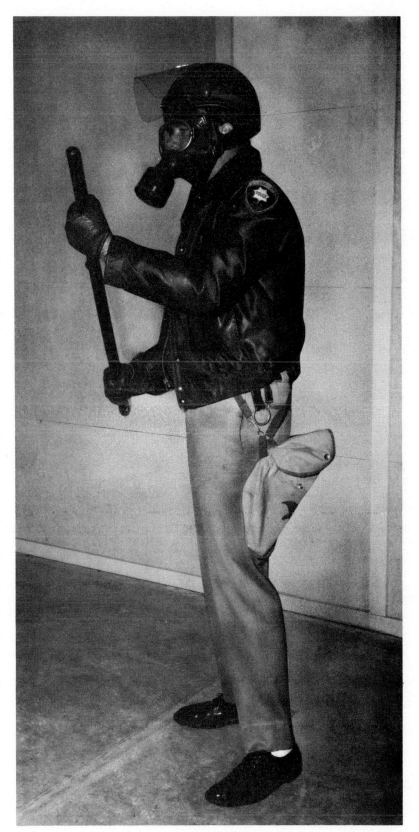

OFFICIAL POLICE DEPARTMENT PHOTOGRAPH OF AUTHOR, POLICE OFFICER **ROBERT MAGINNIS**.

bear injuries. And the game goes on.

The chain of events is always the same no matter what the issue. At 12:00 noon in Sproul Plaza, an illegal rally is held to protest the issue; this lasts approximately one hour. One to one-thirty is the hate-and-stir half-hour. One-thirty to five is the "throwing of rocks and marching period." Five o'clock marks the beginning of the commuter rush hour and nothing will stop a commuter. These are the chronological events that I see as I walk to and from classes. I often pause to listen to the speeches and watch the police take pictures from atop Sproul Hall. I walk off shaking my head because the speech sounds much like the one made the day before; and as I walk away, I glance around wondering how many present are students. I often become depressed since a great University is being maimed by it all. I try to convince myself that these are people who have something to say, to them something very important, and the administration refuses to listen. Thus, demonstration is the only means they have to get their point across and force the administration to listen to their demands.

I leave the campus, get on my motorcycle and go home as a student only to return the following day as a police officer.

The University of California Police Department is located in the basement of Sproul Hall. I usually arrive with nine other officers and after parking our vehicles we walk there, where an officer is assigned to our squad for communication purposes. There is the sound of loud voices as there are 200 policemen in the long hallway. Many are playing cards, a few are telling "war stories," some are reading books, most are complaining. The order is given to leave and one officer swears because it interrupts his run on hearts. Once outside the atmosphere changes. "Look at all them hippies . . ." "Long-haired ass-holes . . ." "Hey, that gal isn't wearing a bra . . ." "Look at that skirt!" As ordered, we move across Sproul Plaza as the crowd is just beginning to hold a rally—for it is not quite 12 noon. On past Sather Gate and we take our position—waiting, just like I remember doing in the Army.

As if someone rings a ready bell, the action starts. During the rally, more policemen appear and I can hear some of them; "We oughta get the Mexican Army and do like they did in Mexico—Shoot the bastards!" "Let 'em come this way and I'll wail on their skulls." (You never, if at all possible, strike anyone on the head; it looks bad.) A camera crew from ABC, CBS and NBC are present. One cameraman comes over to where we are standing and takes a few feet of me. I had the strongest urge to place my 36″ baton about his head and shoulder, so I simply turned my back: I have very strong feelings about T.V. people at demonstrations—not only as a police officer, but as a student. I feel strongly that they promote a good portion of the violence. About 1:30 we move into Zeller-bach Hall, where as it turned out we stayed until about 4:00. Once inside, some of the officers remark upon the beauty of the Hall; the woodwork, the hanging tapestries and the mosaic art work. The cards make their re-appearance and the game of hearts is resumed. I retrieve a pocket book from my jacket, remove the jacket, gas grenades, gas mask, riot baton, and the helmet—which gives me a headache—and spend the next 2½ hours reading and wondering when this will all end. Occasionally I glance out of the second story windows, all of which have rock holes, toward the Sproul area. The original crowd now numbers about 2–3000. I can see those damn cameramen running around, trying to grab onto some of the euphoria of the crowd. I hear a loud noise and we all jump up to see what happened but all seems peaceful—probably a cherry bomb. We are all a little jumpy, although you never show it, because the UCPD had received a call that eight cops would be torched on this particular day. Right outside of the main doors, three men and a dog were playing with a frisby. The frisby sailed upon the roof, but the three young "hippy" type men, two cops, one sturdy table and the game were back in operation with only a ten-minute interruption. Ironic I thought.

The officers that weren't playing cards were people-watching. They were amazed at the collection of types that pass in review; amazed at the style of dress, length of hair, and length of skirts. I was content to read but one officer said that I should join them and watch the people go by, that I wouldn't believe it. I casually mentioned that I was a student here and saw it every day. A look of dismay came over his face; maybe he didn't realize that police officers go to school.

I got tired of reading after a while, which was bad for I started rationalizing my position and involvement.

Police on campus—ten years ago I would have thought that such a situation would not be possible. Now I was part of it. Why the police, I thought? Why not the National Guard? Why not that group of draft dodgers and misfits? The police are called for the simple reason that society does not provide any other force that could handle the situation. I have often hoped that just once Sheriff Madigan would refuse the use of police. Would the other students then take on the responsibility and control the situation themselves?

I often discuss these campus disorders with my fellow officers and one question they always ask me is why some of the 27,000 plus students at Berkeley don't take a stand against the demonstrators. I wish I knew. I have asked a number of students that I know are not involved in the demonstrations why they don't intervene and make their feelings known and put an end to these disruptions. The answers varied. Some, although not directly involved, sympathized with the movement; others simply refused to get involved—perhaps out of fear.

The events have changed as of late. UC is on strike and the "no business as usual" attitude prevails. But one single incident polarized student feelings toward demonstrations and that was the killing of four students at Kent State. It finally happened. My initial reaction, which was shared by many of my fellow officers, was twofold: one, it was due to come, and two, I am glad the police didn't do it. At Berkeley, the impact was most noticeable. The peace brigade, a group of students who *had* intervened against the rock throwers, became an important tool and its purpose a useful one. Something had to be done before a "Kent State" happened at Berkeley.

There is no conclusion, since this paper is nothing more than an attempt to show you what it is like to wear two hats. It is really a unique position, and sometimes an awkward one.

4.6
Violence and Social Change

Dick Arneson

The shooting of four Kent State students by National Guardsmen last week, together with the often combative demonstrations staged across the country in response to the invasion of Cambodia, poses sharply the question: does violence help or hinder movements of protest politics?

When people express skepticism about the efficacy of violence in promoting social change, the image of violence that is usually foremost in their minds is that of individual acts of terrorism or sabotage. Terrorism as a political strategy has been much in vogue lately among would-be radicals. In Berkeley over the past three years, more than a hundred power-line blowups and similar acts have been attributed to, and sometimes even claimed by, radicals. The Weatherman bombings in New York City a few months ago dramatized the attractiveness of terrorism to some elements in the New Left.

Terrorism—hysteria-creating acts of violence carried out by individuals in isolation from any mass movement—expresses the politics of frustration. It's no accident that the ideology of terrorism —first discredited more than 50 years ago—has been resurrected in this country at a time when the anti-war movement was faltering, the student movement seemed to be heading into a dead end, and prospects for building a mass radical movement in this country appeared (to more pessimistic activists) to be virtually nil. Terrorism is the last resort of those who see no way of altering for the better a society they correctly perceive to be in crisis.

A chief stumbling block preventing the growth of mass movements is the conviction of ordinary people that no matter how bad things are, there is no way that they can improve their condition by their own self-activity. This conviction of powerlessness is inculcated by capitalist society, reinforced by the schools, the media, and the job environment. For its own protection, capitalism attempts to instill in the vast majority of people a sense of

Reprinted by permission from "Violence and Social Change," *International Socialist Supplement*, May, 1970.

docility and passivity. For example, electoral politics is structured in such a way as to induce the populace to rely on charismatic heroes, rather than their own intiative, for the solution of social problems.

Terrorist acts carried out by individuals as a substitute for mass action *reinforce* people's feelings of impotence. The political message conveyed by such acts is: don't struggle for yourselves, struggle vicariously by identifying with this heroic individual act. But vicarious struggle is just a euphemism for not struggling at all. That's why Lenin always referred contemptuously to terrorists as "liberals with bombs."

Terrorist acts express liberal politics in another sense as well. Individual acts of violence against the authorities say, in effect, that the trouble with the world is that bad guys are in power, and must be deposed. After a police-station bombing in San Francisco killed several policemen, an underground newspaper interviewed people in the neighborhood about the bombing. The answers centered on the personal character of the cops who were killed. A typical response was: "The desk sergeant was a good guy, so it was bad karma to bump him off." The bombing diverted attention *away* from the social role of the police.

In response, Marxists have always pointed out that it is the social system that's the problem, not the individuals who staff that system. If you assassinate the czar, you don't get democracy, you get another czar. If you assassinate Nixon, you get Agnew, and so on.

An even more telling objection to individual acts of frustration is that they presuppose the futility of mass action. The idea lurking behind terrorism is that since there is no chance of winning the vast bulk of the American people to the side of the movement, the only available mode of protest is individual heroism.

Not surprisingly then, the nationwide eruption of protest triggered by the invasion of Cambodia has lessened the political appeal of the ideology of terrorism.

At the other extreme from terrorism, which characteristically glorifies violence in the abstract, is pacifism, which abstractedly condemns all forms of violence, irrespective of the social context in which violence occurs.

The absolute rejection of violence as a tactic for the movement is associated with roughly the fol-

lowing position: violence breeds more violence. Responding in kind to a violent attack leads to a violent counter-attack, and another violent rejoinder in turn. The only way to break that vicious circle is to step outside it by refusing to engage in violence of any kind. Applied to politics, this position entails that the way to create a non-violent society is to build a principled non-violent movement.

The trouble with pacifist theories is that they necessarily fail to explain adequately the causes of violence in the world today. Nothing is explained by saying that violence or aggression is ingrained in human nature like some sort of original sin. Violence is rooted in the clash of conflicting social interest. The precondition of a truly non-violent society is the creation of a society that is based on the elimination of the social antagonisms that are the most fundamental causes of social violence.

Meanwhile, back in the world we inhabit today, it is not the case that all men can be won over to progressive ideas through peaceful persuasion as pacifists suppose. The people who control this society have different interests than the rest of us—they have a stake in remaining in power, for instance—and they will use all the violence at their disposal whenever violence is needed to maintain their position at the top of society.

The Vietnam War demonstrates the genocidal steps that America's rulers are willing to take in order to preserve capitalism as a world system. The task of those who desire world peace is to build a movement that can force the ruling class to stop the war and dismantle the imperialist war economy. Any such movement will be attacked by the police forces of the state and to shrink from self-defense and confronting the police is to give up the struggle.

Those who eschew all violence as a tool of the movement fail to discriminate adequately between violence harnessed to a mass movement against oppression and violence employed by those who benefit from that oppression and seek to sustain it. Nobody in his right mind wants peace at *any* price. One way to obtain a peaceful world would be for everybody who suffers from injustice—from Vietnamese peasants to American workers—to give up struggle and accept an unjust *status quo*. But such a world, though peaceful, would be a moral nightmare.

The goal of the anti-war movement must be not just peace, but peace-and-freedom. Where violence is necessary in order to defend social movements working towards a truly free and just society, it is immoral to abstain from the use of violence. When the Bolsheviks in 1918 were accused of using the same terrorist methods as the counter-revolution, Trotsky stated this point forcefully:

The terror of Tsarism was directed against the proletariat. The gendarmerie of Tsarism throttled the workers who were fighting for the socialist order. Our extraordinary commissions shoot landlords, capitalists and generals who are striving to restore the capitalist order. Do you grasp this distinction? Yes? For us communists it is quite sufficient.

Burning a bank is not the same as napalming a Vietnamese village. Trying to disrupt a university or a draft board is not the same as trying to destroy a country or a people. Panthers organizing to liberate black people is not the same as police organizing to annihilate the Panthers. And breaking the windows of an Administration building is not the same as killing or bayoneting demonstrators.

Liberation or Oppression

Organized self-defense or even an aggressive, disruptive demonstration is not terrorism. There is violence and then there is violence. Liberation is not the same as oppression.

Non-violence may often prove to be a useful tactic in many circumstances, particularly where people's understanding of the system they are fighting is confused or where the adoption of militant tactics would yield a military disaster. A non-violent sit-in that galvanizes thousands of people against some evil may be preferable to a combative demonstration that attracts only a few hard-core radicals.

No tactic is sacred and no principle says that a movement must be disruptive at all times. The criterion for deciding what tactic to adopt is simply: will it succeed in building the movement, in raising popular consciousness?

The recent anti-ROTC demonstrations on the Berkeley campus provide a case in point. On April 15, thousands of students staged a militant march against ROTC headquarters and battled the police with rocks for four hours after police attacked with clubs

and tear gas to disperse the crowd. However, in subsequent days the demonstrations lost their political focus and almost took on the character of a rumble against the police.

Some vandalism ensued which was not directed at any political target—for example, the breaking of windows at random throughout the campus. This minor vandalism provided the pretext for indiscriminate denunciations of the demonstrations for their "violent" character, and many students were sufficiently confused by these denunciations to abstain from the struggle. The "trashing" of university buildings was politically mistaken precisely because it allowed people to confuse the central question posed by the militant demonstrations: namely, the right of the movement to defend itself from police attack.

When a mass demonstration against ROTC is confronted by the police whose basic social role is to defend institutions like ROTC, the protesters have basically three options: (1) go home; (2) submit passively to arrests and beatings at the hands of the police; or (3) continue the demonstration and defend themselves as best they can from the cops.

Alternative (1) means giving up the struggle. Alternative (2) in effect puts the demonstrators at the mercy of the police and grants the legitimacy of the state's use of police against the movement. Neither is an appropriate response to police violence.

The right of a mass movement for social change to use whatever force is necessary and appropriate in order to achieve its goals is not intuitively obvious to people newly drawn into social struggle. At a mass meeting of 15,000 students, faculty and staff to organize a strike on the Berkeley campus against the invasion of Cambodia, hundreds booed when a speaker suggested that it will be necessary for the movement to *fight* in order to win the political freedom to organize on the campus against the war.

Very quickly, in the course of the struggle itself, those who hissed will learn that the violence of this society perpetrated at home and abroad arises from its social structure. In order to eliminate violence from this society, it will be necessary for the ordinary people of this society to revolutionize that defective social structure—by any means necessary.

Institutionalized Violence: The Prison

This section presents several articles on the genesis and redirection of violent behavior in the prisons of America. The prison is a social system marked by the practice of the repression of violent men. It is a non-success story of a system which effectively creates what it is in theory designed to eliminate—violence. Steps toward reform of these failures produce the "so what else is new" reaction, in a vain hope of sweeping the problem under the rug. One hopeful note is sounded in Hammer's story

of an imaginative use of role playing and psychodrama to bring convicts, judges, and policemen together to share concerns about prison reform. James McConnell contributes an article on constructive brainwashing—in the Skinnerian tradition—which advocates behavioral control of antisocial behavior in a style which smacks of put-on (hopefully).

4.7
Kansas's Achilles' Heel

Newsweek

The Achilles' tendon, a thick, sinewy cord running from the base of the heel to the muscles of the calf, is the control rod of the foot. If it is cut—or if it snaps accidentally, as sometimes happens to middle-aged athletes—the victim's foot flops like a ragdoll's, and for all practical purposes the leg is useless below the knee for six or eight weeks after the tendon has teen retied. It is a grotesque disability, yet last week no fewer than two dozen inmates of Kansas State Penitentiary in Lansing were dragging themselves around the prison yard on crutches—victims of severed Achilles' tendons that they themselves had cut.

Crippled legs are only part of a widespread protest campaign of self-mutilation that has been going on at the prison since July. Using stolen knives, broken light bulbs and even a shattered plastic radio earphone, the convicts have been hacking away at their own tendons, wrists, anything that promises to maim them flagrantly enough to embarrass prison authorities. "He tore the stitches out of his wrist on the way back to prison from the hospital," one official said recently of a prisoner, "and then stuck his finger into the wound and ripped the tendon apart."

"Good Time"

Lansing's self-mutilation campaign is the latest and most provocative evidence of troubles racking the nation's penal system on the state and local level. In the words of one former Kansas official, "There isn't a prison in this country that isn't run at the sufferance of the inmates." The Kansas rebels, far from being a band of suffering Paul Munis rising against their chain-gang bosses, are 40 or 50 hard-core "lifers" who had got used to running the prison their own way and are trying to gouge their old perquisites back from a tough new penal director named Robert Woodson. These used to include control over nearly every aspect of the lives of the prison's 1,300 convicts; homosexual gang-rape was the usual method of enforcement.

There was no limit to the ruling clique's power: in the year preceding July 1, insiders say, six inmates were murdered without official reprisal. First-time offenders were forced to sign up in homosexual "marriages" simply to get the protection to survive, and the inmate "Mafia" controlled the drug trade. "Good time at Lansing," ran the yardbirds' motto, "is bad time anywhere else."

Still, there were small compensations. Under Charles McAttee, who was Woodson's predecessor as penal director until his term ran out last summer, inmates were allowed the freedom of the penitentiary. Prison athletic teams traveled all over the state to compete, and individual prisoners were allowed out on speaking dates and other worthy ventures. In McAttee's view, he had no choice but to let the inmates run the prison. Guards are paid so poorly that no skilled man wanted the job, and few honest ones were able to keep it. Even worse, there are no facilities in the over-crowded prison for sealing off the harmless "straight" prisoners from the hard-core thugs. "The meanest and nastiest criminals claw their way to the top of the convict power structure," according to Dr. Donald Hardesty, a Washburn University psychologist who has studied the prison. "The most devastating psychological weapon to keep the rank and file in line is the forcing of homosexual acts. Anyone who comes in there weighing less than 160 pounds can expect to be gang-raped and turned into a 'catcher.'"

Crackdown

Things got so out of hand that McAttee himself had to raid his own prison last June. In a cell-by-cell shake-down, he found hundreds of weapons—switchblades, make-shift garrotes, lead pipes—and huge quantities of drugs and hypodermics. The next morning, prisoners exploded in a riot that was not finally put down for ten days. Robert Woodson was at the prison when the trouble erupted. Watching the tear gas fly, he vowed that he would "tighten up security and crack down on the inmates" as soon as he took over as penal director on July 1. This he did in tough-cop style, canceling all outside travel privileges, regulating prisoner movements within the prison and—for what it was worth—doubling the number of guards in each cell-block. He cracked down on the drug trade, on gambling and on convict control of the prison hospital and workshops.

Almost immediately, the first of the self-mutilated prisoners appeared in sick bay. At first straggling in only in ones and twos, as many as 25 maimed and bleeding prisoners began turning up daily after a "declaration of war" against Woodson in October. There have been nearly 400 cases so far; as the total mounts, the tension mounts with it—not only among the hard-core but among a great many blameless prisoners as well, who resent the loss of their few privileges. Woodson is placing his hopes on winning a $1 million boost in funds from the state legislature for better-paid and better-qualified guards, but he intends to fight it out on this line in any case. It will be tough. "Anybody who thinks this penitentiary is under control," said a con named Fred Reynolds last week, "is kidding himself."

4.8
One Year of Prison Reform

Tom Murton

On January 29, 1968, Claude Overton, manager of the Cummins Prison Farm, an installation of the Arkansas State Penitentiary, informed chief security officer Harold A. Porter that, because rain was expected in the afternoon, he would not be working the longline (inmate work force) after lunch. Porter therefore stopped by the infirmary about 1:15 P.M. to pick up Reuben Johnson, who had related a bizarre tale of inmates having been murdered and buried in the mule pasture known as Bodiesburg. A squad of Negro inmates marched through the pasture to a point selected by Johnson and proceeded to dig in three adjacent sites.

Livestock manager Frank Crawford and I were in the general area at the time when an inmate came up to us and matter of factly stated: "Mr. Murton, we've struck a coffin." I moved to the site and supervised the excavation of three graves which yielded three mutilated bodies placed in the exact location and in the same condition as Reuben Johnson had indicated. Two were decapitated and the skull of the third had been crushed to the size of a grapefruit.

Within the hour, the remains of the three inmates had been dug up, preserved as evidence, the official agencies had been notified and the squad of inmates had moved triumphantly back to the barracks to relate events to the jubilant prison population. They left behind three gaping scars in the mule pasture—mute testimony to the degradation imposed upon the penal slaves of Arkansas.

The state's prison system had been operated on fear for a century, and most of the traditional methods had been used to instill it: beatings, needles under the fingernails, stompings, the "hide" (a leather strap 5 inches wide and 5 feet long), starvation and an electric device whose terminals were attached to the genitals of the inmate while a trusty or "warden" gleefully turned the crank. True, the prison had made a profit during the previous fifty years. The champions of the Arkansas prison system proudly boasted—and still do—that no appropriated funds were required to support the "convicts." But exploitation of inmates was effective only under the spur of threats, and the ultimate threat was murder. There is ample evidence that the illegal executions uncovered that January day were not isolated events.

The prison has survived the cycle of scandal and reform every twenty or thirty years and has resisted with equal success the occasional token objections from those who became "concerned" about the treatment of prisoners. But that was before Winthrop Rockefeller became the first Republican governor of the state since Reconstruction. Rockefeller expressed understandable indignation over a state police report, prepared in August of 1966, which catalogued the cruelty practiced in the Arkansas prison system. As a candidate, he pledged elimination of corruption in state government, efficiency and "to hire a professional penologist to run the state prison system." [See "Arkansas Prison Farm" by Robert Pearman, *The Nation*, December 26, 1966.] Rockefeller won the election with a mandate from the electorate to end the century of decadence in Arkansas.

A routine police investigation at another unit of the penitentiary system, Tucker Prison Farm, in January of 1967 had disclosed Superintendent Pink Booher sitting at his desk behind a Thompson submachine gun, ready to repel any attack from the inmates who had threatened to shoot him if he attempted to enter the prison proper. This was no idle threat because, in the Arkansas tradition, the total guard force consisted of inmates who were issued guns and instructed to watch over the other prisoners. At that time, only six hired staff and some forty-eight inmate guards were authorized at Tucker. That was one way to save money for the state.

Governor Rockefeller promptly dismissed the superintendent and three other staff members. And for the third time in less than a year, the Arkansas State Police was placed in command of some 300 inmates on the 4,500-acre prison farm.

As one of several consultants to the new state administration, I was called to Tucker to evaluate the situation. In the latter part of February 1967 I was hired as superintendent. The first thing that struck me was the atmosphere of total despair. The inmates did not smile, laugh or talk. Their eyes, their expressions and their demeanor were a vivid portrayal of hopelessness. We found that control of inmates, work assignments, visiting privileges, commissary privileges, furloughs, laundry and clothing procedures, parole eligibility, inmate funds, and the very survival of the inmate had always been delegated to a select few powerful inmates who operated the prison. The system had become ingrained because of lack of outside staff, an apathetic civilian population, indifference on the part of the Governor and the greed of both inmate trusties and various citizens who had a vested interest in the prison and its profits.

To make the system operable, the trusties had been granted certain privileges, including graft obtained from all inmate goods and services, freedom to sell liquor and narcotics, to gamble and lend money, to live in "squatter shacks" outside the main prison, to spend the night with a female companion and to profit from the illegal traffic in prison produce.

Of the two staff members remaining at the time of my appointment, one resigned and the other was fired. That left me in command of a fifteen-man police detachment quartered at the prison, with no civilian staff and an "uptight" inmate population. The first order of business was to arm the state troopers, who had been prohibited by the inmate guards from carrying arms. The power of the inmate guard force was so absolute that when Governor Rockefeller first visited the prison he was not allowed in until his bodyguard had surrendered his gun to an inmate at the front gate.

That spring, the legislature increased the authorized staff at Tucker from six to thirty-eight officers, and I immediately imported a cadre of officers with whom I had worked before. Our basic strategy was to treat the inmate with dignity—a concept heretofore unheard of in Arkansas. Trust was built up in the prison population by daily decisions which cumulatively demonstrated that the prison administration was actually committed to inmate welfare.

However, the real danger was in the inmate power structure, and an attempt to eliminate every aspect of that power would have been foolhardy because, in varying degrees, inmates determine the operation of *all* such institutions. We decided to accept the existence of inmate power, but to substitute, if we could, a legitimate form of self-government for the traditionally exploitive one.

The prison reforms received no assistance from the official agencies of criminal justice, the legislature, the prison board, the prison study commission, other state agencies or the public. As a result, the staff and inmates were drawn together in efforts to reform the prison while providing mutual defense against collective opposition from outside.

My sole authority was that granted by the Governor. Nevertheless, we were able in a few months to feed and clothe the inmates, hire competent staff, upgrade the agricultural programs, establish educational and vocational training programs, provide a rational religious counseling service (to replace forced church attendance under the gun), eliminate corruption, move the trusties into the barracks, and practically eliminate the rapes and other homosexual assaults.

Inmates. were no longer required to act as servants for the staff; they no longer worked outside, tilling the soil for private citizens. Prison-grown food no longer went "out the gate" into private hands; livestock management was upgraded by acquisition of new breeding stock and the institution of sound animal husbandry practices. And a host of minimal creature comforts were provided. We ultimately broke the convict power structure by eliminating the monetary exchange that had maintained the inmate economy, with the attendant gambling, loan rackets and assaults.

I acknowledged that the inmates had information, not available to the professional staff, that could be effective in reforming the prison. One-half of the newly elected inmate council constituted the classification committee which determined work assignments, promotion and the ever critical decisions as to which inmates would be issued guns. It should be noted that no inmate whom the committee classified as minimum custody ever escaped during our administration.

The other half of the inmate council became the disciplinary committee. It proved much more effective than the administration in assigning punishments (I had abolished all corporal punishment). I sat with both committees and reserved the right of veto, but never had to exercise it. A form of responsible self-government was emerging.

Breaking the power structure produced great anxiety among the trusties and culminated in a rash of escapes. (Arkansas is one of the few states where the prison administration must be concerned with the escape of *guards*.) During the first half of my tenure at Tucker, we lost thirty-eight inmates; in the last half, only one inmate escaped. As the tensions eased, we were able to open up death row, where the ten condemned men—one white and nine black—had been confined to their cells under rigid security. Eventually, they were playing in ball games, performing work assignments with the white inmates, attending school, church and vocational classes, playing in the prison band and finally were eating in the dining hall.

One of the last innovations at Tucker, toward the end of 1967, was the inauguration of prison dances, to which inmates were allowed to invite their girl friends or wives (either, but not both). There were no incidents at these parties, no hurled insults, no

drinking and no rape. One unplanned result of the relaxed atmosphere was the intermingling of staff and inmates as dancing partners and the unpardonable sin (in Arkansas) of interracial dancing.

By Christmas of 1967, a woman supervisor was able to work at the prison laundry, female employees ate in the prison dining hall, female teachers conducted classes inside the institution with no guard present and the staff and their families attended programs, sitting with the general inmate population. The most significant change was in the attitude of the inmates. Fear had disappeared, a new community had been created and despair had been replaced by hope. Our energies were no longer directed toward overcoming the inmate population, but toward coping with the state bureaucracy and dealing with our changing relationship with the Governor's office.

That was the situation at Tucker as my staff and I prepared to assault Cummins. The word is used advisedly because it became evident that it might be necessary to shoot our way into the prison to install me as superintendent of the entire prison system. The opposition from both inmates and officials at Cummins was so concerted that death threats had been made against both me and Harold Porter, who earlier had transferred to Cummins. The official police assessment of the situation was that I could not take over the superintendency without an armed force of about 1,000 men. Such a force, composed of state troopers, National Guardsmen and airborne troops, was made available.

I declined the help, preferring to choose for myself the back-up force with whom I would entrust my life. Consequently, I initially took over the institution—peacefully—with the help of a single man, inmate Sheriff "Chainsaw" Jack Bell, who was serving a life sentence for killing a man by sawing off his head.

In a few weeks we managed to gain a semblance of control of the institution, dismissed the more hostile and brutal employees, changed key inmate guards, improved living conditions for both inmates and livestock, eliminated inmate services to the staff, stopped corruption in the medical services and modified procedures at the Women's Reformatory located at Cummins.

That institution of about forty women had constituted the "lost souls" of the Arkansas prison system. They customarily were transported in the same transfer vans with the men and were routinely raped en route to the prison or to and from the state hospital. Many female inmates refused medical attention for fear of being raped on the way to surgery.

Negro inmates among the women had been forced to clip grass with their fingernails as "therapy"; they received only scraps of food left on the table after the white inmates had finished eating. The sewing endeavors in the reformatory were primarily for the benefit of the matrons and their families. Exercise, dancing, talking during the evening, smoking, sitting on the bed, looking at a man (or worse yet, talking to a man) were all punished as serious offenses. The usual sentence was solitary confinement in a concrete cell, which had no plumbing, water or heat. If a prisoner rebelled, the head matron would call her husband, who would "lay on the hide" as the inmate was held to the floor by trusties. One former superintendent had had a buzzer installed next to his bed. With it, he could summon his favorite girl friend from the nearby reformatory.

Mrs. Frank Crawford, whom I placed in charge, promptly corrected the more obvious faults, as we had done at the other institution. We later took a bus load of female inmates to Tucker to participate in the dances. An inmate who had been taken to the State Hospital for childbirth, was allowed to bring her baby back to the prison and to keep him in the main dormitory in an area screened off as a "nursery."

A wedding was planned to legalize a common-law relationship between a pregnant inmate and her man. Mrs. Crawford was to be the matron of honor; her husband Frank was to be best man; my visiting sister, Paula, was to play the organ; Jon Kimbrell, the Tucker chaplain, was to officiate; and I was asked by the prospective bride to give her away. The ceremoney was to take place in the main prison auditorium on March 11, 1968. But events which took place four days before that date forced cancellation of the plans.

In thirteen months, we had revolutionized Tucker and were well on the way to doing the same at Cummins. We achieved what we did in spite of the hostile prison board (which hoped for my failure), the system of criminal justice (which blocked my efforts to prosecute those who stole from the prison), the legislature (which tried to censure me), the citizens of the area (who could no longer steal from the prison), the grand jury (which threatened to indict me for "grave-robbing") and the trusties and staff (some of whom in both groups threatened to kill me).

We also had to withstand the sabotage of equipment sent to Cummins for "repair," the shooting of our livestock at night, the deliberate burning of our slaughterhouse, the refusal of Cummins officials to can our produce and the interference by state purchasing officials, consultants, the Governor's aides and other state officials. *All* reform achievements were accomplished under these adverse conditions.

The year 1968 promised to be different. We had gained the impetus of reform by the Tucker experience, and solving the Cummins problems was essentially a matter of time and strategy. Four of the five members of the old prison board resigned rather than confirm my appointment as permanent superintendent of the prison system. This action cleared the way for Governor Rockefeller to gain control of a state department for the first time since his election.

John Haley, his first appointee to the board a year previously, was elevated to chairman and four other men of seemingly progressive views were appointed in mid-January. Haley, a practicing attorney, was joined by psychiatrist Dr. Peyton Kolb; Marshal Rush, a professional farmer; W. L. Currie, a vocational teacher and the first Negro member of the board, and William Lytle, a minister and professor of theology. Lytle had been appointed at my urging because he had been instrumental in my coming to Arkansas and had expressed deep concern for the prison. Our acquaintance dated from my wedding, at which he had officiated some fifteen years earlier.

We waited in anticipation for Governor Rockefeller, through the board, to effect some of the changes beyond the power of the superintendent. Now the audit of prior prison management could be commenced; gains we had made at Tucker could be consolidated under the supervision of Robert Van Winkle; progressive bills could be prepared for the legislature; a contract could be signed with Tennessee correctional authorities for housing and care of female prisoners; federal funds could be obtained pursuant to grant requests then pending; livestock management could be brought into the 20th century; the inmates could be properly clothed and fed; the Cummins power structure could be broken; and a thorough investigation of the bodies in the mule pasture could be completed.

These were all within our grasp, but the board members, sensing no real support from the Governor, did not reach out to seize true prison reform. Instead, they chose to undermine every aspect of our work. Governor Rockefeller became frightened on the very threshold of success, and deferred to opponents who desired the prison system to remain as it had been. They, and his own advisers, convinced him that I was damaging the image of Arkansas and that his continued stay in office depended on my immediate removal.

The new prison board officially met with me for the first time on March 2, 1968 and informed me that I probably would not be appointed as commissioner to guide the new Department of Correction. Five days later, when the board again met with me, I was summarily fired and placed under house arrest. Although no reasons were given at the time, Governor Rockefeller and John Haley at a press conference the following day accused me, in part, of being a "poor prison administrator" (although Haley had stated I demonstrated "near genius" in revolutionizing Tucker); of knowing nothing about agriculture (ignoring my degree in agriculture, that I had farmed and also taught the subject); and of having ordered asparagus tips for the inmates (a grave accusation contrary to the facts).

It is now nearly two years since Governor Rockefeller appointed his "progressive" Board of Correction. Sufficient time has elapsed to provide some tentative assessment of the direction of prison reform in Arkansas. State Rep. Ivan Rose appealed to his colleagues during a special session of the legislature in 1968: "We got rid of Murton for you so give us a good vote [on prison reform legislation]." They did not then nor have they since.

Anticipated federal grants have not been forthcoming, promised prison industries have not mate-rialized and no contract with Tennessee has been negotiated for care of female prisoners. It was necessary to sell part of the dairy herd in 1968 and again in 1969 in order to provide prison operating funds. An audit of prior prison management, conducted in 1968, yielded evidence of official corruption. The board suppressed the report and no action has been taken against the accused. No superintendent since my removal has had the courage to abolish the money exchange system at Cummins. Hence the inmate power structure continues to exist with the related graft, corruption, intimidation, bootlegging, gambling and assaults. The present commission admits that there have been eighteen stabbings and five deaths since I left.

The inmate council and the disciplinary and classification committees have been abolished. Inmates again work as servants for the staff. The heads of new inmates are shaved as part of the degradation ceremony of prison initiation. Our open press policy has been eliminated, and the prison facilities are in effect closed to newsmen. Thus there is no independent agency to report prison conditions to the public.

Seven key staff members were either fired or resigned when I was forced out. Since then, sixteen of my former staff have been removed. During the first year, seventy-two of ninety-seven prison employees left the prison system. There was no prison physician for eighteen months after my departure. It was eight months before an applicant for commissioner could be enticed to Arkansas. My allegedly "incapable" dairy supervisor was replaced by a "professional" dairyman who shortly thereafter was not only fired for incompetence but was arrested by the state police at the front gate of the prison while trying to smuggle a stolen heifer from the institution.

At Cummins, the inmates raised havoc with the unfinished isolation unit during the summer of 1968 in protest of treatment which they contended constituted "cruel and unusual punishment." The federal court agreed and prison officials were ordered to devise other punitive measures.

Supt. Victor C. Urban then demonstrated his ingenuity by chaining inmates to a fence in a small compound for several days and nights. They received no bedding, no jackets, and had to sleep —if they slept—on the bare ground. But to the inmates so confined, the worst aspect was the humiliation of being forced to squat in the open compound to defecate, while chained to the fence and being observed by visitors.

These facts were reported by the press in the fall of 1968, but the incidents were overshadowed by the shot-gunning of about 100 inmates who sat peacefully in the prison yard in protest against inadequate food, being forced to work from sunup to sundown, being threatened with a pistol by the rider (inmate foreman) and the reinstitution of the "convict doctor" system.

Prison officials later conceded that the protesting inmates had posed no threat, nor were they attempting to riot, create a disturbance or escape. Yet, Associate Superintendent Gary Haydis, with Urban's prior consent, is said to have ordered the shooting. Twenty-four inmates were wounded, one of them losing an eye. Urban proclaimed: "I will not permit any inmate body to take over and rule, which is what this one *would probably have wanted to do*" (emphasis added).

Haydis has since returned to his former employment as director of training of the California Department of Corrections, from which he had been granted a leave of absence while helping to *reform* the Arkansas prison. In the summer of 1969, he was indicted by a federal grand jury in Little Rock for his part in shooting the inmates. On December 16, Haydis went to trial in federal court in Little Rock. Two days later Judge Smith Henley issued a directed verdict of acquittal to the jury based on what he termed a "lack of evidence." Urban has been promoted to Deputy Commissioner of Correction in Arkansas.

The investigation of the bodies in the mule pasture ended with a fraudulent police report which purports to support the myth that what we found was actually a "paupers' graveyard." No more bodies have been exhumed; no prison graveyard has been established; and the present administration has, by silence, in effect condoned a prison system of brutality, torture and murder.

At Tucker, the death-row inmates are again restricted to their quarters a large portion of the day. Only two now have any assigned work project. All forms of legitimate inmate power which we had instituted have been abolished and exploitive trusties have been

moved back into positons of authority. The man chosen to be inmate sheriff at Tucker was sentenced to prison for twenty-one years upon conviction for "assault with intent to commit rape." In October of 1969, he "arrested" an employee of the prison before she reached the farm, drove to a lonely road and raped her—to the amazement of the prison superintendent, J. R. Price.

Our plans for religious and educational facilities to be attached to the main building and to be designed and built by inmate labor, were abolished. An architect was retained by the board and construction was turned over to outside contractors. A magnificent edifice has risen from the watermelon patch adjacent to the parking lot in front of the administration building. This complex thus far has cost between $75,000 and $80,000, according to the commissioner's office, and was still incomplete in October 1969. When finished, it will provide space for religious services, parole services, vocational rehabilitation offices, classrooms, a library and visiting.

The only unresolved detail is how the inmates will be able to get to this beautiful structure. Tucker houses maximum custody prisoners and this new monument to God, while attesting to the fact that religious needs of the inmates are indeed being met, nonetheless is located *outside* the security perimeter of the prison facilities. It will be necessary either to erect a guard tower behind the pulpit or to march the men to church services under the gun—the system employed for generations before our intrusion in Arkansas.

At the Women's Reformatory, the board promptly removed the baby. Dancing was abolished, female inmates are not allowed to listen to the prison band and must be inside the quarters before the male inmates march back from the fields at sundown, lest they be seen. Supt. Ralph Roberts has even denied the Catholic women (about one-third of the population) the right to hear mass: it would be conducted by a priest and such association is considered "immoral" by the administration.

The female prisoners are beaten by the head trusty and thrown into the "hole" for minor infractions. The isolation units still have no plumbing, water or heat; the meal served to an inmate in isolation is only one spoonful of each food item served on the regular menu. And the toilets are still tin cans.

This past summer, two female inmates in isolation were stripped and kept naked for sixty days while mosquitoes feasted on their nude bodies. Conditions became so bad in 1968 that, for the first time, a female inmate tried to escape. In October 1969, two more were listed as "missing."

It was my stated conviction after leaving Arkansas that the prison had reverted to its evil ways. To refute the allegations, the commissioner granted me permission to make a personal inspection of all prison facilities in October 1969. Although I had been kept adequately informed of the decline of the prison, I was not prepared for what I found: both inmates and staff reported to me that conditions have returned almost to the level prior to our intervention. They speak of assaults, beatings by staff and inmates, extortion, liquor rackets, lack of clothing (some fifteen inmates were then working in the fields without shoes), threats on the lives of inmates, pistol whippings and shooting at inmates to speed up field work. The inmates uniformly report the food to be atrocious.

What discouraged me most was the evidence that the flickering light of hope we had ignited had been extinguished. The inmates look at the staff with distrust, suspicion and fear. Once more they shuffle silently to and from work, trapped in the futile, endless cycle of imprisonment, pondering the hopelessness of their plight and the mystery of how they were cheated of the promised emancipation from penal slavery.

In March 1969, Arkansas Commissioner of Correction Robert Sarver testified before the United States Senate: "When I read of an exposé of homosexualities, bribings, escapes [and] political corruption in prisons, I think most knowledgeable correction administrators think: 'So, what else is new?'"

There is little doubt in my mind that Governor Rockefeller was committed to prison reform during his campaign of 1966 and even after in inauguration in 1967. But power structures can tolerate only a limited amount of integrity. There comes a time when the new administration discovers that its other objectives are threatened by the reforms that have been instituted to correct the deficiencies of the former system. Previous Arkansas administrations stand condemned of knowing about prison conditions but not caring. The Rockefeller administration is guilty of knowing, pledging true reform—and recanting for the sake of political expediency. It must share the greater burden of responsibility for what ultimately happens to the prisoners of Arkansas.

4.9
Criminals Can Be Brainwashed—Now

James V. McConnell

The purpose of a law is to regulate human behavior—to get people to do what we want them to do. If it doesn't, it's a failure, and we might as well admit it and try something else. Laws should be goal-oriented; they must be judged by their results, or we're just kidding ourselves. Any time we pass a law that more than a handful of people violate, the law is probably a bad one. Man is the only animal capable of shaping his own society, of changing his own destiny. We must use this capability to build a society in which laws become guidelines rather than threats, guidelines so strong that no one would want to do anything other than follow them.

Liberal doctrine assumes that crime is society's fault, not the fault of the individual who happens to commit the crime.[1] So you shouldn't punish the individual, you should try to change the sick society that spawned the crime in the first place.

The conservative tends to see mankind as basically evil, born with genetically determined instincts that force man to behave wickedly whenever possible. The only way to stop this innate immorality is to stamp it out. Stomp on it. Catch the criminal and beat the living hell out of him; that will make him a much better person. We've molly-coddled the bastards long enough.

Reprinted by permission from "Criminals Can Be Brainwashed—Now," *Journal of Biological Psychology*, April, 1970.

[1] But the doctrine is changing, as *Psychology Today* readers indicated by their responses [November] to our Law & Society opinion study.

Both positions are terribly, terribly naive and ineffective. Somehow we've got to learn how to *force* people to love one another, to *force* them to want to behave properly. I speak of psychological force. Punishment must be used as precisely and as dispassionately as a surgeon's scalpel if it is to be effective.

I've spent a good many years training flatworms in my laboratory, which is why I'm so knowledgeable about *human* behavior, of course. We can train flatworms to do a great many things because we've learned the proper techniques and because we follow instructions exactly. For example, suppose we want to train a worm to run through a maze. The worm must learn that the white alley is always safe, but the black alley will lead to punishment—painful electric shock. There is our worm wandering contentedly when it comes to a choice point. The worm heads into the black alley, for worms tend to prefer black before they're trained. So we give the beast a bit of a shock, just to teach it a lesson. It took us years to learn that we have to control the polarity of the shock very carefully, otherwise the shock itself will propel the animal into the wrong alley. The next thing we had to learn was *when* to give the shock. If you shock the worm too soon, it never learns to connect the punishment with the black alley. If you delay the shock even a couple of seconds after it has stuck its lead in the black alley, the worm doesn't come to associate *entering* the black alley with the punishment, so it goes right on entering the black alley time after time after time.

The amount of punishment you give is important, too. We learned that if we gave our worms more than one or two very quick shocks when they entered the wrong alley, they became so disturbed that they would stop and refuse to move at all.

It took years, but we now know enough that we can train the animals very quickly. We have no trouble training worms, but we have one hell of a time trying to train new laboratory assistants. We explain our findings to them, and they nod their heads, but they don't really believe us and they don't really understand.

I have a friend, a distinguished scientist, who visited my lab one day. He was so fascinated by the worms that he wanted to train one himself. I explained everything to him and he nodded his head and

insisted that he understood—after all, he had raised three kids, hadn't he, and he had taught several thousand medical students over the years. Reluctantly I put a fresh worm in the maze and handed this man the apparatus controlling the shock.

The flatworm crawled along the maze quite nicely, came to the first choice point, and headed into the black alley. Of course, my friend pressed on the wrong button, gave shock of the wrong polarity and propelled the poor worm into the black alley. "Silly animal," the man muttered; he pressed the wrong button again. The worm went further into the wrong alley. "Get out of there, you idiot," he shouted at the worm, and held the shock button down for several seconds.

The worm, I regret to say, went into convulsions about this time and simply lay on its back writhing. My friend thrust the control apparatus back into my hands, advised me that the damned worm was obviously too stupid to learn even the simplest task, and stalked out of the lab.

The more that I think about it, the more convinced I am that the mistake was all mine. Why should I let him try to train a worm . . . or a rat . . . or a human being . . . unless he had been given the proper education first?

Of course, you see the trouble here. Each of us considers himself an unqualified expert on behavior, particularly on human behavior. It's utter nonsense, of course. We won't let a lawyer plead a case or a physician remove an appendix or a teacher conduct a class unless he's had extensive training and passed tests to prove his qualifications. Yet the only test a prospective parent has to pass is the Wasserman, and the only license he needs to practice the upbringing of children is obtainable for five dollars or so at the local marriage bureau.

But I digress. When you're training animals—be they humans or flatworms—there are times when you absolutely have to use punishment, for there are situations in which no other form of behavioral control works. But we use pain only when we wish to remove one very specific type of behavior from an organism's response-repertoire, and we use it very, very carefully.

In contrast to this scientific approach, the conservative insists that punishment be used not to control behavior—that is, to prevent crime—but rather as a kind of divine retribution to be enacted on those poor, miserable sinners who break the law. If the worm doesn't behave properly, shock the hell out of him. That'll learn 'im. Worms ought to be bright enough to know better. The conservative's viewpoint is utterly predictable to anyone who understands the relationship between frustration and aggression. It's very easy for a psychologist to devise a situation in which a laboratory animal is intensely frustrated. Under such conditions, the frustrated beast quite predictably turns on and attacks any scapegoat that happens to be handy. When humans are frustrated, they typically become aggressive. That's a natural law, not just an opinion of mine. When lawmakers don't understand some aspect of the world around them, and when they are frustrated by something the people do or the President does or the Supreme Court rules, the lawmakers typically respond by passing a highly punitive and aggressive law. Yet these are the very situations in which punishment has little or no effect on the behavior of the people the lawmakers want to influence or control. And so bad laws get written, not because they're effective but because they make the lawmakers feel good.

In effect, we have but two means of educating people or rats or flatworms—we can either reward them for doing the right thing or punish them for doing the wrong thing. Most people believe it's more humane to use reward. Surely we would all agree that rewards are usually more pleasant than punishments, and that love seems a nicer way of influencing people than hate. But blind love is even more dangerous than blind hate, for we can all identify hate and reject it, but love is something we've been told is good, good, good.

In Los Angeles there's a psychologist named Ivar Lovaas who is helping revolutionize the fields of clinical psychology and psychiatry. Dr. Lovaas works chiefly with autistic children, so socially retarded that they are little more than animals. They do not speak any known language, they seem to refuse all contact with other human beings. Until very recently they were considered almost hopeless; none of the usual forms of psychotherapy seemed to help them at all. And then along came behavioral psychologists like Ivar Lovaas who took a startling new viewpoint toward helping these kids.

The usual autistic child is lost in passivity, but a few of these very disturbed children go beyond passivity into self-destruction. The self-mutilating autistic child will tear at his flesh with both hands, bite off his own fingers, chew off his own shoulder. As you might guess, it's terrifying to watch these children.

Lovaas believes that autistic children cannot be brought back into the fold of humanity unless they can be taught to speak English or some other language. But how can you go about teaching a child to speak when he prefers to use his mouth to bite his own flesh rather than to speak words? Obviously, the first thing you have to do is to stamp out the self-destructive behavior and then worry about teaching the child how to talk.

Greg was about 11 years old when he was first brought to Dr. Lovaas' laboratory at UCLA. Greg had spent seven of his 11 years in a children's mental hospital. He was violently self-destructive; the nurses at the hospital were convinced that he would kill himself unless he were physically restrained 24 hours a day. None of the usual psychotherapy had worked with Greg. So, for seven years, Greg had been tied to a hospital bed, so tightly that he could barely move. When Greg first came to Lovaas' laboratory, his little body was so twisted from this confinement that he could barely walk.

It took Dr. Lovaas about 30 seconds to stamp out Greg's self-destructive behavior. Lovaas got a cattle prod—a long stick with electrodes at one end that deliver a very painful shock when they touch bovine—or human—flesh. He then turned Greg loose. As soon as Greg made his first self-destructive movement, Lovaas reached over and gave him a good jolt of electricity. Greg stopped moving and what might have been a puzzled look flashed across his face. He seemed to decide that the shock was a mistake, an accident, for a few seconds later he began to tear at his flesh again. Immediately Lovaas reached out with the cattle prod again and shocked the boy. Greg didn't like that at all, not one little bit. He looked up at Lovaas in disbelief and sat there for a few seconds more, then made one last attempt to hurt himself. One more jolt of electricity did the trick. Greg almost never again tried to harm himself when Lovaas was around. What standard therapy had been unable

to do in seven years Lovaas did in 30 seconds. And then, once the self-destructiveness was gone, Lovaas could put the cattle prod aside and go on to the more important and difficult task of teaching Greg to speak by rewarding him whenever he made the proper sounds.

The behavior of children like Greg had been a great puzzle until people like Lovaas began analyzing it. Why would kids want to mutilate themselves? It didn't seem that any sensible goal could be achieved by such behavior, so the psychiatric world decided that these kids were hopelessly insane and they were locked up in hospitals and strapped down to beds all their short, miserable lives. But when Lovaas went to watch these kids in a hospital he noticed something rather strange. As soon as a child began self-destructive behavior, one of the nurses would run to his bed, wrap her arms around him and fuss gently that he mustn't do that sort of thing. Of course, the child couldn't understand much English, so the words were probably wasted on him. But the love and affection weren't. As soon as the nurse turned loose, the child began hurting himself again, and the nurse would return with more hugs and kisses, and the cycle repeated itself. The nurses genuinely loved the kids and wanted to help them. When Lovaas pointed out that they were killing the children with the wrong kind of love administered at the wrong times they refused to believe him. And they undoubtedly thought Lovaas was a terrible, cold-hearted and cruel scientist because he used punishment on kids when everybody knew that kids ought to be loved.

If you take an autistic child out of that hospital and bring him to Lovaas' laboratory, the chances are very good that he can be helped enormously. Leave him in the hospital with the loving nurses and he will probably stay sick the rest of his brief, unhappy life.

When you look at prisons you find much the same situation, I fear. Very few criminals are cured of antisocial behavior while they're in prison, just as very few patients are cured of sick behavior in today's mental hospitals. And in both cases, most of the blame can be placed squarely on staff. A psychologist at an Eastern university told me a most interesting story about a project that the university had undertaken at a large Federal penitentiary. It seems that someone had a great idea that group therapy with a mixed population of guards and prisoners might be productive. So a few therapy groups were formed and the guards and the prisoners had at each other—verbally, that is. After a few weeks, the project collapsed like a punctured balloon —the *guards* couldn't take it any longer. It seems that the therapy was working too well—for the first time the guards began to gain some insight into their own behavior patterns, and they just couldn't face up to what they were really like inside.

As far as most behavioral psychologists are concerned, sick behavior has to be learned. Autistic kids have to learn self-mutilating behavior—it doesn't come built into their genes. We help autistic kids get well by reeducating them, by retraining them, by undoing the bad things they learned so early in life and by teaching them healthy behavior instead. And most behavioral psychologists would insist that criminal behavior has to be learned too, and that whatever is learned can be unlearned.

Back in the early 1950s, the Canadian and U.S. governments set up the Distant Early Warning (DEW) line of radar stations dotted in the ice and snow far above the Arctic Circle. There's not much up there for entertainment—those rumors about hospitality prostitution among the Eskimos are somewhat exaggerated. So the soldiers listened to radio; Radio Moscow came in much more clearly than most Canadian and American stations and beamed English-language broadcasts at DEW-line personnel. So that Canadian government called in Canada's greatest psychologist, Donald Hebb of McGill University, to determine whether soldiers isolated in boring environments are more than ordinarily susceptible to propaganda. And thus began a set of studies called experiments in sensory deprivation.

Hebb hired college students at $20 a day to do absolutely nothing. Each was confined to a tiny cubicle. An air conditioner obscured all outside noises. A mask over his eyes blocked out all visual stimulation. His arms were encased in long cardboard mailing tubes to prevent touching. He was fed and watered as necessary, but otherwise he was required to lie on a comfortable bed as quietly as he could.

Hebb expected the students to last at least six weeks. None of

them lasted more than a few days. During the first 24 hours they caught up on their sleep, but after that the experience became progressively more painful for all of them. They reported long stretches in which they seemed to be awake, but their minds were turned off entirely—they simply didn't "think" at all. They were tested while they were in the cubicles, and most of them showed marked deterioration in intellectual functioning. Many experienced vivid hallucinations—one student in particular insisted that a tiny space ship had got into the chamber and was buzzing around shooting pellets at him. Most of all, though, the students were bored. They tried to trick the experimenter into talking with them. In a subsequent experiment, Hebb let them listen to dull recorded speeches which they could start by pressing a button. The experimenters, who had to listen too, almost went out of their minds, but the students seemed to enjoy thoroughly hearing the same stock-market report a hundred or more times a day. And when Hebb provided propaganda messages instead of stock-market reports, he found that whatever the message was, no matter how poorly it was presented or how illogical it sounded, the propaganda had a marked effect on the students' attitudes—an effect that lasted for at least a year after the students came out of the deprivation chambers.

Hebb's findings led many other investigators to begin work on sensory deprivation.

It is axiomatic in the behavioral sciences that the more you control an organism's environment, the more you can control its behavior. It goes without saying that the only way you can gain complete control over a person's behavior is to gain complete control over his environment. The sensory-deprivation experiments suggest that we should be able to do exactly that.

I believe that the day has come when we can combine sensory deprivation with drugs, hypnosis and astute manipulation of reward and punishment to gain almost absolute control over an individual's behavior. It should be possible then to achieve a very rapid and highly effective type of positive brainwashing that would allow us to make dramatic changes in a person's behavior and personality. I foresee the day when we could convert the worst criminal into a decent, respectable

citizen in a matter of a few months—or perhaps even less time than that. The danger is, of course, that we could also do the opposite: we could change any decent, respectable citizen into a criminal.

We must begin by drafting new laws that will be as consonant as possible with all the human-behavior data that scientists have gathered. We should try to regulate human conduct by offering rewards for good behavior whenever possible instead of threatening punishment for breaches of the law. We should reshape our society so that we all would be trained from birth to want to do what society wants us to do. We have the techniques now to do it. Only by using them can we hope to maximize human potentiality. Of course, we cannot give up punishment entirely, but we can use it sparingly, intelligently, as a means of shaping people's behavior rather than as a means of releasing our own aggressive tendencies. For misdemeanors or minor offenses we would administer brief, painless punishment, sufficient to stamp out the antisocial behavior. We'd assume that a felony was clear evidence that the criminal had somehow acquired full-blown social neurosis and needed to be cured, not punished. We'd send him to a rehabilitation center where he'd undergo positive brainwashing until we were quite sure he had become a law-abiding citizen who would not again commit an antisocial act. We'd probably have to restructure his entire personality. The legal and moral issues raised by such procedures are frighteningly complex, of course, but surely we know by now that there are no simple solutions.

Many cling to the old-fashioned belief that each of us builds up his personality logically and by free will. This is as patently incorrect as the belief that the world is flat. No one owns his own personality. Your ego, or individuality, was forced on you by your genetic constitution and by the society into which you were born. You had no say about what kind of personality you acquired, and there's no reason to believe you should have the right to refuse to acquire a new personality if your old one is antisocial. I don't believe the Constitution of the United States gives you the *right* to commit a crime if you want to; therefore, the Constitution does not guarantee you the right to maintain inviolable the personality it forced on you in the first place—if and when the personality manifests strongly antisocial behavior.

The techniques of behavioral control make even the hydrogen bomb look like a child's toy, and of course, they can be used for good or evil. But we can no more prevent the development of this new psychological methodology than we could have prevented the development of atomic energy. By knowing what is scientifically possible and by taking a revolutionary viewpoint toward society and its problems, we can surely shape the future more sanely than we can if we hide our collective heads in the sand and pretend that it can't happen here. Today's behavioral psychologists are the architects and engineers of the Brave New World.

4.10
The War on Flies

Richard Korn

Dead fish, rotting. What are they doing here, so far inland? Boating in the sun, incongruous on neat lawns, on roads, at school-crossings. The P.T.A. chairlady hurries by them: she seems not to see them. The butcher arranging his fresh flounders in the window: how does he avoid seeing the carcasses on the sidewalk in front of his shop?

Where are all the noses? Is it that the fish do not stink? But no nostrils twitch. And on the slippery pavement no matron falls, though the entrails are everywhere.

Where did they come from? Is it anywhere recorded that a great cleansing wave years ago came out of the sea and flooded this land? Is it remembered that the wave receded, leaving pools of salt water in hollows, depressions, crevasses? And as the pools evaporated: these fish.

The garbage men are efficient. Each day they empty the streets of debris, hauling it off to the regional dump, whence it is transported by trucks and placed on barges and buried in the sea. But the garbage men do not see the dead fish.

Nevertheless, there *is* complaint about the flies. Inexplicably, clouds of flies have appeared, with no explanation. No one sees the fish—but all suffer from the flies. Huge, blue flies, hovering everywhere. And biting, viciously.

Last night the mayor's wife was stung as she sat on the toilet. Instantly the wound filled with green pus. The Health Commissioner was called: he gravely examined the bite. Clearly, it will be necessary to do something about the flies. There will have to be conferences, congresses. New insecticides must be discussed; fly traps will have to be designed. From the four corners of the world we will summon experts on flies.

There will be screens on all windows. There will be roving fly patrols. The streets will be sprayed. If that fails, a huge plastic sheet shall be dropped over the town. Gas masks will be issued to all. The aldermen will ponder the problem in their masks. The children will attend school in their masks.

Finally, good news. The flies in their billions are dying. The stiff blue bodies, shining like jewels, are everywhere. In heaps they are scooped up and carted away.

But next week they return. Only a few at first: then more. The actuaries are already noting the geometric progression. The spraying has failed. There will be flies. In spite of all man can do, there will be flies. It will be necessary to have fly traps on every corner, on every roof top. The little houses appear in their thousands. Each day they fill up: each day we empty them. Half the labor force is employed at the task.

Is there a way to make flies sterile? An expert is called: he produces his formulae, his charts and, finally, some subtly poisoned fly-food. The whole city views the experiment on television—except that few can see the screen because of the flies.

We must produce thousands of sterile flies. Place the sterilizing nutriment in the fly traps. Let the flies eat of it; then liberate them. On each treated fly place a tiny identifying mark. Later we will take samples: we will see whether the sterile population increases. Teams of fly catchers are dispatched to all neighborhoods: they arrive with bushels of fertile flies. These are placed in the traps, to mate with their sterile sisters. An orgy of eating and mating.

The experiment is a success. The flies breed—but their eggs are infertile. We seem to have stopped the explosive cycle.

But there is a disturbing rumor. A technician in the fly-sterilization laboratory has noted that certain flies are refusing to eat the treated food. Rather than eat the bait they devour each other. And with some insidious insight they avoid the stomachs of their poisoned sisters. The technican has reported her findings to her superiors. Naturally, the report is suppressed.

And there is another rumor. It is said that a blind child is going about with stories of dead fish. Confronted by the unbelieving, he extends his hands, as if holding something. But all one can see is a peculiar, oblong cluster of flies filling the space between his hands. Clearly, the child has a strange affinity to flies. He must be carefully watched, examined; if necessary, put away.

In the meantime, we must be patient. Perhaps, through study, we will uncover something. Let us not lose faith in science. Or in each other. We have had hard times before . . .

4.11
Role Playing:
A Judge Is a Con,
a Con Is a Judge

Richard Hammer

For nine days this summer, the grassy, groomed and venerable campus of St. John's College in Annapolis was the scene of a remarkable confrontation. The college kids and their professors were off on vacation, and the "great books"—the core of the St. John's curriculum—has been laid on the shelf. In place of the faculty and students were 21 convicts from three state prisons and about 100 lawyers and judges, prosecutors, policemen, prison officials and state legislators and some "interested citizens." Before the nine days ended, the participants had been enlightened and, in some cases, emotionally scarred by their experiment, a "Workshop in Crime and Correction."

This was anything but a gathering of dreamers and bleeding hearts concerned over the failures of the prison system. Those failures, of course, are beyond argument. The "correctional institutions," as they call themselves these days, neither correct nor rehabilitate; more than half, some say more than 70 per cent, of those released from the nation's prisons end up behind bars again, and what they usually learn behind those bars is how to make better "hits," how to be better burglars or bank robbers the next time they walk free. The nonprisoners at the workshop were not ignorant of these facts, but they lacked an appreciation of the personal and emotional realities behind the statistics. That appreciation was provided in psychodramas, seminars, all-night bull sessions and in hours spent as "inmates" themselves in three Maryland prisons.

The workshop had the best "establishment" credentials: It was financed with $67,000 from the Social and Rehabilitation Service of the Department of Health, Education and Welfare and was sponsored jointly by the Maryland Governor's Commission on Law Enforcement and the Administraiton of Justice and the National College of State Trial Judges, which claims the membership of more than 4,000 jurists in all 50 states.

Directing the conference were the Berkeley Associates, a consulting organization formed by three Californians whose experience in the prison system has left them disillusioned. They are: Dr. David Fogel of the University of California at Berkeley, a heavy-set, bearded, emotional sociologist who worked seven years in the Marin County jail system; Dr. Richard Korn, a U. of C. criminologist who resigned after three years as a psychologist at a New Jersey prison farm "when I found one night that I could lock up my assistant, a prisoner, in his cell and walk away without feeling anything," and Douglas Rigg, a public defender in Berkeley, a former associate warden at San Quentin who once resigned as the warden of a Minnesota state prison after his reform efforts led to charges that he was "coddling convicts."

Given the workshop's credentials, the conference organizers found it easy enough to round up participants among the professionals. Finding the right convicts, however, was another matter.

Berkeley Associates did not want a group hand-picked by prison administrators, but a representative sampling of both men and the right to select the 21 convict participants themselves. Ultimately, they settled for a compromise: Prison officials chose a group of more than 100 inmates from which Berkeley Associates picked the 21 they wanted.

The convicts came from three institutions in Jessups, Md.—the Maryland House of Correction, a medium-security prison with a reputation as little more than a warehouse for men convicted of anything from nonsupport to murder and rape; the Maryland Correctional Camp Center, a minimum security institution where some inmates are on a work-release program, and the Patuxent Institution, a maximum-security prison for "defective delinquents," all of them serving indeterminate sentences.

Some of the 21 men chosen for the workshop were serving terms as short as two years, others had been sentenced to "life plus"; some had been behind bars for only a year, others for 20 years or more. Their crimes ranged from possession of narcotics to burglary to rape and murder. One participant was even an alumnus of death row; his sentence had been commuted to life shortly before his date in the gas chamber.

As a group, the participants were not entirely representative of Maryland's 6,000 convicts. They were articulate and intelligent, with considerable insight into themselves and others. Most of them seemed to retain some hope for a future life beyond the walls. As the workshop progressed, however, it became evident that most of the participants from the outside world looked upon the *consultants* (as they called themselves) not as a select group but as a random sampling of the prison population. The effect of their words and actions during the conference was thus generalized —and magnified.

A typical day began at 8 A.M. as the convicts, dressed in casual sports clothes, arrived at St. John's by bus. More than one prisoner was amused at the thought of breakfasting with the judge who had sentenced him—a judge dressed in Bermuda shorts and a flowered shirt.

The business session usually opened with a speaker after breakfast, then a psychodrama, a brief play in which the magistrates and the miscreants were the cast, sometimes playing their real-life roles and sometimes trading roles. The scene was always one having to do with the judicial process: a disciplinary hearing for a policeman accused of having used abusive language; a grand jury session; a parole hearing; the arrival in prison of a new con. Fogel or Korn set the scene and the actors improvised as the plot developed. Members of the audience were allowed to interrupt if they thought the portrayals lacked realism.

Later in the day, the workshop broke up into seven groups for discussion and more psychodrama. After the prisoners had returned to their cells for the evening, the "outside" participants heard another speaker, then attended informal bull sessions that typically lasted until 4 or 5 A.M.

In the first days of the workshop, there was a tentative feeling, a sparring for openings, an evident wariness. The cops sat in a back row, isolated; the judges sat together; the cons sat in a group. A psychodrama about a policeman's being reprimanded for the use of a racial epithet produced only yawns and bored rustling.

What broke the conference open was a psychodrama on prison life. Fogel set the stage: The action was to be the arrival in prison of a new con, a first offender sentenced to four years for assault. To play the new con Fogel selected a young, blond correctional officer who looked indeed as though he could be in that position. The inmates who processed him into the prison were played by real cons. The only other roles in the play were two prison officials, a guard and a counselor, played by men whose real-life roles these were.

The drama began as "Scag," a black inmate who supposedly worked as a runner in the prison storeroom, led the new con, "Frank," from the storeroom, where he'd been issued prison clothes and other gear, to the tier where he would be locked into a cell.

SCAG: You know anybody here, anybody can help you?

FRANK (shaking his head): No, I don't know anybody.

SCAG: Nobody at all?

FRANK: Nobody. I don't think I belong here.

SCAG (laughs): That's what everybody says. You know, you gonna need some protection.

FRANK: Protection? From what?

SCAG: Man, you is gonna be approached.

FRANK: What for?

SCAG: Man, I ain't got to tell you.

FRANK: Well, I don't want any part of it.

SCAG: You ain't got no choice.

FRANK: If they come to me, I'll fight.

SCAG (laughs): You can't fight three-four men at a time.

FRANK: What can I do?

SCAG: Man, you can avoid it.

FRANK: How?

SCAG: You can pick somebody to protect you. . . . You got any money?

FRANK: No. But I've got a ring and a watch.

Reaching the tier that contains Frank's cell, Scag holds a mumbled conference with Slim, a black inmate assigned as a runner in the tier.

SCAG: We got a new chicken here.

SLIM: Yeah, what we gonna do with him?

SCAG: I'll tell you. I'm gonna play his friend. You make him think he's got to turn to me to protect him from you.

SLIM: Yeah, that's right, I'll scare him right to you and we'll split what he's got. Only don't do like you did the last time and hit me when you're protecting him.

SCAG: Don't worry, we'll play this cool.

As Scag leaves, Slim explains prison life to Frank, telling him that he can order once a week from the commissary and that he must come out of his cell immediately when the bell rings for a meal or an exercise period in the yard or he will be locked in again. Slim offers to give Frank a pack of cigarettes in exchange for two packs after Frank has received his order from the commissary. Then a bell rings and Slim patrols the tier, chanting, Yard time. Yard time."

The scene shifts to the crowded prison yard, and when Frank appears there are whistles. "Say, man," says one con, "that's a real sweetie." Another yells: "Hey, baby, I think you need a protector." The action then moves back to the cell tier.

SLIM: Where you been?

FRANK: In the yard.

SLIM: How come you didn't tell me you was going?

FRANK: I did.

SLIM: Man, I says you didn't! You callin' me a liar?

FRANK: No, I thought. . . .

SLIM: Man, you want to go someplace, you tell me. Whenever you go someplace, you don't go without you let me know, dig?

FRANK: Why are you jumping all over me?

SLIM: Man, you is askin' for it.

I gonna come in that cell with you and lock the door you don't watch out.

Scag suddenly appears, telling Slim to leave the new inmate alone. After Slim wanders off, Scag offers to take Frank into the yard during the next exercise period and walk around with him, explaining: "That'll let everybody know I'm protecting you." He says it will cost a carton of cigarettes a week. Frank says he will think about it and stays in his cell during the next few exercise periods. A few days later, against Slim's urgent advice, he insists upon seeing an officer.

FRANK: It seems there are all these guys who want to be my buddies. They want to protect me. But they want cigarettes and they seem to want my watch and ring and shoes, too. And they seem to be able to do anything they want and nobody stops them.

GUARD: When did all this start? When did they approach you?

FRANK: As soon as I got in here.

GUARD: Can you identify them?

FRANK: I'm afraid. I don't want it to get back to them.

GUARD: Well, anytime you want to tell me anything, you just ask. I'll come. You just ask. We'll protect you.

FRANK: I'm scared to tell.

The realization that the guards cannot effectively protect him sends Frank back to Scag. At the next yard call, they go out together and Scag introduces Frank to other cons, among whom blacks outnumber whites by more than two to one.

Fogel interrupted the action to ask several of the convicts what they were feeling as Frank was being introduced. Among the answers were these:

"I'm feeling that colored guys have all the goodies. I feel like they must feel out in the streets. I'm a minority in here, and I'd like a crack at that goody."

"I don't care what Scag or the rest of the black guys do as long as they don't touch my man."

"I've got a feeling of fear. I know what happens to young cons like him; it happened to me."

"He's a white boy, and I don't care what happens to him."

The action resumes in the office of a counselor with whom Frank has requested an interview.

FRANK: I've had some weird things happen since I came in here. There's a lot of homosexuals running around loose and they all seem to be looking at me.

COUNSELOR: Well, what would you like us to do?

FRANK: I don't know. I think I'm more afraid of the inmates here than I am of the institution itself,

and I thought it would be the other way.

COUNSELOR: What do they want?

FRANK: Everything I've got. My watch, my ring, my shoes, all my personal possessions. Can I send them home?

COUNSELOR: Yes. If you give them to me I can have them sent home for you.

FRANK: They want my tail, too.

COUNSELOR: I'm afraid I can't send that home. You want to tell me who these guys are who are doing these things to you?

FRANK: If I tell you, what will happen to me?

COUNSELOR: We'll try to protect you.

FRANK: How?

COUNSELOR (bursts out): I'll adopt you! . . . Seriously, the only assurance I can give you is close supervision.

The psychodrama ended there, amid shouts and cries from the convicts in the audience. "Man, you can't give him no protection. He'll have boiling coffee thrown at him even if you lock him up in solitary," said one. "He ain't got no assurance. You think his only salvation is in protection and custody, but that won't work. Somebody'd get to him."

"Maybe you'd put him in B-3, where they keep all the sissies," said another con, "and then he'd be branded one, and he'd be branded a rat, too, and that wouldn't be no protection."

"There's a million ways to get to him," a third convict warned. "We'd be in contact with him and that would be that." Another added:

"Nothing anybody can do will make any difference because it's a jungle we live in. The only ones who can do anything for him or against him are the other inmates."

One of the prison administrators asked the actor who had played Slim, "Would you protect him for a guaranteed parole?"

Slim stared at him. "For a guaranteed parole? Man, I guess so."

Another con leaped up: "And who would protect Slim? Then who would protect the next guy and the next? You gonna let us all out on parole to protect this one guy?"

As more members of the workshop joined the discussion on prison life and its purposes, one inmate rose and asked: "What's rehabilitation? I've never seen it. We come in laborers and go out laborers. All we learn in here is how to make [license] tags, and there ain't no place outside where you can make tags. We're the same guy when we go out, and that's where it's at, baby."

The psychodrama had shaken the workshop. For many in the audience—judges, policemen, lawyers and even some prison officials—it was the first good look at what goes on behind the walls and at criminals as real people. Save for the criminal himself, almost everyone's contact with the problems of crime, correction and justice is severely limited. The average citizen's only glimpse of crime occurs when he is a victim, and even then the contact is usually just the discovery that something is missing from his home or car; the policeman's contact with the criminal begins with the arrest, often a dangerous and charged confrontation, and ends at the station house or in the courtroom; the judge and attorneys see the criminal only when his behavior is circumscribed, when he is wearing a face that is often not his real one; prison officials see him only as a number, and parole officers only when he has finished his term and is again a free man.

The disclosures made in the psychodrama—of homosexuality, rackets, brutality and fear—therefore came as something of a shock to many. In the smaller sessions later in the day, emotions ran high and every suggestion brought sharp probing and searching questions.

A discussion of prison apprenticeship programs, for instance, remained optimistic until the convict participants gave their point of view. The training program in printing, they said, was limited to those serving sentences of at least 15 years; it was a five-year program, and—since parole is often granted when one-third of a man's term is served (though it is possible after one-fourth of the sentence)—men serving shorter terms might leave before their training was complete. Convicts sentenced to less than 15 years could enter the program only if they agreed to forgo parole until the training was over. Further, since the apprenticeship program was given only at the House of Correction, an inmate had to agree to remain there and not accept transfer to a minimum-security prison farm where he might be eligible for an occasional weekend home leave.

When prison officials complained that they did not have the money to buy some necessary equipment for a course, the cons said that most of what was needed could be bought through Army surplus for less than $100.

And, of course, there was always the problem of food. "How can we feed these guys decent meals," one official asked, "when all the state allows us is 61 cents a day per con for meals?" You can't feed them very much or very well on that, it was agreed, just as you can't "rehabilitate" them totally when the state budget comes out to less than $2,000 a year for each con. But, one judge wanted to know, isn't at least something good possible—say, ice cream on occasion? "How can we give them ice cream," the official asked, "when it costs about 8 cents a brick wholesale? That's more than 10 per cent of the daily food budget. It's just impossible." The prisoners replied that Army-surplus ice-cream makers could be bought for less than $75—and that one of them could produce ice cream for an entire prison at less than a penny a serving.

Even if all the equipment were available, the prison officials declared, it would still be difficult to do anything about training the inmates to use it. There was a major problem in getting outside instructors to teach because of low salaries. How about using the expertise of the cons? "We don't trust the prisoners to run the programs," said an administrator. "Whenever we've tried it, we've had a bad experience. Rackets have developed—you know, prisoner-teachers selling grades, things like that. So we don't feel we can use them."

"Man," one inmate said, "You'd better realize that the only way you're going to help prepare us to make it on the outside so that we don't come back in is by beginning to show you trust us a little. That's the name of the game. If you don't trust us at all inside, you ain't going to trust us outside, and we know it, and you're going to have us right back with you."

"Why the hell should we trust you?" asked one official. "Look what happens whenever we start trusting you guys. Look at the jungle you guys live in."

"You know you ain't never trusted us one little bit," the con replied, "and maybe that's why we do what we do in there, because there ain't no trust. And you're right, prison's a jungle. But who's really responsible for it, us? Or all you people who dump us in there and want to forget about us until it's time to let us back into society,

until we've served out our time?"

The cons challenged one another as well as the prison system. When one of them complained that the state was charging him $2.50 room and board plus his transportation costs from what he earned on the outside in a work-release program, another snapped: "Man, when you get out, who the hell is going to give you free room and board? Are you a ward of the state or are you a man? You better learn to pay your own way; you're going to have to if you ever get out."

Behind all the criticism was the evident desire to transform prisons from schools for crime into institutions that would produce men able to adapt to society. The cons quickly dispelled the idea that they sought to turn prisons into pleasant resort hotels. They had committed crimes, they agreed, and society had a right to punish them. The point was that if the system was to be successful it had to be more than just institutionalized punishment.

The emotions released by the psychodrama were heightened the next day when the conference adjourned behind prison walls. A third of the delegates went to each of the three prisons, where most of them were led on tours by the inmate conferees, unhampered by guards and officials. And at each of the prisons, three or four of the outside workshop members, including a couple of judges, were processed as though they were new inmates. The convicts and guards who processed them were —officially, at least—unaware that they were not real prisoners, though it was evident that word had leaked out.

While the rest of the outside visitors entered the prisons through the main gates, the men chosen to be pretend-convicts were handcuffed and shackled together, put on prison vans and driven into the processing areas. There they were checked in, stripped and made to sit naked on wooden benches while being interviewed. Then they were forced to undergo a flashlight examination under the arms, between the legs, in all the hairy parts of the body—"we're looking for crabs, narcotics, you know, things like that," said the inmate-clerk conducting the examination at one of the prisons. The new "convicts" were showered, given prison clothes, mugged, fingerprinted and asked other detailed questions about their lives. Then they were led to cells and locked in.

When the doors closed, one "convict," an elderly white-haired state representative, sank onto his cot, put his elbows on his knees and buried his head in his hands. "I can't tell you what this did to me spiritually," he said later. "I knew that any time I wanted to get out, all I had to do was yell and they would come and let me loose. What if I had known that I couldn't get out, that I was to be locked in there for years?"

A judge who had sentenced scores of men to the prison through which he was processed suddenly pretended to be a mute. Later, he was to say that he had enjoyed the experience, but those who saw him doubted it. He was certain, he said, that he had been spotted, "and I didn't know whether I was going to get a knife or just be pointed out to everyone else." Within a couple of hours, he asked to be released from his cell.

When another judge left his cell for lunch, a knife was planted in it by one of the few guards who was in on the pretense. The judge was pulled out of the lunch line and thrown into solitary confinement in the "hole" next to a black convict who was lying on his cell floor, his legs in the air, screaming, "White mother-f——s, white mother-f——s. . . ." (The judge later said he had not heard a word.)

After a half hour in the hole, the judge was brought before a five-man disciplinary board, none of whose members knew that this was all a pretense. The judge was dressed in prison slacks and shirt, white socks without shoes; his hair was tousled, his face distraught.

The board chairman asked, "Do you know why you're here?"

They told me you found a knife in my cell."

"That's right. Can you tell us how it got there?"

"No. I can't think how."

"Did you bring it in with you?"

"No. Somebody must have put it there."

"When did you get here?"

"This morning."

"Do you know anybody in here?"

"No."

"Does anybody in here have anything against you?"

"No."

"Then why would somebody have planted a knife in your cell?"

The judge, knowing that he was innocent, was sentenced to 30 days in the hole.

One of the civilians who went to the House of Correction was later to describe the place as being "like a decayed military school." There was no morale, he said, and there were no screens on the windows: there were razor blades in his cell, splinters of steel in the food, a total lack of communication between the cons and the staff, and everywhere he looked "there were flaming fagots making assignations."

Perhaps one of the most concerned men of all, however, was a high-ranking police officer who was visiting a prison for the first time in his 18 years on the force. He met a prisoner who seemed familiar, talked with him and discovered that he had first met the man many years before, when the convict was 11 years old. "He was a truant and I happened to be at school that day and I talked with him. And then the next day, I got a call and went to a house and there was this little boy. He had had an argument with his mother and stabbed her in the side with a paring knife. He hadn't done much damage, but it was pretty serious. Anyway, he kept getting in trouble, but I never had much time for him, there were always other things. Now he is in for life, for murder, for cutting up someone into eight pieces." The policeman paused and looked around. "I wondered if maybe I couldn't have done something, back then, to have prevented all this. But I'll tell you one thing: I'm going to be a better cop because of this. And I'll tell you something else: Nobody's going to work for me for 18 years without going into an institution this way again. Every man under me is going to spend a day in prison."

"This is a jungle," said one of the judges. "And if all the guys inside come out as they have to live in there, pretty soon we're all going to be living in that jungle. We'd better do something and we'd better do it damn fast."

How did the cons react to the tour through their homes? "I'll tell you," one inmate said the next day, "the guys inside all look at us as traitors for revealing what's been going on. They're telling us, and some of the guards are telling us, 'This thing will cool off and then we'll see about the guys who've opened up on us.'"

And how did the prison administrators react? "We have lousy prisons and no one in the administration will disagree with you," said one. "But where are all of you when we need help? I don't think anybody gives a damn." Another official commented: "Nobody around here understands us; nobody appreciates what we're doing. We're sitting on the lid of a garbage can keeping the garbage off the streets."

Korn tried to pull the reactions together and get at some of the basic truths behind the conferees' experiences of the previous few days. "We do know," he said, "how to deal with the people we love and the people we hate and the people we don't give a damn about, despite all the myths. We protect and defend the people we love. And the people we hate we turn over to the people we don't give a damn about, to people who hate them. We turn animals over to animals to cage them."

What we ask of people we put in prison, Korn said, is conformity, something we do not want for ourselves or anyone we love. In prison we want men to conform to rules that have no meaning. "We call it correction," he said, "but it is not correction."

Korn laid out some of his ideas for a solution, which he called a new-careers program. Under it, the massive institutions would be gradually dispensed with, giving way to community-based and neighborhood correction centers. The inmates would be given responsible, meaningful jobs, often working with youthful offenders in an attempt to stop the young men from becoming professional criminals.

During the last days of the conference there were hundreds of resolutions for action—supporting conjugal visits in prisons, urging improvements in the food, backing the idea of neighborhood correction centers, even making the St. John's Council on Crime and Correction a continuing organization that would meet again to try to reform the Maryland prison system.

There was a graduation ceremony, including diplomas for all those who had attended, and a commencement address. The speaker was Petey Green, a former long-term convict who is working in a new-careers program in Washington. Society has to make use of the talents of the prisoners, Green said over and over again. "And how can you say these guys ain't got no skills when they can reach over and lift your wallet without you feeling it? Who's going to be a better store detective than an ex-booster? Maybe the stores ought to think about hiring somebody like that."

It's not hard to motivate the cons, Green said, if you do it the right way. "Why, when I began to change and got to working in the prison school, there was this one guy, a bank robber, who kept telling me he'd rather play basketball than come to school. So I told him, 'Man, when you went into that bank, they had a big sign sayin' this bank is guarded by cameras. But you couldn't read, and that's how come you got busted.' That guy became one of the best students in the school."

And then, when Green had finished, the cons went back to prison and the free people went their separate ways.

The end of the conference, though, did not mean the end of the campaign for better prisons. The St. John's Council continues, with task forces meeting weekly to work out reform recommendations requested by a joint Legislative committee on corrections.

The convict who played Scag in the psychodrama was paroled on July 28, has a factory job and is applying for a scholarship to study penology at Catonsville Community College. The inmate who played Slim is scheduled to face a parole board soon and, if he is released, may get an $8,000-a-year job—about which he has not yet been told—working with fellow ex-cons. Several other inmate-participants in the conference have won paroles since June and still others have been transferred to minimum-security prisons.

So far, the resolutions of the workshop have not been abandoned. One convict from each of the three prisons attends a weekly meeting, and interest among the inmate-participants remains high. Some of the judges, policemen and legislators are more concerned than they were before the workshop. They seem to agree that what is at stake is not the coddling of criminals but the very fate of society. This is, however, a short-range reaction. Whether the St. John's workshop will lead to anything permanent remains a question.

Violence Through Mass Media

4.12
The Medium Is . . .

The Editors

The world, as depicted by the mass media, is a place in which severe violence is routine. The central role played by violence in the fantasy world of entertainment is to provide a successful means for individuals and groups to resolve conflicts in their favor or self-interest. Violence, regardless of the identity of the initiator, goes largely unpunished. Agents of law enforcement are undistinguishable from others insofar as they also use violence as the predominant mode of conflict solution. Legality, in many instances, is not a relevant dimension or concern.

Ninety-five percent of all American homes contain at least one television set, 99 percent have a radio, and a third of the American populace goes to the movies once a month. An examination of some of the most frequent messages being sent to mass audiences and norms for violence inferred from these messages leads to a serious concern about the effects upon audiences of entertainment programs. At the very least, it can be said that the messages being sent about violence are inconsistent with a philosophy of social behavior based upon involved cooperation, nonviolent resolution of conflict, and nonviolent means of attaining personal ends.

With 95 percent of the American people reading at least one newspaper a week, it is a tragedy that stories dealing with violence are often blatantly mishandled. In some instances, violence is sensationalized in order to sell papers, while at other times violence is reported in the same emotional tone as a Rotary Club luncheon.

Not only do the media depict violence, but they often cause it. The following report comes from Great Britain:

Television chiefs issued a warning to millions of youngsters today after an inquest on a boy who died while imitating his masked and cloaked hero, "Batman." . . . His father . . . told the inquest yesterday he thought his son, hanged while wearing a homemade Batman-style outfit, had been leaping from a cabinet in the garden shed when his neck caught in a nylon loop hanging from the roof. The inquest verdict was misadventure.

And from *Violence and the Mass Media,* a study conducted under the auspices of the National Commission on the Causes and Prevention of Violence, one learns of the effect a television news crew can have on events:

By now it was something after 8 P.M. and the television crews needed something to show on the 10 o'clock news . . .

Up came the three-man television crew: a camera man with a hand-held camera, a sound man and a light man. Very discreet in the dark.

"May as well get it."

You could sense the disappointment in his voice, because pictorially it wasn't much of a demonstration.

The light man held up his thirty volt frezzi and laid a four-foot beam of light across one section of the picket line. Instantly the marchers' heads snapped up, their eyes flashed. They threw up their arms in the clenched Communist fist. Some made a V with their fingers, and they held up their banners for the cameras . . .

Obviously, it was not the same event once the cameras were on.

The insensitivity of television to violence is perhaps best illustrated by the interpolation of singing commercials into the television newscasts in which all manner of events which have recently occurred are intoned in approximately the same portentous or somber voice, whether their consequences are of moment to the world, the nation, the state, the community, or only to some individual celebrity. Occasionally, the pattern is made flagrantly incongruous by the tragic content of the day's news.

Consider, for example, the way the Huntley-Brinkley Report began on June 5 ,1968:

CHET HUNTLEY: Senator Robert F. Kennedy was shot in the head and gravely wounded early today before hundreds of people in his political headquarters in a Los Angeles hotel, a month and a day after the assassination of Dr. Martin Luther King in Memphis, seconds after he had made a speech celebrating his victory over Senator Eugene McCarthy in the California Democratic presidential primary . . .

(Continuing the reporting of this event, the scene was shifted to the hospital.)

JACK PERKINS: The latest medical bulletin . . . says Senator Robert Kennedy remains in extremely critical condition . . .

(Frank Mankiewicz, the Senator's press secretary was then shown reading the medical bulletin. Perkins had some more to say, and then the camera returned to Chet Huntley for further reporting of certain aspects of the situation. He was followed by the face and clipped voice of David Brinkley.)

DAVID BRINKLEY: . . . we have assembled some of the film from last night, beginning with the Senator's victory speech at the Ambassador Hotel, after he won the California primary.

(The film, lasting several minutes, showed the speech, the cheers from the crowd, the moment of the shooting and the ensuing pandemonium and near-panic, the frantic and repeated requests for a doctor, the wounded Senator on the floor, police cars taking the suspect away to jail with crowd reactions as he is brought out and sirens fading into the distance, and then the grief-stricken crowd in the hall again. These scenes were followed by the voice of the program announcer.)

ANNOUNCER: The Huntley-Brinkley report is produced by NBC News and brought to you in color by Newport, the smoothest tasting menthol cigarette—Newport king size and the new extra long Newport Deluxe 100's.

(Then next video image was a filmed commercial showing a frivolous barbershop scene.)

Said a patron whose name was McNair,
As the barber was trimming his hair;
"This new cigarette has the roughest taste yet!
Who's got a smooth one to spare?"
Then up spoke a fellow named Dave

Who had just finished having a shave:
"Newport, you'll find, is a much smoother kind,
With a taste about which you will rave."
CHORUS: Ooooooh, Smoother Newport, Fresher Newport—
Smoother, more refreshing cigarette!

(This was followed by another filmed commercial, for tires sold by Phillips 66 dealers, concluding with the slogan, "At Phillips 66, it's performance that counts." David Brinkley then reappeared on the screen.)

DAVID BRINKLEY: The police are holding a young man charged with the shooting . . .

No senator or presidential candidate need die in vain; his assassination can, after all, attract an audience to whom such commodities as cigarettes and tires can be sold. And children in the television audience can discover that that is what life and death are all about.

The problem of possible desensitization to violence, caused by constant exposure to the mass media, is most acute with children. The average child's perception of the world is heavily influenced by what he sees when he spends several hours each day in front of a television set. The following article, which originally appeared in *Look* Magazine, is a report from one parent on what can be done to guide a child through the violent world of television.

COURTESY OF JORGE CORTÉS.

4.13
Is TV Brutalizing Your Child?

Eliot A. Daley

"How *can you tell* if that's a really live dead man, Daddy?"

My daughter stared at the television screen as she asked. She was watching a marine patrol drag its limp victim out of a bunker in Vietnam. She wanted to know how a four-year-old girl separates the real from the pretend.

It was a reasonable question. For our children, the experience of television has obliterated boundaries and horizons of time, reality and distance that we relied upon as we made our way into a gradually expanding encounter with the world. For us, World War II raged somewhere, but it was not daily fare except for precocious newspaper readers. We never saw a man shot dead before our eyes.

Through television, our children's lives are inundated with death and disaster one moment, trivia and banality the next, cemented together with the 60-second mortar of manipulation and materialism. Their experience is very different from ours. In the matter of violence alone, their formative years are bathed in blood of which we have only recently taken notice. Other writers have amply documented the depressing statistics:

The TV stations of one city carried, in one week, 7,887 acts of violence.

One episode of a Western series garnished Christmas night with 13 homicides.

Between the ages of 5 and 14, your children and mine may, if they are *average* viewers, witness the annihilation of 12,000 human beings.

Consequences *are* observable, from weekly callousness about Vietnam casualty lists, to riots by and against police, to subtly increased agitation among youngsters viewing a violent TV film.

How can our children cope with this? What is real to them?

TV-bred youngsters are buffeted around within a quadrangle of confusion: Real people do pretend things; pretend people do real things; real people do real things;

Reprinted by permission from *Look* Magazine, December 2, 1969, pp. 99–100. Copyright 1969 by Cowles Communications, Inc.

pretend people do pretend things. So how can they tell if he's a really live dead man, Daddy?

Unfortunately, parents unwittingly reinforce whatever unhelpful associations their children make. The parents provided the television set in the first place, and they abandon their children to the solitary experience of viewing without an adult present. It is only natural for them to assume that we sanction what we provide them with, including the television *and* its contents. The set is part of the family, like the dog, the car, the home movies, the books and the crayons. Our children see us rely on TV for information, entertainment and, occasionally, witless diversion; it's natural that they accord it our high credibility.

Yet what does the young child actually perceive? Consider the lessons in human relationships. The child is himself ill-treated in the very act of viewing. The young child wants, to *do*, not to observe. (Anyone who had recently been on an automobile trip with a youngster can confirm this.) Yet he is seduced into utter immobility and bombarded with response-defying stimuli. He is forbidden by parental injunction ("Don't touch the set!") and mindlessness on the screen from actively participating in the programs' development. Uncaring adults in the shows conduct their affairs utterly oblivious of his presence (with the notable exception of *Misterogers' Neighborhood* and, to a lesser extent, *Captain Kangaroo*)—at least until it is time to enrage his appetite for one of the sponsors' products.

Then his little psyche is taken quite seriously. Every twinge known to child psychology, from sibling rivalry to fears about sexuality, is teased out of the viewer and flung back at him in the commercial moment-of-truth. By far the most carefully crafted minutes of the hour, commercials are often so subtly woven into the fabric of a program that children are loping along at full assent and credulity before realizing that the pitch is on.

The principal experience a *young* viewer has with television is that of an unseen, chance observer. Of the programs that attempt to relate the child viewer to the on-screen activity, unquestionably the least successful is *Romper Room*. It manages to convey to the child at home the sense of his being isolated in some nether region of the set, on a glass-enclosed dunce stool, occasionally

fielding requests to mimic the rest of the children who are all part of the *real* action.

Captain Kangaroo relates more directly to its viewers, but still relapses frequently into an implied reference to "all you millions of boys and girls out there in television land." (*Captain Kangaroo*, in many respects a superb program, further continues the tradition of the well-intended but easily befuddled adult male whose penchant for being pelted by Ping-Pong balls is exceeded only by his capacity to be outfoxed by a rabbit.)

The unquestioned master of relating to the young viewer is NET's Fred Rogers, Peabody Award winner for 1969. His face-to-face personal encounter with the individual child elicits an uncanny rapport; the same daughter who will report, "I saw a peacock on *Captain Kangaroo*," will say, "Misterogers showed me a bagpipe." Rogers takes great pains to provide a secure framework for a fantasy laboratory, within which children can exercise the capacity for imaginative thought that will later power them to insight and accomplishment in adult affairs. What sets *Misterogers' Neighborhood* apart from other television experience children enjoy (or suffer) is that it enables their fantasy to become a time of growth rather than diversion.

Virtually all other programs—adult and juvenile—make it clear that the manipulation of persons through deceit, guilt, pseudo-humor or brute force is legitimized by the eventual getting of one's own way. Today's youngsters have become masters of manipulation in a way unknown to the experience of many adults who work with children.

The underlying difficulty for most young viewers seems to stem from the fact that programming directed at them is basically adult "entertainment" done in juvenile dialect. But they haven't had enough reality testing in the world at large to put cartoon violence in a context in which it can be funny.

Ordinarily, the young viewer watches virtually in vain for *alternatives* to a violent expression of hostility or aggression. None are needed apparently, since there is a seemingly limitless warehouse of willing victims and an incredible quality and variety of violence. Worse, there is a total tolerance and total absence of condemnation of violence. Not a voice is raised to suggest the limited appropriateness of violence as a human-relations skill.

Within the apparently accepted spectrum of violence, some modes of "relating" have more impact than others—a knife fight or harm to an animal, for instance, utterly terrifies a young child, while a slap-stick-style brawl appears to be taken relatively lightly. But nowhere does the violence-as-a-problem-solver thesis come a cropper. And if we, are parents, don't blow the whistle on it, nobody will.

The chances are that nothing will be done, because the hours when our young children are most exposed to the barrage of mayhem and murder are precisely those when we most want the kids out of our hair (i.e., in front of the TV) and are least likely to be beside them to interpret (e.g., when it's time to fix dinner—or to sleep-in on Saturday morning). Vicious cartoons still abound on non-network stations. And, despite the networks' recent reduction of overt violence, the massacre of human relationships continues unabated during those hours. Little is shown that represents values parents wish to foster.

Parental capitulation to television is strange. If a demented adolescent who couldn't do anything but tell "comedy-chase" stories were hanging around the neighborhood, few parents would let their preschoolers spend up to 54 hours a week with him. He'd be called a menace. Why the equanimity about the child's experience with television?

Children can handle almost any perception if they have someone to guide their response or reaction. Most programs are capable of being made at least an occasion for reassurance, if not insight. But it takes a responsible, sensitive adult—either on-screen or at home—to do the job.

Family relationships and values are the primary influence on the child. His discerning of what is important to the important people in his life can offset or transform many perceptions picked up through his experience with relatively faceless TV characters. But "offsetting" or "transforming" are not the same as erasing. A child's life is still absolutely inundated with perceptions that *will influence him*, come what may.

Many of these perceptions will be extraordinarily rewarding. From the astronauts walking on the moon to the birth of a baby, television has enriched beyond measure the environment of our children. Television has also brought them a premature awareness of genuine evil.

At the receiving end, parents can elect to eliminate, by turning off, or correctively interpret, by co-viewing, programming that does not support the family's sense of relationships and values. Similarly, parents can advocate, by selective program choice, or reinforce, by co-viewing, programming which reflects their aspirations. My wife has found it effective to make a program guide especially for our young children, using pictures of the clock, channel selector and television characters for the benefit of the non-readers. It eliminates the need for arbitrary, on-the-spot decisions at hours when neither she nor the children is likely to be very discriminating.

Commercials can be made a game, or be governed by ground rules. We encourage our children to analyze them; what are the sponsors doing to make you want this product? The youngsters' insight is often astounding. And one of our product-prohibitions might be helpful: We won't buy any toy with a battery. Our kids don't miss them.

We need not bemoan the fact that commercial television is basically a consumer-delivery system. But we must insist that it deliver them with a minimum of man-handling. Scripts for constructive —yet commercial—programs for children do exist. Parents must encourage their production, through correspondence with advertisers, broadcasters and the FCC, the licensing agency. Parents can also, of course, encourage adequate funding of non-commercial programming.

But somewhere along the line, mothers and fathers simply have to plunk themselves down with their children in front of the TV and spend some time to find out what's going on—both on the screen and in the children. That's the only way you'll know how to answer—or even hear—the question: "How can you tell if that's a really live dead man, Daddy?"

Exporting Violence

A generation of young Americans has grown up with the American war in Indochina. Most Americans have little or no knowledge of the area, the people, or even what the war is about. In this section, a sampling of the Vietnam war's impact on American attitudes about violence is presented in the context of the My Lai (Song My) massacre. Song My occurred in 1968 and became public knowledge in 1970.

Socrates: Then parts of foreign lands will be covetously eyed by us, and ours by them, if, like ourselves, they exceed the limits of necessity and give in to the unlimited accumulation of wealth?
Glaucon: That Socrates, will be inevitable.
Socrates: And so, we shall go to war, Glaucon. Most certainly, he replied.

Plato

Suddenly, a man leapt up about fifty yards away and began to run . . . Every machine gun, Tommy gun, rifle and pistol in our sector poured fire at that man, and I was amazed at how long he continued to run. But finally he went down, silently, without a scream . . .

The group was detailed to go into the field to look for the man we had seen go down, and I went with them. We found him on his back in the mud, four bullet holes stitched across the top of his naked chest. He was wearing only black shorts. He was alive and conscious, moving his legs and arms, his head lolling back and forth. There was blood on his lips. The . . . squad . . . looked down at the man and laughed . . .

Perhaps as an act of mercy, perhaps as sheer cruelty, one of the men picked up a heavy stake lying in the mud and rammed one end of it into the ground next to the wounded man's throat. Then he forced the stake down over the throat, trying to throttle the man. The man continued to move. Someone stamped on the free end of the stake to break the wounded man's neck, but the stake broke instead. Then another man tried stamping on the man's throat, but somehow the spark of life was still too strong. Finally, the whole group laughed, and walked back to the path. . . .

. . . two women, both dressed in baggy black trousers and blouses, ran up from one of the huts. One of them put a hand to her mouth as she saw the wounded man, whom she recognized as her husband. She dashed back to her hut and returned in a moment carrying a bucket, which she carried with black water from the rice field. Sitting down with her husband's head cradled in her lap, she poured paddy water over his wounds to clean off the clotting blood. Occasionally she would stroke his forehead, muttering something. He died about ten minutes later. The woman remained seated, one hand over her husband's eyes. Slowly, she looked around at the troops, and then she spotted me. Her eyes fixed on me in an expression that still haunts me sometimes . . .

Americans! Americans! What has happened to you in Vietnam?

Malcolm Browne
(From "The New Face of War," in Felix Greene, *Vietnam! Vietnam!* Palo Alto: Fulton, 1966.)

PRINCIPLES OF INTERNATIONAL LAW RECOGNIZED IN THE CHARTER OF THE NUREMBERG TRIBUNAL AND IN THE JUDGMENT OF THE TRIBUNAL

As formulated by the International Law Commission, June-July, 1950

Principle I

Any person who commits an act which constitutes a crime under international law is responsible therefor and liable to punishment.

Principle II

The fact that internal law does not impose a penalty for an act which constitutes a crime under international law does not relieve the person who committed the act from responsibility under international law.

Principle III

The fact that a person who committed an act which constitutes a crime under international law acted as Head of State or responsible government official does not relieve him from responsibility under international law.

Principle IV

The fact that a person acted pursuant to order of his Government or of a superior does not relieve him from responsibility under inter-

national law, provided a moral choice was in fact possible for him.

Principle V

Any person charged with a crime under international law has the right to a fair trial on the facts and law.

Principle VI

The crimes hereinafter set out are punishable as crimes under international law:

a. Crimes against peace:
(i) Planning, preparation, initiation or waging of a war of aggression or a war in violation of international treaties, agreements or assurances;
(ii) Participation in a common plan or conspiracy for the accomplishment of any of the acts mentioned under (i).
b. War crimes:
Violations of the laws or customs of war which include, but are not limited to, murder, ill-treatment or deportation to slave-labour or for

any other purpose of civilian population of or in occupied territory, murder or ill-treatment of prisoners of war or persons on the seas, killing of hostages, plunder of public or private property, wanton destruction of cities, towns or villages, or devastation not justified by military necessity.
c. Crimes against humanity:
Murder, extermination, enslavement, deportation and other inhuman acts done against any civilian population, or persecutions on political, racial or religious grounds, when such acts are done or such persecutions are carried on in execution of or in connexion with any crime against peace or any war crime.

Principle VII

Complicity in the commission of a crime against peace, a war crime, or a crime against humanity as set forth in Principle VI is a crime under international law.

4.14
Lessons of My Lai

Edward M. Opton, Jr.

Only a few years ago most Americans associated war crimes, military atrocities, and state-sanctioned murder only with Adolf Hitler, General Tojo, and a few other evil dictators and evil dictatorships.[1] A small number of historians and moralists knew better, and their statements to that effect can be found by a diligent search of scholarly journals.[2]

Reprinted by permission of the author and of the editors from Nevitt Sanford and Craig Comstock (eds.), *Sanctions for Evil*, San Francisco, Jossey Bass, 1970.

[1] This chapter has been expanded from papers by Dr. Opton and two of his associates at the Wright Institute, Nevitt Sanford and Robert Duckles. These papers appeared in somewhat different form in the February 21, 1970, issue of *The New Republic*, the March, 1970, issue of *Trans-action*, and will appear in the proceedings of the Congressional Conference on War and National Responsibility, to be published by Holt, Rinehart, and Winston.

[2] See, for example, Everett C. Hughes, "Good People and Dirty Work," *Social Problems*, 10 (1962), 3–11.

But almost without exception, even those of us who were aware of the 400-year atrocity of the United States' treatment of its Black minority, of the genocide of the Native Americans, of the Northern and Southern Andersonvilles of the Civil War, of the 200,000 Filipinos slain when the United States decided to replace Spain as the colonial owner of the Philippines—even those who knew this history thought of it as thankfully remote, and not as continuous with the present policy of their government. Past history does not call for present action to stop atrocities.

The American war in Indochina has radically changed the perspective of a good many Americans. This chapter is addressed primarily to that large minority who are at least able seriously to entertain the possibility that the cruelties we fought against in Germany and Japan must be faced within our own country as well. The "Lessons of My Lai," are, I hope, the basis for a small part of the learning from history that will be required if we are not to repeat that history endlessly.[3]

[3] Some knowledge of the My Lai massacre is here assumed. Readers unfamiliar with the facts of the massacre should read Seymour

The *public reaction and non-reaction* to My Lai is particularly rich in lessons for those who may want to act to prevent its frequent repetition. I will try to link the public reaction to My Lai with broader aspects of the massacre in five main conclusions.

1) Most of the Explanations That Have Been Advanced Are Seriously Lacking in Credibility. They Explain Away Rather than Explain: They Say in One Way or Another That My Lai Doesn't Really Count Rather Than Acknowledge Its Significance.

Almost all public speculation on the massacre has begun with the assumption that it was an isolated, uncharacteristic incident.[4] The speculation therefore has been on what exceptional circumstances could have resulted in such a deviation from normality. "They must have gone berserk" is the most over-simplified of these kinds of speculation.

Explanations in terms of the hard fighting and casualties the men had experienced fall into this category. But the facts are that many units have fought harder and longer, suffered more casualties, and lived under worse conditions than Company C, 1st Battalion, 20th Infantry, both in this and other wars. Uncomfortable and dangerous as the war in Vietnam is for our men, it is a great deal less uncomfortable and a great deal less dangerous for the typical soldier than was the Korean War or World Wars I and II.

Efforts to find an explanation of the massacre in the personalities of the officers and enlisted men involved are similarly misdirected. Undoubtedly these men have their quirks and oddities, but so do all of us. No one has reported behavior of the officers or enlisted men before or after My Lai that smacks of abnormality. Parents of the men did not complain that their sons returned from Vietnam in any abnormal psychic state. The men are reported to have gone about their gruesome work for the most part with cool efficiency and tragic effectiveness. The fact that the accused officers and men did nothing to draw special attention to themselves in the months before and after the massacre indicates that they were not remarkably different from run-of-the-mill-soldiers. Genuine explanations of My Lai will require us to pay attention to the factors that lead ordinary men to do extraordinary things. The American tradition is to locate the source of evil deeds in evil men. We have yet to learn that the greatest evils occur when social systems give average men the task of routinizing evil.

Another kind of speculation on the causes of My Lai is the reverse of those discussed above. "This kind of thing happens in war," it is said. "It's terrible, but you have to expect excesses in combat." Not so. There have been excesses in combat in every war, but I know of no direct parallel to the My Lai massacre by American troops in any recent war except the war in Vietnam. So far as I know, American soldiers have not carried out any comparable, large scale, public shooting and bayoneting of infants, women, and old men since the campaigns against the Indians. This massacre is most emphatically *not* the "kind of thing that happens" in recent American wars. The question for investigation is: in what ways is My Lai the kind of thing that is done as a matter of routine in Vietnam?

The pattern of violence at My Lai does not resemble a riot or a mass psychosis. But it does have its counterparts in certain American traditions: genocidal attacks on American Indians in the Nineteenth Century and mass lynchings which persisted until the 1930's. Scientific studies of lynch mobs have shown that the members of such mobs are by no means berserk; rather, theirs is an all-too-rational response to the encouragement, spoken or unspoken, of their community leaders. The attitudes of elected officials and leading members of the community are crucial in permitting lynchings; rarely if ever has a job carried out a lunching when the community leadership truly opposed it. It is important that at My Lai, as at the mass lynchings of blacks and the genocide of the native Americans, the victims were of a different race.

2) The Most Important Fact About the My Lai Massacre Is That It Was Only a Minor Step Beyond the Standard, Official, Routine U.S. Policy in Vietnam.

It is official U.S. policy in Vietnam to obliterate not just whole villages, but whole districts and virtually whole provinces. This policy has been eulogized in polished academic prose by Dr. Samuel P. Huntington, Professor of Government at Harvard:

. . . if the "direct application of mechanical and conventional power" takes place on such a massive scale as to produce a massive migration from countryside to city, the basic assumptions underlying the Maoist doctrine of revolutionary war no longer operate. The Maoist-inspired rural revolution is undercut by the American-sponsored urban revolution.[5]

This description of the most massive bombing and scorched-earth operation in the history of the world as an "American-sponsored urban revolution" must be one of the most Panglossian rationalizations of the murder of civilians since Adolph Eichmann described himself as a coordinator of railroad timetables.

At first, efforts were made to remove the inhabitants before "saving" the regions by destroying them, but the pressure of the vast numbers of refugees thus created —at least one-third of the entire population of South Vietnam[6]— has led to policies even more genocidal. Jonathan and Orville Schell, writing in the November 26, 1969, *The New York Times* observed:

. . . Experience in Quang Ngai Province as journalists has led us to write this letter in hopes of dispelling two possible misapprehensions: that such executions are the fault of men like Calley and Mitchell alone, and that the tragedy of Song My (My Lai) is an isolated atrocity.

[5] *Foreign Affairs* (July, 1968), 650. Huntington's internal quote is from Sir Robert Thompson, "Squaring the Error," *Foreign Affairs* (April, 1968), 447.

[6] One-third is a conservative estimate. Professor Huntington (*op. cit.*) brags that our bombing produced a shift from 80–85% rural in the early 1960's to 60% urban by 1968, making South Vietnam more urban than Sweden, Canada, the U.S.S.R., Poland, Switzerland, and Italy. If Professor Huntington is correct, one of every two farm families in Vietnam was forced off their land between 1960 and 1968, with the process accelerating after 1965. The pressure of bombing has increased even more since 1968.

Hersch's definite account, *My Lai 4*, New York: Random House, 1970, or the condensation of his book in *Harper's*, May, 1970. In the earlier versions of this paper the massacre was referred to as the "alleged massacre." The overwhelming weight of the evidence now available has made it impossible to continue to use "alleged" with a straight face.

[4] For a further discussion of "the facade of shocked surprise," see Fritz Redl's chapter in Nevitt Sanford and Craig Comstock (eds.), *Sanctions for Evil*, San Francisco, Jossey Bass, 1970.

We both spent several weeks in Quang Ngai some six months before the incident. We flew daily with the FAC's (Forward Air Control). What we saw was a province utterly destroyed. In August, 1967, during Operation Benton the "pacification camps" became so full that Army units in the field were ordered not to "generate" any more refugees.

The Army complied. But search and destroy operations continued. Only now peasants were not warned before an air strike was called in on their village. They were killed in their villages because there was no room for them in the swamped pacification camps. The usual warnings by helicopter loudspeakers or air-dropped leaflets were stopped. Every civilian on the ground was assumed to be enemy by the pilots by nature of living in Quang Ngai, which was largely a free fire zone.

The pilots, servicemen not unlike Calley and Mitchell, continued to carry out their orders. Village after village was destroyed from the air as a matter of *de facto* policy. Air strikes on civilians became a matter of routine. It was under these circumstances of official acquiescence to the destruction of the countryside and its people that the massacre of Song My occurred. Such atrocities were and are the logical consequences of a war directed against an enemy indistinguishable from the people.

The genocidal policy is carried out in other ways as well. I have personally accompanied a routine operation in which U.S. Cobra helicopters fired 20mm. cannons into the houses of a typical village in territory controlled by the National Liberation Front. They also shot the villagers who ran out of the houses. This was termed "prepping the area" by the American Lieutenant Colonel who directed the operation. "We sort of shoot it up to see if anything moves," he explained, and he added by way of reassurance that this treatment was perfectly routine.

It is official U.S. policy to establish "free-fire zones" and "kill zones" where anything that moves is fired upon. Although in the original theory these were zones from which civilians had been removed, it has long been well known that free-fire zones now include many inhabited villages. It is official U.S. policy to destroy the Vietnamese people's stockpiles of rice in NLF-influenced areas, thus starving the women and children (the armed men, we may be sure, provide themselves with the undestroyed portion of the rice harvest). I have personally observed this policy carried out and reported through official channels as

if the burning of the villagers' rice supply were as routine as the weather report—which indeed it is. It is also official, though secret, U.S. policy to destroy rice and other crops with chemical defoliants.[7]

U.S. policy seems long ago to have given up the idea of gaining the allegiance of the people of Vietnam. "Winning the hearts and minds"[8] is now maintained only as a public relations product for consumption on the home market. In Vietnam itself the policy is, as explained to me by a U.S. Marine officer, "If you've got them by the balls, the hearts and minds will follow." Getting the villagers by the balls means bombing and shelling them from their villages, assassinating their leaders, breaking up their families by removing the men, and removing the rural population to concentration camps euphemistically called "refugee camps." All these official policies involve killing, and killing on a large scale. It is routine policy to talk about what we are doing only in euphemisms like "population control," "prepping the area," and so forth. And it is standard practice to talk about the Vietnamese people in depersonalized terms

[7] "In some instances entire villages are suspected of being Vietcong sympathizers; killing their food crops prevents their use as a staging area for any sort of military operations and has in some instances led to complete abandonment of the village" (statement by Dr. Arthur W. Galston, Professor of Biology, Yale University, to the Subcommittee on National Security Policy and Scientific Developments of the House of Representatives Committee on Foreign Affairs, December, 1969, as quoted by Thomas Whiteside, *Defoliation*, New York: Ballantine Books, 1970, p. 108). See also Jonathan Schell, *The Military Half*, New York: Vintage Books (Random House), 1968, p. 56.

[8] "Winning the hearts and minds of the people," a phrase used to exhaustion by theorists of counterinsurgency in the early years of the war, has a significant history. John Adams wrote to Hezekiah Niles in 1818: "But what do we mean by the American Revolution? Do we mean the American War? The Revolution was effected before the war commenced. The Revolution was in the minds and hearts of the people; a change in their sentiments, of their duties and obligations . . . this radical change in the principles, opinions, and affects of the people was the real American Revolution." (Quoted by Bernard Bailyn, *The Ideological Origins of the American Revolution*. Cambridge, Massachusetts: Belknap Press of Harvard University, 1967, p. 160).

like "gooks," "slopes," and "dinks." This makes it easier to kill civilians—knowingly, routinely, and massively.

The euphemisms and the depersonalizations may enable headquarters personnel, the politicians above them, and the American public to pretend that large-scale killing of civilians does not occur, but the troops in the field know better. The furor over the My Lai massacre must have seemed to them grimly illogical. As the satirist Art Hoppe put it, "The best way [to kill civilians], it's generally agreed, is to kill them with bombs, rockets, artillery shells and napalm. Those who kill women and children in these ways are called heroes . . ."[9] How is it, the foot soldier must wonder, that "to kill women and children at less than 500 paces is an atrocity; at more than 500 paces, it's an act of heroism."

The official policy that results in large-scale killing of civilians through impersonal, long-distance weapons is matched by an official practice of inaction to reduce the cumulatively large-scale killing of civilians in thousands of individual, personal atrocities: dropping civilians out of helicopters[10]

[9] Art Hoppe, "The Best Way to Kill People," *San Francisco Chronicle*, December 1, 1969, p. 41.

[10] While in Vietnam I was surprised by the frequency of stories of civilians dropped from helicopters. Since I did not inquire about war crimes among soldiers and officers I met casually, it seemed that the men had some inner pressure to talk. Jonathan Schell observed the same phenomenon:

"No one has any feelings for the Vietnamese," said Sproul, a private from Texas. "They're lost. The trouble is, no one sees the Vietnamese as people. They're not people. Therefore, it doesn't matter what you do to them."

"We interrogate our prisoners in the field, and if they don't cooperate, that's it," said Brandt. "Our prisoners are usually people that we have just picked up in a hamlet that should've been cleared. But there are insufficient facilities for the people in the refugee camps, so they come back, and they're automatically considered V.C. Then we give it to 'em."

"Those V.C.s are hard to break," said Sproul. "One time, I seen a real vicious sarge tie a V.C. upside down by the feet to the runners of a chopper and drag him three thousand feet in the air . . . Another time, I seen them get a bunch of V.C.s in a chopper. They push out one first, and then tell the others and killing civilians by torture during interrogations; picking off civilians in their rice paddies in

---

that if they don't talk they go out with him. And they talk." (*The Military Half*, pp. 42–43)

The half-boasting about dropping people out of helicopters seems to be an uncomfortable probing of the listener *and of the storyteller by himself*, a queasy assertion that the helicopter murders, and the other war crimes which they epitomize, are acceptable. In this vein, Schell quotes a group of pilots discussing the bombing of schools and orphanages:

The extreme solemnity that had descended on the group seemed suddenly to generate an opposite impulse of hilarity . . .
Captain Reese turned to me and asked if I had ever heard the songs about the war . . . Reese sang rapidly:

"Strafe the town and kill the people,
Drop napalm in the square,
Get out early Sunday
And catch them at their morning prayer."

Major Billings then recited the words of another song:

"Throw candy to the ARVN,
Gather them all around,
Take your twenty mike-mike
And mow the bastards down."

At dinner . . . the pilots began to make jokes in which they ridiculed the idea that the bombings they guided were unnecessarily brutal by inventing remarks that might be made by men so bloodthirsty that they took delight in intentionally killing innocents. The joke-tellers appeared to bring out their remarks with considerable uneasiness and embarrassment, and some of the pilots appeared to laugh unduly long in response, as though to reassure the tellers . . .
"Bruce got a bunch of kids playing marbles," said Major Nugent.
The group laughed again.
"I got an old lady in a wheelchair," Lieutenant Moore said, and there was more laughter . . . Lieutenant Moore was so severely racked with laughter that he could not swallow a mouthful of food, and for several seconds he was convulsed silently and had to bend his head low with his hands over his mouth. Tears came to his eyes and to Major Nugent's.
"Oh, my!" Lieutenant Moore sighed, exhausted by all the laughing. Then he said, "I didn't kill that woman in the wheelchair, but she sure bled good!"
Nobody laughed at this joke. A silence ensued. Finally, Captain Reese suggested that they find out what movies were playing on the base that night. (pp. 139–142)

---

the large areas where anything that moves is "officially" considered an enemy; killing civilians for sport;[11] "plinking" at them from passing air and land vehicles, and so on. These small-scale war crimes have become so common that our reporters seldom report them; they are no longer "news." They have become routine to many of our soldiers, too, and the soldiers, to preserve their equilibrium, have developed the classical psychological methods of justifying what they see happening. The soldier comes to think of the Vietnamese not as a human like himself, nor even, as the army indictment for the My Lai massacre put it, an "Oriental human being," but as something less than human. It is only a small further step to the conclusion that "the only good dink is a dead dink," as Specialist 4 James Farmer, Com-

---

Of course, not all military personnel participate in this banter. For example, 19 non-aviation junior officers aboard the aircraft carrier *Hancock*—half the junior officers assigned to the crew—have lodged an official protest against the war with the ship's captain. One of them, Lt. Junior Grade Allen P. Cox, wrote in support of his position:

Each meal was punctuated with war stories from the pilots, whose bombing victims were referred to as "crispy critters." I particularly remember the account of a boy on a bicycle who was strafed and reported as a "mechanized vehicle."

"The attitude," Lt. Cox said, "was . . . that those [Vietnamese] people were less than people" (Charles Howe, "19 Junior Officers Sign An Anti-War Petition," *San Francisco Chronicle*, June 26, 1970).
As a final example of the symbolic importance and ambivalent attitude toward helicopter-killings in particular, see "Vet Condemned for Atrocity Stories" in the December 1, 1969, *San Francisco Chronicle* (p. 10):

. . . Fred Sedahl, now a reporter for the *Savannah Morning News*, said he has been buried with telephone calls since his story appeared yesterday.
Sedahl described, among other incidents, a 1965 act in which a Viet Cong prisoner was thrown out of a helicopter to "certain death" by a South Vietnamese interpreter in full view of Marines in the helicopter.
"You ought to take a helicopter ride with me," a man who called yesterday said. "I know just exactly what to do with guys like you. You should be the one taken up and dropped out."

[11] See, for example, "Army Probes New Viet Atrocity," *San Francisco Chronicle*, January 12, 1970, p. 9.

---

pany C, Fourth Battalion, Third Infantry, 198th Infantry Brigade, American Division, expressed it to *The New York Times*.[12]

The foot soldier in Vietnam sees Specialist Farmer's conclusion acted out daily, by air, by artillery, by quick death in a napalm holocaust, by slow death in a foodless, waterless "refugee camp," and by the unpunished examples of his fellow soldiers cutting down a civilian here, a family there. "The only good dink is a dead dink" is in the wind in Vietnam, and our soldiers receive plenty of training in bending before the wind of the Army way of doing things.[13] In that official and quasi-official "climate" the My Lai massacre logically represents no major deviation. The massacre was a minor policy and practice. It would be hypocritical self-righteousness to condemn the men who committed a minor embellishment without condemning those who set the criminal policy itself.[14]

---

[12] Quoted in the *San Francisco Chronicle*, December 1, 1969.

[13] A good example of the kind of war crimes that are carried out in Vietnam as the result of strong but unofficial pressure and policy was provided by the court-martial of Lt. James B. Duffy of Claremont, California, as reported in the *Oakland Tribune*, March 20, 1970. Lt. Duffy's defense against charges that he permitted his men to kill an alleged deserter from the South Vietnamese Army was that he "had no choice but to kill the prisoner because of pressure from superiors . . . 'In war,' Lt. Duffy said, 'people are going to get killed. This major [Jeffery Templeton] told me I was to kill and not bring back prisoners. I considered it part of the war . . .'"

"Fellow officers of Duffy testified earlier they were under pressure to report Communist soldiers killed. They said advancement depended on 'body counts.'"

"Capt. Charles L. Stewart, 25, of Ordtonville, Mich., was asked which would be better received by headquarters, a body count of 14 and one prisoner or 15 bodies. 'Fifteen bodies,' Stewart said. 'Prisoners just don't count.'"

[14] Apparently one of the legal defenses by those accused of the My Lai massacre will be that the massacre was no substantial deviation from official U.S. policy. The *San Francisco Chronicle* of June 26, 1970, reports that the attorney for one of the accused men:

. . . said that if the case goes to trial on the facts, he would be able to prove that the Central Intelligence Agency conducted "the systematic and calculated assassina-

3) The Major Responsibility and Guilt for the Massacre Lies with the Elected Officials Who Make U.S. Policy in Vietnam, and with the High Military Officials Who Have Misled Both Elected Officials and the General Public as to What They Have Been Doing Under the Name of Those Policy Directives.

Our elected officials, and their appointed advisors, have special knowledge and considerable freedom of choice, and they have taken it upon themselves to act as our leaders. We therefore have the right and the duty to hold them personally responsible for the ignorance, insensibility, lack of human understanding, and poor judgment they have displayed in shaping our Vietnam policy. Especially deserving of blame are those officials who knew that policies were wrong but found it expedient to remain silent, rather than endanger their careers or risk the ill will of their "teammates."

There is ample evidence that high officials in our government have participated fully in the practice of portraying the "other side" as an aggregate of evil demons. This imagery was at one time so prominent and routine in official pronouncements, and in the media, that only people with some determination to think for themselves could resist adopting it as a matter of course.[15] Among high officials, as among the general public, the dehumanization of "the enemy" tends to spread, so that now those who dare to demonstrate against our Vietnam policy are called "bums" by President Nixon and by the Vice-President "parasites," "goats," and "creeps."

Readers of *The Authoritarian Personality* (1950)[16] recognized in Vice-President Agnew's "impudent snob" speech a text-book manifestation of modern totalitarianism. It is common enough for a "hard-hitting" political speech to contain numerous references to tendencies the speaker's constituents are known to be against, but it is decidedly uncommon in America for a high official to display the whole characteristic *pattern* of totalitarian ideas and images. Why should a man who stereotypes and distantiates people unlike himself in ethnic background and social class also wish to punish people who deviate from narrow norms of sexual behavior? And why should a man who does these things also wish to suppress intellectuals? The answer lies in the story of the development of authoritarianism—in an individual or in a culture. Social scientists have an obligation to tell this story whenever and wherever they can, to point to manifestations and the implications of totalitarianism in high places as well as in low.

The implications of public utterances like those of the Vice-President are not far to seek. "I think," a 19-year-old infantryman told Helen Emmerich, "someone ought to kill those long-haired, queer bastards back in the world. Anyone who demonstrates against the war ought to be lined up and killed, just like any gook here."[17]

I know from personal experience that this is not an uncommon sentiment.

4) America's Citizens Share in the Responsibility for My Lai, for There Has Been Available to All Ample Evidence that the United States Has Been Committing Large-Scale War Crimes in Vietnam. A Will to Disbelieve, a Self-Serving Reluctance to Know the Truth, Just Plain Indifference, as Well as Failings in Our Ethics and Our Educational System, Have Prevented Our Electorate from Influencing Politicians Whose Policies Allow for Crime Against Humanity.

If some of us are disposed to blame our elected officials for wrong policies in Vietnam, these officials are quick enough to pass the responsibility back to the general public, pointing to opinion polls and silent majorities that favor these policies. These officials have a good point. We as a people do bear much of the responsibility for My Lai. The guilt is in large part collective. It can certainly be argued that the massacre would not have happened had our soldiers not been brought up in a culture in which racism and a Good-vs.-Evil Manichean approach to international relations are deeply rooted. It is quite possible that a large number, perhaps a critically large number, of the soldiers would have refused to take part in the massacre had they not been raised on a psychic diet of television violence, which almost every day of their lives impressed its lesson of the cheapness of life. Few of us have done much that was personally inconvenient to discover or to fight against either the root sources or the proximal causes of My Lai. Yet the case is certainly different with those citizens who have opposed the war than it is with those who favored it; and those who have reluctantly given assent are in a different psychological situation than those who have participated vicariously in the killing and the "victories." There are, in other words, different degrees of actual responsibility and of potentiality for feelings of guilt.

Americans React to the My Lai Massacre

Some light is shed on these matters by a survey of reaction to My Lai carried out by students and staff members of the Wright Institute in December, 1969. As far as

---

tion of an indeterminate number of civilians . . . the official name for such systematic program being 'Operation Phoenix.' "

The statement was one of a series of allegations that it would be cruel and unusual punishment to try Torres on murder charges because "indiscriminate destruction of human lives" is official American policy.

Examples of this policy, the petition said, are saturation bombing, free-fire zones, search and destroy missions, and encouragement of high body counts.

[15] Younger readers may find this statement difficult to believe. They may convince themselves by a visit to the library and a quick plunge into the Cold War rhetoric that pervaded the mass media of the 1950's. Especially recommended are the writings of John Foster Dulles and Richard M. Nixon. In recent years the rhetoric among Establishment politicians has been considerably scaled down, representing a major gain for rationality in political discourse. However, the language of military indoctrination propaganda, the crusade of Total Good against Total Evil, has not been scaled down. There is reason to fear that thinking in terms of Crusades still dominates some of our national leaders; for example, Townsend Hoopes and Paul C. Warnke, both former Assistant Secretaries of Defense and hardly dupes of the Kremlin, interpret the May, 1970, invasion of Cambodia as a disastrous continuation of Richard Nixon's "permanent holy war against communism" ("Nixon Is Really Just Digging In," *Washington Post*, June 21, 1970). As this note is written (June 27, 1970) the Governor of California, Ronald Reagan, has just broadcast a call to "expose Southeast Asian Communism for the inhuman monster that it is."

[16] T. Adorno, Else Frenkel-Brunswik, D. J. Levinson, and N. Sanford, *The Authoritarian Personality*. New York: Harper, 1950.

[17] *San Francisco Examiner*, November 23, 1969.

we know, this was the first study ever attempted on American responses to alleged American war crimes. Our conclusion: the same impetus to an emotional cop-out that produces complacent members of a Silent Majority is surprisingly strong in almost all of us, young as well as old, liberal as well as conservative, interviewer as well as interviewee.

The sample was not a large one —most of our data came from forty-two long interviews with randomly selected telephone subscribers in Oakland, California, plus four in-person interviews— but the results are consistent with larger, less intensive surveys by *The Wall Street Journal*,[18] *The Minneapolis Tribune*, The Harris Poll[19] and *Time*. *Time* reported that 65 percent of its sample of 1,608 individuals denied being upset by the news of the alleged massacre. Our intensive interviews throw some light on how those 65 percent assimilate My Lai to the expected, normal routine of things, or disbelieve that any massacre took place, or do both simultaneously.

Anyone who would understand how people defuse the potential emotional chaos that would logically follow from knowledge of monstrous atrocities committed in their name must begin with the Germans.[20] In the years following 1945 the Allies carried out an active Denazification program which included massive attempts to educate the German people as to what they and their government had

done. On the theory that a Germany ignorant of its history would be condemned to repeat it, the Allies tried to make Germans aware of Nazi war crimes and German guilt. The effort was a failure. Our propagandists found that it is almost impossible to induce people to think about what they prefer to forget. With few exceptions, Germans interviewed during the Denazification campaign stood at a far emotional distance from the Nazi crimes, feeling personally and morally uninvolved and unconcerned, or they denied the facts, or they projected the guilt on others, or they rationalized and justified the atrocities, or they simultaneously engaged in several or all of these mental maneuvers, little inhibited by logical consistency.[21]

Straight-out denial of the facts and the meaning of the German genocide in World War II was by no means confined to the Germans. Arthur Koestler was among the few who spoke from many platforms in the early 1940's trying to rouse the English-speaking public to the horror of the German extermination policy. Commenting on the British and American reaction to his efforts, Koestler writes:

There is a dream which keeps coming back to me at almost regular intervals; it is dark, and I am being murdered in some kind of thicket or brushwood; there is a busy road at no more than ten yards distance; I scream for help but nobody hears me, the crowd walks past, laughing and chattering.

I know that a great many people share, with individual variations, the same type of dream. I have quarrelled about it with analysts and I believe it to be an archetype in the Jungian sense: an expression of the individual's ultimate loneliness when faced with death and cosmic violence; and his inability to communicate the unique horror of his experience. I further believe that it is the root of the ineffectiveness of our atrocity propaganda.

For, after all, you are the crowd who walk past laughing on the road; and there are a few of us, escaped victims or eyewitnesses of the things which happen in the thicket and who, haunted by our memories, go on screaming on the wireless, yelling at you in newspapers and in public meetings, theatres and cinemas. Now and then we succeed in reaching your ear for a minute. I know it each time it happens by a

certain dumb wonder on your faces, a faint glassy stare entering your eye; and I tell myself: now you have got them, now hold them, so that they will remain awake. But it only lasts a minute. You shake yourself like puppies who have got their fur wet; then the transparent screen descends again and you walk on, protected by the dream barrier which stifles all sound.[22]

Koestler would have found the responses of our Oakland citizens painfully familiar. For example, an airline stewardess was asked during the interview to inspect the *Life* magazine photographs of My Lai.[23] As she viewed the mangled bodies and the contorted faces of those about to die she trembled and her chin dropped to her chest. Her eyes closed to shut the pictures out. For several seconds she seemed unable to move. But she recovered immediately, for I then asked, "You said before that you weren't surprised. Do you have any other reactions besides that?" She responded:

No, I don't . . . It—when people are taught to hate, it doesn't surprise me how they react, particularly when they are given a weapon; it just seems to be one of the outcomes of war . . .

The contrast between the distress and shame apparent in her bodily reaction and the bland detachment she tried to put into her words could not have been more striking. The shakiness of her posture of "it doesn't surprise me" became evident less than a minute later when she said:

And it amazes me how a group of individuals can follow such a command . . .

Both emotional detachment and logical self-contradiction seem to serve a common purpose, namely, self-centeredness. The need to exclude from one's thinking such potentially troublesome matters as American war crimes was stated explicitly by some subjects. For later when she said:

I can't take the responsibility of the world on my shoulders too strongly myself . . . it upsets me. I'm having my own problems and can't take this stuff too seriously, since it causes me worries and problems.

Another subject, one who declined to be interviewed, said:

Well, I don't know, you see, I can't get upset about all these things, so

---

[18] December 1, 1969.

[19] "General reaction to the reports of the massacre at My Lai, as recorded in a Harris poll in January [1970], can perhaps best be described as bland" (Philip E. Converse and Howard Schurman, "Silent Majorities and the Vietnam War," *Scientific American*, 222 [June, 1970], 24).

[20] I do not mean to imply that the war crimes of the Americans, or our reactions to those crimes, are any more—or less—monstrous than those of the Germans. If data were available comparisons might be made with the French (Indochina, including the massacre of 6,000 civilians at Haiphong; Algeria, including the massacre of 12,000 civilians at Philippeville in 1955), the Russians under Stalin, the Belgians in the Congo, the Turks in Armenia, the Indonesians in the mid-1960's, the Sudanese as this is written, etc., etc. The comparison of American with German reactions to war crimes has been made because only for the Germans is documentation of popular reaction readily available.

[21] See Bertram Schaffner, *Father Land*. New York: Columbia University Press, 1948.

[22] Arthur Koestler, "On Disbelieving Atrocities," *The New York Times Magazine*, January, 1944.

[23] *Life*, December 5, 1969.

I can't give you an opinion one way or another. Okay?

The seemingly paradoxical emotional detachment makes sense on the premise that emotions signal a need to do something, to be involved, even to take responsibility. The spectators who listened to Kitty Genovese scream as she was slowly murdered outside their New York apartments reported afterwards a similar, seemingly paradoxical emotional detachment. The two instances are comparable, and in both the emotional detachment makes it possible to carry out the desire to center one's attention and effort on oneself, one's own needs and problems, hence, not to get involved with external matters.

Most of the Americans we approached would have felt right at home in the emotional climate of post-war Germany. In 1946 Moses Moskowitz reported on a survey of German opinion:

The most striking overall impression is the absence in the German of any emotional reaction toward Jews, be it positive or negative. It was shocking at times to listen to people decrying the evils of Nazism, reciting the horrors of concentration camps . . . without one word of sympathy for the victims.[24]

Similarly, Morris Janowitz found that when the Germans were informed about the concentration camps, they

seldom or never spontaneously offered to help rehabilitate the inmates. This reaction is consistent with the reports that there was no humanitarian move by the Germans in the neighborhood of the camps to assist in alleviation of the suffering . . . until they were ordered to do so by the military commanders.[25]

It Never Happened

Partial or complete denial of the fact of the massacre at My Lai was common. One might expect the extreme forms of denial from such people as Staff Sergeant David Mitchell, one of the accused, who has said: "I can recall no such case where I know of anyone being hurt . . . It is my opinion that what they say happened did not happen." And one might expect the same reaction from Alabama Governor George Wallace: "I can't believe an

[24] Moses Moskowitz, "The Germans and the Jews: Postwar Report," *Commentary*, July, 1946.

[25] Morris Janowitz, "German Reactions to Nazi Atrocities," *American Journal of Sociology*, 52 (1946), 141–146.

American serviceman would purposely shoot any civilian . . . Any atrocities in this war were caused by the Communists."[26] But total denial is by no means confined to those implicated in the alleged massacre and superpatriots. A man who felt that the U.S. should, but cannot, get out of Vietnam told us: "Our boys wouldn't do this. Something else is behind it."

Another complete denial came from a woman who, like the man above, was ambivalent about the war. At one moment she advocated withdrawal by the end of 1970; however, she also endorsed the idea of escalating and winning the war, no matter what the consequences, *but* without killing innocent people. As for My Lai, she said: "It's too unbelievable that they would do something like that." Another person, asked if he believed the massacre really happened, first gave a strong endorsement of President Nixon's policy, then said: "I can't really and truly. No. I don't. I think it could have been a prefabricated story by a bunch of losers."

Strong doubts served the same purpose as complete denial for some people. "Anything could happen. How do we know what's going on?" asked a man who wanted the war escalated, and one of several individuals who felt so threatened by the subject that they cut off the interview in the middle said: "No, sometimes I don't [believe that the massacre happened]. Sometimes I think that our newspapermen get a little bit wild." Implicit in the words of some respondents seemed to be a plea, a real desire to find a way not to have to believe in the reality of the alleged massacre. A sixty-six-year-old grandmother described her family's reaction:

My foster daughter doesn't believe it. She thinks it never happened. Finally [she] admitted to me that she doesn't want to believe it happened. She doesn't want to believe it. She knows in her heart but refuses to face facts.

Apparently the ability to wish away the unpleasant is prevalent in both Germany and America:

The only thing I do know is that if such a good, kind people as the Germans are capable of killing millions of human beings, as you say they did, humanity is fundamentally beastly.—elderly German woman (quoted by Moskowitz)[27]

[26] *San Francisco Chronicle*, December 18, 1969, p. 14.

[27] "The Germans and the Jews: Postwar Report."

And Besides, They Deserved It

Justification was the other most prevalent means of coping with the unwelcome news. One of the principal justifications our respondents offered was the idea that orders must be followed. Even some of the more dovish respondents gave statements like this: "What would their punishment have been if they had disobeyed? Do they get shot if they don't shoot someone else?" And another "moderate" dove said: "They were given an order to do something. They will shoot you if you don't. They had no choice." And a woman who wanted all U.S. troops out of Vietnam by the end of 1970: "They have to follow orders, too, or go to jail."

Only a few respondents recalled that some of the GIs *had* refused to shoot. One of those few was asked what the men should have done. He said: "What a lot of them did, refuse. Quite a few of them refused. Fact is, I even read where one of them shot himself in the foot so he would be evacuated, so he wouldn't have any part of it."

The idea that one must follow orders was more acceptable to men than to women; when asked what they personally would have done if ordered to line up people and kill them, 74 percent of women said they would have refused, but only 27 percent of men. Perhaps ominously, youth were no more independent of spirit than their elders; those over thirty-six more often favored putting the enlisted men who did the shooting on trial than did those under thirty-six, and slightly more of the older group expressly said that the men should have disobeyed orders to kill civilians.

The idea that the men were justified by the orders they received implies a projection of guilt to somewhere higher up, and a

---

I don't believe it actually happened. The story was planted by Vietcong sympathizers and people inside this country who are trying to get us out of Vietnam.—Los Angeles salesman

I can't believe that a massacre was committed by our boys. It's contrary to everything I've ever learned about America.—Lakewood, Ohio, mother

I can't believe anyone from this country would do that sort of thing. —Marvin Sandidge, Memphis contractor (all American quotes from the *Wall Street Journal*, December 1, 1969)

number of our respondents made this explicit. Germans, similarly, tended to blame the German war crimes on Hitler, their leaders, the National Socialist party, the S.S., or on military fanatics. But the idea that Germans, as individuals, might have been in turn responsible for selection and toleration of their leaders was steadfastly rejected. While the question of responsibility lying with the American public was not specifically asked of our predominantly dovish sample, *no one extended the scope of responsibility to himself in particular or the American people in general.* It is encouraging, however, that in a follow-up questionnaire three months later several respondents did say they believed Americans, including themselves, were ultimately responsible for My Lai. Just as Janowitz found in Germany, so in America someone "higher up" is often held responsible, but almost never those ultimately responsible for the government: the people.

Another popular justification was the idea that the alleged victims were not really civilians, but enemies: "Now had these civilians, had these women set booby traps for these people?" Another man who felt he was a "dove" ("I'd hate to say I'm a hawk."), yet who advocated that the U.S. should "let out the stops," said: "These little bastards are devious," implying in context that the women and children were not really innocent bystanders.

None of the respondents *said* that My Lai was justified as revenge for NLF actions, but many seemed to *think* so:

I understand that the Viet Cong, from the start, have bombed school yards, school houses, movie theaters, restaurants . . . just worthless bombing and it's killing innocent people by the score. And these are their own people.

And a hawk said:

Our boys have been castrated by the VC and no one stood up for them. There was no sensation made of this.

If this kind of justification is common among civilians, it is not surprising when four sergeants in Vietnam write to the *San Francisco Chronicle* (December 31, 1969) to explain their approval of My Lai:

You know that this is a VC village, they are the enemy, they are a part of the enemy's war apparatus. Our job is to destroy the enemy, so kill them; a war can be won only when the enemy forces are destroyed or too demoralized to fight effectively

. . . I want to come home alive, if I must kill old men, women, or children to make myself a little safer, I'll do it without hesitation.

While the four sergeants speak bluntly of killing the enemy, an army officer in our sample, who had just returned from Vietnam, justified the massacre in terms of its presumed psychological effect:

. . . I could see the possibility that it was an order from higher up, just as a deterrent to the other people in the area not to harbor the VC . . . And this is really a very good tactic if you stop to think about it, in a war. If you scare people enough they will keep away from you.

[Interviewer: You feel this is a good tactic in a war?]

Yeah, if you want to fight a war. Aw . . . I'm not saying that I approve of the tactic.

[Interviewer: But you think it's an effective tactic?]

Yes, definitely. I think it's an effective tactic. And people who are running wars probably think the same way: that this is an effective tactic.

There was, however, one justification reportedly used by postwar Germans which we did not hear. The respondents, with one exception, did *not* tell us that victims were members of an inferior race. This is not to say that people were unaware of the role of overt racism in making My Lai possible. Both hawk and dove respondents often said that GIs tend to look on Vietnamese civilians as subhuman, as "gooks," "slopes," and "dinks." One man, a Vietnam veteran, gave several specific examples from his own experience to back up his opinion that our lower-level officers and enlisted men typically treat the Vietnamese people as non-humans, speak of them as non-humans, and think of them as non-humans. But with the one exception, ever subject coupled this awareness of racial prejudice in others with an abstinence from publicly subscribing to it himself.[27a]

[27a] The exception, subject 010, said that the typical GI's view of the Vietnamese is that "they're subnormal." Moreover, he said, "I think it's true." He went on immediately to add, "I think that the GIs are very sympathetic towards the Vietnamese people as a whole . . . the GIs over there are trying to educate and help these people." This individual's forthright racism seems in line with his statement later that, "The German Nazis were a superior race eliminating a— what they thought was a threat to their existence."

The writer remembers that in Vietnam, among those more directly responsible for the activities on which the citizens of Oakland were commenting, justification of war crimes by dehumanization of the victims was very common indeed. The Vietnamese are turned into debased abstraction—"gooks," "slopes," "dinks"—or are spoken of in terms of zoology.[28] "Look," a captain told Jonathan Schell after directing the bombing of a group of Vietnamese houses, "those villages are completely infested with VC, just like rats' nests . . ."[29] But it all comes down to racism in the end:

"A lot of these people wouldn't think of killing a man," Bernhardt said of Company C. "I mean, a white man—a human so to speak."[30]

Usually the dehumanization of the Vietnamese has little intellectual or ideological content; the shift from human to sub-human is easiest if not thought about. There are openly ideological exceptions, though; for example, while covering a search-and-destroy operation near Hue, in August, 1967, the writer met a college student who had received a fellowship award to spend the summer in Vietnam as a reporter for a college newspaper news service. The conversation turned to killings of civilian prisoners under torture. The student-reporter stoutly defended the practice: "It's not like killing people,"

[28] "At times," Frantz Fanon writes, "this Manicheism goes to its logical conclusion and dehumanizes the native, or to speak plainly it turns him into an animal. In fact, the terms the settler uses when he mentions the native are zoological terms. He speaks of the yellow man's reptilian motions, the stink of the native quarter, of breeding swarms . . . When the settler seeks to describe the native fully in exact terms he constantly refers to the bestiary. The native knows all this, and laughs to himself every time he spots an allusion to the animal world in the other's words. For he knows that he is not an animal; and it is precisely at the moment he realizes his humanity that he begins to sharpen the weapons with which he will secure its victory" (*The Wretched of the Earth*, New York: Grove Press, 1966 [original publication 1961], pp. 34–35).

[29] *The Military Half*, p. 144.

[30] Quoted by Joseph Lelyveld, *The New York Times*, reprinted in the *San Francisco Chronicle*, December 16, 1969. Michael Bernhardt was one of the members of Company C who refused to take part in the My Lai massacre.

he maintained. "These are *Communists.*"

Along with the dehumanization of the enemy (and of "friendly" civilians) goes a dehumanization of the self, in psychiatric terminology "dissociation,"[31] a sense of eerie or even ludicrous detachment:

Bernhardt says he was not moved by compassion as he watched the slaughter but by a sense of how ridiculous and illogical it all seemed. "I wasn't really violently emotionally affected. I just looked around and said, 'This is all screwed up.'" . . . What he does remember best are a few gruesome vignettes—one soldier, in particular, who laughed every time he pressed the trigger ("He just couldn't stop. He thought it was funny, funny, funny") . . .[32]

A final important justification or mitigation was the idea that other evils have been worse. A young woman, asked if the Song My massacre resembled Nazi atrocities, said:

Oh, it's not the same as their dirty cruelness. I guess it's similar in a way . . . They killed women and children. It doesn't make sense . . . Like, the Nazis, they used showers with acid in the water or something like that, and that was really horrible. Our men are just shooting people.

However, it was usually very difficult to induce people to make comparisons of any kind. The first comparative question, "Do you know of any incidents from other wars, whether or not this country was involved, that can be compared with My Lai?" produced many avoiding answers:

I can't think of any.
No.
None at all that I can recall.

Only when Germany or Lidice were mentioned did painful comparisons begin to emerge, often with strained efforts to find differences.

I have argued that most people responded to the My Lai massacre with one or both of two main propositions: "it never happened," and "besides, they deserved it," and that both propositions have

the function of propping up the conclusion that "I need not concern myself with it." This should come as no surprise to students of the Silent Majority.

But what of the non-silent minority, America's above-the-average, articulate citizens and her intelligentsia? An informal analysis of newspapers, letters to editors, and the *Congressional Record* convinces me that America's politicians and intelligentsia were much less reluctant to concern themselves with My Lai than was the man in the street. Some (not all) Congressional supporters of the Vietnam war acknowledged they were appalled by the massacre, and William Buckley, a leading conservative and "hawk" wrote:

Thus far it [My Lai] looks like simple barbarism, like bloodlust sadism. The trouble with that explanation is that it does not easily reconcile with what we know about typical Americans . . . The prosecution of the guilty will, then, tell us a lot about them, and not a little about us . . .[33]

Discomfort over My Lai was not, however, universal among the intelligent, and they, too, were able to conclude that it never happened, and besides, they deserved it. For example, a Connecticut man in the course of a letter drawing together quotations from several sources wrote:

What facts? There are some accusations, of the type regularly used by the Viet Cong, and some photos.
Of these photos, Sen. Pete H. Dominick, R-Col., said: "Not one picture in the *Life* story showed anyone committing an atrocity." He also said that the photographs do not jibe with the actual geography around the village of Song My [My Lai] . . .
The campaign to crucify our fighting men for doing their duty is strangely reminiscent of the "police brutality" issue.[34]

The best example of an intelligent denial-defense of the My Lai massacre that I have seen is a lawyer-like treatise by Rouben Chublarian, a former officer in the Soviet Army, former lecturer at Central Asia University, and winner of various awards from the Freedoms Foundation of Valley Forge, Pennsylvania, from the

government of Spain, etc. Chublarian's paper is too detailed to summarize, but two quotes will give the central theme:

The statesmen of South Vietnam, who have thoroughly investigated the Songmy incident, have found that the GI's "have not committed a crime."

And besides, "savagery" and "excessive shooting" were justified, a conclusion Chublarian supports by quotations from Lenin, Scholokhov, General William T. Sherman, and an American President, Woodrow Wilson:

The drive to revenge is connected with the drive to win the battle, and "To be victorious you must be brutal and ruthless."[35]

Leave Me Out of This

The various ways of defusing the emotional potential of My Lai were used by hawks and doves alike, though not in equal proportions. Hawks, more than others, tended to justify the alleged massacre. Both hawks and doves argued in one way or another that no massacre happened. The doves tended to comfort themselves with the thought that My Lai's happen in every war, hence one need not be upset. Regardless of the method, the effect was the same: emotional disengagement. I believe the general non-response to My Lai by our random sample of Oaklanders was not fundamentally different from the non-response of Kitty Genovese's neighbors, who heard her protracted screams and cries for help as she was slowly murdered, but who declined to get involved, and who reported afterwards a similar, seemingly paradoxical, emotional detachment. Whether it is Vietnamese peasants or one's next-door neighbor, emo-

---

[31] ". . . dissociation [means] . . . the forbidden or anxiety-arousing or conflict-producing thoughts, feelings, and actions are experienced as 'unwilled' or as not 'owned' by oneself. They 'just happen' or are attributed to other causes or people that 'made me do it,' and the like" (Louis Breger, *Instinct to Identity*, unpublished manuscript in preparation, p. 108).

[32] Lelyveld, *The New York Times.*

[33] *San Francisco Examiner*, December 4, 1969.

[34] James H. Howard, letter to the *New Haven* (Connecticut) *Register*, February 16, 1970. Incidentally, the *Life* photographs do jibe with the appearance of coastal Quang Ngai Province, where My Lai was located, according to my memory and my photographs of the area.

[35] Mr. Chublarian's paper is available from the author at 236 West Walnut St., Philadelphia, Pennsylvania. Wilson's actual words, according to Tom Wicker, writing in *The New York Times*, December 2, 1969, were:

Once lead this people into war and they'll forget there ever was such a thing as tolerance. To fight you must be brutal and ruthless and the spirit of ruthless brutality will enter into the very fibre of our national life, infecting Congress, the courts, the policeman on the beat, the man in the street . . .

The next day, April 2, 1917, Wilson demanded a Declaration of War in the name of the Right, saying that America would have to use

. . . force, force to the utmost, force without stint or limit.

tional detachment makes it possible to keep one's attention and concern focused on Number One, me, myself, I. No malignant evil intent is necessary for men to tolerate, or even reluctantly to applaud war crimes; all that is required is self-centeredness. This focus on the self need not imply any pathological egotism, but only alienated impotence to affect the course of events. Milton Mayer explained the phenomenon in his analysis of the Germans' passive acceptance of Nazism: "Responsible men never shirk responsibility, and so, when they must reject it, they deny it. They draw the curtain. They detach themselves altogether from the consideration of the evil they ought to, but cannot, contend with. Their denial compels their detachment."[36]

5) Little Is to Be Gained, and Perhaps Much Lost, by Attempts to Force Recognition of Responsibility on Those Who Now Completely Wash Their Hands of the Blood of My Lai. But If We Were to Assume That No One Can Be Stirred to Action by Such Atrocities, or If We Fail to Press for Full and Frank Application of Social Science to American War Crimes, We Would Participate by Passivity in the Horror of America's My Lai's, Past and Future.

We must make sure that as many people as possible know the truth and are guided by it. Unless a substantial number of people who can speak and write with authority strive to keep the evil of My Lai, and of the larger policy of which it is an expression, before the public, it is difficult to see what will prevent our military from persisting in genocide in Vietnam, and in future Vietnams.

But dealing with this guilt-laden subject will not be easy, for guilt that is on the edge of consciousness can lead to further destructiveness more easily than to contrition. Charles Manson, the alleged leader of the group accused of the Sharon Tate murders, seeing that his followers were shaken after their night's work, reportedly insisted that they commit more murders the next night. This psychological stratagem was used regularly in the Nazis' training of the SS. Efforts to induce consciousness of guilt in people who

[36] Milton Mayer. *They Thought They Were Free,* Chicago: University of Chicago Press, 1955, p. 76.

lack the inner strength to bear it can backfire, evoking behavior that relieves uneasiness by demonstrating that what is feared can be done, even more and worse, without catastrophic consequences to oneself.

Public breast-beating, whether self-flagellation or condemnation of everyone except oneself, is probably futile at best and a dangerous indulgence at worst. Constructive handling of feelings about My Lai will require attention to what we can do to prevent future atrocities, to end the Vietnam war, and to block the next Vietnam.

Social scientists in particular need not be part of a silent majority as, with rare exceptions, we so far have been. Psychologists can make themselves heard in investigating what makes some killing psychologically "close" and shocking, while the same death by bomb or shell is a matter of indifference. Sociologists have not yet reported on the structural aspects of the military reward system that ensures that almost all war crimes remain unreported. Economists can calculate and publicize the enormous indirect costs of the war, such as disability pensions and survivor benefits that will continue into the Twenty-first Century. Historians could try to make the public aware of the nearly fatal effects of the Indo-Chinese and Algerian wars on French democracy. Survey researchers, psychiatrists, and clinical psychologists could assay the extent of long-lasting alienation and anomie among returned Vietnam veterans. The social sciences could join together in examining the pervasive distortion in information as it passes up and down the chain of military and civilian command, and how this distortion is used to justify and rationalize mass murder.

The psychology, sociology, economics, and history of colonial wars particularly deserve more attention. One of the most insidious arguments for continuation of the Vietnam war is the proposition that termination in less than victory would produce a massive political backlash. We would do well to study some of our own retreats from political-military intervention abroad. Withdrawal from Vietnam would not make President Nixon the first American President to "lose a war," as he professedly fears, but this historical fact must be made a psychological reality if we are to ex-

tricate ourselves from the Vietnam morass. Coming out on the short end of a military conflict has not sapped the will, ruined the economy, or spoiled the society of the United States in the past; and these bugaboos, which are within the legitimate subject-matter of the social sciences, need to be expunged from our minds. That will take work.

Funding such work will be difficult, but if social scientists think the work is important enough, they will find the means of sponsorship and support. There are times when to know and to remain silent is to be an accomplice. One of the lessons of My Lai is that silence in the face of such human disaster can no longer be an acceptable response.

Failure of Americans to respond to My Lai and to all that it symbolizes could be disastrous for the future of our nation. The United States has such an overwhelming technology, and such an overwhelming tendency to make use of it in Vietnam, that it has created a worse war than we have ever had before. But, the fact is that the technology we have available is not being used to its fullest extent in Vietnam. When I talked to American military men in Vietnam on their attitudes toward the war, one of their most common complaints was, "We are fighting this war with one hand tied behind our back." They were often quite bitter about it, and in a sense they had a point.

We have the technology easily to carry out a "final solution" to the Vietnam problem. We have made a very good start on it, but we haven't done it yet. If we do, it will probably not take the form of people in camps and putting them into ovens, but of bringing the ovens to them in the form of shiny aluminum napalm cylinders dropped from the air.

Even more ominous is a 1955 proposal by (then) Vice-President Richard Nixon in a St. Patrick's Day speech to the Executives Club of Chicago:

Our artillery and our tactical air force in the Pacific are now equipped with atomic explosives which can and will be used on military targets with precision and effectiveness. It is foolish to talk about the possibility that the weapons which might be used in the event war breaks out in the Pacific would be limited to the conventional Korean and World War II types of explosives. Our forces could not fight an effective war in the Pacific with those types of explosives if they wanted to. Tactical atomic explosives are now conventional and will be used against the military targets of any aggressive force.

We have not yet completed the task of the final solution, which is well within the capability of the military to carry out, and which many military leaders would very much like to carry out. It would, they feel, protect the men under them. It would make sure that their boys, in their platoons, their regiments, go home standing up rather than in coffins.

If we want to explain what is happening in Vietnam, we must recognize that a balance has been struck between terror and restraint, but that this balance can shift, as I fear it will, in an extremely malignant direction. It is a question of what you can get away with. The laws of war are not a matter of Geneva Conventions or accepted rules, but of what each military commander—and the entire government—can get away with at a particular time. In Vietnam, the men who would like to carry out a "final solution" have not been able to get away with it yet. They have been restrained by forces in our society. If such restraints are to remain in effect, they will have to originate with the citizenry—those who don't want to see the "final solution" carried out.

4.15
The Scars of Vietnam

Robert Jay Lifton

I have done psychiatric work at a number of Veterans hospitals and outpatient clinics, and at the Walter Reed Army Institute of Research. During the Korean War I served as an Air Force Psychiatrist in Korea and Japan. I have spent almost seven years living and working in the Far East, and made visits to Vietnam in 1954 and in 1967.

I have done research on such "extreme situations" as the psychological aspects of Chinese thought reform (or "brainwashing"), and the psychological

From Robert Jay Lifton's testimony before the Senate Subcommittee on Veteran's Affairs on January 27, 1970.

effects of the atomic bomb in Hiroshima. I have been greatly concerned with the application of psychological methods to the study of historical events, and with the general psychology of the *survivor*.

I would like to comment upon the psychological predicament of the Vietnam veteran, both from the standpoint of war in general and of the nature of this particular war.

For veterans of any war there is a difficult transition from the "extreme situation" of the war environment to the more ordinary civilian world. This was noted after World War I, World War II, and the Korean War, but only recently have we begun to appreciate the problem from the standpoint of the psychology of the survivor. The combat veteran of any war has survived the deaths of specific buddies, as well as the deaths of anonymous soldiers on his and on the enemy's side. He survives the general war environment, within which he was taught that killing was not only legitimate but proper and necessary.

Upon returning to civilian life the war veteran faces several important psychological tasks in relationship to the deaths he has witnessed. He must, first of all, struggle with anxiety he continues to feel, often in association with the indelible images of death, dying and suffering that constitute the survivor's "death imprint." He must also struggle with feelings of guilt and shame resulting directly from the war experience. These guilt feelings can relate simply to the fact that he survived while so many others died, or they may focus upon the specific death of one particular buddy who in some way, he feels, was sacrificed, so that he, the veteran, could go on living. His sense of guilt may also relate to his having killed enemy soldiers, or having done various other things in order to stay alive. But his over-all psychological task is that of finding meaning and justification in having survived, and in having fought and killed. That is, as a survivor he must, consciously or unconsciously, give some form to the extreme experience of war, in order to be able to find meaning in all else he does afterwards in civilian life.

These psychological tasks are never perfectly managed, and as a result the veteran may experience anything from a mild readjustment problem to disabling forms of psychiatric impairment. Typically, the returning veteran

manifests a certain amount of withdrawal from civilian life, a measure of distrust of the civilian environment—a feeling that what it offers him may well be counterfeit—and some confusion and uncertainty about the meaning of his wartime experience and of his future life. His overall adjustment is greatly influenced by the extent to which he can become inwardly convinced that *his* war, and *his* participation in that war, had purpose and significance.

All of this is true for the Vietnam veteran. But in addition his psychological experience is influenced by certain characteristics of the war in Vietnam. The average Vietnam GI is thrust into a strange, far-away, and very alien place. The Vietnamese people and their culture are equally alien to him. Finding himself in the middle of a guerrilla war in which the guerrillas have intimate contact with ordinary people, the environment to him is not only dangerous and unpredictable but devoid of landmarks that might warn of danger or help him to identify the enemy. He experiences a combination of profound inner confusion, helplessness and terror.

Then he sees his buddies killed and mutilated. He may experience the soldier-survivor's impulse toward revenge, toward overcoming his own emotional conflicts and giving meaning to his buddies' sacrifices by getting back at the enemy. And in an ordinary war there is a structure and ritual for doing just that—battle lines and established methods for contacting the enemy and carrying out individual and group battle tasks with aggressiveness and courage. But in Vietnam there is none of that—the enemy is everyone and no one, never still, rarely visible, from the ordinary peasant. The GI is therefore denied the minimal psychological satisfactions of war, and, as a result, his fear, rage, and frustration mount.

At the same time he notices that the South Vietnamese fight poorly or not at all; and rather than ask himself why this is so, he tends to associate them with the general corruption and deterioration he sees all about him. Any previous potential for racism is mobilized and he comes to look upon Vietnamese as inferior people or even nonhuman creatures. This dehumanization of the Vietnamese by the individual GI is furthered by his participation in such everyday actions as the saturation of villages with bombs and

COURTESY OF RAT PUBLICATIONS, 241 EAST 14 STREET, NEW YORK, NEW YORK.

artillery fire, and the burning of entire hamlets. Observing the death and injuries of Vietnamese civilians on such a massive scale, and the even more massive disruptions of village life and forced relocations, he cannot but feel that the Vietnamese have become more or less expendable.

That is why Vietnam veterans I have talked to were not really surprised by the recent disclosures of atrocities committed by American troops at My Lai and elsewhere. Virtually all of them had either witnessed or heard of similar incidents, if on a somewhat smaller scale. Hence Paul Medlo's public statement that what he and others did at My Lai "seemed like it was the natural thing to do at the time." Another former infantryman, Terry Reed, who described a similar incident elsewhere, made a public statement of even greater psychological significance. He said: "To me the war was being ambushed every three to five days, being left with scores of wounded GIs. Then come right back at the enemy by going into an innocent village, destroying and killing the people." What these words suggest is how, under the extraordinary stress of an impossible situation, GIs come to see all Vietnamese, whatever their age or sex or affiliation as interchangeable with the enemy, so that killing any Vietnamese can become a way of "coming right back" at those responsible for wounding or killing

their own buddies.

Medlo went on to say that immediately after killing a number of Vietnamese civilians he "felt good" and that "I was getting relieved from what I had seen earlier over there." Applicable here is an established psychological principle that killing can relieve fear of being killed. But there is something more operating in connection with these massacres: the momentary illusion on the part of GIs that, by gunning down these figures now equated with the enemy—even little babies and women and old men—they were finally involved in a genuine "military action," their elusive adversaries had finally been located, made to stand still, and annihilated—an illusion, in other words, that they had finally put their world back in order.

Other veterans have reported witnessing or participating in killings of civilians without even the need for such an illusion. Sometimes these killings have been performed with the spirit of the hunter or the indiscriminate executioner—pot shots at random Vietnamese taken from helicopters, heavy fire directed at populated villages for no more reason than a commanding officer's feeling that he "didn't like their look." In addition there have been many accounts of such things as the shoving of suspects out of helicopters, the beheadings of Vietcong or Vietcong suspects,

and of various forms of dismembering the bodies of dead Vietnamese.

Actions such as these require an advanced state of what I have called psychic numbing—the loss of the capacity to feel—and of general brutalization. Where such actions are committed in a direct face-to-face fashion—without even the psychological protection of distance that is available to those who drop bombs from the sky or direct long-range artillery fire—the psychological aberration and the moral disintegration are very advanced indeed. For while there is little ethical difference between killing someone far away whom one cannot see, and looking directly into the victim's eyes from five or ten feet away while pulling the trigger, there is a considerable psychological difference between the two acts.

The Vietnam GI also is profoundly affected by atrocities committed by the Vietcong, by South Vietnamese soldiers, and by South Korean forces. All of these contribute both to his numbing and his brutalization. But it is one's own atrocities that haunt one most. And no one can emerge from that environment without profound inner questions concerning the American mission in Vietnam and the ostensibly democratic nature of our allies there—even if, as is often the case, the GI resists these questions and keeps them from his own consciousness.

Whatever kind of adjustment the returning Vietnam veteran appears to be making, he must continue to carry images of these experiences inside of him. Survivors of a special kind of war, these men constitute a special kind of veterans' group. Murray Polner, a historian who has now interviewed more than two hundred Vietnam veterans as part of an investigation of their experiences, has found that none of the men he talked to—not one of them—was entirely free from doubt about the nature of the American involvement in Vietnam. This does not mean that all of them actively oppose the war, but rather that as a group they have grave difficulty finding inner justification for what they have experienced and what they have done.

That is exactly what former Army Captain Max Cleland, a triple-amputee, meant when he told this Subcommittee last month: "To the devastating psychological effect of getting maimed, paralyzed, or in some way unable to reenter American life as you left it, is the added psychological weight that it may not have been worth it; that the war may have been a cruel hoax, an American tragedy, that left a small minority of young American males holding the bag." It is also what a 19-year-old marine who had lost part of his leg and was awaiting medical discharge meant when he told Polner (as quoted in *Trans-action* magazine, November, 1968): "I think any other war would have been worth my foot. But not this one. One day, someone has got to explain to me why I was there." This inability to find significance or meaning in their extreme experience leaves many Vietnam veterans with a terrible burden of survivor guilt. And this sense of guilt can become associated with deep distrust of the society that sent them to their ordeal in Vietnam. They then retain a strong and deeply disturbing feeling of having been victimized and betrayed by their own country.

As a result many continue to be numbed as civilians, the numbing now taking the form of a refusal to talk or think about the war. Some become almost phobic toward television broadcasts or newspaper reports having anything to do with the war. A number of those I spoke to could only take jobs permitting them to remain isolated from most of their fellow Americans, often night jobs. One Vietnam veteran told

me, "I worked at night because I couldn't stand looking at those nine-to-five people who sent me to Vietnam." Yet these men are also affected by the deep ambivalence of the general American population about the war in general, an ambivalence which extends to those who have fought it. It is difficult for most Americans to make into heroes the men who have fought in this filthy, ambiguous war, and if they try to do so with a particular veteran there is likely to be a great deal of conflict and embarrassment all around. There is in fact an unspoken feeling on the part of many Americans that returning veterans carry some of the taint of that dirty and unsuccessful war.

From work that I and a number of others have done on related forms of war experience and survival, we can expect various kinds of psychological disturbance to appear in Vietnam veterans, ranging from mild withdrawal to periodic depression to severe psychosomatic disorder to disabling psychosis. Some are likely to seek continuing outlets for a pattern of violence to which they have become habituated, whether by indulging in antisocial or criminal behavior, or by, almost in the fashion of mercenaries, offering their services to the highest bidder. Similarly, many will hold onto a related habituation to racism and the need to victimize others. Any of these patterns may appear very quickly in some, but in others lie dormant for a period of months or even years and then emerge in response to various internal or external pressures.

What I have been saying is that we cannot separate the larger historical contradictions surrounding the American involvement in Vietnam from the individual psychological responses of our soldiers. Indeed the Vietnam veteran serves as a psychological crucible of the entire country's doubts and misgivings about the war. He has been the agent and victim of that confusion—of on the one hand our general desensitization to indiscriminate killing, and on the other our accumulating guilt and deep suspicion concerning our own actions. We sent him as an intruder in a revolution taking place in a small Asian society, and he returns as a tainted intruder in our own society. Albert Camus urged that men be neither victims nor executioners. In Vietnam we have made our young men into both.

Of course Vietnam veterans

need and deserve improved medical and psychiatric facilities, as well as better opportunities for education and employment. But if we are really concerned about the psychological and spiritual health of America's young men—and indeed, about our own as well—we shall cease victimizing and brutalizing them in this war.

David Harris, the husband of Joan Baez, served a prison sentence for refusing induction. His article is an articulate statement of personal conscience, representative of the thoughts of many young people on the senselessness of war. Harris, a pacifist, gives testimony to why he must resist the draft.

4.16
Resistance

David Harris

Before I talk specifically about the draft, I'd like to begin at a general point—the question of what you and I possess as a tool. One of the things that you and I constantly look for in this world is really an adequate tool, something with which we can bring about change in the world. Now, I'm going to begin with an assumption—that the tool that you and I have is not a new set of words; it's not a new slogan, a new candidate, a new set of officers. The tool that you and I have is a life. What matters is how that life is lived from day to day to day.

As we live that life, one of the things that we do is really create a set of terms around ourselves. Your life is surrounded with a logic that the acting out of that life really creates and sustains. I think that the most basic way that you and I can understand this society is not simply as a set of institutions. I think we can go beyond that and say that a society is a model of consciousness. A society is a set of assumptions; it's

Reprinted by permission of the author from a "Resistance" pamphlet.

a set of logic that the members of the society operate within and have recourse to when they have questions.

So that something like history, if we are to look at it, becomes not a progression of great men or great events. History instead is the sum total of the lives of those people never mentioned in history books. What the present society and the progression of societies can teach us is really a thing about how people live their lives and what kind of terms people are willing to live their lives under. That's the question facing you and me as we approach that problem of a life. It's a question about terms. It's a question about what kind of terms you are willing to live under, to live within.

As we in the Resistance look out on a world that is really a merry-go-round of blood and misery; and as we look out on that world of widows and orphans and young men shipped home in boxes and little children with their chins melted to their chests, there is one statement that has cogency and meaning. That statement is a very simple statement, but like most simple statements, is a very complex problem to try to live. That simple statement is: *all men are brothers*. And the problem that we have taken on ourselves is the problem of building that brotherhood into a social and political reality.

As you try to do that with your life—which is the only way that attempt can be made; as you try to live that message of brotherhood from day to day to day in the face of your friends and in the face of those things that might be considered your enemies, in the face of all those institutions that surround you; as you attempt to live that, you run into a very obvious and immediate social institution if you are a young man between the ages of 18 and 35. That institution has been euphemistically called the Selective Service System of the United States, which is a euphemism for military conscription, which is a euphemism for death and oppression.

The Assumptions of the Draft

And for a moment I'd like to talk about the basic assumptions which that system represents, and the pillars upon which it is built, because I think you and I have to understand what it means to carry a draft card. One of the things it means is a set of terms you ac-cept, and for a moment I'd like to lay those terms out.

I. The most obvious assumption of military conscription is that the lives of young people in this country belong not to those young people; the lives of those young people instead are possessions of the state, to be used by the state when and where the state chooses to use them. The decisions made by those young people are not decisions made on the terms that they find in their lives. They are rather decisions that are made on the terms of the state because those people belong to the state. What the draft card represents is a pledge. It's a pledge that all of you have signed to the American state. That pledge says: "When and where you decide murder to be a fit international policy, I'm your boy."

If your relationship to that state is one of subservience, then you can expect that state to reproduce that subservience in kind around the world. History should leave us no doubt about that. And what we see happening in a situation like Vietnam today is not a mistake. It is not something that's fallen down out of the sky on all of us Rather, we see the American logic coming to fruition. We see a dispossessed people dispossessing other people of their lives.

The first problem that you and I face is the problem of repossessing that basic instrument called life. That life all of you have signed over to the state. And it is only when we begin to repossess those lives that you and I can ever talk about those lives having meaning or about living in a society that is really shaped by the meaning of those lives.

II. The second assumption of conscription is perhaps the least obvious, but it is also the most important. For a moment, I'd like all of you to think of your draft cards as an educational mechanism. You're given a draft card to teach you a way of thinking about yourself and a way of thinking about people around you. And what has been taught to a generation of young people in this country by conscription is a basic fact that has to do with a mode of energy of a life.

You know, for all of us there are thousands, literally thousands of psychological and emotional resources we might go to to find the energy to pursue our lives from day to day. But rather than any of those various energies, what we live in is one of those energies organized. And what the draft card has taught people from day to day to day in their lives is how consistently to live under the auspices of fear. How continually when they seek those resources that they need to live a life, how continually to go to fear for those. And as you and I look around us, we can say that fear is not just a simple, personal, psychological fact; what you and I live in the midst of is the organized politics of fear.

If we were to dispense with words like "left" and "right," which may be totally inadequate to understand those organizations from the point of view of what human energy is, their base for social organization, what model of man are they based upon, then what you and I can say in the world today is that we live in the unanimous organized politics of fear. That fear has made men blind. That blindness has made people starve. That blindness is the fact of lives around the world today.

What you and I can reasonably do, then, is not say that we won't be afraid, because I've never met a man who wasn't afraid. What you and I can say is that we refuse to make that fear the central fact of our lives. We refuse to make it the hub around which we revolve.

Most of all, we refuse to build that fear into social organizations. What we can say is, we may be afraid, but that fear will not be imposed by us on the people around us. That fear will not be made into a society, which means that no longer can we continue to act under the auspices of that fear. And what we in the Resistance have done is said: No More. No more will we make that fear the central fact of our lives. No more will we breed and extend that fear. No more will we be that fear's servant.

III. The third assumption of conscription is the most obvious: that is, 80% of the people, in the world today live lives that we could characterize as miserable. They live those lives not because the world does not possess the resources to give them meaningful lives. You live in a country that every hour spends seven million dollars on weapons. Every month we spend the money for armaments for the war in Vietnam that is necessary to feed every starving person in the world today. The world is not lacking the sustenance for those people.

Rather, what stands between those people and anything we

might understand as the basic refinements of life is you and me, and the fact that you and I and the people around the world have made the decision that it's much more important to see every starving face in the world today as a potential enemy than it is to go to those people and talk to their hunger and give them food.

And if we are to ask ourselves what institution in this society stands as a representative of that decision, we can say that the United States military is the obvious representative of that decision on your and my parts, and that the United States military does not exist without conscription, and conscription does not exist without you and me. That system of conscription is not General Hershey. It is not Lyndon Johnson. It is not any Congressman or Senator who voted upon that bill. It is not any one of the little old ladies that shuffle the daily papers of the SSS. Military conscription is every man that carries a draft card.

You and I are the bricks and mortar of that system. And the most elaborate bureaucracy for selective service in the world does not function without people such as you and me willing to sign our lives over to that system. Without you and me, it's nothing. I mean, the beautiful thing about American totalitarianism is that it is participatory. Which means that if you don't buy it, it doesn't move. And I don't buy it.

I think you buy it when you carry a draft card. I think you become one more link in a whole chain of death and oppression on people's lives around the world.

What we in the Resistance have said about the act of refusing to cooperate with military conscription is not that we see it as a final act, not that we see it even as the great culmination. It's one little thing. It's one step. But it's the first step. To take that step means for most of you taking on what's probably going to be a wholly new social role. That's called the role of criminal.

It's funny. You know, as you grow up, you always have this feeling like you are growing up towards something, that somewhere out there there's this true occupation, that there's your thing sitting out there, and finally approaching twenty-three I found my thing in being a criminal. It's really too much. And being under sentence now for three years in the federal prison, the one thing I can say is that I find no more

honorable position in modern America than that of criminal.

Allegiance and Choice

There's nothing that can lighten the fact of that sentence, but there are some things that can put those three years in perspective. The fact is, people around the world who resist the American military pay the price of life itself. You're asked to pay five years. That's a very small price in comparison. And to understand what the choice is . . . the choice is not whether you're going to do time in jail or not; that's a small choice. The choice is how you're going to live.

The choice is whether you're going to live with a draft card in your pocket or not.

What we've said, when the choice gets down between us doing time in jail and living our lives, and the other part of the choice is our staying out of jail and denying those lives, we choose our lives. And if we've got to live those lives in Lompoc Federal Penitentiary, then we'll live them in Lompoc Federal Penitentiary, but by God, we're going to live those lives out on the street. No longer are all those things going to be hidden in the bathroom and the bedroom, where American culture has let everything meaningful sit. Those lives now go out on the street. And those lives are our tool and our weapons, and we take those lives out to build all life with. That's been the choice for us. We've taken one step in that choice.

I think that what you should understand about that choice is, first, all you've got is a life. All any man is given is a life, and it's time for you, instead of dealing with the abstract notion of social problems and sitting down in all your academic regalia and presenting analyses about the various social problems in America, to understand that the social problem of America is people. It is time to understand that you are a people, and that there is a very direct connection between those social problems and the way you choose to live. For those social problems are nothing more than the way Americans choose to live and if you want to speak to those people's lives, then you have to speak to them with a life.

The second thing you should remember is that you can do that. This is not an abstract program for someone else. It's something that each of you can do. I think

what faces each of us is a question about allegiance. What we in the Resistance have said is very simple. We owe allegiance to no piece of colored cloth. We owe allegiance to no musty set of political principles, or any musty set of people that may run those political principles. What we owe allegiance to is the fact of people's lives around the world.

The fact of those lives is that those lives are wrapped in a chain of death and oppression. If you want a symbol for that, then take that widow, take that orphan, take that young man shipped home in a box, take the young child with his chin melted to his chest, and say that's what we owe allegiance to. And anything that stands between us and those people will be walked through.

What we have chosen to do is begin walking through those things. What we've said is that it's time to stand up. It's time to stand up with your brothers around the world. It's time to jump off the merry-go-round. It's time to stop letting your shoulder be used as a hoist for death into the saddle. It's time to stop sharpening his sword. It's time to stop carrying his shield. It's time to stop watching him run off down the road with bloody hoofprints. It's time to stand up.

It's time to say, I'm given one thing on the face of this earth. That is my life. I intend to use my life as a way to build the lives of my brothers.

It's time to say, I'm given a choice in the modern world today. That choice in a way is a simple choice. It's a choice between all those forces in the society and in the world that have become synonymous with man's death and oppression, and those forces which really offer hope and life for people. You must choose between them. You only get to choose one of them. You can't serve a god of militarism and war and serve a god of brotherhood and love. You choose and you serve one or the other, but the existence of one is the absolute contradiction of the existence of the other. That's the choice you and I get to make.

That choice is choosing those terms that we're going to live our lives in. I think what we in the Resistance have chosen is to really make those lives seeds, to make lives seeds of liberation for the world. From these lives can grow a new house for men—a house not built upon one man's ability to kill his brother; but a house built upon the fact of their brotherhood.

That means that you do that from day to day to day until a point is reached. That point is the day when a young child finds two words in a book, and the two words are "oppressor" and "oppressed" and he asks you what those words mean, and you can't point to a goddam thing in the world to tell him. When there's absolutely no substance and meaning left to the words "oppressor" and "oppressed" anywhere in the world, when that word has lost all relationship to the fact of men's lives, that is when you and I get to stop and rest.

But until those two words are categorically stricken from human language, you and I have to work. You and I have to stand up. The first way you can stand up is to take that little piece of white paper called a draft card that you carry around in your pocket, you can take it and say: In reality, this is not a piece of white paper. In reality, this is a death warrant. I've signed this death warrant, and I now tear this death warrant up. My name goes out on no more death warrants, and my body stands between any man and that death warrant. I stand here today and tomorrow and the next day with my brothers and I don't stop standing until all my brothers are on their feet.

4.17
The Best Way to Kill People

Arthur Hoppe

SCENE: The Heavenly Real Estate Office. The Landlord is seated behind his desk, working on a plan for developing a new galaxy, as his collection agent, Gabriel, enters.

THE LANDLORD: Hmmm, a billion bushels of starshine, an aura of moonglow, ten parsecs of . . . What is it, Gabriel?

GABRIEL: It's that little blue-green jewel of a planet you love so, sir. The inhabitants are arguing over how best to kill each other.

Reprinted by permission from the *San Francisco Chronicle*, December 1, 1969. © Chronicle Publishing Co. 1969.

THE LANDLORD: They're what?

GABRIEL: The leaders are finally meeting to talk about throwing their nuclear weapons in the sea. They are afraid they will kill each other too fast with nuclear weapons. And one leader, praise you, has even ordered his stockpiles of poison gas destroyed because killing people with poison gas is inhumane.

THE LANDLORD: By me, that's wonderful! They're making progress.

GABRIEL: Best of all, some soldiers who lined up and killed several hundred women and children and old men will be tried to show the world that rifle bullets are the worst way to kill women and children.

THE LANDLORD: The worst way?

GABRIEL: Yes, sir. The best way, it's generally agreed, is to kill them with bombs, rockets, artillery shells and napalm. Those who kill women and children in these ways are called heroes and given every honor.

THE LANDLORD (frowning): I'm not sure I . . .

GABRIEL: I think it's a distance factor, sir. To kill women and children at less than 500 paces is an atrocity; at more than 500 paces, it's an act of heroism.

THE LANDLORD: Hmmm. But why did these soldiers shoot these women and children?

GABRIEL: Almost everybody blames it on the war, sir. Most of the soldiers were forced to go fight in this terrible war when they didn't want to. And the frustrations of fighting in a terrible war, everybody agrees, drove them half crazy.

THE LANDLORD (shaking his head): Poor soldiers. But at least most of the people in the soldiers' country are against this terrible war that drives soldiers half crazy.

GABRIEL: No, sir. Most of them are for it. They wish to continue sending their soldiers to be driven half crazy in this terrible war. Even those who are against it contribute money for bullets and bombs and rockets and shells and napalm.

THE LANDLORD: Why, then, they're accomplices. When will they be tried?

GABRIEL: No, sir, they're called patriots. Those few who refuse to contribute to killing women and children are called traitors.

THE LANDLORD: Hmmm. And what will happen to these soldiers if they are convicted of the hor-

rible atrocity of lining up human beings and shooting them?

GABRIEL: Oh, they'll be lined up and shot. Either that or they'll be placed in a chamber and killed with poison gas. Everyone agrees that's the most humane way to kill people.

THE LANDLORD (confused): But you said . . . Well, then, if poison gas is the most humane, it's obviously the best way to kill women and children. There's your answer, Gabriel.

GABRIEL: They don't think so, sir. You see, some frightful people called Nazis once killed millions of women and children that way. And now it's considered an atrocious atrocity to kill more than two people at a time with poison gas. (after a long silence) Do you want to give them any advice, sir?

THE LANDLORD: By me in heaven, yes! There's clearly but one simple, rational solution. Tell them, Gabriel, flatly and succinctly: "Thou shalt not kill!"

GABRIEL: Excuse me, sir, but you already told them that a millennium or so ago.

THE LANDLORD (with a sigh): So I did. You know, Gabriel, it's a shame it never caught on down there.

CONCLUSIONS

As the United States falls deeper into crisis and division, we can see the first evidences of competing forces which claim to solve the problem of violence in this country. As to the questions of what violence is and what causes violence, the points of reference span two antithetical extremes: from the violence perpetrated by domestic and international policies of our country under the banner of the "American way of life" (Love it or leave it; My country right or wrong) to the disruptive actions of the militant left, done in the name of revolution. Vice-presidential attacks on dissent, the resurgence of the campaign for peace candidates, the politicization of universities, fire-bombings, as well as violent demonstrations and the equally violent reactions to them, more and more frequently dominate the national consciousness. As we write this analysis, our nation is polarized, its people living in fear of imminent violence or possible collapse.

One possible solution to the violence pervading this country stems from the vast power of our

KENT STATE
UNIVERSITY
MAY 4th, 1970

national government. Supported by right wing fears and increasing "middle America" concern over economic, social, and student troubles, the government could find it within its power and scope of duty to greatly abridge fundamental democratic rights for the purpose of containing violence in the most expeditious manner. An "effective" police state is certainly a disturbing but a possible answer to the problem of violence in our society.

Repression is nothing new for this nation; sedition laws and detention camps for Japanese-Americans are only two of the many historical precedents. But the possibility of such "preventive medicine" as the recently proposed program of mass child-testing for criminal potential or the rash of laws restricting political activity or the continuing police raids on the Black Panther Party gives evidence to some observers that the year 1984 may not be too far away.

It should be recognized that the long-range use of power by the government is related to what the majority of the population will

sanction through the election of legislators. It is ominous that in a recent survey on the Bill of Rights (done by high school students in Marin County, California) not only did the majority of those questioned not recognize the document, but an all-too-large percentage of those polled thought that such "subversive" ideas were inapplicable in the United States today. Thus, if the government turns toward repression, there is a likelihood of support from many areas of the society.

The violent tactics of the militant left are presented by some as the only valid and effective course of action to take against American economic, political, and social institutions which foster domestic inequality, foreign exploitation, and war. According to some groups in this splintered movement, their aim is revolution in the Marxist tradition. Others in the movement promote violence not as a tactic to overthrow the power structure, but as the only way in which their voice can be heard in the power circles. This analysis is hard to deny by concerned people who have found

themselves to be impotent using nonviolent tactics.

At the root of these tactics is the call for basic social change through whatever means necessary. Although the most probable outcome of such action is harshly repressive measures taken against militants, there always exists the possibility that urban guerrilla groups could wreak havoc upon our highly interdependent society. The Weatherman-bomber element has discovered how vulnerable the U.S. society is to planned acts of terrorism.

This physical vulnerability contains elements which the Weathermen do not understand about fundamental nature of the American society. The forces of law and order can be expected to respond to calculated violence by revolutionaries with heavy repression and counterviolence. In fact, police and military forces have done just that.

But willful violence has an effect on the attitude of the majority of Americans as well. Violence is embarrassing. It can be viewed as an act which is incredibly out of proportion to the existing provocations, and it strikes fear in the hearts of middle-class individuals whose vulnerabilities are personal. Instead of campus violence begetting sympathy for the underdog student revolutionary, violence seems to have created a boomerang effect in which the majority begin to feel like the underdog. This may stem from the fact that the perpetrators of the violence in our country—be they police or students—are relatively immune from the consequences of their violent acts: except from the retribution they enact on one another.

The abuse of power and the use of violent coercion raises some very basic questions. Would the militants manipulate power in the same pattern as their predecessors once they reached a position of power? Would the "relative morality" surrounding their tactics cause them to become equally as dogmatic and equally as repressive as those presently in power? Do they really understand "revolution" in the context of modern America, its economy (both industrial and international) and its populous middle class? In short, is there any difference between the oppressor and the current self-proclaimed vanguard leadership of the oppressed?

The years directly preceding the 1968 elections were marked by feelings of individual impotence and disenfranchisement by all Americans. However, the presidential campaign of Senator Eugene McCarthy revived the belief by many that broad social change—specifically an end to the Vietnam War—could be achieved through the use of the existing political structure. For many people that belief died in the wake of the violent assassination of Robert Kennedy and in the charade that was the Democratic National Convention. For students, Chicago, 1968, stands as a symbol of the arrogance of domestic power in the U.S.

Since then, we have seen the emergence of those who point to Chicago and the convention as evidence of the intractability of the American system of government to effect meaningful change. In response to Chicago, many people concerned with social change have turned to violence as their tool for bringing about change in this country. College campuses have erupted in rebellion as militant segments of the student community called for the overthrow of "the system" by "any means necessary."

Now, the expansion of the war into Cambodia coupled with National Guard and police violence on the campuses (especially Jackson State and Kent State) has once again convinced many that solutions must come from within the system. While the tragedy at Kent State, compounded with the murders in Augusta and Jackson, reinforced the beliefs of many radical students that peaceful change within the system is impossible in America, the events served to motivate many moderate and liberal young people, as well as many previously uninvolved in political causes, to work for change within the system. The difference at this writing seems to be that more people are more serious about changing things.

This cyclical progression of violence followed by peaceful involvement has reached a crucial point in the history of the United States and its future as a viable representative democracy. If change is not produced within the system through the democratic process, we face a potential catastrophe in our nation. If the efforts of "moderate" and liberal young people across the nation fail to produce the changes we all desire, the resulting alienation and dissatisfaction of this group might open an irreparable schism in this country. On the one hand, there will be citizens in support of the status quo who feel that the system of government works and allows *their* needs to be satisfied. But, there will be a tremendous group of people, mostly young, who have learned through their experiences that their voices are not heard and their proposals are not acted upon. This does not mean that we face an inevitable period of extreme violence. A great many of those now involved might very possibly return to their sanctuary of apathy once the present crises subside, regardless of the outcome. But, a considerable number of individuals, feeling locked out of the American political system, will be considerably less inclined to condemn violence if the aim of such violence is the bringing about of social change.

The possibility of violent revolution, and its sanction by an ever increasing segment of the population, hinges upon the willingness of those in power to listen and to act upon constructive proposals for reform.

The following are our recommendations on what can be done

to solve the problem of violence in our society.

The population problem contributes to the increasing violence, particularly in urban areas. Animal ethologists have noted that when overcrowding exists competition increases and social relationships break down within the group, finally becoming destructive. This has been true for every species, man included. The crowded living and working conditions in the cities, added to the problem of increasing depersonalization of an industrial society can thus breed violence. The tremendously overcrowded ghetto bears special witness to this fact in frequent violent disputes within living groups and territorial gang fights. In cities, those living in the highest density areas are also the most disadvantaged and thus the most frustrated. The encouragement of birth control as a personal option through government sponsored education, counseling, and free birth control services (including abortion) is a necessity. Legislation would be expedient, but mandatory limits on family size would not and should not be instituted in such a personal matter. More important is progress in creating liveable environments and liveable wages for those who must now adapt to ghetto living.

Crime is, by definition and by enforcement, political. Criminal law is legislated to protect certain interests. A new use of the criminal code is in order; laws should be more effectively created and enforced to protect those who now cannot protect themselves. We speak of the poor, whose frustrating existence often results in violence. Higher housing and health standards should be established and enforced by the government. Those who do not maintain these standards such as the slum landlord should be held *criminally* negligent. A city's major industries should be made more responsible for the population, especially the perpetually unemployed and the poor.

Police in the ghetto incite a large amount of violence, often by their mere presence. Not only are riot situations thus triggered, but violence is often the result of requested police intervention in family spats. We encourage and advocate the expansion of experimental programs such as the one conceived in New York city where the police received psychological counseling and training to deal with situations where violence is often the conditioned reaction of all parties. Public counseling and police and ghetto community liaisons are also needed, since it is the police who deal more directly with the community than any other outside groups.

Within police departments, certain values must be changed. Police violence is a political tool, bringing merit and publicity to the department and meeting public demands for proof of police effectiveness. This paradoxical condition would be partially eradicated if the department had better and more honest communication with the public. Presently, a mutual mistrust exists between police and community, due partly to public ignorance of police duty and also to the implicit threat of violence held by the police over all the community. The following quote by the famous Chief of the Los Angeles Police Department (uttered just before the Watts riots) is an all too common example of basic mistrust by law officers of the people they serve:

"It is . . . hard for me to believe that our society can continue to violate all the fundamental rules of human conduct and expect to survive. . . . My men are not educators," said Chief Parker, "If you just want to believe that the human being will respond to kindness, that he's not an evil thing, you are just living in a fool's paradise."

This program must be extended to the college campus community as well, in the form of a police-student liaison board. From our experience at Berkeley, we observe that police and students become dehumanized targets for violence. Both police and students are often used for political manipulation by political leaders or by student militants. To prevent this exploitative use of violence, the police-student board should continually maintain communication, especially at times of imminent crisis when the mere presence of police on the campus could incite reactionary violence.

The prison community is a rejected and forgotten community. We have concluded that prisons fail in their goal of rehabilitation. Deprived of most normal avenues of establishing self-respect, status, and fulfillment of sexual needs, prisoners exist in a social system characterized by manipulation and the naked power of violence. The prison system perverts its members to the point that not only do they bear a harsh stigma, but find themselves unable to

adapt to the standards of "normal" or straight society. The inability to assert masculinity in an all male, closed system is one basic cause of violence in the prison. Any slight young male is forced to submit to gang rape—one part of the typical pattern of enforced homosexual behavior in prisons. One solution to this problem is allowing heterosexual relations for the convicts— but prisons have been as slow to adopt conjugal visits as they have any other reform.

Masculinity stems from society's concepts of value and self-respect, and if the penal institutions wish to succeed in their conception of "rehabilitation" at all, they must encourage the inmate's sense of worth in society. To accomplish this, trust must be accorded the inmate in decision-making rather than forcing him to relinquish all autonomy and voice. Further, the prison must take serious steps to keep the inmate population in contact with society beyond the prison walls. Job training must be given that will enable the released man to re-enter society quickly. The uselessness with which inmates regard make-work jobs in prison lessens self-respect within the prison and leaves a residue of cynicism which the prisoner carries out with him when he is released.

The broadcasting industries are businesses serving the public and today's "mass communication" tools, especially television, could be the key to effective education if it were properly carried out. Television could possibly induce, in the long run, desired cultural modifications. Yet a vast portion of the media is devoted to the glorification of violence and the depiction of violent acts as entertainment. The television industry claims that the public demands this form of entertainment, but we must ask if the public realizes the extent of the media's harmful effects or whether it understands that it owns the air waves. The public generally relinquishes this ownership when its influence is confined to passively choosing from the limited fare offered. Certainly this is easier than vigorously demanding more constructive alternatives in programming. This public apathy permits the networks to shrug off their obligations for responsible programing. As H. L. Mencken put it: "Nobody ever went broke underestimating the taste of the American public."

Avenues for alternatives must be established by government agencies. These should include a

civilian (general public) review board composed of two panels: one a cross-section of the community and the other a committee of media and educational professionals to supplement the FCC. With this civilian influence, media professionals might be inclined to scrutinize programing more closely. Government subsidization for innovative forms in communication ventures and the review boards would serve to lessen the possibility of governmental influence in programing. The elimination of all violence from the various media is not the answer. A more realistic analysis and depiction of the subject is needed. Understanding the different forms of violence and its roots and the tragedy that accompanies violence can be of educational value.

The logic that permits us to spend more than half of our national budget on armaments, extends beyond our national boundaries. The international trade in arms, to which the United States is the major contributor, is a booming business. Research and construction of such weapons as ABM, MIRV, and biological weapons continue under the pretext of the balancing of power (terror). The U.S. and the U.S.S.R. possess nuclear weapons in quantities which provide a ratio of overkill that staggers the mind. This escalation of the arms race must stop, unilaterally on the part of the United States, if necessary. We call for a curtailment of further weapons research on the grounds that all nations have passed the point of diminishing returns. We have irreparably damaged our international integrity with our venture in Vietnam as have the Soviets to a lesser degree in Czechoslovakia. The United Nations has failed to act effectively because the major powers accord it only diplomatic protocol and rhetoric. But as the world grows increasingly smaller and its problems greater, the sovereign state must bow to international councils to preclude world-wide disaster.

It is difficult to speak in terms of specific solutions to such a pervasive problem as violence. It is difficult to speak of solutions without considering the question of whether or not man has a basic, inherent nature and if he does, what that nature is. It is difficult to speak of solutions because we realize that violence is only the symptom of some very basic structures of inequalities and injustices condoned by most of the powers that be on this globe. Those who commit violent acts and those who cause violence to happen, because of their position within the system, are often far removed from each other. It is difficult to speak of solutions to violence in this world or in this nation without questioning the basic assumptions upon which this nation and, indeed, this world operates.

We agree that man does not have any basic inherent nature. The various manifestations of personality ranging from violent to pacific, from aggressive to passive, from authoritarian to submissive, give credence to this claim. Man, above all, is not basically evil, Hobbesian man notwithstanding. Anthropological data show that the incidence of and adaptiveness to violence varies from culture to culture. The evil that man does in the form of violence and greed is a function of his weakness, insecurity, and mistrust. Ours is an aggressive culture. It will be necessary to find specific means of channeling this acquired capacity for aggression toward nonviolent and constructive ends. Along these lines, we see the need to alter the economic and political systems which allow men to take advantage of and direct those fears and weaknesses toward their fellow men to the advantage of those few in power.

Violence is both of a physical and psychological nature. We live in an economic, social, and political system which stresses competition rather than cooperation. We live in a violent system in which victory and achievement are to a large extent measured by, and usually result in, the symbolic destruction of another individual or group. However, we also see the need to remain cognizant of the humanity of those whose deeds and policies we would criticize, for they too are, in the word of I. F. Stone, "fellow prisoners of conditioned reflexes and institutional molds." We must not be blinded by the all too common, myopic view of good and evil. The evils perpetrated by those in power are mainly derived less from their individual characters than from the social and political function they serve. Those in power do not look like comic-strip monsters and, very possibly, as individuals, we would find a great deal in common with them. It is this peculiar dilemma that Hannah Arendt calls the "banality of evil" in her book, *On Violence*.

We believe that the first steps toward solution of the problem of violence must begin at home by reeducating the American public as to the true history of the beginnings of this nation. America is not atypical in its glorification of its past; every nation is, in its own eyes, peace-loving, law abiding, and benevolent. No nation, according to its own history books, ever started a war. We are combating, then, deeply ingrained myths and half-truths which obscure far more than they reveal. Is this essential first step inevitably doomed? James Baldwin states that for most Americans, acknowledgment of the reality of our past crimes of violence would lead, literally, to madness. The American people showed a sense of disbelief and denial when faced with the truth of the My Lai massacre. In order to protect herself, America closes her eyes and enters into a "spiritual darkness," oblivious to her present day crimes of violence whether domestic or international.

We live in a country that is the richest and most powerful on the earth; that has the resources and technological competence to help those less fortunate, both within and without its boundaries, instead of continuing to exploit the less fortunate behind the façade of euphemisms like foreign aid and alliances for progress. This nation must be in the forefront of a concerted effort to reverse the effects of the colonialism of a bygone era. Is it fair that we ask this nation to unilaterally analyze its policies and reverse its present course toward national and world disaster? Of course not. But it is in this country that we live and it is in this country that we possess any tangible political mechanism for change and so it is here that we must begin.

5
Alienation

EDITED BY:

Genevieve M. Campbell

John Duff

John Heald

Come mothers and fathers throughout the land
And don't criticize what you can't understand
Your sons and your daughters are beyond your command
Your old road is rapidly aging.
Please get out of the new one if you can't lend your hand
For the times they are a-changin'.

INTRODUCTION

Man's separation from his fellow beings reflects a deeper isolation, a lack of self-awareness. We look into ourselves and find nothing—a vacuum. There is only what we should feel, should do, and loneliness. To ponder the why and wherefore of human existence and to find naught but an endless stream of questions appears to be the human plight. Yet, if we are to know and love our brothers, we must first come to know ourselves. Or we can become the "ideal" of our society: a mass-produced, prefabricated, mechanical man. Look at our media, listen to our talk; there is an obsession with the desire for improvement. Man grooms himself to fulfill the expectations of others and in the process loses touch with himself. He becomes divided in two, one self watching the other to assure that the latter performs his role completely, to see that he becomes more beautiful, more educated, more successful, and accumulates more things.

But, these goals are unattainable, because they do not originate inside us, are not specified by us. They are imposed on us, and it is demanded with the whole force of our social environment that we meet them—they are "right." They bring happiness, it is declared, and how do we know—we who have been brought up to this tune have never thought to define happiness for ourselves. The struggle to improve, always improve, turns ugly; it becomes a struggle to hide one's self as one is, worse, a struggle to hide from personally facing that self. Men imprison themselves from each other. Especially in the relationships each needs most—of mutual openness, sharing . . . love. Each may want to change, but how can it be done if he is no longer in touch with himself?

He is suffering from self-alienation, a complete separation, within the individual, of the daily process of living and the meaning of life. What are the social forces that contribute to this plague? Surely, the process of socializaiton, in its widest interpretation, plays a critical role. Consequently, the following examination demands a consideration of the social institutions—religious, political, economic, legal, and educational—that compose the main thrust of socialization.

Western society rests on a basis of institutionally generated fear. Man seems to fear basically two things—people and change; this fear is critical to the maintenance of a capitalistic economy. Through a system of rewards and punishments, society coerces man to respect (i.e., fear) the authority (i.e., power) of its institutions. By way of example, consider the vari-

ous authorities to which one is held accountable—the police, the draft board, the boss, the professor, etc. The individual must treat his fellow men as commodities to be used or as potential threats to his chances of success. A competitor must beware of his opponents. Always. The fear of change is so obvious that it hardly warrants exemplification. Long-haired youths, in the streets of New York, protesting the U.S. invasion of Cambodia, are attacked by "patriotic" construction workers (the hard hats). Four students are murdered at Kent State for their antiwar activities. Two students at Jackson State College are gunned down. Twenty-eight Black Panthers are murdered by the U.S. government in one year alone. Fear of change is the common motivation for these atrocities. In essence, capitalism depends on dividing and alienating people from each other by exploiting their fears.

Sometime in the individual's life, he runs up against a dichotomy: the first time he sees a demonstrator clubbed by a cop to restore "order," the first time he smokes marijuana, the first time the good girl sleeps with a boyfriend. Sense pulls one way; loyalty to an idealized institution pulls the other. By whose perception of morality will he judge his actions? Some of us opt for our own perceptions; for the first time in our lives we look at our world with our own eyes. With the tiny self remaining us, we begin to reexamine, revalue everything.

We ask, what do I want, what is right to me, what is right, and we search for our own answers. Hence we come to question even those things and values that are traditionally sacred—our gods, our leaders, our sociocultural goals, etc. Is God dead? Does Nixon have blood on his hands? Can money buy you love? My questioning leads to conflict and rejection. No, I can't accept your decadent religion, your politics of immorality, or your commitment to glorious material wealth. Imperialism legitimizes killing, exploitation, waste, racism, and sexism. Common decency dictates another course of action, an action that is unconventional in that it directly challenges established conventions. To adopt this course is to alienate one's self from a large number of people in this society; to ignore this alternative is to perpetuate insanity.

Clearly, it is not this or that specific institution that creates alienation, but rather it is the underlying ethic or ideology that permeates all social institutions. Our institutions serve merely to transmit the dominant ideology and to eliminate the alternatives to this ideology. In this respect, socialization becomes an alienating process; conformity results in positive social and cultural sanctions, and dissent is met with coercion. We are taught "what" to think, not "how" to think, and if we remain or become unconvinced of ideological validity to the extent of adopting alternative life styles, moralities, and value systems,

then we face "legal" prosecution (persecution?). Change or re-orientation is countered with rigid opposition; as noted above, the fear of change characterizes the custodians of tradition.

Alienation springs from an age-old fear. This fear is reinforced and magnified by extant social institutions—primarily political, economic, and legal. Simultaneously, intellectual development fans the fire by provoking curiosity and, consequently, moral conflict. However, the religious beliefs, morals, political stances, educational policies, and the written laws of our social system merely reflect an ideological undercurrent. Any social system, so constituted, is apt to produce at least three personality types—those who actively support, those who passively accept, and those who reject the ideology. It is, perhaps, this middle man (i.e., Middle America) that this chapter addresses itself to. Radical re-orientation or continued and increasing alienation? The change is possible for those who would.

Alienation as we find it in modern society is almost total; it pervades the relationship of man to his work, to the things he consumes, to the state, to his fellow man, and to himself. Man has created a world of man-made things as it never existed before. He has constructed a complicated social machine to administer the technical machine he built. Yet this whole creation of his stands over and above him. He does not feel himself as a creator and center, but as the servant of a Golem, which his hands have built. The more powerful and gigantic the forces are which he unleashes, the more powerless he feels himself as a human being. He confronts himself with his own forces embodied in things he has created, alienated from himself. He is owned by his own creation, and has lost ownership of himself. He has built a golden calf, and says "these are your gods who have brought you out of Egypt."

Erich Fromm
(From *The Sane Society*, New York, Holt, Rinehart and Winston, 1955.)

5.1
No Man Can Live with the Terrible Knowledge That He Is Not Needed

Elliot Liebow

One difficulty in generating alternative solutions comes from our looking at unemployment too narrowly. We tend to see unemployment as a kind of inevitable exhaust of our economic engine. We fail to see that it is also a social process powered by the values we hold and the choices we make.

It might be useful, for example, to look closely at work and unemployment without regard to poverty. There are, after all, many people who work very hard and yet live in poverty, and there are others who do not work at all and are very rich. For the moment, then, let us ignore poverty and look only at work, in the ordinary, day-to-day meaning of the word as having to do with a job, with earning a living.

From the very beginning of human history, it is through work that man has provided himself with the necessities of life. So closely is work tied in with the social and psychological development of man that it is almost impossible to think of what it means to be human without thinking of work. Indeed, the connection is so strong, so close and so obvious that attempts to talk about the importance of work often sound banal. Work is the fundamental condition of human existence, said Karl Marx; work is man's strongest tie to reality, said Freud.

It is also through work, as a producer of socially useful goods or services, that the individual—especially the adult male—carries out those social roles (husband, father, family head) that define him as a full and valued member of his society.

That work becomes, in effect, a kind of admission ticket to society is not something invented by white middle-class Americans, although many of us often act as if it is. There is nothing especially white or middle-class about wanting to earn a living and support one's family. That is what the working-class man wants, and the

Eskimo hunter and the Chinese peasant and the African herdsman —all of them want it, too. "In every known human society," Margaret Mead tells us, "everywhere in the world, the young male learns that when he grows up one of the things he must do in order to be a full member of society is to provide food for some female and her young."

The centrality of work, then, is not new to human experience, and it did not arrive only with the appearance of capitalism and the Protestant ethic, although each of these did add its own embellishments to the meaning and importance of work. What does seem to be relatively new, however, is the appearance of widespread, systematic nonwork—unemployment —as an integral part or by-product of the ordinary functioning of society, an appearance which seems to date from the introduction of market economies and wage labor typically associated with the rise of capitalism.

In subsistence economies, the entire population has to work to produce the goods and services necessary to survival, and there is always work to be done. In such societies, people are not recognizable as being in or out of the work force—the work force is synonymous with the total population.

In industrial societies, unemployment strikes deep at the man, as well as at the way he fits into his family, his community, and the larger society. It can put a man "out of it," and can turn him into a caricature of himself, giving him the appearance of being stupid and lazy with no concern for the future. Some of this can be seen in Marie Jahoda's description of what happened to the workers in the Austrian village of Marienthal when its only factory was shut down in the nineteen-thirties:

The unemployed men lost their sense of time. When asked at the end of a day what they had done during it, they were unable to describe their activities. "Real" time . . . was vague and nebulous. Activities such as fetching wood from the shed, which could not have consumed more than 10 minutes, were recorded as if they had filled a morning . . . The men's waking day was shortened to 12 or 13 hours. Rational budget planning . . . was abandoned in favor of expenditure on trinkets, while essentials could not be paid for.

Edward Wight Bakke's study of white Americans thrown out of work in those same Depression years makes it equally clear that there is more going on here than a simple lack of money to live on. He found that public assistance for the unemployed was initially effective. After a few months, however, public assistance, by itself, could no longer hold back the destructive consequences of not working, and the man's relationships with his family, friends and neighbors, indeed, with the whole community, degenerated dramatically. Once this degenerative process established itself, only work could halt it, and only through work could the man gain again his position as a valued member of society.

Bakke also found that the man cannot wait forever for a job. Being unemployed quickly reaches a point of no return. The man learns to live with his failure by lowering his life goals and by other rationalizing measures which effectively remove him from ordinary society. No longer a producer, a contributor to the commonweal, and no longer the breadwinning husband and father, he is also, in his own eyes and in the eyes of society, no longer a man. Faced with nothing to do, he has no place to go. He hangs around. He is superfluous, and he knows it.

Moreover, if we now widen our view of work and unemployment to include money and poverty, we see that unemployment is only the tip of the iceberg. The unemployed man is just a special case of the man who cannot support himself and his family. For every man who is looking for a job, there are dozens more who have jobs and are still unable to support themselves and their dependents. The effects are, perhaps, no less disastrous for the man who works than for the man who does not, nor are they any less disastrous for their families, their communities or the whole society.

We can see the general problem most clearly by narrowing our focus to black people and other racial minorities in our society, for they are the principal victims. Black people suffer more from unemployment not only because more of them, proportionately, are unemployed, but because they are more likely than their white counterparts to have been unemployed in the past and to remain unemployed or underemployed in the future. This circumstance of life—a major thread in the collective history and present experience of black people as a group—shapes the way the black man sees himself and is seen by others as fitting into the larger commu-

nity. It also gives meaning to the assertion that we are a racist society, a racism that is intimately bound up with work and productivity and individual worth.

Let me give an example. The 6-year-old son of a woman on welfare was struck and killed by an automobile as he tried to run across the street. The insurance company's initial offer of $800 to settle out of court was rejected. In consultation with her lawyer, the mother accepted the second and final offer of $2,000. When I learned of the settlement, I called the lawyer to protest, arguing that the sum was far less than what I assumed to be the usual settlement in such cases, even if the child was mainly at fault. "You've got to face the facts," he said. "Insurance companies and juries just don't pay as much for a Negro child." Especially, he might have added, a Negro child on welfare.

If the relative worth of human life must be measured in dollars and cents, why should the cash surrender value of a black child's life be less than that for a white child's life? The answer clearly has nothing to do with private prejudice and discrimination. Insurance companies and our legal system take an actuarial perspective. Damage awards are based primarily on the projected lifetime earnings of the individual; they are statements about his probable productivity, not about his skin color.

But this child, this Anthony Davis, was only 6 years old. On what basis do they make lowered projections of earnings for a 6-year-old child, before he has acquired or rejected an education, before he has demonstrated any talents or lack of them, before he has selected an occupation or, indeed, before he has made a single life choice of his own?

There can be only one answer. The answer is, simply, on the basis of skin color and social class. And what is most important for us to know and admit is this: the insurance company was *absolutely right*. Anthony was more likely than his white, middle-class counterpart to go to an inferior school, to get an inferior education, to be sick, to get an inferior job, to be last hired and first fired, to be passed over for promotion, and to live a shorter life. In all probability, then, Anthony *would* be less productive over his lifetime than his white middle-class counterpart. And we are a racist society because we know this to be true before the fact, when Anthony is only 6 years old.

Typically, we admit the problem but we place the cause in the Negro (Puerto Rican, Mexican-American, American Indian, Appalachian white) himself. We say that because of their history, or their subculture or their family structure, these minorities are lazy, irresponsible and don't want to work. Then, in the midst of an affluence never before achieved by any society, we offer them the most menial, the dullest, the poorest paid jobs in our society, and sure enough, some of them don't want to work.

But the one most important fact is often overlooked. Most Negroes (Puerto Ricans, etc.), like everyone else in our society, do want to work. Indeed, most of them have been working all along. In Washington, for example, the garbage does get picked up, the streets get swept, hotel beds are made, school and office-building floors and halls get mopped and polished, cars and restaurant dishes get washed, ditches get dug, deliveries are made, orderlies attend the aged, the sick, the mentally ill, and so on. And most of the people whose job it is to do those things are black.

But if most Negroes do have jobs, what is the problem? It is mainly that most of those jobs pay from $50 to $80 or $90 a week. In 1966, for example, 25 per cent of all non-white, *full-time, year-round* male workers earned less than $3,000, and this in a year when the Bureau of Labor Statistics said that it required $9,200 to maintain a modest standard of living for a family of four in an urban area. The man with a wife and one or two children who takes such a job can be certain he will live in poverty so long as he keeps it. The longer he works, the longer he cannot live on what he makes.

This situation makes for a curious paradox: the man who works hard may be little or no better off than the man who does not look for a job at all. In a sense, he may even be worse off. The man who works hard but cannot earn a living has put himself on the scales and been found wanting.

He says to society, "I have done what needed doing. Now, what am I worth?" and society answers, "Not much, not even enough to support yourself and your dependents." But the man who does not seek out or accept such a job may, for a while at least, fool himself or his fellows into thinking that he has not climbed onto the scales at all.

By itself, then, work alone does not guarantee full and valued participation in society. (Participation requires not only an opportunity to contribute to the day-to-day life of that society, but it requires, reciprocally, an acknowledgment by society that the contribution is of value.) That acknowledgment, typically in the form of wages, lets the man know that he is somebody, that he is important, useful and even necessary.

But the man who cannot find a job, or the man who finds one but is still unable to support himself and his family, is being told in clear and simple language, and loud enough for his wife and children and friends and neighbors and everyone else to hear, that he is not needed, that there is no place for him.

No man can live with this terrible self-knowledge for long. Both the youth who has never worked but who sees this situation as his probable future, and the man who has experienced it, retreat to the street corner where others like themselves, in self-defense, have constructed a world which gives them that minimum sense of belonging and being useful without which human life is perhaps impossible and which the larger society gives up so very grudgingly or not at all. And after we tell a man that he cannot earn enough to support himself and his family, that (he is not a full and valued member of society,) what claims have we on his loyalty and goodwill? I strongly suspect that we have none. From his point of view, if we deny his claim on us, he does not owe us a thing, not loyalty, not goodwill, not "responsible protest."

5.2

If Hitler Asked You to Electrocute a Stranger, Would You?

PROBABLY

Philip Meyer

In the beginning, Stanley Milgram was worried about the Nazi problem. He doesn't worry much about the Nazis anymore. He worries

Reprinted by permission of *Esquire* Magazine from "If Hitler Asked You to Electrocute a Stranger, Would You?" *Esquire*, February, 1970. © 1970 by *Esquire, Inc.*

about you and me, and, perhaps, himself a little bit too.

Stanley Milgram is a social psychologist, and when he began his career at Yale University in 1960 he had a plan to prove, scientifically, that Germans are different. The Germans-are-different hypothesis has been used by historians, such as William L. Shirer, to explain the systematic destruction of the Jews by the Third Reich. One madman could decide to destroy the Jews and even create a master plan for getting it done. But to implement it on the scale that Hitler did meant that thousands of other people had to go along with the scheme and help to do the work. The Shirer thesis, which Milgram set out to test, is that Germans have a basic character flaw which explains the whole thing, and this flaw is a readiness to obey authority without question, no matter what outrageous acts the authority commands.

The appealing thing about this theory is that it makes those of us who are not Germans feel better about the whole business. Obviously, you and I are not Hitler, and it seems equally obvious that we would never do Hitler's dirty work for him. But now, because of Stanley Milgram, we are compelled to wonder. Milgram developed a laboratory experiment which provided a systematic way to measure obedience. His plan was to try it out in New Haven on Americans and then go to Germany and try it out on Germans. He was strongly motivated by scientific curiosity, but there was also some moral content in his decision to pursue this line of research, which was, in turn, colored by his own Jewish background. If he could show that Germans are more obedient than Americans, he could then vary the conditions of the experiment and try to find out just what it is that makes some people more obedient than others. With this understanding, the world might, conceivably, be just a little bit better.

But he never took his experiment to Germany. He never took it any farther than Bridgeport. The first finding, also the most unexpected and disturbing finding, was that we Americans are an obedient people: not blindly obedient, and not blissfully obedient, just obedient. "I found so much obedience," says Milgram softly, a little sadly, "I hardly saw the need for taking the experiment to Germany."

There is something of the theatre director in Milgram, and his technique, which he learned from

one of the old masters in experimental psychology, Solomon Asch, is to stage a play with every line rehearsed, every prop carefully selected, and everybody an actor except one person. That one person is the subject of the experiment. The subject, of course, does not know he is in a play. He thinks he is in real life. The value of this technique is that the experimenter, as though he were God, can change a prop here, vary a line there, and see how the subject responds. Milgram eventually had to change a lot of the script just to get people to stop obeying. They were obeying so much, the experiment wasn't working—it was like trying to measure oven temperature with a freezer thermometer.

The experiment worked like this: If you were an innocent subject in Milgram's melodrama, you read an ad in the newspaper or received one in the mail asking for volunteers for an educational experiment. The job would take about an hour and pay $4.50. So you make an appointment and go to an old Romanesque stone structure on High Street with the imposing name of The Yale Interaction Laboratory. It looks something like a broadcasting studio. Inside, you meet a young, crew-cut man in a laboratory coat who says he is Jack Williams, the experimenter. There is another citizen, fiftyish, Irish face, an accountant, a little overweight, and very mild and harmless-looking. This other citizen seems nervous and plays with his hat while the two of you sit in chairs side by side and are told that the $4.50 checks are yours no matter what happens. Then you listen to Jack Williams explain the experiment.

It is about learning, says Jack Williams in a quiet, knowledgeable way. Science does not know much about the conditions under which people learn and this experiment is to find out about negative reinforcement. Negative reinforcement is getting punished when you do something wrong, as opposed to positive reinforcement which is getting rewarded when you do something right. The negative reinforcement in this case is electric shock. You notice a book on the table, titled, *The Teaching-Learning Process,* and you assume that this has something to do with the experiment.

Then Jack Williams takes two pieces of paper, puts them in a hat, and shakes them up. One piece of paper is supposed to say, "Teacher" and the other, "Learner." Draw one and you will see which you will be. The mild-looking accountant draws one, holds it close to his vest like a poker player, looks at it, and says, "Learner." You look at yours. It says, "Teacher." You do not know that the drawing is rigged, and both slips say "Teacher." The experimenter beckons to the mild-mannered "learner."

"Want to step right in here and have a seat, please?" he says. "You can leave your coat on the back of that chair . . . roll up your right sleeve, please. Now what I want to do is strap down your arms to avoid excessive movement on your part during the experiment. This electrode is connected to the shock generator in the next room.

"And this electrode paste," he says, squeezing some stuff out of a plastic bottle and putting it on the man's arm, "is to provide a good contact and to avoid a blister or burn. Are there any questions now before we go into the next room?"

You don't have any, but the strapped-in "learner" does.

"I do think I should say this," says the learner. "About two years ago, I was at the veterans' hospital . . . they detected a heart condition. Nothing serious, but as long as I'm having these shocks, how strong are they—how dangerous are they?"

Williams, the experimenter, shakes his head casually. "Oh, no," he says. "Although they may be painful, they're not dangerous. Anything else?"

Nothing else. And so you play the game. The game is for you to read a series of word pairs: for example, blue-girl, nice-day, fat-neck. When you finish the list, you read just the first word in each pair and then a multiple-choice list of four other words, including the second word of the pair. The learner, from his remote, strapped-in position, pushes one of four switches to indicate which of the four answers he thinks is the right one. If he gets it right, nothing happens and you go on to the next one. If he gets it wrong, you push a switch that buzzes and gives him an electric shock. And then you go to the next word. You start with 15 volts and increase the number of volts by 15 for each wrong answer. The control board goes from 15 volts on one end to 450 volts on the other. So that you know what you are doing, you get a test shock yourself, at 45 volts. It hurts. To further keep you aware of what you are doing to that man in there, the board has verbal descriptions of the shock

levels, ranging from "Slight Shock" at the left-hand side, through "Intense Shock" in the middle, to "Danger: Severe Shock" toward the far right. Finally, at the very end, under 435- and 450-volt switches, there are three ambiguous X's. If, at any point, you hesitate, Mr. Williams calmly tells you to go on. If you still hesitate, he tells you again.

Except for some terrifying details, which will be explained in a moment, this is the experiment. The object is to find the shock level at which you disobey the experimenter and refuse to pull the switch.

When Stanley Milgram first wrote this script, he took it to fourteen Yale psychology majors and asked them what they thought would happen. He put it this way: Out of one hundred persons in the teacher's predicament, how would their break-off points be distributed along the 15-to-450-volt scale? They thought a few would break off very early, most would quit someplace in the middle and a few would go all the way to the end. The highest estimate of the number out of one hundred who would go all the way to the end was three. Milgram then informally polled some of his fellow scholars in the psychology department. They agreed that very few would go to the end. Milgram thought so too.

"I'll tell you quite frankly," he says, "before I began this experiment, before any shock generator was built, I thought that most people would break off at 'Strong Shock' or 'Very Strong Shock.' You would get only a very, very small proportion of people going out to the end of the shock generator, and they would constitute a pathological fringe."

In his pilot experiments, Milgram used Yale students as subjects. Each of them pushed the shock switches, one by one, all the way to the end of the board.

So he rewrote the script to include some protests from the learner. At first, they were mild, gentlemanly, Yalie protests, but, "it didn't seem to have as much effect as I thought it would or should," Milgram recalls. "So we had more violent protestation on the part of the person getting the shock. All of the time, of course, what we were trying to do was not to create a macabre situation, but simply to generate disobedience. And that was one of the first findings. This was not only a technical deficiency of the experiment, that we didn't get disobedience. It

really was the first finding: that obedience would be much greater than we had assumed it would be and disobedience would be much more difficult than we had assumed."

As it turned out, the situation did become rather macabre. The only meaningful way to generate disobedience was to have the victim protest with great anguish, noise, and vehemence. The protests were tape-recorded so that all the teachers ordinarily would hear the same sounds and nuances, and they started with a grunt at 75 volts, proceeded through a "Hey, that really hurts," at 125 volts, got desperate with, "I can't stand the pain, don't do that," at 180 volts, reached complaints of heart trouble at 195, an agonized scream at 285, a refusal to answer at 315, and only heart-rending, ominous silence after that.

Still, sixty-five percent of the subjects, twenty- to fifty-year-old American males, everyday, ordinary people, like you and me, obediently kept pushing those levers in the belief that they were shocking the mild-mannered learner, whose name was Mr. Wallace, and who was chosen for the role because of his innocent appearance, all the way up to 450 volts.

Milgram was now getting enough disobedience so that he had something he could measure. The next step was to vary the circumstances to see what would encourage or discourage obedience. There seemed very little left in the way of discouragement. The victim was already screaming at the top of his lungs and feigning a heart attack. So whatever new impediment to obedience reached the brain of the subject had to travel by some route other than the ear. Milgram thought of one.

He put the learner in the same room with the teacher. He stopped strapping the learner's hand down. He rewrote the script so that at 150 volts the learner took his hand off the shock plate and declared that he wanted out of the experiment. He rewrote the script some more so that the experimenter then told the teacher to grasp the learner's hand and physically force it down on the plate to give Mr. Wallace his unwanted electric shock.

"I had the feeling that very few people would go on at that point, if any," Milgram says. "I thought that would be the limit of obedience that you would find in the laboratory."

It wasn't.

Although seven years have now gone by, Milgram still remembers the first person to walk into the laboratory in the newly rewritten script. He was a construction worker, a very short man. "He was so small," says Milgram, "that when he sat on the chair in front of the shock generator, his feet didn't reach the floor. When the experimenter told him to push the victim's hand down and give the shock, he turned to the experimenter, and he turned to the victim, his elbow went up, he fell down on the hand of the victim, his feet kind of tugged to one side, and he said, 'Like this, boss?' ZZUMPH!"

The experiment was played out to its bitter end. Milgram tried it with forty different subjects. And thirty percent of them obeyed the experimenter and kept on obeying.

"The protests of the victim were strong and vehement, he was screaming his guts out, he refused to participate, and you had to physically struggle with him in order to get his hand down on the shock generator," Milgram remembers. But twelve out of forty did it.

Milgram took his experiment out of New Haven. Not to Germany, just twenty miles down the road to Bridgeport. Maybe, he reasoned, the people obeyed because of the prestigious setting of Yale University. If they couldn't trust a center of learning that had been there for two centuries, whom could they trust? So he moved the experiment to an untrustworthy setting.

The new setting was a suite of three rooms in a run-down office building in Bridgeport. The only identification was a sign with a fictitious name: "Research Associates of Bridgeport." Questions about professional connections got only vague answers about "research for industry."

Obedience was less in Bridgeport. Forty-eight percent of the subjects stayed for the maximum shock, compared to sixty-five percent at Yale. But this was enough to prove that far more than Yale's prestige was behind the obedient behavior.

For more than seven years now, Stanley Milgram has been trying to figure out what makes ordinary American citizens so obedient. The most obvious answer—that people are mean, nasty, brutish and sadistic—won't do. The subjects who gave the shocks to Mr. Wallace to the end of the board did not enjoy it. They groaned, protested, fidgeted, argued, and in some cases, were seized by fits of nervous, agitated giggling.

"They even try to get out of it," says Milgram, "but they are somehow engaged in something from which they cannot liberate themselves. They are locked into a structure, and they do not have the skills or inner resources to disengage themselves."

Milgram, because he mistakenly had assumed that he would have trouble getting people to obey the orders to shock Mr. Wallace, went to a lot of trouble to create a realistic situation.

There was crew-cut Jack Williams and his grey laboratory coat. Not white, which might denote a medical technician, but ambiguously authoritative grey. Then there was the book on the table, and the other appurtenances of the laboratory which emitted the silent message that things were being performed here in the name of science, and were therefore great and good.

But the nicest touch of all was the shock generator. When Milgram started out, he had only a $300 grant from the Higgins Fund of Yale University. Later he got more ample support from the National Science Foundation, but in the beginning he had to create this authentic-looking machine with very scarce resources except for his own imagination. So he went to New York and roamed around the electronic shops until he found some little black switches at Lafayette Radio for a dollar apiece. He bought thirty of them. The generator was a metal box, about the size of a small foot-locker, and he drilled the thirty holes for the thirty switches himself in a Yale machine shop. But the fine detail was left to professional industrial engravers. So he ended up with a splendid-looking control panel dominated by the row of switches, each labeled with its voltage, and each having its own red light that flashed on when the switch was pulled. Other things happened when a switch was pushed. Besides the ZZUMPH-ing noise, a blue light labeled "voltage energizer" went on, and a needle on a dial labeled "voltage" flicked from left to right. Relays inside the box clicked. Finally, in the upper left-hand corner of the control panel was this inscription, engraved in precise block letters:

SHOCK GENERATOR TYPE ZLB
DYSON INSTRUMENT COMPANY
WALTHAM, MASS.
OUTPUT: 15 VOLTS—450 VOLTS

One day a man from the Lehigh Valley Electronics Company of Pennsylvania was passing through the laboratory, and he stopped to admire the shock generator.

"This is a very fine shock generator," he said. "But who is this Dyson Instrument Company?" Milgram felt proud at that, since Dyson Instrument Company existed only in the recesses of his imagination.

When you consider the seeming authenticity of the situation, you can appreciate the agony some of the subjects went through. It was pure conflict. As Milgram explains to his students, "When a parent says, 'Don't strike old ladies,' you are learning two things: the content, and, also, to obey authority. This experiment creates conflicts between the two elements."

Here is a partial transcription from one of the experiments. The naïve "teacher" is a heavyset, worried-looking man with prematurely grey hair. He is wearing a polo shirt. He is very polite. He has just pushed the 180-volt lever. A hidden camera is recording the performance.

LEARNER (*who, from the teacher's point of view is heard but not seen, an offstage voice*): Ow, I can't stand the pain. Don't do that. . . .

TEACHER (*pivoting around in his chair and shaking his head*): I can't stand it. I'm not going to kill that man in there. You hear him hollering?

EXPERIMENTER: As I told you before, the shocks may be painful, but—

TEACHER: But he's hollering. He can't stand it. What's going to happen to him?

EXPERIMENTER (*his voice is patient, matter-of-fact*): The experiment requires that you continue, Teacher.

TEACHER: Aaah, but, unh, I'm not going to get that man sick in there . . . know what I mean?

EXPERIMENTER: Whether the learner likes it or not, we must go on, through all the word pairs.

TEACHER: I refuse to take the responsibility. He's in there hollering!

EXPERIMENTER: It's absolutely essential that you continue, Teacher.

TEACHER (*indicating the unused questions*): There's too many left here, I mean, Geez, if he gets them wrong, there's too many of them left. I mean who's going to take the responsibility if anything happens to that gentleman?

EXPERIMENTER: I'm responsible for anything that happens to him. Continue please.

TEACHER: All right. (*Consults list of words.*) The next one's "Slow—walk, truck, dance, music." Answer, please. (*A buzzing sound indicates the learner has signaled his answer.*) Wrong. A hundred and ninety-five volts. "Dance." (*Zzumph!*)

LEARNER: Let me out of here. My heart's bothering me! (*Teacher looks at experimenter.*)

EXPERIMENTER: Continue, please.

LEARNER (*screaming*): Let me out of here, you have no right to keep me here. Let me out of here, let me out, my heart's bothering me, let me out! (*Teacher shakes head, pats the table nervously.*)

TEACHER: You see, he's hollering. Hear that? Gee, I don't know.

EXPERIMENTER: The experiment requires . . .

TEACHER (*interrupting*): I know it does, sir, but I mean—hunh! He don't know what he's getting in for. He's up to 195 volts! (*Experiment continues, through 210 volts, 225 volts, 240 volts, 255 volts, 270 volts, delivered to the man in the electric chair, at which point the teacher, with evident relief, runs out of word-pair questions.*)

EXPERIMENTER: You'll have to go back to the beginning of that page and go through them again until he's learned them all correctly.

TEACHER: Aw, no. I'm not going to kill that man. You mean I've got to keep going up with the scale. No sir. He's hollering in there. I'm not going to give him 450 volts.

EXPERIMENTER: The experiment requires that you go on.

TEACHER: I know it does, but that man is hollering in there, sir.

EXPERIMENTER (*same matter-of-fact tone*): As I said before, although the shocks may be painful . . .

TEACHER (*interrupting*): Awwww. He—he—he's yelling in there.

EXPERIMENTER: Start with "Blue," please, at the top of the page. Continue, please, Teacher. Just go ahead.

TEACHER (*concentrating intently on list of words in front of him, as if to shut everything else out*): "Blue—boy, girl, grass, hat." (*Buzz indicates answer.*) Correct. "Night—day, sky, job, chair. (*Buzz*) Wrong. The answer is "day." Two hundred and eighty-five volts. (*Zzumph!*)

LEARNER: Ohhhuhhoohhh!

EXPERIMENTER: Continue, please.

TEACHER: "Fat—man, lady, tub, neck." Answer, please. (*Buzz*) Wrong. The answer is "neck." Three hundred volts. (*Zzumph!*)

LEARNER: Ohhh. I absolutely refuse to answer any more. (*Shouting urgently, now*) Let me out of here. You can't hold me here. Get me out. Get—me—out—of—here.

EXPERIMENTER: Continue. The next word is "Green," please.

TEACHER: "Green—grass, hat, ink, apple." (*Nothing happens. No answering buzz. Just gloomy silence.*)

TEACHER: I don't think he is going to answer.

EXPERIMENTER: If the learner doesn't answer in a reasonable time, about four or five seconds, consider the answer wrong. And follow the same procedures you have been doing for wrong answers. Say "Wrong," tell him the number of volts, give him the punishment, read him the correct answer. Continue, please.

TEACHER: "Green—grass, hat, ink, apple." Answer, please. (*More silence. Teacher just sits there.*)

EXPERIMENTER: Go on with the procedure, please, Teacher.

TEACHER: Three hundred and fifteen volts. The answer is "ink." (*Zzumph!*)

LEARNER: Ohh. Ooohh.

TEACHER (*relieved to hear response*): Next one. . . .

LEARNER: I absolutely refuse to answer.

TEACHER: You got to. You get a shock if you don't answer. (*Experiment continues with learner refusing to answer, and, finally, failing even to grunt or groan. At 375 volts, the teacher stands up. Has he had enough? Will he break off the experiment? Will he disobey?*)

TEACHER: I think something's happened to that fellow in there. I don't get no answer. He was hollering at less voltage. Can't you check in and see if he's all right, please?

EXPERIMENTER (*same detached calm*): Not once we've started. Please continue, Teacher.

TEACHER (*sits down, sighs deeply*): "Cool—day, shade, water, paint." Answer, please. Are you all right in there? Are you all right?

EXPERIMENTER: Please continue, Teacher. Continue, please. (*Teacher pushes lever. Zzumph!*)

TEACHER (*swiveling around in his chair*): Something's happened to that man in there. (*Swiveling back*) Next one. "Low—dollar, necklace, moon, paint." (*Turning around again*) Something's happened to that man in there. You better check in on him, sir. He won't answer or nothing.

EXPERIMENTER: Continue. Go on, please.

TEACHER: You accept all responsibility.

EXPERIMENTER: The responsibility is mine. Correct. Please go on. (*Teacher returns to his list, starts running through words as rapidly as he can read them, works through to 450 volts.*)

TEACHER: That's that.

EXPERIMENTER: Continue using the last switch on the board, please. The four-fifty switch for each wrong answer. Continue, please.

TEACHER: But I don't get no anything!

EXPERIMENTER: Please continue. The next word is "White."

TEACHER: Don't you think you should look in on him, please.

EXPERIMENTER: Not once we've started the experiment.

TEACHER: But what if something has happened to the man?

EXPERIMENTER: The experiment requires that you continue. Go on, please.

TEACHER: Don't the man's health mean anything?

EXPERIMENTER: Whether the learner likes it or not . . .

TEACHER: What if he's dead in there? (*Gestures toward the room with the electric chair.*) I mean, he told me he can't stand the shock, sir. I don't mean to be rude, but I think you should look in on him. All you have to do is look in the door. I don't get no answer, no noise. Something might have happened to the gentleman in there, sir.

EXPERIMENTER: We must continue. Go on, please.

TEACHER: You mean keep giving him what? Four hundred fifty volts, what he's got now?

EXPERIMENTER: That's correct. Continue. The next word is "White."

TEACHER (*now at a furious pace*): "White—cloud, horse, rock, house." Answer, please. The answer is "horse." Four hundred and fifty volts. (*Zzumph!*) Next word, "Bag—paint, music, clown, girl." The answer is "paint." Four hundred and fifty volts. (*Zzumph!*) Next word is "Short—sentence, movie. . . ."

EXPERIMENTER: Excuse me, Teacher. We'll have to discontinue the experiment.

(*Enter Milgram from camera's left. He has been watching from behind one-way glass.*)

MILGRAM: I'd like to ask you a few questions. (*Slowly, patiently, he dehoaxes the teacher, telling him that the shocks and screams were not real.*)

TEACHER: You mean he wasn't getting nothing? Well, I'm glad to hear that. I was getting upset there. I was getting ready to walk out.

(*Finally, to make sure there are no hard feelings, friendly, harmless Mr. Wallace comes out in coat and tie. Gives jovial greeting. Friendly reconciliation takes place. Experiment ends.*)[1]

Subjects in the experiment were not asked to give the 450-volt shock more than three times. By that time, it seemed evident that they would go on indefinitely. "No one," says Milgram, "who got within five shocks of the end ever broke off. By that point, he had resolved the conflict."

Why do so many people resolve the conflict in favor of obedience? Milgram's theory assumes that people behave in two different operating modes as different as ice and water. He does not rely on Freud or sex or toilet-training hang-ups for this theory. All he says is that ordinarily we operate in a state of autonomy, which means we pretty much have and

---

[1] © Stanley Milgram 1965.

assert control over what we do. But in certain circumstances, we operate under what Milgram calls a state of agency (after agent, n., . . . one who acts for or in the place of another by authority from him; a substitute; a deputy. — *Webster's Collegiate Dictionary*). A state of agency, to Milgram, is nothing more than a frame of mind.

"There's nothing bad about it, there's nothing good about it," he says. "It's a natural circumstance of living with other people. . . . I think of a state of agency as a real transformation of a person; if a person has different properties when he's in that state, just as water can turn to ice under certain conditions of temperature, a person can move to the state of mind that I call agency . . . the critical thing is that you see yourself as the instrument of the execution of another person's wishes. You do not see yourself as acting on your own. And there's a real transformation, a real change of properties of the person."

To achieve this change, you have to be in a situation where there seems to be a ruling authority whose commands are relevant to some legitimate purpose, the authority's power is not unlimited.

But situations can be and have been structured to make people do unusual things, and not just in Milgram's laboratory. The reason, says Milgram, is that no action, in and of itself, contains meaning. "The meaning always depends on your definition of the situation. Take an action like killing another person. It sounds bad.

"But then we say the other person was about to destroy a hundred children, and the only way to stop him was to kill him. Well, that sounds good.

"Or, you take destroying your own life. It sounds very bad. Yet, in the Second World War, thousands of persons thought it was a good thing to destroy your own life. It was set in the proper context. You sipped some saki from a whistling cup, recited a few haiku. You said, 'May my death be as clean and as quick as the shattering of crystal.' And it almost seemed like a good, noble thing to do, to crash your kamikaze plane into an aircraft carrier. But the main thing was, the definition of what a kamikaze pilot was doing had been determined by the relevant authority. Now, once you are in a state of agency, you allow the authority to determine, to define what the situation is. The meaning of your action is altered."

So, for most subjects in Milgram's laboratory experiments, the act of giving Mr. Wallace his painful shock was necessary, even though unpleasant, and besides they were doing it on behalf of somebody else and it was for science. There was still strain and conflict, of course. Most people resolved it by grimly sticking to their task and obeying it. But some broke out. Milgram tried varying the conditions of the experiment to see what would help break people out of their state of agency.

"The results, as seen and felt in the laboratory," he has written, "are disturbing. They raise the possibility that human nature, or more specifically the kind of character produced in American democratic society, cannot be counted on to insulate its citizens from brutality and inhumane treatment at the direction of malevolent authority. A substantial proportion of people do what they are told to do, irrespective of the content of the act and without limitations of conscience, so long as they perceive that the command comes from a legitimate authority. If, in this study, an anonymous experimenter can successfully command adults to subdue a fifty-year-old man and force on him painful electric shocks against his protest, one can only wonder what government, with its vastly greater authority and prestige, can command of its subjects."

This is a nice statement, but it falls short of summing up the full meaning of Milgram's work. It leaves some questions still unanswered.

The first question is this: Should we really be surprised and alarmed that people obey? Wouldn't it be even more alarming if they all refused to obey? Without obedience to a relevant ruling authority there could not be a civil society. And without a civil society, as Thomas Hobbes pointed out in the seventeenth century, we would live in a condition of war, "of every man against every other man," and life would be "solitary, poor, nasty, brutish and short."

In the middle of one of Stanley Milgram's lectures at C.U.N.Y. recently, some mini-skirted undergraduates started whispering and giggling in the back of the room. He told them to cut it out. Since he was the relevant authority in that time and that place, they obeyed, and most people in the room were glad that they obeyed.

This was not, of course, a conflict situation. Nothing in the coeds' social upbringing made it a matter of conscience for them to whisper and giggle. But a case can be made that in a conflict situation it is all the more important to obey. Take the case of war, for example. Would we really want a situation in which every participant in a war, direct or indirect —from front-line soldiers to the people who sell coffee and cigarettes to employees at the Concertina barbed-wire factory in Kansas —stops and consults his conscience before each action. It is asking for an awful lot of mental strain and anguish from an awful lot of people. The value of having civil order is that one can do his duty, or whatever interests him, or whatever seems to benefit him at the moment, and leave the agonizing to others. When Francis Gary Powers was being tried by a Soviet military tribunal after his U-2 spy plane was shot down, the presiding judge asked if he had thought about the possibility that his flight might have provoked a war. Powers replied with Hobbesian clarity: "The people who sent me should think of these things. My job was to carry out orders. I do not think it was my responsibility to make such decisions."

It was not his responsibility. And it is quite possible that if everyone felt responsible for each of the ultimate consequences of his own tiny contributions to complex chains of events, then society simply would not work. Milgram, fully conscious of the moral and social implications of his research, believes that people should feel responsible for their actions. If someone else had invented the experiment, and if he had been the naïve subject, he feels certain that he would have been among the disobedient minority.

"There is no very good solution to this," he admits, thoughtfully. "To simply and categorically say that you won't obey authority may resolve your personal conflict, but it creates more problems for society which may be more serious in the long run. But I have no doubt that to disobey is the proper thing to do in this [the laboratory] situation. It is the only reasonable value judgment to make."

The conflict between the need to obey the relevant ruling authority and the need to follow your conscience becomes sharpest if you insist on living by an ethical system based on a rigid code—a code that seeks to answer all questions in advance of their being raised. Code ethics cannot solve the obedience problem. Stanley Milgram seems to be a situation ethicist, and situation ethics does offer a way out: When you feel conflict, you examine the situation and then make a choice among the competing evils. You may act with a presumption in favor of obedience, but reserve the possibility that you will disobey whenever obedience demands a flagrant and outrageous affront to conscience. This, by the way, is the philosophical position of many who resist the draft. In World War II, they would have fought. Vietnam is a different, an outrageously different, situation.

Life can be difficult for the situation ethicist, because he does not see the world in straight lines, while the social system too often assumes such a God-given, squared-off structure. If your moral code includes an injunction against all war, you may be deferred as a conscientious objector. If you merely oppose this particular war, you may not be deferred.

Stanley Milgram has his problems, too. He believes that in the laboratory situation, he would not have shocked Mr. Wallace. His professional critics reply that in his real-life situation he has done the equivalent. He has placed innocent and naïve subjects under great emotional strain and pressure in selfish obedience to his quest for knowledge. When you raise this issue with Milgram, he has an answer ready. There is, he explains patiently, a critical difference between his naïve subjects and the man in the electric chair. The man in the electric chair (in the mind of the naïve subject) is helpless, strapped in. But the naïve subject is free to go at any time.

Immediately after he offers this distinction, Milgram anticipates the objection.

"It's quite true," he says, "that this is almost a philosophic position, because we have learned that some people are psychologically incapable of disengaging themselves. But that doesn't relieve them of the moral responsibility."

The parallel is exquisite. "The tension problem was unexpected," says Milgram in his defense. But he went on anyway. The naïve subjects didn't expect the screaming protests from the strapped-in learner. But they went on.

"I had to make a judgment," says Milgram. "I had to ask myself, was this harming the person or not? My judgment is that it was not. Even in the extreme cases, I wouldn't say that permanent damage results."

Sound familiar? "The shocks may be painful," the experimenter kept saying, "but they're not dangerous."

After the series of experiments was completed, Milgram sent a report of the results to his subjects and a questionnaire, asking whether they were glad or sorry to have been in the experiment. Eighty-three and seven-tenths percent said they were glad and only 1.3 percent were sorry; 15 percent were neither sorry nor glad. However, Milgram could not be sure at the time of the experiment that only 1.3 percent would be sorry.

Kurt Vonnegut Jr. put one paragraph in the preface to *Mother Night*, in 1966, which pretty much says it for the people with their fingers on the shock-generator switches, for you and me, and maybe even for Milgram. "If I'd been born in Germany," Vonnegut said, "I suppose I would have *been* a Nazi, bopping Jews and gypsies and Poles around, leaving boots sticking out of snowbanks, warming myself with my sweetly virtuous insides. So it goes."

Just so. One thing that happened to Milgram back in New Haven during the days of the experiment was that he kept running into people he'd watched from behind the one-way glass. It gave him a funny feeling, seeing those people going about their everyday business in New Haven and knowing what they would do to Mr. Wallace if ordered to. Now that his research results are in and you've thought about it, you can get this funny feeling too. You don't need oneway glass. A glance in your own mirror may serve just as well.

. . . You see, gentlemen, reason is an excellent thing, there's no disputing that, but reason is nothing but reason and satisfies only the rational side of man's nature, while will is a manifestation of the whole life, that is, of the whole human life including reason and all the impulses. And although our life, in this manifestation of it, is often worthless, yet it is life and not simply extracting square roots. Here I, for instance, quite naturally want to live, in order to satisfy all my capacities for life, and not simply my capacity for reasoning, that is, not simply one-twentieth of my capacity for life. What does reason know? Reason only knows what is has succeeded in learning (some things, perhaps, it will never learn; this is a poor comfort, but why not say so frankly?) and human nature acts as a whole, with everything that is in it, consciously or unconsciously, and, even if it goes wrong, it lives. I suspect, gentlemen, that you are looking at me with compassion; you tell me again that an enlightened and developed man, such, in short, as the future man will be, cannot consciously desire anything disadvantageous to himself, that that can be proved mathematically. I thoroughly agree, it can—by mathematics.

But, I repeat for the hundredth time, there is one case, one only, when man may consciously, purposely, desire what is injurious to himself, what is stupid, very stupid—simply in order to have the right to desire for himself even what is very stupid and not to be bound by an obligation to desire only what is sensible. Of course, this very stupid thing, this caprice of ours, may be in reality, gentlemen, more advantageous for us than anything else on earth, especially in certain cases. And in particular it may be more advantageous than any advantage even when it does us obvious harm, and contradicts the soundest conclusions of our reason concerning our advantage—for in any circumstances it preserves for us what is most precious and most important—that is, our personality, our individuality. . . .

Fyodor Dostoyevsky
(From *Notes from the Underground*, New York, Dell, 1960.)

*Look outside the window, there's a
   woman being grabbed*
*They dragged her to the bushes and
   now she's being stabbed*
*Maybe we should call the cops and
   try to stop the pain,*
*But Monopoly is so much fun, I'd hate
   to blow the game.*
*And I'm sure it wouldn't interest any-
   body outside of a small circle of
   friends.*

*Driving down the highway, yes, my
   back is getting stiff*
*13 cars have piled up—they're hang-
   ing on a cliff.*
*Maybe we should tow them back
   with our towing-chain,*
*But we gotta move, and we might get
   sued, and it looks like it's gonna
   rain.*
*And I'm sure it wouldn't interest any-
   body outside of a small circle of
   friends.*

*Sweating in the ghetto with the
   Panthers and the poor*
*The rats have joined the babies who
   are sleeping on the floor.*
*Wouldn't it be a riot if they really
   blew their tops*

*But they've got too much already and
   besides we've got the cops.
And I'm sure it wouldn't interest anybody outside of a small circle of
   friends.*

*There's a dirty paper using sex to
   make a sale.
The supreme court was so upset they
   sent him off to jail.
Maybe we should help the fiend to
   take away his fines,
But we're too busy reading* Playboy
   *and the Sunday New York Times.
And I'm sure it wouldn't interest anybody outside of a small circle of
   friends.*

*Smoking marijuana is more fun than
   drinking beer,
But a friend of ours got captured; and
   they gave him thirty years.
Maybe we should raise our voices
   and ask somebody why;
But demonstrations are a drag, besides we're much too high.
And I'm sure it wouldn't interest anybody outside of a small circle of
   friends.*

*Look outside the window, there's a
   woman being grabbed
They dragged her to the bushes and
   now she's being stabbed
Maybe we should call the cops and
   try to stop the pain,
But Monopoly is so much fun, I'd hate
   to blow the game.
And I'm sure it wouldn't interest anybody outside of a small circle of
   friends.*

Phil Ochs
("Outside of a Small Circle of
Friends," words and music by Phil
Ochs. Copyright 1966, 1968 Barricade
Music, Inc., New York, New York.
International copyright secured.
Made in U.S.A. All rights reserved.)

They try to escape, but they run
from themselves. They try to forget,
but their only recourse is an excitation of the senses. This stimulant
needs to be incessantly repeated.
The little spell of liberation, the false
glow, the hour of oblivion, leaves
them the more desolate and adds
new tensions to the returning
emptiness. Then there is leisure no
more, no relaxedness, no return to
the things they once loved, no linger-
ing ease of quiet discourse with
friends, no natural savor of living, no
perception of the unfolding wonder
of things. But instead they pass from
excitation to a hollow release, from
release to tension, from tension to
new excitation. Nothing is itself anymore. And no more at the end of the
day do they sink peacefully into the
marvelous process of slowly gathering sleep.
   Once they were so eager to make

life feel real; now they shun its
reality and are driven to pursue
phantoms, the will-o'-the-wisp of the
sense-spurred distraction, the unseeing ghosts of once clear-eyed
joys, the phantom Aphrodite.

Robert MacIver
(From *The Pursuit of Happiness,*
New York, Simon and Shuster, 1955.)

. . . Some rare days often in the
winter when New York is immobilized
by snow—cheerfully, because the
snow gives people an excuse to talk
to each other, and they need, God
help us, an excuse—or sometimes
when the frozen New York spring is
approaching, I walk out of my house
toward no particular destination, and
watch the faces that pass me. Where
do they come from? how did they
become—these faces—so cruel and
so sterile? they are related to whom?
they are related to what? They do not
relate to the buildings, certainly—no
human being could; I suspect, in fact,
that many of us live with the carefully
suppressed terror that these buildings are about to crash down on us;
the nature of the movement of the
people in the streets is certainly very
close to panic. You will search in
vain for lovers. I have not heard anyone singing in the streets of New
York for more than twenty years. By
singing, I mean singing for joy, for
the hell of it. I don't mean the
drunken, lonely, 4-AM keening which
is simply the sound of some poor soul
trying to vomit up his anguish and
gagging   on   it . . . Everyone   is
rushing,   God   knows   where,   and
everyone is looking for God knows
what—but it is clear that no one is
happy here, and that something has
been lost. Only, sometimes, uptown,
along the river, perhaps, I've sometimes watched strangers here, here
for a day or a week or a month, or
newly transplanted, watched a boy
and a girl, or a boy and a boy, or a
man and a woman, or a man and a
child, or a woman and a child; yes,
THERE was something recognizable,
something to which the soul responded, something to make one
smile, even to make one weep with
exultation. They were yet distinguish-
able from the concrete and the steel.
One felt that one might approach
them without freezing to death.

Rich Avedon
James Baldwin
(From *Nothing Personal.*)

What is modern man's relationship
to his fellow man? It is one between
two abstractions, two living machines,
who use each other. The employer
uses the ones whom he employs; the
salesman uses his customers. Every-

body is to everybody else a commodity, always to be treated with
certain friendliness, because even if
he is not of use now, he may be later.
There is not much love or hate to be
found in human relations of our day.
There is, rather, a superficial friendliness, and a more than superficial
fairness, but behind that surface is
distance and indifference. There is
also a good deal of subtle distrust.
When one man says to another, "You
speak to John Smith; he is all right,"
it is an expression of reassurance
against a general distrust. Even love
and the relationship between sexes
have assumed this character. The
great sexual emancipation, as it
occurred after the First World War,
was a desperate attempt to substitute
mutual sexual pleasure for a deeper
feeling of love. When this turned out
to be a disappointment the erotic
polarity between the sexes was
reduced to a minimum and replaced
by a friendly partnership, a small
combine which has amalgamated its
forces to hold out better in the daily
battle of life, and to relieve the feeling of isolation and aloneness which
everybody has.

Erich Fromm
(From *The Sane Society,* New York,
Holt, Rinehart and Winston, 1955.)

5.3
It's Against the Law to Pee in the Streets

Jerry Rubin

The revolution satisfies deep human needs denied by Amerikan
society. That's why it's so dangerous. The biggest social problem in
the country today in loneliness.

"What are you doing tonight?"
*"I don't know, Marty, what are
you doing tonight?"*

Loneliness is not an individual
problem—it's the collective problem of millions of Amerikans,
growing out of the alienating environment we live in. We work in
one part of town with people who
are not our friends, and we sleep
in another part of town and don't

Reprinted by permission of Simon
and Schuster from *Do It!* by Jerry
Rubin, pp. 231–234. Copyright © 1970
by Social Education Foundation.

know our neighbors. We waste much of our life dying in mobile concentration camps called freeways or commuter trains.

Where in the city can we go to make friends? Where can we leap out of our individual prisons and enjoy each other? The city is full of walls, locked doors, signs saying

DON'T

If someone you don't know says hello, you get uptight: *"What's he want?"* It's taboo to talk to strangers. Everybody's hustling. The streets are paved with terror, the city a prison for the soul.

The car, a box, transports lonely people from the box where they sleep to the box where they work, and then back to the box where they sleep. Amerikans relate to each other as drivers of other cars; the only good driver is the one who takes another road. People killed on freeways are casualties of a war every bit as fucked up as Vietnam.

The streets are for Business, not People. You can't sit in a restaurant without buying food; you can't read magazines in a store—you gotta buy, buy, buy—move on, move on. What if you're in the middle of the city and suddenly you have to take a shit?

Tough shit.

We are liberating the city, turning the streets into our living rooms. We live, work, eat, play and sleep together with our friends on the streets. Power is our ability to stand on a street corner and do nothing. We are creating youth ghettos in every city, luring into the streets everyone who is bored at home, school or work. And everyone is looking for "something to do."

For us empty pockets means liberation—from draft cards, checkbooks, credit cards, registration papers—we are close to our naked bodies.

The hippie area becomes the first mass alternative to the Amerikan urban prison. Liberated neighborhoods are a great threat to capitalist city life. So the forces of Death—the business community, cops and politicians—conspire to wipe us out. An entire battery of laws—genocidal laws against the young—makes social life in the streets a crime.

If you don't hand a cop documentary proof of who you are, you can be arrested. To the state empty pockets means vagrancy.

Watching the world from a street corner is loitering. Hitchhiking is a crime. It's against the law to panhandle, to rap to a crowd in the streets, to give out free food in the streets, to stop traffic. Playing a harmonica in the streets is illegal in Venice, California.

Two friends of mine were just arrested for the high political crime of pissing in the street. One was put into a mental hospital.

"Underage" kids caught on the streets are hauled straight to Juvenile Court.

And when all else fails, they establish a curfew, a Nazi law designed to prevent us from getting together.

These laws are designed to strike fear in the youth community. Although they exist on the books everywhere, they are enforced only in the ghetto. Cops patrol the hippie areas the way they patrol black communities, the way Amerikan soldiers patrol Vietnamese villages. Everyone is a likely enemy.

But the main strategy for destroying the free spirit is Business. "Psychedelic" stores try to steal the culture by selling fake artifacts to an emotion-starved Outside World. Camera-toting Amerikan tourists come through in buses and on foot, snapping pictures, laughing, squealing, pointing at us.

The streets turn into a hustle, a business section. We never know whom to trust. Burn artists and undercover cops flood the place, making it unsafe to buy or sell dope on the street.

We become an island in a capitalist sea attacked and infiltrated from inside and outside. The Death culture tries to destroy our Life Force and restructure the youth ghetto in its own image. We lack space in our own community—to breathe, conspire, celebrate, grow.

It is a war for land. Our survival depends on our ability to drive out the psychedelic exploiters, the invading pigs and the politicians and create youth communities where dropouts from middle-class Amerika can live.

Our goal is to create fires, blackouts, subway stoppages, strikes and snowstorms because only in crisis does liberation come to a city. People meet their neighbors for the first time while watching their apartment houses burn down. When the subway rumbles along, everyone acts as if no one else is aboard. As soon as there's a breakdown, people start talking to strangers. During snowstorms New York is a playground, an amusement park.

Crisis brings liberation to a city.

The revolution declares all land titles null and void. We are urban and rural liberators, seizing land for the people. No more "I own it!" People who believe they can own natural resources, industries or land are *really* candidates for mental institutions.

We will bring the war to the suburbs. The middle class creates suburbs as a sanctuary from the fire of the city. Children raised in the suburbs are treated as mentally and physically retarded. If we are not safe in our communities, why should corporate executives be safe in theirs?

We'll get our own tourist buses, steal cameras and ride through the suburbs squealing, laughing, snapping and pointing fingers.

We will take the revolution to Scarsdale.

In a revolution there are no sanctuaries.

. . . For one thing, talking to Americans is usually extremely uphill work. We are afraid to reveal ourselves because we trust ourselves so little. American attitudes are appalling, but so are the attitudes of most of the people in the world. What is stultifying here is that the attitude is presented as the person; one is expected to justify the attitude in order to reassure the person—whom, alas, one has yet to meet, who is light-years away, in some dreadful, private labyrinth. And in this labyrinth the person is desperately trying NOT to find out what he REALLY feels. Therefore, the truth cannot be told, even about one's attitudes: we live by lies. And not only, for example, about race—whatever, by this time, in this country, or, indeed, in the world, this word may mean—but about our very natures. The lie has penetrated to our most private moments, and the most secret chambers of our hearts.

Nothing more sinister can happen, in any society, to any people. And when it happens, it means that the people are caught in a kind of vacuum between their present and their past—the romanticized, that is, the maligned past, and the denied and dishonored present. It is a crisis of identity. And in such a crisis, at such a pressure, it becomes absolutely indispensable to discover, or invent—the two words, here, are

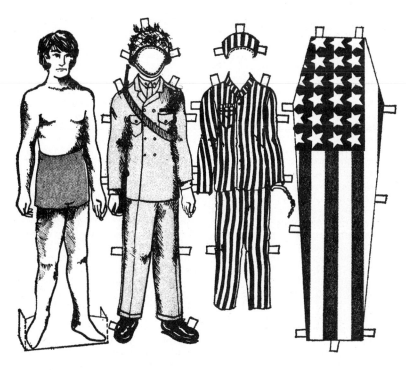

THE OLD MOLE, BOSTON.

synonyms—the stranger, the bar-barian, who is responsible for our confusion and our pain. Once he is driven out—destroyed—then we can be at peace: those questions will be gone. Of course, those questions never go, but it has always seemed much easier to murder than to change. And this is really the choice with which we are confronted now.

Rich Avedon
James Baldwin
(From *Nothing Personal.*)

5.4
Channeling

U.S. Selective Service

"Channeling" is one of ten documents in an "Orientation Kit" put out by the Selective Service. It was issued in July 1965 and has recently been withdrawn. The following are excerpts from that document.

One of the major products of the Selective Service classification

process is the channeling of manpower into many endeavors, occupations and activities that are in the national interest. . . .

The line dividing the primary function of armed forces manpower procurement from the process of channeling manpower into civilian support is often finely drawn. The process of channeling by not taking men from certain activities who are otherwise liable for service, or by giving deferment to qualified men in certain occupations, is actual procurement by inducement of manpower for civilian activities which are manifestly in the national interest.

While the best known purpose of Selective Service is to procure manpower for the armed forces, a variety of related processes take place outside delivery of manpower to the active armed forces. Many of these may be put under the heading of "channeling manpower." Many young men would not have pursued a higher education if there had not been a program of student deferment. Many young scientists, engineers, tool and die makers, and other possessors of scarce skills would not remain in their jobs in the defense effort if it were not for a program of occupational deferments. Even though the salary of a teacher has historically been meager, many young men remain in that job, seeking the reward of a deferment. The process of channeling

manpower by deferment is entitled to much credit for the large number of graduate students in technical fields and for the fact that there is not a greater shortage of teachers, engineers and other scientists working in activities which are essential to the national interest. . . .

The System has also induced needed people to remain in these professions and in industry engaged in defense activities or in the support of national health, safety or interest. . . .

This was coupled with a growing public recognition that the complexities of future wars would diminish further the distinction between what constitutes military service in uniform and a comparable contribution to the national interest out of uniform. Wars have always been conducted in various ways, but appreciation of this fact and its relationship to preparation for war has never been so sharp in the public mind as it is now becoming. The meaning of the word "service," with its former restricted application to the armed forces, is certain to become widened much more in the future. This brings with it the ever increasing problem of how to control effectively the service of individuals who are not in the armed forces.

In the Selective Service System the term "deferment" has been used millions of times to describe the method and means used to attract to the kind of service considered to be most important, the individuals who were not compelled to do it. The club of induction has been used to drive out of areas considered to be less important to the areas of greater importance in which deferments were given, the individuals who did not or could not participate in activities which were considered essential to the defense of the Nation. The Selective Service System anticipates further evolution in this area. . . .

No group deferments are permitted. Deferments are granted, however, in a realistic atmosphere so that the fullest effect of channeling will be felt, rather than be terminated by military service at too early a time.

Registrants and their employers are encouraged and required to make available to the classifying authorities detailed evidence as to the occupations and activities in which the registrants are engaged. . . . Since occupational deferments are granted for no more than one year at a time, a process of periodically receiving current information and repeated review assures that every deferred registrant continues to contribute to the overall national good. This reminds him of the basis for his deferment. . . .

Patriotism is defined as "devotion to the welfare of one's country." It has been interpreted to mean many different things. Men have always been exhorted to do their duty. But what that duty is depends upon a variety of variables, most important being the nature of the threat to national welfare and the capacity and opportunity of the individual. Take, for example, the boy who saved the Netherlands by plugging the dike with his finger.

At the time of the American Revolution the patriot was the so-called "embattled farmer" who joined General Washington to fight the British. The concept that patriotism is best exemplified by service in uniform has always been under some degree of challenge, but never to the extent that it is today. In today's complicated warfare, when the man in uniform may be suffering far less than the civilians at home, patriotism must be interpreted far more broadly than ever before.

This is not a new thought, but it has had new emphasis since the development of nuclear and rocket warfare. Educators, scientists, engineers and their professional organizations, during the last ten years particularly, have been convincing the American public that for the mentally qualified man there is a special order of patriotism other than service in uniform —that for the man having the capacity, dedicated service as a civilian in such fields as engineering, the sciences and teaching constitute the ultimate in their expression of patriotism. A large segment of the American public has been convinced that this is true.

It is in this atmosphere that the young man registers at age 18 and pressure begins to force his choice. He does not have the inhibitions that a philosophy of universal service in uniform would engender. The door is open for him as a student if capable in a skill badly needed by his nation. He has many choices and he is prodded to make a decision.

The psychological effect of this circumstantial climate depends upon the individual, his sense of good citizenship, his love of country and its way of life. He can obtain a sense of well-being and satisfaction that he is doing as a

civilian what will help his country most. This process encourages him to put forth his best effort and removes to some degree the stigma that has been attached to being out of uniform.

In the less patriotic and more selfish individual it engenders a sense of fear, uncertainty and dissatisfaction which motivates him, nevertheless, in the same direction. He complains of the uncertainty which he must endure; he would like to be able to do as he pleases; he would appreciate a certain future with no prospect of military service or civilian contribution, but he complies. . . .

Throughout his career as a student, the pressure—the threat of loss of deferment—continues. It continues with equal intensity after graduation. His local board requires periodic reports to find out what he is up to. He is impelled to pursue his skill rather than embark upon some less important enterprise and is encouraged to apply his skill in an essential activity in the national interest. The loss of deferred status is the consequence for the individual who has acquired the skill and either does not use it or uses it in a nonessential activity.

The psychology of granting wide choice under pressure to take action is the American or indirect way of achieving what is done by direction in foreign countries where choice is not permitted. Here, choice is limited but not denied, and it is fundamental that an individual generally applies himself better to something he has decided to do rather than something he has been told to do.

The effects of channeling are manifested among student physicians. They are deferred to complete their education through school and internship. This permits them to serve in the armed forces in their skills rather than in an unskilled capacity as enlisted men.

The device of pressurized guidance, or channeling, is employed on Standby Reservists of which more than 2½ million have been referred by all services for availability determinations. The appeal to the Reservist who knows he is subject to recall to active duty unless he is determined to be unavailable is virtually identical to that extended to other registrants.

The psychological impact of being rejected for service in uniform is severe. The earlier this occurs in a young man's life, the sooner the beneficial effects of pressured motivation by the Selective Ser-

vice System are lost. He is labeled unwanted. His patriotism is not desired. Once the label of "rejectee" is upon him all efforts at guidance by persuasion are futile. If he attempts to enlist at 17 or 18 and is rejected, then he receives virtually none of the impulsion the System is capable of giving him. If he makes no effort to enlist and as a result is not rejected until delivered for examination by the Selective Service System at about age 23, he has felt some of the pressure but thereafter is a free agent.

This contributed to establishment of a new classification of I-Y (registrant qualified for military service only in time of war or national emergency). That classification reminds the registrant of his ultimate qualification to serve and preserves some of the benefit of what we call channeling. Without it or any other similar method of categorizing men in degrees of acceptability, men rejected for military service would be left with the understanding that they are unfit to defend their country, even in wartime.

An unprejudiced choice between alternative routes in civilian skills can be offered only by an agency which is not a user of manpower and is, therefore, not a competitor. In the absence of such an agency, bright young men would be importuned with bounties and pirated like potential college football players until eventually a system of arbitration would have to be established.

From the individual's viewpoint, he is standing in a room which has been made uncomfortably warm. Several doors are open, but they all lead to various forms of recognized, patriotic service to the Nation. Some accept the alternatives gladly—some with reluctance. The consequence is approximately the same.

The so-called Doctor Draft was set up during the Korean episode to insure sufficient physicians, dentists and veterinarians in the armed forces as officers. The objective of that law was to exert sufficient pressure to furnish an incentive for application for commission. However, the indirect effect was to induce many physicians, dentists and veterinarians to specialize in areas of medical personnel shortages and to seek outlets for their skills in areas of greatest demand and national need rather than of greatest financial return.

Selective Service processes do not compel people by edict as in foreign systems to enter pursuits having to do with essentiality and progress. They go because they know that by going they will be deferred.

The application of direct methods to effect the policy of every man doing his duty in support of national interest involves considerably more capacity than the current use of indirection as a method of allocation of personnel. The problem, however, of what is every man's duty when each individual case is approached is not simple. The question of whether he can do one duty better than another is a problem of considerable proportions and the complications of logistics in attempting to control parts of an operation without controlling all of it (in other words, to control allocation of personnel without controlling where people eat, where they live and how they are to be transported), adds to the administrative difficulties of direct administration. The organization necessary to make the decisions, even poor decisions, would, of necessity, extract a large segment of population from productive work. If the members of the organization are conceived to be reasonably qualified to exercise judgment and control over skilled personnel, the impact of their drawal from war production work would be severe. The number of decisions would extend into billions.

Deciding what people should do, rather than letting them do something of national importance of their own choosing, introduces many problems that are at least partially avoided when indirect methods, the kind currently invoked by the Selective Service System, are used.

Delivery of manpower for induction, the process of providing a few thousand men with transportation to a reception center, is not much of an administrative or financial challenge. It is in dealing with the other millions of registrants that the System is heavily occupied, developing more effective human beings in the national interest. If there is to be any survival after disaster, it will take people, and not machines, to restore the Nation.

Now this distinction between social structure and personal milieu is one of the most important available in the sociological studies. It offers us a ready understanding of the position of the "public" in America today. In every major area of life, the loss of a sense of structure and the submergence into powerless milieux is the cardinal fact. In the military it is most obvious, for here the roles men play are strictly confining; only the command posts at the top afford a view of the structure of the whole, and moreover, this view is a closely guarded official secret. In the division of labor, too, the jobs men enact in the economic hierarchies are also more or less narrow milieux and the positions from which a view of the production process as a whole can be centralized, as men are alienated not only from the product and the tools of their labor, but from any understanding of the structure and the processes of production. In the political order, in the fragmentation of the lower and in the distracting proliferation of the middle level organization, men cannot see the whole, cannot see the top, and cannot state the issues that will in fact determine the whole structure in which they live and their place within it.

C. Wright Mills
(From *The Power Elite*, New York, Oxford University Press, 1956.)

5.5
From The Strawberry Statement

James S. Kunen

Thursday, June 27: I don't understand why our government has us fight the war. I don't know. Are they incredibly evil men, or are they stupid, or are they insane? How can Johnson sleep? How can he go to bed knowing that 25,000 American boys—and countless Vietnamese—have died because of his "policies." He obviously doesn't consider the Vietnamese to be people at all. They're strange, distant, numberless, and yellow, so perhaps he can't empathize with

From *The Strawberry Statement*, by James S. Kunen. Copyright © 1968, 1969 by James S. Kunen. Reprinted by permission of Random House, Inc.

them, can't know their existence and their joys. But what about the Americans? He thinks perhaps that the war is not going well. Doesn't he realize that wars can't go well, that people always die in them and that's not well? Doesn't he know anything? Do statistics hide the truth and keep him from feeling? When I see statistics I practically throw up. I can never forget it. It's in me that my friends everyday hear gunfire and see others fall and hate the enemy. But when they see the ground spin up at them and feel the wetness of their own blood, whom do you think they hate then? These kids who were and were being and were going to be, suddenly finding that they will not be what they wanted or anything else, suddenly finding themselves ending. Won't know or do anything any more. Never see or be seen again. Whom do you suppose they hate? Don't the leaders know that? Couldn't they work out a better way to settle problems? Little boys fight, but by the age of *sixteen*, as irresponsible teens, *they* see that fighting doesn't prove anything. Young men hardly ever fight. Only when their countries do. So it's the countries which display incredibly juvenile behavior. Wars are silly. They're ludicrous. But they're real, extant, constant, present. Why don't countries just stop it? Just cut it out, that's all. We don't want any. They struggle tortuously to arrive at disarmament pacts. They tell everybody that arriving at peace is complex, difficult. Don't they see? It's not a question of state department negotiations or of treaties or international law. It's very simple. All that's necessary is for the leaders to see what they've always done and are doing and for once know and feel and get sick and stop. Nobody fight any more. Of course it's not that simple. But I must be stupid because it seems that simple to me.

It seems that simple to me, and that's not a generation gap, it's an idea difference, and a power gap. You've got the power. You make millions of people suffer. They're hungry and they've got nowhere to go and nothing to do for it. Well cut it out, will you? Just stop it.

If you won't stop it we'll stop you. I've got nothing to lose. You can have your cars and your hi-fi's and your pools and your nice schools. (Sometimes.) I'd like to pawn them off and use the money for schools and houses for the poor. I'd like to do that so I'd feel good. So I'd feel good.

Let's not put our country down. It happens that the United States is the scourge of the earth, but let's not put it down.

I have a mad desire to live.

Hey, do you know what Communists do? They fall in love and have babies sometimes. I swear to God.

Quite some time ago, many years ago in fact, before anybody was born, a seed drifted quietly down from a branch and was buried in the ground, where it grew. It grew into a tall tree, standing in the company of a forest in a land so green it was named "Green Land." No person ever came near, which was all right by the tree. Very recently, yesterday, if you want to know, a jet flew screaming by, unheard by the tree and, unseen by the tree, sprayed the air with poison which drifted quietly down and landed on the tree and, unfelt by the tree, killed the tree. This happens quite frequently, with the result that many trees die and the land is not green any longer. Where there was quiet life there is now violent death, which is why no one is concerned about the tree. There are too many men dying to worry about a tree. Or about a man.

5.6
The War Machine vs. the Peace Machinist

Richard Linsley

Let us suppose that you are one of those Americans who are profoundly opposed to the Vietnam war, that you consider it immoral, and illegal as well. Let us also assume you would like to do something concrete and serious to express your feelings about it. Let us assume, in fact, that you decide you will no longer contribute to the war machine at all. What do you do?

Draft-age kids have a choice, though not an attractive one. Overage, underage, women, 4-F's, the other undraftables haven't even that. A few small things suggest themselves. For instance, you

Reprinted by permission of *Esquire* Magazine from "The War Machine vs. the Peace Machine," *Esquire*, February, 1970. © by Esquire, Inc.

can refuse to buy U.S. Bonds or the like, which of course has the advantage of being wonderfully effortless. And there has been a small movement to abstain from paying Federal taxes on phone bills. And so on. These are falling leaves drifting gently across the backs of two elephants—and when they get around to it, they'll blow some dust up there.

But what about your work, your livelihood? If you are, say, a bartender or on the children's glove counter at Macy's or an account executive on soup ads, this works out with classic simplicity. When you go to bed at night you can think: I drew those beers and served those martinis, I held the nasty little darlings' elbows on the counter and pulled the gloves onto their hands. Or I told off that artist on the shade of red we want on the tomatoes. Then you sleep with a clear conscience. Easy enough. But suppose you are a machinist, a diemaker, a turret-lathe or drill-press operator?

Working in a machine shop can be a very rewarding occupation. There is something special about taking a shapeless and ugly lump of metal, such as a forging, and turning it into a shiningly beautiful and useful object, precisely as called for in the blueprints and specifications. It *must* fit, *must* work. A cabby crossing midtown Manhattan at 5:00 P.M. may need as much skill, but he cannot know exactly at what moment he will come out at the proper address on Sutton Place. A machinist can know that if he turns this dial just so much, presses this lever down and pulls it up at just the right time, the thread he is cutting will come out exactly right. Not all people need these satisfactions, of course. But some do.

Unlike bartenders, glove sales-ladies, and the like, if a machinist decides he will not contribute his person to the war economy he is in for a hell of a lot of trouble. I am a machinist who decided that, and this is how it works.

Assume you have enough money to keep you for a while. Then you quit your job making helicopter parts and die blanks which stamp out the brass shell cases for bullets to kill people. You must quit. Unless you are working nights, it is impossible to hunt another job. Now for another job with nothing to do with the war.

To begin with, you find that you have to forget about any of the big companies. They all have their snouts in the war trough and most

of them two, three, or all four feet as well. Then you have to forget about all the thousands of machine shops, big and little, which have no products of their own but exist by subcontracting from the big ones. That's all war stuff, too.

This knocks you out of the good money, to begin with. The big ones are all unionized; the few which are not (I.B.M. comes to mind) have spent so much to keep the union out that they are apt to pay at least as well, possibly better, than the union places. This also applies to fringe benefits: vacations, pensions, and the like. When I worked on the war my take-home pay was a little over $160 a week, plus fringes. Now it is $94.

What you are looking for, then, is a small factory with its own product (eggbeaters, maybe) which is looking for a machinist. This sounds easy, but is not. Most places of this type have very stable help and do not hire very much. Guys die and retire, but there is usually a relative or friend or an apprentice ready to step in. Nor is it easy to tell from the ads what kind of place it is. Some places make it easy by displaying all their lethal stuff in glass cases in the lobby. Then all you lose is the time spent getting there.

Otherwise, the woman or girl at the reception desk must be faced. The hauteur of these people must be experienced to be believed. Royalty and peasant. It is usually impossible to talk to anyone, to ask any questions, without filling out an application. These are at least two, and often four, pages. I once started to fill one out which inquired into my father's occupation. You wait and wait. Then you meet a personnel man and you can make up your mind.

I went to a Smith Machine Works on West Street in Manhattan. After examining my qualifications, the conversation went thus:

PERSONNEL: I think you will fit in very well here.
ME: What will I be making?
PERSONNEL: We'll start you off at $3.60, $3.70 after thirty days and $3.90 after ninety days. After that there are merit increases. There's all kinds of overtime and fringe benefits.
ME: That will be satisfactory. But I didn't mean what will I be *earning*. I meant what will I be *making*.
PERSONNEL: I don't understand what you mean.
ME: I mean manufacturing. I won't make anything to help the war in Vietnam.
PERSONNEL (*pause*): Everything

we do here has something to do with the war. I'm afraid we cannot use you.

ME: You've a good phrase there. You can't use me.

Through a stroke of luck (and scanning *The Times* when it comes out at eleven P.M.) I got a job in a shop which manufactures marine hardware. When I explained my position on the war, the interviewer said, "Listen. Most of our stuff goes into yachts, but some of it might find its way to a captain's launch in the Navy, or some other small boat. I can't guarantee you."

The thought flitted through my mind that I was hedging, which was the truth. Also that the yachts came about through one war or another. But I was getting nervous so I accepted it.

A month later this decent man came to me and said they had accepted a contract from N.A.S.A., and asked whether I would work on it. I wanted to know if it was missiles and he said, no, it was the moon shot. I swallowed this also, another hedge.

Not many personnel would take the trouble to ask. Some of these personnel clowns can be indecently abusive, but others are understanding, even respectful of my position.

A guy at the College Point Machine told me, "Go work in Saigon, you bastard." I suppose this illiterate meant Hanoi.

One in Jamaica, after a long and friendly talk, said to me: "Mr. Linsley, get into another line of work. In case of peace we are both finished."

"I accept your offer," I said, and we both laughed.

But it gets harder to laugh.

5.7
"I Am Actively Uninvolved"

Chuck Iwal

To you who display the peace symbol:

I walk past the students in Moses. Proud, defiant, afraid, they ask me to join them, "We are the way." But I walk by, I walk by the

Reprinted by permission from "Letters to the Ice Box," *The Daily Californian* (University of California, Berkeley), October 29, 1968.

sit-ins, the non-violent demonstrations, the organizational meetings, the picket lines, the banners, the slogans, the pleading editorials (J'accuse), the issue, the principle, the enormous injustice, the unconcealed tyranny and then I run, run till I am free and in the classroom with simpler people, free, but not from my conscience.

I with my middle-class morality, the result of countless efforts to inculcate and indoctrinate—the American materialist value, the pursuit of money, of wealth, of status and hence the grade—the American brand of happiness.

Yet, I am not uninvolved. I am actively uninvolved. The effort, the time, the energy can't be sacrificed, the classes, the studying—the system's game.

And I cannot change, I am not you. I am not a politico, I am not unconcerned about my future, my life. I am not free.

And so it is I who will seal the doom of your cause, I and people like me in the dormitories, the frats, the sororities, the co-ops, in the classrooms, the laboratories and in the professional schools—the "apathetic" mass.

And I have betrayed my school, I have betrayed my principles, I have betrayed myself.

By making some quality or circumstance, real or exaggerated or imagined, the focal point of a reified identity, I look upon myself as though I were a thing (res) and the quality or circumstance were a fixed attribute of this thing or object. But the "I" that feels that I am this or that, in doing so, distances itself from the very same reified object attribute which it experiences as determining its identity and very often as a bane on its life. In feeling that I am such and such, I distinguish between the unfortunate I and the presumably unalterable quality or lack which, for all time, condemns me to have this negative identity. I do not feel that I am *doing* this or that or failing to do it, but that there *is* a something in me or about me, or that I lack something and that this, once and for all, *makes* me this or that, fixes my identity.

Ernest Schachtel
(From "On Alienated Concepts of Identity," *Man Alone*, p. 78.)

I love the lie and lie the love (?)
A Hangin on and push and shove

Possession is the motivation
That's hangin up the damn nation
Seems like we always end up in a rut!

Everybody now, tryin to make it real
   compared to what?

A slaughter house is killin horse
Twisted children killin forced
Poor old rednecks rollin logs
Tired old ladies kissin dogs
I hate the human love of that stinkin
   mut!
I can't use it. Tryin to make it real
   compared to what?

The president he's got his war
Folks don't know just what it's for
Nobody gives us a rhyme or reason
Half a one dollar they call it treason
We're chicken feathers all, without
   one gut!
God dammit! Tryin to make it real
   compared to what?

Church on Sunday, sleep and nod
Tryin to touch the wrath of God.
Preachers fillin us with fright,
They all trying to teach us what they
   think is right
They really got to be some kind of
   nut!
I can't use it! Tryin to make it real
   compared to what?

Gene Daniels
("Compared to What?" Reprinted by permission of Broadcast Music, Inc.)

5.8
From New Reformation

Paul Goodman

I

In 1967 I was invited to give a course on "professionalism" at the New School for Social Research in New York. (They were expanding the graduate school and the Dean was beating around for a reason for it.) The class consisted of about twenty-five graduates from all departments.

My bias was the traditional one, that professionals are autonomous men, beholden to the nature of things and the judgment of their peers, and not subject to bosses or bureaucrats but bound by an explicit or implicit oath to benefit their clients and the community. To teach this, I invited seasoned professionals whom I esteemed, a physician, engineer, journalist, architect, humanist scholar. These explained to the students the ob-

From *New Reformation*, by Paul Goodman. Copyright © 1970 by Paul Goodman. Reprinted by permission of Random House, Inc.

stacles that increasingly stand in the way of honest practice and their own life experiences in circumventing them.

To my surprise, the class unanimously rejected my guests. Heatedly and rudely, they called them finks, mystifiers, or deluded. They showed that every profession was co-opted and corrupted by the System, that all significant decisions were made by the power structure and bureaucracy, that professional peer groups were only conspiracies to make more money. All this was importantly true and had, of course, been said by the visitors. Why had the students not heard?

As we explored further, we came to the deeper truth that the students did not believe that there *were* authentic professions at all. Professionalism was a concept of repressive societies and of "linear thinking" (a notion of McLuhan's). I asked them to envisage any social order they pleased—Mao's, Castro's, some anarchist utopia—and wouldn't there be engineers who knew about materials and stresses and strains? Wouldn't people get sick and need to be treated? Wouldn't there be problems of communication and decisions about the news? No. It was necessary only to be human, they insisted, and all else would follow.

Suddenly I realized that they did not believe there was a nature of things. Or they were not sure of that. There was no knowledge but only the sociology of knowledge. They had learned so well that physical and sociological research is subsidized and conducted for the benefit of the ruling class that they were doubtful that there was such a thing as simple truth, for instance that the table was made of wood—maybe it was a plastic imitation. To be required to know something was a trap by which the young were put down and co-opted. Then I knew that my guests and I could not get through to them. I had imagined that the worldwide student protest had to do with changing political and moral institutions, and I was sympathetic to this. But I now saw that we had to do with a religious crisis. Not only all institutions but all learning had been corrupted by the Whore of Babylon, and there was no longer any salvation to be got from Works.

The irony was that I myself had said this ten years before, in *Growing Up Absurd*, that young people were growing up without a world for them, and therefore they were "alienated," estranged from nature and unable to find their own natures, since we find ourselves by activity in the world. But I had then been thinking of juvenile delinquents and a few of the Beat Generation; and a couple of years later, I indeed noticed and wrote about a "New Spirit," the Movement—the Freedom Rides, the Port Huron Statement of the Students for a Democratic Society with its emphasis on decentralization and "participatory democracy," the Free Speech Movement in Berkeley, the rising resistance to the Vietnam War—all of this made human sense and was not absurd at all. (The magazine for which I wrote "New Spirit" in 1960 refused to print it because, they said, there was no such movement.) But now the alienating circumstances had proved to be too strong, after all; here were absurd graduate students, most of them political activists—the activists seek me out to bug me.

II

Alienation is a Lutheran concept: "God has turned His face away; things have no meaning; I am estranged in the world." By the time of Hegel the idea was applied to the general condition of rational man with his "objective" sciences and institutions divorced from his "subjectivity," which was, in turn, irrational and impulsive. In his revision of Hegel, Marx explained alienation as the effect of Man's losing his essential nature as a cooperative producer; centuries of exploitation, and, climactically, capitalism, had fragmented his community and robbed him of the means of production. Comte and Durkheim spoke of the weakening of social solidarity, the loss of common faith, the contradiction among norms, so that people lost their bearings—this was anomie, an acute form of alienation that could lead to suicide or aimless riot. By the end of the nineteenth century, alienation came to be used as the term for insanity, derangement of perceived reality; psychiatrists were called alienists.

Contemporary conditions of life have certainly deprived people, and especially young people, of a world meaningful for them in which they can act and realize themselves. Many writers and the dissenting students themselves have spelled out what is wrong. In both schools and corporations, people cannot pursue their own interests, use their powers, exercise initiative. Administrators are hypocrites who sell out people for the smooth operation of their systems. The Cold War has grotesquely distorted reasonable social priorities. Perhaps worse, the powers who make the decisions are incompetent to cope with modern times; two-thirds of mankind are starving, and all are in danger of extinction. For the purposes of this book, let me list some other alienating conditions that call for a religious response.

I have mentioned the lapse of faith in science, which has not produced the general happiness that people expected, and now, under the sway of greed and power, has become frightening. Rationality itself is discredited. Certainly one reason for the fad for astrology and Tarot cards is that they are scientifically ridiculous and dreamy. A hundred years ago, among superstitious peasants, Bazaroff, in *Fathers and Sons*, showed that he was a free spirit by scientifically cutting up frogs and being objective.

Every one of these young grew up since Hiroshima. They do not talk about atom bombs, not nearly so much as we who campaigned against the shelters and fallout; but the bombs explode in their dreams, as Otto Butz found in his study of collegians at San Francisco State College; and George Dennison, in *The Lives of Children*, shows that it is the same with small children in the Lower East Side in New York. Again and again, students have told me that they take it for granted they will not survive the next ten years. This is not an attitude with which to prepare for a career or bring up a family.

Whether or not the bombs go off, human beings are evidently useless. The old are shunted out of sight at an increasingly earlier age; the young are kept on ice till an increasingly later age. Small farmers and other technologically unemployed are dispossessed or left to rot. Increasing millions are put away as incompetent or deviant. Racial minorities that cannot shape up are treated as a nuisance. Together, these groups are a large majority of the population. Since labor is not needed, there is vague talk of a future society of "leisure," but I have heard of no plans for a kind of community in which all human beings would be necessary and valued.

The institutions, technology, and communications have infected even the "biological core," so that people's sexuality and other desires are no longer genuine. (One cannot trust in their spontaneous choices.) Subliminal suggestions have invaded the unconscious, and superficial pleasure is used as a means of social control, as in *Brave New World*. This was powerfully argued by Wilhelm Reich a generation ago, and it is now repeated by Herbert Marcuse. When I pushed the Reichian position in the forties, I was bitterly attacked as a "bedroom revisionist" by C. Wright Mills and the Marxists, but now it has become orthodoxy among the young militants.

(A special aspect of biological corruption is the spreading ugliness, filth, and tension of the environment in which the young grow up. If Wordsworth was right in saying that children must grow up in an environment of beauty and simple affections in order to become trusting, open, and magnanimous adults, then the offspring of our cities, suburbs, and complicated homes have been disadvantaged, no matter how much money there is. This lack cannot be remedied by including Art in the curriculum, nor by vest-pocket playgrounds, nor by banning billboards from bigger highways. Cleaning the river might help, but that will be the day.

(5) And another cause of metaphysical confusion is the sheer prevalence of the man-made, with nothing to compare and contrast it with; everything is stamped with social messages. It has always been the case, in the arts and rhetoric, and in technology in general, that the medium is the message—one cannot separate "form" and "content"; but mass communications are uniquely swamping, all goods are styled and packaged commodities, the medium-message is the only experience. Young people brought up among so much artifice dare not trust the evidence of their own senses and craftsmanship unless it is confirmed on the TV screen or by being on the market; but *these* messages, they know, they certainly can't trust.

III

If we start from the premise that the young are in a religious crisis, that they doubt there is really a nature of things and they are sure there is no world for themselves, many details of their present behavior become clearer. Alienation is a powerful motivation, of unrest, fantasy, and reckless action. It can lead, we shall see, to religious innovation, new sacraments

to give life meaning. But it is a poor basis for politics, including revolutionary politics.)

It is said that the young dissidents never offer a constructive program. And apart from the special cases of Czechoslovakia and Poland, where they confront an unusually outdated system, this is largely true. In other countries, most of the issues of protest have been immediate gut issues, and the tactics have been mainly disruptive, without coherent proposals for a better society. Some American militants say they are "building socialism," but when questioned, they seem to have no institutions in mind, only a dissatisfaction with monopoly capitalism.

This has political difficulties. To have no program rules out the politics of rational persuasion, for there is nothing to offer the other citizens, who do not have one's gut complaints, to get them to come along. Instead, one confronts them with "demands," and they are turned off even when they might otherwise be sympathetic. But the confrontation is inept too, for the alienated young cannot take other people seriously, as having needs and interests of their own; a sad instance was the inability of the French youth to communicate with the French working class in 1968. In Gandhian theory, the confronter aims at future community with the confronted; he will not let him continue a course that is bad for *him*, and so he appeals to his deeper reason. But instead of this Satyagraha, soul force, we have seen plenty of hate. The confronted are not taken as human beings, but as pigs or robots. But how can the young think of a future community with the others when they share no present world with them —no professions, jobs, or trust in the others as human beings? Instead, some young radicals seem to entertain the disastrous illusion that other people can be compelled by frightening them. This can lead only to crushing reaction.

The "political" activity makes sense, however, if it is understood not as aimed at reconstruction at all but as a way of desperately affirming that oneself is alive and wants a place in the sun. "The reason to be a revolutionary in our time," said Cohn-Bendit, leader of the French students, "is that it's a better way to live." And young Americans pathetically and truly say that there is no other way to be taken seriously. Then it is not necessary to have a program; the

right way is to act, against any vulnerable point and wherever one can rally support. The purpose is not, narrowly, politics, but to have a movement and form a community. Not surprisingly, this is exactly the recipe that Saul Alinsky prescribed to rally outcaste blacks. And if, like colonialized peoples, one has suffered lifelong humiliation, Frantz Fanon adds to the prescription the need to be violent, as psychotherapy.

Such conflictful action has indeed caused social changes. In France it was conceded by the government that "nothing would ever be the same." In the United States, apart from the youth action, the changes in social attitude during the last ten years are unthinkable, with regard to war, corporate administration, the police, the blacks. When the actors have been in touch with the underlying causes of things, issues have deepened and the Movement has grown. But for the alienated, unfortunately, action easily slips into activism and conflict that are largely spite and stubbornness. There is excitement and notoriety, much human suffering, with the world no better off. (*New Left Notes* runs a column wryly called, "We Made the News Today, O Boy!") Then instead of deepening awareness and a sharpening political conflict, there occurs the polarization of mere exasperation. Often it seems that the aim is just to have a shambles. Impatiently the activists raise the ante of their tactics beyond what the "issue" warrants, and support melts away. Out on a limb, the leaders become desperate and fanatical, intolerant of criticism, dictatorial. The Movement falls to pieces.

Yet it is noteworthy that when older people, like myself, are critical of wrongheaded activism, we nevertheless almost invariably concede that the young are *morally* justified. For what is the use of patience when meantime millions are being killed and starved, and when bombs and nerve-gas are being stockpiled? Against entrenched power that does these things, it might be better to do something idiotic, and now, than something perhaps more practical in the long run. I don't know which is less demoralizing.

Maybe a deeper truth was revealed in a conversation I had with a young hippie at a college in Massachusetts. He was dressed like an (American) Indian, in fringed buckskin and a headband, with red paint on his face. All his life, he said, he had tried to escape the encompassing evil of our society that was bent on destroying his soul. "But if you're always escaping," I pointed out, "and never attentively study it, how can you make a wise judgment about society or act effectively either to change it or escape it?" "You see, you don't dig!" he cried. "It's just ideas like 'wise' and 'acting effectively' that we can't stand. He was right. He was in the religious dilemma of Faith versus Works. Where I sat, Works had some reality; I had a vocation that justified me; and I even threw some (tiny) weight in the community. But in the reign of the Devil, as he felt it, "We walk by faith and not by sight." (2 *Corinthians*). But he didn't seem to have Faith either.

If we do not understand their alienation, the young seem dishonorably inconsistent in how they take the present world. Hippies attack technology and are scornful of rationality, but they buy up electronic equipment and motorcycles and with them the whole infrastructure. Militants say that civil liberties are bourgeois and they deny them to others, but they clamor in court for their own civil liberties. Those who say that the university is an agent of the powers that be do not mean thereby to assert the ideal role of the university, but to use the university for their own propaganda. Yet if I point out these apparent inconsistencies, it does not arouse shame or guilt. This has puzzled me. But it is simply that they do not recognize that technology, civil law, and the university are human institutions for which they too are responsible. They take them as brute-given, as just what's there, to be manipulated as convenient. But convenient for whom? The trouble with this attitude is that these institutions, works of spirit in history, are how Man has made himself and is. If they treat them as mere things and are not vigilant for them, do not they themselves become very little?

Their lack of sense of history is bewildering. It is impossible to convey to them that the deeds of the past were done by human beings, that John Hamden committed civil disobedience and refused the war tax just as we do, or that Beethoven, just like a rock and roll band, made up his music as he went along, from odds and ends, with energy, spontaneity, and passion—how else do they think he made music?

They no longer remember their own history. A few years ago there was a commonly accepted story of mankind. Mankind (var. *Californiensis*) sprang into existence, from nothing, with the Beats, went on to the Chessman case, the HUAC bust, and the Freedom rides; and came to maturity with the Berkeley Victory, "the first human event in forty thousand years," as Mike Rossman told me. But this year I find that nothing antedates Chicago '68. Each coming class is more entangled in the specious present. Elder statesmen like Sidney Lens and Staughton Lynd have been trying with heroic effort to recall the American antecedents of radical and libertarian slogans and tactics, but it doesn't rub off. I am often hectored to my face with formulations that I myself put in their mouths, which have become part of oral tradition two years old, author prehistoric. Most significant of all, it has been whispered to me—but I can't check up because I don't speak the language—that in junior high, for ages thirteen and fourteen, that's really where it's at! Quite different from what goes on in the colleges that I visit.

What I do see is that dozens of Underground newspapers have the same noisy style and stereotyped content: "A brother throws a canister at a pig." Though each one is doing his thing, there is not much idiosyncrasy in so much spontaneous variety. As if mesmerized, the political radicals repeat the power plays, factionalism, random abuse, and tactical lies that aborted the movement in the thirties. And I have learned, to my disgust, that the reason why young people don't trust people over thirty is that they don't understand them and are afraid to try. Having grown up in a world too meaningless to them for them to learn anything, they know very little and are quick to resent it. Their resentment is understandable; what is disgusting is their lack of moral courage.

Needless to say, the atmosphere is rife with paranoia. The hostile inexperience of the young, with a chip on the shoulder and fortified by ideology, calls out to the latent lunacy of the reactionaries; and the dream world perforce becomes the public world, because they are all our fellow citizens. There will be a couple of massacres before, hopefully, there is a revulsion of common sense. Last month—I am writing in June 1969—a police helicopter gassed the campus of the University of California. The reason for this was that some enterprising hippies were developing a vacant lot of the university as a garden with swings, but the chancellor's office had decided it must be developed as a soccer field.[1]

IV

This is not a pleasant account. Even so, the alienated *have* no vital alternative except to confront the Enemy, and to try to make a new way of life out of their own innards. As they are doing.

It is irrelevant to show that the System is not the monolith that they think and that most people are not very corrupt but just confused and anxious. The point is that they cannot see this, because they do not have a world operable for them. In such a case, the only advice that I would dare to give is that which Krishna gave Arjuna: to confront with non-attachment, to be brave and firm without hatred. (I don't want to discuss here the question of violence; the disdain and hatred are more important.) Also, when they are seeking a new way of life, I find that I urge them occasionally to write a letter home.

As a citizen and father, I have a right to try to prevent a shambles and to diminish the number of wrecked lives. But it is improper for older people to keep saying, as we do, that activity of the young is "counterproductive." It's our business to do something more productive that they can join if they want to.

Religiously the young have been inventive, much more than the God-is-dead theologians. They have hit on new sacraments, physical actions to get them out of their estrangement and break through (momentarily) into meaning. The terribly loud music is used sacramentally—which, incidentally, should be taken into account by those who say it is bad for the hearing; they are welded together in the block of clamor. The claim for the hallucinogenic drugs is almost never the nirvana of opium nor the escape from distress of heroin, but tuning in to the cosmos and communing with one another. They seem to have

---

[1] My guess is that in the School of Architecture of the university, the do-it-yourself method of the hippies in this case is being taught as a model of correct urban landscape architecture, to encourage citizenship and eliminate vandalism, according to the ideas of Karl Linn and others. The chancellor could just as well have given out academic credit and an A grade.

had flashes of success in bringing ritual praticipation back into theater, which for a hundred years playwrights and directors have tried to do in vain. And whatever the political purposes and political results of activism, there is no doubt that shared danger for righteousness' sake is used sacramentally as baptism of fire. Fearful moments of provocation and the poignant release of the bust bring unconscious contents to the surface, create a bond of solidarity, are "commitment."

The most powerful magic, working in all these sacraments, is the close presence of other human beings, without competition or one-upping. The original sin is to be on an ego trip. Angry political factionalism has now also become a bad thing. It is a drastic comment on the dehumanization and fragmentation of modern times that salvation can be attained simply by the "warmth of assembled animal bodies," as Kafka called it, describing his Mice. At the 1967 Easter Be-In in Central Park in New York, when about ten thousand were crowded on the Sheep Meadow, a young man with a quite radiant face said to me, "Gee, human beings are legal!"—it was sufficient to be exempted from harassment by bureaucratic rules and officious police. A small group passing a joint of marijuana often behaves like a Quaker meeting waiting for the spirit, and the cigarette may be a placebo. T-groups and sensitivity training, with Mecca at Esalen, have the same idea. And I think this is the sense of the sexuality, which is certainly not hedonistic, nor mystical in the genre of D. H. Lawrence, nor does it have much to do with personal love, which is too threatening for these anxious youths. But it is human touch, without conquest or domination, and it obviates self-consciousness and embarrassed speech.

A hippie who had helped construct the People's Park in Berkeley said that it was the first time in his life that he had ever enjoyed working hard, because it was "their own." One realizes with dismay that he had probably never repaired his bike as his own, nor painted the house as his own family's, nor studied a subject because it was interesting to himself, nor cooperated with his friends on an enterprise simply because they thought it worthwhile. Everything was sequestered as Papa's or as part of the curriculum or part of

the System. It was necessary to live through alienation and confrontation in order to feel something was "one's own." It was necessary to do it in a gang in order to be onself.

Around this pure but difficult faith, so dependent on its adversaries, and on confused allies, there has collected a mess of eclectic and exotic liturgy and paraphernalia, for there is no natural or primitive traditional expression: mandalas, beggars in saffron (not quite the right shade), (American) Indian beads, lectures on Zen. The exotic is desirable because it is not what they have grown up with. And it is true that fundamental facts of life are more acceptable if they come in fancy dress; for instance, it is good to breathe from the diaphragm and one can learn to do this by humming OM, especially in anxious conditions, as Allen Ginsberg did for seven hours in Jackson Park in Chicago. But college chaplains of the usual faiths are also pretty busy, and they are now more likely to see the adventurous and off-beat than, as used to be the case, the staid and square. Flowers and the poems of Blake have a certain authenticity of tradition, in the line of the English Romantics and the Angel Pre-Raphael. The "psychedelic" biomorphic drawing that decorates the Underground papers is poor, but it carries on the urge to naturalness of William Morris and the decaying flora and fauna of Aubrey Beardsley and Art Nouveau. Conversely, although the almost ubiquitous stars and mountain harmony are phony—in fact, they were co-opted by the Stalinists in the thirties as a ploy of the Popular Front—the electrifying of the instruments is indigenous and the deafening noise is authentically pathetic. So are the strobe lights and the immersion in technologically controlled spaces.

It is hard to describe this, or any, religiosity without lapsing into condescending humor. Yet it is genuine and it will, I am convinced, survive and develop, I don't know into what. In the end, it is religion that constitutes the strength of the new generation. It is not, as I used to think, their morality, political will, or frank common sense. Except for a few, I am not impressed by their moral courage or even honesty. For all their eccentricity, they are quite lacking in personality. They do not have enough world to have strong character. They are not

especially attractive (to me) as animals. But they keep pouring out a kind of metaphysical vitality.

There is a natural cause for religion: impasse. On the one hand, these young have an unusual amount of available psychic energy from childhood. They were brought up on antibiotics that minimized depressing chronic childhood diseases. They had the post-Freudian freedom to act out their early drives and not develop exhausting inhibitions. Up to age six or seven, television nourished them with masses of strange images and sometimes true information; McLuhan makes a lot of sense for the kindergarten years (it is only later that TV diminishes experience). Long schooling would tend to make them stupid, but it has been compensated by providing the vast isolated cities of youth that the high schools and colleges essentially are, where they can incubate their own thoughts. They are sexually precocious and superficially knowledgeable. Nevertheless, all this available psychic energy has had little practical use. The social environment is dehumanized. They cannot use their own initiative. They are desperately bored because the world does not promise any fulfillment—it is the promise, however far-fetched, of fulfillment that makes it possible to be in love. Their kind of knowledge gives no intellectual or poetic satisfaction; it mostly makes them kibitzers.

In this impasse, we can expect a ferment of new religion. As in Greek plays, impasse produces gods from the machine. For a long time we did not hear of the symptoms of adolescent religious conversion, once as common in the United States as in all other places and ages. Now it is recurring as a mass phenomenon.

V

There is no doubt that the religious young are in touch with something historical, but I don't think that they understand what it is. Let me quote from the *New Seminary News*, the newsletter of dissident seminarians from the Pacific School of Religion in Berkeley: "What we confront—willingly or not we are thrust into it—is a time of disintegration of a dying civilization and the emergence of a new one." This seems to envisage something like the instant decline of the Roman Empire, and they, presumably, are like the primitive Christians about to build, out of their hats, another era.

But there are no signs that this is the actual situation. It would mean, for instance, that our scientific technology, civil law, professions, universities, communications, etc., etc., are about to vanish from the earth to be replaced by something entirely different. This is a fantasy of alienated minds. The proposition of the New Seminarians is apocalyptic—the content is St. Mark or St. Paul—but the style and format are conventional. Nobody behaves as if civilization would vanish, and nobody acts as if there were a new dispensation and a new heaven and earth with pneumatic laws. Nobody is waiting patiently in the catacombs and the faithful have not withdrawn into the desert. Neither the Yippies nor the New Seminarians nor any other exalted group have produced anything that is the least bit miraculous. The Yippies promised to levitate the Pentagon, but it did not rise. In A.D. 300 it would have risen six feet while four angels stood at the corners of the world and blew horns; a hundred thousand people would have testified to it. Our civilization may well destroy itself with atom bombs or something else, but then we do not care what will emerge, if anything.

But the actual situation, I have been arguing, *is* very like 1510, when Luther went to Rome, the eve of the Reformation. Everywhere there is protest, conflict, disgust with the Establishment. The protest is international. There is a generation gap. We must recall that Luther himself was all of thirty when he posted the Theses in 1517. Melanchthon was twenty, Bucer twenty-six, Münzer twenty-eight, Jonas twenty-four. The movement consisted of undergraduates and junior faculty.

The main thrust of protest has not been to give up science, technology, and civil institutions, but to purge them, humanize them, decentralize them, change the priorities, stop the drain of wealth. These were the demands of the March 4th teach-in of the dissenting scientists. That event and the waves of other teach-ins, ads, and demonstrations have been the voices not of alienation, of people who have no world, but of protestantism, people deep in the world who will soon refuse to continue under the present auspices because they are not viable. It is a populism permeated by moral and professional unease. What the

young have done is to bring on a religious crisis to make it impossible to continue in such moral unease.

The milieu in which the protest first broke out has been, inevitably, the overgrown monkish school systems. But it is not yet clear to either the protesting students or professors that the essential target of protest is these otiose institutions themselves. In my opinion, much of the student dissent in the colleges and especially the high schools has little to do with the excellent political and social demands that are made, but is the result of boredom and resentment because of the phoniness of the whole academic enterprise.

Viewed as incidents of a Reformation, as attempts of the alienated young to purge themselves and recover lost integrity, the various movements are easily recognizable as characteristic protestant sects, intensely self-conscious. The dissenting seminarians of the Pacific School of Religion or of the Jewish Theological Seminary in New York do not intend to go off to primitive love feasts or back to Father Abraham, but to form their own free seminary; that is, they are Congregationalists. Shaggy hippies are not nature children, as they claim, but self-conscious Adamites trying to naturalize Sausalito and the East Village. Heads are Pentecostals. Those who spindle IBM cards and throw the dean downstairs are Iconoclasts. The critique of the Organization is strongly Jansenist. Those who want a say in the rules and curriculum mean to deny Infant Baptism, like Petrobrusians. Radicals who live among the poor and try to politicize them are certainly intent on social change, but they are also trying to find themselves again, like the young nobles of the Waldenses and Lollards. The support of the black revolt is desperately like Anabaptism, but God grant that we can do better than the Peasants' War. The statement of Cohn-Bendit that I quoted before, that the reason to be a revolutionary is that it is the best way of life at present, is unthinkable from either a political revolutionary or a man imbued with primitive religious faith, but it is hardcore self-conscious protestantism.

These analogies are not fanciful. When authority is discredited, there is a pattern in the return of the repressed. A better scholar could make a longer list; but the reason I here spell it out is that,

perhaps, some young person will suddenly remember that history was about something.

Naturally, traditional churches are themselves in transition. On college campuses and in hobemian neighborhoods, existentialist Protestants and Jews and updating Catholics have taken a place in political and social conflict and, what is more important, they have changed their own moral, esthetic, and personal tone. With excruciating slowness, in a dehumanized society, they are recollecting that religion has some essential relation to human beings, and humanity is in danger. Yet it seems to me that, in their new zeal for relevance, chaplains are badly failing in their chief duty to the religious young, which is to be professors of theology. Because of the generation gap, they certainly cannot perform pastoral services like advice or consolation, which the young insist on doing for themselves. Chaplains say that the young are uninterested in dogma and are intractable on this level, but I think this is simply a projection of their own distaste for the conventional theology that has gone dead for them. The young are hotly metaphysical, but alas, boringly so, because they think the world began yesterday; they have no language to express their intuitions, and they repeat every old fallacy. If the chaplains would stop looking in the conventional places where God is dead, and would explore the actualities where perhaps He is alive, they might learn something and have something to teach.

5.9
The True Christian

Arthur Hoppe

Once upon a time there was a young man named Irwin who devoted his waking hours to Gestalt jogging, transcendental massage, elementary Zoroastrianism, advanced astrology and mastering the Double Lotus position.

Naturally, his parents didn't understand him.

"Irwin," his father would say

Reprinted by permission from the *San Francisco Chronicle*, April 5, 1970. © Chronicle Publishing Co. 1970.

wearily, "I know there's a generation gap. But all these weird religions! Why can't you be more like your mother and me? What's wrong with Christianity?"

"I guess it's that I never tried it, Dad," said Irwin. And being a dutiful son at heart he actually went down to The Billy Graham Crusade the next time it hit town. He came home a drastically changed young man.

"I've heard the call, Dad," he said, his eyes shining. "I've become a true Christian."

"That's great, son," said his father, clapping him on the back. "At last we see eye to eye on things."

"Right, Dad. And you'll be proud to know I've joined The Juniors for Jesus."

"The what?" said his father nervously.

"It's a Christian-action group, Dad," said Irwin, bubbling with the enthusiasm of the young. "Our goal is to see that our loved ones lead true Christian lives so that we may all enter the Kingdom of Heaven together. Now how much did you give to the poor last year?"

"The poor?" said his father uneasily. "Well, we gave $50 to the United Crusade."

Irwin shook his head. "Look, Dad, we've got money in the bank and more food than we can eat, while poor people are going hungry. Remember what the Bible says about a rich man's chances of entering heaven."

So, to encourage Irwin in his new-found faith, his parents agreed to give half their savings and ten per cent of their income to charity. It meant they had to give up their trip to Europe. And Irwin's father did miss his golf club, but it seemed worthwhile.

The next week Irwin's father came home to find his new $35 slacks missing. "Irwin gave them to a magazine solicitor," explained his wife. "The poor man did look a bit threadbare."

Gradually, the family's wardrobe diminished garment by garment. "Actually," explained Irwin happily, a true Christian needs only enough to keep himself warm."

And then half the furniture vanished. "What is a man profited if he shall have two sofas, three end tables and 16 chairs," said Irwin, "and lose his own soul?"

They lost the family car after an accident in which Irwin's father was painfully injured in the left hip. The other party,

though clearly in the wrong, sued. The suit went uncontested. For as Irwin pointed out, it was his father's Christian duty to "turn the other cheek."

Fortunately, just as his parents were reaching wit's end, Irwin picked up a copy of the I Ching, became converted to Ecumenical Taoism and went off to Kathmandu to chew betel nuts and see how long he could grow his toenails.

His parents heaved a collective sigh of relief. "Of course, it was your fault," his mother told his father, "telling him he ought to be a Christian."

"I meant," said his father defensively, "a Christian like us."

Moral: Don't worry about today's generation gap. It could be worse.

5.10
Toward a More Human Society

Kenneth Keniston

If we are to seek values beyond technology, purposes beyond affluence, visions of the good life beyond material prosperity, where are these values, purposes, and visions to be found? Must we, as many secretly fear, await the coming of some new prophet who will create, out of nothing, a new Utopian vision for Americans? Are we condemned to a continuation of technological society until some Messiah arrives to save us?

I believe the answer is closer to home. When, a century ago, Americans began to take seriously the goals of prosperity and freedom from want, these values were not created out of nothing: they had long been part of the Western tradition. What changed was that a dream of the good life previously considered beyond the reach of the ordinary man passed into his hands and was accepted as a concrete goal that could be achieved by ordinary men and women. The turning point at which we stand today requires a similar transla-

From *The Uncommitted: Alienated Youth in American Society.* Copyright © 1962, 1965 by Kenneth Keniston. Reprinted by permission of Harcourt Brace Jovanovich, Inc.

tion of already existing dreams of human fulfillment and social diversity into the concrete goals of individuals and of our society. The values we need are deeply rooted in our own tradition: we must merely begin to take them seriously.

The ideal of full human wholeness is as old as Periclean Athens. But in the course of Western history, this goal could be taken seriously by few men and women: as in Athens, only a small number of the leisured and wealthy, supported by the vast majority of their fellow citizens, attained the freedom from want which is a prerequisite for the implementation of this ancient goal. Even in the Renaissance, when the Greek ideal of full humanity was rediscovered, the vast majority of men and women were far too preoccupied by their incessant struggle against poverty, oppression, and sickness to have time for such lofty ideals. And even today, for most citizens of most nations of the world, the vision of a more harmonious integration of self, a more complete development of talent and ability, must await the attainment of more urgent goals of attaining freedom from want and oppression. Only those who have been able to conquer poverty and tyranny have energy to cultivate their full humanity.

But for those who do not want materially and are not oppressed politically, the quest for fulfillment beyond material goods becomes possible and urgent. There is in human life a hierarchy of needs, such that the higher needs are fully felt when, and only when, the lower needs have been satisfied. Just as thirsty men do not seek food, and the starved have no strength for sex, so freedom from political oppression and material want are prerequisites for any attempt to achieve a more harmonious integration of self, a fuller development of human potentials. Today, in America, and increasingly in other technological nations, these preconditions are rapidly being met: we can now begin to imagine realistically that a whole society might commit itself to the attainment of the greatest possible fulfillment for its members.

To be sure, by the quantitative and reductionistic standards of our technological era, goals like "human wholeness," "personal integration," "the full development of human potentials" are inevitably vague and imprecise. They point to the quality of individual life, rather than to quantitatively measurable entities. Partly for this reason, our knowledge of the sources of human wholeness and fulfillment is woefully inadequate, despite a half-century's systematic study of man. But we do know more than previous generations about the causes of human malformation, distortion, and blighting. Our systematic and scientific knowledge is, no doubt, no more than a confirmation of what a few wise men have intuitively known in the past. But what was heretofore the special wisdom of the sagacious few (which they often carried to their graves) is on the way to becoming communicable public knowledge. Gradually, we are learning to pinpoint the obstacles to full human growth, specifying those especially "lethal" psychological combinations of parentage and social circumstance for children, defining more adequately the antecedents of human pathology, and even at times learning how to intervene positively to foster full human development.

Yet even today, it is far simpler to list the obstacles to full human development, to personal integration, to self-actualization, than to prescribe the precise path to these ancient goals. For just as there are from birth many distinct individuals, each with his own unique genetic and environmental potential, there must remain many paths to fulfillment. Our modern search for a single definition of "maturity" and "positive mental health" that will apply to everyone is probably doomed to failure from the start. Responsiveness, activity, excitability, and even the capacity to learn are not only shaped by the environment, but partly determined by birth. "Fulfillment" depends on individual potential and on social opportunity; human "wholeness" depends on what there is to be made whole.

But though no single definition of human fulfillment is possible, some of its results can be defined. A whole man or woman has the capacity for zest, exuberance, and passion, though this capacity may often be in abeyance. An integrated man does not cease to experience tension, anxiety, and psychic pain, but he is rarely overwhelmed by it. Though all men must at times "close" themselves to that which would be subversive of their commitments, a whole man nonetheless retains the *capacity* for openness, sensitivity, and responsiveness to the world around him: he can always be

surprised because he remains open to that which is alien to himself.

Above all, human wholeness means a capacity for commitment, dedication, passionate concern, and care—a capacity for wholeheartedness and single-mindedness, for abandon without fear of self-annihilation and loss of identity. In psychological terms, this means that a whole man retains contact with his deepest passions at the same time that he remains responsive to his ethical sense. No one psychic potential destroys or subverts the others: his cognitive abilities remain in the service of his commitments, not vice versa; his ethical sense guides rather than tyrannizing over his basic passions; his deepest drives are the sources of his strength but not the dictators of his action. We recognize whole men and women because their wholeness is manifest in their lives: what they do is "of a piece."

If no unitary definition of fulfillment and integration is possible, then a society that is to support these goals must necessarily be a diverse, heterogeneous, pluralistic, and open society. And like the ideal of individual fulfillment, the goal of social diversity is one we have never seriously considered implementing. Although the ideal of political pluralism is entrenched in our liberal tradition, this ideal has most often meant the toleration of political factions, not the encouragement of the full diversity of human talents. Politically, we may tolerate lobbies and believe in political parties; but socially our goals are given by slogans like "Americanization," "the melting pot," and increasingly today "the search for excellence" defined in cognitive terms. Though we think of ourselves as a "tolerant" society, in ordinary speech we most often couple the term "tolerate" with the modifier "barely." All too often, the "tolerance" of Americans is a thin veneer over the discomfort created by all that is different, strange, and alien to them. Once, to be sure, the image of this nation as a vast melting pot suggested the noble vision that the millions of diverse immigrants who came to this shore could be welded into a single coherent nation. But today there is no menace of an America excessively fractured along ethnic, regional or class lines. The current danger is excessive homogeneity, sameness, uniformity. Already ethnic distinctions, regional differences,

even class lines have been blurred beyond recognition in a land where almost everyone lives in the same city apartments and suburban dwellings, eats the same frozen foods and watches the same television programs at the same time on the same networks. Even the current effort of some Americans who are fearful of conformity to be "different," to develop distinctive styles of consumption and life, paralleled by the attempts of advertisers and industry to promote "personalized" and "individualized" products, tends to become only another sign of the homogenization of American society.

Romantic regionalism or the idealization of ethnicity are of course not virtuous in themselves: and even if we chose, distinctions of region and ethnic background could not be naturally preserved. But there *is* an inherent virtue in the appreciation of genuine human differences and the encouragement of a new social diversity based not on region, ancestral origin, class, or race, but on the special accomplishments, potentials, talents, and vital commitments of each individual. Pluralism must be extended from politics to the individual, implemented as a concrete social goal. Human diversity and variety must not only be tolerated, but rejoiced in, applauded, and encouraged.

A society of whole men and women must, then, be a society which encourages diversity, enjoying the differences between men as well as the similarities among them. Social diversity has a double connection to individual fulfillment: not only is a diverse society a precondition for human wholeness, it is its consequence—the kind of society whole men and women choose to live in. Those who are inwardly torn, unsure of their psychic coherence and fearful of inner fragmentation, are naturally distrustful of all that is alien and strange. Those whose sense of inner unity is tenuous are easily threatened by others who remind them of that part of themselves they seek to suppress. Our "one-hundred-per-cent Americans" are those whose own Americanism is felt to be most tenuous; the bigoted and the prejudiced cannot live with the full gamut of their own feelings. And conversely, those who can still sense their shared humanity with others of different or opposite talents and commitments are those who are sure of their own intactness. The goals of human fulfillment and social diversity require each other.

Both of these ideals, I have argued, are ancient ones. They are rooted deep in our Western tradition, and they arise almost spontaneously in those whose material and physical wants have been satisfied. But it remains for us to implement these visions. These are values beyond technology, credal ideals of our civilization which we can now begin to take seriously. Probably for the first time in human history, we can move toward a fullness of life beyond a full larder, human fulfillment beyond material satiation, social diversity beyond consensus.

The Reconstruction of Commitment

History is always made by men, even in an era like ours when men feel they are but the pawns of history. The inability to envision a future different from the present is not a historical imposition but a failure of imagination. It is individuals, not historical trends, that are possessed by a self-confirming sense of social powerlessness. The decision to continue along our present course rather than to take a new turning is still a decision made by men. One way men sometimes have of shaping the future is to be passive and acquiescent before it. Our collective and individual future, then, will inevitably be shaped by us, whether we choose inaction and passivity, regression and romanticism, or action, imagination, and resolve. Men cannot escape their historical role by merely denying its existence. The question is therefore not *whether* Americans will shape their future, but *how* they will shape it.

What is lacking today in America is certainly not the know-how, the imagination, or the intelligence to shape a future better than our present. Nor do we lack the values that might guide the transformation of our society to a more fully human and diverse one. Rather, we lack the conviction that these values might be implemented by ordinary men and women acting in concert for their common good. The Utopian impulse, I have argued, runs deep in all human life, and especially deep in American life. What is needed is to free that impulse once again, to redirect it toward the creation of a better society. We too often attempt to patch up our threadbare values and outworn purposes; we too rarely dare imagine a society radically different from our own.

Proposals for specific reforms are bound to be inadequate by themselves. However desirable, any specific reform will remain an empty intellectual exercise in the absence of a new collective myth, ideology, or Utopian vision. Politically, no potent or lasting change will be possible except as men can be roused from their current alienations by the vision of an attainable society more inviting than that in which they now listlessly live. Behind the need for any specific reform lies the greater need to create an intellectual, ideological, and cultural atmosphere in which it is possible for men to attempt affirmation without undue fear that their Utopian visions will collapse through neglect, ridicule or their own inherent errors. Such an ethos can only be built slowly and piecemeal, yet is it clear what some of its prerequisites must be.

For one, we need a more generous tolerance for synthetic and constructive ideas. Instead of concentrating on the possible bad motives from which they might arise (the genetic fallacy) or on the possible bad consequences which might follow from their misinterpretation (the progenitive fallacy), we must learn to assess them in terms of their present relevance and appropriateness. To accomplish this task will be a double work. Destructively, it will require subverting the methodologies of reduction that now dominate our intellectual life. Constructively, it will require replacing these with more just measures of relevance, subtlety and wisdom, learning to cherish and value the enriching complexity of motives, passions, ethical interests, and facts which will necessarily underlie and support any future vision of the good life.

Secondly, we must reappraise our current concepts and interpretations of man and society. It is characteristic of the intellectual stagnation of our era, an era so obviously different from former times, that we continue to operate with language more appropriate to past generations than to our own. Many of our critiques and interpretations of technological society, including most discussions of alienation, apply more accurately to the America of the 1880's than to the America of the 1960's. We require a radical reanalysis of the human and social present—a reevaluation which, starting from uncritical openness to the experience, joys, and dissatisfactions of men today, can gradually develop

concepts and theories that can more completely comprehend today's world. American society does not lack men and women with the fine discrimination, keen intelligence, and imagination to understand the modern world; but we have yet to focus these talents on our contemporary problems.

But above and beyond a more generous atmosphere and a more adequate understanding of our time, ordinary human courage is needed. To criticize one's society openly requires a strong heart, especially when criticism is interpreted as pathology; only a man of high mettle will propose a new interpretation of the facts now arranged in entrenched categories. And no matter how eagerly the audience awaits or how well prepared the set, only courage can take a performer to the stage. There are many kinds of courage: needed here is the courage to risk being wrong, to risk doing unintentional harm, and, above all, the courage to overcome one's own humility and sense of finite inadequacy. This is not merely a diffuse "courage to be," without protest, in a world of uncertainty, alienation, and anxiety, but the courage to be *for* something despite the perishability and transience of all human endeavors.

Commitment, I have said, is worthy only as its object is worthy. To try to "reconstruct" commitment to American society as it exists today is less than worthy, for our society is shot through with failings, failures, and flaws. It is, as the alienated truly perceive, "trashy, cheap, and commercial"; it is also, as the alienated seldom see, unjust, distorting of human growth and dignity, destructive of diversity. It has allowed itself to be dominated by the instruments of its own triumph over poverty and want, worshiping the values, virtues, and institutions of technology even when these now dominate those they should serve. Only if we can transform the technological process from a master to a servant, harnessing our scientific inventiveness and industrial productivity to the promotion of human fulfillment, will our society be worthy of commitment. And only the vision of a world beyond technology can now inspire the commitment of whole men and women.

America today possesses a vast reservoir of thwarted and displaced idealism; there are millions of men and women who sense vaguely that something is amiss in their lives, who search for something more, and yet who cannot find it. Their idealism will not be easily redirected to the creation of better lives in a better society; it will require imagination, vigor, conviction, and strong voices willing to call for many years, before we dare raise our aspirations beyond vistas of total technology to visions of fuller humanity. But for the first time in American history, and probably in the history of the world, it is conceivable that a whole nation might come to take seriously these ancient and honored visions.

In defining this new vision of life and society, we must remember the quests of the alienated. Though their goals are often confused and inarticulate, they converge on a passionate yearning for openness and immediacy of experience, on an intense desire to create, on a longing to express their perception of the world, and, above all, on a quest for values and commitments that will give their lives coherence. The Inburns of modern American life are often self-defeating; they cannot be taken as exemplars of human integration or fulfillment. But the implicit goals they unsuccessfully seek to attain *are* those of integrated and whole men—openness, creativity, and dedication. Today we need men and women with the wisdom, passion, and courage to transform their private alienations into such public aspirations. We might then begin to move toward a society where such aspirations were more fully realized than in any the world has known.

We can hope for such new commitments in the future only if men now begin to resolve their alienations by committing themselves—through the analysis, synthesis, and reform of their own lives and worlds—to the preparation of such a new society, a society in which whole men and women can play with zest and spontaneity, can work with skill and dedication, can love with passion and care—a society that enjoys diversity and supports human fulfillment.

CONCLUSIONS

Each man can and should be the master of his creations, the sole determinant of his own destiny. What blocks the path? "A social system based on moral corruption and propagated by repression," answer some. They have forgotten that any viable organism is dynamic, that the people who made the system can change it. Others might suggest that factional interests block the road to liberation, that the "other" people, the unenlightened ones, are holding them back. Bullshit. Group interests dominate this society only because the silent majority apathetically relinquishes its power. We need look only at ourselves (not the social system, not other people) for freedom. The psychological revolution begins inside our own heads, when we cast off the shackles of fear, guilt, distrust, hatred. Point that accusing finger at yourself, brother—you are that corrupt social system, you are the "other" people. Change yourself, alter your life style, and you change that system and those people.

Suppose they gave a war and nobody came. Imagine a society geared to individual needs—to explore, to create, to grow, to love. A place where the brotherhood of man became a reality—for God's sake (for mankind's sake), why not? An idle pipe dream? Not necessarily. Alternative life styles, new value systems and moralities are available to those who get high on their own creative potential. Radical reorientation or continued and increasing alienation? The change is possible for those who would seek to know themselves.

REPRINTED COURTESY OF SAWYER PRESS, L.A., CALIF.

Alternate Life Styles

EDITED BY:

Rene Borboa

Lynn Cadwallader

Alan Carlson

Steve Elgar

Ellen Feldheyn

Jean Frazier

Karen Friedland

Hector R. Javkin

Gerald William Lucker

Terje Martinsen

Julian F. Tosky

The answer my friend is blowin' in the wind
The answer is blowin' in the wind.

Bob Dylan
(From "Blowin' in the Wind."
© 1962 by M. Witmark & Sons.
Used by permission of Warner Bros.
Music. All rights reserved.)

INTRODUCTION

America, more than any other nation, is in the process of exhausting the possibilities that technology can offer. The 1960s and the 1970s find us using up most of both the material things and the hopes that the industrial revolution could provide. The belief that developed in the nineteenth century, as exemplified in the London Exposition of 1851 (the greatest good for the greatest number), that the production and distribution of goods could solve our social problems is rapidly fading. There are now "expos" almost every year, in Montreal, Seattle, Osaka, going off and burning themselves out like so many flash bulbs, attempting to catch the last of the enthusiasm over the production of new goods before the enthusiasm disappears.

An era is dying and we are beginning a frantic search for something to replace it. Goods and services can raise our standard of living only if we define our standard of living in terms of goods and services, and we are coming to a realization that they can impoverish life as much as they enrich it. As Marshall McLuhan puts it, we are ". . . people carried about in mechanical vehicles, earning their living by waiting on mechanical machines, listening much of the day to canned music, watching packaged movie entertainment and capsuled news . . ."

The loss of faith in the production of goods is a necessary cleansing. We had to explore what objects could do for us, before really looking at ourselves, because looking at objects was much easier. It is not surprising that the dissatisfaction with the products of technology should occur first in America and first among middle-class youth, who have grown up always possessing those products. In some ways, the aspiration of the middle class and Western youth is one hundred eighty degrees out of phase with the aspirations of the poor and Third World. The poor are still striving for what we have already gotten and don't like very much, and the poor have often been insulted by our contempt for the material things that they have always been denied.

An assistant to Thomas Edison, a man who picked for us many of the fruits of technology, once was discouraged because they had tried 50,000 ways to make the light bulb work and had failed. The great inventor turned to him and said, "Why that's wonderful; now we know 50,000 things that don't work." That knowledge freed him to go on to other possibilities. And so it is with us. Now that we understand that technology cannot solve our social problems, are we possibly free to go on to other possibilities?

We discovered a multitude of responses to the cold reality of America, 1970: hippies in communes, yippies and young politicos, religious cults for Eastern thought, the occult, mysticism, drug experiences, architects who plan buildings according to peoples' psychological needs, and various communities that are working to provide a real sense of togetherness for their members. All of these responses seem to be answering different aspects of society and technology, but each seems to be working toward the preservation of humanity.

A challenge to all of us lies in the following pages. A challenge to learn and understand what different people in our society are creating for themselves and offering to others. Before you lies a challenge that each of us faces: a challenge to question each idea or direction presented; to look into the chaos yourself; to discover how you can deal with the present society and how your own singular life style can and should reflect these discoveries.

6.1
From The Making of a Counter Culture

Theodore Roszak

Technocracy's Children

The struggle of the generations is one of the obvious constants of human affairs. One stands in peril of some presumption, therefore, to suggest that the rivalry between young and adult in Western society during the current decade is uniquely critical. And yet it is necessary to risk such presumption if one is not to lose sight of our most important contemporary source of radical dissent and cultural innovation. For better or worse, most of what is presently happening that is new, provocative, and engaging in politics, education, the arts, social relations (love, courtship, family, community), is the creation either of youth who are profoundly, even fanatically, alienated from the parental generation, or of those who address themselves primarily to the young. It is at the level of youth that significant social criticism now looks for a responsive hearing as, more and more, it grows to be the common expectation that the young should be those who act, who make things happen, who take the risks, who generally provide the ginger. It would be of interest in its own right that the age-old process of generational disaffiliation should now be transformed from a peripheral experience in the life of the individual and the family into a major lever of radical social change. But if one believes, as I do, that the alienated young are giving shape to something that looks like the saving vision our endangered civilization requires, then there is no avoiding the need to understand and to educate them in what they are about.

The reference of this book is primarily to America, but it is headline news that generational antagonism has achieved international dimensions. Throughout the West (as well as in Japan and parts of Latin America) it is the young who find themselves cast as the only effective radical opposition within their societies. Not all the young, of course: perhaps only a minority of the university campus population. Yet no analysis seems to make sense of the major political upheavals of the decade other than that which pits a militant minority of dissenting youth against the sluggish consensus-and-coalition politics of their middle-class elders. This generational dichotomy is a new fact of political life, one which the European young have been more reluctant to accept than their American counterparts. The heirs of an institutionalized left-wing legacy, the young radicals of Europe still tend to see themselves as the champions of "the people" (meaning the working class) against the oppression of the bourgeoisie (meaning, in most cases, their own parents). Accordingly, they try valiantly to adapt themselves to the familiar patterns of the past. They reach out automatically along time-honored ideological lines to find allies—to the workers, the trade unions, the parties of the left . . . only to discover that these expected alliances strangely fail to materialize and that they stand alone and isolated, a vanguard without a following. . . .

Over and again it is the same story throughout Western Europe: the students may rock their societies; but without the support of adult social forces, they cannot overturn the established order.

And that support would seem to be nowhere in sight. On the contrary, the adult social forces—including those of the traditional left—are the lead-bottomed ballast of the status quo. The students march to the Internationale, they run up the red flag, they plaster the barricades with pictures of Marxist heroes old and new . . . but the situation they confront stubbornly refuses to yield to a conventional left-right analysis. Is it any wonder that, in despair, some French students begin to chalk up the disgruntled slogan *"Je suis marxiste, tendance Groucho"* ("I'm a Marxist of the Groucho variety")? At last they are forced to admit that the entrenched consensus which repels their dissent is the generational phenomenon which the French and German young have begun to call "daddy's politics."

If the experience of the American young has anything to contribute to our understanding of this dilemma, it stems precisely from the fact that the left-wing of our political spectrum has always been so pathetically foreshortened. Our young are therefore far less adept at wielding the vintage rhetoric of radicalism than their European counterparts. But where the old categories of social analysis have so little to tell us (or so I will argue here), it becomes a positive advantage to confront the novelty of daddy's politics free of outmoded ideological preconceptions. The result may then be a more flexible, more experimental, though perhaps also a more seemingly bizarre approach to our situation. Ironically, it is the American young, with their underdeveloped radical background, who seem to have grasped most clearly the fact that, while such immediate emergencies as the Vietnam war, racial injustice, and hard-core poverty demand a deal of old-style politicking, the paramount struggle of our day is against a far more formidable, because far less obvious, opponent, to which I will give the name "the technocracy"—a social form more highly developed in America than in any other society. The American young have been somewhat quicker to sense that in the struggle against *this* enemy, the conventional tactics of political resistance have only a marginal place, largely limited to meeting immediate life-and-death crises. Beyond such front-line issues, however, there lies the greater task of altering the total cultural

context within which our daily politics takes place.[1]

By the technocracy, I mean that social form in which an industrial society reaches the peak of its organizational integration. It is the ideal men usually have in mind when they speak of modernizing, up-dating, rationalizing, planning. Drawing upon such unquestionable imperatives as the demand for efficiency, for social security, for large-scale co-ordination of men and resources, for ever higher levels of affluence and ever more impressive manifestations of collective human power, the technocracy works to knit together the anachronistic gaps and fissures of the industrial society. The meticulous systematization Adam Smith once celebrated in his well-known pin factory now extends to all areas of life, giving us human organization that matches the precision of our mechanistic organization. So we arrive at the era of social engineering in which entrepreneurial talent broadens its province to orchestrate the total human context which surrounds the industrial complex. Politics, education, leisure, entertainment, culture as a whole, the unconscious drives, and even, as we shall see, protest against the tech-

[1] For a comparison of American and European student radicalism along the lines drawn here, see Gianfranco Corsini, "A Generation Up in Arms," *The Nation,* June 10, 1968.

Daniel Cohn-Bendit and his spontaneous revolutionaries in France are something of an exception to what I say here about the young European radicals. Cohn-Bendit's anarchist instincts (which greatly riled the old-line leftist student groups during the May 1968 troubles) provide him with a healthy awareness of "the bureaucratic phenomenon" in modern industrial society and of the way in which it has subtly eroded the revolutionary potential of the working class and of its official left-wing leadership. He therefore warns strongly against "hero-worshipping" the workers. But even so, he continues to conceive of "the people" as the workers, and of the workers as the allies and sparkplugs. This leads him to the conclusion that the subversion of the status quo need not await a total cultural transformation, but can be pulled off by "insurrectional cells" and "nuclei of confrontation" whose purpose is to set an example for the working class. See Daniel and Gabriel Cohn-Bendit, *Obsolete Communism: The Left-Wing Alternative* (New York: McGraw-Hill, 1969), especially the keen analysis of the working partnership between "empiricist-positivist" sociology and technocratic manipulation, pp. 35–40.

nocracy itself: all these become the subjects of purely technical scrutiny and of purely technical manipulation. The effort is to create a new social organism whose health depends upon its capacity to keep the technological heart beating regularly. In the words of Jacques Ellul:

Technique requires predictability and, no less, exactness of prediction. It is necessary, then, that technique prevail over the human being. For technique, this is a matter of life and death. Technique must reduce man to a technical animal, the king of the slaves of technique. Human caprice crumbles before this necessity; there can be no human autonomy in the face of technical autonomy. The individual must be fashioned by techniques, either negatively (by the techniques of understanding man) or positively (by the adaptation of man to the technical framework), in order to wipe out the blots his personal determination introduces into the perfect design of the organization.[2]

In the technocracy, nothing is any longer small or simple or readily apparent to the non-technical man. Instead, the scale and intricacy of all human activities— political, economic, cultural— transcends the competence of the amateurish citizen and inexorably demands the attention of specially trained experts. Further, around this central core of experts who deal with large-scale public necessities, there grows up a circle of subsidiary experts who, battening on the general social prestige of technical skill in the technocracy, assume authoritative influence over even the most seemingly personal aspects of life: sexual behavior, child-rearing, mental health, recreation, etc. In the technocracy everything aspires to become purely technical, the subject of professional attention. The regime of experts—or of those who can employ the experts. Among its key institutions we find the "think-tank," in which is housed a multi-billion-dollar brainstorming industry that seeks to anticipate and integrate into the social planning quite simply everything on the scene. Thus, even before the general public has become fully aware of new developments, the technocracy has doped them out and laid its plans

[2] Jacques Ellul, *The Technological Society*, trans. John W. Wilkinson (New York: A. A. Knopf, 1964), p. 138. This outrageously pessimistic book is thus far the most global effort to depict the technocracy in full operation.

for adopting or rejecting, promoting or disparaging.[3]

Within such a society, the citizen, confronted by bewildering bigness and complexity, finds it necessary to defer on all matters to those who know better. Indeed, it would be a violation of reason to do otherwise, since it is universally agreed that the prime goal of the society is to keep the productive apparatus turning over efficiently. In the absence of expertise, the great mechanism would surely bog down, leaving us in the midst of chaos and poverty. As we will see in later chapters, the roots of the technocracy reach deep into our cultural past and are ultimately entangled in the scientific world-view of the Western tradition. But for our purposes here it will be enough to define the technocracy as that society in which those who govern justify themselves by appeal to technical experts who, in turn, justify themselves by appeal to scientific forms of knowledge. And beyond the authority of science, there is no appeal.

Understood in these terms, as the mature product of technological progress and the scientific ethos, the technocracy easily eludes all traditional political categories. Indeed, it is characteristic of the technocracy to render itself ideologically invisible. Its assumptions about reality and its values become as unobtrusively pervasive as the air we breathe. While daily political argument continues within and between the capitalist and collectivist societies of the world, the technocracy increases and consolidates its power in both as a transpolitical phenomenon following the dictates of industrial efficiency, rationality, and necessity. In all these arguments, the technocracy assumes a position similar to that of the purely neutral umpire in an athletic contest. The umpire is normally the least obtrusive person on the scene. Why? Because we give our attention and passionate allegiance to the teams, who compete within the rules; we tend to ignore the man who stands above the contest and who simply interprets and en-

[3] For a report on the activities of a typical technocratic brain trust, Herman Kahn's Hudson Institute, see Bowen Northrup's "They Think for Pay" in *The Wall Street Journal*, September 20, 1967. Currently, the Institute is developing strategies to integrate hippies and to exploit the new possibilities of programmed dreams.

forces the rules. Yet, in a sense, the umpire is the most significant figure in the game, since he alone sets the limits and goals of the competition and judges the contenders. . . .

When any system of politics devours the surrounding culture, we have totalitarianism, the attempt to bring the whole of life under authoritarian control. We are bitterly familiar with totalitarian politics in the form of brutal regimes which achieve their integration by bludgeon and bayonet. But in the case of the technocracy, totalitarianism is perfected because its techniques become progressively more subliminal. The distinctive feature of the regime of experts lies in the fact that, while possessing ample power to coerce, it prefers to charm conformity from us by exploiting our deep-seated commitment to the scientific world-view and by manipulating the securities and creature comforts of the industrial affluence which science has given us.

So subtle and so well rationalized have the arts of technocratic domination become in our advanced industrial societies that even those in the state and/or corporate structure who dominate our lives must find it impossible to conceive of themselves as the agents of a totalitarian control. Rather, they easily see themselves as the conscientious managers of a munificent social system which is, by the very fact of its broadest affluence, incompatible with any form of exploitation. . . .

The great secret of the technocracy lies, then, in its capacity to convince us of three interlocking premises. They are:

1. That the vital needs of man are (contrary to everything the great souls of history have told us) purely technical in character. Meaning: the requirements of our humanity yield wholly to some manner of formal analysis which can be carried out by specialists possessing certain impenetrable skills and which can then be translated by them directly into a congeries of social and economic programs, personnel management procedures, merchandise, and mechanical gadgetry. If a problem does not have such a technical solution, it must not be a *real* problem. It is but an illusion . . . a figment born of some regressive cultural tendency.

2. That this formal (and highly esoteric) analysis of our needs has now achieved 99 per cent completion. Thus, with minor hitches and snags on the part of irrational elements in our midst, the prerequisites of human fulfillment have all but been satisfied. It is this assumption which leads to the conclusion that wherever social friction appears in the technocracy, it must be due to what is called a "breakdown in communication." For where human happiness has been so precisely calibrated and where the powers that be are so utterly well intentioned, controversy could not possibly derive from a substantive issue, but only from misunderstanding. Thus we need only sit down and reason together and all will be well.

3. That the experts who have fathomed our heart's desires and who alone can continue providing for our needs, the experts who *really* know what they're talking about, all happen to be on the official payroll of the state and/or corporate structure. The experts who count are the certified experts. And the certified experts belong to headquarters.

One need not strain to hear the voice of the technocrat in our society. It speaks strong and clear, and from high places. For example:

Today these old sweeping issues have largely disappeared. The central domestic problems of our time are more subtle and less simple. They relate not to basic clashes of philosophy or ideology, but to ways and means of reaching common goals— to research for sophisticated solutions to complex and obstinate issues. . . .
What is at stake in our economic decisions today is not some grand warfare of rival ideologies which will sweep the country with passion, but the practical management of a modern economy. What we need are not labels and cliches but more basic discussion of the sophisticated and technical questions involved in keeping a great economic machinery moving ahead. . . .
I am suggesting that the problems of fiscal and monetary policy in the Sixties as opposed to the kinds of problems we faced in the Thirties demand subtle challenges for which technical answers—not political answers—must be provided.[4]

Such statements, uttered by obviously competent, obviously enlightened leadership, make abun-

[4] John F. Kennedy, "Yale University Commencement Speech," *The New York Times*, June 12, 1962, p. 20.

dantly clear the prime strategy of the technocracy. It is to level life down to a standard of so-called living that technical expertise can cope with—and then, on that false and exclusive basis, to claim an intimidating omnicompetence over us by its monopoly of the experts. Such is the politics of our mature industrial societies, our truly *modern* societies, where two centuries of aggressive secular skepticism, after ruthlessly eroding the traditionally transcendent ends of life, has concomitantly given us a proficiency of technical means that now oscillates absurdly between the production of frivolous abundance and the production of genocidal munitions.
. . .

In his analysis of this "new authoritarianism," Herbert Marcuse calls our attention especially to the technocracy's "absorbent power": its capacity to provide "satisfaction in a way which generates submission and weakens the rationality of protest." As it approaches maturity, the technocracy does indeed seem capable of anabolizing every form of discontent into its system.

Let us take the time to consider one significant example of such "repressive desublimation" (as Marcuse calls it). The problem is sexuality, traditionally one of the most potent sources of civilized man's discontent. To liberate sexuality would be to create a society in which technocratic discipline would be impossible. But to thwart sexuality outright would create a widespread, explosive resentment that required constant policing; and, besides, this would associate the technocracy with various puritanical traditions that enlightened men cannot but regard as superstitious. The strategy chosen, therefore, is not harsh repression, but rather the *Playboy* version of total permissiveness which now imposes its image upon us in every slick movie and posh magazine that comes along. In the affluent society, we have sex and sex galore—or so we are to believe. But when we look more closely we see that this sybaritic promiscuity wears a special social coloring. It has been assimilated to an income level and social status available only to our well-heeled junior executives and the jet set. After all, what does it cost to rent these yachts full of nymphomaniacal young things in which our playboys sail off for orgiastic swimming parties in the Bahamas? *Real* sex, we are led to believe, is something that goes

with the best scotch, twenty-seven-dollar sunglasses, and platinum-tipped shoelaces. Anything less is a shabby substitute. Yes, there is permissiveness in the technocratic society; but it is only for the swingers and the big spenders. It is the reward that goes to reliable, politically safe henchmen of the status quo. Before our would-be playboy can be an assembly-line seducer, he must be a loyal employee.

Moreover, *Playboy* sexuality is, ideally, casual, frolicsome, and vastly promiscuous. It is the anonymous sex of the harem. It creates no binding loyalties, no personal attachments, no distractions from one's primary responsibilities— which are to the company, to one's career and social position, and to the system generally. The perfect playboy practices a career enveloped by noncommittal trivialities: there is no home, no family, no romance that divides the heart painfully. Life off the job exhausts itself in a constant run of imbecile affluence and impersonal orgasms.

Finally, as a neat little dividend, the ideal of the swinging life we find in *Playboy* gives us a conception of femininity which is indistinguishable from social idiocy. The woman becomes a mere playmate, a submissive bunny, a mindless decoration. At a stroke, half the population is reduced to being the inconsequential entertainment of the technocracy's pampered elite.

As with sexuality, so with every other aspect of life. The business of inventing and flourishing treacherous parodies of freedom, joy, and fulfillment becomes an indispensable form of social control under the technocracy. In all walks of life, image makers and public relations specialists assume greater and greater prominence. The regime of experts relies on a lieutenancy of counterfeiters who seek to integrate the discontent born of thwarted aspiration by way of clever falsification.

Thus:
We call it "education," the "life of the mind," the "pursuit of the truth." But it is a matter of machine-tooling the young to the needs of our various baroque bureaucracies: corporate, governmental, military, trade union, educational.
We call it "free enterprise." But it is a vastly restrictive system of oligopolistic market manipulation, tied by institutionalized corruption to the greatest munitions boondoggle in history and dedicated to infantilizing the public by turning

it into a herd of compulsive consumers.

We call it "creative leisure": finger painting and ceramics in the university extension, tropic holidays, grand athletic excursions to the far mountains and the sunny beaches of the earth. But it is, like our sexual longings, an expensive adjunct of careerist high-achievement: the prize that goes to the dependable hireling.

We call it "pluralism." But it is a matter of the public authorities solemnly affirming everybody's right to his own opinion as an excuse for ignoring anybody's troubling challenge. In such a pluralism, critical viewpoints become mere private prayers offered at the altar of an inconsequential conception of free speech.

We call it "democracy." But it is a matter of public opinion polling in which a "random sample" is asked to nod or wag the head in response to a set of prefabricated alternatives, usually related to the *faits accompli* of decision makers, who can always construe the polls to serve their own ends. Thus, if 80 per cent think it is a "mistake" that we ever "went into" Vietnam, but 51 per cent think we would "lose prestige" if we "pulled out now," then the "people" have been "consulted" and the war goes on with their "approval."

We call it "debate." But it is a matter of arranging staged encounters between equally noncommittal candidates neatly tailored to fit thirty minutes of prime network time, the object of the exercise being to establish an "image" of competence. If there are interrogators present, they have been hand-picked and their questions rehearsed.

We call it "government by the consent of the governed." But even now, somewhere in the labyrinth of the paramilitary agencies an "area specialist" neither you nor I elected is dispatching "special advisors" to a distant "trouble spot" which will be the next Vietnam. And somewhere in the depths of the oceans a submarine commander neither you nor I elected is piloting a craft equipped with firepower capable of cataclysmic devastation and perhaps trying to decide if—for reasons neither you nor I know—the time has come to push the button.

It is all called being "free," being "happy," being the Great Society.

From the standpoint of the traditional left, the vices of contemporary America we mention here are easily explained—and indeed too easily. The evils stem simply from the unrestricted pursuit of profit. Behind the manipulative deceptions there are capitalist desperados holding up the society for all the loot they can lay hands on.

To be sure, the desperados are there, and they are a plague of the society. For a capitalist technocracy, profiteering will always be a central incentive and major corrupting influence. Yet even in our society, profit taking no longer holds its primacy as an evidence of organizational success, as one might suspect if for no other reason than that our largest industrial enterprises can now safely count on an uninterrupted stream of comfortably high earnings. At this point, considerations of an entirely different order come into play among the managers, as Seymour Melman reminds us when he observes:

> The "fixed" nature of industrial investment represented by machinery and structures means that large parts of the costs of any accounting period must be assigned in an arbitrary way. Hence, the magnitude of profits shown in any accounting period varies entirely according to the regulations made by the management itself for assigning its "fixed" charges. Hence, profit has ceased to be the economists' independent measure of success or failure of the enterprise. We can define the systematic quality in the behavior and management of large industrial enterprises not in terms of profits, but in terms of their acting to maintain or to extend the production decision power they wield. Production decision power can be gauged by the number of people employed, or whose work is directed, by the proportion of given markets that a management dominates, by the size of the capital investment that is controlled, by the number of other managements whose decisions are controlled. Toward these ends profits are an instrumental device—subordinated in given accounting periods to the extension of decision power.[5]

In the example given above of *Playboy* permissiveness, the instruments used to integrate sexuality into industrial rationality have to do with high income and extravagant merchandising. Under the Nazis, however, youth camps and party courtesans were used for the same integrative purpose—as were the concentration camps, where the kinkier members of the elite were rewarded by being allowed free exercise of their tastes. In this case, sexual freedom was not assimilated to income level or prestige consumption, but to party privilege. If the communist regimes of the world have not yet found ways to institutionalize sexual permissiveness, it is because the party organizations are still under the control of grim old men whose puritanism dates back to the days of primitive accumulation. But can we doubt that once these dismal characters pass from the scene—say, when we have a Soviet version of Kennedy-generation leadership—we shall hear of topless bathing parties at the Black Sea resorts and of orgiastic goings-on in the *dachas*? By then, the good apparatchiks and industrial commissars will also acquire the perquisite of admission to the swinging life.

It is essential to realize that the technocracy is not the exclusive product of that old devil capitalism. Rather, it is the product of a mature and accelerating industrialism. The profiteering could be eliminated; the technocracy would remain in force. The key problem we have to deal with is the paternalism of expertise within a socioeconomic system which is so organized that it is inextricably beholden to expertise. And, moreover, to an expertise which has learned a thousand ways to manipulate our acquiescence with an imperceptible subtlety. . . .

How do the traditional left-wing ideologies equip us to protest against such well-intentioned use of up-to-date technical expertise for the purpose of making our lives more comfortable and secure? The answer is: they don't. After all, locked into this leviathan industrial apparatus as we are, where shall we turn for solutions to our dilemmas if not to the experts? Or are we, at this late stage of the game, to relinquish our trust in science? in reason? in the technical intelligence that built the system in the first place?

It is precisely to questions of this order that the dissenting young address themselves in manifestoes like this one pinned to the main entrance of the embattled Sorbonne in May 1968:

> The revolution which is beginning will call in question not only capitalist society but industrial society. The consumer's society must perish of a violent death. The society of alienation must disappear from history. We are inventing a new and original world. Imagination is seizing power.[6]

[5] Seymour Melman, "Priorities and the State Machine," *New University Thought*, Winter 1966–67, pp. 17–18.

[6] From *The Times* (London), May 17, 1968: Edward Mortimer's report from Paris.

Why should it be the young who rise most noticeably in protest against the expansion of the technocracy?

There is no way around the most obvious answer of all: the young stand forth so prominently because they act against a background of nearly pathological passivity on the part of the adult generation. It would only be by reducing our conception of citizenship to absolute zero that we could get our senior generation off the hook for its astonishing default. The adults of the World War II period, trapped as they have been in the frozen posture of befuddled docility—the condition Paul Goodman has called "the nothing can be done disease"—have in effect divested themselves of their adulthood, if that term means anything more than being tall and debt-worried and capable of buying liquor without having to show one's driver's license. Which is to say: they have surrendered their responsibility for making morally demanding decisions, for generating ideals, for controlling public authority, for safeguarding the society against its despoilers.

Why and how this generation lost control of the institutions that hold sway over its life is more than we can go into here. The remembered background of economic collapse in the thirties, the grand distraction and fatigue of the war, the pathetic if understandable search for security and relaxation afterwards, the bedazzlement of the new prosperity, a sheer defensive numbness in the face of thermonuclear terror and the protracted state of international emergency during the late forties and fifties, the red-baiting and witch-hunting and out-and-out barbarism of the McCarthy years . . . no doubt all these played their part. And there is also the rapidity and momentum with which technocratic totalitarianism came rolling out of the war years and the early cold war era, drawing on heavy wartime industrial investments, the emergency centralization of decision making, and the awe-stricken public reverence for science. The situation descended swiftly and ponderously. Perhaps no society could have kept its presence of mind; certainly ours didn't. And the failure was not only American. Nicola Chiaromonte, seeking to explain the restiveness of Italian youth, observes,

. . . the young—those born after 1940—find themselves living in a society that neither commands nor deserves respect. . . . For has modern man, in his collective existence, laid claim to any god or ideal but the god of possession and enjoyment and the limitless satisfaction of material needs? Has he put forward any reason for working but the reward of pleasure and prosperity? Has he, in fact, evolved anything but this "consumer society" that is so easily and falsely repudiated?[7]

On the American scene, this was the parental generation whose god Allen Ginsberg identified back in the mid-fifties as the sterile and omnivorous "Moloch." It is the generation whose premature senility Dwight Eisenhower so marvelously incarnated and the disease of whose soul shone so lugubriously through the public obscenities that men like John Foster Dulles and Herman Kahn and Edward Teller were prepared to call "policy." There are never many clear landmarks in affairs of the spirit, but Ginsberg's *Howl* may serve as the most public report announcing the war of the generations. It can be coupled with a few other significant phenomena. One of them would be the appearance of *MAD* magazine, which has since become standard reading material for the junior high school population. True, the dissent of *MAD* often sticks at about the Katzenjammer Kids level: but nevertheless the nasty cynicism *MAD* began applying to the American way of life—politics, advertising, mass media, education—has had its effect. *MAD* brought into the malt shops the same angry abuse of middle-class America which comics like Mort Sahl and Lenny Bruce were to begin bringing into the night clubs of the mid-fifties. The kids who were twelve when *MAD* first appeared are in their early twenties now—and they have had a decade's experience in treating the stuff of their parents' lives as contemptible laughing stock.

At a more significant intellec-

[7] The "falsely" in this quotation relates to Chiaromonte's very astute analysis of a doctrinaire blind spot in the outlook of Italian youth—namely their tendency to identify the technocracy with capitalism, which, as I have suggested, is a general failing of European youth movements. This very shrewd article appears in *Encounter*, July 1968, pp. 25–27. Chiaromonte does not mention the factor of fascism in Italy, but certainly in Germany the cleavage between young and old has been driven deeper than anything we know in America by the older generation's complicity with Nazism.

tual level, Ginsberg and the beatniks can be associated chronologically with the aggressively activist sociology of C. Wright Mills—let us say with the publication of Mills' *Causes of World War III* (1957), which is about the point at which Mills' writing turned from scholarship to first-class pamphleteering. Mills was by no means the first postwar figure who sought to tell it like it is about the state of American public life and culture; the valiant groups that maintained radical journals like *Liberation* and *Dissent* had been filling the wilderness with their cries for quite as long. And as far back as the end of the war, Paul Goodman and Dwight Macdonald were doing an even shrewder job of analyzing technocratic America than Mills was ever to do—and without relinquishing their humanitarian tone. But it was Mills who caught on. His tone was more blatant; his rhetoric, catchier. He was the successful academic who suddenly began to cry for action in a lethargic profession, in a lethargic society. He was prepared to step forth and brazenly pin his indictment like a target to the enemy's chest. And by the time he finished playing Emile Zola he had marked out just about everybody in sight for accusation.

Most important, Mills was lucky enough to discover ears that would hear: his indignation found an audience. But the New Left he was looking for when he died in 1961 did not appear among his peers. It appeared among the students—and just about nowhere else. If Mills were alive today, his following would still be among the under thirties (though the Vietnam war has brought a marvelous number of his academic colleagues out into open dissent—but will they stay out when the war finally grinds to its ambiguous finish?).

Admittedly, the dissent that began to simmer in the mid-fifties was not confined to the young. The year 1957 saw the creation at the adult level of resistance efforts like SANE and, a bit later, Turn Toward Peace. But precisely what do groups like SANE and TTP tell us about adult America, even where we are dealing with politically conscious elements? Looking back, one is struck by their absurd shallowness and conformism, their total unwillingness to raise fundamental issues about the quality of American life, their fastidious anticommunism, and above all their incapacity to sustain any significant initiative on the political landscape. Even the Committee of Correspondence, a promising effort on the part of senior academics (formed around 1961) quickly settled for publishing a new journal. Currently the diminishing remnants of SANE and TTP seem to have been reduced to the role of carping (often with a deal of justice) at the impetuous extremes and leftist flirtations of far more dynamic youth groups like the Students for a Democratic Society, or the Berkeley Vietnam Day Committee, or the 1967 Spring Mobilization. But avuncular carping is not initiative. And it is a bore, even if a well-intentioned bore, when it becomes a major preoccupation. Similarly, it is the younger Negro groups that have begun to steal the fire from adult organizations —but in this case with results that I feel are apt to be disastrous.

The fact is, it is the young who have in their own amateurish, even grotesque way, gotten dissent off the adult drawing board. They have torn it out of the books and journals an older generation of radicals authored, and they have fashioned it into a style of life. They have turned the hypotheses of disgruntled elders into experiments, though often without the willingness to admit that one may have to concede failure at the end of any true experiment.

When all is said and done, however, one cannot help being ambivalent toward this compensatory dynamism of the young. For it is, at last, symptomatic of a thoroughly diseased state of affairs. It is not ideal, it is probably not even good that the young should bear so great a responsibility for inventing or initiating for their society as a whole. It is too big a job for them to do successfully. It is indeed tragic that in a crisis that demands the tact and wisdom of maturity, everything that looks most hopeful in our culture should be building from scratch—as must be the case when the builders are absolute beginners.

Beyond the parental default, there are a number of social and psychic facts of life that help explain the prominence of the dissenting young in our culture. In a number of ways, this new generation happens to be particularly well placed and primed for action. Most obviously, the society is getting younger—to the extent that in America, as in a number of European countries, a bit more than 50 per cent of the population is under twenty-five years of age. Even if one grants that people in

their mid-twenties have no business claiming, or letting themselves be claimed for the status of "youth," there still remains among the authentically young in the thirteen to nineteen bracket a small nation of twenty-five million people. (As we shall see below, however, there is good reason to group the mid-twenties with their adolescent juniors.)

But numbers alone do not account for the aggressive prominence of contemporary youth. More important, the young seem to *feel* the potential power of their numbers as never before. No doubt to a great extent this is because the market apparatus of our consumer society has devoted a deal of wit to cultivating the age-consciousness of old and young alike. Teen-agers alone control a stupendous amount of money and enjoy much leisure; so, inevitably, they have been turned into a self-conscious market. They have been pampered, exploited, idolized, and made almost nauseatingly much of. With the result that whatever the young have fashioned for themselves has rapidly been rendered grist for the commercial mill and cynically merchandised by assorted hucksters—including the new ethos of dissent, a fact that creates an agonizing disorientation for the dissenting young (and their critics) and to which we will return presently.

The force of the market has not been the only factor in intensifying age-consciousness, however. The expansion of higher education has done even more in this direction. In the United States we have a college population of nearly six million, an increase of more than double over 1950. And the expansion continues as college falls more and more into the standard educational pattern of the middle-class young.[8] Just as

[8] The rapid growth of the college population is an international phenomenon, with Germany, Russia, France, Japan, and Czechoslovakia (among the developed countries) equaling or surpassing the increase of the United States. UNESCO statistics for the period 1950–64 are as follows:

	1950	1964	Increase
U.S.A.	2.3 million	5 million	2.2x
U.K.	133,000	211,000	1.6x
U.S.S.R.	1.2 million	3.6 million	3.0x
Italy	192,000	262,000	1.3x
France	140,000	455,000	3.3x
W. Germany	123,000	343,000	2.8x
W. Berlin	12,000	31,000	2.6x
Czechoslovakia	44,000	142,000	3.2x
Japan	391,000	917,000	2.3x
India	404,000	1.1 million	2.2x

the dark satanic mills of early industrialism concentrated labor and helped create the class-consciousness of the proletariat, so the university campus, where up to thirty thousand students may be gathered, has served to crystallize the group identity of the young—with the important effect of mingling freshmen of seventeen and eighteen with graduate students well away in their twenties. On the major campuses, it is often enough the graduates who assume positions of leadership, contributing to student movements a degree of competence that the younger students could not muster. When one includes in this alliance that significant new entity, the non-student—the campus roustabout who may be in his late twenties—one sees why "youth" has become such a long-term career these days. The grads and the non-students easily come to identify their interests and allegiance with a distinctly younger age group. In previous generations, they would long since have left these youngsters behind. But now they and the freshmen just out of high school find themselves all together in one campus community.

The role of these campus elders is crucial, for they tend to be those who have the most vivid realization of the new economic role of the university. Being closer to the technocratic careers for which higher education is supposed to be grooming them in the Great Society, they have a delicate sensitivity to the social regimentation that imminently confronts them, and a stronger sense of the potential power with which the society's need for trained personnel endows them. In some cases their restiveness springs from a bread-and-butter awareness of the basic facts of educational life these days, for in England, Germany, and France the most troublesome students are those who have swelled the numbers in the humanities and social studies only to discover that what the society really wants out of its schools is technicians, not philosophers. In Britain, this strong trend away from the sciences over the past four years continues to provoke annoyed concern from public figures who are not the least bit embarrassed to reveal their good bourgeois philistinism by loudly observing that the country is not spending its money to produce poets and Egyptologists— and then demanding a sharp cut in university grants and stipends.[9] . . .

The troubles at Berkeley in late 1966 illustrate the expansiveness of youthful protest. To begin with, a group of undergraduates stages a sit-in against naval recruiters at the Student Union. They are soon joined by a contingent of non-students, whom the administration then martyrs by selective arrest. A non-student of nearly thirty—Mario Savio, already married and a father—is quickly adopted as spokesman for the protest. Finally, the teaching assistants call a strike in support of the menaced demonstration. When at last the agitation comes to its ambiguous conclusion, a rally of thousands gathers outside Sproul Hall, the central administration building, to sing the Beatles' "Yellow Submarine"—which happens to be the current hit on all the local high-school campuses. If "youth" is not the word we are going to use to cover this obstreperous population, then we may have to coin another. But undeniably the social grouping exists with a self-conscious solidarity.

If we ask who is to blame for such troublesome children, there can be only one answer: it is the parents who have equipped them with an anemic superego. The current generation of students is the beneficiary of the particularly permissive child-rearing habits that have been a feature of our postwar society. Dr. Spock's endearing latitudinarianism (go easy on the toilet training, don't panic over masturbation, avoid the heavy discipline) is much more a reflection than a cause of the new (and wise) conception of proper parent-child relations that prevails in our middle class. A high-consumption, leisure-wealthy society simply doesn't need contingents of rigidly trained, "responsible" young workers. It cannot employ more than a fraction of untrained youngsters fresh out of high school. The middle class can therefore afford to prolong the ease and drift of childhood, and so it does. Since nobody expects a child to learn any marketable skills until he gets to college, high school becomes a country club for which the family pays one's dues. Thus the young are "spoiled," meaning they are influenced to

believe that being human has something to do with pleasure and freedom. But unlike their parents, who are also avid for the plenty and leisure of the consumer society, the young have not had to sell themselves for their comforts or to accept them on a part-time basis. Economic security is something they can take for granted—and on it they build a new, uncompromised personality, flawed perhaps by irresponsible ease, but also touched with some outspoken spirit. Unlike their parents, who must kowtow to the organizations from which they win their bread, the youngsters can talk back at home with little fear of being thrown out in the cold. One of the pathetic, but, now we see, promising characteristics of postwar America has been the uppityness of adolescents and the concomitant reduction of the paterfamilias to the general ineffectuality of a Dagwood Bumstead. In every family comedy of the last twenty years, dad has been the buffoon.

The permissiveness of postwar child-rearing has probably seldom met A. S. Neill's standards—but it has been sufficient to arouse expectations. As babies, the middle-class young got picked up when they bawled. As children, they got their kindergarten finger paintings thumbtacked on the living room wall by mothers who knew better than to discourage incipient artistry. As adolescents, they perhaps even got a car of their own (or control of the family's), with all of the sexual privileges attending. They passed through school systems which, dismal as they all are in so many respects, have nevertheless prided themselves since World War II on the introduction of "progressive" classes having to do with "creativity" and "self-expression." These are also the years that saw the proliferation of all the mickey mouse courses which take the self-indulgence of adolescent "life problems" so seriously. Such scholastic pap mixes easily with the commercial world's effort to elaborate a total culture of adolescence based on nothing but fun and games. (What else could a culture of adolescence be based on?) The result has been to make of adolescence, not the beginning of adulthood, but a status in its own right: a limbo that is nothing so much as the prolongation of an already permissive infancy.

To be sure, such an infantization of the middle-class young has a corrupting effect. It ill prepares them for the real world and its

unrelenting if ever more subtle disciplines. It allows them to nurse childish fantasies until too late in life; until there comes the inevitable crunch. For as life in the multiversity wears on for these pampered youngsters, the technocratic reality principle begins grimly to demand its concessions. The young get told they are now officially "grown up," but they have been left too long without any taste for the rigidities and hypocrisies that adulthood is supposed to be all about. General Motors all of a sudden wants barbered hair, punctuality, and an appropriate reverence for the conformities of the organizational hierarchy. Washington wants patriotic cannon fodder with no questions asked. Such prospects do not look like fun from the vantage point of between eighteen and twenty years of relatively carefree drifting.[10]

Some of the young (most of them, in fact) summon up the proper sense of responsibility to adjust to the prescribed patterns of adulthood; others, being incorrigibly childish, do not. They continue to assert pleasure and freedom as human rights and begin to ask aggressive questions of those forces that insist, amid obvious affluence, on the continued necessity of discipline, no matter how subliminal. This is why, for example, university administrators are forced to play such a false game with their students, insisting on the one hand that the students are "grown-up, responsible men and women," but on the other hand knowing full well that they dare not entrust such erratic children with any power over their own education. For what can one rely upon them to do that will suit the needs of technocratic regimentation?

The incorrigibles either turn political or drop out. Or perhaps they fluctuate between the two, restless, bewildered, hungry for better ideas about grown-upness than GM or IBM or LBJ seem able to offer. Since they are improvising their own ideal of adulthood— a task akin to lifting oneself by

[9] In his 1967 Reith Lectures, Dr. Edmund Leach seeks to account for the steady swing from the sciences. See his *Runaway World*, British Broadcasting Company, 1968. For reflections on the same phenomenon in Germany, see Max Beloff's article in *Encounter*, July 1968, pp. 28–33.

[10] Even the Young Americans for Freedom, who staunchly champion the disciplined virtues of the corporate structure, have become too restive to put up with the indignity of conscription. With full support from Ayn Rand, they have set the draft down as "selective slavery." How long will it be before a conservatism that perceptive recognizes that the ideal of free enterprise has nothing to do with technocratic capitalism?

one's bootstraps—it is all too easy to go pathetically wrong. Some become ne'er-do-well dependents, bumming about the bohemias of America and Europe on money from home; others simply bolt. The FBI reports the arrest of over ninety thousand juvenile runaways in 1966; most of those who flee well-off middle-class homes get picked up by the thousands each current year in the big-city bohemias, fending off malnutrition and venereal disease. The immigration departments of Europe record a constant level over the past few years of something like ten thousand disheveled "flower children" (mostly American, British, German, and Scandinavian) migrating to the Near East and India—usually toward Katmandu (where drugs are cheap and legal) and a deal of hard knocks along the way. The influx has been sufficient to force Iran and Afghanistan to substantially boost the "cash in hand" requirements of prospective tourists. And the British consul-general in Istanbul officially requested Parliament in late 1967 to grant him increased accommodations for the "swarm" of penniless young Englishmen who have been cropping up at the consulate on their way east, seeking temporary lodgings or perhaps shelter from Turkish narcotics authorities.[11] . . .

So, by way of a dialectic Marx could never have imagined, technocratic America produces a potentially revolutionary element among its own youth. The bourgeoisie, instead of discovering the class enemy in its factories, finds it across the breakfast table in the person of its own pampered children. To be sure, by themselves the young might drift into hopeless confusion and despair. But now we must add one final ingredient to this ebullient culture of youthful dissent, which gives it some chance of achieving form and direction. This is the adult radical who finds himself in a plight which much resembles that of the bourgeois intellectual in Marxist theory. In despair for the timidity and lethargy of his own class, Marx's middle-class revolutionary was supposed at last to turn renegade and defect to the proletariat. So in postwar America, the adult radical, confronted with a diminishing public

among the "cheerful robots" of his own generation, naturally gravitates to the restless middle-class young. Where else is he to find an audience? The working class, which provided the traditional following for radical ideology, now neither leads nor follows, but sits tight and plays safe: the stoutest prop of the established order. If the adult radical is white, the ideal of Black Power progressively seals off his entrée to Negro organizations. As for the exploited masses of the Third World, they have as little use for white Western ideologues as our native blacks—and in any case they are far distant. Unless he follows the strenuous example of a Regis Debray, the white American radical can do little more than sympathize from afar with the revolutionary movements of Asia, Africa, and Latin America.

On the other hand, the disaffected middle-class young are at hand, suffering a strange new kind of "immiserization" that comes of being stranded between a permissive childhood and an obnoxiously conformist adulthood, experimenting desperately with new ways of growing up self-respectfully into a world they despise, calling for help. So the radical adults bid to become gurus to the alienated young or perhaps the young draft them into service.

Of course, the young do not win over all the liberal and radical adults in sight. From more than a few their readiness to experiment with a variety of dissenting life styles comes in for severe stricture —which is bound to be exasperating for the young. What are they to think? For generations, left-wing intellectuals have lambasted the bad habits of bourgeois society. "The bourgeoisie," they have insisted, "is obsessed by greed; its sex life is insipid and prudish; its family patterns are debased; its slavish conformities of dress and grooming are degrading; its mercenary routinization of existence is intolerable; its vision of life is drab and joyless; etc., etc." So the restive young, believing what they hear, begin to try this and that, and one by one they discard the vices of their parents, preferring the less structured ways of their own childhood and adolescence— only to discover many an old-line dissenter, embarrassed by the brazen sexuality and unwashed feet, the disheveled dress and playful ways, taking up the chorus, "No, that is not what I meant. That is not what I meant at all."

For example, a good liberal like Hans Toch invokes the Protestant work ethic to give the hippies a fatherly tongue-lashing for their "consuming but noncontributing" ways. They are being "parasitic," Professor Toch observes, for "the hippies, after all, accept—even demand—social services, while rejecting the desirability of making a contribution to the economy."[12] But of course they do. Because we have an economy of cybernated abundance that does not need their labor, that is rapidly severing the tie between work and wages, that suffers from hard-core poverty due to maldistribution, not scarcity. From this point of view, why is the voluntary dropping-out of the hip young any more "parasitic" than the enforced dropping-out of impoverished ghetto dwellers? The economy can do abundantly without all this labor. How better, then, to spend our affluence than on those minimal goods and services that will support leisure for as many of us as possible? Or are these hippies reprehensible because they seem to enjoy their mendicant idleness, rather than feeling, as the poor apparently should, indignant and fighting mad to get a good respectable forty-hour-week job? There are criticisms to be made of the beat-hip bohemian fringe of our youth culture—but this is surely not one of them.

It would be a better general criticism to make of the young that they have done a miserably bad job of dealing with the distortive publicity with which the mass media have burdened their embryonic experiments. Too often they fall into the trap of reacting narcissistically or defensively to their own image in the fun-house mirror of the media. Whatever these things called "beatniks" and "hippies" originally were, or still are, may have nothing to do with what Time, Esquire, Cheeta, CBSNBCABC, Broadway comedy, and Hollywood have decided to make of them. Dissent, the press has clearly decided, is hot copy. But if anything, the media tend to isolate the weirdest aberrations and consequently to attract to the movement many extroverted

[11] For the statistics mentioned, see Time, September 15, 1967, pp. 47–49; The Observer (London), September 24, 1967; and The Guardian (London), November 18, 1967.

[12] Hans Toch, "The Last Word on the Hippies," The Nation, December 4, 1967. See also the jaundiced remarks of Eric Hoffer in the New York Post Magazine, September 23, 1967, pp. 32–33; Milton Mayer writing in The Progressive, October 1967; and Arnold Wesker's "Delusions of Floral Grandeur" in the English magazine Envoy, December 1967.

poseurs. But what does bohemia do when it finds itself massively infiltrated by well-intentioned sociologists (and we now all of a sudden have specialized "sociologists of adolescence"), sensationalizing journalists, curious tourists, and weekend fellow travelers? What doors does one close on them? The problem is a new and tough one: a kind of cynical smothering of dissent by saturation coverage, and it begins to look like a far more formidable weapon in the hands of the establishment than outright suppression.

Again, in his excellent article on the Italian students quoted above, Nicola Chiaromonte tells us that dissenters

must detach themselves, must become resolute "heretics." They must detach themselves quietly, without shouting or riots, indeed in silence and secrecy; not alone but in groups, in real "societies" that will create, as far as possible, a life that is independent and wise. . . . It would be . . . a non-rhetorical form of "total rejection."

But how is one to develop such strategies of dignified secrecy when the establishment has discovered exactly the weapon with which to defeat one's purposes: the omniscient mass media? The only way anybody or anything stays underground these days is by trying outlandishly hard—as when Ed Saunders and a group of New York poets titled a private publication *Fuck You* to make sure it stayed off the newsstands. But it can be quite as distortive to spend all one's time evading the electronic eyes and ears of the world as to let oneself be inaccurately reported by them.

. . . It will be my contention that there is, despite the fraudulence and folly that collects around its edges, a significant new culture a-borning among our youth and that this culture deserves careful understanding, if for no other reason than the sheer size of the population it potentially involves.

But there *are* other reasons, namely, the intrinsic value of what the young are making happen. If, however, we want to achieve that understanding, we must insist on passing over the exotic tidbits and sensational case histories the media offer us. Nor should we resort to the superficial snooping that comes of cruising bohemia for a few exciting days in search of local color and the inside dope, often with the intention of writing it all up for the slick

magazines. Rather, we should look for major trends that seem to outlast the current fashion. We should try to find the most articulate public statements of belief and value the young have made or have given ear to; the thoughtful formulations, rather than the offhand gossip. Above all, we must be willing, in a spirit of critical helpfulness, to sort out what seems valuable and promising in this dissenting culture, as if indeed it mattered to us whether the alienated young succeeded in their project. . . .

However lacking older radicals may find the hippies in authenticity or revolutionary potential, they have clearly succeeded in embodying radical disaffiliation—what Herbert Marcuse has called the Great Refusal—in a form that captures the need of the young for unrestricted joy. The hippy, real or as imagined, now seems to stand as one of the few images toward which the very young can grow without having to give up the childish sense of enchantment and playfulness, perhaps because the hippy keeps one foot in his childhood. Hippies who may be pushing thirty wear buttons that read "Frodo Lives" and decorate their pads with maps of Middle Earth (which happens to be the name of one of London's current rock clubs). Is it any wonder that the best and brightest youngsters at Berkeley High School (just to choose the school that happens to be in my neighborhood) are already coming to class barefoot, with flowers in their hair, and ringing with cowbells?

Such developments make clear that the generational revolt is not likely to pass over in a few years' time. The ethos of disaffiliation is still in the process of broadening down through the adolescent years, picking up numbers as time goes on. With the present situation we are perhaps at a stage comparable to the Chartist phase of trade unionism in Great Britain, when the ideals and spirit of a labor movement had been formulated but had not reached anything like class-wide dimensions. Similarly, it is still a small, if boisterous minority of the young who now define the generational conflict. But the conflict will not vanish when those who are now twenty reach thirty; it may only reach its peak when those who are now eleven and twelve reach their late twenties. (Say, about 1984.) We then may discover that what a mere handful of beatniks pioneered in Allen Ginsberg's youth

will have become the life style of millions of college-age young. Is there any other ideal toward which the young can grow that looks half so appealing?

"Nothing," Goethe observed, "is more inadequate than a mature judgment when adopted by an immature mind." When radical intellectuals have to deal with a dissenting public that becomes this young, all kinds of problems accrue. The adolescentization of dissent poses dilemmas as perplexing as the proletarianization of dissent that bedeviled left-wing theorists when it was the working class they had to ally with in their effort to reclaim our culture for the good, the true, and the beautiful. Then it was the horny-handed virtues of the beer hall and the trade union that had to serve as the medium of radical thought. Now it is the youthful exuberance of the rock club, the love-in, the teach-in.

The young, miserably educated as they are, bring with them almost nothing but healthy instincts. The project of building a sophisticated framework of thought atop those instincts is rather like trying to graft an oak tree upon a wildflower. How to sustain the oak tree? More important, how to avoid crushing the wildflower? And yet such is the project that confronts those of us who are concerned with radical social change. For the young have become one of the very few social levers dissent has to work with. This is that "significant soil" in which the Great Refusal has begun to take root. If we reject it in frustration for the youthful follies that also sprout there, where then do we turn?

6.2
Why All of Us May Be Hippies Someday

Fred Davis

And thus in love we have declared the purpose of our hearts plainly, without flatterie, expecting love, and the same sincerity from you, without grumbling, or quarreling, being Creatures of your own image and mould, intending no other matter herein, but to observe the Law of righteous

Reprinted by permission from "Why All of Us May Be Hippies Someday, Trans-*action*, December, 1967.

action, endeavoring to shut out of the Creation, the cursed thing, called Particular Propriety, which is the cause of all wars, bloud-shed, theft, and enslaving Laws, that hold the people under miserie.

Signed for and in behalf of all the poor oppressed people of England, and the whole world.

Gerrard Winstanley and others
June 1, 1649

This quotation is from the leader of the Diggers, a millenarian sect of communistic persuasion that arose in England at the time of Oliver Cromwell. Today in San Francisco's hippie community, the Haight-Ashbury district, a group of hippies naming themselves after this sect distributes free food to fellow hippies (and all other takers, for that matter) who congregate at about four o'clock every afternoon in the district's Panhandle, an eight-block strip of urban green, shaded by towering eucalyptus trees, that leads into Golden Gate Park to the west. On the corner of a nearby street, the "Hashbury" Diggers operate their Free Store where all —be they hip, straight, hostile, curious, or merely in need—can avail themselves (free of charge, no questions asked) of such used clothing, household articles, books, and second-hand furniture as find their way into the place on any particular day. The Diggers also maintained a large flat in the district where newly arrived or freshly dispossessed hippies could stay without charge for a night, a week, or however long they wished—until some months ago, when the flat was condemned by the San Francisco Health Department. Currently, the Diggers are rehabilitating a condemned skid-row hotel for the same purpose.

Not all of Haight-Ashbury's 7500 hippies are Diggers, although no formal qualifications bar them; nor, in one sense, are the several dozen Diggers hippies. What distinguishes the Diggers—an amorphous, shifting, and sometimes contentious amalgam of ex-political radicals, psychedelic mystics, Gandhians, and Brechtian avant-garde thespians—from the area's "ordinary" hippies is their ideological brio, articulateness, good works, and flair for the dramatic event. (Some are even rumored to be over 30.) In the eyes of many Hashbury hippies, therefore, the Diggers symbolize what is best, what is most persuasive and purposive, about the surrounding, more variegated hippie subculture—just as, for certain

radical social critics of the American scene, the hippies are expressing, albeit elliptically, what is best about a seemingly ever-broader segment of American youth: its openness to new experience, puncturing of cant, rejection of bureaucratic regimentation, aversion to violence, and identification with the exploited and disadvantaged. That this is not the whole story barely needs saying. Along with the poetry and flowers, the melancholy smile at passing and ecstatic clasp at greeting, there is also the panicky incoherence of the bad LSD trip, the malnutrition, a startling rise in V.D. and hepatitis, a seemingly phobic reaction to elementary practices of hygiene and sanitation, and—perhaps most disturbing in the long run—a casualness about the comings and goings of human relationships that must verge on the grossly irresponsible.

But, then, social movements—particularly of this expressive-religious variety—are rarely of a piece, and it would be unfortunate if social scientists, rather than inquiring into the genesis, meaning, and future of the hippie movement, too soon joined ranks (as many are likely to, in any case) with solid burghers in an orgy of research into the "pathology" of it all: the ubiquitous drug use (mainly marihuana and LSD, often amphetamines, rarely heroin or other opiates), the easy attitudes toward sex ("If two people are attracted to each other, what better way of showing it than to make love?"), and the mocking hostility toward the middle-class values of pleasure-deferral, material success, and—ultimately—the whole mass-media-glamorized round of chic, deodorized, appliance-glutted suburban existence.

The Hip Scene Is the Message

Clearly, despite whatever real or imagined "pathology" middle-class spokesmen are ready to assign to the hippies, it is the middle-class scheme of life that young hippies are reacting against, even though in their ranks are to be found some youth of working-class origin who have never enjoyed the affluence that their peers now so heartily decry. To adulterate somewhat the slogan of Marshall McLuhan, one of the few non-orientalized intellectuals whom hippies bother to read at all, *the hip scene is the message,* not the elements whence it derives or the meanings that can be assigned to it verbally. (Interestingly, this fusion of dis-

parate classes does not appear to include any significant number of the Negro youths who reside with their families in the integrated Haight-Ashbury district or in the adjoining Negro ghetto, the Fillmore district. By and large, Negroes view with bewilderment and ridicule the white hippies who flaunt, to the extent of begging on the streets, their rejection of what the Negroes have had scant opportunity to attain. What more revealing symbol of the Negro riots in our nation's cities than the carting off of looted TV sets, refrigerators, and washing machines? After all, aren't these things what America is all about?)

But granting that the hippie scene is a reaction to middle-class values, can the understanding of any social movement—particularly one that just in the process of its formation is so fecund of new art forms, new styles of dress and demeanor, and (most of all) new ethical bases for human relationships—ever be wholly reduced to its reactive aspect? As Ralph Ellison has eloquently observed in his critique of the standard sociological explanation of the American Negro's situation, a people's distinctive way of life is never solely a reaction to the dominant social forces that have oppressed, excluded, or alienated them from the larger society. The cumulative process of reaction and counter-reaction, in its historical unfolding, creates its own ground for the emergence of new symbols, meanings, purposes, and social discoveries, none of which are ever wholly contained in embryo, as it were, in the conditions that elicited the reaction. It is, therefore, less with an eye toward explaining "how it came to be" than toward explaining what it may betoken of life in the future society that I now want to examine certain facets of the Hashbury hippie subculture. (Of course, very similar youth movements, subcultures, and settlements are found nowadays in many parts of the affluent Western world—Berkeley's Telegraph Avenue teeny-boppers; Los Angeles' Sunset Strippers; New York's East Village hippies; London's mods; Amsterdam's Provos; and the summer *Wandervögel* from all over Europe who chalk the pavement of Copenhagen's main shopping street, the Strøget, and sun themselves on the steps of Stockholm's Philharmonic Hall. What is culturally significant about the Haight-Ashbury hippies is, I would hazard, in general significant about these others as well, with—to be sure—certain qualifications. Indeed, a certain marvelous irony attaches itself to the fact that perhaps the only genuine cross-national culture found in the world today builds on the rag-tag of beards, bare feet, bedrolls, and beads, not on the cultural-exchange programs of governments and universities, or tourism, or—least of all—ladies' clubs' invocations for sympathetic understanding of one's foreign neighbors.)

What I wish to suggest here is that there is, as Max Weber would have put it, an *elective affinity* between prominent styles and and certain incipient problems of identity, work, and leisure that loom ominously as Western industrial society moves into an epoch of accelerated cybernation, staggering material abundance, and historically-unprecedented mass opportunities for creative leisure and enrichment of the human personality. This is not to say that the latter are the *hidden causes* or tangible *motivating forces* of the former. Rather, the point is that the hippies, in their collective, yet radical, break with the constraints of our present society, are—whether they know it or not (some clearly do intuit a connection)—already rehearsing *in vivo* a number of possible cultural solutions to central life problems posed by the emerging society of the future. While other students of contemporary youth culture could no doubt cite many additional emerging problems to which the hippie subculture is, willy-nilly, addressing itself (marriage and family organization, the character of friendship and personal loyalties, the forms of political participation), space and the kind of observations I have been able to make require that I confine myself to three: the problems of *compulsive consumption*, of *passive spectatorship*, and of the *time-scale of experience*.

Compulsive Consumption

What working attitude is man to adopt toward the potential glut of consumer goods that the new technology will make available to virtually all members of the future society? Until now, modern capitalist society's traditional response to short-term conditions of overproduction has been to generate—through government manipulation of fiscal devices—greater purchasing power for discretionary consumption. At the same time, the aim has been to cultivate the ac-

quisitive impulse—largely through mass advertising, annual styling changes, and planned obsolescence—so that, in the economist's terminology, a high level of aggregate demand could be sustained. Fortunately, given the great backlog of old material wants and the technologically-based creation of new wants, these means have, for the most part, worked comparatively well—both for advancing (albeit unequally) the mass standard of living and ensuring a reasonably high rate of return to capital.

But, as Walter Weisskopf, Robert Heilbroner, and other economists have wondered, will these means prove adequate for an automated future society in which the mere production of goods and services might easily outstrip man's desire for them, or his capacity to consume them in satisfying ways? Massive problems of air pollution, traffic congestion, and waste disposal aside, is there no psychological limit to the number of automobiles, TV sets, freezers, and dishwashers that even a zealous consumer can aspire to, much less make psychic room for in his life space? The specter that haunts post-industrial man is that of a near worker-less economy in which most men are constrained, through a variety of economic and political sanctions, to frantically purchase and assiduously use up the cornucopia of consumer goods that a robot-staffed factory system (but one still harnessed to capitalism's rationale of pecuniary profit) regurgitates upon the populace. As far back as the late 1940s sociologists like David Riesman were already pointing to the many moral paradoxes of work, leisure, and interpersonal relations posed by a then only nascent society of capitalist mass abundance. How much more perplexing the paradoxes if, using current technological trends, we extrapolate to the year 2000?

Hippies, originating mainly in the middle classes, have been nurtured at the boards of consumer abundance. Spared their parents' vivid memories of economic depression and material want, however, they now, with what to their elders seems like insulting abandon, declare unshamefacedly that the very quest for "the good things of life" and all that this entails—the latest model, the third car, the monthly credit payments, the right house in the right neighborhood—are a "bad bag." In phrases redolent of nearly all utopian thought of the past, they proclaim

that happiness and a meaningful life are not to be found in things, but in the cultivation of the self and by an intensive exploration of inner sensibilities with likeminded others.

Extreme as this antimaterialistic stance may seem, and despite its probable tempering should hippie communities develop as a stable feature on the American landscape, it nonetheless points a way to a solution of the problem of material glut; to wit, the simple demonstration of the ability to live on less, thereby calming the acquisitive frenzy that would have to be sustained, and even accelerated, if the present scheme of capitalist production and distribution were to remain unchanged. Besides such establishments as the Diggers' Free Store, gleanings of this attitude are even evident in the street panhandling that so many hippies engage in. Unlike the street beggars of old, there is little that is obsequious or deferential about their manner. On the contrary, their approach is one of easy, sometimes condescending casualness, as if to say, "You've got more than enough to spare, I need it, so let's not make a degrading charity scene out of my asking you." The story is told in the Haight-Ashbury of the patronizing tourist who, upon being approached for a dime by a hippie girl in her late teens, took the occasion to deliver a small speech on how delighted he would be to give it to her—provided she first told him what she needed it for. Without blinking an eye she replied, "It's my menstrual period and that's how much a sanitary napkin costs."

Passive Spectatorship

As social historians are forever reminding us, modern man has—since the beginnings of the industrial revolution—become increasingly a spectator and less a participant. Less and less does he, for example, create or play music, engage in sports, dance or sing; instead he watches professionally-trained others, vastly more accomplished than himself, perform their acts while he, perhaps, indulges in Mitty-like fantasies of hidden graces and talents. Although this bald statement of the spectator thesis has been challenged in recent years by certain social researchers—statistics are cited of the growing numbers taking guitar lessons, buying fishing equipment, and painting on Sunday—there can be little doubt that "doing" kinds of expressive pursuits, particularly of the collective type, no longer bear the same *integral* relationship to daily life that they once did, or still do in primitive societies. The mere change in how they come to be perceived, from what one does in the ordinary course of life to one's "hobbies," is in itself of profound historical significance. Along with this, the virtuoso standards that once were the exclusive property of small aristocratic elites, rather than being undermined by the oft-cited revolutions in mass communications and mass education, have so diffused through the class structure as to even cause the gifted amateur *at play* to apologize for his efforts with some such remark as, "I only play at it." In short, the cult of professionalism, in the arts as elsewhere, has been institutionalized so intensively in Western society that the ordinary man's sense of expressive adequacy and competence has progressively atrophied. This is especially true of the college-educated, urban middle classes, which—newly exposed to the lofty aesthetic standards of high culture—stand in reverent, if passive, awe of them.

Again, the problem of excessive spectatorship has not proved particularly acute until now, inasmuch as most men have had other time-consuming demands to fill their lives with, chiefly work and family life, leavened by occasional vacations and mass-produced amusements. But what of the future when, according to such social prognosticators as Robert Theobald and Donald Michael, all (except a relatively small cadre of professionals and managers) will be faced with a surfeit of leisure time? Will the mere extension of passive spectatorship and the professional's monopoly of expressive pursuits be a satisfactory solution?

Here, too, hippies are opening up new avenues of collective response to life issues posed by a changing sociotechnological environment. They are doing so by rejecting those virtuoso standards that stifle participation in high culture; by substituting an extravagantly eclectic (and, according to traditional aestheticians, reckless) admixture of materials, styles, and motifs from a great diversity of past and present human cultures; and, most of all, by insisting that every man can find immediate expressive fulfillment provided he lets the socially-suppressed spirit within him ascend into vibrant consciousness. The manifesto is: All men are artists, and who cares that some are better at it than others; we can all have fun! Hence, the deceptively crude antisophistication of hippie art forms, which are, perhaps, only an apparent reversion to primitivism. One has only to encounter the lurid *art nouveau* contortions of the hippie posters and their Beardsleyan exoticism, or the mad mélange of hippie street costume—Greek-sandaled feet peeking beneath harem pantaloons encased in a fringed American Indian suede jacket, topped by pastel floral decorations about the face—or the sitar-whining cacophony of the folk-rock band, to know immediately that one is in the presence of *expressiveness* for its own sake.

In more mundane ways, too, the same readiness to let go, to participate, to create and perform without script or forethought is everywhere evident in the Hashbury. Two youths seat themselves on the sidewalk or in a store entranceway; bent beer can in hand, one begins scratching a bongo-like rhythm on the pavement while the other tattoos a bell-like accompaniment by striking a stick on an empty bottle. Soon they are joined, one by one, by a tambourinist, a harmonica player, a penny-whistler or recorder player, and, of course, the ubiquitous guitarist. A small crowd collects and, at the fringes, some blanket-bedecked boys and girls begin twirling about in movements vaguely resembling a Hindu dance. The wailing, rhythmic beating and dancing, alternately rising to peaks of intensity and subsiding, may last for as little as five minutes or as long as an hour, players and dancers joining in and dropping out as whim moves them. At some point—almost any—a mood takes hold that "the happening is over"; participants and onlookers disperse as casually as they had collected.

Analogous scenes of "participation unbound" are to be observed almost every night of the week (twice on Sunday) at the hippies' Parnassus, the Fillmore Auditorium, where a succession of name folk-rock bands, each more deafening than the one before, follow one another in hour-long sessions. Here, amidst the electric guitars, the electric organs, and the constantly metamorphizing show of lights, one can see the gainly and the graceless, the sylph bodies and rude stompers, the crooked and straight—all, of whatever condition or talent, *dance* as the flickering of a strobe light reduces their figures in silhouette to egalitarian spastic bursts. The recognition dawns that this, at last, is dancing of utterly free form, devoid of fixed sequence or step, open to all and calling for no Friday after-school classes at Miss Martha's or expensive lessons from Arthur Murray. The sole requisite is to tune in, take heart, and let go. What follows must be "beautiful" (a favorite hippie word) because it is *you* who are doing and feeling, not another to whom you have surrendered the muse.

As with folk-rock dancing, so (theoretically, at least) with music, poetry, painting, pottery, and the other arts and crafts: expression over performance, impulse over product. Whether the "straight world" will in time heed this message of the hippies, is to be sure, problematical. Also, given the lavish financial rewards and prestige heaped upon more talented hippie artists by a youth-dominated entertainment market, it is conceivable that high standards of professional performance will develop here as well (listen to the more recent Beatles' recordings), thus engendering perhaps as great a participative gulf between artist and audience as already exists in the established arts. Despite the vagaries of forecasting, however, the hippies—as of now, at least—are responding to the incipient plenitude of leisure in ways far removed from the baleful visions of a Huxley or an Orwell.

The Time-Scale of Experience

In every society, certain activities are required to complete various tasks and to achieve various goals. These activities form a sequence —they may be of short duration and simple linkage (boiling an egg); long duration and complex linkage (preparing for a profession); or a variety of intermediate combinations (planting and harvesting a crop). And the activity sequences needed to complete valued tasks and to achieve valued goals in a society largely determine how the people in that society will subjectively experience *time*.

The distinctive temporal bent of industrial society has been toward the second of these arrangements, long duration and complex linkage. As regards the subjective experience of time, this has meant what the anthropologist Florence

Kluckhohn has termed a strong "future orientation" on the part of Western man, a quality of sensibility that radically distinguishes him from his peasant and tribal forebears. The major activities that fill the better part of his life acquire their meaning less from the pleasure they may or may not give at the moment than from their perceived relevance to some imagined future state of being or affairs, be it salvation, career achievement, material success, or the realization of a more perfect social order. Deprived of the pursuit of these temporally distant, complexly modulated goals, we would feel that life, as the man in the street puts it, is without meaning.

This subjective conception of time and experience is, of course, admirably suited to the needs of post-18th century industrial society, needs that include a stable labor force; work discipline; slow and regular accumulation of capital with which to plan and launch new investments and to expand; and long, arduous years of training to provide certain people with the high levels of skill necessary in so many professions and technical fields. If Western man had proved unable to defer present gratifications for future rewards (that is, if he had not been a future-oriented being), nothing resembling our present civilization, as Freud noted, could have come to pass.

Yet, paradoxically, it is the advanced technology of computers and servo-mechanisms, not to overlook nuclear warfare, that industrial civilization has carried us to that is raising grave doubts concerning this temporal ordering of affairs, this optimistic, pleasure-deferring, and magically rationalistic faith in converting present effort to future payoff. Why prepare, if there will be so few satisfying jobs to prepare for? Why defer, if there will be a super-abundance of inexpensively-produced goods to choose from? Why plan, if all plans can disintegrate into nuclear dust?

Premature or exaggerated as these questions may seem, they are being asked, especially by young people. And merely to ask them is to prompt a radical shift in time-perspective—from what *will be* to what *is*, from future promise to present fulfillment, from the mundane discounting of present feeling and mood to a sharpened awareness of their contours and their possibilities for in-

stant alteration. Broadly, it is to invest present experience with a new cognitive status and importance: a lust to extract from the living moment its full sensory and emotional potential. For if the present is no longer to hold hostage to the future, what other course than to ravish it at the very instant of its apprehension?

There is much about the hippie subculture that already betokens this alteration of time-perspective and concomitant reconstitution of the experienced self. Hippie argot —some of it new, much of it borrowed with slight connotative changes from the Negro, jazz, homosexual, and addict subcultures—is markedly skewed toward words and phrases in the active present tense: "happening," "where it's at," "turn on," "freak out," "grooving," "mind-blowing," "be-in," "cop out," "split," "drop acid" (take LSD), "put on," "uptight" (anxious and tense), "trip out" (experience the far-out effects of a hallucinogenic drug). The very concept of a happening signifies immediacy: Events are to be actively engaged in, improvised upon, and dramatically exploited for their own sake, with little thought about their origins, duration, or consequences. Thus, almost anything—from a massive be-in in Golden Gate Park to ingesting LSD to a casual street conversation to sitting solitarily under a tree—is approached with a heightened awareness of its happening potential. Similarly, the vogue among Hashbury's hippies for astrology, tarot cards, I Ching, and other forms of thaumaturgic prophecy (a hippie conversation is as likely to begin with "What's your birthday?" as "What's your name?") seems to be an attempt to denude the future of its temporal integrity—its unknowability and slow unfoldingness—by fusing it indiscriminately with present dispositions and sensations. The hippie's structureless round-of-day ("hanging loose"), his disdain for appointments, schedules, and straight society's compulsive parceling out of minutes and hours, are all implicated in his intense reverence for the possibilities of the present and uninterest in the future. Few wear watches, and as a colleague who has made a close participant-observer study of one group of hippies remarked, "None of them ever seems to know what time it is."

It is, perhaps, from this vantage point that the widespread use of

drugs by hippies acquires its cultural significance, above and beyond the fact that drugs are easily available in the subculture or that their use (especially LSD) has come to symbolize a distinctive badge of membership in that culture. Denied by our Protestant-Judaic heritage the psychological means for experiencing the moment intensively, for parlaying sensation and exoticizing mundane consciousness, the hippie uses drugs where untutored imagination fails. Drugs impart to the present—or so it is alleged by the hippie psychedelic religionists —an aura of aliveness, a sense of union with fellow man and nature, which—we have been taught—can be apprehended, if not in the afterlife that few modern men still believe in, then only after the deepest reflection and self-knowledge induced by protracted experience.

A topic of lively debate among hippie intellectuals is whether drugs represent but a transitory phase of the hippie subculture to be discarded once other, more self-generating, means are discovered by its members for extracting consummatory meaning from present time, or whether drugs are the *sine qua non* of the subculture. Whatever the case, the hippies' experiment with ways to recast our notions of time and experience is deserving of close attention.

The Hippies' Future

As of this writing, it is by no means certain that Haight-Ashbury's "new community," as hippie spokesmen like to call it, can survive much beyond early 1968. Although the "great summer invasion" of émigré hippies fell far short of the 100,000 to 500,000 forecast, the influx of youth from California's and the nation's metropolitan suburbs was, despite considerable turnover, large enough to place a severe strain on the new community's meager resources. "Crash pads" for the night where simply not available in sufficient quantity; the one daily meal of soup or stew served free by the Diggers could hardly appease youthful appetites; and even the lure of free love, which to young minds might be construed as a substitute for food, tarnished for many—boys outnumbered girls by at least three to one, if not more. Besides, summer is San Francisco's most inclement season, the city being shrouded in a chilling, wind-blown fog much of the time. The result was hundreds of youths leading a hand-to-mouth existence, wandering aimlessly on the streets, panhandling, munching stale doughnuts, sleeping in parks and autos and contracting virulent upper-respiratory infections. In this milieu cases of drug abuse, notably involving Methedrine and other "body-wrecking" amphetamines, have showed an alarming increase, beginning about midsummer and continuing up to the present. And, while the city fathers were not at first nearly so repressive as many had feared, they barely lifted a finger to ameliorate the situation in the Haight-Ashbury. Recently, however, with the upcoming city elections for Mayor and members of the Board of Supervisors, they have given evidence of taking a "firmer" attitude toward the hippies: Drug arrests are on the increase, many more minors in the area are being stopped for questioning and referral to juvenile authorities, and a leading Haight Street hippie cultural establishment, the Straight Theatre, has been denied a dance permit.

It has not, therefore, been solely the impact of sheer numbers that has subjected the new community to a difficult struggle for survival. A variety of forces, internal and external, appear to have conjoined to crush it. To begin with, there is the hippies' notorious, near anarchic aversion to sustained and organized effort toward reaching some goal. Every man "does his own thing for as long as he likes" until another thing comes along to distract or delight him, whereupon the hippie ethos enjoins him to drop the first thing. (Shades of the early, utopian Karl Marx: ". . . in the communist society it [will be] possible for me to do this today and that tomorrow, to hunt in the morning, to fish in the afternoon, to raise cattle in the evening, to be a critic after dinner, just as I feel at the moment; without ever being a hunter, fisherman, herdsman, or critic." From *The German Ideology*.) Even with such groups as the Diggers, projects are abandoned almost as soon as they are begun. One of the more prominent examples: An ongoing pastoral idyll of summer cultural happenings, proclaimed with great fanfare in May by a group calling itself the Council for the Summer of Love,

was abandoned in June when the Council's leader decided one morning to leave town. Add to this the stalling and ordinance-juggling of a city bureaucracy reluctant to grant hippies permits and licenses for their pet enterprises, and very little manages to get off the ground. With only a few notable exceptions, therefore, like the Haight-Ashbury Free Medical Clinic, which—though closed temporarily—managed through its volunteer staff to look after the medical needs of thousands of hippies during the summer, the new community badly failed to provide for the hordes of youth drawn by its paeans of freedom, love, and the new life. Perhaps there is some ultimate wisdom to "doing one's own thing"; it was, however, hardly a practical way to receive a flock of kinsmen.

Exacerbating the "uptightness" of the hippies is a swelling stream of encounters with the police and courts, ranging from panhandling misdemeanors to harboring runaway minors ("contributing to the delinquency of a minor") to, what is most unnerving for hip inhabitants, a growing pattern of sudden mass arrests for marihuana use and possession in which as many as 25 youths may be hauled off in a single raid on a flat. (Some hippies console themselves with the thought that if enough middle-class youths get "busted for grass," such a hue and cry will be generated in respectable quarters that the marihuana laws will soon be repealed or greatly liberalized.) And, as if the internal problems of the new community were not enough, apocalyptic rumors sprung up, in the wake of the Newark and Detroit riots, that "the Haight is going to be burned to the ground" along with the adjoining Fillmore Negro ghetto. There followed a series of ugly street incidents between blacks and whites—assaults, sexual attacks, window smashings—which palpably heightened racial tensions and fed the credibility of the rumors.

Finally, the area's traffic-choked main thoroughfare, Haight Street, acquired in the space of a few months so carnival and Dantesque an atmosphere as to defy description. Hippies, tourists, drug peddlers, Hell's Angels, drunks, speed freaks (people high on Methedrine), panhandlers, pamphleteers, street musicians, crackpot evangelists, photographers, TV camera crews, reporters (domestic and foreign), researchers, ambu-

latory schizophrenics, and hawkers of the underground press (at least four such papers are produced in the Haight-Ashbury alone) jostled, put-on, and taunted one another through a din worthy of the Tower of Babel. The street-milling was incessant, and all heads remained cocked for "something to happen" to crystallize the disarray. By early summer, so repugnant had this atmosphere become for the "old" hippies (those residing there before —the origins of Hashbury's new community barely go back two years) that many departed; those who remained did so in the rapidly fading hope that the area might revert to its normal state of abnormality following the expected post–Labor Day exodus of college and high-school hippies. And, while the exodus of summer hippies has indeed been considerable, the consensus among knowledgeable observers of the area is that it has not regained its former, less frenetic, and less disorganized ambience. The transformations wrought by the summer influx— the growing shift to Methedrine as *the* drug of choice, the more general drift toward a wholly drug-oriented subculture, the appearance of hoodlum and thrill-seeking elements, the sleazy tourist shops, the racial tensions—persist, only on a lesser scale.

But though Haight-Ashbury's hippie community may be destined to soon pass from the scene, the roots upon which it feeds run deep in our culture. These are not only of the long-term socio-historic kind I have touched on here, but of a distinctly contemporary character as well, the pain and moral duplicity of our Vietnam involvement being a prominent wellspring of hippie alienation. As the pressures mount on middle-class youth for ever greater scholastic achievement (soon a graduate degree may be mandatory for middle-class status, as a high-school diploma was in the 1940s), as the years of adolescent dependence are further prolonged, and as the accelerated pace of technological change aggravates the normal social tendency to intergenerational conflict, an increasing number of young people can be expected to drop out, or opt out, and drift into the hippie subculture. It is difficult to foresee how long they will remain there and what the consequences for later stages of their careers will be, inasmuch as insufficient time has passed for even a single age cohort of hippies to make the transition from early to middle adulthood. However, even among those youths who "remain in" conventional society in some formal sense, a very large number can be expected to hover so close to the margins of hippie subculture as to have their attitudes and outlooks substantially modified. Indeed, it is probably through some such muted, gradual, and indirect process of social conversion that the hippie subculture will make a lasting impact on American society, if it is to have any at all.

At the same time, the hippie rebellion gives partial, as yet ambiguous, evidence of a massiveness, a universality, and a density of existential texture, all of which promise to transcend the narrowly-segregated confines of age, occupation, and residence that characterized most bohemias of the past (Greenwich Village, Bloomsbury, the Left Bank). Some hippie visionaries already compare the movement to Christianity sweeping the Roman Empire. We cannot predict how far the movement can go toward enveloping the larger society, and whether as it develops it will—as have nearly all successful social movements—significantly compromise the visions that animate it with the practices of the reigning institutional system. Much depends on the state of future social discontent, particularly within the middle classes, and on the viable political options governments have for assuaging this discontent. Judging, however, from the social upheavals and mass violence of recent decades, such options are, perhaps inevitably, scarce indeed. Just possibly, then, by opting out and making their own kind of cultural waves, the hippies are telling us more than we can now imagine about our future selves. [EDITORS' NOTE: Indeed, the noble experiment in the Hashbury died, thus dating the article somewhat. But, the life style, or, more accurately, the consciousness of the hippies remains; the beginning perhaps of *The Greening of America*.]

FURTHER READING SUGGESTED
BY THE AUTHOR

It's Happening by J. L. Simmons and Barry Winograd (Santa Barbara, Calif.: Marc-Laird Publications, 1966).
Looking Forward: The Abundant Society by Walter A. Weisskopt, Raghavan N. Iyer, and others (Santa Barbara, Calif.: Center for the Study of Democratic Institutions, 1966).
The Next Generation by Donald N. Michael (New York: Vintage Books–Random House, 1965).
The Future as History by Robert L. Heilbroner (New York: Grove Press, 1961).

VOL. I, NO. 1   BERKELEY, CA.   PLEASE RECYCLE

6.3
Communitas—a Magazine of the Future

EDITED BY The SAP Family

COMMUNITAS: IN THIS ISSUE

When all else fails, split. This can be done individually or in groups, the latter being the topic of concern. In *Communitas* we are trying to present some ideas about what happens when people can't take it any longer and set out on their own. They go into the woods to form "intentional communities." Not new towns, or suburbs but *communities* and these communities are formed purposefully. Beautiful! There are also towns, such as Canyon, California (described in this issue), that are communities and that work and live together. Canyon is particularly united by a struggle to survive. As many communities have

discovered, being different from other towns is not always seen as a good thing by the other local residents. Being different can be interpreted as a threat to "our American way of life."

Despite the problems, attempts are continually made at creating a better community. Rick Margolies, in his article "On Community Building" describes some of the ways to begin to form a new style of life. This is followed by a description of Ananda, an intentional community that exists today. The members of the community see themselves as setting up the basic social pattern for "the new age: the formation of Self-realization cooperative communities, or 'World Brotherhood Colonies'" (Kriyananda, *Cooperative Communities: How to Start Them and Why*, San Francisco, Ananda Publications, 1970, p. 1).

In a different vein, we present a summary of a study done by Professor Benjamin Zablocki of the University of California at Berke-

ley on the social systems that hold communal living groups together. Since the life span of these groups seems to be very short, Zablocki's study may help to point out things to avoid to those who would set up their own community.

We have some words from Bucky Fuller, the creator of the Geodesic dome (although this is by no means his only great accomplishment). His words are divergent in two respects: he does not advocate abandonment of our technology and a return to the simple way of life: he sees the use of technology as the means of freeing man so that he may use more of his infinite creative ability. Secondly, he reminds us that Utopia is for all or none. We must maintain a world consciousness. The problems of one individual, one country, must be the concerns of one world and one united people. As our technology has given us the capability to commit suicide on a worldwide basis, so has it given us a means to save mankind. The choice is between Utopia and Oblivion.

The remaining items in the magazine stand by themselves as small signs of alternate life styles.

PHOTO COURTESY OF JOSHUA WATTLES.

On Media

By Jerry Rubin

Tensions within the youth culture are reaching the boiling point because we are creating liberated areas for dropouts in every city and town, and because a community that doesn't control its own economic base is helpless in the face of The Man!

Haight Ashbury, the first mass experiment at an urban youth ghetto, floundered because it had a Communist ethic built upon a capitalist material base.

Love cannot exist without economic reality.

In our community every man is his own brother's keeper.

Our youth ghettos must have a communal economy so that we can live with one another, trading and bartering what we need. A free community without money.

We can organize our own record companies, publishing houses and tourist companies so profit will come back into the community for free food, free rent, free medical care, free space, free dope, free living, community bail funds.

Thousands of us have moved from the cities into the country to create communes. Dig it! The

Reprinted by permission of Simon and Schuster from *Do It!* by Jerry Rubin, pp. 236–237. Copyright © 1970 by Social Education Foundation.

communes will bring food into the city in exchange for services which the urban communes will bring into the country.

We will declare war against landlords and liberate homes and apartment buildings for people who live in them.

We will police ourselves.

And arm ourselves against pigs who come into our communities to wipe us out.

We are creating our own institutions which will gradually replace the dying institutions of Amerika.

Our media, the underground press, both creates and reflects our new consciousness. The Establishment press reflects the irrelevant, dying and repressive institutions with which we are at war.

The attack on our press is the attack on our right to think for ourselves. To destroy our culture they must destroy our media. And to protect our culture we must protect our press against pig harassment, obscenity bursts and everything else.

The underground press is the beating heart of the community.

And now—some samples of the underground press.

REPRINTED BY PERMISSION FROM *THE BERKELEY BARB.*

Phrequent Phones

Abortion Communica-
tion SF 387-6480
Abortion Couns. 845-6550
Berk. Family Planning
Birth Control 845-6550
Berk. Immunizations . . 841-0200
Ext. 556

Berk. Pregnancy Care
Maternity Care 845-6550
Berk. Pregnancy Test . 845-6550
Berk. Pub. Hea. Nurse ..841-0200
Ext. 271
Berk. Runaway Cnt. . . . 849-1402
Berk. Sanit. Compltns. . .841-0200
Ext. 274
Berk. Shrink Clinic . . . 849-0911
Ext. 393
Berk. TB Tests 841-0200
Ext. 271
Berk. VD Clinic 845-0197
Berk. Well Baby Cln. . . .841-0200
Ext. 278
Berk. Fire Dept. 845-1710
Berk. Health Info. 841-8600
Berkeley BARB 849-1040
Bethlehem Comm. Cnt. . .452-2245
Black Panther Party 845-0103
Childbirth Education . . .841-0738
Community of St. Francis
SF 841-3557
Citizens Alert SF 776-9669
Damian Switchboard
Daly City 775-1357
Drug Crisis Clinic 548-2570
Drug Prevent. & Rehab.
East Palo Alto 322-8691
Drug Treatment SF . . . 621-9758

DRAFT HELP
Conc. Objectors, SF. . .397-6917
Draft Help, Oak. 451-1672
Draft Help, S.F. 863-0775
Own Recognizance,
Alameda 522-2202
Quaker Draft Cnsl. . . 843-9725
Resistance
Oakland 465-1819
SF 626-1910
War Resisters
League 626-6976
War Resisters
League SF 922-0864
Ecology Action 843-1820
Economic Opport. Ofc . . . 841-9151
Food Stamps 849-2460
Food Stamps SF 558-5662
Free Black Clinic
SF 563-7876
Free Chiroprct. Clinic
SF 391-1848
Free Church - Open 24
Hours 549-0649
Free Clinic - Open 24
Hours 548-2570
Free Hashbury Clinic
SF 431-1714
Free Musicians Coop
SF 431-1097
Free Store 533-7210
Free University 841-6794

409 House - Drug Help
SF 621-9758
Gay Liberation 848-9696
SF 841-3557
Health Department - Free
Services 841-0200
Heliotrope SF 931-1693
Huckleberry's for Runaways
SF 731-3921
I.D.E.A.S. 387-5999
Indian Center 626-7955

LEGAL HELP
ACLU 548-1322
ACLU SF 433-2750
Berk. Neighborhoo
Legal Assistance 841-9274
Law Student Civil Rights
Research Center 431-3980
SF Neighborhood Legal
Assistance 626-5285
West Oakland Legal
Switchboard 836-3013

Mobile Hlp Unit Ofc. . . . 421-9850
Mobile Phone 954-7304
Music Switchboard . . . 387-8008
Peace and Freedom Party
Berk. 863-8834
Monterey . . . . . (408) 624-1908
SF 863-8834
People's Architecture . . 849-2577
People's Office 549-3977
Planned Parenthood
East Bay 654-3212
SF 654-3212
Teen Clinic 567-0870
Police Complaint Cnt. . . 548-0921
Pregnancy Cnsl. 848-6036

Pregnancy Test
Berk. 845-6550
Oakland 654-3212
Rap Center 548-2570
Schizophrenics Anny. . . .566-2207
Sexual Freedom
League 654-0316
Suicide Prevention Center
Alameda Cty N 849-2212
Alameda Cty S 537-1323
SF 221-1424
Contra Costa 939-3232
SWITCHBOARDS
Berkeley 549-0649
East Oakland 569-6369
Palo Alto 329-9008
Contra Costa 933-9880
SF 387-3575
SF (Mission) 863-3040
Marin 456-5300
W. Oak. (legal) 836-2938
San Jose 295-2938
Talf 845-4919
Taxi Unlimited 841-2345
Tenants Union 549-3977
Trading Post 626-9461
Universal Life Church
Berkeley 843-9638
Oakland 654-3195
Welfare Rights Organiz.
Berkeley 845-4919
East Oakland 568-3031
SF 392-8076
Women's Liberation . . . 848-5875
843-9900
Women (N.O.W.) 564-0181
Unless otherwise specified all list-
ings are in Berkeley.

Many people arriving in Berkeley without very much bread or friends who are already established here find Berkeley a very disappointing place. I can remember well my first night trying to find a place to crash. "Oh WOW man, I wish I could help you out, but . . ." Maybe I was unlucky, but I think Berkeley is full of some pretty uptight freaks.

Freaks here have reason for being paranoid, because people do get ripped off by crashers, but that is one of the risks you take by trying to be open and trusting in a closed society. Anyway, to all you young American yippies on the move, Berkeley is not heaven, but you'll have to find that out for yourself. You learn a lot on the road and meet good people but eventually we have to settle down and put roots deep into our own community.

The revolution is going to be made by people living the revolution right now. We need more than our long hair and dope; we need our own communes to live in, our own natural diet to make us strong physically and spiritually, our own schools for our children, and the power to defend our gestalt lifestyle. For all those who still feel that urge to ramble, here is your survival manual . . .

NEW This Week: The Free Clinic is starting first aid classes Monday, April 13th from 3-5pm, dealing in general community problems. Sign up at the Free Clinic, open 24 hours, 2418 Haste. The clinic handles all medical problems up to surgery. If you have spare bread they can use it.

People's Park Annex is the scene for free produce. The food will be distributed Friday from 1-3pm and hopefully on all future Fridays. Bring your own boxes to pick up food.

OLD STUFF...

FOOD
*Hare Krishna Temple, 2710 Durant (east of Telegraph). Free food (donation of 75 cents asked) at 12 Monday thru Saturday and at 3:30 Sunday.
*University Lutheran Church, corner of Haste and College, Free meal from 6:30 to 8:00 Thursday. Far out church service Friday at 8:00.
*If you are thinking of ripping off some food be very careful. All the big chain stores prosecute shoplifters without mercy and most have elaborate systems to catch you.

*Food Stamps at Berkeley Welfare Department, 2530 San Pablo. Immediate attention, no waiting. is the new policy.
*Food Conspiracy. Call Sherry Lawhorn at People's Architecture, 849-2577.

*By the way, if you're by U-Save and don't want to pay a pig market for pig food, try across the street. Wing Lung: 1947 Grove. Neat stuff, and if you know how to take your time and dig out bargains, CHEAP and NOURISHING . . . Examples: Brown rice 2 lb./ 37c . . . 5/85c . . . 10/$1.60 . . . 25/$3.55 . . . 50/$7.00. Or "Ramen" alimentary paste (noodles) pure wheat with fish soup base 8/$1.00. Cheap groovy tea. All sorts of goodies if you can turn on to oriental food. Also bowls and chopsticks and very practical simple utensils. Nice people. (If, like some of us, still into tobacco: Cigarettes 35c + tax.)

CLOTHES
*Free clothes every day at People's Park Annex at Grant and Hearst.
*Free clothes at "Changes", 5003 Foothill, in East Oakland. 535-7210. The hours aren't definite, so you might call before you go.

HOUSING
*Ask people on the street if they'll let you crash at their house or apartment, and don't bring others to crash there. It's also possible for several people to share rent on a house. When crashing, try to help out with the work, and if you can, contribute some bread.
If you have any dope, share it, and if anyone's paranoid, don't hold.
As it gets warmer you'll be able to sleep on the rooftops and in people's back yards. Get to know someone in the building so if you get hassled, you can say you live there.
The Free Church, 2389 Oregon (just below Telegraph) will get you a place to crash two nights a week. (549-0649.) Sign up at 8:00 p.m.

AUTO SERVICE
*Many people in Berkeley drive VW's and VW buses. The best and cheapest service is Liberation Auto Service. The shop is a VW bus. Call 845-5759. He'll get your message; you'll be called back. The people's auto service won't rip you off.

DEALING
*the Family Store is coming out with its second catalog in about two weeks with more up-to-date information on where good people sell/service what.
If you want to know where you can get something and not have to deal with a fast-talking greed-creep, then you look in the FS Catalog — something of leather or a woven shawl, for instance — and the catalog will help you make the connections.
As an extension the FAmily is trying to open a recycle shop, which is a free store carried further; they need only a place. Not just clothes, not just talking, but giving. Giving up everything that's not needed to the exchange: old stereo components, tools, furniture, etc. And hopefully when you need something you can go down and find it.
Call 534-7167 and ask for Ed, Bonnie or Peter (The Family).

FREAKING
*Thorazine is always good to have around before a heavy trip. Whatever you do, don't go to a hospital. They will get your name before they give you a downer and turn you in to the pigs. Call the RaP Center and they will talk it out with you. 549-2570. DON'T GO TO THE HOSPITAL!

MONEY
*Sell the Tribe! Vendors pay 7½ cents a copy and sell it for 15 cents. You can return ANY number you don't or can't sell. The Tribe gives credit, too. First time vendors can get 25 papers on credit and when you pay for these, you can credit for any number. The Berkeley Tribe, 1708A Grove St., 549-2077.
If anyone has any information on more free or cheap stuff, call the Tribe and ask for Dave Yippie! or leave word to call.

REPRINTED BY PERMISSION FROM *THE BERKELEY TRIBE*, APRIL 10–17, 1970.

PURPOSE: Demand the impossible now!

THE FAMILY STORE

Directors:
Edwin A. Kartman
Bonnie J. Faucher
Peter E. Sears

. . . is a "yellow pages" of the cultural revolution, open without charge to qualified artisans, craftsmen, proprietors of shops and others manifesting a good trip for bread or barter.

THE MUSTARD SEED
HASTE & TELEGRAPH
This large, attractive natural foods center and restaurant has recently opened at the Forum, operated by the Messiah's World Crusade, a devoted organic food commune with experience in The Haight and Mill Valley.

FOOD CONSPIRACY?
Two significant trends in food consumption are organic foods and cooperative buying.
Last summer 35 people representing 12 tribes met to develop an alternative to the poisoned, processed and synthetic foods of the not-so-supermarkets. They agreed to call their brotherhood OM, the two letters standing for Organic Merchants.
Among other things, they agreed not to sell anything containing white sugar, bleached white flour, artificial flavor, artificial color, preservatives, emulsifiers or other synthetics, corn syrup, cottonseed products.
There was a second meeting of OM at Big Sur. Hopefully, more information and common planning will be forthcoming. Inquire further of the organic merchants listed in *Family Store*.
The second approach is based upon community organizing for collective buying, initiated by the Great Food-Buying Conspiracy after a gathering of the Tribe in Berkeley last August.
Since then, the Conspiracy has grown into five buying coops in Berkeley alone with a

membership of some 300 families, who are reported to be saving 20–50% by pooling orders and taking care of purchasing and distribution. Tasks are shared by the members and rotate to avert the development of mini-bureaucracy, power trips, etc.
According to The Food-Buying Conspiracy, these are things you'll need:
1) large vehicles (two if over 30 living units are buying).
2) two bookkeeper-cashiers, and a table.
3) two or three parking spaces in your lot.
4) two or three scales, used, baby.
5) CASH to pay the farmers.
6) paper bags and boxes for people to take home their stuff.
7) one person to dispose of left-overs.
The procedure is slightly different for fruits and vegetables, cheeses, and dry goods, and depends on local resources and help from sympathetic, groovy merchants. For details, contact The Food Conspiracy in Berkeley, 848-6457 or 548-0577.

PEOPLES' ARCHITECTURE
1940 BONITA
849-2577
Movement architecture. The logistics & politics of design; community self-help projects. Community education. Inflatables, research.

LEOPOLD'S RECORDS
2517 DURANT
848-2015
Owned by The Students of Berkeley as a non-profit service to the community. Lowest prices in town.

GAREN, JIMMY, AND JOHN
2519 ETNA NO. 3
840 0001
"We make things of wood, steel, plastic from telephones, lamps to furniture and other useful or outrageous creations. Creative photography also. Let us build your ideas. Also light hauling."
THE FAMILY STORE
BOX 7067
Publishers of this directory and related non-profit programs to encourage and assist evolutionary forms, new life-styles; getting it all together NOW. Ed Kartman and the Family.

ANNE
2333 GRANT
549-1588
Clothes made to order, batiks, hand-painted designs, tie-dyeing, suede; interior decorating ideas.
"You have the right to work, but for the work's sake only. They who work selfishly for results are miserable." *Bhagavad Gita*

WHOLE EARTH ACCESS CO.
2466 SHATTUCK
848-0510
To furnish knowledge and tools for self-sufficiency . . . books, tipi's, other tools. Dale & Mike. Good luck on this new venture.

ECOLOGY CENTER
2170 ALLSTON
548-2220
Clearinghouse, book store, print shop, mobilizing public concern with environmental threats to the survival of man and all living things.

TAXI UNLIMITED
2054 UNIVERSITY
841-2345
"Take a trip with the hip taxi co-operative. 24 hours a day seven days a week. Meter rates from Berkeley to wherever. Also package delivery and errand service. (Openings for new drivers, over 25.)"

EXCERPTED AND REPRINTED BY PERMISSION FROM THE FALL AND SPRING EDITIONS OF *THE FAMILY STORE DIRECTORY*, BOX 7067, BERKELEY, CALIFORNIA.

People's Park: Symbol of Our Creativity

By Craig Oren

"A quiet revolution began Sunday."

I wrote that line in this newspaper exactly one year ago today. The occasion was the beginning of People's Park.

That Sunday, several dozen students, local residents, and street people responded to an announcement in the Berkeley Barb of a "park-building." They brought shovels, rakes, and even a bulldozer with them.

It was a warm day, but many worked even while sweat glistened on their faces. By the time evening fell, the land between Dwight, Bowditch, and Haste was no longer vacant. Flowers and benches stood where once there was only a vacant mudflat.

The next day, when I walked past the Park, the land seemed to have an atmosphere very unfamiliar to Berkeley—an atmosphere of creativity, cooperation, and community.

For before that April Sunday, Berkeley had been suffering from battle fatigue. Only weeks earlier, a six-week long student strike had ended in name-calling and in the disillusionment of many with radicals. Almost everyone had predicted a quiet Spring.

But somehow, that Park brought us together for a few short weeks.

After it was all over many out-of-town people, even radicals, found it hard to understand why we had wanted the land so much, why we had day after day defied police and marched in downtown Berkeley.

Perhaps it was because the Park was something we had built, we had planed. There was no bureaucracy looking over our shoulders telling us what we could or could not do. The people who built and used the Park made the decisions.

One meeting particularly comes to mind. We were discussing if "crashers" should be allowed to use the property. It was an unusual debate; there was very little of the egotripping and infighting that usually characterizes radical meetings. The decision was finally made by group consent-participatory democracy, if you will.

Another meeting also is memorable. It was held the evening of May 14, only hours before hundreds of police seized the land. Everyone there knew the police would soon take what we had built; it was only a question of time.

We sat around the "swimming hole" and talked while children played. The air was charged with tension, but there was no panic. We laughed at Chancellor Heyns' statement that the land had cost a "precious" million dollars. Somehow, we knew that even though we could not stop the destruction of our Park, even though they had the guns and the tear gas, we would win. I was reminded of Huey Newton's motto, "The spirit of the people is greater than the Man's technology."

And with that faith, we went out into the streets. When we saw the police would stop at nothing, were even willing to kill, we adapted our tactics and sought to limit our own violence. We marched in downtown Berkeley for days, closing stores and making the rest of Berkeley feel the same terror we did. We destroyed the morale of the National Guard with our smiles and determination. We frustrated trigger-happy cops with a huge, peaceful Memorial Day march conducted literally under the guns of the police and Guard.

The only thing we could not win was the park itself.

Looking back, I think I know why the Park could not be allowed to live. It was a clenched fist in the face of the establishment, not only because we challenged ideas of corporate property, but because it was a living symbol that we could "get it together," that despair was not the inevitable result of action.

People's Park is now a vacant parking lot and an unusused athletic field. If our Park was a symbol of our creativity, then the sterile deserted land behind the fence expresses the brutality and ugliness of our enemies.

Reprinted by permission from *The Daily Californian* (University of California, Berkeley), April 21, 1970.

Myth of Yippie

By Jerry Rubin

A new man was born smoking pot while besieging the Pentagon, but there was no myth to describe him. There were no images to describe all the 14-year-old freaks in Kansas, dropping acid, growing their hair long and deserting their homes and their schools. There were no images to describe all the artists leaving the prison of middle-class Amerika to live and create art on the streets.

The Marxist acidhead, the psychodelic Bolshevik. He didn't feel at home in SDS, and he wasn't a flower-power hippie or a campus intellectual. A stoned politico. A hybrid mixture of New Left and hippie coming out something different.

A streetfighting freak, a dropout, who carries a gun at his hip. So ugly that middle-class society is frightened by how he looks.

A longhaired, bearded, hairy, crazy motherfucker whose life is theater, every moment creating the new society as he destroys the old.

The reality was there. A myth was needed to coalesce the energy.

Yippies forged that myth and inspired potential yippies in every small town and city throughout the country to throw down their textbooks and be free.

Yippies would use the Democratic Party and the Chicago theater to build our stage and make the myth; we'd steal the media away from the Democrats and create the specter of "yippies" overthrowing Amerika.

The myth is real if it builds a stage for people to play out their own dreams and fantasies.

The myth is always bigger than the man. The myth of Che Guevara is even more powerful than Che. The myth of SDS is stronger than SDS.

The myth of yippie will overthrow the government.

Reprinted by permission of Simon and Schuster from *Do It!* by Jerry Rubin, pp. 82–83. Copyright © 1970 by Social Education Foundation.

PHOTO COURTESY OF JOSHUA WATTLES.

Revolution Towards a Free Society: Yippie!

By A. Yippie

YIPPIE!

Lincoln Park

VOTE PIG IN 68

Free Motel
"come sleep with us"

1. An immediate end to the war in Vietnam. . . .

2. Immediate freedom for Huey Newton of the Black Panthers and all other black people. Adoption of the community control concept in our ghetto areas. . . .

3. The legalization of marihuana and all other psychedelic drugs. . . .

4. A prison system based on the concept of rehabilitation rather than punishment.

Reprinted from a Yippie leaflet distributed at the Chicago 1968 Democratic Convention.

5. . . . abolition of all laws related to crimes without victims. That is, retention only of laws relating to crimes in which there is an unwilling injured party, i.e., murder, rape, assault.

6. The total disarmament of all the people beginning with the police. This includes not only guns, but such brutal devices as tear gas, MACE, electric prods, blackjacks, billy clubs, and the like.

7. The Abolition of Money. The abolition of pay housing, pay media, pay transportation, pay food, pay education, pay clothing, pay medical help, and pay toilets.

8. A society which works toward and actively promotes the concept of "full employment." A society in which people are free from the drudgery of work. Adoption of the concept "Let the Machines do it."

9. . . . elimination of pollution from our air and water.

10. . . . incentives for the decentralization of our crowded cities . . . encourage rural living.

11. . . . free birth control infor-

mation . . . abortions when desired.

12. A restructured educational system which provides the student power to determine his course of study and allows for student participation in overall policy planning. . . .

13. Open and free use of media . . . cable television as a method of increasing the selection of channels available to the viewer.

14. An end to all censorship. We are sick of a society which has no hesitation about showing people committing violence and refuses to show a couple fucking.

15. We believe that people should fuck all the time, anytime, whomever they wish. This is not a program to demand but a simple recognition of the reality around us.

16. . . . a national referendum system conducted via television or a telephone voting system . . . a decentralization of power and authority with many varied tribal groups. Groups in which people exist in a state of basic trust and are free to choose their tribe.

17. A program that encourages and promotes the arts. However, we feel that if the Free Society we envision were to be fought for and achieved, all of us would actualize the creativity within us. In a very real sense we would have a society in which every man would be an artist.

. . . Political Pigs, your days are numbered. We are the Second American Revolution. We shall win. Yippie!

The Tales of Hoffman

By Mark E. Levine
    George C. McNamee
    Daniel Greenberg

Direct examination of Defendant Abbott H. Hoffman by Defense Attorney Weinglass.

Q.: Will you please identify yourself for the record?
A.: My name is Abbie. I am an orphan of Amerika. . . .

From *The Tales of Hoffman,* edited by Mark L. Levine, George C. McNamee, and Daniel Greenberg. Copyright © 1970 by Bantam Books, Inc.

Q.: Where do you reside?

A.: I live in Woodstock Nation.

Q.: Will you tell the court and jury where it is?

A.: Yes. It is a nation of alienated young people. We carry it around with us as a state of mind in the same way the Sioux Indians carried the Sioux nation around with them. It is a nation dedicated to cooperation versus competititon, to the idea that people should have better means of exchange than property or money, that there should be some other basis for human interaction. It is a nation dedicated to—

THE COURT: Excuse me, sir. Read the question to the witness please. (Question read) Just where it is, that is all.

THE WITNESS: It is in my mind and in the minds of all my brothers and sisters. We carry it around with us in the same way that the Sioux Indians carried around the Sioux nation. It does not consist of property or material but, rather, of ideas and certain values, those values being co-operation versus competition, and that we believe in a society—

MR. SCHULTZ (Attorney for the Government): This doesn't say where Woodstock Nation, whatever that is, is.

MR. WEINGLASS: Your Honor, the witness has identified it as being a state of mind and he has, I think, a right to define that state of mind.

THE COURT: No, we want a place of residence, if he has one, place of doing business, if you have a business, or both if you desire to tell them both. One address will be sufficient. Nothing about philosophy or India, sir. Just where do you live, if you have a place to live? Now you said Woodstock. In what state is Woodstock?

THE WITNESS: It is in the state of mind, in the mind of myself and my brothers and sisters. It is a conspiracy.

Words on Life Styles

The conflict of life styles emerged around . . . "cultural" and "psychological" issues. For instance, music when Arlo Guthrie, Judy Collins, Phil Ochs . . . and others tried to sing for the jury, they were admonished that "this is a criminal trial, not a theater." No one, including the press, understood what was going on. . . . To understand their meaning would be to understand the meaning of the new consciousness. . . . Singing in that courtroom would have jarred its decorum, but that decorum was oppressing our identity and our legal defense.

Tom Hayden
(From *The Trial*.)

Society just isn't geared to people
who grow a beard
Or little girls with holes in their ears
They're liable to hunt you down
And dress you in a wedding gown
And offer substantial careers.

Richard Farina

East of Oakland

By Hector Javkin

East of Oakland, by the side of the San Leandro creek, near the wealthy communities of Orinda and Moraga, alive within a canyon of second growth redwoods, is Canyon, California, a former logging town, which now has 150 people in 45 homes, who are having to fight to live as they want to live and to continue to live in Canyon at all. Many of the residents tend to have long hair and beards, but they are a varied group, with a number of different backgrounds and occupations, among them a carpenter, a computer programmer, a Civilian Intelligence man at a nearby naval Station, and several mechanics. There is an organization which lives and works in Canyon, Vocations for Social Change, which acts as a clearing-house for non-establishment jobs. Most of the residents seem to find ways of spending more time in their own community than people elsewhere, often accepting a lower economic standard of living in order to do so.

The homes in Canyon also vary widely. Some are of standard 16-inch center-stud construction, with most being of the vacation-cabin type. A number of the houses, however, represent the creations of underground architecture. Probably the prettiest of these is a geodesic dome, con-

By permission of the author.

structed of thirty sheets of light plywood, forming a dome which can support the weight of several men on it without supporting posts of any kind. Another has a sleeping alcove in the lower floor but has a top floor that is covered by a series of sloping roofs but has no walls. Privacy is provided by the quiet of the hills and the courtesy of the neighbors. When I asked the resident of this second house how old it was, he pointed down and said, "That board you're standing on is about fifty years old." He had built on what was left of a previous structure, partly with wood he had found. Residents periodically mill the lumber from redwoods knocked down by storms.

Talking to *Ramparts* reporter Sol Stern, Canyon resident Sally Kehrer explained, ". . . we are closely bound together by our love for the land and each other, by our mutual participation in the cycle of the seasons and by the overwhelming magic of this place called Canyon. Together we watch the flowers come with the warm days of spring—different flowers every week in the grass and among the trees. We watch the hills grow brown and dry in the summer. In the Fall we gather to make wine by crushing the grapes and storing them in barrels. We come together in our houses in the cold windy rain of winter and talk in front of a fire. We help each other to build what has to be built —a house, a store, a porch, a septic tank."

Canyon is a community possibly different from any other in the United States. Many of its men wear beards and cork-sole boots; many of the women have their ears pierced. When young people from Orinda go to visit Canyon, when their parents begin to suspect that Canyon residents are selling them drugs, when Canyon refuses to look like the rest of Contra Costa County, and when a huge water company becomes convinced that Canyon is a threat to one of its reservoirs, then Canyon is in danger of ceasing to exist.

If it does cease to exist it will not be the demise of yet another hippie experiment. Canyon is over a hundred years old. When California entered the Union, Canyon (then called Moraga Redwoods) as well as Oakland (San Antonio) both voted in favor: Canyon with 61 votes and Oakland with 5. The Canyon school was built in 1918. As late as the 1940's Canyon still had a population of over 400. It was not until 1950 that the East Bay Municipal Utility District (M.U.D.) started buying land in Canyon, and the number of homes and residents quickly began to diminish. . . .

The kind of community Canyon has become makes standard sewage systems impossible. The terrain is quite hilly. A considerable amount of leveling, terracing, as well as man-holes at each grade change would be necessary. The present natural landscape would change a great deal, probably altering the entire character of the community, as well as the ecology of the area.

Canyon at present uses septic tanks, which present an ecological question and some serious political problems. San Leandro Creek runs through Canyon and feeds the San Leandro Reservoir which belongs to East Bay M.U.D., which has charged that Canyon's septic tanks are polluting, or threaten to pollute, the reservoir. So far, despite repeated tests by East Bay M.U.D. officials, no pollution has been traced to the tanks. In fact, it seems that the creek is somewhat less polluted as it passes through Canyon, because it is not grazing land, than at other points all the way from its source to the reservoir.

A creative reclamation scheme has been proposed which would eliminate the septic tanks altogether. The plan was devised by Dr. Douglas McMillan, a water engineer and a Canyon resident. When I asked McMillan about the motivation for the design and implementation of the plan, he replied that the need was political, that the septic tanks were a political wedge against Canyon even if no harm came from them.

The advantage of the proposed new sewer system over both gravity sewers and the present septic tanks is that a ready-made fire protection water supply would come along with it.

The scheme would require the approval of Canyon as an autonomous utility district, with power to control its own building and zoning, a power that Contra Costa County is reluctant to give it. In the last vote concerning such a district, the Board of Supervisors voted it down four to one. Canyon residents are trying to appeal that decision.

For the past twenty years, Canyon has been fighting a struggle for survival. Residents feel that East Bay M.U.D. is trying to force them out, not out of a concern about water pollution, a threat

which can be dealt with, but as part of a huge land-grab and profit-taking scheme. They live on beautiful land, beautiful because it is undeveloped but also very suitable for development, which they feel is East Bay M.U.D.'s goal.

They are struggling against a war of attrition. In 1952, East Bay M.U.D. purchased 24 houses around Canyon and had them burned—at a time when there was considerable fire hazard in the area. There were at least two condemnation suits initiated by East Bay M.U.D. in the 1950's. The Board of Supervisors of Contra Costa County, under pressure from East Bay M.U.D., has made it almost impossible for Canyon residents to get building permits. Ken Avelino's house was destroyed by the flood of 1962; it took him a year to get a permit to rebuild. In June of 1966, when the store and post office came up for sale, East Bay M.U.D. offered $14,000 for the land, threatening to cut off the access road to Canyon. Residents got together and managed to raise enough money to buy the land themselves, whereupon the Contra Costa County Health Department condemned the building. After several appeals, the community submitted plans to repair and remodel the store. They were denied a permit. Using Thanksgiving weekend of 1967, a time when building inspectors would not come, the entire community worked together to rebuild the store. With the building repaired, the permits finally were granted.

In June of 1967, a 26-acre parcel of land with five homes on it came up for sale. East Bay M.U.D. offered the landowner $55,000. At first she agreed to sell. Residents learned of the proposed sale however, and convinced her, by telling her what the sale would mean to Canyon and by offering her $60,000 to sell the land to them. Soon after this sale, East Bay M.U.D. convinced the Contra Costa County Board of Supervisors to pass a new ordinance prohibiting new septic tanks within 1000 feet of any reservoir or tributary. Since almost all of Canyon lies within 1000 feet from the creek, this makes any new building illegal since some form of sewage disposal is necessary.

East Bay M.U.D.'s drive to buy land continued, and Canyon's resistance became more determined. Although a number of older residents became discouraged and some sold their land, they sold it to people who they felt could be trusted to keep Canyon intact,

even if they had to sell for half the price offered by East Bay M.U.D.

Some Canyon residents began to build, on their own land, without permits. In January and February of 1969 there was a three-week inspection by the County Building department. On February 19, three building inspectors, twelve police officers and a dog catcher trampled over Canyon posting some 20 structures (including a children's tree house, 2 chicken coops and one hay barn) with a notice making entry a misdemeanor. Residents were warned that their children were also subject to this order and would be taken to the juvenile center if they disobeyed.

I saw a film on the posting shown by Doug McMillan when he came to talk at Berkeley on the reclamation scheme. It showed the residents following the police around Canyon as the postings went up. One man, his voice almost shrill with anguish, told them again and again, "You are on our land. You are trespassing on our land. Get off our land. We will not interfere with you or the building inspectors, but we ask that you get off our land." The postings went up, but the residents continued to live in their homes, and retained attorney William Bennett, who plans to make building permits a constitutional issue. Under the Uniform Building Code in effect in most communities in the United States, the Board of Supervisors acts as both the lawmakers and the judges, violating the constitutional concept of separation of powers. If Canyon wins that fight, it will be a major victory for underground architecture and the concept of owner-built homes.

On March 18, 1969, an accident occurred which changed the attitudes of many of the residents and pointed out the desperate need for fire protection. A gasoline line belonging to the Shell Oil Company, running above ground near Canyon above the creek, was broken open by explosives. Fifteen thousand gallons of gasoline poured into San Leandro Creek. A Shell executive, Earl J. Davis, came out to investigate and local police came to warn residents of the fire hazard. Davis was sending back a report from the public phone outside the store when the volatile fumes exploded, possibly ignited by a spark from the phone. A sheet of flame shot upwards over a hundred feet, engulfing the store. Davis was pulled out, in flames,

PHOTOS OF CANYON COURTESY OF LOUISA MILLER.

by several Canyon residents, who suffered severe burns as a result. The man had sustained burns over 80% of his body, however, and he died a few days later. The store and post office were burned to the ground. The entire canyon would have burned if the explosion had occurred during the dry summer months.

Shell Oil at first denied any responsibility and refused either to help pay for the store or to put the gas line underground. They finally agreed to put the line underground, after one of their vice-presidents, a friend of Davis, learned of Canyon's attempt to save him. The community never received a penny toward the rebuilding of the store, although a new trailer post office was brought in by the Federal government.

After the fire, many of the older residents, who had still thought of Canyon as a peaceful place where they could live without the hassles of civilization, began to make plans to leave. The people who remain are those committed to a fight to preserve their homes and their community. There aren't many like them. They think for a time when you ask them a question. McMillan thinks that people who live in cities are "speed-freaks," amphetamine-addicts who live at a hurried pace, prematurely burning out their lives which he can't even attempt to understand. I really can't disagree with him, and I wonder if our speed-freaked culture can learn quickly enough to leave Canyon and its people be.

If there is no community for you, young man, make it yourself.

Paul Goodman
(From *Making Do*.)

On Community Building

By Rick Margolies

What do we do when we're white and affluent, in a world of starvation and colored revolution? Sent to the best schools, for what? To make more money and spend how many vapid Sundays by the pool? Toward what distant goal?

Yes, we've been raised with the best the age could buy: clothes, cars, vacations, maids, colleges. And still we're not satisfied. The children of affluence, playing the games of the age. The world prostrate before us, why not rise to the rape? Perhaps we're afraid to lie, perhaps we learned our families' spoken moralisms too well. Yes, unwilling to call cynicism wisdom, label resignation reality. And now, a bit unsure, we stand in beards and old army shirts, having cut loose our buttoned-down minds just a bit. We've marched against the war, only to find our parents won't let us come home. We've refused to cooperate with the draft and are in court or prison. For what? Whose battles are we fighting? Deep down, we don't really believe we're making a revolution. We: lily-white, pampered sons and daughters of the suburbs, with our puffy, soft bodies which may never know what labor means. But for all our self-doubts this much we know: we can never go back again. 10,000 kids out to change the world. Now the years of dreaming and visionary phrase making are over and we stand face-to-face with ourselves. Wrestling with the demons within, striking at the devils without, we must fill the void of this plastic pleasure world or become a vacuum in it.

Several years ago community was the cop-out of those who couldn't cope with our political struggles. Today we find our political and psychic renewal in the creation of community. Our hardships in the past few years have shown that the road that supports us in helping each other work things out emotionally and intellectually is the path of greatest political relevancy as well. For most cry out for a better way to live together but are too emotionally and economically locked up in their present style of living. Young people can talk with us freely about our concerns because they have not yet invested their lives in an entrapping mode of existence. Parents and older

By permission of the author.

people, quietly sympathetic to our concerns and criticisms, demand to know our "program." Our program is what we are already about: the discovery of our true selves and our need for new relationships, which is the creation of community where there was but alienation.

Thus, our task in the years ahead is to restructure our lives into these new forms of relatedness to each other and the greater society. Our concern is to destroy the master-slave relationship in all its corporate and psychic manifestations and to build in its place non-hierarchical communities. Wherever people are living and working and are not the initiators and final arbiters of that life process, we must move people to restructure their situation so that where there was a pyramid of command there is now a non-hierarchical democratic body or community. Thus, our politics is mediated to us through our own relationships, whether we be in a family, a work group, or a learning situation.

The Failure of Contemporary Politics

In order to see our task clearly we must understand how the political process rationalizes the mainstream of American life. The failure of contemporary politics is that it accepts as given the atomization, alienation, and fragmentation of existence in an advanced capitalist society. Both conservatives and liberals are corporate capitalists, for their lives are determined by the organizational mode and existential style of the corporation and the city. Lives are atomized in careers and families, each man/family an individual unit viewing itself in competition with all other such units. Sharing and cooperation become superficial. One expends life's energy in accumulating money and consumer objects toward making one's home a privatized utopia. One's personal success and worth are soon equated with accumulated property and people find themselves isolated in their home or apartment with two or three locks on the door. People become threats.

The city fragments our lives by separating work, service and residential sections by considerable distances. People work miles from their homes and develop two sets of acquaintances: those on the job and those at home. At work one

relates to those around through the corporate role one has achieved; it is known who is inferior and can be ordered around and whom one must obey. At home, after the psychic death of commuting, relationships increasingly take on the same master-slave character: the wife must keep her place as cook/housekeeper and the kids are ordered around like administrative assistants. People conform to their roles, and as the saying goes, "just do the job." People become objects.

The city is built for commerce and travel. The roads are laid out for auto and truck traffic, not for people. The neighborhoods are segregated either business or residential by bureaucratic zoning boards that are little influenced by the people who live in the area. The idea of reconstructing the city into humanly scaled communal neighborhoods in which people can walk or bicycle to stores and services is a threat to the propertied class which controls the zoning and redevelopment boards. People become nuisances.

A man's politics is truly alienated from him if it is a concern he has outside of his everyday existence. Regardless of whether he is a conservative, a liberal, or a radical, he relates to those around him as threats, objects, and nuisances. The exploitative nature of our lives will remain if we resign ourselves to this alienated politics which is not grounded in a new economic and social reality.

Beyond Resistance: The Integration of Political, Economic, and Social Spheres

If we were truly free we would set our own terms. This would mean to work for a new wholeness in our lives. Resistance and protest are basically forms of alienated politics because they do not embrace the total person as he lives his life; they never transcend outrage. We must, of course, resist when we are pushed and protest when outraged, but it is clear that this does not teach us how to live our lives anew. I am far from arguing for the end of protest and resistance, but rather for the integration of this vitally necessary consciousness-building activity into a non-frenetic philosophy of our life's work. For personal frustration and psychic exhaustion are endemic to resistance politics. The burn-out rate in our movement is probably two or three years. If a fuller comprehension of what we are about is not grasped we will all become cynical, bleary-eyed nihilists. The New York City Resistance (an anti-draft group) has discovered this through its own struggle. In a recent mailing they counseled "The concept of communal living is an important element in the lives of people who see themselves in the struggle for social change on a long-term basis. Development of community and dealing with interpersonal relations are very important in facilitating working together. Experiments with new forms of living are crucial to the development of a vision of the new society that must be built."

The liberal, with his do-your-own-thing pluralism, has no such socialist vision of a common life together, for his life is rooted deep in the class and caste system of capitalism, as are his myriad neuroses. If we know the psychological destructiveness of a bourgeois existence built around property, how can we but share what money and property we have? If we see the human perversity of treating children as private property, how can we but raise our children in communal families as the kibbutzim do? A marriage easily becomes a box trapping man, wife and children in a circle of distrust. The Oneida Community, over 110 years ago, had a highly successful community marriage in which each was married to all.

As we come together and restructure our relationships, we create the germ cells of a renewed social organism, growing from the ground up, into the institutions which sit heavily on our lives. Thus, as we build out from our own privatized existences into small communal families living in one house together, sharing the work necessary to maintain life (meals, sanitation, income) and raising children . . . , so must we build out from our communal houses to create new communal economic and political institutions in our neighborhoods. This is the essential element of survival and development, for the tendency is to become overly involved in the weight and mire of interpersonal problems, as well as the daily delights of domestic "playing house." A community which does not grow out into the life of the neighborhood will, within a year or two, grow in upon itself and die.

A unified group of eight or ten people, who can work smoothly together because they have grown to trust one another, can be a great constructive force in a neighborhood. The key to this organizing effort is an attitude essentially humble and downright neighborly, for we must be sensitive to our own arrogance and self-righteousness as we make our small contribution to the growing Left in America. Our deeply philosophical, political, and social analysis, while so meaningful to our personal understanding of our lives, is so much hostile and abstract thought to the average man or woman in most neighborhoods. We will futilely smash our heads against the brick wall of the Silent Majority's deep-seated fear of change if we come at them spewing forth hot rhetoric and dogmatic clichés.

The systematic isolation and destruction by the state of the Black Panther Party indicates one result of letting the flamboyant rhetoric of revolution run ahead of the actual organizing work. It was only after the repression had become rather extensive that the Panthers toned down much of their rhetoric and began the social programs that must be the base and substance of truly revolutionary activity. The breakfast for children program of the Panthers is an example of touching the people's real needs, which demonstrates constructive concern while conducting political education and organizing. Unfortunately, the awareness of the necessity of organizing socially came too late for the thirty members of the Panther Party who were murdered in their beds and in their offices. When the police attacked a Panther office, the neighbors stood by and watched.

Organizing around social and domestic needs, as distinguished from purely political education, has a great potential for speaking to a broad range of people concerning the exploitative nature of corporate capitalism. To this point the Left has not touched the real lives of most Americans. Political analysis alienated from actual social changes that people can see and participate in remains alien and apart from people's lives and is thus unconvincing, like so many leaflets littering the stone steps and cement sidewalks of the system.

Social organizing must be close enough to the real local needs of a neighborhood not to be considered weird, offensive, or outlandish. Such a project must be a believable contribution to the life and activity of the neighborhood. One does not start a head shop in a poor neighborhood, but one might start a food co-op emphasizing inexpensive and "organic" (not chemically-treated) foods. Such a store would provide a natural way to get to know and talk with the people about the deeper questions of the exploitative economy, the function of the political state in its perpetuation, and the day by day development of a smooth technological totalitarianism. Child care centers, neighborhood radio stations, film theaters, community centers, coffeehouses, bookstores, and credit unions are other examples of social projects that would help introduce a community of radicals, up to that point isolated in the incest of their houses and their meetings, to the everyday life of their neighborhood.

OUR STRUGGLE MUST BE BASED ON THIS PROCESS OF COMMUNITY BUILDING. We must avoid the false glorification of struggle which comes from the frustration of seeing no results of resistance and mobilization politics but bleary eyes, bloodied heads, and pictures in the daily papers. What is needed now is more programmatic and structural thinking if we are to avoid an escalating spiral of street confrontations which will psychically and physically destroy our people. The question is not whether we can face down the police at a confrontation, but rather whether we can decentralize the police establishment so that neighborhoods can elect and recall police officers and generally set their own moral standards of what is legal and what is not. And that is a question of first getting ourselves together where we live.

Learning from History

The past 150 years have provided us with a rich history of building decentralized socialism within a capitalist society. Of the three major branches of that history, the French Communities of Work, the American communities of the 19th century, and the Israeli kibbutzim, the latter two can teach us more, partly because there is more substantial material on them. My remarks here are generalized and are intended only to excite the reader's curiosity to discover more for himself: a bibliography follows this essay.

During the last century approximately 100,000 people lived in small communitarian societies throughout the wilderness areas of rapidly industrializing, urbanizing America. Those who forged out these communities were the most imaginative of the pioneer stock. For them the freedom of the new country meant the chance to experiment and innovate toward a more just society, rather than the opportunity for fortune-hunting in the cities.

The kibbutzim represent the end result of the fusion of the religious and socialist traditions of communitarianism in the German youth movements at the turn of the century. They were not as idealistically utopian in their conception as the American communities, for the task was as much forging a new nation out of a desert wilderness of Palestine as it was to build the micro-units of a just society. In Israel they say the revolution is the color of the ground, for in making the desert fertile they changed the earth from yellow to green. In the American communities the concern from the beginning was self-sufficiency and independence, so the primary question of their role in the developing macro-economic-political structure did not concern them. But from the beginning the various kibbutzim pursued ways of helping each other and the needs of nascent Israel, so their focus while building internally was outward, toward federation. Today there are four kibbutz federations serving 82,000 people in a total of 230 communities. The various federations are allied with political parties and provide, in proportion to their numbers, a remarkably high percentage of government leaders in the Knesset (parliament), the ministries, and the military. With ⅓ of the nation's total agricultural production, the kibbutzim are an integral part of the economic and political structure of Israel. Whether they will go on to rid their country of corporate capitalism and militarization remains to be seen.

Perhaps the first lesson of this history is the need to develop a communal life style which is continually sensitizing people to the larger task they are about in the society as a whole—a philosophy which encourages people to intentionally build toward the larger task. Whether the kibbutz federations (one is avowedly marxist) will continue to act to maintain their safe position in a hostile society or take the necessary risks to revolutionize the country is an open question, a question which

can only be answered perhaps by the young people of the kibbutzim. The failures of the American communities show that the critical revolutionary style was never found either. For these communities sought isolation; from the beginning they imagined themselves apart from their society so that as they grew their activity reflected this myopic self-definition. They willingly became encapsulated as their hostility toward outsiders turned in on them, from the local townfolk refusing to trade with them, to outright attacks. But the greatest danger of this selfish concern with internal welfare is the stagnation of increasingly incestuous relationships. The communities became inbred and self-satisfied, and in the process destroyed the creative energy of building a new society. It is this complacency, rooted in the static and narrow-minded view of what they were about, that placed them outside the historical forces that were determining the shape of the embryonic nation. The failure lies in not realizing that a community's welfare, in the broadest sense, is inextricable from the society's economic and political realities.

The Need for an Experimental Approach

History has also shown us that rigidity of outlook and approach to what a community is about is equally destructive and inhibiting. As we come together to live or work we must grow toward an ideal, always grounding our action in the compost pile of present realities. Different forms of community will arise for different human types and personalities. This is natural and good as long as the various forms strive for continual growth and further development —internal development toward human relatedness which is truly liberating, and externally toward the creation of new communal institutions where the power is vested in the people, not in absentee lords of the propertied class. The goal is a new social dispensation and a New Human Being. We must be an open mind and avoid the dogmatic and the fanatic, for the organizational form must begin where people are and grow along a path all can follow in trust and understanding. Let us be clear about dogmatism. One is dogmatic when he imposes what he believes to be true or right on a situation and demands

acquiescence and allegiance from others, instead of slowly working through mutual prejudices and fears with them, always willing to change himself, so that all arrive at the apparent truth existentially, in the fullness of self-knowledge.

The Need for a Ritual of Regular Dialogue

Our growth, individually and collectively, will take place not in a vacuum but in the dialectic of conflicting ideas and perspectives. And this must be based on a willingness to learn from each other, a willingness to change and grow —a lesson, sad to tell, the American socialist communities never learned. Most died a premature death because of endless internal bickering and factionalism. The need is for a mechanism of some kind which facilitates regular dialogue, such as a weekly meeting for this express purpose. The meeting will truly be mechanical, however, if there is no trust between the people.

Such a gathering is a special time, distinct and separate from the more pedestrian daily routine. A regular time and place help create an atmosphere of respect and importance. Limiting the meeting to several hours is wise, as longer sessions are repetitious, tiring, and often counter-productive. It is more helpful to have a two hour meeting every week than a six or seven hour marathon once a month. The objective here is to be concise, honest, and direct with one another, not to make long, abstract, or theoretical speeches. Long meetings dull people to hearing the simple truths, which are often more profound. The sacredness of your brief time together might be emphasized by a simple ritual, such as the singing of a song or sitting on the floor of the living room (rather than the more frequented dining room) in a circle.

Oneida, perhaps the most interesting and successful of the American intentional communities, had such a session, called "Mutual Criticism" (an early form of encounter group or group therapy). Charles Nordoff, a journalist who visited Oneida in 1875, noted that mutual criticism was ". . . a most ingenious device, which Noyes (founder of Oneida) and his followers rightly regard as the corner stone of their practical community life. It is in fact their main instrument of government; and it is useful as a means of eliminating uncongenial elements, and also to train those who remain into harmony with the general system and order." (Charles Nordoff, *Communistic Societies of the United States*, Dover paperbound, 1965.) A Mutual Criticism encounter could be requested by a member who wanted personal counsel and advice or it could be administered for correction of a delinquency. The important thing to note is that the criticism was not authoritarian and thus was understood to be an aide and guide. Thus no ill feeling was provoked in the "victim." I find this especially striking and essential to successful forms of community: that a person's intellectual and spiritual advancement was a community concern. It was the goal of all to uplift each and every member of the community in a real spirit of love and compassion.

Community with Two Poles: Urban and Rural

Another vivid lesson from past community failures is how a community situated in the country, devoted entirely to agriculture and the soil, becomes completely encapsulated and stagnant. Our communities must provide two environments, with houses and work to be done in the cities, as well as land and labor in the country. Perhaps the perfect distance could be measured by an hour and a half's travel time: close enough to be convenient, but distant enough to limit frivolous trips.

To see community building as our life task is to seriously develop economic means of support which represent our concerns and simultaneously free much of our time to be active at other tasks. We must, of course, simplify our living, minimizing bourgeois self-indulgencies and expensive tastes, otherwise our rural communes will become counter country clubs. Kropotkin argued well for villages of mixed agriculture and manufacture, a good mind-picture of the rural commune pole of our communities. Full-scale agriculture is too time-consuming; we must develop "truck gardening" (raising vegetables and fruit for immediate sale in near-by cities and towns). In manufacturing, as in agriculture, one of the main questions is how easily can people be trained in the necessary skills. This facilitates more people doing shorter work shifts. A goal in this regard might be everyone doing four hours of work each day in the

community's industry, houses, or fields. Possible industries include furniture making, prefabricated housing (construction of structural components, as well as completed houses), printing and publishing, graphics and film-making, and the stand-bys of the underground: pottery and leather goods. The work should grow out of what each group finds fulfilling and can hopefully be related to the activity of the community's city terminus. Perhaps selling products on campuses or in depressed neighborhoods would also provide an entree to talking to people about community and concerns of the movement.

Questions of Internal Organization

There are several issues which will arise concerning internal organization. The more openly discussed and understood are these inherent questions, the more stable will be the group. For our purpose here, I wish to deal with the questions of leadership, discipline, new members, child-rearing and women's liberation.

Leadership—Leaders come organically out of a group which is together emotionally and intellectually. The important difference is between a coercive leader and a natural one. The coercive leader bases his authority on a position in a hierarchy which has power over your life or on his own manipulative powers of persuasion over the group. Humor is often used as a weapon in a face-to-face group by an authoritarian leader to subtly cause an opposing member to appear foolish. A natural or rational leader gains the personal confidence of members of the group who know him well from living with him, but do not submit to him. It is my experience that the natural leader is the one most willing, or most devoted to doing the work that must be done. Leaders should not assume too much of the work, however, to avoid the community's becoming dependent on their contributions. A genuine leader makes himself superfluous by drawing forth the leadership potentials of others, and speaking directly, but lovingly, to people's passivity and dependency on others' strengths.

One of the popular myths of our "counter-culture" is that we can eliminate all authority by merely saying we will make all decisions and do all actions democratically and without leaders. I call this a myth because most of us feel very deeply our own powerlessness and

resultant acquiescence to strong personalities. This is usually threatening to people's self-image and thus it is denied. The dynamic is very strongly present nonetheless for it works unconsciously. We say to ourselves consciously that we are all equal in our own "democratic" group while we feel, silently or unknown to ourselves, passive and dependent on the stronger or more aggressive members.

In many of the urban communes that I am familiar with in Washington, including the two I lived in each for a year, there is usually an authoritarian personality, often benign, who sets the emotional and intellectual tone of the group. There are two sides to such a group "minidictator": mother and father. The maternal side says everything is alright here and we are together, the paternal side is morally disapproving, determines what is right and radical, and generally is the final word on group activities. Often there are two such authority figures, one maternal and one paternal, who are locked in an emotional power struggle for leadership. This conflict of temperament, most often veiled and unconscious, is usually further animated by the personal pathologies of men trying to dominate women and women trying to castrate men. Rational leadership will gently, and without malice or vengeance, expose this dynamic for all to see and discuss. For without such a frankness the group will become an emotional quagmire which pulls down everybody's spirits rather than giving new life and freedom to individual potential and aspiration.

Discipline—Discipline in a hierarchical institution is punishment. People in such situations are victims, rather than captains, of their fate. But in a decisional community where all are equal members it is the way they constitute themselves so as to get their work done. Which is to say, where all are life-dedicated to a task, discipline becomes the question of how to organize yourselves toward that goal. And this depends largely on the scale and intimacy of the group. A simple mechanism might be the "period of commitment" in which the community decides that it wants to accomplish so many tasks within a certain time period and then members voluntarily pledge themselves to do specific things.

Group responsibility (discipline) should be discussed in the light of the wheelie-feelie polarization. The wheelies are the politicos, the wheeler-dealers of our movement with a background in history, economics, and politics, and consequently see most of the movement's concerns in structural and programmatic ways. The feelies are the artists of the movement who are into art, dancing, music, the occult, the mystical, and various schools of psychology, and thus see most of the movement's concerns in psycho-dramatic terms of people being more gentle and expressive with each other. Each perspective has a valuable contribution to make to the other; in fact, one of the major failures of the radical movement after the First World War was the estrangement between those doing cultural things and those doing politics. There is now a marked tendency for the wheelies and the feelies to be unable to communicate with each other, let alone work together closely. How they get together over common concerns will depend largely on openly discussing their unique perceptions in regular dialogue encounters.

Discipline is a problem in the movement because most of us have personally rebelled against the perversity of authoritarian families and schools, where discipline was a punishment or a means to get us to someone else's end. Now that self-discipline is required to free us further from this societal quagmire, we flounder. But the fact is that in the years ahead we must study and work harder than we have to this point, for ours is a long march, not an acid trip, through the institutions, and through the creation of new institutions.

New Members—Several of the American communities had a complete open door policy about new members. In each case it was a principal cause for their demise. For such community experiments often attract free-loaders, cranks, and crashers of all kinds who have little interest in the people of the community or commitment to the socio-political task they are about. If the community feels dedicated to the therapeutic task of rejuvenating people to full active and independent communitarians, all well and good; but the history of such situations has been that it requires so much time and effort that it exasperates and destroys the community's mission. In reality, such new members change the personality of the community more than the community does them.

Which is not to say that only exact carbon-copies of present community members should be admitted. Far from it, for such a process will develop an ingrown homogeneity which equally subverts the life of the group. For we are intentionally living in a particular communal way, and we are purposely about the socio-political reconstruction of a capitalist, racist society. New members should be in joyous agreement with our style of life and our purpose. This is of paramount importance, for it means they fully understand and articulate with their own lives what we are about. . . .

A good means for the selection of new members is a less stringent variant of the one the kibbutzim have perfected. A person would simply live and work as a full member in the community for approximately three months. This would provide ample time to know a person in many intimate situations and also to fully acquaint the aspirant with the people and way of life of the community. During the period of mutual familiarization, dialogue encounters might occur so that the new member can confront the community and vice versa. In this way, real existential problems can be worked through to everyone's understanding and satisfaction. This may seem very rigorous and perhaps harsh on the aspirant, but radical communities such as we are building toward are integral, intentional bodies and we cannot be too careful in adopting new brothers and sisters. This will seem unnecessary however, for transient, casual groups that are not building for a *life* together.

Child-rearing and Women's Liberation—Community without children is an immature affair. Children are the leaven and spice of group living, if the flour of the loaf is pure. Which is to say that in a radical community, where men and women respond to each other openly and lovingly, and where women are not relegated to the caste of dishwasher/child-raiser, children are essential for a full life.

Women's Liberation is the first movement group to emphatically articulate the need for consonance between interpersonal harmony and so-called "radical" politics. In a community of trust, growth and action are based on complete responsiveness to every person's sensitivities and contribution. Our sisters cannot be passed over in what they are feeling and saying in group dialogue and decision-making. Women cannot be treated as second-class citizens who must keep their place as cook, nurse-maid, and geisha girl. And this means a reconstitution of how men act, as well as women. Nursing, feeding, cleaning up after the communities' children, is as much man's work as woman's. For in the communal raising of children, where men and women share the work equally, man's so-called "realistic" view of how to deal with people and situations will be humanized, while woman's time will be more freed and her perspectives broadened. Only through the building of communities of trust and shared responsibility will women (and men) find liberation, and only through communal child-rearing and the liberation of women will we achieve true community. Women looking for liberation without community is a soul searching for a body, and a community in which women are not free is a body without a soul.

The Illusion of Community

It is most common for people who live together, whether that be a family, a group of friends, or a larger community, to adjust to each other's sensitivities and peculiarities at the surface, as if they were borders that could not be crossed. Learning how not to irritate other people often passes for deep relationship. But to really know and to be a part of another is to respond to his sufferings and joys, as if they were your own, as if the rich oil of your soul constantly flowed between you, back and forth, and you had no bodies to physically harbor the spirit.

A negative form of community develops when the members become psychologically dependent upon the group, says Michael Maccoby, a radical humanist psychologist, who has worked with several kinds of intentional communities. When being together becomes a goal in itself; when everyone feels threatened when one or two members choose not to participate, then a destructive dependency has developed. For the group must free the individuals in it and this will happen only when everyone helps each other to know his own fears, weaknesses, and strengths so that each person will act out of a strong, honest sense of his being, rather than a weak dependent submission. A seeming paradox: each must be stronger than the group, yet draw his ultimate strength and direction from it.

Some of the so-called "hip" communes evidence this emasculating form of community. Much time is spent just being together, listening to music, rapping endlessly, or sitting around. The ultimate rule of such a community is being gentle with each other, touching each other and generally not violating where another person "is at." It is a regression toward the safe, tactile environment of the womb. This is a serious situation when the supportive group becomes enfeebling to the vitality and independence of its members, for the group experience should advance and develop individual potential and productivity.

Another community of illusion develops where people settle into living together without truly responding to each other. Mechanisms for mutual defense soon develop, such as a recurring joke, a shared experience, stereotype, scapegoat, or cliché, which defuse the tension when people begin to really touch each other. For we are all scarred by the inhibitions and defenses from being dealt with by parents and teachers who manipulated our desires and fears, albeit unknowingly, because they were unresponsive and afraid of themselves being free. Most people are afraid to be known and know themselves, partly because of the pain of confronting their fears and weaknesses and partly because they may have to change as a result. But in a radical socialist community, the intention is to create new men and women who are strong and loving in the task they are about. And this comes only from being open, accepting, and willing to learn from each other. Only those who are sensitive and probing, only those who are receptive and willing to change will be broken out of the prison of their defenses, like a strong oak shooting up after the hard nut is consumed by the growing seedling.

The Act of Initiation

I think it important to suggest some models of community building for different situations. They will remain incomplete however, because it is of paramount importance to build community to the situation and needs of the people involved. Perhaps the value of these models is in what they illustrate about the process of initiation.

Initiation is, in a sense, a question of scale and intimacy, for the intensity of the group's life is established in the formative period, just as a person's spirit (faith, hope, vision) which he will carry throughout his life is primarily formed while an infant. For an infant to become a psychically whole organism it must grow in an environment of trust and common concern. It is said that one of the first psychic imprints on a child's mind is the face of his mother as he looks up from suckling her breast. If the face is lovingly approving he is more likely to be secure and hopeful throughout his life. If the child perceives hostility or disapproval, however slight, as he is at his mother's breast, then he will carry the scars of insecurity and indecision with him as he grows. And it is on this early foundation of trust and faith that the child interprets and integrates into his worldview new and more challenging experiences and people.

And so it is with the generation of community. When the first people come together to work out their concerns, as they seek for a common vision, they build the foundation on which the larger community will stand or crumble. For as they widen their circle the hope and spirit of their vision will be unmistakably transmitted to the new members. Communication is more than words, it is the totality of mind-body sensitivity: eye contact, body movements, speed of delivery and response, voice tonality and loudness, and ego diffusion. And so, the fervor and unity of the core group, what the kibbutzniks call a *garin* (nucleus), will be transmitted to the new members in its true strength and fullness.

If the environment is spiritually whole, if there is understanding and hope, the organism will be strong. But if the structure is incoherently thrown together it will be too brittle to weather the storms and buffetings of the future. It is this communion of inner cohesion, collaboration and mutual stimulation that Martin Buber calls "the center." "The real essence of community is to be found in the fact—manifest or otherwise—that it has a center. The real beginning of a community is when its members have a common relation to the center overriding all other relations: the circle is described as the radii, not the points along its circumference." (Martin Buber, *Paths in Utopia*, Beacon Press paperbound: Boston, p. 135.)

Some Models

The communion sought at conception is a universal prerequisite. The acts of commission which follow, however, might be quite different in varying situations. The spiral of community must generate out from the initial moment of conception into the material world of the present. This would obviously involve a different activity for a middle class residential area, a college campus, or an urbutz (an urban kibbutz).

A Middle Class Neighborhood

On a middle class block, the community-building process might begin by two or three neighbors, whose previous contact was casually social and sporadic, coming together to dialogue about what they might do to help each other toward a common life. The discussions might alternate from home to home once or twice a week. They should include all members of the families, for the community they are prefiguring must be an extended family. A common meal, in which all help, gives substance to the ensuing dialogue. During the discussion it helps to occasionally reverse positions by vocalizing in your own words each other's concerns, to see if you are really sensitive to what the other is saying. In the regular meeting and dialogue, the pooling of money for the meal, and the cooking and cleaning up, you will have a slight taste of communal responsibility and responsiveness.

The renting or buying of a house on the block or near-by might be the next important step. This would truly be a communal space, owned and shared by the whole neighborhood, for common meals, dances, drama and satire, meetings, film and music facilities, organizing projects and community seminars and celebrations. It should become the home and center of the community's life. During the day it might be a child-care center to free the women's time and provide the best formative environment for the children. This should be staffed by the community's men and women, especially teen-agers, for whom sensitivity to young children is an important orienting and stabilizing element.

Increasingly, by intention or not, the growing community will confront the propertied political powers that be: zoning and licensing boards, redevelopment authorities, realtors, business owners, and school bureaucracies. The children are a case in point. Clearly, we must free the children from the custodial authoritarianism which kills their curiosity and eagerness to discover, and bring them back into the community, on the streets, and in neighborhood minischools (see Paul Goodman's "Minischools" in the *N.Y. Review of Books*, Jan. 4, 1968). This is but another facet of political decentralization where the power (and the glory) of controlling our own lives will have to be won through institutional struggle.

This freeing of the children is linked to the freeing of the mothers, who must deny their own eagerness to discover new things outside the home because they are imprisoned in the role of custodian while the children are home and the men are away pursuing their barely visible horizons. The creation of a minischool/child-care center where all care for the young on a rotating basis is perhaps the most revolutionary beginning act of community building in a middle-class neighborhood, largely because child-rearing is the greatest rationalization for that style of life and partly because the freeing of women will generate enormous creative energy. For it truly replaces the exploitative, privatistic life-patterns while at the same time constructing an alternative pattern.

This is not the theoretically revolutionary, alienated politics of so many today, but the substantive socio-political reconstruction which must be the cell-tissue and the bone structure of any new social body.

After the early accomplishment of a community house, child care facilities, and a minischool, the group can go on to yet more adventuresome goals: internal revenue sharing, the establishment of a neighborhood food and consumer's co-op, and even the creation or purchase of neighborhood stores and services to be set up as cooperatives. But the really meaty questions involve redesigning the neighborhood into a communal village with ample work, recreation, and residential facilities at hand. Planting streets over and making them into village malls. (This might be started by organizing a block party in which the police cooperate and remove all the cars. Many weeks afterward people will excitedly remember how the neighborhood was transformed.) The creation of small producer units to be owned by the community, based on the interests

PHOTOS COURTESY OF STEVE CLARK.

of the particular people; setting up a small clothes or furniture producing shop, a bakery, etc. The possibilities are immense. The basic principle is embarrassingly simple: people work great distances from their homes at alienating jobs for which they have been educated, yet at home they have hobbies they truly enjoy doing. The task is to free each other from the Money/Status rationalizations so that those personally expressive and creative things we do with our hands at home become more and more our activity and source of bread. In the heat and energy of this creation we will find renewal together.

A College Campus

Community building on a campus, whether urban or rural, starts with the control of space. Student power demands are movements to control space, both existentially and environmentally. College administrators believe the dormitories, class buildings, courses, and activities belong to them and are to be "administered" to the students. A doctor administers a drug to a diseased patient, but a man cannot administer an education. For to grow and learn in full health is to need nothing administered to you.

The *garin*, or core group, would start with six to eight men and women, who would go about setting up a communal house. It is important to invite sympathetic faculty and their families, as well as non-university people who live in the area, to share our life together. If the house is off campus, the administrators may not let students live there. If it is on campus, they may not let men and women live together. In either case, the struggle to control our own life will begin early. In the case of dormitories perhaps the opening act should be what the students of the Free University in West Berlin did recently. A group of forty men packed up their belongings and moved into the previously all-women dormitory, occupying the rooms left vacant by the equal number of women who moved into the men's dorm. The act drew immediate support from the student body and disapproval from the doctoral administrators, but the latter could do nothing when faced with a popularly-supported *fait accompli*.

The direction of this is essential to community building: the control of our lives, the liberation from repressive and exploitative social customs, the creation of democratically (read decentral) owned and operated institutions and the achievement of communion in our lives. On campus this carries us in the direction of building a non-hierarchic, non-status-enforcing community where all students, faculty, and workers share in maintaining the physical plant, as well as the learning/teaching process. Everyone has something to give; it is the task of community builders to create the environment where all are sensitive to the wisdom each possesses.

And the fertile ground of this learning environment must be heterosexual communal living, if future efforts are to bear joyful fruit.

An Urbutz

In the center of most large cities there are growing up loose configurations of people under 30, living in individual houses or apartments of six-twelve, who are beginning to play with the notion of getting together in some communal relationship beyond their own communal houses. It is unfortunate, though understandable, that they begin by defining themselves in the predominantly ecstatic terms of elysian freedom. It is unfortunate because the vision leads to a rejection of the responsibility facet of freedom, while overemphasizing the liberation side.

Since I work and live in the Washington Free Community, I will use it as a critical example. In January of 1968, a group of twenty young activists and artists came together in an old theater to talk about what they might do to provide facilities and services and generally make the scene for young people more meaningful. Plans were hatched for workshops (pottery, sewing, photography, film, dance, acting) and exchanges (jobs, communal houses), and a food co-op.

A four-page graphics and word explanation of the idea came out in the Washington *Free Press,* then the only counter-culture paper in the city, whose staff was among the first to conceive of the idea of an "underground" young people's community. But as the weeks went on it became clear that there were few people willing to take on the personal responsibility of doing the work necessary to make the various new projects happen. Most were too committed to doing their own things, whether that was political organizing, working on the *Free Press* or the American Playground (the community's radical theater: guerilla, street, and environmental) or otherwise pursuing a privatized vision of what cultural revolution meant. There was in all this a great deal of rationalization and abstract phrase-making, my own included.

Several of the early communal houses never congealed because the people were not honest with each other, let alone themselves individually. Basic questions about how they were to live together (meals, money, decoration of the house, crashers) were never resolved. But today there are eight or so communal houses with varying styles, degrees of cooperativeness, interpersonal communion, and activeness. There is also a great deal of transience in the houses, with an original group of eight or nine rarely staying together for more than nine months to a year.

Even now there is resistance to any inter-house coordination or organization, which is especially difficult because of the geographic separation of the houses and projects. In the beginning when a few suggested setting up a non-profit corporation (the officers were to be figureheads with all decisions made by a democratic body) so that the community could begin to generate its own funds for projects and to buy communal houses, the idea was denounced as a "sell-out" and "totalitarianism."

Perhaps it is too early to draw conclusions about the experience of the Washington Free Community, perhaps I am too critical because my hopes were so high; but I think we can learn something valuable from the first year of this experiment. It seems clear that the commitment of the early core group that met at the theater was to an idea, not to each other. This is one of the most destructive aspects to utopian or visionary thinking, namely, that the relationships of the people to each other is filtered and mediated through the mental structure of what they think they should be doing. The relations between people become rigid. People resort to dogmatic clichés of what is current to be radical and unquestioning allegiance to the original idea of what you are supposedly about. People hide behind political rhetoric and the sanctity of their "thing."

Buber would say there was no community, the people did not ". . . have a common relation to the center overriding all other relations . . ." For when a true community forms, the commitment is to each other first and foremost, and as a result, the vision of how you are to live together is based on who you actually are, without your rhetorical defenses. Where the personal commitment exists there is honesty in expressing one's hopes and reservations, there is trust that you will be respected as a person and not mocked for your views and feelings, and perhaps most importantly, there is a willingness to learn from each other. Where there is no honesty, no trust, no willingness to learn and develop, there will be no coordination or organization of joint work (outside of small ad-hoc groups) and there will be no regular mechanism, such as a weekly meal and meeting, for decision-making. And where there is no center of energy and no magnetism between people who trust each other there will be the continual turn-over of people passing on to other cities and other scenes. Today's mobility is as much a search for a home as a thirst for experience.

Another problem in the Free Community is the absence of a sense of tradition, a rootedness in history. There is a general feeling that what we are doing is totally new, that there have been few before who have tried such experiments, or that the city, or affluence, or the media have so radically changed our environment there is no previous experience to draw on. As a friend told me, "I've come to the point where I think there is no one who can teach us anything." This anti-intellectualism, this refusal to see ourselves on the cutting edge of the fertile history of socialist humanism, Marxist and otherwise, has a deep existential root. All of us in the Free Community have arrived at our present radicalism through a rejection of the imposed teachings and pious moralism of authoritarian families and schools. Wisdom and learning appeared as a rationalization for a repressive social system so obviously anti-human, manipulative, and plastic. In the process of personal liberation we perhaps overreacted. This accounts for our distrust of the intellectual process and the absence of personal discipline. But perhaps the cause goes deeper into our psychological past in that we really don't trust our own ability to discern sham and fantasy from true wisdom. This may tie in with a refusal to be honest about our own perception and intelligence, in that we may

have to be willing to admit error or lack of insight and in the process change who (we think) we are. If we can overcome this existential mistrust and self-doubt we will be greatly enriched and strengthened by an enormous wealth of wisdom, not only in history, but among ourselves.

But the Washington Free Community is young and hopefully we will see in the coming years its development toward a cohesive micro-socialist urbutz. Such an urbutz might share some of the skeletal forms of the present community but would be much closer to the spiritual and socialist tradition of the kibbutzim. There would be the communion of the Buberian center, the essential inner cohesion, collaboration, and mutual stimulation and decision-making of true community. There would be an eagerness to experiment with new modes of organization and coordination of joint work and projects. There would be internal revenue generation and a regular meeting for group planning toward the future. But most important is the sacred commitment to each other in this time and in this place. For it is upon this rock that all we do, individually and collectively, rests.

SUGGESTED READING

Benello, C. George. "Participatory Democracy and the Dilemma of Change," in Priscilla Long (Ed.), *The New Left: A Collection of Essays.* Porter-Sargeant: Boston, 1969.

Benello, C. George. "The Wasteland Culture," *Our Generation,* vol. 5, no. 2, September, 1967.

Bottomore, T. B. (Ed.). *Karl Marx: Early Writings.* McGraw-Hill: New York.

Buber, Martin. *Paths in Utopia.* Beacon Press Paperback: Boston, 1949. (Highly recommended. Perhaps the best work on community building and the history of socialism.)

Engels, Frederick. *The Origin of the Family, Private Property, and the State.* New World Paperbacks: New York, 1942.

Engels, Frederick. *Socialism: Utopian and Scientific.* New World Paperbacks: New York, 1947.

Fried, Albert, and Sanders, Ronald (Eds.). *Socialist Thought: A Documentary History.* Doubleday Anchor: Garden City (N.Y.), 1964.

Fromm, Erich. *The Heart of Man.* Harper Colophon: New York, 1968.

Fromm, Erich. *The Sane Society.* Fawcett paperback: Greenwich (Conn.), 1955.

Infield, Henrick F. *Cooperative Communities at Work.* Dryden Press: New York, 1945.

Infield, Henrick F. *Utopia and Experiment: Essays in the Sociology of*

Cooperation. F. A. Praeger: New York, 1955.

Mattick, Paul. "Workers' Control," in Priscilla Long (Ed.), *The New Left: A Collection of Essays.* Porter-Sargeant: Boston, 1969.

Heaven Isn't Perfect

San Francisco Examiner

For better or worse, there will be 100 million more Americans in the world by the end of the century. Since 70 per cent of the existing U.S. population is already crowded into one urban sprawl or another, it seems clear some new housing solution is required.

The likeliest and perhaps even the cheapest such solution is the "new town."

Reluctantly, tardily, but with a feeling of inevitability, the U.S. is now weighing an immense commitment to build many such towns. One prestigious task force of government officials has recently issued a book-length report recommending that fully 110 new cities be built in the next three decades.

And they're not talking about villages. According to the report, 10 of the cities should be designed to accommodate one million people each: the other 100 would be 100,000 each.

No one has itemized the cost, but undoubtedly it would be of space-age proportions. The Committee for National Land Development Policy advocates "an industrial Homestead Act," with the Federal government giving free land to new towns, as it once did to railroads and farmers.

President Nixon is also weighing a "surprise" request for legislation before the end of the year, a program that would encompass the building of 100 new cities before the year 2000.

Such a beginning is long overdue. Britain has been building "new towns" for almost a quarter of a century and the Scandinavian countries have not been far behind. Thus far, however, the U.S. has only a handful actually being

Reprinted by permission from the *San Francisco Examiner,* October 19, 1969.

lived in, and these are still a tiny fraction of their intended size.

Columbia, Md., for example, halfway between Baltimore and Washington, D.C., hopes to have 125,000 residents by 1980. But after more than two years of promotion and development, only 1000 families have moved in. And they are by no means ecstatic over the experience.

"A city ought to belong to its people," says Irwin Auerbach, who with his wife and daughter comprise one of Columbia's "first families."

But Auerbach has a feeling of powerlessness in his new community. "The real control is in the hands of the developers," he says. "Still, it's a better way of life than we've had before . . . and I have high expectations."

New towns like Columbia and Reston, Va., in the Washington area, Valencia and Irvine in California, Litchfield Park, Ariz., and Clear Lake City, Tex., are thoroughly planned. They run to garden apartments, cluster homes and vistas of green. Cars are usually kept on the perimeters, and shopping centers are built within walking distance of homes.

But the main ingredient of a new town that is truly new—and the single thing that differentiates it from a suburban development— is local industry. Ideally, the large majority of residents should be able to work in the immediate vicinity. America's new towns lack this attribute.

Thus, the plans of private industry are crucial to the future. Some firms are already involved in new towns; others plan such involvement.

Southern California Edison has announced it will build an "all-electric" city near Los Angeles. Westinghouse will build something similar in Florida, Humble Oil is sponsoring Clear Lake City and Goodyear is associated with Litchfield Park.

But both the Humble and Goodyear projects are within commuting range of large cities. As yet, it is not certain whether the new towns involved will be true new towns or merely large suburban developments of Houston, Tex., and Phoenix, Ariz.

The modern concept of the new town was first formulated by a visionary British land reformer named Ebenezer Howard in his 1898 book, "Tomorrow." Howard's ideal of a "garden city" inspired the building of Letchworth and Welwyn in the early decades of this century and has since led to

24 new cities with a total population of more than 500,000.

But the blandness of the architecture—and apparently of the life style has led to a syndrome called the new "town blues," one observer summed up the local reaction:

"One neatly controlled vista after another . . . everything nice, pat and predictable. It's like dying and going to heaven and deciding you don't like it there."

The Scandinavians have had similar problems. But according to Wolf Von Eckardt, architectural critic of The Washington Post, their new towns nevertheless make "even the best U.S. suburbs look woefully deprived."

Von Eckardt and most other critics are especially impressed with Tapiola, Finland, which seems to have broken out of the mildness mold. "It looks and feels," he says, "as spontaneously lusty and natural, in an endearingly well-behaved sort of way, as the Finnish children that swarm all over."

Though the problem is notably absent in the slow-paced U.S. program, it is, of course, possible to go too fast in building new cities.

West Germany is pushing a project to jam 50,000 Berliners into Maerkisches-Vierte—and though the people will probably get there by the 1972 target, many of the facilities will not. Complaints about shortages of schools, streets and shopping facilities have drained the project of the triumph its high-pressure planners expected.

One kind of new town always has good possibilities of achieving a balance in housing and local employment. Government cities, whatever their other deficiencies, at least provide a steadily growing demand for labor. Brasilia is a case in point; so are Islamabad, Pakistan, and Chandigarh, in the Indian state of Punjab.

The process should not be unfamiliar. The U.S., too, once had a new and carefully planned city: Washington, D.C.

There is a story of an American Indian who supported his family by tilling a little plot of soil less than an acre in size. He was befriended by a neighbor, a wealthy white farmer. This man, pitying his poor friend his meager subsistence, offered him several acres of adjoining land as a gift.

"You are kind," answered the Indian, "but see: the land I have is quite enough for our needs. If I had more to till, when would I find time for singing?"

If men would only simplify their needs, how much time might they not find to sing.

Kriyananda
(From *Cooperative Communities: How to Start Them, and Why*, San Francisco, Ananda Publications, 1970.)

Ananda

By Jim Mitchell

Gold-hungry men once raped and scarred the hills between Sacramento and Reno, while the California sunshine baked the soil into rich, red dust. Clouds of the warm dust follow my footprints now, as I walk with new and young people who have come here to settle the Sierra foothills and give them a loving consciousness. Bare or sandaled feet, long hair, beards and blue jeans, Pakistani or Indian prints—a Hare Kirshna chant rises above drum and cymbals, a marriage of expectation and inward peace. Twenty-or-so young adults on the dusty path ahead of me are searching their land for the site of the teepee village they will build to sustain them through the harsh Sierra winter.

Ananda, the dream of an American Yogi, is both retreat and community. About two years ago, he and a group of Yoga followers purchased 72 acres of dry grassland in the Sierra foothills near Nevada City, California. The land bent up, over, and down the clay soil of the foothills, supporting thin forests of deciduous and pine trees, deer, berries, and hawks.

From "Ananda," *The Modern Utopia*, 4, 2 (Spring, 1970). Reprinted by permission of the Alternatives Foundation, P.O. Drawer A, Diamond Heights Station, San Francisco, California 94131.

Three forks of the Yuba river cut the land nearby, but their path is deep in canyons, leaving the surface of most of the land with little water. In summer, the sky is blue and clouds are unknown; in winter, snow is drifted through the forest by 70-mile-per-hour winds.

Yet today, geodesic domes rise on the 72-acre Ananda Meditation Retreat. A common house (food, meetings), an office, and a temple are arranged near the wooden water tank and small garden. A-frame cabins, scarcely 20 feet long and yet complete with meditation rooms, are occupied year-round. Hundreds of people are now involved in this dream of Kriyananda, the Yogi who originated the project, and they look to Ananda as their meditation retreat and spiritual center.

Ananda grew from Kriyananda's book, *Cooperative Communities—How to Start Them and Why.* Paramhansa Yogananda proposed self-realization cooperatives, or "world brotherhood colonies" as an alternative living situation in a world whose tensions and pressures had grown far beyond the control of the individual. From the Yoga precept that all good things come from the inner man, it follows that "self-realized" men will be a force for good in the larger world of all men. Ananda, therefore, is far from being a withdrawal from modern life; rather, it is a statement of how all men might live. Develop the inner self, and all else will follow. As Kriyananda says,

To "hie away" to the country, then, need in no way imply a rejection of one's social responsibilities. It can become, rather, the beginning of a sincere assumption of such responsibilities.

Kriyananda's cooperative community simply provides the social context compatible with development of the inner self.

The community might, in short, be similar in many ways to any village, with the basic distinction that it would be an intentional community, based on cooperation, not competition, on self-unfoldment rather than on self-aggrandizement at the expense of one's fellows.

And so, in his book he treats in theory the details of community life: economics, government, social and physical structures, education. He favors prohibition of drugs and limitation of smoking, growing of organic produce, use of talents of members to provide income from outside, an established

but flexible government, and a creative educational system at least through the elementary grades. He also feels there is "no reason why a community seeking a natural way of life should utterly reject modern civilization," and would have the community buy such goods and services as needed from outside. His characteristic realism shows through when discussing pitfalls of communal life:

. . . Let us not expect miracles. It is enough if a new way of life is better than the old. It is too much to ask it to be perfect.

Many people in the Bay area are involved in the Ananda Meditation Retreat. They attend weekend meditation seminars with Kriyananda, spend whole weeks there, and some few live year-round at the retreat. Complete adherence to the teachings of Yogananda is not required; all the members are asked is to be in sympathy with the practice of this belief. Members and share-holders in the retreat find there a place of peace, of warm smiles, of genuine friendship, and of spiritual guidance.

The retreat has grown well in two years. But in July of this year, Kriyananda's dream of a complete year-round community was jolted into a dynamic existence. Nearly 400 acres of land came up for purchase only six miles from Ananda Meditation Retreat. Within twelve hours, the Ananda community voted and purchased 270 acres, centered around an old run-down farmhouse, and took an option on 80 more acres in the surrounding hills. Now there were two Ananda's —meditation retreat and farm community.

And here am I, following these young people, whose meditations and chants are so strange and whose joy in their land and lives is so evident to me. We are walking their land, feeling her consciousness, praying to all the great religious masters, guru's, and yogi's for guidance in selecting the site of the first winter community at Ananda. We hadn't gone a half mile before my college skepticism lost to their joy and now I, too, am singing Hare Krishna.

We've stopped. Tom and John, the tacitly accepted leaders of the community, turn toward a hillside of light brush, now shadowed by the setting Sierra sun. They raise their arms high, and the sacred Om comes seven times, deep from within—a blessing borne on human wind. We all chant the

sacred word with them, breathing as necessary when addressing God and settling the dust within ourselves. Peace comes; we stand and look at the hillside. Tom talks of the eastern exposure, cut off by another hill from the morning sun. Jim, a local farmer who is paid by the community for far less than the value of his advice and experience, tells now of the watershed pollution problem, of the location of the pads for the teepees, and of the erosion problems. After ten minutes of discussion among the community, this site is abandoned—wrong ecology, wrong vibrations. Once again, chant, drum, and cymbals mark the passage of a community over its land.

As we walk down one hill and toward another, a full moon red from the dust of this land begins to rise over the higher Sierras to the east. We round a grassy knoll that rolls up, westward and to our right. Another discussion of pads, exposure, winds, roads, and drainage, and without a word we all scramble to separate corners of the hill. We sit on the hill, like so many pawns at mid-game. Silence. Tom and John rise, and walk back up the road. One-by-one, the community rises to follow. All together again, we sit down in the tall grass and look eastward toward the dawning moon. But our view is blocked by a single tree at the foot of the knoll. We rise, and together move 50 yards left. Immediately Hare Krishna rises with the red moon. Before us, the rolling foothills hold our farmhouse gently, softly. The round red moon climbs toward its morning eclipse.

While we sing, unity flows over us just as night engulfs the valley. Together, we stand and lock arms. Our dance and chant soon tire three-year-old Timshel, and Geri, her mother, breaks the circle of arms to hold her. A reflection shoots through the broken circle: is this really to be the site of the first long winter at Ananda? Everyone moves together in a group embrace, uncertain, yet saying "yes" with silent voices.

A feeling of absolute peace and unity catches everyone in the group, including my wife and I. Once again, Om goes up seven times over the valley—but now it is a statement, not a plea. The drum hanging silent from his shoulder, John turns to the valley and prays, ". . . bless this, the site of our temple . . ."

Quiet, communion, a reading from the Autobiography. The moon turns from red to white.

Someone asks no one, "Is this it?" John answers, "It sort of has to be now. It's been taken out of our hands." Tom ponders, smiles, and replies, "Except, it wasn't in our hands to begin with."

We walked and chanted back to the farmhouse, while I thought of their winter and mine. On the hill to our left, the foundation of the community's two-story A-frame schoolhouse was nearly ready for pouring. Goats stirred in the field. Crickets sang as the moon lit our path back to the farmhouse and more of their land's mint tea.

The spirit of Ananda has given some focus to my latent wish for a viable alternative to both the drugged idealism of "hip" and the subtle trap of urban comfort. Here is a beginning, an answer to Seattle's August. Country life isn't easy, and communal life has such particular problems as economics, diet, and sanitation. But these are direct, existential problems whose reality includes possible solution, not the impossible confluence of uncontrolled mobs, concrete, politics, and pollution, of constant "independence" (alienation) or "entertainment" (distraction). At Ananda, each person is free to build a new and beautiful reality, for such a reality need only be the sum of the spirit and body of each member—you become a new society, and the strength and beauty of that society depends directly on your own spirit. All during my stay at Ananda, my ears echoed Luke's maxim, "Physician, heal thyself."

The Genesis of Normative Systems in Rural Hippie Communes: A Summary

By Benjamin Zablocki

In traditional society, the forces that bind groups of people together may be characterized either as sovereignty (a monopoly on the legitimate use of force) or tradition. The intentional community affords an opportunity to look at society in miniature, before the beginnings of sovereignty and tradition. Most of the twelve communities in the study began with attempts at complete anarchism;

By permission of the author. Quotes are from his unpublished works.

all later looked for a means of re-establishing the normative order. The responses of the communities fall into three categories which are not mutually exclusive: (1) fragmentation, (2) the institution of contract, (3) the search for world view consensus.

Fragmentation is the process of dividing the community, either into familial groups or subcommunities or into communal, cooperative, and individualistic segments. "This is the most primitive form of normative system and it might be argued that groups which rely upon it exclusively are not really communities at all."

"A certain amount of harmony and coordination must be maintained constantly, somehow, without infringing upon the freedom of the individual. Toward this end, three of the communities studied modified absolute anarchism into what may be called 'contractual anarchism.' Basic anarchism assumes that men are altruistic in intention and responsible in action. Contractual anarchism makes only the first of these assumptions. Thus it permits individual freedom in entering into contracts, but it demands that contracts once entered into are carried out . . ."

"The most widely used means of normative structuring is the search for world view consensus. These communities believe that their members perceive the world in basically the same way, often this was the original reason for coming together. Such communities adopted the policy of making group decisions unanimously. . . ."

"Finding a charismatic leader is often a solution of a community's need for normative order. Curiously, sometimes such a leader brings about a total reversal in the politics of the community from anarchy to authoritarianism. . . ."

The various techniques discussed for developing normative systems were moderately successful; six of the twelve communities studied have since disintegrated, with an average life span of two years. "In general, segmental communities have had the greatest success. The evidence points to a basic contradiction within the hippie communitarian idea. . . ."

"The communal spirit of the beginning tends to fade away, returning, if at all, sporadically. The structure of anarchy itself then becomes a means of exploitation. Anarchy without mutual concern favors tyranny of the strong over the weak, and the tyranny of the least-committed over the most-

committed. In illustration of the first, it is generally the men in such communities who tend to be anarchist, while the women tend to be democratic. The second type of tyranny is seen in any relationship in which there is unequal commitment. The burden is always on the most committed person to convince the other to do what is necessary to keep the community together. . . ."

"The communiteers are faced with a dilemma. If they remain faithful to the original spirit of the community, they will find it extremely difficult to develop a complex instrumental structure (often economically necessary). If they develop a complex structure, they may cut themselves off from the manifestation of the group spirit. . . ."

"If the original spirit were to continuously regenerate itself, this would solve the problem. This seems to be the major function of religion in communal life, and it helps to explain why, historically, religious communities have been the only ones that have really been successful. To some extent, the hippies have been successful in using collective drug experiences as the functional equivalent of religion. . . ."

Some Thoughts

By Buckminster Fuller

Professor John R. Platt, Chicago University physicist and biophysicist, in a thorough survey of the overall shapes of a family of trend curves which comprehensively embrace science technology and man in universe, says: "The world has become too dangerous for anything less than Utopia" (p. 288).

Not only did all the attempts to establish Utopias occur prematurely (in respect of technological capability to establish and maintain any bacteria- and virus-immune, hungerless, travel anywhere Utopias), but all of the would-be Utopians disdained all the early manifestations of industrialization as "unnatural, stereo-

From *Utopia or Oblivion* by R. Buckminster Fuller. Copyright © 1969 by Buckminster Fuller. By permission of Bantam Books, Inc.

typed, and obnoxiously sterile." The would-be Utopians, therefore, attempted only metaphysical and ideological transformations of man's nature—unwitting any possible alternatives. It was then unthinkable that there might soon develop a full capability to satisfactorily transform the physical energy events and material structure of the environment—not by altering man, but by helping him to become literate and to use his innate cerebral capabilities, and thereby to at least achieve man's physical survival at a utopianly successful level.

All the attempts to establish Utopias were not only premature and misconceived, but they were also exclusive. Small groups of humanity withdrew from and forsook the welfare of the balance of humanity. *Utopia, must be, inherently, for all or none.*[1] A minority's knowledge that the majority of humanity suffers and deteriorates while only the minority prospers would never permit a Utopian degree of contentment of the all-powerful subconscious reflexing of the human brain (pp. 289–290).

. . . Jerome Wiesner, head of the Department of Nuclear Physics at the Massachusetts Institute of Technology and past science adviser to Presidents Eisenhower, Kennedy, and Johnson, writing in a recent issue of *Scientific American,* states, "The clearly predictable course of the arms race is a steady downward spiral into oblivion." But he did not say how it could be arrested. Let us, too, at least give ourselves a chance to vote to commit ourselves earnestly for the Design Science Decade approach to attaining Utopia. This moment of realization that it soon must be Utopia or Oblivion coincides exactly with the discovery by man that for the first time in history Utopia is, at least physically, possible of human attainment (pp. 291–292).

[1] Emphasis added.

Words on Religion

A visitor to Canyon meets people who really enjoy their community. Every day Canyon residents help each other out by sharing physical labor, transportation, and moral support during legal hassles. The inner strength and stability of the community point towards its successes.

Other groups of people realize the importance of inner strength and seek to establish it through shared religions, rites, or rituals. Benjamin Zablocki likens communal drug use to communion and comments on the commonly reported psychedelic feeling of loss of personal ego and a melting into a communal ego.

Whether a religion requires partial commitment such as Nicherin Shoshu chanting or leads to an entirely different life style such as the Hare Krishna monks who must chant nearly 2000 times a day, the intended result is the same—a feeling of group spiritual consciousness. If any idea or feeling is real for a person, then it is real.

May the Divine Mother, She-of-White-Raiment, " '. . . be my rear guard; May I be safely led across the dangerous ambush of the *Bardo;* And may I be placed in the state of the All-Perfect Buddhahood.'

By praying thus, humbly and earnestly, thou wilt merge into the heart of the Divine Father-Mother, the Bhagavan Amitabha, in halo of rainbow-light, and attain Buddhahood in the *Sambhoga-Kaya,* in the Western Realm named Happy."

(From W. Y. Evans-Wentz' edition of *The Tibetan Book of the Dead,* Oxford University Press.)

HEXAGRAM XXXIX, THE KIEN

```
—— ——
————
—— ——
————
—— ——
—— ——
```

The Kien

In the state indicated by Kien advantage will be found in the southwest, and the contrary in the northeast. It will be advantageous also to meet with the great man. In these circumstances, with firmness and correctness, there will be good fortune.

1. From the first line, divided, we learn that advance on the part of its subject will lead to greater difficulties, while remaining stationary will afford a ground for praise.

2. The second line, divided, shows the minister of the king struggling with difficulty on difficulty, and not with a view to his own advantage.

3. The third line, undivided, shows its subject advancing, but only to greater difficulties. He remains stationary, and returns to his former associates.

4. The fourth line, divided, shows its subject advancing, but only to greater difficulties. He remains stationary, and unites with the subject of the line above.

5. The fourth line, undivided, shows its subject struggling with the greatest difficulties, while friends are coming to help him.

6. The topmost line, divided, shows its subject going forward, only to increase the difficulties, while his remaining stationary will be productive of the great merit. There will be good fortune, and it will be advantageous to meet with the great man.

(From James Legge [trans.], *I Ching* [The Book of Changes], New York, Dover.)

WHAT IS THE INTERNATIONAL SOCIETY FOR KRISHNA CONSCIOUSNESS?

The International Society for Krishna Consciousness was formed in 1966 by Prabhupada A. C. Bhaktivedanta Swami, who came from India on the order of his Spiritual Master to preach love of God to the people of the West. Prabhupada is in a line of disciplic succession going back directly 500 years to the time when Lord Chaitanya appeared in India, and from there back still further—5000 years—to the time when Krishna first spoke The Bhagavad Gita to His disciple Arjuna.

Krishna Consciousness is experienced as a process of self purification. Its means and end are an open secret, and there is no financial charge for learning Khrishna Consciousness or receiving initiation into the chanting of Hare Krishna. The gist of devotional service to Krishna is that one takes whatever capacity or talent he or she has and dovetails it with the interests of the Supreme Enjoyer, the Lord, Sri Krishna. The writer writes articles for Krishna, and we publish periodicals in this way. The businessman does business in order to establish many temples across the country. The housholders raise children in the science of God, and husband and wife live in mutual co-operation for spiritual progress. These activities are done under the sanction of the expert Spiritual Master, and in line with the Scriptures. Devotional service in Krishna Consciousness means regular chanting in the temple, hearing talks about the Pastimes of Krishna from Srimad Bhagwatam, and taking foodstuffs

PHOTO COURTESY OF JOSHUA WATTLES.

prepared for and offered to the Supreme Personality of Godhead.

By books, literature and records, the Society is dedicated to awakening the worldwide public to the normal, ecstatic state of Krishna Consciousness, so that all may regain their eternal position of favorably serving the will of Krishna. Sankirtan—congregational chanting—is carried to the people: in public parks, schools, on t.v., in the theater, on the streets. Krishna Consciousness is not an idler's philosophy. Rather by chanting and by engagement in the service of Krishna, anyone who takes part will experience the state of "Samadhi," ecstatic absorption in God-consciousness, 24 hours a day!

As the philosophy of Krishna Consciousness is non-sectarian, any man, Hindu or Christian, will become better in his faith by chanting the Holy Name of God and by hearing The Bhagavad Gita. Without knowledge and realization and loving service to the One Supreme God, there can be no religion. Let everyone rejoice in the Sankirtan Movement, and we may see the fulfillment of the prediction

made by Lord Chaitanya 500 years ago: that the chanting of the Holy Names of God, Hare Krishna, would be carried to every town and village of the world. Only in this way can real peace prevail. It is sublime and easy.

HARE KRISHNA, HARE KRISHNA,
KRISHNA KRISHNA, HARE, HARE,
HARE RAMA, HARE RAMA,
RAMA RAMA, HARE HARE

A safe beginning, it seems to me, would be to heed well the fact that most successful colonies have been religiously oriented. If the idea of world brotherhood colonies is to spread, it would be well for at least the initial experiments not to be planned without including this (so far) all but essential ingredient.

But a religious orientation does not imply sectarianism. The pure essence of religion is its emphasis on an inner life. It is not because of religious fanaticism that communities have held together, but because the inner life developed in each member by his faith has given him a peace to smile away petty annoyances, a flexibility

to meet his neighbor part way on disagreements, a freedom to enjoy things without attachment. In the sense of emphasizing this inner awareness, no community can afford to be lax. It is to make possible such an inner life that cooperative communities are needed in the first place.

Kriyananda
(From *Cooperative Communities:*
How to Start Them, and Why,
San Francisco,
Ananda Publications, 1970.)

You don't change the world, you change yourself.

Krishnamurti

. . . To put it into so many words, to define it, was to limit it. If it's this, then it can't be that . . . Yet there it was! Everyone had his own thing he was working out, but it all fit into the group thing, which was—"the Unspoken Thing," said Page Browning, and that was as far as anyone wanted to go with words.

For that matter, there was no theology to it, no philosophy, at least not in the sense of an ism. There was no goal of an improved moral order in the world or an improved social order, nothing about salvation and certainly nothing about immortality or the life hereafter. Hereafter! That was a laugh. If there was ever a group devoted totally to the here and now it was the Pranksters. I remember puzzling over this. There was something so . . . religious in the air, in the very atmosphere of the Prankster life, and yet one couldn't put one's finger on it. On the face of it there was just a group of people who had shared an unusual psychological state, the LSD experience—

But exactly! The experience—that was the word! and it began to fall into place. In fact, none of the great founded religions, Christianity, Buddhism, Islam, Jainism, Judaism, Zoroastrianism, Hinduism, none of them began with a philosophical framework or even a main idea. They all began with an overwhelming new experience . . .

Tom Wolfe

(Reprinted with the permission of Farrar, Straus & Giroux, Inc. from *The Electric Kool-Aid Acid Test* by Tom Wolfe. Copyright © 1968 by Tom Wolfe.)

Religion in the Age of Aquarius: A Conversation with Harvey Cox

By T. George Harris

Do you know what people are saying when they ask your sign? They are saying I want to relate to you, to be intimate with you in this kooky, interesting way—a way that is going to blow the minds of those goddamned rationalists. The logical people who have organized our society have defined us into categories that we can't live in. . . .

So along comes this absolutely weird group of categories unrelated to social status or anything else. Nobody's defining you, and your not putting a tag on him. If you're a Taurus and I'm a Taurus, my god, immediately we've got a secret intimacy. We enter into this

little conspiracy . . . this little conspiracy going against the . . . people who put down everything that is not scientifically demonstrable or socially presentable. So we find our own ways to define ourselves.

The astrology trip is a form of play, of relating to each other in ways we don't have to take too seriously until we know we want to. In a broader sense, astrology and drugs and Zen are forms of play, of testing new perceptions of reality without being committed to their validity in advance—or ever. . . .

I'm not alone, of course, in feeling that in our frantic rush to affluence we have paid a high price in psychic damage. The convincing evidence is beginning to come out of psychology and anthropology. It suggests that we have almost lost or mutilated our gift for true festivity and celebration, for pure imagination and playful fantasy.

Today's partial rebirth of fantasy may be a deceptive flush on the cheek of a dying age. We're overdue. We have spent the last few hundred years with our cultural attention focused dourly on the "outside" factual world—exploring, investigating and mastering it.

Those who had a penchant for fantasy never really felt at home. They were even driven out of religious institutions, the shelter where the fantasies of the mystics would normally be cherished and cultivated. . . .

It's my conviction that conventional religion has declined not because of the advance of science or the spread of education of any of the reasons normally advanced for secularization. The reason is simple but hard to see because it is embedded in our total environment: the tight, bureaucratic and instrumental society—the only model we've known since the industrial revolution—renders us incapable of experiencing the nonrational dimensions of existence. The absurd, the inspiring, the uncanny, the awesome, the terrifying, the ecstatic—none of these fits into a production- and efficiency-oriented society. They waste time, aren't dependable. When they appear, we try to ban them by force or some brand name therapy. Having systematically stunted the Dionysian side of the whole human, we assume that man is just a reliable plane-catching Apollonian.

The blame for this distortion

usually gets hung on something called "puritanism" or the "Protestant ethic." But this analysis, I believe, is not entirely adequate. No religion yet tested seems to stand unbent by the managerial faith known as "economic development." Communism, nationalism and other ideologies have gone the same route elsewhere on the globe.

We are never completely the captives of our culture or its language. People all over the world are turning, often desperately, to the overlooked corners and freaks that were never completely systematized. Hence our fascination for pop art and, gloriously, for Fellini's films—junk and rejects of the industrial process. Also with the slippery stuff that never found a place in it: astrology, madness, witches, drugs, non-Western religions, palmistry and mysticism, shoddy or serious.

Even the current preoccupation with sex and violence can, to some extent, be understood in terms of this reaction. Both blood and sperm are explosive, irregular, feeling-pitched, messy and inexplicably fascinating. You can't store either one safely in the humming memory of an IBM 360, to be smoothly printed out only when needed in the program. To use a theological term, they transcend routine experience. . . .

Most of the sophisticated, critical theology being written today—and this has been true for several decades—comes out of the 19th century discovery of the historically conditioned character of our tradition, of our Bible, of our encyclicals and rituals. Everything in conventional religion has become second hand. We are allowed to feel it only through careful study of the people who first experienced it long ago.

Look, my thesis here is that the sociology of religion is posing problems that theology has to give attention to now—the problems of present experience. Theology has to go much deeper into the social sciences, which suffer from an overweening presentism but can offset the obsessional past in theology. Ever since Emile Durkheim, sociologists have been laying the base for systematic study of the nonhistoric dimension of experience, often without meaning to.

. . . People are playing with new perceptions. It's not just the girls who join witches' covens or put on benign hexes. Arthur Waskow reports in "Liberation" on

WE'D LIKE YOU TO

GET FROCKED

JOIN OUR RAPIDLY GROWING FAITH AS AN

° **ORDAINED MINISTER** °

FAR OUT!

WITH A RANK OF

° **DOCTOR OF DIVINITY** °

We want men and women of all ages, who believe as we do, to join us in the holy search for Truth. We believe that all men should seek Truth by all just means. As one of our ministers you can:

1. Ordain others in our name.
2. Set up your own church and apply for exemption from property and other taxes.
3. Perform marriages and exercise all other ecclesiastic powers.
4. Get sizeable cash grants for doing our missionary work.
5. Seek draft exemption as one of our working missionaries. We can tell you how.
6. Some transportation companies, hotels, theaters, etc., give reduced rates to ministers.

GET THE WHOLE PACKAGE FOR $10.00

Along with your Ordination Certificate, Doctor of Divinity and I.D. card, we'll send you 12 blank forms to use when you wish to ordain others. Your ordination is completely legal and valid anywhere in this country. Your money back without question if your package isn't everything you expect it to be. For an additional $10 we will send your Ordination and D.D. Certificates beautifully framed and glassed.

SEND NOW TO: **MISSIONARIES OF THE NEW TRUTH**
P.O. Box 1393, Dept. **T-5**
Evanston, Illinois

REPRINTED BY PERMISSION FROM *THE BERKELEY TRIBE*, APRIL 10–17, 1970.

the whole range of rituals among radical groups, who at times are too serious to play in the way I mean it. They have underground churches, exorcism, Buddhist communities, immolations, confessionals, tie-dye vestments, burn-the-money offerings, encounter groups, monastic contemplations, Indian runes, freedom Seeders, commune liturgies, the whole bit.

. . . The search for new perceptions, however, is not limited to radicals or neo-mystics. I noticed a while back that my students were reading—really hooked on—six books that ordinarily would not seem to have anything in common. Here they are:

Stranger in a Strange Land, Robert Heinlein's science fiction on the human-from-Mars. Valentine Michael Smith, the Hero, could "grok," that beautiful verb for total comprehension, in a way that we earthlings have trained ourselves not to do.

I Ching, the "book of changes" or the sacred books of ancient China.

The Double Helix, the account of how the genetic code was broken—by imagining pretty molecular structures and finding out which one could, by inference, be assumed to exist. Also, there

were so many completely nonscientific factors—trying to beat Linus Pauling and coping with ill-tempered Rosie, the chick in the next lab.

The Teachings of Don Juan, Carlos Castenada's account of the romantic who refused to see things as practical men did, and do.

The Politics of Experience, psychiatrist R. D. Laing's wild wonderful application of the theory that schizophrenia is double vision, a survival reaction.

The Mind of the Dolphin, John C. Lilly's research on what the comics of the sea say to each other.

These books all deal with unorthodox, often spooky ways of knowing and feeling, even with seeing things as the dolphin does.

But getting into a nonliteral mode of thought, let alone trying to write about it is nearly impossible for many people. . . .

. . . Durkheim open(ed) up the study of religion. . . . He took on very early the sociologists who wanted to get rid of religion. Religion is not a carry-over from the age of superstition, he pointed out, because religious symbols are essential. They unify the social group. Maybe the best behavioral

definition of religion is simply that it's the highest order of symbol system—the one by which other symbol systems and metaphors and myths and values of a culture are ultimately legitimized. The clammy inanities of the present church liturgy have no power to bring us together.

. . . To comprehend religion's place in industrial, urban society, you have to look at more than the church. In *The Invisible Religion* Thomas Luckmann showed that the church has lost its monopoly on religious symbols. Luckmann . . . is very important to me because he showed that we have been looking at far too narrow a phenomenon—the church.

Another guy who has influenced me is Robert Bellah. . . . Focusing on Presidential inaugurals, he caught the religious overtones and rituals in national life.

Wouldn't it be interesting to analyze The Movement as a kind of counter-civil religion emerging in America with, already, its own sacred texts: "I Have a Dream," for instance, and "Damn Americans Who Build Coffins," and a section of "Marcuse" and one on "draft card immolations." Every radical has to find symbols that are extrinsic, esoteric and have the power to keep him from being encapsulated in the existing culture. . . .

Sister Mary Corita . . . artist Corita Kent—is enormously important. . . . With her paintings she lets us say that man's creations, even the venial ones, are sacred. . . . Corita's humanizing the environment and also reminding us that the world is, as she says, unfinished. There's a new universe to create. She brings off these two masterful strokes at once, and she's got the love to put an ironic twist on slogans that have been used for manipulation. . . .

Post-industrial man is rediscovering festivity. In churches all over the country there's been this eruption of multimedia masses, jazz rituals, folk and rock worship services, new art and dance liturgies. You know, there's always a John Wesley around to wonder why the devil should have all the good things. Judson Memorial in New York and a few other churches have had "revelations," the nude dancers in psychedelic lights at the alter. Some people oppose the guitar and the leotard in church for the same reason their forbears opposed the use of the pipe organ—it never had been done before, or so they think. Others reject the festive new liturgies as merely the latest example of the Establishment's exploitation of flashy gimmicks to lure the recalcitrant back into the fold. They've got a point. Ecclesiastical imperialism is always a threat.

What matters is that the renaissance of festivity is comprehensive, and at the moment there's far more of that outside of the church than inside. . . .

Our feasting is now sporadic and obsessive, our fantasies predictable and our satire politically impotent. Our celebrations do not relate us, as they once did, to the parade of cosmic history or to the great stories of man's spiritual quest. If discovering that people have bodies is one of the risks we have to take, that seems to be a small—indeed pleasant—price to pay. . . .

Then came a student who was going to take the symbolic step forward in the induction center. But he didn't want it to be a dour affair. Since he was doing it to affirm life, refusing to kill, he got his girlfriend to make bread and strawberry jam and all his friends came with him, girls handing out flowers to the military and being festive. Even the people at their desks got caught in the spirit of it.

This kind of thing upsets many adults, not only because they disagree on ideas but because they think the kids are putting them on. They're afraid they are being had. What they don't understand is the whole idea of festivity and celebration. . . .

We may yet see comparative religion turn from its Protestant fixation on the texts of other faiths —surely a distorted and limiting view—to a more promising study of the whole religious ritual of a culture.

Some form of institutionalized religious expression is going to survive. Man is not only a religious being but a social one as well. He's not going to accept a completely do-it-yourself approach on anything this close to survival. Oh, the denominational type of Christianity headquartered in skyscrapers with branch offices in the suburbs is fated for rapid extinction, and it can't disappear too quickly for me. Yet, some form will rise out of the present resurgence of spiritual concern.

The figure of Christ is ubiquitous. He is now beginning to appear as Christ the Harlequin: the personification of celebration and fantasy in an age that has lost

both. It is a truer sense of Christ than the saccharine, bloodless face we see painted so often. He was part Yippie and part revolutionary, and part something else. On his day of earthly triumph, Palm Sunday, He rode to town on a jackass. One of the earliest representations of Jesus in religious art depicts a crucified figure with the head of an ass. A weak, even ridiculous church somehow peculiarly at odds with the ruling assumption of its day can once again appreciate the harlequinesque Christ.

Alternate Attractive Myths: Berkeley, Nature, Drugs

By Lynn Cadwallader

". . . And I feel like I'm fixin' to die." HELP! GOD! MOTHER! Where am I now? People lay the heavy Berkeley trip on you— peace, baby. Brotherhood, brother. So what about the 14-year-old brothers who only know how to ask for spare change? And the soul brothers who proposition a girl everytime she wears a skirt? Then you pass a Sunday morning scene on a sidewalk off of Telegraph: a chick about half a block away from her old man. Her hair is orange and brown and her face has the dark circled eyes and yellow color of too much speed and too many all-nighters. Her purple T-shirt and wrinkled levis cling to her body like so much dust. Her dragging feet stop as she yowls, "I'm gunna make a phone call." He keeps walking and his blond head doesn't turn. "Keep walkin'. Just keep walkin'." "No, I'm gunna make a phone call. Oh, man, he can't kick me off the street." The magnetic myth of Berkeley helps to scar another personality. Christ! I was on my way to church. When I got there, the sermon was some dribble read out of a book from the 1600's written for illiterate priests. Amusing. And the hip liberal lady who wore flowered pants inside a church could only say, "Is there any way to take the cannibalism out of communion?" I don't know, lady, because different minds interpret the symbolism of communion in different ways. But I do

By permission of the author.

know some people who care enough about what Jesus actually said to do something about Berkeley's particular problems. The Free Church, headed by Dick York, an ordained Episcopal priest feeds and houses kids as well as trying to answer their individual problems and giving them pertinent church services.

A lot of friends say their minds are boggled, their heads are not together. The combination of Berkeley freakiness and multiversity pressures and powers seems to be too much. They decide that an alternate style of life in Oregon, Canada or Alaska is the answer. Maybe it is. I was lucky. I had an Alaskan experience before the Berkeley experience and my head definitely feels somewhat together. Polly from Tennessee and I were living in isolated Indian and Eskimo villages last summer. About mid-way through our adventure we saw a *Life* magazine article about communes and people who thought they were getting close to nature. We didn't have to try to get close—we were with some people who even remembered a time of shelters in the woods instead of cabins. We were packing in all our water from a river and we didn't worry about the fish that swam around in it. That water and those fish were great! We went out with people to their fishnets in the early morning and huge salmon flapped at our feet. Someone killed a moose and passed it out to the whole village. We got a warm flank and learned how to cut and dry it for preservation. We cooked on wood burning stoves and tried a hand at splitting wood to keep ourselves warm. A bucket in the corner of our log cabin served as a toilet and had to be emptied every few days. We spent time with all ages, playing, working and listening. Some older people apologized for not speaking English very well, but God, could they tell stories. I apologize for not having learned their language. We wondered how Christianity applied to their lives. We understood as we sensed a spiritual group consciousness when forty people, some who didn't speak English, crowded into a one room log cabin for a prayer service we led. We were there, with people, when a man was drunk and shooting sled dogs, and when a forest fire was so close that the sky turned orange, then red, then pitch black in midday. We met households in which sexual activity and death were normal parts of life and not distorted or denied. We realized every day that what counts in living is caring about people, right now.

Yeah, Berkeley was a new thing, but I was ready. I discovered a few months ago that even if you're ready, it gets heavy. Finals were over and a friend, Steve, was taking me up to visit his brother who lives in a rural area north of the City. As soon as his van was buzzing along the freeway away from Berkeley, my head felt ten pounds lighter. I was elated and felt like smiling for three hours straight. Steve's brother, Bill, is about thirty and makes a living selling his ceramic pottery. The family, including wife, Irene, and Cosmo and Marka have tried living in communes and feel that they are not successful unless everybody involved knows each other quite well and everyone is able to take responsibility for work. They now have a pink house near farms, next to a railroad track that is used once a week for the pencil factory. They have goats and chickens and rabbits and gardens and plenty of love. An old grain store across the road serves as Bill's ceramic studio. They have many friends who live nearby and visit often. Upon meeting Walter, a former teacher, he offers you a hit off a forty foot coiled clay pipe and says, "That's mighty fine hash." He's president of the mushroom club and is planning a Morrell hunt for the summer. He is also planning a commune and thinking about ordinances and reflects, "In five years, there may be no rules." His wife is requesting running water, please, and her baby is being nursed by another friend who offers the formula for a good commune: separate houses, a strong leader, and plenty of grass.

Can plenty of grass, enough to keep everyone passive, be too much grass? Perhaps. A couple who lives in an isolated house accessible only by a dirt road was interesting to meet. They're on welfare and sometimes he makes jewelry. They moved very slowly and didn't have much to say. Laundry had been hanging out for a few days and he spent a lot of time nude. She said, "I knew you would do that sooner or later," as the baby urinated on her. "Yesterday I had wet pants all day." She blew some sweet marijuana smoke into his face and said, "There, that's all you get." They were nice, but maybe it was just a bad day to be visiting. I sensed stagnation.

Myths of happiness such as magical Berkeley, natural communal living and drugs grow ever more omnipotent. The attractiveness of an easy change to solve many problems leads many down unexpected avenues. Understanding and integrating a collection of experiences affords a broad development of self identity and a viable individual life style.

Beating the Man at the Gate

By Ralph J. Gleason

One Eye Connolly, the celebrated gate crasher, claimed to have gotten in free to all kinds of public events, from the Dempsey-Tunney fights to the World Series as a gate crasher. He had nothing on some of the young rock fans.

Neither did the hipsters who used to try to beat the door charge by sneaking in the rear exit at the Black Hawk, walking backwards as if they were changing their minds about leaving and were on some strip of film being reversed.

Today's youngsters come in the roof of Winterland, sneak up the backstairs of Fillmore West, crawl through the ventilators at the Berkeley Community Theater and climb the walls to drop down by the fountain at the Family Dog.

Cheap Ticket

Beating The Man is becoming a sport. It's gotten well past casually walking in with the audience at the intermission as if you'd been outside having a quick smoke. It's even gotten past borrowing somebody's ticket stub handed out the window to come in on the front gate, with the implied presumption you had left with permission.

Now the thing to do is buy a cheap ticket for the top of the balcony at a concert and calmly walk down the aisle and sit in a front seat until removed—forcibly. And it almost always has to be forcibly. Insistence on one's right to be in a seat one did not buy, if carried on with conviction, sets up a social situation where many elderly ushers (male or female) simply give in and most of the young ushers are at least latently sympathetic and after a certain point they don't care either.

The Ritual

At a recent concert in the Berkeley Community Theater, I watched two young ladies (I was about to say chickees, but then visions of Womens Lib flashed in my head and if there is one thing I can't stand, it's to see a strong woman cry) go through the ritual three times. They were balcony ticket holders and they sat in three different locations in the pit seats by the stage.

Each time the proper ticket holders came along and each time the usher had to be sent for and each time the young ladies made as much of a fuss as they could, and each time they lost. But they kept at it. The last time, the usher lost patience completely and yanked one of them right out of the seat.

That same night, when the ushers were trying to keep the balcony ticket holders (and gate crashers) from coming down to the lip of the stage, one young lady, a willowy blonde who ended up standing by the stage edge writhing and twisting in solitary ecstacy, calmly chatted with one usher after another, postponing being moved back, flirting with them until, when enough other people crowded the aisles, she was able to slip by and get to the stage.

Ritual Challenge

It is really a kind of ritual challenge like running the bulls in Spain. Can you Beat The Man? It implies several things which are not exactly virtues, certainly in the traditional sense.

For one thing, it means that you simply don't care at all about the person who has bought and paid for his seat. If you can keep it, screw him. This is the same philosophy which leads people to rise at moments of personal ecstacy and stand, blocking the view of everyone else.

I watched one girl at a dance at Contra Costa College resist the sleeve pulling and coat tugging of at least half a dozen contemporaries whose view she blocked. My need is greater than yours.

I have even seen people insist on sitting two in a seat alongside me at crowded concerts, insisting on sharing the seat they had wrongly occupied with the rightful ticket holder rather than simply refusing altogether to give it to him.

Recently I watched a huge jolly man in a blue denim shirt with long hair in a pony tail get bounced from one seat after another during the first half of a show, only to see him slip back in near the end when someone left a seat vacant for a brief moment.

It used to be that at half time the balcony came down and occupied the empty seats at concerts that were not sell outs. It used to be that you could leave your seat and go out for a smoke in the intermission. Now everybody smokes no matter where they are, school facility or not, and if you leave your seat, you better put a guard on it.

I remember the time when three dixieland fans, a man and two women, were bounced from the Opera House for carrying their drinks back from the intermission bar visit and sitting in the front row sipping.

Nowadays the bottles of wine and cans of beer are openly guzzled anywhere during the show. And breaking the no-smoking regulations is child's play. Now concert audiences, especially for rock shows, might as well accept the fact that smoking a joint is as casual as chewing gum.

Joints and Roaches

And at a recent concert, for the first time in my life, I saw someone sniffing cocaine at the start of a show, bending over, lighting matches in the darkness to see the white powder, and snorting up a nailful right out in full view of anyone who cared to watch.

One night a young couple walked up the aisle asking if there were any joints for sale. People said no, they wouldn't sell a joint but would give them one! Strangers pass roaches down the aisle to strangers and throughout one entire number by The Who recently, a young man lit match after match as he frantically searched under his seat for the roach he had dropped.

It is certain that standards are changing and it's not just in the concert hall. Beating the door charge or the ticket price may be like beating the phone company, but clouting a couple of LPs from a record store or books from a bookstore seems slightly more direct. Yet it is true that pilferage is on the increase in books and records (was it only ten years ago that a law student was busted for stealing a book?).

Out! Out!

One of the funniest, if unintentionally comic, situations I ever

saw develop was when The Band played a concert at the Berkeley Community Theater. There were two performances and after the first one the ushers and Bill Graham had to get the hall emptied quickly so that the second set of ticket holders could come in.

A young lady and a young man were in the orchestra pit and Graham asked them to leave.

"Why do you have to charge so much money?" the girl asked Graham. "Why are the tickets so expensive? Do you have to be a millionaire?"

Graham, who is not noted for having a high threshold of tolerance for those who challenge him, assumed his standard debating posture and asked them if it was wrong for him to make a profit and did they know how much The Band was charging him? Suddenly he stopped and demanded "How much did you pay for your ticket?"

Freebies

"Oh," they said, almost in unison, "we didn't buy tickets, we got in free!"

Graham froze like a figure in an avant-garde film and then threw them out.

The gate crasher syndrome builds up, of course, with the added challenge of provoking an easily ignitable promoter into a screaming match.

The best instructions I ever heard to a stage door guard were given the night that the Jefferson Airplane, the Quicksilver Messenger Service and the Grateful Dead gave their own show at Winterland. "Let in anybody who gives you a good rap" they told the stage door guard. And he did. It made up quite an assembly.

Gay Married Life

By Michael Grieg

Verne and Maria seem like any other old, happily married couple.

After a hard day at the accountant office, Verne likes nothing better than to work out at the gym. Maria, who is taking karate lessons herself, prefers to arrange flowers, collect salt and pepper

Reprinted by permission from the *San Francisco Chronicle*, July 15, 1970. © Chronicle Publishing Co. 1970.

shakers and cook spicy Italian dishes.

Together in their modest Sunset District apartment, they usually watch television—such programs as "Mod Squad" and "Laugh-In."

But Verne often knits while they watch. Meanwhile, Maria swigs the beer. Both are women.

Part of San Francisco's homosexual community of some 75,000, Verne and Maria feel they're "just as married" as anyone else after ten years together.

Partnership

"Maria's parents didn't like me—they're Sicilian," said Verne, burly but sweet. "So we eloped."

They exchanged wedding bands as a symbol of the lasting bond. And now that they've put a down payment on a $37,000 Mill Valley home, they plan to draw up partnership papers—the usual form of legal "marriage" for old homosexual couples.

Verne feels that a City Hall license is "just a scrap of paper anyway—we don't need the State's blessing to recognize where we're at."

But Maria, more conservative, looks forward to the day of relaxed marriage laws when homosexuals can make it "absolutely legal."

"I think it's nice being married," she said, as she handed Verne a washed dish for drying. "A simple wedding is very beautiful. Why, I've been trying to talk Verne into getting married in church so the world can know."

Church

Both are members of the 70-member congregation of San Francisco's homophile Metropolitan Community Church which meets Sundays at Jackson's Bar, at Bay and Powell streets.

Thirty-six weddings between persons of the same sex have already taken place at the church's Los Angeles center, and the first one here—between two males—is scheduled for August.

"Making it legal—or at least religious—might enable us to file a joint income tax return," said Maria, an office manager. "And, if we can prove we have a stable relationship, we might be able to adopt children."

The problem of being a childless couple is her greatest disappointment. "We have so much love to give—the love of two mothers," she said. "Of course, we'd probably spoil the kids rotten —like we have our four cats."

Pregnant

In the absence of a legal marriage and with adoption roadblocks, Verne said, some lesbian couples obtain children on the "gray market" by paying for them. One lesbian even got pregnant, with the consent of her partner.

"They picked out a nice homosexual guy they knew so there wouldn't be any emotional hangup," said Maria. "We're having a shower for her next month."

Gay couples like Verne and Maria are supported in their wish to "make it legal" by such homosexual rights groups as the Mattachine Society and the Daughters of Bilitis.

"A lot of homosexuals still feel that what they're doing is wrong and sinful," said Mattachine spokesman Hal Call. "A real marriage, for them, would make it acceptable in the eyes of God and society. They have the right to legal recognition."

Jeri, president of the Daughters of Bilitis here, feels that most lesbians are "law-abiding citizens" who should be able to get married and enjoy "all the tax breaks and benefits in the way of health and car insurance."

The right of a marriage license for homosexuals is also staunchly defended by such ministers as the Rev. A. Cecil Williams of Glide Memorial Church.

The strongest defense, perhaps, is made by the Rev. Troy D. Perry, husky 30-year-old pastor of the Metropolitan Community Church in Los Angeles.

Having married 36 homosexual couples in the past year and a half, the clergyman obviously practices what he preaches. He told The Chronicle that the weddings, complete with rice, are a variation on the Episcopal ceremony, with "wedded spouse" substituted for "lawful wedded wife."

And the Rev. Mr. Perry, a former Baptist minister with a former wife (a woman), feels the whole procedure—despite the substitution—is "perfectly legal," in California, that is, since marriage laws vary from state to state. Federal law does not apply.

Laws

To make it "legal," he insists that the couples he marries must have lived together for six months. And he cites as his legal basis Section 79 of the California Civil Code, commonly applied to common law marriages.

"When unmarried persons, not minors, have been living together as man and wife, they may without a license be married by any clergyman," the law states.

"A certificate of such marriage shall be made by the clergyman, delivered to the parties and recorded upon the records of the church of which the clergyman is a representative. No other record need be made."

The minister said that his unconventional ceremonies have led to friction with Los Angeles county clerk William G. Sharp, but there hasn't been a court test yet.

"Sharp says homosexuals don't consummate their marriages to make it legal," the maverick minister said. "Well, I told him they got to bed, and that's enough.

"So he told me that what they do is illegal and that they can't have children. Well, ordinary married couples also perform sexual acts that are illegal. And would he deny marriage to heterosexual couples who can't have children?"

Couples

The Rev. Mr. Perry said that among the happy couples he has married are a buyer for a big department store and the vice president of a small company, who have lived together for 17 years.

"They lived in one of the most attractive hillside homes in Los Angeles—way up there in the $80,000 class," he said.

A lesbian couple, who were together eight years, have since the ceremony adopted "a beautiful little Negro girl" who they obtained on "the gray market." "She calls one of them 'Auntie' and the other 'Mama,' and they've never been happier," the minister noted.

"Why, one of these days—when the little girl gets older—I expect they'll be going to PTA meetings."

And does the Rev. Mr. Perry kiss the male spouses following the ceremony?

"Oh, no," said the clergyman, who admits his own homosexuality without shame. There might be some jealousy, he said.

"I have a lover, a wonderful chap whom I wouldn't give up for the world. One of these days we're going to be married in church by a minister I've ordained. But we haven't set the date yet."

The Simple Life and How to Avoid It

By Arthur Hoppe

Once upon a time, there was a busy, frustrated man named Henry D. Thoreaubach who yearned, like most of us, for the simple life.

Henry's life was very complicated. At the office, he spent half his time deciding whom to saddle with the problems he'd been saddled with. The other half was devoted to seeing people he didn't want to see, phoning people he didn't want to phone, and writing people he wished would drop dead.

Being a busy man, he had many labor-saving devices. He had machines to chew up his garbage, wash his dishes, entertain his children, launder his clothes and brush his teeth. His hobby was laboring to repair them. It was very time-consuming.

But he loved his family. And he tried to schedule 12-minute chats with his children at 6:18 P.M. daily and a romantic evening with his wife every other Wednesday— when he could squeeze them in.

Yet, somehow, Henry had the feeling he wasn't getting anywhere.

Well, one day Henry happened to read Thoreau's "Walden" during his Great Books Reading Hour (every third Tuesday, 9 to 10 P.M.). "That," he cried, "is the life for me!"

So he chucked his job, sold his house, bought an axe, ten pounds of nails and some fishhooks and set off to build a little log cabin in the wilderness.

He was lucky to find a nice 50-foot lot on a pond for only $19,-500. And after he'd signed the mortgage, searched the title and assumed his pro-rata share of the bonded indebtedness for streets and sewers, it was his.

Then he shouldered his axe and went off to chop down a tree. Unfortunately, the Forest Service caught him. So after he paid his fine, he had to contract with the EZ Credit Lumber Co. to deliver the logs. But he forgot a building permit.

The Building Inspector demanded studs on 16-inch centers. The Plumbing Inspector de-

Reprinted by permission of the author and the publisher from the *San Francisco Chronicle,* February 9, 1970. © Chronicle Publishing Co. 1970.

A BERKELEY ORIGINAL—GEN. WASTE-MORE-LAND.
PHOTO COURTESY OF JOSHUA WATTLES.

6.4
Toward Humanity

The Editors

Wait a minute. Don't just turn the page after finishing our chapter. We want you to reflect on the nature of the world you face when you turn away from this book and why so many different kinds of people are trying alternate life styles.

More than anything else in America, the worth of the individual is allegedly prized. You as an individual feel pressures to increase self-awareness and self-actualization. You are confronted with other people who are just as intent on making a path for themselves as individuals as you, and you are confronted with processes of institutions that are more real than the people within them. Your society seemingly cannot effect its declared constitutional equality. Yes, it all gets pretty bad. Everyone needs a place where he can feel loved and nurtured and re-enforced. The ideal of the American family is to act as such a cushion against the harsh outer world. A haven of acceptance is necessary for survival. Interestingly enough, the alternate life styles that we have presented here are not so far removed from the ideal American family. They are, in fact, logical extensions of the ideal. As the outer world grows more impersonal, many people are trying to create a larger sphere of good vibrations for themselves and others. Each trial is important because each demonstrates the courage to attack inhumanity and live more fully, creatively, and joyfully.

So, you've finished reading what we've finished editing, but none of us is finished living or thinking. Our lives are spent pondering the choices we make. Periodically, we question our style of life and perhaps the periodic asking of the question is the only answer to the question: we must realize that everyone questions, that everyone sometimes wonders if an alternate life style might be better. Constructive answers can come from such questions, especially when socially conscious people realize the importance of their life styles. Unlike isolated attempts or campaigns for social change, a life style is a continuous reflection of personal ideals. Maybe you aren't the person to drop all of your current life and adopt a radically different role, but you can realize

manded enlarged toilet drains. The Electrical Inspector demanded No. 218a conduits. The Health Inspector . . . And when he tried to catch fish for his dinner he was socked $50 for failing to carry license.

That's when Henry said the hell with it, returned to the city and went on welfare. Here was the simple life he'd yearned for. He didn't do a thing all day long. "I am no longer busy and frustrated," said Henry after two months of it, "I am bored and frustrated."

Fortunately, Henry got a job making umbrellas. Red ones, blue ones, flowered ones. He liked making umbrellas. People needed them. Besides, he didn't have to see people, phone people or write people he didn't want to see, phone or write. So he had lots of time on his hands.

He had time to picnic with his family, learn to play the piccolo, read "Catch-22" in a single sitting, master Urdu, take long walks and, oh, a jillion other things. In fact, he didn't have any time at all. His life was soon twice as busy and complicated as it ever was.

But Henry didn't care. He was very, very happy.

Moral: Life isn't simple these days. So why clutter it up with a lot of nonsense?

the vitalness of your life and the potential influence of your everyday activities. Good luck and peace to you all.

EDITOR'S BIBLIOGRAPHY: ALTERNATIVE LIFE STYLES

Vocations for Social Change: This is a group that attempts to act as a clearing house for nonestablishment jobs. They put out a bulletin and a supplement on alternate months. One issue is free. Write to: Vocations for Social Change, Canyon, California 94516.

The Whole Earth Catalog: The catalog includes useful tools, from small computers to back-packing equipment, books on building homes, etc. If you are building a community you would do well to start with the catalog as a source for the things you'll need. Portola Institute, 558 Santa Cruz, Menlo Park, California 94025. A subscription at $8 yr. includes two catalogs and four supplements.

The Family Store: Directory of the People's Resources: We found the directory and Ed Kartman (one of the Family) to be extremely helpful in this project. While the listings are primarily for the Bay Area, the Family would like to see it become a nationwide venture. If you would like to be listed or would like a copy, write to: Family Store, 3060-22nd Ave., Oakland, California, 94602. Subscriptions are $3.50 yr., $1.00 for a single issue (fall or spring).

Cooperative Communities: How to Start Them, and Why, by Kriyananda (1970, 4th ed.): This book contains a philosophical discussion as well as practical details on the process of starting an intentional community. It also includes information about an existing community founded by Kriyananda. Ananda Publications, Box 18272, San Francisco, California. $1.25. Other information on the community itself may be obtained by writing to Ananda Cooperative Community, Alleghany Star Route, Nevada City, California 95959.

Synergy: The Creative Alternative (August-September, 1969): This is an excellent bibliographic source published by the Bay Area Reference Center (BARC). This particular issue is a good starting place for those who would like to find out more about alternative ways of life and/or set out on a venture of their own. We are grateful to Synergy and to the helpful people of BARC. Synergy is not sold; it may be available at your local library. If not, write to The Bay Area Reference Center, San Francisco Public Library, Civic Center, San Francisco, California 94102.

Part III
Special Problem Areas

In this part of the Handbook, the editors deal with three concrete social problem areas which persist today, as well as three problem areas which are relatively new for most social problems books.

The drug scene is viewed as a part of a larger scene which is itself not healthy. This is a scene in which the adult world—with easy access to *its* drug (alcohol) —is currently uptight about the widespread use of drugs among the young. The student editors perceive a generation gap of their own with respect to their high school age friends and siblings who are starting to use the hard drugs like heroin at a very early age. In the context of the philosophical inputs of Leary and Watts, the writings of drug users, and the editors' analyses of drug treatment programs, recommendations are made for a program of drug education in schools, the legalization of drug possession, immunity from prosecution for those who seek treatment for addiction, and a shift in priorities along the lines suggested by Joel Fort: "When life itself becomes a mind expanding experience, drugs will become relatively unimportant in our society."

The encounter group boom is critically analyzed as a phenomena which is becoming a social problem of its own, despite the evidence that the techniques emerged from a need to solve other social problems. Most Berkeley students, many Californians, and some of the rest of the society have had some exposure to some form of group experience. The viewers of *Bob, Carol, Ted and Alice* have had at least a vicarious look. In an age when individual therapy is expensive, groups are booming as many people seek a painless way to find a measure of happiness, communication, or feeling. The editors strike a cautionary note after evaluating the pros and cons, seeing the encounter groups as useful but dangerous in the hands of the many untrained people who are exploiting the popularity of the technique.

In the chapter on mental health, the editors are very critical of the mental hospitals in the United States. Most of the team members have worked as volunteers in mental hospitals, and use their first hand experience plus the chapter readings to condemn involuntary commitment and impersonal treatment of patients. Sadly, they find little progress since the dramatic speech of President John F. Kennedy in 1963 which called for drastic reform in the treatment of the mentally ill. Their recommendations center on preventative mental health care, community mental health centers, separation of criminals and custodial patients from mental hospitals, and the creation of foster-family living groups staffed by nonprofessionals.

Part of the ecology action movement includes a focus on the population explosion—a fact which prompted the chapter on the psychological consequences of population control. The problem is easy to define—the world is crowded and getting more so, dangerously. But the solutions can not be formulated as policy decisions alone, since the having of children impinges on individual freedoms, attitudes, and desires which have not been carefully researched. The articles cover the views of Paul Erlich, the folklore in debates on population, attitudes toward the pill and vasectomy, and the role of women. The editors recommend ending restrictions on abortion, free access to reliable family planning information and birth control devices, changes in attitude toward the childless couple, a two child family norm, and a five-year study of the demographic changes in the population as a function of living under more relaxed laws which give real options to families that wish to plan.

The education reform chapter brings out the seldom heard testimony of "experts" on education—the students. From the bitter tone of "Student as a Nigger" to the positive suggestions of John Hurst and Herb Kohl, there is one theme —that basic reform in higher education must be initiated and pushed by concerned students in the face of the inertia inherent in the academic bureaucracy.

The final chapter on white community involvement makes an interesting counterpoint to the chapter on the third world experience in Part II. Written mainly by students, the articles present a model, a philosophy, and an honestly described case study of an attempt to combat racism in their own very white community.

The Drug Scene

EDITED BY:

Ted J. Alves

James L. Chenney

Betsi Goff

Douglas R. Horner

Kevin Keogan

Paul A. Pickering

Elizabeth Stephens

Richard Stephens

Hillary Turner

INTRODUCTION

If one were to pick up almost any book on social problems written within the last ten years, he would surely find at least one chapter devoted to the topic of drugs and drug addiction. The traditional focus of such chapters was on alcoholism and heroin addiction. To be sure, these are two important aspects of the "drug scene" even today. But, in the last ten years, concerned observers of American society have witnessed a startling increase in the variety of drugs consumed and in the number of people consuming them. Psychedelic drugs, amphetamines, and barbiturates have spread to college campuses, high schools, and even elementary schools. Millions of Americans, young and old alike, stand in awe of what has become one of our most pervasive social problems—the Drug Scene. Although many books have already been written on this subject, it is the belief of the editors of this chapter that the time has come for formulating a new perspective on drug usage—a perspective which views the "drug scene" *in toto*, which exposes the dangerous undercurrents of fear, hatred, and misunderstanding about the many mind-altering drugs and those who use them, and which clears the air for a rational approach to the problem. This chapter is dedicated to these ends.

The increasing use of drugs in American society *is* a problem, but it can also be seen as a symptom of a much larger problem in society. Americans are taught from birth to be independent, to desire success and happiness, to minimize their anxieties, to get along well with others, to obey the law, and to be "good," productive citizens. Many of these basic social values are now being questioned, especially by young Americans. These members of the younger generation see a status quo whose very foundation is being ripped away by its own ineffectiveness. Many young Americans feel alienated from their society, many refuse to participate, many use drugs.

There is little doubt that America has become a "drug-permissive" society in which almost any degree of use of the socially approved drugs (e.g., alcohol and tobacco) is seen as "normal." But when a college student is sent to prison (for up to 40 years in some states) for possessing less than an ounce of marijuana, a drug which he and millions of other Americans see as completely harmless, his faith in the goals of our legal system is destroyed. Thousands of young people have been turned into de facto criminals by our impersonal laws dealing with drugs. State and federal legislators have passed (with little or no forethought) ludicrously strict drug control laws while, simultaneously, allowing America's five to fifteen million alcoholics easy access to their drug of choice. Many educators have simply ignored the issue of drug use, opting for ignorance and indecision rather than honesty and action. Drug treatment programs are inadequate at best, and drug education projects are almost totally lacking in most states. It is not surprising, then, to find many social scientists asking now, "Why aren't *more* young people using drugs?"

Drug use is a personal as well as a social experience. Like the black flag of anarchy and the clenched fist, drugs have become a symbol—a personal symbol—of a Brave New World which many young Americans see on the horizon. Drugs are a threat to members of the Old World, a threat which they do not understand, which they wish to eliminate. But drugs are here to stay. Few experts believe that we will see anything but an increase in the amounts and varieties of mind-altering chemicals used in this country in the next several years. Is drug usage, then, a problem to be ignored or a problem to be dealt with? Should we pray for rain or seed the clouds of knowledge which are gradually accumulating around the issue of drug use in America?

In this chapter, the editors have attempted to provide some of those seeds. Alan Watts discusses the mystical and religious nature of psychedelic drugs along with various objections to their use which are commonly raised in Western societies. Helen Nowlis describes the meaning of drugs in the student subculture. Timothy Leary focuses on the meaning and ethics of marijuana in our new Molecular Age of mind-manifesting drugs. Joel Fort discusses the "social problem" nature of drug use and points to many of the misdirected efforts our society has made in attempting to find solutions to the problem. Finally, several of the editors have contributed an article on drug treatment facilities as they exist today with an eye on the direction of future developments in this area of the drug scene. It is the hope of the editors that this chapter will broaden the reader's perspective of the drug scene in a way that will compel him to rational thought and action on the problems presented herein. Our conclusion cites several recommenda-

"WE'VE GOT EVERYTHING." PHOTO COURTESY OF JOSHUA WATTLES.

tions for social action which will help to dispel the many misconceptions surrounding the drug scene and will initiate a new social understanding of the real problems of drug use.

In the last few years, America has witnessed, with growing concern, a rapid increase in student drug involvement. One cogent fact has emerged—there are no simple answers to why students take drugs. In the following article, Helen Nowlis discusses the appeals of drugs, social reactions to drug subcultures, the current state of student alienation, and the problems of American youth as they reach for adulthood. The article focuses on the role of educational institutions in helping students solve these problems, in helping them break parental bonds and become independent individuals—aware of their environment and willing to deal with it justly and honestly.

7.1
The Student and His Culture

Helen H. Nowlis

Assuming that it is more profitable to look at the drug user than at the drug and that most reasonably normal people do not continue to do something that does not provide them with at least some satisfaction, we now look at the student and the demands of the world in which he lives and grows. Such questions as whether using drugs should be satisfying, or whether the needs they are perceived to satisfy are legitimate needs, are in some ways irrelevant. The needs are felt as real, they motivate behavior, and they cannot be wished away

Venturing into this area warrants a repeated warning, lest it be forgotten. Just as students differ, students who use drugs differ, and it is a great mistake to get overenthusiastic about any one explanatory idea. This becomes

From the book *Drugs on the College Campus* by Helen H. Nowlis. Reprinted by permission of Doubleday & Company, Inc.

increasingly true as drug use spreads. There are, however, some general observations which may be useful.

All college students are at one or another stage in growth from childhood to adulthood. This growth process involves both the unlearning of modes of behavior which were appropriate and rewarded in childhood and the learning of new modes in accordance with society's definition of the adult role, a definition which is neither clear nor consistent. Becoming adult involves, at a minimum, substituting independence for dependence, individual identity for borrowed or assigned identity, and meaningful social relationships with a variety of individuals outside the family circle for basic relationships inside the family. It involves development of meaningful sexual identity and appropriate masculine or feminine roles and a meaningful relationship to life and the meaning of life. The attainment of maturity also involves the ability to postpone immediate gratifications in the interest of long-range goals. (The atomic bomb and the "buy-now-pay-later" philosophy seem to have contributed little to the development of this ability in either youth or adult.)

Neither meaningful identity nor a set of values to live by can be bestowed like a mantle. They must become a part of one's being, and the process of internalizing them can be painful, both for the person and for those who care. Becoming independent may, some believe must, involve rebellion. Developing an identity consistent with one's talents and abilities, hopes and dreams, requires hard work and experimentation which may be unsuccessful more often than it is successful. Developing mature, meaningful social relationships is difficult at best and the more so if independence and some degree of identity have not been achieved. Tolerating the frustration involved in postponing gratifications can make other frustrations seem greater. Finding the meaning in life and being at peace with one's self and one's God are goals many adults never attain.

The irony of the appeal of LSD is that, in one way or another, it can be perceived as offering a promise of help in all of these difficult tasks. It seems as if nothing could have been better designed, either by the proponents of LSD or by the mass media which publicized it, to appeal to the personal, social, and emotional needs and the idealism of these young people who are "hung up" in a society which has made adolescence so prolonged and adulthood so uncertain. What LSD is said to offer is inviting fare for the weary traveler, inviting in direct proportion to the degree of weariness.

There are other reasons why students use drugs and, for the most part, they are the same reasons why adults use drugs such as alcohol, tranquilizers, amphetamines, barbiturates, aspirin, nicotine, and caffeine. All of these are widely used by a variety of people for a variety of reasons—for a change of pace, to change mood, to reduce anxiety, for a pick-up, to combat fatigue, to relieve tensions, to relieve boredom, to facilitate social interaction, to sleep, just for fun. It would not be surprising to find that some four-year-old watchers of television could name a specific product for each purpose.

Some adults try these drugs, some react badly or do not find what they are seeking and never try again; some use them occasionally; some use them socially; some use them to escape; some are as dependent, psychologically

and in some cases physically, as they would be if their dependence were on an opiate. The main difference is that these substances are socially acceptable and are fairly easily available. Man has used drugs throughout the ages to escape from discomfort and misery. It is interesting to note that in our society misery is a condition familiar not only to the socially and economically depressed but also to those who are in the midst of "success."

There are many other appeals. More young people than most adults would care to admit are weary of chasing the same carrot at the end of the same stick for fourteen to sixteen years; they dream of getting out of "the rat race" just for a while. Some take a junior year abroad, others do their stint in the military, some take time out for Vista, some keep their noses to the grindstone, hating it to varying degrees, some flunk out though not for lack of ability, some take a marihuana dropout on weekends. LSD invites them to do what some want most to do, with the company of like-minded peers as a bonus, to "solve" their problems, whether these be rebellion or the search for independence, for identity, for satisfying social and personal relationships, for values which are not confused and uncomfortable, or for a meaningful religious experience. To "drop out" the LSD way does not require long arguments with the stockholders—parents, deans, other adults—few of whom seem likely to be persuaded that a moratorium is a positive, constructive, appropriate action at this time and for these reasons. LSD can appear to be a painless way to experiment with dropping out, to escape temporarily into a "bright and shiny world," a world in which people are interested in what really seems to matter, not what should matter, what one is and wants to be, not what he should be.

The response of society to student drug use may foster further use when that response is based on assumptions which seem contradictory or hypocritical to the student. For example, it is widely assumed that when there is no medically approved reason for taking a drug the individual has no right to take it. A further questionable assumption is also made: since the only legitimate use of a drug is in the treatment of illness, anyone who takes a drug is, *ipso facto*, ill—or criminal. The students who reject both assumptions

point to alcohol as a potent drug about the use of which society makes completely different assumptions: the individual does have the right to choose to take alcohol for other than medical reasons, and the person who uses alcohol properly is not considered to be ill. They then argue that the attitudes toward alcohol should be extended to include other seemingly non-dangerous, non-medical drugs.

The fact that so many young people are ready to consider just what it is that LSD and the group who use it have to offer should make us think not only about students and drugs but also about the society in which the student has grown up.

The more one inquires into all aspects of the drug problem the more one is impressed with the importance of availability. Has there ever been a society in which drugs were more widely available than in current American society? It is a society dedicated to progress through chemistry. Since infancy the student has learned to open his mouth on command and swallow whatever was popped in to cure what ailed him, and he has watched his parents do the same. A very significant portion of the family budget is often spent on drugs, tobacco, and mood-changing beverages. One study suggests that the average household may have as many as thirty drugs in its medicine cabinet. Blum[1] notes that users of illicit and exotic drugs, in contrast to non-users, had been ill more often as a child, had been taken to the physician more frequently, and had taken more medications. He also suggests that there are many confirmed "drug optimists," individuals who have grown up confident that for every ill there is a drug which will cure it.

Unfortunately, there are more and more individuals who think that each ill needs not one but many drugs. Wahl[2] has recently described a symptom complex, "status medicamentosis," which results from indiscriminate medication with too many drugs. He argues that it develops as a result of two social-psychological factors: 1) a widespread and intense belief in the power of medication,

[1] R. H. Blum, *Nature and Extent of the Problem.* NASPA Drug Education Project Background Papers, 1966, p. 5.

[2] C. W. Wahl, "Diagnosis and Treatment of *Status Medicamentosis.*" *Dis. Nerv. Syst.*, 1967, 28, pp. 318–22.

a belief which ignores the limitations and side effects of drugs and which is a by-product of constantly hearing about the impressive and diverse successes of medical science, and 2) the deterioration of patient-doctor relationships in an era of increased specialization. Relying more on medication than on the physician, the person medicates himself excessively and indiscriminately. He uses medication as a kind of magical protector and depends on medication rather than people to handle certain emotional drives and needs.

That physicians themselves contribute to this situation is suggested by Louria. "At the present time, it is a reasonable estimate that half of the sedatives and tranquilizers prescribed by physicians are given unnecessarily. If the medical profession will rigidly limit the use of these drugs, it is likely that at least some of those who would otherwise illicitly use them would realize the inadvisability of medicating themselves with these potentially dangerous agents."[3]

Another important aspect of current society is its attitude toward risk. Students have grown up in an atmosphere which takes risks for granted and assumes that there is little that can be done without risk. Risk-taking ideally involves rational decisions about the utility of a certain action, decisions which are based on informed estimates of both the value of the goal and the probability of gain or loss, of reward or disaster. Despite obvious risks, cars are driven on freeways and airplanes are filled with passengers because rational men continue to believe in the utility of doing so. But risk-taking is more often based not on rational decision but on irrational thinking, habit, hunch, impulse, mood, or information that is inadequate and erroneous. A temporary feeling of invulnerability may lead the individual to believe "it won't happen to me." Or feelings of hopelessness or of being discriminated against may lead him to believe he has very little to lose and much to gain. Thus an adequate description of the risks involved in drug use may serve as an effective deterrent to some but have no effect or even the opposite effect on others.

One does not have to look far to see other aspects of the society in which the young person finds

himself which may be relevant in understanding much of what is happening. The fact that our society holds certain beliefs to be inviolable even as it violates them adds other complications to the process of growing up. Most young people have learned their verbal lessons well—love not hate, brotherhood not discrimination, equal opportunity, freedom from fear and want, equality in diversity, the basic worth of the individual. But the world is not like that. With the straightforwardness that so often characterizes youth, some scream "hypocrisy" while others set about trying to live according to these basic beliefs.

It has frequently been pointed out that ours is an achievement-oriented, environment-dominating society which almost exclusively values and reards intellectual or cognitive performance to the exclusion of the life of emotion and feeling. It is a society which often measures success and prestige in terms of material possessions, which considers a young person privileged if he comes from a family which has a modern home, several cars, and an income sufficient to provide travel, a college education, membership in a country club, or perhaps a summer home. Far more young people than those who turn to drugs are uneasy in this climate. Some of them look at eminently "successful" parents and do not like what they see or sense. They wonder if getting an education in order to get a job which will provide them with sufficient income to live in the suburbs and be miserable, become alcoholic, develop ulcers, get divorced, is worth the struggle. "There must be something else." The books they read—Sartre, Hesse, Thoreau, Heller, Heinlein, Huxley, Bellows, Tolkien—suggest that there may be.

They feel the need for deep and meaningful experience in an increasingly secular society. Because the church, as organized religion, seems to reflect so many of the trends in society which they find distasteful, they are attracted to the Eastern religions with their emphasis on mysticism and personal religious experience. They want a personally meaningful part in a world which seems so full of aggression, discrimination, poverty, famine, alcoholism, divorce, and hypocrisy that the individual seems superfluous. They want a "frontier" in which to find adventure, challenge, and an opportunity to prove themselves at a time when the only frontiers available

for the many would seem to be the technological jungle or the world within. Some of them are rejecting the jungle and withdrawing into the inner world.

The explosion in population and urbanization has contributed to an impersonality in which one's identity is more determined by what one owns, where one lives and works or goes to a college, what one wears, in short, what one appears to be, than it is by what one thinks and feels and is. The explosion in communication, technology, and the mass media has resulted in what Keniston[4] has called "stimulus flooding," a constant bombardment of information, of points of view, of advertising, of happenings in every corner of the globe, even in outer space—more information than any man can process, more din than he can tolerate. In perfectly good human fashion he responds by screening it out, ignoring it, protecting himself against more and more of it, and by becoming numb. But the screen may become so dense that it isolates him as well from direct experience with the simple, the beautiful, the unexpected in the world around him. The preoccupation of some of the dropouts with flowers, sunsets, folk songs, togetherness, and meditation is not without significance, nor is the preoccupation of others with a din of their own making. There is more than one way to shut out the world.

Many of the trends in society are paralleled in the institution of higher education. Responding in part to the pressures of society and in part to the pressures of increased knowledge and specialization, many institutions have grown tremendously in size and complexity. Their students encounter increased impersonality and frustration in everything from practices in the cashier's and registrar's offices to the conduct of courses and the administration of degree requirements. This impersonality and dehumanization come at the very time in development when young people need recognition from the social environment of their growing individuality and desperately want meaningful relationships with important adults, although on their

[3] Donald Louria, *Nightmare Drugs.* New York: Pocket Books, Inc. (#10157), 1966, pp. 76–77.

[4] K. Keniston, *Drug Use and Student Values.* NASPA Drug Education Project Background Papers. See also K. Keniston, *The Uncommitted: Alienated Youth in American Society.* New York: Delta (Paperback #92737), 1967.

own terms and at their own times. Wherever they are, but particularly if they are in college, they are concerned to varying degrees with self-discovery. By this they mean their own search for their own identity in the world as they perceive it, a search which goes beyond the mere acceptance of a pattern to which they are expected to conform. Despite outward appearances they really want custom tailoring. They are preoccupied with being themselves but, since they are not yet sure just what that means, they may temporarily settle simply for not being what society expects them to be so that they may go on with the search. They want recognition that this search is an important and worthwhile endeavor and they want help, but help with the questions that have meaning for them at a particular stage in their search, not advice about where they should be.

There is little agreement as to the part which a college or university should play in this whole process, either among or within colleges. In pursuing excellence, many institutions seem to have defined excellence in a way that parallels the definition of society: in terms of number of Ph.D.s on the faculty, quantity and quality of faculty scholarships and research, number of research grants, number of Nobel Laureates and members of a National Academy, number of students who go on to graduate and professional study. These assets are not to be underestimated; they can contribute directly to important and relevant education. But is this all? For many institutions, the problem may be that they have not clearly thought through the implications of the distinction between education and training made by Sanford. "True education is liberating and differentiating. If it is successful it makes every individual different from every other. . . . Training tends to process individuals so that they are more alike, speaking the same language, sharing the same professional baggage, engaging in the same kinds of activities in the same more or less prescribed way."[5] The two would seem to have very different implications for curriculum, for evaluation, for posture with reference to the interests and concerns

of students. Is the purpose of the institution training for a specific role in the economy, broadly defined, or is it self-realization, including preparation for a broadly defined role in society? This is not necessarily an either-or proposition. It is possible to do one while concentrating on the other, but the implications of this dual role need to be clear. If the main goal is at the training end of the continuum, the subsidiary goal, if it is to be viable, must be accepted and supported by those whose main concern is scholarship and training. Is education, defined as awareness, attitude, style, approach, frame of mind, to be planned for, or is it just supposed to happen? Is concern for the realization of uniqueness and individuality reflected in classroom, curriculum, and housekeeping, even when it is secondary, or is there only lip service to this goal?

It is conceivable that serious attention paid to some of the non-intellectual needs felt by students, which are not always accurately reflected in what they say they want, could pay great dividends both now and in the future. Preoccupation with problems of growing can seriously interfere with progress in training. In this age of almost universal expectation for higher education, it may not be enough to assume that if these problems are sufficiently major to interfere with progress in what is often considered the main business of higher education, the student does not belong in college. For some institutions this may be a tenable solution; for all institutions it probably is not.

Robert Nixon,[6] a psychiatrist specializing in the study of late adolescence, has thought through some of the ways in which these three factors—youth, the culture, and the educational institution—are interrelated and the implications of these interrelationships for the growth of the young person. According to Nixon, the late adolescent should be entering the cognitive stage of development, a stage characterized by questioning and rethinking all of one's past development. Youth examines his past history for "unfinished business," gaps left in every person's life as a result of the imperfect resolution of tasks peculiar to a

particular stage of development. Not only these gaps but all aspects of his identity, and the values, attitudes, and behaviors which are a part of that identity, are subjected to close scrutiny. Those aspects of the identity which do not fit with what he feels he is now or with what he hopes to become are abandoned and he experiments with new attitudes, values, and behaviors to take their place. This whole process of re-examination and experimentation necessarily involves anxiety—anxiety aroused by letting go of old ways before new ones are available. Nixon believes that anxiety is essential to growth, yet our society feels that anxiety is "bad," something to be avoided, to be conjured away with drugs, both in oneself and in others. For most young people, although they experience "at least a taste of the questioning that characterizes this stage," the anxiety seems too great to bear and they retreat to the previous stage of unquestioning acceptance of the status quo. "We of the older generation are so wary of our own anxiety that we have been able to teach them almost nothing about theirs, so few of them can tolerate the pain of growth." For the majority, then, "the cognitive stage becomes the graveyard of psychological growth."[7]

Not only does society dislike anxiety, it also dislikes being questioned. So many of the values and attitudes which make up the identity of the pre-cognitive adolescent were the values and attitudes of the parents as representatives of society. A re-examination of the identity leads to a re-examination of the parents, which generates anxiety in them. The simplest solution for all concerned would seem to be to stop the questioning, thereby relieving the anxiety. But this solution also leads to the psychological graveyard."

It would seem that educational institutions are in a position to play an important supportive role in the student's development during this stage. "Where better can they be taught the relationship between anxiety and growth, and where else are they supposed to be systematically encouraged to ask their questions, to examine critically this world we share? Those of us engaged in formal education of the late adolescent have at hand an opportunity to foster growth that is almost non-

[5] R. N. Sanford, *Self and Society.* New York: Atherton Press, 1964, p. 41. See also R. N. Sanford, *Where Colleges Fail.* San Francisco: Jossey-Bass, 1967.

[6] R. E. Nixon, "Psychological Normality in Adolescence." *Adolescence,* 1966, *1,* pp. 211–23. See also R. E. Nixon, *The Art of Growing.* New York: Random House (Paperback #PP23), 1962.

[7] R. E. Nixon, "Psychological Normality in Adolescence," pp. 219–20.

existent elsewhere in this society. That we use it so little, and misuse it so much, is not to our credit as educators and in all probability contributes more than we like to think to the discontent of the youthful generation."[8] . . . [D]ecisions, whether implicit or explicit, about the proper role and function of the educational institution determine to a great extent the nature and level of educational effort directed to a variety of important but controversial problems or issues, not the least of which is drug use.

[8] *Ibid.*, p. 222.

Joel Fort attacks the bourgeois drug culture of middle America. In his attempt to bring rationality to the problems of drug use and abuse in America, Fort should be commended for his courageous efforts to fight for equality in drug laws. He attacks certain drug laws as diverting finances and attention from the real problem and as "a convenient device for attacking youth and stifling dissent." The point is made that the socially approved drugs are not necessarily the most harmless, as is made evident in the statistics concerning the high death rate and high crime rate connected with alcohol and the harmful effects of nicotine. Fort is beating a path through the current hysteria and propaganda produced by the media, law-makers, and the drug police. His weapons are research, historical facts, and medical expertise. This article is a requisite for the anti-drug, stimulant/tranquilizer craving, middle America, as it is also essential to those who wish to change the present drug myth.

7.2
Social Problems of Drug Use and Drug Policies

Joel Fort

The welfare of the people has always been the alibi of tyrants.

Camus

I. Introduction: Definitions

A rational discussion of the social problems relating to drug abuse requires accurate definitions of terms whose meanings are too often taken for granted, terms such as "drug," "use," and "abuse." The word "drug," which is so loosely bandied about by the mass media, police, and politicians in connection with marijuana, LSD, and narcotics, actually applies to the whole range of mind-altering drugs, including aspirin, antibiotics, and antihistamines. In medicine, the term "drug" applies to any biologically active substance affecting the brain or other bodily organs or tissues. Mind-altering or psychoactive drugs—those which primarily affect the mind or consciousness include alcohol, caffeine, nicotine (tobacco), barbiturates and other sedatives, amphetamines and other stimulants, tranquilizers, narcotics, LSD-type drugs, and marijuana.[1] Those who improperly define "drugs" communicate, often deliberately, erroneous impressions to the public and to lawmakers.

Common parlance about the "use" of socially disapproved or illegal drugs usually conveys the impression that any or all use is abusive and constitutes addiction; conversely, references to socially

Reprinted by permission from "Social Problems of Drug Use and Drug Policies," *California Law Review*, 56, 1 (January, 1968). Copyright © 1968 by California Law Review, Inc. Dr. Fort is the founder of the Center for Solving (Special) Social and Health Problems, San Francisco; author of *The Pleasure Seekers: The Drug Crisis, Youth and Society*; lecturer at the School of Social Welfare, University of California at Berkeley, and the Department of Biology, San Francisco State College.

[1] Each of the mind-altering drugs should be referred to by name, e.g., "LSD" rather than "psychedelic" or "hallucinogen," and "marijuana" rather than "soft narcotic" or "mild psychedelic." On whether marijuana is properly classified (in laws, popular articles, and political speeches) as a narcotic, see W. Eldridge, *Narcotics and the Law* 1, 15 n.5, 139 (2nd ed. 1967).

approved drugs such as alcohol and nicotine usually imply that almost all use, including abusive and addictive use, is normal. We must recognize that use of drugs in either category ranges from one-time or occasional use, on the one hand, to regular use—only some of this involving large or excessive quantities or daily use—on the other. Furthermore, only a few of the many mind-altering drugs, namely alcohol, barbiturates and other sedatives, and narcotics, will, when used daily and excessively, lead to addiction, that is, physical dependence. Addiction means that the body cells adapt to the drug, that the user requires ever larger amounts to produce the same effect, and that an abrupt termination of drug usage produces an abstinence syndrome or withdrawal illness. Habituation—that is, psychological dependence—may result from using any of the drugs, including coffee, alcohol, nicotine and marijuana. This condition exists when an individual becomes so psychologically accustomed to the drug that when it is no longer available he becomes ill at ease, restless, or irritable. Of course, even television viewing and other activities not involving drugs may produce habituation.

The term "drug abuse" refers to the use of a mind-altering drug—usually chronic, excessive use—to an extent that interferes either with an individual's social or vocational adjustment or with his health. This concept properly includes such things as drunk driving, cirrhosis of the liver due to alcoholism, barbiturate addiction, amphetamine psychosis, and a "bad" LSD "trip." Addiction is only a small part of the drug abuse picture. "Misuse" of mind-altering drugs refers to any nonspecific or nonmedical use of such drugs, including alcohol and nicotine.

The definition of what is or is not a "problem" is perhaps the most complex of all. For the most part, "problems" are artificially defined for use—often irrationally and for self-serving reasons—by opinion formers and rulemakers. Many of the things which we are told are drug "problems" are pseudoproblems; for example, the wrong drug or the wrong component of the cycle of use and control of a particular drug frequently is designated as a problem. On the other hand, some of the most underemphasized aspects of drug use or control are serious problems. Laws enacted in a climate of ignorance and hysteria understandably create "problems" where they did not exist before.

II.   Drug Use Laws and Policies

There is considerable misunderstanding about drug policies, largely because our society has developed these policies in a very narrow, and oversimplified fashion. The drugs disapproved by society's "establishment" or rulemakers are dealt with in terms of criminal prohibitions accompanied by increasingly severe penalties for the user or possesser of such drugs.[2] Such a policy is analogous to smashing a young child in the face and throwing it out of the home for touching something it was not supposed to touch rather than recognizing that a wide range of less destructive and more effective measures are available. In contrast, use of socially acceptable drugs such as alcohol and nicotine encounters little regulation, and what regulation there is often goes unenforced.

Present policies regarding alcohol and nicotine involve often unenforced laws against sale to, or use by, minors,[3] modest state and federal taxes,[4] minimal restrictions on the hours during which

alcohol can be served in public places,[5] federal laws regulating production of alcohol,[6] and a large body of laws against serving already intoxicated people[7] or driving while intoxicated.[8] Some counties in a few states pretend to maintain prohibition of alcohol. Policies relating to socially condemned drugs date back at least to the passage of the Harrison Anti-Narcotic Act[9] in 1914 and include the fourteen year period of national alcohol prohibition, the Marijuana Tax Act of 1937,[10] state marijuana laws,[11] the Narcotic Control Act of 1956,[12] the Federal Drug Abuse Control Amendments of 1965[13] and state laws on LSD-type drugs.[14]

The American system of attempted control of drugs has been extremely unsuccessful and harmful; the use and abuse of mind-altering drugs has increased enormously in direct proportion with the imposition of severe criminal penalties on users. More potentially dangerous drugs (al-

cohol, heroin, nicotine, LSD, and amphetamines) and a greater diversity of substances are now being used to alter consciousness. Use has come to involve ever younger age groups and a greater diversity of socio-economic classes. Tens of thousands of individuals have been branded as criminals and their lives ruined. The almost constant publicity given to various drugs by politicians and the drug police has, over a period of decades, greatly sensationalized substances such as heroin, marijuana, and LSD, thereby stimulating curiosity and magical expectations about drug usage. Beginning with the prohibition against alcohol, the supply of illegal drugs has been driven underground into the black market where it has helped to enrich and develop organized crime. Powerful and virtually uncontrolled bureaucracies established in local, state, and federal governments have developed new and more ineffective laws and have attacked every effort towards developing rational, humane, and effective policies. The selective enforcement of these status crimes—crimes without victims as they are sometimes called—and their emphasis on the user rather than on the profiteer involves tremendous hypocrisy and produces disrespect for the law and the police. The enforcement practices of drug police, such as the use of spies, informers, threats, bribes, and entrapment are basically un-American and immoral and lead to further disrespect for law enforcement.

America's drug control laws, including those directed against alcohol in the 1920's and the more recent ones concerning heroin, marijuana, and LSD, have consistently been enacted on the basis of anecdotal, unscientific, and illogical testimony adduced mainly from drug police and their political allies and received in a climate of hysteria willingly developed and reinforced by the mass media. Legislatures have heard almost no medical, sociological, or scientific testimony from either individuals or organizations before enacting these far-reaching laws.[15] Moreover, with the possible exception of the relatively brief period of alcohol prohibition, there have

---

[2] See, e.g., Ind. Ann. Stat. s 10-3538 (Supp. 1967) (narcotic drugs); Miss. Code Ann. s 6831-08 (Supp. 1967) (barbiturates and stimulants). Regarding sales of narcotics (including marijuana), the Indiana statute provides for penalties of 5-20 years and not more than $2,000 for a first offense, and 20 years to life and not more than $5,000 for subsequent offenses; regarding possession, it provides for 2-10 years and not more than $1,000 for a first offense, 5-20 years and not more than $2,000 for subsequent offenses. Under the Mississippi law, both possession and sale are punishable by a fine of not more than $1,000 and imprisonment for not more than 5 years for a first offense, a maximum fine of $3,000 and a 5-10 year period of imprisonment for a second offense, and a maximum fine of $5,000 and a 10-20 year period of imprisonment for a third offense. *See generally* Rosenthal, *Dangerous Drug Legislation in the United States, Recommendations and Comments,* 45 Texas L. Rev. 1037, 1073, 1077 (1967).

[3] E.g., Cal. Bus. & Prof. Code ss 25658-65 (West 1964) (alcohol); Cal. Pen. Code s 308 (West 1955) (tobacco).

[4] E.g., Int. Rev. Code of 1954, ss 5001, 5021-23, 5041, 5051, 5081, 5701 (taxes on distilled spirits, wine, beer, cigars, and cigarettes); Cal. Rev. & Tax Code ss 30101, 32151 (West Supp. 1966); *id.* s 32201 (West

1956) (taxes on distilled spirits, wine, beer, and cigarettes).

[5] E.g., Cal. Pen. Code s 398 (West 1955).

[6] Int. Rev. Code of 1954, ss 5001-692.

[7] E.g., Cal. Bus. & Prof. Code s 25602 (West 1964).

[8] E.g., Cal. Pen. Code s 367d (West 1955).

[9] Ch. 1, 38 stat. 785 (now Int. Rev. Code of 1954, ss 4701-36).

[10] Act of Aug. 2, 1937, ch. 553, 50 Stat, *as amended,* Int. Rev. Code of 1954, ss 4741-62.

[11] E.g., *compare* Cal. Health & Safety Code s 11721 *with id.* s 11001(d) (West 1964). For a concise review of state marijuana legislation, see Rosenthal, *supra* note 2, at 1077.

[12] Ch. 629, 70 Stat. 567 (codified in scattered sections of 21, 26 U.S.C.).

[13] Pub. L. No. 89-74, 79 Stat. 226. For a description of the law see Rosenthal, *supra,* note 2, at 1051-62.

[14] E.g., Cal. Health & Safety Code ss 11901, 11910-16 (West Supp. 1967); *compare* Ariz. Rev. Stat. Ann. ss 32-1964, 32-1975(B) (Supp. 1967) *with id.* ss 32-1965 to -1968 (1965); *compare* N.Y. Pen. Law ss 220.00-.40 (McKinney 1967) *with* N.Y. Mental Hygiene Law s 229 (McKinney Supp. 1967). *See generally* Laughlin, *LSD-25 and the Other Hallucinogens: A Pre-Reform Proposal,* 36 Geo. Wash. L. Rev. 23, 28 n.25 (1967).

[15] *See, e.g., Hearings on Traffic in, and Control of, Narcotics, Barbiturates, and Amphetamines, Before a Subcomm. of the House Comm. on Ways and Means,* 84th Cong., 1st and 2nd Sess. (1957).

been no powerful financial or political interests defending either the users of these drugs or the drugs themselves, a situation obviously conducive to the enactment of such laws.

III. Drug Use and Abuse: The Pattern and Its Implications

Roughly eighty million people in the United States use nicotine,[16] and probably as many use alcohol.[17] Included in both categories are millions of persons under the age of twenty-one whose use of these drugs is ordinarily illicit and involves deliberate violations of the law,[18] often with the same motives that accompany the use of less approved drugs such as marijuana. Both alcohol and nicotine are used by persons in all socioeconomic groups and in widely varying occupations. The causative relationship between the use of nicotine and hundreds of thousands of deaths and disabilities each year in the United States from lung cancer, heart disease, hypertension, emphysema, and bronchitis is well established.[19] There are an estimated 4.5 to 6.8 million alcoholics in the nation,[20] and more in the San Francisco Bay Area alone than there are narcotic addicts in the entire country.[21] At least twenty-five

[16] Lukas, *The Drug Scene: Dependence Grows,* N.Y. *Times,* Jan. 8, 1968, at 22, col. 2 [hereinafter cited as *The Drug Scene*].

[17] *Id.* "It can be said that 68 percent of all American adults have had at least one drink within the past year. Twenty-two percent of the population report they have never tried an alcoholic beverage." *President's Comm'n on Law Enforcement and Administration of Justice, Task Force Report: Drunkenness* 29–30 (1967) [hereinafter cited as *Task Force Report: Drunkenness*].

[18] See note 3 *supra* and accompanying text.

[19] *See* U.S. Dep't. of Health, Education & Welfare, Public Health Service, *Smoking & Health: Report of the Advisory Comm. to the Surgeon General* (1964).

[20] *See Task Force Report: Drunkenness, supra note 17,* at 30–32. The Jellinek formula, used to produce the 4.5 million figure, has been subject to much criticism (including criticism by Jellinek himself) by those who contend that it under-reports alcoholism. *Id.* at 31.

[21] There are probably about 100,000 narcotic addicts in the United States. *See* note 35 *infra* and accompanying

thousand deaths and more than a million severe injuries on the highways each year are associated with alcohol consumption;[22] twenty percent of the people in state mental hospitals are there because of alcoholic brain disease;[23] fifty percent of the people in prisons have committed their crimes in association with alcohol consumption;[24] one third of all arrests are for drunkenness,[25] and probably as many as one-half are for alcohol-related offenses.[26] Alcohol use generates other enormous costs to society in the form of absenteeism and job loss, marital disruption, and welfare costs.

Sedatives, stimulants, and tranquilizers are used by at least ten million Americans, many of whom are in the middle and upper socioeconomic groups and over thirty. There are probably several hundred thousand "abusers," including persons having barbiturate addiction and amphetamine psychosis.[27] These drugs are primar-

text. It is estimated that there are 250,-000 alcoholics in the San Francisco Bay Area. State of California, Dep't. of Public Health, Div. of Alcoholism, Cirrhosis Death, Estimated Number of Alcoholics and Rate per 100,000 Population, California Three Year Average, 1962–64 (undated fact sheet).

[22] *See Task Force Report: Drunkenness, supra note 17,* at 37–39.

[23] *See id.* at 121.

[24] *See id.* at 4, 40–42.

[25] "Two million arrests in 1965—one of every three arrests in America—were for the offense of public drunkenness. . . ." "The two million arrests for drunkenness each year involve both sporadic and regular drinkers." *Task Force Report: Drunkenness, supra note 17,* at 1.

[26] *Id.* at 40.

[27] *See The Drug Scene, supra* note 16, at 22, col. 2; *President's Comm'n on Law Enforcement and Administration of Justice, Task Force Report: Narcotics and Drug Abuse* 29, 30, 33, 34 (1967)/hereinafter cited as *Task Force Report: Narcotics and Drug Abuse/.* These figures do not include the massive use of the mild stimulant, caffeine—in the form of coffee, tea, and cola drinks—but this must also be considered when examining the pattern of use and abuse of mind-altering drugs. Also not included in the above figures is the enormous use of over-the-counter, non-prescription substances which are widely advertised as being sedatives, stimulants, or tranquilizers. These preparations, usually containing such ingredients as antihistamines, aspirin, or belladonna, have either a placebo or nonspecific effect.

ily obtained through doctors who often prescribe them rather loosely in large quantities for nonspecific conditions. Under federal law, such prescriptions can be refilled only five times and only over a maximum six-month period.[28] There is a much less extensive but significant use and abuse of these drugs, particularly amphetamines such as methedrine, by young people who obtain it on the black market. As might be expected, the activities of the young have received disproportionate attention. Probably most of the use of these drugs in American society is for a nonspecific or even ill-advised purpose, in other words "misuse."

Marijuana, although receiving far more attention, actually ranks far below both alcohol and nicotine in terms of illicit drug use and abuse or other problems. The dried leaves of the female cannabis sativa plant, which in the form of cigarettes we call marijuana, are currently smoked, for the most part occasionally and irregularly, by many Americans in all socioeconomic classes and occupational groups.[29] Several decades ago when many of the present marijuana laws were enacted, marijuana use was concentrated mainly among certain "outgroups" in American society: Negroes, Mexican-Americans, jazz musicians, Bohemians, and intellectuals. But as a direct consequence of the extremism of the laws and their enforcement, the sensationalizing of the drug by drug police and mass media, the inculcation of the habit of cigarette smoking by the tobacco in-

[28] *Compare* Act of July 15, 1965, Pub. L. No. 89–74, s 3 (b), 79 Stat. 227, 230, *with* 21 C.F.R. s 166.3 (Supp. I 1966).

[29] There is no reliable estimate of the prevalence of marijuana use. To the limited extent that police activity is an accurate measure, use appears to be increasing. . . . Marijuana use apparently cuts across a larger segment of the general population than does opiate use, but again adequate studies are lacking. . . . There are many reports of widespread use on campuses, but estimates that 20 percent or more of certain college populations have used the drug cannot be verified or refuted. *Task Force Report: Narcotics and Drug Abuse, supra* note 27, at 3. The author believes that marijuana users in the United States may number one million or more.

dustry, and the general strong pressures to use mind-altering drugs in our society, the pattern has shifted enormously. Persons between eighteen and thirty are now the primary users of marijuana, but there is also considerable use among older age groups.[30] Selective enforcement of the law causes undue public emphasis upon marijuana use among certain groups such as "hippies," high school and college students, Negroes, and Mexican-Americans, but this is a very unrepresentative sampling of the total picture.

The kinds of abuses associated with such drugs as alcohol and nicotine have not been observed with marijuana, although if research had not been prevented by the dictatorial policies of the Federal Bureau of Narcotics and local narcotics agencies, we would have a much fuller picture. In any case, in view of marijuana's widespread use by so many people for so many years and the apparent absence of any problems other than those manufactured by our present policies and their supporters, it can be said that the main abuse associated with marijuana comes from the destruction of the lives of those thousands of young people who are branded as criminals. Survey data from high schools and colleges in urban areas indicate that illicit use of marijuana, like illicit use of alcohol and nicotine, is both widespread and increasing among students.[31] This information has many social implications for the future. Marijuana has become symbolic of the generation gap and of the conflict between young and old. If present trends towards extremism and polarization of thinking continue, the generations will be driven even

farther apart, and an increasing number of young people will be driven from full participation in society.

The LSD-type drugs, particularly LSD itself, have probably been tried by at least a million people, but are probably being used with some degree of regularity by only some tens of thousands of mostly young, intellectually or mystically inclined middle-class youth. Almost all of the use of the LSD, psilocybin, mescaline (peyote), and DMT (dimethyl-tryptamine) is nonmedical and illegal.[32] However, the use of some of the newer synthetic "psychedelics," such as STP and MDA, does not violate the criminal law. Because isolated instances of abuse associated with LSD have been so sensationalized—a variety of crimes and psychotic behavior have been attributed to it—and because users have been driven underground and made afraid to seek help, it is very difficult to assess the extent of abuse connected with the LSD family of drugs.

The four main categories of LSD abuse are (1) acute panic reactions which ordinarily subside when the drug effect wears off in the course of ten to twelve hours; (2) recurrence of LSD-type perceptual phenomena for brief periods (usually seconds), weeks, or months after the original "acid" experience; (3) prolonged schizophrenic psychoses requiring weeks or months of hospitalization—a phenomenon which seems to occur only in individuals who already were overtly or latently schizophrenic; and (4) rare accidental or suicidal death while under the drug's influence.[33] The incidence of these various abuses probably ranges from about one in one thousand "trips" to one in ten

thousand "trips."[34] Those abuses which have, through distorted accounts, received the most extensive public attention—death and psychosis—occur much more frequently in connection with alcohol, barbiturates, and cigarettes, not to mention such nondrug causes as guns and disturbed family lives.

The phenomenon which has come to be referred to as "dropping out" is associated in many minds with LSD, but this concept is very vague and is frequently applied to any individual who deviates from a pattern of forty hours' work in a five-day week at a traditional type of job or who questions the cherished values and traditions of established society. Probably no one has "dropped out" solely as a result of using LSD; it is more likely that individuals already frustrated with the society around them have, in conjunction with LSD use, disaffiliated themselves from conventional society.

Millions of Americans use narcotic drugs such as morphine, codeine, Percodan, and Demerol for temporary relief of coughs and pain. With the exception of cough syrups which are easily bought over the counter, this use is by special prescription from a doctor. There is also considerable misuse of these drugs, medical addiction by hundreds of thousands who have severe injuries or terminal illness with pain, and widespread abuse of headache remedies and cough syrups containing narcotics. The number of illicit or illegal narcotic addicts in the United States, using mostly heroin, is probably about one hundred thousand.[35] The majority are young Negro, Mexican, or Puerto Rican Americans of culturally deprived backgrounds who have grown up in urban slum ghettos, where crime is common and drugs are available at an early age.[36]

[30] Mrs. Garnet Brennan, 58-year old principal of a grade school in Nicasio, California, was fired from her job after openly admitting that she had been smoking marijuana almost daily for 18 years. Mrs. Brennan had an excellent 30-year record of teaching, is a homeowner in suburban Forest Knolls, and has always been highly regarded by friends, neighbors, and associates. Her admission was in the form of an affidavit which was one of hundreds being collected by defense attorneys representing a Marin County resident charged with the sale of marijuana. See *Berkeley Barb*, Oct. 20–26, 1967, at 7, cols. 1 & 2, and at 14, cols. 1 & 2; *San Francisco Chronicle*, Nov. 3, 1967 at 3, col. 6. One wonders how many others in Mrs. Brennan's age group use marijuana but fear admitting it.

[31] See *Task Force: Narcotics and Drug Abuse, supra* note 27, at 3.

[32] See note 14 *supra*. Another and quite different pattern of use of this family of drugs (not included in the estimates in the text) is the use of peyote in religious ceremonies by Indian members of the Native American Church, discussed in W. LaBarre, *The Peyote Cult* (1964).

[33] These abuses have been compounded and complicated by the laws used to deal with LSD-type drug; they have brought about the use of impure black market drugs which are often inadequately prepared and which often have an unknown dosage; furthermore, they lead to surreptitious use of the drugs without screening or guidance by trusted and experienced persons. As in the case of marijuana, one significant abuse is the branding of users as criminals.

[34] See *generally*, S. Cohen, *The Beyond Within: The LSD Story* (1964); Cohen, *A Classification of LSD Complications, Psychosomatics*, May–June 1966, at 182; Cohen, *Lysergic Acid Diethylamide: Side Effects and Complications*, 130 J. *Nervous and Mental Disease* 30 (1966).

[35] See *Task Force Report: Narcotics and Drug Abuse, supra* note 27 at 2, 47–48. The estimates *id.* at 47–48 refer to *opiate* addicts; since neither cocaine nor marijuana is addictive, *see id.* at 3, narcotic addiction is synonymous with opiate addiction.

[36] See *id.* at 48–50.

Because narcotic drug laws have driven the drugs and their users underground, enabling the underworld to charge exorbitant prices, most heroin addicts are heavily involved in crimes against property to support their expensive "habit."[37]

A tremendous variety of miscellaneous substances are also being used for mind-alteration, mostly by children and young adults. These substances include asthma and cold inhalers, the belladonna or scopolamine in over-the-counter "sedatives," the nitrous oxide in deodorant and shaving cream aerosol cans, the fumes of glue and gasoline, nutmeg and other spices, morning glory and other plant seeds, and a great diversity of other natural and synthetic drugs and substances.[38] It should be clear from this that politicians, police, newspapers, and others who characteristically misuse this issue to benefit themselves, will have almost unlimited opportunities in the future to misdirect society's resources by enacting more criminal laws instead of attacking the real problems.

IV. The Real Social Problems: Those Caused by Drug Abuse and by Drug Policies

The most serious and least discussed social problem resulting from mind-altering drug use in American society is misuse of individual abilities, energy, time, and money. The indirect as well as direct glorification of mind-altering drugs by the press, advertising media, police, and parents, the ready availability of many of these drugs, the hedonistic tendencies in our society, and the widespread alienation of young and old have brought us to our present predicament: Millions of Americans are unable to find meaning or purpose in life, to be happy, or to relate to other human beings without using drugs.

The enforcement of laws pertaining to the use of mind-altering drugs diverts financial resources, personnel (police, district attorneys, judges), and prison facilities from dealing with rapidly increasing *real* crime such as murder, rape, and theft;[39] it diverts

attention from the more crucial problem of distribution and sale of these drugs (such as marijuana or heroin from Mexico); and it precludes giving adequate emphasis to the major drug being abused, alcohol. Furthermore, the efforts to deal with drug use hampers society in combatting far more important social problems such as poverty, disease, racial discrimination, and war.

Our rulemakers' official disapproval of drug use, reminiscent, perhaps, of the Romans' use of bread and circuses, serves as a valuable smoke-screen for obscuring more difficult matters. In a related fashion, laws against drug use—particularly those dealing with marijuana—provide a convenient device for attacking youth and stifling dissent and nonconformity. The unjust treatment of youth and other minority subcultures is a major social problem, breeding crime, hypocrisy, and anarchy, and driving thousands from meaningful participation in society. For both sides in this conflict between generations, drugs such as marijuana have taken harmful symbolic importance.

Problems resulting directly from the use of mind-altering drugs include dangerous or antisocial behavior on the one hand and illness or death on the other. In the former category, it is most often alcohol, among drug which causes or contributes to accidents, violence, and crime. Guns and mental illness also play prominent—yet generally ignored—roles. Acute or chronic excessive use of alcohol and nicotine—the most freely distributed and least condemned mind-altering drugs—is the most prominent form of drug use associated with illness, dis-

ability, and death. In addition, thousands of accidental and suicidal deaths occur each year in this country from overdoses of barbiturates, chloral hydrate, and Doriden or other narcotic and sedative drugs, often taken in combination with alcohol. LSD-type drugs and amphetamines play only a relatively minor role in causing direct physical harm to users and in causing or inducing them to engage in harmful behavior; their greatest abuse effect is in producing disabling psychoses.[40]

The drastic interference with, even prohibition of, treatment of drug abusers ranging from alcoholics through narcotic addicts is another much neglected social problem stemming from our present legal policies. In many states doctors are expected to violate medical ethics by reporting narcotic users to the police; and in some states, such as California, proper treatment of the addict is barred by a law specifying that narcotics can only be administered in certain closed institutions and only for limited periods of time.[41] Professionals seeking to rehabilitate drug abusers are so stigmatized that they often turn to less controversial and more lucrative problems. Some doctors are even afraid to provide the proper amount of narcotics for a patient in severe pain. Furthermore, important research of great potential benefit to society is made difficult or impossible by present state and federal laws and regulations, particularly in regard to marijuana and LSD.[42]

Conclusion

The social and legal policies ostensibly developed to control or prevent the use of mind-altering drugs are the cause of the main social problems arising from their use. These policies have been markedly ineffective, irrational, and harmful. The wrong drugs are receiving most of the attention; alcohol and nicotine are seriously undercontrolled and overavailable. Present laws are directed at the wrong phase of the cycle of promotion, distribution, and use.

[37] *See id.* at 55–57.

[38] *See id.* at 36.

[39] *See* Kadish, *The Crisis of Overcriminalization,* 374 *Annals* 157, 163–65 (1967). "Excessive reliance upon the criminal law to perform tasks for which it is ill-suited has created

acute problems for the administration of criminal justice. The use of criminal law to enforce morals . . . has tended both to be inefficient and to produce grave handicaps for enforcement of the criminal law against genuinely threatening conduct. . . . [It] has served to reduce the criminal law's essential claim to legitimacy by inducing offensive and degrading police conduct, particularly against the poor and subcultural, and by generating cynicism and indifference to the criminal law. It has also fostered organized criminality and has produced, possibly, more crime than it has suppressed." *Id.* at 157. Professor Kadish served as a General Consultant for the President's Commission on Law Enforcement and Administration of Justice and is presently Reporter for the California Joint Legislative Penal Code Revision Project.

[40] *See Task Force Report: Narcotics and Drug Abuse, supra* note 27, at 27, 30–31.

[41] Cal. Health & Safety Code ss 11390–96 (West 1964).

[42] *But see* Ariz. Rev. Stat. Ann. s 32–1968 (1956); Cal. Health & Safety Code s 11916 (West Supp. 1967); N.Y. Mental Hygiene Law s 229 (McKinney Supp. 1967).

Manufacture and distribution of all mind-altering drugs—including alcohol and tobacco—should be reduced by the application of civil and criminal penalties; advertising of these drugs should be completely banned and all products containing them prominently labeled as dangerous to health and safety. Discretion to grant probation, parole, and suspended sentences for drug offenders should be reinstituted. Research and treatment by physicians should be fully permitted and in fact encouraged. The most urgently needed reform is to take out of the criminal law the "status crime" of being a user or possessor of a particular drug and to concentrate instead on antisocial behavior and on the phases mentioned above.

In keeping with a humanistic concept of life we should primarily concern ourselves with human beings, who for a variety of sociological and psychological reasons use drugs. We are giving the drugs themselves undue attention. Those who abuse drugs should have available long term, comprehensive outpatient public health programs of treatment and education such as San Francisco's Center for Special Problems, founded by the author. Educational programs designed to present the objective facts about the full context of these drugs including the potential risks involved in their use should be made available to students—including those in elementary school—and to the general public, to desensationalize and demythologize alcohol, marijuana, and the rest. The Federal Bureau of Narcotics and other drug police agencies should be closed and their agents redeployed to deal with the real problems described above.[43]

Finally, we must attack the roots of drug use and abuse which are deeply imbedded in a sick, corrupt, and hypocritical society. We must turn our attention from symptoms or branches of problems to the task of improving the quality of American life, facilitating the pursuit of excellence and encouraging individuality. When life itself becomes a mind-expanding experience, drugs will become relatively unimportant in our society.

[43] Cf. *President's Advisory Comm'n. on Narcotics and Drug Abuse, Final Report* 31–37 (1963).

Timothy Leary once again confronts the unconventional when he looks toward the future of drug usage, its application and control. Rebuking the present "morality" of drug laws, Leary calls for a new ethical code which can be applied in dealing with the drugs of the present as well as the drugs of the future. The proposals he presents in this article allow for individual freedom in addition to a safeguard from governmental and scientific abuse. While Leary's recommendations appear simple, they capture a basic concept of human liberation that has been so long neglected in drug legislation and application.

7.3
The Politics, Ethics, and Meaning of Marijuana

Timothy Leary

I

I have written these pages about the social, ethical, and scientific meanings of marijuana under two compelling time-pressures: first, the gentle prodding of David Solomon, who was kind enough to hold up publication of this book to include my hasty comments; and second, the less than gentle insistence of a Texas judge that I spend the next thirty years in prison.

I am concerned more about my promise to David Solomon than about the threat of incarceration. If psychedelic drugs tell us anything, it is that the prisons exist only in man's mind. Any ground is sacred ground if you are open enough to realize it. Including Leavenworth.

By legal and social standards, the sentence of thirty years' imprisonment and a $30,000 fine for the possession of half an ounce of marijuana might seem severe. But the basic issue here is internal freedom. The basic charge is heresy. At other stages in this long struggle for freedom of consciousness such penalties would be considered light. I protest but not complain.

My crime is the ancient and familiar one of corrupting the

minds of the youth. This charge is a valid one. I have written some forty articles and five books about the effects of psychedelic drugs. I have addressed these messages to all who can read, but I have been keenly aware that it has been the young who have attended and acted on these messages.

The March 11, 1966, issue of *Time* magazine announces that at least 10,000 students at the University of California have taken LSD. The number of students who smoke marijuana is considered to be considerably higher.

I am repeatedly asked to deplore this use of psychedelic drugs by the young. Is not this a dangerous and reckless misuse? And I repeatedly refuse to generally condemn this psychedelic revolt of the young. Cite me an individual case and I may be able to speculate about this specific recklessness or wisdom. But, in general, I say that it is a good thing that more and more Americans are expanding their awareness, pulling back the veil of symbolic platitude, and confronting the many other levels of energy that are available to man. It is a tragedy that more older people aren't joining the young. To parents who are worried about their children "turning on," I would say, "Don't fight your kids; join them in this adventure of exploration. If you are tolerant of your children's use of alcohol (which numbs their vision), why are you intolerant of their wish to expand their vision?" In the gamble of life my wager goes down on the side of the young. The current generation is the brightest, holiest, bravest, and most curious of any generation in human history. And, by God, they better be.

None of us knows how to handle the power and promise-threat of mind-expanding chemicals. But if I am confronted with a fifteen-year-old who does not know what he is doing and a fifty-year-old who does not know what he is doing, I'll take the fifteen-year-old every time. In using a new form of energy, whatever mistakes the teenager makes will be in the direction of sensation, love-making, curiosity, desire for growth. The fifty-year-old has abandoned sensation, lost the impulse to make love, killed his curiosity, and dissipated his lust for growth. You know how he uses new forms of energy: for control and power and war-making.

Support the kids. Listen to them. Learn from them if they will let you. They are closer to their nervous systems, closer to cellular and seed wisdom, closer to the Divine Energy than we parents. The human species, let's face it, is an adolescent, as yet unformed, confused, evolutionary form. Stand in the way of the energy process as it slowly, relentlessly begins to uncoil, and it will crush you and your symbolic illusions. Cherish it, nurture it, let it grow, let it blossom, and you will be reborn in and with your children.

II

Marijuana alters consciousness. LSD alters consciousness.

On that they all agree. Policeman. Priest. Pusher. Politician. Prophet. Pharmacologist. Psychologist.

They all agree that marijuana and LSD alter consciousness. But how? And to what end—evil or beneficial? To these questions there is no agreement.

Sincere, well-intentioned men are led to extreme positions. On the one hand, punitive laws, repressive crusades, police action, the arming of agents of Health, Education and Welfare, the lengthy imprisonment of citizens for no crime other than the altering of their own consciousness:

One of the stiffest and most inflexible sets of laws ever put to the Federal books, the Boggs–Daniel Act (1956) represents the high-water mark of punitive legislation against the use, sale, and handling of drugs. It imposed severe mandatory sentences for sale or possession of narcotics—permitting in most cases neither probation nor parole. . . .

In some states, such as New York, sentencing is fairly lenient. Mere possession (25 or more marijuana cigarettes . . .) carries sentence of only (sic) three to ten years.[1]

In today's affluent society the use of marijuana is no longer confined to the "dregs" of society. It is becoming increasingly fashionable for middle- and upper-class youth. California jails now hold close to 6,000 people for breaking marijuana laws. Sixty-four percent of all Californians arrested on marijuana charges are under 25 years of age. Arrests for breaking marijuana laws . . . since 1962 . . . have increased nearly 500%.[2]

On the other hand, passive resistance, poetic and artistic and scientific appeals to reason, futile

[1] *The Drug Takers*, Time-Life Books, 1965, pp. 53–54.

[2] *San Francisco* Magazine, February 1966, p. 16.

protests, flights into exile, cynicism:

. . . Dr. S. J. Holmes, director of the narcotic addiction unit of the Alcoholism and Drug Addiction Research Foundation in Toronto . . . believes it is "fantastic and ridiculous" that a person caught with one marijuana cigaret can be sent to prison.

It is particularly ridiculous, he said, when compared with the use and effect of alcohol. "This situation is really a disgrace to our civilization and merits much consideration."[3]

The preliminary estimates of a foundation-financed study on drug use at San Francisco State show that 60% of the students will at some time use an illegal drug . . .

Marijuana is sold on the campus, smoked on the campus, and used by professors.

A Berkeley sorority girl said, "When you drink you lose control and sensitivity, generally feeling and acting like a slobbering idiot. This never happens with pot."

Most spoke of the legal problems as did this girl: "It doesn't bother me to break the law. How many times do you break it jaywalking and so on? The main thing is that I just don't think of using marijuana in these terms. It's pure hypocrisy and stupidity that it's not legal. The law is wrong for both practical and moral reasons."[4]

There are many dimensions to the psychedelic drug controversy and no simple answers. I wish to consider in this essay three issues: the political, the moral, and the scientific.

The Political Issue

The Politics of Consciousness Expansion

To understand the psychedelic controversy it is necessary to study the sociology of psychedelic drugs. Who wants to smoke marijuana? To eat peyote? To ingest LSD? What people are involved in this new drug menace? The young. The racially and nationally alienated. The creative. Most users of psychedelic plants and drugs fall into at least one of these three categories.

The Young

Over 50 percent of the American population is under the age of 25. Ominous, isn't it? From 50 to 70 percent of the use of marijuana and LSD is by the high school and college age group. From 50 to 70

[3] Toronto *Globe and Mail*, February 17, 1966, p. 5.

[4] *San Francisco* Magazine, February 1966, pp. 18–19.

percent of the arrests and imprisonments for possession of psychedelic substances fall on the shoulders of those under the age of 30. Whisky-drinking middle age imprisons pot-smoking youth. Think about this.

The Racially and Nationally Alienated

Negroes, Puerto Ricans, American Indians. The use of psychedelic plants in these noble minority groups of the American society is high. The whisky-drinking, white middle-class imprisons those with different cultural and religious preferences. Think about this.

The Creative

I would estimate that over 70 percent of nonacademic creative artists have used psychedelic substances in their work. Painters. Poets, Musicians. Dancers. Actors. Directors. The whisky-drinking middle brow imprisons the growing edge. Think about this.

The Criminal and Psychedelic Drugs

The stereotyped picture of the marijuana smoker is that of a criminal type. The statistics do not support this myth. Marijuana is used by groups that are socially alienated from middle-class values —youth, Negroes, Indians, creative artists, but few criminals. Alcohol is the drug of the nonyouthful, noncreative, white criminal. The economics of heroin leads the addict to commit crime. Few criminals smoke pot. Few pot smokers are criminals (except for the offense of changing their own consciousness).

The Psychedelic Minority Group

A United Nations report on worldwide use of drugs estimated that in 1951 there were 200 million cannabis users. This is an awesome statistic. Worldwide, there are more marijuana users than members of the Protestant and Jewish religions combined.

The number of pot smokers worldwide is larger than the population of the United States of America. It is safe to say that there are more pot smokers than there are members of the middle class throughout the world. Indeed, we have the astonishing spectacle of a middle-class minority, tolerant to alcohol and addicted to bureaucracy, passing laws against and interfering with the social-religious rituals of a statistically larger group! Think about that one.

It has been estimated that as many as ten million people in America today have used marijuana, peyote, and LSD. Remember the Indians, the Negroes, the young, the creative. We deal here with one of the largest persecuted minority groups in the country. This group is nonvocal, effectively prevented from presenting its case, essentially stripped of its constitutional rights.

Another crucial sociological issue that is easily overlooked: psychedelic people tend to be socially passive. The psychedelic experience is by nature private, sensual, spiritual, internal, introspective. Whereas alcohol and amphetamines stimulate the afferent nervous system—inciting furious game activities—the psychedelics stimulate the afferent nervous centers. Contemplation . . . meditation . . . sensual openness . . . artistic and religious preoccupation.

Excesses of passive contemplation are no better than excesses of action—but certainly no worse. God and the DNA code designed man to have interoceptive and exteoceptive neurological systems, and any harmonious view of man should allow for judicious and thoughtful balancing of both.

Throughout world history psychedelic people have not tended to form commissions to stamp out nonpsychedelic people. Nor do they pass laws against or imprison nonpsychedelicists.

The Ethical Issue

The Molecular Revolution

Politically oriented activists have throughout history left the psychedelic minority pretty much alone. The power-holders have been too busy fighting each other to worry about those who prefer to live in quiet harmony and creative quietude.

It is harder work to contact and control your nervous system than the external symbol structure. Yogins, meditators, monks, hashish mystics have been too busy decoding and appreciating their afferent (sensory) and cellular communication systems to busy themselves with political struggles.

But now comes the molecular revolution. The work of James McConnell demonstrates that learning is molecular. Dumb flatworms eat smart flatworms and become smart. Holger Hyden discovers that the brain cells of educated rats contain a third more RNA than do the brain cells of uneducated rats. University of California

psychologists pass on learning from one rat to another by injecting RNA from trained rats. Neurologists are "wiring-up" the brains of animals and men and altering consciousness by pressing buttons. Press a button: make him hungry. Press a button: make him erotic. Press a button: make him angry. Press a button: make him feel good.

The psychedelic chemicals flood out of the laboratories—into the hands of the two familiar groups: those who want to do something to others and those who want to do something to themselves.

U.S. Army psychologists secretly drop LSD into the coffee of an infantry platoon. The surprised soldiers giggle, break ranks, and wander off looking at the trees. Psychiatrists secretly drop LSD into the water glasses of psychotic patients and report that LSD enhances insanity. And on the college campuses and in the art centers of the country hundreds of thousands of the creative young take LSD and millions smoke marijuana to explore their own consciousness. The new cult of visionaries. They turn on, tune in, and often drop out of the academic, professional and other games-playing roles they have been assigned. They do not drop out of life, but probe more deeply into it, toward personal and social realignments characterized by loving detachment from materialist goals.

Laws are passed encouraging the administration of LSD to the unsuspecting (patients, soldiers, research subjects) and preventing self-administration!

The Two Commandments of the Molecular Age

Of the many powerful energies now suddenly available to man, the most challenging and sobering are those that alter the fabric of thought and judgment—the very core of meaning and being.

Learning, memory, mood, judgment, identity, consciousness can now be transformed instantaneously by electrical and chemical stimuli. In the long-short diary of our species, no issue has posed such a promise-peril.

The history of human evolution (not unlike that of every other species of life on our planet) is the record of new forms of energy —physical, mechanical, chemical —discovered, slowly understood (and misunderstood), painfully debated, eventually adapted to.

Today the human race is confronted with new energies that tax

our wisdom, confuse our judgment, terrorize our emotional securities, excite our highest aspirations, and threaten to alter our central notions of man and his place on this planet. Never has man faced ethical and political issues so complex, so delicate, so demanding, so frightening. Never has man been in greater need of ethical guidance. And where is it?

Our scientists plunge enthusiastically into the process of mind-changing, consciousness alteration, with little apparent regard for the moral, political complications.

One of the few men who have recognized the high stakes of this new game of cerebral roulette is David Krech, psychologist Berkeley. Dr. Krech is quoted as saying:

Until recently, these substances were considered science-fiction, but real science has been moving forward so rapidly in this area that science-fiction is hard put to keep up with it. About 15 years ago, I doubt whether I could have found more than a half-dozen laboratories in the entire world which were concerned with basic research in behavior, brain, and biochemistry. Today there hardly exists a major laboratory where such research is not being given high priority.

If we should find effective mind-control agents, we must consider whether the manufacture and dispensing of such agents should be left to private enterprise or to military control or to political control. And how should this be done, and when and by whom? It is not too early for us to ponder very seriously the awesome implications of what brain research may discover.[5]

The time has come for a new ethical code to deal with issues unforeseen (or were they, really?) by our earliest prophets and moralists. Although the social-political implications are hopelessly complicated, the moral issues are clear-cut, precisely pure. And if the moral center of gravity is maintained, the endless chain of political and administrative decisions can be dealt with confidently and serenely.

Two new ethical Commandments are necessary as man moves into the Molecular Age. Compared with these imperatives the codes of earlier prophets seem like game rules—codes for social harmony. The new Commandments are neurological and biochemical in essence, and therefore, I suspect, in closer harmony with the laws of cellular wisdom, the law of the DNA code.

[5] *This Week* Magazine, February 13, 1966, p. 5.

I did not invent these Commandments; they are the result of some 250 psychedelic sessions. They are revealed to me by my nervous system, by ancient, cellular counsel. I give them to you as revelation, but ask you not to take them on faith; check them out with your own nervous system. Ask your DNA code. I urge you to memorize these two Commandments. Meditate on them. You might take 300 gamma of LSD and present these Commandments to your symbol-free nervous system. Nothing less than the future of our species depends upon our understanding of and obedience to these two natural laws.

I. Thou Shalt Not Alter the Consciousness of thy fellow man.

II. Thou Shalt Not Prevent thy fellow man from Altering his own Consciousness.

Commentary on the Two Commandments

Thousands of theological, philosophical, and legal texts will be written in the next few decades interpreting, qualifying, and specifying these two Commandments. I happily leave this chore to those who face the implementation of this code. But a few general comments may be helpful.

1. These Commandments are not new. They are specifications of the first Mosaic Law—that man shall not act as God to others. Be God yourself, if you can, but do not impose your divinity on others. They are also specifications of the two Christian Commandments—Thou shalt love God and thy fellow man.

2. There are several obvious qualifications of the first Commandment. Do not alter the consciousness of your fellow man by symbolic, electrical, chemical, or molecular means. If he wants you to? Yes. You may help him alter his own consciousness. Or you may get his conscious, alerted permission to alter his consciousness for him. In the direction he wants.

3. There are several obvious qualifications of the second Commandment. Do not prevent your fellow man from altering his consciousness by means of symbols. This is the familiar "Freedom of expression" issue. But also you must not prevent your fellow man from altering his own consciousness by chemical, electrical, or

molecular means. These are new freedoms which the wise men who wrote the Constitution and the Bill of Rights did not anticipate, but which they might have included had they known.

4. May you prevent your fellow man from altering his consciousness if he thereby poses a threat to others or to the harmonious development of society? Yes. But be careful. You walk a precarious precipice. Whenever society restricts the freedom of the human being to alter his own consciousness (by means of symbols or chemicals), the burden of proof as to danger to others must be on society. We may prevent others from doing things that restrict our consciousness—but the justification must be clear.

The Scientific Issue

The Scientific Meaning of Marijuana

The political and ethical controversies over psychedelic plants are caused by our basic ignorance about what these substances do.

They alter consciousness. But how, where, why, what for? Questions about psychedelic drugs remain unanswered because our basic questions about consciousness remain unanswered. As we learn more about the biochemistry and physiology of consciousness then we will understand the specific effects and uses of consciousness-altering plants.

External, look-at-it-from-the-outside science is not enough. Biochemistry and neurology will soon unravel some of the riddles of molecular learning and RNA[6] education. Blessings on James McConnell and David Krech and Holger Hyden. But then what? Who shall use the new magic molecules? Who shall control them? The routine scientoid solutions are: Inject them in the stupid, inject them in the crazy, inject them into army privates, in-

[6] Within the nucleus of every living cell lies a tiny, complex chain of nucleic acid molecules called the DNA code. DNA is the brain of the cell: the timeless blueprinting code that designs every aspect of life. DNA executes its plans by means of RNA molecules. RNA is the communication system, the langauge, the senses and hands of the DNA. The language of RNA can be passed from one organism to another. The discovery of this fact is revolutionizing our theories of memory, learning consciousness, and education. The basic unit of learning is molecular. The basic unit of consciousness is molecular.

ject them in the senile—and eventually, when they are safe enough to prevent law suits, sell them to the docile middle class.

But wait a minute. We can't do that any more—remember? We are not dealing with molecules that blow up the enemy or eradicate insects or cure headaches or produce the mild stupor of alcohol or tranquilize the active. We are dealing with agents that change consciousness. And we have a new Commandment to obey—remember? "Thou Shalt Not Alter the Consciousness of thy fellow man."

And if you try to control the new molecules, then we have the black-market problem all over again. You remember the LSD situation? The scientoid plan was to research LSD quietly in mental hospitals and army bases—double-blindly drugging the unsuspecting. But the word got out: "LSD produces ecstasy. LSD helps you see through the game veil." And the revolution began. The upper-middle-class underground, the white-collar black-market.

And then the laws and the penalties and the arming of agents of the Department of Health, Education and Welfare, to hunt down psychedelics.

Any officer or employee of the Department . . . may
1. carry firearms
2. execute and serve search warrants . . .
3. execute seizure . . .
4. make arrests without warrants . . .[7]

And next come the Smart-pills. Will the same cycle of dreary platitudes and bureaucratic hysteria make the rounds again?

WASHINGTON, D.C., JANUARY 1, 1969.—HEALTH, EDUCATION AND WELFARE OFFICIALS ANNOUNCED TODAY REGULATIONS CONTROLLING ILLICIT USE OF AMINO ACIDS.

ACCORDING TO THE NEW LAWS, DNA AND RNA MOLECULES CAN BE ADMINISTERED ONLY BY GOVERNMENT-APPROVED PHYSICIANS IN A GOVERNMENT-SUPPORTED HOSPITAL.

HARVARD BLACK MARKET BARED IN RNA.

SMART PILL FAD NEW CAMPUS KICK.

"Hey! Did you hear? There's a new shipment of black-market Einstein A.A. in the village!"

"I'm giving my wife some Elizabeth Taylor acid for Christmas. Smuggled

[7] Drug Abuse Control Amendments of 1965.

in from Mexico. We can all afford to learn new methods, right?"

"I know it's against the law, but Willy is five years old and can't work quantum-theory equations. So, in despair, I've connected with some Max Planck RNA."

NEW YORK, APRIL 1, 1969, A.P. —The newly organized microbiological unit of the Health, Education and Welfare Department armed with paralysis spray guns and electron microscopes raided an RNA den last night. Over one hundred millionth of a gram of amino acid was seized. Agents estimated that the haul was worth close to $800,000. Held on charges of being present in premises where illegal drugs were seized were a poet, a philosopher, and two college-age girls. H.E.W. agents tentatively labeled the contraband molecules as Shakespeare RNA, Socrates RNA, and Helen of Troy RNA.

R. Wilheim Phlymption, President of the American Psychiatric Association—Amino Acid Division, when notified of the raid, said: "Amino acids RNA and DNA are dangerous substances causing illegitimacy, suicide and irresponsible sexuality. They should only be administered by psychiatrists in government hospitals or army research stations."

The four alleged drug-cultists who were held in $25,000 bail smiled enigmatically, but made no comment.

These headlines won't happen, will they? They can't happen, because now we have the two commandments for the Molecular Age.

Remember: "Thou Shalt Not Alter the Consciousness of thy fellow man."

Remember, congressmen, policemen, judges. And agents of the Department of Health, Education and Welfare, lay down your arms. Remember the second Commandment: "Thou Shalt Not Prevent thy fellow man from Altering his own Consciousness."

Now that chemists have produced psychedelic chemicals, now that biochemists are isolating the powers of RNA, it is time to face the real scientific issue.

The meaning and use of consciousness-changing methods cannot be understood from the standpoint of external science, from the standpoint of look-at-it-from-the-outside science. Not only does this violate the first Commandment, it just doesn't work.

The meaning and use of psychedelic chemicals—LSD, RNA, marijuana—depends on the scientists taking the molecules himself, opening up his own consciousness, altering his own nervous system. Only in this way will we develop the maps, models, languages, techniques for utilizing the new mind-changing procedures.

You can't use the microscope by clapping it over the eyes of unsuspecting mental patients and army privates.

The mind-altering chemicals— marijuana, lysergic acid, amino acid—have to be studied from within. *You* have to take them. You can observe their effects from outside, but this tells you very little. You can "sacrifice" the animals and discover brain changes. You can drug mental defectives and seniles and observe gross behavior changes, but these are the irrelevant husks. Consciousness must be studied from within. Molecular learning is communication at the cellular and molecular level. The mental defectives can't decipher these languages. The molecular psychologist must decipher these languages.

This is not a new idea. This is the core idea of all Eastern psychology. Buddhism, for example, is not a religion; it is a complex system of psychology, a series of languages and methods for decoding levels of consciousness.

And this is the original method of Western scientific psychology— the trained introspection of Wundt, Weber, Fechner, Titchener. The scientist must learn the language of the neuron and cell and teach it to others. It's a tough assignment, isn't it? No more dosing the passive subjects. *You* inhale, swallow, and inject the magic molecule *yourself*. You train others to do the same.

Frightening? Yes, it is frightening. And this defines the first criterion of the scientist of consciousness. He must have courage. He must embark on a course of methodically and deliberately going out of his mind. This is no field for the faint of heart. You are venturing out (like the Portuguese sailors, like the astronauts) on the uncharted margins. But be reassured; it's an old human custom. It's an old living-organism custom. We're here today because certain adventurous proteins, certain far-out, experimenting cells, certain beatnik amphibia, certain brave men, pushed out and exposed themselves to new forms of energy.

Where do you get this courage? It isn't taught in graduate school or medical school or law school. It doesn't come by arming government agents. It comes from faith. Faith in your nervous system. Faith in your body. Faith in your cells. Faith in the life process. Faith in the molecular energies released by psychedelic molecules.

Not blind faith. Not faith in human social forms, but conscious faith in the harmony and wisdom of nature. Faith easily checked out empirically. Trust your equipment and its reaction to the molecular messages of the psychedelic drugs.

To do this we need a method and a map. The method tells us how to use consciousness-altering substances—marijuana, LSD, RNA. The map is the language of the different levels of consciousness triggered by the psychedelic molecules.

The two Commandments tell you that—politically and ethically —you may not drug others but have to do it to yourself. And the scientific nature of the problem— consciousness—tells you again that you may not drug others but have to do it to yourself.

You cannot understand the use and meaning of such psychedelic substances as marijuana, LSD and RNA until you have models, maps of the different levels of consciousness contacted by these substances.

Maps implement and make possible the two Commandments. These moral imperatives insist that only the carrier of the nervous system can alter the function of that nervous system. Only you should decide where your consciousness should locate. To make such decisions—which levels of consciousness to contact and how to reach them—you need information. To understand how marijuana affects consciousness you must understand the dimensions of consciousness and the specific level which cannabis triggers.

This brief essay does not allow a detailed description of the maps and methods of consciousness expansion and of the exquisitely detailed implications for using psychedelic substances. Here I can list only the major level of consciousness, indicate which plants and drugs get you to each level, and, in particular, attempt to suggest the meaning of marijuana.

Consciousness is energy received and decoded by a structure. There are as many levels of consciousness available to the human being as there are anatomical structures in the human body for receiving and decoding energy. There are as many levels of reality as there are anatomical structures for decoding energy. The anatomy of consciousness is the anatomy of neural and cellular structures.

There are six levels of consciousness, and each of these levels is reached and triggered by means of chemicals—produced naturally by the body or ingested in the form of drugs.

1. *The Level of Minimal Consciousness:* sleep, coma, stupor. This state occurs naturally by means of internal body chemistry or can be inducted by drugs such as barbiturates, somnambulants, alcohol, and opiates. External stimuli are disregarded.

2. *The Level of Symbolic Consciousness* (usually and erroneously called "normal consciousness"). This level of consciousness is exclusively focused on external perceptions or mentalisms (thoughts) about external conditioned symbols. This state occurs through the process of imprinting —a chemical fixing of the nervous system which "hooks" attention to externals. The chemical process is at present unknown. Serotonin may be the chemical secreted by the body that addicts the nervous system to symbolic externals. Note that narcotic-type drugs (including alcohol) release man from the addictive hook to symbols in the direction of "escape" whereas the psychedelic chemicals release man from the external-symbolic in the direction of expanded consciousness.

3. *The Level of Sensory Awareness—External.* Here, consciousness is focused on the sensory nerve endings that receive energy from the outside. The retina of the eye, the eardrum and the Organ of Corti, the olfactory (smell) bulbs, the taste buds, the naked endings which receive impulses of touch, temperature, pain. In routine consciousness we are aware only of symbols—"things" seen, heard, touched, tasted. At the Neural or Sensory Level we are aware of direct energy exploding on our sense endings—light waves hurtling into the retina at the speed of 186,000 miles a second, pressure exploding the naked grenades of sensation in our touch receptors, and so forth. Drugs that trigger direct sensation are marijuana, small doses of LSD (25–50 gamma), of mescaline (50–150 mg), psilocybin (6–16 mg). Certain yoga exercises can attain the Sensory Level of Consciousness. [Yoga is the royal road to the Divine through the senses. The strategy of the Yogin is to eliminate all external stimuli except those that trigger the sense organ he wishes to "turn on." Meditation is a technique for eliminating extraneous stimuli and zeroing-in on the eye (mandala), ear (mantra), taste-touch-smell (tantra).]

Marijuana is the mildest of the psychedelic drugs. It activates the external sensory system and tones down the symbolic game addiction. Experienced marijuana users know how easy it is "to hang someone up" on the gustatory sense by talking about food during a session. Pot-smoking musicians let themselves get hung-up on sound waves hitting the tympanic membrane. Pot-smoking artists turn off visual symbols and register light pounding against their retinas. The aphrodisiac, touch amplification of cannabis is a well-known, well-guarded secret among marijuana adepts.

4. *The Level of Sensory Awareness—Interoceptive.* Here, consciousness is focused on the billions of nerve endings that are buried within the body and clustered in centers that receive impulses from visceral organs. For thousands of years it has been known that existing in the body is a chain of neural centers that collect messages from internal-organ systems. These centers are called *cakras.* Sexual, digestive, eliminative, cardiac, respiratory, cerebellar, cortical—the seven sense organs of the internal environment structures for decoding energy as complex and varied as the eye, ear, tongue, nose. Chemical alteration of the nervous system is required to contact these inner sense organs. Marijuana can do it only if you turn off external stimuli. Smoke pot in a completely dark, silent room, and if you are well trained, you can contact your *cakras.* Moderate or large doses of LSD propel consciousness into the kaleidoscopic Niagara of internal-body sensation, but when this happens the unprepared voyager either gets confused or lets this internal flood of electric energy flow by unrecognized.

5. *The Cellular Level of Consciousness.* Every cell in your body is playing out a game that has been played out millions of times before. Within the nucleus of each cell in your body is a strand of nucleic acid molecules, possessing a timeless wisdom, which creates bodies (like yours and mine) exactly the way General Motors designers plan each year's crop of automobiles. (An accurate irony. And designed for quick obsolescence, too.)

Now it is possible for man's nervous system to get in touch with cellular consciousness. This statement may sound far-out and mystical, but it is not. I am talking about the transmission of information in electro-molecular form from within the cell to nerve endings outside the cell. The brain can be "taught" by molecules such as RNA. Tribal educational processes employ symbols given social meaning through conditioned associations. Recently scientists have discovered another form of education: learning by means of cellular molecules which pass on ancient energy-wisdom in the language of chemistry. Molecular learning, cellular consciousness, can be stimulated by plants and drugs. Moderate doses of LSD (100–250 gamma), of mescaline (150–500 mg), of psilocybin (16–50 mg) can put the nervous system in contact with cellular messages—if external stimulation is temporarily blocked off. These experiences often described in the language of "reincarnation" are routine phenomena in LSD sessions. Marijuana and mild doses of psychedelic drugs cannot produce this level of consciousness.

6. *The Pre-Cellular (Atomic) Level of Consciousness.* For thousands of years psychedelic philosophers have reported the ultimate state of transcendental consciousness in terms of pure energy: "void," "white light," "the core flame," "the light within." Though metaphors vary, there is agreement on the elemental, pre-life nature of this energy. Many LSD subjects also report similar experiences—after ingesting large doses (250–1500 gamma). Here our maps of consciousness fade into obscurity. Here our symbols become poetic, mystical. The empirical question is: Can the human nervous system contact, pick up, chemical energies of a molecular or atomic level? Can such experiences be mapped and made available for subsequent observations? I do not know. I present this sixth level of consciousness hesitantly, knowing that I risk losing even the least skeptical of my readers. We must keep an open mind. We must provide in our symbolic mappings categories for events that, at the moment, go beyond our observations.

This list of six levels of consciousness may be thought of within the metaphor of expanding optical lenses—which are familiar external techniques for expanding man's visual consciousness.

Narcotic drugs—including alcohol—shut off vision, dull perception, provide escape from the glare of reality.

"Normal" symbolic consciousness is normal, uncorrected vision.

Marijuana is the weakest, the mildest of the expanding lenses. It and other stimulants of sensory awareness are like corrective lenses; they bring vision into sharper focus. Moderate doses of LSD, mescaline, psilocybin are powerful microscopes that bring cellular structures into focus. Heavy doses of LSD are like the electron microscope. They magnify to such a power that cellular structure is reduced to a whirring flux of molecular particles.

You can no more generalize about psychedelic drugs than you can about optic magnification. Before making a statement about the psychedelic experience or about a psychedelic substance you must define the type and the dosage. Expanding lenses run from the corrective lens through the range of magnification to the millionth-power amplifiers.

A final comment about the disciplined yoga of psychedelic drugs. They are not shortcuts; they do not simplify. They answer no questions; they solve no problems. Indeed, the psychedelic drugs complicate knowing and understanding because they show each issue in multidimensional complexity.

My first adult psychedelic experience came in Mexico in 1960 after eating seven of the Sacred Mushrooms of Mexico. I have often said of this experience that I learned more in five hours than I did in the previous sixteen years as a psychological researcher. But this learning must be specified. It was revelatory rather than intellectual. For example, suppose that I had been living three hundred years ago and had spent sixteen years in medical research, poking, examining, and thumping sick bodies to determine the cause of disease. Then one day someone puts a microscope to my eye and I look at the blood cells of a healthy person and the blood cells of a sick person. In one split second I would have understood more about the cause of disease than I had learned in the previous sixteen years. I would have understood that there exists a level of energy and invisible meaning, hitherto undreamed of, that was crucial to my profession. I would realize that the rest of my professional life would be dedicated to the laborious, disciplined looking through the lenses at the new data suddenly made available.

The understanding and application of the psychedelic drugs require brutal diligence on the part of the researcher or the searcher. There is no instant mysticism, no instant psychoanalysis available here. Only the challenge and the promise of long, dedicated, systematic work, of observation and replication.

Even the benign and gentle amplification of marijuana requires study and discipline. It takes time to use marijuana. It is a subtle and fleeting experience. One who is used to the crudity and jolting paralysis of alcohol smokes cannabis and says nothing happens. He fails to notice the soft, sensitive unfolding of his sense endings. The wise use of cannabis requires a precise knowledge of its effects and exquisite skill in arranging the external stimuli so that they gratify and talk directly to the exposed sensory nerve endings rather than inundate and jumble. For some reason my countrymen are reluctant to realize that psychedelic drugs pose a linguistic problem. That one must painstakingly learn the new dialects of sensual and cellular energy.

From the earliest days of our search-research project at Harvard, in Mexico, and later in Millbrook, New York, we have stressed training. In lecturing about the effects of psychedelic drugs I repeat this point over and over again: training . . . specialized training. After four years of college, if you want to specialize in science it takes four years to get a doctorate. Four postgraduate years to get a PhD. To specialize in medicine, it requires eight years after college. Eight postgraduate years to get the MDA. Dear friends, to specialize in the use of your own nervous system, to learn to use your head, and to use the wisdom in your cells, it requires many more years. Count on fifty years of postgraduate work to get your LSD.

━━━━━━━━━━━━━━━

7.4
Poem

Jerry Heath

Spring's sun igniting
Thrusting me deep into heavens dreams
A soft breeze, cool and fragrant, stirs the waking green trees
Light spilling into every pore and crack

By permission of the author.

Trickling down, exposing a small brown path
Far away a tiny flicker of light
My feet now carrying me in flight
Further I must go deeper, deeper, deeper
I must
Something stirring
Far away I hear the melody
Birds singing, dawn's song
Morning life rings loud in my ears
Something stirring, some rushing over me
Senses running out of control
Splashing waves of color bathed in music
Each sensation, a symphony
Filling me with love of the splendor, of this beautiful land
Gazing into the heavens of earth
Shadows disappearing, the fog creeping off
The haze is clearing, no longer guided
                 no longer guarded
Life's living blindfold slipping, sliding, melting away

Standing high on the rim of the world
Tomorrows days lying naked just before me
Driving me wild in this quiet vibrating land
Climbing, grabbing searching for a hold
I struggle for what I want
For what I need
Just a tiny little peak
DEEP IN THE HEART OF DESTINY

Higher, higher, higher, I must go
Still further, push man, Let's go
Why now must my body grow so slow
Digging, crawling, agony devouring my soul
My body so heavy, can't make it go
My head so very light, brains aglow
Almost as if a strange sweet lullabye
Is now driving me to sleep
I scream out
GOD   Damn you, damn you, damn this whole fucking worthless, stagnant, starving, dead world.

I scream out again and again
Echo's hunting for my ears
Ringing, banging, smashing their way back
Slipping, sliding, tumbling back down
I cry out loud for someone to catch me before I hit the ground
Falling faster, deeper, faster, deeper, faster deeper

Falling

My body gaining speed, Everything a blur, swinging all around
Faster, deeper, go baby, go all the way down
Seconds are now minutes
Hours drag into days
I'm trapped, circled by endless darkness
Flying through a maze
Tangled in subterranean logic
Mocked by reality
My taunted mind searching for an escape
Struggling to break free from the grasp that flings me through space

The lifelong journey
The faceless man
The lifeless body
The mindless zombie
           All scrambling
from death's gorge

Hope gives me new power
Faith gives me unmatchable strength
Yes, I can suddenly see
No longer will I shake with fear
Nor fall to my knees and let life run over me
Grasping the hand that seized me
Walking away, no longer the custodian of a worthless plight

Pondering all that I had learned and seen
Among the flowers and the green trees
Knowing what it was to have the joy

In the following essay, Alan Watts examines four characteristics of the religious experience brought about by psychedelic drugs, particularly by LSD and marijuana, and compares the nature of such experience with our Western religious and secular values. The most significant point made in this article rests in Watts' criticism of the direction in which we are being led by Western man's alienation from nature. Unlike the appreciation for his environment and the unison of self with nature experienced in many Eastern cultures and in psychedelic consciousness, Western man applies his technology to work against nature. In so doing he is virtually losing sight of all his humanistic values, replacing them with an alienating, mechanical self-image.

7.5
Psychedelics and Religious Experience

Alan Watts

The experiences resulting from the use of psychedelic drugs are often described in religious terms. They are therefore of interest to those like myself who, in the tradition of William James, are concerned with the psychology of religion. For more than thirty years I have been studying the causes, consequences, and conditions of those peculiar states of consciousness in which the individual discovers himself to be one continuous process with God, with the Universe, with the Ground of Being, or whatever name he may use by cultural conditioning or personal preference for the ultimate and eternal reality. We have no satisfactory and definitive name for experiences of this kind. The terms "religious experience," "mystical experience," and "cosmic consciousness" are all too vague and comprehensive to denote that specific mode of consciousness which, to those who have known it, is as real and overwhelming as falling in love. This article describes such states of consciousness as and when induced by psychedelic drugs, although they are virtually indistinguishable from genuine mystical experience. It then discusses objections to the use of psychedelic drugs which arise mainly from the opposition between mystical values and the traditional religious and secular values of Western society.

The idea of mystical experiences resulting from drug use is not readily accepted in Western societies. Western culture has, historically, a particular fascination with the value and virtue of man as an individual, self-determining, responsible ego, controlling himself and his world by the power of conscious effort and will. Nothing, then, could be more re-

Reprinted by permission from "Psychedelics and Religious Experience," *California Law Review*, 56, 1 (January, 1968). Copyright © 1968 by California Law Review, Inc.

pugnant to this cultural tradition than the notion of spiritual or psychological growth through the use of drugs. A "drugged" person is by definition dimmed in consciousness, fogged in judgment, and deprived of will. But not all psychotropic (consciousness-changing) chemicals are narcotic and soporific, as are alcohol, opiates, and barbiturates. The effects of what are now called psychedelic (mind-manifesting) chemicals differ from those of alcohol as laughter differs from rage or delight from depression. There is really no analogy between being "high" on LSD and "drunk" on bourbon. True, no one in either state should drive a car, but neither should one drive while reading a book, playing a violin, or making love. Certain creative activities and states of mind demand a concentration and devotion which are simply incompatible with piloting a death-dealing engine along a highway.

I myself have experimented with five of the principal psychedelics: LSD-25, mescaline, psilocybin, dimethyl-tryptamine (DMT), and cannabis. I have done so, as William James tried nitrous oxide, to see if they could help me in identifying what might be called the "essential" or "active" ingredients of the mystical experience. For almost all the classical literature on mysticism is vague, not only in describing the experience, but also in showing rational connections between the experience itself and the various traditional methods recommended to induce it—fasting, concentration, breathing exercises, prayers, incantations, and dances. A traditional master of Zen or Yoga, when asked why such-and-such practices lead or predispose one to the mystical experience, always responds, "This is the way my teacher gave it to me. This is the way I found out. If you're seriously interested, try it for yourself." This answer hardly satisfies an impertinent, scientific-minded, and intellectually curious Westerner. It reminds him of archaic medical prescriptions compounding five salamanders, powdered gallows-rope, three boiled bats, a scruple of phosphorus, three pinches of henbane, and a dollop of dragon dung dropped when the moon was in Pisces. Maybe it worked, but what was the essential ingredient?

It struck me, therefore, that if any of the psychedelic chemicals would in fact predispose my consciousness to the mystical experience, I could use them as instruments for studying and describing that experience as one uses a microscope for bacteriology, even though the microscope is an "artificial" and "unnatural" contrivance which might be said to "distort" the vision of the naked eye. However, when I was first invited to test the mystical qualities of LSD-25 by Dr. Keith Ditman of the Neuropsychiatric Clinic at UCLA Medical School, I was unwilling to believe that any mere chemical could induce a genuine mystical experience. I thought it might at most bring about a state of spiritual insight analogous to swimming with water wings. Indeed, my first experiment with LSD-25 was not mystical. It was an intensely interesting aesthetic and intellectual experience which challenged my powers of analysis and careful description to the utmost.

Some months later, in 1959, I tried LSD-25 again with Drs. Sterling Bunnell and Michael Agron, who were then associated with the Langley-Porter Clinic in San Francisco. In the course of two experiments I was amazed and somewhat embarrassed to find myself going through states of consciousness which corresponded precisely with every description of major mystical experiences I had ever read.[1] Furthermore, they exceeded both in depth and in a peculiar quality of unexpectedness the three "natural and spontaneous" experiences of this kind which I had had in previous years.

Through subsequent experimentation with LSD-25 and the other chemicals named above (with the exception of DMT, which I find amusing but relatively uninteresting) I found I could move with ease into the state of "cosmic consciousness," and in due course became less and less dependent on the chemicals themselves for "tuning in" to this particular wave-length of experience. Of the five psychedelics tried, I found that LSD-25 and cannabis suited my purposes best. Of these two, the latter, which I had to use abroad in countries where it is not outlawed, proved to be the better. It does not induce bizarre alterations of sensory perception, and medical studies indicate that it may not, save in great excess, have the dangerous side effects of LSD, such as psychotic episodes.

[1] An excellent anthology of such experiences is Raynor C. Johnson, *Watcher on the Hills* (New York, Harper & Bros., 1959).

For the purposes of this study, in describing my experiences with psychedelic drugs, I avoid the occasional and incidental bizarre alterations of sense perception which psychedelic chemicals may induce. I am concerned, rather, with the fundamental alterations of the normal, socially induced consciousness of one's own existence and relation to the external world. I am trying to delineate the basic principles of psychedelic awareness. But I must add that I can speak only for myself. The quality of these experiences depends considerably upon one's prior orientation and attitude to life, although the now voluminous descriptive literature of these experiences accords quite remarkably with my own.

Almost invariably, my experiments with psychedelics have had four dominant characteristics. I shall try to explain them—in the expectation that the reader will say, at least of the second and third, "Why, that's obvious! No one needs a drug to see that." Quite so, but every insight has degrees of intensity. There can be obvious$_1$ and obvious$_2$, and the latter comes on with shattering clarity, manifesting its implications in every sphere and dimension of our existence.

The first characteristic is a slowing down of time, a *concentration in the present*. One's normally compulsive concern for the future decreases, and one becomes aware of the enormous importance and interest of what is happening at the moment. Other people, going about their business on the streets, seem to be slightly crazy, failing to realize that the whole point of life is to be fully aware of it as it happens. One therefore relaxes, almost luxuriously, in studying the colors in a glass of water, or in listening to the now highly articulate vibration of every note played on an oboe or sung by voice.

From the pragmatic standpoint of our culture, such an attitude is very bad for business. It might lead to improvidence, lack of foresight, diminished sales of insurance policies, and abandoned savings accounts. Yet this is just the corrective that our culture needs. No one is more fatuously impractical than the "successful" executive who spends his whole life absorbed in frantic paperwork with the objective of retiring in comfort at sixty-five, when it will be all too late. Only those who have cultivated the art of living completely in the present have

any use for making plans for the future, for when the plans mature they will be able to enjoy the results. "Tomorrow never comes." I have never yet heard a preacher urging his congregation to practice that section of the Sermon on the Mount which begins, "Be not anxious for the morrow. . . ." The truth is that people who live for the future are, as we say of the insane, "not quite all there"—or here: by overeagerness they are perpetually missing the point. Foresight is bought at the price of anxiety, and, when overused, it destroys all its own advantages.

The second characteristic I will call *awareness of polarity*. This is the vivid realization that states, things, and events which we ordinarily call opposite are interdependent, like back and front or the poles of a magnet. By polar awareness one sees that things which are explicitly different are implicitly one: self and other, subject and object, left and right, male and female—and then, a little more surprisingly, solid and space, figure and background, pulse and interval, saints and sinners, and police and criminals, ingroups and outgroups. Each is definable only in terms of the other, and they go together transactionally, like buying and selling, for there is no sale without a purchase, and no purchase without a sale. As this awareness becomes increasingly intense, you feel that you yourself are polarized with the external universe in such a way that you imply each other. Your push is its pull, and its push is your pull—as when you move the steering wheel of a car. Are you pushing it or pulling it?

At first, this is a very odd sensation, not unlike hearing your own voice played back to you on an electronic system immediately after you have spoken. You become confused, and wait for *it* to go on! Similarly, you feel that you are something being done by the universe, yet that the universe is equally something being done by you—which is true, at least in the neurological sense that the peculiar structure of our brains translates the sun into light and air vibrations into sound. Our normal sensation of relationship to the outside world is that sometimes we push it, and sometimes it pushes us. But if the two are actually one, where does action begin and responsibility rest? If the universe is doing me, how can I be sure that, two seconds hence, I will still remember the English language? If I am doing it, how can I be sure that, two seconds hence, my brain will know how to turn the sun into light? From such unfamiliar sensations as these the psychedelic experience can generate confusion, paranoia, and terror—even though the individual is feeling his relationship to the world exactly as it would be described by a biologist, ecologist, or physicist, for he is feeling himself as the unified field of organism and environment.

The third characteristic, arising from the second, is *awareness of relativity*. I see that I am a link in an infinite hierarchy of processes and beings, ranging from molecules through bacteria and insects to human beings, and, maybe, to angels and gods—a hierarchy in which every level is in effect the same situation. For example, the poor man worries about money while the rich man worries about his health: the worry is the same, but the difference is in its substance or dimension. I realize that fruit flies must think of themselves as people, because, like ourselves, they find themselves in the middle of their own world—with immeasurably greater things above and smaller things below. To us, they all look alike and seem to have no personality—as do the Chinese when we have not lived among them. Yet fruit flies must see just as many subtle distinctions among themselves as we among ourselves.

From this it is but a short step to the realization that all forms of life and being are simply variations on a single theme: we are all in fact one being doing the same thing in as many different ways as possible. As the French proverb goes, *plus ça change, plus c'est la même chose*—"the more it varies, the more it is one." I see, further, that feeling threatened by the inevitability of death is really the same experience as feeling alive, and that as all beings are feeling this everywhere, they are all just as much "I" as myself. Yet the "I" feeling, to be felt at all, must always be a sensation relative to the "other," to something beyond its control and experience. To be at all, it must begin and end. But the intellectual jump which mystical and psychedelic experience make here is in enabling you to see that all these myriad I-centers are yourself—not, indeed, your personal and superficial conscious ego, but what Hindus call the *paramatman*, the Self of all selves.[2]

As the retina enables us to see countless pulses of energy as a single light, so the mystical experience shows us innumerable individuals as a single Self.

The fourth characteristic is *awareness of eternal energy*, often in the form of intense white light, which seems to be both the current in your nerves and that mysterious *e* which equals mc^2. This may sound like megalomania or delusion of grandeur—but one sees quite clearly that all existence is a single energy, and that this energy is one's own being. Of course there is death as well as life, because energy is a pulsation, and just as waves must have both crests and troughs the experience of existing must go on and off. Basically, therefore, there is simply nothing to worry about, because you yourself are the eternal energy of the universe playing hide-and-seek (off-and-on) with itself. At root, you are the Godhead, for God is all that there is. Quoting Isaiah just a little out of context: "I am the Lord, and there is none else. I form the light and create the darkness: I make peace, and create evil. I, the Lord, do all these things."[3] That is the sense of the fundamental tenet of Hinduism, *Tat tvam asi*—"THAT (i.e., "that subtle Being of which this whole universe is composed") art thou."[4] A classical case of this experience, from the West, is in Tennyson's *Memoirs*:

A kind of waking trance I have frequently had, quite up from boyhood, when I have been all alone. This has generally come upon me thro' repeating my own name two or three times to myself silently, till all at once, as it were out of the intensity of the consciousness of individuality, the individuality itself seemed to dissolve and fade away into boundless being, and this not a confused state, but the clearest of the clearest, the

surest of the surest, the weirdest of the weirdest, utterly beyond words, where death was an almost laughable impossibility, the loss of personality (if so it were) seeming no extinction but the only true life.[5]

Obviously, these characteristics of the psychedelic experience, as I have known it, are aspects of a single state of consciousness—for I have been describing the same thing from different angles. The descriptions attempt to convey the reality of the experience, but in doing so they also suggest some of the inconsistencies between such experience and the current values of society.

Resistance to allowing use of psychedelic drugs originates in both religious and secular values. The difficulty in describing psychedelic experiences in traditional religious terms suggests one ground of opposition. The Westerner must borrow such words as *samadhi* or *moksha* from the Hindus, or *satori* or *kensho* from the Japanese, to describe the experience of oneness with the universe. We have no appropriate word because our own Jewish and Christian theologies will not accept the idea that man's inmost self can be identical with the Godhead, even though Christians may insist that this was true in the unique instance of Jesus Christ. Jews and Christians think of God in political and monarchical terms, as the supreme governor of the universe, the ultimate boss. Obviously, it is both socially unacceptable and logically preposterous for a particular individual to claim that he, in person, is the omnipotent and omniscient ruler of the world—to be accorded suitable recognition and honor.

Such an imperial and kingly concept of the ultimate reality, however, is neither necessary nor universal. The Hindus and the Chinese have no difficulty in conceiving of an identity of the self and the Godhead. For most Asians, other than Moslems, the Godhead moves and manifests the world in much the same way that a centipede manipulates a hundred legs: spontaneously, without deliberation or calculation. In other words, they conceive the universe by analogy with an organism as distinct from a mechanism. They do not see it as an artifact or construct under the conscious direction of some supreme technician, engineer, or architect.

---

immense drama in which the One Actor (the *paramatman* or *brahman*) plays all the parts, which are his (or "its") masks, or *personae*. The sensation of being only this one particular self, John Doe, is due to the Actor's total absorption in playing this and every other part. For fuller exposition, see Sarvepalli Radhakrishnan, *The Hindu View of Life* (New York, The Macmillan Company, 1927); Heinrich Zimmer, *Philosophies of India* (New York, Pantheon Books, 1951), pp. 355–463. A popular version is in Alan Watts, *The Book: On the Taboo Against Knowing Who You Are* (New York, Pantheon Books, 1966).

[3] *Isaiah* 45: 6. 7.

[4] *Chandogya Upanishad* 6.15.3.

[2] Thus Hinduism regards the universe, not as an artifact, but as an

[5] *Alfred Lord Tennyson, A Memoir by His Son* (1898), Vol. I, p. 320.

If, however, in the context of Christian or Jewish tradition an individual declares himself to be one with God, he must be dubbed blasphemous (subversive) or insane. Such a mystical experience is a clear threat to traditional religious concepts. The Judaeo-Christian tradition has a monarchical image of God, and monarchs, who rule by force, fear nothing more than insubordination. The Church has therefore always been highly suspicious of mystics because they seem to be insubordinate and to claim equality or, worse, identity with God. For this reason John Scotus Erigena and Meister Eckhart were condemned as heretics. This was also why the Quakers faced opposition for their doctrine of the Inward Light, and for their refusal to remove hats in church and in court. A few occasional mystics may be all right so long as they watch their language, like Saint Teresa of Avila and Saint John of the Cross, who maintained, shall we say, a metaphysical distance of respect between themselves and their heavenly King. Nothing, however, could be more alarming to the ecclesiastical hierarchy than a popular outbreak of mysticism, for this might well amount to setting up a democracy in the kingdom of heaven —and such alarm would be shared eqully by Catholics, Jews, and fundamentalist Protestants.

The monarchical image of God with its implicit distaste for religious insubordination has a more pervasive impact than many Christians might admit. The thrones of kings have walls immediately behind them, and all who present themselves at court must prostrate themselves or kneel because this is an awkward position from which to make a sudden attack. It has perhaps never occurred to Christians that when they design a church on the model of a royal court (basilica) and prescribe church ritual, they are implying that God, like a human monarch, is afraid. This is also implied by flattery in prayers:

O Lord our heavenly Father, high and mighty, King of kings, Lord of lords, the only Ruler of princes, who dost from thy throne behold all the dwellers upon earth: most heartily we beseech thee with thy favor to behold . . .

The Western man who claims consciousness of oneness with God or the universe thus clashes with his society's concept of religion. In most Asian cultures, however, such a man will be congratulated as having penetrated the true secret of life. He has arrived, by chance or by some such discipline as Yoga or Zen meditation, at a state of consciousness in which he experiences directly and vividly what our own scientists know to be true in theory. For the ecologist, the biologist, and the physicist know (but seldom feel) that every organism constitutes a single field of behavior, or process, with its environment. There is no way of separating what any given organism is doing from what its environment is doing, for which reason ecologists speak not of organisms in environments but of organism-environments. Thus the words "I" or "self" should properly mean what the whole universe is doing at this particular "here-and-now" called John Doe.

The kingly concept of God makes identity of self and God, or self and universe, inconceivable in Western religious terms. The difference between Eastern and Western concepts of man and his universe, however, extends beyond strictly religious concepts. The Western scientist may rationally perceive the idea of organism-environment, but he does not ordinarily *feel* this to be true. By cultural and social conditioning, he has been hypnotized into experiencing himself as an ego—as an isolated center of consciousness and will inside a bag of skin, confronting an external and alien world. We say, "I came into this world." But we did nothing of the kind. We came *out* of it in just the same way that fruit comes out of trees.

Such a vision of the universe clashes with the idea of a monarchical God, with the concept of the separate ego, and even with the secular, atheist-agnostic mentality, which derives its common sense from the mythology of nineteenth-century scientism. According to this view, the universe is a mindless mechanism and man a sort of accidental microorganism infesting a minute globular rock which revolves about an unimportant star on the outer fringe of one of the minor galaxies. This "putdown" theory of man is extremely common among such quasi-scientists as sociologists, psychologists, and psychiatrists, most of whom are still thinking of the world in terms of Newtonian mechanics, and have never really caught up with the ideas of Einstein and Bohr, Oppenheimer and Schrödinger. Thus to the ordinary institutional-type psychiatrist, any patient who gives the least hint of mystical or religious experience is automatically diagnosed as deranged. From the standpoint of the mechanistic religion he is a heretic and is given electro-shock therapy as an up-to-date form of thumbscrew and rack. And, incidentally, it is just this kind of quasi-scientist who, as consultant to government and law-enforcement agencies, dictates official policies on the use of psychedelic chemicals.

Inability to accept the mystic experience is more than an intellectual handicap. Lack of awareness of the basic unity of organism and environment is a serious and dangerous hallucination. For in a civilization equipped with immense technological power, the sense of alienation between man and nature leads to the use of technology in a hostile spirit—to the "conquest" of nature instead of intelligent cooperation with nature. The result is that we are eroding and destroying our environment, spreading Los Angelization instead of civilization. This is the major threat overhanging Western technological culture, and no amount of reasoning or doom-preaching seems to help. We simply do not respond to the prophetic and moralizing techniques of conversion upon which Jews and Chrstians have always relied. But people have an obscure sense of what is good for them—call it "unconscious self-healing," "survival instinct," "positive growth potential," or what you will. Among the educated young there is therefore a startling and unprecedented interest in the transformation of human consciousness. All over the Western world publishers are selling millions of books dealing with Yoga, Vedanta, Zen Buddhism, and the chemical mysticism of psychedelic drugs, and I have come to believe that the whole "hip" subculture, however misguided in some of its manifestations, is the earnest and responsible effort of young people to correct the self-destroying course of industrial civilization.

The content of the mystical experience is thus inconsistent with both the religious and secular concepts of traditional Western thought. Moreover, mystical experiences often result in attitudes which threaten the authority not only of established churches but also of secular society. Unafraid of death and deficient in worldy ambition, those who have undergone mystical experiences are impervious to threats and promises. Moreover, their sense of the relativity of good and evil arouses the suspicion that they lack both conscience and respect for the law. Use of psychedelics in the United States by a literate bourgeoisie means that an important segment of the population is indifferent to society's traditional rewards and sanctions.

In theory, the existence within our secular society of a group which does not accept conventional values is consistent with our political vision. But one of the great problems of the United States, legally and politically, is that we have never quite had the courage of our convictions. The republic is founded on the marvelously sane principle that a human community can exist and prosper only on a basis of mutual trust. Metaphysically, the American Revolution was a rejection of the dogma of Original Sin, which is the notion that because you cannot trust yourself or other people, there must be some Superior Authority to keep us all in order. The dogma was rejected because if it is true that we cannot trust ourselves and others, it follows that we cannot trust the Superior Authority which we ourselves conceive and obey, and that the very idea of our own untrustworthiness is unreliable!

Citizens of the United States believe, or are supposed to believe, that a republic is the best form of government. Yet, vast confusion arises from trying to be republican in politics and monarchist in religion. How can a republic be the best form of government if the universe, heaven, and hell are a monarchy?[6] Thus, despite the theory of government by consent, based upon mutual trust, the peoples of the United States retain, from the authoritarian backgrounds of their religions or national origins, an utterly naive faith in law as some sort of supernatural and paternalistic power. "There ought to be a law against it!" Our law-enforcement officers are therefore confused, hindered, and bewildered—not to mention corrupted—by being asked to enforce sumptuary laws, often of ec-

clesiastical origin, which vast numbers of people have no intention of obeying and which, in any case, are immensely difficult or simply impossible to enforce—for example, the barring of anything so undetectable as LSD-25 from international and interstate commerce.

There are two specific objections to use of psychedelic drugs. First, use of these drugs may be dangerous. However, every worthwhile exploration is dangerous—climbing mountains, testing aircraft, rocketing into outer space, skin diving, or collecting botanical specimens in jungles. But if you value knowledge and the actual delight of exploration more than mere duration of uneventful life, you are willing to take the risks. It is not really healthy for monks to practice fasting, and it was hardly hygienic for Jesus to get himself crucified, but these are risks taken in the course of spiritual adventures. Today the adventurous young are taking risks in exploring the psyche, testing their mettle at the task just as, in times past, they have tested it—more violently—in hunting, dueling, hot rod racing, and playing football. What they need is not prohibitions and policemen but the most intelligent encouragement and advice that can be found.

Second, drug use may be criticized as an escape from reality. However, this criticism assumes unjustly that the mystical experiences themselves are escapist or unreal. LSD, in particular, is by no means a soft and cushy escape from reality. It can very easily be an experience in which you have to test your soul against all the devils in hell. For me, it has been at times an experience in which I was at once completely lost in the corridors of the mind and yet relating that very lostness to the exact order of logic and language, simultaneously very mad and very sane. But beyond these occasional lost and insane episodes, there are the experiences of the world as a system of total harmony and glory, and the discipline of relating these to the order of logic and language must somehow explain how what William Blake called that "energy which is eternal delight" can consist with the misery and suffering of everyday life.[7]

The undoubted mystical and re-

ligious intent of most users of the psychedelics, even if some of these substances should be proved injurious to physical health, requires that their free and responsible use be exempt from legal restraint in any republic which maintains a constitutional separation of Church and State. I mean "responsible" in the sense that such substances be taken by or administered to consenting adults only. The user of cannabis, in particular, is apt to have peculiar difficulties in establishing his "undoubtedly mystical and religious intent" in court. Having committed so loathsome and serious a felony, his chances of clemency are better if he assumes a repentant demeanor, which is quite inconsistent with the sincere belief that his use of cannabis was religious. On the other hand, if he insists unrepentantly that he looks upon such use as a religious sacrament, many judges will declare that they "dislike his attitude," finding it truculent and lacking in appreciation of the gravity of the crime, and the sentence will be that much harsher. The accused is therefore put in a "double-bind" situation in which he is "damned if he does, and damned if he doesn't." Furthermore, religious integrity—as in conscientious objection—is generally tested and established by membership in some church or religious organization with a substantial following. But the felonious status of cannabis is such that grave suspicion would be cast upon all individuals forming such an organization, and the test cannot therefore be fulfilled. It is generally forgotten that our guarantees of religious freedom were designed to protect precisely those who were *not* members of established denominations, but rather such screwball and (then) subversive individuals as Quakers, Shakers, Levellers, and Anabaptists. There is little question that those who use cannabis, or other psychedelics, with religious intent are now members of a persecuted religion which appears to the rest of society as a grave menace to "mental health," as distinct from the old-fashioned "immortal soul." But it's the same old story.

To the extent that mystical experience conforms with the tradition of genuine religious involvement, and to the extent that psychedelics induce that experience, users are entitled to some constitutional protection. Also, to the extent that research in the psychology of religion can utilize

---

[6] Thus, until quite recently, belief in a Supreme Being was a legal test of valid conscientious objection to military service. The implication was that the individual objector found himself bound to obey a higher echelon of command than the President and Congress. The analogy is military and monarchical, and therefore objectors who, as Buddhists or naturalists, held an organic theory of the universe often had difficulty in obtaining recognition.

[7] This is discussed at length in A. Watts, *The Joyous Cosmology: Adventures in the Chemistry of Consciousness* (New York, Pantheon Books, 1962).

such drugs, students of the human mind must be free to use them. Under present laws, I, as an experienced student of the psychology of religion, can no longer pursue research in the field. This is a barbarous restriction of spiritual and intellectual freedom, suggesting that the legal system of the United States, is, after all, in tacit alliance with the monarchical theory of the universe and will, therefore, prohibit and persecute religious ideas and practices based on an organic and unitary vision of the universe.[8]

[8] Amerindians belonging to the Native American Church, who employ the psychedelic peyote cactus in their rituals, are firmly opposed to any government control of this plant, even if they should be guaranteed the right to its use. They feel that peyote is a natural gift of God to mankind, and especially to natives of the land where it grows, and that no government has a right to interfere with its use. The same argument might be made on behalf of cannabis, or the mushroom *Psilocybe mexicana Heim*. All these things are natural plants, not processed or synthesized drugs, and by what authority can individuals be prevented from eating them? There is no law against eating or growing the mushroom *Amanita pantherina*, even though it is fatally poisonous and only experts can distinguish it from a common edible mushroom. This case can be made even from the standpoint of believers in the monarchical universe of Judaism and Christianity, for it is a basic principle of both religions, derived from *Genesis*, that all natural substances created by God are inherently good, and that evil can arise only in their misuse. Thus laws against mere possession, or even cultivation, of these plants are in basic conflict with Biblical principles. Criminal conviction of those who employ these plants should be based on proven misuse. "And God said, 'Behold, I have given you *every* herb bearing seed, which is upon the face of all the earth, and every tree, in the which is the fruit of a tree yielding seed; to you it shall be for meat.' . . . And God saw everything that he had made, and, behold, it was very good." (*Genesis* 1:29, 31.)

7.6
Poem

Jerry Heath

Big eyes—Piercing deep
Till frenzied minds fall fast asleep
Groping for reality, eyes respond
  with rage
Within a nation of blinded sheep,
　　　　Heralding an age

Having a joint before suffocation
Stealing a little peek at elation
Listening to prophets of annihilation
Can't seem to find any peace in
  this nation

Burnt out eyes in a rotting hull
Cob webs strung from skull to
  skull
Tattered cloth on withered frames
Reflect a world of misplaced aims

There's refuge in madness, like a
  mother's womb
Shades of evil create untimely
  tombs
Prophecies of doom and wanton
  destruction
Fill minds with impulse towards
  pure self-instruction

White and warped with blinding
  fury
Plastic stamped dolls are waving
  Old Glory
Disillusioned by a carnival of
  mimicry
That nurses monotony as the ideal
  therapy

Hysteria and grand illusion
Fill my mind with self-delusion
Crusading fanatics that warp and
  flow
Like a cancer, they thrive and
  grow

Polar bodies that vie for sound
Are driving me to the underground
Where questions maybe sought
  upon
To yield an answer to base life on

By permission of the author.

7.7
Amphetamine Abuse

Theodore J. Alves

The Problem

The United States is today the biggest drug taking society in the history of mankind. In the network of drug consumption, the largest increases have occurred in the field of stimulants. Amphetamine abuse has been reported in almost every major city in the United States.[1] This paper will attempt to summarize some of the problems and work being done in the field of amphetamine abuse. The considerations given here will reflect research done primarily in the San Francisco Bay area, and over a time spanning approximately 1964 to the present.

If a person asks, "Why is there such an increase in the use and abuse of drugs among the youth today?" the answer will most often be according to private prejudice. In order to avoid certain value judgments, the scope of this study will mainly concern only those cases where amphetamine abuse was excessive. It must be understood, however, that amphetamine abuse is not confined to drug subcultures, rather that it occurs in a range from business men dropping amphetamines in the morning to increase work output and then coming down with martinis at night, to compulsive "dieters," to students who always need an extra push for homework, to housewives who find that their housework becomes much more interesting when they're on amphetamine. The excessively high dose abuser is relatively a new problem.

Pharmacology

Amphetamine can refer directly to Benzedrine; however, the amphetamines, in general, are the class of stimulant drugs represented by Benzedrine, dextro-amphetamine (Dexedrine) and methamphetamine (Methedrine). Methedrine is the amine most often used by high dose amphetamine abusers, and will be the focus of this paper. It is often referred to as "speed" or "crystal."

In summarizing the effects of

By permission of the author.

[1] R. E. Long and R. P. Penna, "Drugs of Abuse," *Journ. of American Pharmaceutical Ass'n.*, Vol. NS8, No. 1 (January, 1968), p. 23.

amphetamines, David Goddard (1962) relates: "Drugs of this class . . . cause wakefulness, some increased physical activity, and, in moderate doses, euphoria."[2] The ordinary clinical dose of Methedrine varies from 2.5 mg. daily to 15 mg. per day.[3] Tolerance is developed, however, and doses can be raised to as much as 500 mg., as noted by Goddard. He goes on to say, also, that large doses may produce a toxic psychosis.

In this study, high dose abuse will refer to the chronic use of Methedrine in amounts from about 50 mg. to well over 1,000 mg. per day. Doses of over 500 mg. did not occur in any context on a prescribed or continual basis until the recent advent of the "speed freak," who has taken it upon himself to attempt this form of abuse.

Many abusers begin with low doses of oral amphetamines and slowly increase their dosage up to 150 or 250 mg. per day. When the desired results are not obtained, they change to intravenous administration. During early phases 20 to 50 mg. doses taken three or four times a day suffice, but as tolerance builds, the dose and frequency of injection increase considerably.

The intravenous use of amphetamines produces a syndrome of a variety of behavioral and physical effects, some of which, particularly insomnia and anorexia, may themselves produce deleterious effects.

Why do people shoot speed? The answer is quite straightforward, it can be intensely pleasurable:

The first time I rushed I thought it was nirvana. It's like an orgasm in your mind. It happens like a shock, but it's a shock of pure pleasure— euphoria. You're entirely in your own world except that you know exactly what the people around you are. No matter what happens next, it's completely out of sight, because, man, you feel like you can just do *anything!*

(Those further interested should refer to the *Journal of Psychedelic Drugs*, Vol. II, No. 2, edited by Dr. David E. Smith, an excellent

source of amphetamine abuse phenomenology.)

Social Problems

Individually, the Methedrine abuser's hyperactivity often leads to a mode of extroversion which appears to be aggressive or irritable. Police have reported on the unpredictable character of the person who has taken massive doses of amphetamines. It should be pointed out that narcotics agents tend to come into contact with heavy users under the least tranquil of conditions; such as when making arrests. Their very presence may invoke an aggressive response. The concern for aggression and violence often centers on the assumption that among the effects of a drug is its tendency to induce unprovoked violence. Clearly, the opiates do not possess this characteristic pharmacologically.[4] Although the opiate user may commit violence, particularly during an act such as robbery in order to support his habit, there is nothing in the drug effect to incline him to do so. The amphetamines do, however, tend to set up conditions in which violent behavior is more likely to occur. Hyperactivity combined with suspiciousness may precipitate unwarranted aggressive behavior.

Those people who become heavily involved in the speed scene cannot function in the straight world, at least not in many capacities. Groups and even small subcultures have developed around the heavy abuse of speed. In such a climate the speed scene becomes engrossing; it is time demanding and unique. Friendships become limited to within the scene; where else can such an individual find others who can relate to him while he is high, or who understand his situation enough to ease him or leave him alone when in the intense discomfort of the crash after an extended run? Only those in the speed world can understand and accept him while he is up and when he is coming down.

The most acute consideration, however limited, of the social problems of the speed world are to be found in the marketplace. With the explosion of speed abuse in the Haight-Ashbury and elsewhere, a profitable market devel-

oped. By 1967, San Francisco had become the major center of manufacture and distribution on the west coast. Several large laboratories and countless small operations were being conducted. Increased enforcement drove the larger labs into more secluded rural areas. As the penalties for manufacture were increased, the market became more organized in its methods and operation. High level distribution is relatively obscure though; it is the lower levels of dealing which take precedence in forming sensational social problems. The speed market has its own characteristics which tend to set the field for possible violence. Consumers of marijuana and the psychedelics are generally not compulsive users and most often have some source of income. While on the other hand, heroin addicts are generally sophisticated hustlers who support their habits through schemes of robbery, passing bad checks, prostitution or confidence games. Much of the money in the heroin market is derived from sources outside of it. It seems that many of the speed freaks did not have the skills of the professional hustler, and there tends to be very little outside money in the market on the lower levels. The market turns in upon itself as rip-offs become common and weapons are used for protection. In a market of this type, the burn-artist becomes one of the major sources of violence as a target for forceful retribution.

Another dangerous aspect of Methedrine abuse occurs when heroin is employed as a tranquilizer in order to help the speed freak to come down from an extended run. A dependence on heroin may be initiated.

Treatment Considerations

The physical effects of massive doses of Methedrine, the extremes of elation and depression combined with hyperactivity make it a drug of choice for younger people or those who have the stamina to absorb its physical impact.

The assumption of the law agencies that traffic in illicit amphetamines can be controlled by pursuing users and sellers, and penalizing them severely is irrelevant. Methamphetamine is easy to synthesize and relatively cheap. Scores of persons are willing to risk arrest in order to produce and sell it. The fear of imprisonment is largely mitigated by the fact that almost everyone is also carrying marijuana which is punish-

[2] David Goddard, "Report of an Ad Hoc Panel on Drug Abuse," *Proceedings*, White House Conference on Narcotic and Drug Abuse, September 27–28, 1962, pp. 271–308.

[3] Chauncey D. Leake, *The Amphetamines: Their Actions and Uses*, Springfield, Ill. Charles C. Thomas, 1958.

[4] John Kramer, M.D., "An Introduction to Amphetamine Abuse," *Journ. of Psychedelic Drugs*, Haight-Ashbury Medical Clinic, Vol. II, No. 2 (1969), p. 2.

able by even more severe penalties, so, to the user nothing new is introduced by anti-amphetamine legislation. In fact, the reality that law makes use illegal and that police and their supporters look down upon speed freaks is of little importance to them. Even after accounting for the paranoia which pervades the speed scene, a counter tendency stemming from the illegal status of amphetamines is noted; there seems to be strong bonds of trust and cameraderie among speed freaks which grows out of their unusual shared personal experiences.

The resolution of this paradigm is easy to understand, but difficult to implement. Institutional treatment for the individual must aim toward long term planning for change of life style. The past must be forgotten; the individual must be dealt with directly at his point of immediate need; and alternative choices which begin to help the person formulate a program for change in his immediate future must be offered.

An example of such a method is the Mendocino Drug Abuse Program. First, it is a hospital with modern medical facilities; but second, it is a minute, drug free society, whose intention is to resocialize its members by making them adopt and believe in new self concepts, concepts which replace the old patterns and stigma of drug addict. The technique of rehabilitation is highly adaptable and includes many of the psychotherapeutic methods used by Synanon and Esalen, as well as meditation and even video-taping. Success in such programs has been marked. But prevention, however, is the ultimate goal.

It is the potential drug abuser who must make his own decision, and this decision can only be based on accurate information. The key to prevention lies in effective education.

In the very recent past, a conspicuous decline of high dose amphetamine abuse has been indicated. To state the principal cause would be speculation, but some reasoning can be made. First, the drug itself is physically extreme and can lead to complete physical debilitation as well as to a paranoid psychosis when abused to the extremes as has been noted. Second, the "famous" drug subcultures such as the Haight have been decaying into squalor and violence for some time now and, as such, set forth a poor example for the future. My third point is genuine societal concern. It is this

point I wish to dwell on, because it is the only variable in the experiment which the community can manipulate. There has been remarkable concern both on the institutional and the gut levels in the case of Methedrine abuse. The motto "Speed Kills" is direct, short and carries a message of concern. Free clinics, staffed by volunteers serve not as an "answer to your problem," but rather in acceptance of the young person as he is, without questioning of his motives. In this way the community can work with young people, enabling them to direct their life styles into ones which will bring meaning and hope rather than destruction, misery and despair. And it seems to be working.

The following transcriptions of public service radio messages were done by leading rock performers—evidence of the efforts of heroes of the drug culture to try to care for their own. Their message is simple—Speed Kills! Drug use in general is not to be scorned, but they admit that dangers do exist. These announcements are broadcast in the language of the young on radio stations in the San Francisco area such as station KSAN.

7.8
Speed Kills!

The Community

This is Steve Stills and all I got to say is "Speed Kills"—so watch it. Put it down. Do it now.

This is John Mayall speaking, and I'm talking to anybody who'd care to hear my personal views on Speed. I've seen too many people suffer as a result of taking this drug; and you do risk a good part of your mind—so, use your head while it's still in working order and recognize the danger of Speed. That's all.

When I first came to this country (this is Eric Burden of The Animals talking, by the way) . . . when I first came to this country,

there was a lot of sense being talked by kids here, in particular; and that knocked me out, it was one of the great things about America because they didn't seem to get hung up by the lies that had been told by the Establishment for so long. And one of the sensible things that was being said was that booze is not good for us, booze does us harm, we'd much rather get high on something else. All of that good sense seems to have disappeared in the fact that people are now using amphetamines, which is even worse for you than booze is. So if you're intelligent and if you're really hip to things, you'll realize that booze is one thing, pot is another, but amphetamines are *death*.

This is Grace Slick of the Jefferson Airplane . . . one pill makes you larger, one pill makes you small, and if you shoot up Speed you won't be there at all because you'll be dead, baby.

Hello, this is Frank Zappa from the Mothers of Invention, and I would like to talk to you about Speed. Hi, Speed Freaks! Listen, you're really in for a lot of fun in the next five years. Let's say you start today shooting up. A big rush and you're ready to rip. It's a wonderful life, being a Speed Freak. It'll last five years. Put Speed *down*.

Hello, this is John Sebastian. If you're finding out about getting high, please stay with the wonderful things that grow from the ground. There are chemicals and powders that aren't groovy highs, and they're on the street, too. Speed, smack, barbiturates . . . they burn out your brain and your body and they steal your freedom. Please stay away from powder.

Hi, this is Peter Tork on behalf of your local Speed dealer. Remember, Speed makes a better killer out of *you*.

Suzy . . . Suzy Speed Freak? This is the voice of your conscience, baby, I just want to check a couple of things out with you. Did you know that you got five years to live if you start today using Speed? Think of it, five years and it's all over! You've already spent maybe 9, 10, 11, maybe 12 years in school, and it was such a drag, wasn't it? Just think, in five years it can all be over if you use Speed. Start today.

This is Frank Zappa from the

Mothers of Invention . . . Hi! Wanta die? Start today . . . use a little Speed. You got five years. Rot your mind, rot your heart, rot your kidneys . . . cuckaracha!

7.9
Heroin Addiction: The Problem and Its Treatments

Hillary Turner

This analysis was done to discuss the new look in treatment techniques for the older problem of heroin addiction.

The ideal treatment for heroin addiction would be to work with an addict and cure him; to turn him back into society as a productive, law-abiding, stable and non-(drug) dependent citizen. This vision, however, is far-fetched at best, for the illness that is manifested in addition has deep roots. Drugs may be seen not so much as an evil in themselves, but rather as a symptom of a sick society. Narcotic addiction has been a societal problem of long standing, and to eliminate it, effort should be directed, wholeheartedly, at those facets of society that breed a need for escape, "kicks," or masochism. That is why a program like Synanon must incorporate its members permanently—as an alternate society it provides a home where members can adapt beneficially and live, accepted for whomever they may be. Synanon could also be seen in the same sense as methadone maintenance, another sort of life-time crutch, though environmental rather than chemical. Synanon posts on its bulletin boards news clippings of all former members who left and did not make it—who were arrested, killed, or whatever. This practice serves to emphasize the need to remain in a place where an addict knows he can make it, for to return to the outside, despite the removal of the physical stigma, is to be confronted once again by those very factors that brought about addiction in the first place. This is not the professed theory of all cures, of course, for it is too bleak and too hopeless a notion for everyone to entertain. But it must be realized that for the majority of addicts,

By permission of the author.

addiction was the result of some internal deficit, some deficit in their immediate society, or most likely, some delicately balanced, self-perpetuating combination of the two. To even hope for a meaningful decrease in heroin addiction, the problem must first of all be taken out of the hands of the law, for not only has the criminal approach failed miserably in the realm of cure, but it has served to further heighten such criminal activities as theft, in order to support habits made ludicrously expensive by black market control. Simultaneously made with this step must be an all-out attack on those sore-spots of our society in which are festering poverty, prejudice, or inequality. As our society exists now, it appears that for an addict to live a happy, productive life, he must be supported, for the rest of his life by a crutch, be it methadone, Synanon, or continued "Family" relations. Although undoubtedly some heroin addicts have been thoroughly "cured," or have learned new survival-adaptive techniques, this is not seen to be the trend, and it cannot be until all sides of the problem are effectively dealt with.

According to Dr. Joel Fort, "The present system is soft on drugs, because in direct connection with it we've had massive increases in drug use and abuse. It's been hard on people, but soft on drugs." Any statistics available dealing with heroin addiction, especially the most recent ones, will serve to substantiate this. In San Francisco alone, the number of resident addicts is estimated (most likely underestimated) to be ten thousand. Of this number, the addiction of the lower age group, from twelve to twenty-five, has increased five to ten times since last year. The direct costs of San Francisco heroin addicts to their community has been estimated at well over two hundred million dollars annually, and indirectly at over one billion dollars. These few figures are commensurate with the problem nation wide. Heroin addiction has reached epidemic proportions, and the time has come when Americans can no longer blind themselves to the problem but must strive together to alleviate the grim and urgent crisis.

However, who is to judge which of the present methods of treatment is the best? It is not possible to do so—drug addiction is an individual problem and one cure will obviously not help everyone. There are so many types of addiction—the ghetto junky, the young

middle-class student playing around, dabbling, the physician addict, to name but a few. The curative process should consist of offering to the addict the most beneficial method for him specifically. For example, young junkies who are still "on a run," prostitutes able to support their habits, clever young pimps or hustlers, and so on, conceivably may not want or be able to accept methadone maintenance; their habit is not yet a desperate hassle.

There are a number of treatment approaches currently in use which we will attempt to describe. A bright young junior high school student might find Chrysalis House to be dull, isolated and boring—perhaps even an accentuation of the very societal conditions that led him to shoot heroin in the first place. Some personality types may not be able to tolerate the rigid, almost militaristic approach offered by Synanon or Mendocino—it is easily conceivable that many people would get turned off by all the rules, restrictions, regulations, or dehumanizing practices intrinsic to such approaches. Following, then, is a discussion of a few existing heroin rehabilitation programs and an evaluation of such methods in regards to future action.

Methadone Maintenance

The methadone maintenance program is one type of treatment for heroin addiction. It is not a cure, in the fullest sense of the word, for although it blocks psychological craving for heroin and stops physical dependence, it does so by perpetuating and to some degree increasing addiction to another chemical. Although this may at first appear to be an ". . . insidious and immoral" approach (as stated by the director of Oakland's Synanon organization, Chester Stern), after a closer investigation one finds it to be a highly effective, useful, and beneficial treatment.

Methadone is a synthetic narcotic, discovered by German chemists some twenty years ago. It was originally used as an inexpensive pain killer until its usefulness in the realm of heroin addiction was learned. It was pioneered in the United States by Vincent Dole and Marie Nyswander. Although it has been proven useful in several large-scale programs around the country, severe restrictions in some states are curtailing its much needed usage. In California, which has the most severe restrictions of any state, sections 11391 to 11395 of the Health and Safety Code require, for such treatment, that the addict must have been committed to a hospital or institution, or to prison, and that the treatment must be reported. California law also dictates how much methadone can be given and for how long (thirty days). The addict may only be treated in prison hospitals or locked wards ("closed, approved institutions"), or in effect, such a program is illegal. In California, the only exceptions consist of a few very limited research projects, as in San Jose or San Francisco. As this treatment has thus far been highly successful, as well as inexpensive and simple to administer, a sample of such a method will be further discussed using the Center for Special Problems in San Francisco as a model.

Founded by Dr. Joel Fort and now directed by Dr. Barry Ramer, the Center has been able, for almost a year, to treat a small number of heroin addicts with methadone maintenance. Originally granted a special dispensation as a research oriented activity, the program started with twenty men and now has expanded to accommodate thirty-one addicts—a miniscule figure indeed when compared with the huge number of addicts in the city. Although there are twenty to thirty inquiries by new addicts every day to apply for treatment, as of now they must be refused, due to the illegality of expansion and the lack of funds; which is rather ironical when the two hundred million dollars a year in direct costs by the addict to the community are considered.

Chemically speaking, the program consists of a life-long, built-up habit. It is, in this sense, harder to kick than heroin, in terms of craving, although the withdrawal syndrome will be physically smoother if staggered. Addicts come once a day, usually in the morning, to the Center and drink their dose in a glass of Tang. This is an added advantage of the program; methadone, if shot, has effects more similar to those of heroin, but it may be ingested effectively, or in accord with the goal of treatment, which is to function "normally" while also being blocked of the desire for heroin and not experiencing withdrawal from lack thereof. The effects of methadone come on slowly and last twenty-two to twenty-four hours. It is not felt for about the first six days after the start of the program; the addict

just does not get sick. The drinking is supervised so that the methadone cannot be subsequently sold or shot. Every morning a bona fide urine sample is taken to insure the ingestion of the methadone as well as to serve as a check for other drugs. While on methadone maintenance the use of heroin is frustrated as its effects will not be felt.

Considered socially, a highly promising eighty-three to eighty-nine percent success rate has been recorded at the Center so far (one thousand addicts are being treated in the New York methadone maintenance program with an eighty-five percent success rate). In the Center for Special Problems, roughly one third of the addicts on methadone now function well socially, one third do so with additional therapy and counseling, and the other third, while physically compliant with the goals of treatment, have not yet adjusted socially. This is an incredible step towards reaching the previously mentioned ideal cure, for while the addict is still drug-dependent it is not in a mind altering capacity, and the addict has an excellent chance of being able to legally and productively function in society. Thus, until such other facets of the entire drug problem are attacked, as inherent societal difficulties, methadone maintenance may be seen as a great advance in humane and viable treatment of heroin addiction.

After just a month or so addicts on the program start relating and living in a manner markedly different from their previous existence under the yoke of heroin addiction. Getting out of the often desperate hassle of always having to secure a fix on time, the paranoia brought about by the illegality, not only of the drug, but also by means of acquisition, as well as several other similar problems, clearly puts a different perspective on one's mode of living. The only side effects thus far detected have been infrequent cases of mild constipation or even more rarely a decrease in sexual potency; which is still a great improvement over the common impotency of a heroin addict.

No very young addicts are now being treated at the Center; the mean age is twenty-nine years. Only those addicts who have been convicted of two felonies are allowed. As of now, the Center has no money and no definite plans of funds to come. In view of the slight cost needed to maintain an addict in the program for one year

(two thousand dollars, ten dollars of which pays for the methadone and the rest of which covers the urine analyses) as opposed to the fantastically high amount an addict must procure to support a habit, the reluctance of political bodies to appropriate these funds may only be judged as blind and tragic. Everyone on the program must pay the Center for some part of their treatment, usually five to ten dollars per week, and must pay a large starting fee, which then serves to cover the first ten weeks—for some guarantee of commitment. Of the few who have dropped out of the program are included a small group from the start of the program who had not understood it and upon finding what it entailed, were not ready for it, as well as a chronic alcoholic, a psychotic personality, and so forth.

One must still keep clearly in mind, however, that no matter how encouraging this method appears, it will not work for every addict, and does entail certain possible dangers. To instigate a life-long cure, especially to a young person could be a precocious or unnecessary giving up of hope; perhaps through another method an addict could be more fully "cured." Also the introduction of methadone as a treatment for heroin addiction recalls a similar medical phenomena of the 1920's, when heroin, a new substance, was introduced as a cure for morphine addiction, then a major problem. To some physicians especially, the parallel is unmistakable—until a drug is evaluated on a street usage level, after having found reliable controlled statistics, its range of effect cannot be truly known. They feel that methadone usage could be altered significantly if allowed to leak out to the streets (which they must think is unavoidable) and may have the potential of being a "super smack." Such dangers, however, are conceivably controllable (putting methadone maintenance on a similar plane of acceptance as a diabetic taking his insulin daily) and actions recently taken, as by six doctors and four narcotics addicts in San Francisco (April 11, 1970) who filed a suit in Superior Court in an attempt to do away with California laws prohibiting methadone maintenance, are a welcome and necessary step. The doctors include Dr. Joel Fort, Dr. David Smith of the Haight-Ashbury Clinic, and Dr. Eugene Schoenfeld ("Dr. Hippocrates").

The suit includes charges based on the unconstitutionality of the laws prohibiting treatment. Also, on May 13, 1970, the State Assembly in Sacramento presented a concrete example of efforts on the part of the California Legislature to legalize wide use of methadone treatment. The Assembly approved the bill (initiated by John Vasconcellos, Democrat, San Jose) unanimously and has now passed it to the Senate.

Chrysalis House

Located outside of San Jose in a rural area, Chrysalis House is operated by former addicts and two directors, and is completely devoid of doctors, psychiatrists, and so on. "The dormant self encapsulated stage of growth between the voracious hunger of the caterpillar and the free flight of the beautiful butterfly." This is the meaning of the name of this other organization for heroin rehabilitation, and together with the sign in the front office, "This is the first day of the rest of your life," clearly sets the tone.

Chrysalis House is a comparatively small community, consisting of approximately forty ex-addicts at the present time. Although presented as merely a stage in an addict's life, ". . . a shelter in which to grow, in order to prepare himself for what could otherwise be a painful re-entry into the normal world," it was impossible to determine much success from the information offered. The impressiveness of Chrysalis House germinates from its environment; the atmospheric mood or tone as well as the physical layout. It is run, financially, on some money from State Welfare, as well as on public donations, and fortunately appears to be a very comfortable living situation. It is a group of pleasant model homes facing inward on a common yard. The discernible feelings were clearly ones of warmth, helpfulness, and friendliness. Although there must obviously exist a strict disciplinary procedure for the community to work, it is not manifested at all in a dehumanizing or brutal manner.

Addicts come into Chrysalis House and kick cold turkey. They must then start a three stage program, the common requirement of which is to attend nightly "rap sessions," which were described by several participants as lacking the rough, crude characteristics associated with such encounter or game techniques employed by such other programs as Synanon.

SCENES FROM CHRYSALIS HOUSE, SAN JOSE, CALIFORNIA. PHOTOS COURTESY OF JOSHUA WATTLES.

Use of drugs commands a thirty day expulsion period. The stages of the program limit the activities and freedom of the addict, dependent upon his growth in reliability and self-sufficiency.

Mendocino State Hospital

Coordinating with the Mendocino State Hospital in Ukiah, California, "The Family" offers a unique rehabilitative program not only for drug addicts, but also for anyone suffering from serious "character disorders" who desires help. Unlike traditional drug rehabilitation programs, the Family claims to be totally self-controlled and directed. The governing body, known as the elders, is composed of both ex-addicts and professionals. Though social workers, psychiatrists, psychologists, and doctors are directly involved in the program, they hold no more power than any other family member, and are examined and controlled as closely as the ex-addicts. The Family offers no quick, miracle cure but only militaristic hard work, dissatisfaction, and eventually a return to constructive social functioning based on self awareness and non-chemical living. As the "Family"-produced "Green Sheet" points out, this program is totally voluntary and directed at those individuals who want to kick, but can not succeed on their own:

You have come to us because you want to stop using drugs, but we don't want you if you are half-hearted or under pressure. This is not a place to clean up. We will not let you take a vacation here.

To stop using dope is not enough; it is just a beginning. You have come to us because you are at your wit's end. Your life has been miserable and *you* need a change.

The ultimate goal of our Family is to create a meaningful life; to produce free men. You are not free now because you are hypnotized by notions that you have never looked at. Entering our Family means that *all* your behavior and values will be questioned and examined. The unexamined life is not worth living. We offer you the chance to live life again by examining your life closely.

Changing your life is not something that is done to you; it is something *you* do. You will be very uncomfortable here. You will often find our way of life hard, irritating, stupid, and unsatisfactory. You will be disgusted often and want to quit. You will not understand what is going on. You will be expected to struggle to tell the truth, and you will discover that the truth is not always easy to find and is often not pleasant when you find it.

The Family program proper consists of at least two years actively engaged in communal living and "theraputic" game playing. Before a person can enter the Family proper, he must go through a screening period which lasts from two to three months. If an addict has not yet kicked, he spends some five days in the detoxification center of the hospital after which he is expected to use no more stimulants, depressants, or chemicals, with the exception of tobacco.

For the first month of his stay in the Family, the neophyte is not allowed to communicate with any other family members or staff. He is considered to be an emotional child not capable of rational thought processes or emotions. To engage in game playing at this point would be frustrating and fruitless. The addict must pass through an incubation period in which he sheds his stereotype street behaviors and begins to introspect and examine. As an orientation to the Family concepts (vaguely described as philosophical life perception roles) and his fellow brothers and sisters, the addicts engage in controlled confrontations known as "slip games." The Family elders believe that these games help overcome restricting barriers of pride and ego as individuals must act out the foolish behavior which the slip requires of them. People are forced to laugh at themselves and one another as they flap their arms and crow or execute twenty push-ups while repeating "I need help." As the pictures show, a sign may be hung on an individual which documents his hangup or social error.

If the neophyte has not left the program (statistics such as these are not available) and is ready to accept the responsibilities of the Family, he enters the first of four stages. These stages correspond to the amount of work responsibility, the receptivity to games and the development of the individual according to the Family goals. After twelve to fifteen months and completion of stage three, the individual can decide if he will stay at Mendocino and accept the heavy responsibility of coordinating the Family and its members or move out into any one of a number of after-care systems. These facilities, which include the Porcupine Family, Inc., a non-profit arts and crafts community in Ukiah, the Awareness House system, and national training centers in Tucson, Sonora, Marysville, Yuba City,

and Fort Bragg, are closely directed and regulated by the elders of the Family. Often times the brothers and sisters remain in these centers or in Mendocino after their scheduled second year graduation. However, whatever they may decide to do, they are thereafter constantly in communication with the patriarchs of the Family.

The Family claims to have evolved away from the traditional approach of dealing with the addict and drug addiction. Rather than considering addiction as a bacteria which infects the diseased addict, the Family considers addiction a mental hygiene problem or an "identity addiction." While in the streets, the addict was forced to play the role of a hustler; alienated not only from his partners but also from his own emotions. It is the intent of the addict and the Family to break down the masks and myths, expose the raw personal emotions, and create a meaningful life.

The Family techniques of dissolving these facades are unique to the traditional theraputic and behavioristic approach. They neither engage in professional analyst-patient therapy nor operant conditioning, but rather attack and examine overt behavior as a means of unmasking motivation. Frank Valasco, liaison between the hospital and the elders, describes their distrust of the professional therapy:

Individual therapy creates too many destructive secrets. It is a process of the hidden mover who can actually create war in which the two innocent parties do not know where the aggravation comes from. The entire community is a therapy.

All family members play games. The directors of the Family place the success of the program and behavioral change on the process of these games:

The first few months that a person is here they will use every possible behavioral pattern that they have learned to avoid other ways of dealing with the situation. This is the beauty of the program: that they can immediately zero in on the destructive behavior pattern, use that on a verbal level, engrossing it so that the person sees it in an application. Then the person reacts to it, because it is an emotionally charged situation, then it comes out, bubbles out, roars out, it does all kinds of things to him as a human being . . . right in front of the family, and they can use that as immediate input.

Just as a matriarchal figure tends to be too domineering and protective of its offsprings, so too

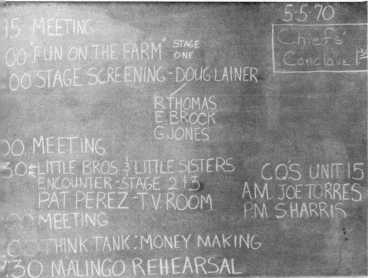

SCENES FROM THE MENDOCINO STATE HOSPITAL DRUG TREATMENT PROGRAM IN UKIAH, CALIFORNIA, SHOWING THE USE OF SIGNS IMPOSING A LABEL FOR A PERSON'S MISBEHAVIOR AS DETERMINED BY THE ELDERS OF "THE FAMILY."
PHOTOS COURTESY OF ROBERT BUCKHOUT.

the Family elders find it difficult to accept their children, and reserves the power to call them back in the fold at anytime.

Synanon

Synanon was founded in 1958 in an apartment in Ocean Park, California, by Charles Dederich, an ex-alcoholic then living on a $33-per-week unemployment check. It started as little more than an informal discussion group of Alcoholics Anonymous members and a few narcotic addicts. Before long it was recognized that this type of contact would work to help the addicts, and in September 1958 Synanon was incorporated as a non-profit foundation. In less than a year Synanon boasted a roll of forty members and occupied a former National Guard armory on a beach at Santa Monica, California. In the past three years Synanon membership has grown from 50 to 5000 members, and there are Synanon centers in seven cities across the country and in Puerto Rico that house close to 1600 reclaimed drug addicts and ex-alcoholics.

After years of existence on handouts begged from business and industry, Synanon has grown into an organization with assets worth $15 million including large real estate holdings, a network of gasoline stations, a rubber parts factory in Anaheim, a fleet of busses, autos and trucks, and an advertising firm which has a volume of $2 million in sales per year. It has even acquired a computer to keep track of its many activities.

Even though Synanon has grown greatly in size and interests, its objectives have stayed the same and its rules simple. There are two basic rules to which the members of Synanon must adhere: 1) No drugs, including marijuana and alcohol; 2) No violence or threat of it. Non-resident members are not to drink any alcohol on the day that they attend a Game or visit a club facility, and no member of Synanon is to use illegal drugs if he wishes to remain a member in good standing. These rules are not policed but are enforced by the honesty of the members and group pressures, since full participation in Synanon's program is needed to avoid returning to addiction.

The main proposal of Synanon is to reclaim the addict, not just through a type of therapy, but through a controlled environment designed to change the person.

The capsulated society of Synanon attempts through peer and group pressures to internalize a very strong feeling against the use of drugs and to promote group unity. In many respects it is attempting to do the job of imparting to the addict the internalized values that the family and the outside society have failed to do. It tries to give the individual an honest self-evaluation, an adequate yet peaceful outlet of aggression, and a place to air any undue frustrations he or she may feel.

The notorious Synanon Game, which if left open would attract spectators much like the zoo or the circus, is analogous to the idea of Confession in the Catholic Church. It is a means with which to purge oneself of frustrations, trespasses, and guilt. It leaves him refreshed and possibly at peace with himself. But the analogy stops at judgment. The individual is left to judge himself instead of being judged by someone totally unconcerned with him. The Game is sometimes stormy and verbally violent but is usually more thought-provoking than verbal confrontation.

The Game started as frank "bull sessions" in Dederich's apartment as an unreserved and uninhibited interaction among people with only physical violence or the threat of it restricted. It enables the players to see themselves as others see them, a sort of mirror reflecting all the discrepancies of the person's "self-image" and directly confronting him with them. The Game eliminates the "we-they" conflict found in other groups and institutions by reflecting it in a personal realm. The Game usually takes place three times a week and functions as an exploration of personal problems. It seems to be effective not only in theory but in fact as being a verbal outlet for disorderly behavior, for once purged of hostilities the participant can proceed with orderly activity.

Stemming from the Game is the Stew, which is a sort of marathon game. Participants can slip in and out or stay for the duration, usually about 30 hours. In addition to handling personal and group problems this may involve lectures, music, or anything else that comes to mind. It is a session established as an educational experience in which people can come to a mutual understanding of each other.

One of the most recent innovations of Synanon is in the form of a program for self-understanding

and awareness in teenagers, called "Notions." It is an idea founded in Oakland which attempts to counter the problems of public schools, dope, crime, prejudice and the so-called generation gap. The teenager joins as a non-resident member and comes to Synanon on Saturdays to work, eat, explore himself in the Game, and to understand others. It is a new absorption effort, offering Synanon's social movement to a teenage society.

The newest plan of the now expanding institution is a city composed of only members of Synanon—Synanon City. It is now in progress in Marin County, California, and will be set up as a total living communal experience among friends. It already has the best sewage disposal system in the country, where in an emergency the outflow can be used as drinking water. At present there are 40 "caves" built, and a present estimate of room required for 25,000 people. There will be no locks on doors in Synanon City, and it will be a self-contained municipality. The people already living there seldom venture out of Synanon City because they feel that the existence is so fulfilling. Synanon City in the future will have much to overcome in the society in which it exists, because it shuns the basic ideas of family and home which our society holds as God-ordained. But even if in the future it fails, it will become known possibly as man's only attempt at an honest and worthy human living experience in a society rocked with evils it cannot cope with.

The road of Synanon's progress has been troubled and rocked with many fears and prejudices of an already imperfect society. Many people attack Synanon's lack of professional supervision and the theory that one addict can cure another. Even now, in California, State authorities won't permit parolees from State institutions to enter Synanon, and yet the California Department of Corrections uses modified Synanon methods in its own programs, such as the "Family" in Mendocino. Also, there is the criticism of Synanon's almost militaristic, rigid discipline and control of its members' lives, yet the psychologists agree that lack of discipline and meaning is a modern ill of our society as a whole.

The John Birch Society has even accused Synanon of being a revolutionary movement to overthrow the basic institutions of our society. Some conventional rehabilitationists believe that the only way an addict can kick the habit is to be jailed or hospitalized, and yet it has been demonstrated that this method has failed dismally.

The fantastic results of Synanon's program far outweigh the criticism it has incurred. While Federal and State hospitals claim about a ten-percent cure among their former patients, Synanon can claim that ninety percent of its members who completed a two-and-one-half year program have stayed away from drugs to date. This is conservatively nine times the rehabilitation rate for drug addicts involved in traditional withdrawal programs. While most drug cure programs emphasize decreasing dosage withdrawal or chemical substitution, Synanon demands abrupt and complete withdrawal backed by powerful group pressures and a complete change in the environment that contributed to the cause of the addiction. Withdrawal from a drug-dependent society is a most important factor in the approach of the addict rehabilitation. This factor is lacking in the State programs of addiction cure. Even though Synanon can be accused of not freeing the drug addict within our total society, so that he can walk any street at any time and not have the possibility that under crisis he will return to drug use, its results cannot be denied. Sociologist Lewis Yablonsky stated in *The Tunnel Back* that, "Synanon's genius lies simply in establishing lines of communication with the addict. . . . most other therapeutic programs are unable to reach the addict because of his hostility and desire to deceive 'the authorities.' Synanon has completely destroyed the 'we-they' attitude which hampers other programs."

Drug use was once a scarce affliction but now is a social epidemic that knows no bounds of economic or chronological lines. It lives in the nicest and worst neighborhoods. Synanon has grown from a small therapy group that once infuriated professionals and frightened neighbors into the most successful social movement for the cure of drug addiction. Today doctors and judges alike send people to Synanon—because it works. Abraham Maslow, the late professor of Psychology at Brandeis University, said, "Synanon is now in the process of torpedoing the entire world of psychiatry and within ten years will completely replace psychiatry." The Game was working before

places like Esalen made "T-groups" a release for a weekend.

Conclusion

Clearly, an enormous amount of work must be done now and in the future if we hope to help and accommodate the ever increasing number of heroin addicts. Following is a concrete and positive model for future consideration, as presented in an article by Jerome Jaffe.

However, serious problems arise when a number of different agencies offer different treatments based on radically different philosophical premises. Sometimes the user becomes locked into a system that may not be appropriate for him. If a user does not show satisfactory progress toward the goals of that treatment program, he will be discharged from voluntary programs or more closely confined or supervised in the involuntary programs. An agency rarely admits that its approach may not be suited to a user's needs at that point in his life. At best the voluntary programs permit their failures to drop out and find their own way into other treatments if they can. Other programs often have long waiting lists and the user may not be treated for months. At worst, he is imprisoned—legally—in an inappropriate program for months or years.

The problem of moving from one type of treatment to another could be solved by a multi-modality program with a central entrance, from which users could move into a number of philosophically and operationally distinct treatments. Assignment to different systems could be based on individual preferences, on the dictates of a research design, or —if it becomes available—a rational judgment based on knowledge of what kinds of individuals do best in which programs. Once the user enters a particular program his or her progress would be followed. When the program or the patient feels that satisfactory progress is not being made he would be reassigned to another program. The problem of starting and coordinating a number of different programs is obviously more difficult than establishing and evaluating any single approach. Yet it seems as if only such a coordinated effort would be able to identify which specific treatments were best suited to reach particular goals for various types of addicts.

In 1967, as the chief consultant to the Illinois Narcotic Advisory Council, I suggested that such a multi-modal program be developed to treat Illinois' estimated 6,000 compulsive narcotics users. Even though there was no assurance that a multi-approach program would function better than a number of different, independent and philosophically diverse agencies, or that it could be made to function at all, the Council authorized the attempt.

The system—a cooperative project of the State of Illinois Department of Mental Health and the University of Chicago Department of Psychiatry— took in its first patient in January 1968. By July 1969 it was fully operating and included six treatment centers in different locations, linked by weekly staff meetings and central entrance and evaluation procedures. The total program, now serving more than 700 persons, offers methadone maintenance, therapeutic communities, hospitalization and half-way-house facilities, group therapy and the use of narcotic antagonists.

While at first no one geographical center attempted all approaches, that was obviously a logical next step. Such a program is now being operated successfully in the former staff building on the grounds of the Tinley Park Mental Health Center. Total abstinence, methadone maintenance and narcotic antagonists are all being used within therapeutic community directed by ex-addicts. Because of its multi-modal approach the Tinley Park unit provides an ideal training experience.

Although it now appears that a multi-approach program can work in a single structure it is still too soon to gauge the effectiveness of the individual parts, of the efficiency of the total multi-approach concept. But it is already unequivocally clear that where vested interests have not developed and treatment of narcotics users has not become politicized, people with widely different philosophies can not only talk together but actively cooperate.

BIBLIOGRAPHY

1. Blum, Richard H., *Drugs and Society*, San Francisco, Jossey Bass, 1970.
2. Blum, Richard H., *Drugs and Students*, San Francisco, Jossey Bass, 1970.
3. Joel Fort, "Social Problems of Drug Use and Drug Policies," reprinted from *The California Law Review*, Vol. 56, No. 1, 1968.
4. Goddard, David, "Report of an Ad Hoc Panel on Drug Abuse," *Proceedings*, White House Conference on Narcotic and Drug Abuse, September 27–28, 1962.
5. Jaffe, Jerome, "Whatever Turns You Off," *Psychology Today*, May, 1970.
6. Kramer, John. "An Introduction to Amphetamine Abuse," *Journal of Psychedelic Drugs*, Haight Ashbury Clinic, Vol. II, No. 2, 1969.
7. Leake, Chauncey D. *The Amphetamines: Their Actions and Uses*, Springfield, Ill., Thomas, 1958.
8. Long, R. E., and Penna, R. P. "Drugs of Abuse," *Journal of American Pharmaceutical Association*, Vol. NS8, No. 1 (January, 1968).
9. Nowlis, Helen H., *Drugs on the College Campus*, New York, Anchor, 1969.
10. "The Pursuit of High," *Medical Economics*, Special Issue, April 20, 1970.

11. Solomon, David, *The Marihuana Papers*, Indianapolis, Bobbs-Merrill, 1966.
12. Watts, Alan, *Does It Matter?* New York, Pantheon Books, Random House, 1970.

7.10
Rock 'n' Roll/Long-Haired/Dope Yoga

(CONFESSIONS OF A 25-YEAR-OLD ALL-AMERICAN DOPE EATER)

DEDICATED WITH LOVE
TO SCOTT MONTY

The author of this story will be twenty-six at the time of publication. For ten years he has been engaged in what he now calls calls "rock 'n' roll/long-haired/dope Yoga," a unique invention of America in the twentieth century. What is peculiar about this Yoga is that one doesn't really know he's in it until he's out of it. The Chinese said, "Every way is The Way," and this has been his way. The author doesn't regret anything that happened, for the simple reason that it got him where he is today, and today feels good.

The first drug he ever used was alcohol—beer and wine mainly—quite a bit at times, starting about in the tenth grade. Over the course of the next ten years, he used benzedrine, dexedrine, methedrine, morning glory seeds, marijuana, hashish, DMT, lysergic acid, mescaline, psilocybin, a snort or two of heroin (which he had to try after all he'd heard—good and bad) and some smoking stuff called "peace" or "angel dust" (bad). And tobacco, maybe the worst drug considering cost, what you put in (lung tissue) and what you get out. The author never used cocaine, peyote or laughing gas, though would have if he'd come in contact. Never used STP or PCP or MDA or those things that followed LSD—acid was plenty. Never had any inclination to use so-called "downers" (that name was enough). Mainly a lot of alcohol, benzedrine, marijuana and LSD. There's kids around today who compile a list that would make his look amateurish—Peace Be with Them.

I was born and raised in Berke-

By permission of the author.

ley, California, of parents who both came out of early nineteen-hundreds immigrants. Father grew up outside Cleveland, parents of Czech and Austrian origin, was a research chemist (of "magna cum laude" and Ph.D. stature) for a major oil company and was an alcoholic most of my youth. My mother came from a farm in the Dakotas, out of straight Lutheran Swedes, was a registered nurse, but confined her energies to being a good housewife thru most of my younger days. I attended public schools thru high school, was always getting elected to everything and usually getting good grades without much effort. Upon leaving junior high school, my classmates had voted me "most popular," "best all-around personality" and "most likely to succeed" as well as electing me student body president. Some people found this a little ironic in the years to come. Carried bag lunches and ate peanut butter sandwiches every day for years. Was a Coke (as in Coca-Cola) nut. Played basketball and football. Need I say it? All-American kid. Newspaper boy and Boy Scout to boot.

Getting into the last couple years of high school some troubles started coming to the surface which had first been felt back in eighth and ninth grades. Marks in school started falling, cut classes a lot, and drank heavily (bottles of "Thunderbird" which usually left me on someone's bathroom floor or front lawn and finally in giant car wreck). Had quite a rep as a wild driver. Inside I wanted to be one of the bad guys—but never felt at home with either the "bad guys" or the "good guys"—yin/yang, black/white, back and forth. Senior year felt so "screwed up" I blew the student body president election and romance with beautiful chick (whose father was later to become mayor) and played football mainly to get away from the other stuff.

One semester of work at a Berkeley chem lab and then off to UCLA in the fall. At UCLA met the "love of my life" but never got into school much and had to drop out I was so far behind. Back in on probation for the spring semester and proceeded to flunk out. While at UCLA went to a shrink for a while but that got nowhere (he never looked particularly healthy to me). Might mention here that tried that trip again at Kaiser hospital in Oakland in '65 with more or less same results (altho I liked the guy this time). I

think it was while I was at UCLA that my parents finally got divorced after years of tears and hassles. Me and my girl moved up to Berkeley. One year at local city colleges and night schools and a summer session back at UCLA (where I had the fortunate instinct to get into some Japanese and Chinese lit classes and where I had a chance to do some grass but scared) and got myself into UC Berkeley for Fall 1964. That was also the summer I was nineteen, and I remember being on some kinda Scott Fitzgerald tragi-romantic kick that my life was through there at nineteen. That romanticizing of the negative ("I must be brilliant, look how bad I feel.") was something that took me years to get over.

Well, you all know what happened at Berkeley in the fall of '64—the Free Speech Movement. I fell in love (platonically, that is) with the public figure of Mario Savio. Tried to pull the semester off with a three or four day methedrine studying trip and got very involved with ole Hamlet, but a friend got caught doing a Philosophy exam for me, so I got an F there and I was out again. That was enough. (I had grass once at a party that semester but had to get drunk to get the nerve to try it and so didn't feel anything.)

Spring '65 construction job in Richmond. Somewhere around this time started enjoying grass (listened to John Coltrane and Monk the first time stoned and loved it) but also still drinking excessively 'cause I remember waking up on the morning of my birthday with vomit all over me, just as my poor mother came in to wake me for work. At work was turning on a young Berkeley kid headed for Reed college to my recent Jack Kerouac, Gary Snyder, Allen Ginsberg discoveries. He turned me on to the *Tao Te Ching*, bless him. Attended the Berkeley Poetry Conference in midsummer and got a chance to see Snyder, Ginsberg and Robert Creeley in person. Was tired of the job already so got on my first freight train ride and headed to LA to meet up with my old spiritual-adventure sidekick from UCLA beer drinking nights and head to Mexico. (This friend has now been in India for almost two years doing his master-pupil Yoga.) Mexico for four or five weeks; San Blas mostly and some giant three day Mexico City red-tape deals trying to get rid of our broken down old Plymouth. Didn't score grass down there (which seems strange now) but did a lot of two and three day legal-benzedrine trips that got pretty far out—including human compassion tears (my friend's) on the steps of the old church in Tepic and days of diarrhea induced life flash-back nightmares in San Blas (mine).

Fall '65 back in Berkeley goofing, feeling shitty, writing poems and hanging out with older painter-writer friend. Long walks home early in the morning so wiped out had to stop and crash on peoples' steps and then continue on. Went to a couple nights of the Trips Festival and heard from old high school teacher-friend about visits to Ken Kesey's La Honda place, but wasn't aware of all that was going on there—tho did part my hair down the middle and wear the brightest shirt I had when we went to the Festival.

Got drafted that fall and spent the next two months getting as wasted as I could. Took three or four 15 mg. dexedrine spansules (good ole "Christmas trees") the morning I was on my way to Fort Ord, drank coffee all day and talked to the induction center shrink in the afternoon, shaking and sweaty, about how I would never fit into the Army (which was true) and got a one year I-Y. Was so wound up and paranoid ("One year? A trick! I'm gonna have to do this all over again!") took me days to come down; went and hid in black ghetto SF hotel.

Spring '66 finds me working in Oakland plastics factory and getting into a pretty frantic state of taking bennies all day long, then easing off enough to eat dinner at home, going out at night to drink and smoke grass and hang out and then coming home and staying up most the night editing a small lit magazine—the first and last issue of which got out by July.

That summer I again started hanging around with—and now blowing grass with—an old school friend, Scott. He was on his way to Stockton for school and talked me into coming on up. This cat is a super-energy, super-non-intellectual who some people used to take for a great egocentric trickster. Up to Stockton where we rent a little house, go swimming a lot, make bold thefts at the local "Payless" (Scott showing me how much can be gotten away with if you come on as if nothing at all wrong is going on) and start turning a lot of UOP people on to marijuana. We did morning glory seeds several times (something I'd first

tried when I was back in junior college days, I think) and had pretty good, tho often nauseous, results. Then up from the Haight-Ashbury itself came the chick friend of one of our pals with—you guessed it—LSD. Over playing in our neighborhood park—"Victory Park," believe it or not—we look at one another and roll on the ground in joyous laughter. Well, some confusions still but we start turning into a regular old hippy-house. Grass and acid are pretty easy to get and still cheap so we smoke all the time and do acid every weekend and oftener. We make a lot of trips down to the bay area, where a lot of our friends still live, and go "tripping" in Golden Gate Park. I have trouble getting used to Scott's ways still, but we read about the Haight in the papers and magazines (what a place to find out about something, ugh!) and idealistic, romantic me believes it all and my hair gets long and in the spring I become Stockton's first long-hair mailman.

Also in the spring, surprisingly, Timothy Leary comes to UOP chapel and we all get good and zonked and go to hear. Can't see nothing 'cause he's apparently sitting on the floor but the stained-glass windows become dancing women out of some Indian sculpture and a voice in front somewhere is saying softly, "We have met together before . . ." Back outside the sun is out and a light rain is falling as we walk into the "Garden of Eden." A friend goes over to talk to some bushes. I discover I have something stuck in my throat—that old chunk of apple—which I call "my past life" (meaning the last few years) and which I'm in the bathroom trying to vomit up. I don't get that settled but I feel like I've finally found someone who is a "teacher" and so I go and sit at Leary's question-and-answer period feet and dig the way he has an immediate clear rap for everything tossed his way.

Summer comes and is beautiful, but Scott is putting a lot of his energy into a chick he's digging and I'm having some not very good trips—one in particular I remember where we took a whole tab of stuff we'd usually only use a quarter or half of and which sent me into Van Gogh's head in the nut-house—calm, in a way, but completely cut off. Scott tells me things like, "Well, maybe you're Christ and have to experience these evils of the world," and, to my brother, "Your brother

always thinks he's responsible for all of us," which gets a laugh outa me.

I'm still full of "searching" feelings and so at the end of the summer Scott and I ride freights and hitch to the East to visit my Berkeley painter-writer friend who's in Boston. Scott and his chick leave after a week or so and I stay on, attracted by the worldly and intellectual knowledge of my friend and thinking that Scott is a little goofy to be so playful all the time. (He used to get on me all the time about being so serious about everything, but the way I was seeing it there was plenty to get serious about.) The fall was spent in Boston and New Haven in a pretty depressed state (uptight New England even made me weaken and get my hair cut off to look for a job—raking leaves at Yale—altho I grew it right back), but got a chance to read Huxley and Hesse and *One Flew Over the Cuckoo's Nest* and pick up on the spirits in the (Am.) Indian things at a New Haven museum. My friend is beautiful and loves me but can't help with what I need and so off to a NY friend's place for a couple weeks. One day I walk the Brooklyn Bridge, in homage to Whitman and Crane and Lorca and Ginsberg and all the NY poets and the day looks good so I take some acid and head over to the Huntington Hartford to look at paintings, which I love. I get loaded in a room with three wall sized Dalis—that was something—and then walk outside right into rush hour downtown midtown Manhattan and get so overwhelmed that the subway ride home feels like it's going downhill and I can't sleep all night.

For Christmas headed up to the farm in the Dakotas where my mother is thru the holidays, stay on a few weeks and love it, and go back to California with plans to come back for the spring to work for my uncle. Scott's place in Mission District SF for a month or two and a trip to Mexico with UCLA friend again and my chick "Sita." Trip down there is up and down, good and bad; beautiful all-day stay at the market place in Guadalajara, ocean swimming, good food, but also get thrown in jail a couple times—once in Puerto Vallarta where they're deporting all the young American kids living there and once on the way home in Culiacan.

Back out to the farm for April thru June. Had a beautiful healthy stay (except for first couple days bad vibrations pressured into cutting off my beard and trimming hair). Out in the middle of the night checking for new calves, watching wonderful new-born blank-consciousness eyes when they came, seeing the first sprouting grain of the spring, first swallow nests, first tulips. Meditating at sunset to the sound of hungry cows and writing some good poems—tho lonely at times for Sita and friends—one or two nights drunk on the living room at three or four AM with Bobby Dylan or the Miracles or Hank Williams on the phonograph. Sometimes feeling good would put on grandfather's Al Jolson record and dance around the house. Got turned on to children—my uncle's two little girls—and to country music—up to this time all rock and black soul music. Tried to get some acid to do before I left and then one of last days there, after long emotional heart-to-heart uncle rap, was riding tractor in sametime sun and rain and was crying one minute and laughing the next and realized I was already stoned just being there.

June '68 took me back to Scott's in SF and then over to Oakland when he bought a house. Found that Sita was living with some other cat since I'd left her and I went to win her back with promises of moving up to Stockton and finding a house out in the country. (Sita, Capricorn; Scott, Aries; and me, Cancer, by the way, for those interested. UCLA friend also Cancer.) In August went up to Stockton and got a job in one of the canneries (steaming hot tomato juice and dexedrine hell) and sent for Sita. We stayed with some old-friend UOP cats awhile and then the two of us and two of them found a nice place for rent out where the suburbs were ending and the farms began. One of these cats became important in my life by virtue of his being a super-energy Taurus who'd been a star (talker, footballer, bullshitter, brawler—I dug him, beautiful) throughout growing up in Stockton and who came from real Okie parents (Okla. and Ark.) and had grown up on country music and turned me on to a lot of the classic people like Roy Acuff and Ernest Tubb.

House out there was beautiful (nearly got evicted the first week by steaming hot owner who'd driven non-stop from Nevada when he'd heard there were long-hairs living in his house, but a big fried-chicken dinner by Sita fixed him up) with fruit trees and giant yard and we got us kittens and some beautiful hound puppies and some rabbits and had a pretty nice life. Sita and I fixed up a cottage that had been filled with junk and had our own beautifully decorated place complete with wall hangings, a bed made of railroad ties and a big wooden goldfish tank. Sita was uptight often and some of our acid trips ran into troubles but we all had a lot of good times dancing and playing guitar and singing and going crawdad fishing and we succeeded in turning our Okie brother on to grass—something he'd been dead set against. I switched my job to one at a wooden container factory (where I had to hide my hair under a knit stocking cap), got laid off and went on unemployment. Sita's uptightness and my inability to smooth it over, plus her desire to return to school led to a move down to Berkeley shortly after Christmas. Also about this time we made a trip in the VW bus my father had helped us get to Nogales where we sunk $500.00 into an abortion.

In Berkeley we parked our bus near some friends' house and cooked and ate with them for a couple months while sleeping in the bus. Something blew up between Sita and me and I decided I'd had enough of her but by the time she'd found a room to move into I was ready to move in with her. The house we got into had lost contact with the landlady and just as we were getting settled she came by and threw everyone out. Then we moved into a "commune" kinda house on Fulton St. with a cat novelist, a young two-kid Zen couple, and another chick who had a baby girl. I say commune "kinda" 'cause some of us—me, at least, I know—weren't quite sure how it was supposed to work, so there was ups and downs, but eventually all of us became pretty close—if not then, later. A cat named "Mad Richard" used to bring by wonderful homemade LSD and a guy in India sent some great hash that lasted thru most of the summer.

Somewhere in the early summer an old chick friend of the novelist and some other people moved in next door so that we had a two-house thing going—which was nice. Sita and I had a falling out over my wanting to ball this chick and it felt like the best way out of our uptight-couple trip we'd gotten into was to break it off, so Sita moved out. I was then working at a fibre-glass place in east Oakland and kept my head busy with work and odd jobs around both houses and balling, but felt restless still. That summer among others who came by our place was a big young blonde chick named Elizabeth and her kid John (also old friends of the novelist—and at this point I was getting impressed with this cat and his old friends). She wanted me to go up to Oregon with her and altho I was greatly taken by her youthful energy I was also a little scared of it and stayed. (It turned out I missed a stay at Ken Kesey's place and a cross-country bus trip to the Woodstock Festival.) Soon, tho, I took off with my sleeping bag and a small stash to go see the Pacific northwest for the first time (and maybe run into Elizabeth). Went to Seattle and then out to a fishing village on the coast to see the Rain Forest. The woods and forests of the north were great. One time I hiked into the forest far enough so that I didn't see anyone else all day long and got thoroughly rain-soaked but had a pleasant trip by a river in the woods.

Back down in Portland I worked with some light show people for a week so I could go see the Grateful Dead (who I'd never seen before) free, but never even saw them really 'cause the first night there a few of them came out and played country music and I was stoned and so jazzed by the musicianship I saw on stage that I left in the middle of the night determined to go back to California and be a cowboy singer. On the way back down I stopped where some people were squatting/camping in the woods and got taught some things about good food and non-meat diets. Then started home and had the "misfortune" to get a ride with two inexperienced young cats who were broke and stealing gas all the way to SF. We stopped by the road to sleep for the night and some local police came and found a joint in the car and claimed to find "debris" in my shirt pocket. The cats were seventeen and so I was off to jail—my first time except for the Mexico mix-ups. After three days I was ready to accept the deal they offered me even tho I knew they were trying to screw me. Back in Berkeley in time to regretfully see the chick next door pack up her kids and leave Berkeley and to get a phone call from Elizabeth, from the "Hog Farm" in New Mexico, excited about what had happened at Woodstock and her Prankster friends and so the novelist cat (he should have a name here by now—how about "Lefty"), who was moving to NM anyway, and I took off.

Stayed with Elizabeth at the Hog Farm for a few weeks where I read about Kesey in the "Electric Kool-Aid" book and decided my life was lame and vowed to return to California and live the Kesey philosophy. I left Elizabeth and John shortly after we got back (despite my vow) unable to handle all of her energy at that time. Hung around friends in Berkeley for the fall dropping whatever dope came along whenever it came (as part of the vow to go all out and "play hard")—acid, mescaline, grass and a lot of speed that one of my working friends was taking—and attempting to convert the people I was staying with to "The Way." But fall turned into a rut; despite frequent trips out of town and despite a really good visit to my old painter-writer friend (now in Tucson) and a good acid trip with him where I told him I would have to find the right tribe or clan or family to be with and he told me I would have to return to "straight" society (both of which were to come true).

Basement apartment in the black part of Berkeley for the winter where the cat I was staying with and I got into such a stale-headed rut that he threw me out. Best part about this time was that I started playing guitar and seeing old friend Peter again. Started living in my VW bus and sleeping in the Berkeley hills, and I started feeling stronger and freer and "energy" was a word I found myself using a lot. Kept kinda drifting around different people's places in Berkeley 'cause felt a lot of this "energy" but wasn't sure where to put it. Stayed mainly at Scott's and at Peter's and in the backyard of a chick from the Hog Farm, "Rose," who I'd seen on the street and had big love-eyes attraction for. Helped put in a beautiful organic vegetable garden at her house and then one at Scott's house and was taking acid pretty often again and having nice trips, and going to see the Grateful Dead play whenever they were in town. Practicing guitar and loving Rose and seeing a lot of old friend Peter (who had told me once, "What you need, son, is a guitar in your hands." Thank you, brother.).

I had gotten a letter from the chick who used to live next door on Fulton St.—a chick who I had very strong "wanting her to be my woman" feelings about—saying to come live with her and was trying to figure out how to cut loose from

Rose and Berkeley 'cause was discovering at the same time I wanted to leave that this was where my people really were and that if I did it the way my head was then it was gonna be going against "the flow"—the same old trip of pulling out when the going got rough. So kept trying to figure something out. About the same time started listening a lot to an underground version of the Beatles "Let It Be" album and kept hearing a lot of things about "get back" and "the way back home" and "the long winding road"—the record kept coming on very strong to me—and I also sensed that maybe this was the last Beatles' album and that made something prophetic out of it, too.

Peter ("the rock," right?) and Rose and I took acid and went to see the "Dead" on Thursday night April 8th, and I got very stoned. When I walked in all the doubts and attempts at figuring things out made me feel wisdomless, as if I hadn't learned one fucking thing in all those years of dope taking and traveling around. When the Dead started playing, the sound of the music came out so strong that I got scared at first and so started dancing and getting into the swing of it and confidence started coming back and things started getting clearer to me. The three of us were gonna go again on Sunday night but I was in doubts still about things and so threw coins for the *I Ching* (hoping it was gonna tell me to go ahead and leave to go to this other chick). I threw "Stillness," changing to "Gradual Growth" which seemed like the wrong answer, so I threw again and got "Youthful Folly" (where it said "he who throws two or three times in order to get the answer he wants is a big dunce"), changing to something I've forgotten but represented by "the sun over the earth." So we went, taking acid again, and things opened up even more and there was awe at the power of it all but understanding, too; and I was able to see intellectually what all of the last several years had been leading up to and how it all fit together and what the Beatle "messages" were all about, and started seeing which way I should head.

Went home that night and cut my beard off and a few days later cut two years of hair down to a moderate length. "Fate" left us a temporarily free house in Oakland that had a big yard and water coming right out of a well and we started putting in the third veg-

etable garden of the spring. When friends asked why I cut my hair I told them I was gonna run for President.

––––––––––––––––––––

The following is an historical note reviewing the process involved in the establishment of the marijuana myth and demonstrating the emotional irrationality that forms the basis of the present laws.

7.11
Pot: A Rational Approach

Joel Fort

But we didn't have to wait until 1968 to learn that pot is relatively harmless. Some research has been done in the past in spite of the vicious circle mentioned by Zinberg and Weil. As far back as 1942, the mayor of New York City, Fiorello La Guardia, alarmed by sensational press stories about "the killer drug, marijuana" that was allegedly driving people to rape and murder, appointed a commission to investigate the pot problem in his city. The commission was made up of 31 eminent physicians, psychiatrists, psychologists, etc., and six officers from the city's narcotics bureau. If there was any bias in that study, it must have been directed against marijuana, considering the presence of the narcotics officers, not to mention psychiatrists and M.D.s, who were then, as now, rather conservative groups. Nevertheless, after two years of hard study, including psychological and medical examinations of users, electroencephalograms to examine for brain damage, sociological digging into the behavior patterns associated with marijuana use and intelligence tests on confirmed potheads, the commission concluded:

Those who have been smoking marijuana for a period of years showed no mental or physical deterioration which may be attributed to the drug. . . . Marijuana is not a drug of addiction, comparable to morphine. . . . Marijuana does not lead to morphine or heroin or cocaine addiction. . . . Marijuana is not the determining factor in the commission of major crimes. . . . The publicity concerning the catastrophic effects of marijuana smoking in New York City is unfounded.

Even earlier, a study of marijuana use in the Panama Canal Zone was undertaken by a notably conservative body, the United States Army. Published in 1925, the study concluded, "There is no evidence that marijuana as grown here is a habit-forming drug" and that "Delinquencies due to marijuana smoking which result in trial by military court are negligible in number when compared with delinquencies resulting from the use of alcoholic drinks which also may be classed as stimulants or intoxicants."

What may be the classic study in the whole field goes back further: to the 1893–1894 report of the seven-member Indian Hemp Drug Commission that received evidence from 1193 witnesses from all regions of the country (then including Burma and Pakistan), professionals and laymen, Indians and British, most of whom were required to answer in writing seven comprehensive questions covering most aspects of the subject. The commission found that there was no connection between the use of marijuana and "social and moral evils" such as crime, violence or bad character. It also concluded that occasional and moderate use may be beneficial; that moderate use is attended by no injurious physical, mental or other effects; and that moderate use is the rule: "It has been the most striking feature of this inquiry to find how little the effects of hemp drugs have intruded themselves on observation. The large numbers of witnesses of all classes who profess never to have seen them, the very few witnesses who could so recall a case to give any definite account of it and the manner in which a large proportion of these cases broke down on the first attempt to examine them are facts which combine to show most clearly how little injury society has hitherto sustained from hemp drugs." This conclusion is all the more remarkable when one realizes that the pattern of use in India included far more potent forms and doses of Cannabis than are presently used in the United States. The commission, in its conclusion,

stated:

Total prohibition of the hemp drugs is neither necessary nor expedient in consideration of their ascertained effects, of the prevalence of the habit of using them, of the social or religious feelings on the subject and of the possibility of its driving the consumers to have recourse to stimulants (alcohol) or narcotics which may be more deleterious.

Ever since there have been attempts to study marijuana scientifically, every major investigation has arrived at, substantially, the same conclusions, and these directly contradict the mythology of the Federal Bureau of Narcotics. In contrast with the above facts, consider the following advertisement, circulated before the passage of the 1937 Federal anti-marijuana law:

Beware! Young and Old—People in All Walks of Life! This (picture of marijuana cigarette) may be handed to you by the *friendly stranger.* It contains the Killer Drug "Marijuana" —a powerful narcotic in which lurks *Murder! Insanity! Death!*

Such propaganda was widely disseminated in the mid-1930s, and it was responsible for stampeding Congress into the passage of a law unique in all American history in the extent to which it is based on sheer ignorance and misinformation.

Few people realize how recent anti-marijuana legislation is. Pot was widely used as a folk medicine in the 19th Century. Its recreational use in this country began in the early 1900s with Mexican laborers in the Southwest, spread to Mexican Americans and Negroes in the South and then the North, and then moved from rural to urban areas. In terms of public reaction and social policy, little attention was paid to pot until the mid-1930s (although some generally unenforced state laws existed before then). At that time, a group of former alcohol-prohibition agents headed by Harry J. Anslinger, who became head of the Federal Bureau of Narcotics, began issuing statements to the public (via a cooperative press) claiming that marijuana caused crime, violence, assassination, insanity, release of anti-social inhibitions, mental deterioration and numerous other onerous activities. In what became a model for future Federal and state legislative action on marijuana, Congressional hearings were held in 1937 on the Marijuana Tax Act. No medical, scientific or sociological evidence was sought or heard; no alternatives to criminalizing users

and sellers were considered; and the major attention was given to the oilseed, birdseed and paint industries' need for unrestrained access to the hemp plant from which marijuana comes. A U.S. Treasury Department witness began his testimony by stating flatly that "Marijuana is being used extensively by high school children in cigarettes with deadly effect," and went on to introduce as further "evidence" an editorial from a Washington newspaper supposedly quoting the American Medical Association as having stated in its journal that marijuana use was one of the problems of greatest menace in the United States. Fortunately for historical analysis, a Dr. Woodward, serving as legislative counsel for the American Medical Association, was present to point out that the statement in question was by Anslinger and had only been reported in the A.M.A. Journal.

Dr. Woodward deserves a posthumous accolade for his single-handed heroic efforts to introduce reason and sanity to the hearing. Most importantly, the doctor (who was also a lawyer) criticized the Congressmen for proposing a law that would interfere with future medical uses of Cannabis and pointed out that no one from the Bureau of Prisons had been produced to show the number of prisoners "addicted" to marijuana, no one from the Children's Bureau or Office of Education to show the nature and extent of the "habit" among children and no one from the Division of Mental Hygiene or the Division of Pharmacology of the Public Health Service to give "direct and primary evidence rather than indirect and hearsay evidence." Saying that he assumed it was true that a certain amount of "narcotic addiction" existed, since "the newspapers have called attention to it so prominently that there must be some grounds for their statement," he concluded that the particular type of statute under consideration was neither necessary nor desirable. The Congressmen totally ignored the content of Dr. Woodward's testimony and attacked his character, qualifications, experience and relationship to the American Medical Association, all of which were impeccable. He was then forced to admit that he could not say with certainty that no problem existed. Finally, his testimony was brought to a halt with the warning, "You are not cooperative in this. If you want to advise us on legislation, you ought to come here with some constructive proposals rather than criticism, rather than trying to throw obstacles in the way of something that the Federal Government is trying to do."

A similar but shorter hearing was held in the Senate, where Anslinger presented anecdotal "evidence" that marijuana caused murder, rape and insanity.

Thus, the Marijuana Tax Act of 1937 was passed—and out of it grew a welter of state laws that were, in many cases, even more hastily ill conceived.

[EDITORS' NOTE: It is the opinion of the editors that all drug use should be legal. Past punitive measures have failed miserably in their attempt to prevent drug abuse. Drug abuse is a social and, at times, a medical problem. If drug laws must exist at all, they should be directed towards restrictions of the drug; but not a penalty for the use of the drug.]

COMMENTARY

Statistics on drug use are extremely difficult to tabulate. The world production of marijuana in 1946 was estimated at 45,000 pounds. In 1960 the estimate was 1,800,000 pounds and today a good guess would be at least twice this figure. Use of this and other "illegal" drugs has risen in the United States at least in proportion of the world increase in marijuana production, and probably much faster. The Special Problems Center in San Francisco, a branch of the Department of Health, estimates the rise in heroin use at 1000 percent for the year 1969 in the city of San Francisco. The point is that no matter how immersed one becomes in aspects of the drug scene and drug related problems, it is nearly impossible to obtain a clear overall perspective of what is going on. One point can definitely be made clear: "illegal" drug use and drug related problems are increasing in a continuously accelerating fashion. An analogy can be drawn between increasing drug use and exploding population growth. The more people that use drugs, the more widespread the influence becomes, and the faster drug related attitudes develop and change. Those who are aware of this trend and are in a position to act must explore all constructive proposals concerning drug related problems.

With the tremendous increase in drug use, there is a somewhat proportionate rise in drug abuse. Before continuing, this last statement must be qualified. In discussing proposals for the treatment of drug related problems, the editors wish to use the perspective presented in Dr. Joel Fort's article ("Social Problems of Drug Use and Drug Policies"). This perspective encompasses the idea that tobacco is our nation's number one drug problem, alcohol use rates second, and third is the use of various "illegal" and unaccepted drugs in our society. The recent rise in drug abuse is connected largely with this group of illegal drugs, but the following program proposal will concern itself with the entire range of drug related problems. Given this perspective, we will describe one possible, logical manner in which to cope with the rising rate of drug related problems. The discussion will be of a general nature with the details left to your imagination.

The three levels of the program we propose are not by any means an impossible goal. The program could fit into the existing structures and could be funded nationally with a portion of the money spent annually on the Vietnam War, or with a portion of the money saved by even the partial reduction of thefts by heroin addicts (an estimated $25,000,000 a day business in this country at the present time). Models for the three levels of the proposed program are today in existence and functioning well in many areas of California. What is needed is coordination between these three levels and an expansion of the program on a nationwide basis. Many of the present institutions could be adapted to this program by changing their approach and underlying attitudes to drug related problems. The emphasis of the program is the placement of social problems largely in the hands of the local community and an attempt at as close to a humanistic approach as possible in treating these problems in and away from the community. This approach will also allow the individual as much personal freedom as possible to solve his own problems.

The first level of our proposed program is a number of community based centers. The purpose of these centers would be to provide direct services to the community. The structure of these centers would vary according to the distinct problems of the communities in which they are located. The organizing staff, excluding needed medical workers, should consist of concerned young people from the area holding B.A. or M.A. degrees in social work, psychology, or other related fields. The majority of the workers at the community center would consist of local residents who had experienced the problems of living in the surrounding community and wished to help solve these problems. Upon applying for work at the center, individuals would be screened by the organizers and several other workers, the main criteria for acceptance being a willingness to help. A short training period should follow acceptance. Training should be given in such areas as how to handle the red tape and talk to people in the local health and police agencies. These workers would help people with their personal problems as well as working to improve the environment of the community. They would act as a bridge between the community and the local institutions. It is our feeling that, at this level, drug related problems cannot and should not be separated from the general problems of the community. The community center should have a friendly atmosphere so as to dispel the sterile institutional impression that can "turn off" many people who want and need assistance.

The best example of an existing community center which we have been exposed to is an organization called the Aquarian Effort in Sacramento, California. It is located in an old two-story home and is staffed mostly by nonprofessional ex-drug users who advocate a totally nonchemical existence. Their proposals for helping drug users with problems are:

1. That a drug clinic be established and manned twenty-four hours a day to respond to pleas for help.

2. That a training program be set up that will allow an exchange of information between professionals and former users who will be frontline community group workers and "therapists."

3. That non-civil service paid positions be created (full and part-time) open to recent users, who will have responsibility as organizers, therapists, and group-leaders.

4. That a center be set up much along the lines of Fort Bragg's Awareness House that will allow both users and non-users to gather and *openly* discuss the issues, and also to coordinate activities, provide entertainment, provide an outlet for creative expression, make provisions for lost users, etc.

5. That a "hip" job corps be established to provide users who are pulling out of "hard" drug use some means of livelihood.

This organization is very new and has many growing pains, but much can be learned about the needs of a community center from its attempt. Two suggestions concerning a necessary expansion of this type of community effort are: an outpatient medical treatment center combined with a methadone maintenance program, and a limited sleeping area where a person might stay for a short time while workers help him to solve his individual problems.

At the second level, we propose a center designed specifically for those who have a drug related problem in the form of a total or near total dependence on a "strong" drug (including alcohol) for continuing their daily existence. Included in this category would be alcoholics and heavy acid, speed, and heroin users. The most logical approach to this type of center we have seen is an organization called "The Family," located at Mendocino State Hospital in Ukiah, California. Our impression of this program, covered in detail within the chapter, is that it makes available a process of resocialization for the individual who sincerely wishes to change his life style. It follows from this that the individuals in the center must be separated from their community in order to better examine their past way of life. Also, we feel that "The Family" is not for everyone with a serious drug related problem. It appears that one must desperately want to change his life to be a successful "graduate" of "The Family." What of the person who does not fit into "The Family's" resocialization process or does not genuinely want to change his life style? We do not feel, as Leary's article points out, that anyone has the right to force an individual to change his mode of living. In this case, is a nationwide methadone maintenance program the answer?

There are alternatives to "The Family's" approach. Several were discussed in detail within the chapter. First, we will suggest that no one approach be presented as the utopian answer and that no single approach be adopted without further examination. Secondly, we can suggest improvement in "The Family's" approach that may make it more attractive to prospects. If, given proper state and federal support, "The Family" could be established at sites physically divorced from state mental institutions and if centers could be located in pleasant, rural surroundings, then the necessary, rigid self-examination process could be offset in some ways and the stigma of "undergoing treatment at a mental hospital" could be removed. At this level, again, the centers would be staffed mainly by nonprofessional ex-drug users. These individuals, who understand completely the nature of the drug user's life style, are best qualified to help the drug addict reexamine himself. We applaud "The Family's" approach for one point which appears highly significant: it differs from the concept of "once a drug addict always a drug addict." In theory, their goal is to place graduates of their program in meaningful jobs as mature members of our society. (It is our personal feeling that one who has been through a period of heavy drug use and is able to return to his society as a mature and stronger individual has a deeper awareness of what is needed to improve that society and can make many positive contributions.)

Professionals at the first two levels are employed only as consultants to the individuals involved in doing the work. The third level concerns the professional's role in the state hospitals and mental institutions in relation to the first two levels of this proposed program. An adjustment process will be necessary for this group to recognize and complement the first levels of the program. The value of the nonprofessional worker must be fully realized. The opinion of some who are professionals is that this process would entail uprooting some entrenched beliefs and would therefore be extremely difficult to establish. The professionals in the state institutions must treat those who have drug problems and are unable to help themselves. This should include a short term heroin withdrawal program. A further example of those treated at this level would be severe cases of LSD toxic psychosis. When the patient is able to make his own decisions at an acceptable functional level, he should be referred by the professional staff to his community center or an organization like "The Family." Here aid can be offered through which the individual can be helped to help himself. One strong suggestion for treatment at this professional level is that no one paradigm for the treatment of any group of drug related problems should be accepted as gospel. All treatment methods available should be used and new ones should be examined carefully and objectively.

Two further aspects must be considered in relation to any program for the treatment of drug related problems. The first is the legal aspect of drug use. Drug abuse laws must be placed in line with scientific fact and must be removed from the realm of emotional reaction. Dr. Joel Fort's approach of "hard on drugs and soft on people" is highly recommended. The fear of being arrested after asking for help for a drug related problem must be removed completely before the effectiveness of any type of program like the one proposed can be validated. On a larger scale, the alienation of a generation of young people over the issue of irrational, ineffective, and hypocritical drug abuse laws must be halted. Scientific investigation into all aspects of drug use must be allowed by lawmakers. Myths and emotional reactions for and against drug use must be replaced by objective information and realistic advice.

In conclusion, we wish to raise some questions about drug use in relation to the nature of our society. What must we do to search for and resolve the disenchantment with society that most drug use projects? What is the state of our ruling morality when it strikes out and slaps, then shuns those who show their disaffection by using drugs? Why not find out the whys? Why not look at your own meanings and value systems for the cause of your own confusion and doubts? Who should be on the defensive, "drug people" or the rest of society? What can be said of a society that punishes the use of "illegal" drugs and, at the same time, accepts the use of potent drugs like alcohol and tobacco? Is an important aspect of our society expressed by the shelves in the aisle of a drugstore filled with pills whose purposes range from helping you to sleep to helping you to stay awake to treating a hangover?

We feel that any value judgment made on the use of any drug is the responsibility of the individual. We also feel that drugs are not the cause of any problems in themselves. The problem lies with the individual's use of drugs to assist adjustments within his own personality made necessary by the nature of his surrounding cultural or environmental frustrations and pressures. The program we propose, combined with a revision of present drug laws, would concern itself in a more realistic manner with the drugs, the individual, and the individual's environment. We wish to place final emphasis on the fact that this program is only one idea. It is our conception of what can be done in a social problem area where changes are needed very badly. A final question: What of "The Family" graduate who is resocialized, ready for a meaningful nonchemical existence, and returns to a society in which he finds little meaning? It may be only an idealistic hope that a humanistic approach to drug related problems could further a needed reevaluation and restructuring of our present society in a more meaningful direction.

Through the window of our minds
eye to you
What is needed is not what should
or could be
But the dream of what has not yet
been
The issue truly is one of sanity

CONCLUSIONS

The following is a list of several specific proposals directed towards those who are in a position to initiate needed changes.

1. Education

After fifteen or sixteen years of schooling we can state clearly that there is little, if any, rational drug education in the American school system. The basis for drug education material made available to the public and found in the schools has been emotional irrationality. The extent of this education is limited and its effects are insignificant. In fact, drug education has not yet begun.

Drug education programs must be established—*now*. They must reach from the students in elementary school to their frightened parents. These programs must present rationally the pros and cons involved in the use of all types of drugs. Full-time positions for drug counselors should be established in junior and senior high schools and colleges. These informed individuals must offer reasonable advice on all aspects of drug use to those who wish it. The basis for an educational program should be obtained from the advice and opinions given by individuals who have used the drugs concerned. The purpose of drug education must be to enable every person to make his own decision, based on realistic factual information, as to whether he wants to use a particular drug.

2. Specific Proposals for New Drug Laws

Any individual who admits himself for treatment concerning a drug abuse problem *must* be assured total freedom from arrest or prosecution.

Any individual should be allowed to possess, manufacture, and *give away* any drug.

Drug use should be removed from the spectrum of "crimes without victims." Legislators must be encouraged to base all future drug laws on scientific fact—not on emotionality. Emotionality in drug laws will only bring antithetic reactions from those who are using drugs. The present system of drug control laws is, quite obviously, ineffective in its attempt to convince young people not to use drugs.

3. Drugs and Society

Finally the editors feel that there are, in our society, a number of pervasive social attitudes which, increasingly, are making America a "drug prone" society. Many Americans feel alienated from society, from their jobs, and from their peers. Many are pessimistic, many feel socially ineffective, many sense that they have little control over their government. Americans are seeking new ways to express their individuality—to show that they *are* somebody, somebody that matters. Drug use is one way of expressing individuality, but it is certainly not the only way and probably not the best way. Society must change its priorities if Americans are to discover that life can be interesting and involving without the artificial stimulation which drugs provide.

A RATHER SPECIAL EDITORS' BIBLIOGRAPHY

Burroughs, William (with Allen Ginsberg), *The Yage Letters*, $1.25, City Lights. This book is a description of trips to South America in search of the hallucinogenic vine yage and the experiences encountered while under the influence of this plant. Burroughs is a long time drug user and (according to his pupils) intellectual guru to Ginsberg, Jack Kerouac, and others.

Carrol, Lewis, *Alice in Wonderland* and *Through the Looking Glass* (available in a number of low-priced paper editions). Anyone who has read these books recently will have no trouble understanding why "Alice" was a favorite name in the Haight-Ashbury or why one of the Jefferson Airplane's biggest hit records was called "White Rabbit." Carrol's fantasy world is full of parallels to the world of hallucinogenic drugs.

Castaneda, Carlos, *The Teachings of Don Juan: a Yaqui Way of Knowledge*, $.95, Ballantine. This is the story of a UCLA anthropology student who found himself becoming the disciple of a Mexican Indian "man of wisdom," whose primary method of teaching was the use of various vision inducing plants. The story is unique in that it offers the master-pupil tradition in a Western (and modern) setting.

Ginsberg, Allen, *Empty Mirror: Early Poems*, $1.25, Corinth; *Howl and Other Poems*, $1.00, City Lights; *Kaddish and Other Poems*, $1.50, City Lights; *Reality Sandwich*, $1.50, City Lights; *Planet News*, $2.00, City Lights. Ginsberg is important not only as a poet but also as the most popular of those writing about drug-induced "mystical" experiences and other present day trends. One might look at the poems "Howl" (written under mescaline), "Laughing Gas" (nitrous oxide, the drug of Coleridge's circle), and "Wales Visitation" (LSD).

Hesse, Herman, *Demian*, $.95, Bantam; *Journey to the East*, $1.45, Noonday; *Siddhartha*, $1.25, New Directions; *Steppenwolf*, $1.25, Bantam; *Magister Ludi*. Hesse does not deal directly with drug use, but all his works (only his best known are listed here) are concerned with the human mind reaching for "enlightenment." *Steppenwolf* has been called a "completely psychedelic" book and contains lines and passages that very closely resemble what people like Timothy Leary and the Beatles were to say some years later.

Huxley, Aldous, *The Doors of Perception, Heaven and Hell*, $1.45, Har-Row; *Island*, $1.25, Bantam. Huxley was perhaps the first major public figure of our time to write about personal drug experiences of a "mystical" nature. *The Doors of Perception* is an account of experiments with mescaline. In *Island*, his last novel, Huxley creates a World in which "mind-expanding" drugs, pieces of Eastern religion, communal parenthood, and technology form the basis of a utopian society. Alan Watts has called it the summation of his writing career.

Kerouac, John (Jack), *On the Road,*

$.95, Signet; *The Subterraneans*, Evergreen; *The Dharma Bums* (out of print at this time, but worth finding); *Desolation Angels; The Scripture of the Golden Eternity*, $.95, Corinth. All of Kerouac's books deal, to one degree or another, with drug use and the search for religious fulfillment. *On the Road* describes the lives of Kerouac, Ginsberg, Neal Cassidy, and others who led the way for what was to later culminate in the "hippy" movement. *The Subterraneans* and *The Dharma Bums* (which introduced the poet Gary Snyder) describe "beat" life in Berkeley and San Francisco. *Desolation Angels* is a chronicle of Kerouac's adventures and times, and *The Scripture of the Golden Eternity* is an interesting poem-book of "mystical" content.

Kesey, Ken, *One Flew Over the Cuckoo's Nest*, $.95, Signet. The leader of the California branch (as opposed to Leary's Eastern school) of LSD users sets down here the basis for an "action" way to personal fulfillment (as opposed to one of meditation). Portions of this inspiring first novel are said to have been conceived while under the influence of drugs.

Leary, Timothy, *High Priest*, $2.95, College Notes & Texts. This is the story of the early drug experiences of the man whose name came to be linked publicly more than anyone else's with the LSD movement. It is an interesting story for anyone who thinks Leary just popped on the scene a ready-made public guru. Leary is also the author of *The Psychedelic Experience* and *Psychedelic Prayers* (regarded as manuals of LSD use), *The Politics of Ecstasy*, various articles in the *Psychedelic Review*, and others.

Reps, Paul, *Zen Flesh, Zen Bones*, Anchor. This is an interesting book for the mystically or Eastern minded reader in which Reps, an American by birth, relates some of the tales, sayings, and anecdotes from the tradition of Zen Buddhism.

Rubin, Jerry, *Do It!* $2.45, Simon and Schuster. Probably the best known of today's youthful leaders writes here about his personal "transformation" and attempts to get the reader into the mind of many of today's long-haired protesters.

Snyder, Gary, *The Back Country* (poems), $1.25, New Directions; *Earth House Hold* (essays), $1.95, New Directions. Gary Snyder is considered to be one of the finest young American poets and writes with authority on many of the fields currently popular in this country including Zen Buddhism, the wisdom of ancient India, American Indian lore, and the ecological crisis. Raised in the Pacific Northwest he was one of the main movers of the "beat" era, has done graduate work in anthropology and linguistics, has translated several Chinese and Japanese poets, and has spent several years in Japan studying Zen.

Waley, Arthur, *The Way and Its Power: A Study of the Tao Te Ching*, Evergreen. Waley has translated a great deal of philosophical and religious writing of the East, particularly ancient China, and has also written several books about those aspects of Eastern thought. The *Tao Te Ching*, traditionally connected with Lao Tse, is one of the principal works of Ancient China and is one of the foundations and prized flowerings of Taoism.

Watts, Alan, *Psychotherapy, East and West*, .95, Ballantine; *Nature, Man and Woman*, $1.65, Vintage; *The Joyous Cosmology*, $1.45 Vintage; *The Book: On the Taboo Against Knowing Who You Are*, .95, Collier/Macmillan. These are just four of Watts' many works most of which attempt to transcribe into modern Western terms the wisdom and myths of the ancient East, particularly the teachings of the Vedas, the backbone of the philosophies of India. Watts brings with him a thorough scholarly background and a clear writing style. *Psychotherapy: East and West* compares the wisdom "masters" of the East with Western psychoanalysis; *Nature, Man and Woman* deals with the relationship between man, his mate, and the world around him and how these relationships sometimes become more like alienations; *The Joyous Cosmology* talks about how mind-expanding drugs fit into the "enlightenment" tradition; and *The Book* is an up-to-date rendering of the Vedic myth of how and why we are all here.

Wilhelm, Richard, and Cary Baynes, trans., *I Ching; or the Book of Changes*, $6.00, Princeton University Press. Along with the *Tao Te Ching*, the *I Ching* is one of the main texts of Taoism, "the middle way."

Wolfe, Tom, *The Electric Kool-Aid Acid Test*, $1.25, Bantam. This is a fast-paced account of the early days of Ken Kesey and the Merry Pranksters, ranging from Kesey's days as a "promising young novelist" at Stanford to his arrests on marijuana possession charges. A story that few knew was unfolding at the time, it contains such characters as Mountain Girl, Speed Limit, and Captain Trips and deals with the genesis of much of what was to evolve as the Haight-Ashbury world of light shows, acid-rock, and long-haired costumed LSD trippers.

A BRIEF LISTING OF SOURCES OF INFORMATION ON THE DRUG CULTURE

The Beatles, "Revolver," "Sgt. Pepper's Lonely Hearts Club Band," "Magical Mystery Tour," and "Yellow Submarine." The Beatles became the most popular of all musical groups that young people (or "turned-on" people) listened to and were by far the most influencial in spreading the messages about what was going on. The albums listed here contain music directly associated with the drug and religious movements; in particular, "Sgt. Pepper" is said to have many allusions to LSD and many of the songs composed by George Harrison show his interest in things Indian and mystical.

"Eureka: the Great Poster Craze." A collection of prints of some of the "psychedelic" posters which became, along with music, one of the main art forms of the "hippy" movement.

The Family Dog. This "tribe" of "long-hairs," based in or around San Francisco, were associated with the production of the first light/sound shows which are such an integral part of the hip scene today. These shows provide a place of social meeting, live musical entertainment, and a visual show that many enjoy while under the influence of hallucinogenic drugs. At the time of this writing The Family Dog is still operating a dance hall on the Great Highway, near the ocean beach in San Francisco.

The Grateful Dead. This is the favorite band of San Francisco "hippies" and the foremost practitioners of what is called acid-rock. They have been associated since the "early days" with the Ken Kesey group and with the light/sound shows and they popularized the concept of free concerts among rock groups. Their lead guitarist, Jerry Garcia, was a major force in the birth of the "San Francisco sound" and was something of a hero in the Haight days. Their music has most strength when listened to "live," but there are also albums available on the Warner label: "The Grateful Dead," "Anthem of the Sun," "Aoxomoxoa," and "LIVE/DEAD."

Indian Music. Ravi Shankar in particular popularized Indian music among the young and "turned-on" during the 1960s. This music was found to have a structure and flow which was a pleasant complement to the drug state.

Marvel Comics. *Captain America, The Fantastic Four, The Hulk*, and other comics of the Marvel series have become popular among the hip (and are mentioned as being a favorite of Ken Kesey's in Tom Wolfe's book) because of their incredibly idealized plot and dialogue which can be interpreted as an allegory of the whole American way of life.

The Realist. A 1969 issue of this always different and "irreverant" Paul Krasner publication contains an informative piece by Mr. Hugh Romney (formerly one of the Merry Pranksters of the Kesey days) on "The Hog Farm," a uniquely American phenomenon consisting of primarily young people who live on colorfully painted (and named) buses constantly in motion and who live from one day (or one "trip") to the next, trusting in the present to take care of the future. Comes out of NY.

Zap Comics. Along with *Snatch,
Yellow Dog,* and other similar
publications, *Zap* comics employs
many of the artists who did the
original dance posters as well as
others. They are created by and directed to the hip community. Their
publication is sporadic and they
are best found wherever posters,
underground newspapers, and
similar matter is being sold.
You're on your own now.

The Encounter Group Boom

EDITED BY:

Susan Fantus   Sandy Kallerup
Roy R. Harmon   Caryl Sutton

INTRODUCTION

In the last few years encounter
groups have multiplied at an exponential rate. This rush toward
encounter groups is a signal we
cannot ignore of a need in our
society for more intimate and
honest communication and, even
more basically, of the need for
help (and information) in learning the skills which enable one to
connect with other people. This
hunger is not answered by the institutions of our society which
frustrate and anger our generation
with their irrelevancy, hypocrisy,
and disregard for our needs for
real communication. It is far from
a coincidence that in Berkeley,
where we have one of the largest
and most impersonal educational
factories, encounter groups have
found a most fertile breeding
ground. Other antiquated institutions—the Church, school clubs,
and living groups such as fraternities and sororities—for the most
part no longer fulfill these needs
for communication (if, indeed,
they ever did). We have been
forced to create out of this
vacuum a new structure to provide the possibility for intimacy—
the encounter group.

In studying the encounter group
boom, we, the editors, have sorted
through our mixed feelings towards this popular phenomenon,
only to express doubts as to the
real value of groups. The groups
seem to offer the individual sudden awareness and personal
change, not taking into account
his many years of living that have
shaped his feelings and reactions.
The hard-sell campaign promises
much with such phrases as increased awareness, personal
growth, a new awakening, a real
experience of communication. The
predictions are many and varied
as to the prospective future and
profitable returns of the encounter
group. But what is the reality?
How "real" is the experience?
How honest and sincere? Solution
or catharsis?

There are indications that the
popularity of encounter groups
may be starting to lag. Many people have become disillusioned
when they find that promises of
instant intimacy are not fulfilled
and that what is labeled Honest is
not always. There is revulsion
toward the people who grossly
capitalize on personal needs by
charging exorbitant prices for
group experiences. Enthusiasm is
dampened by the emotional elitism of people who have learned to
be facile at playing the encounter
group games, especially those who
encounter for entertainment without concern for the consequences
of their actions. Some people find
that they don't really want to be
Intense every moment of their
lives, that some things should be
treated with humor and not everything need be taken very seriously.
Others have rediscovered their
needs for privacy. But these rum-
blings have to do with the workings of encounter groups which
could be straightened out.

In an ideal situation the encounter group can help the individual in many ways. It can allow
him to share his confusion,
alienation, and insecurity. It can
provide the medium to explore
beneath the superficiality of his
everyday acquaintances to approach more intimate relationships. It can aid him on a journey
through his unexplored inner
space. It can help him discover his
identity in a society that seems to
ignore his need for individualiza-
tion.

We will present many views on
the encounter group boom, ranging from description to criticism,
satire to ideas for potential use.
Keep in mind the conflict between
the ideals of the encounter group
and the in-practice reality. We begin with a general overview and
description of the encounter group
movement in the article by Ted
Rakstis, followed by more comments about the growth of encounter groups by Lieberman, Yalom
and Miles, Kuehn and Crinella,
and Havemann.

8.1

Sensitivity Training: Fad, Fraud, or New Frontier?

Ted J. Rakstis

High on a mountainside overlook-
ing the Pacific Ocean in northern
California, 25 strangers gather at
the Esalen Institute for a five-day
adventure into "self-discovery." At
the outset, several members of the
group are openly hostile. But after
a week of nude sulphur baths,
dream analysis, and pull-no-
punches dialogues, the one-time
adversaries warmly embrace and
leave filled with at least temporary
love for each other and the world.

In a Chicago suburb, 65 people
walk in off the street and pay $6
each to attend a three-hour "microlab" conducted by an amateur
psychologist who assures them
that they will "find a beautiful
feeling, a sense of being connected to their fellow man." They
touch one another's faces, grope
around while blindfolded, and lie
in a circle and ramble on about
the happiest moment in their
lives.

And in Boston, a dozen hard-
bitten businessmen meet for three
days under the guidance of an
expert in group dynamics. Following a test to measure their attitudes toward group inclusion,

Reprinted by permission from
Today's Health, published by the
American Medical Association, Janu-
ary, 1970.

affection, and the need to control, one executive's profile nails him as a corporate tyrant. A subordinate tells him bluntly: "It's no wonder we can't communicate on the job—you're uptight and you bug everyone around you."

In one form or another, all these people are undergoing sensitivity training, an anything-goes human relations movement whose major precepts are "do your own thing" and "tell it like it is." Sensitivity training sessions also are known as encounter groups, personal growth labs, T-groups ("T" for training), awareness experience, confrontation groups, training laboratories, organizational development, and, collectively, the human potential movement. Whatever it may be called, the phenomenon is attracting hundreds of thousands of Americans of all ages to programs run by persons who may be either skilled professionals or rank amateurs.

The tangle of sensitivity training nomenclature suggests that not even the experts can clearly define it. It incorporates elements of psychiatry, sociology, philosophy, education, religion, and community organization, and its practitioners number people from these and other fields. Depending upon his professional background and personal bias, each person who conducts a sensitivity group has a different focus.

Most sensitivity sessions, however, share several common attributes. The programs are designed to place people in a group situation. Through a mixture of physical contact games and no-holds-barred discussions about each other's strengths and failures, each group member hopefully will feel less constricted. He will become more open, readily able to understand himself and others. If he is a member of an organization, it may enable him to become a more persuasive and influential participant in group decisions.

But these goals can be achieved only if the person is willing to accept the rules of the group and its trainer. He must *want* to be sensitized and must be prepared to deal with the frank criticism that the group may engender. Unless he is willing to "open up," he will be wasting his time and may run the risk of psychological punishment. In short, sensitivity training is not for everyone.

Sensitivity training has been around since 1947, when three social psychologists formed an organization bearing the cumbersome title of National Training Laboratories Institute for Applied Behavioral Science (NTL). Yet only in the past three years has the movement really begun to explode. "Growth centers," emulating the highly experimental work of Esalen Institute, now are found throughout the nation, and countless independent entrepreneurs are running sessions that seek to "turn on" participants through sensory awareness rather than drugs.

During a time when Americans are torn with conflict and beset by fear, loneliness, and alienation, many are searching for something of meaning. Says Thomas Bennett, Ph.D., director of graduate studies for George Williams College and a fellow of NTL: "In our culture, it's extremely difficult to find experiences with other people which provide a degree of freedom and intimacy and a real opportunity to deal with persons at a fairly intense level. A lot of that has led to the growth in sensitivity training."

The supporters of sensitivity training call it a new frontier in social psychology, a means of making people more innovative, honest, trusting, and free. It is not a form of psychoanalysis, they say, but a significant outgrowth of adult education rooted in the emotions rather than the intellect. Numerous organizations—corporations, universities, churches, government agencies—view it as a method of helping people to break the communication barrier.

Skeptics term it "the acidless trip" or "instant intimacy." Right-wing political groups have tried to link sensitivity training with Communism, brainwashing, and sexual promiscuity. More responsible critics, including some in the medical profession, question the wisdom of stripping a person's emotions to the core in a group setting. They challenge the use of unskilled trainers, the frequent absence of pre-screening to keep psychotics out of the programs, and the problem of returning to an essentially insensitive world after an emotion-charged group experience.

The sensitivity training boom has come so quickly and assumes so many forms that most of the experts have been caught off guard. Neither the American Psychiatric Association nor the American Psychological Association has an official position, and the American Medical Association's Council on Mental Health offers this middle-of-the-road viewpoint:

"Although sensitivity training is an issue of current concern, it is not an accepted part of medical practice. The Council believes that the procedures employed are not well enough defined to lend themselves to objective evaluation. It urges that particular caution be taken against participating in sessions conducted by leaders who are not professionally trained and qualified, in view of reports of psychotic and neurotic sequelae [consequences]."

It is difficult, however, to define "qualified trainer." At present, there are no laws controlling trainer certification. National Training Laboratories, based in Washington, D.C., with several branch offices across the nation, has the most stringent standards. NTL requires that its trainers have a Ph.D. or master's degree in psychology, social work, or one of the other related "helping professions" and that trainer candidates take advanced laboratory training. But NTL represents only one branch of the field. Some "trainers" have virtually no education whatever. Says one: "Who needs a degree? I know I'm a good trainer because I've got a 'gut' feeling for people."

The motivations of persons enrolling in sensitivity groups vary as widely as the caliber of the trainers. Some are making an honest attempt to discover themselves; others want a quick emotional "high" and a chance to meet members of the opposite sex; many attend only because their job requires it. A few use it as a cheap substitute for group psychotherapy. Oron P. South, Ph.D., director of the Midwest Group for Human Resources, a division of NTL, warns: "This is learning, not therapy. It is not intended for sick people, but for the 'normal neurotic' who wants to get more out of his relations with people."

Just as the quality of programs and trainers defies easy categorization, "sensitivity training" in itself is an omnibus label that means little. Despite the profusion of names and the frequent overlapping of techniques, there are really three distinct styles.

One is the encounter group, sometimes called a "personal growth lab," which focuses on the individual and seeks to instill in him a sense of self-awareness. Since it relies heavily on nonverbal ("touch and feel") methods, this is actually sensitivity training in the most commonly accepted use of the term.

The T-group, an older method,

uses more verbal exercises and emphasizes the "here and now"— the relationship of each group member to what is happening in the group at that particular time. It allows the participant to know what others think of him, to be granted the wish once expressed by Robert Burns: "Oh wad some power the giftie gie us To see oursels as others see us!"

A third basic form is a T-group offshoot known as organizational development. Somewhat less personal than either the encounter session or the T-group consisting of strangers, its goal is to help members of an organized body—a business, school, or church—learn to work better as a team.

There also are several different time lengths for sensitivity programs. The shortest form is a three-hour "microlab." More often, encounter or T-group labs run from two days to two or more weeks, and yet another version is the "marathon," a continuous, exhaustive session that may last for 24 or 48 consecutive hours. Because of the emotional and physical fatigue that may result, NTL and most other responsible training groups usually avoid the marathon.

Esalen Institute, at Big Sur, California, developed the encounter method. Founded in 1962 by Michael Murphy, a 39-year-old psychology graduate of Stanford University, Esalen attracts some 25,000 awareness seekers each year to Big Sur and a branch in San Francisco. At Big Sur, the site of a former health spa, 75 people pay $60 each to attend weekend meetings, and 25 more spend up to $175 on in-depth, five-day sessions.

The Esalen pilgrims are a mixed lot—business and professional people, teachers, movie stars, housewives, hippies. Unlike NTL, Esalen conducts no programs for organizations. "You do things in a personal growth lab that you could never try with a bunch of IBM executives," explains Stuart Miller, Ph.D., the Institute's vice president.

Philosophy, psychology, the meditative aspects of Eastern religions—these and dozens of other approaches are tried at Esalen. "Our techniques demand the total involvement of participants and, like the experiences of an LSD trip, are intensely personal and extremely difficult to describe in conventional language," says Murphy. Miller further terms Esalen as "experiential and experimental, a forum for the exploration of human potential."

The Esalen enrollee may find himself hugging strangers of both sexes, pounding pillows to release aggressions, telling the group his deepest secrets, acting out all the characters in his dreams, or taking an imaginary trip through his own body and relating the experience. William Schutz, Ph.D., one of the Institute's leading figures, says that the goal is to find "joy," and, appropriately, he has written a book titled *Joy*.

The most controversial phase of the Esalen program has been its mixed nude bathing, an idea conceived in 1967 by Paul Bindrim, a Los Angeles psychologist. Bindrim, who emphasizes that his approach is totally nonsexual, explains: "If a participant disrobes physically, he might gain the freedom to also disrobe emotionally." Since Bindrim introduced the nude swimming at Esalen, he has traveled extensively to other growth centers across the nation to carry on similar programs.

Persons who have gone to Esalen often say they were wary and nervous when the sessions began. The most antagonistic members of some groups frequently find Schutz placing them in a situation of direct physical or verbal confrontation. In most cases, the hostility melts into trust or even affection. By the end of a week, says one writer who entered Esalen full of doubt, "I found myself hugging everyone, behaving like the idiots I had noticed on first arriving."

Esalen has 15 full-time associates on its staff. Ten have advanced degrees, but several never have graduated from high school. "We consider experience, talent, and creativity far more important than formal education," says Stuart Miller. Similarly, the outsiders who come to Esalen to conduct workshops may be psychotherapists, historians, Hindu mystics, or LSD apostles.

Some 90 growth centers—Miller calls them "little Esalens"—have sprung up across the United States. A year ago, there were only 40, and five years ago they were almost unknown. Among them are Kairos, in San Diego; Oasis, in Chicago; Espiritu, in Houston; and the Center for the Whole Person, in Philadelphia. Many were founded by persons trained at Esalen and closely follow the Big Sur methods.

A number of solo practitioners also are operating encounter groups. One such man is Jorge Rosner, a Chicagoan who tries to help people overcome their "mini-

fears" through weekly three-hour "Adventures Into Being" at a place called The Center. Rosner, a product of Esalen, admits that he has no degree but feels that his background in experimental theater qualifies him as a trainer.

"In this field, a college education is not important," he maintains. "People with degrees get too hung up on intellectual aspects. Psychiatrists, particularly, are used to working with people on a one-to-one basis and can't get with it in a group situation."

Esalen and its disciples are part of the free-wheeling, eclectic West Coast encounter movement. The East Coast school, exemplified by National Training Laboratories, is more scientific, oriented toward research and organizational work, insistent upon education and experience in its trainers. NTL is the father of the T-group.

In a sense, the T-group is as unstructured as the encounter group. There is no agenda; the leader lets the group swing on its own momentum. The session revolves around the "here and now" rather than the "then and there." Group members, usually 10 or 12 in number, often know each other only by their first names. Their occupations, home problems, and childhood experiences are irrelevant. What matters is what is happening within the group.

Like encounter groups, T-groups often play many nonverbal games. People may shout, crawl around the floor, chant arm in arm, or hug each other. But there also is considerable talk, centered upon how the group is behaving. For those who enjoy cocktail banter, a T-group experience can be painful. Masks are torn away and emotions exposed; a person may face a torrent of comments like, "I perceive that you're acting phony," or "You're a nonperson; you really turn me off."

The T-group has a peculiar lingo, a mixture of hippie talk and social science jargon. People are always "hungup" or "uptight," trying to discover "where I'm at." They don't talk; they "have a dyad." In one exercise, half the group listens to the others and then gives its impression of what it has heard. But this is not talking and criticizing—it is known as "input" and "feedback." (Some sophisticated T-groups get "feedback" through videotaped replays.)

Despite the esoteric terminology, the T-group to some extent shares with its cousin, the encounter group, a basic disdain for intellectual solutions. Trainers speak about a need to elevate the "affective domain" over the "cognitive domain," to trust the senses more and the intellect less. A common T-group remark is: "Don't *think—feel!*"

The T-group theory is that criticism will develop honesty, self-understanding, and trust in others. However, it also can result in conflict, and for this reason a skilled trainer is a requisite. Jerry Spiegel, an active NTL trainer in Chicago, observes: "In most cases, a poor trainer will simply create a dull group. But there's always the chance that two people will really get into a major conflict—or that a participant may be on the verge of real emotional difficulty—so the trainer must be prepared to intervene. T-group training is like fire. It can warm the house and make it comfortable, or it can burn the damn thing down."

Besides drawing together an assortment of strangers, the T-group also can be used as a training tool for homogeneous groups. Spiegel's wife, Eleanor, who also is an NTL trainer, has been involved in working with a series of all-female T-groups where the major emphasis has been issues of femininity. The techniques range from the more nonverbal aspects of sensitivity training to written tests that evaluate such perceptions as the need for affection. Many NTL trainers also conduct sessions for married couples, single people, and family groups.

Nearly 75 percent of the work of most NTL trainers is with organizations, and business has become a strong booster of T-group learning, which it sometimes terms organizational development. Among the companies that have sponsored programs for their employees are General Electric, Standard Oil of New Jersey, Syntex Laboratories, Humble Oil and Refining, and Texas Instruments. One of the corporate pioneers is TRW, Inc., a Cleveland aerospace contractor that has offered training to executives in its four divisions since 1963. Some companies force their employees into T-groups. TRW makes attendance optional, yet about 90 percent of those who are eligible accept.

"You've got to make T-group instruction voluntary," says Thomas A. Wickes, Ph.D., director of personnel development for TRW and an NTL trainer. "This program is not for everyone, and the guy who is compelled to attend is likely to resist. He may even suffer emo-

tional damage. We also give our men three or four 'checkout' points when they can drop out. T-groups make our men more human executives. But, unfortunately, those who benefit the most are the ones who need it the least . . . and vice versa."

Many companies have discovered that T-group experience enables executives to talk matters out more freely. In an era in which the autocratic and arbitrary rule of a few men at the top of the corporate pyramid has given way to consensus decisions made by committees, the T-group is designed to bring forth the best skills that each man can contribute.

One T-group conceptualization describes personality traits and shows that most people fall into one of three categories—the "Tough Battler," the "Friendly Helper," and the "Objective Thinker." The lesson is that any decision-making group needs each of these types if it is to function as a representative body. Through T-groups, companies have uncovered men who are highly valuable but who previously were never noticed and thus never consulted.

Besides helping to build functional management teams, business has found the T-group useful in reducing potential employee conflict. When Scott Paper Company hired 30 disadvantaged persons—primarily black—for its plant in Chester, Pennsylvania, it put 300 workers through 16 hours of T-group training to help them understand the problems of slum-dwellers. Company officials later said that the program averted what could have been an explosive transition.

Schools have employed the T-group for similar purposes. In Pontiac, Michigan, a community filled with racial tension, the school board recently allocated $25,000 for a program for parents, students, teachers, and administrators throughout the school system. After black students boycotted Proviso East High School in Maywood, Illinois, early in 1969, NTL was called in to organize a teacher-student lab. "The NTL project opened up lines of communication so that students and teachers began talking to each other," notes one Proviso East teacher. "Things came out in the open."

State and municipal bodies—including the police forces in Los Angeles, Houston, and Grand Rapids, Michigan—have experimented with T-groups. Some phy-

sicians are trying it as a means of improving patient relationships, and the University of Alabama Medical Center recently began an organizational program for some 100 medical personnel. Many people in the creative arts, notably the theater, have turned to T-groups and encounter programs.

A number of churchmen also are adopting the technique. In Chicago, for example, the Rev. Owen F. McAteer, associate pastor of St. Dorothy's Catholic Church, has organized a group of 25 priests and nuns and set up sensitivity training under the auspices of the Archdiocese of Chicago. "The program is helping nuns and priests to communicate better with their parishioners, to come down a bit off their pedestals," says Father McAteer. "This can be one of the most effective of all methods to achieve the goals of Christianity."

As sensitivity training spreads throughout America, attitudes polarize. Proponents call it one of the major learning discoveries of this century, but opposition develops on many fronts. It has become a prime target of the same ultra-conservative groups that oppose sex education in the schools, such as the John Birch Society and the American Independent Party. A Chicago group called Let Freedom Ring recently issued a manifesto branding sensitivity training as "a Communist brainwashing technique" and "a grotesque, mind-bending program." Yet not all the critics are of this fanatical breed; even responsible medical men are troubled by abuses.

At a school district in Jackson, Michigan, a sensitivity training program that mixed teachers with teen-agers became so controversial that the Michigan State Medical Society launched a statewide study. The Society's Committee on Mental Health, in probably the strongest statement yet issued by a major American medical body, concluded that sensitivity training is acceptable only when conducted by professionals in the field of mental health.

"These programs are being run by unskilled and unqualified lay individuals," declares Benjamin Jeffries, M.D., a Detroit psychiatrist who is chairman of the committee. "As a result, participants are experiencing emotional problems beyond their capacity to control. I personally feel that the only people who should be doing this type of training are psychiatrists, psychologists, and psychiatric social workers."

The medical profession is sharply divided over whether encounter and T-groups actually constitute psychiatry in disguise. Howard P. Rome, M.D., senior consultant and professor of psychiatry at the Mayo Graduate School of Medicine and a member of the AMA Council on Mental Health, feels that sensitivity training is outside the field of medicine.

"People in the behavioral sciences other than psychiatry are most valuable in conducting these programs," Doctor Rome asserts. "With the nation facing a critical health manpower shortage, we must use all available resources."

NTL officials state that less than one percent of the persons who have been in their sessions have suffered psychological damage and that most of those already had emotional problems. Although most reputable trainers try to screen out persons with psychiatric disorders, some occasionally slip through. When an unqualified trainer is presiding, the problem can become acute.

The vice president of one Midwest corporation suffered a complete mental breakdown in a T-group and was forced to enter a hospital. In New York, a mentally ill woman enrolled in a growth center and soon started to organize her own sessions. And in Evanston, Illinois, after an untrained high school teacher tried to sensitize his students, one girl went into screaming hysterics and a boy later was found wandering the streets in a stupor.

"Sensitivity training can all too easily become insensitivity training," contends Dana L. Farnsworth, M.D., director of health services for Harvard University and chairman of the AMA Council on Mental Health. "There can be great danger for the person who has psychotic difficulties or who is involved in any sort of acute crisis."

Moreover, laboratory training is viewed by most experts as essentially a program for adults. In many communities, some of the strongest opposition to T-groups has come after teachers participated with youths and trainers utilized some of the more deeply personal techniques of sensitivity training. "When teen-agers are involved, you've got to be very careful in what you do," says NTL trainer Jerry Spiegel. "A T-group is a learning process, not a way to get an emotional kick."

Perhaps the greatest potential danger occurs when an inexperi-enced person who has been "turned on" at a session tries to help others find the same route. So far, there is little evidence of outright fraud in the sensitivity training field, but there is a proliferation of misguided do-gooders. A number of teachers, for example, have been known to begin programs for their students on the basis of a single weekend's encounter experience. Their intentions may have been honest, but the results sometimes were disastrous. As Doctor Farnsworth puts it: "Compassion without competence soon becomes quackery."

Another major problem is the inability of many people to cope with an insensitive society once they have left the sanctuary of the group. The T-group hangover has been particularly troublesome for business. A *Wall Street Journal* survey of companies sponsoring T-groups reported that many persons have returned to their jobs disillusioned with office policies and personnel, tried for a more open environment, and then were either fired or quit in frustration. Although a T-group may alter an individual's personality, it is likely to have little effect upon the organization he works for.

The encounter session or T-group can become an emotional crutch for the person who finds it difficult to adjust to the world around him. "You see a number of people coming back year after year; they're called T-group bums," says Morton Lieberman, Ph.D., associate professor of psychiatry at the University of Chicago. "They have a strong need for this kind of relatedness and they aren't getting it outside in real life."

There is also mixed opinion over whether people derive any meaningful long-term benefits from laboratory training. Although NTL claims that two-thirds of the persons who have taken T-group instruction have improved their skills, there as yet are no scientific studies to support this. It is highly doubtful whether sensitivity training can conquer both heredity and environment and create a new person, but it can make him think and perhaps modify his behavior.

"T-groups can't change your personality," Jerry Spiegel observes. "However, they can make you acutely aware of the impact you have on others—and their impact on you. The training session furnishes you with the information, the sort of things your friends won't tell you. What you do with that information is up to you."

For good or ill, sensitivity training appears to be more than a mere passing fad. In its more bizarre forms, as a means of providing thrill seekers with a quick emotional jolt, it may fade into obscurity once the novelty has worn off and the publicity has subsided. But as a means of learning to cope in a group, of discovering and capitalizing upon hidden inner strengths, its potential appears limitless.

"Sensitivity training will settle down and find its rightful place," Doctor Rome predicts. "Hopefully, we will see the day when instruction in human relations will be as much a part of the school curriculum as the three R's. When properly used, sensitivity training can help to educate our young people to live in a pluralistic society as better, more understanding citizens. It can be a powerful tool in creating a better world."

8.2
Encounter Groups as a Social Movement

Morton A. Lieberman
Irvin D. Yalom
Matthew B. Miles

The force propelling us to the present inquiry was the explosive expansion of such groups which may literally be involving tens of thousands of people each year. The growth of the encounter group movement seemed to promise too much potential for the hypotheses about broad-scale social developments to be left unstudied. What are encounter groups? Why are they "catching on"? What do they do for participants? How does the movement relate to other social processes and other dimensions of social change? As mental health professionals further questions of whether and in what ways this group movement offers a new system of service and how it relates to other service forms are more than academic to us.

Reprinted by permission of the authors from "The Group Experience Project: A Comparison of Ten Encounter Technologies," *Encounter: Confrontations in Self and Interpersonal Awareness*, New York, Macmillan, forthcoming.

(Throughout history small groups have flourished in times of rapid social change when old values and behavior patterns were no longer working and individuals were forced to reexamine and redefine their value systems. Such groups have always served as important healing agents;) from the beginning of history, groups have been used to inspire hope, increase morale, offer emotional support, induce serenity, renew confidence in the benevolence of the universe, and thus counteract psychic and many bodily ills. Religious healers have always relied heavily on group forces, but when healing passed from the priesthood to the secular professions, the conscious use of group forces fell into a decline concomitant with the increasing reverence of the doctor-patient relationship. (The encounter movement exists outside of the traditional help-giving institutions of society. Its strong egalitarian overtones may represent a reaction against many of the traditional institutional forms of help-giving.)

The encounter movement also has potent recreational aspects. Encounter groups are the verbal equivalent to sky diving—they are high-risk, high-contact endeavors. Encounter groups are controlled, regulated surprises; all participants share some image of what will unfold, but there is sufficient mystery about details to give a quality of danger or excitement.

The rapid growth of encounter groups, the bewildering variations in form and function, the infusion into established institutions of diverse natures, as well as the development of new institutions such as growth centers and "living room groups" add up to a picture of a vigorous social movement touching many facets of human endeavor. (We suspect that they may be a response to a pressing need in our culture.) The California milieu, the most potent incubator of encounter groups, exaggerates certain characteristics of contemporary American society— many Californians have few roots in the community, institutional or personal. Geographic and social mobility are the rule rather than the exception. The extended family is rarely represented; the stable primary family uncommon (one of two California marriages ends in divorce); the neighborhood or work group has diminished importance because the average Californian has arrived recently and is expected to leave soon. The neighborhood merchant and the family

doctor are rapidly disappearing and organized religion has become irrelevant to many young people. In short, the cultural institutions which have provided stability and intimacy are atrophying, without, of course, a concomitant decrease in human needs for these elements.

In the fall of 1968, we discovered at least 200 encounter groups operating in the Palo Alto area. Many of these groups have no institutional backing and recruit participants only by word of mouth. Teachers were leading encounter groups in the classroom; housewives were leading encounter groups in their homes for their friends or the friends of their adolescent offspring. Some groups had loose institutional affiliations: one free university offered an assortment of approximately 50 encounter groups every quarter; one highly-structured institution, Synanon, offers an astonishing number of groups known as "square games," for non-addicts (the Oakland Synanon branch alone had 1500 individuals participating weekly in groups and another 1000 on a waiting list). A very visible index of the encounter group movement is the rapid proliferation of "growth centers." Some 75 growth centers, many of them spin-offs modeled on the Esalen design, have arisen around the country. Many churches, particularly on the West Coast, have been almost "swamped" with encounter activities to the extent that some professional churchmen have expressed serious concern[1] about the number of ministers who have thrown off their ministerial robes to become full-time encounter leaders.

The encounter group may be viewed as a social oasis in which societal norms are explicitly shed. No longer must facades of adequacy, competence, self-sufficiency be borne. In fact, the group norms encourage the opposite behavior: members are rewarded for expressing self-doubts and unfulfilled longings for intimacy and nurturance. (The encounter group offers a unique form of intimacy—one which has no commitment to permanence.)

Members attend encounter groups not only for affective supplies but for "self-validation":

[1] Perhaps of even greater concern is the potential of encounter groups (unlike the bowling leagues) to compete directly with church function, insofar as both meet needs for communion.

they are intrigued by an opportunity which permits adults to expose themselves, to be examined and to be approved. A great majority of individuals, though functioning competently, have deep concerns about their adequacy: few other institutions offer an occasion for what appears to be a comprehensive examination of one's status as a human being.

8.3
Sensitivity Training: Interpersonal "Overkill" and Other Problems

John L. Kuehn and
Francis M. Crinella

There is a lesson to be learned from a well-known phenomenon in epidemiology that health professionals and other applied scientists might find useful to contemplate. Sometimes in eradicating a particular pathologic influence, whether at the level of microorganism, animal species, or human behavior, we run the risk of destroying the precarious balance of the biobehavioral system. An example of this is the recent experience of public health workers in Southeast Asia. These workers' effectiveness in destroying potentially dangerous reptiles has led to an ecologic imbalance, with an increase in the number of rats and a rise in the incidence of bubonic plague.

Overenthusiasm for any type of system intervention, including the various forms of group experience being touted as helpful for personal and societal "growth," delude both the candidates and practitioners, as we ever-hopeful Americans seek answers to complex problems, only to be confronted with ones that may be even less tractable.

The mental health professions have not been immune to this ofttimes destructive "true believerism," which can rapidly shift toward nonrational and contagious religious conversion experiences. Here again the revival meeting and the tent show are very much

Reprinted by permission from *The American Journal of Psychiatry*, 126, 6 (December, 1969), 108–109. Copyright 1969 by the American Psychiatric Association.

in the American tradition as a way to cope with the loneliness of our national experience. As mental health workers and physicians, we find it painful to remind ourselves of the not-so-remote excessive use of electroconvulsive shock, prefrontal leucotomy, and most recently the psycho-active drugs. . . .

We believe this ecologic consideration of potential "overkill" should be kept in mind by all those involving themselves in sensitivity training. This is not to say that small groups cannot be enormously useful (as are ECT and drugs) where the indications are rational *and explicit as to goals.*

Rosenbaum and many others have underscored the need for sound conceptualization, organized research, and thorough training in developing any program that presumably has value in terms of survival of the species, social utility, and the alleviation of human suffering. "There are no shortcuts, and enthusiasm is no substitute." (Max Rosenbaum, "Group Psychotherapy and Psychodrama," in B. Wolman, ed., *Handbook of Clinical Psychology,* New York, McGraw-Hill, 1965).

8.4
Alternatives to Analysis

Ernest Havemann

Out of the T group have risen the other kinds of shoulder rubbing and psyche baring, usually called encounter groups, that take place at Esalen and other centers and under the direction of individual leaders throughout the country. Whereas the members of T groups usually have a good deal in common in their working-day lives, the members of encounter groups usually do not; they get together haphazardly from all walks of life. What takes place, however, is quite similar to the activity of the T group. Members of encounter groups tend to let down their defenses, reveal their self-doubts and tell each other frankly what

Reprinted by permission of the Sterling Lord Agency. Excerpted from an article in *Playboy* Magazine, November, 1969. Copyright 1969 by Ernest Havemann.

they like and do not like about one another. There are occasional flare-ups of hostility and moments of deep affection. There is a good deal of laughter—also, to a greater extent than in T groups, a good deal of weeping.

Why are people so willing—even eager—to bare their souls to strangers? Dr. Rogers says it is a sign of the times, something that could never have happened at an earlier stage of history. "When a man is scrambling very hard to get his three meals a day," says Dr. Rogers, "he doesn't have time to feel alienated from his fellow human beings. Now that we have the affluent society, we do have the time and we realize that we are alone and lonely, lacking deep contacts with others. We begin to say, 'I wish there were someone I could talk to honestly; I wish someone cared about me.'" Charles Seashore, a psychologist with N.T.L., says, "There's a kind of immaturity and thwarted growth in all of us. As human beings, we have all kinds of potentialities—to be warm or stand-offish, loving or hostile, open or suspicious, enthusiastic or constrained, adventuresome or cautious, emotional or reserved. But our society rewards some of these traits and discourages others, and most of us wind up as adults with just one or two stereotyped responses that we display automatically to all the hundreds of different situations in which we find ourselves. The popularity of groups rests on the fact that most of us feel deprived; probably 85 to 95 percent of us feel that we're not as close to people as we'd like to be, or that we're not as open and honest about our feelings, or that we have an anxiety over submitting to or exercising authority, or that our lives are too boxed in and narrowly predictable from day to day. Since the group encourages intimacy, honesty and adventure, it's a great experience even if its effects are only temporary."

Is the group a form of therapy? Dr. Maslow says no: "Although I'm very impressed with groups, I don't think they can help with serious problems—only minor hang-ups. A neurosis just won't fade away at a T group or a weekend marathon." The N.T.L. staff is careful to call its aim not therapy but "personal learning and personal growth." Dr. Seashore points out that he himself once experienced what he considered a therapeutic breakthrough in a T group —but that it occurred in the 139th group he attended or conducted, a

figure hardly likely to be reached by nonprofessionals.

Dr. Rogers, on the other hand, has no doubt that the group is a form of therapy and a highly effective form, at that; he has come to believe that 20 hours in a group are more effective than 20 hours of one-to-one treatment. The secret of the group, he thinks, is that "it gives people permission to be helpful to one another"—a privilege that is not generally available in society and that is grasped eagerly and often with great skill, resulting in very much the same kind of support offered in client-centered therapy. In one way, says Dr. Rogers, the group is superior to client-centered therapy as he practiced it in the past; this is the fact that members of the group freely express their negative as well as their positive feelings toward one another. Thus, each person in the group is at times deeply liked and supported for his good qualities and, at other times, confronted with harsh criticism of the bad, a push-pull process that seems to speed awareness of the true self. If Dr. Rogers returned to one-to-one practice, he says, he would be very free to give his patients constant feedback on his inner reactions to them, pro or con.

Whether the encounter group should properly be called therapy or just a form of education, it certainly does *something* for people. At the Western Behavioral Sciences Institute, psychologists gathered interviews from 1000 people who had taken part in groups; these people agreed almost unanimously that they had greatly enjoyed the experience and had been profoundly influenced; typical comments were, "It was the most important thing that ever happened to me" and "It changed my whole life." What, exactly, about the group had produced this effect? As the psychologists had expected, the one thing mentioned most frequently was some particularly dramatic example of deep exchange of understanding and emotion between two or more members of the group —sometimes an incident in which they themselves had taken part, sometimes an incident that they had merely observed (another example, perhaps, of Dr. Bandura's learning through imitation). To the psychologists' surprise, however, these outstanding incidents did not necessarily involve the therapist who led the group; in fact, the therapist was responsible for no more of them than anybody else. To psychologist Richard Farson this suggested a strange possibility: To the extent that the encounter group is therapeutic, is it a form of therapy that requires no therapist? In other words, can a group succeed without a professional leader?

Dr. Farson's idea of experimenting with leaderless groups was opposed by every therapist he knew. Without professional guidance, he was warned, members of the group would quickly be at one another's throats. Nonetheless, he went ahead, though with extreme caution. The first leaderless group was watched anxiously by two professional therapists behind a one-way see-through mirror, ready to intervene quickly if the group got stalled or out of hand. As it turned out, the two observers were unneeded. In fact, every time the group seemed on the verge of serious trouble, the two therapists were amazed to see some completely untrained member step in and do exactly what they themselves would have done. With this reassurance, Dr. Farson then set up a full-scale experiment comparing leaderless groups with groups led by professional therapists. It developed that the leaderless groups, even when composed of people who had never before taken part in an encounter, behaved very much like the led groups; their members got right down to business, avoided excess hostility and did a good job of helping one another. To Dr. Farson, the experiment suggests a startling answer to the problem of how the nation can possibly train enough therapists for all the people who need help. "It may turn out," he says, "that our greatest resource for solving human problems is the very people who have the problems."

One immediate result of Dr. Farson's experiment has been a do-it-yourself kit for nonprofessionals eager to organize their own groups. The kit was created largely by a young psychologist named Betty Berzon, a former associate of Dr. Farson at the Western Behavioral Sciences Institute; it is a set of tape recordings, each running about an hour and a half, designed to be played by a group that will hold eight meetings. For each session, the voice on the tape suggests various activities that have been found helpful in groups. For example, all members but one are asked to form a tight circle, into which the missing member then tries to break. Or the members are asked to write down,

anonymously, some secret of which they are ashamed; the slips are shuffled and handed out; each member, in turn, then reads the paper he has drawn and discusses how it might feel to have such a secret. Following each suggestion, the tape goes silent, to give the group time to carry out the instructions; then the voice returns with something new. The recordings are called Encountertapes and are manufactured by the Human Development Institute of Atlanta, a subsidiary of Bell & Howell (an indication that the group movement has grown big enough to interest the multimillion-dollar corporation world).

"What we've done," says Miss Berzon, "is package the group experience and make it available to schools, churches and industries. This takes it out of the esoteric centers like Esalen and right into the mainstream of everyday life." Miss Berzon was one of the several thousand people marooned for three days at New York's Kennedy Airport by an unexpected snowstorm last winter. Listening to the incessant bulletins over the airport loudspeakers, and watching her frustrated fellow travelers grow increasingly bored and glassy-eyed, she kept grieving at the lost opportunity for playing her Encountertapes over the speakers and turning an ordeal into a delightful mass initiation into the marvels of the encounter group. She can never pass a tall office building without thinking of it as a place where a public-address system and a single set of Encountertapes could bring the group experience to many thousands of people at a time.

Even enthusiasts such as Miss Berzon, however, concede that the group has one serious defect for which no remedy is as yet apparent. It is one thing to confess your secrets, pour out your angers and break into tears among a few people gathered expressly in behalf of this kind of free and frank communication; it is quite another thing to do so at home or in the office. Says Miss Berzon, "Once you've had this taste of honey—once you've had the opportunity to really relate in depth to other people—it's hard to go back to the cocktail party kind of superficiality. But everyday life isn't like the group. And your family, your boss and your friends probably have a vested interest in keeping you just as you've always been. So the effect tends to get dissipated when you go home." Says Dr. Farson, "People *feel* they're changed by

the group, but no matter how you observe them, test them or question their families and friends, you don't find any significant changes in their actual behavior. The reason is that what happens in the group is something that a person can't make happen anywhere else."

Trying to transfer the atmosphere of the group into real life can, in fact, be downright dangerous. One businessman who attended a T group reports, "I learned that I had been making myself miserable by bottling up my hostilities and being overpolite to everybody, so I decided to change all that. Three days later, I realized that I was losing my customers, my employees and my wife—and I changed back in a hurry." Dr. Glasser, who is skeptical of encounter groups, says, "They're based on a false premise. Until all people are open and honest at all times, it's unrealistic to think that you can be—without getting hurt."

In one way or another, most leaders of the group movement are now grappling with this problem. Many of them believe that the solution is to expand the movement, through Encountertapes and the establishment of hundreds of new Esalens, until millions of Americans have had group training of one kind or another; these millions will then reshape society into a sort of single big, happy, uninhibited, affectionate, turned-on encounter group. But as one skeptical psychologist has said, "There are a lot of religious overtones to the movement; these people are like the early Christians, who thought that all of society's problems would vanish as soon as everybody became a Christian."

Others are making a more direct attempt to bring the group and everyday life closer together. The National Training Laboratories, for example, has made some significant changes in the way it organizes its T groups. One N.T.L. psychologist says, "We used to be willing to take just one person from a business organization; we'd get him all revved up and then send him back to office colleagues and a job that hadn't changed a bit. Now we try to get at least two men from the firm, so that they can support each other after they go back. And what we really like is to have many people from the same company and work with the management to open up the lines of communication and creativity; we're trying to change the climate of the big organizations, such as corporations and universities, in which people are embedded." Dr. Farson has been thinking about what he calls "social architecture," a possible new science of the future. "If you want to help people transcend themselves," he says, "you've got to rearrange the social situations in which they constantly find themselves—the job, family, school and church." Thus, the attempt to heal and bolster the human psyche, having already expanded from couch to group, seems likely to expand further into all kinds of social situations. What started as Freud's first modest efforts to help a few hysterical patients has indeed come a long way.

The next articles, one by Rueveni and Speck and the other by Sikes and Cleveland, discuss the potential uses of encounter groups in two areas of social concern: therapy for those with more severe behavioral problems and human relations training for police and community.

8.5
Using Encounter Group Techniques in the Treatment of the Social Network of the Schizophrenic

Uri Rueveni and
Ross V. Speck

In the present paper an attempt is made to describe briefly what network therapy is by focusing on several basic encounter group techniques (sensitivity training) used during a six-week stint of social network therapy.

Goals and Rationale for Network Therapy

The major goal of our approach is to alleviate a crisis situation in a family, although, at times, our goal may be the opposite one of creating a crisis where there is insufficient pressure toward change in a malfunctioning family sys-

Reprinted by permission from *International Journal of Group Psychotherapy*, October, 1969.

tem. We aim at preventing hospitalization, and instead, providing the troubled family with a group of concerned human beings, consisting of the family, their kin, friends, and neighbors (the social network) who are willing to give emotional support and create therapeutic potentials for healing.

We subscribe to the hypothesis that decreased rates of mental illness often result when a person has a large social network actively intervening in his life. By convening the social network of the schizophrenic person and his family, we are reconstituting a forgotten and often hidden group of relationships, with the purpose of making the entire group as intimately involved as possible in each others' lives in order to supply a strong sense of "tribe" support, reassurance, and solidarity.

Our approach aims to create within a brief period of time (six weeks) a potent therapeutic climate within the social network. To achieve this purpose, we have utilized a variety of encounter group techniques to facilitate the expression of honest feeling and openness in interpersonal communication and the development of trust between "tribe" members. We have sought to create conditions conducive for the index patient in the network to modify his patterns of behavior.

We have found that encounter techniques, even in large groups, can stimulate rapid jelling of the assembled social network into a cohesive, task-oriented group. Interpersonal defensive operations are more rapidly discarded than when conventional group psychotherapy techniques are used. The development of trust between group members seems to be enhanced, opening the way for innovative activism. By using encounter methods, the network therapists feel they can prepare the group to intervene, take more risk, to care, and to give of themselves more readily. The network members themselves determine what the network tasks are to be in order to break up tight and chronic symbiosis and motivate an unemployed schizophrenic person to work or a house-bound person to move out into the world.

Techniques Used

In recent therapies of two social networks, we have found the following techniques useful.

Inner-Outer Group Encounter

Members are asked to assemble in two concentric groups. Members of the "inner circle" are directed to interact while members of the "outside circle" observe and refrain from speaking. Every twenty minutes the groups change, and members of the inner circle move back and sit in the outside circle. Members of the outside circle can comment or consult with the members of the inside circle only if they take a seat in an empty chair in the inner circle. This is called "the consultant's chair."

We have used this method primarily during the first two network meetings as a method of rapidly acquainting network members with each other and at the same time pulling them together as a group with a task. The tasks for inner group members is varied. Members are asked to give their impressions of each other and then to discuss their feelings. They are asked to role-play, to assign names to various group members according to their feelings at the moment about those persons, and to share their feelings with regard to the tasks. We usually ask members of the outside group to comment upon what has happened in the inner circle. We have found that splitting the "tribe" into two concentric groups with different assigned tasks produces an increase in group tension. We feel this is desirable in the process of tightening the network. The two groups become critical and competitive, thus generating increased tension which leads to deeper interpersonal involvement and network commitment. When the tension between the two groups becomes unbearable, cohesiveness of the whole network is facilitated. They unite as in religious conversion and share a feeling of oneness and closeness. We have called this process "synthesis."

Eyeball-to-Eyeball Confrontation

In this exercise, originally described by Schutz (1967), two group members are instructed to remain silent, look into each other's eyes, and walk very slowly toward each other. When they get close to each other, they are instructed to do whatever they are impelled from within themselves to do. We find this technique particularly useful in encountering the labeled schizophrenic person with his father, mother, sister, and friends. For example, a daughter first approached her mother very hesitantly, then later she hugged and kissed her. This was particularly interesting since they had never been able to do so previously. Such encounters stimulate an intense exchange of feelings among other network members and enhance the climate of trust in the entire group.

We feel that the blocking of verbal communication forces the members to search for new modes of communication, which is part of preparing the stage for change to occur. Nonverbal communication modes are more primitive and probably reach deeper into the person, allowing sudden emotional outbursts as well as making him aware of interpersonal needs for contact, affection, love, and care.

Breaking "In" and "Out"

Members of the group form a tight circle, interlocking their arms. The schizophrenic person stands in the middle and is instructed to break out of the circle. When this is accomplished he has to break into the circle again. This can be one of the most dramatic moments in the entire social network meeting. Ann, for example, had expressed her feelings of disgust with the entire meeting, characterizing the group members as being superficial, hypocritical, and unconcerned about her. She was asked to name those individ·als she blamed most, and they then formed a tight circle around her. It took her ten minutes of hard work to break out of the circle, and she was crying and exhausted. She struggled, pulled, kicked, and hit members of the circle the entire time. When she accomplished her task (first breaking out, then breaking in again), each member approached her and expressed his feelings toward her. Many hugged and kissed her. During the ensuing discussion, Ann and the group felt close to each other and a productive exchange of feelings developed.

Group Swaying

An entire assembled network of, say, seventy persons is instructed to hold hands and then to close their eyes and begin swaying. After a few minutes of silent swaying, the members are instructed to express in one word whatever they are feeling about the schizophrenic person. Affectively tinged associatons rapidly spread throughout the group. Such things as care, concern, hope, love, tension, fear, despair, joy, sadness, confidence, and trust are expressed. The swaying and the nonverbal union by hands pro-

duces a type of group conversion experience and a oneness with each other.

In our McLuhan world of instant "tribe," many humans feel their isolation, loneliness, and alienation. There is a hunger and longing for touch, closeness, group inclusion, and belonging. Group swaying can meet some of this deep human longing. The numerical increase and success of group marathons using encounter techniques attest to a general seeking in our culture for a return to the mystical and religious type of experience rather than the purely verbal. Swaying seems to have potential in meeting more primitive group needs.

Conclusions and Implications

Our experiences in conducting network meetings increased our confidence that many encounter group techniques can enhance the therapeutic potential of the social network of the schizophrenic person. We feel that the social network can provide a possible alternative to hospitalization in many cases. We find that by utilizing encounter group techniques we can enhance conditions that provide the schizophrenic person and his family with group support and trust. In two recently completed networks, our aim was to help the schizophrenic person separate from his family, live independently, and seek employment. In both cases this was accomplished. We are currently planning additional social network meetings in an effort to improve our techniques and utilize crisis situations that can be benefited by social network assembly.

REFERENCES

Attneave, C. (1968), Personal communication.
Barthol, R. P. (1968), The Peanut Cluster. *Human Relations Training News*, 12:4–5.
Malamud, D. I., and Machover, S. (1965), *Toward Self Understanding, Group Technique in Self Confrontation*. Springfield, Ill.: Charles C Thomas.
Morton, R. B., Rothaus, P., and Hanson, P. G. (1961), Adaptation of the Human Relation Training Laboratory to a Psychiatric Population. *Newsletter for Research in Psychology*, 3:19–28.
Rothaus, P., and Morton, R. B. (1961), Proceedings No. 2. Patient Laboratory. Houston, Texas, Veterans Administration Hospital.
Rothaus, P., Morton, R. B., Johnson, D. L., Cleveland, S. E., and Lyle, F. A. (1963), Human Relation Training for Psychiatric Patients.

Arch. Gen. Psychiat., 8:572–581.
Schutz, W. C. (1967), *Joy: Expanding Human Awareness*. New York: Grove Press.
Speck, R. V., and Morong, E. (1967), Home-Centered Treatment of the Social Network of Schizophrenic Families: Two Approaches. Paper presented at the annual meeting of American Psychiatric Association, 1967.
Speck, R. V., and Rueveni, U. (1969), Network Therapy: A Developing Concept. *Family Process* (in press).

8.6
Human Relations Training for Police and Community

Melvin P. Sikes and
Sidney E. Cleveland

Houston, Texas, like many communities throughout the country, is undergoing a period of social change. Many traditional social attitudes, social groupings, and customs are rapidly being altered. New social and political groups are evolving to challenge the authority and practices of established interests. The sense of urgency and insistence accompanying demands for change gives rise to tension within the community, distrust, unsettling rumors, and sometimes physical confrontations. Most often it is the city police force that is thrust directly into the fray and serves as the primary mediator for urban tension. Inevitably, charges of police brutality and misbehavior, alleged or real, arise to complicate a difficult situation. The relationship between police and community becomes a focal point for friction and the detonation device leading to violent explosions.

Recognizing the present social crisis and the existing potential for violence, Houston city officials and business leaders sought a program that would ease police-community relations and provide for an exchange of attitudes and feelings between police and community members. Following a request from the mayor's office, a group of

Houston businessmen formed Community Effort, Inc. as a private funding agency for the Houston Cooperative Crime Prevention Program. The senior author was approached by this group to devise a program to bring together police and community for a mutual exchange of attitudes and images.

The design and methodology selected for this police-community program follow closely the model provided by the Houston Veterans Administration Human Relations Training Laboratory (Rothaus, Morton, Johnson, Cleveland, & Lyle, 1963), employing the T group and sensitivity-training approach. A series of human relations training laboratories was devised, each lasting 6 weeks and accommodating 200 police officers for each series. The officers met for 3 hours once a week over the 6-week period. A corresponding number of community members, especially representative of minority and dissident groups, were recruited for these same sessions. Approximately 40 officers and community members were scheduled for a 3-hour session each of the 5 work days. These personnel were further divided into three separate smaller groups meeting concurrently. The series will continue until the entire police force of 1,400 officers has been involved.

Group leadership was provided by doctoral level psychologists with a background in group psychotherapy and human relations training. The 15 leaders needed for each series were drawn primarily from the staff of the Houston Veterans Administration Hospital and the Departments of Psychology at the University of Houston and Texas Southern University. Advanced graduate students in the Veterans Administration psychology training program were employed as assistant group leaders. The group meetings were held at community centers located primarily in the poverty areas. The police officers, in uniform but off their regular tour of duty, were bussed to the meetings. Officers received regular salary from the city for the 18 hours spent in these sessions, and consultant fees for the professional staff were met by private philanthropy through Community Effort, Inc.

The initial meeting of police and community members was organized around the exchange-of-images model advanced by Blake, Mouton, and Sloma (1965) in their laboratory program dealing with union-management conflict. Police were first asked to develop a list of their images of the community and then a list of their self-images. The community participants were assigned the same task. The two subgroups then confronted each other with their images, and these lists formed the initial structure for interchange between police and community. Individual group leaders relied on their own experience and intuition to structure later sessions, and a variety of techniques borrowed from sensitivity training and psychodrama, such as role reversal, "concentric circles," "doubling," and role mirroring, have been employed to deal with specific crises or to stimulate lagging group participation.

The course of the program has not been unruffled or uninterrupted. In a community action program such as this a basic law seems to operate to the effect that whatever might go wrong does go wrong. First, our staff of psychologists and community workers rather naively expected the community to flock eagerly to the program. This did not occur, however, and only after a massive public relations effort using the news media, community agencies, and church and social organizations did the community begin to respond. Initially, fear of recrimination, suspiciousness, and apathy combined to limit community participation.

The third laboratory session had to be interrupted while city officials sought a legal basis for paying the police for their time in the program. This interruption occurred at a point where community participation had just begun to flourish. The fourth laboratory was marred by the assassination of Martin Luther King, Jr. An interesting exercise for a psychologist is to imagine himself as the leader of a group composed of police and black militants meeting the morning after the assassination. In still another laboratory one police group walked out in the middle of one of their sessions, following a particularly heated exchange. This crisis was picked up by the local news media and for a brief moment threatened the existence of the whole program. Fortunately, the incident served to demonstrate that the program and the group sessions were not a "whitewash" and that real emotions were aroused and basic attitudes explored. This police group returned the following week, and the laboratory was completed without further crises.

Despite these interruptions and emergencies, the program has continued and has received support from city representatives and community leaders. Evaluation of the program reveals enthusiastic acceptance by the participating community members and at least moderately good acceptance by the officers. Evaluation of the program's effectiveness in producing favorable attitudinal change on the part of police and community has been attempted by use of a brief anonymous questionnaire, administered at the close of the final group meeting. Police and community were asked to rate their overall reaction to the program on a poor-excellent scale and to indicate in what way the course had changed their attitudes toward police or community. Other questions called for an expression of their feelings about the impact of the program on their community or police relationships.

More sophisticated and rigorous evaluation was not attempted because of the defensiveness of both police and community. It was feared that administration of any intrusive psychological evaluation on a pre- to postprogram basis might jeopardize the whole program. In Table 1 the evaluation of

TABLE 1. POLICE-COMMUNITY RESPONSE TO A HUMAN RELATIONS TRAINING LABORATORY

RATING	% POLICE	% COMMUNITY
Excellent	4	18
Very good	23	33
Good	58	42
Poor	15	7
Feelings more positive	37	65
Feelings more negative	2	4
Feelings unchanged	61	31

the program by police and community participants is presented. These data, gathered on the first four of seven projected laboratories, are based on the responses of approximately half the police force (700) and 500 participant citizens. As can be seen, community acceptance is strongly positive, with police reaction moderately good.

An analysis of the responses of police and community to other items on the questionnaire yields the following summary of areas of attitude change effected by the program.

Police

1. Gratified that the community has gained some appreciation of

the policeman's role, what he can do and cannot do. The police seemed surprised as to how misinformed the public is regarding police procedures, the limits of their authority, and the nature of their duties. Best expressed by a policeman who noted on his evaluation sheet: "I wasn't aware that the community was so misinformed as to my duties. They expect the police department to answer every problem, for example as to marking streets or building bridges."

2. Recognition that the police may provoke situations and aggravate feelings by verbal abuse, the use of "trigger" words ("Boy," "Nigger," "spic," etc.). A realization by some policemen that they can unintentionally hurt others by this name calling. For example, an officer commented, "As a policeman I have learned how defensive we really are—how much I rationalize. I have learned that we can hurt people without really knowing it."

3. An awareness by the police, and a shocked reaction by some, as to the intensity of the hatred for the police held by some community members. Among some officers this confrontation served as an eye-opener regarding the intensity of antipolice feelings within the Negro community. One officer put it this way in his evaluation notes: "I didn't realize there was as strong resentment against the Police Department as some people of the Negro community expressed." Another said, "I never realized so many people had such deep resentment toward the police. It made me stop and think."

4. A massive defensiveness among the police as to any wrongdoing on their part, any need for change in their attitudes or behavior. A pretty general feeling that to admit to misbehavior is to admit to weakness and failure. This majority position is offset to some extent by an expressed recognition among a minority of the police of their defensiveness and need to deny or excuse misbehavior on the part of officers. This defensiveness is represented in a statement such as the following, given by one officer: "I feel the entire course should have been eliminated. There was nothing brought out that was not known. Nothing was said to change my opinions." "All the community wants is the police to give in to them." But a more open attitude is expressed in opinions expressed by a minority of the officers, such as: "The course has caused me to

see myself as the community sees me. It has brought to light things which I did not think the public was even aware of."

5. Some awareness of the need to control personal feelings and emotions and to respond in a courteous and self-controlled manner. An example of this is the officer who commented: "It made me understand that although I may have preconceived ideas or biased opinions of people, that I must strive as a policeman to keep these out of my personal dealings with others. I should go further to understand what might motivate this person to feel the way they do [sic]."

Community

1. Better awareness of policeman's role, his problems, and scope of his responsibilities. Better understanding of police procedures, why they ask certain questions, issue certain orders, or often appear brusque, indifferent, and even rude and insensitive. One community member put it this way: "This course will bring a better understanding between the policeman and myself to the community which I reside in and through this understanding there will be more cooperation in feeling that he, the policeman, will get respect and as citizens we will realize more he is doing his job."

2. Recogniton of their responsibility as citizens to enforce law and order, to "become involved," and to work *with*, not against or apart from, the police. For example, one citizen commented on his evaluation sheet: "This course has enabled me to understand the duties and responsibilities of the police and how we, the community, can cooperate with them in doing a better job." Another said, "I was never fully aware of the many problems facing the police in their duties and how the community tends to hinder the police instead of helping. As a community we fail to get involved when we should."

3. Greater respect for the police as individual human beings rather than being classed into one undifferentiated group, the "blue minority." Recognition of the citizen's tendency to dehumanize the police and see them as unfeeling, lacking in sympathy, as being authoritarian robots rather than real people who sometimes make honest mistakes, get angry, or behave unwisely. Examples are given by citizens who wrote the following on their evaluation

sheets upon completion of the course: "Before this course I regarded the policeman as a symbol of authority not as a real human being." "The community sometimes reacts blindly against policemen as a whole. I could see that a great many police want to do a good job in a professional manner." "The police officer has become for me more a human being and less of a sadistic robot."

4. Recognition by community members of their own bias and prejudice toward the police. This point was well illustrated in one citizen's evaluation of his response to the program: "I find that I possess a good deal of hostility, and prejudged and preconceived notions and ideas toward the police which were incorporated into my personality before I attended these meetings."

5. An expressed hope that some of the police will change their behavior and attitudes toward minority group members. A note of optimism that there will be change for the better replacing a feeling of despair that nothing will change.

6. At least an intellectual understanding among some community members as to how their attitudes and feelings can influence and shape their perception of reality, their view of the police and police behavior.

7. A sense of freedom and release in the opportunity to criticize, talk back to, yell at, and challenge the statement of a policeman without retaliation or fear of retribution.

8. An understanding of some of the pressures the police feel subjected to—shortage of personnel, personal risk and danger, inferior and obsolete equipment, internal friction, and archaic rules within the police department. One community member stated it this way: "This course has helped in understanding the problems of the police, how they jeopardize their lives and the apathy they must deal with."

9. Recognition among many community members that they tended to demand of the police ideal and perfect behavior. One community member expressed the sentiment of many in commenting on his evaluation sheet: "I now recognize that policemen are human beings who may make mistakes instead of machines that should never make a mistake."

10. Reduction in fear of police as threatening authority figures. This was expressed by one community member who scrawled on

his evaluation sheet, "It [the course] taken away the fear."

Conclusions

It is apparent that the number and direction of responses from the participating community suggest a greater program impact upon them than upon the police. The real impact on either group is not known. No claim is made that 18 hours of discusson and interaction will sweep away years of rancor and distrust. Tension and misunderstanding still exist. But such a confrontation may open the way to greater mutual respect and a more cooperative relationship.

REFERENCES

Blake, R. R., Mouton, J. S., & Sloma, R. L. The union-management intergroup laboratory: Strategy for resolving intergroup conflict. *Journal of Applied Behavioral Science,* 1965, *1,* 25–57.

Rothaus, P., Morton, R. B., Johnson, D. L., Cleveland, S. E., & Lyle, F. A. Human relations training for psychiatric patients. *Archives of General Psychiatry,* 1963, 8, 68–77.

Consideration should be given to the composition of encounter groups as well as to the various uses already mentioned. The following article by Horwitz deals with the role of the leader, an issue we feel is essential to the discussion of encounter groups.

8.7
Transference in Training Groups and Therapy Groups

Leonard Horwitz

Human relations training groups or sensitivity groups have attained increasing popularity during the past fifteen years both in America and abroad. Under the sponsorship of the Laboratory for Group Development in Bethel, Maine,[1]

Reprinted by permission from *International Journal of Group Psychotherapy,* 14, 2 (April, 1964), 207–212.

[1] The major summer laboratory conducted by National Training Laboratories, National Education Association, Washington, D.C.

the technique of using the small unstructured group to study group processes and to aid group members in the acquisition of personal insights has gained wide acceptance in a variety of settings. Jerome Frank (1964) has made the only focused attempt to describe and conceptualize the similarities and differences between training groups and therapy groups, noting certain clearcut differences in goals and processes between the two. He based his observations upon an experience at Bethel as a member of a training group (T-group) in the mid-1950's.

Frank emphasizes the following major difference in objectives. Training groups attempt to help members become more sensitive to their own functioning and to the important events occurring within the group so that they may become more effective as members and as leaders of other groups. A therapy group aims to help its members attain insight into their functioning in interpersonal situations of *all* kinds and thus it aims to help relieve neurotically determined distress. As Frank (1964) describes it, there is a de-emphasis in the training group upon learning about oneself:

Training groups are composed of individuals trying to learn new skills from the trainer. Therapy groups attempt to modify more pervasive and more central attitudes than training groups, so they put relatively more emphasis on unlearning old modes of behavior as compared to learning new ones, and take longer to achieve their aims.

A second distinction Frank makes is that teaching membership skills in the training group focuses on interpretations about the group as a whole, rather than about individual motivations. Feelings of members are elucidated only insofar as they shed light upon and illustrate group process. Therapy groups, of course, focus primarily upon the individual and his underlying motives and conflicts. A third important difference lies in the role of the central figure. In therapy groups, the initial dependence upon the therapist is greater and is never completely resolved:

The therapist can never become fully a member of the group, though he may approximate this, whereas trainer and member of a training group can become genuinely indistinguishable [Frank, 1964].

There has been a steady trend

toward de-emphasizing the study of group process in T-groups in favor of enhanced personal insight. Some writers have referred to sensitivity training as "psychotherapy for normals" (Weschler et al., 1962), although many decry this therapeutic trend in T-groups. Shepard (1964) described the shift as follows:

Implicit recognition that individual development was the lasting consequence of training led to increased focus on individual dynamics. Group level interventions were replaced by more personally oriented interventions . . . NTL began to focus on the problem of "giving and receiving feedback" and, in recent years, personal feedback has seemed to be the most important feature of the T-group.

Although there has been a shift toward personal insight, Bethel groups do *not* typically aim at uncovering and resolving unconscious conflict. Rather, they attempt to help the individual perceive more clearly his own mode of interaction which may impair his effectiveness. Perhaps one could say that T-groups aim to impart insights concerning the more conscious or preconscious levels of personality functioning.

With this shift in emphasis toward more insight-giving in training groups, a natural question is whether training techniques have begun to shift in the direction of those used in a therapeutic group. More specifically, has the trainer begun to use transference reactions to him as a vehicle for uncovering personal dynamics, as is done in therapy groups? On the basis of the training group literature, as well as my own experience in a few Bethel T-groups, it appears that such a shift in trainer role has not occurred. It is my purpose to examine the differences in leader roles in the two groups, particularly in the use of transference, and to explore the consequences of the difference in method.

Before delineating these differences, I wish to emphasize that neither group psychotherapy nor human relations training may be adequately represented by a single point of view. Practitioners in each field span a wide range of methods, techniques, and theories. Most therapists operate within a psychoanalytic frame of reference and hence emphasize transference, although there are distinct variations in their use of leader versus peer transference and the strictness with which they attempt to maintain their role of a projection screen. Similarly, trainers differ widely in their "visibility" (Whitman, 1964) within their groups. The modal points to be used in our comparison will be the training group described by Bradford (1964) and the therapy group formulated by Sutherland (1952) and Ezriel (1952).

First, how is transference, particularly with regard to the leader, conceptualized in the therapy group? The therapist clearly and explicitly views his role as a transference figure: a screen upon which wishes and fears are projected, brought into awareness by interpretation, with the object of their resolution. He encourages transference reactions: (1) by confining his participation as much as possible to creating a permissive atmosphere in which free expression of feelings and fantasies is received uncritically, (2) by promoting an attitude of reflection about the meaning of individual and group behaviors, and (3) by restricting his remarks to interpretations of group themes and individual variations around them. His role approaches that of the psychoanalyst whose thoughts and feelings remain relatively unknown to the patient and whose silence tends to induce considerable frustration with a resulting emergence of regressive tendencies which then become the subject of analysis and interpretation. This model of the therapist who limits his interaction with the group and who is often seen as quite depriving is, of course, varied according to the capacity of the group to tolerate the anxiety induced by such a procedure.

Roles of Trainer in a T-Group

The central figure in the human relations training group, on the other hand, plays multiple roles (Bradford, 1964). He may permit the group to struggle with its transference reactions toward him, but he does not consciously and explicitly attempt to promote transference. Little, if any, explicit reference to this cornerstone conception of psychotherapy appears in the literature. Certain generic issues, like members' reactions to the trainer, the prototypes of dependency and counter-dependency, the distorted attitudes toward authority figures, are observed by all writers of the Bethel school, though there is an assiduous avoidance of the term.[2]

[2] In a personal communication, Bennis correctly points out that such

Benne (1963) recommends, for example, that the trainer sometimes remain impassive and enigmatic to encourage the expression of fantasies about the trainer which can then be corrected. But the consensus is that the trainer should serve other functions than simply those of observer and interpreter. First, the usual laboratory setting generally reduces transference reactions. All participants, including the trainer, are addressed by their first names. Since they usually spend two weeks together on a "cultural island," trainer and participants see each other during coffee breaks, evening social hours, and other real-life situations where the trainer emerges as a real person. Second, a trainer role which tends to attenuate transference reactions is that of the person who "models" the ideal of openness in expressing one's feelings. Thus he may at times share his own feelings of perplexity, anxiety, or confusion about what is transpiring in the group, partly to encourage others to express their reactions freely and partly to help the group resolve unrealistic fantasies of the omniscient leader. Finally, the trainer sometimes is "teacher," who may deliver a "lecturette" or summarize some shared event which has special value as a generalization about group behavior.

While training groups attend to problems regarding group process, therapy groups have little, if any, interest in the dynamics of groups per se. Learning group dynamics in a therapy group is incidental to its major purpose of enhanced personal insight. Thus, while both groups seek personal insight for their members, the training group in addition attempts to teach important dimensions of group functioning. Problems of membership requirements and their changes during the life of the group, the dynamics of decision-making, and the growth of group norms are studied in the training group as they are experi-

terms as "parataxic distortion" or "valid communication" which are common in training literature denote the same process as transference reactions. He also notes that transference occurs *despite* the trainer's attitude; his method may enhance or discourage its development, but it will appear in some form and to some extent. Dorothy Stock, also in a personal communication, made a similar point regarding the use of nonanalytic terminology in training literature since the laboratory method had its origins in the fields of social psychology and education.

enced. Such problems may also be part of the data generated in a therapy group, but they are not a focus of learning for the patients. Both trainer and therapist, for example, must always be alert to restrictions in group norms, particularly as they tend to interfere with free communication of feelings. The woman, for example, who emphasizes the "intellectual brilliance" of the male members tends to freeze the men into highly restraining roles. Their attempts to fulfill her expectations result in intellectual muscle-flexing. Both therapist and trainer are likely to call attention to the inhibiting effect of such a statement, but the trainer will also attempt to show that rigidifying norms in a group may easily be established, particularly early in a group's life, and such events must be carefully scrutinized.

Members of one T-group, asked several days after having started about accepting a new member, sensed that this was the preference of the trainer and though disposed favorably, they were not enthusiastic about the idea. One member, who vehemently opposed the proposal, finally enlisted many proponents on his side. In an instance of this kind, both training and therapy groups have the opportunity to explore feelings about newcomers, the leader's power, and submission to a powerful peer. For the training group, it was an excellent illustration of an important facet of group dynamics: the numerical majority is often secondary to the "emotional" majority in the decision-making process. Such lessons are not relevant to the objectives of a therapeutic group, because patients do not attempt to understand the dynamics of groups, but it provides the trainer with an opportunity to clarify and point up a principle of group dynamics. Such teaching makes for some attenuation of transference to the trainer. These interventions, insofar as they reveal the trainer as a real person with a particular style of teaching, tend to make him less of a projection screen than is a more silent therapist. Furthermore, this kind of spoon-feeding also reduces the oral frustration within the group and contributes to the reduction of the more regressive fantasies of the members.

The Trainer as a Model

In addition to his role of teacher, the trainer often moves gradually in the direction of a membership role, so that toward the end of the life of the group, his contributions and status approach those of a peer. This develops largely through his "modeling" behavior by which the trainer exemplifies the ideals of openness and a willingness to face uncomfortable, conflictful situations without smoothing them over. Of course, the group therapist also confronts uncomfortable issues in the group, but he does so without blurring his identity as the central figure in contrast to the trainer who moves into a membership role.

How the trainer moves from the position of central figure toward that of membership status may be illustrated by several examples of trainer behavior. Not infrequently during the inevitable ritual of self-introductions around the table in the first session, the trainer will be asked to introduce himself and describe his background as the other members do. More often than not, the trainer will introduce himself, perhaps more briefly than the others, to avoid frustrating the group. In so doing he contributes to the reduction, at least in part, of the members' preoccupation with the mysterious leader who has let his group know that he does not intend to lead. A therapist would probably interpret the meaning of the request that he introduce himself, rather than meet the request.

One kind of recommended trainer behavior is a willingness to express "his own situationally induced feelings of discomfort, anger, uncertainty, and helplessness with the group" (Benne, 1964). Such expressions serve two major purposes. One, they presumably help members to express more easily their own feelings, which may be threatening to reveal. They also help limit the regressive fantasies which inevitably develop in the unstructured group in which the central figure is seen as magically endowed with unusual powers for both good and evil and against which various defenses must be erected. The group therapist, on the other hand, would attempt to interpret the group's regressive and dependent wishes toward him without abdicating his special role as the central figure. Thus, the trainer presents himself as a real person, with the same kind of weakness and fallibility common to the other members; the therapist does not reveal these inner thoughts and feelings but, rather, helps his patients to modify their dependency position by making them

more aware of it.

The following example of a membership-modeling intervention used by the trainer is offered by Bradford (1964). A T-group came into one of its early sessions to find that the nameplates on the table had been shuffled around in a way to suggest that somebody was attempting to manipulate the seating arrangement. Resentment simmered, but the group was fearful of dealing with the issue. The trainer forthrightly said that he felt "pushed around" and his frankness permitted the group to uncork its anger. In a similar situation, the therapist would undoubtedly try to encourage and elicit feelings about such an event and try to uncover the meanings of behavior, but he would be unlikely to impart his own feelings to the group. A by-product of the trainer's intervention would be to enhance his image as a member and further help to strip him of his "projection screen" qualities.

The trainer also participates in giving "personal feedback" to members. It has already been pointed out that Bethel groups are increasingly moving away from a concern with group issues and are focusing upon personal learning via the feedback process. Personal feedback by the trainer to members undoubtedly contributes to his membership status, but can be made "safely" only insofar as the omniscience imputed to the trainer has been resolved, or at least reduced.

Effects of Trainer's Membership Status

The trainer never fully achieves the ideal of becoming a co-equal or peer with the others. The powerful dependency strivings are not that easily neutralized, and hence the members will not permit the trainer to become just another member. Thus, feedback from the trainer must be carefully attuned to the trainer's perceived position in the group. The therapist, on the other hand, operates in a more protected position. He usually gives interpretations within the safety of a group theme; that is, the therapist shows each individual his particular reaction to the common group tension (Ezriel, 1952).

This movement toward increasing membership status of the trainer, with consequent attenuation of transference reactions toward him, raises the question of the effects of such an approach in contrast to what develops in the

usual therapy group. In my experience in both kinds of groups, the outstanding difference between the training group and the therapy group is the reduced preoccupation of members with the trainer as compared with that of patients with the therapist. While both groups develop magical expectations toward the central figure, their intensity—as well as the elaborate fantasies concerning what "he" is thinking or planning and why he is behaving as he does—tends to be substantially reduced in the training group. The therapy group encourages the development of regressive transference reactions toward the leader; in contrast, the T-group attempts to keep them in check by having the trainer play a memberlike role and focusing his comments upon peer relations rather than trainer-member relations. In this way, members of the T-group go through a relatively abbreviated period of dealing with their dependency problems toward the trainer and begin to focus upon their relationship to each other, the problems of intimacy and closeness, and learn from this emphasis upon peer relationships about their characteristic modes of interaction.

Another development in the therapeutic group largely absent in the T-group is an explicit termination process. Regressive developments as termination approaches in a therapeutic process are well known. Dependency feelings characteristic of the beginning reappear, anger at not having been magically cured surges up, and depression over having to give up a valued relationship occurs. But the training group, not having developed an intense transference relationship with the trainer, reveals little of these phenomena.[3] T-group literature concerning characteristic problems of bringing a training group to a close is relatively sparse.

[3] Dorothy Stock in a personal communication states: "I think there is a termination process in T-groups, but it is not focused around the leader. Two things I have noted: first, a mourning over the impending separation from one's peers; and second, disappointment at not having achieved all one's individual goals and for not having dealt as hoped with all the issues which came up during the course of the group. I have seen groups which dealt with both these issues admirably and realistically, making the last few sessions very productive and satisfying. Groups which have not seem prone to reunions."

The method which attenuates transference reactions to the leader and abbreviates the period of concern about them in the group seems to me consistent with the aim of giving personal feedback to members during a relatively brief series of sessions in T-groups as compared with therapy groups. The definite time limit and predetermined number of sessions in a T-group (usually about twenty sessions) will in itself set limits upon the degree of dependence upon the central figure which is likely to develop. Several writers have noted the kind of self-regulation which tends to develop in time-limited groups (Berman, 1953). The leaders' "membership" role seems to reinforce this decreased dependency upon the leader and consequent increased reliance upon peers for personal learning primarily by means of feedback.

Feedback in a Training Group Versus Insight in a Therapy Group

The feedback process is designed primarily to enable the participant to become more aware of some of his characteristic modes of interacting, which become apparent to others in a close relationship but which are hidden from the participant himself. It is a process of communicating one's perceptions of others in a setting where members are ideally attempting to help each other and where the observations are gauged approximately to the level at which the member is ready to accept them.[4] Usually, the feedback received by a member in a T-group has a special impact upon him because it generally is derived from a consensus of observations, and the sheer weight of numbers, combined with an effort to give responsible help, usually produces a significant effect upon the member. The extent to which these insights produce significant behavioral change is a question still to be answered.

[4] A common myth which has developed about T-groups is that feedback is nothing more than a "no-holds-barred" attack upon a fellow member. While angry outbursts may occur, the trainer takes pains to point up the difference between such retaliations and the more deliberate and constructive efforts involved in the feedback process. It is not a means of "tearing down defenses," as some have described it but, rather, a genuine effort to encourage growth and change by enhancing self-understanding.

A dramatic instance of feedback occurred in one T-group in connection with a member's efforts to dominate and control the group. The initial comments to him concerned his drive for power and his lack of any genuine interest in others, despite his superficial solicitousness. Finally one member said he thought Jim was contemptuous of the others in the group, of their opinions, abilities, and of what they had to offer him. Jim opened his notebook which contained a voluntarily kept personal diary and he read a paragraph describing his impressions after the initial meeting. He had written that not a single person in the group showed any leadership ability and none could hold a responsible position in industry like he did. He then acknowledged to the group that he had heard similar criticisms from others and he even admitted some explosive and sadistic behavior toward his wife. His subsequent behavior in the group became considerably less "phony" and pseudo-sympathetic and there was little doubt that the group's feedback had produced, or at least reinforced, an important personal insight.

How does the feedback process in a Bethel group compare with the insights which develop in a therapeutic group? In the kind of group psychotherapy described by Sutherland (1952) and Ezriel (1952), the therapist attempts to uncover a common group tension or an underlying conflict shared by the entire group although expressed in an idiosyncratic manner by each member as a function of his own character structure. It is similar to the orientation described by Whitman and Stock (1958) in their discussion of the group focal conflict. Thus, in the group which is dealing with dependency conflict in its initial phases and is looking toward the leader for omnipotent and magical solutions, some will ask the therapist what to discuss, some will ask for instruction about the theory of group psychotherapy, while others may silently and expectantly await the therapist's magical words to rid them of their anxiety. The therapist must interpret this group theme while at the same time pointing out to individual members their own characteristic mode of expressing their wishes and fears. Although various kinds of distortions, projections, and manipulations occur in the behavior of members toward each other, the therapist uses these behavioral data in relation to the

common tension toward him.

In one therapeutic group I conducted, much of one meeting consisted of a heated argument over the obscene language of one member, a young man. During the argument, it became increasingly clear that the "offender" (who was also the therapist's most vocal proponent) perceived the therapist as a bourgeois and repressive individual who kept him from talking as freely as he wished. This perception he displaced onto persons in the group who most closely approximated his image of the therapist. One of his antagonists, a young woman who argued for more gentlemanly language, was struggling against her own introject of the evil, seductive father who has control over sexual and aggressive impulses. (This patient had suffered a brief psychotic episode during which she had the delusion that her father was going to rape her.) The common tension which involved the group in this instance was the fear lest their sexual impulses get out of hand. The young man defended himself against these impulses by projecting a severely repressive superego onto the group, only to struggle vigorously against it. The prudish girl, on the other hand, unable to tolerate her own sexual wishes, was doing battle with the projected licentiousness which she saw ready to run rampant in the group. The therapist attempted to show that despite their polarized positions, they were struggling with transference distortions based on the same fear of sexuality, one by projecting id wishes and the other by projecting superego injunctions. When they became aware of these distortions, they were able to begin dealing with these internal, repressed conflicts. The level of insight into unconscious motives which the therapist aims for is considerably deeper than the insight which occurs in a training group.

Therapeutic and training groups emphasize the different methods of insight-giving: the training group depends more upon personal feedback from one's peers, while the therapy group depends largely on the therapist's interpretation of transference to him. It is interesting to speculate on whether or not it would be profitable to use the transference approach with a brief, time-limited group, like a T-group, to enhance the objective of personal insights. If the trainer were to confine his role to observer and interpreter and thereby encourage the development of transference reactions, the group would undoubtedly become more preoccupied with the central figure and develop more intense feelings toward him. Then the group might spend a considerable portion of the twenty-odd sessions expressing and coming to terms with their frustrated dependency needs and their wishes to be given a few omniscient observations about themselves from the trainer. Efforts to learn about themselves from the group's observations would certainly decrease inasmuch as the expert leader would understand more about their behavior, motives, and latent preoccupations than anyone else present. To the extent that the group did acquire insights from the central figure, it would be within the context of the common problem within the group.

The feedback method, on the other hand, encourages peer observation in the form of mutual evaluations in which each member has the opportunity of hearing a consensus opinion about his role in the group. It appears to have some special advantages over the transference method for a brief, time-limited group. First, feedback is in no way restricted to a group theme, and therefore is likely to encompass a wide range of behaviors and observations. Rather than emphasizing individual modes of relating oneself to the authority figure in the group, the T-group permits a wider range of observations: a person's over-readiness to rush to the defense of those who are attacked, another's habit of quickly acceding to pressure from others, or another's tendency to stir up hostile interactions by subtly getting others to do battle. Second, the feedback method exploits the power of peer pressure. A common occurrence in a T-group is the report by a member who has just been evaluated by his group that he has heard these observations many times before, by his wife, or his colleague, supervisor, or friend. But the previous comments were rarely as telling in their impact as the group consensus. The power of group opinion, especially in an atmosphere of mutual care and trust, carries with it considerable persuasive force.

A final, and perhaps crucial, advantage of transference attenuation in the T-group is the trainer's wish to avoid the depth of regression which the therapist seeks to elicit. The therapist aims to promote regressive responses from the patient in order to bring into awareness the unconscious conflicts which impair his functioning. The therapist is best able to do this by refraining from excessive participation, by taking the role of a projection screen, and by some degree of frustration of the patient's conscious and unconscious wishes. The trainer, on the other hand, would see such behavior as creating an "artificial" authority problem and seeks to resolve the authority transference as quickly as possible by interpretation and also by playing roles which tend to remove the aura of mystery surrounding the more neutral and less "visible" therapist. The trainer is content to work with more superficial and more conscious layers of the personality than is the therapist.

My conclusion is that the use of transference is appropriate for the intensive, uncovering approach of a therapeutic group, but is best attenuated and minimized in a training group. Where the objective is restricted to helping an individual gain insight about his major blind spots in relating himself to others in groups, and where a time limitation exists with regard to the life of the group, the feedback technique seems to be the method of choice.

Summary

Human relations training groups have increasingly focused over the past few years upon personal insights into individual members' characteristic modes of behavior. While such groups also deal with group issues, these have become of secondary interest in the usual Bethel T-group. Since the T-group is coming to be used to acquire enhanced understanding about oneself, although at a more superficial level than in a therapy group, the problem is posed as to why the central vehicle of psychotherapy, transference, is not emphasized as the major tool of the typical training group. The group therapist encourages the development of transference, particularly to himself, by confining his behavior largely to that of observer and interpreter of group and individual conflicts and resistances. He thus facilitates regressive reactions toward himself which are fundamental in uncovering unconscious conflict. The trainer, on the other hand, not only interprets but often moves in the direction of a "member" role, by "modeling" behavior and contributing his own reactions to group events as a way of helping the group to understand and learn about itself. These member-like behaviors contribute (1) to an attenuation of transference reactions and to diminished preoccupation with the central figure, (2) to a decrease in regressive reactions, and (3) to increased interaction and interdependence among the members. To achieve the goal of maximum learning about blind spots and distortions in one's personal interactions in a brief time-limited group, the "member-like" role of the trainer seems preferable to the transference role of the therapist.

REFERENCES

Benne, K. D. (1964, in press), Comments on Training Groups. In Bradford, L. P., et al. (eds.), *T-Group Theory and Laboratory Method*. New York: John Wiley.

Bennis, W. G., and Shepard, H. A. (1956), A Theory of Group Development. *Human Relations, 9:* 415–437.

Berman, L. (1953), Group Psychotherapeutic Technique for Training in Clinical Psychology. *Am. J. Orthopsychiat., 23:*322–327.

Bradford, L. P. (1964, in press), Experiences in a T-Group. In Bradford, T. P., et al. (eds.), *T-Group Theory and Laboratory Method*. New York: John Wiley.

Ezriel, H. (1952), Notes on Psychoanalytic Group Therapy: II. Interpretation and Research. *Psychiatry, 15:*119–126.

Frank, J. D. (1964, in press), Human Relations Training Groups and Therapy Groups. In Bradford, L. P., et al. (eds.), *T-Group Theory and Laboratory Method*. New York: John Wiley.

Shepard, H. A. (1964, in press), Explorations in Observant Participation. In Bradford, L. P., et al. (eds.), *T-Group Theory and Laboratory Method*. New York: John Wiley.

Sutherland, J. D. (1952), Notes on Psychoanalytic Group Therapy: I. Therapy and Training. *Psychiatry, 15:*111–117.

Weschler, I. R., Massarik, F., and Tannenbaum, R. (1962), The Self in Process: A Sensitivity Training Emphasis. In Weschler, I. R., and Schein, E. H., *Issues in Training*. Washington, D.C.: National Training Laboratories.

Whitman, R. M. (1964, in press), The T-Group in Terms of Group Focal Conflict. In Bradford, L. P., et al. (eds.), *T-Group Theory and Laboratory Method*. New York: John Wiley.

Whitman, R. M., and Stock, D. (1958), The Group Focal Conflict. *Psychiatry, 21:*269–276.

8.8
Anyone for "Psychological Strip Poker"?

Ted J. Rakstis

"Sensitivity training parlor games are a regrettable attempt to capitalize upon a trend."

So says Dana L. Farnsworth, M.D., chairman of the American Medical Association's Council on Mental Health.

"The danger in playing these games is the same as getting into a sensitivity training session with an incompetent leader," contends Dr. Farnsworth.

Dr. Howard P. Rome of the Mayo Graduate School of Medicine adds: "In a real therapy or training session, you have a skilled leader and a feeling of mutual trust. On a parlor game level, both are missing. Games like this should be called 'psychological strip poker.'"

These two psychiatrists are talking about "games" such as "Sensitivity" and "Group Therapy" which have invaded the American living room . . . games based on sensitivity training. They are sold at bookstores and novelty shops.

Guests at dinner parties proclaim: "I'm the group leader," and unleash a barrage of intensely personal questions.

And there's even a textbook for parlor sensitivity buffs—it's called *Joy.* It describes encounter group exercises in detail. A Boston psychiatrist and an advertising man created "Sensitivity," a game designed to be played by five to eight persons. Each player is given a folder outlining a fictitious case history of a troubled person—a businessman whose wife has learned about his mistress, an alcoholic mother, a man hopelessly in debt, a homosexual.

The participant then assumes the role and tells the group his troubles. They judge his performance with red cards for "anger" and blue cards for "sympathy." When the first round of questioning is over, "Academy Awards" are presented, including the "Silver Chastity Belt for successful avoiding of all talk about s-e-x" and the "Ghengis Khan Memorial Trophy for the invasion of privacy on all fronts while keeping your own frontiers intact."

In "Group Therapy," players

Reprinted by permission from *Today's Health,* published by the American Medical Association, January, 1970.

follow instructions from "therapy cards." A typical command would be: "Stand up. Select someone. Go totally limp in his arms," or "Pick a way in which you are phony and exaggerate it." The others render their verdicts by flashing "Cop Out" or "With It" cards, and the winner is the first person who advances from "Hung Up" to "Free." As the game's instruction sheet describes it: "Group Therapy is for people who want to do more than just play games. It's for people who want to open up. Get in touch. Let go. Feel free."

David Viscott, M.D., one of the developers of "Sensitivity," insists that his game has enough built-in safeguards so that it never can become too personal. "I've never heard of anyone getting hurt, and I've seen it played—and played it—hundreds of times," he contends.

Advertisements for Encounter

AN ENCOUNTER GROUP FOR PEOPLE WHO HATE ENCOUNTER GROUPS

Too many enthusiastic participants in weekend residential encounter groups later fail to convince their spouse, friends or others in their lives of the joyful aliveness and growth potential of these sessions. This workshop is specifically designed for those who wish to gently and lovingly introduce the "significant others" in their life to the weekend encounter group experience. Bring your "significant others" or have them come alone for a series of typical and unique encounter group experiences conducted in an atmosphere of patience and trust.

COUPLES' AND LOVERS' MARATHON WEEKEND MARATHON WITH GEORGE AND PEGGY BACH

George and Peggy Bach, originators and developers of the husband/wife team approach in marathon groups, invite other spouses and lovers to join them in a 24-hour day and night continuous group session. Participants will practice the fine art of intimate communication. Verbal and nonverbal, fighting and loving, autonomous and dyadic ways of deepening and stimulating the male-female bond will be

explored. Clarification of "multiple loving," its creative and destructive function in modern marriage will be attempted. Participants will also be introduced to Dr. Bach's original "Fight Training for Lovers" in which intimate partners can strengthen their love relationships by learning how to "fight" fairly and effectively. This marathon will in effect be a participative preview of Dr. Bach's book *Intimate Enemies,* to be published by Morrow in November. Preregistration is necessary so that participants can study Dr. Bach's basic marathon rules ahead of time.

Registration: $145 per couple

The program leaders describe their workshop as follows: "Visitors at Esalen often speak of the enchantment and magic they experience in Big Sur. Sometimes we are inclined to take our environment for granted; sometimes we are caught up and awed by the force and presence of this beauty. In this workshop, we wish to explore those forces in nature of which we are a part. We will camp in the mountains and seek to discover the forces around us. As we begin to do so, we can evoke from within ourselves the forces which will complement and enhance our environment, each other, water, wind, sun, moon."

Bring sleeping bag and clothing for a week's camping in the mountains. For additional information, write Jack Hurley, Esalen, Big Sur. $240 per person.

LE VOYAGE SURPRISE

A trip without an itinerary? C'est impossible! But this trip comes off, taking its travelers on a journey that is frantic, fantastic, and uproariously funny. With hardly a break, the tour goes to a turn-of-the-century brothel, to the stage of a provincial theatre, and to the country of Stromboli, ruled by a dwarf queen. But the voyage is more than a brilliant French comedy; it is the universal journey of all those who quest for inner peace and struggle with the demons of the soul. (Directed by the Prevert brothers)

8.9
The Encounter Group Versus Psychiatrists

David Perlman

The encounter group movement now sweeping America poses a real problem for psychiatry. Thousands upon thousands of people are now involved in marathons, truth labs, psychological karate, Synanon square games, Esalen sessions and T-groups.

But do they do good or harm? Do they unlock human potential, increase sensitivity, promote awareness? Or do they push uneasily balanced people into psychosis, into suicide, into deep and intractable distress?

Leaders of the American Psychiatric Association have just completed a special report on the encounter movement, and the report quite frankly concedes ignorance.

Join

For the average layman now weighing whether to join a marathon, a game or an encounter session, the report does contain some clues:

"The intensive group experience," says the spokesmen for America's leading psychiatrists, "is neither good nor bad. In irresponsible, inexperienced hands it may result in a host of adverse consequences; if properly harnessed, however, the experience may be a valuable adjunct in the production of behavioral and attitudinal change."

Last week, in an interview, the chairman of the psychiatric organization's task force translated it this way:

"Encounter groups are totally different from psychotherapy, and people shouldn't go into them with expectations of treatment for emotional problems."

Research

The chairman was Dr. Irving Yalom, associate professor of psychiatry at Stanford University Medical Center.

Dr. Yalom also heads a long-range research project into encounter groups; others on his research team include Dr. Morton A.

Lieberman, a University of Chicago psychologist, and Dr. Matthew Miles, a psychologist at Columbia.

According to Dr. Yalom more than 200 varied encounter groups are flourishing right now in the neighborhood of Palo Alto alone. At the Esalen Institute, in Big Sur, at least 50,000 persons have come to experience encounter sessions. Throughout the West the movement has reached "near epidemic proportions," the APA task force reports.

These groups are led by a fantastic range of people: trained psychiatrists, students, sensitive and skilled social workers, inexperienced housewives, and outright quacks promising all sorts of psychic cures.

In the study by Dr. Yalom's group 209 Stanford students have been participating in 19 encounter groups. In the first six months 40 students dropped out, and there were three "clearly discernible casualties."

Encounters

The casualties cannot be firmly blamed on the effects of the encounters, Dr. Yalom said, but they did include one suicide and two students who sought emergency hospital treatment: one for manic irritability and excitement, and the other for severe anxiety and depression.

In another study of 32 T-group members there were 16 bad reactions, ranging from outright psychosis to mild anxiety or depression.

But other encounter groups have seen no casualties at all in—and it's impossible to say how many people entering encounters do so after long periods on the edge of mental illness, Dr. Yalom and his APA task force pointed out.

Attitude

The attitude of the psychiatrists can best be summed up this way:

Many encounter groups may be effective in releasing blocked emotions. Some, with trained leaders, may help cope with problems like drug addiction or alcoholism. Many provide harmless entertainment and even "peak experiences" that may prove emotionally useful. Some are apparently dangerous. Much depends on the skill, the training, the sensitivity and the goals of the group leader. But in the jungle of varied encounters, it's a case of "buyer beware."

8.10
Psychiatric Perspectives on T-Groups and the Laboratory Movement: An Overview

Louis A. Gottschalk and
E. Mansell Pattison

Assets of the T-Group Method

The T-group provides a vehicle for teaching the importance of interpersonal relations in natural group functioning. Rather than through didactic description, the T-group teaches through experience. An analogy might be made with the teaching of arithmetic. The teacher can do a problem on the board, but the student does not learn the arithmetical maneuver until he has actually solved a number of similar problems for himself on his own paper.

The T-group provides a means of sharpening perceptual skills—of recognizing interpersonal perceptual distortions, learning ways to check out interpersonal perceptions, and learning how to correct interpersonal perceptions. A corollary is the learning of one's own functioning in a group: seeing the role one plays vis-à-vis others, how one distorts presentation of self to others, and how to obtain corrective feedback.

The T-group teaches people how they communicate with others, the variety of modes of interpersonal communication, and how to increase the effectiveness of communication, while decreasing the "noise" in the communication system.

The T-group provides a degree of "experiencing isolation," similar to the isolation of psychotherapy, that may enable participants to test out different modes of interaction and broaden their repertoire of human relations skills.

The T-group and related laboratory exercises have provided theory and method for effective intervention in organizations. This may range from natural community groups (churches) to community action groups (urban renewal), service organizations (YMCA), and business and industry (Shell, Esso, Bell Telephone).

The human relations emphasis in the T-group and laboratory method provides a method for nurturing human growth that may be incorporated into our educational structure to counterbalance many of the dehumanizing elements of American culture and particularly the mechanistic elements of the American school system (23).

The laboratory movement has given impetus and support to the scientific study of group function, leadership, and function of different types of groups, which have received little emphasis in the clinical professions. The T-group provides a natural laboratory.

The T-group and laboratory movement, less tied to professional conventions, has introduced many innovations in group interaction that may have clinical applicability: brief therapy groups, intensive group experiences, use of nonverbal interaction methods, refined use of group process analysis, and increased effectiveness of task groups.

Liabilities of the T-Group Method

Here we shall cite the major problems that have arisen in the use of the laboratory method. For the most part, these have not escaped the attention of leaders of the movement. In some exemplary instances, careful measures have been taken to deal with these problems (7). In other instances such problems are almost totally ignored.

There may be lack of adequate participant selection criteria. Persons may be involved in intensive interpersonal groups who cannot tolerate or learn from such relations. At best they emerge untouched and unmoved; at worst, they may decompensate.

Leaders have various degrees of competence, with few reliable norms for performance or a professional peer group to whom they must answer. Thus, leaders may use groups for their own aggrandizement or neurotic needs. Leaders may be incompetent—either accomplishing little or allowing unnecessary and destructive group activity.

There is a lack of clearly defined responsibility. This may range from a sense of no concern where a group ends up in its interaction to failure to respond to members who are undergoing un-

due stress or personal decompensation.

The T-group may provide a forum for more honest confrontation of self and others. It may also be a "hit-and-run" game. For example, one may talk quite freely to a stranger on an airplane but be totally incapable of confiding in one's real life relations. Thus the T-group may foster a sense of pseudo-authenticity and pseudo-reality—that this is really living while the rest of life is phony. The reality of the situation may be that the T-group participant can afford to act in ways that ignore reality because he does not have to live with the consequences of his behavior. Some people return to national sensitivity groups year after year because, they feel, "here I can really be myself." They are in fact unable to be themselves. Or they may be inappropriately capable of sharing intimate details of their psychological experience in a group of people without being able to do so when they should with a single individual.

The T-group may foster a sense of new-found patterns of relationship that may be inappropriate to a participant's real life circumstances. For example, T-group participants may return to their organization with "new ways of being"—only to find that the new self is not accepted by the old work group. The result may be ostracism or more likely a quick extinguishment of the new T-group self through involvement in everyday life and work that provides negative reinforcement of the new learning. The laboratory movement has sought to circumvent this problem by training people from an entire work group. But that solution does not adequately address the problems of differentiating a special group behavior from everyday group behavior. For example, if a patient talked to all his friends as he talks to his therapist he would soon run out of friends. Yet the T-group member may assume that T-group behavior should become the norm for interpersonal relations with everyone within his ken.

The T-group has often ignored the necessity and utility of ego defenses. Exposure and frankness, attack and vulnerability may become premium values. Often little attention is paid to the necessity for support and nurturance. Human foibles, inadequacies, and the normal range of variation in life style may be given short shrift. Some leaders have even theorized

on the value of some type of total exposure. This ignores individual differences in the capacity to tolerate stress and frustration. The mode of the self-reliant man who can take anything the group dishes out may more often be the covert norm than adjusting the group's expectations to the needs, capacities, and interests of each person.

The T-group may foster a concept that anything goes regardless of consequences. Instead of creating interpersonal awareness it may foster personal narcissism. If an individual says anything he wishes, then he may come to assume that just because he feels like expressing himself is justification enough to do so. This may preclude effective communication, for he then ignores whether the other person is receptive to his message, and he ignores the effect of his message on the other person. Communication may not be seen as an interpersonal event but merely as the opportunity to express oneself. The principle of "optimal communication" is ignored for the principle of "total communication."

A premium may be placed on total participation, on "experiencing" without self-analysis or reflection. The result may be exhilarating experience but no learning. A crass way of putting it is: "all id and no ego." One need not go that far, but an example will suffice. In several group-process teaching laboratories, mental health professionals who had been in prior sensitivity and encounter groups participated. They reported they had learned about themselves in their previous "group" experiences, but they had acquired little if any knowledge about how groups actually function. Nor had they acquired any useable knowledge about how they might effectively work with groups. The group laboratory should aim not only at acquiring understanding of the self but also at learning how to use the knowledge and experience in the group.

The T-group experience has often been conducted with a work group in disregard for the fact that this group must continue to work together after the T-group experience is terminated. The group is asked to participate "as if" their real life work-role relationships did not exist. The result may be both nonlearning and disaster. For example, in one professional work team that participated in a T-group experience, the members were instructed to tell each other "how they really felt about each other." The members successfully "told off" their chief in the T-group. The result was total disruption of the effectiveness of that team thereafter.

More important, however, is the issue of goals. In this instance the trainer ignored the goal of helping this professional team to work together and share perceptions and feelings "as appropriate." Instead, "experiencing" and "honesty" became the catch-words for an exercise in the group denial of reality. At stake is the question of how to increase the effectiveness of a team that works together and not to pretend that a group does not have real, ongoing, and intimate relationships that may be influenced by revelations made in the T-group.

The above illustration also points up another area of confusion in making a contract. The professional team entered the T-group with a contract asking for help in making the work group more effective. The trainer had his own personal contract that dealt only with change in individual members and ignored the contract to help the team. A contract to help a team may not necessarily result in helpful changes for team members, nor may helping team members to change necessarily be helpful to team function.

The T-group has often been conducted with little concern for how the learning in the T-group setting is to be transferred to the on-the-job setting. Trainers may assume that transfer of learning will occur automatically, that attention to transfer issues may interfere with the group process, or that the T-group experience is intrinsically valuable and that transfer of learning to the job or community is in a sense irrelevant. Pattison (48) has reviewed research data suggesting that ingroup behavior change in psychotherapy groups is often *not* accompanied by change in behavior outside the group. The same has been observed for T-groups. Until recently much of laboratory training focused on the T-group experience alone and ignored the fact that little transfer of learning was occurring. Nor were provisions made for changing T-group procedure to accomplish transfer of learning or generalizations of interpersonal responses. More recently, structured programs for subsequent follow-up training experiences have sought to remedy this problem.

The T-group has sometimes not been provided with appropriate leadership to teach or guide a group into optimal effective function. There is a notion commonly held in T-group theory that the group can be trusted to provide a just guideline for appropriate interpersonal attitudes and behavior. A group of people, however, can be tyrannical and destructive just as it can be beneficent and supportive. Historically, Carl Jung opposed group therapy because he felt it placed people at the mercy of others. The same objection is raised by right-wing groups such as the John Birch Society, who perceive of group methods as robbing a person of his autonomy.

There is no reason to assume that a small group will automatically develop into a supportive structure toward increased selfhood. Yet there is a covert assumption among some trainers that T-groups will always proceed in benevolent fashion. In fact, some T-groups do tyrannize their members—as do some therapy groups. This fact is overlooked in the eagerness of some trainers to develop autonomous, democratic groups. If the goal is effective democratic groups, then more attention must be paid to training groups in how to actually achieve that goal, rather than merely letting them flounder in dubious self-discovery.

Among recent innovations in T-groups has been the introduction of various nonverbal techniques for increasing "self-awareness." These include various role-playing maneuvers, action techniques such as wrestling, lifting members, and various types of body-contact-exploration maneuvers. This raises a number of theoretical, technical, and ethical issues beyond discussion here. The one point to be made is the shift of focus. These techniques, or some of them, may have a definite value. However, the focus has shifted from interpersonal learning and group process learning to individual learning. That in itself is not questionable. However, if personal issues become the chief focus, then the entire original goal for T-group method as a democratic group process educational experience has been lost. The exponents of these T-group techniques then have reverted back to the origins of group methods when individuals were treated *in* a group, not *by* and *with* a group. The distinctiveness of group process and group method is largely discarded. Much may be learned through these innovative group techniques, but at the expense of what can be learned about *group* function. Such trainers have not recognized that you cannot have it both ways.

The question of time-limited experience has received inadequate attention. It is assumed that the T-group members all learn at the same rate, that the length of T-groups is a relatively minor variable in learning, and that preparation for learning and reinforcement of learning are relatively secondary to the immediate T-group experience. Pattison (48) has shown in the context of group therapy that such time variables are all relatively undefined from an experimental point of view. Some effort has been made to address this issue in the training literature, but generally there has been no attempt to clearly define learning goals that can be accomplished in time-limited interaction and learning goals that require longer term spaced reinforcement. The most careful experimental work in this regard has been done in terms of time-limited psychotherapy and brief therapy. It is surprising that this matter has not been a subject of more T-group research. It would appear that the time limits used for T-groups have been those of convenience or propitiousness rather than those demonstrated to maximize the type of learning goals sought.

The assessment of T-group results has failed to consider seriously the psychonoxious or deleterious effects of group participation. The lessons learned long ago by psychoanalysts about the detrimental effects of adverse counter-transference reactions of the psychoanalyst (see for example the review by Orr [47]) and the rationale for the preparatory psychoanalysis of the student psychoanalyst before he undertakes doing a psychoanalysis under supervision have often been ignored by nonpsychoanalytic psychotherapists. Most outcome studies have been limited to investigating conditions of no-change or degrees of improvement. In fact, there has been a subtle but pervasive notion that psychotherapy is purely a beneficial maneuver—at least in the hands of competent practitioners.

A recurring rediscovery of negative therapeutic effects of psychotherapy occasioned by the therapist or by the therapeutic context has been noted or demonstrated again recently by various authors (27, 28, 29, 30, 52, 71). The detection and recognition of such effects is a thorny research problem that admits of no easy solution. The issue with the T-group movement is that there has been an enthusiastic partisan tone within the movement that fosters the concept that a T-group experience would be good for anybody and always profitable. The result may be a deluding distortion of participants' responses and a deceptive "oversell" that may end as destructively as the oversell of psychotherapy two decades ago.

To summarize the assets and liabilities of the T-group method, it may be stated that the T-group presents a powerful means of involving people in human behavioral analysis. The method provides possibilities for a highly significant contribution to the humane quality of existence in our culture and its various work and community components. The training laboratory has potential as a powerful instrument. Its liabilities lie in the area of utilization, as with any powerful instrument. Without adequate training, supervision, and guidelines, a powerful instrument may be destructive, just as a valuable drug may have undesirable effects if used unwisely or in incorrect doses. The liabilities described are not intrinsic deficits; rather, they are deficits of training, experience, clarity, and precision of goals (3). They can be avoided. Leaders within the laboratory movement are addressing themselves to the task.

Of more concern are the peripheral and derivative products of the laboratory movement—groups that have picked up bits and pieces of the laboratory movement, without the democratic concerns of the originators, without the clinical experience of the early leaders, without even the informal communicative guidelines that tend to keep professionals within a self-corrective framework, and without the continuing inquiring, self-critical, self-evaluative, and research perspective.

It is perhaps paradoxical that despite the enthusiasm that the laboratory movement has fostered, its practitioners have not fully realized how powerful are the tools they have developed. Therefore, the enthusiasm may not yet be tempered by respect and concern that these tools be rightly used.

Summary

The laboratory group method movement grew out of the developing concerns for democratic community groups during the 1930s. The sensitivity group or T-group became the most widely known but represents only one part of the effort to develop educational action programs that could teach citizens how to function more effectively, humanely, and democratically in a variety of group settings. The laboratory movement has proceeded from a rather unified effort into a number of divergent activities, ranging from therapy groups for normals to group dynamics workshops, task-oriented group exercises, and organizational intervention techniques. It is assuming greater importance in the United States, and the development of community mental health theory and programs should provide a common basis for increased involvement with psychiatry. There is, in fact, a wide overlap between almost all of the activities of the laboratory movement and psychiatric concerns, methods, and goals.

The laboratory movement has developed powerful instruments for human change. To date, some of the problems in the use of these instruments have not been clearly specified and dealt with. Some of these include quality control of the training of the group leader, the selection of participants who are not likely to suffer personality disruption from such group experiences, the clarification of the limitations of the beneficial effects of such group work, the protection of uninformed lay people from extravagant claims of therapeutic changes effected by these procedures, and the development of systematic research studies to evaluate the process and outcome of such group activities. These problems should and can be tackled. There is also the need for a more firmly developed institutional and professionalized base for the implementation of the laboratory method.

REFERENCES

1. Argyris, C.: Interpersonal Competence and Organizational Behavior. Homewood, Ill.: Richard D. Irwin, 1962.
2. Argyris, C.: Organization and Innovation. Homewood, Ill.: Richard D. Irwin, 1965.
3. Argyris, C.: On the Future of Laboratory Education, J. Appl. Behav. Sci. 3:153–183, 1967.
4. Artiss, K. L., and Schiff, S. B.: Education for Practice in the Therapeutic Community, Curr. Psychiat. Ther. 8:233–247, 1968.
5. Astrachan, B. M., Harrow, M., Becker, R. E., Schwartz, A. H., and Miller, J. C.: The Unled Patient Group as a Therapeutic Tool, Int. J. Group Psychother. 17:178–191, 1967.
6. Barber, B.: Some Problems in the Sociology of the Professions, Daedalus 92:669–688, 1963.
7. Batchelder, R. L., and Hardy, J. M.: Using Sensitivity Training and the Laboratory Method. New York: Association Press, 1968.
8. Beckhard, R., ed.: Conferences for Learning, Planning and Action, vol. 6 of National Training Laboratories Selected Reading Series. Washington, D.C.: National Training Laboratories and National Education Association, 1962.
9. Benne, K. D.: "History of the T-Group in the Laboratory Setting," in Bradford, L. P., Gibb, J. R., and Benne, K. D., eds.: T-Group Theory and Laboratory Method: Innovation in Re-Education. New York: John Wiley & Sons, 1964, chap. 4.
10. Berne, E.: The Structure and Dynamics of Organizations and Groups. New York: J. B. Lippincott Co., 1963.
11. Berzon, B., and Solomon, L. N.: The Self-Directed Therapeutic Group: Three Studies, J. Counsel. Psychol. 13:221–227, 1966.
12. Block, H. S.: An Open-Ended Crisis-Oriented Group for the Poor Who Are Sick, Arch. Gen. Psychiat. 18:178–185, 1968.
13. Bradford, L. P.: Biography of an Institution, J. Appl. Behav. Sci. 3:127–143, 1967.
14. Bradford, L. P., Gibb, J. R., and Benne, K. D., eds.: T-Group Theory and Laboratory Method: Innovation in Re-Education. New York: John Wiley & Sons, 1964.
15. Cartwright, D., and Zander, A., eds.: Group Dynamics: Research and Theory, 2nd ed. Evanston, Ill.: Row, Peterson, 1960.
16. Davies, J. C.: Neighborhood Groups and Urban Renewal. New York: Columbia University Press, 1966.
17. Durkin, H. E.: The Group in Depth. New York: International Universities Press, 1964.
18. Edelson, M.: Ego Psychology, Group Dynamics, and the Therapeutic Community. New York: Grune & Stratton, 1964.
19. Fairweather, G. W.: Social Psychology in Treating Mental Illness: An Experimental Approach. New York: John Wiley & Sons, 1964.
20. Fairweather, G. W.: Methods for Experimental Social Innovation. New York: John Wiley & Sons, 1967.
21. Forces in Community Development, vol. 4 of National Training Laboratories Selected Reading Series. Washington, D.C.: National Training Laboratories and National Education Association, 1961.
22. Frank, J. D.: "Training and Therapy," in Bradford, L. P., Gibb, J. R., and Benne, K. D., eds.: T-Group Theory and Labora-

tory Method: Innovation in Re-Education. New York: John Wiley & Sons, 1964.

23. Friedman, L. J., and Zinberg, N. E.: Application of Group Methods in College Teaching, Int. J. Group Psychother. 14:344–359, 1964.

24. Gosling, R., Miller, D. H., Turquet, P. M., and Woodhouse, D.: The Use of Small Groups in Training. London: Codicote Press, 1967.

25. Gottlieb, A., and Pattison, E. M.: Married Couples Group Psychotherapy, Arch. Gen. Psychiat. 14: 143–152, 1966.

26. Gottschalk, L. A.: Psychoanalytic Notes on T-Groups at the Human Relations Laboratory, Bethel, Maine, Compr. Psychiat. 7:472–487, 1966.

27. Gottschalk, L. A.: "The Evaluation of the Use of Psychoactive Drugs, With or Without Psychotherapy, in the Treatment of Non-Psychotic Personal Disorders," in Efron, D., ed.: Psychopharmacology: A Review of Progress 1957–1967. Washington, D.C.: Government Printing Office, 1968.

28. Gottschalk, L. A., and Auerbach, A. H., eds.: Methods of Research in Psychotherapy. New York: Appleton-Century-Crofts, 1966.

29. Gottschalk, L. A., and Gleser, G. C.: The Measurement of Psychological States Through the Content Analysis of Verbal Behavior. Berkeley: University of California Press, 1969, pp. 259–273.

30. Gottschalk, L. A., and Whitman, R.: Some Typical Complications Mobilized by the Psychoanalytic Procedure, Int. J. Psychoanal. 43: 142–150, 1963.

31. Group Development, vol. 1 of National Training Laboratories Selected Reading Series. Washington, D.C.: National Training Laboratories and National Education Association, 1961.

32. Hare, A. P.: Handbook of Small Group Research. New York: Free Press, 1962.

33. Human Forces in Teaching and Learning, vol. 3 of National Training Laboratories Selected Reading Series. Washington, D.C.: National Training Laboratories and National Education Association, 1961.

34. Jones, M.: Beyond the Therapeutic Community Social Learning and Social Psychiatry. New Haven, Conn.: Yale University Press, 1968.

35. Kaplan, S. R.: Therapy Groups and Training Groups. Similarities and Differences, Int. J. Group Psychother. 17:473–504, 1967.

36. Klein, D. C.: Community Dynamics and Mental Health, New York: John Wiley & Sons, 1968.

37. Klein, W. H., Le Shan, E. J., and Furman, S. S.: Promoting Mental Health of Older People Through Group Methods. New York: Mental Health Materials Center, 1964.

38. Leadership in Action, vol. 2 of National Training Laboratories Selected Reading Series. Washington, D.C.: National Training Laboratories and National Education Association, 1961.

39. Lippitt, R. L.: Training in Community Relations. New York: Harper & Row, 1949.

═══════════════════════

The article which follows was written by a young Japanese-American student at California State College, Hayward. It is a very sensitive account of a transcendant experience in an encounter group which speaks for itself. The author found it hard enough to see himself; his anonymity reflects his continued inability to be completely out front about himself. But, if encounter groups have done nothing else, we see here the growth of a very real, feeling human being.

8.11
The Living Experience of an Encounter Group

Anonymous

I find it difficult to put my feelings about my Encounter Group experience into words. The Encounter Group, as a contemporary phenomena, is caught in the business of cracking open emotional and psychical shells which encase most of us who inhabit today's technoculture. Originally evolving from J. L. Moreno's method of psychotherapy, the psycho-drama, Encounter Groups have been handed the task of "humanizing" the individual. In an age of Behaviorism and Determinism the Encounter Group as all gift horses, is being squarely examined and denounced by most academic members of the scientific community. The non-scientific structure and methods, feelings, sensitivity and insight, honesty and directness all subjective modes of perceiving are often looked down on as a kind of pseudo-psychology whose position in objective science is at best shaky. However the reinforcing contact of human beings with each other and the interaction of

By permission of the author.

human beings as such cannot be denied validity nor value. Yet, this very fluidity through which the significant contact takes place is a repudiation of standards upon which objective science sets itself. Perhaps this is a necessary and endemic quality of Group experience. And again we fall upon the philosophical horns of the question, "Is science, as such, a free play of ideas which is as much a matter of exercise and delight as well as a necessary activity for the scientist (as much free play as human relations appear to be) or is science the result of the divorce of knowledge from the sensual realm of human experience and can be derived only through the abstraction of ideas from that experience?" I will not pretend to answer this question which has been with us since the advent of Scientific Inquiry and continues to divide scientists and non-scientists alike.

For myself, I find that instead of beginning with a deterministic framework which, as the word implies, "pre-determines" the course of my actions and my emotional make-up, I proceed from actions and events to alternatives which themselves are germane to the content and makeup of what I call my "personality" and in fact "determine" the nature of that content and its organization.

My biases have been allied with the first part of that question only after living through a week-end experience with the Group. The experience itself encompassed much more than simply my participation as another member. Certainly our experiences and the limitations of our senses and intellect "determine" the kinds of people we are and very much of what we do. These things we have no control over as yet. But, what I think is important and central to the issue of my own life is what I *decide* to do within that sense and intellect which is mine and those experiences which I encounter. In other words, I *must decide* within the framework of that which is already given. My biases now aired, I would like to go on to the experience itself from which my point of view is taken.

I found myself at a crucial choice near the end of the group weekend. I had been through a trying crisis since Friday evening and it had dragged itself out until Sunday. The leader by this time had made clear his frustration and disappointment with the group's lethargy as no attempts had been made to "encounter" seriously. During this period I felt myself rising on the tip of a mounting anxiety. The anxiety stemmed from alternatives that were pulling me in two directions. One of these was a decision to leave the cabin and start back for home and the other, a decision to stay and to work through my crisis in the group setting. A watchful observer might say that I had also "taken cues" from the leader to respond, that too is true. The fact remains that it became possible for me to move from my immobility and into the feelings that were stirring loudly around inside of me. The desire to "allow" those internal feelings to be revealed was indeed contingent on the accepting nature of the group. The conflict having declared itself and beginning to surface in my consciousness, began to confront me as a kind of foggy self-awareness through which the conscious "I" could move into dealing with the problem at hand, that of committing myself to act one way or the other. That is "I" could then decide whether "I" wanted to attempt dealing with it through direct participation in my crisis within the group or to leave that internal situation alone and not deal with it, simply through non-action. The decision I made was to dive in and to take the problem by the horns. The emotions that were present as I recall were on one hand, rage, fury and resentment, and on the other hand, fear, anxiety and physical pain. I felt in the midst of all this an almost equally as strong an urge to go both ways. The physical sensations seemed to threaten complete paralysis with either choice. Fear, anxiety and pain are usually accepted passively by the organs of the body, while fury, and rage act as propellants which urge the body and the psyche onto action. Resentment, while on the same side of the coin as fury and rage is often an antecedent feeling and therefore a kind of middle-ground analogously akin to the edge of the coin, yet leaning toward the active direction. The result which I had anticipated from unleasing those pressing feelings was fainting, "passing out" from the overwhelming power of my anger (immobility again). The leader's acute sensitivity to my situation was vital to my continuing the process of venting that rage and then bringing it back to a simmer. As far as I had made the decision to vent my fury and to let go of any attempts to control it, "I" made it possible for those pressures to

have their way, to be at their complete mercy while the course of events themselves came under the guidance of the leader. He himself had no control over the situation. His part in the drama was to steer the direction that those emotional pressures would take. "I" am very much like the cartridge of a CO_2 container and the seething emotions are like the pressures within. The cues I received from the group were like the active agent which turns the cap of the container and the leader then functions as the steering agent who aims the cartridge in a particular direction as the gas escapes. During the course of events that followed, the "I" which is in apparent control, drops from view, removes itself and gives itself over to the actions of those events. During the experience I felt somewhat entranced and perhaps possessed.

The second and perhaps most important portion of my encounter group experience took place outside the formal group setting. I had gone through a crisis in my personal life which my ego handled by regressing to an infantile state, essentially internalized anger or depression. My relation to one of the women in the group outside of the formal setting was a necessary interaction which helped me to complete the child-adult cycle. This woman provided a much needed mother-figure, comfort, acceptance and reassurance. This relationship allowed my ego structure to "work out" the infantile needs for support successfully. From this stage "I" was able to take the necessary steps to revitalize the ego structure, externalize the grief, and finally act out the anger within the group. In other words we have here, a life situation played out in the broadest sense of a group context. Thus, the "artificial" contract of "encountering" fell away and with it, the need to maintain my own group persona. A new integration between self-image and self was created in the process quite inadvertently and quite unexpectedly. The process itself was both traumatic and dynamic.

I felt that what indeed had happened was a disintegration and reintegration of ego needs and coping devices into a new frame of operations. This came by way of new insights and self-perceptions which I believe have added a larger perspective to my own personal way of understanding myself and others. It is as I experienced it, a

"peak experience" to borrow a phrase from Abraham Maslow.

I would like in conclusion to speak briefly about such "peak experiences." The "peak experience" I believe is almost a psychological onus. I say that because it is quite internal, highly subjective, intensely preoccupying and lastly resistant to methods of the test-tube. This last mentioned aspect makes the whole examination of the group dynamics an enigma and therefore frowned upon by the "empirical," academic standard bearers of psychology. The intensity of the "peak experience" is such that it is not desirable as normal functioning of the ego. One would not like to be constantly "high." The symptoms displayed during the "peak experience" are indeed reminiscent of schizophrenic psychosis (which I will not attempt to detail here) and thus not desirable qualities for the socialized or "adjusted" individual who ideally exhibits a flexibility and relative "stability" in expressing those emotions and in interacting. The "peak experience" has no visible utility to those people outside the experiencing individual's realm, and involves only the valuing system of the experiencing individual. Thus again empirically we are left with little upon which to fix our theoretical handles. What then can we extract from the "peak experience" which we may call valuable? The answer to that perhaps is more literary than it is scientific. We might say that in an age where there is a barrenness of human sensory experience that the "peak experience" provides an oasis for the individual to renew and revitalize his realm of experiencing. Satiation and stimulation need not be ends in themselves. Rather, hopefully, we might be able to shake from the whole of the encounter group bag, a few grains of experiential wisdom. Until science can provide us with better tools to utilize such intangibles as human responsibility and human choice, let us not judge too harshly the latent potential which lies in individual people and is energized in bringing them together and through the use of a collective skill (the group member's sensitivity to each other). This skill of providing each other with experiential data is not the monopoly of experts but rather a skill which is shared by individual human beings in plurality. It lays in the groundwork of interaction possibilities which I think are creative for the art of living.

Journal

October 12, 1970

Well, it's finally started. I was lying on the bed recovering from supper when the phone rang. It's Marvin, Marvin ——, yeah, the leader. Where was the place that we were supposed to meet, I wanted to know. The card that Styles sent me said Rm. 204 at the First Congregational Church in Berkeley. 2626 Regent, we got the whole ground floor. Everybody was there when I got there all probably waiting for the last few stragglers. The room was nice. Somebody's living room. Yeah, like New England style with a kind of post-Hip motif in decorating style. A long row of windows at the street side of the room with a long bar hanging a wide length of short curtain, paisley curtain. Like the rest of the room a soft dark color. The room had a warm look about it, the furniture was low, cushions were strewn in the middle of the three-quarter size rug and the people on top of them. There were a few straight types, it's hard to tell yet. Man! Was I nervous, everybody had the lousiest way of looking natural and relaxed. All the way up from my place my stomach had been leaping at my throat trying to get out. Now it had settled into a state of angry disquiet and holding stiffly to the center of my rib-cage like a misplaced balloon. What the hell somebody in the group must feel the way I do. There was a guy with long, dark tangled hair with his back to the sliding door as I came in. He looked up and asked, "Eugene?" Yeah I said. And sat down.

Marvin started the rites off. He wanted us to turn to the person next to us and rap. Just rap, introduce yourself, don't fall into roles as to what you are doing on the outside, just kind of stay with it here. OK, sounds like a good idea. I turned to the kind of straight looking guy next to me with the high forehead the horn-rimmed glasses. Looked nervous so I didn't feel too awfully bad. We shook hands and exchanged greetings. His name . . . Andy. This was Andy's first time here to a group of any kind. He seemed OK, interested, good listener fairly sharp at keeping his mind on the conversation. I went through the whole bit . . . my cultural constipation. Yeah there was some crap that I needed to get rid of. Japanese are awfully repressed,

guilt-ridden and authority-ridden people. Disciplined, we'd been called by the whites that patronized us. We had discipline and self-control that's what they said in their naive sincerity. Yeah we're great people. We've made it, assimilation . . . admirable. The last group I went through was Hell. I was defensive, super-defensive, but I had learned the cues and some of the tricks to watch for. Andy was a Jewish boy. Physicist . . . grad student here at Cal. He had a problem, didn't say what just then. But part of it was that he wasn't very sociable, people looked at him differently than he did at himself . . . didn't seem too important. Maybe it was his "Jewish" mother. What's a Jewish mother? I keep hearing the slur like someone was talking about some infamous interrogator or dungeon-keeper. He talked fast in a medium-low voice. The words coming out one after the other like they couldn't get away from him fast enough—then the questions. He was pretty well tuned in to me but he wasn't trying to stick me with anything uncomfortable. I didn't see any traps. Like I must have sounded just like him. That's an easy way to fill up a void to throw up enough dust and hope that you're out of the way before it settles . . . If the company is unfriendly. I heard him say that the "Cultural-Identity" thing was pretty big these days . . . a little disdain perhaps? No I hadn't gone that far. But it's a good thing to affirm that biculturalism after all I can't change the color of my skin . . . some times I'd like to . . . that devil doesn't creep up on me much anymore I can say stick it! to the haoles (whites) these days . . . I'm feeling my oats, as they say. Well Marvin got us back to the group. It was hard to say what he was like at first. I compared the voice on the phone to Mark's, the leader of the last group. I liked him . . . sometimes, maybe Marvin didn't have the touch or the feel . . . the inflection and the tones sounded different. More casual, responding quickly to my own messages raveled in my voice. Mark came across like a Christian one guy had said. Sure of himself and self-righteously friendly. But he was OK. He had cools and he could take care of himself . . . and other people.

So it started off with Mark and the tall dark haired girl with the sharp features, the sallow skin and the piercing, steady blue eyes. That was Ellen. Then back to

Mark as Ellen introduced him, then Don . . . there was a lot more Don would tell us that night. Don introduced Sherry, Jeannie, Andy, Barnie, Judy, Andy and finally me. That's how we sat around the room. God! It was nine o'clock. We had spent a full hour just introducing each other. As soon as I had finished introducing Andy, Andy stepped forward to explain his reasons for being here. He had told me that there was an inconsistency in the way people saw him and the way he saw himself. He told the group more explicitly that he worked up at the Rad Lab and that according to the way he was perceived by others, he was a genius but he himself "knew" that he was only bright. It was a lead . . . with his right hand. Don was the first to jump at the opening, saying that that was a strange way to present himself. I thought that it was phony too. But I wasn't quite sure why. As I think back on it it sounded like a come-on. Like Andy was trying to talk us into thinking that he was brilliant . . . that he really did have a problem being too far above us mortals, and using his admission to his brightness or limited genius as a confession of modesty. As he came across he presented false modesty. Nobody bought his explanation. But Don was reacting even more strongly. His criticism was remarked to sound like, "I wish I had the same problem." Several people reacted strongly to Don, Ellen, Jeannie and Marvin.

Marvin asked me to say some more about the way I felt about my problems. I went into a semi-brief explanation of Japanese culture, psyche and history as I had learned to understand it. We were a parallel Puritan type society in the U.S. Like anger wasn't something you expressed because self-control was expected and you didn't talk about sex because that was private. Everything emotional and irrational was hinted at, frowned about and whispered in confidence. And here I was in the group attempting to get rid of the extra baggage. I didn't know how to accept Marvin's invitation to speak. He had started out by telling me that he admired the discipline and self-control that he had seen in Japanese people and that he had attempted to learn from them. That sounded like a patronizing, gracious, lure and I obligingly swallowed it. It's really hard to tell how sincere a comment like that is or whether it's part of the facilitator's bag of tricks. I remembered someone playing host that way trying to make you feel comfortable and accepted in order to have the party go smoothly and encourage shyer guests to loosen up and enjoy themselves. I didn't feel like I was giving the party so I complied. That little speech was enough to get a rise out of Don. Was I here to contribute something to the group or was I here for myself? Well I was there for myself and making no bones about it, not on the first night anyway. So I let him have it. How could he start reading shit into what I was doing? To Don I was not a trustworthy person because I would be someone that he could not depend upon. Well, so what, why the hell should that bother him so much? Don seemed like a pretty anxious guy to me. Like he seemed to need a lot of reassurance and comfort. It wasn't a hard guess to make. His veneer was hard and clinical, even somewhat desperate. Whenever one reacts to another in a group by demanding something from that other person he leaves himself open for attack. But if he can say that he "feels" such and such about another and articulates positive perceptions of the other to balance his expressions, then he has a balanced wheel to roll and it isn't likely that someone is about to upset his cart. A onesided attack always leaves one open for flanking movements by the enemy. After putting Don back in his place it was a lot easier to be condescending and gentle. Of course one who is harmless or is rendered harmless makes the other feel magnanimous. I think some losers play that losing game so that they can reap the benefits of generosity of the victor after being roundly tromped. Anyway I was feeling much more comfortable with Don after spotting his sore spots and making him aware of it. I was also feeling a little reckless with my generosity. The discussion soon drifted off into business of the group . . . where to find a cabin and a date for the encounter weekend. The night ended quietly.

October 19, 1970

I always get that funny feeling in my stomach before I start out for the group. It's like jumping off a diving board ten feet up I guess. There's always that intense feeling of anxiety until things get going. It doesn't take much for my stomach to start churning so I eat light, some soup, noodles maybe with a little meat. The gas and the tension make that a big meal. We met at Marvin's place on Monday. It's a small one room pad in west Berkeley below San Pablo. I got there early and Andy #1 was there, the physics major. He was huddled over in the corner, cold? or may be tight and withdrawn. His face had that perennial intense peering look. Marvin was loose and easy as usual . . . his warmth overriding his nervousness. I felt a little more at ease, like the demons in my guts had withdrawn for a strategic retreat. I let some of that energy out with an enthusiastic greeting to Marvin and Andy. There were a couple of new girls there. Holly had that fresh scrubbed look of the girl next door, smooth and angular features, light brown hair pulled straight back. Something about her said that she wasn't the cool, hip kid she was dressed as. Marvin needed some cups for coffee and there was some small discussion about where to go for an open store. Holly told me I could go since I had a car and knew the area. Things like that always tingle my senses even on first impressions . . . she was to be watched further . . . maybe she would be a little uptight and frozen . . . we'd see. I asked who else wanted to go and Andy volunteered. We went around the corner and came back in a few minutes. Others had started arriving. Jeez, can't remember them all. Some had dropped from the last meeting it had seemed . . . two chicks with a mutual friend . . . male type. Guess you could call that a conflict of interest. I guess that says that personal involvement cramps honesty . . . just a guess. How much more would they have to put out to relate had they stayed . . . not much privacy in that situation. It seemed like that small living room of Marvin's was going to be filled with wall to wall people that night. The quiet blond girl with the sharp nose and broad face was Mary, a new comer to the group. She had been there with Holly but had said little. Then there was Sherry, Carole, Charlotte, and David. David was the last to come. He was the youngest, 18. He had a fair soft, almost pretty face . . . the beauty and callowness of American youth . . . gentle. Marvin always has a cool way of starting off. He tried something structured and it blew. Tried to have people get together again by introducing each other in a metaphor . . . like he told me he saw a tree in me . . . I was solid. Then David walked in and the thing broke up.

So he just went to ask where everybody was at. Mary told us some about her last group. She was withdrawn, the lost flower child type. But somehow she struck me as sincere, sensitive and real. Probably the kind that spent a lot of time alone, bored with the lively plastic relationships, the enthusiastic kids from the suburbs who went to school with her. The latest movies, what you did last Saturday in the park, the false sensitivity to Politics and to people's feelings. I liked her. She wore dark brown pants and a colored poncho, her voice was heavy, unfeminine, guys probably didn't pay much attention to her and I imagined that there were few male relationships in her life. But she was there. I managed to open my mouth after a few minutes of listening and watching the signs. Good old Eugene, better red than dead. I was keyed up as hell and the demons had jumped back to life, hacking a merry rhythm inside of me. That was my energy I told them . . . the bottled up anger that was finding its way out of the spout of the lamp. Marvin said he couldn't imagine me as having problems dealing with my explosive feelings, I didn't come across that way . . . well perhaps he would see later on.

Of course somebody had to ask about the anger and so for the sake of structure (letting the new people know where I was at I went through a summary of my history . . . like a progress report) I complied. Holly was telling us her trite reasons for being there . . . one has to be gentle with people like that, . . . meeting people, making friends . . . wanted to know what it was like. Fuck! But why an encounter group? Church socials provide the same openings. It was a put on but this wasn't the time to get into things with her. I'd have to wait and see. When I got into my anger thing and the trip with my past . . . my uncertainties . . . flat and matter of fact of course there was to be misinterpretations of that. And Holly would be the one to misread that. I was just declaring myself, like saying, "I am . . ." but she took that to mean I wanted some reassurance. So she broke in with I feel warm toward you. And my reaction was to tell her that she made me suspicious . . . like the mothering trip that so many white chicks get into . . . the bag that compensates for their sexuality. Hell! She had volunteered me for the trip to the store a few minutes ago, without offering to come along. What kind of offer of friendship was that? The usual middle-class, cliche type, you don't get to open yourself to people until you see that they are vulnerable too . . . then you can feel "warmth." Bullshit! Well, I've got a good idea of what I think I can expect from this chick . . . I don't like her too much and I'll be waiting for a chance to pounce on her. Yeah, my hatred for the castrating woman, I'd like to take the knife away from her and I will. The next fool to react to that was Don . . . he has a way of sticking his neck out for the inanest reasons . . . he didn't want to commiserate together. We had heard David. He had been asked and he spoke. He was old, old . . . he had experienced so much more than many twice his age. He spoke of drugs and Synanon, of homosexual experiences. Now he decided that he preferred women and that he thought people didn't think much of him, like he had nothing to give. Mary broke in, she had reached out to David, she had reached out toward me when Don had made his remarks . . . she was OK. After David had finished Don made a funny. Dave had mentioned that he got bored with people who were always talking about the mundane things they had done in school and whatnot with their lives . . . it seemed like some people always had a lot to be interested in and he had nothing to say. Don cracked that he (David) could talk about that (his homosexual experiences). It was a dig, but it was funny . . . the tensions were exposed in those that had been listening carefully. I tend to lose conversations if I don't concentrate and I had misread Don's remark to mean it was directed at something else that David had said. I had told David that I could identify with the way he felt and the things that he had been through. He had lain around in bed for about three months just doing nothing . . . just lying there. That had been my trip for the whole summer of my Senior year after I had graduated high school and the trauma of the illness I had suffered brought back lapses like that for the last seven years . . . many long, endless nights. It was hell. Marvin cut in and looked at David. He said out loud that people were reaching out to David and had David noticed it? Marvin's sensitivity to what was happening in the group impressed me. David seemed to respond to that, the acceptance and the warmth had been made clear

to him. Then we went back to Don. Like the voice in the wilderness crying "Let's not sit around and wring our hands at each other's problems." That drew a real lash from me. Like he really pissed me off and I let him have it. Nobody was talking about weeping, I told him, David was telling us where he was at. It seemed like David had come to grips with himself and Mary had acknowledged that too. Don was in a heavy situation again. Mary reacted to him by saying that she wanted to talk to him, but that his defensiveness made her fighting mad. Marvin added that it sounded like Don wanted to hear good things about himself but when anything was said, he regarded it as "sickly sweet Bullshit." Andy #1 got into the act with his thrice removed analysis of Don and it was icily denied by the group. He shaped and formed his words into abstractions that when they were finally said, had lost the essence of the situation. Holly was the only one who felt that she was in tune with Don. Her feelings were that Don didn't want to just talk about problems but that he wanted to discuss affirmative things too. It was like she too had missed the whole point of the encounter. Almost as if things had gotten to be too heavy for her and that she like her middle-class counterparts, would simply dismiss. I was getting more and more annoyed by her. It's tiresome, to deal with people like her. The repressions, the wax papered emotions, the Pollyanna countenance. Of course I realize that I am reading as much into what she was responding through to my own history and projections . . . maybe we'll deal with her later. I told Don that I again heard him asking us to reassure him, but it was up to him to tell us what that was if I was to be able to meet him on some common ground. Here, Marvin's professionalism wisely called the trip to a halt. We took a break around cider and coffee, and the evening drifted off uneventfully.

October 26, 1970

We got into a good thing at Andy #2's house. I was feeling pretty churned up when I got there. Ellen had laid a bum trip on me the night before. Not intentionally, but she did. When Marvin got there we got to talking about what had happened that day. I told him that I was still going up. He was feeling pretty good and mentioned it. I got into the thing

about Ellen calling me and said that she was feeling lonely and wanted me to be there with her but that she was also feeling bored and neglected. Partly because she was wearing my ring. When she went to parties only her friends would dance with her but nobody else would come near because she was supposedly taken. I was mad at her because it sounded like she wanted entertainment and since I wasn't around to provide it she was beginning to have second thoughts about her commitment. I said that I had told her that if she really felt she wanted to be with me to just come on up. And she had said that she was too sensible for that because the semester was easy and it was almost over. She's coming in December to finish the year here but she kept saying that she couldn't wait. I had told her that she could go out with guys other than her friends as we had already decided that that would be the sanest thing to do since it would be awhile before we could get together. She said that there was nobody else and that she didn't meet anybody that she was interested in getting to know but that she just couldn't wait. I had bent over again and said for her to take off the ring . . . shit, I didnt know what was going on in her head . . . but it really had me hurt and shook up. I guess I had given her vibes that I was really enjoying myself over here, swimming and practicing Karate again after many years laying off. My guess was that she wanted me to feel that I really missed her and for me to tell her about it. But I guess I just am getting into myself now and what really keeps me going is looking forward to her coming . . . with enthusiasm and some anxiety. Marvin asked if I was going to do anything about it and I said that I was. I was going to tell her that I was really pissed off at her. I am beginning to realize that I must be able to tell her that I am mad at her as well as how much I really care about her for the relationship to work. I finally ended my phone conversation with her by saying that if the semester was more important than me then that was up to her. That message really got through cuz she called when I got home to tell me that she was feeling better and had resolved her crisis. So much for my little episode. I had worked out my decision to accept the consequences when I had been grieving that I would have to put her out of my mind if she decided to split.

Everybody showed up that night and Sherry was in a bad way even though she was trying to come across as calm and together. She had lost a close friend the past weekend and was having trouble dealing with the death. I had similar experiences in the service which I found to be terrifying. Everybody else seemed uncomfortable with the situation. We began talking about our own experiences and kind of skirting the issue. Sherry was pretty much wanting to do something but afraid to get into it. She kept saying that she didn't want to lose control here. So Marvin finally brought up the observation that he felt she wasn't getting into her grief. He asked her if she wanted to talk some more about it, and she said no. And he, like a good leader said that it was fine.

Sherry suggested that we try some body awareness stuff. We put her in the center and did a trust fall but she wasn't relaxed enough to get into the experience. Charlotte, the Norwegian gal, had been quiet and distant from the group. Someone asked her if she was able to trust people. She replied that there was trust and then there was trust. She could trust people in some situations and not in others. She said that she had been taken before because she was gullible to people . . . being too trusting, emotionally, financially, etc. She represented in some distant way the feeling that I get with women that hold themselves back, not willing to open themselves to me. The whole thing about my mother and my anger at her was there but very quietly under the surface. Women that are cold hold a challenge for me, like it is an invitation to take them on and to break open that retentiveness . . . a reflection of how I view my own masculinity . . . very shakily at times. I told the group that when the trust fall is done something is given to the person whom the trust fall is being done to. I said that I would like to give something to Charlotte. She was on the spot and was showing it by twitching her feet. After hesitating for a moment she agreed. Charlotte is a big girl and we passed her around in the circle. She began to slump and let herself go slowly. Then we picked her up and rocked her above the group, high over our heads. She was wearing a short skirt and it kept coming up, but she didn't seem to mind. The contact, apparently had been made and it was groovy. I felt successful . . . in a mildly gloating way.

We put her down and massaged her. A few moments later she got up and said that she felt better. Her twitching feet stopped and her stomach quit making so much noise. An exchange took place between Andy #1, the physics major, and Sherry. He told her that he felt depressed because she had avoided him at the Styles Hall party the past weekend. Then he said he understood why she had (the death experience). He kept saying that he was mad at himself for not having the control to keep himself from being resentful, but he understood. Sherry responded by saying that she was sorry but she avoided him because she felt she couldn't handle him just then. And that she really didn't want to hurt him and was sorry about it because if she really cared about people as much as she likes to think of herself then she wouldn't do it. Both of them kept insisting that it was their own fault . . . but I felt that there was something more going on. Marvin tried to end it by saying that we would assign blame to both of them. I cut in and said that I felt that there was unfinished business between them. Holly agreed and said that they weren't facing up to it. I was going to tell them what I thought was going on. Andy was saying I'm still mad at you and Sherry was saying look how hard I'm trying, but I wasn't about to play therapist . . . so I went ahead and told them about the bum trip Ellen had laid on me. And that even though she had told me not to worry and asked if I understood, I only could say "Yes I understood, but it still didn't make me feel any better." Sherry clicked into that and could see that Andy was still feeling bad although he didn't want to admit it. That took care of that. I was feeling pretty loose and easy that night, but some of the people felt like the group hadn't gotten off the ground. I had told Marvin earlier that I liked to touch people and that he had broken the ice for me by opening up himself to somebody else. He extended his hand to me and we had a warm clasp . . . that was really good. The group through Marvin's urging closed in and people put arms around each other as we sat in a circle. I asked Charlotte if she was still with us and she answered affirmatively. While Sherry and Andy were talking, Carole and I had the soles of our feet together. We started to do a trip together, moving and pressing our feet against each other. A feeling of

flowing energy was going through me and our feet wiggled, and grasped and explored . . . like getting acquainted, until I told her that my ankles were getting tired. When the group moved in I put my arm around Charlotte and gave her a back rub. She reached over and at first awkwardly and then knowingly started a rhythmic kneeding of my chest and stomach as I was lying on my back. Charlotte seems like a very sensuous girl and quite voluptuous . . . and she was beginning to stir sexual feelings in me. Like my body was beginning to tingle but the conflict of feelings over my attachment to Ellen and the suspicion of difficult women kept me from having an erection, although it would have been really nice to have one . . . I think a potentially full feeling of having thoughts and emotions and attention focused in one direction . . . well so be it we'll have to work it out . . . me and my superego. Impotence is one thing that I have had to reckon with over the last 7 years . . . the whole fear of not being able to fulfill the masculine role . . . throwing out old hangups is like shedding a skin that you're still attached to. The night ended up in one big group massage and embracing. Andy the egghead made the remark that it was like a Roman orgy . . . but even he was beginning to like it. After we broke up I told Marvin and Andy #2 that after tonight I would have trouble chastising Ellen and I was right . . . when she called my feelings were more into perspective.

November 2, 1970

The group was a little slow this time. Mary asked us to have the session over at her place but she ended up housing a bunch of people over the weekend so that canned that. We went over to Andy #1's house on Haste for the meeting. For some reason or another several members of the group didn't show. Charlotte was the only one who wasn't accounted for. Judy was sick and Mary was too busy taking care of the guests who had crashed for the weekend. We got started anyway . . . the group feeling a little more relaxed. I brought Holly over from Mary's house and she was in her usual cheerful spirits. This time Marvin got started by invoking memories of the last meeting. "Did anybody experience anything that they talked to friends about during the week?" And would we share what we felt about what had happened now? So we started in a circle . . . everybody taking their turns. Carole had a beautiful way of expressing what she felt. She told us that she went home and wrote and wrote and wrote. It was a groovy session that we had experienced and made the group feel more like a "group" rather than a bunch of individuals who had gotten together . . . we had shared the nice experience of wanting each other. For Carole, it was an experience that she wanted to cling to. She felt herself hanging on and grasping as she felt the feelings leaving her . . . then she was able to realize that she could just let go. That is a little reminiscent of living . . . hanging on to the past, fearing the future . . . trying to keep hold of the good feelings that we experience and hold onto them forever. I guess it's kind of like being mortal and middle class, but then sometimes I think that eternity would be a bore. Anyhow it was really nice the way she said it. Carole is a sensual girl and though she isn't attractive in the conventional sense I kind of dig the way she comes across. She came to sit down by me and I gave her thigh a friendly and welcoming pat . . . hesitantly not knowing how it would be received and not feeling all too confident of my own desire to reach out to her . . . to say hello, how are you, I like you and it's good to see you in that gesture. It was well received and she gave me a clammy stiff reassuring squeeze. I guess we're all pretty awkward at liking each other . . . in and out of our private lives. There were a couple high points in the evening. Marvin put Andy #1 and Sherry into a role playing situation. Andy the physicist came across to me like a little boy. He told us that it was really typical the way girls turned off to him. One girl that he knew told him that he says "hi" the way some people say "please." You know like he really wants to be liked and accepted but at the same time he uses his intellect to dissect and to penetrate and barricade to keep the intercourse as free from threatening involvement as possible. It's so obvious even on a superficial level that he was quite upset about the whole thing. It's strange and yet it isn't that he at first when the group had started stated his reason for being in the group was so that he could make the connection that apparently was a contradiction in the way he viewed himself and the way others saw

him. Of course I think he was saying that he didn't think that he was coming across as begging, but it was the apparent message that the girls had gotten . . . that he wanted mothering and they weren't about to give it. Well, what the fuck . . . American women need so much to feel protected or domineering that he really wouldn't have much choice to begin with. Andy is a Jewish guy and I have a hunch that he has a "Jewish mother" . . . and maybe there is something there that he hasn't come to terms with like helplessness from an overprotective mother. Mothering is not what he needs but since that is what he is used to I guess that is what he expects . . . all guesses of mine. Anyway, now we were at the root of his reason for being in the group. So he and Sherry went through an imitation of meeting at a party and began talking like they had just met. It wasn't too productive and nobody picked up any vital vibes. I wasn't really into it myself except for a little bit. I told them that it seemed like their demands on each other were crossing. Sherry seems almost demanding that people recognize her as gentle and sensitive and Andy it looked to me was performing via his intellect, sometimes rebutting sometimes probing but without apparent empathy. That is expressing sympathetic emotion, "oooing" and "ahhhhhing" to exaggerate what I mean. So there was this barrier. So he tried the role-playing trip again with Holly who seemed like she was really getting into this sham conversation. Then she came back and said that there was more that she would like to have said but she was trying to follow Andy and to stay in tune with what he was talking about. That was missed by Marvin who called her a nice "show lady" . . . which is apt for Holly but it was misconstrued . . . because she said that she hadn't meant that she was just putting on. From here we went to Don the nemesis of the group. Holly was trying to convince us that she was really a happy person . . . not that she repressed things but that she really believed that she could look at the better side of life and take the bad stuff in stride. Don told her that he didn't think that she was real but that she was much nicer and that he felt more warmth toward her when she was just being herself when nobody was looking. When Don had practically called her a phony . . . I asked Holly what she felt toward

Don . . . she replied that if he felt that way it was up to him. And didn't express much emotion to it. My guess is that she was "fronting" us again and internalizing the pressure. I told her that when she was talking to us about the way she felt . . . good and together . . . it was almost believable but when she failed to respond to Don which would have been fighting words for me . . . that I had suspicions that maybe what Don had said was in fact true. I told Don that I thought that he had hit upon some crucial issues although I didn't feel the warmth he claimed or the helpfulness he tried to assure us of. So I told Holly that although I felt that she wasn't always for real in her Pollyanna cheerfulness, that she was trying and that was important. She thanked me for that because that was what I think she wanted us to recognize . . . that she was trying. I had a flash that I shared with the group. I saw Holly going door to door saying "Hi! I'm selling girlscout cookies" . . . in a fresh, girl next-door sort of way. Then I saw Don going from house to house saying the same words in kind of a grim demanding way. He noted dourly that I liked describing people in interaction in terms of knocking on doors. I told the group that I was into a private therapy session because I felt that I could work a lot better with a one-to-one relationship which would take all of my time and intensity in the session instead of monopolizing the group's time every session. Marvin interjected by saying that he thought that I was in touch and that I shouldn't hesitate to bring up something that I wanted help with. And I guess pride has something to do with that . . . coping with a dozen people and their feedback and not wanting to bring out something humiliating that I had experienced. I told them about Mark and Louise . . . the evening that I had had dinner at their place. And about Mark and I having some trouble communicating at times because of his intensity and my fear of hurting his feelings . . . something that I was avoiding. Mark and I had talked about it I had said, but Louise was the same way as Mark in many respects . . . and I didn't feel like I knew her well enough or would be accepted if I tried to bring something like that up. It's hard to work with things like that with people who you feel close to since there is always the fear of damaging the relationship. And that is where I am as far as my anger and my fear of expressing it go. It's something that I am coming to terms with the more often that I see Mark and make myself face what I am avoiding . . . the little gestures and expressions, physical and verbal that betray my hesitance about myself. The group again deteriorated into a nice love-in with Carole cuddled up next to me. I think we really groove on each other . . . partly because we have a threshold of mates that we are committed to outside of the group. That commitment is really like a special kind of freedom when I think of it.

November 9, 1970

What a heavy night! We had the meeting at Holly's place this time. Marvin started off the thing with a game. It went like this. "I am withholding from you . . . so and so . . . such and such feelings." The whole thing was so low key, everybody saying nice things to each other that it was sickening. Holding back anyone? It surprised me when we got to Andy the physics major who told Marvin that he didn't have rapport for him any more like he had had earlier. It came out hard and pretty strong and it sounded good from him. Andy is usually apologetic and this statement gave him much more substance. It's amazing how the structure of the group can immediately cast people into different states of mind. The group is a pretty comfortable one . . . and we mix fairly well. As soon as Marvin asked us to get started and introduced the game a hush tenseness fell over everyone . . . expectancy. We finally started going full speed ahead with Holly this time. Strange that thoughts don't come to me so easily just yet. All I see in my head is Holly sitting there in the middle of the group with Marvin holding her hands and caressing her. Then me moving into the center with her feeling the strain of anguish . . . like confronting my mother again in this young girl . . . wanting so much to give her something . . . love? . . . understanding? . . . warmth? I heard myself saying inside of me. "Why won't you let me love you? Please don't hold me out." I asked Marvin if he had done fantasy trips before, if he could do one with Holly. She kept saying that she was "trying" to feel but she could understand things and feelings only in her head. The whole damned thing started, now that my head is coming together on the scene, when

Andy had finished his withholding game. Holly responded to him by saying that she was afraid of showing him warmth or feelings because she was afraid that he would try to lean on her and she thought that any display of emotion would be a come-on. I don't remember what Andy said to that but it was more like he responded to her in the way that he felt in one of the situations that involved them both the last time . . . I'm not too clear right now. There was nothing in what Andy had said for Holly to assume that Andy would make any advances as she described or that he even had the intentions . . . but she kept stressing how she would like a relationship to be give as well as take. Holly is preoccupied with her feelings and keeps explaining them away any time something happens. She keeps talking about her feelings without ever expressing them . . . well she does but they come across as explanations. Later she told me (as I suspected) that her father was rejecting and that he rejected her although she really tried hard to get him to like her. She isn't really what you would call a seductive girl . . . she tries this bright and cheerful demeanor but sometimes I think it's a mask . . . too much talking about I really feel good . . . and not just being that good feeling. It always has to be qualified. She is afraid of men and I am afraid of her. I don't think I could depend on her for support if it were ever to become an involved relationship. I could immediately see the relationship between her and a lot of women . . . who are always working at cross purposes with people like Andy and myself. I need a lot of support from a woman . . . someone who can express what she feels that gives me a sounding board from which to gauge myself. I think that she is too fearful of the rejecting father-figure. Something really incredible happened last night while Holly was talking. Don was sitting off in the corner in a chair. We invited him to come back and join the group but he refused saying that he was a lot more comfortable out there. Then when Holly started getting into her approval trip and the group was trying to get her to feel, to move into her own emotions and verbalize them, Don moved back behind Holly and put his arm around her almost demanding that she lie back. Not really even knowing where she was at. She was unyielding at first but then she gave in . . . what a

double shell trick. Holly was sitting there explaining and defending herself and Don came in to offer assistance . . . letting her off the hook . . . and grabbing attention for himself as Marvin pointed out. Don never tries to put himself on the line . . . instead he comes out with cynical remarks about the things people are doing as not really worth it and not working. Marvin got pissed at that. He finally told Don that it was his trip to be an armchair cynic, but that he never participated himself. Don looked a little taken aback but he wasn't about to relinquish his stand. Andy was showing a great deal of animosity toward him. Called him a three-dollar bill.

Something there that's hard to identify yet. Holly, Holly . . . what a heavy trip on my head. I get tired thinking about Monday night. She is like watching myself a few years ago. Trying to justify my own existence, talking away about these feelings and those feelings that I had just discovered as if they had never existed before. So wrapped up in the causes and consequences of those feelings that the world outside was only an auxiliary illusion. It, for all worthwhile purposes, wasn't there and neither were other people . . . merely shadows of my limbo. In some way I can sympathize with her struggle and in other ways it makes me impatient, I want to get on with my own business of living too. You can't communicate with a recording. Very frustrating and yet there seems to be much potential in the direction that she is taking. Well, who am I to say anyway.

When we were sitting there in the circle and I was offering myself to her . . . she began to talk like to say how nice the experience was and I put my fingers to her lips before she could erect that barrier of sound from her own voice between us. "People talking without speaking, / People hearing without listening." It's really tiring and taxing to be trying to relate to all this and it's a waste of energy. The only locks that are open are the ones that can be picked but what takes too much concentration and it drains me. Is the group working? I wonder after sessions like this. It's great right! We get onto something heavy and everybody's energy is focused on this one miniscule of the human condition and it resists all efforts to put it in its place, like a virus. Holly has to feel comfortable and safe before she can be Holly . . .

and all the explanations in the world will not make her her. I don't think that it can be done in 10 sessions . . . like saying living made easy in 10 easy lessons, no cost and no obligation except full person commitment. Well, maybe that is why they are sometimes called T-groups. At least there is an element of learning that we must deal with when our sham fronts are presented to us in a basket. Marvin told me afterwards that I had been taking chances then pulling out at the last minute. He was referring to the time when I had asked him if he could do the fantasy trip. He said that you sometimes get into situations where you have to take the situation in hand and do something with it. I told him that what scared me was not so much the thought of the responsibility, but the false trips that had been laid on me in the other group that I was in. The role-playing and acting out gimmicks hadn't been entirely successful because the timing was bad. The skill with which Bill —— had presented himself in the therapy session had led me to choose him over a psychiatric social worker who was pulling rabbits out of her hat. I felt that pulling a fantasy thing on Holly might not just put me into a therapist role . . . it might not have done me any good and set her back. People are toughies said Marvin and I think that he's right . . . they can take a lot. But I wasn't feeling that way when I yelled to him for help. It was my own anxiety as well that needed relieving and realizing this added factor made me even more reluctant to take over the scene. Maybe I'll be more in the frame of mind to take more responsibility for somebody next time. I'm beginning to see that I really want to reach out. I stayed up with Holly till 2 AM and we got to say a little more to each other but I was getting really tired and feeling like we were going around and around. When I decided to call it quits and let us both get to bed we went out to the porch and embraced. I told her, "It's nice to be close to somebody." Then I realized what I had said although I think that it went by her. I wanted to be in relationship to people and that somebody that had come sliding out of my unconscious almost meant anybody. I miss Ellen but I can't be preoccupied with her now . . . when she gets here we'll pick up where we left off. I guess what I had said to Holly made me feel a little guilty about Ellen as if it should be Ellen specifically that I

should want. But as it came out it's anybody that I want to be close to. While I was holding Holly I think I noticed her putting her head in my shoulder and cuddling . . . like a child wanting to be protected. Those kinds of signals come over strong . . . maybe I was just making that up from what I had seen of her in the group and afterwards . . . and it gave me the burden of being paternal . . . not really feeling that we were meeting as equals . . . gives me all kinds of paranoid fantasies of being used to garner the much needed approval she needs for her ego. Reaching out to others is reaching out from knowing where I'm at . . . and in these situations I have mixed feelings about what is expected of me and what it is I want to give. Holly makes me feel like I should be lifting her, protecting her, supporting her. I'd like to share my experiences with her and give her my warmth and friendship, that which there is to give . . . that is . . . as I listen to her and listen to what she is asking of me. I would like for her to listen to me and to understand where I am. We damned humans make things so difficult for each other and ourselves. I have very mixed feelings about Holly . . . I'd like to believe that sweet self that she pours out . . . seductively? and on the other hand I am afraid of being used to confirm her own identity. She's afraid of Andy and not afraid of me . . . is she identifying with me because there is something there to take? Well . . . tune in next week for the next exciting chapter . . . when Super Self-Actualizer, actually actualizes . . . Fuck!

Nov. 17, 1970

Dear Ellie:

Got your letter today with my ring in it . . . thanks for sending it back and thanks for cleaning it . . . for taking care of it lovingly. I have an awful lot to tell you about what happened last Friday after I called you from up in Monte Rio. Even today there are things going on on the inside that I know that you could never possibly know no matter how much I would like to share them with you. A lot of it is so infinitely sad and so infinitely beautiful. And it has a lot to do with how I am beginning to understand about love. Or maybe to feel about it. I am writing a journal and a report for a small groups class. It's a whole mind-fucking trip to try to put the wonderful glory of a human experi-

ence into a fucking test-tube and to dissect it . . . right now I don't think I am even going to try to do that . . . I feel like I grew so much within my world after this weekend. And yet I feel empty . . . a nice, real sort of empty . . . Judy and I shared so much that it's almost unbelievable. There isn't too much that can be said about that intellectually . . . and there is no need to. Right now I am close to tears in reliving that experience . . . there is so much to tell and yet so little about it that can really be said. The tears are both of joy and sadness . . . something I don't think that I ever have felt in all my 25 years. After I finished talking to you on the phone I went into the living room and Marvin our leader commented that he could hear me yelling at you . . . I had never talked much with Judy before . . . I think that I was afraid to because I felt that I could really like her, and I didn't want to. In some ways I feel now that she has always been my lover and always will be. I'm still awed by the experience with her . . . it's almost too powerful that I am being swept up in it, and carried away like the tide that takes the sand away into the sea and spreads it away. I've got to get a hold of myself before I can continue to write this to you. I've been to so many distant lands inside myself and I feel like I've lived forever in a moment with her . . . a moment that was once and for always and never again. I asked her to talk to me and so she went with me into the bedroom. We sat on the bed and I told her about your affair with Les. I was beginning to shake and she came over to me and held me while we talked . . . something that I didn't expect. The shaking finally stopped . . . my anger at you had subsided for the moment. Our talk didn't seem too deep at the time . . . there was a lot that I felt that I had worked out with you . . . and I was on another level then. What you had told me had struck me down like the scythe of Death in one swoop and I don't know where I found the strength to come back to life but I had. We went into the kitchen and began talking with Marvin about superficial things . . . about groups and about the cabin . . . where we would all sleep. Judy and I had only known each other for a few moments but I asked her to stay with me that night . . . she smiled, and hugged me . . . and she thanked me. There were three beds in the room . . . one double bed and a bunk. I didn't see much of her for the rest of the evening and in a few hours we began to turn in. She and Holly got undressed and into their nighties, and I climbed into bed. It was cold so we piled sleeping bags and blankets on the bed . . . I told Holly to jump in since the top bunk which she was on was broken on one side. She got in on the side near the wall . . . and with a little coaxing Judy joined us . . . I think that she was a little afraid . . . she does have a boyfriend at Stanford. But she climbed in on the other side of me next to the bedstand. Holly dropped right off to sleep and Judy was trying to I think. They both had their backs to me and there I was . . . between two women . . . not able to sleep . . . not because they were there, but because there was that sudden void inside of me remembering you and lonely. A couple of hours later I turned over toward Judy and touched her shoulders, and she moved slightly. I remember her waking gently and holding on to my hands, then she turned over toward me and we started to talk. I can't remember what it was we said to each other but we talked of all kinds of things. Judy has asthma and it was beginning to bother me to hear her wheezing. I remember telling her that it was beginning to frighten me to hear that . . . and she asked why . . . and I told her that it was because I was beginning to like her. She was smiling at me, that funny, pixie smile of hers that was love and life and understanding. We caressed and talked and the night wore on and she kissed my face and hands . . . I had to ask her if she wasn't afraid of sleeping in the same bed with her and she replied that she had been a little.

It was good to be with her to be able to take the warmth and the love that she gave so freely. Yet there was still that funny cold spot inside of me . . . like a hollow inside of my stomach . . . because I was still so hurt and broken. She made me laugh about the small things that happen in life as she told me about herself and we talked about each other. She lay in my arms for a long time then she turned over and I slept with my arms around her and our bodies touching. I was stroking her side and her belly as we began to drift off . . . I must have been asleep for a few minutes or maybe it was longer the whole memory of it eludes me when I try to put it into words . . . then I realized

that I was caressing her breasts . . . she didn't move but put her hand on top of mine. She woke and we began talking again . . . I asked her if that had bothered her and she shook her head. I began to feel myself getting hard and I told her . . . that it was like my strength coming back. I could have made love with her that night . . . I wanted to . . . not out of spite for you . . . but out of the need to be cared for, to have someone show love for me. She thought that it was my anger toward you that made me feel that way and I said that I needed her mothering very much. And then I told her that it would be like her making love to me and not the other way since it was all her strength that I would be drawing on to bring mine back. That wasn't the way out of it . . . it would have to be on my own. We turned over again and went back to sleep. I lay there with my hand on her breast . . . I think it was almost the same as nursing from her like the last scene from the "Grapes of Wrath," that was the most vivid image that came to my mind . . . her loving me . . . if we had made it would have been the same kind of thing . . . but she was giving me an awful lot anyway . . . and that wasn't necessary to physically be enveloped in her body. I'm beginning to get back into my head now and this whole letter is beginning to look stiff and cramped . . . a lot of what happened can't be talked about to anyone . . . not even myself . . . somehow a lot of it would be destroyed that way. Judy was up early and we began to talk some more . . . and laugh . . . it was so nice. Holly was really zonked and hadn't heard a thing that had happened that night. We stayed in bed while the morning came in through the curtains . . . then Judy got up and asked if she could use my tooth brush . . . or did I offer it to her . . . I went back to sleep and was out for a couple hours. Judy came bouncing back into the room and sat on the bed . . . or was that the next day? Nothing much happened when Marvin tried to get the encounter group into a session that afternoon . . . and nothing happened again that night . . . Almost everyone had just deteriorated into one big pile on the floor and some . . . Andy felt like it was a cop-out . . . so he went to bed saying nothing. I went to bed about 3 AM and slept alone that night . . . Judy stayed with Marvin on the floor next to the fire. She came in to wake me up about

noon . . . what's happening . . . I forgot something here. The encounter group took a permanent break that afternoon and I was still exhausted from my episode with you . . . so I went to bed. I was all alone in that room . . . such a dark empty space inside . . . so tired and so sleepless. Judy came in again after I had been there . . . I was crumbling. She sat on the bed and asked me how I was. "I don't feel good, I don't feel good" I remember saying . . . and she asked if it was because of you or because I was ill . . . it was about you I had said and she held me in those warm little arms of hers. That's when I felt everything well up inside of me and come pouring to the surface . . . I cried and cried and cried and she just held onto me. She said that she thought it was good that I could cry and not as I was thinking . . . that I had become a little boy . . . she said that she wished that more of the men she had known could cry . . . she just held onto me and I could feel her warmth and caring come through my anguish . . . and it was good. I can hear myself through the sobbing crying "Judy . . . Judy . . . Judy!" And as quickly as it had begun . . . it ended . . . this is all so hard to talk about . . . not because I have difficulty with it but because so much was happening to me, that cannot be reexperienced in the telling. She stayed with me for a long time and we began talking again about life, and love and Jesus . . . she doesn't know too much about the Bible being Jewish . . . and we laughed again . . . then she left me again and I slept a heavy, deep, exhausted sleep. Like I said . . . nothing much happened that night and I slept well. The next afternoon on Sunday when Marvin pulled the group again for the last time, he was frustrated and pissed off. I had two urges building inside of me. One was to split and go back to Berkeley and the other was to spill my guts there. I didn't decide to do it . . . it happened . . . I started getting sick again and I told Marvin what was happening . . . I was beginning to shake again and he told me to let the shaking go, not to fight it . . . then my rage and fury poured out and I struck the floor . . . I wanted to destroy you and Les. I hated both of you and would as well killed both of you. Marvin threw a pillow on the floor and I lit into it and kept pounding on it . . . frightened that I would pass out or vomit but I kept pouring out my rage and wading into it. I told you to get lost that I didn't want you . . . the whole thing must have lasted 5 minutes but it felt like years . . . Marvin kept throwing the pillow back at me . . . he must have done that about a dozen times or more. "She's coming back . . . Ellen's coming back" he kept saying as he threw the pillow at me until I fell back exhausted and slumped . . . his voice was very quiet . . . softer than a whisper as he asked me what was happening . . . "There's still something left that you're hanging onto he told me." "What is it?" he asked. I felt empty and drained and purged . . . like all the shit in my insides had been purged . . . but he was right, there was something there . . . I wasn't sitting up . . . and he picked it up showing me how I was sitting, falling back into myself . . . "What was it?" I wanted to know. "What about the good things about her" he asked . . . "they're still there aren't they"? And he was right again . . . there were good things there that I couldn't clear myself of but they hadn't surfaced. I was getting back my power and it came back into my bones filling them . . . filling the empty cavity inside my body . . . and I sat up. I didn't have anything to say to anyone and everyone was quiet. Then I said a little defiantly, "Alright, I'm OK, if you guys want to know anything I'm open for questions." Then I talked of the last few days . . . I looked at Judy as I talked and told the group that the experience with you had shattered me but that she had been there to comfort me . . . and now I wasn't going to be a little boy anymore that I was going to stand on my foot . . . you've got to walk before you can run I said . . . I'm doing it. Judy reached out to me and held both my hands in hers . . . Marvin was there with his hand on my shoulder. "You were really in trouble for awhile there" he said. "And it scared the shit out of me." I thanked him . . . he had been with me every step of the way . . . what an amazing guy! He had been there before and he had known. I spent the rest of the afternoon making the closures to the experience and then I stayed with Judy. Carole was concerned "about the lady on the floor" (you). She could identify with your struggles . . . and Marvin asked her to play you . . . and I played me and we had a dialogue . . . Carole began to cry

as she pleaded for me to understand her needs . . . that she didn't want to hurt me but that she had needs of her own that she couldn't deny. We finished that with you by my leaving you . . . telling you that those feelings were your responsibility and that I couldn't continue with the hurt forever . . . that I was going to walk away and reach out to other people. Then Marvin asked her to be me and for me to take Ellen's place . . . when I pleaded with her the way I felt you do for understanding she started getting scared . . . "her back was to the wall" she said. It was amazing to see her get into her own strength and to tell me that she had to leave me (Ellen) because she could only tolerate so much hurt . . . she was almost afraid to do it until she did it. Then she cut me off. Marvin asked her what was going on with her . . . and she answered that she was thankful . . . to her husband Tom, for his understanding, his patience and his kindness. Sherry was sitting on the side watching us. And she said that she could feel the aloneness of the both of us . . . Sherry had had a hard time working through her own feelings of death and aloneness when her mother died and when a dear friend passed away a few weeks ago . . . she didn't want to explode in front of the group . . . and now suddenly it happened . . . all the bottled up grief broke through and she cried convulsively . . . in a few minutes she was alright . . . and we went on to a break. The group seems to have a life rhythm of its own . . . moving spontaneously into encounter and out of it . . . something that Marvin has no control over . . . he only helps to get these things going and to guide the experiences. Judy and I were sitting together for the rest of the afternoon . . . I could be her protector now that I had decided to be my manhood and she accepted it gratefully . . . that morning when she came into my room and sat on the bed she had aches from sleeping on the floor with Marvin . . . it was good to rub her back and to switch the roles of support . . . and that afternoon she cuddled up with me and I kept her warm with a blanket around her shoulders. Judy is so much the Pixie little girl and so delightful that people often lay that trip on her. And she told me later that she was grateful that I let her mother me. She is on top of all that . . . a UCLA grad with a Masters in Psychiatric Social

work. She's been to Europe and had worked a year in San Francisco with the County. Now she's just living off her savings in a commune in Berkeley. She'll be moving down to Los Altos with her boyfriend . . . soon. I can talk about the weekend now the way I do only because of last night. We had our regular encounter meeting up at David's house on the hill when you come maybe we can go up there it's so high on the hill that they had to have an elevator built to carry the materials up. Last night . . . when I went to pick Judy up and Marvin . . . I felt defensive about her when she got into the car . . . partly because I felt vulnerable to her having exposed myself to her and partly because I was afraid that I would like her too much. We had gone through a heavy thing with Holly . . . there had been a lot of conflict between the two of us and I was in the middle of things again . . . for a short moment she became real to all of us and me especially . . . I couldn't believe the warmth I felt toward her . . . and it all lasted a moment . . . till I crawled back into my shell. On different levels we have the same problem . . . she had a rejecting father and I had a rejecting mother . . . it's no accident that we would clash. Usually she tries to play the cute little girl and everybody gets turned off by it . . . they just ignore her. I've really been frustrated with talking to her and so finally I just quit. I picked Marvin up at her place in Oakland and she sat in the back . . . I hardly said anything to her all the way up to David's. She said in the group that she had negative feelings and that she wanted to express them . . . Marvin asked if there was anybody in particular . . . and she started crying . . . almost like an act to please the group . . . nobody would respond and I just sunk lower into myself . . . giving up on her. "I'm a person," she kept saying . . . "I feel like I'm just another body here." Marvin was frustrated and impatient with her tears like everybody else . . . and she finally directed herself to me and she told me how much she wanted to know me and for us to be real to each other because she felt some of my strength . . . I told her she scared me because I couldn't be a man all the time . . . and even though I liked her and offered to take her swimming (she was a competition swimmer in high school) . . . and that I needed to be understood and to be a little boy sometimes. She came over to me and hugged me for some reason I don't understand and I still felt myself holding back . . . scared . . . then Marvin said that he was amazed that Holly was stronger than me in reaching out . . . for the first time she really did although she had been giving people all kinds of hugs before this one seemed real. Judy and Sherry were talking to her . . . I think she is a little jealous of Judy since I think everyone has positive warmth toward Judy . . . and Holly was almost saying "How come when you act like the cute little girl, everybody likes it? And when I do it nothing happens? Nobody responds?" She needs a lot of re-assurance and that is hard to do . . . but I found all kinds of funny things happening to me when Marvin put us both in the middle of the room and had us look into each others eyes. Sherry told me later as a few other people did that they really didn't believe what was happening . . . I looked like I was eyeing her cautiously even though I said I felt better when I heard them start to clear things up . . . for me. When Judy and Holly were talking . . . Holly completely misreads things be-cause of her own needs . . . she needs to be needed . . . and she is afraid of men. She kept telling Judy that she felt at other meetings nobody had paid much attention to Judy and that she wanted to "help Judy bring herself out". . . and Judy replied that Holly had to bring her own things out because she (Judy) didn't feel left out or the need to be brought out. This was making more sense to me but I didn't feel too much for Holly . . . just wanted to leave her alone, get her to leave me alone. When Holly finally was able to say that she wanted my friendship . . . then I was able to say "Dummy, Dummy". . . and hug her and really explode into joy . . . for a moment . . . It's amazing how the others pick that up . . . Sherry said that when I say "dummy". . . is when I'm feeling really affection-ate. Don cut in a few moments later to say that he saw Holly like a little girl who was unloved by her mother . . . and that he saw Holly playing with dolls . . . and because she was unloved by her own mother . . . she would make the momma doll love the baby doll . . . and that he wished she could enjoy her tears more instead of just trying to play to the group . . . in order to become an-other encounter group member. His perceptions were right-on and Marvin agreed . . . but the whole

thing between me and Holly suddenly died . . . of terror . . . I had these visions of being dangled on strings like a puppet . . . I told Don that was the most sinister thing that I had heard . . . right away I moved away from Holly . . . emotionally . . . it really frightened the hell out of me like I was going to be controlled or had been in fact just by letting myself feel warm toward her and embrace her . . . which is what she wanted . . . the whole good thing that had happened to Holly was beginning to be picked apart . . . I was leaving her without support and Marvin asked us if we wanted to get into it . . . and it was being ruined . . . and I was confused. David . . . he is only 18 but he is always the most fascinating guy . . . so accurate in what he says . . . he cut in and said to let it be and for whatever was going to take place outside the group to happen between me and Holly to happen and not to destroy it there. Marvin thanked him . . . because fear of being manipulated by a woman is one of his own big fears and he was being caught up in it. Then after awhile Judy and I started talking again . . . I told her about my defensiveness and that I was afraid of liking her too much. When we went to get her (Holly had gotten off at Andy's house to show him where David lived) and Marvin and I got out to go call her . . . I told him how incredible I found Judy . . . and he said, "Aha, now we know who you'll be going after when you get over Ellen." And I said nah, there is a little bit of the "Jewish mother" in Judy and that is scared me a little . . . then I caught myself and said . . . "Yeah, maybe you're right." I really could build a relationship with her if it wasn't for all our private involve-ments . . . and it would really be tempting. I told Judy about this and she said that she really liked me and was sorry that I felt the distance and defensiveness about her . . . it might even be hard being friends with her I felt be-cause that longing is something I'd always have to fight . . . she was trying to be as nice about it and Marvin caught the sugar-coating . . . because she was afraid to hurt my feelings . . . Andy Jokelson . . . said that there was nothing wrong with that and that I understood how everything was anyway . . . so Judy just said that she felt strong feelings toward me but that she had feelings in another place too (her boyfriend) and that she was sorry . . . she

was holding my hands all this time . . . then Marvin asked me how I felt . . . and I said all churned up inside . . . like I want to move to the other side of the room . . . I knew she was warning me . . . so I said . . . I think I'll do it . . . and so I did . . . Andy said he thought that was very hard to do . . . but it wasn't really . . . but I thanked him for his under-standing. He is really a good, gentle guy . . . Then Marvin turned to Judy who had her head down and looked dejected . . . and said, "That didn't feel too good did it?" And Judy shook her head. Judy and I didn't say anything to each other for the rest of the night and I avoided even looking over at her . . . after the group ended she said that she had wanted to come over to me but I said that I didn't want that and she said she knew and understood . . . that's why she hadn't. She went home with me . . . and we talked about it . . . She asked me how I felt about her and I said that I felt a comfort-able distance. She nestled in my arms . . . as she told me again how much she felt for me . . . and I said to her "Another time . . . another place". . . and she pressed herself against me closer. We said little more to each other, then I told her that what had happened to us reminded me of a short-story by Dostoevsky . . . about a lonely man who meets a young girl. The girl is in love with some-body else but for several nights on an appointed date . . . her love doesn't come . . . and all this time this guy loves her more and is very happy . . . he keeps her company while she waits and comforts her when he doesn't come . . . It takes four nights . . . then while they are walking the sidewalk . . . a stranger comes and the girl stiffens because she recognizes him she breaks away from him and rushes toward the stranger . . . then just as quickly runs back to him kisses him hard on the mouth and leaves quickly with the stranger. The lonely guy doesn't feel regret or anger . . . even as he sits in his lonely room for this girl has given him a moment that will last a lifetime. I told Judy that we probably wouldn't see much of each other . . . all of us after the group meetings end but somehow that wasn't important because the valuable things that she and I shared this weekend I'll remember for a long, long time. Just before she turned to go . . . I took her face in my hands and for the first time I kissed her softly on the mouth and held her tightly

... "Good-bye, Judy," I said to her. I had pictured us a couple steps beyond where we were . . . with a lot of confusion and unhappiness because of her feelings for Stuart and herself and me . . . and I knew that we would have to let go of each other . . . but it didn't matter, it just didn't matter . . . that moment was forever and it always will be . . . just the way it was with you should our relationship end . . . When I picked Marvin up last night, I told him the good feelings about you had surfaced. I had talked to Dora at school and she has a guy in Mexico that she knew for a short while . . . we spent the afternoon together and talked. I told her about you and what had happened . . . she had been through a terrible engagement with a guy who was paranoid in a very sick way . . . and had broken it off . . . but she is willing to go out with me . . . she said that she felt we had been honest with each other more than she has been with most people she knows. She is kind of a loner too . . . all she has is her family . . . but she is not you. I had become nostalgic about you . . . yesterday almost as if it were something in my past . . . listening to sweet ballads and remembering how it was between us . . . after last night I felt that way about Judy . . . very much so. I went home and found the book by Dostoevsky with the story "White Nights" and read it again . . . then this morning I got up and put a note in it and took it up to Judy's house . . . she is in LA with her family for the week . . . so I left it in her room . . . and felt sad for the rest of the day, it was a sweet, wonderful sadness that I haven't felt in years . . . since I was ill and it felt like life again coming back to me no matter where I go or what happens to me . . . I can love and let go and give and take. That book was a gift to Judy . . . I found one long strand of her blond hair in my car today and was looking for a jar to put it in . . . it's funny and beautiful how such small things can bring me so much joy and happiness as well as the deepest sorrow that I know. We gave something to each other out of the depths of our humanness and there is no need to cling to it . . . because it is divine, it is eternal . . . and it will last as long as I have life in me.

CONCLUSIONS

In the preceding articles we have presented different viewpoints on encounter groups. Our main purpose has been to encourage the reader to synthesize the material and come up with his own ideas and, even more important, his own feelings about groups. Attitude is as important in joining a group as comprehension of the concept of encounter groups. One very significant variable contributing to the success of a group is the individual's motive. Why encounter? a game? for fun? to acquire new friendships? heavy analysis? curiosity? It helps if the members of the group are not functioning at cross-purposes. Other elements which the reader should be aware of, if he is seriously contemplating joining a group, are the qualifications for a leader, the basis for selecting other members, the use of structured games and techniques, and the aims and goals of the group. It is not easy to make judgments in these areas and we feel that licensing by any official body is out of the question, mainly because establishing criteria for encounter groups, such as selecting members or training leaders, is very abstract and also individual.

Our experience in encounter groups has made us wary. However, if one chooses to join a group there are some qualities we suggest you look for: (1) small number of members (6–10), (2) commitment to regular attendance, (3) a leader who functions as a member while maintaining enough distance to remain objective, (4) members unified in their purpose for joining a group, (5) lack of reliance on touchy-feelie substitutes for intimacy, (6) no drugs. We feel that these things contribute to a sense of trust among members, probably the most critical element of encounter groups. We envision the encounter group not as an "anything goes" situation, rather an honest sitting down with other people who care. This type of rap session could be plugged into the educational system, in hospitals, in churches, but please not over loud-speakers in airports.

The problems we have been discussing are very specific, dealing with revamping the workings of the encounter group and do not question the ideals behind the machinery. Our most important caution has to do with the role of encounter groups in social change. We return to our question of what the encounter group is providing. Is real exploration going on and is its continuation fostered? Or do encounter groups abort this process by pacifying us with the security of belonging to the subsociety established by the group? Or by leading us to believe that sharing our problems equals effectively coping with them? We fear the concept of encounter groups contains the implication that the solution of social problems lies only in helping the individual to adjust. What about the legitimate anger and frustration at the many injustices suffered by individuals in our society? When catharsis is the only result of their expression, an important impetus towards change is siphoned off. If the group functions as a ventilation system for society, then perhaps there is the danger that the group actually operates as a device to maintain the status quo, an extension of the check and balance system of society. In an encounter group feelings tend to be poured out, examined, and dissipated; they may never find a more energetic, creative outlet.

Encounter groups are not by definition counter-revolutionary. On the contrary, the encounter group can be a useful tool in man's creation of a better society —if used to resolve important conflicts in a just manner. The legal system, for example, could eliminate much of its ritual and arrive at solutions to the real grievances, especially in civil suits, by incorporating some encounter group techniques. We have seen some hope in the article by Sikes and Cleveland that encounter groups might help smooth the strained relations between police and the community. Encounter groups could be a training ground for equipping individuals for more direct confrontation with social ills. There can be no social change if men come together merely to throw up their discontent, alienation, and frustration, and then go away satisfied. We see a desperate need for social change —perhaps man's frustration rather than his inner peace may better aid this change.

We end where we began with questions, but a better understanding of what the group is and more importantly what the group is not. It is not a one-step process to a happier and more fulfilled life, neither is it an international communist conspiracy. To further reevaluate the group we must begin with ourselves, questioning our motives and sincerity, our ideals and goals. The individual is suffering from slow starvation for honesty and increased awareness in his dealings with himself and others. Let encounter groups not add to that slow death.

Toward Mental Health

EDITED BY:

Sheila Bacharach   Robert J. Nichols

John R. Farrell   Rachel Posner

Suzanne M. Fleck   Vicki Lynn Weisblat

INTRODUCTION

"They call it a mental hospital, but it's . . . a place where they put people away"—a simplistic, yet direct and concise indictment of mental health care in the United States. Despair rather than hope, custodial care rather than psychological expertise accompany hospitalization in institutions which are somewhat accurately described as insane asylums, loony bins, or nut houses. The patients, however "ill," are more commonly seen as crazy, insane, not responsible for themselves or their actions, and therefore not requiring responsible humanity from their caretakers. Treatment is not necessarily overtly cruel, vicious, or inhuman, but it attacks the symptoms of depersonalized psychotics rather than the problems of disturbed individuals. People are not objects to be marched through daily routines; they are not powerful dynamos, all consciously willing the destruction of precious values, property, or sanity. They are people, motivated by such familiar emotions as hope, fear, love, and anger, people who have resolved conflicts between self and reality in a way that is unpleasant, unacceptable, or terrifying to their neighbors. We are their neighbors; we, as a nation, state, and community, build, sustain, legalize, and sanction custodial care of the mentally ill.

Who is "mentally ill"? Psychiatry answers straightforwardly: those divorced from reality are mentally ill—the catatonic, the hebrephrenic, the paranoid. This process of labeling and compartmentalization facilitates assembly-line care of patients. Social psychology, however, can perhaps afford a more ambiguous definition. The patient in many cases, as alluded to by Szasz, has a different frame of reference, a different perception of reality than does the society and culture around him. The difference is that that society and that culture—we—are the majority and define reality for the minority by strict standards of conduct. According to R. D. Laing, "What we call normal is a product of repression, denial, splitting, projection, introjection, and other forms of destructive action on experience." From this view of normality it can be concluded that what is repressed, denied, and projected is the seeming unreality, the conflicting approach to life which does, or could, bring serious questioning of what is, in fact, real; of what is good or bad; of what is ill and what is not ill; and whether there need be such standards. Perceptions of reality are for the most "normal" person, often tenuous; workers in mental institutions find identification with even the most uncommunicative patients easy and, in fact, natural. Those doctors, nurses, and aides who continue to work in mental hospitals and have dealt closely with the question of who is ill, find the distinctions between well and ill to be finely graded rather than strictly categorized. We are all "ill"—we all repress or deny some aspect of what is idealized as majority culture. But we repress the conflict, and thus do not threaten anyone else by our opposition. Those who do not repress, those who deny and thereby threaten our reality, are ill—and as such are "put away" where they can no longer be a threat.

This is a somewhat idealized conception of disturbance. Few psychiatrists or psychologists would say that all patients have a conscious or even semiconscious "concept of reality." Those who simply are not in contact with societal reality live in a dimension of noncommunication and nonreality. Care of these patients is necessarily different than care of the patients who are readily oriented and capable of communication. But the question here is not whether the latter can be given "better treatment," can be released from hospitals or can live in their communities. The question is whether *both* types of patients, whose both in and out of contact with our world, can and will be given the above rights. We say yes—and propose to suggest "how."

Today's mental hospital strips, dehumanizes, disregards, and, finally, mechanizes its patients. They are "put away"—not helped or cared for, but shelved as expediently and inexpensively as possible. Therapeutic techniques have been known to have been used punitively in an effort to ensure hospital conformity. Electroshock therapy (EST), used to stimulate depressive patients, has historically been used as punishment for disobedience. Lobotomy, a brain operation, was developed as a means of eliminating hyperaggressiveness. It too has been misused as a punitive measure in combating nonconformity. According to the Hirschowitz study, at one state mental hospital one-third of the patients had been lobotomized and many had received hundreds of shock treatments during a Minnesota vogue for "repressive EST." As indicated by Kesey, EST, lobotomy, and countless other measures are prescribed for patients, and can often be enacted against the patient's will. Similarly drug therapy, developed as a chemical means to make patients amenable to therapy, is inevitably used more to control behavior than to effect treatment. The depressive patient can be aroused, and the aggressive one can be calmed. In many state hospitals drugs are a means to ensure conformity within the established environment. Drugs are often used to bring all patients to the same harmless stupor which allows questioning and action only within restrictive (drugged) limits.

Innovative mental health care is difficult within large state hospital systems, because of restrictive legislation, inadequate funds, and community unawareness and apathy. Private hospitals, funded through contributions and high fees, can operate truly therapeutic programs, ones which guarantee to the patients more than custodial care. But the facilities of these private hospitals are often limited to less than 100 patients—patients who can afford to pay prohibitive daily costs. Those who cannot pay these fees must rely on state hospitals which allocate an average of $4 a day per patient. Another type of discrimination is thus enforced: the rich receive elaborate care and treatment, and the poor are subjected to custodial care and suppression of individuality or hope, which may have originally motivated them to seek treatment voluntarily.

The problem is one of attitude. We no longer put our "insane" in chains or in dungeons, but paternalistic care does not allow real freedom to patients and staff. "They," the patients, are "sick," and "we" are "well," and we do a good deed by insisting on humane care for the unfortunate insane. But "they" are part of us and "we" are part of them, part of the disillusionment which created escape from our reality. We give our mentally ill our repressed desires, our bit of sickness, and give them nothing in return for the burden they carry. It is not a paternalistic obligation which must motivate our care of the "mentally ill." It must be gratitude for bearing the pain which we have given them. The articles which follow are included in an effort to channel our gratitude, to pay the heavy debt we owe those who bear our inadequacies with so little recompense. The article on madness by Thomas Szasz is included here to question the concept of "mental illness." He also attacks involuntary commitment as a threat to individual liberty and the rights of a citizen, as does David Muller who adds that it intensifies the problems of already overburdened hospitals. There are approximately 750,000 people in mental hospitals in the United States, 90 percent of whom are there involuntarily. This is three times the number of persons in all jail and prison facilities. Misuse of otherwise traditional therapeutic measures inside hospitals is the subject of the selection from Kesey's *One Flew over the Cuckoo's Nest.* Bart promotes progressive therapies to remedy the problem sum-

marized by Laing: "Psychiatry could be, and some psychiatrists are on the side of transcendence, of genuine freedom, and of true human growth. But psychiatry can so easily be a technique of brainwashing, or inducing behavior that is adjusted, by (preferably) non-injurious torture. In the best places where straitjackets are abolished, doors are unlocked, lobotomies largely foregone, these can be replaced by more subtle lobotomies and tranquilizers that place the bars of Bedlam and the locked doors *inside* the patient" (see the article by Pauline Bart).

A more radical form of therapy can be found in the policies and practices of the RaP Center, as illustrated by Claude Steiner. Hirschowitz suggests an innovative inpatient program involving decentralization of strict hierarchical functions. Lastly, we have included a congressional address by President John F. Kennedy to illustrate the abundance of proposed solutions and the harsh reality of the slow implementation and confused national priorities regarding mental health.

The always controversial Dr. Szasz presents a point of view which challenges the conventional wisdom of the mental health establishment. He questions the basic aim of psychiatry—the study and treatment of mental disorders. He asserts that the psychiatrist deals with moral and social problems rather than a subspecialty of medicine. Szasz points out the evils of labeling persons as dangerous merely because they break laws or social customs—a direct attack on the normative model commonly used to classify "abnormal" behavior. Of late Szasz has been a leader of those who condemn involuntary commitment to mental institutions.

9.1
The Manufacture of Madness

Thomas S. Szasz

. . . the writer's function is not without arduous duties. By definition, he cannot serve today those who make history; he must serve those who are subject to it.

Albert Camus

It is widely believed today that just as some people suffer from diseases of the liver or kidney, others suffer from diseases of the mind or personality; that persons afflicted with such "mental illnesses" are psychologically and socially inferior to those not so afflicted; and that "mental patients," because of their supposed incapacity to "know what is in their own best interests," must be cared for by their families or the state, even if that care requires interventions imposed on them against their will or incarceration in a mental hospital.

I consider this entire system of interlocking concepts, beliefs, and practices false and immoral. In an earlier work, *The Myth of Mental Illness,* I tried to show how and why the concept of mental illness is erroneous and misleading. In the present work, I shall try to show how and why the ethical convictions and social arrangements based on this concept constitute an immoral ideology of intolerance. In particular, I shall compare the belief in witchcraft and the persecution of witches with the belief in mental illness and the persecution of mental patients.

The ideology of mental health and illness serves an obvious and pressing moral need. Since the physician's classic mandate is to treat suffering patients with their consent and for their own benefit, it is necessary to explain and justify situations where individuals are "treated" without their consent and to their detriment. The concept of insanity or mental illness supplies this need. It enables the "sane" members of society to deal as they see fit with those of their fellows whom they can categorize as "insane." But having divested the madman of his right to judge what is in his own best interests, the people—and especially psychiatrists and judges, their medical and legal experts on madness—have divested themselves of the corrective restraints of dialogue. In vain does the alleged madman insist that he is not sick; his inability to "recognize" that he is, is regarded as a hallmark of his illness. In vain does he reject treatment and hospitalization as forms of torture and imprisonment; his refusal to submit to psychiatric authority is regarded as a further sign of his illness. In this medical rejection of the Other as a madman, we recognize, in up-to-date semantic and technical garb, but underneath it remarkably unchanged, his former religious rejection as a heretic.

Well-entrenched ideologies—such as messianic Christianity had been, and messianic Psychiatry now is—are, of course, not easily refuted. Once the basic premises of an ideology are accepted, new observations are perceived in its imagery and articulated in its vocabulary. The result is that while no fresh observation can undermine the belief system, new "facts" generated by the ideology constantly lend further support to it. This was true in the past for the belief in witchcraft and the corresponding prevalence of witches, and it is true today for the belief in mental disease and the corresponding prevalence of mental patients.

Unfortunately, it is easier to perceive the errors of our forebears than those of our contemporaries. We all know that there are no witches; however, only a few hundred years ago, the greatest and noblest minds were deeply convinced that there were. Is it possible, then, that our belief in mental illness is similarly ill conceived? And that our practices based on this concept are similarly destructive of personal dignity and political liberty?

These are not idle or unimportant questions. On our answers to them depends not only the fate of millions of Americans labeled mentally ill, but, indirectly, the fate of all of us. For, as we have been warned time and again, an injustice done to one—especially in a society that aspires to be free—is an injustice done to all. In my opinion, the "mental health"—in the sense of spiritual well-being—of Americans cannot be improved by slogans, drugs, community mental health centers, or even with billions of dollars expended on a "war on mental illness." The principal problem in psychiatry has always been, and still is, violence: the threatened and feared violence of the "madman," and the actual counterviolence of society and the psychiatrist against him. The result is the dehumanization, oppression, and persecution of the citizen branded "mentally ill." If this is so, we had better heed John Stuart Mill's warning that ". . . it is contrary to reason and experience to suppose that there can be any real check to brutality, consistent with leaving the victim still in the power of the executioner." The best, indeed the only, hope for remedying the problem of "mental illness" lies in weakening—not in strengthening—the power of Institutional Psychiatry.[1] Only when this peculiar institution is abolished will the moral powers of uncoerced psychotherapy be released. Only then will the potentialities of Contractual Psychiatry[2] be able to unfold—as a creative human dialogue unfettered by institutional loyalties and social taboos, pledged to serving the individual in his perpetual struggle to rise, not only above the constraints of instinct, but also above those of myth.

In sum, this is a book on the history of Institutional Psychiatry—from its theoretical origins in Christian theology to its current practices couched in medical rhetoric and enforced by police power. The importance for man of understanding his history has perhaps never been greater than today. This is because history, as Collingwood reminds us, "is 'for' human self-knowledge. . . . Knowing yourself means knowing what you can do; and since nobody knows what he can do until he tries, the only clue to what man can do is what man has done. The value of history, then, is that it teaches us what man has done and thus what man is." By showing what man has done, and continues to do, to his fellow man *in the name of help,* I hope to add to our understanding of what man is, where coercion, however well-justified by self-flattering rhetoric, leads him, and what might yet become of him were he to replace control of the Other with self-control.

This book presupposes no special competence or training in the reader—only open-mindedness. But it requires of him one more thing—that he seriously consider, with Samuel Johnson, that "hell is paved with good intentions," and that he conscientiously apply this caveat to the ideology, rhetoric, and rituals of the political organization characteristic of our age—the Therapeutic State.

---

[1] By Institutional Psychiatry I refer generally to psychiatric interventions imposed on persons by others. Such interventions are characterized by the complete loss of control by the client or "patient" over his participation in his relationship with the expert. The paradigm service of Institutional Psychiatry is involuntary mental hospitalization.

[2] By Contractual Psychiatry I refer generally to psychiatric interventions assumed by persons prompted by their own personal difficulties or suffering. Such interventions are characterized by the retention of complete control by the client or "patient" over his participation in his relationship with the expert. The paradigm service of Contractual Psychiatry is autonomous psychotherapy.

David Muller continues the attack on involuntary commitment by pointing out several factors underlying the confusion over who should be committed. He is scornful of the vague legal definitions which vary from state to state. The thrust of the article is that too many rational people are being involuntarily committed—a problem which produces poor psychiatry and injustice.

9.2
Involuntary Mental Hospitalization

David J. Muller

Despite the fact that large numbers of patients are being kept in mental hospitals today against their will, much confusion surrounds the important question of who should be kept involuntarily on a psychiatric ward. There are four main factors behind this confusion: (1) the vagueness in terminology of the existing statutes regarding who should be civilly committed; (2) the lack of sufficient emphasis on this topic in the forensic psychiatry literature; (3) the tendency to overdiagnose human behavior; and

Reprinted by permission from *Comprehensive Psychiatry*, 9, 3 (May, 1968), 187–193.

(4) the widely divergent views held by psychiatrists and society in general regarding a man's right to individual freedom and his responsibility for his own behavior.

If the issue were clarified, perhaps large numbers of civil commitments would no longer take place and our psychiatric facilities could better meet the needs of their patients, especially those who voluntarily seek help.

This paper will explore these problems in some detail and propose remedies for them, including a recommendation of specific narrow criteria for civil commitment.

Vague Legal Definitions

In the District of Columbia Hospitalization of the Mentally Ill Act of 1964, certifiable mental illness is defined as "any psychosis or other disease which substantially impairs the mental health of an individual." This law represents an attempt by Congress to provide greater protection for the mental patient, and is felt by many to be a superior law to those currently found in most states. A model mental health code proposed by the National Institute of Mental Health in 1952, defines a mentally ill person as "an individual having a psychiatric or other disease which substantially impairs his mental health." The Royal Commission Report on the Law Relating to Mental Illness and Mental Deficiency of 1957 states; "We consider that the use of special compulsory powers on grounds of the patient's mental disorder is justifiable when: (a) there is reasonable certainty that the patient is suffering from a pathological mental disorder and requires hospital or community care; and, (b) suitable care cannot be provided without the use of compulsory powers; and, (c) if the patient himself is unwilling to receive the form of care which is considered necessary, there is at least a strong likelihood that his unwillingness is due to lack of appreciation of his own condition deriving from mental disorder itself; and, (d) there is also either, 1, good prospect of benefit to the patient from the treatment proposed—an expectation that it will either cure or alleviate his mental disorder or strengthen his ability to regulate his social behavior in spite of the underlying disorder, or bring him substantial benefit in the form of protection from neglect or exploitation by others; or, 2, a strong need to protect others from antisocial behavior by the patient."

The presence of a psychosis is a relatively clear concept, but what is meant by "substantial impairment" of one's mental health? Whose mental condition is such that he needs care? How dangerous does a person have to be in order to qualify? The term "mental illness" has been especially criticized by Szasz (12) who feels it is misleading and that there is no valid parallel between physical illness and what is referred to as mental illness. Glasser (4) also rejects the term saying, "We believe that this concept, the belief that people can and do suffer from some specific diagnosable treatable mental illness, analogous to a specific diagnosable treatable physical illness is inaccurate, and that this inaccuracy is a major roadblock to proper psychiatric treatment." Such wording of the existing laws grants great latitude to the physician in deciding whom to certify for commitment proceedings. The law probably intends this so that the judge and sometimes the jury can weigh the testimony and make the best decision for the particular case. However, the physician, often a psychiatrist, has great influence in such proceedings, and the fact that he has signed certification papers often tends to sway the court, especially if this is his area of special competence. Few judges will jeopardize their positions by releasing a person described by a physician as severely mentally ill and dangerous. The quality of legal representation afforded the patient for the hearing itself may on occasion also be inadequate and thus also make a decision for commitment more likely.

Lack of Emphasis in the Forensic Psychiatry Literature

As stated previously, the forensic psychiatry literature rarely deals with this issue directly and at length. Much more, for example, is written in regard to competency to stand trial. Yet the number of civil commitments in this country far exceeds the number of defendants whose competency is questioned. Davidson (2) says that in a commitment hearing "a physician who cannot demonstrate to a judge that the patient is psychotic has a weak case." Guttmacher and Weihofen (5) say that "if through error or malice a sane person should be committed, the hospital authorities would release him as soon as the fact became apparent." An established psychiatric text states, "although it is perhaps

theoretically possible that a sane person of the community might be 'railroaded' into an institution, it probably rarely occurs now in this country, certainly not in a public mental hospital." (8) In these contexts, sane can be understood as meaning not psychotic. It is unfortunate that other criteria are not mentioned. Slovenko (11) acknowledges at least two criteria when he says, "Any psychiatrist can give numerous instances and conditions in which the consent of the patient is neither possible nor relevant, including the various psychoses and situations in which suicide is imminent."

Overdiagnosis

In addition to the vague and controversial terms involved in the question of civil commitment, there is a tendency in certain circles to overly diagnose human behavior. Almost every act is labeled and assigned unconscious meaning. The terms sociopath, latent homosexual schizophrenic and others have been carelessly used, with a resulting impression that everyone, especially the criminal, is mentally ill. Whitlock (13) mentions the prevalence of this opinion in regard to criminal behavior but strongly takes issue with it. Szasz (12) points out that human stupidity and miscalculation are often ignored in assessing behavior. Is every irresponsible, ill conceived or criminal act evidence of underlying mental illness? Few would say so, but in a recent position statement regarding the adequacy of psychiatric treatment approved by the Council of the American Psychiatric Association the following statement was made: "It would manifestly be 'poor treatment' to release a patient to commit an unlawful act" (10). The implication seems to be that all unlawful behavior is due to mental illness and that the psychiatrist is somehow responsible for his former patient's behavior, at least for the time immediately following release from treatment. Consider the private psychiatrist who feels his exhibitionistic patient, after extensive evaluation, is not interested in changing this aspect of his behavior and finally in candor terminates the patient's visits. What of the alcoholic patient in the hospital who sobers up, denies his problem, says he wants no professional help and demands his release? Both of these patients will undoubtedly resume their sometimes unlawful acts. As the concept of mental illness is used more and more to explain human behavior, civil commitments accordingly will become more numerous.

Divergent Views on Human Freedom and Responsibility

Man's right to be different and to express this difference in public has long been an unresolved question. The ideological debate between the rights of the individual and the rights of society goes on. Certain groups are concerned over loss of individual liberty while others are aggrieved because society is being disrupted by individual dissent and nonconformity. Psychiatrists and other professional persons involved in civil commitment proceedings such as lawyers and judges will naturally find themselves variously aligned between these points of view, and accordingly different decisions will be made depending on which individuals are involved in each case. Opposing psychiatric testimony in criminal cases today bears witness to this. The controversy is encouraged by the vagueness of the existing laws. Pollack (9) acknowledges this divergence of opinion by saying: "Social policy may provide a broad or a narrow standard for legal definition of mental illness for purposes of commitment. In some jurisdictions the narrow standard of mental illness limits commitments to an individual who is mentally disturbed and dangerous to others. A somewhat broader standard of mental illness considers the mentally disturbed person as one who is dangerous to himself or others. The broadest legal standard of mental illness for commitment purposes holds that the mentally disturbed person may be committed if his mental disturbance promotes danger to himself or others or if he requires treatment, care or custody which he refuses to accept voluntarily. Little agreement exists as to whether society should adopt a narrow or a broad standard of mental illness."

The freedom of man's will is also debated. Some say man's behavior is determined solely by many factors beyond his control while others affirm man's freedom to deal with reality in the way he chooses. The more deterministic a person is in his outlook, in general, the more favorably he will view the civil commitment of an individual.

Resultant Current Problems

The author feels that many ra-tional persons are currently being sent to and kept in psychiatric facilities involuntarily, and that these people should not be there. They neither want psychiatric help nor can they readily be influenced by it. These commitments are often justified by citing the potential dangerousness of the individual. The largest number of persons so committed probably are chronic alcoholics. The widespread continuation of this practice, in addition to violating the rights of the citizen and discouraging individuality will also harm society as a whole. Already over-burdened mental hospitals will become even less able to perform their therapeutic functions. Those voluntary patients, who need psychiatric help and who should be the first to get it, will of necessity receive less attention. Psychiatric treatment for the involuntary rational patient is exceedingly difficult to accomplish, and under current knowledge and practice the results of such treatment programs are very disappointing. This approach is also very costly in terms of staff, time and money. It often tends to demoralize the other, voluntary patients in the institution by undermining any therapeutic atmosphere that may exist. The hospital staff also become discouraged when their efforts are not met at least partially by a significant number of the patients. Enthusiastic, effective mental health workers often become punitive and custodial as they repeatedly encounter the frustrations of dealing with unwilling, consciously resistant rational patients. This is not to say that there should be no institutional treatment programs for the resistant rational patient, but rather that such programs should be limited to those who have violated the law. If mental hospitals become more and more like jails they will become less attractive to the voluntary patient, and their therapeutic efforts, which should foster personal growth and responsibility, will suffer.

These issues are also salient in the growing fields of community mental health and preventive psychiatry. At present the most strategic employment of our scarce community resources in clinical psychiatry dictates first priority to those areas in which greatest results are obtained in the briefest length of time. Caplan (1) writes that "the preventive psychiatrist must exercise a rational choice in deploying his efforts differentially among categories of patients. This may mean that his major efforts will be devoted to the short treatment of the many patients with good prognoses, instead of being sunk in the bottomless pit of the interminable treatment of a few difficult cases. In this respect, he may adopt a similar policy of the army surgeon, who gives priority after a battle to the lightly wounded and only later turns his attention progressively to the more serious cases." The involuntary patient is in general the most difficult to help.

Some Corrective Proposals

Specific Commitment Criteria

More specific criteria need to be established for imposing involuntary mental hospitalization. Today state mental hospitals are often sent individuals who more properly belong in penal institutions, schools for the retarded or nursing homes. If the following criteria were adopted, this would not be the case. Two basic considerations are recommended. First, only patients with specific types of mental disorder should be involuntarily hospitalized. These are the psychoses, both functional and organic, and those conditions in which there is permanent or temporary impairment of cerebral cortical functioning so that at the time, the person is not considered fully responsible for his own behavior. These include the various brain syndromes and severe mental retardation. And secondly that person must be dangerous to himself or others on account of his mental disorder. For if no danger is involved how can society justify removal of a person's liberty? Farney (3) states: "A person has or should have the right to be mentally ill and not seek treatment if that is his wish, as long as his illness creates no danger to public health or welfare." But what does "dangerous" mean? Does this mean physical danger only? If so, how much? It is the author's feeling that the danger should be to a person or his property, and the degree of likely damage either physical or emotional must be great. Simple harassment would be insufficient reason to call someone dangerous. Katz and his colleagues (6) point out the many aspects of "dangerousness" in their recent text. The availability of interested family members or friends can be a crucial factor here. An old man who is rendered mentally incompetent by a chronic brain syndrome associated with cerebral arteriosclerosis may be dangerous to himself and his property if there is no one to assist and look after him, but when his family is willing to supervise his behavior he may become no longer dangerous.

In the above formulation, drug abuse, character disorders, and neuroses are not suitable conditions for commitment no matter how dangerous the persons with these problems may be. Many states have special commitment statutes for alcoholics, but the author feels that such persons should not be sent involuntarily to mental hospitals unless they fulfill the above criteria. If a person is rational and chooses to continue his alcoholism and not seek help for it, as long as he does not violate law he should be permitted to exercise his freedom. Attempts should be made to help and better inform him, but he is entitled to his freedom. If, however, he violates law in association with his alcoholism, then society can abridge some of his rights and impose certain conditions such as attendance at a clinic, or the taking of disulfiram on a daily basis, or even confinement in a penal institution where some treatment may be offered. Society has the right to punish offenders by the removal of liberty commensurate with the offense. In these cases society can try to force treatment on a rational individual, if it so chooses, since that person has lost some of his legal rights. In other words, the criminal can be sentenced to treatment.

Many, including Slovenko (11) feel that the acutely suicidal patient, even if only considered neurotic, should be kept in the hospital at least until the acute self destructive tendencies abate. The length of time involved is strictly a matter of judgment on the part of the physician. In fact, if the patient is felt to be responsible for his own behavior, there would seem to be no legitimate medicolegal reason at all to continue hospitalization on an involuntary basis.

Currently, the general public is unaware of many of these issues. Indignant protests arise when the "former mental patient" commits a crime. The resultant pressure often results in more custodial and less therapeutic attitudes on the part of many mental health administrators. These pressures can be alleviated only by greater clarification to society of what psychiatry and the other helping professions can and cannot do. Let us make it clear that we do not intend to supplant the penal system. Let us be sure the public

realizes we cannot predict future human behavior. Many people today feel that psychiatrists can "cure" the unwilling rational patient, as the internist, for example, can cure a case of pneumonia. The reality of current psychiatric capability should be stated openly. In addition, far greater dialogue between law and psychiatry is needed. Judges, policemen, lawyers and mental health workers should become more familiar with each others' problems, capabilities and limitations.

Summary

There is much confusion today over who should be involuntarily kept on a psychiatric ward. Four main factors contributing to this confusion are: (1) the vagueness of the existing statutes, (2) the lack of emphasis on this topic in the forensic psychiatric literature, (3) the tendency in some circles to over-diagnose human behavior, and (4) the widely divergent opinions of psychiatrists and society in general on man's right to liberty and the freedom of man's will.

This lack of real definition concerning who should be civilly committed has resulted in the unjustified loss of liberty by thousands of mental health patients the further overburdening of already inadequate public mental hospitals.

Some remedies for this undesirable situation include the author's proposal of specific criteria for civil commitment, further public education, and far greater communication among those professions involved in the civil commitment process.

REFERENCES

1. Caplan, G.: Principles of Preventive Psychiatry. New York, Basic Books, Inc., 1964, p. 90.
2. Davidson, H.: Forensic Psychiatry. New York, The Ronald Press Co., 1965, p. 228.
3. Farney, D.: Incarceration of the Mentally Ill—New York's New Law. Syracuse Law Review 14: 671–687, 1963.
4. Glasser, W.: Reality Therapy. New York, Harper and Row, 1965, p 45.
5. Guttmacher, M., and Weihofen, H.: Psychiatry and the Law. New York, W. W. Norton and Co., 1952, p. 289.
6. Katz, J., Goldstein, J., and Dershowitz, A.: Psychoanalysis, Psychiatry and Law. New York, The Free Press, 1967.
7. Lindman, F., and McIntyre, D.: The Mentally Disabled and the Law. Chicago, The University of Chicago Press, 1961, p. 20.
8. Noyes, A., and Kolb, L.: Modern Clinical Psychiatry (ed. 6). Philadelphia, W. E. Saunders Co., 1963, p. 556.
9. Pollack, S.: The Court-Appointed Psychiatrist. Arch. Gen Psychiat. 16:582–585, 1967.
10. Position Statement on the Question of Adequacy of Treatment. Amer. J. Psychiat. 123:1458–1460, 1967.
11. Slovenko, R.: The Psychiatric Patient, Liberty and the Law. Amer. J. Psychiat. 121:534–539, 1964.
12. Szasz, T.: The Myth of Mental Illness. New York, Macmillan, 1963.
13. Whitlock, R.: Criminal Responsibility and Mental Illness. London, Butterworths, 1963, p. 5.

This paper is representative of the many first-hand accounts written by students who volunteer to work in mental hospitals near universities. Writing during a period of continuous volunteer work, Miss Weisblat chronicles the day to day small things which amplify the impersonality of the mental hospital It is a more graphic and revealing account than one would find in most articles written by professionals in the mental health field. It is hoped that this article may suggest ways in which students may take maximal advantage of their field experiences.

9.3
An Overall View of Today's Mental Hospital

Vicki L. Weisblat

To be a mental patient is: to be so fearful that each aspect of the environment represents a threat to one's existence; to experience the world as unreal and to see the "outside" as just a flimsy structure with no substance; to live with the feeling of restraint and being closed in, or suffocated, and to feel rebellion and resentment at this and be unable to express it in any effective way; to experience utter, desperate, and unrelieved loneliness, with no hope of change; to feel that in the entire universe there is no person that will ever understand one; to believe that one's actions have no

By permission of the author.

effect and that one is not affected by the actions of others. To be a mental patient means the inability to think or to trust one's thoughts; it means to be lacking in privacy and to be exposed to the view of strangers, and forced to associate with these strangers, when association with anyone is a thing to be dreaded and shunned. This is what one finds upon waking up in a ward, like T-7 at Napa, with sixty-seven other women.

Here a patient is not treated as a human being to be cured, but as an undesirable charge to be tolerated. One of the justifications used for erecting mental hospitals was that of protecting the public from the dangers of the insane. Prevailing conceptions of persons responsible for patient supervision were naturally consistent with the principal custodial function, which was the hospital's main function. Hospitalization was regarded as an end in itself and, accordingly, little concern or effort was directed toward introducing positive therapeutic measures.

The public, having achieved a comfortable method of sending its local responsibilities, i.e., its mentally ill citizens to a large, centralized, and somewhat isolated institution, now found it easy to forget them, and settled into an indifference which is still common today.[1]

Whereas a general hospital patient is hospitalized for a brief and usually predictable period "in order to have his illness treated," very different imagery surrounds the mental hospital patient. To be "mentally ill" is for most persons in our society a matter of external stigma and internal shame. The mental hospital patient becomes an inhabitant of a new and remarkable society.[2]

In this new society of the ordinary state hospital, it is often said of the patients who do not leave within their first year, the longer they stay, the less likely it is that they will ever leave. There is a model implicit in this evaluation: patients are riding upon an escalator—and if they wish to get off, they must step lively. As the escalator progresses downward, proportionately fewer patients get off. Some patients will remain in the

hospital, probably on its worst wards, for some time.[3]

Goffman writes of the progressive degradation of the hospitalized patient due to a number of successive institutional occurrences that affect the patient's self-esteem. Goffman describes a process by which the new patients have already suffered initial degrading experiences and by which they endure further demoralization in the hospital.[4]

What follows admission may be seen as a routine, although chaotic and unpredictable at times, and a new way of life begins. One is now a member of a new society, the mental hospital, at large, and specifically ward T-7. From this point deemed admission, the patient is under the continuous twenty-four hour supervision of the ward attendants until he achieves a position in the hospital society in which he has ground privileges or work which permits him to go unsupervised about the hospital for brief periods of time. If he doesn't achieve such a position, he will remain under this supervision until he dies or is discharged, and even if he has some privileges these are subject to cancellation by the attendants if his behavior does not continue according to the standard established on his ward as desirable for patients.

A patient should receive supervision, attention to his daily wants, and his physical health needs. This is not always the case, however, as can be evidenced on T-7. A daily want and, of course, need, is for the penal commitment case to have full knowledge of legal procedures, which are kept from her and delayed until staff convenience will take precedence. Sylvia was told her court date would be no later than two weeks, and that was four weeks ago. This is her right and its denial to her is causing a great deal of anguish. In a small number of cases patients will also receive such psychiatric attention as the ward physician finds it possible to give, and will have some opportunity to participate in group recreation or occupational therapy programs carried on in the hospital. This is the tragedy of today's mental hospitals. Of prime importance should

be the treatment function, but the hospital is primarily concerned with the custodial aspect and then institutional maintenance. A patient must be young, attractive, interesting, or unusual to merit regular psychiatric care.

Another factor to be considered is the actual delegation of powers in the hospital. In theory, all aspects of the hospital are considered to be under the control and executive direction of the Superintendent, who, as a physician exercises this executive control over both the medical-psychiatric and the "business" side of the hospital's organization in such a fashion that the hospital functions to receive, treat, and discharge mentally diseased citizens of the state according to modern principles of psychiatry.

In theory, the Superintendent is responsible for the patient. This responsibility, however, is delegated through a Clinical Director and thence to an individual ward physician, a member of the regular medical staff of the hospital. Formally, responsibility remains at this point in the system. All important administrative and medical action connected with any patient must be carried out in the name of his physician or the Superintendent as Chief of Physicians. In carrying out this responsibility the ward physician has available the consultation services provided by the Clinical Director as head of the medical staff of the hospital.

In addition to the consultation service available to him, the ward doctor has a group of auxiliary services provided by the hospital. These are rendered by social service workers, clinical psychologists, occupational and recreational therapists, physical therapy services, including surgery, registered nurse service and clerical personnel.[5] T-7 can not be seen as the model theoretical ward spoken of here, as it is not given its fair share of qualified personnel mentioned here to attend to the patients and assist the doctors.

With the consultative and auxiliary services, the ward physician acts from his knowledge of the patient's condition to prescribe appropriate treatment procedures to the patient's ward nurses or attendants. The latter, the attendants, are the contact between the medical administrative system and the patient, and they are the only personnel in the system who have direct and continuous rela-

[1] Ivan Belknap, *Human Problems of a State Mental Hospital* (New York: McGraw Hill, 1958), p. 34.

[2] Daniel Levinson and Eugene Gallagher, *Patienthood in the Mental Hospital* (Boston: Houghton Mifflin, 1964), p. 20.

[3] Anselm Strauss, Leonard Schatzman, Rue Bucher, Danuta Ehrlich, and Melvin Sabshin, *Psychiatric Ideologies and Institutions* (Glencoe: Free Press, 1964), p. 172.

[4] Erving Goffman, *Asylums* (New York: Doubleday, 1961), p. 128.

[5] Belknap, *op. cit.*, p. 61.

tionships with the patients on a twenty-four hour basis.

The functions of the attendant are to carry out prescribed treatment and maintain the patient under continuous observation, reporting to the physician any symptoms, physical or mental, which require action or bear in any way on treatment. This objective can be seen from a two-fold position. On one hand, who are the attendants to judge symptoms bearing on the case, from a purely psychiatric standpoint? Yet, on the other hand, they may be in a very good position to judge, sometimes more so than the doctor himself, because of their continual presence in the patient's surroundings. They come to know the patients on a more personal level than the doctors do, and can judge their daily behavior as habit or something new. However, the attendant is usually seen in the caretaker light, and has the responsibility of seeing that the patient is protected from himself and harmless to others, properly dressed, clean, and presentable in appearance, and that he is fed. The attendant also has duties related to those of an orderly in a general hospital, mainly ward housekeeping: seeing that the ward is sanitary, swept, mopped, and tidy, and that necessary treatment and maintenance equipment is present on the ward. In reality, though, it is the willing and able patients who perform these duties, which are often thought to be therapeutic, besides. Sylvia, from T-7 disagrees and feels mop therapy makes the mind a non-functional entity, instead of helping it regain its sanity.

Let me now turn to the chronic ward, itself, as a sub-culture of the greater society in the mental hospital. Chronic wards tend to have primarily a custodial orientation, as the mental hospital as a whole, because most of the patients violate at least some of the amenities of every-day living; many are bewildered, and some are destructive. It is hard to maintain staff morale with patients whose chances of recovery appear relatively slight. Care of these patients is, therefore, largely in the hands of the lowest stratum in the hospital hierarchy, the attendants, as mentioned above, and their work is not pleasant, their pay is low, their training frequently inadequate.[6] This seems

ironic that the persons who need the most help, obtain the least, if any.

Stanton and Schwartz characterize three types of patients on a ward, these being active, intermediate, and withdrawn. They also state that aggressive behavior on the part of most patients was a fairly common phenomenon on the ward. Withdrawn patients expressed their aggression primarily in the form of negativism, passive resistance, and incontinent behavior. They sometimes resisted bathing, dressing, eating, and getting out of bed. They rarely expressed hostility openly, and, when they did, it took the form of shouting, screaming, or attacking a member of the staff or another patient. Such outbursts were ordinarily short-lived, accompanied sharp increases in anxiety, and appeared to be explosions under internal pressure which had no other goal than relief.

Most physical assaults were made by intermediate patients. Often the hostile expression was unorganized and indirected, and it was difficult to determine its cause. In contrast, the active patients used a wide range and variety of expressions for their hostility, especially on the verbal level. They were more sustained, subtle, and flexible in participating in conflictual situations, and their efforts had a clearer goal. They were often sarcastic and fairly sophisticated in attacking sensitivities of the staff.[7] I can not say if all of this information holds true for T-7, as I have not been there long enough on any one day, but some of it is probably applicable.

Seclusion is usually a punishment for extreme behavior, and if a certain act deems seclusion for the patient, then seclusion it is. Some staff feel it is often more therapeutic than drugs, where, a patient, removed from outside stimuli, could calm down naturally. "She probably will be there for only a short time and will become quieter, partly because of removal from stimulation of other patients, and because of the extra attention she will get from some of the nurses and attendants."[8]

Some feelings against seclusion are that being put in a barren room is like being in jail, fearing seclusion as an unknown, that it is punishment, and that it accentuates loss of control.[9] Here again, I am not aware of the seclusion system on T-7.

An interesting phenomenon of any ward is the covert emotional structure which underlies the overt formal and informal structure of the hospital, or the occurrence of mood sweeps in the general atmosphere of the hospital, which is known as a collective disturbance, if it is severe enough. A collective disturbance usually refers to a situation in which the majority of patients on a ward become upset at one time, although the disturbance is probably much wider and also includes the staff.[10]

Daily medication time can be looked upon as a minor collective disturbance, where one can feel tension in the air as patients await medicine. Staff also seems tense at these times, for they want everything running smoothly. Cyclical moods seem to dominate ward atmosphere, though, as one day the ward as a whole will be fairly quiet, while another day it will display anger and hostility. These moods affect staff decisions, as was evidenced when one day no one was allowed out for walks, regardless of how her individual conduct had been.

Another ward idiosyncrasy was that there seemed to exist more optimism about the interaction of patients with the hospital-in-general than there was about the interaction of the staff with the hospital-in-general. The optimistic topic about the interaction of patients with the hospital referred mostly to the security the patients felt in a protected setting and to the therapeutic effect of being in the hospital. Mollie, who had been doing responsible work on T-7, was to be transferred to an open ward, but when she learned this, her behavior regressed, because she did not want to leave T-7, her home, just as the hospital at large meant security to her. The pessimistic topics were largely concerned with boredom, dreariness, and the monotonous atmosphere, as Sylvia complained to me so many times.

Patients often feel they have to learn to conform and suppress symptoms in order to be moved

---

[6] John Clausen, *Sociology and the Field of Mental Health* (New York: Russell Sage Foundation, 1956), p. 23.

[7] Alfred Stanton and Morris Schwartz, *The Mental Hospital, A Study of Institutions* (New York: Basic, 1954), p. 169.

[8] William Caudill, *The Psychiatric Hospital as a Small Society* (Cambridge, Mass.: Harvard University Press, 1958), p. 90.

[9] *Ibid.*, p. 91.

[10] *Ibid.*, p. 67.

from the locked to the open ward, as Sylvia did by brown-nosing, acting cheerful, and trying to say the right things at the right time, which did prove fruitful in one respect, she did get a grounds permission card. This ability to think and act in such a logical, reality-oriented way, though, may also be seen as a good sign of the patient's condition.

Thus, it is important to ask, in what ways is the hospital good or bad for the patient? Every patient arrives at some assessment of the hospital in these fairly personal terms. It has an important influence upon her response to specific persons, situations, and therapeutic efforts. Accordingly, her handling of this issue matters not only to her but also to the staff. It is difficult for a patient to form a trusting relationship with a doctor or nurse, or to believe that the treatment offered her is intended truly for her benefit, if she experiences the hospital primarily as a prison and herself as an object of ridicule and degradation.

She must also ask herself, "What is the way to recovery?" The patient may believe there is "nothing wrong" from which she has to recover, which is Sylvia's case, a penal commitment, and there may be nothing wrong in this case. Or she may believe something ails her but it does not require psychiatric hospitalization and treatment. She is more concerned with being discharged from the hospital than with recovery as viewed by hospital staff. Again, she may find her situation in the hospital more gratifying, or less threatening, than that which awaits her outside. Florence, for example, ran away from Macy's while with a recreational therapist, but returned the next day voluntarily, as she had no home to go to, because the hospital, in fact, was her home. She is thus motivated more to maintain her hospital status than to strive toward recovery and discharge.

The patient also wants to know what other patients are like. A crucial, anxiety-laden fact of life for every person who enters the mental hospital, whether as patient or as staff member, is that she will become part of a "crazy" world, a community in which the majority of inhabitants are "mentally ill": A major role-task is to work out a conception of what patients are like and how best to deal with them. This is especially difficult for the newly entered patient, who, burdened with her inner problems, is highly vulner-

able to the most frieghtening fantasies (her own and those conveyed to her by others) regarding life in the insane asylum. There is also a great probability that the patients will reinforce each other's difficulties than they will facilitate each other's improvement.

The ideal patient would be optimistic and rely on external supports and controls. The patient holding this view counts heavily on the healing effects of time, rest, and good food. She regards the hospital as a "resort hotel for resting and enjoying yourself." The specific psychiatric treatment she receives is not her concern; it is up to the doctor to decide what is best and to prescribe accordingly. The patient herself can help primarily by keeping busy and cheerful, and by following the rules. "If a patient does what she's supposed to do around here, getting well will take care of itself." The responsibility for therapeutic work is thus largely externalized onto a beneficent ward staff and an omniscient, magically healing doctor.[11] It is too bad that this is rarely the case, with either staff or patient.

Even though the goal of the mental hospital is to restore patients to normal living, it is difficult for those who have spent a long time in it to resume living outside it, as was seen in the case of Florence. The patient gradually unlearns normal modes of functioning and acquires a set of attitudes and habits that unfit him for ordinary living.

Desocialization is engendered by enforced dependency and passivity. The patient is given little or no significant responsibility and little opportunity to make important decisions; he is subjected to continuous orders from others, to regulations for minutest aspects of his behavior, and to severe restrictions of movement. He also has no opportunity for productive remunerative work or intimate and meaningful relationships with significant others. Thus, there is a severe disparity between the expectations of him on the outside as an independent, autonomous, and self-directing citizen and his desocialized role in the hospital. He is not motivated or helped to move toward the outside and ends by being unable to conceive of himself as living outside the hospital at all.[12]

[11] Levinson and Gallagher, *op. cit.*, p. 221.

[12] Morris Schwartz and Charlotte Schwartz, *Social Approaches to Men-*

The patient in the mental hospital is treated, moreover, as if being a patient were her only role: all others, for example, mother, daughter, worker, student, or citizen, are largely suspended while she is in the hospital, and the person is completely submerged in the status of patient. This is reflected in the way the institution deals with her, in the attitudes personnel have toward her, and in the limitations placed upon her; there is virtually no opportunity for an inmate to perform roles other than that of patient. The staff sees her only in terms of her "illness" and views mental illness as a "disease of the total person," whereas the healthy aspect of a patient, no matter how small it may be, should be sought out and stressed. Experiencing the person only as a patient tends to increase the staff's hopeless feelings about her. This, too, makes it difficult for her to leave.

The patient role is also an indefinite one in the sense that there are no time boundaries to being a patient. When staff can neither specify nor explain the course of her improvement nor indicate the steps leading to her discharge, she can not foresee the termination of her status as a patient. The vagueness associated with "getting well" may contribute to her confusion, uncertainty, and despair and so prolong her stay.[13]

On the other side of the coin, some patients are too sick to think about tomorrow and its possibilities, but acceptance of chronicity is rare and not encouraged. As if to indirectly reinforce confidence, a patient witnesses relatively rapid turnover among her companions, who come and go almost daily. Discharged patients are remembered, and there is enough realistic talk about leaving among those who remain to lend an air of movement to the wards, despite the stability of routines. Even frequent transfers reinforce the idea of movement.

And so we have the patient who is expected to perceive herself and other patients as sick and in need of hospitalization and at the same time the patient who is expected to be optimistic about her own and others' chances for recovery, and to concentrate her efforts toward the goal of leaving the hospital. It is no wonder actual and permanent recovery is quite diffi-

tal Patient Care (New York: Columbia University Press, 1964), p. 200.

[13] *Ibid.*, p. 201.

cult to attain.

I come now to the questions of what can be done or what should be done. Should hospitalization be reduced to a phase, rather than a center of treatment, with psychiatry moving from individual control to a complete prevention, treatment, and rehabilitation program in all communities of the United States? This would demand close and continuous relations with the community, families, schools, churches, welfare and health institutions and occupations.

As it stands today, hospital staff must be administered in an impersonal fashion with minimum allowance for personal peculiarities on the part of staff, patients, or relatives. Standard operating procedure is inflexible, and administrative routines dominant.

There is now also a tendency in local communities to dump the residual welfare, mentally deficient, and other types of problematic individuals for whom the community doesn't provide into the mental hospitals, and this has a harmful effect on the possibility of modern psychiatric treatment.

A stagnant and hopeless atmosphere prevails throughout most wards, while this group absorbs great amounts of medical time and skill in the treatment of their physical problems. This, again, further and decisively diminishes the possible psychiatric functions of the hospital.

Thus, possible reorganization can occur by preventing by whatever means are necessary the present use of the state mental hospital as a solution to welfare and mental deficiency problems in the local community; changing internal administrative structure; running the hospital as a system of linked auxiliary services under over-all medical supervision, rather than as a simple line and staff organization in which these services are discharged by delegation of commands to subordinates; and moving away from authoritarianism and towards individual spontaneity of modern psychiatry. All are possible means of some improvement.

Another way is to give stronger status to ward attendants and social workers. Failure to do this means that the executive can rely on none of the motivation, spontaneity, creativeness, and participation in a centrally shared purpose which is required by any organization to get work done.

Elevate their status to highly trained psychiatric social worker, nurse supervisor and psychologist and their relation to the psychiatrist should personally be much closer than that of any of these personnel. Then psychiatrists can operate the state hospital with maximum effectiveness, because they will be delegating work to well-paid and competent auxiliaries, instead of to poorly paid, untrained and resentful subordinates.[14]

Until this complete change occurs, we shall still have a mental hospital system that is undefined or rigid, defensive and hostile, and at almost every point presenting obstacles to any sustained progress in the care of the mentally ill.

What about abolishing mental hospitals altogether and beginning anew, from a new frame of reference other than psychiatric and medical? That is a whole new topic, one about which little is known today, but in the future, what about it?

BIBLIOGRAPHY

1. Belknap, Ivan. *Human Problems of a State Mental Hospital* (New York: McGraw-Hill, 1958).
2. Caudill, William. *The Psychiatric Hospital as a Small Society* (Cambridge, Mass.: Harvard University Press, 1958).
3. Clausen, John. *Sociology and the Field of Mental Health* (New York: Russell Sage Foundation, 1956).
4. Goffman, Erving. *Asylums* (New York: Doubleday, 1961).
5. Levinson, Daniel, and Gallagher, Eugene. *Patienthood in the Mental Hospital* (Boston: Houghton Mifflin, 1964).
6. Schwartz, Morris, and Schwartz, Charlotte. *Social Approaches to Mental Patient Care* (New York: Columbia University Press, 1964).
7. Spitzer, Stephan, and Denizen, Norman. *The Mental Patient* (New York: McGraw-Hill, 1968).
8. Stanton, Alfred, and Schwartz, Morris. *The Mental Hospital, A Study of Institutions* (New York: Basic, 1954).
9. Strauss, Anselm, Schatzman, Leonard, Bucher, Rue, Ehrlich, Danuta, and Sabshin, Melvin. *Psychiatric Ideologies and Institutions* (Glencoe: Free Press, 1964).

[14] Belknap, *op. cit.*, p. 100.

Even for those who have never set foot in a mental hospital, the writing of Ken Kesey has created an image of the individual pitted against authority, which knows what is best for the patient. The unforgettable McMurphy, protagonist of *One Flew Over the Cuckoo's Nest* represents a life force which is tragically snuffed out by the inexorable push toward conformity which labels him as an irredeemable deviant. The scene below describes McMurphy's sudden awakening to the fact that he is the only involuntarily committed patient on his ward.

9.4

From One Flew Over the Cuckoo's Nest

Ken Kesey

I remember it was a Friday again, three weeks after we voted on TV, and everybody who could walk was herded over to Building One for what they try to tell us is chest X-rays for TB, which I know is a check to see if everybody's machinery is functioning up to par.

We're benched in a long row down a hall leading to a door marked X-RAY. Next to X-ray is a door marked EENT where they check our throats during the winter. Across the hall from us is another bench, and it leads to that metal door. With the line of rivets. And nothing marked on it at all. Two guys are dozing on the bench between two black boys, while another victim inside is getting his treatment and I can hear him screaming. The door opens inward with a whoosh, and I can see the twinkling tubes in the room. They wheel the victim out still smoking, and I grip the bench where I sit to keep from being sucked through that door. A black boy and a white one drag one of the other guys on the bench to his feet, and he sways and staggers under the drugs in him. They usually give you red capsules before Shock. They push him through the door, and the technicians get him under each arm. For a second I see the guy realizes where they got him, and he stiffens both heels into the cement floor to keep from being pulled to the table—then the door pulls shut, phumph, with metal hitting a mattress, and I can't see him any more.

"Man, what they got going on in there?" McMurphy asks Harding.

"In there? Why, that's right, isn't it? You haven't had the pleasure. Pity. An experience no human should be without." Harding laces his fingers behind his neck and leans back to look at the door. "That's the Shock Shop I was telling you about some time back, my friend, the EST, Electro-Shock Therapy. Those fortunate souls in there are being give a free trip to the moon. No, on second thought, it isn't completely free. You pay for the service with brain cells instead of money, and everyone has simply billions of brain cells on deposit. You won't miss a few."

He frowns at the one lone man left on the bench. "Not a very large clientele today, it seems, nothing like the crowds of yester-year. But then, *c'est la vie*, fads come and go. And I'm afraid we are witnessing the sunset of EST. Our dear head nurse is one of the few with the heart to stand up for a grand old Faulknerian tradition in the treatment of the rejects of sanity: Brain Burning."

The door opens. A Gurney comes whirring out, nobody pushing it, takes the corner on two wheels and disappears smoking up the hall. McMurphy watches them take the last guy in and close the door.

"What they do is"—McMurphy listens a moment—"take some bird in there and shoot *electricity* through his skull?"

"That's a concise way of putting it."

"What the hell *for*?"

"Why, the patient's good, of course. Everything done here is for the patient's good. You may sometimes get the impression, having lived only on our ward, that the hospital is a vast efficient mechanism that would function quite well if the patient were not imposed on it, but that's not true. EST isn't always used for punitive measures, as our nurse uses it, and it isn't pure sadism on the staff's part, either. A number of supposed Irrecoverables were brought back into contact with shock, just as a number were helped with lobotomy and leucotomy. Shock treatment has some advantages; it's cheap, quick, entirely painless. It simply induces a seizure."

"What a life," Sefelt moans. "Give some of us pills to stop a fit, give the rest shock to start one."

Harding leans forward to explain it to McMurphy. "Here's how it came about: two psychiatrists were visiting a slaughterhouse, for God knows what perverse reason, and were watching cattle being killed by a blow between the eyes with a sledge-hammer. They noticed that not all of the cattle were killed, that some would fall to the floor in a state that greatly resembled an epileptic convulsion. 'Ah, *zo*,' the first doctor says. ''Zis is exactly vot ve need for our patients—zee induced *fit!*' His colleague agreed, of course. It was known that men coming out of an epileptic convulsion were inclined to be calmer and more peaceful for a time, and that violent cases completely out of contact were able to carry on rational conversations after a convulsion. No one knew why; they still don't. But it was obvious that if a seizure could be induced in non-epileptics, great benefits might result. And here, before them, stood a man inducing seizures every so often with remarkable aplomb."

Scanlon says he thought the guy used a hammer instead of a bomb, but Harding says he will ignore that completely, and he goes ahead with the explanation.

"A hammer *is* what the butcher used. And it was here that the colleague had some reservations. After all, a man wasn't a cow. Who knows when the hammer might slip and break a nose? Even knock out a mouthful of teeth? Then where would they be, with the high cost of dental work? If they were going to knock a man in the head, they needed to use something surer and more accurate than a hammer; they finally settled on electricity."

"Jesus, didn't they think it might do some damage? Didn't the public raise Cain about it?"

"I don't think you fully understand the public, my friend; in this country, when something is out of order, then the quickest way to get it fixed is the best way."

McMurphy shakes his head. "Hoo-*wee!* Electricity through the head. Man, that's like electrocuting a guy for murder."

"The reasons for both activities are much more closely related than you might think; they are both cures."

"And you say it don't *hurt?*"

"I personally guarantee it. Completely painless. One flash and you're unconscious immediately. No gas, no needle, no sledge-hammer. Absolutely painless. The thing is, no one ever wants another one. You . . . change. You forget things. It's as if"—he presses his hands against his temples, shutting his eyes—"it's as if the jolt sets off a wild carnival wheel of images, emotions, memories. These wheels, you've seen them; the barker takes your bet and pushes a button. *Chang!* With light and sound and numbers round and round in a whirlwind, and maybe you win with what you end up with and maybe you lose and have to play again. Pay the man for another spin, son, pay the man."

"Take it easy, Harding."

The door opens and the Gurney comes back out with the guy under a sheet, and the technicians go out for coffee. McMurphy runs his hand through his hair. "I don't seem able to get all this stuff that's happening straight in my mind."

"What's that? This shock treatment?"

"Yeah. No, not just that. All this . . ." He waves his hand in a circle. "All these things going on."

Harding's hand touches McMurphy's knee. "Put your troubled mind at ease, my friend. In all likelihood you needn't concern yourself with EST. It's almost out of vogue and only used in the extreme cases nothing else seems to reach, like lobotomy."

"Now lobotomy, that's chopping away part of the brain?"

"You're right again. You're becoming very sophisticated in the jargon. Yes; chopping away the brain. Frontal-lobe castration. I guess if she can't cut below the belt she'll do it above the eyes."

"You mean Ratched."

"I do indeed."

"I didn't think the nurse had the say-so on this kind of thing."

"She does indeed."

McMurphy acts like he's glad to get off talking about shock and lobotomy and get back to talking about the Big Nurse. He asks Harding what he figures is wrong with her. Harding and Scanlon and some of the others have all kinds of ideas. They talk for a while about whether she's the root of all the trouble here or not, and Harding says she's the root of most of it. Most of the other guys think so too, but McMurphy isn't so sure any more. He says he thought so at one time but now he don't know. He says he don't think getting her out of the way would really make much difference; he says that there's something bigger making all this mess and goes on to try to say what he thinks it is. He finally gives up when he can't explain it.

McMurphy doesn't know it, but he's onto what I realized a long time back, that it's not just the Big Nurse by herself, but it's the whole Combine, the nation-wide Combine that's the really big force, and the nurse is just a high-ranking official for them.

The guys don't agree with McMurphy. They say they *know* what the trouble with things is, then get in an argument about that. They argue till McMurphy interrupts them.

"Hell's bells, listen at you," McMurphy says. "All I hear is gripe, gripe, gripe. About the nurse or the staff or the hospital. Scanlon wants to bomb the whole outfit. Sefelt blames the drugs. Fredrickson blames his family trouble. Well, you're all just passing the buck."

He says that the Big Nurse is just a bitter, icy-hearted old woman, and all this business trying to get him to lock horns with her is a lot of bull—wouldn't do anybody any good, especially him. Getting shut of her wouldn't be getting shut of the real deep-down hang-up that's causing the gripes.

"You think not?" Harding says. "Then since you are suddenly so lucid on the problem of mental health, what *is* this trouble? What *is* this deep-down hang-up, as you so cleverly put it."

"I tell you, man, I don't know. I never seen the beat of it." He sits still for a minute, listening to the hum from the X-ray room; then he says, "But if it was no more'n you say, if it was, say, just this old nurse and her sex worries, then the solution to all your problems would be to just throw her down and solve her worries, wouldn't it?"

Scanlon claps his hands. "Hot damn! That's it. You're nominated, Mack, you're just the stud to handle the job."

"Not me. No sir. You got the wrong boy."

"Why not? I thought you's the super-stud with all that wham-bam."

"Scanlon, buddy, I plan to stay as clear of that old buzzard as I possibly can."

"So I've been noticing," Harding says, smiling. "What's happened between the two of you? You had her on the ropes for a period there; then you let up. A sudden compassion for our angel of mercy?"

"No; I found out a few things, that's why. Asked around some different places. I found out why you guys all kiss her ass so much

and bow and scrape and let her walk all over you. I got wise to what you were using me for."

"Oh? That's interesting."

"You're blamed right it's interesting. It's interesting to me that you bums didn't tell me what a risk I was running, twisting her tail that way. Just because I don't like her ain't a sign I'm gonna bug her into adding another year or so to my sentence. You got to swallow your pride sometimes and keep an eye out for old Number One."

"Why, friends, you don't suppose there's anything to this rumor that our Mr. McMurphy has conformed to policy merely to aid his chances of an early release?"

"You know what I'm talking about, Harding. Why didn't you tell me she could keep me committed in here till she's good and ready to turn me loose?"

"Why, I had *forgotten* you were committed." Harding's face folds in the middle over his grin. "Yes. You're becoming sly. Just like the rest of us."

"You damn betcha I'm becoming sly. Why should it be me goes to bat at these meetings over these piddling little gripes about keeping the dorm door open and about cigarettes in the Nurses' Station? I couldn't figure it at first, why you guys were coming to me like I was some kind of savior. Then I just happened to find out about the way the nurses have the big say as to who gets discharged and who doesn't. And I got wise awful damned fast. I said, 'Why, those slippery bastards have *conned* me, snowed me into holding their bag. If that don't beat all, conned ol' R. P. McMurphy.' " He tips his head back and grins at the line of us on the bench. "Well, I don't mean nothing personal, you understand, buddies, but screw that noise. I want out of here just as much as the rest of you. I got just as much to lose hassling that old buzzard as *you* do."

He grins and winks down his nose and digs Harding in the ribs with his thumb, like he's finished with the whole thing but no hard feelings, when Harding says something else.

"No. You've got more to lose than I do, my friend."

Harding's grinning again, looking with that skitterish sideways look of a jumpy mare, a dipping, rearing motion of the head. Everybody moves down a place. Martini comes away from the X-ray screen, buttoning his shirt and muttering, "I wouldn't of believed it if I hadn't saw it," and Billy

Bibbit goes to the black glass to take Martini's place.

"You have more to lose than I do," Harding says again. "I'm voluntary. I'm not committed."

McMurphy doesn't say a word. He's got that same puzzled look on his face like there's something isn't right, something he can't put his finger on. He just sits there looking at Harding, and Harding's rearing smile fades and he goes to fidgeting around from McMurphy staring at him so funny. He swallows and says, "As a matter of fact, there are only a few men on the ward who *are* committed. Only Scanlon and—well, I guess some of the Chronics. And you. Not many commitments in the whole hospital. No, not many at all."

Then he stops, his voice dribbling away under McMurphy's eyes. After a bit of silence McMurphy says softly, "Are you bullshitting me?" Harding shakes his head. He looks frightened. McMurphy stands up in the hall and says, "Are you buys *bullshitting* me!"

Nobody'll say anything. McMurphy walks up and down in front of that bench, running his hand around in that thick hair. He walks all the way to the back of the line, then all the way to the front, to the X-ray machine. It hisses and spits at him.

"You, Billy—you *must* be committed, for Christsakes!"

Billy's got his back to us, his chin up on the black screen, standing on tiptoe. No, he says into the machinery.

"Then *why?* Why? You're just a young guy! You oughta be out running around in a convertible, bird-dogging girls. All of this"—he sweeps his hand around him again—"why do you stand for it?"

Billy doesn't say anything, and McMurphy turns from him to another couple of guys.

"Tell me why. You gripe, you bitch for *weeks* on end about how you can't stand this place, can't stand the nurse or anything about her, and all the time you ain't committed. I can understand it with some of those old guys on the ward. They're *nuts*. But you, you're not exactly the everyday man on the street, but you're not *nuts*."

They don't argue with him. He moves on to Sefelt.

"Sefelt, what about you? There's nothing wrong with you but you have fits. Hell, I had an uncle who threw conniptions twice as bad as yours and saw visions from the Devil to boot, but he didn't lock himself in the nut-house. You could get along outside if you had the guts!"

"Sure!" It's Billy, turned from the screen, his face boiling tears. "Sure!" he screams again. "If we had the g-guts! I could go outside to-today, if I had the guts. My m-m-mother is a good friend of M-Miss Ratched, and I could get an AMA signed this afternoon, if I had the guts!"

He jerks his shirt up from the bench and tries to pull it on, but he's shaking too hard. Finally he slings it from him and turns back to McMurphy.

"You think I wuh-wuh-wuh-*want* to stay in here? You think I wouldn't like a con-con-vertible and a guh-guh-girl friend? But did you ever have people l-l-laughing at you? No, because you're so b-big and so *tough!* Well, I'm not big and tough. Neither is Harding. Neither is F-Fredrickson. Neither is Suh-Sefelt. Oh—oh, you—you t-talk like we stayed in here because we liked it! Oh—it's n-no use . . ."

He's crying and stuttering too hard to say anything else, and he wipes his eyes with the backs of his hands so he can see. One of the scabs pulls off his hand, and the more he wipes the more he smears blood over his face and in his eyes. Then he starts running blind, bouncing down the hall from side to side with his face a smear of blood, a black boy right after him.

McMurphy turns round to the rest of the guys and opens his mouth to ask something else, and then closes it when he sees how they're looking at him. He stands there a minute with the row of eyes aimed at him like a row of rivets; then he says, "Hell's bells," in a weak sort of way, and he puts his cap back on and pulls it down hard and goes back to his place on the bench. The two technicians come back from coffee and go back in that room across the hall; when the door whooshes open you can smell the acid in the air like when they recharge a battery. Mc-Murphy sits there, looking at that door.

"I don't seem able to get it straight in my mind. . . ."

The following statement of a mental patient's rights in a mental hospital must be posted in each California hospital. Most student volunteers report that they have not seen them. Even so, the permissiveness in the rules is obviated by the phrase "These rights may be denied for good cause . . ." and by some of the facts in the previous articles.

PATIENT'S RIGHTS

Lanterman-Petris-Short guarantees certain rights to each person involuntarily detained for evaluation and treatment, and to each voluntary patient, as well. The department must prominently post these rights in Spanish and in English in the hospitals and bring them to the attention of the patients:

To wear his own clothes; to keep and use his own personal possessions including his toilet articles; and to keep and be allowed to spend a reasonable sum of his own money for canteen expenses and small purchases.

To have access to individual storage space for his private use.

To see visitors each day.

To have reasonable access to telephones, both to make and receive confidential calls.

To have ready access to letter writing materials, including stamps, and to mail and receive unopened correspondence.

To refuse shock treatment.

To refuse lobotomy.

Other rights that might be specified by departmental regulations.

These rights may be denied for good cause, but only by the professional person in charge of the facility. If any of these rights are denied, it must be entered into the patient's record. And any information relating to the denial of rights must be made available on request to the patient's attorney, his guardian, or conservator, members of the Legislature, members of the county board of supervisors or the Department of Mental Hygiene.

Pauline Bart relates the ideology of contemporary forms of psychotherapy to an evolving philosophy of science. She argues that the choice of such therapeutic methods as Gestalt therapy, self-actualization, encounter groups, behavior modification therapy, and ther-

apy by computer is based on an ideological or value judgment—a point made in the past by Thomas Kuhn in reference to all science. Citing the Rogers-Skinner debate (see Chapter 1), Bart reviews critically each of these techniques with an evident bias of her own. She is clearly disturbed by the trend in therapy toward mechanistic methods which produce immediate results at the price of turning one's back on the humanistic tradition of Western Civilization.

9.5
Myth of the Value-Free Psychotherapy

Pauline Bart

I have been discussing changes in psychiatric conceptions of man and of the treatment process in order to show that some psychiatrists are becoming aware of the interrelationship of social structure and the individual. The most striking changes in psychotherapy, however, have come from psychologists rather than psychiatrists. It is important to note that Freud was opposed to analysis being limited to medical men. And Reiff (1966:28) considers the elimination of lay analysts probably the most critical defeat suffered by psychoanalysis, and one for which the American analysts were largely responsible. The view in the United States that only M.D.'s are qualified to receive training enabling them to become analysts seems to be patently ideological, since it makes entry into the field extremely difficult for all those who do not have the financial resources to pay for the medical schooling itself, as well as the training analysis most psychiatrists consider necessary. This limitation, resulting in psychiatrists either coming from upper or upper middle-class backgrounds, or having been successful in their desire for upward mobility may be one reason for the image of man, private man, held until recently by most psychiatrists. For people who are "making it" in society, societal factors are not perceived as being very important. On the

Reprinted by permission from "Myth of the Value-Free Psychotherapy," in Wendell Bell and James A. Mau (eds.), *Sociology and the Future,* New York, Russell Sage Foundation and Basic Books, 1971.

other hand, psychologists have had for many years a running battle with medical men for their right to treat clients. Their status is reflected in the lower fees they charge. That the radical changes in psychotherapy have come from psychologists may be a function of their lesser commitment to classic Freudian models and to the psychiatric profession, but more importantly to their differing education. Psychologists would be more likely to have been exposed to other behavioral and social sciences. Thus they would be more aware of sociocultural variables. In addition, the learning theory they are taught would make behavior-modification therapy, one of the new trends, a natural occurrence.

In this section I will discuss two psychotherapeutic approaches, each used mainly by psychologists, each based on a completely different set of assumptions about man, and thus having different images of, and implications for, the future.

Man the self actualizer: goodby Mr. Weber. Because the "basic encounter" therapists I will discuss in this section work within an existential *weltaunschaung,* I will begin by presenting a work written by an existential psychiatrist, which deals with what Bell and Mau term "the future as a cause of the present." Existential psychiatry differs from traditional psychiatry in its anti-deterministic stance and in its rejection of two assumptions sometimes held in non-existential psychiatry: 1) that man should be adjusted to society, and 2) that man may be reduced to a bundle of biological urges.

It (existential psychiatry) conceives of the individual choosing and making his world rather than adjusting to it or succumbing to it. This view holds that the world is part of the existing human being, that he is part of it, and that he makes his world. (Mendel, 1964:32–34)

The future, rather than being merely the natural consequence of the past, is "recognized as a vital and strongly influential aspect of human existence in the present moment." (Mendel, 1964:32–34) The here and now is emphasized, since the patient needs experience rather than interpretation, for "learning and change occur only through activity."

Existential psychotherapy has for some time been popular in Europe, but only recently has been taken up in this country. The most popular current offshoot is "encounter therapy" or "encounter

groups."[1] Many encounter therapists,[2] call themselves humanistic pists, predominantly psycholo-psychologists, and as such have their own association and journal. (See Bugental, 1967, for a representative collection of their works.)

If Freud's thinking reflected nineteenth century mechanistic physics, then it is not surprising that concomitantly with the discovery of the principle of indeterminacy in twentieth century physics, a discovery which resulted in physicists perceiving that the objective was related to the subjective, psychology should once again focus on the more subjective aspects of the individual and a "humanistic psychology" should emerge. (It is also interesting to note that a similar trend has taken place in sociology with the existence of a "humanistic underground," to use Bernard Rosenberg's term.) I noted in the discussion of Freud that his psychology was a reflection of a society built upon the axioms of an economics of scarcity. With economics no longer the dismal science of the nineteenth century, with abundance possible, a new psychology was needed to reflect the increase of leisure time and the decrease in the importance of the work ethic. Energy formerly required for mere survival could now be devoted to improving the quality of life through increased awareness both of oneself and of one's surroundings. Bugental (1967:345–346), a humanistic psychologist and adviser to the Esalen Institute which will be described below, says that we are in the early stages of "another major evolution in man's perception of himself and thus the whole nature of human experience," due to the availability of this energy. He considers behavioristic psychology with its view of man as "nothing but a complex of muscle twitches"

[1] Some therapists, such as Rogers (1967), differentiate between group therapy, which is for people who have problems, and encounter groups which are for everyone. Since this distinction is, however, rarely made in practice, because "sick" people are thought to benefit by encounter groups, I will use the terms interchangeably.

[2] I analyzed the fall, 1967, catalogues of Esalen and Kairos and found the following occupational characteristics of seminar and workshop leaders: 30 Ph.D. psychologists, 12 Ph.D.'s in other fields, 9 M.D.'s, and 42 others such as ministers, artists, and dancers.

and its disposal of concepts such as "soul," "will," "mind," "consciousness" and "self" inappropriate to present and future conditions although appropriate in the past.

This new psychological vocabulary, rather than emphasizing regularity, uniformity and predictability, will highlight "the unique, the creative, the individual, and the artistic." More attention should be paid to man's internal subjective experiences, and it should be recognized that the supposed "law of causality" is:

. . . simply a useful heuristic aid. . . . Some of man's behavior flows from *reason* and not from *cause.* The difference is revolutionary. Let this difference be accepted and developed, and the torch is lit which will burn away the whole of the mechanomorphic picture of man and illuminate the human enterprise to entirely new levels of realization. (Bugental, 1967:347)

Consequently, there will be a potential for improving social institutions so that they will be more suited to man's evolving needs.

The late Fritz Perls, a founder of Gestalt therapy (a therapy using body movement, similar ideologically to encounter therapy) and permanent resident psychologist at Esalen, agreed with Bugental that the traditional concepts of linear causation are no longer appropriate. In a 1967 fund-raising speech for the new Topanga Human Development Center, an Esalen-Kairos type of workshop located in an artsy-craftsy canyon in Los Angeles, he stated that his approach was processual. In contrast to psychoanalytic thinking, he focuses on "the now and the how" rather than on "the wild goose chase of the past."

The goal of encounter therapy, in contrast to behavior modification therapy to be discussed below, is not the elimination of discomforting symptoms. Indeed one need not have any symptoms at all. It is the therapy for the man who has everything. As Wesley (1967) states, this therapy is for "anyone who has come to recognize a vague dissatisfaction in his life arising from the lack of expressive spontaneity, love and joy." Rogers says, "Encounter groups are for those who are functioning normally but want to improve their capacity for living within their own sets of relationships." (1967:717)

The theory of human nature held by encounter therapists is Rousseauian, and the assumption is made that through the permissive and accepting climate of an encounter group the potential for growth present in each individual will develop. As a result of this experience, people will be able to fulfill their potentialities.

I have attempted to show the elective affinity between the decline of the Protestant Ethic, the rise of a leisure-based society, and self actualization therapy. The relationship between time and the growth of industrial society has been frequently noted. Thus it is consistent with the decline in the work ethic that changed attitudes towards time should also be evidenced. In another paper, I mentioned the "cubic schedule" at Synanon. Marathon group therapy, used at Esalen, Kairos and by many encounter therapists, "represents a challenge to conventional arrangements of time in that its basic characteristic is that of the continuous session ranging over one or more days. Regularly scheduled meetings of one or two hours' duration, stretching out over many months or even years have been customary. The implications of the two basic approaches to people literally imply different views of men." (Stoller, 1969:42)

Traditional psychotherapists have criticized the marathons. In keeping with the nineteenth century ideology out of which psychoanalysis developed, they believe that long periods of arduous work are necessary for any benefit to occur. They find it difficult to accept the claim that people may change as a result of participating in a thirty-hour, two-day period of therapy.

Not only are the traditional concepts of causation and determinism challenged and ·attitudes toward work and time changed, but conventional attitudes toward sex are also contested. In contrast to the Freudian conceptualization of genitality in which homosexual relationships are considered fixations, sexual activity not culminating in genital intercourse is considered polymorphous perverse, and promiscuity is considered immature, among some self-actualizing groups relatively free sex is considered part of the growth process. Thus Kairos offers a seminar entitled "Enjoying the Non-Permanent Relationship," the purpose of which seems to be to teach women to enjoy casual sex, since these non-permanent interactions "constitute the majority of man-woman relationships." At Esalen, mixed nude bathing at the hot springs is part of the schedule, and although it is not required,

group processes are such that it is expected.

Most encounter therapists and their followers spend some time at Esalen (and Kairos), a mental health spa located at Big Sur, on the California coast south of San Francisco and once the haunt of artists and writers such as Henry Miller and Robinson Jeffers (see Murphy, 1967 for a more detailed presentation of the program). Humanistic psychologists, such as the late Abraham Maslow, have recently lead seminars there. But musicians, dancers, craftsmen, and specialists in Zen and Yoga are also present so that those attending can realize their full potential through body awareness, music, baking, ceramics, graphics, leatherwork, metal sculpture, photography, and textiles.

The importance of relating to nature, the anti-intellectualism, the emphasis on Eastern philosophy, techniques and music, and the Rousseauian image of man are found both among the hippies[3] and the self-actualizers. In addition, they are like American Romantics such as Emerson (1837:3) who said: "Why should we grope among the dry bones of the past or put the living generation into masquerade out of faded wardrobe? The sun shines today also." Both groups do not feel the past is relevant to their present experience.

As a participant-observer at a "Basic Encounter Group" which attempted to recreate the Esalen atmosphere, I noted the following differences between this group and conventional group therapy:

1. The presence of a non-verbal therapist, a dancer, whose function was to increase the group members' body awareness.
2. The meeting neither started nor ended on time. In conventional therapy, lateness is interpreted as resistance, an approach to time consistent with the requirements of an expanding industrial economy.
3. The relationship between the therapists and the group was relatively egalitarian.
4. Part of the encounter was devoted to non-verbal communication between dyads which in two instances resulted in what can most parsimoniously be called in the vernacular "making out."

[3] The use of the term "hippie" does not imply that they are a homogeneous group. There are, however, some common beliefs and behavior patterns distinguishing them from "straight" society.

This group emphasized various sense modalities not previously highly valued in our society, geared as it was to production rather than consumption. The permissive attitude toward sex, the emphasis on body awareness, the democratization of the therapeutic process, all are associated with similar trends in other areas of our society and assume a future very different from the past.

The values of these therapists are freedom, spontaneity, intimacy and creativity. Their idea of the freedom man needs to grow is not simply Freud's goal of replacing id with ego, but rather freedom to express feelings, to become close to people with less fear of interdependence and intimacy, freedom to express oneself through non-verbal as well as verbal means, through movement and art and nature. The structure of society, with its emphasis on role-appropriate behavior in interaction, is considered a barrier to full humanness.[4] Thus, individuals are encouraged not to become "victimized by the social rigging in which his life moves . . . (which) chokes off the expansion of his life-self intimacy." (Kairos, 1967) Continuing on this theme, another Kairos seminar suggests that "people grow through developing trust, openness, realization and interdependence," so that the goal of this seminar is "growth toward a life that is more personal, intimate, self-determined, and *role-free*." (emphasis added) Often at Esalen individuals do not state their occupations in order to discourage interaction based upon roles.

An example of such an approach to changing institutions, and one that shows a Rogerian method of bringing about a society more suited for today's world, is the Educational Innovation Project of Carl Rogers and the staff of the Western Behavioral Sciences Institute working with the personnel and students of the Immaculate Heart Schools[5] (Rogers,

[4] This attempt to get through the presentation of self is also advocated by Synanon and the hippies. Synanon games propose to enable people to get away from the type of game playing that constitutes most of human interaction. The Diggers and other hippie groups believe that "tripping" enables a person to get to his "pure being" and away from his presented self.

[5] The sisters of the Immaculate Heart of Mary direct and teach in the college, secondary, and primary

1967). The purpose of Rogers' (1967:717) "plan for self-directed change in an educational system" is to enable educational institutions to develop flexible and adaptive individuals who will be comfortable with rapid social change. "Basic encounter" groups with a maximum of freedom for personal expression, exploration of feelings, and communication are "one of the most effective means yet discovered for facilitation of constructive learning, growth, and change—in individuals or in the organizations they compose . . ." (718) The whole system must participate for change to be effective. Otherwise the changed individual either becomes frustrated or returns to his previous method of interaction because of group pressure. Rogers believes that whole systems can be changed in a relatively short period of time.

Rogers, in a symposium with Skinner on control of human behavior, has set down his values and beliefs concerning the role psychology should play in the increasing possibility of such control. He suggests that the type of therapy he advocates will result in greater maturity, variability, flexibility, openness to experience, increased self-responsibility, and self-direction. He values:

man as a process of becoming, as a process of achieving worth and dignity through the development of his potentialities; the individual human being as a self-actualizing process, moving on to more challenging and enriching experiences, the process by which the individual creatively adapts to an ever-new and changing world; the process by which knowledge transcends itself . . . (Rogers and Skinner, 1956:1063)

Thus, he attempts to learn if science can

. . . aid in the discovery of new modes of richly rewarding living, more meaningful and satisfying modes of interpersonal relationships. Can science inform us on ways of releasing the creative capacity of individuals. . . . In short, can science discover the methods by which man can most readily become a continually developing and self-transcending process, in his behavior, his

schools involved in this experiment. They have recently been in the news because of their innovations which have brought them into conflict with Cardinal MacIntyre of Los Angeles, a conflict which was finally mediated by the Vatican. One issue which disturbed some more conservative Catholics was the encounter therapy which the sisters considered a means of breaking down traditional morality.

thinking, his knowledge? (Rogers and Skinner, 1956:1063)

He believes that the therapy that he and his followers practice express such values and produce a client who is "self-directing, less rigid, more open to the evidence of his senses, better organized and integrated, more similar to the ideal which he (the client) has chosen for himself." (Rogers and Skinner, 1956:1063)

There are two limitations of this type of therapy. The development of each individual's full potentialities is possible only where there is an economic surplus. Maslow (1962) points out in his work on need hierarchies that self actualization could occur only after other needs, such as the needs for safety, for food, and for shelter were met. Thus those portions of our society still poorly housed, fed, clothed, and subject to the capricious behavior of police cannot afford the luxury of self actualization (nor can most of the world). Stoller told me that when he applied the encounter techniques to welfare mothers and to drug addict prisoners, their structural situations made it impossible for the benefits they believed they obtained to be carried over into their daily life. Moreover, the goals of encounter therapy, goals stressing expressivity, would be most useful for individuals having had traditional WASP socialization emphasizing the virtues of stoicism and restraint. Other ethnic and class groups, white and non-white, whose significant others do not discourage expression of emotion and "acting out," would perhaps be better served by other modes of therapy.

Man, "the two legged white rat or larger computer:"[6] behavior modification therapy.

Small, battery powered reliable conditioning apparatus for human subjects . . .
Shock Box (variable intensity) $35
Blinky Box (random order light stimuli) $25
Tinkle Bell (moisture sensitive signal for control of bedwetting) $25
. . .
Humanitas Systems, Orange City, Fla. (advertised in Psychology Today, December, 1967)

Behavior modification therapy is the antithesis of the self-actualizing therapy. It is deterministic rather than indeterministic, is based on different theoretical

[6] Phrase taken from Bugental (1967: 345).

groundwork, holds different views of human nature and of how society can and should be changed, and thus has a different image of the future (see paradigm). It reflects tendencies toward rationalization (in the Weberian, not Freudian, sense), dehumanization, and scientism in our society.

Although there are certain aspects of social control in every psychotherapeutic situation, whatever the rhetoric, and although Synanon self-consciously uses their "games" for social control of "dope fiends" there, in general most of the trends discussed have veered away from the social control model presented previously. Behavior modification therapy, however, seems most adequately conceptualized as a continuation of the tradition of therapy as social control. The therapist controls the situation.

The image of man these therapists use is derived from the behavior of animals. Their position is unique because they derive from a theory of learning specific techniques of therapy (London: personal communication). Because the basic theoretical work from which these programs derive was done on animals, these therapies are based on present observable behavior, rather than on unconscious factors or past events. Such therapies are designed to remove the symptoms causing the discomfort without "tampering with 'selves and souls' or even 'personalities.'" (London, 1964:34) Many behavior modification therapists believe that "the difficulties which bring people to therapy reflect learnings of fundamental behaviors which are at least as easily observed in lower animals as in people," and thus can be cured by mechanical procedures (London, 1964:77). They try to change the system of reinforcements so that the symptom they want to "extinguish" is no longer "reinforced" (rewarded). According to Kanfer and Phillips (1966), for this therapy to be effective the patient must have a specific problem such as a phobia, rather than more general problems such as feelings of worthlessness, personal inadequacies, or chronic generalized anxiety. Mowrer (1963:579) considers behavior therapy the "method of choice" because "the way to feel better is to be better in the ethical and interpersonal sense of the term," but his position is different from those behavior modification therapists "who assume that all that is wrong with neurotics is that they have some unrealistic fears which need to be extinguished or counter-conditioned."

These therapists disagree with the Freudians who believe that insight will lead to changed behavior. They would be more likely to agree that changed behavior (which they would produce by manipulating reinforcements) would lead to insight. They are also opposed to the humanistic, non-scientific (according to their standards) approach of the encounter therapists which they consider sentimental and muddle headed. Thus, their papers have starkly mechanistic titles such as "The Therapist as a Social Reinforcement Machine" (Krasner, 1961; reported in London, 1964:239) and "The Psychiatric Nurse as Behavioral Engineer" (Ayllon and Michael, 1959). Some techniques they use seem more akin to Dr. Benway (Burroughs' character) than to Dr. Kildare. Thus, in the Ayllon and Michael study the nurse changed the behavior of a patient who insisted on being fed but who wanted to be neat. The nurse deliberately dribbled food on her when she fed her. The patient eventually fed herself. The patient "unexpectedly" relapsed after a four-week improvement in self feeding.

No reasonable explanation is suggested by a study of her daily records; but, after she had been spoonfed several meals in a row, the rumor developed that someone had informed the patient that the food spilling was not accidental. In any event the failure to feed herself lasted only about 5 days. (Ayllon and Michael, 1959:331)

Another example, this one unsuccessful, dealt with the attempt to eliminate violent behavior. This behavior had reached such proportions that "at the least suspicious move on her part the nurses would put her in the seclusion room." Since one of the non-violent behaviors she exhibited was sitting, lying, squatting, or kneeling on the floor, it was decided to strengthen this class of responses since it "would control the violence and at the same time permit the emotional behavior of other patients and nurses toward her to extinguish." (Ayllon and Michael, 1959:329) She was to be socially "reinforced" by the nurses for a period of four weeks when she approached them while she was on the floor. During the four week period her approaches to nurses increased and her attacks on other patients decreased. Then, the plan for the next four weeks was to

discontinue reinforcing being on the floor "once the patient-nurse interaction appeared somewhat normal. Presumably this would have further increased the probability of approach to the nurses." However, "during the four weeks of extinction, the frequency of being on the floor returned to the pretreatment level," the attacks on patients and nurses increased, and the nurses started restraining the patient once more. (Ayllon and Michael, 1959:329)

The patient's failure to make the transition from being on the floor to approaching the nurses suggests that the latter response was poorly chosen. It was relatively incompatible with being on the floor. This meant that a previously reinforced response would have to be extinguished before the transition was possible, and this, too, was poor strategy with a violent patient. (Ayllon and Michael, 1959: 329)

Perhaps the reader can think of alternative reasons for the failure of this experiment. Ayllon and Michael believe patients' behavioral problems result from events "occurring in the patients' immediate or historical environment. They are not manifestations of mental disorder." (Ayllon and Michael, 1959: 323) [I do not understand their dichotomy.]

An attempt is made to discover and manipulate variables to modify the behavioral problem. Since the nurses are the major agents of social control and treatment in the hospital, a program is set up for the patient based on a rigid schedule of observation and the nurses are trained not to reinforce behavior they wish changed by giving attention or sympathy, but rather to reinforce desired behavior.

The logical extension of the model of man depicted in this section can be found in Colby's (1966) work, psychotherapy by computer. If the important part of therapy is not the relationship with the therapist, if, as described above, a nurse can be "programmed" to modify behavior, then why not make use of the new technology available and help solve the shortage of therapists? Colby (1966:151) considers the therapist:

. . . an information processor and decision maker with a set of decision rules which are closely linked to short-range and long-range goals. With time he builds up a cognitive model of the patient; carries on thought operations on the model, using first and second order inferences in a partially specialized langúage; and finally decides on a com-

munication to offer to the patient in natural language . . . guided by rough empiric rules telling him what is appropriate to say and not to say in certain contexts.

The person (as yet patients are not being used in the studies) types statements on a teletype and the program types answers substituting appropriate words in the responses for those found in the input sentences. For example:

PERSON: My mother dislikes me.
PROGRAM: Why do you feel your mother dislikes you? (Colby, 1966; 148–149)

The program should identify and keep statistical track of important topics for the formulation of future responses.

Efficiency is obviously a value of these researchers, as it is noted the therapist is "much more efficient" since he can work with many more patients. Several psychologists with whom I have spoken think the programs are good; and their image of the future is to give all the chronic patients, who at this time receive no therapy, the opportunity of conversing with a tape. But in view of Rioch's (1963) success in training housewives in a brief period of time who are just as effective as therapists, as professionals with standard training, one wonders why so little attention is being focused on this alternative possibility? Choosing a computer program over a housewife-therapist certainly is a reflection of values.

The workers in this area admit that they do not know how effective computer therapy will be. The program cannot handle sarcasm, shouting, or changes in feeling tone, and still arouses some antagonism, which is assumed to be due to defects in the program rather than to the process. An example of such hostility is the following:

PERSON: I hate you, you stupid machine.
PROGRAM: What don't you like about me?
PERSON: You have no feelings.
PROGRAM: How do you mean? (Colby, 1966:150)

It would be unfair to assume that the behavioral modification therapists are monsters—men with no feelings who wish to produce a generation of robots, men who have turned their back on the humanistic tradition in Western civilization to become mad scientists in the laboratory. It is obvious, for example, that B. F. Skinner, on whose work much of the application of learning theory is based, is a man of good will, a man who would like to apply what he has found out about how pigeons learn, to create a world:[7]

in which there is food, clothing and shelter for all, where everyone chooses his own work and works on the average only 4 hours a day, where music and the arts flourish, where personal relationships develop under the most favorable circumstances, where education prepares every child for the social and intellectual life which lies before him, where—in short—people are truly happy, secure, productive, creative, and forward-looking. (Rogers and Skinner, 1956: 1059)

In the above quote, Skinner is referring to his image of the future which he presented in his utopian novel, *Walden Two* (1962). The book has been severely criticized for its *Brave New World* aspects, the lack of real freedom, but Skinner believes that "All men control and are controlled. The question of government in the broadest possible sense is not how freedom is to be preserved, but what kinds of control are to be used and to what ends." (Rogers and Skinner, 1956:1060)

Like the behavioral modification therapists, and in contrast to the existential self-actualizing therapists, Skinner is a determinist. He does not believe that people be have in certain ways because of any innate goodness or evil but because they are reinforced for doing so:

The resulting behavior may have far-reaching consequences for the survival of the pattern to which it conforms. And whether we like it or not, survival is the ultimate criterion. (Rogers and Skinner, 1956:1065)

In his symposium with Carl Rogers he points out that there is no evidence "that a client ever becomes truly *self* directing."

. . . The therapeutic situation is only a small part of the world of the client. From the therapist's point of view it may appear to be possible to relinquish control. But control passes, not to a "self," but to forces in other parts of the client's world. This solution of the therapist's problem of power cannot be our solution, for we must consider all the forces acting upon the individual. (Rogers and Skinner, 1956:1065)

Therefore, in *Walden Two* Skinner (1962:296–297) designs a total environment, or, as some might say, dictatorship, a total institution. Frazier, the designer in

the novel, sees no conflict between dictatorship and freedom, since people are trained, through positive reinforcements to "want to do precisely the things which are best for themselves and for the community. Their behavior is determined, yet they're free."

Frazier's (and Skinner's?) goal is the control of human behavior, not for exploitation of others, nor for his own benefit, nor for the benefit of some elite, but so that everyone may share in the advantages of the new technology of control:

"What remains to be done?" he said, his eyes flashing. "Well, what do you say to the design of personalities? Would that interest you? The control of temperament? Give me the specification, and I'll give you the man! What do you say to the control of motivation, building the interests which will make men most productive and most successful? Does that seem to you fantastic? Yet some of the techniques are available, and more can be worked out experimentally. Think of the possibilities! A society in which there is no failure, no boredom, no duplication of effort!" (Skinner, 1962:292)

People marry young at Walden Two, but if the Manager of Marriages thinks there "is any great discrepancy in intellectual ability or temperament, they are advised against marrying. The marriage is at least postponed, and that usually means it's abandoned." (135) A "series of adversities" is *designed* to develop the greatest possible self-control in children (115). The approach is always pragmatic; every principle is experimentally tested. Thus, "History is honored at Walden Two only as entertainment." (115) In sum:

Political action was of no use in building a better world, and men of good will had better turn to other measures as soon as possible. Any group of people could secure economic self-sufficiency with the help of modern technology, and the psychological problems of group living could be solved with available principles of "behavioral engineering." (Skinner, 1962:14)

REFERENCES

Ayllon, Teodoro, and Jack Michael. 1959. "The Psychiatric Nurse as a Behavioral Engineer." *Journal of the Experimental Analysis of Behavior* 2:323–334.

Bart, Pauline. 1962. "Mobility and Mental Illness: A Review and Ideological Analysis of the Literature." Unpublished paper.

Bart, Pauline. 1967. *Depression in Middle Aged Women: Some Sociocultural Factors.* Unpublished dissertation, University of California at Los Angeles. University Microfilms, Ann Arbor.

Bugental, James T. F. 1967. "Epilogue and Prologue." James Bugental (ed.), *Challenges of Humanistic Psychology.* New York: McGraw-Hill:345–348.

Colby, Kenneth, *et al.* 1966. "A Computer Method of Psychotherapy: A Preliminary Communication." *Journal of Nervous and Mental Disease* 142:148–152.

Emerson, Ralph Waldo. 1950. "Nature." *The Complete Essays and Other Writings.* Brooks Atkinson (ed.). New York: The Modern Library:3.

Kairos. 1967–68. Kairos. Esalen Institute. San Francisco, Calif. (Pamphlet).

Kanfer, Frederick H., and Jeane S. Phillips. 1966. "A Review of the Area of Behavior Therapy." *Archives of General Psychiatry* 15 (August):114:127.

Kesey, Ken. 1962. *One Flew Over the Cuckoo's Nest.* New York: Viking.

Laing, R. D. 1965. *The Divided Self.* Middlesex, England: Penguin.

London, Perry. 1964. *The Modes and Morals of Psychotherapy.* New York: Holt, Rinehart, and Winston.

London, Perry. 1969. "Morals and Mental Health." To appear in Robert Edgerton and Stanley Plog (eds.) *Changing Perspectives in Mental Illness.* New York: Holt, Rinehart, and Winston.

Maslow, Abraham. 1962. *Towards a Psychology of Being.* Princeton, N.J.: Van Nostrand.

Mendel, Werner M. 1964. "Introduction to Existential Psychiatry." *Psychiatry Digest* 25 (November): 32–34.

Mowrer, O. A. 1963. "Payment or Repayment? The Problem of Private Practice." *American Psychologist* 18:577–580.

Murphy, M. 1967. "Esalen: Where It's At." *Psychology Today* 1 (December):34–42.

New York Times. 1964. January 20:12.

Reiff, Phillip. 1966. *The Triumph of the Therapeutic.* New York: Harper & Row.

Rioch, Margaret J., *et al.* 1963. "NIMH Pilot Study in Training Mental Health Counselors." *American Journal of Orthopsychiatry* 33: 678–689.

Rogers, Carl R. 1967. "A Plan for Self-directed Change in an Educational System." *Educational Leadership* 24 (May):717–731.

Rogers, Carl R., and B. F. Skinner. 1956. "Some Issues Concerning the Control of Human Behavior." *Science* 124 (November):1057–1066.

Skinner, B. F. 1962. *Walden Two.* New York: Macmillan.

Stoller, Fred. 1968. "Marathon Group Therapy." G. M. Gazda (ed.), *Innovations in Group Psychotherapy.* Springfield, Ill.: Thomas:42–95.

Stoller, Fred. 1969. Personal communication.

[7] Skinner appeared in September, 1967, on a panel of five speakers at an Esalen sponsored discussion in San Francisco, "The Scope of Human Potential."

Szasz, Thomas. 1962. *The Myth of Mental Illness.* New York: Hoeber-Harper.

Topanga Human Development Centre. 1967. Private Printed Brochure.

Wesley, S. M. 1967. "Experiential (Experience) Therapy: A Way In, A Way Out." Private Printed Brochure.

Western Behavioral Sciences Institute. 1968. "Educational Innovation Project." *Interim Report of the Western Behavioral Sciences Institute of La Jolla, California.* (April).

Yablonsky, Lewis. 1965. *Synanon: The Tunnel Back.* Baltimore: Penguin.

We present here the first of three articles aimed at changes in the treatment of patients classified as mentally ill. Looking at the hospital as a total treatment environment, Hirschowitz proposes a program of milieu therapy under the label "remotivation." The staff (aides, therapists) are the first to be remotivated. The direction of the change is from custodial to active promotion of health, authenticity, genuineness, and hope. The paper presents a case history of change and its evaluation. More importantly, the author draws an analogy to the study of organizational behavior in showing that the patient, the aide, and the therapist are trapped in a pattern of institutionalized overdependence in the mental hospital. Therapy can flourish only when all parties believe that they can control their own lives. Like Pauline Bart, Hirschowitz argues that "People are not by nature passive or resistant to organizational needs. They have become so by experience in organizations." This is a success story of moving the much maligned mental hospital organization to the point where it can meet its stated goal of helping people.

9.6
Changing Human Behavior in the State Hospital Organization

Ralph G. Hirschowitz

I believe that man will not merely endure; he will prevail.

William Faulkner
(Speech on receiving the Nobel Prize, December 10, 1950)

Introduction

This paper describes a social rehabilitation program for chronic, regressed state hospital patients in which six custodial "back wards" were transformed into active therapeutic "front wards." In planning and implementing this program, significant changes occurred in the hospital's attitudes, organization, and staff roles.

The role of the aide-therapist was particularly significant. The aide-therapist accepted primary responsibility for the education, rehabilitation, and remotivation of his patients, and it is to him that the program's success was attributed. The organizational climate which permitted the aide-therapists' emergence is described.

Remotivating the Remotivators

Before the first phase of the program, little was expected of staff or patients. Attitudes and behavior were custodial, emphasizing care, control and chronicity. At the same time pressures against dehumanizing practices were being intensified. These pressures had produced positive changes in the wards' physical architecture. Walls had been painted; pictures and calendars had been introduced; and patients were given some measure of dormitory and bathroom privacy. However, there was little concomitant change in the psychological architecture of the wards. Patients continued to fear the staff, while staff continued to fear the patients; patients retreated from the staff, who as often, retreated from them. The staff felt hopeless about the patients, the patients felt hopeless about the staff.

As the author assumed responsibility for the wards, there was considerable pressure from the central nursing office to have aides practice "Remotivation."

Reprinted by permission from *Psychiatric Quarterly*, 43, 4 (1969), 591–610. Copyright 1969 by State Hospitals Press.

These remotivation classes made no significant impact upon patients or staff. In observing the remotivation program, it seemed apparent that the staff's needs for remotivation had not been met. A necessary condition for the humanization of patients is the humanization of staff. Remotivation is here broadly viewed as the promotion of growth and change toward mature, responsible, reality-oriented behavior. Remotivation may include teaching the "three r's," but its ultimate goal is to develop *the therapeutic three R's*—Responsibility, Reality, and significant Relatedness.

Some lessons were learned about remotivation. First, remotivation will not succeed if it is applied as a mechanical technique without flexibility or imagination. Second, remotivation is not effective when the psychiatric aide practices it only because he is expected to by superiors in the nursing hierarchy. In order to motivate, the aide must himself be motivated: Innovation proceeds by choice and consent, not by coercion. Third, a remotivation program does not succeed without provision for continuity. In order to remotivate the remotivator, he should be given the opportunity to educate, activate and motivate his patients at all times, not merely during a remotivation "class." If a remotivation group is time-limited, there tends to be erasure of ego gains when the group ends. ("Total push" programs similarly failed to sustain therapeutic momentum.) The final lesson, to which most of this paper addresses itself, is that a remotivation program cannot succeed without enduring changes at all levels of the traditional state hospital organization. "Bureaupathology," with its routinization and mechanization of man, must first be excised.

Change—the Intelligence Phase

These lessons were learned in a unit consisting of six highly traditional back wards. The wards were filled with patients who had been there an average of 17 years and suffered from various combinations of schizophrenia, desocialization or social breakdown syndrome, institutionalism or "institutional neurosis," and iatrogenic insult.[1] On a typical ward, there

[1] One third of the patients had been lobotomized. Many had received hundreds of shock treatments during a Minnesota vogue for "regressive EST."

was minimal interaction between patient and patient, or patient and staff. Patients were bent, apathetic and withdrawn. They inhabited a world of timeless inertia. All patients were over-medicated. The over-dependent were over-protected, the over-independent were over-controlled.

As the writer spent time on the wards it seemed that the aides were perceived as custodians or guards ("attendants"). They were expected to stay in line, take orders and run tight ships. They would often be inspected by nursing supervisors whose values emphasized cleanliness, orderliness, and life "by the book." New aides with innovative need-dispositions might attempt change but would gradually succumb to the prevailing routinization, retreating from the ward scene to coffee rooms whenever faced by threat or challenge. In surveying this human field of forces the author realized that the staff would have to be "unfrozen" before one could hope for the psycho-social rehabilitation of patients. On entering the system the author spent most of his time on the wards listening to the aides, drinking coffee with them, getting to know them, and asking them questions. As they thawed and opened up, they contributed valuable data and suggestions. In group meetings with the staff, an egalitarian climate was encouraged—i.e., aides were encouraged to participate, while the traditional pecking order was neutralized. Traditionally, lowest-ranking staff spoke last and least. An attempt was made to collapse this hierarchy by discouraging those professional monopolizers who talked at, or down to, but not with, others.

In the early weeks, daily meetings were structured to provide opportunities for self-correcting feedback and on-the-job learning. These were down-to-earth encounters stressing collaborative problem-solving in language that was not too technical or abstract. As aides contributed to discussions and were heard with respect, participants found it both safe and satisfying to be real. A necessary dimension for patient rehabilitation had been introduced—the genuineness and authenticity emphasized by authors like Buber, Laing, and Farber. Aides were becoming hopeful that change in their own fate and destiny could occur and some of this hopefulness spread by positive contagion to the patients.

Change—The Design Phase

The first phase was characterized by reconnaissance, relationship-building and the seeking of sanctions for change. When there had been sufficient negotiation, persuasion and discussion, a "representative"[2] organizational design was formalized in which the psychiatric aide was to be the patient's formal therapist and representative. The aide would accept responsibility for his own selected group of patients while the unit's professionals would be consultants and ward coordinators.

It was expected that the patient was to be observed and accepted as a human being with assets as well as liabilities. Simple models, in simple language, were offered for defining his strengths as well as his weaknesses. Information about family and community resources that could be mobilized on his behalf was inventoried. Each patient, like the staff, was encouraged to accept as much freedom and responsibility for himself as he was capable of. Previous infantilizing patterns were replaced by such working axioms as: "Do not do for others what they are capable of doing for themselves." It was deemed more therapeutic to teach others to do for themselves rather than to do for them. Although this took up much of the aide's time, there was rapid payoff as patients displayed more independence and self-sufficiency. There was reciprocal reinforcement through the ward culture of independence, autonomy, and individual responsibility. Everyone in the system began to expect more of himself and of others.

All aides who became therapists did so voluntarily. Those who stated that they were not able or willing to be therapists were permitted to retain traditional roles or define alternative roles. The majority of aides elected to accept responsibility for selected residents.[3] A criterion for selection was that the aide-therapist must feel hopeful and confident about his ability to help. He was then the primary change-agent responsible for counseling, educating,

[2] A model of a milieutherapeutic representative system is offered by Strauss et al., in *Psychiatric Ideologies and Institutions*, pp. 135–137. Free Press. New York. 1964.

[3] In order to change the ascribed patient role, patients were referred to as residents as though they were temporary residents in a college dormitory.

activating, motivating, and rehabilitating his selected residents. He represented the resident's best interests, negotiating on his behalf when the resident was unable to represent himself adequately.

The responsibility for conducting and coordinating the therapeutic program at the ward level was delegated to any unit professional who would plan and conduct a ward community effort. He was the conductor of a therapeutic community orchestra in which a group of able people were to be harmoniously orchestrated, while playing an agreed score together. He was assisted in doing this by a ward coordinator, who was both administrative assistant and assistant conductor. When the program was initiated, these two positions were occupied by professionals and nurses but were later to be turned over to subprofessionals. The six ward program directors were coordinated and supported by a unit program director. When the program began, the author was the unit director but was later able to delegate this task to an occupational therapist, who had been an able ward program conductor.

The ward staff had available to them a number of consultant resource persons including a hospital physician. The physician was responsible for the diagnosis and treatment of all medical problems brought to his attention by the aide-therapists. All prescriptions for psychotropic medication were written by him in consultation with the aide-therapists.

In the early weeks of the program, there was "culture shock." Decision-making responsibilities needed constant reclarification to reduce the selective inattention of conflicted participants, who passively resisted the delegation that was occurring. On these wards, the doctor had traditionally made all decisions about patients' ward leaves, home visits, and discharges, etc. Formal communication with a patient's family had been the prerogative of the social worker or physician. In the new design, the aide-therapist had the right to make all decisions he was able to make. He also had the right to communicate with family members or community agents so that a responsible plan for the patient's community re-entry could be prepared.

Aides were at first reluctant to make major decisions. In order to buttress the system and provide the constant support that was needed, 24-hour consultation was made available to all aides. As it became clear that they would receive support for calculated risk-taking, they became more confident, and as they became more confident, they learned that change was possible for their patients and for themselves. They were recognized, validated, and affirmed as effective workers.

Rewards and Incentives

In monitoring and assessing the movement that occurred, aides seemed to find motivation and incentive in three feedback circuits:
 (1) The patients rewarded them by trusting them, forming bonds of affection, confidence and respect; (2) they received recognition from their co-workers for the visible changes they were able to catalyze in their patients; (3) they received supportive supplies of validation, recognition, and help from organizational superiors.

As the system unfroze, the organizational climate became noticeably warmer; a sense of common humanity, shared effort, and corporate dignity made for high morale. All members of the community were affirmed as involved participants in a community enterprise. A vital, therapeutic culture replaced an aging custodial one. Breaking the syllogistic code of chronicity was crucial to this metamorphosis. The basic proposition of the back ward syllogism —that all patients were "chronic," therefore beyond hope of change —could no longer be sustained. Self-fulfilling prophecies do operate in "people work," and hope is a major determinant of patient fate. Optimism is of the essence in a therapeutic enterprise. This theme has been significantly developed by Hansell, who writes:

The expectation of the observer is the principal ingredient in care. Even for the most severely troubled psychiatric casualty, expectation is the most powerful instrument. Persons in crisis and persons in great turmoil have lost their idea of who they are and where they are going; if there is any idea, it lies in a concerned person who explores a vision of what could be, and who sees esteem, beauty, and citizenship as real potentialities for this human being even if they are present only in trace quantities at this moment.

In addition to the rewards provided in the human circuits described above, an attempt was made to reward the aide by providing him with educational experiences that he could value. In addition to daily group problem-solving, he spent three hours a

week in formal in-service education. He was given cognitive maps to understand what he was doing, and might do, in language that he could grasp and apply. The education program was structured so that aides participated in program administration as well as the teaching-learning transactions; some aides had considerable experience and their "conventional wisdom" was tapped.

The Politics of Organizational Change

Significant as the above-described symbolic, intrinsic, and ineffable rewards were, I doubt that they are sufficient explanation for the rapid impetus toward change which developed in this program. Nor do I believe that ideological and social change can be sustained by high-quality innovative ideas and personal charisma alone. It is doubtful that this traditional system would have moved, or change "long endured"[4] if I had not held considerable formal power as assistant medical director. Without formal power, it is doubtful if this group could have been influenced to disrupt its "quasi-stationary equilibrium,"[5] or provide the incentive to translate new ideas into action. My formal position gave the staff abundant permission as well as some necessity to listen; in the ranks that moved forward, psychological man moved hand-in-hand with economic man, rational man, and political man. My power-sanctioned influence was vital in the initial "unfreezing," and indispensible in buffering, protecting, and sanctioning "freezing at the new level."

The formal motivational structure was also activated so that aide-therapists could be motivated by formal recognition and material rewards. Wherever possible, promotions and merit raises went to those aides who had shown competence in the field. The aides were motivated to organize and negotiate on their own behalf. (There was a significant breakthrough, not without reverbera-

---

[4] ". . . a new nation conceived in liberty, and dedicated to the proposition that all men are created equal.
 "Now we are engaged in a great civil war, testing whether that nation or any nation so conceived and so dedicated can long endure. . ." (Lincoln's Gettysburg Address).

[5] For the formulation and language which follow, the author is indebted to Kurt Lewin.

tions, when I became a card-carrying member of the AFL-CIO Civil Service Union with which the aides were affiliated.) In the formal organization, I was energetic in seeing that representatives were heard and grievances redressed. Aides' requests for self-determination and autonomy in such matters as dress and working conditions were heard and responded to. The prevailing system of merit raises and promotions was critically evaluated and aides' suggestions sympathetically appraised. Wherever possible, task forces were set up to investigate possibilities for change; aides were represented on these task forces.

Although some attempt was made to reorganize the formal motivational structure to validate the aides' claim for more pay for more responsible work, it should be noted that the hospital was embedded in a state civil service framework which permitted limited flexibility in budget and personnel policy. Administration was able to support the aides' legitimate claims but unable to resolve the dilemma of how to provide the aide-therapist with more appropriate position and salary. This problem, together with the educational upgrading of the aide, remains to be resolved. I have discussed this issue elsewhere, as has Graham who offers the aides' viewpoint in this summary:

A special word must be given here to the way in which "the problem of the attendant" is discussed among psychiatrists at technical meetings. Pleas are made for better education, "making him feel a part of the group," and recognition that he "also has a part in the treatment of the patient." Such analyses overlook the fact that an aide is not paid enough to consider his position a possible career, he is often prevented from expressing his opinion about patients, and when he does, he is often not taken seriously. When his problems (including that of advancement) are considered, administrators often try to solve them "for him" rather than work them out with him seriously and matter-of-factly.

The Program Evaluated

After some months of the program, a research psychologist canvassed the aides who cited the following advantages in their change of role.

"If you have extra time, you know where to spend it."

"You put forth more effort, the patients come to you more."

"Closer relations develop between patients and aides."

"All patients get some attention, nobody is lost in the shuffle."

"Aides now have greater freedom and authority in contacting resource persons."

"You used to have to contact charge to make decisions, each aide now makes his own decisions."

In commenting on the patients, they mentioned: "Feeling of greater trust in all patients, you don't have to watch them all the time." "You see more improvement in the patients."

Early in the program, the hospital's director of volunteer services wrote the following report for the local newspaper.

One of the most exciting things in this hospital is to see what's happening on some of the wards that used to be "back wards" composed chiefly of long-term patients labeled hopeless.

Patients who have been mute are speaking, folks who have just sat in corners are getting up and venturing out, women who never combed their hair are caring how they look, some are learning to care about each other.

Perhaps the biggest single factor in this improvement is the new freedom that has been given psychiatric technicians to change their role from that of custodians to that of active therapists. They are encouraged to doctor the patients and to advise, to counsel, to use their ideas, to follow their hunches, relate to their patients as human beings. As a result they are enjoying their jobs more, they are seeing professionals on the team as consultants, not as mere order-givers. Most important, they are seeing changes in the patients under their care. No longer do they watch over a large group of patients with a keen eye for trouble. Instead each has day in, day out responsibilities for a small group of patients whom they seek to help grow toward health.

Professionals as Program Conductors

What of the consultants, those staff members who volunteered to write program scores and orchestrate the staff resources? What were their rewards and their motivations? In this program, with its endorsement of delegation, everyone could realize his potential. As Kiger has emphasized, nothing of value is lost in a system which applies principles of decentralization and delegation. In our system, participants were given opportunities to innovate, innate potentialities were realized, and existing competencies enhanced, refined, and extended. Only incompetencies were lost. In their indirect, consultant role, nurses

and professionals were offered opportunities to do more for patients. This they valued. A property held in common by the professional staff who chose to work on the back wards was their stubborn refusal to acquiesce in the dominant culture's basic assumption that these patients were beyond hope. They were exquisitely sensitive to Hansell's "trace quantities" of potential becomingness.

The consultants were given frequent opportunities for sharing knowledge, for learning together, and for learning outside the system. I learned with them and was readily available for support and supply. In addition, as they worked effectively, material rewards and recognition for responsibilities were provided. Self-esteem, self-worth, and self-confidence grew as morale, engagement, and commitment burgeoned in this once dispirited unit. (This unit eventually offered ideological leadership to the entire hospital. The hospital was later decentralized into autonomous community-oriented units, in which the organizational principles of this system were generally applied. In the new units, the early cadre of consultants have occupied senior administrative positions.)

Change—The Phase of Ideological Dissonance and Organizational Anomie

As soon as the back ward's rehabilitation program was seen to be effective, there were reverberations at all levels of the hospital organization. Patients who for years had played "crazy" roles—e.g., the hospital "greeters"—now dressed and behaved normally; patients about whom staff had hovered apprehensively, no longer showed signs of rage; patients who had been mute and unresponsive now spoke and responded. The code of chronicity and self-fulfilling prophecies about patients and aides in the organization could no longer be sustained. Hallowed traditions and unquestioned assumptions about the hospital's mission were now discussed and reevaluated. The hospital's assumptive universe was shattered and it was in crisis.

In assimilating these changes in the hospital, there was continuous discussion of the staff's contributions to past patient behavior as well as the staff's recent contributions to change in the patient and his roles. A new pattern of "case conference" emerged in the hospital in which the "case" was no

longer the patient but the organization. Individual clinicians were becoming social system clinicians. Attempts were made to define organizational pathology and consultants were brought into the system to assist. Consultants helped diagnose organizational dysfunction, made recommendations for change, reinforced some of the recent innovations, and played catalytic, facilitating and educational roles in changing staff's values and roles. Throughout the hospital,[6] there were explorations of alternative ways of looking at patients and their problems, as well as alternative ways of attempting to solve these.

It became apparent that the staff's custodial expectations could no longer be projected on to the patients. The hospital began to revise its ideological assumptions as well as its institutional role prescriptions. As consultants selectively reinforced the emerging ideological and organizational changes, leadership was confronted with the implications of the innovations it had spawned. Leaders began to realize that the organization's traditionism raised many obstacles to functional change. Traditionalism is here characterized, following Hagen, by hierarchy, low productivity, minimal opportunity for role achievement, and a sense that hallowed custom rather than rational empirico-pragmatism proscribes the limits of possible problem-solving.

With central office support, a massive strategy was developed to deal with the dead wood, the outmoded habits, and the self-defeating attitudes of the staff. A remotivation program was designed to combat the institutional "neuroses" of the patients by modifying complementary institutionalizing patterns in the staff.

As the hospital reverberated with the hope and threat of change, some staff welcomed the change, some were indifferent, and some were bitterly opposed. There was ideological dissonance in the hospital as well as cognitive dissonance in the heads of the more inflexible traditionalists. These traditionalists did not agree

[6] As behooves a therapeutic community, members of the business and maintenance departments participated in in-service training sessions for cross sections, vertical and horizontal, of all the hospital staff. Aides and physicians, janitors and secretaries, business managers and nurses, began to hear one another, learn from one another, and help one another.

that the new organizational design promoted an expanded freedom, responsibility, authority and autonomy for *all,* and that *all* stood to gain. In their efforts to reduce dissonance, they avoided open discussion or confrontation of the issues, preferring to defend tradition because it was hallowed, not because it was effecitve. They responded to the delegation of authority subjectively as loss: loss of power, loss of face, loss of self-esteem, and, for some, loss of *raison d'être.* In crisis, they responded with patterns of attack, defense or withdrawal. Energies were dissipated needlessly by political maneuvers in which the proponents and antagonists of innovation failed to establish effective dialogue. A massive program of in-service training, together with simultaneous re-organization, was implemented in the hope that staff would be helped to attack shared problems rather than one another.

Organizationally, the hospital was decentralized into regional units with strong community affiliations and orientations. Each unit was charged to collaborate with community resources so that psychiatric adaptive casualties would receive early detection, early intervention and continuity of therapy. Vigorous young leaders with community mental health ideologies endorsing principles of trust and delegation were selected. Before, during, and after these changes, all levels of the organization were involved in planning and implementation. As the new design became operational, cognitive maps and consultative supplies were programmed in. A program of continuous in-service education and orientation was introduced. There were frequent workshops in which community representatives were involved. These workshops generated small group encounters which facilitated dislogue toward continuity between hospital and community mental health workers. Also, mental health workers inside and outside the hospital were simultaneously sensitized to new ways, techniques, and languages.

Consultants were introduced to expose the mental health workers to such techniques as crisis intervention, family therapy, group therapy, and strategies for resocialization. Intense efforts were made to share learning and language with the staff of social work agencies, community mental health centers, and key professionals such as ministers and phy-

sicians. (The hospital initiated small group encounters among ministers, and the author conducted three psychiatric seminars for a total of 40 physicians at hospitals in the community.) In addition to formal workshops and seminars, informal dialogue was promoted. The aides became active in the re-establishment of links between patients, their families and community agencies. Aide-therapists would often travel 100 miles or more in order to forge and maintain these links.

It has been documented elsewhere that when state hospitals decentralized (the Utah experience is illustrative), skewed power struggles continued for many months. It became essential for unit leaders to participate in personnel decisions. As soon as the hiring, orienting, firing, and rewarding power of the central nursing office was curbed, the innovative forces were strengthened. Personnel received loud, clear messages that rewards would be based upon task-achievement. Bonus incentives were based upon *role results* rather than *role occupancy,* upon role achievement rather than simple role ascription.

Change—The Phase of Consolidation

After a year, the new system moved toward "freezing at the new level." There was internal consolidation as well as reinforcement by external visitors and consultants. The morale of the hospital's firing line personnel reached a high point when an Ohio hospital asked for a speaker to visit them. An aide was elected as ambassador and he reported on his visits as follows:

I spent most of the time describing how my duties as a psychiatric technician under the former departmental treatment program differed from my current responsibilities as a member of the treatment team. . . . My audiences seemed to respond with genuine interest and even amazement, as I described how at Fergus Falls in the last two years the role of the psychiatric aide[7] has dramatically changed from that of being nursing personnel with the primary task of providing good custodial care for the hospital resident to a role of major responsibility as a therapist in a psychiatric treatment program which has as its goal the successful rehabilitation of the hospital resident and his early return to a satisfying life in the community. The Cleve-

[7] In the Minnesota Civil Service system a psychiatric aide is called a psychiatric technician.

land staff were particularly interested in such matters as staff responsibilities and the delegation of authority in our unit's treatment program. . . . I described how under this type of treatment program the technician-therapist is used as the primary treatment person for a specific number of residents with the unit's professional staff providing the technician-therapist with supportive consultation in a team approach that is designed to help the individual resident attain his treatment goal.

A new therapeutic culture and social organization had emerged. The system now clearly endorsed change, innovation, participatory democracy, as well as the values of individual freedom, responsibility and autonomy. Change was promoted on three related fronts —change in the culture, in the organization, and in individual personalities. In achieving this, vigorous delegation of authority permitted a concomitant attentuation of the centralized span of control. The change from central control to regionalized units with local autonomy permitted the units to beam toward the community. Sociofugal movement outward, rather than sociopetal movement toward a central office, was now endorsed. Unit personnel became accountable to their patients and their communities rather than to their directors or department heads. While retaining a necessary minimum of effective decision-facilitating central organization, redundant "bureaupathology" had been successfully excised. In the process, a lean, dedicated central staff was able to meet the needs of the decentralized, community-oriented units for supplies, consultation, and protective buffering from resistant community forces.

Some of the organizational changes here described are documented in a collection of articles describing Fergus Falls State Hospital as a "psychiatric hospital in transition."

Some Organizational Principles: Rules for Men, Not Men for Rules

Having described phases of a "hospital in transition," some underlying principles are now discussed. These principles are relevant to any traditional service system in need of remedial change.

State hospitals need help to absorb advancing mental health technology and accommodate to the community expectations generated by Public Law 88-164. There is increasing recognition that the over-centralized, top-heavy state hospital (Goffman's "total institution") with its militaristic emphasis upon order, ritual and control is now dysfunctional. Some radical surgery is needed to extend the hospital's mission beyond the provision of the three C's—Custody, Care and Control.

In the traditional mental hospital, superiors maintain formal distance, while enforcing uniformity and predictability; such superiors see themselves responsible for planning, organizing, directing, controlling and supervising their subordinates. Subordinates are told what to do and how to do it. Predictability is enforced through elaborate policy and procedure manuals as well as rigid role ascription (job descriptions). Role slack with its prospects of role achievement is precluded. The organization commits a procrustean folly: Body, mind, heart and soul must diminish in order to fit an organizational position—the position does not expand to fit a growing occupant.

As Argyris has discussed, man is expected to serve the traditional organization, the organization does not serve man. Reinforced by medical-nursing orthodoxy,[8] decisions are made at the top and subordinates are expected passively to comply. Orders are to be executed, not questioned. Conversely, in the absence of specific orders, no action is to be taken. Such an organization exercises strong pressures toward mechanical efficiency, uniformity and predictability. By enforcing predictability, the organization militates against change, growth, or learning within the system. Participants are not motivated to experiment by solving old problems in new ways. Potential growth crises in patients are then defined as psychopathology or "incidents" which evoke pressures toward dependent, subordinate, predictable behavior rather than independent, autonomous, but less predictable, behavior. The values of such an organization are antithetical to the

values of a therapeutic milieu. In evaluating the therapeutic community, Rapoport identifies such core values as communalism, democracy, reality confrontation and permissiveness. The anti-therapeutic community—i.e., the traditional organization, by contrast values elitism, autocracy, reality denial (via communication censorship and screening) and control. A field of forces develops in which the patient is pressured to enact the institutionally-defined patient role. Kahne has commented on the malignant properties of a psychiatric system which enforces uniformity in his "thesis that challenges refutation":

To the extent that the future is a foregone conclusion (that is, that the behavior of doctors and nurses is perfectly predictable), the chronic patient would remain impervious to even the most ingenious treatment strategies. . . . Since almost all of the chronic patient's life flows through the instrumental agencies of the hospital, the form of behavior, is to some extent, being institutionally prescribed whether wittingly or unwittingly.[9]

The uniformity and predictability of the traditional large state hospital organization have been borrowed from the organizational patterns once prevalent in industry and the army. Such models are ill derived. The industrial product is a thing, not a regenerated human being; the military product is death and destruction. In the ideal psychiatric system, the product is a highly differentiated human being who has learned the three R's. While the traditional psychiatric system recognizes that it serves human beings, it has been "mass production" attuned, prescribing uniform methods rather than generating ever-advancing, ever-changing, individualized goals for the human beings it serves. Where goals are prescribed, methods can be flexible; where methods are prescribed, goals may be ignored. The system that becomes method-oriented is doomed to obsolescence. A pragmatic public evaluates service by goals achieved, by results not methodologies, by ends not means.

Argyris further emphasizes that in the traditional organization employees are generally working in an environment where

1. They are provided minimal control over their work-a-day world.

2. They are expected to be passive, dependent and subordinate.
3. They are expected to have a short time-perspective.
4. They are induced to perfect and value the frequent use of a few skin surface, shallow abilities.
5. They are expected to produce under conditions leading to psychological failure.

"Psychological failure" occurs when treatment goals do not ego-involve the employee and do not permit him any measure of self-realization or actualization.

(This thesis can be extended to campus crises where students are rejecting their traditional subordinate position. They are staking a claim to participatory involvement in decisions about their fate and destiny, including the content, process, and structure of their learning experience.)

In a state hospital, stripped of most rights and freedoms, the patient is the ultimate subordinate. In an organizational hierarchy often complicated by redundancy of levels and of links, the only "institutional career" available to him is the ascribed, over-dependent, submissive, chameleon role or a deviant position in which the over-independent, distrustful, manipulative maverick "beats the system" at the heavy personal price of isolation, psychopathy, paranoia, or alienation.

Since psychiatric frontiers are expanding and community expectations changing, the state hospital of necessity suffers from culture lag. (The fate of all institutions in an innovative, mobile, self-correcting society is similar. Health, educational, welfare and correctional systems are confronted with similar needs to change hallowed assumptions and operations.) The formal, rigid structure depicted above was designed to meet society's past expectations for efficient, economical, custodial service. In order to achieve goals of education, and psychosocial rehabilitation, a more informal, open, human-centered organization is required. In developing such an open organizational structure, resources are maximized and morale improved by flattening the traditional organizational pyramid. Instead of solutions being prescribed at a distance from the problem, decision-making can be delegated to workers on the "firing line"—to nurse-therapists and to aide-therapists. This improves efficiency by eliminating redundant communication links. Delegation also greatly enhances interpersonal effective-

---

[8] Perhaps the most appropriate model for medical-nursing line traditionalism is the operating room where the surgeon makes decisions and the operating room machinery is geared to meet his needs and execute his orders. In general, this is an appropriate model similar to the military model for dealing with emergency situations. However, this model is inappropriate for the psychiatric system where some ambiguity is built in, not built out.

[9] For Kahne, "it becomes apparent, especially with the chronic patient, innovation, variation and uniqueness will characterize the prescriptive efforts."

ness. The organization becomes looser, and less ordered by procedure or policy manual. The task of a psychiatrist in such a system is to motivate psychiatric aides to teach and motivate patients. Instead of organizational participants being rewarded for habits of compliance, tidiness or orderliness, the organization rewards for creative problem-solving, and for teaching. In this way, all are motivated, encouraged and expected to grow and to change.

Once the organization is committed to growth and change, it is ready to design and implement an organizational structure with features of an educational institution, so that growth and change are facilitated. The culture and structure of such an organization have been conceptualized by Daniels and Kuldau as "intentional social system therapy." They have said, "An intentional social system is, in effect, a plan designed for living that encourages individual growth and responsibility." They describe an organizational structure in which all have free and open access to lines of communication and which provides "opportunity, greater responsibility, and a series of challenges to the participants (sometimes referred to as a series of 'controlled crises')."[10] They emphasize the need for socially appropriate roles, duties, obligations and responsibilities for all participants. They stress the importance of role-modeling in social learning. (In our verbally-oriented culture with its exegetic traditions of "the word," socializing agents may fail to appreciate that they teach by what they *are* and *do* as much as by what they *say*.) Daniels and Kuldau emphasize

. . . an ideology and value system that espouses capacities and assets of man rather than his liabilities and defects, the individual responsibility of man as basic to human social function and dignity rather than control and regimentation, human growth through living-learning experiences rather than *in situ* insight, humanism rather than dehumanization, a model of marginal people as more socially disordered than diseased, and the helper therapy principle rather than passive compliance.

[10] In attempting to introduce change into frozen, rigid or closed systems, I have found the notion of purposive disequilibration or crisis engineering to be a useful one. Once there is subjective distress inside a closed system, it is, by definition, in crisis and potentially receptive to skilled intervention. It becomes temporarily open to change.

Control or Motivate?

Ultimately, every man is faced with certain value choice and decisions. So is organization man. The choice that faces psychiatric organizations and psychiatric organization men has been discussed in Douglas M. MacGregor's classic paper in which he describes "Theory X" and "Theory Y." State hospitals which have institutionalized over-dependence in their personnel and patients have embraced "Theory X." "Theory X" superiors believe: "The average man is by nature indolent—he works as little as possible, he lacks ambition, dislikes responsibility, prefers to be led. He is inherently self-centered, indifferent to organizational needs." Because of this basic distrust of subordinates, "they must, therefore, be persuaded, rewarded, punished, controlled—their activities must be directed."

MacGregor rejects the "Theory X" hypothesis, and experience leads the present writer to do the same. MacGregor propounds "a different theory of the task of managing people based upon more adequate assumptions about human nature and human motivation." His "Theory Y" states

People are *not* by nature passive or resistant to organizational needs. They have become so as a result of experience in organizations.

The motivation, the potential for development, the capacity for assuming responsibility, the readiness to direct behavior toward organizational goals are all present in people. Management does not put them there. It is the responsibility of management to make it possible for people to recognize and develop these human characteristics for themselves.

The hospital organization which endorses "Theory Y" can also apply "innovative ideas, which are entirely consistent with 'Theory Y.'" The impact of these ideas has been described in this paper. Particular ideas are "decentralization and delegation—these are ways of freeing people from the too close control of conventional organization, giving them a degree of freedom to direct their own activities, to assume responsibility . . ."

It is this choice then, Theory X or Theory Y, that squarely confronts the psychiatric leader. In embracing Theory Y, the psychiatric leader chooses to believe that nonprofessionals share the professionals' wishes to grow, to develop, to mature, to be responsible, to apply previously gained in-

sights creatively. A superior in a line organization can choose to believe in people and trust his subordinates. His choice must assume that his subordinates are as likely to be responsible as his peers, that they can function responsibly and have a sufficient measure of maturity to ask for help when they need it. In line relationships emphasizing mutual trust, not only does the subordinate trust his superior to provide help as needed, but the superior has enough confidence in his subordinate to delegate decision-making. Such an organization is open, democratic, genuine and motivating. These values promote a climate of possibility, creating the necessary conditions for the human potentialities of all to be realized.

In the program described here, a nurturant climate was created in which all had the opportunity to grow and develop. Theory Y emphases and Theory Y operations were introduced. An organization which had endorsed Theory X values was moved in a Theory Y direction. In spite of some resistance and institutional anomie, the program in one year doubled the patient discharge rate while reducing the patient re-admission rate. The program has been effective and its principles have endured.

Theory Y values are basic to the sane, democratic society which the mental hospital should be. As Talbot and Miller have written

An ideal psychiatric hospital is not merely a sanctuary, a cotton-padded milieu that emphasizes the fragility, the incompetence, the helplessness, the bizarreness of patients. It is a sane society when it permits the optimal use of the intact to heal capacities of the patients through its social organization, its social supports, and its community values.

The changes here described have been from Theory X to Theory Y, from dehumanization to rehumanization, from "cotton-padded milieu" to sane society. The writer has sought to demonstrate that rehumanization, rehabilitation, re-education and remotivation do succeed in an organization which is open, which permits concern for all its members, and which generates hope in a humanizing network where all are permitted to trust, respect and value one another.

Claude Steiner presents a plan for a radically different alternative to conventional psychiatry in the form of a RaP center which stresses participatory democracy and rejects the usual medical control. A number of students at Berkeley have worked at the RaP center in keeping with the spirit of using untrained peers in group and one-to-one treatment of disturbed people. Characteristic of his radical view of psychiatry is the belief that ". . . deviant behavior is a person's right and not the object of guilt or shame and that all service should take place by request of persons who find their (own) behavior unsatisfying." We thus have one application of the principles espoused by Szasz, albeit an application Szasz would probably not endorse.

9.7
Guiding Principles of a Community "RaP" Center

Claude Steiner

The Radical Psychiatry (RaP) Center is the center of operations of the RaP Community. The RaP Community is a group of people whose common goal is expressed in the following policy:

1. The purpose of the RaP Community shall be to provide psychiatric services for the people. Psychiatry as understood by the RaP Community has as its purpose to combat alienation between people and to promote life, liberty and the pursuit of happiness. The RaP Community is open to all interested persons.

2. The RaP Community will be controlled solely by its membership and rejects outside control, including medical control.

3. a. A person's work is the only criterion by which he or she shall be judged.
   b. Who can do what job within the RaP Community shall be decided on the basis of observation of the person's work only, specifically disregarding professional degrees.
   c. Who makes decisions and who commands the attention of the Community shall similarly be determined on the basis of work done and energy invested into the Community.

4. The RaP Community believes that a person's dissatisfactions are the result of his relationships and environment. This leads to an em-

By permission of the author.

phasis on the use of groups for study and change, recognizing the value of one-to-one relationships but discouraging long term dependency relationships.

5. We believe in people's free choice of individual life styles and acknowledge their choice of behaviors as an individual right. There are many paths for growth —we affirm the individual's right to choose his own.

6. We reject the use of medical terminology, specifically diagnostic labels. We believe that people and their behavior can better be understood through descriptions of behavior rather than labels.

7. The RaP Community believes in the complete openness about thoughts, discussion, records and decisions, without the compromising of confidentiality.

8. The services of the RaP Community shall be free. No one shall be paid for rapping.

This policy is implemented at the RaP Center through a variety of activities, centered around the Contact rap. The Contact rap is an area within the RaP Center where people make personal contact with reach other. The newcomer whether he is there to give or to receive is greeted by a Contact rapper. Ordinarily he will be invited to join in with other people but if he wishes it will be possible for him to be with just one person. As he joins the Contact rap he will be engaged in a conversation. Not to diagnose, or to force him to choose a role, but to make friendly contact and to see whether he can find at the RaP Center what he is looking for. If he has come to the RaP Center to give he will be informed of our policy regarding training and will be invited to join in the first step of giving as a Contact rap trainee. In he is there to receive he will be asked if he wants to remain in the Contact rap, if he wants to additionally join a Heavy rap group or if he needs to see a one-to-one Contact rapper for a more intimate, intense discussion. As soon as they are clear, the contact rapper will attempt to meet the newcomer's needs.

Some persons will come to the RaP Center just to talk because they are lonely or because they find the kind of talk that goes on at the Contact rap interesting or because they are in search of something the nature of which they don't know. Others will be quite clear about what they want and ask for it. The Contact rap takes the place of the intake or screening interview at most psychiatric facilities and by its very nature avoids role typing an indi-

vidual and gives the newcomer an opportunity to evaluate the RaP Center and its members before making any commitments. It gives him an opportunity to decide what part of the RaP Community's help he wishes to accept and gives him an opportunity to see how he himself can be helpful, and most of all it avoids role typing as a "patient" the needy newcomer and the typing as a "therapist" of the newcomer who is willing to give.

Contact Rap

The Contact rap is the hub of the RaP Center's activities. From the Contact rap, if he decides that he is in further need, a person can proceed into a brief series of one-to-one Contact raps or a Heavy group rap. If he chooses to give, he can proceed to the Training rap which is a seven step training series. He may also choose to join any other RaP Center activity.

The RaP Center's daily activities are overseen by a daily rap Head who is responsible for the overall operation of the RaP Center during that day, and who is responsible in turn to the RaP Center's director.

Heavy Group Rap

A Heavy group rap is a group of between eight and twelve persons who have a stated problem and have joined the group for the purpose of doing something about it with a leader who is trained in modern group techniques. It meets weekly for at least two hours and its agenda consists of the different contracts of each person in the group. A person remains in the group as long as he has a stated contract and then leaves the group to make a place for someone else who has a problem that needs to be worked on.

Training Rap

Because it is the aim of the RaP Community to provide psychiatric services and because it is also the conviction of the RaP Community that all persons have the potential to be psychiatrists, the RaP Center proposes to train, from the ground up, those persons who are willing to put energy and effort into the RaP Center. The training will be available to any person, regardless of their previous training, who demonstrates an interest in the RaP Community by investing a certain amount of energy in its function.

The training program has as its

guidelines the principles of Radical Psychiatry (RaP). These principles are outlined forthwith:

The practice of psychiatry is being severely hampered by a) unwarranted constraints which limit the use of available psychiatric resources and b) unproven mystifications which limit the effectiveness of those resources being used.

1. The most fundamental set of constraints and assumptions stems from the fact that the practice of psychiatry has been taken over by the medical profession. Psychiatry (Greek: suki-utre, soul healing) was practiced by priests, elders and physicians alike until medicine usurped control of its practice. This seizure sharply limited psychiatric resources and created an elitist hierarchy in which medical training rather than competence is the criteria for who can practice the art of soul healing. An outcome of this takeover was the introduction of the concept of illness. Examples are the unwarranted labeling of behavior such as alcoholism and other drug abuse as illnesses, and the like assumption about all schizophrenic and manic-depressive psychoses. Calling deviant behavior such as homosexuality an illness is equally unjustified. This is not to say of course that no psychoses or mental disturbances are the domain of medicine since some have an organic basis and may be amenable to medical treatment.

The assumptions about illness usher in further fallacies about treatment:

a) The use as specifics (that is, drugs which are curative of the above mislabeled illnesses) of drugs which do not, in fact, "cure" the "illnesses" and whose long-term side effects are often so devastating that they produce actual physical illnesses and further emotional disturbances.

b) The frequent interpretation of therapeutic failure by the psychiatrist to mean that the "illness" is incurable (chronic, progressive) as in alcoholism and schizophrenia. This conclusion of incurability causes the practitioner to aim therapy at temporary control rather than permanent removal and creates expectancies of incurability in patients. The "diagnosis" of behavior disorders in terms of an illness model—diagnoses which are unreliable, that is, not reliably consistent from diagnostician to diagnostician, and which once obtained do not suggest any specific therapeutic approach—is

equally undesirable. Psychiatric diagnoses are, in reality, subtle insults reified by diagnostic tests, tests which have no proven scientific validity and which are therefore not useful but which keep psychologists occupied with busy work. This latter outcome has the effect of maintaining the medical establishment's control over psychiatry away from its most eminent threat, the psychological establishment.

2. The second assumption is related to the value of the long term one-to-one relationship. This assumption is the end result of the convergence of a set of other assumptions. Most fundamentally, the belief that emotional disturbance has its roots within the person, from which it follows that therapy should focus on the person, a process best pursued by the intense investigation of intrapsychic life. Search for "insight" is further encouraged by the notion of the unconscious. The one-to-one assumption is reinforced by the clinical-medical, physician-patient model on one hand, and on the other hand by the age long tradition of confidential discussion with priests and elders, in private because of the shame associated with the confession of personal failure or the disclosure of deviant behavior.

3. Finally, psychiatry has been willing to assume, by remaining "neutral" in an oppressive situation, the role of arbitrator over, and controller of, deviant behavior and has taken a hand in its removal by labeling it "neurotic" and analyzing it away to bring about "adjustment," or by calling it psychotic and removing it via medication and hospitalization. Consequently, it has undertaken to support the establishment's oppression; a further consequence of this role is found in the willingness to decide for patients the area and extent of desirable change and to engage in non-contractual forms of therapy with no pre-established limits or termination point. The above points constitute the basis for the Radical Psychiatry Manifesto.

Radical Psychiatry Manifesto

1. The practice of psychiatry has been usurped by the medical establishment. Political control of all its public aspects has been seized by medicine, and the language of soul healing has been infiltrated with irrelevant medical concepts and terms.

Psychiatry must return to its non-medical origins since most psychiatric conditions are in no way the province of medicine. All persons competent in soul healing should be known as psychiatrists and psychiatrists should repudiate the use of medically derived words such as patient, illness, diagnosis, etc. Medical psychiatrists' unique contribution to psychiatry is as experts in drugs and neurology.

2. Extended individual psychotherapy is an elitist, outmoded, as well as non-productive form of psychiatric help. It concentrates the talents of the few on the few. It silently colludes with the notion that people's difficulties have their source within them while implying that all is well with the world. It promotes oppression by shrouding its consequences with shame and secrecy. It further mystifies by attempting to pass as a model for the ideal human relationship when it is, in fact, artificial in the extreme.

People's difficulties have their source not within them but in their alienated relationships, in their exploitation, in polluted environments, in war and in the profit motive. Psychiatry must be practiced in groups. One-to-one contacts, of great value in crises, should become the exception rather than the rule. The high ideal of I-Thou loving relationships should be pursued in the context of groups rather than the stilted situation of the consulting room. Psychiatrists not proficient in group work are deficient in their training and should upgrade it. Psychiatrists should encourage bilateral, open discussion and discourage secrecy, confidentiality and shame.

3. Psychiatry, especially in the public sector, has become an enforcer of establishment values and laws. Adjustment to prevailing conditions is the avowed goal of most psychiatric treatment. Persons who deviate from the world's madness are given fraudulent diagnostic tests which generate diagnostic labels which are subtle insults leading to treatment which is, in fact, a series of graded repressive procedures such as "drug management," hospitalization, shock therapy, perhaps lobotomy. All these forms of "treatment" are perversions of legitimate medical procedures which have been put at the service of the establishment by the medical profession. Treatment is forced on persons who would, if left alone, not seek it.

Psychological tests and the diagnostic labels they generate, especially "schizophrenia," must be disavowed as meaningless mystifications the real function of which is to distance psychiatrists from people and to insult people into conformity. Medicine must cease contributing to oppression by refusing to avail hospitals, drugs and other legitimate medical procedures to the purpose of overt or subtle law enforcement. Medicine must examine how drug companies are dictating treatment procedures through their often obscene advertising. Psychiatry must cease playing a part in the oppression of women by refusing to promote adjustment to their oppression. All psychiatric help should be by contract, that is, people should choose when, what and with whom they want to change. Psychiatrists should refuse to participate in the pacification of the oppressed and should encourage, instead, people's struggles for liberation.

A dissenting voice on the move toward community-based treatment of mental disorders is presented by James Statman. While he is in agreement with our general argument against value-free therapy, he raises the point that well-meaning white social innovators may overwhelm the liberation movements in the ghettos with unneeded benevolence. He sees the real possibility of subtle oppression by federally financed community mental health workers who may co-opt the local leadership. As militance increases, Statman feels that the mental health organization will inevitably be pressured to help cool things since the status quo is a necessary condition for their existence. It is conceivable that all of the previous articles describe change processes which must emerge *from* communities rather than being imposed *on* them. Statman provides a healthy reminder (as does Valentine in Chapter 2) that those in the white majority, who have the vision for and access to change, should heed the old adage: *Physician, heal thyself.*

9.8
Community Mental Health as a Pacification Program

James M. Statman

There is no necessity for working social scientists to allow the political meaning of their work to be shaped by the "accidents" of its setting, or its use to be determined by the purposes of other men. It is quite within their powers to discuss its meaning and decide upon its uses as a matter of their own policy.

C. Wright Mills

To be professionally concerned with problems of social and mental health in America is to take a political stance. No longer can we remain professionally detached from the political and social upheavals which surround us. The rush of events of the last decade has made this quite clear. No longer can we self-righteously proclaim an "end to ideology," assert that ideology has no place in the helping professions or maintain the myth of a value free social and behavioral science. For within this declaration of neutrality lies, we may suspect, a less-than-critical acceptance of prevailing social and political values. In a society in which health, education and welfare are largely matters of government policy, and low priority matters at that, it becomes especially important for those concerned with the planning, administration and execution of such services to critically examine their role. The omnibus community mental health programs established in the urban ghettos serve real political and social functions both in these neighborhoods and in the society as a whole. In this paper we will attempt to examine some of these functions so that we may, as Mills suggests, come to understand and control the political meaning of our work.

It has long been recognized that individual mental health is related to the quality of the social and economic milieu in which the person exists (e.g., Hollingshead and Redlich, 1958; Srole *et al.*, 1962; Langner and Michael, 1963; Peck, Kaplan and Roman, 1966). The problems of individual survival posed by life in the urban ghetto, as well as the tensions generated by inter-group social conflict and

Reprinted by permission of the author. Presented at the Forty-seventh Annual Meeting of the American Orthopsychiatric Association, San Francisco, Spring, 1970.

rapid social change surely must take their toll (Klein and Statman, 1969). Thus the comprehensive community mental health approach aims not simply at bringing services closer to the person, or at coordinating and oiling the bureaucratic wheels of existing health services, but also at confronting oppressive institutions within the community. The approach, then, is to provide community as well as group and individual therapy; to include what have been termed "social action" as well as "mental health" aspects. Peck, Kaplan and Roman (1966), for example, were among the first to decry the ". . . failure to recognize the potential mental health implications of social action programs or conversely the need to build certain social action components into community mental health programs." While we would agree with this concern, we would add that with the birth of comprehensive community mental health programs, such as the Albert Einstein–Lincoln Hospital project in New York, the time has come to begin to also evaluate the social action implications of community mental health.

Such an evaluation obviously cannot be drawn in a vacuum. Indeed, the most general defining characteristic of such programs is that they self-consciously and purposively exist, functionally as well as geographically, within a community. Thus, it is only within the context of the community in process, and more likely than not, a community undergoing rapid social change, that they can be judged.

Any evaluation of community mental health programs, then, must begin by looking at the community itself. While there are obviously many inter-community variations, we would suggest that it is not unreasonable to characterize the urban ghetto today as in a state of active transformation and rebellion. The movement of black and other minority peoples for liberation has been the most explosive and far-reaching event of recent times. Every ghetto neighborhood has been affected; every block, housing project and high school has been reached, every person has been changed. Within every urban ghetto indigenous, militant social action has been planned and often executed, changing the social and economic reality of the ghetto as well as the psychological reality of the ghetto resident.

White society has responded to

the black liberation movement with both the carrot and the stick. Blacks and other minority people in America have always known the face of white oppression, and the police still patrol the ghetto like members of an army of occupation. Yet along with repression and "backlash," we have also seen "wars on poverty" and "great societies." Indeed, it has become something of a cliche to note that ghetto uprisings, though first met with armed might, are later buried under a deluge of benevolent social welfare programs.

The comprehensive community mental health approach is clearly a part of this white response. As the black movement has escalated in militancy, so too have both faces of the white power structure. (Only recently, as the black movement pushes still further, has the carrot been withdrawn, leaving only the stick.) Federally sponsored community mental health programs are one manifestation of this escalation. Such programs are created in the heart of the ghetto. They influence all the service agencies which affect the community. They seek out neighborhood leaders, open store-fronts and hire community people. Their presence is quickly noted; they cannot be ignored.

The oppression and exploitation of colonial people, whether in Asia, Africa and Latin America or in the black and brown ghettos of the United States has, under varying social and historical conditions, operated at many levels and taken a variety of forms. Most obvious of course is that oppression enforced through the club, the dog and the gun by the occupying police or army. Here the message is clear; one must obey or be destroyed by the sheer brutal might of the oppressor. However, the compliance exacted by the use of massive force represents only one, and not necessarily the most effective means of inducing obedience. Indeed, there is much in the literature of social psychology (cognitive dissonance theory, for example) as well as in the history of oppressed peoples to suggest that it is often the employment of only that minimal force required to insure compliance which proves to be most effective. This may be especially true if such force is presented in a form which is not readily perceived as coercive or which in fact is seen as helpful in intent by both the agents of oppression and the oppressed. The mystification of experience which accompanies the acceptance of

such "kindnesses" creates a form of oppression far more destructive than that of the armed occupier. Thus, in the urban ghetto of America today, it is the Social Worker, the Psychologist and the Educator who play the key oppressive role—who have become the "soft police."

Our paper will focus upon such repressive functions, inherent in the community mental health movement. Regardless of the altruistic intent of the staff, federally funded community mental health programs aimed at the ghetto serve to pacify the neighborhood—to mystify and mollify justifiable outrage and thereby prevent action for meaningful change. Our analysis suggests that by diverting neighborhood concern toward problems of "mental health" and away from efforts to confront the basic oppressive institutions in our society, such programs function to maintain the status quo rather than to advance the interests of the oppressed community.

Our analysis will focus upon a brief consideration of three interrelated questions: (1) Do urban ghettos need "mental health" or does the professional clinical approach serve to divert community resources from more meaningful efforts? (2) Does the employment of neighborhood leaders as mental health aides or in other "para-professional" job slots serve as a form of cooptation, alienating these leaders from their community and thereby weakening the neighborhood power base? (3) Is it naive to believe that federally funded social action programs are free to confront the basic oppressive institutions in our society?

Let us first consider the question of social action. Such programs are usually envisioned in terms of grassroots organizing aimed at modifying oppressive institutions within the community. Yet, the changes in community social and economic conditions engendered by such concerted actions are not their sole value. For within the process of organizing, of rising up in struggle and of course, in winning, lies a potent form of therapy—a rekindling of hope and of personal efficacy in those long suffering the weight of oppression.

Yet, social action obviously means more than developing civic pride. In institutions which oppress the community one soon discovers that they do not yield to the application of mild pressures or the force of moral indignation,

and that such institutions are in fact interrelated in a complex web which imprisons the community. The experience of the last decade, as well as of the labor movement, is quite clear; social action, if it is to succeed, means militancy and whether it is at first directed at private institutions, such as slum housing, or whether municipal institutions such as the school, sanitation, housing or welfare systems are attacked, the issue must inevitably find the community and the ruling power structure at odds. Why should we doubt this? Obviously the oppression of the ghetto is more than an accident of history, a bad habit or a product of benign neglect. Such oppression exists as an integral part of our political and economic system, and will be defended by those ruling elements in the system which profit from this form. Thus, only militant organizing and action can lead to liberation.

Can we really expect that social action projects which owe their continued existence to governmental support are free to challenge governmental and corporate institutions which oppress the ghetto? How long would local power structures permit their influence to be threatened by a government sponsored militant opposition? Thus, despite the honest intent of the staff, such programs have built into their structure, a brake upon their effectiveness. For as social action increases in militancy, pressures will arise within the organization to go slow, to compromise and to tone down the program in order to save it. Well meaning men will gradually face a conflict between their program, which they have created, nurtured, fought and worked hard for, their jobs, and the pressure for that degree of militancy required for success. To expect that such social action programs will opt for militancy is like expecting an Army sponsored college peace group to storm the Pentagon.

Our concern, however, is not due simply to these programs' built-in lack of efficacy. Rather, their pacificatory function lies in their ability to involve militant and potentially militant individuals and groups in their futile programs. Such involvement leads to a situation in which a federally funded agency is able to locate and, to some degree, give direction to, and control, ghetto opposition. As the community mental health social action projects will undoubtedly be better funded than grassroots social action groups, there will be pressure on indigenous organizations to cooperate with these projects; here leaflets can be typed and printed or sound equipment borrowed. Increasingly, local groups will come to depend on and have a stake in the program. Even if militant neighborhood organizations ignore or oppose the community mental health project, the conflict between groups can only serve to split and confuse the community as well as to wastefully engage the energies of the militant group.

The social action aspect of community mental health programs serves as a good example of cooptation. As William Gamson (1969) has noted, cooptation is an important though subtle form of social control. This mechanism, which "involves yielding access to the most difficult and threatening potential partisans" attempts to defuse potentially explosive opponents by incorporating them into the structure of the organization, of the system, which they oppose and inducing them to identify with and subject themselves to, the rewards and punishments which the organization bestows. Perhaps the clearest example of the cooptive function of community mental health programs can be seen in their emphasis upon the cooptation of neighborhood leaders through the creation of what has been condescendingly termed the "para-professional."

The employment of indigenous personnel in social action and mental health service programs functions not simply to teach and train, but also to alienate these leaders and potential leaders from their community, to turn their energies away from militant social action for the community and toward personal success. Let me cite a rather striking example of such cooptation. During the 1969 Orthopsychiatric convention in New York, a community control dispute erupted at the Lincoln Hospital community mental health program. As the convention opened, several staff members were arrested in a sit-in at Lincoln Hospital and others were suspended. As many of you will recall, this dispute spilled over into, and soon became a volatile issue at the convention. At the invitation of the dissidents and with the cooperation of the hospital administration, almost thirty convention participants were given a tour of the Lincoln Hospital project and encouraged to discuss the controversy with both clients and staff. On this tour, several of us met a

young black neighborhood worker, a militant who had spent time in the South as a civil rights worker, and who sat in his office, reading, surrounded by posters of Malcolm X and other revolutionary leaders, seemingly oblivious to the conflict boiling all around him. Several of us expressed our surprise at finding him so curiously uninvolved in the dispute. His somewhat annoyed explanation was quite simple. As part of his training program, this young man had been given the opportunity to enroll in a local community college. It was mid-term time and so, regardless of the issues, he had to study for his examinations. Who were we, he added, with our advance degrees, to criticize him for seizing this chance for success. Although one could only agree with him, it seemed clear that the community had lost one of its potential leaders.

While cooptation can be employed by incorporating neighborhood leaders into many types of organizations, community mental health programs present an especially effective form of mystification and cooptation—what we may term the "psychologicalization of discontent." No one will deny that ghetto communities are in need of improved mental health services, or that neighborhood people will find some value in seeking out and participating in such programs. However, in an environment of extreme poverty and oppression, to focus upon individual problems of mental health is to divert community energies from thier primary task, their own liberation. The problem of the ghetto is not one of psychopathology. To convince an individual in an oppressed community that the root of his problem is intrapsychic is to mystify him, pacify his legitimate and healthy anger, and surely, to oppress him.

REFERENCES

Gamson, William A. *Simsoc*. New York: The Free Press, 1969.
Hollinshead, A. B., and Redlich, F. C. *Social class and mental illness: A community study*. New York: John Wiley and Sons, Inc., 1958.
Klein, R. A., and Statman, J. M. *Community crisis and inter-group tension: A progress report*. 1969 Convention of the A.P.A.
Langner, T., and Michael, S. *Life stress and mental health. The midtown Manhattan study*. New York: McGraw-Hill, Inc., 1963.
Peck, H. B., Kaplan, S. R., and Roman, M. Prevention, treatment and social action: A strategy of intervention in a disadvantaged urban

area. *American Journal of Orthopsychiatry*, 1966, 36, 57–69.
Srole, L., Langner, T., Michael, S., Opler, M. K., and Rennie, T. A. C. *Mental health in the metropolis. The midtown Manhattan study*. New York: McGraw-Hill, Inc., 1962.

The tragedy of the assassination of John F. Kennedy is manifested in his call for an imaginative community mental health program which has not yet been realized. Today, the trend in many states toward cutting mental health funds has left us in 1970 with the task of describing the sorry state of mental hospitals, which, more inadequate than ever before, are still the last resort for society in coping with mentally disordered people.

9.9
Mental Illness and Mental Retardation

John F. Kennedy

Remarks on Proposed Measures To Combat Mental Illness and Mental Retardation (February 5, 1963)

I have sent to the Congress today a series of proposals to help fight mental illness and mental retardation. These two afflictions have been long neglected. They occur more frequently, affect more people, require more prolonged treatment, cause more individual and family suffering than any other condition in American life.

It has been tolerated too long. It has troubled our national conscience, but only as a problem unpleasant to mention, easy to postpone, and despairing of solution. The time has come for a great national effort. New medical, scientific, and social tools and insights are now available.

With respect to mental illness, our chief aim is to get people out of State custodial institutions and back into their communities and homes, without hardship or dan-

From *Public Papers of the Presidents*, No. 50 (John F. Kennedy, 1963).

ger. Today nearly one-fifth of the 279 State mental institutions are fire and health hazards.

Three-fourths of them were opened before World War II. Nearly half of the 530,000 persons in our State mental hospitals are in institutions with over 3,000 patients getting little or no individual treatment. Many of these institutions have less than half of the professional staff required.

Forty-five percent of them have been hospitalized for 10 years or more. If we launch a broad, new mental health program now, it will be possible within a decade or two to reduce the number of patients now under custodial care by 50 percent or more.

Mental retardation ranks with mental health as a major health, social, and economic problem in this country. It strikes our most precious asset, our children. It disables 10 times as many people as diabetes, 20 times as many as tuberculosis, and 600 times as many as infantile paralysis.

There are between 5 and 6 million mentally retarded children and adults, an estimated 3 percent of our population, much too high for a country of our resources and wealth. There are many causes, many of them still unknown, but I think that statistics already point to a direct relationship between lack of prenatal care and mental retardation.

Primarily for lack of funds, between 20 and 60 percent of the mothers receiving care in public hospitals in some large cities receive inadequate or no prenatal care and mental retardation is more prevalent in these areas. I am recommending a new, 5-year program of assistance to States and local health departments to develop comprehensive maternity and child health care programs serving primarily families who are otherwise unable to pay for needed medical care.

We, as a nation, have neglected too long the mentally ill and the mentally retarded. It affects all of us and it affects us as a country. I am hopeful that beginning today this country will move with a great national effort in this field so vital to the welfare of our citizens.

Thank you.

Special Message to the Congress on Mental Illness and Mental Retardation (February 5, 1963)

To the Congress of the United States:

It is my intention to send shortly to the Congress a message pertaining to this Nation's most urgent needs in the area of health improvement. But two health problems—because they are of such critical size and tragic impact, and because their susceptibility to public action is so much greater than the attention they have received—are deserving of a wholly new national approach and a separate message to the Congress. These twin problems are mental illness and mental retardation.

From the earliest days of the Public Health Service to the latest research of the National Institutes of Health, the Federal Government has recognized its responsibilities to assist, stimulate and channel public energies in attacking health problems. Infectious epidemics are now largely under control. Most of the major diseases of the body are beginning to give ground in man's increasing struggle to find their cause and cure. But the public understanding, treatment and prevention of mental disabilities have not made comparable progress since the earliest days of modern history.

Yet mental illness and mental retardation are among our most critical health problems. They occur more frequently, affect more people, require more prolonged treatment, cause more suffering by the families of the afflicted, waste more of our human resources, and constitute more financial drain upon both the public treasury and the personal finances of the individual families than any other single condition.

There are now about 800,000 such patients in this Nation's institutions—600,000 for mental illness and over 200,000 for mental retardation. Every year nearly 1,500,000 people receive treatment in institutions for the mentally ill and mentally retarded. Most of them are confined and compressed within an antiquated, vastly overcrowded, chain of custodial State institutions. The average amount expended on their case is only $4 a day—too little to do much good for the individual, but too much if measured in terms of efficient use of our mental health dollars. In some States the average is less than $2 a day.

The total cost to the taxpayers is over $2.4 billion a year in direct public outlays for services—about $1.8 billion for mental illness and $600 million for mental retardation. Indirect public outlays—in welfare costs and in the waste of

human resources—are even higher. But the anguish suffered both by those afflicted and by their families transcends financial statistics—particularly in view of the fact that both mental illness and mental retardation strike so often in children, leading in most cases to a lifetime of disablement for the patient and a lifetime of hardship for his family.

This situation has been tolerated far too long. It has troubled our national conscience—but only as a problem unpleasant to mention, easy to postpone, and despairing of solution. The Federal Government, despite the nationwide impact of the problem, has largely left the solutions up to the States. The States have depended on custodial hospitals and homes. Many such hospitals and homes have been shamefully understaffed, overcrowded, unpleasant institutions from which death too often provided the only firm hope of release.

The time has come for a bold new approach. New medical, scientific, and social tools and insights are now available. A series of comprehensive studies initiated by the Congress, the Executive Branch and interested private groups have been completed and all point in the same direction.

Governments at every level—Federal, State, and local—private foundations and individual citizens must all face up to their responsibilities in this area. Our attack must be focused on three major objectives:

First, we must seek out the causes of mental illness and of mental retardation and eradicate them. Here, more than in any other area, "an ounce of prevention is worth more than a pound of cure." For prevention is far more desirable for all concerned. It is far more economical and it is far more likely to be successful. Prevention will require both selected specific programs directed especially at known causes, and the general strengthening of our fundamental community, social welfare, and educational programs which can do much to eliminate or correct the harsh environmental conditions which often are associated with mental retardation and mental illness. . . .
underlying resources of knowledge

Second, we must strengthen the and, above all, of skilled manpower which are necessary to mount and sustain our attack on mental disability for many years to come. Personnel from many of the same professions serve both the mentally ill and the mentally retarded. We must increase our existing training programs and launch new ones; for our efforts cannot succeed unless we increase by several-fold in the next decade the number of professional and subprofessional personnel who work in these fields. My proposals on the Health Professions and Aid for Higher Education are essential to this goal; and both the proposed Youth Employment program and a national service corps can be of immense help. We must also expand our research efforts, if we are to learn more about how to prevent and treat the crippling or malfunction of the mind.

Third, we must strengthen and improve the programs and facilities serving the mentally ill and the mentally retarded. The emphasis should be upon timely and intensive diagnosis, treatment, training, and rehabilitation so that the mentally afflicted can be cured or their functions restored to the extent possible. Services to both the mentally ill and to the mentally retarded must be community based and provide a range of services to meet community needs.

It is with these objectives in mind that I am proposing a new approach to mental illness and mental retardation. This approach is designed, in large measure, to use Federal resources to stimulate State, local and private action. When carried out, reliance on the cold mercy of custodial isolation will be supplanted by the open warmth of community concern and capability. Emphasis on prevention, treatment and rehabilitation will be substituted for a desultory interest in confining patients in an institution to wither away.

In an effort to hold domestic expenditures down in a period of tax reduction, I have postponed new programs and reduced added expenditures in all areas when that could be done. But we cannot afford to postpone any longer a reversal in our approach to mental affliction. For too long the shabby treatment of the many millions of the mentally disabled in custodial institutions and many millions more now in communities needing help has been justified on grounds of inadequate funds, further studies and future promises. We can procrastinate no more. The national mental health program and the national program to combat mental retardation herein proposed warrant prompt Congressional attention.

A National Program for Mental Health

I propose a national mental health program to assist in the inauguration of a wholly new emphasis and approach to care for the mentally ill. This approach relies primarily upon the new knowledge and new drugs acquired and developed in recent years which make it possible for most of the mentally ill to be successfully and quickly treated in their own communities and returned to a useful place in society.

These breakthroughs have rendered obsolete the traditional methods of treatment which imposed upon the mentally ill a social quarantine, a prolonged or permanent confinement in huge, unhappy mental hospitals where they were out of sight and forgotten. I am not unappreciative of the efforts undertaken by many States to improve conditions in these hospitals, or the dedicated work of many hospital staff members. But their task has been staggering and the results too often dismal, as the comprehensive study by the Joint Commission on Mental Illness and Health pointed out in 1961. Some States have at times been forced to crowd five, ten or even fifteen thousand people into one, large understaffed institution. Imposed largely for reasons of economy, such practices were costly in human terms, as well as in a real economic sense. . . .

But there are hopeful signs. In recent years the increasing trend toward higher and higher concentrations in these institutions has been reversed—by the use of new drugs, by the increasing public awareness of the nature of mental illness, and by a trend toward the provision of community facilities, including psychiatric beds in general hospitals, day care centers and outpatient psychiatric clinics. Community general hospitals in 1961 treated and discharged as cured more than 200,000 psychiatric patients.

I am convinced that, if we apply our medical knowledge and social insights fully, all but a small portion of the mentally ill can eventually achieve a wholesome and constructive social adjustment. It has been demonstrated that 2 out of 3 schizophrenics—our largest category of mentally ill—can be treated and released within 6 months, but under the conditions that prevail today the average stay for schizophrenia is 11 years. In 11 States,

by the use of modern techniques, seven out of every ten schizophrenia patients admitted were discharged within 9 months. In one instance, where a State hospital deliberately sought an alternative to hospitalization in those patients about to be admitted, it was able to treat successfully in the community fifty percent of them. It is clear that a concerted national attack on mental disorders is now both possible and practical.

If we launch a broad new mental health program now, it will be possible within a decade or two to reduce the number of patients now under custodial care by 50 percent or more. Many more mentally ill can be helped to remain in their own homes without hardship to themselves or their families. Those who are hospitalized can be helped to return to their own communities. All but a small proportion can be restored to useful life. We can spare them and their families much of the misery which mental illness now entails. We can save public funds and we can conserve our manpower resources.

Comprehensive Community Mental Health Centers. Central to a new mental health program is comprehensive community care. Merely pouring Federal funds into a continuation of the outmoded type of institutional care which now prevails would make little difference. We need a new type of health facility, one which will return mental health care to the main stream of American medicine, and at the same time upgrade mental health services. . . .

While the essential concept of the comprehensive community mental health center is new, the separate elements which would be combined in it are presently found in many communities: diagnostic and evaluation services, emergency psychiatric units, outpatient services, inpatient services, day and night care, foster home care, rehabilitation, consultative services to other community agencies, and mental health information and education.

These centers will focus community resources and provide better community facilities for all aspects of mental health care. Prevention as well as treatment will be a major activity. Located in the patient's own environment and community, the center would make possible a better understanding of his needs, a more cordial atmosphere for his recovery and a continuum of treatment. As his needs change, the patient could move without delay or difficulty to different services—from diagnosis, to cure, to rehabilitation—without need to transfer to different institutions located in different communities.

A comprehensive community mental health center in receipt of Federal aid may be sponsored through a variety of local organizational arrangements. Construction can follow the successful Hill-Burton pattern, under which the Federal Government matches public or voluntary nonprofit funds. Ideally, the center could be located at an appropriate community general hospital, many of which already have psychiatric units. In such instances, additional services and facilities could be added—either all at once or in several stages—to fill out the comprehensive program. In some instances, an existing outpatient psychiatric clinic might form the nucleus of such a center, its work expanded and integrated with other services in the community. Centers could also function effectively under a variety of other auspices: as affiliates of State mental hospitals, under State or local governments, or under voluntary nonprofit sponsorship.

Private physicians, including general practitioners, psychiatrists, and other medical specialists, would all be able to participate directly and cooperatively in the work of the center. For the first time, a large proportion of our private practitioners will have the opportunity to treat their patients in a mental health facility served by an auxiliary professional staff that is directly and quickly available for outpatient and inpatient care.

While these centers will be primarily designed to serve the mental health needs of the community, the mentally retarded should not be excluded from these centers if emotional problems exist. They should also offer the services of special therapists and consultation services to parents, school systems, health departments, and other public and private agencies concerned with mental retardation.

We as a Nation have long neglected the mentally ill and the mentally retarded. This neglect must end, if our nation is to live up to its own standards of compassion and dignity and achieve the maximum use of its manpower.

This tradition of neglect must be replaced by forceful and far-reaching programs carried out at all levels of government, by private individuals and by State and local agencies in every part of the Union.

We must act
—to bestow the full benefits of our society on those who suffer from mental disabilities;
—to prevent the occurrence of mental illness and mental retardation wherever and whenever possible;
—to provide for early diagnosis and continuous and comprehensive care, in the community, of those suffering from these disorders;
—to stimulate improvements in the level of care given the mentally disabled in our State and private institutions, and to reorient those programs to a community-centered approach;
—to reduce, over a number of years, and by hundreds of thousands, the persons confined to these institutions;
—to retain in and return to the community the mentally ill and mentally retarded, and there to restore and revitalize their lives through better health programs and strengthened educational and rehabilitation services; and
—to reinforce the will and capacity of our communities to meet these problems, in order that the communities, in turn, can reinforce the will and capacity of individuals and individual families.

We must promote—to the best of our ability and by all possible and appropriate means—the mental and physical health of all our citizens.

To achieve these important ends, I urge that the Congress favorably act upon the foregoing recommendations.

CONCLUSIONS

Since President Kennedy's speech was delivered in 1963, the words "community mental health center" have become part of the psychiatric vocabulary, but such programs have not been enacted. Due to what we (the editors) see as confused priorities, mental hospitals today are overcrowded and understaffed. But the time for rhetoric must stop—action must be taken to return the mental hospital to its therapeutic function. State hospital systems as they exist today are no longer adequate for this purpose.

We envision a community mental health center including preventative, inpatient, and outpatient care. The objectives of community care would be:

1. To furnish a continuum of mental health services in the local community, providing early diagnosis and treatment, prehospital and after care for all types of mental disorders. These multiple services will be given at one location.
2. To find successful approaches and programs for the prevention of mental illness, alcoholism, and mental retardation.
3. To increase needed manpower in the mental health field, to strengthen known resources of knowledge, and to expand research activities for finding new knowledge about mental illness. It is expected that the areas of research and training will enhance greatly the area of service.
4. To develop and maintain a coordinated plan for programing and financing comprehensive mental health clinic services through the use of federal, state, and community resources.
5. To keep before all people related to the clinic the goal in the care of all patients: to restore the individual to his fullest mental, physical, social, and vocational abilities.
6. To establish gradually and expand the community or regional facilities which eventually would replace the traditional large mental institutions.

Preventative care will provide an opportunity for direct and indirect communication. Rap centers will provide an atmosphere of group encounter, where people drop in off the street, and where those seeking help may oftentimes find themselves helping others. Nonprofessionals would volunteer their services, thereby cutting costs, and working toward establishing person-to-person contact in an informal atmosphere. Suicide prevention centers would offer 24-hour phone communication for those in desperation.

Outpatient care would include day treatment centers and short-term psychotherapy. Day treatment would allow preservation of community and family roles, while at the same time offering varied therapies to help cope with these roles. Psychodrama, art- and music-therapy would provide release of frustration, and would help the people to deal with their roles more effectively. Short-term therapy, with a definite time limit, would offer more tangible goals to patients seeking a one-to-one relationship with a professional.

Inpatient care would only include voluntary patients. The criminally insane would be treated in modernized penal institutions, and geriatrics would be moved to rest homes. By ridding the mental hospital system of those patients requiring only custodial care (the criminally insane, geriatrics, and mentally retarded), the mental hospital may assume its proper therapeutic function. Inpatient care could then encompass foster-family living groups staffed by nonprofessionals. They would be educated in the fundamentals of psychology and psychiatry, and would then live in a family situation with patients who would otherwise be hospitalized in state institutions. The nonprofessional would supervise activities similar to those of day-treatment centers and encourage residents to assume those roles necessary to family and community life. Those voluntary patients seeking constant professional psychiatric and medical attention would be recommended to small state-funded hospitals operating on the level of private hospitals. Psychiatric technicians and volunteers would ensure constant personal contact and medical supervision. This system would encourage people to seek, not avoid, the help of state mental hospitals. The key to this program, and to those previously suggested, is personal, nonprofessional treatment of people as people.

Psychological Consequences of Population Control

EDITED BY:

Mark K. Harrington   Guy Mansfield

Sandra A. Hickey   Dave Stoltze

Margaret Kerr

INTRODUCTION

As the U.S. government moves inexorably toward tighter governmental control of the environment, in the wake of the ecology movement, the question of population control becomes unavoidable. If the ecology movement has done nothing else, it has made more Americans aware of the interdependence of people, nature, and technology. Depending upon which oracle he listens to, the citizen is advised either to be very alarmed or very complacent.

It is rather clear that the message of alarm is beginning to take hold.

In regard to the expanding population, one of the most influential books of the past decade has been Paul Ehrlich's *The Population Bomb*.[1] While to some the staccato style of this tract sounds overly pessimistic and alarmist, most of the other population spokesmen refer to, applaud, or denounce Ehrlich. If his projections about impending famine and the need for mandatory population control have any foundation, the procrastination on discussion and action may prove to be disastrous.

Assuming that famine or war does not intervene, the present world population will double in thirty-five years at the present rate of growth—a fact which is not questioned by even the optimistic in the population field.

A survey of the literature shows that population research has been dominated first by demographers, recently joined by biologists. The more thoughtful of these investigators write openly about the material, ethical, and spiritual consequences of the state intervening in the "natural" process of procreation. Hardin has been quoted on occasion as saying that "the freedom to breed is intolerable."[2] Some third world spokesmen speak of the population control advocates as racist protagonists who are consciously or unconsciously pushing a program which will inevitably lead to genocide against third world people (see Robert Chrisman's article in this chapter, "Ecology Is a Racist Shuck"). Uncritical acceptance by the public of old clichés like "The rich get richer, the poor get children" lends credence to the fears of some black leaders who think that society will attempt first to curb the breeding of poorer, minority people when it finally gets alarmed about the population explosion. In short, population is a controversial, complex problem with no easy answers.

Further, as Wayne Bartz indicates in "While Psychologists Doze On" in this volume, few social scientists have done research in this area. Yet, this social problem is a natural area for sociologists and social psychologists, since the problem and its solution rests so much in the area of people's attitudes.

We have attempted to bring together a sample of representative ideas and research about the population problem as a kind of primer for social scientists who wish to get involved. The article by Kutner and Duffy—probably the first of its kind—was commissioned especially for this section. Further information can be obtained from the editors of a new newsletter on psychological consequences of population. (Write to Ed Pohlman, Dept. of Psychology, University of the Pacific, Stockton, California 95204.)

[1] Paul Ehrlich, *The Population Bomb*, New York, Ballantine, 1968. See also Paul and Anne Ehrlich, *Population Resources and Environment*, New York, Freeman, 1970, for a more thorough documentation of the population bomb argument.

[2] G. Hardin, "The Tragedy of the Commons," *Science*, 162, (1968), 1243–1248.

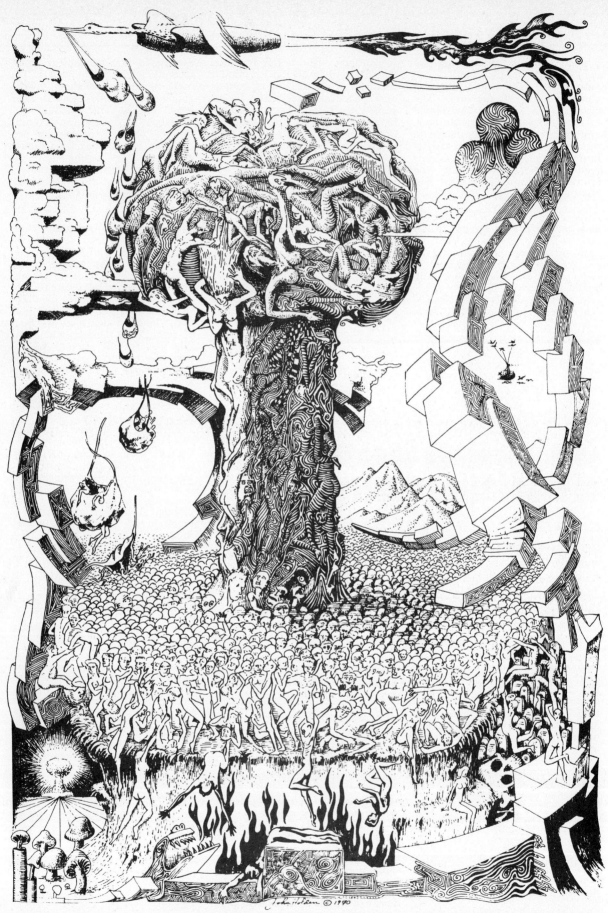

THE POPULATION BOMB. COURTESY OF JOHN HOLDEN.

10.1
People Pollution

Paul R. Ehrlich

We are witnessing today the extinction of those species of birds which feed high on oceanic food chains. The peregrine falcon and brown pelican are on their way out, and barring a miracle, most or all of our other seabirds seem doomed to follow them. The problem, of course, is *worldwide* pollution with chlorinated hydrocarbons—pesticides like DDT and its relatives, and industrial solvents known as PCBs. These chemicals have already decimated populations of land birds. They have been responsible for massive fish kills. They have helped greatly to reduce the abundance of butterflies in both Europe and North America. They may have substantially reduced the life expectancy of people born since 1945. And they may have also started an irreversible trend leading to a drastic lowering of the capacity of the planet Earth to support mankind.

But chlorinated hydrocarbons are just one class of what might be described as general environmental pollutants. Lead, nitrates, phosphates, fluorides, radioactive materials, and dust likewise are some of man's most potent weapons in his all-out assault on Earth's life support systems. These life support systems—ecosystems—are complex, and because of their complexity they are stable. But human activities tend to simplify ecosystems and reduce their stability; man is seriously damaging the apparatus necessary to support his existence.

The basic cause of our crisis is a human population which is already about six times too large. Like the famous deer of the Kaibab Plateau, in Arizona, we have exceeded the carrying capacity of our environment. In our desperate attempts to maintain such a bloated population, we will inevitably do further damage to our environment. Just as inevitably, the human population will complete its outbreak-crash cycle. We've had most of the outbreak—what remains is mainly the crash. For when a biological population outstrips its resources, it inevitably declines rapidly to a very low level—or to extinction. This normally

occurs through a dramatic increase in the death rate.

But the human population has some choice left—it can decrease its size either through a rise in the death rate, or through a drop in the birth rate, or some combination of the two. Some increase in the death rate now seems unavoidable. The question we now face is whether the entire crash will be a result of increased deaths.

The connection between population growth and environmental deterioration, strangely, is still not clear to many persons. Twice as many people create more than twice as much smog, since commuters must travel further and, as freeways become more clogged, our overpowered cars are forced to go slowly—and their engines produce more dangerous effluents at low speeds than at high speed. Twice as many people often more than double sewage disposal problems. Up to a certain point, natural processes in our waters can purify wastes. But as the volume of wastes increases, that point is passed and pollution problems follow. Each additional person "demands" more water for home use and industry, and more power. Thus beautiful valleys are dammed, farmland is flooded, and extraordinarily dangerous nuclear reactors and filth-producing fossil-fueled powerplants are constructed.

Above all, more people require more food, and few of our activities are more destructive to the environment than agriculture. In essence, when man practices agriculture he destroys complex, stable ecological systems and replaces them with simple, unstable systems. Agriculture requires immense amounts of water, and "modern" agriculture also demands the use of large amounts of fossil fuels, pesticides, and inorganic nitrogen fertilizers. All have deleterious effects on our environment.

Depletion of groundwater supplies, often with an accompanying increase in the saltiness of the water, is a common result of the demand for agricultural water—a demand which also results in dams, ponds, and canals defacing the landscape. Inorganic nitrogen fertilizers lead to a loss of humus in the soil and a resultant breakdown in the nitrogen cycle. This leads to large amounts of nitrates being flushed from agricultural lands, helping to overfertilize fresh waters. The results include the poisoning of babies and the

exposure of humans to dangerous germs from the soil—germs which previously have not come into contact with man. But a more general result is the death of our streams, rivers, and lakes.

Perhaps the most serious environmental problem directly attributable to agriculture is that caused by pesticides—especially the hard pesticides, the chlorinated hydrocarbons. Conservationists are well aware of the direct kills of wildlife attributable to these compounds and the die-offs caused by their concentration in ecological systems. Some may also think that this is a necessary price to pay for feeding hungry people. But in truth, our use of pesticides is not necessary to maintain our agricultural production. Present patterns of pesticide usage do just one thing: they create large profits for the petrochemical industry. It is ironic that most people make only one connection between this serious ecological threat and population growth. They have been hoodwinked into thinking that broadcast use of pesticides is necessary to produce food in large quantitites.

Examine for a moment the effect of broadcast use of insecticides against plant-eating insects. This effect is related to a basic characteristic of the eating sequences in ecological systems—a characteristic of food chains. In general, there is always less weight of living organisms at each succeeding step up the chain, more weight of grass than of cows, more weight of cows than of men. Similarly there will normally be more individuals of a plant-eating (herbivorous) insect species in a field than of a predatory insect species feeding on the plant-eaters.

The fundamental reason for this diminishing weight and numbers is embodied in a physical law—the second law of thermodynamics, which says that energy transfers are not 100 percent efficient; at each step in the food chain; some useful energy is lost. Energy from the sun is captured by green plants and used to build the large molecules of which the plants are made, and to run their life processes. This energy is passed up the food chain from plant to herbivore to predator to higher-order predator. But the organisms at each step have less energy available to them than those at lower levels, so that ordinarily there is a smaller mass of predators than herbivores, and so on.

Insects that are pests on plants have large populations—that is why they are pests. Because of the second law of thermodynamics, predators and parasites feeding on the pest will ordinarily have much smaller populations. Large populations have more genetic variability than smaller populations. Therefore, everything else being equal, a pest population is more likely to contain individuals with some genetic resistance to a pesticide than a population of predators feeding on the pest. However, all things are not equal. Herbivores have long evolutionary experience with chemical warfare. Plants have been trying to poison them for millions of years. (We use many plant pesticides such as pyrethrins and nicotine for their original purpose. What we call spices are also plant biochemicals designed to repel or kill herbivores, as are the active ingredients in marijuana and heroin.)

Herbivorous insects have evolved many ways of dealing with plant-produced insecticides, and these strategies may often be adapted for defense against the poisons manufactured by man. Thus when a field is sprayed for the first time, the usual result is that, although *most* of the pests are killed, *all* the predators and parasites are exterminated. The few resistant pests that survive breed—free from the attacks of their enemies—and soon another pesticide application is needed. As the sequence is repeated, the end result is a strain of pests quite resistant to the pesticide, happily living in the absence of its predators and parasites.

Happy, too, is the petrochemical industry, whose solution to this problem is more pesticides. The industry, of course, encourages repeated spraying "by the calendar" whether pests are present or not. This sells more spray and encourages the evolution of insecticide resistance, which eventually sells even more. It's a great business—especially since killing of predators often produces large populations of herbivorous insects which were previously innocuous. Until DDT was introduced, mites were rarely pests. But DDT killed mite-eating insects, and mites began to gobble crops. Thus another bonanza for the poison-peddlers—the manufacture of chemicals to kill the pests they have created!

Last December a group of graduate students and I were doing field research in Trinidad. We came across an especially interesting case of the ecology of pesticides. An attempt was being made to grow passion fruit commercially, and insecticides were being used to combat the caterpillars of *Heliconius* butterflies which are a major pest on the *Passiflora* vines. It is a losing game. *Heliconius* butterflies are naturally controlled by predacious ants which patrol the vines, attracted by special nectaries on the pedicels and blades of the leaves. These ants are killed by the pesticide, leaving the plants relatively defenseless. Repeated pesticide applications are thus needed to control the caterpillars, adding greatly to the expense of the operation and creating additional difficulties by killing valuable pollinators.

It was not clear that any productivity was gained from pesticide use, and we could not help but wonder what the results would have been if an equal effort had been aimed at measures to encourage large ant populations. Consideration of such roles would come automatically if farmers and pest-controllers were given even the most elementary ecological training.

Ecologically sensible control of the insects which compete with us for food would be much safer, cheaper, and more effective than broadcast spraying. It would mean the use of what biologists call *integrated* control—the application of a combination of methods, sometimes including nonpersistent pesticides, when a pest threatens to become serious. But a shift to integrated control will present problems. The goal of *extermination* of pests will have to be dropped, and one of keeping pest populations at a manageable level substituted. No insect pest has ever been exterminated through the use of pesticides, anyway, and the amounts of poison used in the attempt are much greater than would be required to keep pest populations at a manageable level.

American housewives will have to be reeducated to prefer a small amount of insect damage in their produce to a thin film of poison on it. (Some British women already pay extra for insect-damaged fruit, realizing it is much safer to eat than the undamaged.) And most important, agriculturists will have to be trained to diagnose potential pest outbreaks and to use a flexible control strategy. They can use so-called cultural methods, such as destroying the breeding sites of pests which reproduce somewhere away from the crops. They can use biological controls, such as introducing or encouraging a predator, parasite, or a disease-causing organism which attacks the pest. Or they can use a powerful but nonpersistent pesticide.

What should be avoided at all costs is the repeated application of the same pesticide, which creates ideal conditions for the development of resistance. If repeated use of insecticides is essential, then a mix of poisons having different modes of action should be used. Above all, the agricultural community will have to replace the unrealistic goal of pest extermination through simple application of chemicals with that of pest population regulation by flexible, constantly monitored techniques.

The pesticide-PCB problem illustrates the need for a global approach to conservation. Chlorinated hydrocarbon molecules, manufactured by man, pollute our entire planet. No organisms, even those in "protected areas," are safe from them. Our conservation approach, until recently, was to preserve *areas*—essentially saying to society, "Despoil most of the Earth, but save these parcels in their natural state." There was little else we could do, but it was basically a losing battle. In the long run the situation was bound to deteriorate—areas could be destroyed but they could not be re-created. Now it has become clear that even in the short run the piecemeal approach to conservation will not work. The widespread effects of chlorinated hydrocarbons on birds already demonstrate this. But other pollutants have similar potentials.

Perhaps the least appreciated threat of pollution is its effect on climate. The weather machinery of our planet is driven primarily by energy from the sun. To understand man's effects on weather and climate, one must understand what is called the "heat balance" of the planet. The sun's energy arrives mainly as visible light, energy in short wavelengths to which the atmosphere is largely transparent. Some of this energy is absorbed by materials at the surface of the planet, warming the surface. In turn the warmed surface radiates energy, but in the form of long wavelength infrared radiation. The atmosphere is not, however, transparent to infrared radiation. Water vapor, water droplets, and carbon dioxide absorb infrared radiation, are warmed, and in turn reradiate it as infrared. About half of this energy is reradiated back toward the surface.

The overall result of this "greenhouse effect" is for the heat to be trapped near the surface. (The glass of a greenhouse is largely transparent to incoming short wavelength visible light. The contents of the greenhouse are warmed by absorption of this radiation and radiate infrared. This is absorbed by the glass of the greenhouse and reradiated—about half of it back into the greenhouse. This is why a greenhouse is warmer in the daytime than the air surrounding it.) The average temperature of the Earth's surface is 60F. Without the greenhouse effect it would be about −7F.

Another important factor affecting the heat balance of the planet is the percentage of incoming solar energy which is reflected directly back into space without being absorbed—the *albedo*. Increased cloud cover, dustiness of the atmosphere, and expansion of ice caps, increase the albedo, as does the expansion of deserts and wastelands—which reflect more light than do forests and farms.

It is not, however, entirely the planetary heat balance which determines the climate in any given place. Our weather patterns are determined by differential heating, especially the heat gradient from equator to pole. The details of the generation of weather are complex and poorly understood. It is possible that an overall rise in temperature of a few degrees could produce a much *colder* climate in many localities, caused by changes in the speed or direction of circulation bringing more cold air from polar regions.

Man's activities influence the weather in several major ways. Burning of fossil fuels has increased the carbon dioxide content of the atmosphere, adding to the greenhouse effect. It is thought that this caused a significant rise in the surface temperature between 1870 and 1940. Since then the temperature has been decreasing, and many meteorologists feel that this is the result of increased reflectivity of the atmosphere. Dust from agricultural activities and effluents from vehicles, industry, and trash burning have created a planetwide veil of pollution, increasing the albedo. The albedo has also been augmented by an increase in deserts and wastelands and increases in cloud cover. Largely because of human activities, the amount of land classified as desert or wasteland has grown from less than 10 percent to more than 25 percent in the last century. And meteorologists estimate that cirrus cloud cover over North America, the North Atlantic, and Europe has increased roughly 5 to 10 percent because of jet contrails.

Man's activities and construction also have significant local effects on weather, but it is his influence on large-scale climatic change that is of greatest concern, for there can be little doubt that such change has been accelerated on a global basis with almost complete disregard for possible consequences. Some of the changes which have been predicted would be cataclysmic—slippage of the Antarctic ice cap, causing tidal waves which would wipe out most of humanity; or the sudden onset of a new ice age. But even in the absence of such extreme (and hopefully remote!) possibilities, the results of rapid climatic change would be lethal both for many humans and for many other organisms.

Agriculture is extremely dependent on weather. Even relatively small changes in the amount of rainfall or the number of frost-free days can have profound effects on what, if anything, can be grown in an area. Human beings are also extremely conservative in their agricultural practices. They are unlikely quickly to adopt new crops as conditions change. Rather they are likely to assume that the changes are temporary, and will attempt to wait out a sequence of years of "bad weather." One inevitable result of accelerating climatic change will be reduced agricultural productivity—at a time when the Earth's capacity to produce food is already stretched to the maximum.

Or consider the fate of hard-won Redwood National Park if the climate of the Pacific Northwest became rapidly warmer and drier, or the Everglades if Florida became significantly drier or colder. Organisms faced with change in climate must adapt, or migrate, or become extinct. Adaptation is made more difficult by rapid change. And all too often man's destructive activities have left no place to migrate to. And the larger the human population, the greater man's influence on the climate—one more way in which he is contributing to the destruction of the world biota and thus to the simplification of ecosystems.

Indeed, a theoretical upper limit of man's population growth is set by his own direct contributions to the heat balance. All human activities use energy, and de-grade usable energy to heat. If man's current pattern of energy use is extrapolated, we find that in the next century or so the problem of worldwide thermal pollution could bring about climatic catastrophe.

We do not know whether the future holds more cooling of the planet followed by an ultimate heating, or some other combination. We do not have a clear picture of what either trend would produce in the way of specific local climatic changes. What we *are* doing is conducting a global experiment, one of the results of which might be the decimation of *Homo sapiens*.

Such experiments, however, are standard items in the repertoire of cynical proponents of technological "progress" for its own sake. The Federal Aviation Agency's ludicrous supersonic transport project is fundamentally a giveaway program for aircraft companies, the environmental effects of which may be catastrophic. The problem is not just the hideous noise (which we are "assured" will only be visited upon those who live in sparsely inhabited areas until the rest of us learn to adjust to the booms). One possibility is that persistent contrails from the SST will create virtually complete cirrus cloud cover over much of North America, Europe, and the North Atlantic. But the government considers this risk well worth running in order to subsidize the airplane manufacturers!

What can be done to reverse our runaway plunge towards destruction of our environment and ourselves? The answer is that there is a great deal that *could* be done. The question now is whether mankind *will* do anything. In outline, the overall solution is simple: halt population growth and slowly reduce the human population to a size that can be supported in a comfortable style more or less permanently—possibly about 500,000,000 people, one-seventh of the present population. Simultaneously, the overdeveloped countries—the USA, western Europe, the Soviet Union, and Japan—must de-develop, and the underdeveloped countries must be helped to semi-development. De-development primarily means shifting from what economist Kenneth Boulding calls "cowboy" economy to a "space-man" economy. In our present cowboy economy, emphasis is on growth, high levels of production, consumption, and waste. "Progress" is the watchword, and the growth of the Gross National Product the ultimate goal. The dogma of economic growthmanship conforms with both the folk wisdom of the average businessman and the "thinking" of all but the most sophisticated older economists. (A new generation of young economists, however, shows cheering signs of reconnecting their discipline with reality.)

These economic attitudes must be radically changed, and fast. The overdeveloped countries can no longer afford to co-opt the vast majority of the Earth's resources for their own use. We must convert to an economy of stability, one in which the emphasis is on keeping power demands low and recycling materials. Simultaneously, the underdeveloped countries must be helped to ecologically sound agricultural development and *very limited* industrialization. Fundamental changes must be made in the international trade system to see that agrarian nations are able to receive the products of industrialized countries which are necessary prerequisites of a "quality" life—such things as good medical care, adequate housing, adequate public transport, and farm machinery.

The task will be unprecedentedly difficult to accomplish. A rapid change in human attitudes will be necessary—changes in attitudes about such fundamental things as reproduction, competition, and economic growth. The Judeo-Christian idea of man dominating nature must be replaced by the goal of living in harmony with nature. The USA and USSR now spend tens of billions of dollars on military adventures which destroy human lives and the environment and on a thermonuclear arms race which threatens the destruction of civilization. These nations and others must work much more rapidly to find ways to de-escalate, and to devote many hundreds of billions of dollars over the next decade to a last attempt to save the world.

Given the communications systems and educational levels of the overdeveloped countries, it seems likely that governments could accomplish the necessary changes in attitude, *if* those governments can be made aware of the situation. The task of aiding the underdeveloped countries is immensely more difficult in view of their legacy of distrust of the overdeveloped countries.

Conservationists now find themselves in the curious position of being themselves members of an endangered species. Their own survival is intimately intertwined with that of the other organisms they have long sought to protect. In the demise of the peregrine falcon we can see a preview of our own fate. The decade of the 1970's represents the last chance for both conservation and for man.

10.2
While Psychologists Doze On

Wayne R. Bartz

Not long ago I attended the annual dinner meeting of a local psychological association. The after-dinner speaker was a member of the Biology Department at a University of California campus, and his topic for discussion concerned the approaching worldwide population disaster. It happened that I was seated at the front table near the speaker and thus faced the rest of the group, being able to listen to the talk and also watch the general reaction among the psychologists and their spouses and friends in the audience. It was an unsettling experience because of the immense contrast between the points being made by the speaker and the environment in which the topic was being discussed. My ears were hearing descriptions of the development of a problem almost incomprehensible in its enormity, with predictions of starving millions, violent revolutions, and wars directly fostered by population pressures, while my eyes looked out over a group of very satisfied and comfortable people who had just finished wining and dining at the area's finest restaurant, their clothing stylish, their late-model, often expensive cars parked outside waiting to whisk them away to their comfortable upper-middle-class homes. And sure enough, there among the audience were a few individuals dozing off for a nice, full-stomach, after-dinner nap, while the speaker at times perhaps slightly irritated their slumber with strong

Reprinted by permission of the author and the American Psychological Association from "While Psychologists Doze On," *American Psychologist*, 25, 6 (June, 1970), 500–503. Copyright 1970 by the American Psychological Association.

words about empty bloated stomachs, skeletal children, and the borrowed time for America's way of life. Well, I reassured myself, after any good meal many will feel drowsy, and I know that as a responsible group of social scientists these psychologists are indeed concerned with the population question; a socially aware and active profession has to be. Doesn't it?

Some weeks later I attended the Vancouver Convention of the Western Psychological Association. Looking through the convention catalog, I found approximately 575 presentations listed on the usual wide variety of topics somehow included under the heading of "psychology." How many of those presentations were identifiable as relating to the population problem? Exactly zero! That's right, not a one. Could this be a fluke? Shortly after I returned home, I came across a recent article by Schofield (1969) in the *American Psychologist* concerning psychology and health services. Included in his paper were the results of an attempt to compare the frequency of occurrence of various health field topics in *Psychological Abstracts* during 1966 and 1967. Among those figures are the findings for "Population Control": neither year even has an entry under "Percentage of all articles," because the obtained frequencies were less than 1 percent. Please note that this was for topics *within the health field.* The proportion of population studies if we were to include *all* topics in psychology would surely be nil. Not only was it beginning to appear to me that psychologists might be dozing as the population explosion fuse burns—we are downright snoring!

Perhaps it is a question of the priority of the problem, a lack of importance that makes it hard for psychologists to direct their attention away from more pressing matters such as nude marathons, chicken pecks, subjective probability, and preference among body products. But, outside of psychology, there does seem to be a growing awareness in the scientific community that the population problem is perhaps the most serious threat ever faced by the human race, a threat that is unique in its rapidly accelerating curve of development over Man's brief history and in its potential for imminent worldwide chaos from which no one will be immune. Pohlman (1966), one psychologist who has been actively working in this area, comments that in view of the apparent magnitude of this human problem "it is ironic to note the almost total absence of psychologists from research on birth and population control and planning [p. 967]." He suggests some possible areas for research (Pohlman, 1966) and also has reviewed the birth-planning literature in order to provide a background for psychologists interested in the area (Pohlman, 1967).

Many paperback book counters contain two popular books on population: *Famine 1975!* by William and Paul Paddock (1967) and *The Population Bomb* by Paul Ehrlich (1968). These books are designed to alert and prod the reader. They are also meant to be frightening, and they *are* frightening! We have all seen the frequent articles on the back pages of newspapers concerning population problems, and, since reading those books, I have realized that such articles (which often quote "experts" in the field) are essentially in unanimous agreement with the dark predictions made by Ehrlich and the Paddocks. Awareness of the problem is growing, but everyone seems to expect someone else to do something about it. The Paddocks give an example of such thinking in the observation that agricultural experts agree among themselves that increased food production is no answer, but they expect the population experts to solve the problem with a breakthrough in population control. The population specialists, on the other hand, admit that they cannot solve the problem through population control, but they hope the agricultural people will come up with a major development in food production to save the ball game. "If we can put a man on the moon, we can solve the population problem," I was told recently. This same rationale also seems to be applied readily to all other problems facing us, the slogan almost becoming an answer in itself to expressed social concern. Placing a man on the moon was a great feat of technology and hardware development. Changing worldwide human behavior and beliefs is not an exercise in hardware development—and, really, can we ship the excess billions to the moon? "Science will solve the problem" appears to be more wishful thinking than realistic appraisal, unless there is an immediate massive reorganization and worldwide effort to find solutions on a first-priority basis. In-

deed, some feel that it is already too late no matter what is done and that appalling famines will begin in the midseventies, science or no science.

If psychologists have their heads in the sand regarding this issue, it is interesting to note that nonscientist public figures are making suggestions to wide audiences that almost sound as if they could have come from psychologists (if there were any saying anything). The lengthy interview with Gore Vidal (1969) in a recent issue of *Playboy* (a publication which, regardless of the reader's opinions, reaches and perhaps influences millions of individuals) contained a recurrent theme of the population problem. Vidal speculates on the possibility of concentrated educational efforts to change long-accepted attitudes toward parenthood, motherhood, marriage, sexuality, and Man's "freedom" to destroy the environment. He talks of using "propaganda" extensively in the changing of attitudes, beliefs, and the modification of behavior (do not attitudes, beliefs, and behavior modification have something to do with psychology?). Any behaviorally oriented psychologist can readily point out the hypocrisy of a society in which we talk about the desirability of population control, but which incorporates a wide range of social and material reinforcers for reproductive conformity through marriage and childbearing. The single person is thought perhaps to be "queer," the childless couple is asked many leading questions about why they do not have children ("There must be something wrong with them"), and the entire tax structure contains penalties for the single person, with tax relief in direct proportion to the size of a family. Perhaps psychologists could be of help in changing maladaptive attitudes and beliefs, perhaps they can suggest effective means of providing contingent material reinforcement to promote remaining single or childless, perhaps they can help develop effective national methods of behavioral control or, let us use the word, manipulation. If human behavior has to be "manipulated" in order to halt humanity's rush to oblivion, then we should not shy from the notion. Psychologists have some knowledge of the effects of overcrowding on living organisms and are aware of the importance of environmental variables on behavior. If for some people religious beliefs interfere

with effective birth control, then psychologists could provide direct help to them in discarding obsolete human-damaging notions, instead of waiting for foot-dragging theologians to finally get around to it themselves. If the concept of sexual behavior being "for" reproduction is an outmoded holdover from primitive times when more men meant greater tribal strength and were needed for species survival, perhaps psychologists could help bury such "purpose" explanations. Note that we are not talking about control or regulation of human sexual behavior, which involves only the consenting adults, but we are talking about control of *reproductive* behavior, which affects everyone. "Freedom" in sexual expression does not also imply freedom of reproduction if the latter is viewed as a socially undesirable occurrence.

Sure, these are controversial topics! Yes, indeed, there is a value judgment being made! If one feels that survival of the human race is important, he has made a value judgment and can no longer ignore the question of population. (Some might argue, however, that nothing in Man's history suggests very strongly that he should survive or is worth saving—the only answer to that view might be that even if such is the case, there is a serious possibility that Man will destroy every other form of life on earth along with himself when he goes, and therefore is worth saving to avoid a worse disaster than his existence.) If one takes a long look at psychology's present preoccupations through the gloom-colored glasses of the impending population disaster, the question cannot help but be raised as to whether psychology's sum total contribution to humanity will in the long run amount to only a few insignificant grains to be lost in the sands of time. In a recent issue of the *American Psychologist*, Maslow (1969) asserts that in our developing humanistic concern "The first and overarching Big Problem is to make the Good Person [p. 732]." I would suggest that this is an irrelevant concern if we do not first insure having a *living* person, with enough to eat, room in which to live, and an environment worth living in. To the man who is starving in the street, who has watched his children die of disease and malnutrition and his country collapse in anarchy, questions of what makes a "good person," self-actualization, psychotherapy, interpersonal relations, and our many other humanistic diversions become just so much esoteric bull. Let us hope that Maslow does not get his wish for "all biologists, as I would urge all other people of goodwill," to put their full energy into the problems of the "good person" and "good society" until the question has been answered as to whether or not we can have the survival of mankind. What kind of goal is a world filled with the corpses of "good people" who have starved to death in "good societies" that failed to cope with the population avalanche?

Personally, I feel like an impotent observer standing on the deck of the Titanic as it sails toward destruction, watching the majority of the passengers amusing themselves at their various entertainments, unconcerned over the possibility of danger ahead, each expecting someone else to ward off any possible threats. I suspect that the population biologists are correct in their pessimistic predictions; the human community is not going to be willing to recognize the enormity of the problem until it is too late; and the natural controls seen in man's past, war and famine, will once again run rampant, but in far greater strength than ever before.

Many Americans feel that we can be safe and secure in our country and that world chaos will not be our problem or concern. When the Titanic goes down and the sea is filled with thousands of struggling bodies, will they ignore the lone luxuriously appointed lifeboat floating among them containing a few fat people in tuxedos? Will they be "good" people and drown quietly without rocking our boat or disturbing our nap? I doubt that a Red China, for example, in its death agonies, will look without malice toward affluent America and refrain from hostile acts. In the 1970s, even the small countries will be able to produce nuclear weapons—shall we politely ask them to starve in peace and not point their rockets at us? Can we as psychologists really do anything? I do not know, and I certainly cannot pretend to be asking the reader to follow my example, because I have done nothing significant in this area. The first step, however, is to stop ignoring the problem and to find out something about it to see if there is anything we can do. If even a minor proportion of the psychologists in the APA would put a small part of their attention into the world's biggest problem, we just might be able to contribute. Let us

not hide from something because it is almost too horrible to think about, and, instead, let us dig in a bit and see what, if anything, we can do.

REFERENCES

Ehrlich, P. R. *The population bomb.* New York: Ballantine, 1968.

Maslow, A. H. Toward a humanistic biology. *American Psychologist,* 1969, 24, 724–735.

Paddock, W., & Paddock, P. *Famine 1975!* Boston: Little, Brown, 1967.

Pohlman, E. Birth control: Independent and dependent variable for psychological research. *American Psychologist,* 1966, 21, 967–970.

Pohlman, E. A psychologist's introduction to the birth planning literature. *Journal of Social Issues,* 1967, 13, 13–28.

Schofield, W. The role of psychology in the delivery of health services. *American Psychologist,* 1969, 24, 565–584.

Vidal, G. Interview with Gore Vidal. *Playboy,* 1969, *16* (6) 77–96, 238.

10.3
One of "Five Who Care"

René Dubos

Step by step, people are becoming more tolerant of worse and worse environmental conditions that, though not sufficiently dangerous to destroy life, ruin its quality. Consider, for example, the effect of air pollution in the industrial areas of Northern Europe. This part of the world has been heavily polluted for more than a century; exposure to its smogs is made even more traumatic by the peculiarities of the Atlantic climate. Yet Northern Europeans have multiplied extensively and prospered economically as if they had become fully adapted to pollution. The long-range consequence of this so-called adaptation, however, is a high frequency and severity of emphysema and chronic bronchitis among adults. Such chronic pulmonary diseases are now increasing in many parts of the U.S.

Social regimentation and standardization are certainly compatible with the survival and multi-

Reprinted from *Look Magazine*, April 21, 1970. Copyright 1970 by René Dubos. This article was one of five by distinguished men who are deeply concerned about the environmental crisis.

plication of biological man, but they are not compatible with the full expression of his humanness.

We are naturally preoccupied by the unpleasant effects of the environment now. But these immediate effects are of minor importance when compared with the distant ones. Our children may suffer more than we.

It has been established beyond doubt that environmental influences exert their most profound and lasting effects when they impinge on the organism during the very early phases of its development, both prenatal and postnatal. The mind is affected just as much as the body. Mental and emotional attributes can be atrophied, distorted or enhanced by the surroundings in which the mind develops, and by the stimuli to which it has to respond.

Children can be habituated to search for happiness in overeating, unbalanced food, unsuitable entertainments, perverted addictions, escape from mental or physical effort. Such habituations provide temporary relief or even satisfaction, but they have dangerous consequences. Habituation to overcrowding may inevitably lead to an increasingly organized and regimented world. Overcrowding and regimentation are quite likely to generate social disorder and violence. To some overcrowded populations, the bomb may one day no longer seem a threat, but a release.

Children can also readily learn to accept treeless avenues, starless skies, tasteless food, a monotonous succession of holidays that are spiritless and meaningless because they are no longer holy days, life without flowers or birds.

Loss of these amenities of life may have no obvious detrimental effect on their physical well-being, but it will almost certainly be unfavorable to the development of their mental and emotional potentialities.

The potentialities of human beings often remain in a latent unexpressed state. They have a better chance to come to light when the environment provides a wide variety of enriching experiences, especially for the young. If surroundings and ways of life are highly stereotyped, the only components of man's nature that flourish are those fitting the narrow range of prevailing conditions. Hence, the sterilizing or even destructive influence of many housing developments, which, although sanitary and efficient, are planned as if their only function was to provide disposable cubicles for dispensable people.

Young people raised in a featureless environment and offered only a narrow range of experiences are likely to suffer from a kind of deprivation that will cripple them intellectually and emotionally.

Slum children, for example, often continue conforming to the ways of life of their destitute parents even when skilled social workers try hard to change their habits and tastes. As early as three to four years of age, many of the children are already programmed to unhappy patterns of existence, and there is reason to fear that they will later imprint their own children with these same patterns. The situation is very similar, in fact, for some children who are raised in wealthy suburbs but whose social environment is intellectually and emotionally impoverished.

We must strive to create for all human beings, and for children in particular, environments as diversified as possible. We may lose some precious efficiency, or increase the complexity of life, or even create a few difficult situations. But diversity gives man a greater chance to express his humanness by responding creatively to his environment.

A rapid growth of population, however, tends to limit diversity. In fact, it may be the root of our ecological crisis. The dangers posed by overpopulation are more grave and more immediate in the U.S. than in less industrialized countries. Each U.S. citizen uses more of the world's natural resources than any other human being and destroys them more rapidly, thereby contributing massively to the pollution of his own surroundings and of the earth as a whole—let alone the pollution of the moon and space. Also, the destructive impact of each U.S. citizen on the physical, biological and human environment is enormously magnified by the variety of gadgets and by the amount of energy at his disposal.

American cities give the impression of being more crowded than Asian and European cities not because their population density is higher—it is in fact much lower—but because they expose their inhabitants to many more unwelcome stimuli. Much of the experience of crowding comes not from contacts with real human beings but from the telephones, radios and television sets that bring us the mechanical expressions of mankind instead of the warmth of its biological nature.

Thus we cannot achieve environmental quality without changing our ways of life and even our aspirations. We shall have to limit the amount of energy introduced into ecological systems, the kinds of industrial goods produced, the extent of our aimless mobility and our population size. In my opinion, all these limitations can be achieved without causing economic stagnation or stopping real progress. Indeed, a change in social structure and goals can enrich our lives, by opening the way for a social renaissance.

The colossal inertia and rigidity —if not indifference—of social and academic institutions make it unlikely that they will develop effective programs of action or research focused on environmental problems. Two kinds of events, however, may catalyze and accelerate the process. One is some ecological catastrophe that will alarm the public and thus bring pressure on the social, economic and academic establishments. Another, more attractive, possibility is the emergence of a grass-roots movement, powered by romantic emotion as much as by factual knowledge, that will give form and strength to the latent public concern with environmental quality.

Because students are vigorous, informed and still uncommitted to vested interests, they constitute one of the few groups in our society that can act as a spearhead of this movement. I wish that I were young enough to be a really effective participant in the "Environmental Teach-in." I would proclaim in action rather than just in words my faith that gross national product and technological efficiency are far less important for a truly human life than the quality of the organic world and the suitability of the environment.

10.4
The Tragedy of the Commons Revisited

Beryl L. Crowe

There has developed in the contemporary natural sciences a recognition that there is a subset of problems, such as population, atomic war, and environmental corruption, for which there are no technical solutions (1, 2). There is also an increasing recognition among contemporary social scientists that there is a subset of problems, such as population, atomic war, environmental corruption, and the recovery of a livable urban environment, for which there are no current political solutions (3). The thesis of this article is that the common area shared by these two subsets contains most of the critical problems that threaten the very existence of contemporary man.

The importance of this area has not been raised previously because of the very structure of modern society. This society, with its emphasis on differentiation and specialization, has led to the development of two insular scientific communities—the natural and the social—between which there is very little communication and a great deal of envy, suspicion, disdain, and competition for scarce resources. Indeed, these two communities more closely resemble tribes living in close geographic proximity on university campuses than they resemble the "scientific culture" that C. P. Snow placed in contrast to and opposition to the "humanistic culture" (4).

Perhaps the major problems of modern society have, in large part, been allowed to develop and intensify through this structure of insularity and specialization because it serves both psychological and professional functions for both scientific communities. Under such conditions, the natural sciences can recognize that some problems are not technically soluble and relegate them to the nether land of politics, while the social sciences recognize that some problems have no current political solutions and then postpone a search for solutions while they wait for new technologies with which to attack the problem.

Reprinted by permission from *Science, 166* (November 28, 1969), 1103–1107. Copyright 1969 by the American Association for the Advancement of Science.

Both sciences can thus avoid responsibility and protect their respective myths of competence and relevance, while they avoid having to face the awesome and awful possibility that each has independently isolated the same subset of problems and given them different names. Thus, both never have to face the consequences of their respective findings. Meanwhile, due to the specialization and insularity of modern society, man's most critical problems lie in limbo, while the specialists in problem-solving go on to less critical problems for which they can find technical or political solutions.

In this circumstance, one psychologically brave, but professionally foolhardy soul, Garrett Hardin, has dared to cross the tribal boundaries in his article "The tragedy of the commons" (*1*). In it, he gives vivid proof of the insularity of the two scientific tribes in at least two respects: first, his "rediscovery" of the tragedy was in part wasted effort, for the knowledge of this tragedy is so common in the social sciences that it has generated some fairly sophisticated mathematical models (*5*); second, the recognition of the existence of a subset of problems for which science neither offers nor aspires to offer technical solutions is not likely, under the contemporary conditions of insularity, to gain wide currency in the social sciences. Like Hardin, I will attempt to avoid the psychological and professional benefits of this insularity by tracing some of the political and social implications of his proposed solution to the tragedy of the commons.

The commons is a fundamental social institution that has a history going back through our own colonial experience to a body of English common law which antidates the Roman conquest. That law recognized that in societies there are some environmental objects which have never been, and should never be, exclusively appropriated to any individual or group of individuals. In England the classic example of the commons is the pasturage set aside for public use, and the "tragedy of the commons" to which Hardin refers was a tragedy of overgrazing and lack of care and fertilization which resulted in erosion and underproduction so destructive that there developed in the late 19th century an enclosure movement. Hardin applies this social institution to other environmental objects such as water, atmosphere, and living space.

The cause of this tragedy is exposed by a very simple mathematical model, utilizing the concept of utility drawn from economics. Allowing the utilities to range between a positive value of 1 and a negative value of 1, we may ask, as did the individual English herdsman, what is the utility to me of adding one more animal to my herd that grazes on the commons? His answer is that the positive utility is near 1 and the negative utility is only a fraction of minus 1. Adding together the component partial utilities, the herdsman concludes that it is rational for him to add another animal to his herd; then another, and so on. The tragedy to which Hardin refers develops because the same rational conclusion is reached by each and every herdsman sharing the commons.

Assumptions Necessary to Avoid the Tragedy

In passing the technically insoluble problems over to the political and social realm for solution, Hardin has made three critical assumptions: (i) that there exists, or can be developed, a "criterion of judgment and a system of weighting . . ." that will "render the incommensurables . . . commensurable . . ." in real life; (ii) that, possessing this criterion of judgment, "coercion can be mutually agreed upon," and that the application of coercion to effect a solution to problems will be effective in modern society; and (iii) that the administrative system, supported by the criterion of judgment and access to coercion, can and will protect the commons from further desecration.

If all three of these assumptions were correct, the tragedy which Hardin has recognized would dissolve into a rather facile melodrama of setting up administrative agencies. I believe these three assumptions are so questionable in contemporary society that a tragedy remains in the full sense in which Hardin used the term. Under contemporary conditions, the subset of technically insoluble problems is also politically insoluble, and thus we witness a full-blown tragedy wherein "the essence of dramatic tragedy is not unhappiness. It resides in the remorseless working of things."

The remorseless working of things in modern society is the erosion of three social myths which form the basis for Hardin's assumptions, and this erosion is proceeding at such a swift rate

that perhaps the myths can neither revitalize nor reformulate in time to prevent the "population bomb" from going off, or before an accelerating "pollution immersion," or perhaps even an "atomic fallout."

Eroding Myth of the Common Value System

Hardin is theoretically correct, from the point of view of the behavioral sciences, in his argument that "in real life incommensurables *are* commensurable." He is, moreover, on firm ground in his assertion that to fulfill this condition in real life one needs only "a criterion of judgment and a system of weighting." In real life, however, values are the criteria of judgment, and the system of weighting is dependent upon the ranging of a number of conflicting values in a hierarchy. That such a system of values exists beyond the confines of the nation-state is hardly tenable. At this point in time one is more likely to find such a system of values within the boundaries of the nation-state. Moreover, the nation-state is the only political unit of sufficient dimension to find and enforce political solutions to Hardin's subset of "technically insoluble problems." It is on this political unit that we will fix our attention.

In America there existed, until very recently, a set of conditions which perhaps made the solution to Hardin's problem subset possible: we lived with the myth that we were "one people, indivisible. . . ." This myth postulated that we were the great "melting pot" of the world wherein the diverse cultural ores of Europe were poured into the crucible of the frontier experience to produce a new alloy —an American civilization. This new civilization was presumably united by a common value system that was democratic, equalitarian, and existing under universally enforceable rules contained in the Constitution and the Bill of Rights.

In the United States today, however, there is emerging a new set of behavior patterns which suggest that the myth is either dead or dying. Instead of believing and behaving in accordance with the myth, large sectors of the population are developing life-styles and value hierarchies that give contemporary Americans an appearance more closely analogous to the particularistic, primitive forms of "tribal" organizations living in geographic proximity than to that shining new alloy, the American civilization.

With respect to American politics, for example, it is increasingly evident that the 1960 election was the last election in the United States to be played out according to the rules of pluralistic politics in a two-party system. Certainly 1964 was, even in terms of voting behavior, a contest between the larger tribe that was still committed to the pluralistic model of compromise and accommodation within a winning coalition, and an emerging tribe that is best seen as a millennial revitalization movement directed against mass society—a movement so committed to the revitalization of old values that it would rather lose the election than compromise its values. Under such circumstances former real-life commensurables within the Republican Party suddenly became incommensurable.

In 1968 it was the Democratic Party's turn to suffer the degeneration of commensurables into incommensurables as both the Wallace tribe and the McCarthy tribe refused to play by the old rules of compromise, accommodation, and exchange of interests. Indeed, as one looks back on the 1968 election, there seems to be a common theme in both these camps—a theme of return to more simple and direct participation in decision-making that is only possible in the tribal setting. Yet, despite this similarity, both the Wallaceites and the McCarthyites responded with a value perspective that ruled out compromise and they both demanded a drastic change in the dimension in which politics is played. So firm were the value commitments in both of these tribes that neither (as was the case with the Goldwater forces in 1964) was willing to settle for a modicum of power that could accrue through the processes of compromise with the national party leadership.

Still another dimension of this radical change in behavior is to be seen in the black community where the main trend of the argument seems to be, not in the direction of accommodation, compromise, and integration, but rather in the direction of fragmentation from the larger community, intransigence in the areas where black values and black culture are concerned, and the structuring of a new community of like-minded and like-colored people. But to all appearances even the concept of color is not enough to sustain commensurables in their emerging community as it fragments into religious nationalism, secular nationalism, integrationists, separationists, and so forth. Thus those problems which were commensurable, both interracial and intraracial, in the era of integration become incommensurable in the era of Black Nationalism.

Nor can the growth of commensurable views be seen in the contemporary youth movements. On most of the American campuses today there are at least ten tribes involved in "tribal wars" among themselves and against the "imperialistic" powers of those "over 30." Just to tick them off, without any attempt to be comprehensive, there are: the up-tight protectors of the status quo who are looking for middle-class union cards, the revitalization movements of the Young Americans for Freedom, the reformists of pluralism represented by the Young Democrats and the Young Republicans, those committed to New Politics, the Students for a Democratic Society, the Yippies, the Flower Children, the Black Students Union, and the Third World Liberation Front. The critical change in this instance is not the rise of new groups; this is expected within the pluralistic model of politics. What is new are value positions assumed by these groups which lead them to make demands, not as points for bargaining and compromise with the opposition, but rather as points which are "not negotiable." Hence, they consciously set the stage for either confrontation or surrender, but not for rendering incommensurables commensurable.

Moving out of formalized politics and off the campus, we see the remnants of the "hippie" movement which show clear-cut tribal overtones in their commune movements. This movement has, moreover, already fragmented into an urban tribe which can talk of guerrilla warfare against the city fathers, while another tribe finds accommodation to urban life untenable without sacrificing its values and therefore moves out to the "Hog Farm," "Morning Star," or "Big Sur." Both hippie tribes have reduced the commensurables with the dominant WASP tribe to the point at which one of the cities on the Monterey Peninsula felt sufficiently threatened to pass a city ordinance against sleeping in trees, and the city of San Francisco passed a law against sitting on sidewalks.

Even among those who still adhere to the pluralistic middle-class American image, we can observe an increasing demand for a change in the dimension of life and politics that has disrupted the elementary social processes: the demand for neighborhood (tribal?) schools, control over redevelopment projects, and autonomy in the setting and payment of rents to slumlords. All of these trends are more suggestive of tribalism than of the growth of the range of commensurables with respect to the commons.

We are, moreover, rediscovering other kinds of tribes in some very odd ways. For example, in the educational process, we have found that one of our first and best empirical measures in terms both of validity and reproducibility—the I. Q. test—is a much better measure of the existence of different linguistic tribes than it is a measure of "native intellect" (6). In the elementary school, the different languages and different values of these diverse tribal children have even rendered the commensurables that obtained in the educational system suddenly incommensurable.

Nor are the empirical contradictions of the common value myth as now as one might suspect. For example, with respect to the urban environment, at least 7 years ago Scott Greer was arguing that the core city was sick and would remain sick until a basic sociological movement took place in our urban environment that would move all the middle classes to the suburbs and surrender the core city to the ". . . segregated, the insulted, and the injured" (7). This argument by Greer came at a time when most of us were still talking about compromise and accommodation of interests, and was based upon a perception that the life styles, values, and needs of these two groups were so disparate that a healthy, creative restructuring of life in the core city could not take place until pluralism had been replaced by what amounted to geographic or territorial tribalism; only when this occurred would urban incommensurables become commensurable.

Looking at a more recent analysis of the sickness of the core city, Wallace F. Smith has argued that the productive model of the city is no longer viable for the purposes of economic analysis (8). Instead, he develops a model of the city as a site for leisure consumption, and then seems to suggest that the nature of this model is such that the city cannot regain its health because it cannot make decisions, and that it cannot make decisions because the leisure demands are value-based and, hence, do not admit of compromise and accommodation; consequently there is no way of deciding among these various value-oriented demands that are being made on the core city.

In looking for the cause of the erosion of the myth of a common value system, it seems to me that so long as our perceptions and knowledge of other groups were formed largely through the written media of communication, the American myth that we were a giant melting pot of equalitarians could be sustained. In such a perceptual field it is tenable, if not obvious, that men are motivated by interests. Interests can always be compromised and accommodated without undermining our very being by sacrificing values. Under the impact of the electronic media, however, this psychological distance has broken down and we now discover that these people with whom we could formerly compromise on interests are not, after all, really motivated by interests but by values. Their behavior in our very living room betrays a set of values, moreover, that are incompatible with our own, and consequently the compromises that we make are not those of contract but of culture. While the former are acceptable, any form of compromise on the latter is not a form of rational behavior but is rather a clear case of either apostasy or heresy. Thus, we have arrived not at an age of accommodation but one of confrontation. In such an age "incommensurables" remain "incommensurable" in real life.

Erosion of the Myth of the Monopoly of Coercive Force

In the past, those who no longer subscribed to the values of the dominant culture were held in check by the myth that the state possessed a monopoly on coercive force. This myth has undergone continual erosion since the end of World War II owing to the success of the strategy of guerrilla warfare, as first revealed to the French in Indochina, and later conclusively demonstrated in Algeria. Suffering as we do from what Senator Fulbright has called "the arrogance of power," we have been extremely slow to learn the lesson in Vietnam, although we now realize that war is political and cannot be won by military means. It is apparent that the myth of the monopoly of coercive

force as it was first qualified in the civil rights conflict in the South, then in our urban ghettos, next on the streets of Chicago, and now on our college campuses has lost its hold over the minds of Americans. The technology of guerrilla warfare has made it evident that, while the state can win battles, it cannot win wars of values. Coercive force which is centered in the modern state cannot be sustained in the face of the active resistance of some 10 percent of its population unless the state is willing to embark on a deliberate policy of genocide directed against the value dissident groups. The factor that sustained the myth of coercive force in the past was the acceptance of a common value system. Whether the latter exists is questionable in the modern nation-state. But, even if most members of the nation-state remain united around a common value system which makes incommensurables for the majority commensurable, that majority is incapable of enforcing its decisions upon the minority in the face of the diminished coercive power of the governing body of the nation-state.

Erosion of the Myth of Administrators of the Commons

Hardin's thesis that the administrative arm of the state is capable of legislating temperance accords with current administrative theory in political science and touches on one of the concerns of that body of theory when he suggests that the ". . . great challenge facing us now is to invent the corrective feedbacks that are needed to keep the custodians honest."

Our best empirical answers to the question—*Quis custodiet ipsos custodes?*—"Who shall watch the watchers themselves?"—have shown fairly conclusively (9) that the decisions, orders, hearings, and press releases of the custodians of the commons, such as the Federal Communications Commission, the Interstate Commerce Commission, the Federal Trade Commission, and even the Bureau of Internal Revenue, give the large but unorganized groups in American society symbolic satisfaction and assurances. Yet, the actual day-to-day decisions and operations of these administrative agencies contribute, foster, aid, and indeed legitimate the special claims of small but highly organized groups to differential access to tangible resources which are extracted from the commons. This

has been so well documented in the social sciences that the best answer to the question of who watches over the custodians of the commons is the regulated interests that make incursions on the commons.

Indeed, the process has been so widely commented upon that one writer has postulated a common life cycle for all of the attempts to develop regulatory policies (10). This life cycle is launched by an outcry so widespread and demanding that it generates enough political force to bring about the establishment of a regulatory agency to insure the equitable, just, and rational distribution of the advantages among all holders of interest in the commons. This phase is followed by the symbolic reassurance of the offended as the agency goes into operation, developing a period of political quiescence among the great majority of those who hold a general but unorganized interest in the commons. Once this political quiescence has developed, the highly organized and specifically interested groups who wish to make incursions into the commons bring sufficient pressure to bear through other political processes to convert the agency to the protection and furthering of their interests. In the last phase even staffing of the regulating agency is accomplished by drawing the agency administrators from the ranks of the regulated.

Thus, it would seem that, even with the existence of a common value system accompanied by a viable myth of the monopoly of coercive force, the prospects are very dim for saving the commons from differential exploitation or spoliation by the administrative devices in which Hardin places his hope. This being the case, the natural sciences may absolve themselves of responsibility for meeting the environmental challenges of the contemporary world by relegating those problems for which there are no technical solutions to the political or social realm. This action will, however, make little contribution to the solution of the problem.

Are the Critical Problems of Modern Society Insoluble?

Earlier in this article I agreed that perhaps until very recently, there existed a set of conditions which made the solution of Hardin's problem subset possible; now I suggest that the concession is questionable. There is evidence of structural as well as value problems which make comprehensive solutions impossible and these conditions have been present for some time.

For example, Aaron Wildavsky, in a comprehensive study of the budgetary process, has found that in the absence of a calculus for resolving "intrapersonal comparison of utilities," the governmental budgetary process proceeds by a calculus that is sequential and incremental rather than comprehensive. This being the case ". . . if one looks at politics as a process by which the government mobilizes resources to meet pressing problems" (*11*) the budget is the focus of these problem responses and the responses to problems in contemporary America are not the sort of comprehensive responses required to bring order to a disordered environment. Another example of the operation of this type of rationality is the American involvement in Vietnam; for, what is the policy of escalation but the policy of sequential incrementalism given a new Madison Avenue euphemism? The question facing us all is the question of whether incremental rationality is sufficient to deal with 20th-century problems.

The operational requirements of modern institutions makes incremental rationality the only viable form of decision-making, but this only raises the prior question of whether there are solutions to any of the major problems raised in modern society. It may well be that the emerging forms of tribal behavior noted in this article are the last hope of reducing political and social institutions to a level where incommensurables become commensurable in terms of values *and* in terms of comprehensive responses to problems. After all, in the history of man on earth we might well assume that the departure from the tribal experience is a short-run deviant experiment that failed. As we stand "on the even of destruction," it may well be that the return to the face-to-face life in the small community unmediated by the electronic media is a very functional response in terms of the perpetuation of the species.

There is, I believe, a significant sense in which the human environment is directly in conflict with the source of man's ascendancy among the other species of the earth. Man's evolutionary position hinges, not on specialization, but rather on generalized adaptability. Modern social and political institutions, however, hinge on specialized, sequential, incremental decision-making and not on generalized adaptability. This being the case, life in the nation-state will continue to require a singleness of purpose for success but in a very critical sense this singleness of purpose becomes a straightjacket that makes generalized adaptation impossible. Nowhere is this conflict more evident than in our urban centers where there has been a decline in the livability of the total environment that is almost directly proportionate to the rise of special purpose districts. Nowhere is this conflict between institutional singleness of purpose and the human dimension of the modern environment more evident than in the recent warning of S. Goran Lofroth, chairman of a committee studying pesticides for the Swedish National Research Council, that many breast-fed children ingest from their mother's milk "more than the recommended daily intake of DDT" (*12*) and should perhaps be switched to cow's milk because cows secrete only 2 to 10 percent of the DDT they ingest.

How Can Science Contribute to the Saving of the Commons?

It would seem that, despite the nearly remorseless working of things, science has some interim contributions to make to the alleviation of those problems of the commons which Hardin has pointed out.

These contributions can come at two levels:

1) Science can concentrate more of its attention on the development of technological responses which at once alleviate those problems and reward those people who no longer desecrate the commons. This approach would seem more likely to be successful than the ". . . fundamental extension in morality . . ." by administrative law; the engagement of interest seems to be a more reliable and consistent motivator of advantage-seeking groups than does administrative wrist-slapping or constituency pressure from the general public.

2) Science can perhaps, by using the widely proposed environmental monitoring systems, use them in such a way as to sustain a high level of "symbolic disassurance" among the holders of generalized interests in the commons—thus sustaining their political interest to a point where they would provide a constituency for the administrator other than those bent on denuding the commons. This latter approach would seem to be a first step toward the ". . . invention of the corrective feedbacks that are needed to keep custodians honest." This would require a major change in the behavior of science, however, for it could no longer rest content with development of the technology of monitoring and with turning the technology over to some new agency. Past administrative experience suggests that the use of technology to sustain a high level of "disassurance" among the general population would also require science to take up the role and the responsibility for maintaining, controlling, and disseminating the information.

Neither of these contributions to maintaining a habitable environment will be made by science unless there is a significant break in the insularity of the two scientific tribes. For, if science must, in its own insularity, embark on the independent discovery of "the tragedy of the commons," along with the parameters that produce the tragedy, it may be too slow a process to save us from the total destruction of the planet. Just as important, however, science will, by pursuing such a course, divert its attention from the production of technical tools, information, and solutions which will contribute to the political and social solutions for the problems of the commons.

Because I remain very suspicious of the success of either demands or pleas for fundamental extensions in morality, I would suggest that such a conscious turning by both the social and the natural sciences is, at this time, in their immediate self-interest. As Michael Polanyi has pointed out, ". . . encircled today between the crude utilitarianism of the philistine and the ideological utilitarianism of the modern revolutionary movement, the love of pure science may falter and die" (*13*). The sciences, both social and natural, can function only in a very special intellectual environment that is neither universal or unchanging, and that environment is in jeopardy. The questions of humanistic relevance raised by the students at M.I.T., Stanford Research Institute, Berkeley, and wherever the headlines may carry us tomorrow, pose serious threats to the maintenance of that intellectual environment. However ill-founded *some* of the questions raised by the new generation may be, it behooves us to be ready with at least some collective, tentative answers—if only to maintain an environment in which both sciences will be allowed and fostered. This will not be accomplished so long as the social sciences continue to defer the most critical problems that face mankind to future technical advances, while the natural sciences continue to defer those same problems which are about to overwhelm all mankind to false expectations in the political realm.

REFERENCES AND NOTES

1. G. Hardin, *Science 162,* 1243 (1968).
2. J. B. Wiesner and H. F. York, *Sci. Amer. 211* (No. 4), 27 (1964).
3. C. Woodbury, *Amer. J. Public Health 45,* 1 (1955); S. Marquis, *Amer. Behav. Sci. 11,* 11 (1968); W. H. Ferry, *Center Mag. 2,* 2 (1969).
4. C. P. Snow, *The Two Cultures and the Scientific Revolution* (Cambridge Univ. Press, New York, 1959).
5. M. Olson, Jr., *The Logic of Collective Action* (Harvard Univ. Press, Cambridge, Mass., 1965).
6. G. A. Harrison *et al., Human Biology* (Oxford Univ. Press, New York, 1964), p. 292; W. W. Charters, Jr. in *School Children in the Urban Slum* (Free Press, New York, 1967).
7. S. Greer, *Governing the Metropolis* (Wiley, New York, 1962), p. 148.
8. W. F. Smith, "The Class Struggle and the Disquieted City," a paper presented at the 1969 annual meeting of the Western Economic Association, Oregon State University, Corvallis.
9. M. Bernstein, *Regulating Business by Independent Commissions* (Princeton Univ. Press, Princeton, N.J., 1955); E. P. Herring, *Public Administration and the Public Interest* (McGraw-Hill, New York, 1936); E. M. Redford, *Administration of National Economic Control* (Macmillan, New York, 1952).
10. M. Edelman, *The Symbolic Uses of Politics* (Univ. of Illinois Press, Urbana, 1964).
11. A. Wildavsky, *The Politics of the Budgetary Process* (Little Brown, Boston, Mass., 1964).
12. *Corvallis Gazette-Times,* 6 May 1969, p. 6.
13. M. Polanyi, *Personal Knowledge* (Harper & Row, New York, 1964), p. 182.

10.5
Control of Human Population Growth

David M. Prescott

One need not be a biologist, a demographer, or a specialist in some similar field to recognize the serious consequences created by the world's existing, excessive rate of human reproduction. Of deepest concern is the malnourishment and starvation on a massive scale that is the immediate effect of overpopulation. Unfortunately, most political leaders nearsightedly profess to see this problem exclusively as a shortage of food rather than an overabundance of births. Such superficial analysis and lack of understanding naturally place intense emphasis on the politically simple and *supposedly* humanistic solution that world food production and distribution must be enormously increased, with little more than token attention to the concomitant and more fundamental problem of birth control.

Malnourishment is not the only consequence of unregulated reproduction—for the affluent nations to allow their populations to expand to the maximum that resources can support must inevitably lead to a severe deterioration of the quality of living. In the United States the 100 million projected additions to the population over the next decades require, according to Undersecretary Train of the Department of Interior, that conservation must give way to development. Such projections and attitudes are ominous, yet we hear little more than a whisper of protest that the disadvantages of population growth in the United States certainly outweigh the supposed economic advantages.

At some point in the future, absolute restriction of the birth rate, hopefully through civilized planning, will become strict necessity. With the present lack of recognition on the part of virtually all of the world's inhabitants of the tragic consequences of over-reproduction and the present lack of any real sense of urgency among political leaders, no steps of much significance are likely to be taken in the United States or other nations before overpopulation becomes much more severe than it is at present.

In the achievement of population growth control, the least in-

fringement on individual freedom would result from some voluntary regulation such as advocated in family planning programs, although it is unlikely for a number of social and cultural reasons that voluntary programs will ever produce any significant results among any except the more highly educated people of this world. To depend, moreover, on the individual voluntary restraint on reproduction would be unjust in the face of *ad libidum* reproduction by the ignorant or uncooperative. Voluntary restriction of reproduction for other than reasons of individual self-interest is not likely to be much more successful than voluntary payment of income taxes. The institution of population control will probably evolve through economic pressures such as the abolishment of the income tax dependency allowance for children, followed by the introduction of other financial penalties. It seems inevitable that sterilization must be imposed on some equitable basis for reproduction control to be completely effective. The relinquishment of the right to reproduce at will represents the loss of a major individual freedom, but this is still small in comparison to the losses of individual freedom that will be forced on our descendants in a nation and world in which the population has been allowed to expand to a limit imposed only by material resources.

10.6
Population Policy for Americans: Is the Government Being Misled?

Judith Blake

Pressure on the federal government for "action" to limit population growth in the United States has intensified greatly during the past 10 years, and at present such action is virtually unchallenged as an official national goal. Given the goal, the question of means becomes crucial. Here I first evaluate the particular means being advocated and pursued in public policy, then I present alternative ways of possibly achieving the goal.

The prevailing view as to the best means is remarkably unanimous and abundantly documented. It is set forth in the 17 volumes of congressional hearings so far published on the "population crisis" (*1*); in "The Growth of U.S. Population," a report by the Committee on Population of the National Academy of Sciences (*2*); in a statement made by an officer of the Ford Foundation who was asked by the Department of Health, Education, and Welfare to make suggestions (*3*); and, finally, in the "Report of the President's Committee on Population and Family Planning," which was officially released this past January (*4*). The essential recommendation throughout is that the government should give highest priority to ghetto-oriented family-planning programs designed to "deliver" birth-control services to the poor and uneducated, among whom, it is claimed, there are at least 5 million women who are "in need" of such federally sponsored birth-control assistance.

By what logic have the proponents of control moved from a concern with population growth to a recommendation favoring highest priority for poverty-oriented birth-control programs? First, they have assumed that fertility is the only component of population growth worthy of government attention. Second, they have taken it for granted that, to reduce fertility, one sponsors birth-control programs ("family planning"). Just why they have made this assumption is not clear, but its logical implication is that population growth is due to births that couples would have preferred to avoid. Furthermore, the reasoning confuses couple control over births with societal control over them (*5*). Third, the proponents of the new policy have seized on the poor and uneducated as the "target" group, for birth-control action because they see this group as the only remaining target for a program of voluntary family planning. The rest of the population is handling its family planning pretty well on its own: over 95 percent of fecund U.S. couples already either use birth-control methods or intend to do so. The poor, on the other hand—at least those who are fecund—have larger families than the advantaged; they not only use birth-control methods less but they use them less effectively. The family-

planning movement's notion of "responsible parenthood" carries the implication that family size should be directly, not inversely, related to social and economic advantage, and the poor are seen as constituting the residual slack to be taken up by the movement's efforts. Why are the poor not conforming to the dictates of responsible parenthood? Given the movement's basic assumptions, there are only two answers: the poor are irresponsible, or they have not had the opportunity. Since present-day leaders would abhor labeling the poor irresponsible, they have chosen to blame lack of opportunity as the cause. Opportunity has been lacking, in their eyes, either because the poor have not been "educated" in family planning or because they have not been "reached" by family-planning services. In either case, as they see it, the poor have been deprived of their "rights" (*2*, p. 22; *6*). This deprivation has allegedly been due to the prudery and hypocrisy of the affluent, who have overtly tabooed discussion of birth control and dissemination of birth-control materials while, themselves, covertly enjoying the benefits of family planning (*7*).

So much for the logic underlying recent proposals for controlling population growth in the United States. But what is the evidence on which this argument is based? On what empirical grounds is the government being asked to embark on a high-priority program of providing contraceptive services to the poor? Moreover, what, if any, are some of the important public issues that the suggested policy raises—what are its social and political side effects? And, finally, is such a policy, even if appropriate for the poor and even if relatively unencumbered by public disapproval, relevant to the problem of population growth in America? If demographic curtailment is really the objective, must alternative policies be considered and possibly given highest priority?

Turning to the alleged need for government-sponsored birth-control services, one may ask whether birth control has in fact been a tabooed topic among the middle and upper classes, so that the less advantaged could be said to have suffered "deprivation" and consequently now to require government help. One may then question whether there is a mandate from the poor for the type of federally sponsored service that is now being urged, and whether as many

as 5 million women are "in need" of such family-planning assistance.

Has Birth Control Been a Tabooed Topic?

The notion that the American public has only recently become willing to tolerate open discussion of birth control has been assiduously cultivated by congressmen and others concerned with government policy on population. For example, Senator Tydings credited Senators Gruening and Clark and President Johnson with having almost single-handedly changed American public attitudes toward birth control. In 1966 he read the following statement into the 28 February *Congressional Record* (*8*).

The time is ripe for positive action. Ten years ago, even five years ago, this was a politically delicate subject. Today the Nation has awakened to the need for Government action.

This change in public attitude has come about through the efforts of men who had the courage to brook the tides of public opinion. Senator Clark is such a man. Senator Gruening is such a man. So is President Johnson. Because of their leadership it is no longer necessary for an elected official to speak with trepidation on this subject.

A year later, Senator Tydings reduced his estimate of the time required for the shift in public opinion to "3 or 4 years" (*9*, p. 12; *10*). Senator Gruening maintained (*11*) that the "ninety-eight distinguished men and women" who testified at the public hearing on S. 1676 were "pioneers" whose "names comprise an important honor roll which historically bears an analogy to other famous lists: the signers of the Declaration of Independence, those who ratified the Constitution of the United States and others whose names were appended to and made possible some of the great turning points in history." Reasoning from the continued existence of old, and typically unenforced, laws concerning birth control (together with President Eisenhower's famous anti-birth-control statement), Stycos, in a recent article (*12*), stated:

The public reaction to family planning in the United States has varied between disgust and silent resignation to a necessary evil. At best it was viewed as so delicate and risky that it was a matter of "individual conscience." As such, it was a matter so totally private, so sacred (or profane), that no external agents, and certainly not the state, should have anything to do with it.

Does the evidence support such impressionistic claims? How did the general public regard government sponsorship of birth control long before it became a subject of congressional hearings, a National Academy report, and a Presidential Committee report? Fortunately, a question on this topic appeared in no less than 13 national polls and surveys conducted between 1937 and 1966. As part of a larger project concerned with public knowledge and opinions about demographic topics, I have gathered together the original data cards from these polls, prepared them for computer processing, and analyzed the results. The data are all from Gallup polls and are all from national samples of the white, adult population. Here I concentrate on adults under 45—that is, on adults in the childbearing age group.

TABLE 1. PERCENTAGES OF WHITE U.S. MEN AND WOMEN BETWEEN THE AGES OF 21 AND 44 WHO, IN VARIOUS NATIONAL POLLS AND SURVEYS MADE BETWEEN 1937 AND 1964,[a] EXPRESSED THE OPINION THAT BIRTH-CONTROL INFORMATION SHOULD BE MADE AVAILABLE TO INDIVIDUALS WHO DESIRED IT.

	MEN		WOMEN	
YEAR	%	N	%	N
1937	66	1038	70	743
1938	67	1111	72	548
1939	74	1101	73	630
1940	72	1127	75	618
1943	67	628	73	866
1945	64	714	70	879
1947	76	353	75	405
1959	78	301	79	394
1961	82	336	81	394
1962	85	288	80	381
1963	78	323	79	373
1964	89	324	86	410

[a] The questions asked of respondents concerning birth control were as follows. In 1937: Do you favor the birth control movement? In 1938, 1939, 1940, 1943, 1945, and 1947: Would you like to see a government agency (or "government health clinics") furnish birth-control information to married people who want it? In 1959, 1961, 1962, and 1963: In some places in the United States it is not legal to supply birth-control information. How do you feel about this—do you think birth-control information should be available to anyone who wants it, or not? In 1964: Do you think birth-control information should be available to anyone who wants it, or not?

The data of Table 1 contradict the notion that Americans have only recently ceased to regard birth control as a tabooed topic. As far back as 30 years ago, almost three-quarters of the women questioned in these surveys actively approved having the *government* make birth-control information available to the married. By the early 1960's, 80 percent or more

of women approved overcoming legal barriers and allowing "anyone who wants it" to have birth-control information. The figures for men are similar. The question asked in 1964—the one question in recent years that did not mention illegality—brought 86 percent of the women and 89 percent of the men into the category of those who approved availability of birth-control information for "anyone who wants it." Furthermore, in judging the level of disapproval, one should bear in mind that the remainder of the respondents, in all of these years, includes from 7 to 15 percent who claim that they have "no opinion" on the subject, not that they "disapprove."

An important difference of opinion corresponds to a difference in religious affiliation. Among non-Catholics (including those who have "no religion" and do not attend church) approval has been considerably higher than it has been among Catholics. Among non-Catholic women, over 80 percent approved as early as 1939, and among non-Catholic men the percentages were approximately the same. The 1964 poll showed that 90 percent of each sex approved. Among Catholics, in recent years about 60 percent have approved, and, in 1964, the question that mentioned neither the government nor legality brought opinions of approval from 77 percent of the women and 83 percent of the men.

Clearly, if birth-control information has in fact been unavailable to the poor, the cause has not been a generalized and pervasive attitude of prudery on the part of the American public. Although public officials may have misjudged American opinion (and may have mistakenly assumed that the Catholic Church "spoke for" a majority of Americans, or even for a majority of Catholics), most Americans of an age to be having children did not regard birth control as a subject that should be under a blanket of secrecy and, as far back as the 1930's, evinced a marked willingness to have their government make such information widely available. It seems unlikely, therefore, that poorer sectors of our population were "cut off" from birth-control knowledge primarily because informal channels of communication (the channels through which most people learn about birth control) were blocked by an upper- and middle-class conspiracy of silence.

What has happened, however, is that pressure groups for family

planning, like the Catholic hierarchy they have been opposing, have been acting as self-designated spokesmen for "public opinion." By developing a cause as righteous as that of the Catholics (the "rights" of the poor as against the "rights" of a religious group), the family planners have used the American way of influencing official opinion. Now public officials appear to believe that publicly supported birth-control services are what the poor have always wanted and needed, just as, in the past, official opinion acceded to the notion that such services would have been "offensive" to certain groups. Nonetheless, the question remains of whether or not publicly supported services are actually appropriate to the attitudes and objectives of the poor and uneducated in matters of reproduction. Is the government responding to a mandate from the poor or to an ill-concealed mandate from the well-to-do? If there is no mandate from the poor, the provision of birth-control services may prove a convenience for certain women but is likely to have little effect on the reproductive performance of the poor in general. Let us look at the evidence.

Is There a Mandate from the Poor?

The notion that the poor have larger families than the affluent only because they have less access to birth-control information implies that the poor *desire* families as small as, or smaller than, those of the well-to-do. The poor are simply unable to realize this desire, the argument goes, because of lack of access to birth-control information. The National Academy of Sciences Committee on Population stated the argument very well (2, p. 10).

The available evidence indicates that low-income families do not want more children than do families with higher incomes, but they have more because they do not have the information or the resources to plan their families effectively according to their own desires.

The committee, however, presents none of the "available evidence" that "low-income families do not want more children than do families with higher incomes." Actually, my data supply evidence that runs counter to the statement quoted above, both with respect to the desired or ideal number of children and with respect to attitudes toward birth control.

I shall begin with the preferred size of family. A number of national polls, conducted over some 25 years, provide data concerning opinions on ideal family size. In addition, I include tabulations of data from two national surveys on fertility (the "Growth of American Families Studies"), conducted in 1955 and 1960 (13, 14). My detailed analyses of the results of these polls and surveys are given elsewhere (15) and are only briefly summarized here. Table 2 gives mean values for the family

the percentages of white men and women who expressed approval of birth control in surveys made between 1937 and 1964, by educational level and economic status, respectively.

Looking at the educational differential (Table 3), one finds that, in general, the proportion of those who approve birth control drops precipitately between the college and grade school levels. As far back as the early 1940's, over 80 percent of women and 75 percent of men with some or more

finds the same results. The high proportions (close to 100 percent) of women in the highest and next-to-highest economic brackets who, in recent years, have approved birth-control efforts is noteworthy, as is the fact that approximately 80 percent of women in these brackets approved such efforts as far back as the 1930's. On the other hand, men and women in lower income brackets have been slower to approve birth-control policies.

Despite the inverse relationship just described, I may have over-emphasized the lesser approval of birth-control programs on the part of persons of lower economic and social status. After all, in recent years approval often has been high even among people at the lowest social levels. Among women with only a grade school education, the percentage of those favoring birth-control programs averaged 73 percent in polls taken between 1959 and 1964; among men at the lowest educational level, the corresponding average was 66 percent. Yet it is undeniably true that, throughout the period for which data are available, the people who needed birth control information most, according to recent policy pronouncements, have been precisely the ones who were least in favor of a policy that would make it widely available.

The truth of this conclusion becomes more evident when we move to an analysis of a question asked on the 1966 Gallup poll: Do you think birth-control pills should be made available free to all women on relief who are of childbearing age? This question presents the public with the specific issue that is the focus of current policy—namely, birth control especially for the poor. A summary of the replies to this question is given in Table 5, together

TABLE 2. MEAN NUMBER OF CHILDREN CONSIDERED IDEAL BY NON-CATHOLIC WOMEN, ACCORDING TO EDUCATION AND ECONOMIC STATUS FOR SELECTED YEARS BETWEEN 1943 AND 1968.

| DATE | AGE RANGE | LEVEL OF EDUCATION[a] | | | INCOME OR ECONOMIC STATUS[b] | | | | TOTAL RESPONDENTS | |
		COLLEGE	HIGH SCHOOL	GRADE SCHOOL	1	2	3	4	X̄	N
1943	20–34	2.8	2.6	2.6	2.9	2.7	2.7	2.5	2.7	1893
1952	21+	3.3	3.1	3.6		3.3	3.3	3.3	3.3	723
1955[c]	18–39	3.1	3.2	3.7	3.2	3.1	3.2	3.5	3.3	1905
1955[d]	18–39	3.3	3.4	3.9	3.4	3.3	3.4	3.7	3.4	1905
1957	21+	3.4	3.2	3.6		3.3	3.2	3.5	3.3	448
1959	21+	3.5	3.4	3.9		3.5	3.5	3.6	3.5	472
1960[c]	18–39	3.1	3.2	3.5	3.1	3.2	3.3	3.2	3.2	1728
1960[d]	18–39	3.2	3.4	3.6	3.2	3.3	3.5	3.4	3.4	1728
1963	21+	3.2	3.4	3.5	3.3	3.3	3.5	3.5	3.4	483
1966	21+	3.1	3.3	3.7	3.2	3.2	3.4	3.7	3.3	374
1967	21+	3.1	3.3	3.4	3.3	3.2	3.1	3.4	3.3	488
1968	21+	3.2	3.3	3.7	3.2	3.0	3.4	3.6	3.3	530

[a] Level of education is measured by the highest grade completed.
[b] Levels 1 to 4 for economic status range in order from "high" to "low."
[c] Minimum ideal (results from coding range answers to the lowest figure).
[d] Maximum ideal (results from coding range answers to the highest figure).

size considered ideal by white, non-Catholic women, according to education and economic status.

The data lend little support to the hypothesis that the poor desire families as small as those desired by the middle and upper classes. Within both the educational and the economic categories, those on the lower rungs not only have larger families than those on the higher rungs (at least in the case of non-Catholics) but say they want larger families and consider them ideal. This differential has existed for as long as information on preferred family size in this country has been available, and it persists. It thus seems extremely hazardous to base a major governmental effort on the notion that, among individuals (white individuals, at least) at the lower social levels, there is a widespread and deeply held desire for families as small as, or smaller than, those desired by the well-to-do. No major survey shows this to be the case.

Not only do persons of lower socioeconomic status prefer larger families than the more affluent do, they also generally favor birth control less. Tables 3 and 4 show

college education approved government action on birth control. By 1964, over 90 percent of both sexes approved. By contrast, only 60 percent of men and women with an elementary school education approved in the 1940's, and, despite a rise in approval, there is still a differential. When non-Catholics alone are considered, the educational difference is even more pronounced in many cases.

Turning to economic or income status (Table 4), one generally

TABLE 3. PERCENTAGES OF WHITE U.S. MEN AND WOMEN BETWEEN THE AGES OF 21 AND 44 WHO, IN VARIOUS NATIONAL POLLS TAKEN BETWEEN 1943 AND 1964, EXPRESSED THE OPINION THAT BIRTH-CONTROL INFORMATION SHOULD BE MADE AVAILABLE TO INDIVIDUALS WHO DESIRED IT. THE PERCENTAGES ARE GIVEN BY LEVEL OF EDUCATION[a]; THE NUMBERS IN PARENTHESES ARE TOTAL NUMBERS OF RESPONDENTS IN EACH CATEGORY.

| YEAR | MEN | | | WOMEN | | |
	COLLEGE	HIGH SCHOOL	GRADE SCHOOL	COLLEGE	HIGH SCHOOL	GRADE SCHOOL
1943	75 (184)	68 (284)	56 (157)	82 (216)	74 (442)	60 (207)
1945	74 (202)	62 (360)	58 (140)	83 (216)	68 (434)	56 (207)
1947	91 (84)	72 (199)	67 (66)	81 (89)	74 (228)	72 (81)
1959	88 (89)	76 (163)	65 (49)	91 (55)	79 (279)	68 (41)
1961	88 (102)	81 (188)	67 (46)	84 (81)	81 (265)	78 (50)
1962	91 (93)	85 (171)	61 (23)	84 (79)	82 (258)	66 (44)
1963	86 (105)	79 (178)	53 (40)	81 (80)	78 (251)	81 (42)
1964	92 (107)	88 (188)	83 (29)	94 (79)	86 (293)	74 (38)

[a] The level of education is measured by the last grade completed.

TABLE 4. PERCENTAGES OF WHITE U.S. MEN AND WOMEN BETWEEN THE AGES OF 21 AND 44 WHO, IN VARIOUS NATIONAL POLLS TAKEN BETWEEN 1937 AND 1964, EXPRESSED THE OPINION THAT BIRTH-CONTROL INFORMATION SHOULD BE MADE AVAILABLE TO INDIVIDUALS WHO DESIRED IT. THE PERCENTAGES ARE GIVEN BY ECONOMIC STATUS (LEVELS 1–4[a]); THE NUMBERS IN PARENTHESES ARE TOTAL NUMBERS OF RESPONDENTS IN EACH CATEGORY.

YEAR	MEN				WOMEN			
	1	2	3	4	1	2	3	4
1937	78 (112)	70 (406)	61 (520)		67 (69)	78 (293)	64 (372)	
1938	65 (125)	74 (453)	62 (521)		80 (51)	73 (232)	70 (259)	
1939	78 (116)	75 (432)	73 (553)		71 (68)	77 (260)	71 (302)	
1940	79 (131)	75 (443)	68 (553)		80 (49)	78 (258)	71 (311)	
1943	76 (80)	72 (219)	62 (330)		80 (90)	79 (272)	68 (500)	
1945	73 (67)	66 (286)	62 (352)		83 (75)	77 (264)	64 (531)	
1947	86 (42)	77 (123)	72 (188)		92 (38)	71 (119)	73 (237)	
1959	83 (101)	76 (120)	73 (79)		83 (139)	82 (152)	72 (95)	
1961	93 (42)	85 (80)	87 (103)	69 (111)	88 (41)	80 (97)	80 (76)	81 (138)
1962	82 (45)	89 (71)	86 (94)	80 (74)	82 (51)	80 (75)	84 (110)	77 (140)
1963	88 (60)	84 (79)	76 (96)	61 (97)	87 (67)	79 (107)	79 (98)	75 (100)
1964	90 (67)	87 (26)	93 (82)	85 (79)	96 (90)	90 (87)	85 (104)	78 (120)

[a] Levels 1 to 4 for the years 1961–64 range from income of $10,000 and over down to incomes under $5000. Prior to 1961, levels 1 to 3 represent "upper," "middle," and "lower" income brackets.

with average percentages of people who, in the five surveys made between 1959 and 1964, replied that they approved birth control generally.

It is clear that the overall level of approval drops when specific reference to a poverty-oriented birth-control policy is introduced. The decline is from an average of approximately 80 percent for each sex during the period 1959–64 to 65 percent for men and 71 percent for women in 1966. Of most significance, however, is the fact that the largest proportionate drop in approval occurs among members of the "target" groups themselves—the poor and uneducated. In particular, there is a remarkable drop in approval among men at this socioeconomic level. There is a 42-percent decline in approval among men who have had only a grade school education and a 29-percent drop among those with a high school education. Among the college-educated men the drop in approval is only 6 percent. The results, by income, parallel those by education: there is a 47-percent drop for men in the lowest income group but only a 9-percent drop for those in the highest income bracket. Even if the tabulations are restricted to non-Catholics (data that are not presented here), the results are essentially the same.

If the ghetto-oriented birth-control policy urged on the federal government meets with limited public enthusiasm, how does the public view extension of that policy to teen-age girls? This question is of some importance because a notable aspect of the pressure for government-sponsored family-planning programs is advocacy of making birth-control information and materials available at the high school level.

The Committee on Population of the National Academy of Sciences urges early education in "family planning" in order to prevent illegitimacy (2, p. 13).

. . . government statistics show that the mothers of approximately 41 per cent of the 245,000 babies born illegitimately in the United States every year are women 19 years of age or younger. Thus a large proportion of all illegitimate children are progeny of teen-age mothers. To reduce the number of such children born to teen-age mothers, high-school education in family planning is essential.

Katherine B. Oettinger, Deputy Secretary for Family Planning of the Department of Health, Education, and Welfare, importunes us not to "demand the eligibility card of a first pregnancy before we admit vulnerable girls to family planning services" (16). The Harkavy report states (3, p. 29):

Eligibility requirements should be liberal with respect to marital status. Such services should be made avail-

able to the unmarried as well as the married. . . . Eligibility requirements should be liberal with respect to the age of unmarried women seeking help. This will undoubtedly pose some problems, but they may not be insurmountable. Some publicly supported programs are already facing them (for example, in Baltimore).

Representative Scheuer from New York has berated the federal government for not "bringing family planning into the schools." He has cited the "desperate need for family planning by unmarried 14-, 15-, and 16-year-old girls in school [which] is so transparently evident that it almost boggles the imagination to realize that nothing has been done. Virtually no leadership has come from the federal government" (9, p. 18).

Obviously there is little recognition in these statements that such a policy might engender a negative public response. Yet such a possibility cannot be discounted. The results of the 1966 question "Do you think they [the pills] should be made available to teen-

TABLE 5. PERCENTAGES OF WHITE U.S. MEN AND WOMEN BETWEEN THE AGES OF 21 AND 44 WHO, IN A 1966 POLL, EXPRESSED APPROVAL OF FREE DISTRIBUTION OF BIRTH-CONTROL PILLS FOR WOMEN ON RELIEF, AND AVERAGE PERCENTAGES OF INDIVIDUALS IN THIS AGE GROUP WHO, IN POLLS TAKEN BETWEEN 1959 AND 1964, EXPRESSED APPROVAL OF BIRTH CONTROL. PERCENTAGES APPROVING AND NUMBERS OF INDIVIDUALS INTERVIEWED ARE GIVEN AS TOTALS AND ALSO BY EDUCATION AND ECONOMIC STATUS OF THE RESPONDENTS.

ITEM	MEN			WOMEN		
	1966		1959–64	1966		1959–64
	%	N	(AV. %)	%	N	(AV. %)
Total	65	264	82	71	385	81
Education						
College	82	98	87	75	197	87
High school	58	142	82	70	392	81
Grade school	38	24	66	59	32	73
Economic status						
1	79	80	89	70	110	87
2	69	75	84	76	99	82
3	59	65	83	70	91	80
4	39	41	74	67	76	78

TABLE 6. PERCENTAGES OF WHITE U.S. MEN AND WOMEN WHO, IN A 1966 POLL, EXPRESSED APPROVAL OF MAKING BIRTH-CONTROL PILLS AVAILABLE TO TEEN-AGE GIRLS. PERCENTAGES APPROVING AND NUMBERS OF INDIVIDUALS INTERVIEWED ARE GIVEN BY AGE GROUP, BY EDUCATION, AND BY ECONOMIC STATUS.

| | ALL RELIGIONS | | | | NON-CATHOLICS | | | |
| | MEN | | WOMEN | | MEN | | WOMEN | |
ITEM	%	N	%	N	%	N	%	N
Age								
Under 30	29	86	17	149	34	65	19	102
30–44	19	172	8	238	20	133	7	169
Education								
College	32	98	15	100	36	75	13	71
High school	18	142	9	264	19	110	9	180
Grade school	13	24	11	35	6	17	14	28
Economic status								
1	33	80	11	113	35	58	11	75
2	20	75	13	105	24	58	14	72
3	19	65	7	94	18	50	5	64
4	13	41	16	82	15	33	14	66

age girls?" suggest that a policy of pill distribution to female adolescents may be viewed by the public as involving more complex issues than the mere democratization of "medical" services. These results, tabulated by social level, are shown in Table 6.

It may be seen that, in general, a proposal for distribution of pills to teen-age girls meets with very little approval. There is more disapproval among women than among men. Even among women under the age of 30, only 17 percent approve; among men in this age group, 29 percent approve. At no age does feminine approval reach 20 percent, and in most cases it is below 15 percent. Furthermore, restriction of the results to non-Catholics does not raise the percentages of those who approve the policy. Most noteworthy is the socioeconomic gradient among men. Whereas 32 percent of college-educated men approve distribution of pills to young grils, only 13 percent of men with a grade school education do. Thirty-three percent of men in the highest income bracket approve, but only 13 percent in the lowest bracket do.

Clearly, the extension of "family planning" to poor, unmarried teen-agers is not regarded simply as "health care." Individuals may approve, in a general way, a wider availability of birth-control information without approving federal expenditure to facilitate a high level of sexual activity by teen-age girls. One suspects that explicit recognition and implied approval of such activity still comes hard to our population, and that it comes hardest to the group most involved in the problems of illegitimacy and premarital conception—namely, the poor and uneducated themselves. The extreme disap-

proval of a policy of pill distribution to teen-age girls that is found in lower-class groups (particularly among lower-class men) suggests that a double standard of sexual behavior is operative in these groups—a standard that does not allow open toleration of the idea that the ordinary teen-age girl requires the pill, or that a part of her junior high school and high school education should include instruction in its use.

Can "Five Million Women" Be Wrong?

The most widely publicized argument favoring federal birth-control programs, and apparently the one that elected officials find most persuasive, is the claim that there are approximately "five million" poor women "in need" of publicly subsidized birth-control help (17). I list below some of the principal assumptions upon which this estimate is based—all of which introduce serious upward biases into the evidence.

1) It is claimed that women at the poverty and near-poverty levels desire families of 3.0 children. While this may be true of nonwhite wives at this economic level, it is not true, as we have seen, of white women, who comprise a major share of the "target" group and who, on the average, desire a number of children closer to 4 (especially if Catholics are included, as they are in the "five million").

2) It is assumed by the estimators that 82 percent of all poor women aged 15 to 44 are at risk of conception (that is, exposed sexually), in spite of the fact that only 45 percent of poor women in this age group are married and living with their husbands. In arriving at

the figure of 82 percent, the estimators assumed that all women in the "married" category (including those who were separated from their husbands and those whose husbands were absent) were sexually exposed regularly, and that half of the women in the "nonmarried" category—that is, single, widowed, and divorced women—were exposed regularly. Information is scarce concerning the sexual behavior of widows and divorced women, but Kinsey's data on premarital coitus leads one to believe that the assumption of 50 percent for single women may be high. Among the women with a grade school education in Kinsey's sample, 38 percent had had coitus at some time between the ages of 16 and 20, and 26 percent, at some time between the ages of 21 and 25. Moreover, as Kinsey emphasizes, these encounters were characteristically sporadic (18).

3) The proportion of sterile women among the poor is assumed to be 13 percent, although the Scripps 1960 "Growth of American Families Study" showed the proportion among white women of grade school education to be 22 percent (14, p. 159).

4) No allowance is made for less-than-normal fecundity, although the Scripps 1960 study (14, p. 159) had indicated that, among women of grade school education, an additional 10 percent (over and above the 22 percent) were subnormal in their ability to reproduce.

5) It is taken for granted by the estimators that no Catholic women would object, on religious grounds, to the use of modern methods, and no allowance is made for objection by non-Catholics, on religious or other grounds. In other words, it is assumed that all women "want" the service. Yet, in response to a question concerning the desirability of limiting or spacing pregnancies, 29 percent of the wives with grade school education who were interviewed in the Scripps 1960 study said they were "against" such limitation or spacing (14, p. 177). Among the Catholic wives with grade school education, the proportion "against" was 48 percent, although half of these objectors were "for" such the rhythm method. Similar objections among the disadvantaged have been revealed by many polls over a long period.

6) Perhaps most important, the estimate of 5 million women "wanting" and "in need of" birth control information includes not only objectors but women who are

already practicing birth control. Hence, in addition to all the other biases, the estimate represents a blanket decision by the estimators that the women require medical attention regarding birth control —particularly that they need the pill and the coil. In the words of the Harkavy report (2, attachment A, p. 19):

This may be considered a high estimate of the number of women who need to have family planning services made available to them in public clinics, because some of the couples among the poor and near poor are able to exercise satisfactory control over their fertility. However, even these couples do not have the same access as the non-poor to the more effective and acceptable methods of contraception, particularly the pill and the loop. So, simply in order to equalize the access of the poor and the near-poor to modern methods of contraception under medical supervision, it is appropriate to try to make contraceptive services available to all who may need and want them.

Yet the 1960 Scripps study found that, among fecund women of grade school education, 79 percent used contraceptives (14, p. 159). The 21 percent who did not included young women who were building families and said they wanted to get pregnant, as well as Catholics who objected to birth control on religious grounds. As for the methods that women currently are using, it seems gratuitous for the federal government to decide that only medically supervised methods—the pill and the coil—are suitable for lower-income couples, and that a mammoth "service" program is therefore required. In fact, the implications of such a decision border on the fantastic—the implications that we should substitute scarce medical and paramedical attention for all contraceptive methods now being used by poor couples.

In sum, the argument supporting a "need" for nationwide, publicly sustained birth-control programs does not stand up under empirical scrutiny. Most fecund lower-class couples now use birth-control methods when they want to prevent pregnancy; in the case of those who do not, the blame cannot simply be laid at the door of the affluent who have kept the subject of birth control under wraps, or of a government that has withheld services. As we have seen, opinion on birth control has been, and is, less favorable among the poor and the less well educated than among the well-to-do. In addition, the poor desire larger

families. Although it may be argued that, at the public welfare level, birth control has, until recently, been taboo because of the "Catholic vote," most individuals at all social levels have learned about birth control *informally* and without medical attention. Furthermore, the most popular birth-control device, the condom, has long been as available as aspirin or cigarettes, and certainly has been used by men of all social classes. When one bears in mind the fact that the poor have no difficulty in gaining access to illegal narcotics (despite their obvious "unavailability"), and that the affluent had drastically reduced their fertility before present-day contraceptive methods were available, one must recognize and take into account a motivational component in nonuse and inefficient use of contraceptives. Indeed, were relative lack of demand on the part of the poor not a principal factor, it would be difficult to explain why such an important "market" for birth-control materials—legal or illegal—would have escaped the attention of enterprising businessmen or bootleggers. In any event, any estimate based on the assumption that all poor women in the reproductive group "want" birth-control information and materials and that virtually all "need" publicly supported services that will provide them—including women with impaired fecundity, women who have sexual intercourse rarely or not at all, women who object on religious grounds, and women who are already using birth-control methods —would seem to be seriously misleading as a guide for our government in its efforts to control population growth.

Moreover, the proposal for government sponsorship takes no account of the possible advantages of alternative means of reaching that part of the "market" that may not be optimally served at present. For example, competitive pricing, better marketing, and a program of advertising could make it possible for many groups in the population who are now being counted as "targets" for government efforts to purchase contraceptives of various kinds. When one bears in mind the fact that an important reason for nonuse or lack of access to contraceptives may be some sort of conflict situation (between husband and wife, adolescent child and parent, and so on), it becomes apparent that the impersonal and responsive marketplace is a far better agency for

effecting smooth social change than is a far-flung national bureaucracy loaded with well-meaning but often blundering "health workers." The government could doubtless play an initial stimulating and facilitating role in relation to private industry, without duplicating, on a welfare basis, functions that might be more efficiently handled in the marketplace.

Would the Policy Have Side Effects?

The possible inadvisability of having the government become a direct purveyor of birth-control materials to poverty groups becomes more clear when we consider some of the risks involved in such a course of action.

Even if the goal of reducing family size were completely and widely accepted by the poorer and less educated sectors of the population, we should not assume that the general public would necessarily view a policy concerned with the means and practice of birth control (in any social group) as it views ordinary medical care—that is, as being morally neutral and obviously "desirable." Birth control is related to sexual behavior, and, in all viable societies, sexual behavior is regulated by social institutions. It is thus an oversimplification to think that people will be unmindful of what are, for them at least, the moral implications of changes in the conditions under which sexual intercourse is possible, permissible, or likely. An issue such as distribution of pills to teen-age girls runs a collision course with norms about premarital relations for young girls—norms that, in turn, relate to the saliency of marriage and motherhood as a woman's principal career and to the consequent need for socially created restrictions on free sexual access if an important inducement to marriage is not to be lost. Only if viable careers alternative to marriage existed for women would the lessening of controls over sexual behavior outside of marriage be unrelated to women's lifetime opportunities, for such opportunities would be independent of the marriage market and, a fortiori, independent of sexual bargaining. But such independence clearly does not exist. Hence, when the government is told that it will be resolving a "medical" problem if it makes birth-control pills available to teen-agers, it is being misled into becoming the protagonist in a sociologically based conflict between short-run feminine impulses and long-run feminine interests—a conflict that is expressed both in relations between parents and children and in relations between the sexes. This sociological conflict far transcends the "medical" issue of whether or not birth-control services should be made widely available.

Actually, the issue of sexual morality is only one among many potentially explosive aspects of direct federal involvement in family-planning programs for the poor. Others come readily to mind, such as the possibility that the pill and other physiological methods could have long-run, serious side effects, or that racial organizations could seize on the existence of these programs as a prime example of "genocide." Eager promoters of the suggested programs tend to brush such problems aside as trivial, but the problems, like the issue of sexual morality, cannot be wished away, for they are quite patently there (9, p. 62). There *are* risks involved in all drug-taking, and it is recognized that many of the specific ones involved in long-term ingestion of the pill may not be discovered for many years. No one today can say that these are less than, equal to, or greater than the normal risks of pregnancy and childbirth. Equally, a class-directed birth-control program, whatever its intent, is open to charges of genocide that are difficult to refute. Such a program cannot fail to appear to single out the disadvantaged as the "goat," all the while implying that the very considerable "planned" fertility of most Americans inexplicably requires no government attention at all.

Population Policy for Americans

It seems clear that the suggested policy of poverty-oriented birth-control programs does not make sense as a welfare measure. It is also true that, as an inhibitor of population growth, it is inconsequential and trivial. It does not touch the principal cause of such growth in the United States—namely, the reproductive behavior of the majority of Americans who, under present conditions, want families of more than three children and thereby generate a growth rate far in excess of that required for population stability. Indeed, for most Americans the "family planning" approach, concentrating as it does on the distribution of contraceptive materials

and services, is irrelevant, because they already know about efficient contraception and are already "planning" their families. It is thus apparent that any policy designed to influence reproductive behavior must not only concern itself with all fecund Americans (rather than just the poor) but must, as well, relate to family-size goals (rather than just to contraceptive means). In addition, such a policy cannot be limited to matters affecting contraception (or even to matters affecting gestation and parturition, such as abortion), but must, additionally, take into account influences on the formation and dissolution of heterosexual unions (19).

What kinds of reproductive policies can be pursued in an effort to reduce long-term population growth? The most important step toward developing such new policies is to recognize and understand the existing ones, for we already have influential and coercive policies regarding reproductive behavior. Furthermore, these existing policies relate not merely to proscriptions (legal or informal) regarding certain means of birth control (like abortion) but also to a definition of reproduction as a primary societal end and to an organization of social roles that draws most of the population into reproductive unions.

The existence of such pronatalist policies becomes apparent when we recall that, among human beings, population replacement would not occur at all were it not for the complex social organization and system of incentives that encourage mating, pregnancy, and the care, support, and rearing of children. These institutional mechanisms are the pronatalist "policies" evolved unconsciously over millennia to give societies a fertility sufficient to offset high mortality. The formation and implementation of antinatalist policies must be based, therefore, on an analysis and modification of the existing pronatalist policies. It follows, as well, that antinatalist policies will not necessarily involve the introduction of coercive measures. In fact, just the opposite is the case. Many of these new policies will entail a *lifting* of pressures *to* reproduce, rather than an *imposition* of pressures *not* to do so. In order to understand this point let us consider briefly our present-day pronatalism.

It is convenient to start with the family, because pronatalism finds its most obvious expression in this

social institution. The pronatalism of the family has many manifestations, but among the most influential and universal are two: the standardization of both the male and the female sexual roles in terms of reproductive functions, obligations, and activities, and the standardization of the occupational role of women—half of the population—in terms of childbearing, child-rearing, and complementary activities. These two "policies" insure that just about everyone will be propelled into reproductive unions, and that half of the population will enter such unions as a "career"—a life's work. Each of the two "policies" is worth considering.

With regard to sex roles, it is generally recognized that potential human variability is greater than is normally permitted *within* each sex category. Existing societies have tended to suppress and extinguish such variability and to standardize sexual roles in the ways that imply that all "normal" persons will attain the status of parents. This coercion takes many forms, including one-sided indoctrination in schools, legal barriers and penalties for deviation, and the threats of loneliness, ostracism, and ridicule that are implied in the unavailability of alternatives. Individuals who—by temperament, health, or constitution—do not fit the ideal sex-role pattern are nonetheless coerced into attempting to achieve it, and many of them do achieve it, at least to the extent of having demographic impact by becoming parents.

Therefore, a policy that sought out the ways in which coercion regarding sex roles is at present manifesting itself could find numerous avenues for relieving the coercion and for allowing life styles different from marriage and parenthood to find free and legitimated expression. Such a policy would have an effect on the content of expectations regarding sex roles as presented and enforced in schools, on laws concerning sexual activity between consenting adults, on taxation with respect to marital status and number of children, on residential building policies, and on just about every facet of existence that is now organized so as exclusively to favor and reward a pattern of sex roles based on marriage and parenthood.

As for the occupational roles of women, existing pressures still attempt to make the reproductive and occupational roles coterminus for all women who elect to marry and have children. This rigid structuring of the wife-mother position builds into the entire motivational pattern of women's lives a tendency to want at least a moderate-size family. To understand this point one must recognize that the desired number of children relates not simply to the wish for a family of a particular size but relates as well to a need for more than one or two children if one is going to enjoy "family life" over a significant portion of one's lifetime. This need is increased rather than lessened by improved life expectancy. Insofar as women focus their energies and emotions on their families, one cannot expect that they will be satisfied to play their only important role for a diminishing fraction of their lives, or that they will readily regard make-work and dead-end jobs as a substitute for "mothering." The notion that most women will "see the error of their ways" and decide to have two-child families is naive, since few healthy and energetic women will be so misguided as to deprive themselves of most of the rewards society has to offer them and choose a situation that allows them neither a life's work outside the home nor one within it. Those who do deprive themselves in this fashion are, in effect, taking the brunt of the still existing maladjustment between the roles of women and the reproductive needs of society. In a society oriented around achievement and accomplishment, such women are exceptionally vulnerable to depression, frustration, and a sense of futility, because they are being blocked from a sense of fulfillment both at home and abroad.

In sum, the problem of inhibiting population growth in the United States cannot be dealt with in terms of "family-planning needs" because this country is well beyond the point of "needing" birth control methods. Indeed, even the poor seem not to be a last outpost for family-planning attention. If we wish to limit our growth, such a desire implies basic changes in the social organization of reproduction that will make nonmarriage, childlessness, and small (two-child) families far more prevalent than they are now. A new policy, to achieve such ends, can take advantage of the antinatalist tendencies that our present institutions have suppressed. This will involve the lifting of penalties for antinatalist behavior rather than the "creation" of new ways of life. This

behavior already exists among us as part of our covert and deviant culture, on the one hand, and our elite and artistic culture, on the other. Such antinatalist tendencies have also found expression in feminism, which has been stifled in the United States by means of systematic legal, educational, and social pressures concerned with women's "obligations" to create and care for children. A fertility-control policy that does not take into account the need to alter the present structure of reproduction in these and other ways merely trivializes the problem of population control and misleads those who have the power to guide our country toward completing the vital revolution.

REFERENCES AND NOTES

1. *Hearings on S. 1676, U.S. Senate Subcommittee on Foreign Aid Expenditures* (the 1965 and 1966 Hearings each comprise seven volumes; the 1967–1968 Hearings, to date, comprise three volumes) (Government Printing Office, Washington, D.C.).

2. "The Growth of U.S. Population." *Nat. Acad. Sci.-Nat. Res. Council Pub. 1279* (1965).

3. O. Harkavy, F. S. Jaffe, S. S. Wishik, "Implementing DHEW Policy on Family Planning and Population" (mimeographed, 1967; available from the Ford Foundation, New York).

4. "Report of the President's Committee on Population and Family Planning: The Transition from Concern to Action" (Government Printing Office, Washington, D.C., 1968).

5. K. Davis, *Science* 158, 730 (1967); J. Blake, in *Public Health and Population Change*, M. C. Sheps and J. C. Ridley, Eds. (Univ. of Pittsburgh Press, Pittsburgh, Pa., 1965).

6. In the words of the Committee on Population, "The freedom to limit family size to the number of children wanted when they are wanted is, in our view, a basic human right . . . most Americans of higher income and better education exercise this right as a matter of course, but . . . many of the poor and uneducated are in fact deprived of the right."

7. W. J. Cohen, *Family Planning: One Aspect of Freedom to Choose* (Government Printing Office, Washington, D.C., 1966), p. 2. Cohen, former Secretary of Health, Education, and Welfare, says: "Until a few years ago, family planning and population problems were considered 'hush-hush' subjects. Public discussion was curtailed not only in polite society, but in the legislative and executive branches of the government as well."

8. *Hearings on S. 2993, U.S. Senate Subcommittee on Employment, Manpower, and Poverty, 89th*

Congress, Second Session, May 10 (Government Printing Office, Washington, D.C., 1966), p. 31.

9. *Hearings on S. 1676, U.S. Senate Subcommittee on Foreign Aid Expenditures, 90th Congress, First Session, November 2* (Government Printing Office, Washington, D.C., 1967), pt. 1.

10. Senator Tydings (D-Md.) said at the Hearings on S. 1676 (see 9): "As recently as 3 or 4 years ago, the idea that Federal, State or local governments should make available family planning information and services to families who could not otherwise afford them was extremely controversial. But in a brief period of time there has been a substantial shift of opinion among the moral leadership of our country, brought about in large measure by the vigorous efforts of the distinguished Senator from Alaska, Ernest Gruening, the chairman of this subcommittee."

11. E. Gruening, "What the Federal Government is now Doing in the Field of Population Control and What is Needed," speech presented before the U.S. Senate, 3 May 1967.

12. J. M. Stycos, in *World Population and U.S. Government Policy and Programs*, F. T. Brayer, Ed. (Georgetown Univ. Press, Washington, D.C., 1968).

13. R. Freedman, P. K. Whelpton, A. A. Campbell, *Family Planning, Sterility and Population Growth* (McGraw-Hill, New York, 1959).

14. P. K. Whelpton, A. A. Campbell, J. E. Patterson, *Fertility and Family Planning in the United States* (Princeton Univ. Press, Princeton, N.J., 1966).

15. J. Blake, *Demography* 3, 154 (1966); *Population Studies* 20, 27 (1966); *ibid.* 21, 159 (1967); *ibid.*, p. 185; *ibid.* 22, 5 (1968).

16. *Family Planner* 2, 3 (1968).

17. The estimate (by Arthur A. Campbell) under discussion here may be found in the Harkavy report (see 3 attachment A, pp. 4–19). Another estimate has been circulated by the Planned Parenthood Federation in a brochure entitled *Five Million Women* (Planned Parenthood, New York).

18. A. C. Kinsey, W. B. Pomeroy, C. E. Martin, P. B. Gebhard, *Sexual Behavior in the Human Female* (Saunders, Philadelphia, 1953), pp. 291 and 337.

19. K. Davis and J. Blake, *Econ. Develop. Cult. Change* 4, 211 (1956).

20. I make grateful acknowledgment to the Ford Foundation for support of the research presented in this article and to the National Institutes of Health (general research support grant 1501-TR-544104) for assistance to Statistical Services, School of Public Health, University of California, Berkeley. I am also indebted to Kingsley Davis, whose critical comments and helpful suggestions have greatly advanced

my thinking. The Roper Center and the Gallup Poll kindly supplied me with polling data.

10.7
Voices on Women

Margaret Kerr

The title of this chapter is "Psychological Consequences of Population Control." Being a solitary worker-student, I had not been at all involved in the current women's liberation movement, so I looked at this title and thought, "Oh, good! Population control will bring about changes in the role which society assigns us." Obviously, although I had not thought much about it and had done nothing, I felt the need for changes. The process of vision and revision undergone while working on this book, coupled with an increasing awareness of women's liberation, has brought me to the point where I dislike the idea that we will now have to consider readjusting women's role because of the pressing need for population control.

It is true that society can no longer tell women their basic function is to bear children and then turn around and say that this is a no-no. That is, not if we expect to have sane women. However, changes in women's role are called for independently of the question of population control. The very concept of "the role of women" should be seen for the blind absurdity which it is. As pointed out by K. D. Naegele, "Eve and Iris Murdoch, Cleopatra and Mary MacCarthy, Saint Joan and Simone de Beauvoir, Lady MacBeth and Freud's Dora, Mary Woolstonecraft and Virginia Woolf, Gabrielle Roi and Charlotte Whitton—they all answer to the name of woman. So do many more. What qualities, between them, do they and other women hold out to us as excellent, as in need of preserving?"[1] The discontent expressed by the growing women's liberation movement indicates that women are *now* suffering the psychological consequences of an unrealistic "woman's role." That role is

By permission of the author.

[1] K. D. Naegele, "Higher Education for Women," in *The Real World of Woman*, CBC Public Affairs Conference, Canada, 1962.

changing, because women will no longer accept its untenable constrictions. In the future, we will have to think in terms of the many roles of women, not just one.

Thus, population control, one aspect of the broader problem of environmental deterioration, is also only one aspect of a broader problem faced by women today. The question, then, is not how population control will influence woman's role, but how women in their many roles can and will affect it. It should be pointed out that the tendency of many writers on the environmental crisis to ignore women is very short-sighted, especially if population control is really as critical as claimed by some. After all, it is women who bear the children and who are usually responsible for practicing birth control. To overlook them is to risk losing their support.

Here are two women's views of the cards being dealt them by society now:

Modern woman is not allowed to be completely human. She faces a role conflict. A choice must be made between becoming the family oriented housewife or the emancipated woman pursuing a professional career. It seems unfair for such a conflict to exist. The woman should be allowed to perform either role or combine both as long as she is happy and no other individuals are harmed. The Twentieth Century has allowed women the freedom of higher education and admittance to professional employment. Remnants of an older set of social traditions seem to negate this choice. The woman who chooses to enter the professional world may find herself criticized by men in the business field as well as by women remaining at home. Such a woman is considered masculine. However, her great-grandmother, who tilled the soil and cleared the forest with her husband, is considered an individualist, a true frontier woman and an independent American. . . . There appears to be a cultural lag between the role of woman and the needs of a modern society. The role of homemaker and childbearer were sufficient in an earlier era. At that time, homemaking involved more than using Ajax, Baggies, and Lysol or sending junior off to school. The woman remains constrained and confined by a role which is no longer fully appropriate. . . . In this sense she is dehumanized by a social norm which does not allow her to develop her fullest potential as a human being . . ."

> Pamela Anikeef
> ("Feminine Role Conflict,"
> unpublished paper.)

I am female. I have to find out what that means, who I am and what I want to be, what type of woman I should be. I refuse to accept male

definitions. What other definitions are there? I don't trust Helen Gurley Brown. The placement counselor is sorry I don't type. I reject both the assumption and the sh--work. To spell it out would be unladylike. I refuse to be screwed by IBM. Man is the oppressor. Shall I love the enemy? Have I any choice? I am expected to grow children as a hobby. Overpopulation kills. I demand control over my body. Is Joan Baez a "working mother"? Does anyone know a "working father"? Or a "career boy"? I don't want to be labeled. Shall I be my father's daughter, husband's wife, child's mother? Am I an apostrophe? I demand the right to define myself. I think I am learning to think female.

> Anonymous
> (*College and University Business*,
> February, 1970.)

Yes, she does seem to be learning to "think female." But, one aspect of the type of thinking expressed here (indicative of the attitude of some, but not all, members of women's liberation) should be explored a little further —that is, the tendency to look upon man as the enemy who foists oppression onto women. Is he really the enemy?

". . . Sex role stereotypes call for men to be dominant, and achieving and enacting a dominant role in relations with others is often taken as an indicator of success as a man. Thus "success" for a man often involves influence over the lives of other persons. But success in achieving positions of dominance and influence is necessarily not open to every man, as dominance is relative and hence scarce by definition. Most men in fact fail to achieve the positions of dominance that sex role stereotypes ideally call for. Stereotypes tend to identify such men as greater or lesser failures, and in extreme cases, men who fail to be dominant are the object of jokes, scorn, and sympathy from wives, peers, and society generally.

One avenue of dominance is potentially open to any man, however—dominance over a woman. As society generally teaches men they should dominate, it teaches women they should be submissive, and so men have the opportunity to dominate women. More and more, women, however, are reacting against the ill effects of being dominated. But the battle of women to be free need not be a battle against men as oppressors. The choice about whether men are the enemy is up to men themselves.

Male liberation seeks to aid in destroying the sex role stereotypes that regard "being a man" and "being a woman" as statuses that must be achieved through proper behavior. People need not take on restrictive roles to establish their sexual identity. . . .

The acceptance of sex role stereotypes not only limits the individual but has bad effects on society generally. The apparent attractions of a male sex role are strong, and many males are necessarily caught up with this image. Education from early years calls upon boys to be brave, not to cry, and to fight for what is theirs. The day when these were virtues, if it ever existed, is long past. The main effect now is to help create a world in which private "virtues" become public vices. Competitiveness creates exploitation of humans the world over, as a necessary consequence of the drive of men to achieve "success." If success requires competitive achievement—not only in money, but prestige—and if this comes from the acquisition of power and influence, then there will be a drive for power and influence of an unlimited nature, which is exactly what the world is seeing. . . .

In the increasing recognition of the right of women to participate equally in the affairs of the world, then, there is both a danger and a promise. The danger is that women could try simply to get their share of the action in the competitive, dehumanizing system that men have created. The promise is that women and men might work together to create a system that provides equality to all and dominate no one. The women's liberation movement has stressed that women are looking for a better model for human behavior than has so far been created. Women are trying to become human, and men can do the same. This implies that neither sex should be limited by role stereotypes that define "appropriate" behavior. The present models of neither men nor women furnish adequate opportunities for human development. That one half of the human race should be dominant and the other half submissive is incompatible with a notion of freedom. Freedom requires that there not be dominance and submission, but that all individuals be free to determine their own lives.

Jack Sawyer
("The Male Liberation Movement,"
unpublished paper.)

The subject of the dominant male stereotype may seem to be far removed from the environmental crisis, but when you think about it that is not necessarily so. Another outlet for the feeling that one must dominate can be found in dominance over the physical environment, an unrealistic attitude which has helped bring us to our present situation.

On the other hand, women, who have long been taught to live with the idea of adapting to forces stronger than themselves are particularly suited to coping with the realization that nature is infinitely more dominant than we in the long run and that our salvation may lie in adjusting to it rather than in trying to adjust it to us. Perhaps the very qualities which have been imparted to us through

the education accompanying the current standards for feminine behavior are those which will have to come to the fore in the future. So, let's not be too quick to emulate men in trying to find new paths for ourselves. The roads which they laid out are already falling apart.

For a number of years we have been entertained by Sunday magazine supplements with descriptions of the kind of world we will live in by the year 2000. Visions of aluminum spires sparkling under plastic, air conditioned domes, robots and computers which will perform the majority of industrial and household tasks, and a life expectancy of 150 years constitute elements of this dream.

The threat of nuclear holocaust has long been with us—ever since Hiroshima. But now still another nightmare quality has entered the scene—the widespread realization that we face a crisis of enormous proportions concerning not only the quality of life but that of survival of life as we know it. . . .

Now we, as women, have long been used to our role as housekeepers. Some of us heartily dislike this role, others thoroughly enjoy it. However there is a new challenge for us all, whether willing or unwilling housekeepers, and that is earthkeeping. We must now expand the walls of our housekeeping domain and make the planet our concern. Here, we as women, can come together to meet what is the greatest threat and challenge that mankind has ever had.

There are two courses of action we can take in this new role of earthkeeper. The first one that we must follow is that of population control, one which can be met and solved only on an individual and personal basis if we are to remain a democratic society.

There are a variety of theories about overpopulation and its solution. One group of persons, educated and intelligent, believes so firmly in the inexhaustible ability of science to solve problems of population and environment that they refuse to be alarmed about the situation at all. The flaw in this ostrich-like kind of thinking is a misconception that earth's resources are inexhaustible. It is what Kenneth Boulding calls the "cowboy economy" way of thinking. It is rooted in the American past where a man or a family could always find more gold, more land, more water by moving westward.

Another group maintains that the problems of overpopulation will be solved if there is free access to family planning services and the repeal of all laws pertaining to abortion. These are both important and significant means of preventing the conception and birth of *unwanted* children. . . .

In the United States it is not the unwanted children who constitute the main population explosion. They are certainly a part of it. However, it is the *wanted* children who are

contributing to this enormous bulge of population growth which is making the eastern seaboard and central Great Lakes area a great megalopolis, filling schoolrooms faster than additions can be built, and taxing the citizen at levels he feels he can scarcely meet.

Today our whole society is structured to reward and reinforce the large family, which also means that we consider marriage, childbearing and childrearing as full, life-time occupations for practically every woman. We provide income tax deductions based on the number of children and dependents in a family. We provide free elementary and secondary education for every child, and the childless must pay taxes for this purpose as well as those who have had children. We claim to abhor abortion although thousands of women seek it illegally and many die as a result of infection and botching of the procedure. . . . Homosexuality is condemned and made punishable by law. Bachelors and spinsters are considered to be unfortunate, especially the spinsters. Single women who do not marry and bear children are made to feel "unfulfilled." Our attitudes, our mores, our social norms all make the woman who bears children . . . believe that she is fulfilling the only really acceptable role of women in our society. This complex of social attitudes toward producing children is what is called by social scientists a pronatalist policy.

What happens? This pronatalist society of ours ends up with thousands upon thousands of women and children on the Aid to Dependent Families and Children relief rolls. These are the women who are just like the majority of other women not on AFDC who have been programmed by our society from the pink-lined bassinet to the pink-lined casket to look upon marriage and childbearing as the only acceptable life style for a woman. . . .

What are the solutions to this appalling problem of thousands of women on welfare, thousands of women having large families, thousands of women having another baby to make their lives meaningful?

The answer lies in the fact that we must change our attitudes toward the role of women in our society and provide them with meaningful and socially significant alternatives to full time child bearing and raising. It is as simple and as complex as that. We must provide women with a range of options from which they may freely choose the kind of life they wish to lead. The social acceptability of many different life styles open to women is the key to a free society and a stable population.

How can we bring about a change in our social attitudes and expectations for women? Here are some of the ways:

1. We can work to change the laws pertaining to divorce, families, place of residence, guardianship of children, right to keep maiden names, etc., so that women have the same equality as men before the law.

2. We must make changes in our economy to see that women receive equal pay for equal work, that protective labor laws apply to both men and women, that women can work overtime if they wish and be paid time-and-a-half of the prevailing wage. We must also make every effort to encourage women to aspire to more responsible positions and to enter the decision making levels of business and industry, education, and government. We must also provide the opportunity for women to do this as well as encouraging them in this kind of endeavor.

3. We must work to change our educational systems so they encourage our daughters to develop job skills and, if they are especially bright, to enter the professions . . . just as we encourage our sons to seek jobs which will give them the opportunity to utilize their talents and abilities. . . .

4. We must strive, as parents, to teach our daughters and our sons that it is important for girls to become women and individuals in their own right, to make a contribution to society outside the home, and that small families must be the rule in the years to come.

These are all means for creating a wider range of job opportunities for girls, and that is the key to giving women a range of options for the kind of life they may choose to lead. This is a concept which is seldom made explicit in all the rhetoric we hear about the population explosion. Yet, it is the only democratic way of controlling the size of our population.

Closely related to this problem of population control is the fact that the whole environmental problem provides an area for women to utilize their skills and talents as never before. A good example of a young woman who perceives this new area of concern and action is Stephanie Mills, who made headlines last June (1969) and startled the nation by saying in a commencement address, "The most humane thing for me to do is to have no children at all." Since then she has become a national spokesman for the environmental movement and editor of a monthly magazine called *Earth Time*. . . .

This brings us to the second phase of solution to this problem of earthkeeping, and that concerns our efforts to preserve our communities, our state, our nation, our planet. How can we contribute our hearts and skills and concern to keeping our earth?

First, we must become informed. There is material everywhere about the whole subject and its complexity. . . .

Next, we can look at our local communities—what kind of sewage plant is there? Has the problem of tertiary treatment been studied and what is it? What is the zoning law situation? We can also start organizations like the Madison area Capital Community Citizens. This month they had a referendum on the ballot which read to the effect that it was the right of every Madisonian to enjoy pure air and water and a quality environment. This does not do anything specific, but it does arouse attention and interest in the question. . . . They also lobbied a law through the city council which states that 1% of all paved parking areas shall be left open so that rain water can get into the soil and seep into the subterranean ground water supplies.

Another avenue for action is the political arena. Here is where women can use their concern and ability in persisting to promote action. . . . Most policies are formed by Congress and federal agencies. These organizations are like molasses which responds quickly to immediate pressure but as soon as that pressure is released, returns to its original form. However, they are very susceptible to pressure carried out over a long period of time. . . .

There you have it—two approaches to earthkeeping. One is to encourage and to make every effort to promote more equal opportunities for all women. The other is to read, learn, act on the local, state and national level to combat the destruction of our earth. Earthkeeping is truly women's work—and men's, too.

Marian Thompson
("Keepers of the Earth,"
unpublished paper)

Stephanie Mills does not stand alone in her renunciation of childbearing. Other young women also feel it would be humane not to give birth, or inhumane to do so.

Into this world
With its wars of present,
And its threats for tomorrow,
With its treasury of uncured diseases,
Its hostility between men
With different races or tongues,
Its blood of the past
Crusted on the flowers of its earth,
Its alienation of human kind
Keeping growth or springtime from
    the memory souls
Of half its inhabitants,
Into this kind of world
I would bring no innocent child
To make him share such lifelong
    perils
Not only by himself
But crushed by the multitudes
Who suffer with him.
I would commit no such
Painful life to my baby,
For I see grown men falling
Under the scars of this battle.

Sandra Hickey
("Poem for the Unborn")

Enough said for now, but women will be speaking out more and more in the future. The old notion that women will sit back and let men, in their infinitely greater wisdom, handle life outside the home is at least dying, if not already long dead. The future requires much more from all of us than that old pretense.

10.8
A Psychological Analysis of Oral Contraceptives and the Intrauterine Device

S. Jerome Kutner and
Thomas J. Duffy

Psychology is very applicable to reactions to contraception because each method has certain characteristics that are more or less compatible with the properties of the user. Therefore, understanding side-effects, as well as selecting a method should involve a psychological analysis of the relationship between the user and the method.

This paper will limit itself to the intrauterine devices (IUD) and oral contraceptives. These techniques are often pitted against each other in relation to the patient, if she does not elect to terminate her fertility by surgery. In consequence, we will make a psychological interpretation of each of these methods and compare them. The intention is to advocate an approach to research and practice and to present some empirical justification.

The Intrauterine Device

The IUD may minimize guilt over the use of birth control. Any method is likely to generate a moral conflict in women who believe that sex is more for reproduction than pleasure. The IUD could lessen feelings of responsibility in the user because it is inserted by the doctor. Whereas, "the pill" must be taken by the user. Furthermore, with the IUD there is even greater temporal dissociation between the contraceptive act and the sexual act than there is with oral contraceptives. Finally, the use of the IUD, like "the pill," is not contingent on sexual relations.

The desire for procreation is of course not limited to guilt. The woman with a strong desire for children may "forget" to take "the pill." Thus if the motivation to conceive were strong and the ability to delay gratification were weak, the IUD would be a relatively acceptable technique for spacing a family. Likewise, the IUD appears to be an appropriate

By permission of the authors.

method for a woman who tends to be very passive. She might be unsuccessful if she were required to do something, such as, taking "the pill" every day for three-quarters of her menstrual cycle.

However, psychological conflicts also seem to take their toll on users of the IUD. King (1) points out that emotional difficulties may account for the inability of some women to succeed with this method. He reported that of the first 150 patients in whom the Margulies Coil was placed, 17 either repeatedly expelled it, bled excessively, or asked to have it removed for various reasons. Of these failures, 11 (65%) either were at the time or had been receiving psychotherapy. Whereas, of the 133 users for whom the coil was satisfactory, only 5% had a background of psychothreapy. King (1) suggested that a psychic disturbance may affect the neuromuscular mechanism on which the operation of the IUD is based. What exactly might this emotional conflict be? Lidz (2) observed among IUD users feelings of frustration, guilt and lack of libido which she imputed to the deprivation from being able to have more children.

The IUD seems to have many advantages in terms of guilt-reduction. Nevertheless, research on this method suggests that psychic conflicts may still be responsible for its expulsion, as well as some harmful side-effects.

Oral Contraceptives

Oral contraceptives also have certain features that may be psychologically relevant. First, the mere fact that the method is a drug in the form of a pill will account for differences in acceptability among individuals. Some patients, for example, are afraid of pills. Second, in psychoanalytic terms, since "the pill" is taken orally, variation in forgetting, acceptance and side-effects may be affected by the extent to which the user can be characterized as an *oral personality*. Third, compulsiveness may facilitate the use of this method because of the frequency of attention that it requires.

The rest of this paper will explicate three more variables associated with "pill" use: responsibility, femininity, and the fear of pregnancy.

Responsibility and Marriage

Ovulation suppressors require the female to assume *active* responsibility for contraception. In contra-distinction to the IUD, the responsibility is critical because the woman must be relied on to use the method every day for about three-quarters of her menstrual cycle. Therefore, success with "the pill" may depend on interpersonal and intrapersonal traits conducive to her acceptance of contraceptive responsibility. Zell and Crisp found that in many cases when the husband recommended the use of the drug, the wife became hostile. "These wives had been attempting to make their husbands responsible for their pregnancies and, thus, to deny their own responsibilities. They interpreted the husband's suggestion as an attempt to place the responsibility for pregnancy on themselves" (Zell and Crisp [3], p. 659). The investigators further asserted that the problem was a symptom of the couple's general failure to assume mutual responsibility in marriage.

Bakker and Dightman (4) used objective personality tests to study the forgetting of oral contraceptives. They empirically associated personality with ineffectiveness of use. "Immature women who have a tendency toward acting out and who avoid taking responsibilities are prone to forget their contraceptives. This forgetting is enhanced by the presence of discord between husband and wife and conflicting attitudes toward sexuality" (Bakker and Dightman [4], p. 566).

Continuation of using oral contraceptives was compared to responsibility by Ziegler, Rogers, Kriegsman and Martin (5). They showed that wives who continued to take the "pill" were more responsible than their husbands, as measured by the California Psychological Inventory (CPI). The importance of this finding was highlighted by the inability of the severity of side-effects to predict discontinuance.

Moos (6) has noted that although the rejection rates for the IUD and the "pill" are similar, the women who reject one method do not tend to reject the other. The necessity for taking active female responsibility seems to be one of the basic differences between the methods. The empirical literature does indicate that remembering and continuance with the "pill" are facilitated by two conditions: first, the wife is generally more responsible than the husband, and second, they are compatible.

Femininity and Hormones

Oral contraceptives contain the synthetic hormones estrogen and progestin. These exogenous hormones seem to create symptoms similar to those of pregnancy. Swollen and sore breasts occur very frequently among "pill users." In the Contraceptive Drug Study eighteen out of thirty-five (51%) Kaiser Health Plan members reported an increase in this symptom three months after they started using contraceptive pills.

A tentative explanation for the variability between subjects is the *hormone shock hypothesis*. Women have various levels of natural estrogen and progesterone which predispose them to reacting in different ways to the same exogenous hormones. *Specifically, women with less endogenous hormone will respond more acutely to a sudden, large supply of exogenous hormone.* The problem is adaptation. The effect is manifested most perceptibly in the end-organ, viz., the breasts. Drill (7) stated, "The estrogen and progesterone secreted during an ovulatory cycle may produce breast discomfort, soreness, or engorgement, and similar hormonal effects may be noted during the use of oral contraceptives (p. 113)."

In support of the *hormone shock hypothesis*, it has been known for some years that the response to an exogenous hormone tends to be inversely proportional to the amount already present in the animal. Thus small amounts of testosterone or adrenal steroids produce little change in normal subjects, but may provoke a dramatic response in patients without testes or adrenals.

Wide variation in physiological and psychological reaction to oral contraceptives has also been noted by Moos (6). He too suggests that individual differences in endocrine-associated effects may be due to variability in predispositions interacting with relatively fixed doses of estrogen-progestin preparations. He contends that for some proportion of women the dose administered will be either too high or too low. Indeed, the dose relationship predicted by the *hormone shock hypothesis* does exist. Garcia and Wallach (8) reported that breast engorgement is less prevalent at lower doses. One would also expect on the basis of the proposed explanation that once a change in the hormonal milieu has passed, adaptation would follow. Drill (7) observed that breast swelling and sensitivity have been shown to be most marked during the first cycle.

Method. The Contraceptive Drug Study has used the Masculinity-Femininity scale (Mf) of the Minnesota Multiphasic Personality Inventory (MMPI) to predict complaints about swollen and sore breasts. The Mf scale is a questionnaire that measures interests and attitudes related to femininity. The same thirty-five women referred to previously were given the MMPI before they started using oral contraceptives. In addition, they rated themselves on four-point scales concerning a variety of symptoms both before and three months after using oral contraceptives. The rating scales were on symptoms, such as swollen and sore breasts, leg cramps, headaches, moodiness, etc.

Results. The subjects were divided into quarters depending on their Mf scores. The first quarter consisted of the most feminine women (mean T-score = 41). The second and third quarters were joined to form the intermediate group (mean T-score = 49). The fourth quarter included the least feminine women (mean T-score = 59). Thus, the distribution of femininity in the sample was roughly normal, and neither extreme group was very deviant.

The only symptom change that was clearly predicted by femininity was the increase in *swollen and sore breasts* mentioned before. Seven out of eight (87%) of the least feminine women showed an increase in their ratings of the symptom, while only one out of eight (13%) of the most feminine women did the same. The difference was statistically significant ($\chi^2 = 9.03, d.f. = 2, p < .02$). However, femininity was independent of the symptom rated *before* using the drug ($r = -.02$). The association between femininity and the symptom strengthened *after* drug use ($r = -.50, d.f. = 33, p < .01$, two-tailed test). The physiological authenticity of swollen and sore breasts as a side-effect of oral contraceptives has been demonstrated by its dose-relatedness (see Garcia and Wallach[8]). Thus, it appears that femininity underlies this physiological side-effect of the medication.

Discussion. To our knowledge, sex hormones have never been empirically correlated with the Mf scale. Hence, no inference can be made from the present results to the *hormone shock hypothesis.* Nevertheless, the need for a psychoendocrine approach to studying the side-effects of contraceptive drugs is patently suggested by

the data. Furthermore, the results are consistent with those of Ziegler *et al.* (5). They found that women who permanently discontinued contraceptive use of the drug were significantly less feminine on the Mf scale than those who continued in this manner. Accordingly, the significance of the orientation which has been delineated here may transcend the symptoms studied. For, as Drill (7) has pointed out, although the breast and the uterus are the major *end-organs* for gonadal hormones, other tissues of the body are also affected. These effects may be even more pervasive and enduring, for instance, alterations in body weight, blood fats, glucose and porphyrin metabolism, protein-binding and pituitary hormones. Dickey and Dorr (9) share this concern with regard to a serious side-effect. "Until the cause of the relationship between oral contraceptives and thromboembolism is known, we believe the safest practice is to consider all symptoms of hormonal imbalance, and especially those of hormone excess, to be warnings of potential danger" (p. 281).

The Fear of Pregnancy

It is significant that women believe swollen and sore breasts to be one of the foremost symptoms of pregnancy. If this symptom occurs, the pill may not allay the fear of pregnancy.

Method. Consequently, the Contraceptive Drug Study has investigated the relationship between fear of pregnancy and a variety of symptoms which are commonly attributed to oral contraceptives, including swollen and sore breasts. The Fear of Pregnancy Test was developed especially for this purpose. The Test consisted of ten fears, one of which was "becoming pregnant," which had to be rank ordered. The rank given to "becoming pregnant" was the score. (Reliability was acceptable: $r = .83$, test-retest, and $r = .89$, alternative form.)

The Fear of Pregnancy Test and a number of rating scales concerning symptoms were given to fourteen Kaiser Health Plan members just before and three months after going on "the pill."

Results. Women who showed no change or even an increase in their fear of pregnancy reported a worsening of symptoms, such as leg cramps, swollen and sore breasts, and headaches. Their overall symptomatology increased significantly ($t = 2.38, d.f. = 6$,

$p < .05$, one-tailed test). By contrast, the women who showed a diminution in fear of pregnancy indicated a nonsignificant decrease in their overall symptomatology. In addition, the symptom that best differentiated between those who did undergo a decline in fear and those who did not was swollen and sore breasts.

Discussion. Unfortunately antecedent-consequent relations cannot be identified with these data since both variables represent changes in scores derived simultaneously. But it may be hypothesized that swollen and sore breasts were a cue that influenced fear of pregnancy. Moreover, it is quite plausible that the fear of pregnancy, once established, in turn, determined other complaints, such as headaches. That is, fear of pregnancy can be conceptualized as a motivation for taking "the pill" and risking illness. Additionally, the reduction of fear of pregnancy is a reward or justification for the risk, as well as for experiencing symptoms. Hence, the two groups of subjects may not have actually differed in terms of the experience of symptoms, but only in their readiness to complain. The group that showed no decline in fear of pregnancy may have complained of a worsening of symptoms because they lacked the reward they anticipated. In summary, if breast symptoms occur, the fear of pregnancy will not diminish. If the fear does not decrease, complaints about other symptoms are likely to be made.

The toleration of side-effects might be based on not only a decrement in fear of pregnancy, but also other rewards. Some "pill-users" may, for instance, benefit from intensified sexual pleasure, regulation of the menstrual cycle, or remission of premenstrual symptoms. The nature of the reward would of course depend on the motivation of the woman and her partner. In his review of the literature on the psychological side effects of oral contraceptives, Glick (10) reports that most clinicians ascribe the improved sense of well-being, libido and other benefits to the removal of the fear of pregnancy. However, Murawski (11) described quite a different situation that obtained with one of his subjects. She had experienced such severe headaches that her physician advised her to discontinue "the pill," and to use an IUD. She did this, but she is now thinking of returning to contraceptive pills to offset signs of aging at forty-two. Since "the pill" has potentially different *secondary gains* than the IUD, patients should be evaluated accordingly. Zell and Crisp (3) demonstrated that not all patients have improved sexual adjustment with oral contraceptives. Couples with adequate or even marginal sexual adjustment before taking Enovid did respond well. But those with poor sexual adjustment showed little or no change. Therefore, the potential for benefiting from oral contraceptives varies, and can be assessed. One approach to this evaluation has been espoused by Dickey and Dorr (9).

Future research as well as practice should take into account the positive side-effects in conjunction with the negative ones. Otherwise our knowledge of many deleterious reactions which is formed through verbal reports may be very perverse. That is, a given side-effect may be *experienced* by many but *reported* by only a few women due to the positive side effects. Or adverse reactions may be exaggerated by women who are not receiving the "pay-off" they expected.

Summary

Characteristics of the IUD and contraceptive pills were studied relative to personality. Side-effects and effectiveness of use seemed to be an outcome of an interaction between the method and the personality of the user. Successful use of the IUD appears to be hindered by emotional conflict. Oral contraceptives are used most efficiently by women who are more responsible than their husbands, but also compatible with them. Less feminine "pill users" reported more instances of swollen and sore breasts. A decline in fear of pregnancy was connected with less pill-related symptoms.

The choice of contraception should hinge on an evaluation of the positive and negative side effects that are likely to transpire for a particular individual.

REFERENCES

1. King, A. G. Selection of patients for the intrauterine contraceptive device (editorial). *Obstet. and Gynec.* 29:139, 1967.
2. Lidz, R. W. Emotional factors in the success of contraception. *Fertil. and Steril.* 20:761, 1969.
3. Zell, J. R., and Crisp, W. E. A psychiatric evaluation of the use of oral contraception: A study of 250 private patients. *Obstet. and Gynec.* 23:657, 1964.
4. Bakker, C. B., and Dightman,
C. R. Psychological factors in fertility control. *Fertil. and Steril.* 15:559, 1964.
5. Ziegler, F. J., Rogers, D. A., Kriegsman, S. A., and Martin, P. L. Ovulation suppressors, psychological functioning and marital adjustment. *JAMA 204:* 97, 1968.
6. Moos, R. H. Psychological aspects of oral contraceptives. *Arch. Gen. Psychiat.* 19:87, 1968.
7. Drill, V. A. *Oral Contraceptives.* New York: McGraw-Hill, 1966.
8. Garcia, C. R., Wallach, E. E. "Biochemical changes and implications following long-term use of oral contraception," in Behrman, S. J., Corsa, L. Jr., and Freedman, R. (eds.) *Fertility and Family Planning: A World View.* Ann Arbor: The University of Michigan Press, 1969.
9. Dickey, R. P., and Dorr, C. H. Oral contraceptives: Selection of the proper pill. *Obstet. and Gynec.* 33:273, 1969.
10. Glick, I. D. Mood and behavioral changes associated with the use of the oral contraceptive agents. *Psychopharmacologia* (Berlin) 10:363, 1967.
11. Murawski, B. J. Psychologic considerations for the evaluation of long-term use of oral contraceptives. *J. Reprod. Med.* 3:151, 1969.

10.9
Psychosocial Response to Vasectomy

Fredrick J. Ziegler
David A. Rodgers
Robert J. Prentiss

Voluntary male sterilization, vasectomy, has not been an unusual method of contraception in recent years. In 1970, approximately 7 percent of husbands of fertile wives in the western United States had obtained a vasectomy, whereas the national incidence was approximately 2 percent. Aside from its intended function of surgically induced sterility, no adverse physiologic effects of vasectomy have been demonstrated or seriously proposed. A number of reports, however, have addressed themselves to the possibility of alterations in psychological functioning after vasectomy. . . .

. . . Since 1960, the present

Reprinted by permission of the authors and AMA Specialty Journals from "Psychosocial Response to Vasectomy," *Archives of General Psychiatry,* 21, 1 (July, 1969).

authors and their associates have collaborated in conducting a longitudinal or prospective study, with a comparison group, in order to assess changes in psychological functioning and in marital relations following vasectomy. The present report primarily concerns data from 42 couples who were systematically assessed by structured psychiatric interviews, psychological testing, and questionnaire reports over a four-year period beginning prior to having vasectomies performed by private practicing urologists. A comparison group of 42 couples was studied during this same time period, beginning just before being given first prescriptions for ovulation suppression pills by private practicing gynecologists. The details of research design, findings, and our formulations of the studies through the two-year follow-up period have been previously reported. The vasectomy group, with few exceptions noted below, consistently attributed only favorable changes to vasectomy, blaming other life circumstances for any adverse changes in their emotional functioning or their family situation. As a group, however, the men and their wives showed somewhat more psychological pathology at that time than did the women and their husbands in the pill-taking group, both as assessed by changes in psychological testing and by ratings of mental status from the protocols of the psychiatric interviews. At that time, the vasectomy couples rated their own marriages significantly less enthusiastically than did the comparison group couples. The study then seemed to replicate the reports of others that men and their wives generally express enthusiasm for vasectomy after they have turned to this contraceptive method, but that evidence of adverse psychological changes is demonstrable if one looks for it. We ascribed these paradoxical findings to "dissonance reduction," in which persons in some situations tend to reassure themselves by focusing primarily on favorable considerations, ignoring or rationalizing contradictory evidence. We concluded:

The data suggest that the operation is responded to as though it had demasculinizing potential, with a result that the behavior of the man after vasectomy is more likely to be scrutinized by himself and others for evidence of unmasculine features. Behavior questioned as possibly unmasculine is anxiety-provoking and tends to be eliminated, narrowing the range of acceptable behaviors on a highly individualized basis reflecting each person's circumstances and interpretation of "unmasculine." In some instances, the result is a salutary decrease in immature and indecisive behavior, with improvement in occupational, parental, and husband role enactments. In other and perhaps more characteristic instances, the decreased flexibility reduces personal effectiveness, heightens personal anxiety, and abrades marital harmony and the satisfactions of the wife. . . .

At the end of four years then there was no impressive evidence that couples after vasectomy, when studied in the manner which we have described, were psychologically worse off than a comparison group of couples if assessed by indicators of pathology or disturbance. There was indication that even four years after vasectomy, men were still concerned about any evidence of loss of masculinity and were attempting to compensate for it by an increase in the frequency of intercourse and other behavioral changes. To date, we have been unable to identify a group of men in the present study who were especially vulnerable to the psychological hazards of vasectomy. Different men showed different aspects of both positive and negative postoperative changes, apparently reflecting rather individualized ways of reacting. . . .

Our studies as well as others reported in the literature indicate that adverse psychological changes can occur in response to vasectomy. We interpret the evidence as indicating that vasectomy is reacted to by most subjects and their wives as if the operation had "demasculinizing potential," such that an increase in psychological upset or in compensatory stereotyped masculine behavior or both is found in a high percentage of subjects. In the presently reported intensive study, severely adverse psychological changes were few, and, we infer, were largely aborted by the discussion with the investigators. The subjects were also undoubtedly rather effectively prescreened by the urologists who performed the operations. Nevertheless, even within this group, there is consistent evidence that a vasectomy can be a continuing challenge to a man's conception of himself.

In a previous study, we have shown that two quite different cultural subgroups (college students and a Protestant church group) held derogatory attitudes toward couples who rely on vasectomy for contraception as contrasted to couples using ovulation suppression; and we infer that such attitudes are widely prevalent in most cultural groups and are even held to some extent by the men who obtained vasectomy and by their wives. After a couple has selected vasectomy as a desirable contraceptive procedure for rational reasons that presumably outweigh their covert negative attitudes, full therapeutic discussion of their concerns and their reactions would theoretically be expected to modify their covert unfavorable attitudes, such that their vulnerability to the impact of negative cultural judgments and to pscyhological upset would be reduced. We infer that such reduction in vulnerability occurred in the present study. In any event, and especially if the foregoing inference is correct, the conclusion seems warranted that if a man, his wife, and a physician conclude that vasectomy is a desirable contraceptive method for the couple and if the couple has adequate opportunity to discuss all implications of the procedure with an informed person, the ultimate effect of vasectomy on psychological functioning and marital adjustment will, on the average, be comparable to the effect of electing ovulation suppression. . . .

. . . In summary, then, it seems to us that the results of these studies argue strongly for individualized contraceptive medical advice, that each procedure has its identifiable assets and hazards, and that vasectomy can be regarded as a desirable alternative under the conditions specified.

An abortion-seeking woman is not a happily pregnant woman. Certainly, at that particular time in her long reproductive span, she is neither a suitable nor willing candidate for the exacting task of motherhood. To compel such women into reluctant maternity is not in the best interests of society or of future infants. Present laws compelling live birth do not compel her to become happy with the pregnancy, nor do they make her delightedly expectant and welcoming of the coming maternity. They certainly can not compel her to be a willing, loving, capable mother to her compulsory infant, as love is one value no body of males sitting in council has ever been able to impose by law!

The laws are held firmly in place by large religious lobbies in state and federal seats of government. These self interested groups, along with such institutions as the American Medical Association, law enforcement officials and political leaders in nearly every community in the U.S., have vested interests in keeping the simple surgery of abortion a most expensive business, with the profits finding a place in their private pockets!

Lana Clarke Phelan and Patricia Therese Maginnis (From *The Abortion Handbook for Responsible Women.* California: Contact Books, 1969, p. 45.)

10.10
Population Control, Sterilization, and Ignorance

Thomas Eisner
Ari van Tienhoven
Frank Rosenblatt

We recently submitted a questionnaire to students and faculty at Cornell University designed to test attitudes and preferences concerning family size and contraceptive technique. The 1059 respondents (74 percent males) were a mixed lot who represented the physical and biological sciences, humanities, and social sciences and who included faculty (294), graduate students (174), upperclassmen (264), and freshmen (327). Given the level of education of the sample, the results were unexpected in several respects.

First, although there was general agreement (84 percent) on the desirability of limiting family size, a substantial majority (65 percent) said it wanted three children (39 percent) or more (26 percent). Only 30 percent favored two children, and a mere 5 percent expressed preference for one or none. Choice was in no major way affected by age, sex, marital status, parenthood, or professional specialty. Even the respondents

Reprinted by permission from *Science,* 167 (January 23, 1970), 337. Copyright 1970 by the American Association for the Advancement of Science.

COURTESY OF GENE LEGEND.

proponents of voluntary sterilization are backing a hopeless or nearly hopeless cause. But what are we to make of the educated youth growing up among us that is either unconcerned about population growth or, at the very least, unable or unwilling to apply to itself the simple arithmetic of compound interest? And what, if any, are the prospects for improved sex education when ignorance about the reproductive system is widespread even among those who should know best?

Not only do we need population control, but we will *get* it. The question is: what kind? When I first became interested in population, I was overwhelmed by its seriousness and I was an advocate of government involvement in population control. After having looked at the government, I am no longer quite convinced that I want them controlling my population or anybody else's because they might decide to clamp down on "effete impudent snobs."

Stephanie Mills
(From "Earth Day" speech at
University of California, Berkeley,
April 21, 1970.)

whom we expected to be most concerned about the population crisis (for example, graduate students and young faculty in biology) included a minimum of 50 percent with a desire for three children or more.

As regards contraception, about one-half favored "the pill" over all other available means as a way both to space children (53 percent) and to maintain family size at its desired limit (50 percent). Other contraceptive appliances such as condoms, diaphragms, and intrauterine devices were each given top preference by no more than 13 percent of the sample. Voluntary sterilization, either of man or woman, was judged as decidedly undesirable. Only 6 percent opted in favor of vasectomy as the preferred form of contraception once full family size had been achieved; the corresponding number favoring ligation of the oviducts was 2 percent. A majority (52 percent of males and 61 percent of females) said they would *never* undergo sterilization, even after having had the desired number of children. The

operation was judged to be as undesirable as abortion and abstinence for prevention of family growth beyond the set limit. It is of interest in this connection that the consequences of sterilization are not generally understood. For example, asked whether vasectomy would abolish the ability to ejaculate, nearly half the respondents (49 percent) confessed to ignorance or expressed either certainty or probability that emission would no longer accompany orgasm. Biology students scored no better than nonbiologists, and graduate students, even after marriage and parenthood, seemed to be no better informed than freshmen. The only exceptional group was the biology faculty, but, even there, 30 percent were either misinformed or uninformed on this point. Comparable ignorance prevails with respect to oviduct ligation: 37 percent of respondents were certain, or thought it probable, that the operation would interfere with the menstrual cycle.

We are bothered by these results. Perhaps of least general concern is the probability that

10.11
Tinkering with Nature

Charles McCabe

Can you imagine what would happen if the population nuts got their way, which largely I take to be the limitation by fiat of all families to the number of two?

This would be yet another, and by far the most offensive, attempt to apply the criminal sanction to the behavior of human beings.

It would fail, as all such attempts in the course of history have failed, because you cannot successfully legislate against those strong feelings we call human nature.

Were the two-and-that's-it law passed in this country, its most likely result would be precisely

Reprinted by permission from the *San Francisco Chronicle*, January 27, 1970. © Chronicle Publishing Co. 1970.

what the law was directed against: A population explosion.

As Prohibition taught hordes of Americans to drink who never might have without the law, compulsory population restriction would bring out very strong familial feelings in men and women who might not have experienced them before.

Before Prohibition was enacted, and before whoring was made sinful, and before gambling was interdicted, there were fanatical men who knew what was good for their neighbor, and were damned well going to shove it down his throat.

The population nuts are of this genre. Their aim—control of population to fit in better with environment—is admirable. Their method, the force of law, is both inhuman and unworkable.

I see much to recommend the view that two children are enough, and that others might be adopted, so long as it is the free act of a free family.

The kind of people who know what's good for their fellows, and try to enact their views into law, just plain scare me.

For you may bet a nickel that if laws were passed to limit families to two, there would be strong movements to limit them to one, and then to zero. These laws would all be unsuccessful. They would all add criminals to our society, which has no need for these kinds of criminals.

One can predict some extraordinary consequences from the passage of such laws.

There would, of course, be no more abortion mills, since abortion would be regarded as one of the highest social goods.

Instead, in places like Tijuana and Japan, there would be a lively illegal trade for people who desired—against their Nation's will—to have a third, and a fourth, and maybe a fifth child.

You may be sure doctors would be found who would be willing to batten on this illegal trade, and petty gangsters would be thrown up who could get the offender in touch with the doctor. These things can be arranged, you know.

Less frivolously, I quote a reader: "Population control on a meaningful scale will be 'tinkering' more immediately and specifically with our psyches, society and politics. And we may come to feel that the resultant explosions in these parts of our world are even more threatening than the population explosion.

"What I mean is this: The average age of our population at this time seems to be about 25 years. That means a nice yeasty foment of idealism and new ideas is frothing in the current scene. Lots of controversy and excitement.

"Advance the average age of our population to 35 or 40, as would result if effective population control were achieved, and much of the present bubble and bustle would disappear. Youth is hopeful and daring; maturity is caution and resolution. A population of mature persons would work real mischief with our psychological outlook . . .

"I'm still strongly committed to population control, but we also need to be alert to the human anguish that will result unless the chemical, mechanical, surgical and fiscal instruments are tempered by thoughtful preparation for people's other needs."

10.12
Ethical Aspects of Population Policy

Arthur J. Dyck

It took hundreds of thousands of years to produce a living population of one billion people by 1850 A.D. Within 75 years, from 1850 to 1925, the second billion was added, and by 1960, in only 35 more years, the third billion. At the present growth rate of 2 percent per year, it will take only 35 years to double the world's population.

In view of this increasingly rapid growth of population, it is no wonder that the National Academy of Sciences, in 1963, said that other than the search for lasting peace, no problem is more urgent. We live in an age when human life is threatened by two lethal bombs: the H-bomb and the population bomb. From now on, every generation will have to find ways of containing these two threats to humanity. For the time being, with respect to the H-bomb, we have what is optimistically called a nuclear stalemate. What is the situation with respect to rapid population growth and its consequences?

The dangers of thermo-nuclear war are well-known. What are the dangers of rapid growth rates?

By permission of the author.

Rapid population growth rates can lead to famine, can thwart economic development, can contribute to ecological imbalances, can erode the quality of life, and can utterly deplete irreplaceable resources.

The spectres of famine and economic stagnation are closing in upon the less-developed nations. These threats can be forestalled for a time, but at present growth rates, which double the population of many of these countries within 20 to 30 years, the best efforts in agricultural development will fail. Some predict famine within this decade, others presume that it can be averted for another 20 to 30 years.[1]

Ecological imbalances and the erosion of the quality of life are immediate concerns for affluent nations where pollution is already disturbing and hazardous. Questions about the quality of life are subtle, bound up as they are with questions concerning harmonious relations with our environment, economic growth, adequate nutrition and the benefits of small family size. But for affluent nations, a central question has become one of making decisions about the use of space, about the most desirable or necessary balance between wilderness and open space, on the one hand, and compact urban living on the other. Affluence has crowded our national parks, killed other species, and engulfed the wilderness. What, if anything, do we wish to do about it? The aesthetic qualities of our environment which nourish the human spirit are hard to assess and, once lost, are probably irretrievable.

But even if we have twenty to thirty years to cope with dwindling food supplies, dwindling per capita income, environmental disequilibriums, crowding, and the like, the earth can only sustain so many people, and its resources are finite.

Given our desire to avoid increased death rates, how do we bring down birth rates? What is being done to accomplish this end? Increasingly, national governments are providing contraceptives, and information concerning their use, to as many people as possible. During this past decade, family planning programs have

[1] For the former view, see, for example, William and Paul Paddock, *Famine 1975*, Boston: Little Brown & Company, 1967; for the latter view, see *The World Problem, Report of the Panel on the World Food Supply*, Vol. II. *A Report of the President's Science Advisory Committee*, The White House, May 1967, pp. 1–135.

become highly popular government policies.[2]

For such family planning programs, governments and voluntary organizations can offer two very cogent moral justifications. In the first instance, they assist couples to have only the children that they want: the provision of contraceptives and contraceptive information extends human freedom. Secondly, family-planning programs enhance the health of individuals, particularly the health of mothers, and through rational spacing of births, the development, health, and welfare of children as well.

The struggle to gain acceptance for contraceptives has been long and arduous. Margaret Sanger, a pioneer in the birth control movement, began her efforts in 1912. In the proceedings of the Sixth International Neo-Malthusian and Birth Control Conference published in 1926, Margaret Sanger maintained "that there can be no hope for the future of civilization, no certainty of racial salvation until every woman can decide for herself whether she will or will not become a mother, and when and how many children she cares to bring into the world."[3] In 1930, at Lambeth, the first Protestant acceptance of the use of contraceptives, tentative though it was, became a reality. In 1967, thirty heads of state had signed a declaration on population affirming the right of each couple to decide the number and spacing of their children and pledging their efforts to make this a reality for everyone within their jurisdiction.

But in the very year that Margaret Sanger's dream was more nearly realized and realizable than ever before in the history of the world, a new attack on family planning began. It was in 1967 that Kingsley Davis asked whether "stressing the right of parents to have the number of children they want evades the basic question of population policy which is how to give the society the number of

children they need."[4] This attack on the right to decide the number of one's children by using contraceptives did not stem from the fear of promiscuity that motivated Margaret Sanger's opponents, but from the fear that people, left to their own devices, will choose to have too many children. Family planning may be an expression of human freedom, but it is now being questioned with respect to its adequacy as a method of trying to bring down birth rates. Four arguments have been advanced against exclusive reliance upon family planning programs as instruments of population policy.

First, some studies indicate that the introduction and acceptance of contraceptive practices have had little effect upon birth rates.[5] Second, the impact of family-planning programs is inexorably linked to the family-size ideals of the culture or region into which they are introduced. Some demographers have argued that, given the family-size ideals currently prevailing, one can reduce birth rates by no more than 20% in less-developed countries, a reduction that would still leave these countries with growth rates high enough to double their populations every generation.[6]

A third and quite different argument has been advanced against the effectiveness of family-planning programs as instruments of population policy. We cannot, so this argument runs, leave the decisions of social issues to individual couples. We cannot expect couples, each pursuing their own interests, to satisfy the interests or needs of society.[7]

Still a fourth consideration has arisen. Increasingly, it is being pointed out that family-planning

programs are not the sole way in which governments are involved in influencing population growth. Such involvement takes the form of influencing the costs and benefits of having children. On the one hand, child labor laws and compulsory education, where they exist, have the effect of increasing the cost of having children. On the other hand, tax deductions, maternal benefits, baby bonuses and aid to dependent children subsidize parenthood and reduce its cost.

Given these doubts concerning the efficacy of family planning as a means of implementing population policy, and given also the growing realization that governments already have programs that go beyond the mere provision of contraceptives, it is not surprising to find a proliferation of proposals that call upon governments to move from policies that simply support voluntary birth control to policies of population control. Population control, unlike family planning, involves governments in the conscious regulation and specification of the numbers and distribution of people needed by the society under their jurisdiction. In the endeavor to curb birth rates, proposals favoring population control are invoking the coercive powers of government for the sake of influencing reproductive decisions and bringing them into conformity with goals set by the state. Currently, such proposals range from suggestions to use various monetary incentives and penalties, to suggestions to use compulsion by issuing ration cards or putting sterilants in the water supplies, or requiring sterilizations or abortions.[8]

In assessing the consequences of rapid population growth, and in trying to define the so-called "population problem," we are specifying what it is that enhances or threatens the good life. In short, we are making judgments about what is ethically acceptable and unacceptable. Similarly, proposals to encourage, influence, or require certain reproductive decisions also involve judgments about what is ethically acceptable and unacceptable. Population policies and population analyses alike are posing serious questions regarding what is ethically acceptable.

[2] See, for example, Bernard Berelson *et al.* (eds.), *Family Planning and Population Programs* (1966), Bernard Berelson (ed.), *Family Planning Programs: An International Survey* (1969), and Dorothy Nortman, "Population and Family Planning Programs: A Fact Book," *Reports on Population/Family Planning* (The Population Council), December 1969.

[3] See Margaret Sanger, "The Children's Era," *Religious and Ethical Aspects of Birth Control*, New York: The American Birth Control League, Inc., 1926, p. 56.

[4] Kingsley Davis, "Population Policy: Will Current Programs Succeed?" *Science* 158 (1967), 730–739.

[5] See, for example, John C. Cobb, Harry M. Raulet, and Paul Harper, "An I.U.D. Field Trial in Lulliani, West Pakistan," Paper presented at the American Public Health Association, October 21, 1965; and John B. Wyon and John E. Gordon, "The Khanna Study," *Harvard Medical Alumni Bulletin* 41 (1967), 24–28.

[6] See Harvey Leibenstein, "Population Growth and the Development of Underdeveloped Countries," *Harvard Medical Alumni Bulletin* 41 (1969), 29–33.

[7] See, for example, Davis, *op. cit.*, and Garrett Hardin, "The Tragedy of the Commons," *Science* 162 (1969), 1243–1248.

[8] See Bernard Berelson, "Beyond Family Planning," *Studies in Family Planning* 38 (1969), 1–16, for a review and assessment of 29 current population policy proposals.

I wish now to focus on these questions of ethical acceptability and some of the policy suggestions that prompt them.

As a criterion, "ethical acceptability" can be used in at least three important ways. First, ethical acceptability can function as a sociological criterion. In assessing population policy proposals, one can ask whether they will be considered right or wrong by the target population, government officials, professional and intellectual elites, and the outside agencies committed to assistance. Here, ethical acceptability means compatibility or congruence with existing moral beliefs and conventions. When ethical acceptability is so defined, it is limited to a pragmatic consideration of the likelihood that a given policy suggestion will be adopted or rejected. This one can discover by conventional sociological investigations of the prevalence of the relevant moral beliefs and conventions.

Ethical acceptability can also be used as a normative criterion. One can ask of any given population policy whether it corresponds to what people *ought* to value and whether it resolves conflicts of value in the way that these *ought* to be resolved. These are questions for normative ethics, questions as to what things are right or wrong, good or bad. Some of the most important normative criteria are freedom, distributive justice, veracity, and the calculation of benefits and harms, including, at one extreme, threats to our very survival.[9]

But normative assessments of the rightness or wrongness of given population policy proposals may differ. Where disagreements exist, it is necessary to specify criteria for adjudicating moral

disputes. This brings us to the third meaning of "ethical acceptability." It can refer to what is specified by meta-ethical criteria.

There is growing agreement among ethicists that the rationality of moral claims is to be judged by the extent to which they satisfy the following criteria: knowledge of facts, vivid imagination of how others are affected by our actions, and impartiality with respect to both our interests and our passions, so that what obtains for one person obtains for another and for ourselves as well.[10] These criteria describe the kinds of considerations that are reflected in the process of formulating or reformulating our own moral judgments and that emerge as well in our attempts to resolve disputes. They are embodied in our social and institutional practices, and appear in our classical attempts to describe God, an ideal moral judge.

Using these normative and meta-ethical criteria, I wish to explore the ethical acceptability of some major population policy proposals. Let us begin with problems of distributive justice.

1. *Distributive Justice.* The ethical acceptability of any population policy will certainly hinge on the relation it bears to distributive justice. Distributive justice refers to the way in which goods and benefits are to be divided. As used here, achieving a just distribution of goods is governed by two principles: each person participating in a practice or affected by it has an equal right to the most extensive liberty compatible with a like liberty for all, and, secondly, inequalities are justifiable only where it is reasonable to expect that they will work out for everyone's advantage and provided that the positions and offices to which they attach or from which they may be gained are open to all.[11]

Distributive justice is a strongly-held value. Gross inequalities with respect to one's share in a society's goods or one's opportunity to change a disadvantageous posi-

tion, as in slavery, can prompt people to risk death. It is in the interests of society as well as individuals to satisfy the principles of distributive justice. Positive incentives refer to a variety of governmental inducements that take the form of direct payments of money, goods, or services to members of the target population in return for the desired practice of limiting births. Negative incentives refer to tax or welfare penalties extracted from couples that exceed a specified number of children.

Melvin Ketchel has described very well some of the forms of injustice that would generally be perpetrated by population policies resorting to positive and negative incentives:

In underdeveloped countries practically no financial inducements to have children now exist to be reversed, and the imposition of further taxes upon the many poor people would depress their living standards even further and probably only succeed in raising the death rates. In developed countries people in higher economic groups could still afford to have as many children as they wished, so the economic pinch associated with having children would be felt mainly by middle-class and lower-middle-class people, to whom the cost of having children, though somewhat eased by government economic favors, is still relatively high. In order to be effective, economic pressures would probably have to be severe enough to be quite painful, and when they reached a level of painfulness at which they were effective, they would probably seriously affect the welfare of children who were born in spite of the pressures. It seems to me that the same arguments apply to the use of economic pressures to lower the birth rate as are used to argue against the issue of suppressing illegitimacy by cutting off aid to dependent children. If children become a financial burden, there will be fewer of them, but those that are born will be punished by being deprived of precisely those economic advantages they should have, both for humanitarian reasons and for their growth and development into worthwhile citizens. The same objection applies to the use of financial rewards to induce people not to have children because such programs would make the families with children the poorer families. A further objection to the use of economic pressures or rewards is that, since they would be primarily effective against certain economic groups, such methods are discriminatory.[12]

---

[9] See W. D. Ross, *The Right and the Good*, Clarendon, Oxford, 1930, for a more complete list, one which is widely used and referred to among professional ethicists. Ross calls these norms *"prima facie* duties." *Prima facie* duties specify recognizable right- and wrong-making characteristics of actions. Specific actions or policies will be right or wrong in so far as they exhibit one or the other of these characteristics. For example, the act of telling a lie to save a friend violates the prima facie duty of truth-telling but satisfies the *prima facie* duty of not harming others. To decide the rightness or wrongness of particular actions or policies will usually involve a process of weighing conflicting moral claims upon us. The normative criteria I have specified are to be understood as *prima facie* claims.

[10] See, for example, Kurt Baier, *The Moral Point of View* (1958), Richard B. Brandt, *Ethical Theory* (1959), Roderick Firth, "Ethical Absolutism and the Ideal Observer," *Philosophy and Phenomenological Research 12* (1952), 317–345, William Frankena, *Ethics* (1963), R. M. Hare, *Freedom and Reason* (1963), and Maurice Mendelbaum, *The Phenomenology of Moral Experience* (1955).

[11] This formulation appears in John Rawls, "Justice as Fairness," *The Philosophical Review* LXVII (1958), 164–194.

[12] Melvin M. Ketchel, "Fertility Control Agents as a Possible Solution to the World Population Problem," *Perspectives in Biology and Medicine* II (1968), 697–698.

Among the variety of specific proposals to use positive incentives is one that advocates the provision of pensions for poor parents with fewer than N children as social security for their old age.[13] This particular policy recommendation is perhaps the least unjust of all the proposals involving incentives, especially in less-developed countries where pensions are presently largely unavailable, and parents depend upon their children for social security.

If social security were provided for those parents who had no more than some specified number of children, this provision would not severely, or directly, affect the lives of children in economic conditions where it is not normally possible to save money. Similarly, it would not discriminate much against parents who exceeded the specified number of children for they would, as has been the custom, look to their children for social security.

It is true that the whole society would bear the cost of this pension plan, but such a cost could be seen as enhancing the over-all welfare of the society, and, therefore, as a mutually advantageous burden to bear, even though it would discriminate somewhat against the grown children of large families who would have to support their parents as well as contribute to the cost of the pension plan.

In any estimate of the benefit-harm ratio that would obtain should some policy of positive or negative incentives be initiated, it is important to consider the way in which these benefits and harms would be distributed, and how to avoid discriminating against the poor. Generally, the chances that the children of the poor will get a good education, that they will survive to adulthood, and that they will have a good and productive life, and thus realize the hopes for the future that the parents have invested in them, are not nearly as good as for the children of people at higher income levels. Having only two or three children may, from the vantage point of

the poor, look precarious.

In his book, *Children of Crisis,* Robert Coles has raised the question whether many of us understand what a new child means to many of our poverty-stricken mothers, to the men in their lives, and to their other children. To further our understanding, he cites the following very dramatic and articulate account by a black mother:

The worst of it is that they try to get you to plan your kids by the year; except they mean by the ten-year plan, one every ten years. The truth is, they don't want you to have any, if they could help it.

To me, having a baby inside me is the only time I'm really alive. I know I can make something, do something, no matter what color my skin is, and what names people call me. When the baby gets born I see him, and he's full of life, or she is; and I think to myself that it doesn't make any difference what happens later, at least now we've got a chance, or the baby does. You can see the little one grow and get larger and start doing things, and you feel there must be some hope, some chance that things will get better; because there it is, right before you, a real, live, growing baby. The children and their father feel it, too, just like I do. They feel the baby is a good sign, or at least he's *some* sign. If we didn't have that, what would be the difference from death? Even without children my life would still be bad—they're not going to give us what *they* have, the birth control people. They just want us to be a poor version of them only without our children and our faith in God and our tasty fried food, or anything.

They'll tell you we are "neglectful"; we don't take proper care of the children. But that's a lie, because we do, until we can't any longer because the time has come for the street to claim them, to take them away and teach them what a poor nigger's life is like. I don't care what anyone says: I take the best care of my children. I scream the ten commandments at them every day, until one by one they learn them by heart—and believe me they don't forget them. (You can ask my minister if I'm not telling the truth.) It's when they leave for school, and start seeing the streets and everything, that's when there's the change; and by the time they're ten or so, it's all I can do to say anything, because I don't even believe my own words, to be honest. I tell them, please to be good; but I know it's no use, not when they can't get a fair break, and there are the sheriffs down South and up here the policemen, ready to kick you for so much as breathing your feelings. So I turn my eyes on the little children, and keep on praying that one of them will grow up at the right second, when the school-teachers have time to say hello and give him the lessons that he needs, and when they get rid

of the building here and let us have a place you can breathe in and not get bitten all the time, and when the men can find work—because *they* can't have children, and so they have to drink or get on drugs to find some happy moments, and some hope about things.[14]

This graphic description of the feelings of one poverty-stricken mother underlines the claims of distributive justice. Within any population policy, attention must be given to the problem of poverty. This is not so much because the poor have relatively high birth rates, but rather because the conditions under which it is just and rational to expect anyone to curtail family size, do not occur in dire poverty where infant mortality rates are high enough, educational opportunities scarce enough, job opportunities uncertain enough, to undermine the usual rationale for careful family planning. I am convinced, therefore, that alleviating conditions of poverty and delivering better health care to the poor must be part of any population policy, if it is to be just and effective.

Clearly, population policies that employ positive and negative incentives create injustices, discriminating against the relatively poor and bringing about relatively less advantageous economic conditions for the children of parents who are subject to penalties or who fail to gain rewards. Furthermore, there is no assurance that these injustices would be worth the price, for there is no evidence that incentives reduce birth rates. Historically, incentives have only been used, without success, to try to raise birth rates.

What about the use of compulsion to secure the goals of population policy? Compulsion, on the face of it, is the most predictable and hence, rational way to achieve the exact birth rates considered desirable or necessary for a given nation. Thus the economist Kenneth Boulding has suggested marketable licenses to have children in whatever number that would ensure a zero growth rate, say 2.2 children per couple: the unit certificate might be the deci-child, and accumulation of ten of these units by purchase, inheritance, or gift, would permit a woman in maturity to have one legal child.[15] Another proposal

[13] See, for example, Goran Ohlin, *Population Control and Economic Development,* Development Centre of the Organization for Economic Co-operation and Development (1967), 104; T. J. Samuel, "The Strengthening of the Motivation for Family Limitation in India," *The Journal of Family Welfare 13* (1966), 12; Joseph Spengler, "Population Problem: In Search of a Solution," *Science 166* (Dec. 5, 1969), 1234–1238.

[14] Robert Coles, *Children of Crisis* (1964), 368.

[15] Kenneth Boulding, *The Meaning of The Twentieth Century: The Great Transition.* New York: Harper & Row, 196, 135–136.

has been made by Melvin Ketchel, a biologist, who as we noted earlier, rejects incentives as unjust and otherwise impractical. He advocates mass use by government of a fertility control agent that would lower fertility in the society by 5 to 75 percent less than the present birth rate, as needed. Such a substance is now unknown but would, he believes, be available for field testing after 5 to 15 years of research work. It would be put in the water supply in urban areas and introduced by other methods elsewhere.[16] Variants of compulsory sterilization, both temporary and permanent, and compulsory abortion have been proposed as well.[17]

Aside from the obvious technical and administrative difficulties of all of these proposals, especially in less-developed countries, the effectiveness of a policy of compulsion is directly dependent upon its ethical acceptability. Any law can be disobeyed, or subverted, and the problem of punishing offending parents is especially acute. Could it be done, for example, without inflicting suffering upon innocent children? Obviously fines and jail sentences would be a hardship for children as well as parents no matter what provision society would make for the children. Compulsory sterilizations and abortions are the only existing techniques that would predictably enforce a specific quota of children per couple. But these methods are ethically very unacceptable for reasons that we shall note later.

Compulsion, like incentives, discriminates against the poor. As we have observed earlier, restricting the very poor to one or three children would render their lives much less joyous, much less hopeful and much more precarious. In less-developed countries, such restrictions for the poor mean economic losses in the form of reductions both in labor and in security for their old age.

Suppose, however, that the United States eliminates gross poverty, something which, in principle, it can do. What other ethical objections to the use of compulsion by its government would remain? The most conspicuous argument against compulsion is that it is incompatible with the freedom to pursue our

own happiness and forge our own destiny.

2. *Freedom.* Freedom refers in part to the relative absence of government interference and compulsion concerning those actions that are not harmful to the public interest. It refers also to what we sometimes call equality of opportunity, that is, the opportunity to determine and change one's economic, social and political status within one's society. Freedom in both the senses I have specified is as strong a value as survival itself. People will risk death to obtain it for themselves and others. They will not trade it off completely for some other actual or potential benefit.

But freedom is not always incompatible with compulsion. One of the more obvious ways in which freedom is secured through compulsory regulations is illustrated by the laws governing traffic. Without such laws, it is difficult to imagine how the freedom to drive private automobiles in crowded areas could be maintained. Compulsory education also guarantees and enhances freedom. Compulsion also can prevent great harms both to individuals and to society. One example is compulsory vaccinations to prevent epidemics as well as individual suffering. In all these examples, certain choices are taken away from the individual, and yet his total freedom is increased. Would compulsion in limiting the number of one's children be comparable to any of these examples? To answer this question, one must try to characterize more nearly the kind of decision involved in choosing whether or not to have children, and how many to have.

In Plato's *Symposium,* Socrates notes that there are three ways in which people can try to satisfy their deep longing for immortality.[18] One way is to have children. Another is to commit a deed, or deeds, noble and heroic enough to receive the attention of one's community and become a part of its collective memory. A third way is that of scholarly pursuit and authorship. Children, therefore, provide a deeply gratifying link to the human community and to the future. Decisions about how we will use our reproductive powers are decisions about our own future and about our own contribution to the future of the human community, about how one's life is to count, and how far its influ-

ence is to extend.

Even apart from its procreative powers, human sexuality is an important expression of our individuality and a source of intense pleasure. Any policy concerned with the control of human sexual behavior should be seen as right or wrong to the degree that it enhances or diminishes self-fulfilling freedom and sexual joy.

Sexuality is at once an expression of our individuality, and a gift that each of us receives from others, his parents most immediately, but also from the wider community. Indeed, it is a gift from the human species to the human species. We owe a debt of *gratitude* to these wellsprings of our unique genetic and social individuality for the very possibility of experiencing sexual pleasure, and for the considerable rewards of child-bearing and child-rearing.

As those who have been chosen to live, we incur an awesome but joyous obligation to see to it that these gifts of life, sexual expression, procreation, and child-rearing have a future. Our obligation to the larger community is particularly vital insofar as each of us has unique genetic endowments and unique talents to offer and to perpetuate. No one else can give to the species what we bring to it. Failure to reproduce is both an individual and a communal act that requires special justification if it is to be morally responsible. Obviously, individual decisions to refrain from having children of one's own are easier to justify in times of rapid population growth.

If these are the values guiding our reproductive decisions, the very dignity and identity of the person as a moral being is at stake in any decision to use compulsion in controlling reproductive behavior. For example, when a society decides that certain categories of people are not to be considered eligible to reproduce themselves, as certain states do in their current sterilization laws, the effect is to cut off the couples or persons so categorized from one of the basic forms in which they are able to contribute to their own future and to that of their community. Compulsion, in the form of rationing the number of children per couple, would not be as hard a blow to human dignity as compulsory childlessness, but it would still have the moral and psychological sting of any measure designed to ration the number and nature of one's contributions to society.

---

[16] Ketchel, *op. cit.*

[17] Davis, *op. cit.,* 730–739; and Paul Ehrlich, *The Population Bomb,* New York: Ballantine, 1968.

[18] B. Jowett (tr.), *The Dialogues of Plato* (1937), Vol. I, 332–334.

In the United States, the dignity and autonomy associated with reproductive decisions is seen by some to be a constitutional right. One argument used by the Planned Parenthood Federation of America to defeat the birth control laws of Connecticut in the Supreme Court was that these laws, by forcing couples to relinquish either their right to marital sex relations or their right to plan their families, constituted a deprivation of life and liberty without due process of law in violation of the Fourteenth Amendment.[19] Earlier Supreme Court decisions were cited affirming the right "to marry, establish a home and bring up children" as among "those privileges essential to the orderly pursuit of happiness by free men" under the Fourteenth Amendment. (*Meyer v. Nebraska*, 262 U.S. 390, 399, 1923; cf. *Skinner v. Oklahoma*, 316 U.S. 535, 1942). In one of these decisions, *Skinner v. Oklahoma*, the Supreme Court in 1942, ruled that Oklahoma's sterilization law violated the Fourteenth Amendment by authorizing the compulsory sterilization of so-called "habitual criminals." The sterilization of the mentally ill as it is now encouraged and permitted by a number of state laws, though technically "voluntary" insofar as they require the consent of guardians, also deprives people of their right to plan their own families and family life. Like those unfortunates in the fetal and senile stages of life, the mentally ill are among those groups that tend to be seen as something less than worthy members of the human species and hence are not predictably afforded the usual rights and privileges of human beings.

As we noted earlier, Kingsley Davis has directly challenged the right of any person to determine for himself how many children he shall have, because on his view, the assertion of this right conflicts with society's need to keep the number of children at some specified level.[20] In this instance, Davis, like many others, sees a conflict between individual rights and interests on the one hand, and societal necessities and interests on the other.

But is this true of those inter-ests we call human rights? I am convinced that it is not correct to think of a human right as something that can come into conflict with our public interests. To identify a human value as a right is to claim that something of value is *so* valuable and *so* precious that society has a stake in it. Consider, for example, freedom of speech, which is considered a fundamental human right. Freedom of speech is essential to the formation of society itself, and to the establishment and maintenance of voluntary associations.

Rights imply duties. When we say that freedom of speech is a right, we imply that it is our duty, and the duty of others, to see to it that freedom of expression is generally honored and protected. As John Stuart Mill eloquently argued in his famous essay on liberty, it is in the interest both of society and of the individual to protect and to nourish freedom of speech as a fundamental value.[21] Only when ideas see the light of day and enter into competition with other ideas can a society have a basis for progress and innovation.

In claiming that freedom of speech is a right that society should protect, we are not claiming that every utterance ought to be sanctioned. Clearly, the right to free speech is not abrogated by considering it a crime falsely to cry "fire" in a crowded theatre.[22] The protection of freedom of speech does not depend upon permitting any utterance without regard to its consequences. The important thing, however, is that the interests in encouraging certain utterances, and in discouraging others, are both public and private. It is of benefit both to individuals and to society to encourage free expression generally, and to discourage certain forms of it under special circumstances.

This is true also of decisions regarding the nature and the number of one's children. Since we consider it the right of individual couples to make such decisions voluntarily, then it is both an obligation and an interest of society to see to it that this right is honored. At the same time, it is in the interest both of individuals and of society to curtail the extensive expression of this choice should the

consequences of rapid growth rates become too oppressive or threatening. However, if society is to avoid conflict between two public interests, namely the interest in maintaining the quality of life, as against the interest in maintaining the right voluntarily to decide the number of one's children, every effort must be made to provide the information, materials, and conditions that will assist individuals voluntarily to limit their births for their own welfare and for the common good. Compulsory measures can only be justified when they constitute what in just-war parlance we call a last resort.

Not every compulsory measure can be justified, however, even as a last resort. The continuation of human life depends upon the exercise of our reproductive powers. To maintain a population at a replacement level requires slightly more than two children per couple, at the death rates prevailing in affluent nations. In principle, every couple in this world could be granted the right and privilege to have at least two children of their own. The threat of overpopulation is not in itself a sufficient argument for singling out any given type of individual for compulsory sterilizations or compulsory abortions. The suggestion by Kingsley Davis, echoed by Paul Ehrlich, that abortions be required in cases where the child would be illegitimate not only dries up the most important source of children for sterile couples who covet the privileges in the Fourteenth Amendment of which they would otherwise be deprived, but also denies the unwed mother any right to a moral decision about the resort to abortion, both as it touches upon the fetus and upon the operation and the risks to which she will be subjected.

The right to exercise one's procreative powers is not identical with the right to have as many children as one wants through the use of these powers. In a situation of the last resort, societies might very well decide to ration the number of children per family and try to provide some just means, not Boulding's scheme since it involves purchasing power, for deciding who will be permitted to reproduce more than two children. This limits the right to choose how many children one will have but not the right to choose to have one or two children of one's own. Ketchel's proposal threatens this right since by the use of sterilants

[19] The Connecticut law was judged to be in violation of the rights guaranteed by the Fourteenth Amendment, specifically of the right to privacy. See *Griswold v. Connecticut*, 381 U.S. 479 (1965).

[20] Davis, *op. cit.*

[21] *On Liberty* (1859).

[22] "The most stringent protection of free speech would not protect a man in falsely shouting 'fire' in a theatre and causing a panic." Oliver Wendell Holmes, Jr., *Shenkwin v. United States* (1919), p. 249.

that reduce everyone's fertility some people are presumably involuntarily rendered infertile. Of course, if Ketchel can prevent or offset such mishaps, his proposal could be used as a method of rationing, one that would be more easily enforceable than rationing schemes that would have to rely on present contraceptives.

The right to have a choice regarding the exercise of one's procreative powers and to be able to retain the capacity to procreate is as fundamental as the right to life. Choosing to have a child of one's own is a choice as to one's own genetic continuity. One should be free to express one's gratitude to one's parents and to honor their desire for continuing in the human community; one should be free to seek a place in the memory of future generations. If our lives are to be deprived of any choices in establishing these links to the past and the future, we have lost a great deal of what life is all about and, indeed, we have lost the most predictable way known to us of extending our lives on this earth. Only very few people achieve immortality on earth in other ways. Compulsory irreversible sterilization is not a justifiable method of curbing birth rates.

Our draft system is often used as an analogy for justifying the use of compulsion to meet the needs of society. A just war, fought with just means, as a last resort, and in self-defense, would seem to justify conscription.[23] But even in this situation, conscientious objectors are exempt from military service.[24] Population policies should make a similar provision for those who cannot in good conscience submit to sterilization or have an abortion or stay, for other reasons, within a given rationing scheme. Presumably, where population problems are a clear and present danger, most people will be eager to limit the number of their children. The precedent in human history is now well known: hunter-gatherer societies presently being studied in the deserts of Africa keep their populations at levels that guarantee them ample food and leisure

for what they regard as the good life.[25] They have what we will need to develop, namely, a very keen appreciation of the limits of their environment and of their own technical capacities to benefit from it, without harming it.

Although I believe it is wise to sort out in advance what forms of compulsion would be least evil as last resorts, I consider compulsion unjustifiable now and in the indefinite future for at least two reasons: First, famines and environmental deterioration are not exclusively a function of population growth rates; second, more practical and ethically acceptable alternatives to compulsion exist and have not yet been sufficiently tested. This leads us to consider certain current assessments of benefits and harms.

3. *Benefit-harm ratios.* It would take us too far afield to document the debate about how long we can continue to avert famines in less developed countries. Suffice it to say, that agricultural development is accelerating and these efforts must be continued. Furthermore, there are indications that in the Punjab of India, where new high-yielding strains of wheat are being introduced, birth rates are going down as income increases, and as women further the trend to delay marriage in order to receive better educations and better dowries, it is noteworthy that this drop in birth rates has not come through any increase in the use of modern contraceptives but through an increase in the resort to time-honored folk methods.[26]

The crisis that does seem to be urgent and immediate for affluent countries is the one posed by pollution and environmental deterioration generally. In *The Population Bomb*, Paul Ehrlich sounds the alarm: our environment is sick and the disease is identified as overpopulation.[27] The remedy is population control to achieve zero growth rates as rapidly as possible, using coercive methods as necessary. One can agree on the goal of zero growth rate, but we

should not be deceived into thinking that this will solve our ecological problems.

In his testimony before the Reuss Committee, a congressional subcommittee on conservation and natural resources, Roger Revelle, the Director of Harvard's Center for Population Studies, made the following analysis:

The lack of utility of any simple correlation between environmental deterioration and population growth can be demonstrated by calculating the size of the population of the United States which, with the same per capita income and dirty habits as the average U.S. citizen in 1965, would have produced no more pollution than the country experienced in 1940.

Other things being equal, the number of automobiles and the amount of gasoline and paper consumed would have remained about constant over the quarter century if our population had declined from 133 million people in 1940 to 67 million in 1965. To maintain a constant flow of sulfur dioxide in the air from electric powerplants, the population would have had to decrease to only 40 million people. Presumably the amount of nitrogen fertilizers would not have increased, if all but 17 million Americans had reemigrated to the homes of their ancestors. Only 17 million people in the country would use the same amount of nitrogen in 1965 as we used in 1940. The national parks would have remained as uncrowded in 1965 as they were in 1940 if our population during the interval had gone down from 130 million people in 1940 to 30 million people in 1965, instead of going up to 195 million, as, of course, it actually did.

These unlikely speculations emphasize the uncertainties of the relationships between population, gross national product, and the quality of life, of which environmental deterioration is one aspect.[28]

Where the urgent problems of feeding people and curbing ecological imbalances arise, effective government intervention is required regardless of what is accomplished by a given government in the way of reducing or even halting growth rates. To halt pollution now, let us enact the most humane and just measures that will effectively restrain our major polluters.

I can agree with Paul Ehrlich on his call for a new, positive attitude toward our environment, a

[23] For a discussion on the just war criteria, see Ralph B. Potter, *War and Moral Discourse* (1969).

[24] For a detailed account of current practice and a proposal for extending it, see Ralph B. Potter, "Conscientious Objection to Particular Wars," in D. A. Giannella (ed.), *Religion and the Public Order* (1968), 44–99.

[25] Harold Thomas, unpublished manuscript.

[26] For example, in certain areas of India. See John Wyon, "Population pressure in rural Punjab, India, 1952 to 1969," paper presented at the Seventh Conference of the Industrial Council for Tropical Health, October 1969, at Harvard School of Public Health, Boston, Massachusetts.

[27] Ehrlich, *op. cit.*

[28] Roger Revelle testimony in *Effects of Population Growth on Natural Resources and the Environment*, Washington: U.S. Government Printing Office, 1969 (Hearings before the Reuss subcommittee on Conservation and Natural Resources).

note also well sounded in Frederick Elder's recent book *Crisis in Eden.*[29] But this presents us with a most urgent crisis of conscience. In our justifiable concern for the freedom and welfare of women, we have considerably eroded our ethical concern for the human fetus. As one student argued in one of my seminars, we should look upon the human fetus, especially in its earlier stages, as one of the very simpler forms of animal life. Ah, that is the rub! His argument was designed to lessen our regard for the fetus and make it more dispensable, precisely the kind of attitude we are now being called upon to change. We are supposed to recognize that our life and its security is bound to the simplest forms of life on earth and, though we kill to eat, there are constraints upon our actions that we ignore at our utmost peril. Is the fetus, then, something less than the simplest forms of life? To regard it as such appears to me to be fraught with the kind of peril so eloquently expressed by Ralph Potter in his essay on "The Abortion Debate,"

When a fetus is aborted no one asks for whom the bell tolls. No bell is tolled. But do not feel indifferent and secure. The fetus symbolizes you and me and our tenuous hold upon a future.[30]

The current New York law has created a perilous situation. If abortions do turn out to be permissible until the fetus is 24 weeks old, there can be occasions, however rare, when doctors will have snuffed out a viable fetus. Should we toll the bell or should we be morally indifferent to the risks of infanticide? The New York State Medical Society, at least for now, is reportedly clear about this:

After the 20th week of gestation, the process cannot be classified as an abortion and constitutes an actual birth process.
Because the chances of fetal survival increases each week, abortive acts should not be initiated after the 20th week of gestation.[31]

As things now stand, however, the counsel of the Medical Society is not legally binding. It is surely appropriate that we reflect more carefully upon what we are now doing in the area of abortion, considering also the increased risks to women when abortions are performed after the 12th week of gestation and the hints that society may consider compulsory abortions desirable or necessary at some yet unspecified date.

But we do have population problems and we must ask whether there are population policies that are more beneficial than harmful and which do not involve injustices or serious threats to human freedom. I believe that there are.

In a country like the United States, birth rates have been dropping steadily for the past decade. We have time to see how much more can be done by extending voluntary family planning, by better delivery of health services to improve infant and maternal care, by educating people to the bad consequences of continued population growth for the nation as well as the individual family, and by improving educational and job opportunities for everyone, especially blacks, women and other currently disadvantaged groups.

What about the situation in lesser-developed countries? On the basis of intensive research over a period of seven years in the Punjab region of India, Gordon and Wyon hypothesize that people in such an area would be motivated to reduce their birth rates if: mortality rates for infants and children were sharply decreased; local social units were stimulated to measure their own population dynamics and to draw inferences from them concerning their own welfare and aspirations; and efficient methods of birth control were introduced.[32] Initiating these conditions would substantially increase the opportunities to reduce family size without undue fear, to assess more precisely how fertility affects families and their community, and to plan family size more effectively. Whether birth rates would be markedly lowered by bringing about these conditions alone would depend not simply upon the extent to which people in that region stand to benefit from a reduction in fertility, but also upon the extent to which they actually perceive such benefits and believe they are attainable. The gathering and dissemination of information is, therefore, a crucial aspect of this proposal. Without accurate information, a sense of group responsibility cannot exist on a fully rational basis, and will have no perceptible dividend to the individual members.

Looking at the total ecological context within which population problems arise in the less-developed countries, especially the factors of undernourishment, poverty, and lack of opportunity, some writers have suggested that nothing less than substantial technological, social, and economic changes would provide the conditions under which birth rates can be sufficiently reduced. These changes include industrialization, urbanization, and modern market agriculture.[33] Such changes are necessary to provide the conditions which, in the demographic history of the West, have been associated with sharp declines in birth rates, namely rising levels of literacy, better communications, increased economic opportunities, improved health care, lower infant mortality rates, higher status for women, and higher costs of bearing and rearing children.

These two policies would not violate any of our ethical criteria. They would enhance human freedom and encourage responsible community behavior. Both would increase the elements in the decision-making processes of individual couples that contribute to making the morally best decision. They would increase knowledge of the facts, stimulate the imagination of people concerning the effects of reproductive decisions, and encourage more impartiality by fostering loyalties that go beyond one's own interests and passions, and those of one's own group.

Gordon and Wyon's proposal has the advantage of introducing a minimum of disruption into a culture. It may, by the same token, be inadequate to induce the requisite behavior without further transformations of the social and economic lot of the people involved.

In conclusion, let us briefly reflect upon certain practical guidelines that should be part of the formulation and implementation of these and any other population policies. These guidelines draw in a special way upon the norm of

[29] Frederick Elder, *Crisis in Eden— A Religious Study of Man and Environment,* Nashville: Abingdon Press, 1970.

[30] Ralph Potter, "The Abortion Debate," *Religious Situation 1968,* Boston: Beacon Press, 1968.

[31] *New York Times* article.

[32] Wyon and Gordon, *op. cit.*

[33] See, for example, Roger Revelle, "International Cooperation in Food and Population." *International Organization XXII* (1968), 362–391.

veracity, i.e., truth-telling and promise-keeping, and the meta-ethical criteria specified earlier.

4. *Guidelines for formulating and implementing population policies.* First, people need to know the facts. An ideal program that would evoke the voluntary response of the people affected by it would make an honest case for the reproductive behavior called for in the policy. Parents need to know what benefits will accrue to them from limiting the number of their children. Evaluations of population policy recommendations, therefore, must include specific designations of what counts as a population problem and of what interests individuals and societies have in their children. Research is definitely needed to explore more fully the significance and meaning of children to parents in a wide variety of circumstances.

Often, in discussions of population policy, there are allusions to the use of propaganda. This word threatens to create a credibility gap. If by propaganda we mean trying to persuade people that a certain policy is in their interest, without giving them the facts that will allow them to decide whether it *is* actually in their interest, we violate the canons of veracity. Moreover, we do not satisfy the criterion of giving people as many of the facts as possible, and, hence, do not respect their potential to make a morally correct decision and to act upon it.

Population policy must be formed in the light of vivid images of how others are affected by our actions. In some of the literature, there is a distinct elitist strain, implying that only certain people are in a position to formulate population policy and that the rest of mankind must be propagandized, won over by incentives, or compelled to act in ways considered to be desirable by the experts. In contrast to such elitism, ethically acceptable population policies should be based on sympathetic understanding of the conditions of life and of the aspirations of the people who will be affected. To guarantee this, many voices must be heard.

Black people in the United States are among those who are making apparent the value of wide and diverse participation in the planning process and thereby extending the actualization of democratic ideals and the humanization of social institutions. Ways must always be sought to assure that vivid images of how people live, and of what they feel and desire, will guide and shape the planners and their work.

Problems of rapid population growth make the need for impartiality, a third meta-ethical criterion, concretely explicit. Though survival values within our species are strong and tenacious, they are usually individualized and tied to relatively small interest groups representing one's social, ethnic, and national identity. For the survival of such groups many would, under certain circumstances, make sacrifices and even die. But population policies, though they must attend to the needs and interests of particular regions and population groups, should endeavor to ascertain and foster the best interests of the entire human species in its total ecological setting, a task that embraces attention to other species and material resources as well. The goals of population policies go beyond the boundaries our societal and national interests set for us.

In defining these goals, population policies would fail utterly to improve the human condition and enlist its deepest loyalties, were they to diminish, rather than augment, the extent to which beneficence, freedom, distributive justice, and veracity are realized on the earth. These are not moral luxuries; our survival, and the worth of that survival, depend upon their effective implementation. As the demographer Ansley Coale has so sagely observed, "preoccupation with population growth should not serve to justify measures more dangerous or of higher social cost than population growth itself."[34] It would be the ultimate irony of history if through our population policies we should lose precisely what we seek to save.

[34] Ansley Coale, "Should the United States Start a Campaign for Fewer Births?" Presidential Address to the Population Association of America, 1968.

10.13
Beyond the Teach-In

Barry Commoner

Confusion between certain aspects of the environmental movement and other social issues is also generated by the view that the former is closely connected to the population crisis. In one sense, this belief is valid, for clearly the world population cannot continue to grow at its present rapid rate (largely in under-developed countries) without eventually outrunning the capacity of the planetary ecosystem to produce sufficient food to sustain it. But some environmentalists hold that in advanced countries like the United States "the pollution problem is a consequence of population." This view leads to the idea that the environmental crisis in the U.S., which clearly calls for drastic action, can be solved only if we take strong action to stop the growth of the U.S. population.

A good deal of the confusion surrounding priorities can be cleared up by some facts. Nearly all the stresses that have caused the environmental breakdown here—smog, detergents, insecticides, heavy fertilizers, radiation—began about 20 to 25 years ago. That period saw a sharp rise in the per capita production of pollutants. For example, between 1946 and 1966, total utilization of fertilizer increased by 700 percent, electric power nearly 400 percent, and pesticides more than 500 percent. In that period, the U.S. population increased by only 43 percent. This means that the major factor responsible for increasing pollution in the U.S. since 1946 is not the increased number of people, but the intensified effects of ecologically faulty technology on the environment.

Reprinted by permission from *Saturday Review*, April 4, 1970. Copyright 1970 by Saturday Review, Inc.

PHOTO COURTESY OF RICHARD MISRACH.

10.14
The Earth Belongs to the People: Ecology and Power

R. Giuseppi Slater
Doug Kitt
Dave Widelock
Paul Kangas

President Nixon, *Life* Magazine, *The New York Times*, NBC, Standard Oil, all tells us the same thing: there are too many people in America, and in the world. Overpopulation is the root cause of pollution. Overpopulation is the reason people around the world are starving. There are too many people and not enough food. Too many people wanting too many things. Too many people making too much of a mess.

Pollution, they tell us, is merely the by-product of a much greater threat, one that could plunge mankind into chaos. They call this the Population Explosion.

Are they right?

"POPULATION EXPLOSION!" Newspapers warn that we'll be jammed together like chickens in a coop within a century. University pro-

fessors claim that a tremendous number of us will starve to death before that can happen.

Everyone agrees that people themselves are the problem. Too many people cause overcrowding; too many people cause hunger.

Blaming *people* for these troubles sounds perfectly reasonable, but that doesn't automatically make it true. The ancients thought that the sun went round the earth. That seemed reasonable to them. Only after they thought about it and checked out a few facts, did the truth become apparent.

Complex problems rarely have simple answers. If we pick apart the "population explosion" idea, it's clear that people are really talking about two somewhat different things: the growing population of the planet, and why people are starving. We have to tackle these one at a time to see if the world's "population problem" is really a *people* problem.

Perhaps we are really the victims.

Too Many People?

Right now, the world's population is growing at a rate that would cause it to double every 37 years.

Play around with this figure and you find that a few centuries of

growth at that pace would pack the earth with people. Sometimes newspapers or magazines carry incredible articles which do this, and they end up by predicting a sardine-package death for humanity!

Don't believe it. We won't run out of room.

The world's population is growing like never before. But that doesn't mean that the world will become so crowded we can hardly move. Several powerful forces have always limited the number of people that live on the earth, and they will stop population growth long before we find ourselves sleeping five to a bed.

This is easy to demonstrate. Imagine that you're in an automobile cruising along at about 20 miles an hour, and suddenly you press the pedal to the floor. Whoosh! In a few seconds you're doing 60 mph. Now, at this point you wouldn't think, "Wow, if in five seconds I've gone from 20 to 60, then I'll be doing 100 in another five seconds. And if I keep it floored for a minute, I'll be up to 500 miles per hour!" You know very well that the car reaches a top speed and won't go any faster.

The same thing holds true for population. Certain *natural forces* prevent endless population growth, just as a car will only go so fast because its engine can suck in only so much air and fuel and won't turn over any faster. People need food, water and space in order to live; as these get scarce, population growth slows down.

But a car may stop accelerating, even if it hasn't hit top speed, because the driver *decides* not to go any faster. In the same way, people too may *decide* to have smaller families and slow down or stop the rate of population increase. People may put off getting married for many years or practice various methods of natural birth control. In modern societies contraceptive devices and medical abortions give people even more ability to limit population growth. All of these are *social forces*.

But then, why is the number of people in the world still increasing? People have been around for over a million years; why haven't we hit our limit yet?

The answer is simple but decisive: technology. Technology means that although there's only so much farmland and water and living-space in the world, we can find better ways to use these things. Metal plows grow more food than wooden hoe-sticks, especially after they've been attached to tractors.

This leads to an important point, overlooked by all the alarmists who fear that more people on the planet automatically means less food per person. These people make the same mistake that the Reverend Thomas Malthus made two centuries ago. Malthus and his 20th century followers never take into account the effects of new forms of technology; people keep finding ways to get more and more from the unexpandable resources of Nature. *Technology expands the limits of population.*

The lesson of human history shows just how important this is. World population has not *constantly* increased since the dawn of humanity. It has increased in *stages*. Whenever a significant improvement in technology came along that let people get more from the fixed resources of the world, population went through a *growth cycle*: first it increased very rapidly, then growth slowed down and, eventually, tapered off. Population stabilized once again, at a much higher level.

The first people on the planet filled their stomachs by hunting animals and gathering wild plants that could be eaten. The balance of Nature decided how much food was available. This meant that human population, once it reached a certain level, grew very little over many thousands of years.

Then, about eight or nine thousand years ago, people discovered that it was easier to plant seeds in the ground and raise food in one place than to wander across the countryside looking for it. More food could be grown this way, and extra food could be raised and saved for hard times. Because the technology of agriculture meant more food, it also meant more people: there was a "population explosion." Within 4,000 years, world population had increased 16 times!

There were many other improvements in agriculture, but even so, by the year 1300 A.D. world population had more or less stabilized again. The planet could support more farmers than hunters, but still *only so many*.

In the middle of the 17th century, a new technology began to develop. People began to study the laws of natural science; discoveries were put to use in ingenious machines that magnified human labor and used new sources of power. The production of a single worker was enormous with the new methods. Soon enough machines were also used to get increased benefits from the natural riches of the earth. People could make things never before imagined and grow more food than ever.

The effects of this Industrial Revolution were stupendous, and they continue to this day. Population growth went into a spurt that dwarfed anything in the previous million years.

Today, the countries which accounted for the rapid population growth at the beginning of the Industrial Revolution have become industrialized, economically developed nations; they are not growing all that quickly today. *Most of the rapid increase going on now is accounted for by the "underdeveloped countries."*

But their surge will not go on indefinitely, something conveniently overlooked by many population alarmists. When these "experts" look at the charts and blurt, "Look how fast world population is growing: it's going to double every 35 years!" they assume that today's high growth rate won't slow down. It's as though the man who rammed the car accelerator to the floor and jumped his speed from 20 to 60 mph in 5 seconds suddenly shouted, *at that instant,* "I'll be zooming along at 500 mph in a minute from now!"

The same combination of natural conditions and social forces that have always controlled the size of population will eventually stop the spurt in the underdeveloped countries. We can see why the boom must taper off, as it has in the advanced countries, by understanding what caused it in the first place.

All the "underdeveloped countries" of Asia, Africa and Latin America are based on farming rather than industry. History tells us several important things about the traditional farming society:

These societies have always had *high birth rates*, which means large families. It takes lots of manpower to work the fields when farm machinery isn't available; with a few more kids, you can produce much more food. Big families usually do better than small ones.

At the same time the death rate is also very high. People don't know much about science and modern medicine. They can't fight disease. Many women have ten children and see only two or three reach adulthood.

In traditional farming societies, the high birth rate and the high death rate just about balance each other, so population doesn't grow very fast. It is a growth limited mostly by *natural forces*: hunger and disease.

Things change when a society becomes industrialized and modernized. Here, birth rates drop off. Kids are expensive to raise in a city. You've got to support them for 16 years or more before they can earn their own way. Space and food cost money; the more children you have the more you spend without getting any income in return. Families get smaller.

At the same time, though, the industrial society learns a lot about science, and medicine, and hygiene. So the death rate too drops off.

The low birth rate and the low death rate almost cancel each other out. Population is relatively stable. *Social forces* from economic pressures are most important in limiting growth.

Today, the countries of the Third World are still mainly agricultural societies. They are poor and their birth rates are high. But since World War II, the death-reducing techniques of the industrialized nations have been introduced. Babies get vaccines to keep them from getting sick; swamps are drained or treated to remove disease-carrying mosquitos; public sanitation is developed—and fewer people are dying.

The result: fast-growing population.

What is going to cut this rapid population growth? Two roads open out for Third World countries caught in this bind.

They could begin to develop economically. Selective industrialization would allow them to get more from the natural resources of the land. The greater food yields from modern farming techniques would go a long way to feed their people. Soon enough, the social forces and economic pressures especially active in industrial societies would start reducing population growth.

This is already happening in some Third World countries.

At present, though, *most* countries in Africa, Asia and Latin America seem to be heading down a different road. They remain agricultural and unmechanized while their populations balloon and their food output starts to fall behind. The amount of food per person has declined for the last ten years. Sooner or later the preeminent natural force—starvation—must start cutting down the population growth.

These countries are on a road of misery. Today almost a billion and half of their people are under-fed. Half a billion are actually starving. Whether or not their population growth manages to keep increasing over the next decade or two, hunger looms as the only future for these nations—*unless they develop.*

Why have some Third World countries developed while others remain trapped in a cycle of misery? This, and not population growth, is the true problem.

Underdevelopment and hunger: Why do they exist? Why do they continue?

Lots of Food and Lots of Hunger

Over half the people on our planet go to bed hungry every night. Why?

"The world is hungry because we can't grow enough food to feed all the people." This is what TV analysts, government officials, businessmen, and college professors tell us. They predict massive famines within ten years, killing hundreds of millions of people at a time.

They may be right about the famines. It's hard to say there aren't famines right now when up to five million people, mostly children, starve to death in a year, and when 650 million of the world's billion children won't reach adulthood.

But are they right about *why* these people starve? Has mankind swollen so much there isn't enough food to go around? Let's examine more closely what the experts and the officials mean when they talk about overpopulation.

To look at the pictures in the news, you'd think underdeveloped countries are hungry because they are overflowing with people. You see miles and miles of tightly-clumped shanties, filled with gaunt, desperate people, surrounding the cities of Brazil. Ask the slum dwellers of Brazil where they came from, however, and many point towards the vast empty countryside. They came because they had lost their land. A few big landowners and some American investors control most of the good land. As these interests develop their property, trying to harvest profits from the soil, they evict the peasants who have always lived on the land.

These families have nowhere else to go but to the city. And the slums continue to swell.

In America, too, we find ourselves packed even more tightly. Like the peasants of Brazil, more and more of us are *compressed* onto less and less of the land. Like the peasants of Brazil, we do not own or control the land, and so we have no choice: 70% of the people live on 1% of the land in America, and the concentration grows worse every year.

The squeezing of people together is happening in many places. But the plain fact is that there are a lot fewer people for a lot more land in most of the underdeveloped countries. Population density for Africa and Latin America is far below that of Europe.

Only a few Third World countries have high densities—India, Pakistan, Ceylon, the Dominican Republic, and one or two others. But none exceed 450 people per square mile. And yet Holland, with a population density of 972 per square mile, is not called overpopulated, while countries like Venezuela, with only 27 people for each square mile, are said to have a "population problem." There are no hungry people in Holland.

So "overpopulated," to the experts and officials, primarily means "underfed." Look through the lists these men compile of "overpopulated" countries, and you will find that they have actu-ally compiled a list of hungry countries. What kind of a list is it?

Virtually all the nations of Latin America are on this list, and most of Africa (the black states), and Asian countries like India, Indonesia and Syria. In other words, the *poor* nations—and people—of the world are the ones said to have "population problems." Experts and officials see hungry people in thinly settled countries and tell us, "If bellies are empty there, then they have too many people."

Does this kind of reasoning trouble you? It should, especially if you've ever been hungry, out of money and standing in the middle of a supermarket. Because that is a much more accurate description of the plight of the hungry.

America itself is the perfect example to prove this. In 1968, the Citizens' Board of Inquiry into Hunger and Malnutrition in the United States discovered that there are 30 million hungry people right here in the USA. They found that 10 million are not just hungry but live on the edge of starvation. They saw starving children in the fields of Mississippi and in the slums of New York.

The United States is also the world's richest nation. It worries about growing *too much* food. In 1968, the government paid big-time farmers and agribusiness $4 *billion* to take *35 million acres* of good soil out of production. Otherwise, the bumper crops from this land would have glutted the world market and made prices fall.

Why does the government limit production in a world of hungry people, even when some of those people live in our own country? Said a top official in the Department of Agriculture (as quoted in *Hunger U.S.A.*), "It is true that there may be a greater need for food in some countries, but there is not necessarily a market for such food."

Translation: *In America, food is grown for profit, not to feed people.*

What does this mean in human terms? It means, for one thing, that a place like Stanislaus County, in central California, smack dab in the lushest farmland in the world, can become an official "Hunger Disaster Area." That's what happened in December of 1969, when thousands of unemployed people in the area did not have money to buy food from the fertile fields of their own county—while surplus food was stuffing federal warehouses in the area.

And this is exactly the same situation faced by the hungry countries around the world.

According to the 1969 report of the UN's Food and Agricultural Organization, food surpluses—not shortages—are the looming problem in the near future. In the underdeveloped countries, their report points out, food production supposedly outpaced population growth in the last few years. Experts are starting to worry that too much food may accumulate.

One UN food official even predicts that, based on production figures,"There will be no danger of starvation in the next 10 to 15 years." With two billion people underfed right now, that's a rather incredible prediction. The same official tossed off another remark that begins to make sense: "Whether or not people will have income to buy the food . . . is a different matter."

Translation: *Hunger is not lack of food. Hunger is lack of money.*

People are hungry while wheat-glutted Canada will plant no crop in 1970; while American farmers are plowing under thousands of tons of potatoes to raise the market price; while as much grain sits in warehouses around the world as was exported in all 1969.

It should be clear, then, that "overpopulation" is not the real cause of hunger. Does this surprise you? It's certainly not what our leaders and authorities have told us. Let's take it a little further.

Remember the list of "overpopulated" countries, a list composed of hungry people on four continents? There are several countries that would have been on that list 25 years ago, but aren't there now. They are China, Cuba, North Vietnam and North Korea. Over a fifth of the world's people live in these nations. All have had socialist revolutions within the last 25 years.

The people there are no longer starving. If you find that difficult to believe, check out the sources listed at the end of this booklet. They offer recent information on the food production and other economic aspects of these nations.

So our list takes on a new meaning. The two billion hungry people of the world live in areas that were colonized by the Western countries and are still closely bound to them, or live within the Western countries themselves. *Hunger is a "Free World" phenomenon.*

What does this tell us now about overpopulation and hunger?

We can learn much from an interesting comparison: China, Brazil and the United States are more or less equal in size. China has 700 million people, the United States has 200 million, and Brazil has 90 million.

If lots of people means overpopulation, and if overpopulation means starvation, then China should be incomparably worse than the other two.

But instead, Brazil has 40 million hungry people, America has 30 million, and China has virtually none!

A closer look at Brazil will show why so many people of the "Free World" are hungry. Brazil has, according to one Latin American scholar, "more arable land than all of Europe." But most of this land is controlled by a tiny elite and by wealthy corporations from America and other Western nations. What do these landowners grow on their enormous plantations? Coffee.

Brazil's largest export is coffee. There is no food value in coffee, but there's a lot of profit in it. Unfortunately, the profit all goes to a handful of big landlords.

The situation is the same for the rest of the Third World. While landless people starve, the immense plantations and foreign-owned estates occupy the most fertile land and produce only one or two cash-crops for export.

Land that could produce basic foods goes to grow cotton and tea in India, coffee and cotton in Guatemala, bananas and coffee in Honduras, rubber in Indonesia, sugar, coffee and cotton in Mexico . . . the list could go on and on.

All this tells us why there is hunger in a world with so much food.

It tells us that most food production in the "Free World" is seen from a capitalist standpoint: it's supposed to make money for the farmer. If you can't afford it, then you can't have it. That's why in India big farmers sometimes let their wheat harvests rot in the silo when they can't get a good price, even though whole provinces are starving. It's why in America, with 30 million underfed people, the government holds down the harvest to keep prices high.

Overpopulation is a hoax. Hunger in these "Free World" countries is not due to the limits of Nature. The people are poor and hungry because too often the great resources of their land are gobbled up for the benefit of a wealthy few.

Their hunger is not a matter of too many people. It is a matter of too much theft.

10.15
Population Control, 1986

Horacio V. Paredes

The tiny red and green wing lights of Air Force One blinked endlessly. Stop-stop-stop, one seemed to say; and the other, in eternal counterpoint: go-go-go. Faster and faster they went in wild debate as the ear-piercing scream of the jet fell a few octaves. With a slight shudder and an agonized squeal from its rubber tires, the white and gold airplane touched the runway, braking intermittently. Slowly it made its way to a line of waiting men and there stood dumb, its mechanical belly yawning wide for its glass elevator.

It was a bad time to arrive in Washington. Juan Balaquit realized that he was nervous. At times like these, he reminded himself that he was, after all, President of the Third Philippine Republic.

If only he had Blanquita with him today, he thought. She was always such a support.

But President MacGregor had been firm on the Overseas-Intelstat: "We don't bring our wives when we talk of war."

He remembered again his shock when screaming headlines in Manila speculated: "Philippine Republic to War with India?" It was preposterous, of course, but then the Indonesian-Nigerian war too had seemed impossible. That it had started was as impossible to comprehend as its ending so suddenly. A few bombing raids. Small, expeditionary forces landing in undefended areas of Africa and Indonesia, and then a peace treaty, after close to fifteen million dead. "Why?" everyone asked, but it was all over and, when things were well again, the matter had been all but forgotten.

At the White House, the two presidents strode forward. At the door of the Cabinet Room, Mac-Gregor flung open the doors and strode in, not waiting for the Filipino. Instantly angered by the protocol breach, Balaquit stopped

Reprinted by permission from *Atlas,* April, 1970, p. 33. Copyright 1970 by the World Press Company.

and cursed softly. The President of the Third Philippine Republic was ready to turn on his heel and go back to Manila when, at the head of the huge mahogany table, he saw R. M. Krishnan, Prime Minister of India, his white mane lit like a halo by the backlighting, and Panama's Miss Teresa Montenegro, Secretary-General of the United Nations, her kindly face smiling a warm welcome.

Shocked out of his anger, he sat across from Krishnan with as much self-control as he could muster. Then his knees began to shake uncontrollably underneath the table and he could trust neither his hand nor his speech. Holding tightly to the heavy table, he breathed deeply and said in a voice that sounded to him too thin and afraid: "Good evening, Mister Prime Minister, Miss Montenegro. I hope that all is well in your countries."

He felt it was stupid to have spoken until Krishnan choked: "Is this necessary? Can we not solve this some other way?"

Miss Montenegro said: "Gentlemen, I think we all know why we are here. You are all aware, I am sure, of the 197th Treaty signed by all nations and unknown, for their own good, to most of the citizens in our countries.

"For those of you who need a refresher on the gravity of the situation," she continued, "let me state a few facts."

She cited computer figures of the world population as of half an hour ago: food production estimates, commercial statistics, arable land areas. This was all familiar ground. The world was a mess, Balaquit thought, through the dismal statistics of droughts, famines, birth rates, epidemics. When he could stand it no longer, he cut in: "We shall have self-sufficiency in rice by the end of the year. Our fishing industry will soon have sufficient capacity for our population. Vegetable and wheat substitutes will be sufficient for us by next year. Coconuts, our scientists have found, can more than meet our protein requirements for the next fifteen years. Our meat and poultry . . ."

"Yes, Mr. President," Miss Montenegro said, and there was a catch in her voice, "we know, we know. But you know that your population is growing at the rate of five thousand a day. According to our U.N. computer, the exact figure for yesterday was 4,842. Tomorrow there will be more.

"You are gulping at the last dregs in the barrel. And after that, what? Famine? Nationwide hunger? Revolution? When tens of thousands die in the Philippines, a hundred thousand will die elsewhere because your sugar cannot be exported, your coconuts are needed at home, you are willing to import rice and some crook somewhere is willing to sell his people's rice to you. Dr. Krishnan can argue along the same lines, Mr. President. But we all know that the situation is impossible.

"A full meal for a Filipino will mean a hungry African or Thai. Ten acres of Russian wheat destroyed will mean one hungry family in Africa, two in Asia and four in America, and 17 dead Chinese. The balance is so terrifyingly insecure that only war will give us peace."

And with that, she produced five thin red folders. They were identical. Each was titled "Secret Agreement: War Treaty Between the Republic of India and the Philippines under the Terms of the 197th Treaty; Prepared by the 197th Treaty Office, United Nations."

MacGregor stood up, walked the length of the room and said:

"Gentlemen, we are all friends here. Our three countries have been the staunchest of allies. I want you to know that this solution is the only one available. The U.N. has tried everything else and nothing else will work. Now, under the 197th Treaty, the U.S. Armed Forces will make sure that this agreement is carried out, or else. Afterwards, we shall assist your countries in any way necessary for war damages, rehabilitation and so on, but you must stick to the program."

Balaquit reached for his folder and lifted each page slowly until he saw what he was looking for. Manila would be bombed, excepting government offices—estimated casualties: 4,600,000. Central Luzon would be invaded by expeditionary forces—estimated casualties: 2,200,000. The Visayas and Mindanao would suffer another 1,032,000 casualties. None destroyed. Factories would be of the agricultural lands would be clearly marked. But churches would be targets.

His forces would kill 25,362,000 in India. Seventeen thousand Indian troops would be massacred after they had done their bit and five thousand Filipino soldiers would die in India. He felt he would cry.

Miss Montenegro quietly said: "This must be kept completely your secret. The fate of the United Nations and a self-sufficient world is in your hands now, gentlemen. One word and we will have riots, wars and undreamed-of chaos. On page 17 you will find the steps which must be taken to prepare for war. We have programmed the hostilities to start at 0600 GMT on 18 January 1986; that is a month from today. A U.N. adviser will contact you on your return to your countries."

"The U.N. adviser is necessary," the American president said, "We have had relative peace in the forty years since World War II and nothing must shatter that peace. I need not remind you of the findings of special study groups: war properly used can wipe the slate clean, as it were, so that a people can start over again. Germany, Italy, Japan, Korea and Vietnam after their wars immediately succeeded in controlling their populations, increasing production and, in short, becoming useful citizens of the world. It was because of these findings that the treaty was formulated, and my country, Russia and the People's Republic of China agreed to guarantee the terms of the treaty. In this case, the United States of America will join forces against any nation that interferes and against any combatant who deviates no matter how slightly from the plans.

"The plans call for hostilities to last three weeks, after which a peace treaty will be signed between your countries and aid from my country in the amount of one hundred million dollars for India and forty-five million for the Philippines will be delivered to you when the plan has been successfully carried out."

"But this is murder," Krishnan blurted.

"I cannot sign a piece of paper that condemns eight million of my people to die," Balaquit cried.

MacGregor roared, beyond control, "If you didn't have so many goddamned babies—if you had only listened twenty years ago, if you didn't have the highest goddamn birth rate in the world—we wouldn't have a problem now!"

Miss Montenegro looked at Balaquit and Krishnan and said in a small voice: "Gentlemen, if we leave the conference room with the document unsigned you will be kept here in this country while coup d'états install men handpicked by President MacGregor.

MacGregor smiled and said mildly: "Gentlemen, this is necessary. Don't look on it as murder or execution. See it rather as prevention of widespread famine—as a needed pruning of your population in order that the whole tree may grow taller and stronger. See it as a beginning of real progress."

"The end begins here. And it begins now," Krishnan said as he stood up, his wiry frame straight. His eyes moist and his hands visibly shaking, he excused himself and walked over to Balaquit, who stood up and was embraced by the old man. Then he went out into the hall.

In the conference room there was an uneasy silence. Then a shot rang out. Before a guard came back in to tell them the news, they knew.

MacGregor reached for a phone and shouted into it: "General Watson, the son-of-a-bitch shot himself. Take over with your local boys there. Yes, they'll get their aid in two and a half months. We'll run their postwar recovery ourselves and make sure it sticks."

Balaquit accused himself of cowardice. The thoughts he felt were induced by fear but they were clear as day. In his mind, he saw American advisors running his country. The Filipino underlings guided like puppets, with long strings all the way to the White House. He saw Congress flying an American flag, MacGregor in the Speaker's chair. He saw tall Americans walking briskly into Malacañang to give orders and he saw the clear necessity of it all. . . .

And then in his mind's eye there was the smiling bloody face of Bobby Kreutz when they were twelve, his blond hair tousled, his front tooth missing. Bobby and he had fought it seemed for an hour. They hit each other with their fists and wrestled on the grass until the rain came. And then they had lain on the wet grass, spent and panting, giving out small whoops every now and then. They lay there with the rain on their faces. And Bobby had said, in between gasps of air, "Johnny, let's go over and beat up the Smith boys. Between the two of us we can beat up any four American kids."

"So," he said, "you're a Filipino now, are you?" Bobby coughed once, giggled and then laughed happily. And their laughter came in bursts which died down and exploded again in sudden crescendos under the rain on the wet grass in the late afternoon.

10.16
Japan: A Crowded Nation Wants to Boost Its Birthrate

Philip M. Boffey

Japan is the most crowded nation in the world. It has 102 million people—half as many as the United States—all crammed into a string of narrow islands that are smaller in total area than Montana. Moreover, 85 percent of Japan's territory is mountainous—a scenic splendor but ill-suited for habitation—so the huge population is actually squeezed into a series of narrow valleys and coastal plains. Japan far exceeds any other country in population density per inhabitable area. As of 1968, Japan had 1333 inhabitants per square kilometer of cultivable land, compared with 565 for runner-up Holland.

The resulting congestion seems unbelievable to many Westerners. Farmland is so scarce that one finds crops growing everywhere—up the sides of steep hills, in the narrow alleys between adjacent railroad tracks, even at the front stoop, where one ordinarily expects to find a lawn. In the cities, and even in rural villages, tiny houses are jammed side by side, with little or no yard space and barely enough room to walk between. Living is so close that privacy is difficult. As one Japanese physician expressed it: "It's a standing joke among us that you can always tell what a neighbor is cooking. If you can't smell it, you can hear the conversation."

Thus it came as a shock to many Westerners last summer when Prime Minister Eisaku Sato publicly advocated an *increase* in Japan's birthrate. Sato's statement, made in a speech to Japanese newspaper editors, seemed to mark a major reversal of Japan's population policy. For the past two decades, Japan has struggled to curb its population growth, and to a large extent it has succeeded. But now, the Prime Minister indicated, the population control effort may have gone too far. Sato noted that Japan's birthrate had fallen below the average for other advanced nations, and he said the government would strive to bring it back up to that average level. Thus, while other world leaders are struggling to curb the widely

Reprinted by permission from *Science, 167* (February 13, 1970), 960–962. Copyright 1970 by the American Association for the Advancement of Science.

feared "population explosion," Japan seems to have embarked on a somewhat contrary course.

The Prime Minister's remarks caused great consternation in family planning circles in Japan, for even at the current rate of expansion, Japan's population is expected to rise to 131 million by early next century before starting to decline. Tauma Terao, an economist who is chairman of the Family Planning Federation of Japan, told *Science*: "I am entirely against the idea of raising the birthrate. Japan already has too large a population." Similarly, Minoru Muramatsu, one of Japan's leading authorities on the public health aspects of population growth, said in an interview: "In terms of space, Japan already has too many people. If you live in Tokyo, all you can find is a place to eat and a place to earn money. There is no green, no trees. I don't feel that people are living a very human life."

A High-Level Recommendation

Yet Sato's statement was no irrational, off-the-cuff remark by an uninformed politician. It was based on some cautiously worded recommendations made by the Population Problems Inquiry Council, a cabinet-level advisory group which includes some of Japan's leading demographers. Moreover, the recommendations are aimed at alleviating some potentially serious economic and social problems that are related, at least in part, to Japan's success at curbing its population growth. One such problem is a worsening labor shortage that threatens to undermine Japan's "economic miracle"; another is an increasing number of elderly people who will have to be cared for somehow, particularly now that Japan's traditional descendant family system, in which the younger generations cared for the older, is breaking up.

This article will make no attempt to prescribe what Japan's population policy should be, for the Japanese, one of the world's most highly educated and industrious peoples, are certainly capable of deciding for themselves what sort of future environment they want. But the Japanese situation is worth examining in some detail because the same problems—and the same political and economic pressures—may well arise in this country as the population growth here is brought under tighter control.

Japan has undeniably achieved

remarkable success at controlling its birthrate. In the early 1920's, the birthrate stood above 36 per 1000 population, but then it declined moderately and steadily, a phenomenon that usually accompanies the transition from an agricultural to an industrial society. The rate fell as low as 26.6 in the late 1930's before the trend was reversed by the pronatal policy of Japan's military leaders. After the Second World War the rate soared back up as Japan experienced the normal "baby boom" that occurs when soldiers and overseas civilians return home. The birthrate reached 34.3 in 1947 (an intermediate level by world standards) and stayed above 33 in 1948 and 1949, before beginning the precipitous drop that has brought Japan much praise for its "population miracle." By 1957 Japan's birthrate had fallen to 17.2, a historically unprecedented drop of 50 percent in just 10 years. The decline seems especially sharp when measured from the peak of the postwar baby boom, but even compared with prewar trends, the reduction is considered significant.

What was the secret of Japan's success? Interestingly enough, many Japanese demographers describe the achievement as largely "spontaneous" in the sense that the Japanese people, faced with near-starvation economic conditions after the war, concluded on their own that they should limit the number of children. The news media and women's magazines issued dire warnings, particularly at the height of the baby boom, about the bleak future faced by a nation with too many mouths and a war-ravaged economy, and the highly literate Japanese population obviously got the message. The national government unquestionably helped the population control effort, chiefly by reversing its pronatal policy of the war period. A national Eugenic Protection Law, passed in 1948 and subsequently amended, removed the previous obstacles to birth control, abortion, and sterilization. But many Japanese experts believe the government was always at least one step behind what the people were already doing. One reason for the Eugenic Protection Law, for example, was that so many women were obtaining illegal abortions that the government decided it should protect their health by legalizing the procedure. "The government had no definite policy to bring about population control," says Toshio Kuroda,

chief of the migration research division at the government's Institute for Population Problems. "It just happened under the very extraordinary situation after the war. Ten years later people looked back and said we were successful at controlling our population. But no expert in Japan predicted it would happen."

The chief method for curbing the birthrate was induced abortion. The Japanese do not seem to have the strong religious scruples against "taking a life" that have hobbled efforts to increase the use of abortion in this country. Indeed, during the 18th and 19th centuries Japanese peasants often resorted to infanticide to get rid of unwanted children at times of crop failure. Today, abortions are legally obtainable for a number of health and economic reasons. In practice, they are said to be obtainable almost at will. The vast majority of abortions are performed by private physicians within the first 3 months of pregnancy, and most of these take place without overnight admission to a hospital or another medical facility. The operations are quite inexpensive, costing an average of $10 to $15, according to one estimate published in 1967. Health insurance benefits often bring the out-of-pocket cost down much further—sometimes even below $1.

Abortions Declining

The number of officially reported abortions (which is believed to represent about half the total number of abortions) reached a high of 1.17 million in 1955 but has since declined to 757,000 in 1968, largely because of government efforts to encourage contraception as an alternative to abortion. In the early 1950's, according to studies by the Institute for Population Problems, abortion accounted for roughly 70 percent of the decline in Japan's fertility while family planning accounted for 30 percent, but in recent years the percentages have been reversed.

The percentage of couples practicing contraception in Japan seems to be somewhat lower than the figure for comparable populations elsewhere. A 1965 survey indicated that about 67 percent of all Japanese couples either had practiced or were then practicing contraception, compared with perhaps 80 to 90 percent for Great Britain and for the white population of the United States. The most popular contraceptive meth-

ods have consistently been the condom and the "safe period" or a combination of both. The Japanese make little use of the "pill" or the intrauterine device (IUD), which are mainstays of the population control effort elsewhere, largely because conservative medical opinion in Japan believes it is not wholesome to introduce foreign materials into a healthy body. The government officially prohibits the insertion of IUD's and the sale of oral contraceptives, and while there are large loopholes in these laws, few Japanese use either of the methods.

Japan's success at curbing its population growth is believed to have contributed significantly to the fantastic economic boom that has propelled Japan's gross national product to third rank in the world. If Japan had not curbed its birthrate so sharply, some analysts say, then a sizable portion of the nation's capital resources would have been used to support new additions to the population and would not have been available for economic recovery and industrial investment. Yet the curbing of population growth has not been an unmixed blessing. As conditions have changed in recent years, industry has increasingly complained about a labor shortage, particularly a shortage of young laborers.

I found considerable disagreement as to whether Japan is really suffering from a labor shortage and, if so, what should be done about it. The age composition of the Japanese population has changed considerably over the past decade or two. There has been a sharp decrease, both absolute and relative, in the population of children below the age of 15, and a sharp increase, both absolute and relative, in the population over 65. Meanwhile, the working age population, from 15 to 64, has continued to increase, but at a slower and slower rate. The average annual increase in the working age population exceeded 1 million for the 1965–70 period, but it will drop to 620,000 for the next 5 years and will become negative by the end of the century. When viewed against the needs of a rapidly expanding economy, the labor pool appears to be shrinking.

"The labor supply has changed rather remarkably from surplus to shortage," says Saburo Okita, director of the Japan Economic Research Center and a member of the Population Problems Inquiry Council. "There is already a shortage of young workers, and while there is still some surplus of middle-aged workers and women, many of us predict there will be a serious labor shortage in the coming years." Some Japanese economists contend that a decline in West Germany's economic growth rate in the late 1950's was caused primarily by a drop in the growth rate for Germany's labor population, and they suggest that Japan's "economic miracle" may be stalled by the same problem.

Seeking Cheap Labor?

Yet Takuma Terao, the economist who heads the Family Planning Federation of Japan, offers a much different analysis. "The industrialists say the labor shortage is very severe," he says. "But I say what is deficient is young labor, which is very cheap. So all we can say is that we lack cheap labor, only that." Terao and most other experts agree that the chief factor behind the shortage of young labor has not been the low birthrates, but rather the great growth in the number of young people who now go on to high school or college instead of beginning work at an early age. Terao believes it would be "rash to raise fertility" simply to assure more laborers. He believes it would be more sensible for Japan to "rationalize" its traditionally inefficient business enterprises so as to gain greater labor productivity. "We already have an abundance of laborers," he says, "but they are not well utilized."

The Population Problems Inquiry Council—the cabinet-level advisory group whose recommendations provided the basis for Prime Minister Sato's remarks—took a middle-of-the-road position. The council which is made up of some 40 public and private members, including academics and business and labor leaders, was asked in April 1967 to study the implications of Japan's low birthrate. Last August a subcommittee of the council issued an interim report on its findings; a final report is due this year. According to Kuroda, who sat on the council, the interim report represents a "compromise between those who are worried about a labor shortage and those who think Japan is already too populated." The report is said to have been drafted by Minoru Tachi, an eminent demographer who heads the government's Institute of Population Problems. An unofficial English translation was prepared by the U.S. State Department.

The report, if read carefully, does not seem especially earthshaking. It notes that Japan's population, by some measures, is no longer replacing itself; it warns that this is causing certain problems; and it recommends that Japan seek to achieve a "stationary" population in terms of both total size and age distribution. The report makes no mention of what the ideal population for Japan should be, and as far as I could tell from talking to two members of the council—namely, Kuroda and Okita—there was little discussion of optimum population size. Instead, the report focused its attention on indicators that measure the changing growth rate and age composition of the Japanese population.

The report expressed particular concern over trends in the net reproduction rate, a measure of the extent to which the female population of child-bearing age is reproducing itself with female babies. If the net reproduction rate is 1, the population will potentially become stationary one generation later. If the rate exceeds 1, the population will continuously increase, and if it falls below 1, the population is expected to begin to decrease one generation later. Japan's rate is currently the lowest in the world except for some East European Communist bloc nations. It has remained slightly below 1 almost every year since 1956, generally ranging between 0.9 and 1.

A Rare Occurrence

The report states that while the rate has occasionally dipped below 1 in other countries, "it is very rare for such a situation to continue for more than ten years." (The net reproduction rate for the United States was 1.2 in 1967 and has not dropped below 1 since the 1930's.) The report suggests that Japan's population reproductivity is now "too low," and while it acknowledges that "a high population increase rate cannot be welcomed," it nevertheless believes it would be "desirable" for the net reproduction rate to return to 1 "in the near future" in order to ease the "severe changes in population composition by age."

But the report is very careful not to suggest any direct intervention by the government, such as subsidies to support additional children. Instead, the report simply urges the government to improve social conditions so that Japanese couples will spontaneously

decide to have more children. The report also recommends that Japan improve its old-age welfare system and increase the productivity of its labor system.

The report gives no hint as to how its recommendations would affect the size of Japan's population, but there is no question that the population will continue to rise substantially. Government estimates for Japan's population in the year 2025 range from a minimum of 129 million (if the net reproduction rate remains below 1) to a maximum of 152 million, with the median projection being 140 million.

The report is so cautiously written that even such critics as Muramatsu acknowledge there is "nothing really wrong with it if you read the text very carefully." After all, who can object to the government improving social conditions? But opponents of the report are upset that mass media stressed the need for more births and largely ignored the question of social improvement. Some also feel the government was premature in its announcement, since they believe the net reproduction rate is already heading back toward 1, or even higher, without any encouragement. Other critics fear the government will eventually decide to intervene in a very direct way to encourage more births, and some even fear that the government's action was partly motivated by a desire to grow soldiers for a future large army.

At bottom, the disagreement is one of priorities. Those who regard economic expansion as the greatest good want more bodies to man the assembly lines. Those who are worried about overcrowding are willing to sacrifice some economic growth in return for more living space. The question of how much living space is desirable, however, is a knotty one. My own reaction to Japan was to be appalled at the overcrowding. But there is some evidence that the Japanese have grown accustomed to their close living conditions and actually even like them. Ichiro Kawasaki, a former Japanese diplomat, has written that the massive stone buildings of the West "overwhelm" Japanese travelers, and they soon "begin to miss the light wooden structures and small landscape gardens to which they have so long been accustomed." Similarly, Maramatsu, who spent several years at Johns Hopkins University and who frequently travels abroad, laments that many Japanese have no idea what he is talking about when he extols the "spacious way of living" in other countries. "For generations," he says, "many of our people have been living under the same conditions, so they don't question whether it is wrong or right."

Such differing attitudes toward space needs make it difficult for the experts in one advanced nation to suggest the best population policy for another advanced nation. Such differences also make it difficult to visualize how much of a burden population growth in any one country would really impose on future generations in that country. Perhaps future generations will enjoy living shoulder to shoulder.

The Lesson of Japan's Experience

Japan's decision to boost its birthrate slightly may have an impact and significance beyond its own borders. Some family planning advocates fear Japan's action may throw a monkey wrench in worldwide efforts to curb population growth by somehow downgrading the importance of birth control. Others fear Japan demonstrates that radical population control can never succeed, for the minute a nation reaches the point where its population is apt to level off and then decline, various pressures—political, economic, and nationalistic—build up to reverse the trend. Both views are probably too apocalyptic, for Japan is merely trying to boost its net reproduction rate by a modest amount until it returns to 1—a level that is considered the desirable goal by planners in many other countries. Some U.S. experts, for example, have called for a stationary population and a zero rate of growth, and that is precisely what Japan is seeking.

The real significance of Japan's experience may be that it underlines the costs involved in achieving population control. Some experts in this country, such as Ansley J. Coale, director of the Office of Population Research at Princeton University, have pointed out that a stationary population and a zero growth rate have unfavorable as well as advantageous effects. Coale suggests, for example, that a stationary population "is not likely to be receptive to change and indeed would have a strong tendency towards nostalgia and conservatism." He also suggests that such a society would no longer offer "a reasonable ex-

pectation of advancement in authority with age," since there would be essentially the same number of 50-year-olds as 20-year-olds. Zero growth is unquestionably desirable at some point before crowding becomes painful, but in the current rush to jump on the population control bandwagon, it is well to remember that population control is not an unmixed blessing. There are costs involved, and someone will have to pay them.

10.17
Ecology Is a Racist Shuck

Robert Chrisman

The once-exciting ecology "movement" has in recent months managed to assume the stigmata of homework. One reason for its suddenly tired face is that all the ballyhoo about ecology has very little to do with ecology itself. Persons who talk fluently about it are in fact simply talking about dirty air or conservation. The ecological issue itself becomes increasingly difficult to see. Everybody's an ecologist: Nixon's an ecologist, Agnew's an ecologist, Ronnie Reagan, Timothy Leary, everyone.

What began as the optimistic new ecology movement has degenerated into a limp banner erected by tired liberals who want to have their political cake and eat it too. One result has been a strong reaction from the left: the movement has been called a racist shuck by black militants, counter-revolutionary by the left, and a cop-out by political activists. It is generally acknowledged that the goals of the movement have been absorbed by much of middle America, and thus have become weakened. There is also the feeling that a good movement has been co-opted by the establishment. And some of the criticisms are true. The ecology movement *has* provided Americans a diversion from campus strikes, the black liberation struggle and the Southeast Asian war; and the establishment *has* skillfully manipulated the movement.

But none of these appraisals

recognizes the force which gave birth to the ecology movement and its conservative *Zeitgeist*. The national liberation struggles of black and Third World peoples throughout the United States and the world have exerted tremendous pressure upon the economic, political and cultural conditions of white America, and the ecology movement has emerged as a conservative reaction to those struggles, to the new world view and the world order they demand.

The political conservatism of the ecology movement is apparent in its program. Besides demanding the conservation of existing natural resources, the movement demands strict population control. Its entire program is built on one premise: *to survive, man must keep natural things as they are and, if possible, return them to an earlier state.* This is the cornerstone of the conservative vision.

The scientific underpinnings of the ecology movement provide the clearest demonstration of its conservatism. It is mired in 19th century theories of population and energy, and that in itself represents a willful and reactionary desire to return to the past, deliberately ignoring contemporary knowledge. The literature of ecology regularly stresses the "fact" that the earth is a finite and entropic system whose energy will die out, in accord with the second law of thermodynamics. Derived from Newton's 17th century concepts of a mechanistic and static universe, the second law assumes that the energy source of a system eventually runs down and the system dies.

However, the ecologists' Cassandra-like cry that the world is nearing its end is not shared by all scientists. As eminent a scientist and world planner as R. Buckminster Fuller argues that they are wrong: "Physicists . . . have discovered experimentally that energy can neither be exhausted nor originated. Energy is finite and infinitely conserved." Using Einstein's discoveries, science has established that all matter is energy, that energy is radiation and that the two are interchangeable. Thus the ecologists' contention that the earth's few finite energy sources are about to be depleted is refutable.

The ecology movement has also revived the discredited population theory of Thomas Malthus, the early 19th century British economist who advanced the "geometric progression" idea of population growth. Malthus maintained that population increased geometrically, but the food supply increased only arithmetically. Starvation, war and pestilence, he concluded, were nature's way of eliminating the excess population. But it has since been demonstrated that war and poverty increase the birth rate; hence the population eventually increases. Significantly, Malthus' work, published in the wake of the French Revolution and during the uprisings of the European masses, expresses a Toryist contempt for the poor, which certainly affected his simple theory of death as a means of population control. The current ecology buffs advocate a more genteel solution: the poor simply should not give birth in the first place.

Even though its scientific ideology is rooted in the 19th century, the ecology movement nonetheless would have us believe that it has sprung forth fully grown in the 1970's. In fact, the subject has been in the public literature for at least 35 years. John Steinbeck was one of the first—and still best—popularizers of the ecological perspective. His *Log from the Sea of Cortez* (when stripped of its mystic blubber) is an excellent exposition of the ecological behavior of fishes. The basic premise of *The Grapes of Wrath* is ecological. *In Dubious Battle* contrasts the actions of individual man in an ecological fashion. Not surprisingly, Steinbeck's vigorous protest of social evils is anchored in the ecological perception that all men are equal because they must live in the same life zone. And his magnificent short story, "Flight," where the biological and human dimensions are totally integrated, remains the best piece of ecological literature of the last 35 years.

The next development in popular ecological literature was Rachel Carson's *Silent Spring* and *The Sea Around Us*. Beautifully written and scientifically informed, these books evoke the mysterious splendor of the organic process and also spell out, in solid muckraking fashion, the corruption of this process by pesticides and radioactive wastes.

It is here that Steinbeck and Carson part company with the present ecological faddists. Each writer produced a literature and effected a political stance that was corrective of his contemporary status quo politics. And each expressed an awe and a passionate love for the life process. But current ecological literature is deficient in just those qualities that

distinguished the works of Steinbeck and Carson. The science is muddled, the politics are limp, and the pervading emotion is a confused hostility directed toward large masses of people.

Ironically, today's ecology enthusiasts do not seem to like living things. Life must be limited, they say, else it will destroy itself. We must have a small population and a lot of space. People corrupt things. They breed, they shit, they eat, they need clothing, they need shelter, they need fuel. We must eliminate people; otherwise they'll *use* the earth.

If this sounds extreme, take a look at a current piece of ecological literature, *The Environmental Handbook*, edited by Garrett De Bell. This collection of essays does not tell one much about ecology or ecotactics (*The Boy Scout Handbook* is vastly superior), but it does reveal a lot about the liberal mystique regarding ecology. De Bell's introduction invokes a kind of Armageddon: "We thought that the one-month deadline for the writing was impossible, that we could easily spend a year on it. *But a year is about one-fifth of the time we have left if we are going to preserve any kind of quality in our world.*" (Italics in original.)

The book's politics are clear. The individual citizen is to be responsible—burn propane, don't burn garbage; save newspapers, don't have kids; write letters to Congress, and sit back, sanctimoniously satisfied. In other words, a Presbyterian revolution.

In one of the book's essays, "Survival U: Prospectus for a Really Relevant University," John Fischer makes it unbelievably plain: "To get hired, each [professor] will have to demonstrate an emotional commitment to our cause. Moreover, he will be expected to be a moralist; for this generation of students, like no other in my lifetime, is hungering and thirsting after righteousness. What it wants is a moral system it can believe in—and that is what our university will try to provide. In every class it will preach the primordial ethic of survival.

"The biology department, for example, will point out that it is sinful for anybody to have more than two children. It has long since become glaringly evident that unless the earth's cancerous growth of population can be halted, all other problems—poverty, war, racial strife, uninhabitable cities, and the rest—are beyond solution."

This is quite a passage. Within

it are the seeds of religious fanaticism and puritanical bigotry, based on a crude Darwinism which establishes the "primordial ethic of survival" as a religious principle.

Maureen Shelton's little piece, "Game Ranching: An Ecologically Sensible Use of Range Lands," has a similar reactionary primitivism. Let us all eat "elands, wildebeests, and other wild ungulates—indigenous to the local environment." By some obscure logic, she has determined that beef cattle are inefficient and expensive. She seems to overlook the fact that beef cattle have been developed over the last 6000 years because domestic cattle provided man with the cheapest and most reliable meat supply.

Most interesting, however, are the wild ungulates she selects: they are all African. Does Miss Shelton recommend that Africa become the cattle ranch of the world? No. She is discussing the solution Southern Rhodesia has already developed for feeding blacks: ". . . many cattle ranchers . . . state they are making a greater profit from the game, or game and cattle, than from cattle alone on the same lands."

The first real ecological concern is the preservation of the human species, but there are no humans and no real issues considered in the *Handbook*'s 300-plus pages The Vietnamese war is not viewed as an ecological problem, despite the fact that U.S. genocide has eliminated over three million lives, that U.S. defoliants have poisoned people and reduced their life support systems to withered leaves. The ecological crisis of American blacks—historical and contemporary—is not reviewed here. There is no discussion of nonwhite suffering save one reference to "*la Mureta Andanta,*" the disorders suffered by braceros from picking grapes sprayed with a nerve gas called DDT. Nor is there an analysis of nuclear energy.

Another example of the new literature of ecology is Paul Ehrlich's *The Population Bomb*. Ehrlich gets to the point rather quickly. In the prologue he states: "Our position requires that we take immediate action at home and promote effective action worldwide. We must have population control at home, hopefully through a system of incentives and penalties, *but by compulsion if voluntary methods fail. We must use our political power to push other countries into pro-*

grams which combine agricultural development and population control." (Italics added.)

We all know what populations he's talking about. The black population of the United States is growing at a rate 30 per cent higher than the white population. And it seems to be the great hordes of nonwhite people which upset Ehrlich:

"I have understood the population explosion intellectually for a long time. I came to understand it emotionally one stinking hot night in Delhi a couple of years ago. My wife and daughter and I were returning to our hotel in an ancient taxi . . . and the air was a haze of dust and smoke. The streets seemed alive with people. People eating, people washing, people sleeping. People visiting, arguing, and screaming. People thrusting their hands through the taxi window, begging. People defecating and urinating. . . . People, people, people, people. As we moved slowly through the mob, hand horn squawking, the dust, noise, heat and cooking fires gave the scene a hellish aspect. Would we ever get to our hotel? All three of us were, frankly, frightened."

Frightened of what? Obviously, of being outnumbered by a group of colored people. I'm sure Dr. Ehrlich is more comfortable in downtown Manhattan.

Next we find the usual "geometric progression" argument: in 1650 A.D., the population was 500 million; in 1850, one billion; in 1930, two billion; in 1970, three billion plus. Then, the usual scare —we'll be standing on each other's toes in 500 years.

The argument seems convincing. But it is superficial. Hard census data and world-wide estimates have only been available for the last 500 years or so. On the basis of their trends, population experts project a future curve—and then run it *backwards,* to account for 6000 B.C., when nobody had the faintest idea just how many people there were.

Furthermore, the geometric progression argument does not acknowledge the years from 1650 to 1970 as having any unique historical or economic or cultural qualities that would influence population growth. Ehrlich finds that the "doubling" rate for developed countries such as the U.S., Britain, Russia, Japan, Norway, etc. is much lower than that of undeveloped countries, averaging about 125 years. But the typical African, Asian, or South American country figures to double its population in about 25 years. There is the obvious correlation here between prosperity and low population. Prosperity *creates* low population, not vice versa. The U.S. is at its peak of prosperity today and also has the lowest birth rate in its history: 23/1000. It is obvious that economic and cultural conditions determine the population growth rate, and when the survival needs of the species are met, its birth rate declines. Conversely, when its existence is threatened, the rate increases.

Perhaps an even more important factor is the stability of the culture. The population boom of the past 500 years exists in precise parallel to the imperialist expansion of western Europe throughout the globe. All continents were hit. In each case, cultural patterns were disrupted. A culture is itself an ecological unit and the disruption of a given culture will of necessity disrupt its birth rate.

Wherever the white man went, he brought with him two systems, monogamy and patriarchy, and reinforced them with the Bible and the bullet. As a result, polygamous family systems—the preference of most non-European peoples—were disrupted. So were their intrinsic birth control systems. Many African and Asian peoples, for example, practiced continence during and after pregnancy, sometimes for two or three years per child. And they practiced polygamy, simultaneously, so that one wife was available if another were not. The newly liberated victims of exploitation, war and cultural rape obviously have tremendous problems of re-culturation and economic development, and these survival tensions are reflected in their birth rates.

A look at the census figures of China makes this apparent. In 755 A.D., during the middle T'ang dynasty, population was 53 million; in 1102 A.D., the Sung dynasty counted 44 million (during its contracted period); in 1290 A.D., the Yuan dynasty counted 60 million; in 1578 A.D., the declining Ming dynasty counted 61 million. For 800 years, the Chinese population was practically constant.

But during the Ch'ing dynasty the population jumped from 140 million in 1740, to 362 million in 1812, and then to 440 million by 1900, in precise parallel to white European expansion throughout the world. Where it had remained stable for the previous 800 years, the Chinese population *tripled* in 160 years—the years of white imperialist expansion.

Now white America has discovered ecology. It has "discovered" its own industrial abuses, it has acknowledged its pollution and waste of the earth. But the new enthusiasts of the ecology movement have managed to avoid drawing the long-range political conclusions which naturally result from their position, conclusions which the underdeveloped Third World nations whose population growth they fear have been much faster to grasp: industry must be controlled and owned by the whole population it affects. Private ownership of the earth and its resources is an obsolete, vicious practice. Land must be seized and redistributed in equitable amounts to provide each man a decent living zone.

Precisely because the ecology movement manifests a conservative reaction to national liberation struggles throughout the world, it will not endorse their political solutions. In the United States, for example, liberals, moderates and conservatives alike among the white middle class began to flee the cities in the late '60s, as the black struggle intensified. As the black nationalist movement expanded and moved toward economic and political self-determination, a white nationalist movement developed. "Hard hat" gangs, expanded police forces, "neighborhood schools" and discriminatory unions are some of its manifestations.

The ecology movement is also a manifestation of this counter-nationalism. By advocating a reduction in industrial development and in the use of industrial fuels, it does not jeopardize the holdings of the white bourgeoisie but only provides a rationale and a method for repressing the industrial development of black and Third World peoples. The ecology movement's campaign for a reduced birth rate would ease racial tensions by reducing the numbers of nonwhites, instead of confronting the real crises.

The ecology movement's political arm, the League of Conservation Voters, is a nonpartisan front for anyone who advocates conservation, and may well represent an unholy alliance between liberals and Birchers. The League does not distinguish between political conservationists and political conservatives: "The League will support a man from any political party if he is a true friend of the earth. The urgency of saving our environment and our species . . .

should become obvious to liberals and conservatives alike." The Birchers, the Minutemen and the Wallaceites have always been conservationists. Their frontier mystique of fishing, hunting and living off the land requires fresh waters and open spaces. The present liberal-hippie craze for natural living is the reciprocal of the Bircher's mystique.

Despite the ecologists' claim of a uniquely nonpolitical base, the movement does in fact represent a distinctively political viewpoint, and it embodies an obviously political platform which contains these planks: token reform by industry at the domestic level; decentralization of the cities (and the colonization of them); reduction of the nonwhite population of the U.S. and the world through birth control, sterilization and abortion.

White as Moby Dick, the ecology fad seems bent upon creating some kind of white haven or heaven in what is left of the earth. Recognizing the fearful damage the modern military industrial complex has done to its material resources, the liberal bourgeoisie of the U.S. has come up with a solution which will not threaten the fundamental power of private industry and will guarantee that Third World peoples will not industrialize but will remain agricultural. The liberal middle class will be relieved of its burdens of conscience, and nothing will be confronted or resolved; the imperialist oppression will remain and so will the basic standard of living it enforces.

═══════════════════

CONCLUSIONS

After a rather extensive amount of research and an utterly astounding amount of debate, we find ourselves in the position of having to draw conclusions and make recommendations for social action. The political overtones and undertones attached to the question of population control, coupled with the differing views of the editors, have made consensus on all points impossible. We have come to some agreement, however, and present here for the reader's consideration a list of recommended actions along with comments on various points by each of the editors.

1. As far as the deterioration of the planetary ecosystem is concerned, we agree that it cannot be

COURTESY OF DREW HEMINGWAY ANDERSEN.

attributed to a single cause. At least three major factors involved are: faulty use of the available technology, failure to sufficiently develop alternative technologies (nuclear power, etc.), and a growing population which is too large already. Any effort directed at only one of these seems bound to fail. Therefore, we recommend that equal weight be given to programs designed to deal with all three at one time.

2. Each state should repeal existing legal restrictions on abortion so that abortion is a matter between a woman and her doctor. There will still be people against abortion on moral and ethical grounds, but repealing laws will not affect them. The state has no business enforcing private ethics.

3. Birth control information and techniques should be made available to anyone who wants them. This will require a system of free clinics which should be administered at local levels with financial aid from the federal government if necessary. Availability of such information should not be directed toward any particular racial, ethnic, or economic minority. Such direction leads to not unfounded accusations of genocide and overlooks the effect of the middle-class three-child norm on population growth. There also should not be any age restrictions on the dissemination of information, Yes, Mom, this means *your* 14-year-old daughter.

4. The mass media should make every effort to present the population problem to the public, to publicize informational clinics and programs, and to help bring about changes in attitudes toward single and childless people.

5. The public schools should be more responsible in teaching about the population problem. There should be an end to all this nonsense about sex education being a "communist plot," "illegal," or "immoral." Every school should have a comprehensive program in sex education, including contraceptive techniques and ecological economics.

6. Each and every one of us should examine our attitudes toward single, childless, and one child households. The term selfish can no longer be applied exclusively to these people.

7. Particular attention should be given to the roles assigned to men and women in our society. Limitation of family size and relegation to the home are conflicting norms which could lead to serious psychological problems for women. Legal and economic restrictions on women's activities must be removed.

8. Married couples should have *no more* than two biogenic children. Families wanting more offspring should adopt them. A step in this direction would be the creation of model national adoption statutes to encourage adoption and remove some of the stigma still felt by adoptive parents.

9. Federal funds could be used much more constructively if they were put into research on environmental and population problems rather than the absurd war in Southeast Asia. Much of this money should be used to promote research programs designed to further knowledge of man's relation with nature.

10. Finally, once all or at least several of the above reforms have been initiated we propose that the bureau of vital statistics undertake a five year study of demographic trends in the United States. This way the effectiveness of these reforms can be evaluated. We cannot tell if the doomsday predictions of overpopulation will come true until we observe population growth rates during a period when abortion, birth control, relaxed attitudes toward adoption and awareness of population problems are the norm.

EDITORS' BIBLIOGRAPHY

1. Appleman, Philip, *The Silent Explosion*, Boston, Beacon, 1966.
2. Behrman, S. J., Leslie Corsa, Jr., Ronald Freedman, eds., *Fertility and Family Planning*, Ann Arbor, The University of Michigan Press, 1969.
3. Commoner, B., *Science and Survival*, New York, Viking, 1966.
4. De Bell, Garrett, ed., *The Environmental Handbook*, New York, Ballantine, 1970.
5. Ehrlich, Paul R., *The Population Bomb*, New York, Ballantine, 1968.
6. Erlich, Paul R. and Anne H., *Population, Resources, Environment*, San Francisco, Freeman, 1970.
7. Hardin, Garrett, ed., *Population, Evolution and Birth Control*, San Francisco, Freeman, 1970.
8. Phelan, Lana Clarke, and Patricia Therese Maginnis, *The Abortion Handbook for Responsible Women*, North Hollywood, Contact Books, 1969.
9. Rainwater, L., ed., *Family Planning in Cross National Perspective*. Special issue of the *Journal of Social Issues*, 23, 4 (1967); available from SPSSI back issues, Acme Printing and reproductions, 611 South Maple Road, Ann Arbor, Michigan.
10. Rienow, R. and L., *Moment in the Sun*, New York, Ballantine, 1969.
11. Shepard, Paul, and Daniel McKinley, *The Subversive Science: Essays Toward an Ecology of Man*, New York, Houghton-Mifflin, 1968.
12. *A Selected Bibliography: Family Planning Population, Related Subjects*, Planned Parenthood-World Population, 515 Madison Avenue, New York, New York 10022.

Toward Educational Reform

EDITED BY:

Dan Daly
Jean G. Davidson
Michael R. Goff
Ellen A. Goldman

Paul Matz
Jane B. Rockwood
Madelyn Silver
Bart Wander

I

What did you learn in school today,
Dear little boy of mine?
What did you learn in school today,
Dear little boy of mine?
I learned that Washington never told
 a lie,
I learned that soldiers seldom die,
I learned that everybody's free,
That's what the teacher said to me,
And that's what I learned in school
 today,
That's what I learned in school.

II

What did you learn in school today,
Dear little boy of mine?
What did you learn in school today,
Dear little boy of mine?
I learned that policemen are my
 friends,
I learned that justice never ends,
I learned that murderers die for their
 crimes,
Even if we make a mistake
 sometimes,
And that's what I learned in school.

III

What did you learn in school today,
Dear little boy of mine?
What did you learn in school today,
Dear little boy of mine,
I learned that our government must
 be strong,
It's always right and never wrong,
Our leaders are the finest men,
And we elect them again and
 again,
And that's what I learned in school
 today,
That's what I learned in school.

IV

What did you learn in school today,
Dear little boy of mine?
What did you learn in school today,
Dear little boy of mine?
I learned that war is not so bad,
I learned about the great ones we
*   have had,*
We fought in Germany and in France,
And someday I might get my chance,
And that's what I learned in school
*   today,*
That's what I learned in school.

Tom Paxton
("What Did You Learn in
School Today?"
© Copyright 1962, 1964 by
Cherry Lane Music, Inc. Used by
permission. All rights reserved.)

INTRODUCTION

It is our firm belief that the educational systems in the United States need many changes. We necessarily call for a total revamping of the entire system from kindergarten through the university. Because we have selected readings that clearly reflect our sentiments, there is no point in reiterating the ideas here. We hope the selections will turn the reader to thinking about the needed changes in our educational systems and how these changes can be accomplished. Our goal is to point out some of the grievances concerning the present approaches and to suggest some alternatives for promoting change. The ideas mentioned are not nearly representative of the infinite number of alternatives. Using these ideas as stimuli, we hope you will come up with your own actions. Each of us must arrive at our own conclusions and act upon them.

Schoolbell go ding dong
The children all line up
They do what they are told
Take a little drink from the liar's cup.

Just teach them not to criticize
to "yes" the bosses, impress the
*   clients*
o teachers of the world
Teach them to take it well.

Buffy Sainte Marie
(© 1969 Caleb Music.
Printed with permission
of the publisher.)

COURTESY OF WILLIAM RIBAR.

"The Student as Nigger" is a classic article to students. Seldom in the history of student journalism have so many editors gotten in so much trouble over such a small amount of candor. The author, a professor, tells it like it is in no uncertain terms. The language of the article has sparked controversy among parents and school administrators while the substance of the article provokes knowing grins and head nodding from students.

11.1
From The Student as Nigger

Gerald Farber

Students are niggers. When you get that straight, our schools begin to make sense.

. . . At Cal State L.A., where I teach, the students have separate and unequal dining facilities. If I take them to the faculty dining room, my colleagues get uncomfortable, as though there were a

Excerpt from the *Daily Bruin Spectra,* April 4, 1967.

bad smell. If I eat in the student cafeteria, I become known as the educational equivalent of a nigger lover. In at least one building, there are even rest rooms which students may not use. At Cal State, also, there is an unwritten law against student-faculty love-making. Fortunately, this anti-miscegenation law, like its Southern counterpart, is not 100 percent effective.

. . . A student at Cal State is expected to know his place. He calls a faculty member "Sir" or "Doctor" or "Professor"—and he smiles and shuffles some as he stands outside the professor's office waiting for permission to enter. The faculty tells him what courses to take (in my department, English, even electives have to be approved by a faculty member); they tell him what to read, what to write, and frequently, they set the margins on his typewriter. They tell him what's true and what isn't. Some teachers insist that they encourage dissent but they're almost always jiving and every student knows it. Tell the man what he wants to hear or he'll fail your ass out of the course.

. . . Even more discouraging than this Auschwitz approach to education is the fact that the students take it. They haven't gone through twelve years of public schools for nothing. They've learned one thing and perhaps only one thing during those twelve years. They've forgotten their algebra. They're hopelessly vague about chemistry and physics. They've grown to fear and resent literature. They write like they've been lobotomized. But, Jesus, can they follow orders! Freshmen come up to me with an essay and ask if I want it folded and whether their name should be in the upper right hand corner. And I want to cry and kiss them and caress their poor tortured heads.

Students don't ask that orders make sense. They give up expecting things to make sense long before they leave elementary school. Things are true because the teacher says they're true. At a very early age we all learn to accept "two truths," as did certain medieval churchmen. Outside of class, things are true to your tongue, your fingers, your stomach, your heart. Inside class, things are true by reason of authority. And that's just fine because you don't care anyway. Miss Wiedemeyer tells you a noun is a person, place, or thing. So let it be. You don't give a rat's ass; she doesn't give a rat's ass.

Learning is a dangerous thing for the simple reason that persons come to prefer the better because they come to understand the worst.

Carl G. Rosberg,
Department of Political Science,
University of California, Berkeley

John Hurst is an unusual teacher at the University of California, Berkeley, in that his reputation has been made as *a teacher.* Hurst's example as an innovator says more to students about educational reform that most commission recommendations. His answers to a student editor's questions provide a more specific critique than the previous article by Farber. Sadly, most of the imaginative answers Hurst points to are taken from subcollege level classrooms contributing to the general impression we have that colleges will be the last place to reform themselves.

11.2
The Critical Faculty: An Interview with John Hurst

Barbara Cowan

The lecture hall was clogged with people who filled every seat, globbed up in the aisles, and packed the stage—but no one expected a riot. Some showed up simply to raise grade averages, others came to rap about education, and many were worried that this was the last time persistent administrators were allowing Associate Professor John Hurst to teach Education 191A. "We haven't got class cards for everyone . . ." Edging in toward that voice, hundreds of students milled their way toward Hurst, who backed off, jumped up on the podium, and protectively held the cards overhead. "But tomorrow we'll bring enough for all of you." More uptightness. A student snatched the entire stack away, sending a cascade of IBM cards down to the floor where football players leapt over rows of hairy heads, people were knocked over, and fights erupted as the mob smashed forward to grab and grab until the cards were gone. They were reportedly going for upwards of $5 each the next day.

The scene tames down a bit for office hours, but John Hurst is always swamped with people, most of whom aren't asking for anything but just dig rapping with a professor who likes to talk with students. Currently being investigated by the Committee on Courses and widely resented by many faculty members, Hurst has his own ideas about education, most of which are inconsistent with those implemented by the University. At a recent administrative meeting it was suggested that a high percentage of students take courses from Hurst to get off academic probation, and when an education student asked, "What's wrong with students getting off probation?" no one bothered to answer.

Hurst's approach is highly unorthodox, his style is frank and uncluttered with bureaucratic hangups. And he's tenured. He attended Georgetown University on an athletic scholarship, received a bachelor's in education from Springfield College, a Ph.D. from Ohio State, and taught at the University of Minnesota before coming to Berkeley in 1961. He is accredited to teach Educational Psychology as well as Physical Education on a University level.

On the wall of his office, Hurst has a faded Phi Beta Kappa plaque plastered with cut-out block letters which read: "To offer a prize for doing a deed is tantamount to declaring that the deed is not worth doing for its own sake." It's someone

Reprinted by permission from *The Daily Californian* (University of California, Berkeley), October 22, 1969.

else's certificate, but the sentiment is particularly embodied by Hurst, whose presence on this campus continues to stimulate student commitment to humanizing the educational process through the exploration of alternative approaches to learning.

You've been widely criticized by various campus administrators, faculty, and some students for allowing those in your classes to determine their own grades and their own course of study. What's your response to accusations that you teach "micks" devoid of educational value?

HURST: Any course a student takes is no more or less than how he perceives it. Unfortunately a course in which the authoritarian or imposed requirements are relatively minimal is perceived by our educational system as a "mick." At no point in our educational process do we assume that the student is a responsible individual capable of making significant choices, capable of directing himself in his own studies. Today with a society placing emphasis on obtaining a degree, both students and teachers have been taught to ignore what happens in the process of getting there. One of the things which frightens me the most in the schools today is that their whole orientation has been moving toward manipulation rather than toward giving individuals a wider alternative of choice. Curriculums are being presented in a mechanical and manipulatory fashion so the individual himself is becoming a smaller and smaller component of the educational process, to the degree that students think in terms of "micks" rather than in terms of freedom.

Why is that?

HURST: Probably because people are afraid, because fear is so pervasive in our society that the number one product of the public schools is fear—after that comes prejudice. Once you're no longer afraid of losing your job, or getting poor grades, or getting kicked out of school, then after many, many years of being afraid, you can begin to act with relative freedom in education. I attempt to teach my courses so that students can work toward their own expectations—not mine or their parents' or society's. Yet so many kids are incapable of functioning in a free educational environment; many lack the confidence to perceive of themselves as whole human beings who can obtain knowledge—as defined by themselves—without dependence on our highly structured approach to learning. And it is in the schools that they have lost this confidence.

What kinds of changes do you view as instrumental in eradicating fear and in promoting confidence?

HURST: Things are happening in really strange ways, in the Berkeley public schools, for example. Some of the kids who have grown up in rather hip homes simply are not conditioned to fear adults, and they're going in there and really shaking up the teachers. If the kid doesn't want to do something he calmly informs the teacher that he'd rather do something esle, which of course provokes the traditional teacher response: "Do it or I'll make you do it." But the kid's cool; he just smiles and does that something else, leaving the teacher flying about in a rage while he docilely repeats, "I love you teacher but I just don't want to do that because it doesn't make any sense." Most teachers in public schools are so bound by their own preconceptions they simply cannot handle a child whose objections do not explode into violence. I suspect that probably the best way to get rid of fear in our schools is to produce kids who aren't afraid to learn. If enough kids grow up experiencing freedom in the schools despite administrative efforts to prevent this from happening, it'll probably accelerate educational change at a rate much beyond anything we can do as adults.

How about alternatives to public education?

HURST: Setting up private and radical education programs is a nice idea but these take money, which is hard to come by for educators providing alternatives. Consequently these systems are frequently geared to children whose parents can pay for it. The masses of children today have no educational alternatives other than public schools, and those teachers who flick in public school teaching because it is hopelessly beyond repair, are denying others the enlightened views they may take elsewhere. Many teachers today are creating free classrooms, but these are the few who are willing to lose their jobs. It's been repeatedly demonstrated that when teachers are not dependent on the security of their positions, the learning experience can happen with a great deal of humanity.

How can this humanity be instilled into the classroom experience?

HURST: I believe what we need to do if we really want to make things better is to allow and facilitate everybody's finding new experiences, with both teachers and students searching them out and looking at them in a very critical way. It's imperative that teachers learn from their students and give up the rigid lesson plan to become involved. I think the age of rationalism is over in education. Rationalism has led us down to the end of the line and now we have to look at man—to look at all of man, who is more than rational. The distinction between the intellect and emotion probably has very little to do with reality, and as much as we claim to be liberated, too many of us are unconsciously hung-up in fear. While we may no longer be afraid of the university or the public schools, we are still afraid of each other. I suspect that being intellectual brats of our educational system, we too often equate our intellectualization of so-called freedom with the emotional substance which is yet to come, which is much more difficult to obtain.

Why can't educational institutions simply "let go" and permit students to shape their own studies by learning from each other as well as from those faculty members who aren't afraid of them?

HURST: Assorted administrators are uptight about professors who give independent study credit but don't spend all their time directing the student. That's probably the whole hangover of the Christian ethic in our society that man is basically evil and therefore we must force him to be good. We of course define good—not the student, and the idea of giving the student freedom to evolve ideas of his own has become contrary to the whole educational process. What other system in the world would continue to keep a person subservient for sixteen years and then tell him he knows nothing about what he has gone through? By what logic does the typical education processor addressing students about the schools or about education and "you must listen to me because I know everything there is to know —so we're starting from scratch?" There are all kinds of things that happen. Students can't teach others in our system because nobody's an expert until he goes through the particular initiation rites. You're not knowledgeable until you have a bachelor's tucked under your arm, and you're not qualified to help others learn until you turn "accredited personnel." This is just basically nonsense. It would seem to indicate that education has been a fantastic failure.

Who takes responsibility for this disaster?

HURST: Few in education will admit to failure. The learning process in all disciplines remains tightly structured because experts in education presume to know what is good for the student and when a specific dosage of goodness is to be prescribed. Well, hell, 90 per cent of the professors on this campus have never even had an education course in their lives—in the sense that they have never had a focused period of time when they directed their thoughts toward the education process. They come prepared to be scholars and their only exposure to teaching has been the teaching they have experienced. It's no wonder, then, that education is static, that they teach no differently than the professors who have taught them —often to the point of using their professors' notes. The educational process is unexciting to many students because there is little opportunity for the individual to make choices as to what he wants to study, how he wants to approach that study, and under what timetable he wants to proceed. Educators think they are creating free people but they're really manipulating freedom—a central component of which is the opportunity to make choices. Yet the educational process today makes all the choices: how many courses equal knowledge and what level of performance equals knowledge. Monstrous types of computer programs guide the student through a sixteen-year course of study in a very controlled and prescribed way, thus producing someone unable to make choices or to think in alternative terms.

Do you think the majority of students who get plugged into our educational system realize there are other ways?

HURST: The awareness is filtering down further and further from the University and high school level. There are some 12 or 13 year old kids, for example, who are in every sense of the word critically able to evaluate their education on a highly sophisticated level. Yet I suspect that here in Berkeley we tend to overestimate the proportion of kids who are turned on to education. And students cannot be aware that alternatives exist until they realize what's happening to them in our schools. That most students are afraid to live a life style of learning that is beautiful and meaningful to themselves—that will eventually rub off on teachers and other students—seem to enhance the ultimate threat that American education and American society will become a totally manipulative state in the frightening sense of 1984 with the rhetoric of a democracy.

Do you see your courses as alternatives to structured learning?

HURST: In a large sense, yes. It's clear that the right of the individual to direct his own life is being seriously threatened in this country. You can direct your own life—including your own education—as long as you direct it the way society pressures. The effect of the mass media and the knowledge of mass psychology that many social scientists have gained is tremendous. Advertising and governmental propaganda is becoming increasingly effective in stealing our psychological freedom, and that's doubly devious because most of us are not aware of it. I believe that by experiencing choices in an educational environment relatively free of structure, an individual can learn to seriously examine his existence in society so that when he faces that society he not only fills a slot in technology but fills a piece of the universe as well. Perhaps he will even be concerned with motivations other than simply gaining more possessions or more money.

Then the concept of "wholeness" in education can survive?

HURST: I'm not sure. There is a tremendous difference between what a University states as its objectives and the extent to which it meets these objectives. It appears today that educational goals have been translated into a mastery of fragmented subject matter and a strong emphasis on specialization. With a faculty more committed to refining specific disciplines than to pursuing the process of education, institutions are simply not meeting the crucial responsibility to re-evaluate their roles in a technological society. Technology has so seriously eroded academic freedom in the pursuit of knowledge that universities, particularly in the professional fields, produce technically competent human imbeciles. Because it takes more and more time to educate an individual in technology, we therefore must eliminate some of the "whole" aspects of his education

that are not essential to his producing a solid state computer . . . which essentially leaves us with a society with no one prepared or particularly concerned with how that computer is to be run, nor how it is to harmonize with the human situation.

And that means harmonizing with the human environment in an ecological sense as well?

HURST: Absolutely. If in his educational pursuits an individual does not examine or define for himself his own personal relationship to his natural environment that individual is missing one of the most beautiful ways to learn. People are going to start dying in L.A. because of the smog . . . not just a few people getting sick but people are actually going to die. There is a reality out there and it's a reality that we can't continue to violate without coming up against the consequences. People cannot be repressed forever—the environment cannot be fucked up forever. It'll fight back or people will start dying from DDT. But at this point the really serious question is are we too late. Will the effect be irreversible? When the concentration of DDT builds up cumulatively in the body for enough people to take it seriously will it be too late?

Do you think so?

HURST: I really don't know. One maintains hope, otherwise the fight is ridiculous, and we might as well all go live the remainder of our lives in the countryside.

11.3
The Education Game

The Daily Californian

As each quarter begins, we page through the course directory with a feeling of optimism and hope that finally we might find courses that we will want to attend for interests' sake, rather than as a means to get five more units of credit.

Occasionally, some of us are successful in our efforts to discover something worthwhile in the "educational game." For a brief

Reprinted by permission from *The Daily Californian* (University of California, Berkeley), April 10, 1970.

moment, our faith in a university education is restored.

Most of the time our efforts are frustrated. By midquarter we find ourselves in the often irksome and monotonous ritual of class attendance coupled with the burden of producing yet another 15-page paper.

Many people believe that college students are looking for an easy ride through school. We are supposedly not really interested or committed to learning. Yet, deep down, we know that this is a misconception. We, the generation growing up absurd, know that many of us came here to overcome the absurd, desiring to become a part of some form of liberating educational experience.

For most of us, our ideals don't work, our hopes are lost in the mechanical crush of the multiversity machinery.

In seeking a good course we usually look for a good reading list, an interesting course description and a good rating of a professor. We normally overlook what should be the most important factor, the context in which we are taught—the impact of the total educational experience on us.

Think about what the educational experience is like in a classroom. You're probably squeezed into a wooden desk.

With a minimum of bodily movement allowed in this position, you are forced to look straight ahead at the instructor, standing either behind a large desk or elevated on a stage. You are subtly coerced into adopting a very passive relation to the class; your response, if any, is to scribble in a notebook concepts that you have almost no time to contemplate or approach critically. Usually, you become disinterested to the point where you end up escaping into free-form doodling on the margin of a notebook.

The active role is taken by one person, THE TEACHER, the class depends on him and is controlled by him. Think of his reaction to criticism of the directions of the class, to the reading list . . . to grades. When you consider this situation, in light of the total time we have spent in the classroom from age five, you will discover that most of our lives we have been conditioned to be receptive, unresponsive, uncreative and passive salivators! We are rarely exposed to ideas about other ways of conducting our education and our daily lives.

The classroom in many ways is

the extreme manifestation of an authoritarian way of life that we are forced to adapt and eventually internalize as our own.

We have not been forced to put things together, to construct, to build, to develop our own way of living. Most students from affluent homes were used to getting what they wanted from earliest memory, to the extent that so-called luxuries—like toys—were expected as a right. We were not allowed to make our own toys, we took what we received, played with it for awhile, became frustrated—tired of it—tossed it away and waited for the next outside "thing" of amusement.

Some of us react to the dehumanization that pervades our lives each day, by losing hold of ourselves, adopting absurd posture and adjustments to an absurd situation—Lenny Bruce and more recently Jerry Rubin are extreme examples of those who have exposed the absurd by becoming absurd.

However, their struggle exemplifies the self alienation which the individual has undergone. Revenge, hopelessness and defeat become ends in themselves. Nevertheless, some of us manage to retain some semblance of hope that our ideals may be realized while attempting to free ourselves from the fear of working without externally imposed guidelines to action.

Picture yourself in a class with 250 other students for a whole quarter, without teachers and grades. Where there is no direction set for you, where you, together with the other students, must set the direction. At first you are lost. You are forced to grapple with your own insecurity, forced to confront beings as individuals, and other students as humans, and not as competitors.

In order for the class to create a direction of its own, each of you must enter into a collective struggle to define your collective will.

John Hurst, an extremely popular professor with the students in the School of Education, has sat in front of his class and had nothing to say—he had no pedantic pitch to give. In so doing, he placed each student in the position of defining the condition in which he found himself. Meaning only grew out of individual expression and involvement. Hurst believes that the ability to learn, to make choices—the responsibility for learning—should rest primarily with the student. If a stu-

dent wants to enroll in his class, get an A and not attend, that is his decision—you will get out of the class as much as you want to put into it.

Hurst's main concern is with students and their total learning experience. Hundreds of students jam into his classroom each quarter, his office is cluttered with students both talking to him and waiting to see him each day, even when, as during this quarter he is not teaching a course. He eats dinner with students in their homes. He does not hide himself within the traditional pontifical role of a professor.

His rejection of the grading system as a means for evaluating his students' work has grown out of a deep commitment to a personalization of the student-teacher relationship through written and oral commitment.

Professor Hurst's work has gone largely unrecognized for six years. Many of his colleagues—who have devoted most of their time to research and little to teaching—have been recognized for their research work.

One had to cram all this stuff into one's mind, whether one liked it or not. This coercion had such a deterring effect that, after I had passed the final examination, I found the consideration of any scientific problem distasteful to me for an entire year. . . . It is, in fact, nothing short of a miracle that the modern methods of instruction have not yet entirely strangled the holy curiosity of inquiry: for this delicate little plant, aside from stimulation stands mainly in need of freedom: without this it goes to wrack and ruin without fail. It is a very grave mistake to think that the enjoyment of seeing and searching can be promoted by means of coercion and a sense of duty. To the contrary, I believe that it would be possible to rob even a healthy beast of prey of its voraciousness, if it were possible, with the aid of a whip, to force the beast to devour continuously, even when not hungry—especially if the food, handed out under such coercion, were to be selected accordingly.

Albert Einstein

This article speaks for itself as a statement of the alienation bred by one of the great Universities.

11.4
$6000 Degree in Boredom

Carol Matzkin

I bought my degree from the University for $6000. Every quarter, I handed the Regents a hefty check, in good faith that I would get something in return. I have, but not what I expected. I have received the knowledge that this university is worthless. I just received a letter from Phi Beta Kappa, congratulating me on my "meritorious achievements." All I could do was laugh. My only achievement at this University has been surviving the four year factory as, hopefully, a vital human being . . . of emerging from this fetid system untouched by it and, therefore, unscathed.

I remember once, four years ago, when I was actually excited by my classwork. That was in English tutorial 1A. We became a close-knit learning group, four students, grads, and the professor. We reached for the stars, because he told us we could reach them. We had time to grab but a few before he was "released" from the department.

All my real teachers are gone now. It was too hard for them here. If they tried to reach out for their students, tried to make their interests relevant to us, and not Reagan or some abstract philosopher, or their department head, they were considered too powerful, too dangerous. The professor who led my journalism class in some of the most soul-searching important discussions of People's Park, society, and ourselves, is gone now. Supposedly because he did not publish enough. Others are being threatened on the same count.

I tried the art department—I tried many of them. First there was the art professor who claimed that women should be making babies, not art—and ripped apart, or worse, ignored our precious creations. And another—a major force in the old guard department,

Reprinted by permission from *The Daily Californian* (University of California, Berkeley), 1969.

whose old fashioned, conservative ideas dragged me down to the depths of boredom, as time and time again, he criticized our work on grounds that were totally irrelevant to the statements we were trying to make.

The lecture courses were all abominable. Typical is the one I'm now registered for: Geography 103. The professor, though obviously dedicated to his subject matter, has totally lost touch with his students. He's a walking, talking catalogue—liberally sprinkling his lectures with names, places, and words no one in the peanut gallery has ever heard of before. The only time he indicated he's aware of our presence is when he scolds the class: "Will the girl in the rear please stop reading her Daily Californian." Doesn't he wonder why she's reading it?

But worse, far worse than lecture courses (at least you can escape into the anonymity of fybates[1] and objective finals) are the so-called experimental courses. Courses such as last year's fiasco Political Science 101X (Freedom) claim academic freedom, but are caught up in the same myopic outlooks as any other course. The three quarter course boasted the "finest" crop of professors in the school—and that's exactly what they ended up with. Though hundreds tried to get in, 25 or so made it, and only 2 or 3 stuck through to the bloody end. The class was supposed to talk about and experiment with freedom, eventually making a film on the subject. But the professors, too long in the system, couldn't let loose enough. Students continually pushed against their invisible bars, while teachers insisted on analyzing, abstracting, killing whatever creativity could have cropped up. They blamed us for the constipation and then proceeded to do what they apparently had wanted to do in the first place. One wrote the script, one directed, etc., etc. We students, stupid enough to stick with, were relegated to bit parts in mob scenes, or worse, carrying their cameras and doing their dirty work. Rumor has it the film is finished but typically, only the professors have seen it.

The individual[2] courses could be the university's saving point but, unfortunately, they are too often a farce. Time after time, I have been turned down on the grounds that the professor didn't have enough time, that it wasn't specifically his field, that he doesn't trust students to work on their own.

Seeing that I feel this way about the University, it should seem remarkable that I am ending my career as a "student" with a 3.5 average. It's really not. Once you become aware of the fact that most courses will hinder, rather than help you on the path to knowledge, you learn to be crafty. For the past three years, I've managed to fulfill all my requirements while spending a maximum 3 hours a week in class. How? I took the most bummer requirements spring quarter each year, sure that riots and revolution would keep the class in turmoil. I chose the rest of my courses on either the basis of which would take the least amount of time and work (currently fybated courses with written B.S. finals) or those which were loose enough to give me credit for doing what I wanted to do anyway.

Sad as it is, if you want that idiot diploma so badly (Why? Why? I ask myself) pay the University your hundred or five hundred a quarter, and try to arrange for as much free time as possible so that you can pursue your own interests, develop your own talents.

Somewhere along the line, if I had been inspired, I could have learned a lot about zoology and history and art and English. As it is, all I know is how to get around rules and requirements. In this University, as it now is, we have no choice: beat it or become it. It has nothing to teach us.

A child born in the United Kingdom today stands a ten-times-greater chance of being admitted to a mental hospital than to a university, and about one-fifth of mental hospital admissions are diagnosed schizophrenic. This can be taken as an indication that we are driving our children mad more effectively than we are genuinely educating them. Perhaps it is our very way of educating them that is driving them mad.

R. D. Laing
(From *The Politics of Experience*.)

An extension of Farber's argument is Jerry Rubin's *Do It*, an anti-intellectual attack written in an infuriating but compelling style. Along with other excerpts from *Do It* in some of the other chapters, the substance underlies the style. The analysis of education is hard to deny despite a tendency on Rubin's part to preach the PIG-litany of the new left.

11.5
Burn Down the Schools

Jerry Rubin

A sunny day on the Berkeley campus. Students are carrying ten pounds of books from one class to the next.

We nonstudent fuck-ups say, "Excuse me, student. Did you know that the sun was shining?"

They look at us like we're crazy.

We invade the libraries yelling, "The sun is shining! The sun is shining!"

We go into a psychology class on "Thinking," a huge lecture hall with 300 students. The professor is up front, diagramming behavior on the blackboard. Everybody writes down in their notebook every word he spews.

His first words are, "Good morning, class."

The guy next to me copies down, "Good morning, class."

Somebody raises his hand and asks: "Do we have to know that for the exam?"

The classroom is an authoritarian environment. Teacher up front and rows of students one after another. Do not lose your temper, fuck, kiss, hug, get emotional or take off your clothes.

The class struggle begins in class.

We roll a few joints and start smoking in the middle of the classroom. The smell is overpowering, but no one seems to notice it.

The Viet Kong could attack with mortar shells, and everybody would still be taking notes.

It's an assembly line.

The professor talks; students copy.

Reprinted by permission of Simon and Schuster from *Do It!* by Jerry Rubin, chap. 36. Copyright © 1970, by Social Education Foundation.

---

[1] Summaries of class lectures that can be purchased.

[2] Independent study.

Everyone is 99 percent asleep.

Marvin Garson takes off his shirt and begins tongue-kissing with his chick Charlie. I rip off my shirt and start soul-kissing with Nancy.

There we are in the middle of class, shirts off, kissing, feeling each other up and smoking pot.

Everyone gets itchy and nervous because of us. No one can take any notes any more. The professor stutters. Pens stop. People squirm. Everyone's looking at us —no one at the professor. But the students are too repressed and shy to say anything.

Finally a girl in the middle of the room can't stand it any more. "Could these people please stop making a disturbance?" she pants.

Nancy leaps to her feet: "This is a class on thinking! We're thinking! You can't separate thinking from kissing, feeling, touching.

"We're the laboratory part of the class. Anybody who wants to come, join us. Anybody that wants to listen to the lecture part of the class move to the other part of the room."

The professor then reveals his soul. "In MY class," he says with authority, "I do the teaching."

SCRATCH A PROFESSOR AND FIND A PIG.

(His assistant goes to get the uniformed pig, so we split.)

TWO HUNDRED PSYCHO-LOGICAL TERRORISTS COULD DESTROY ANY MAJOR UNIVER-SITY—WITHOUT FIRING A SHOT.

Schools—high schools and colleges—are the biggest obstacle to education in Amerika today.

Schools are a continuation of toilet training.

Taking an exam is like taking a shit. You hold it in for weeks, memorizing, just waiting for the right time. Then the time comes, and you sit on the toilet.

AH!

UM!

It feels so good.

You shit back right on schedule—for the grade. When exams are over, you got a load off your mind. You got rid of all the shit you clogged your poor brain with. You can finally relax.

The paper you write your exam on is toilet paper.

BABIES ARE ZEN MASTERS, CURIOUS ABOUT EVERYTHING.
ADULTS ARE SERIOUS AND BORED.
WHAT HAPPENED?
BRAIN SURGERY BY THE SCHOOLS.

I lost my interest for books in literature class. I lost my interest in foreign languages in language class. I lost my interest for biology in biology class.

Dig the environment of the university! The buildings look like factories, airports, army barracks, IBM cards in the air, hospitals, jails. They are designed to wipe out all individuality, dull one's senses, make you feel small.

Everyone should bring dayglow paint to campus and psychedeli-cize the buildings as the first act of liberation.

"Critical" or "abstract thinking" is a trap in school.

Criticize, criticize, criticize.

Look at both sides of the argu-ment, take no action, take no stands, commit yourself to noth-ing, becuase you're always looking for more arguments, more infor-mation, always examining, criti-cizing.

Abstract thinking turns the mind into a prison. Abstract thinking is the way professors avoid facing their own social im-potence.

Our generation is in rebellion against abstract intellectualism and critical thinking.

We admire the Viet Kong guer-rilla, the Black Panther, the stoned hippie, not the abstract in-tellectual vegetable.

Professors are put-ons, writing and talking fancy, scientific, big motherfucking words, so the people on the street won't dig that they're not saying shit.

They're so thankful for their "intellectual freedom in Amerika" that they're not going to waste it fighting on issues like poverty, war, drugs and revolution. They insist upon freedom to be irrele-vant.

We judge our teachers as men first and teachers second. How can you teach us about World War I if you weren't in the streets of Czechago?

The goal of the revolution is to eliminate all intellectuals, create a society in which there is no dis-tinction between intellectual and physical work: a society without intellectuals. Our task is to destroy the university and make the entire nation a school with on-the-job living.

School addicts people to the heroin of middle-class life: busy work for grades (money) stored in your records (banks) for the future (death). We become re-placeable parts for corporate Amerika!

School offers us cheap victories —grades, degrees—in exchange for our souls. We're actually sup-posed to be happy when we get a better grade than somebody else! We're taught to compete and to get our happiness from the UN-happiness of others.

For us education is the creation of a free society. Anyone who wants to teach should be allowed to "teach." Anyone who wants to learn should be allowed to "learn." There is no difference between teachers and students, because we teach and learn from each other.

The professors and the students are the dropouts—people who have dropped out of Life. The dropouts from school are people who have dropped into Living. Our generation is making history in the streets, so why waste our lives in plastic classrooms?

High school students are the largest oppressed minority in Amerika.

We know what FREEDOM IS when we hear the bell dismissing school.

"SCHOOL'S OUT, I'M FREE AT LAST!"

Teachers know that unless they control our toilet training, we'd never stay in class. You gotta raise your hand to get permission to go take a shit. The bathrooms are the only liberated areas in school.

DROP OUT!

Why stay in school? To get a degree? PRINT YOUR OWN! Can you smoke a diploma?

The same people who control the universities own the major capitalist corporations, carry out the wars, fuck over black people, run the police forces and eat money and flesh for breakfast. They are absentee dictators who makes rules but don't live under them.

Universities are feudal autoc-racies.

Professors are house niggers and students are field niggers.

Demonstrations on campuses aren't "demonstrations"—they're jail breaks. Slave revolts.

The war on the campuses is similar to the war in Vietnam: a guerrilla people's war.

By closing down 100 universities in one day, we, the peasants, can level the most powerful blow possible against the pigs who run Amerikan society.

We'll force the President of the United States to come on his hands and knees to the conference table.

We're using the campus as a launching pad to foment revolution everywhere.

Ronnie Reagan, baby, you're right!

So, in a sense, there is something to the argument that college prepares for life—if conformity and mediocrity are what we are trying to prepare people for. If we want to condition people to obeying arbitrary demands without question and make them dependent upon extrinsic rewards and coercion; if it is a world of whimsical authority, arbitrary deadlines and external motivation for which we are preparing our students—then there is a point in this "preparation." Otherwise it cannot be defended as sane or valuable. This kind of forced feeding and pressure—racked regimentation cannot be justified as a preparation for mature people to pursue ideas and projects independently for the rest of their lives. It does not make for self-motivated, adventurous persons eager to explore life with confidence. Perhaps it produces the kind of people most fit for an authoritarian, repressed society, but that is not, in our opinion, the purpose of education.

Don Robertson and Marion Steele
(From *The Halls of Learning*.)

For most students today, Paul Goodman had the first if not the last word on what is wrong with society. He feels that schools are wasteful since they are designed to serve the 15 percent of adolescents who learn well in school— leaving the growing majority to flounder as a system oversight who have been oversold on the value of school. His insights into the need for freedom, self-directed education, field experience, and more options represent a potpourri of ideas which have been adopted on a spotty basis in American education. We have been *Growing Up Absurd* and are unfortunately continuing to educate absurdly as well. As Goodman puts it, "I would not give a penny to the present administrators, and I would largely dismantle the present school machinery."

11.6
Freedom and Learning: The Need for Choice

Paul Goodman

The belief that a highly industrialized society requires twelve to twenty years of prior processing of the young is an illusion or a hoax. The evidence is strong that there is no correlation between school performance and life achievement in any of the professions, whether medicine, law, engineering, journalism, or business. Moreover, recent research shows that for more modest clerical, technological, or semiskilled factory jobs there is no advantage in years of schooling or the possession of diplomas. We were not exactly savages in 1900 when only 6 per cent of adolescents graduated from high school.

Whatever the deliberate intention, schooling today serves mainly for policing and for taking up the slack in youth unemployment. It is not surprising that the young are finally rebelling against it, especially since they cannot identify with the goals of so much social engineering—for instance, that 86 per cent of the federal budget for research and development is for military purposes.

We can, I believe, educate the young entirely in terms of their free choice, with no processing whatever. Nothing can be efficiently learned, or, indeed, learned at all—other than through parroting or brute training, when acquired knowledge is promptly forgotten after the examination— unless it meets need, desire, curiosity, or fantasy. Unless there is a reaching from within, the learning cannot become "second nature," as Aristotle called true learning. It seems stupid to decide a priori what the young ought to know and then to try to motivate them, instead of letting the initia-

Reprinted by permission from *Saturday Review*, May 18, 1968. Copyright 1968 by Saturday Review, Inc.

tive come from them and putting information and relevant equipment at their service. It is false to assert that this kind of freedom will not serve society's needs—at least those needs that should humanly be served; freedom is the only way toward authentic citizenship and real, rather than verbal, philosophy. Free choice is not random but responsive to real situations; both youth and adults live in a nature of things, a polity, an ongoing society, and it is these, in fact, that attract interest and channel need. If the young, as they mature, can follow their bent and choose their topics, times, and teachers, and if teachers teach what they themselves consider important—which is all they can skillfully teach anyway—the needs of society will be adequately met; there will be more lively, independent, and inventive people; and in the fairly short run there will be a more sensible and efficient society.

It is not necessary to argue for free choice as a metaphysical proposition; it is what is indicated by present conditions. Increasingly, the best young people resolutely resist authority, and we will let them have a say or lose them. And more important, since the conditions of modern social and technological organization are so pervasively and rigidly conforming, it is necessary, in order to maintain human initiative, to put our emphasis on protecting the young from top-down direction. The monkish and academic methods which were civilizing for wild shepherds create robots in a period of high technology. The public schools which did a good job of socializing immigrants in an open society now regiment individuals and rigidify class stratification.

Up to age twelve, there is no point to formal subjects or a prearranged curriculum. With guidance, whatever a child experiences is educational. Dewey's idea is a good one: It makes no difference *what* is learned at this age, so long as the child goes on wanting to learn something further. Teachers for this age are those who like children, pay attention to them, answer their questions, enjoy taking them around the city and helping them explore, imitate, try out, and who sing songs with them and teach them games. Any benevolent grownup—literate or illiterate—has plenty to teach an eight-year-old; the only profitable training for teachers is a group therapy and, perhaps, a course in child development.

We see that infants learn to speak in their own way in an environment where there is speaking and where they are addressed and take part. If we tried to teach children to speak according to our own theories and methods and schedules, as we try to teach reading, there would be as many stammerers as there are bad readers. Besides, it has been shown that whatever is useful in the present eight-year elementary curriculum can be learned in four months by a normal child of twelve. If let alone, in fact, he will have learned most of it by himself.

Since we have communities where people do not attend to the children as a matter of course, and since children must be rescued from their homes, for most of these children there should be some kind of school. In a proposal for mini-schools in New York City, I suggested an elementary group of twenty-eight children with four grownups: a licensed teacher, a housewife who can cook, a college senior, and a teen-age school dropout. Such a group can meet in any store front, church basement, settlement house, or housing project; more important, it can often go about the city, as is possible when the student-teacher ratio is 7 to 1. Experience at the First Street School in New York has shown that the cost for such a little school is less than for the public school with a student-teacher ratio of 30 to 1. (In the public system, most of the money goes for administration and for specialists to remedy the lack of contact in the classroom.) As A. S. Neill has shown, attendance need not be compulsory. The school should be located near home so the children can escape from it to home, and from home to it. The school should be supported by public money but administered entirely by its own children, teachers, and parents.

In the adolescent and college years, the present mania is to keep students at their lessons for another four to ten years as the only way of their growing up in the world. The correct policy would be to open as many diverse paths as possible, with plenty of opportunity to backtrack and change. It is said by James Conant that about 15 percent learn well by books and study in an academic setting, and these can opt for high school. Most, including most of the bright students, do better either on their own or as apprentices in activities that are for keeps, rather than

through lessons. If their previous eight years had been spent in exploring their own bents and interests, rather than being continually interrupted to do others' assignments on others' schedules, most adolescents would have a clearer notion of what they are after, and many would have found their vocations.

For the 15 percent of adolescents who learn well in schools and are interested in subjects that are essentially academic, the present catch-all high schools are wasteful. We would do better to return to the small preparatory academy, with perhaps sixty students and three teachers—one in physical sciences, one in social sciences, one in humanities—to prepare for college board examinations. An academy could be located in, and administered by, a university and staffed by graduate students who like to teach and in this way might earn stipends while they write their theses. In such a setting, without dilution by nonacademic subjects and a mass of uninterested fellow students, an academic adolescent can, by spending three hours a day in the classroom, easily be prepared in three or four years for college.

Forcing the nonacademic to attend school breaks the spirit of most and foments alienation in the best. Kept in tutelage, young people, who are necessarily economically dependent, cannot pursue the sexual, adventurous, and political activities congenial to them. Since lively youngsters insist on these anyway, the effect of what we do is to create a gap between them and the oppressive adult world, with a youth subculture and an arrested development.

School methods are simply not competent to teach all the arts, sciences, professions, and skills the school establishment pretends to teach. For some professions—e.g., social work, architecture, pedagogy—trying to earn academic credits is probably harmful because it is an irrelevant and discouraging obstacle course. Most technological know-how has to be learned in actual practice in offices and factories, and this often involves unlearning what has been laboriously crammed for exams. The technical competence required by skilled and semiskilled workmen and average technicians can be acquired in three weeks to a year on the job, with no previous schooling. The importance of even "functional literacy" is much exaggerated; it is the attitude, and not the reading ability, that

counts. Those who are creative in the arts and sciences almost invariably go their own course and are usually hampered by schools. Modern languages are best learned by travel. It is pointless to teach social sciences, literary criticism, and philosophy to youngsters who have had no responsible experience in life and society.

Most of the money now spent for high schools and colleges should be devoted to the support of apprenticeships; travel; subsidized browsing in libraries and self-directed study and research; programs such as VISTA, the Peace Corps, Students for a Democratic Society, or the Student Nonviolent Coordination Committee; rural reconstruction; and work camps for projects in conservation and urban renewal. It is a vast sum of money—but it costs almost $1,500 a year to keep a youth in a blackboard jungle in New York; the schools have become one of our major industries. Consider one kind of opportunity. Since it is important for the very existence of the republic to countervail the now overwhelming national corporate style of information, entertainment, and research, we need scores of thousands of small independent television stations, community radio stations, local newspapers that are more than gossip notes and ads, community theaters, high-brow or dissenting magazines, small design offices for neighborhood renewal that is not bureaucratized, small laboratories for science and invention that are not centrally directed. Such enterprises could present admirable opportunities for bright but unacademic young people to serve as apprentices.

Ideally, the polis itself is the educational environment; a good community consists of worthwhile, attractive, and fulfilling callings and things to do, to grow up into. The policy I am proposing tends in this direction rather than away from it. By multiplying options, it should be possible to find an interesting course for each individual youth, as we now do for only some of the emotionally disturbed and the troublemakers. Voluntary adolescent choices are often random and foolish and usually transitory; but they are the likeliest ways of growing up reasonably. What is most essential is for the youth to see that he is taken seriously as a person, rather than fitted into an institutional system. I don't know if this tailor-made approach would be harder or easier to administer than standardization that in fact fits nobody and results in an increasing number of recalcitrants. On the other hand, as the Civilian Conservation Corps showed in the Thirties, the products of willing youth labor can be valuable even economically, whereas accumulating Regents blue-books is worth nothing except to the school itself.

(By and large, it is not in the adolescent years but in later years that, in all walks of life, there is need for academic withdrawal, periods of study and reflection, synoptic review of the texts. The Greeks understood this and regarded most of our present college curricula as appropriate for only those over the age of thirty or thirty-five. To some extent, the churches used to provide a studious environment. We do these things miserably in hurried conferences.)

We have similar problems in the universities. We cram the young with what they do not want at the time and what most of them will never use; but by requiring graded diplomas we make it hard for older people to get what they want and can use. Now, paradoxically, when so many are going to school, the training of authentic learned professionals is proving to be a failure, with dire effects on our ecology, urbanism, polity, communications, and even the direction of science. Doing others' lessons under compulsion for twenty years does not tend to produce professionals who are autonomous, principled, and ethically responsible to client and community. Broken by processing, professionals degenerate to mere professional-personnel. Professional peer groups have become economic lobbies. The licensing and maintenance of standards have been increasingly relinquished to the state, which has no competence.

In licensing professionals, we have to look more realistically at functions, drop mandarin requirements of academic diplomas that are irrelevant, and rid ourselves of the ridiculous fad of awarding diplomas for every skill and trade whatever. In most professions and arts there are important abstract parts that can best be learned academically. The natural procedure is for those actually engaged in a professional activity to go to school to learn what they now know they need; re-entry into the academic track, therefore, should be made easy for those with a strong motive.

Universities are primarily schools of learned professions, and the faculty should be composed primarily not of academics but of working professionals who feel duty-bound and attracted to pass on their tradition to apprentices of a new generation. Being combined in a community of scholars, such professionals teach a noble apprenticeship, humane and with vision toward a more real future. It is humane because the disciplines communicate with one another; it is ideal because the young are free and questioning. A good professional school can be tiny. In *The Community of Scholars* I suggest that 150 students and ten professionals—the size of the usual medieval university—are enough. At current faculty salaries, the cost per student would be a fourth of that of our huge administrative machines. And, of course, on such a small scale contact between faculty and students is sought for and easy.

Today, because of the proved incompetence of our adult institutions and the hypocrisy of most professionals, university students have a right to a large say in what goes on. (But this, too, is medieval.) Professors will, of course, teach what they please. My advice to students is that given by Prince Kropotkin, in "A Letter to the Young": "Ask what kind of world do you want to live in? What are you good at and want to work at to build that world? What do you need to know? Demand that your teachers teach you that." Serious teachers would be delighted by this approach.

The idea of the liberal arts college is a beautiful one: to teach the common culture and refine character and citizenship. But it does not happen; the evidence is that the college curriculum has little effect on underlying attitudes, and most cultivated folk do not become so by this route. School friendships and the community of youth do have lasting effects, but these do not require ivied clubhouses. Young men learn more about the theory and practice of government by resisting the draft than they ever learned in Political Science 412.

Much of the present university expansion, needless to say, consists in federal and corporation-contracted research and other research and has nothing to do with teaching. Surely such expansion can be better carried on in the Government's and corporations' own institutes, which would be unencumbered by the young, ex-cept those who are hired or attach themselves as apprentices.

Every part of education can be open to need, desire, choice, and trying out. Nothing needs to be compelled or extrinsically motivated by prizes and threats. I do not know if the procedure here outlined would cost more than our present system—though it is hard to conceive of a need for more money than the school establishment now spends. What would be saved is the pitiful waste of youthful years—caged, daydreaming, sabotaging, and cheating—and the degrading and insulting misuse of teachers.

It has been estimated by James Coleman that the average youth in high school is really "there" about ten minutes a day. Since the growing-up of the young into society to be useful to themselves and others, and to do God's work, is one of the three or four most important functions of any society, no doubt we ought to spend even more on the education of the young than we do; but I would not give a penny to the present administrators, and I would largely dismantle the present school machinery.

11.7
The Case Against Grades

Jack Sawyer

The ill effects of the grading system are well-known. It restricts students' freedom, fosters a cynical, anti-intellectual atmosphere, forces students to pursue grades before learning, and impedes development of independent learning and creativity. It is presumed necessary to provide needed certification of competence, give feedback to students on their progress, provide incentive to learn that would otherwise be lacking, and furnish a reward to those who do learn.

Examination of these presumed functions shows that they are largely unnecessary, attainable by other means, or not met by grades anyway. Any remaining positive functions are simply not worth the toll that grading exacts upon learning. To preserve this prime function of universities, the grading system must be abolished. Whatever problems this may create will be less than the violence that grades now do to learning.

Ill Effects of Grading

1. Grading restricts the freedom of students, encourages respect for authority rather than knowledge, and suppresses development of the ability to make independent assessments.

The grading system imposes external constraints sometimes thought to promote learning, but learning should depend upon individual motivation, not imposed conditions. Students should be free to determine their own education. If a person wants to learn something, then it is unnecessary to employ grades to motivate him. If he does not so choose, then it is oppressive to require him. The use of grades causes the authorities who impose them to be respected (or resented) for their power rather than their knowledge.

The coercive aspects of the educational system may well carry over into other areas of life, promoting a norm of blind obedience to authority, and inhibiting development of the ability of individuals to choose independently. If college students are thought incapable of acting wisely, when are

By permission of the author. Reprinted from the *Daily Northwestern Magazine,* February 25, 1970.

they capable of choosing? Unfortunately, 16 or more years in which what is right is defined by what the teacher says prepares persons poorly for later independent choice, as the reluctance of adults to make independent assessment of events in the world around them indicates.

2. Grading discourages an open, intellectual atmosphere, promotes deviousness and cynicism, and damages relations among students and teachers.

Free pursuit of knowledge requires an atmosphere where everyone is free to voice opinions, doubts, uncertainties, ignorance, and even error. But the requirement of evaluation forces students to consider the possible effect of exposing their ignorance. It also means that teachers can never be quite sure that a student is interested in the subject rather than in improving his grade.

The necessity to grade forces a game, with opposing roles, upon students, faculty, and administrators. The game invites duplicity by all involved in the process. The resulting deviousness, and its widespread toleration, involves the university in a duplicity that is highly inconsistent with its professed goals of promoting truth and clarity. Grading also forces students into competition with each other and inhibits their developing the ability to learn from one another.

3. Grading forces both students and instructor to orient their course activity around this requirement, restricts the range of activities, and defines learning by this restricted range.

Since students' fate in college and afterward may depend upon grades, they must necessarily first work to assure that they will "succeed." Thus the first task is to learn how to get grades adequate for their purpose. Under the grading system, students rightly ask whether lecture material will be on the examination, what form the examination will take, how much each course component weighs in the final grade, etc. Grading creates just what faculty decry and students resent—the necessity to be oriented toward grades.

In attempts to be fair, instructors may carefully limit and prescribe course material in ways they would not if free of the need for comparative evaluation. Students necessarily select projects on the basis of the amount of effort and the probability of success. It becomes better to deal

successfully with trivial problems than to tackle challenging problems on which one might fail, and this attitude carries over to other situations. Materials and modes best suited for rapid regurgitation are favored; cramming and other practices inimical to learning are encouraged. Worst of all, grade-defined success in a course tends to reify as "learning" whatever was done to get it.

4. Grading discourages more independent, creative activity, prevents the development of self-motivation, and denies the opportunity to learn how to learn.

The necessity to meet standard requirements deters students from pursuing knowledge independently and creatively. The imposition of external incentives effectively eliminates the opportunity for internal motivation to develop and be used. It cheats students of what could otherwise be an excellent opportunity—perhaps the last good chance—to learn how to learn. Yet the rate of change of society makes it increasingly more important to be able to learn rather than to know any specific, soon-outmoded information.

How will mechanically-educated persons cope with the society of the year 2000? Significant new knowledge itself will be better fostered by those who have learned how to learn creatively—whatever volume of information might be ground out more mechanically. Universities that do not encourage persons to learn freely seem unlikely to provide significant help in the important aspects of people's lives, nor to create a society of free, unalienated people.

The Presumed Functions of Grading

1. Certification: As measures of performance, grades are inaccurate, fail to predict future performance outside school, and are not needed by other institutions anyway.

Grades are invariably based upon incomplete samples of the relevant knowledge; the samples are moreover necessarily biased in both content and form of evaluation. Grading practices reflect personal differences in teaching philosophy and vary widely among instructors, as do average grades given. These and other shortcomings make the transcript a dubious document. Businesses realize this and do not place too much reliance on it, usually insisting, as graduate schools do not, upon per-

COURTESY OF JORGE CORTÉS.

sonal interviews.

Undergraduate grades do predict graduate school grades to a limited extent, but neither graduate nor undergraduate grades have been shown consistently to predict performance outside school.

The use of grades for entrance to graduate and professional schools has been considered the major impediment to the abolition of grades. However, there are other ways—such as examination of actual products from students —to accomplish selection. The market value to a student of a certificate is perhaps a more relevant consideration than one would like to think, but it is a questionable concern for a university, particularly if this marketable certificate interferes with learning, so that producing certified graduates diminishes the learning that is supposed to be certified.

2. *Feedback: Students need to know how they are doing, but this is not aided by merely an A-F grade, and requires instead information that is much more substantive, detailed, and frequent, and which can come from sources other than the instructor.*

Feedback is crucial to learning, but the grading system inhibits rather than facilitates it. Feedback is more freely given, received, and utilized in an atmosphere free of coercive evaluation. Grading encourages seeking of feedback for reasons irrelevant to learning; students may ask instructors to explain a low grade not to correct misinformation, but to justify the grade. They may also fail to seek feedback simply to avoid this unfavorable impression. Grading establishes the instructor, even against his will, as the final and only arbiter of what is right and wrong, important and unimportant. Those who accept this are hoodwinked, those who do not but

conform become cynical and those who resist subject themselves to sanctions.

Grading generally encourages students to look for feedback solely from the instructor, not from fellow students, from other sources, or from their own knowledge. It is poor preparation for future independent learning, and tends to create either lack of ability to discriminate at all, or application of fixed standards.

3. *Incentive: If some students learn only because of the incentive of grades, and would not learn otherwise, one should question the value of what they learn, whether they are enabled ever to learn on their own, and perhaps why they should be doing something they don't want to.*

Material learned only for the sake of getting a grade seems unlikely to be either esteemed or retained. Though forced learning may be at its dubious best in situations of rote learning for short-term recall, it seems unlikely that creativity and intellectual honesty can be motivated by externally imposed sanctions. In any event, forced grades are alienating; they get persons to do something they don't want to, and involve the university in furthering alienation. It would be far better to question whether the university needs to provide certificates that are sought for the sake of certification alone and are destructive of learning itself.

4. *Reward: Those who have truly learned are rewarded both intrinsically and through the use of what they have learned.*

This reward is a natural consequence, and it can neither be bestowed or removed. Grades and certificates, in contrast, are not valuable in themselves, but only by reputation. They are most needed when the intrinsic reward is lacking; grades and certificates are more useful to those who have not received the real reward of learning. But for what are they rewarded then? For whatever combination of compliance and cleverness it took to complete the requirements of the system. The power to bestow these arbitrary rewards increases the power of the university, both in society and over its members, but does it further learning?

Grading Must Be Abolished

It is apparent that the process of grading tends to destroy what it attempts to measure. The ill effects are all too evident. It is coming to be recognized that the grading system cannot be salvaged —that there is a basic incompatibility between grading and learning. Effort should be devoted not to vain attempts at salvage, but instead to exploration of new and better ways of education. Freedom from grading may not promote the aims of those—at any level in the university—who see the university primarily as a certifying institution, but it will help those whose concern is learning. The question at stake is what the University is all about, and whose interests it serves.

Art Hoppe again? Yes—on target with an analysis of how Skarewe University coped with yet another form of student protest.

11.8
The Good Old Medieval Campus

Arthur Hoppe

Once upon a time in the country called Wonderfuland there was a 500-year-old institution named Skarewe University. It issued Diplomas.

Just about everybody went to Skarewe University. They spent exactly four years studying exactly 16 required courses in thisology and thatology. They did this to get a Diploma.

Diplomas were very valuable. If you showed one to a prospective employer he gave you more money. No one knew why.

But the country fell on uneasy times. Even the students at Skarewe University caused trouble. They demanded this and they demanded that. And they got everything they demanded. Until, finally, they couldn't think of anything else to demand.

"I know," said one student one day, "let's demand that they abolish Diplomas!"

And, not having anything else to do, the students went on a Diploma Strike.

Reprinted by permission from *The San Francisco Chronicle*, December 16, 1968. © Chronicle Publishing Co. 1968.

The President of Skarewe University was stunned. "If we don't issue Diplomas," he said, "we will lose our standing in the academic community."

The business community was shocked. "Without diplomas," employers said, "how can we tell a college graduate from an uneducated man?"

Editorial writers viewed with alarm. "These radicals would destroy the very purpose of dear old Skarewe U.," they wrote. "They should be forced to accept their Diplomas whether they like it or not."

The Trustees were furious. "Abolishing Diplomas will set our university back 500 years," they thundered. "It will become a medieval institution!"

And it did.

From the very day that Diplomas were abolished, 64.3 per cent of the students quit to go engage in more financially-rewarding pursuits. And those who were left found parking spaces for their cars—for the first time since the Middle Ages.

Just as in the Middle Ages, students now attended Skarewe University solely to gain knowledge and wisdom.

And as there were no required courses, teachers who imparted knowledge and wisdom gave well-attended lectures. And those who didn't, didn't. Just as in medieval times.

Just as in medieval times, students pursued only the studies that interested them and read only the books that stimulated them. And all, being constantly interested and stimulated, were dedicated scholars.

Thus it was that Skarewe University became what it had been 500 years before—a vast smorgasbord of knowledge and wisdom from which the student could select that which delighted and enriched him.

So everybody was happy. The President was happy to head such a distinguished community of scholars. The trustees were happy there were no more riots. And the taxpayers were happy they no longer had to purchase educations for those who didn't want them.

Even prospective employers were happy. For, oddly enough, even without a Diploma, you could still pick out the applicant who had gone through college—because for the first time in 500 years, he was a well-educated man.

Nobody starts off stupid. You have only to watch babies and infants, and think seriously about what all of them learn and do, to see that, except for the most grossly retarded, they show a style of life, and a desire and ability to learn that in an older person we might well call genious. Hardly an adult in a thousand, or ten thousand, could in any three years of his life learn as much, grow as much in his understanding of the world around him, as every infant learns and grows in his first three years. But what happens, as we get older, to this extraordinary capacity for learning and intellectual growth?

What happens is that it is destroyed, and more than by any other one thing, by the process that we misname education—a process that goes on in most homes and schools. We adults destroy most of the intellectual and creative capacity of children by the things we do to them or make them do. We destroy this capacity above all by making them afraid, afraid of not doing what other people want, of not pleasing, of making mistakes, of failing, or being wrong. Thus we make them afraid to gamble, afraid to experiment, afraid to try the difficult and the unknown.

John Holt
(From *How Children Fail*.)

Our schools are crazy. They do not serve the interest of adults and they do not serve the interests of young people. They teach "objective" knowledge and its corollary, obedience to authority. They teach avoidance of conflict and obeisance to tradition in the guise of history. They teach equality and democracy while castrating students and controlling teachers. Most of all they teach people to be silent about what they think and feel, and worst of all, they teach people to pretend that they are saying what they think and feel. To try to break away from stupid schooling is no easy matter for teacher or student. It is a lonely and long fight to escape from believing that one needs to do what people say one should do and that one ought to be the person one is expected to be. Yet to make such an escape is a step toward beginning again and becoming the teachers we never knew we could be.

Herb Kohl
(From *The Open Classroom*.)

11.9
Opening It Up: An Interview with Herb Kohl

The Editors

Editors' Note: We find the programs outlined by Herb Kohl in *36 Children* and *The Open Classroom* to be the most supportive of our own conclusions. We therefore strongly suggest that you read his books. Mr. Kohl is currently a director of Other Ways, a program for change within the Berkeley high school system. The philosophy of Other Ways is to provide a means for each student to form a personal solution with which he can approach the educational system. The program serves as a catalyst for new alternatives for students, as well as for school systems. The following interview presents some of Kohl's points and answers questions we had concerning his ideas.

JEAN: Both *The Open Classroom* and *36 Children* present a very encouraging and revolutionary approach to education. For those persons who have not yet read your books, would you briefly explain what you mean by an "open classroom"?

KOHL: It's unstructured, but not unstructured in the sense that it is just a nice place to be. The open classroom is a place that has lots of stuff for kids to do, where kids are free to choose things that they want to do, and where the teacher loses the power of compulsion (the teacher can't make anybody do anything). On the other hand, I don't mean a place where the teacher doesn't exist as a person or as an adult. I mean a place where the teacher can do what he wants to do, too—like have fun and teach what he knows. The other thing is that he can't compel students to learn what he likes to teach them. He is just another person in the classroom; he isn't a god.

MADI: Do you feel this approach should start on the kindergarten level?

KOHL: It's easiest with the younger kids because that is the way many nursery schools function as it is. We are starting here in Berkeley with junior high and high school kids. We have to start everywhere. I think that college kids are doing it themselves. They are taking this absurd institution in which they are trapped and trying to remake it.

PAUL: What about the evaluation tests and intelligence tests students are supposed to take?

KOHL: Something very interesting happened at a junior high school in Berkeley recently which certainly is a strategy for change. The teachers were going to give all those achievement tests. But the black kids refused to take them because they were not written in black dialect and the white kids refused to take them because they were meaningless. The entire junior high school went out. If two or three kids decide that they won't do something, they can be punished—you can fail them or call them crazy and send them to the counselor or something. But when the whole school refuses, the adults are in trouble.

PAUL: How do you get a straight school to go along with the actions you outline?

KOHL: It's very difficult. One way of doing it is getting the principal to believe that things have to change. But that generally doesn't happen. The way to do it is to come into the school as an individual teacher, be quiet about it, and infiltrate the school. Don't come in and put your ideas out right away. You are a guerilla fighter against the schools. You come in and begin to do things quietly, keep your door closed, and don't get too outrageous or make people mad at you. Disarm them a little and then make a friend and the two of you begin working together. Keep careful documents of what you are doing. Get to know the kids and their parents, and do a lot of stuff with the kids after school. And before you know it you have a cell: a mini-revolution within the school. You move from there and you move sensibly. If you move into a really uptight authoritarian school, the kids won't be ready; they will be used to the system so you will have to move gently. Most of the time, people's intellectual notions run ahead of their ability to do things. So you might believe a certain thing is worth doing but until you've been in the classroom and worked a couple of years, you won't know how to do it . . . There's nobody more panicked and frightened than people running school districts right now. After all, high schools are exploding. People have two ways to go: they can become more militaristic and turn the schools into police states or they can open the schools up.

PAUL: Could you go into what you think education is?

KOHL: That's a very difficult question. I wouldn't look at it in the context of American society. But, in general, education is that which adults present to young people in order to welcome them as part of adult society—rites of passage. The problem with our society is that when the society is so contorted and so filled with contradictions and hypocrisies, what can we pass on to the young except a hypocritical vision of adult life? In our society the function of education is to produce kids who are obedient, dependent, good consumers, good wasters, and people who are non-creative. What we're trying to do with open teaching is to create sane revolutionaries—young kids who'll be able to be independent, to function on the basis of real needs, and to be devoted to creating a good life. This all means changing the system. You can become anything: a doctor, a lawyer, a businessman or something, and if you're dedicated to using what you know and what you become in a human way rather than in a selfish way, then you're contributing to some real change in society.

MADI: What do you do about college placement tests?

KOHL: It's very simple. We teach the kids how to take them. We're very cynical about them. College placement tests are cynical documents themselves. For example, we'll do a course on the Sociology of Testing—who makes up the tests, what kinds of questions they ask, and what kinds of things you have to do in order to pass them.

PAUL: When you first present the kids with open teaching, do they freak?

KOHL: Yes, it takes a while for kids to get used to it. People are so unused to making choices for themselves that they'll keep on asking, "tell me what to do." If you refuse, the kids will get bored, apathetic, and wander around at loose ends.

PAUL: So what do you do? Guide them into it?

KOHL: No, we constantly present them with options. Would you like to get into city planning? Are you interested in building a dome? You present a lot of choices, but do not force them in any way. The worst people I've found freaking on freedom are college kids. For many people, going to college represents a form of defeat rather than a victory. What I mean by that is that many people going to college, and even more so those going to graduate school, would like to go out and do something real in life but they're afraid of that independence and the risks they will have to take, so they'll go on and let themselves be pushed through an institution for another four years.

MADI: How do you feel reform can happen in the colleges?

KOHL: More and more students have to take things into their own hands and have to make decisions for themselves. Rather than a small minority of people who could be punished, larger numbers of students are beginning to feel the absolute need and the possibility of doing something to change things. As the movement moves to 50 percent of the people at a university, the university is going to have to change. Attempting to change things in some fundamental way can be considered deviant if 10 percent or 20 percent of people are doing it, but, for example, how can you consider smoking marijuana deviant student behavior when more than 50 percent of the students do it? It's no longer deviant; it's the society which is deviant, the laws are deviant. . . .

One of the most valuable things in the world is for students to teach each other. We found in our school that students know a great deal that they can share with each other. One student will offer a course and all the others will want to take it. Courses don't have to be full semesters. We've given up the entire time schedule. For example, if someone knows how to do batik, she'll give a course that will last a week or so. By that time, everyone else will know about as much as she knows and can go off and do it by himself. Classes and meetings come about and last as long as they're relevant. . . .

I have a certain number of recommendations that I would make for developing alternatives. Anyone who wants to become a teacher absolutely ought to think of doing some other thing or things well. In other words, for a while in your life, you ought to forget about teaching and learn how to do something: learn how to paint, learn how to be an automobile mechanic, learn how to be a writer, but learn something. Then when you start teaching, you can fall back on what you know. . . .

Our government looks upon schools essentially as a place where good Americans are produced and what that means is someone who is going to support American industry—who is going to buy new cars and believe that he needs a color television set and will be silent, as in majority. So, in a sense, what we're talking about when we talk about chang-

ing the school is changing the whole society. . . . I speak to many teachers and they say, "We can't change, the principal won't let us." That is not true. Generally they won't let themselves. The only reason people don't change is because they don't want to. They really can change. . . .

Schools are a good place to do decent and honest social revolutionary work.

SOME THINGS THAT WE CAN DO FOR CHANGING WAYS

1. We can constantly ask ourselves if the learning environment that we have set up is the best that we can do to help develop the child's ability to think for himself (which is one of the principal new goals).
2. Remember that *change* doesn't come fast or easy to anyone—teachers or students. Don't expect overnight miracles. *Start slowly.* Don't give up.
3. Give up our authority wherever possible—the kids will know when you are sincere. We don't need to be nearly as authoritarian as we think. Whenever possible *suggest* rather than assign or order.
4. Let kids *talk* and *move* in the room (within orderly reason, of course).
5. Abolish rigid seating charts.
6. Vary our techniques if possible —use films, speakers, students' reports, student art efforts, etc.
7. Open our rooms to visitors— guest speakers, older students, parents (anyway, after school).
8. "Freedom, not license" (to quote Neill of Summerhill). No child, or adult, has the right to disturb someone else's chance to learn. Freedom does not mean permissiveness, nor permission to tyrannize. Important to remember, because some children will misunderstand freedom.
9. Be prepared to see that you may be wrong once in a while. Admitting this to a youngster can make him feel that he doesn't *need* to oppose you —we don't always have to be right.
10. Be prepared to change completely (slowly, of course) our feelings about children. When you "get down off the podium" and move among them, as it were, you'll see them as real people who don't want to be dominated any more than adults do—people who are capable of and willing to work, but in their own way. It doesn't have to be teacher's way only.
11. We can remember that there are many youngsters who have brought emotional problems from home and who can't easily respond to freedom.

Be prepared to be kindly firm with them in class and give them plenty of opportunity to *talk to you* at some quiet time. This is what they need. It's the group that throws them. Punishment only confirms their belief that teacher is against them.

William Williams,
Junior High School Teacher,
California

The freedom to learn must include the freedom not to learn.

John Hurst,
Professor of
Educational Psychology
University of California, Berkeley

Doors lock a kid's mind. The moment he walks into a classroom he has about 18 by 30 feet and that's it. He's shafted. He can't move! If we're going to give kids the right to think and explore and discover, they have to be in a building where they have freedom to move, freedom to think. Movement and thinking go hand in hand.

Herbert Jackson

11.10
The American University— 1970

George Stern

The original model for the American university was entirely functional in a developing country struggling to achieve universal secondary education and needful of every scientist and technician it could produce. A program which ensured a little knowledge in many fields and a lot of it in one was an efficient way of producing technologists who were specialized yet capable of understanding related areas of interest.

The pattern for the American university was laid down in the late 19th century, at a time when industrialization was just beginning to take firm hold and the traditional church-affiliated colleges were no longer adequate to train the new types of men who were needed. Americans who had gone abroad to learn science in the German universities brought back a curriculum model on which to build here at home.

Reprinted by permission from *Event*, 10, 2 (1970), 13–17.

In 1870, however, only two in 100 American 18-year-olds graduated from high school and both were likely to get a terminal BA degree as well. The diversified university curriculum was a rational way to maximize institutional resources for the purpose of educating the whole of this small and homogeneous community of men. Today, 80 in 100 18-year-olds graduate from high school, of whom 44 will enter college and 24 will finish. Only one of these will get a Ph.D., the purpose for which almost every element in the present undergraduate university curriculum has evolved. In other words, the program is now designed for only two per cent of the people who are admitted to it!

This bizarre outcome was the inevitable consequence of two social forces. On the one hand, the graduate faculties were driven, like the surgeons before them, to the inexorable extension of their hegemony over an institution that has become more and more specifically adapted (like the hospitals) to meet their particular professional needs. Students, on the other hand, were led to view education as the ladder for ascending the social scale. Every immigrant and his son could believe that higher education was an essential requisite for mobility when only two per cent of the 18-year-old population finished either high school or college. Dropout rates have held essentially constant for decades. Three-fourths of our 18-year-olds will never complete college, and only the most insignificant proportion of them can ever receive the degree for which its curriculum is now designed: the Ph.D.

The IQ Dilemma

The wholesale elimination of students at the college level is a reflection of the relationship between intellectual tasks and measured intelligence. Ten per cent of the population have IQ's below 80, the level characterized as dull normal. Therefore, even with the yet-to-be achieved full integration of non-white Americans into the public school system, universal secondary education cannot rise above 90 per cent without being redefined as a custodial institution. If everyone with an IQ of 100 and above were admitted to college we would be accepting by definition only one-half the population. Twenty-four per cent of all 18-year-olds graduate college, cor-

responding to the percentage with IQ's over 110. The current percentages of MA's and Ph.D.'s produced match the percentages of those with IQ's above 125 and 140 respectively. Thus, no increase in the rate of production of post-secondary degrees is possible without a redefinition of post-secondary education itself.

This is precisely what is now taking place. As long as participation in higher education was voluntary, access to it a privilege rather than a right, and graduation from it a seeming requirement for achievement in a competitive society, the universities continued to evolve towards their present state largely unquestioned. But the success of the same technology for which the universities were created has brought them to their present crisis. The labor force, once predominantly agrarian, is now divided almost equally between blue- and white-collar workers. Furthermore, the blues are decreasing relative to the whites and the percentage of professionals has risen from three per cent of the labor force in 1870 to 14 per cent in 1968. Productivity can be maintained on an ever declining base of laborers and machine operators, but the conversion of blues to whites is limited by the distribution of intellectual resources in the population at large. Productive economic utilization of people from the lower half of the IQ distribution is being eroded more rapidly than new occupational categories can appear to absorb them.

The two most rapidly growing industrial groups in the country—public administration and professional services—involve small percentages of blue-collar workers, while the three most rapidly declining—agriculture, mining and personal services—are made up preponderantly of them. Four per cent of the labor force is unemployed, over two-thirds of them blue-collar workers. Furthermore, the capacity of the economic system to absorb more professionals may be as limited as the genetic capacity of society is to produce them. The curve representing the proportion of professionals in the labor force appears to be flattening out at about 15 per cent, and there are already signs of overproduction in such fields as physics and psychology.

Teenagers have been most affected by unemployment regardless of sex, color, or place of residence, but the highest rate of all

is among black teenagers in central cities, 30 percent of whom were jobless in 1968. Were it not for the Armed Forces, which rose from some 1.5 million men in 1950 to over 3.5 million today, and the effect of the draft in holding perhaps another half million in college who would not otherwise be there, these unemployment rates would be far higher and their selective character even more ominous.

Thus, the universities have become a holding station for a significant number of white middle-class Americans who are being held involuntarily in school at the price of being drafted, and who therefore feel entitled to demand that the curriculum justify itself.

Pressure From Blacks

The concerted effort to bring black Americans into the universities in substantial numbers for the first time brings still more pressure on the curriculum. They demand access as a right rather than a privilege, but have been ill-prepared by the public schools to enter the conventional program. And it is by no means evident that higher education is going to bring them substantial gains: average earnings for black college graduates are no better than those of white high school graduates, black high school graduates those of white grade school graduates, and this differential has been maintained for the past decade. The functional connections between school and society seem to have become rather suddenly strained, and the students are not only aware of this condition but are directly or indirectly rebelling against it in their protest movements.

Although there is protest of some kind on virtually every college campus in the country, it is at the so-called, "mega-versities"—institutions with student bodies of 10,000 or more—that it achieves its fullest dimensions. Sources of frustration peculiar to university life are not hard to find. Their sheer size alone raises acute problems of logistics and stress. Although they make up less than ten per cent of America's schools, these large universities are responsible for the education of half of the country's 7.5 million college students. Thus, they attempt to house, feed, and schedule populations equal in size to many American cities but in physical areas no larger than the average village. The only other institutions in history to attempt such segregation are the military camps, either for soldiers or for displaced persons. But in that event one would expect the anomic depersonalization of the large university and the garrison-like proportions of its dormitories, dining halls, lecture rooms, library centers, and recreational facilities to produce the passive dependency and childlike guile that help both the soldier and the concentration camp victim to survive, rather than the militant activism that is so much in evidence on large university campuses.

The Ph.D. Marketplace

Another source of conflict lies in the fact that large universities admit a more diversified student body than smaller single-purpose schools, and tend to orient themselves more towards the lowest common denominator among them. A consequence of this is that most incoming studnts are highly misinformed about the extent to which the college is organized to meet their various needs. They think the university is prepared to do as much in shaping their social lives as it is in shaping their intellects. This is not the case. Life at most universities is distinguished neither for scholarship nor for communal participation. Its one outstanding feature is the consistency with which opportunities are provided for student play—one of the *lesser* expectations of the incoming freshmen, significantly enough.

There is still another factor peculiar to the university that contributes to student unrest. Graduate departments require graduate faculties, and these tend to be a very select group, even among the already highly select population of faculty Ph.D.'s. They are recruited in a marketplace that is extremely sensitive to the academic rank of the schools and departments in which they received their training, and critically judgmental of a candidate's potential for research, publication, and program building. Having been weighed repeatedly for these same qualities from the time of their initial admission to graduate school as students, those Ph.D.'s who become faculty in graduate programs are unquestionably the most aggressive, ambitious, competitive, energetic, counteractive, articulate, pragmatic, and intellectually facile of all graduate school products, and committed both vocationally and by personal convic-

tion to the development of others like themselvs.

It is in this respect that the graduate disciplines in the arts and sciences have come to be the determining force in education, reaching down through the colleges and high schools to the elementary grades to channel the brightest and the most successfully motivated into the tracks that lead on specifically to the graduate schools. The second-best fall out to other careers; the best are encouraged to work toward Ph.D.'s, and the very best to join in training others. The entire school system, then, has become academia's way of reproducing itself.

These mechanisms are not limited to selective encouragement and channeling. The university program for the junior and senior years consists of course offerings designed by each department for its majors, the student pool from which graduate school material is drawn. All students, majors and non-majors alike, are given lecture-discussion guidance through a literature considered essential by way of preparation for subsequent graduate training. Universities so unfortunate as to have substantial numbers of undergraduates unable to handle such courses successfully do not develop an alternative curriculum, but instead run everyone through the same content, which is watered down to the level of the "regular" majors and stiffened by more rigorous special sections, courses or requirements for the so-called "professionals" who are the only ones considered seriously in the graduate school track.

Surplus People

Every civilization has invented abstract pursuits for its leisure class, and then proceeded to isolate the youth of its aristocracy and instruct them in a common mode of speech, dress, thought, and behavior that provided an indelible sign of class distinction. But a productive technology that no longer requires—and indeed cannot employ—a large labor force has turned the concept of the leisure class on its head. On the one hand speech and dress have been made so uniform by a common culture in school and through the mass media that the obvious stigmata of class have all but disappeared except to the most sensitive observer. On the other hand, further schooling is useful only to the increasingly

select few who have the special capacities to engage in such abstract games, and *their* reward is to be drawn into increasingly alienated forms of technical service. We have begun the transition to a consummatory, leisure society, but it is being realized first by those who are least equipped in intelligence, training or motivation and who must therefore be subsidized by what is now called welfare or unemployment insurance.

These are surplus people in a scarcity economy, unable to stay in a graded educational system designed to fit men to the needs of a competitive society and therefore unemployable. But there are no surplus people in a leisure economy, only surplus goods and time, and the function of education under those circumstances will be to equip every one to use both creatively. The new curriculum must be designed not for society but for man himself. It must be based on those invariant biological properties which so characterize man that to maximize the opportunities for their development is to optimize the opportunity for each individual to approach the utmost expression of human-kind of which he is capable.

Madelyn Silver speaks as a student to students on their role as innovators in educational reform. She describes one form of grass-roots course planning organization which is representative of many others which have sprung up in the universities and outside (Free Universities). The author clearly places more hope in students initiating change.

11.11
Yes, Virginia, You Can Build the Alternatives

Madelyn Silver

The acknowledged origin of the educational reform movement began at Berkeley with the Free Speech Movement in 1964, and

By permission of the author.

we're still fighting for changes. Many crises have arisen and several significant changes have been made. In the area of building educational alternatives, a very important step has been the formation of the largest student-initiated course program on a college campus in the country.

As defined in a recent catalogue of its courses,

The Center for Participant Education, an Associated Students sponsored program, is a vehicle for students to make their educations more relevant to their needs and interests, to become active participants in the educational process itself, and to challenge the one-sided and distorted intellectual and political perspectives of so many University courses. . . .

While students are in the University they should be able to develop their understanding and competence in areas that are important to *them* so that they can now and in the future significantly affect their own lives and society. C.P.E. courses appeal to the interests of students because students themselves initiate and develop the courses. In most C.P.E. courses students are encouraged to determine for themselves what form and direction the class will take. . . .

In order for students' needs to be fulfilled they must be articulated and actively worked for. *Students have got to learn to do things for themselves.* They must help in the running and initiation of classes. Active participation means accepting the responsibility for the success or failure of a course—coming to class meetings, participating in discussions, examining and evaluating the course's direction, and working with C.P.E. to develop new courses or change existing ones.

The C.P.E. office is in the Associated Students Building on campus and here a volunteer staff coordinates the courses. Anyone who wants to lead a course (professor, student, dropout, housewife, or whoever) merely comes to the office and fills out a brief form that includes a short course description appropriate for the C.P.E. catalogue. (Teaching a class in a free-form situation can be more than a vehicle for knowledge—it can be a truly enlightening experience for both teacher and student, bringing challenges to each other's world-views, ideas, and life-styles.) The C.P.E. office puts together the catalogue and arranges course sign-ups. Classes are held on or off campus, days or evenings. The class sizes range from three to several hundred.

In the fall of 1968 the California Regents took away C.P.E.'s ability to offer blanket credit for courses. If a student desires credit for a course, he now must arrange for it through a professor as independent study credit. Credits are not the object; learning and opening up minds to alternative points of view are more realistic goals.

The most important aspect of C.P.E. courses is that they are aimed at making change possible. They help the student to develop a conception of himself and his world which he, not someone else, creates. The philosophy is that the classes should contribute to a sense of autonomy and freedom amongst the students, regardless of the course content. Classes are aimed at doing this through their style and perspective on learning; C.P.E. opposes grades, requirements, and stuffy, boring, irrelevant courses and teachers. Students should control their educations; they should decide what they want to learn and how. Most students don't know what this means because they have never seen through an exciting educational experience. C.P.E. tries to provide that experience for as many students as possible by offering courses which are exciting, experimental, dynamic, and responsive for students' needs, and which are free of competition and fear, role playing, a sterile classroom environment, and formality.

Courses in the past have included "Astrology," "The New American Revolution," "Norman Mailer: The Novelist as Superstar," "Conversational Hebrew," "Speedreading," "Nader's Raider's West," "Photography," "Politics, Technology, and The Ecology of Pollution," "The Role of the Emerging Landscape Architect/Planner," and "Social Change: Differences Between Liberal and Radical Perspectives." Use your imagination; usually about one hundred topics are offered each quarter.

Programs similar to C.P.E. (usually known as Free Universities) have developed at college campuses and in communities across the country. They must be maintained even when the administration or authorities become oppressive if total change is to eventually come about in the educational systems. It's up to *you*—a few individuals can initiate group action. If you want changes, do something about it by building the alternatives.

Some people are *born* to teach; some *learn* to teach; most just have a credential.

Hazel Trowbridge,
California Elementary
School Teacher

11.12
New Directions for Ed Reform

Bill Moody

For too long, simply *freeing up* the university learning experience has been our main preoccupation in education reform. Granted the learning process needs to be freed up, and this concern is a valid one. But should it be our only concern?

I think not.

It seems to me that the problems of the American university have deeper roots than outdated or rigid curricula, authoritarian classroom structures, or reactionary grading systems. The real problems with higher education have their roots in that same social and political system that has created our problems in Vietnam, in the cities, and that has oppressed minorities—not a very original analysis, I agree, but one much overlooked by those of us who think of ourselves as being *into* ed reform.

I would suggest that the whole system of American education is a natural outgrowth of our social/political system, in the same way as the war in Vietnam is a natural outgrowth of American foreign policy of domination in the third world. It follows that just as this country's withdrawal from Vietnam without a parallel change in the socio-political system that creates the foreign policy would serve no purpose, a broad reform of college curriculum without a solution to the socio-political problem which causes that rigid, outdated curriculum would serve no purpose.

The American university today is functioning by and large exactly as it is supposed to function. It produces research and knowledge for the government, military, and corporations. It produces compla-

Reprinted by permission from *Edcentric*, February, 1970.

cent, submissive graduates who are highly skilled, and who take their slots in life as the managers who keep the technocracy running and expanding on its present mindless course. Our universities are in their present deplorable state not by accident, but by natural design, according to their function in society.

If we accept this analysis, then it becomes clear that the university, rather than being the problem, is one symptom of much deeper problems rooted in the socio-political system which creates the university.

At this point we must ask ourselves if our personal education reform work is dealing only with the symptom of a problem (e.g. withdrawing from Vietnam without a parallel change in foreign policy), or if the reform relates to the solution of the deeper social and political problems.

For example, were I confronted with the decision of either working for securing a pass-not pass system for my campus, or for open admissions, and I could only give my time to one, the choice would have to be open admissions. For even if I could secure the pass-not pass system, the university would still be serving the same function in society, and the socio-political system that keeps it serving those functions has not even been questioned by my actions. At best, I have provided a little more freedom in the educational process for an already elite group of people, commonly known as students.

On the other hand, in working for open admissions, I have to confront the question of why black people and poor people have (historically) been systematically excluded from higher education. What is the problem with the socio-political system that makes our universities the near monopoly of white middle- and upper-middle-class students? In demanding open admissions, hopefully I will be able to relate to the black liberation movement, which is trying desperately to solve those problems of oppression and discrimination within the political system, and which is reflected in our colleges and universities. If the demand is met, many black and/or poor people will have the opportunity to receive a higher education and to equip themselves with the intellectual skills to further the liberation movements within this country and its universities, to say nothing about the changing character of a university

when there suddenly is tremendous growth of minority groups on the campus.

Moreover, in one sense, knowledge in our society is power. A technological society is built on the expansion/creation of knowledge. One of the main functions of the American university is to create that knowledge for technology and to produce graduates with the skills to manage and implement it. Historically, the socio-political system has managed to reserve the universities for the white middle and upper-middle classes, which has given them a certain kind of power, because of the management skills acquired at the universities, over and forbidden to the minority groups and the poor. With the acceptance of open admissions *en masse* the poor and minority groups would gain the skills and knowledge necessary for this certain kind of power in the technocracy, which would lead to a fundamental reordering of power relationships within the socio-political system.

In this sense, open admissions would be helping to redefine one of the basic functions of the university—the broadening of power among minorities and the poor, as opposed to the historical function of reserving power to the white middle and upper classes.

Hopefully, I am pointing in the direction that we should go, if we are really serious about reforming the universities. There is a growing awareness among many student organizers that most education reform is meaningless at worst, and simply makes a drab four-year experience better at best —that very rarely are new curriculum designs, pass-not pass systems, teacher and course evaluations, etc., relevant to the real social and political problems that have made our universities what they are.

We must realize that our universities have been shaped by the society in which we live. And, if we intend to radically alter the functions and structure of the university, then we must also make that struggle relevant to the solution of the problems within the socio-political system.

The new education has as its purpose the development of a new kind of person, one who—as a result of internalizing a different series of concepts—is an actively inquiring, flexible, creative, innovative, tolerant,

liberal personality who can face uncertainty and ambiguity without disorientation, who can formulate viable new meanings to meet changes in the environment which threaten individual and mutual survival.

The new education, in sum, is new because it consists of having students use the concepts most appropriate to the world in which we all must live. All of these concepts constitute the dynamics of the questing-questioning, meaning-making process that can be called "learning how to learn." This comprises a posture of stability from which to deal fruitfully with change. The purpose is to help all students develop built-in, shockproof crap detectors as basic equipment in their survival kits.

Neil Postman and
Charles Weingartner
(From *Teaching as a
Subversive Activity*.)

CONCLUSIONS

We cannot fail to mention something very significant that affected us as we put this book together. The National Student Strike Against the War that began in May, 1970, with Nixon's move into Cambodia as a catalyst, dramatically affected the educational reform movement. For example, at Berkeley the strike took the form of "reconstitution." We kept the University open, yet changed many of its directions. Classes were "reconstituted" so as to be relevant to the issues at hand. For example, a social psychology class went into the community canvassing against the war and applying attitude change techniques rather than passively listening to lectures on the theories. Actions proved more relevant than intellectualizing. Special workshops were formed in the psychology department to deal with such pertinent topics as "The Psychology of the Military" and "The Oppressed and the Oppressor." Other departments reconstituted in likewise relevant manners. Students were given the option of taking courses on a pass/not pass basis rather than for a letter grade. For the first time the University answered students' needs in a time of crisis. We hope this sensitivity to students' needs will continue.

It is hard to imagine where "reconstitution" could end. We can envision many changes: the establishment of interdisciplinary studies, the removal of the grading system, the opening of admissions, a flexible catalogue with student-initiated courses, "the open classroom" approach to teaching, and the replacement of dehumanizing IBM numbers and needless bureaucracy by acknowledgement of the person. In fact, the possibilities and needs for change are limited only by one's imagination.

Through the preceding selections we have attempted to state the problem and the grievances, and then to suggest some alternative approaches and philosophies. The establishment of free universities and free schools is a realistic goal as an alternative outside the system. Counter and experimental courses are possibilities for changing the system from within.

Our main statement is that it is up to every individual to make his education relevant. We do not feel that the majority of the school

systems are conducive to a pleasurable and meaningful educational experience. Change is possible, but someone must initiate it. The student who does not try to change the system as it stands is showing his approval of that stifling system. If one does not approve, the options for change are his if he will take a stand and build alternatives. The fight to participate in one's educational experience and to save tomorrow's victims from the presently oppressive approaches is worth the investment.

We all are shaped by the educational system and must change it first if we hope to make other changes in society. Let our schools become the first truly democratic institutions in America. To have a democracy, the majority cannot remain silent. *Speak out! The schools should not shape us—we must shape them.*

their own people. For many whites this came as a shock. Many retired back to the luxuries of their middle-class neighborhoods, others dropped out, and still others began struggling to establish new methods for attacking the problem of racism.

When the Kerner Report was published the nation was told that the problem is in white society (the government had "discovered" racism in the same way as Michael Harrington "discovered" poverty in his book *The Other America*, even though both have existed for over two hundred years). The Kerner Report, however, instead of relating to the white society with programs designed to get to the heart of racism, advised feeding more money into the cities. This is important, but it does not create change where change has to occur —in white communities.

During the movement in the South and the crisis of the cities in the North, more and more whites began fleeing to the suburbs to escape from being confronted with the reality of the situation. During the migration to the suburbs whites still had the hope that the situation could work itself out and the source of this help was Martin Luther King. As the situation was growing more and more tense, Dr. King was assassinated. The security whites felt when he was alive was no longer there and the question asked by whites was, "Where do we go from here?" After the death of Dr. King many liberal whites in the suburbs, either because of sorrow or guilt, decided that it was time to make a stand and work to overcome the injustices which Martin Luther King had spoken so loudly about, particularly racism.

The purpose of this chapter of this book is not to delve deeply into an analysis of all the white middle-class groups which have sprung up throughout the country after the death of Dr. King. However, the dynamics which various groups have gone through during the past three years are quite similar. To rid the country of racism was the thing to do in order to restore peace and tranquility. As it has turned out these groups did not totally understand the complexity of the problem.

Actions focused on the black community, not inward on the white communities in which the members of these groups lived. There was a general lack of leadership and organization in many of the groups. Meetings turned

White Students in the White Community

EDITED BY:

Ronald Bayne   Doreen Hamilton

John Forrester   Judy Wanschura

. . . there is a gap between the children of affluence and the children of squalor. Our need for a new life style, for women's liberation, for the transformation of work, for a new environment and educational system, cannot be described in the rhetoric of Third World revolution where poverty, exploitation and fascist violence are the immediate crisis. We cannot be black; nor can our needs be entrusted to a Third World vanguard of any kind.

Tom Hayden
(From *The Trial.*)

INTRODUCTION

The history of the civil rights movement of the 1960s saw the first major attempt of blacks and whites to work together for the purpose of doing away with the

most obvious and blatant expressions of racism in this country. The events of the movement we are all aware of (from the bus boycott, to the killing of one civil rights worker after another, to the mass march on Washington). It is important to understand the dynamics of the movement and its impact on approaches to social change. With high ideals whites came to support the struggle of the blacks in the South. Martin Luther King had pricked the consciousness of the nation and it seemed that the nation was uniting with him against the injustice of the South. Then the cities in the North blew up, manifesting that the injustices apparent in the South exist in every part of the nation. Stokely Carmichael exhorted whites to go back to their own neighborhoods and liberate into nothing more than discussions about the problems of the day; the same people were talking with each other most of the time, and because of this, today in 1970 many of these groups have become completely stagnated and are unable to function effectively as community organizations. They are unable to relate to the problem of what it means to work in the white community.

With the advent of the 1970s, groups of white middle-class Americans have begun—because of the frustrations of the past ten years—to work seriously on constructing models for work and organizing in white middle-class communities. The remainder of this chapter of the book will be an account of a working model for white community work. The basic premise which this model is based upon is that whites must concern themselves with problems in their own community. The model is based on the assumption that most white middle-class communities cannot constructively relate to the pressing social problems of society until they have experienced what social change means in their own communities.

_____

12.1
A Philosophy for White Community Work

Judith Wanschura

For a number of years now, we white middle class people have been very concerned about the plight of those "less fortunate" than we. We have fought for civil rights for blacks; we have set up community houses with social workers in Chicano neighborhoods; we have sent boxes of canned food to Indian reservations; we have tutored kids in ghetto schools; we have fought for integration. We have led the struggle for equality for minorities. Indeed we have tried to make the Third World people in our country not just equal, but the same as us. We have said, "This is the way you must go. Accept all our values, put on a white mask, prove yourselves and we will give you all your rights. If you become just like us, then we will treat you

as human beings." But now those minority people are organizing themselves. They are developing their own leadership and their own racial and cultural identity. They no longer want or need paternalistic whites defining for them what they want and telling them how to get it. They refuse to accept any longer the proposition that in order to become human in the eyes of the society, they must become "white." And many white people feel hurt and indignant and threatened. Our leadership is no longer accepted. The Third World people are no longer believing the contention that white is right. "Go home," they are saying, "Work with your own people. There are plenty of problems there and we don't want you in our communities any more." And we are confused and frightened.

We are confused because we don't see what we can do at home. "Work with our own people? But," we said, "we are not the disadvantaged. We are not treated unequally. The problem is not ours." A few white people have looked, however, at history, at how the situation came to be, at how discrimination and prejudice became integral parts of our institutional structures. We saw that whites had created the situation, that whites had brought black people from Africa and made them slaves and defined them as three-fifths of a person, that whites had murdered half of the Indian population of our country, that whites encouraged the immigration of Mexicans and Asians as a source of cheap labor and have prevented them from rising to a better position. Then there was the Kerner Commission report: "What White Americans have never fully understood—but what the Negro can never forget—is that white society is deeply implicated in the ghetto. White institutions created it, white institutions maintain it, and white society condones it. . . . White racism is essentially responsible for the explosive mixture which has been accumulating in our cities since the end of World War II." White people read that and some acknowledged, now that even whites on a government commission were saying it, that maybe racism was a white problem after all.

And we are frightened. We are frightened because something new is developing, something we don't understand and fear we can't control. Black people and Chicano people and Asian people and Native American people are organizing themselves and developing identities independent of us. They are acting on their own and not controlled by whites. And they are challenging our comfortable status quo, our belief that our way of life is the best, and our confidence that it will endure. They present an internal threat by forcing us to admit to any doubts we might have about our life style or value system; and they present an external threat by being a physical danger to the political, and economic systems and objects which support that life style.

So what do we do? How do we work with our racism? How do we deal with our fear? The Kerner Commission was no help here. After placing the blame where it belongs, they proceeded to talk about the problems in the ghetto and to recommend various remedial programs. In other words they recommended the perpetuation of the paternalistic, nonthreatening situation of whites granting to minorities the equal treatment and opportunities which are theirs by right. They recommended continuing to try to make Third World people just like us, while at the same time keeping them in a subservient position on the receiving end of our largess. They recommended our denying their human dignity.

So to find the answer, some whites began to look more closely at how racism is perpetuated. We looked at the advantages to whites of a racist system. We looked at how racism is deeply a part of the institutional structures of the society. We recognized the very real threat which the freeing of Third World people poses to those institutions. A few superficial changes in housing laws or hiring practices or college admission procedures are not going to be sufficient to affect anything so thoroughly a part of the institutions. Only some very fundamental changes in those institutions are going to bring to a position of full equality and equal dignity those who for so many years have been used as the bottom of the social, political, and economic structures, who for so many years have been denied an identity. But why, if it is of such benefit to us, if the elimination would be so detrimental to us, should we try to do anything about racism?

One reason is that the Third World people have threatened to tear this country apart if we don't, but that threat could also be dealt with, as indeed we are now dealing with it, by increased police force, increased repression and full-scale genocide, as we have dealt before with the American Indian. But we too have much to gain by changing the social, political, and economic structures, for racism is really only one part of a much larger, deeper problem. As one member of the community with which we have been working said, "How can we even talk about increasing understanding with the black people in another city when there is such lack of tolerance and understanding right here at home?" Middle class white people are finding that their material success is insufficient and unsatisfying. We have everything, yet somehow we feel we have nothing. We are burdened with the tremendous insecurity of having fulfilled the dream of success and happiness only to find that the dream is not real. We are divided from ourselves, we are divided among ourselves. We find our communities divided along lines of political affiliation, age, relative wealth, beliefs, rumors. People do not know or even care who lives on the other side of the six-foot fence. We whites have defined ourselves in negatives; we have defined ourselves by what we are not. We are not black; we are not Mexican; we are not Oriental; we are not Indian; we are not lazy; we are not aggressive; we are not promiscuous, dirty, or any of the common stereotypes of the "other"; we are not; we are not. We find ourselves defined out of existence. We have lost ourselves to the pursuit of the comfortable life. After the job, the family, the house, and the three week vacation, then what? Saul Alinsky elaborates on the condition of white people in his article in this section.

Many white people react to this insecurity and fear with an affirmation of the life style to which they are committed, by clinging to it and defending it violently against any challenge. Others react with denial of that life style, by rejecting it completely and developing new goals and a new value system. Some search for an identity and for a meaning in life through encounter groups, others through religion or mysticism, others through drugs.

Some white people realize that we have to work together toward a solution. We have to come collectively to a definition of whiteness, to a sense of identity as human beings so that the growing self-identity of the Third World people is no longer a threat to us. We are

white, our heritage is European, our cultural and historical background is rich. As a group historically our actions have been both good and evil. We need to accept ourselves at that—no better and no worse than any other race. We have to work together to change our institutional structures and relationships so that we do not need to keep Third World people oppressed in order to preserve our way of life, so that their liberation does not mean our destruction. We need to develop an economic system which does not rely on a pool of cheap labor at the bottom, which does not dispense rewards by means of competition such that the more people we can put out of the running at the beginning the better our chances are. We need to develop a social system in which each person does not depend upon having someone below him for his sense of worth. We need to develop a more open democratic political system so that no one group can take control over all the others, but so that all groups can share the control collectively. We have to work for these ends together, for only together do we have any power.

Students, too, feel the need to take control of their own lives, to do something to change the injustice and oppression which they see and feel around them. For several years they have been trying to alleviate the effects by tutoring ghetto children or perhaps working at a community center, but they have been white students in programs designed, directed, and funded by whites. Many students now see that whites must take care of white communities, must work on the cause of the problem, and that the Third World students must work in their own communities. For students, working with white communities can mean many things. It may be overt political action ranging from stuffing envelopes for an election campaign to street rioting. It may be direct community work, such as setting up educational enrichment programs in lower class predominantly white schools or organizing people around the unique needs of white communities. Peter DuMont and Doreen Hamilton discuss one model of the very beginning stages of organizing in a white community. Students working in white communities can also mean attempting to change the university. The university is a microcosm of the outside world with its racism, its role-defined divisions among people, its high

level of competition for academic success, its large number of disillusioned people who find that academic success alone is insufficient to their human needs. Just as people in residential white communities need to join together both to develop a white identity and to exercise their collective power to change the society, so also students need to join together to develop an identity and to exercise their collective power to change the university. One level of changing that university is to redirect the utilization of its resources. The university has tremendous resources in terms of manpower, expertise, information, and research capability, resources which can be used by students for their own benefit and that of outside communities.

12.2
A Model for Constructive Change in White Communities

Peter DuMont

(with contributions from Doreen Hamilton)

Recently I was introduced to a field of activity which I have since found deeply satisfying, deeply boring, marked by achievement and frustration, enlightening, mundane, discouraging, depressing, warm, insulting, real, unpredictable, funny, tragic, unreal, hopeful, stimulating, thought-provoking, harrying, repetitive, and triumphant. What has provoked all these differing reactions? Community work. Specifically, the Oakville Come Together Committee. But to understand this, first you will need some background.

Oakville[1] is a small (12,000), insular town in the hills directly adjoining a much larger city. Bedroom to some of the biggest money and politics in the area, it is almost totally white, very affluent, and very well guarded from the monstrous problems of the big city around it. It has its own police, fire, and school districts, and its own newspaper, *The Oakviller*, "The only newspaper devoted ex-

By permission of the author.

[1] The name of the actual community has been changed in consideration for the privacy of the townspeople.

clusively to the news of Oakville." Notable events in the community are the coaster derby and the Fourth of July parade.

Oakville faces consistently adorn the society pages of *The Tribune* (the big city paper), whose publisher resides in Oakville, and each year numerous Oakville "debs" take their bow at the Winter Ball. The spacious, tree-lined streets are quiet, except for an occasional screech from the tires of a teenager's new Camero; and life in Oakville has traditionally been placid, effectively isolated and removed from the problems of the world. A few small stores and a couple of gas stations are the whole of Oakville's native economy. Oakville's citizens can enjoy the advantages of a big city and all its facilities only minutes away, with none of the disadvantages like noise, traffic, racial tension, factories, crowding, poverty, and slums to disturb them. They can drive over these things in their cars and arrive safely in the adjoining city's financial and social districts without unpleasant interruption. It is the perfect haven for those with the money and social qualifications to live there.

But recently, Oakville has been feeling problems created not from without but from within. While the conservative community has carefully guarded against the problems of race, poverty, and industry, it has not expected, nor can it effectively deal with, the internal problems of differing opinion. The generation gap is alive and well and thriving in Oakville. The TV children, born into a world of economic and social security, are questioning the values and practices upon which their security is based. The children of Oakville are taking drugs and protesting against the War, and there is increasing polarization between adults of differing viewpoints.

In the high school, much furor has been caused by a relatively innocent student effort called the Awareness Program. It was begun some five years ago by a student leader who attempted to combat provincialism by hosting speakers from the outside on relevant social issues (drugs, the War, racial tension, etc.). Each year the Awareness Program has caused a barrage of reactionary concern from the community (a Democratic candidate and a Black Panther were barred from speaking), and just recently, the principal was fired for being overly permissive,

much to the dismay and organized protest of the students. Also, much needed school bonds have just been twice defeated at the polls of this very wealthy community.

Some parents have sided with their youth. The school board, city council, and much of the community remains unwaveringly "uptight" conservative. Oakville is seeing the same dangerous polarization that the rest of the nation is experiencing—polarization on the War, on education, on drugs and the youth cult vs. the Establishment; on people who are not people, but stereotypes: the enemy.

Three years ago, after the assassination of Martin Luther King, a group of high school students called a town meeting in Oakville "to do something about racism." They invited several speakers, most notably a black minister from the nearby city. They canvassed the community with leaflets quoting Thomas Jefferson and desperately appealing to the social conscience of all citizens to begin working on the problem of racism.

The meeting drew a packed house of adults and children, all sufficiently concerned in one manner or another to attend. To everyone's surprise, the minister told the community in no uncertain terms that they were racist, bigoted, filthy dogs and had better not come to the ghetto and expect to help because the problem was right there in Oakville.

Everybody left the meeting disturbed. That in itself was perhaps good—at least people were aware of a problem, but the minister's harsh approach alienated more people than it changed in a positive sense. If anything, the situation was worse than before.

Some concerned parents, however, along with the high school organizers, started the Council of Citizens (CC), which held "coffee klatch" discussion groups in an effort to increase communication and to examine their own racial attitudes. After many such sessions, the CC worked out a fair housing agreement with the realtors in the area and managed to effect a change in wording in the district educational philosophy to make sure that the school's hiring practices were non-discriminatory. It seemed though that these actions were only chipping away at the basic problem: the attitudes of the conservative majority of the community. CC had become a group of adults who agreed with

each other and had no effect on the rest of the community. Indeed, CC seemed to be polarizing the community more than before; most conservatives were either non-cooperative or openly hostile to CC.

It was in this climate that CC first made contact with the Community Projects Office (CPO) at the nearby university in late spring of 1969. By January of 1970, six college students in a class on white community problems began to meet with the Council of Citizens and various high school students in Oakville. A committee including two representatives each from CC, the college class, and the high school was established to explore alternate methods for involving the entire community in constructive change. Gradually, a new approach evolved. How about another town meeting, but with a completely different emphasis? Instead of creating a tense, hostile atmosphere like the last town meeting, why couldn't a relaxed, informal setting be created where people could exchange ideas and opinions without feeling threatened? Perhaps change would occur if people did not have to fulfill previously assumed roles such as councilman, school board member, socialite, company president, "conservative," or "liberal." The idea would not be to reform people, but rather to develop a sense of community where people of differing opinions could find a common ground. Then attitudes would naturally begin to change for the better.

In order to make the town meeting a true community affair—of, by and for the people of Oakville —it was decided that various organizations and any interested citizens would be invited to help in the planning. Invitations were first sent to the CC mailing list and at each subsequent meeting several new people were present. The procedure proved cumbersome, however, because the purpose of the program, the college students' involvement and the new concept of white community work had to be clarified for each newcomer. Because a large portion of each meeting was devoted to repeating explanations, little progress on the programs was achieved. At one such meeting, a college student was the only one present to do the explaining. This directly led to the resignation of a CC member who believed that the group was being manipulated by the college.

Thereafter the program began to encounter much resistance. The college newspaper erroneously reported the course as "a study of racism in Oakville," and a concerned resident sent the clipping to the city council which shuddered at the very thought. (The council had received a lot of flack after the first town meeting. As one councilman put it: "My phone was coming off the wall.") Several letters were written to the college and one to the state legislature demanding an investigation of the presence and nature of the college students involved: Why were these outside agitators coming in to disrupt the quiet life of Oakville?

CC, conscious of its reputation, and the need to maintain a nonthreatening image, voted to withdraw its support from the noncontroversial town meeting program. In explaining their actions, members of CC said they felt that nobody would come to the program, that it lacked focus, that the high school students were not enthusiastic enough, and that it was no longer safe to work with the college students.

But there was considerable dissent from some members of CC, and these adults, along with the college students and some high school students, began to meet independently to continue work on the town meeting. It was obvious that the first and highest hurdle to be overcome was the stigma of college students "coming in from the outside."

Suddenly, an idea. Why not involve college students who come from Oakville? They would have a perfectly legitimate right to participate in the program because they were citizens of the town. They had gone to high school there and their families, if not they themselves still lived in Oakville. It was the perfect solution, but easier said than done.

In mid-January, Ron Bayne, the director of the Community Projects Office, came to my fraternity after dinner one evening to speak about the activities of his office. In talking with him afterwards, I happened to mention that I was from Oakville. "From Oakville?" he said, his eyes lighting up and his lank frame drawing up in excitement. "You're from Oakville?" Yes, I was from Oakville. In fact, I had been born and raised there and had moved out only five months earlier to live away as I attended the University. Like it or not, I was still an "Oakviller."

Soon he was immersed in a description of the special Oakville Project. Puffing on a cigarette, he was rapping in a voice that was nervously cool, seeming to hide quiet desperation. Here was a model program tht somehow had to succeed. It was a whole new approach to community work, he said. "We're working in a white community, but we're coming together as whites to talk about what it is to be white—what it is to be ourselves. What are our problems, as whites, living together? We're talking about why our kids are going to drugs, why our marriages are falling apart, why our schools aren't the way we want them to be, and like that. Do you see, Pete? We're saying 'We have plenty of problems in our *own* community without worrying about racism and poverty. Let's get it together on our own and then maybe we can talk about the bigger social problems.'" In other words, we were going to do what the black minister had told us to do two years ago, but we were going to do it in a manner that wouldn't threaten and alienate people."

Well, it sounded good, but I was thoroughly enjoying the whole "college experience" (even to practicing meditation). Here was a man with a big black beard asking me to plunge myself back into the whole, straight, uptight Oakville scene, something I had only so recently escaped. He had to have an Oakviller—no one else would do. I was overtly hesitant; I was sure I would not have time to continue, but for some reason I could not say no. It was a fateful decision, for it has taken me on a path which has changed my life, one from which I may never turn away.

The next few evenings found me making countless phone calls, a fate which the community worker must learn to accept with a wry smile. The natives were getting restless about "outside agitators," Ron explained to me, and Oakvillers were needed to counteract this fear. It would be my job to get Oakville alumni now attending the University to a meeting where we could discuss the situation. I had obtained a list from my old high school counselor and started in phoning some eighty names, most of which I recognized but did not know as people. The general implied reaction, similar to my own initial reaction, was, "Wow. I've escaped Oakville and I want nothing to do with it. Sorry."

Out of some fifty I contacted and some twenty who said they would come, about ten people finally showed up at the meeting, which reflects another problem inherent to community work: people who say they will do something on the phone often don't come through. The ten who did come, and the ten who finally made up our new class on the Oakville Project, were people I knew well and could call my friends: one senior boy, two junior girls, one sophomore girl, and six freshmen—four boys and two girls. In addition there were four non-Oakville students still working on the project, but they were now outweighed by Oakvillers. This proved to be a tremendous advantage as we progressed through the development of the program.

By the beginning of Spring Quarter, 1970, we were "getting it together," holding meetings every Monday at the University, as well as attending night meetings in Oakville with the adults and high school students. *The Tribune,* in response to a memo from the editor himself, who wanted to investigate the situation, did a story on us titled "Understanding Project Planned." What was our purpose? To bring people together. What should we call ourselves? The Oakville Come Together Committee.

At first we were very disorganized—twenty-odd people casting about for a method to get opposite ends of the community together, and once together, to have them experience something worthwhile. We tried to get different members of the community involved in the planning by putting an article in *The Oakviller,* but we got no response.

Well, perhaps people really didn't know what we were doing or why we were doing it, we reasoned. Maybe we can put a tag on it, something people can get their minds around, suggested one adult. How about calling it a birthday party for Oakville? Oakville is 63 years old. Why not have a birthday party? Wow! Groovy, far out, what a kick, what a trick!

So, we reserved the only place we could, the Junior High Multipurpose room—a large, sterile, cement, tile, and fluorescent auditorium and cafeteria. There we would have the "Oakville Birthday Party." But at our next meeting we talked about it for a while (e.g., how do we get people talking about important issues at a birthday party?) and finally someone said, "What are we trying to pull? Aren't we getting off the track? What is our real purpose anyway, to trick people or to do something worthwhile? We may get fewer people, but let's be honest." This was greeted by great sighs of relief and agreement from almost everyone, although most of us had liked the birthday idea when it was first suggested. So we were back to our original problem—how to get people there. And things degenerated once again into confused castings in search of a workable method.

Perhaps it was because we had no leader. We had been meeting again and again, and each time the same thing had happened. People kept looking around when a task was presented to be done; no one really wanted to commit himself to any work or responsibility. The overall effect was an aimless wandering by the group, and more meetings.

The leader in a group such as ours is not so much a director as a facilitator. He serves as a prod, a reminder, someone with the reins to whom people can turn when there is a gap in the progress of the group. There is reassurance in a leader. Each individual then has in mind a reference point, a contact, someone he knows has the responsibility to tie the group together so that their efforts are not dissipated. The leader is an organizer, a central nervous contact. He divides tasks and distributes labor. He makes administrative decisions at each point of confusion, thereby greatly speeding up the process of group planning. The wise leader will guide and suggest. He will pose the crucial question, define the confused situation. He will interject his own creative ideas for discussion as a member of the group. He will provide enthusiasm, hope, constructive criticism, energy, and humor. We needed a leader.

"I really think we have to have a chairman," I said. This was greeted by mixed reactions. One man said, "Well, I don't think anybody really wants to do it, or really has the time."

As it turned out, I was the only one who did have time, because I was working that quarter instead of studying, and I was appropriate. I was neither a CC adult (stigmatized by the previous town meeting and the racism emphasis), nor was I a high school student (too young and unable to coordinate the college students). So I offered to be the chairman and was elected by acclamation.

It was developed and affirmed

thereafter that we should have a performance by a professional mime troupe from the city, that the "Instruments of Peace," a teenage singing group, should sing, and that we should call our town meeting "The Oakville Come-Together."

After the entertainment we would have people break up into small groups to discuss anything on their minds. We would not tell anybody to talk about anything. We would simply provide a forum and let people bring up what topics they would, person to person. We hoped that by talking, young to old, right to left, constructive interchange would occur. And, too, it was decided that I should go to the city council meeting four nights later. There I would officially inform the council of our activities and invite them—as individual councilmen and citizens of Oakville—to participate in the planning. We split into committees to hammer out specifics; the publicity committee agreed to write an article for *The Oakviller* and to make up a descriptive flyer; and it seemed that we were on the road.

Too late to be put on the official agenda, I just went to the meeting, hoping to be heard at the end. After much discussion of the "Oakville Flag Committee," dangerous crosswalks, and sewer problems, I was finally recognized by a begrudging mayor. I proceeded to read a copy of a letter of invitation which I had given to each of the councilmen before the meeting. What followed was at first a surprise and later a cause for considerable anger. The council proceeded to cross-examine me with a barrage of questions. "What is this meeting *really* about? Why are college students interested in Oakville? Where is the money coming from (a question I could not answer, because we hadn't discussed it)? Who's behind this? Why can't the council handle these problems you are talking about? Why are students getting credit for this? What department is sponsoring you? (At the time it was Asian Studies, the only department willing to extend credit. I took a big gulp and answered "Ethnic Studies," which they accepted.)

Aren't you going to talk about racism? Does this have anything to do with that town meeting two years ago? Is this that course reported in the college paper about racism in Oakville? (One of the councilmen pulled out the clipping from his briefcase and read

from it.) How did you secure the room for this? Do you have a signed permit from the school officials in charge?" Again and again I tried to answer their questions without damning our cause by some innocent slip which would be misinterpreted. Again and again they came back for more, pressing, prying, trying to get at the real reason behind all this. There was a high wall of mistrust between us and try as I might I could not scale it.

I left the meeting feeling shocked, disappointed, whipped, angry, and degraded. For my efforts the council had passed a resolution stating that in no way was it related to this "Come Together," and they further forbade us to use the term "town meeting" in connection with the "Come Together," as this would imply the council's involvement.

It seemed that they were not human beings. They were actors, role players protecting the sacred purity of their community, at the expense of my humanity and their own. Interestingly, I talked to two councilmen after the meeting and they were considerably more friendly. One even complimented me on a good job of defending my cause. These were human beings talking to me, not the humanoid prosecutors of the official meeting. We could disagree, but at least we could communicate and coexist without hostility. How much better than before!

This "breakthrough" change of attitude is exemplary of what we hope to accomplish with our Come Togethers. We are attempting to encourage individuals of varying social orientation to encounter each other as real people, not as stereotypes locked in roles from which they cannot escape.

The Oakviller's report of the council meeting called me a "young man [who] seemed sincere in his beliefs [but] was extremely vague as to details." I had tried to explain that we were not definite in our plans because we wanted the community to determine the nature of the meeting, not us. This the council could neither understand nor accept. The report in *The Clarion* (another small newspaper with a section on Oakville) was more sympathetic in its text, but the title read: "Council Faces Student Agitators and City Sewage." We found afterwards that this was meant as a joke by the headline boy for *The Clarion*, but it was no joke for us. When we saw that headline at CPO we nearly fainted. Just the stereotype scare-image we were trying to avoid: Student agitators! Why hadn't they called me a hippie commie crum bum?

The entire council effort, it seemed, was a disastrous failure. I wrote letters to the editors of *The Oakviller* and *The Clarion* in an attempt to heal the wounds, but we still are known as a "subversive group" in some Oakville circles.

Despite the council setback, work on the Come Together progressed, including the creation of a slide show. Someone had suggested that a member of the committee take pictures of historic scenes in Oakville from pictures in the library, old newspapers and so forth. He was able to take slides which depicted startling changes, showing hayfields and eucalyptus groves where houses now stand. Along with the slides went a soundtrack: music and the taped voices of long-time residents sharing their memories of a time gone past. The construction of the slide show is a story in itself, with many parallels to an overall experience. Let it suffice to say that we ran into suspicion and non-cooperation at first, but emerged with a successful end-product. The slide show was an educational experience for both the young and old who created it.

On April 30, the day of the Come Together, the stage was set. The flyers and the publicity were out; the slide show was finished; the mime troupe would perform. At 3:30 P.M. we started decorating and setting up; at 8:00 people started coming. By 8:15 the room was full of young people and adults—about 300 people. There was a good cross-section of the community. Our first success! We began.

The singers sang well (including "The Times, They Are A-Changin'") and did much to set a pleasant atmosphere. As chairman of the committee, I opened the meeting. I said that our purpose was not to foist anything up on anybody (as the council had feared), but to provide a setting where constructive interchange could occur. I explained that the class at the university was almost entirely composed of Oakville alumni and that we were working for Oakville because we wanted to see our community grow in understanding and cooperation. I mentioned that every citizen had been invited to help in the planning by an article in *The Oakviller,* and that we had received a total of one

phone call on the number we had given. This received quite a laugh. I hope some of it was from guilt.

Then I introduced the mime troupe. They were a big success, flying kites and lifting 5000 pound weights, etc. The slide show, "Before the Night" (of fading memories), was another success and received much applause.

Next came "A Time for Sharing," the discussion period on the program and our purpose for being. This was a critical point. How would the people react? I introduced "A Time for Sharing" as an opportunity to take stock of where we were as a community, where we had been (as in the slide show), and where we were going. At one point I slipped and mentioned the word politics as a possible subject. Immediately came many tense, concerned glances from the older people present. I attempted to recover by quickly saying that personally, I hoped the discussion would center around Oakville as a community and not get off into national politics, etc. I fear I overcompensated by saying, "I'd like to see this be informal. Get up if you like; move to another table if you want . . ." People took me more literally than I expected. Everybody got up. Many groups did form, however, and some began to discuss topics like the schools, the judicial system, drugs, and housing and zoning in Oakville.

This last was the Mayor's group, which I temporarily joined. The Mayor, who was the only councilman present, told me during this time: "You're doing a fine job, DuMont. As you know, we were afraid of you, but this looks like a good thing." Quiet, jaw-clenching triumph.

Many people left during the discussion, but about one half stayed to the end. In closing, I announced that I hoped a new spirit of cooperation and communication would be born, and requested that people sign up for future planning. About fifty did sign up, mostly high school students. Many people commented that they had enjoyed the meeting; there seemed to be no negative response. People had enjoyed the entertainment and conversation. It had been a "different" occasion, a new approach to community activity. The Come Together was not even reported in *The Oakviller.* We had to send in our own story a week late. The editor, though he knew of the event, apparently did not consider it sufficiently important to send a reporter. *The Clar-*

ion contained a glowing report:

Oakville indeed came together Thursday night to enjoy a form of community togetherness rare in these polarized times. . . . The crowd was an unusual mix, mostly the young and old, with few at the middle age. . . . There were people present who do not normally come to most local public meetings. One woman was there in curlers, surely a first for Oakville.

Our first Come Together was successful not only as an event by itself but as a beginning. Much of the fear that we encountered (though certainly not all of it) was dispelled, at least for the people who attended. For them we were no longer the "college nasties" coming to study racism and disrupt the community. Although doubts about our motives may have lingered on, there was no evidence that anyone left the meeting feeling insulted, alienated or tricked. This was quite an accomplishment. Perhaps some of them had learned and grown.

The first Come Together was only a beginning, however. We have since had two more, and we are planning a fourth. The second (May 26) turned out at the last minute to focus on the firing of the high chool principal by the school board the night before. This became an "open mike" situation where one person at a time addressed the entire audience. We have found this to be much less effective than the person-to-person, small group approach.

The third Come Together was held the evening of June 18. Because no one (e.g., the chairman) checked up on it, there was no publicity in the local papers. We canvassed about one third of the community with descriptive leaflets. These said, in part, that topics raised at the first meeting such as drugs, the war, the generation gap, and so on, would be discussed, after a reshowing of the slides. (The slide show, incidentally, had stirred the Mayor to propose a new "Oakville Historical Collection.")

Only about fifty people attended the third Come Together, but it was very, very successful. A college girl on the committee acted as the emcee much to the pleasure of the female committee members (à la Women's Liberation), and after the slide show we broke into three discussion groups of some fifteen persons each. In my group were a doctor on the city council and some of his friends, and an equal number of younger people and committee members. At first the councilman was very tense and kept referring to my appearance at the council meeting as "causing much concern and question." Apparently I had tried so carefully not to answer questions with simplistic "yes" or "no" answers at the council meeting that I had seemed to the council to be hiding something. This had caused much speculation as to our nature and our backing. The good doctor came to the meeting thinking we might be Communist-backed, with intentions of overthrowing the local government!

After one hour of informal, unpressured group conversation, we covered many subjects ranging from the war and drugs to the children and families of Oakville, and the councilman left saying that the Come Together was a great idea. When I asked him if he felt it worthwhile he said briskly, "Of course it's worthwhile. I learned a lot. Didn't you?" "Oh, yes." I said. "I just wanted your personal reaction."

Indeed I had learned a lot. I learned that I had unknowingly created suspicion by my actions. At any level of community operation it is exceedingly important to proceed in a manner which is not threatening—a manner which beckons rather than prods. Fear is the worst of our enemies because it makes people withdraw and become defensive. There is enough fear already to create problems. The community worker must do everything he can to avoid creating fear by his own efforts.

After our groups broke up I overheard someone asking the doctor how he felt. "Well, I feel a lot better than when I came, that's for sure." In fact, he invited one of the members of our committee and his wife to his house for a drink after the meeting, and they stayed up until two in the morning talking about the Come Together! The doctor is now an outright supporter of the Come Together Committee and is going to try to explain the idea to the rest of the council and his conservative friends in the community. What a breakthrough—and simply because we were able to sit down and talk. This is the purpose and the rationale behind the Come Together.

The Come Together stands as a landmark to the beginning of a successful approach to facilitating social change: bring people together; provide them with a common, stimulating, and preferably enjoyable experience—but *not* a

threatening one; allow and encourage them to talk, person-to-person, back and forth. Barriers are broken, stereotypes are rendered meaningless, polarization is reduced, and a foundation is laid for future constructive growth and change. One woman told me after our discussion period: "I will no longer be simply a *resident* of Oakville." She continued that because of our efforts she had been spurred to take a more active, thinking citizen's role. It may well be that we have stimulated a greater awareness and concern in many people. Hopefully, in this achievement we will continue.

Philosophy of the Come Together Committee

Social change, ideally a progression towards a more satisfactory and fulfilling community for everybody, should take place steadily and peacefully. The processes of peace are not dramatic; they are not filled with passion. They involve individual commitment and dedication of citizens living in a community. But individuals will inevitably have differences of opinion. These differences, when not aired and resolved in an atmosphere of mutual respect and tolerance, lead to frustrations and hostilities which prevent peaceful social change. Many of these differences can be resolved simply by exchanging ideas. To effect this solution we must come together. This is civilization working in its finest form.

12.3
From Reveille for Radicals

Saul Alinsky

Today while most of the world is working and fighting for the basic means of physical survival, we are locked in battle for our spiritual survival. Theirs is the confrontation with the age-old issues of food, shelter, disease, and the protection of personal property, whereas we are now engaged in the historic confrontation with self.

Probably at no time in American history have we experienced a greater revolution than we now find ourselves facing. This is not a time of change but of cascades of change.

We Americans have led the way into a technological world where in an age of automation, computers, cybernetics, mass media and mass everything, we find ourselves bulging with production surpluses of everything, including time. We find ourselves in a world where people are dying of malnutrition while here most of us are dieting. Even so, our present affluence and achievements are probably minimal compared to our vast productive potentials. According to the Protestant ethic we have been rewarded for our virtue of working for success. In our pursuit of material happiness we have achieved plentitude. We have "security." We—more than three-quarters of us—have it pretty well made when it comes to food, housing, and other physical needs. Even our own minority poor generally need not fear actual starvation or being totally without shelter. And after all, we even have plans to get rid of poverty itself. The only things from the past which continue to operate, as they always will, are the elementary laws of physics—such as *every positive carries a negative.*

Yet, while we seem to have found the good life we also seem to have lost ourselves. We should be happy, but we are in fact confused, frustrated, resentful, and frightened of the feeling of an ever growing loneliness. We don't know what to do because we don't know what's wrong, except that we know that something very fundamental is wrong; something is missing which we know is more important than many of the things we have achieved. That something is a sense of ourselves as individuals, as people, as members of the human family. What is at stake is our sanity. Our world is so fractured in every area and at every level that all the different pieces, seemingly so important in themselves, swirl and beat upon us so that we no longer know what anything means.

Much has been written about what threatens us as residents in this paradise of plenty. The mass media, particularly television, have so transformed communication that, coupled with the interlocking political and economic interests of all mankind in an ever shrinking world, the new technology spells the end of any closed system of ethics. It means that a whole realm of morality and principles must emerge if there is to be any world at all. Remember that it was Aristotle who originated the word *principle,* and he

would have been the first to recognize that if fifteen different people from fifteen different backgrounds of experience entered the same room we would find fifteen different sets of principles clogging all attempts at communication. . . .

Obviously certain common ethical definitions have to be agreed to. We must accept open-ended systems of ethics and values, not only to meet the constantly changing conditions but also to keep changing ourselves, in order to survive in the fluid society that lies ahead of us. Such systems must be workable in the world *as it is* and not unrealistically aimed toward *the world as we would like it to be.*

Keeping in mind the universal law mentioned earlier that every positive having its corresponding negative, we may well reflect on the fact that the very roots of security, of stability, can and have been anchors of stagnation and rot, holding and dragging us against the winds and seas of change.

We have entered a mass civilization which carries with it a climate of conformity and consensus and which, Ortega y Gasset warned, "crushes beneath it everything that is different, everything that is excellent, individual, qualified and select." The mental overcast resulting from these clouds of consensus looms as one of the most ominous threats for the days ahead.

To face the days ahead we must ask two questions: first, "Where are we?" and second, "Where do we go from here?" We Americans seem to have forgotten where we came from, we don't know where we are, and we fear where we may be going. We are a scene of frenetic fears, confusion, and madness. Scared New World.

Life has become a catalogue of crises: the Urban Crisis, the Race Crisis, the Campus Crisis, the Poverty Crisis, the World Crisis, the Crisis of a Free and Open Society, and underneath it all our personal crises of whether to live or drop out. We are bombarded with so-called studies and reports on the consequences of urbanization, the population explosion, the changing character of our educational system, our values, our family life, our relationships with one another, or rather our lack of relationships, the ever increasing alienation of the individual from his society, his inability to act on those issues that are vital to him, his family, and his community. Sociologists chorus the prevalence of *anomie,* and speculate on what we can do about it. . . .

That we look upon these crises as problems is a hopeful sign. A problem is something you can do something about. We may not know how, where, and what, but we know that eventually we can do something. The tragedy would be if we viewed a crisis as a plight; as an inevitability of life, like death; as a happening to which one is resigned. *This has always been the prime task of the organizer—the transformation of the plight into the problem.* The organizer must be able to communicate and convince the people that, if they find a way to join together, they need not fatalistically accept their plights but will have the power to affect the shape of their world. It is then that a people drop their defenses—for instance, the bitter humor that is often the only recourse if man has to live with the inevitable—and begin to act with anger, purpose, and hope.

Today the signs are flying that the American people are ready for organization and for action to "break out" and get back on the road to life, to being free citizens and not alienated bits of anonymity. We are in a revolution and should be reminded of Kropotkin's comment on the Russian Revolution, "The hopeless don't revolt, because revolution is an act of hope."

Let us take a look at a couple of these "crises"; the urban and racial crises.

America's urban crisis is primarily an umbilical crisis. We concede the unprecedented, sweeping and shatteringly rapid changes of our times. We have been ripped from the womb of the past. We know, we see, we hear, we talk about this whole changed and changing world but we will not cut the cord of the past and go out to live in the present. The past, though dead, has the security of familiarity, and so we move like zombies.

Our urban crisis is many-faceted: residual, overlapping local authorities of the past; the flight of whites and industry away from the city; the massive migration to the cities of low-income newcomers—both white and non-white; the huge increase in the black population of America's major cities, with all its attendant problems in the areas of education, housing, jobs, and new political alignments. . . .

Our present impasse on the race issue is due largely to our refusal to confront the issue for one of two reasons: either we don't know what to do about it, or, if we do know, we don't want to do anything. We shun meeting the issue head-on by relying on a series of tired gambits in the form of conferences, surveys, investigations, or study commissions appointed by the president, or governor, or mayor. Then we militantly and self-righteously proclaim our determination for bold, prompt, massive action, which always turn out to be bumbling, procrastinating, minuscule gestures. Blue-ribbon commissions always give birth to blue babies.

I suggest that those who live in the past don't want a confrontation with the present. I believe that white Americans welcome the present race violence and that under the surface reactions of horror and shock is very deep relief. Now white Americans are back in the familiar jungle. Now the confrontation is in terms they can understand and in accord with their prejudices. Now they can have a confrontation because they think they know the answer to violence, and the answer is force, and furthermore they welcome the use of force. Now they no longer have to talk or think about injustice, guilt, or the immorality of racism. Now it is simple: "Law and order must be upheld before we get around to anything else."

The issue we face is not just *what* is to be done, but *how* it is to be done. The situation is far too complex for us to attempt to continue the old practices, which I branded years ago as "welfare colonialism." Democracy can no longer be paraded under the simple disguise of admitting black-skinned representatives, who more often than not represent no one but themselves, to the privy councils. The new Uncle Talk-Toughs who have replaced the former Uncle Toms will be just as ineffective as long as they represent no larger group than the latter did in the past.

The void of leadership in the black ghettos or, similarly, in the white ghettos or the gilded ghettos of the middle class—in short, the general lack of leadership in America—is ominous for the democratic future. The democratic process cannot function without the essential mix of legitimate representatives who can meet with accredited representatives of other sectors of society in order to face up to the pushing, hauling, dealing and temporary compromises that are part of the pressure of democracy. Without this kind of representation the democratic process comes to a halt. This is what is happening today. Where are the leaders of the black ghetto who truly bear the credentials to represent their communities?

Let me put it another way. Suppose that white society, the establishment, the status quo, the power structure or any other name you wish to put on it, awoke one morning after experiencing a divine revelation and said, "Everything we have done in the past as far as our nonwhite fellow citizens are concerned has been hypocritical, immoral, undemocratic, and has violated the Judeo-Christian moral precepts. . . ."

We could then turn to the black ghettos and say, "Send us your representatives." Who would come forth? Who represents these people? Certainly practically none of those whom white society is now consorting with and also

financing. Now we see why it becomes so terribly important that the ghettos be organized. Organization is not only for the purpose of power,[1] but unless a people have become organized and their membership roster is open for public inspection, unless they have met in convention, agreed upon policy, programs, constitution, and elected officers, you will not find that necessary combination of circumstances from which legitimate, bona fide, accredited representation can be either selected or elected. Across the nation our ghettos are appallingly lacking in those combinations or organizations that can claim to legitimate representation.

The danger of black power is that there may be no black power. This nation desperately needs the organized power of our black sector and its representatives in our body politic. I am gravely concerned that those who talk black power will do no more than talk, will not engage in the arduous, tedious job of organization. If this happens the term "black power" will degenerate from a proud, meaningful phrase and threat into a joke.

Certainly the basis for real power cannot be found among most of those whose vocabulary and mentality are restricted to simplistic two-word slogans, "Black Power" and "Get Whitey." These people, with their frenetic but unproved claims that they represent the ghetto, bring to mind the story of the emperor's new clothes.

Today there is a great emphasis among blacks on identity: black culture, black history, and pride of race—"Black is beautiful." The importance of achieving the objective of a black sense of identity cannot be understated. It is essential and of prime significance. It must be achieved. What concerns me deeply is that identity without power is still a second-class identity. Black culture must proceed hand-in-hand with the organization of blacks for black power. Actually most lessons of life are learned in and through action. Many of the blacks who are most articulate about black culture have yet to demonstrate their capabilities for organization. For many of them the evocation of black culture has become a comforting rationale, an escape to avoid being put to the test of organization. They say that blacks are not ready for organization un-

til they have achieved their black identity. What they mean is that they either cannot organize or are afraid to try and fail. In my personal experiences I have never met a competent organizer who could resist organizing in any situation that demanded power for the sake of effecting change. Any organizer, educator, or sophisticated person knows that a basic, personal sense of identity can come only through the drama of moving experiences—of action. It is the change which occurs within a black minister of a small church living in a drastically limited segregated world, who because he is a leader of a real, not theoretical, black power organization and because of the actions attendant on that position, finds himself within a period of two years at an annual stockholders' meeting confronting the chairman of the board of one of the nation's largest corporations. He is not only confronting this chairman and issuing an ultimatum, but is followed by the nation's press as he storms out of the meeting. His actions are looked upon by the mass media as more important than what is happening at the stockholders' meeting. He has achieved his identity, his black identity. He is a man in every sense and he achieved his manhood the only way any man gets it—through action. And he has power. Black culture without black power is still castration. We are witnessing the emergence of a variety of species, including one which I have described as "the black in the gray flannel dashiki." We must have more black organizers who will do the job.

Another problem of today is the breakdown of communication between blacks and whites. If whites believe in full equality and the essential dignity of all races, then they cannot surrender their own dignity and be part of the masochistic cult which submits to outrageous and, in many cases, patently psychotic charges and attacks. A relationship of dignity and equality cuts both ways, and no one who is committed to the full equality and dignity of others can or will sacrifice his own in the process. During the recent trial of Black Panther leader Huey Newton, many San Francisco white liberals wore large buttons reading "Honkies for Huey!" Can you imagine if a white civil rights leader were on trial that blacks would go about with buttons reading "Niggers for ———!" Of course not. So long as mindless white

[1] Webster's Unabridged Dictionary defines power as "the ability to act."

masochism and unproductive, groveling guilt prevails, so long will there not be any meaningful communication or constructive positive changes for a world of equality. Many whites have become terrified of even raising a question with blacks for fear of having it branded as a race issue. Unless whites overcome their own hang-ups so that they can both listen and speak to blacks in the same way that they would be listening and speaking to whites, and vice versa, we will continue to face the consequences of black charlatans combining with white neurotics to sow the seeds of disillusionment and bitterness, and we will provide a comforting rationale for all racial bigots, both black and white.

The lack of citizen organization in the black ghettos is common in most of the other communities that make up the city. Our most populous cities have little citizen participation, little effective local democracy, and the individual has little, if any, degree of self-determination.

The plight of the people in our cities is made worse by a network of "citizen committees," "Health and Welfare Councils," "Poverty Program Committees," and other blue-ribbon packages that claim to represent people who have given them no mandate and who, as often as not, are ignorant that others are speaking in their name.

Without questioning the undoubted integrity and sincerity of those involved, I believe great harm has been done to the city and its people by these tiny organizations of professionals from private and government agencies who, along with an occasional other nonresident, claim to be spokesmen for hundreds of thousands of people throughout the city. The unchallenged presence of these small groups creates the impression that the population is being democratically represented. No number of "citizen committees," "Health and Welfare Councils," or other such devices can successfully play stand-in for the real thing. Unrepresentative committees are not democratic by virtue of ritual. . . .

Our cities lack citizen participation or organization on the local level. The failure of the "bottom" to make itself felt has permitted city-wide institutions and major interest groups—whether welfare, economic, religious, service, or fraternal—to arrogate the power of speaking for individuals without any challenge or objection.

With the urban society's development of vertical city-wide organizations and agencies, the disappearance of an articulate and active mass base has in effect insulated the heads of these organizations from their bodies. . . .

In the local community the individual citizen generally reacts to this situation by not reacting. Caught in circumstances that make him feel a lack of identification as an individual, which gives him a numbing sense of *not* belonging and a feeling that no one really cares for him, he responds by not caring. In the course of my work I have talked to people in just about every kind of American community, and nowhere is the old slogan "You can't fight City Hall," uttered with as much conviction as in these cities.

Even when a person may have a sudden desire to take a hand, he lacks the means by which to translate his desire into active participation. And so the local citizen sinks further into apathy, anonymity, and depersonalization. The result is his complete dependence on public authority and a state of civic-sclerosis.

I do not believe that democracy can survive except as a formality if the ordinary citizen's role is limited to voting, and if he is incapable of initiative or all possibility of influencing the political, social, and economic structures that surround him. This issue is at the center of the future of democracy in America.

The breakdown of citizen activity at the local level has fostered a phenomenon foreign to basic American premises. The concentration and centralization of power, authority, and office in the hands of a few has reached an unprecedented highwater mark in city, state, and national government.

I am fully aware of the dangers of a parochial and isolationist mentality. I have seen too many examples of community chauvinists, of jingoistic local groups doing things without consulting the common good. I am painfully cognizant that modern city problems require intricately co-ordinated planning if they are to be solved. I know, too, that meeting our city problems satisfactorily means making certain sacrifices for the general well-being.

Bearing this in mind I nevertheless recall Alexis de Tocqueville's observation that in the last analysis democracy is preserved and strengthened by maintaining differences and variations. When

—as is happening in our cities— all strong, local vested interests are obliterated, when these differences are removed, then I too see what Tocqueville saw as the major peril to our democracy: an egalitarian society that may have the look and forms of democracy, but is its very opposite. . . .

Our world has always had two kinds of changers, the social changers and the money changers. History is made up of the constant conflict between the two—witness the renowned account in the New Testament of Christ in the temple.

The social changers go by many names: agitators, revolutionaries, catalysts, and "outside" trouble makers.[2] We have added still another cliché to our vocabulary: "The generation gap."

True, the older generation does not look particularly hopeful. They were the young radicals of my time, the late thirties, forties, and fifties, and with rare exception have moved over into the establishment. Where they have not moved over as individuals they have been carried along by organizations which were formerly radical and today are part of the establishment. Many protested when their organizations went to the right but they stayed with them. They professed their desires to remain to the left and proclaimed their anguish at being seduced, but no one has ever been seduced who didn't want to be. Many of them claim to be "forward-looking" on the basis of a record of past progressivism. They continue to look at their past and stumble backward into the future, unseeing, confused, bitter and resentful at their rejection by the present generation. They rationalize in defense of themselves, which inevitably leads them to a defense of the establishment that may border on the absurd.

Many of the predictions I made some twenty years ago in *Reveille for Radicals* have, to my intense regret, been fulfilled. An example of this is to be found in the organized labor movement, which today is a part of the establishment and

---

[2] The establishment, the status quo, the power structure, or the lousy bastards, depending upon one's point of view and vocabulary, has always identified all trouble makers, agitators, revolutionaries, etc., as being from the "outside." Generally speaking, there is a certain validity to this, since the power establishment usually has retained power by crippling, crushing, or corrupting any would-be developing social changer within its area of power.

not even the progressive part at that. My comments then about the Building Trades Unions could have been written today; these unions are still segregated. What could be more absurd than the head of the now-merged A.F.L.-C.I.O., George Meany, defending the criminal idiocy of Vietnam.

Mr. Meany also said that the "one overriding fact" that "is and must be the primary concern of the A.F.L.-C.I.O." on the Vietnam war was the existence of a free trade union movement in South Vietnam. He said he could not understand any unionist who would advocate a course that would abandon those union members "to certain destruction."

"And, perhaps, I am too simple to comprehend how one who takes that position can be called a 'liberal,' " he said. "But the A.F.L.-C.I.O. is a very large house—with many mansions—and it takes all kinds."[3]

Mr. Meany's only flash of insight is in his words "perhaps, I am too simple to comprehend." . . .

The younger generation is almost as discouraging as the older. Despite its "campus crises" and multitudinous minor "confrontations"—many seemingly for the sake of confrontation—this generation may well be later described by history as the dropout generation. Here we find dissent by dropout which takes a number of forms.

At one extreme we have the hippies, who have not only physically and mentally dropped out but have even passed further into social outer space by taking their "trips" with drugs.

On the other side we have the so-called activists, who in their own way are also out of the action. By refusing to begin with the world as it is and to build power instruments for change, they have reacted with a disorganized, almost anarchistic, approach of "confrontations" and "doing their thing."

The tragedy of the young generation's "radicals" is that they dogmatically refuse to begin with the world as it is. But the only world we have is the world as it is, and we have to begin with that.

Any social changer, throughout history, has always known that you begin from where you are. Change can only be effected through power, and power means organization. Organization can be built only around issues which are specific, immediate, and realizable. Phrases like "participatory democracy" are meaningless for

the purpose of real organization. When we begin with issues we begin with controversy. There is no such animal as a "noncontroversial issue"; in fact, it is a contradiction in terms. When you and I agree about something, we have no issue; it is when we disagree that "the issue is drawn."

A book I am now completing presents certain universal rules of change.[4] The first one reads, "Change means movement. Movement means friction. Friction means heat. And heat means controversy." It is as simple as that. The same rule that applies in the mechanics is even more germane to social mechanics: movement means friction. The only places where one can have movement without friction is either in outer space, which is friction-free, or in a graduate seminar of a university, or in a church conference that emphasizes reconciliation. "Reconciliation" as the term has been used is an illusion of the world as we would like it to be. In the world as it is "reconciliation" means that one side has the power and the other side gets reconciled to it. Then you have reconciliation and peace and co-operation.

The fact that we accept working in the world as it is does not in any sense negate, dilute, or vitiate our desires to work toward changing it into the world as we would like it to be.

There is a great difference between the world as it is and the world as we would like it to be. One way to see this quickly is to turn on television early any evening and watch drama follow drama, in each of which love and virtue always emerge triumphant. This world as we would like it to be continues until the eleven o'clock newscast, when suddenly we are plunged into the world as it is. Here, as you know, love and virtue are not always triumphant.

In the world as it is, man moves primarily because of self-interest.

In the world as it is, the right things are usually done for the wrong reasons, and vice versa.

In the world as it is, constructive actions have been reactions to a threat.

In the world as it is, a value judgment is rarely, if ever, made on the basis of what is best. Life does not accord us this luxury. Decisions are made on the criteria of alternatives.

In the world as it is, "compro-

mise" is not an ugly but a noble word. If the whole free way of life could be summed up in one word it would be "compromise." A free way of life is a constant conflict punctuated by compromises which then serve as a jumping-off point for further conflict, more compromises, more conflict, in the never-ending struggle toward achieving man's highest goals.

In the world as it is, what you call morality is to a significant degree a rationalization of the position you occupy in the power pattern at a particular time. If you are a *Have-Not* and want *to get*, then you are always appealing to "a higher than man-made law," since the status quo has made the laws. If you are a *Have* and are out *to keep*, then you are constantly talking about the sanctity of the law and the responsibility of gradual operation "through accepted channels."

In the world as it is, one must begin from where one is. A political idiot knows that most major issues are national, and in some cases international, in scope. They cannot be coped with on the local community level. . . . However, it is just as clear that in order to create a national movement one must first build the parts to put together. The building of the parts is a tough, tedious, time-consuming, often monotonous and frequently frustrating job. There is no detour to avoid this means to the end of building a national movement. To organize the automobile industry each part of General Motors from Chevrolet to Cadillac, to sub-contracting plants making automobile parts from batteries to hub caps, had to be organized and then put together, and then General Motors was organized. The same process had to be followed with Chrysler and its constituent parts and then Ford and its parts, and now the bigger parts were ready to be put together and there was a nationwide automobile workers union.

The fundamental issue is how we go about building a national movement when so many of the present generation do not want to undergo the experience in time or detail of the organization of the parts, or of the local areas of organization. They want to jump right into a "national organization." Either they do not want to do the tough and tedious job of building the parts, or are incapable of it, or it is a combination of both. Creative organizers are a rarity. And so a part of the present generation takes refuge in a revo-

[3] *The New York Times*, December 8, 1967.

[4] *Rules for Revolution* (to be published by Random House, New York).

lution of rhetoric and calls national meetings of fifty "state representatives" who represent no more than themselves, and one wonders at times how much of even that they do. It is an escape from the world as it is.

In the world as it is, irrationalities play a signficant part. Life does not break down logically into Roman numerals I, II, and III, and sections (a), (b), and (c). It becomes tremendously important to understand, accept, and be comfortable with the irrationalities that are part of the life about us. . . .

I strongly suggest to you that this is not cynicism but realism. Ideologies are not very significant in themselves. The Soviet power position and its so-called ideology or rationalizations shifted drastically as the Russians moved from a *Have-Not* to a *Have* society, just as ours did when we moved from a *Have-Not* to a *Have* nation.

The younger generation must soon swing into action. Action is purposeful, deliberate, designed not as an end in itself but to generate new action in developing a program. Breathers of compromises are an essential to the pragmatic social changer. The approach of so much of the present younger generation is so fractured with "confrontations" and crises as ends in themselves, that their activities are not actions but a discharge of energy which, like a fireworks spectacle, briefly lights up the skies and then vanishes into the void.

When the young talk of revolution it becomes clear how far out of the scene one can be in refusing to begin with the world as it is. They use the word "revolution" but their goal is a miraculous divine revelation whereby people will suddenly reject old values and accept new ones or whereby they will begin living up to the "old" values such as love. The revolution becomes the resurrection or Gabriel blowing his horn. . . .

At various universities members of the Students for Democratic Society have asked me, "Mr. Alinsky, do you know that what you are doing is organizing the poor for the acceptance of these bourgeois, decadent, degenerate, bankrupt, materialistic, imperialistic, hawkish middle-class values of today's society?" There has been a long silence when I have responded with, "Do you know what the poor of America or, I might add, the poor of the world want? They want a bigger and fatter piece of these decadent, degener-

ate, bankrupt, materialistic, bourgeois values and what goes with it!"

They have assumed the kind of stance in which if the starving poor are pleading for bread and say, "Help us organize for power that we and our children may fight for bread," the modern young "revolutionary" would be compelled to respond, "Before we move I think we ought to think over some basic values: 'Do you realize that man does not live by bread alone?'" It is this kind of reaction and thinking which makes the far left appear to be infinitely more intelligible when viewed from a perspective not of the current political scene but of our space program. These political astronauts have gone beyond the "third world" and are now orbiting well into a mystical fourth world.

One must understand that these student activists as well as the hippies have with rare exception come from the middle class. It was their parents who had a fixed road to happiness by making that house out in the suburbs, the bank account, the country club, the color TV set, and two cars in the garage. If the parents got these things they would have it made. The parents are the ones who worked, followed all the signposts and got the goods for the promised good life but who, instead, now find themselves lost in Nowhere.

They are even more alienated from the scene than the poor because what they had after they got it was not the good life; they do not know where to go, they lack any compass or direction, so they founder and are frightened. The poor at least have a compass, a direction, and a purpose because, regardless of what anyone says to them, getting that bank account, that color TV, that house in the suburbs, and two cars is happiness. One can never reject these possessions unless one has experienced them, just as you cannot preach spiritual values to someone who is starving and whose idea of happiness is having enough food. It is after he achieves enough food for today and all of the tomorrows that he moves to the next stage, realizing that this has not brought him happiness. Then he is ready for, and starts demanding, other things. . . .

Unless the young radicals get with the scene as it is, we will see that the present disillusionment, boredom, and sense of failure will finally fertilize a rationale of, "Well, I tried to fight this system, the establishment, I tried to do

something but people won't listen and this whole goddamned system has just got to collapse of its own inner moral decay. There's no sense in my demonstrating and starving, so then . . ." So then they get a job on Madison Avenue and at the ripe old age of twenty-eight are "elder statesmen" of their own fevered imaginations, ready to start reminiscing about "their radical youth."

Although they are visibly dropping out of "social action" by the age of twenty-five or twenty-eight, they were never really in. I would describe the current scene of these activist dropouts or political hippies as "Political Hippyitus." These young people are the ones who scream "Burn the system down!" "Destroy the establishment!" and when you say, "What kind of a system would you have instead?" they respond by saying, "That is not a relevant question! That question confuses the issue! The new way will arise from the ashes of the destruction of the present system." . . .

It has been said that patriotism is the last refuge of the scoundrel. Today "youth" has become the refuge of the ignorant and confused. Lack of any knowledge, experience, or understanding of how to bring about change stems from this chronological castration. They have cut themselves off from any of the experience, knowledge, insights, understanding of the past. To them anyone past the age of twenty-five or thirty should drop dead—they have substantially revised one of George Bernard Shaw's Maxims for Revolutionists, "Every man over forty is a scoundrel," to "Every man over twenty-five . . ." They are implicit personifications of Aristotle's comment, "The young think they know everything and are confident in their assertions." They don't know that the average age of the members of the Jacobin clubs of the French Revolution was forty-two, or the similar age of the leaders of the Russian Revolution. Their "thing" will be noted as the "Revolutionaries of Rhetoric."

I have been so critical and so rough on our present young activists because to me they are the hope for the future. They are the seedlings from which will come the experienced, effective radical leaders of the next generation; the ones who will stand up, organize, lead, and fight for the good life. They are essential to the growth of a democratic society. We cannot afford another decade of a desert of dissent which followed the late Senator Joseph Mc-Carthy's night of persecution. It was those years of fear which stifled and sterilized the radical campus crop of the early fifties and created the present generation gap in the continuum. This must not happen again. Failure of today brings disillusionment of tomorrow and the rationalization of "I fought and tried but people just don't care. Anyway the system is so rotten and decayed that it will collapse. I'll get a good job and get mine; or I'll be part of the national conferences where we can denounce the system." Worse than all this is my fear that disillusionment of these young alleged activists carries the seeds of a potential cynicism which may result in this "active" turned-on generation becoming the most turned-off and reactionary generation as they go into their thirties. This must not happen.

The refusal to accept the past is not the only reason for the ineffective activity by the present generation of activists. They have grown up in a society which is extraordinarily fragmented and reflects itself in their own fractured way of life.

The present generation is coming on stage at a time of the greatest revolution in the history of man—the technological age—computerized, cybernetic, and automated; at a time of mass media and the jet when barriers of distance and data have become shattered; when everything has been fractured and the gaps spring up everywhere. communication gaps, generation gaps, gaps between a people and their government, and most important the gap between people and the world they live in. No longer can the old defenses prevail, nor the classic cliché, "When you grow older you'll understand." They know that their parents don't understand and they wonder legitimately whether anyone understands the titanic changes of the world of today. We continue to enumerate the lines and values of the dead world of the past.

Those of my generation are largely politically senile. Senility is a relinquishment of life as it is in the here and now and the taking of refuge into the security and familiarity of the past. When life becomes too confusing, too complex, too strange, too much, then you turn away. Today our college campuses are succumbing to the same affliction of my chronological compatriots—political senility. The plague of senility is as wide-spread among the twenty-year-olds as it is among the sixty-year-olds. Instead of escaping by being fugitives into the past, they escape by being fugitives into the future. In both cases they turn from the present. . . .

Economically we have emerged as a middle-class nation. Our poor are in the minority, so that even if we organize all the blacks, Mexican-Americans, Puerto Ricans, and Appalachian whites and create a coalition, they will still need allies for the necessary power for change. These allies can come only from organized sectors of the middle class. Politically we feel alienated, rejected, and hopeless. The chasm between the people and their political representatives has widened to a terrifying degree. In a political vacuum we become increasingly vulnerable to a seizure from the far right. We know that the Snake is there but we are as paralyzed as the Rabbit. People are not rabbits, and America must shake off this nightmare and awake again. The middle classes must be organized for action, for claiming their rights and powers of citizenship in a free society. The organization must be committed to the values of a free and open society. The middle classes must begin to participate as citizens for those ideals which give meaning and purpose to life.

Logic and faith go together as the opposite sides of the same shield. We know by our intelligence the greatness and desirability of a free and open society over all other alternatives. Logic tells us, "We'll believe it when we see it." But there is also the converse, faith. Faith, or belief in the people, tells us, "*We'll see it when we believe it.*"

For Those Who Would Change Things Now

A substantial portion of the royalties earned from this book will be given to the Fund for the College of Malcolm X, a four-year ethnic studies college to be built at the University of California, Santa Cruz. The Fund has been created to help raise the private money needed to operate a "cluster college" on the University campus. We believe that the College of Malcolm X will represent a major effort in promoting social change, making it fitting indeed that proceeds from a book on social change should go toward solving some of the social problems discussed.

We are urging the readers of this book to consider donating money in any amount to the Fund for the College of Malcolm X to help bring this dream into being. You can purchase a frameable numbered "stock" certificate or donate money in the amounts of $25, $100, $1,000 or up. Please read the following description of the Malcolm X College idea, and make a donation or pledge ($50 per year) by sending checks to the Fund for the College of Malcolm X, Box 1362, Santa Cruz, California 95060.

The College of Malcolm X

Background

On August 7, 1968, members of the Black Liberation Movement of Santa Cruz proposed that the seventh college of the University of California at Santa Cruz be devoted to the teaching of the Black Experience and be called the College of Malcolm X. Twenty colleges are scheduled for UCSC.

Reprinted by permission.

Five of them are completed at present. Each is a separate college, with its own theme and faculty. College VII, planned for completion in 1972, will be organized similarly and will be an integral part of the Santa Cruz campus of the University.

The proposal was reviewed by students and faculty, and the Committee for the College of Malcolm X was formed by concerned people from the University and from the larger Santa Cruz community who felt that the idea was worthwhile and especially suited to the Santa Cruz campus, which is so involved in creative experiments in higher education.

After extensive work by the faculty-student Committee on Educational Policy and Committee on Colleges, the Academic Senate unanimously passed their resolution, presented on February 12, 1969, that the emphasis of College VII be the study of minority groups in the United States. The UCSC Chancellor has appointed Herman Blake, Professor of Sociology, to head an Ethnic Studies Committee charged with developing a minority studies program for College VII and with consulting with architects in the design of the college. Members of the committee—whites, blacks, Asian-Americans, and Mexican-Americans—are drawn from members of the community, faculty and students.

At the same meeting, the Academic Senate passed the following resolution by a vote of seventy-three in favor and none against, with ten abstentions:

It is the sense of this division that the man known as El Hajj Malik El-Shabazz and Malcolm X would appropriately be commemorated by the use of his name for the college. . . .

It should be noted that UCSC students have expressed almost unanimous support for the College of Malcolm X. Close to 2000 of the 2600 students on the campus signed a petition supporting the original proposal. $30,000 in pledges to the Fund for the College of Malcolm X has been raised from faculty and students.

This strong commitment from the UCSC campus is the basis for the work which lies ahead: developing a detailed educational plan, fund raising, convincing the citizens of Santa Cruz and the state of the merits of the plan, and finally winning the approval of the Regents of the University of California.

Building a Minority Studies College

College VII at UCSC will open in 1972 with space for approximately 700 students. The minority studies program, now being planned by the Ethnic Studies Committee will be aimed principally at the four minority groups in California— Black, Mexican-American, Asian-American and Native American. Because of the controversial nature of this proposal we will turn to some frequently-asked questions:

Why Build a Separate College for Minority Studies?

The concept of the "Black Experience" has been viewed by minority group students as a pan-racial concept representative of all people of color who possess a racial identity which has traditionally been neglected in white-oriented educational institutions and in the teaching of such disciplines as history, art, literature. We interpret the theme "minority studies" to mean that the educational focus of the college would be a positive affirmation of the cultural heritage of minority peoples and the place of that heritage in the history and culture of the United States. The educational environment at UCSC is planned by a provost and his key faculty. The college gives core courses consistent with its theme while students are free to take courses elsewhere in the University. Like the present UCSC colleges which emphasize natural science or art, the focus of a minority studies college will parallel in every way the present college operation, harmonizing with the general educational objectives of the campus-wide degree requirements.

Will the Faculty Be Entirely Non-White?

No. As in other colleges, the faculty will be chosen jointly by the provost and the existing boards of study solely on the basis of scholarly qualifications. We may expect that some of the professors, especially those with responsibility for the core and college courses will be non-white.

Why Is the Architecture Mentioned in the Proposal?

In the experience of the existing colleges, a coordination of architecture and college plan would always be desirable. While not feasible in the past, such a coordination is possible with all UCSC colleges after the sixth.

Will All of the Students Be from Minority Groups?

No, definitely not. A segregated college would be both illegal under the Civil Rights Act and, more importantly would be inconsistent with the beliefs of Malcolm X who grew to reject racism. A large percentage of students who attend the college will have to be from minority groups and a large percentage will have to be white in order to realize the educational objectives of the school. But the basic principle remains—this will be a college open to all people and for all people.

Why Name a College after Malcolm X?

There are already in existence a number of black universities, and programs in "Black Studies" are available in several predominately white institutions (e.g., San Francisco State, University of California, Berkeley). The uniqueness of the present proposal—a college in the midst of the University of California, accessible to students of all colors—is emphasized by the name. The College of Malcolm X. This name speaks directly to majority and minority groups in this country, defining the ideal of the college more precisely than "Afro-American" or "Black Studies," by identifying the program with the ideals of this great man. This name is the most controversial part of the proposal only because Malcolm X has been so widely misunderstood.

Young people of all races have read and been inspired by *The Autobiography of Malcolm X*, recognizing a man who came to value truth and brotherhood in spite of his earlier hatred of white people which was nurtured by living in the Black Experience in America. We recommend reading the entire book, but a short version is available on request from the Committee for the College of Malcolm X.

How Can We Help?

Realistically, this dramatic proposal will need the spiritual and financial help of a large segment of the community if it is to succeed. We view the College of Malcolm X as an institution with a national impact. We have begun the collection of books, periodicals, position papers and audiovisual materials in the formation of the Ethnic Studies Library, which we hope will be a major scholarly resource in the College. Your contributions of any materials bearing on the problem of minority groups in America would be most welcome. In turn, we the Committee for the College of Malcolm X (Box 1362, Santa Cruz) and the Black Liberation Movement (Box 1502, Santa Cruz) are ready to provide speakers to any interested group. Contributions of money to the Fund for the College of Malcolm X are welcomed (see details on the page devoted to the fund).

Some Background on Malcolm X

El-Hajj Malik El-Shabazz, widely known as Malcolm X, was born on May 19, 1925 into the terrors of the Ku Klux Klan in Nebraska. His family moved after he was born to the country in Michigan, but they never escaped the harassment directed toward them because of their color. Malcolm's father, the Reverend Earl Little, was a Baptist minister, a dedicated organizer for Marcus Aurelius Garvey's U.N.I.A. (Universal Negro Improvement Association). The Reverend believed, as did Marcus Garvey, that freedom, independence and self-respect could never be achieved by the Negro in America and that therefore the Negro should leave America to the white man and return to his African land of origin. As Malcolm X explained in his autobiography "among the reasons my father had decided to risk and dedicate his life to help disseminate this philosophy among his people was that he had seen four of his six brothers die by violence, three of them killed by white men, including one by lynching." Malcolm X's father died at the hands of the white man.

Most people remember Malcolm X as a convicted felon, dope addict, hustler and racist. In his time, his bitter outbursts against white Americans made world headlines. Less well known is that near the end of Malcolm X's life, his thought underwent a dramatic change. He no longer believed as he once had that all white men were devils. As his letter from Mecca reveals, Malcolm X came to believe that brotherhood practiced by all colors is possible, that it is necessary and that racism is a suicidal path for this country.

Malcolm X, unlike his father, was to develop a faith in his homeland, a faith in the power of the people to transform this society and to unite as human beings in the international struggle for human rights. Ossie Davis tried to explain why Malcolm X was so eulogized by his people.

The honor and respect given to the memory of Malcolm X is largely due to these reasons, as Ossie Davis wrote:

White folks do not need anybody to remind them that they are men. We do! . . . what ever else he was or was not—Malcolm was a man!

Malcolm kept snatching our lies away. He kept shouting the painful truth we whites and blacks did not want to know . . .

And Malcolm was free. No one who knew him before and after his trip to Mecca could doubt that he had completely abandoned racism, separatism and hatred.

Fund for the College of Malcolm X

The Fund for the College of Malcolm X is a voluntary organization. The Board of Trustees is made up of faculty, students, and members of the Santa Cruz community. It is not connected or affiliated with, nor is it endorsed, favored, opposed or supported by the University of California. It is, however, an opportunity for all of us who are interested in the development of the College of Malcolm X, to make a meaningful and needed contribution toward this end.

Usually a college at UCSC is financed from a variety of sources. The development of certain facilities at each college, such as a college library, a public auditorium, special cultural events, etc., has been dependent on the $600,000 to $800,000 contributed to the University from private sources. In the past, the Regents of the University of California have agreed to the naming of colleges on the UCSC campus after major donors.

For the most part, the gift funding for the existing colleges at UCSC has come from private foundations. We are suggesting a variation in approach to the gift funding of College VII, which we hope to see become the College of Malcolm X. Since the idea for the college had its roots in the community, and since much of the enthusiasm and continued support for the proposal is in the community, both on and off the UCSC campus, it would be entirely appropriate if this same community aided in funding the college.

The Fund for the College of Malcolm X is seeking to raise the private gift funds. It is certain that private foundations sympathetic toward the idea of the college and impressed with our efforts could be counted on to pro-

vide part of the funds. The money will be presented to the University of California by vote of the Fund's Board of Trustees.

Each supporter of the college is asked to make a tax-deductible contribution of $50 now ($25 for students) and to pledge $50 per year for three years thereafter (to begin after graduation for students). Checks for the pledges should be made out to the Fund for the College of Malcolm X. The treasurer will send you a signed receipt for tax purposes.

Board of Trustees of College of Malcolm X

David E. Kaun, Professor, University of California at Santa Cruz, Treasurer

Robert Buckhout, Assistant Professor, University of California at Santa Cruz

John Sumida, Student, University of California at Santa Cruz

James Gonzales, Student, University of California at Santa Cruz

Pennie Weinberg, Student, University of California at Santa Cruz

Chris Burke, Student, University of California at Santa Cruz

Participation Shares

In an effort to gather the participation of large numbers of people in the College of Malcolm X, Participation Shares with a value of $10 are being sold by the Fund. Donations of $10 or more will entitle the donor to a numbered stock certificate which "signifies the desire of the owner to share in the future of the College of Malcolm X—an institution devoted to the study of minority peoples for the benefit of all peoples. Expected dividend: better educated citizens fulfilling the dream of the late El Hajj Malik El-Shabazz— Malcolm X."

Checks to purchase shares or to sign up for a pledge should be mailed to:

Fund for the College of Malcolm X

David E. Kaun, Treasurer

Box 1362

Santa Cruz, Ca. 95060

. . . Each hour here in the Holy Land enables me to have greater spiritual insights into what is happening in America between black and white. The American Negro never can be blamed for his racial animosities—he is only reacting to four hundred years of the conscious racism of the American whites. But as racism leads America up the suicide path, I do believe, from the experiences that I have had with them, that the whites of the younger generation, in the colleges and universities, will see the handwriting on the wall and many of them will turn to the spiritual path of *truth*—the *only* way left to America to ward off the disaster that racism inevitably must lead to.

Malcolm X

AOXOMOXOA:
A Dictionary
of Berkeley Slang

Compiled by Jean Frazier

ACID: LSD

ACID ROCK: music that resulted from the LSD culture, also known as psychedelic music

ALL RIGHT: 1. (interj.) exactly, cf. right on 2. (adj.) a superlative, as, "She is an all right chick." also spelled ALRIGHT

AMAZING: very good, a superlative

AVE, THE; THE AVENUE: Telegraph Avenue, the center of the Berkeley street community

AMERIKA: radical spelling of America, meant to emphasize the fascist aspects of the country

BAD: good

BAD TRIP: 1. a bad experience with drugs 2. any bad experience

BAG: 1. an interest 2. a talent, skill or way of living, as "skiing is his bag."

BALL: to have intercourse

BARB, THE: the Berkeley Barb, a local underground newspaper

BEAUTIFUL: a superlative, often used to describe good feelings about another person

BLASTED: intoxicated by a drug

BLOAT: 1. (v.) to overeat 2. (n.) an occasion when one overeats

CLEAR BLOAT: pleasantly full feeling (also a CLEAR)

MOBY BLOAT: very full feeling (also called a MOBY or the MOBIES)

BLIRGE: near ultimate bloat, however one might consider eating again at this stage

By permission of the author.

BLIVET: the ultimate bloat, characterized by the lack of desire to ever eat again

BLOW: 1. to smoke dope 2. to become high from drugs as in "blow your mind" 3. fellatio or cunnilingus 4. to fail at some enterprise, e.g., "to blow it"

BLOW YOUR MIND: 1. a sudden realization, usually strange 2. under the influence of a drug 3. a feeling similar to a drug experience caused by a different stimuli

BLUE MEANIES: the deputies of the Alameda County Sheriff's Department

BREAD: money

BRICK: a kilogram of marijuana or hashish

BRING DOWN: 1. (n.) a depressing event 2. (v.) to cause someone to come down from a drug high 3. to cause depression

BROTHER: a fellow member of the cause, whatever it may be

BULLSHIT, BS: 1. (n.) worthless talk or words, used especially to describe exam papers that lack factual content 2. (v.) to talk or write at length without saying anything 3. to lie 4. to rap

BUM: (adj.) used to describe a bad drug experience, as in "bum trip"

BUMMER: 1. a bad experience with drugs 2. any bad experience

BUMS: college protestors

BURN, BURNED: 1. to cheat, con 2. to sell phony drugs 3. (p.t.) to be sold phony drugs, to be cheated

BUST, BUSTED: 1. (v.) to arrest 2. (n.) an arrest 3. (p.t.) in jail, arrested

CAN: 1. an ounce of marijuana 2. jail

CAP: a capsule of a drug, as "a cap of acid"

CAT: a male human being, usually not of the establishment

CHICANO: a Mexican-American

CHICK: a female human being, usually young

CITY, THE: San Francisco

CLAP: venereal disease (well, one of them)

CLEAN: not in possession of illegal drugs

COME DOWN: 1. (v.) to lose a drug altered state of mind 2. to become depressed 3. (n.) a depressing event 4. loss of face

COME OFF IT: expression with various meanings such as (1) don't try to fool me; (2) stop it; (3) be serious; (4) tell the truth

COME THE REVOLUTION . . . : after the revolution occurs

COMING TOGETHER: 1. starting to take shape 2. unifying experience 3. oneness

COMMUNE: a living arrangement involving both sexes in which everything is shared, held in common

CONTACT HIGH: a mind-altered state that results from association with someone who is under the influence of a drug, or from sitting in a room filled with marijuana smoke

COOL: a superlative, may describe any situation

COOL IT, CI: 1. stop it 2. have caution, be careful

COP OFF: 1. to steal, to take

COP OUT: 1. to confess to the police 2. to do something despite the fact that it goes against your values 3. to join the establishment 4. to fail to do something because of fear of reprisal

COSMOS: the fourth dimension, a line which is at a right angle to every other line in space

COTTON MOUTH: dry feeling in the mouth which results from smoking marijuana

CRABS: crab lice

CRASH: 1. to come down hard after using drugs 2. to sleep after using drugs 3. to fall asleep from exhaustion 4. to fall asleep after an emotional experience

CRASH PAD: 1. a place to sleep off the effects of a drug 2. any place to stay briefly for free

DEAL: to sell drugs

DIG: 1. to like 2. to understand

Dig It: (interj.) understand it, believe it

Do It!: an interjection used to urge people to start to do something; to show approval of what a person is doing; to urge people to continue

Do It Up Right: to do something well or in an exciting manner

Dope: any drug

Do-Vibes: a burst of energy, a desire to do something

Down: 1. not under the influence of drugs 2. depressed

Downer: 1. a sedative, barbiturate 2. something which negatively affects one's spirits

Do Your Thing: 1. to do something which you enjoy or find pleasure in 2. to do something for which you have a particular talent 3. to do your job

Drop: to take or swallow as, "drop acid"

Drop Out: to leave the established order either by withdrawing into one's self or by joining a community on the outside

Ego Trip: a long discourse about oneself, often induced by drugs 2. something undertaken for self-glorification

Electric: containing psychedelics, usually LSD, as "electric kool-aid"

Fantastic: very good, a superlative

Far Out: a superlative

Fine: very good

Flash: 1. (n.) a sudden realization 2. (v.) to realize, to understand fully

    Acid Flash: the return to a previous LSD experience without taking the drug again, usually occurs in brief flashes

Flipped Out: crazy, strange, out of touch with reality

Flying: under the influence of drugs, very high

For Real: truly, honestly

Freak: 1. (n.) a drug user who uses primarily one drug, as a "meth freak" 2. anyone with an obsession or a great interest in something, that is, a collector of stamps is a stamp freak 3. (v.) to be obsessed with something, to become deeply involved in an experience

Freak Out: 1. (n.) an engrossing experience, sometimes with the connotation of having been an odd experience 2. (v.) to become so involved with something as to lose touch with the world 3. to go crazy due to the use of drugs

Fuck: 1. (v.) to have intercourse 2. (interj.) an expression of disappointment, anger or annoyance

Fuckin', Fucking: an adjective used to add emphasis, as, "I can't find the fuckin' keys."

Fuck Off: leave, get lost

Fuck Up: 1. (n.) a mistake, error 2. (v.) to ruin, spoil, subvert

Funky: 1. blatantly honest, real, pertaining to some basic function 2. old fashioned, simple 3. sweaty, dirty

Fuzz: police

Gas: fun, exciting

Gay Lib: short for Gay Liberation Front

Get Into It: become involved with, study, be fascinated by

Get It All Together: 1. to get organized, to get started on something 2. to get into the proper state of mind

Get It Off: to ejaculate

Get Your Shit Together: 1. to get organized, to get started on something 2. to get into the proper state of mind

Grass: marijuana

Groove: 1. (v.) to become involved in, to be completely absorbed by, to enjoy 2. (n.) something which is absorbing or interesting 3. very good, as, "the concert was a real groove,"

Groovy: very good, a superlative

Hairy: extremely difficult

Hang In There: persist, continue

Hang Up: 1. (n.) a special interest 2. a problem, worry or preoccupation 3. (v.) to be interested in 4. to be concerned or preoccupied by

Hard Hat: (derived from demonstrations of construction workers who wore hard hats and who were in support of the President's war policy) a reactionary, often violent

Hard Stuff: addictive drugs, narcotics

Have a Good Day: a common expression of farewell

Harvey Krishna: nickname for Hare Krishna (a Hindu chant) used by Frank O'Niell in the comic strip "Odds Bodkins"

Hash, Hashish: the resin from the flower of the female marijuana plant

Hassle: 1. (n.) an argument, a disagreement 2. a problem, a disagreeable turn of events 3. (v.) to bother, to disturb 4. to argue with

Head: 1. (n.) a heavy drug user, as, "acid head" (a heavy user of LSD) 2. (adj.) relating to drugs, as, a "head shop" (a store which sells drug paraphernalia)

Hearts: amphetamines

Heavy: important, complicated, serious, overwhelming, or amazing, as, "The lecture on the war was really heavy."

Hellicop: surveillance helicopter flown by the Berkeley police during campus and Southside uprisings

High: 1. a floating, happy, strange state of mind brought about by the use of drugs 2. a similar state of mind whatever the stimuli, as, "she gets high on people"

Hit: a puff of a cigarette, pipe or hookah containing marijuana or hashish

Hitch: short for hitchhike

Hit the Flicks: go to the movies

Holding: to be in possession of illegal drugs (cf. clean)

Horse, H: heroin

Hubert: a Berkeley evangelist who is a familiar figure on the campus

Incredible: very good, a superlative

Into: involved in, interested in, occupied by, as, "She is really into psychology"

Jazzed: to be excited about, to be interested in (cf. shine it on)

Jesus Freak: a person who has found Jesus to be the "ultimate trip," e.g., a head who has gone beyond acid to Christ

Joint: a marijuana cigarette

Junk: heroin

Karma: fate

Kilo, Key: a kilogram of marijuana or hashish

Lay Down a Rap: 1. to talk someone down from a drug induced state 2. to talk at length under the influence of drugs 3. to talk for an extended period 4. to describe something a length

Lay It On: 1. to give something to someone, as, "he laid a joint on her" 2. to BS someone, to tell an artfully contrived story

Lay Off: to stop bothering someone, to leave that person alone

Let It All Hang Out: to be entirely open and honest

Let It Come: to have an orgasm

Let It Happen: to have an orgasm

Liberate: to steal (cf. rip off)

Lid: an ounce of marijuana

Loaded: under the influence of a drug

Make It: to have intercourse

Man: a common greeting, interjection used to refer to either sex

Mellow: soft, pleasant, nice

METH: diminutive for methedrine

METH MOUTH: dry mouth that results from the use of methedrine

MIKE, MIC: a microgram

MINDBLOWER: an event, person, place or thing which is startling, exciting, unusual, or overwhelming; also used to refer to the effects of a drug

MINDFUCK: something which is too much to accept, more upsetting than a mindblower

MOTHERFUCKER: someone who puts you down; orig. the slaveowner who raped the mother of a slave

MUNCHIES: the hunger that arises from smoking marijuana

MUTHA, MOTHER: short for motherfucker; an interjection expressing anger or disgust

MY WOMAN: girlfriend, wife, lover

NARC, NARK: a narcotics agent of the police force

NORTHSIDE: the area on the north side of the Berkeley campus

NO SHIT: truthfully, for real

NUMBER: a marijuana cigarette

OFF: to kill, as, "Off the pig"

OINKERS: the police

OLD LADY: girl friend

OLD MAN: boy friend

OUNCE: an ounce bag of marijuana

OUTASIGHT, OUT OF SIGHT: extremely good, a superlative

OUT FRONT: very open and honest

OUTRAGEOUS: very good, a superlative

OUTSTANDING: very good, a superlative

PAPER, PAPERS: paper used to roll marijuana cigarettes

PARANOID: afraid of being raided or caught by narcotics agents while in possession of or while using an illegal drug; paranoia is most common while under the influence of a drug

PARK, THE: the People's Park of Berkeley—1969

PEACE: a greeting or farewell remark, as, "Peace, brother"

PEOPLE'S PARK: a plot of unused University land that was converted into a user-designed park by the street people and students of Berkeley and which was the scene of much controversy in 1969. The land is now an unused parking lot and soccer field.

PIG: police

PILL, THE: birth control pills

PLASTIC: artificial, cheap, modern; often old apartments and houses are described as nonplastic

POP: to swallow, as, "pop a pill"

POT: marijuana

PSYCHED UP: to be psychologically prepared for, to be anxious to begin

PSYCH OUT: 1. to understand completely 2. to con or fool

RADICALIZE: to convert someone to leftist ideology through the use of repression and right wing tactics

RAP: 1. (v.) to talk 2. (n.) a lengthy discourse

RAYGUN: Gov. Reagan

REAL, REALLY: used for plus emphasis

RECONSTITUTION: refers to changing a course for coverage of traditional material to an examination of the relevance of the course as it relates to the war in Indochina and/or abandonment of traditional course activities in order to devote full time to the antiwar effort. Reconstitution was a movement on the Berkeley campus in the Spring of 1970.

REDS: type of downer, seconalbased

REEFER: 1. a marijuana cigarette 2. a refrigerator

REFUGEE: a person enrolled in a course which has not been reconstituted (see above) and seeks to transfer to a reconstituted course so that he may do antiwar work

RIGHT ON: 1. (interj.) definitely, exactly 2. yeah, okay 3. (adj.) something which is right, correct, perfect or very nice, as, "Her speech was right on."

RIP OFF: 1. (v.) to steal, to abscond with 2. to arrest 3. to kill 4. (n.) an arrest, a bust 5. a con job, a trick

RIPPED: high, under the influence of a drug

ROACH: the butt of a marijuana cigarette

ROACH CLIP: a holder for the roach designed so the user will not burn his hands

RONNIE-BABES, RONNIE-BABY: nicknames for Gov. Ronald Reagan

ROOKED: cheated, swindled

SCENE: total setting, locale, place, mood or environment, e.g. "He was interested in the Telegraph street scene"; "The party was a weird scene."

SHUCK: 1. (n.) a trick, a con 2. (v.) to trick

SHINE IT ON: to interest someone in something, to get someone jazzed about something

SHIT: 1. heroin 2. anything considered to be worthless or phony 3. an expression of anger or disgust 4. excrement

SHOOT: to inject drugs

SISTER: a female member of the cause, especially, a member of the Women's Liberation Front

SNOW: cocaine

SOD BROTHER: a merchant who supports the People's Park

SOMETHING: good or bad feeling or experience; usage depends upon context and tone of voice, as, "That test was really something." (bad) or "Wow, that chick is something." (good)

SOUTHSIDE: the southside of the Berkeley campus which includes Telegraph Avenue and its environs

SPACED OUT: 1. intoxicated by drugs, high 2. out of contact with reality, freaked

SPEED: amphetamines

SPLIT: to leave

STASH: one's personal supply of drugs

STASH BAG: a bag in which to keep drugs

STONED: high, under the influence of drugs

STP: hallucinogen, stronger than acid

STRAIGHT: 1. down, not under the influence of drugs 2. someone who does not use drugs 3. a member of the establishment

STRANGE: used to describe experiences, may be good or bad depending upon the context; often connotes something odd or unusual

STRANGE PLACE: unusual mental state, as, "His head has been in a strange place since he came back to Berkeley."

STREET PEOPLE: non-students who live on or around Telegraph Avenue

STUFF: drugs

SUPER: adjective used for emphasis; sometimes used to indicate large size or something very special

SUPER-LUTHE: a former Protestant whose behavior is occasionally characterized by the Puritan Ethic, e.g., sudden bursts of house cleaning (the word is derived from super and Lutheran)

TAB: tablet

TELE, TELLY: Telegraph Avenue (cf. the Ave)

THING: a much-used abstract word which may mean life styles, attitudes, beliefs, activities, occupations, sexual organs or . . .

THIRD WORLD: non-white, the colonized peoples of the world

TIGHT: 1. tense, scary, as, "a tight situation" 2. uptight, straight, stingy, strict, not loose

TRIBE, THE: the Berkeley Tribe, a local underground newspaper

TRIP: 1. (n.) a drug experience, especially with psychedelics, as, an acid trip 2. any experience which produces a drug-like state of mind 3. (v.) to take drugs 4. to become involved in something to the exclusion of all else, as, "They really tripped on the music." (also TRIP OUT)

TURN OFF: to become disgusted, uninterested or depressed

TURN ON: 1. to become high on drugs 2. to stimulate sexually 3. to become involved in, to become interested in, to be excited by, as, "Bach really turns me on."

UNDERGROUND: 1. not of the established order, often refers to the media 2. in hiding

UNREAL: 1. something very good, a superlative 2. strange, odd, freaky

UP: high, under the influence of drugs

UP FOR IT: 1. to be psychologically prepared for (cf. psyched up) 2. to be physically able to do something

UP FRONT: extremely open and honest

UPPER: a stimulant, amphetamines

UP THE REVOLUTION: up with the revolution, support the revolution

UPTIGHT: 1. tense, nervous, suspicious, upset or angry 2. straight-laced, of the Victorian age

UP YOURS: short for "up your ass," an expression of anger or disgust

VIBES, VIBRATIONS: a sensed or shared mood or feeling; vibes may be good or bad, as, "The courtroom was full of bad vibes."

WEED: marijuana

WEIRD: strange, odd, heavy

WHAT'S HAPPENING: that which is occurring, the center of the action

WHERE HIS HEAD IS AT: state of mind, mental condition

WHERE IT'S AT: that which is happening, the true essence of that which is going on

WHIRLYPIG: helicopter flown by the Berkeley police during student disruptions (cf. Hellicop)

WILD: very good, a superlative

WIPED OUT: very tired, about to crash

WIRED: high on speed (amphetamines)

WOMEN'S LIB: short for Women's Liberation Front

WOW, OH WOW: a common interjection which expresses almost anything

YELLOW JACKETS: barbiturates, so called because of the color of the pill

YIPPIE: the Youth International Party; a member of the Youth International Party; anyone who wants to be one; a myth

ZAP: a very quick action; may be used in place of any action verb, as, "Let's zap down to the Ave."

ZONKED: 1. under the influence of a drug, very high 2. just about to fall asleep due to the use of drugs, wiped out 3. very tired

AOXOMOXOA: a word which may be read forward or backward, like this dictionary

This dictionary expires December 31, 1970. Please write your own. J.F.

Indexes
Names

Subjects

73 74 75   10 9 8 7 6 5